V-Ray 5 for 3ds Max 2020

VOLUME 2

Revitalize your architectural visualizations by bringing new levels of realism to your day and night interior scenes. This book features full-color, step-by-step tutorials to develop a firm understanding of the processes and techniques involved in creating jaw-dropping 3d visualizations for top marketing agencies.

This second volume includes day and night lighting of an atrium scene using seasoned tools and techniques to deploy V-Ray 5 and 3ds Max 2020. It has never been quicker and easier to create the industry's top-of-the-range 3d marketing visuals.

The book starts with an overview of the best techniques to approach clients via emails, calls, meetings, and social media. There are also key insights into the best practices of handling projects, pricing, contracts, invoices, pre-production, production, post-production, etc.

The subsequent step takes users through the installation of V-Ray 5 and the process of accessing the V-Ray Material browser dialog.

Throughout the book, users are taken through VRayMtl functions such as Diffuse, Roughness, Reflect, Glossiness, Metalness, Refract, IOR, Abbe number, Fog color, Translucency, BRDF, Coat, Sheen and Bump.

Users will also learn how to use procedural maps such as VRayBitmap, VRayTriplanarTex, Bricks, Metals, Carpaint, VRayDisplacementMod, VRayUVWRandomizer, VRayMultiSubTex, VRayPointCloudColor, VRayDirt, VRayAerialPersepective, VRayLightMtl, VRayMtlWrapper, VRayOverrideMtl, VRay2SidedMtl, VRayBlendMtl and VRayEdgesTex.

Users will have a rare insight into all functionalities of a V-Ray camera, VRayLight objects, Render settings, Frame buffer, Global switches, IPR options, Bucket and Progressive image samplers, Image filters, Global DMC, Color mapping, Brute force GI, Light cache, Color management, Distributed rendering, Render elements, V-Ray image file format, VFB History settings, VFB Lens Effects, LightMix, Film tonemap, Hue/Saturation, Lookup Table and much more.

Finally, users will embark on the amazing journey of utilizing the previous chapters to create eye-catching 3d marketing visuals through the meticulous process of pre-production, production and post-production of both day and night scenes/lighting. The tips and tricks section will extensively cover key sections about Verified views for planning applications, Parametric modeling with AdvArray, anima®, project manager plug-in, Verge3d, Webrotate 360, Accucities 3d city models and much more.

V-RAY 5 FOR 3DS MAX 2020

DAY & NIGHT INTERIOR WORKFLOWS FOR PARAMETRIC DESIGNS

VOLUME 2

JAMIE
CARDOSO

CRC Press
Taylor & Francis Group
Boca Raton London New York

CRC Press is an imprint of the
Taylor & Francis Group, an **informa** business

First Edition published 2023
by CRC Press
6000 Broken Sound Parkway NW, Suite 300, Boca Raton, FL 33487-2742

and by CRC Press
4 Park Square, Milton Park, Abingdon, Oxon, OX14 4RN

CRC Press is an imprint of Taylor & Francis Group, LLC

ISBN: 978-1-032-41890-2 (hbk)
ISBN: 978-1-138-78038-5 (pbk)
ISBN: 978-1-315-77080-2 (ebk)

DOI: 10.1201/9781315770802

Typeset in Minion Pro
by codeMantra

Access the Instructor & Student Resources: https://www.routledge.com/9781138780385

Contents

Preface

V-Ray rendering engine was created by the Chaos group in 1997. It was originally available as a rendering plug-in for 3ds Max only, and later integrated into other platforms such as cinema 4D, Maya and Sketchup.

At the start, it was competing with other rendering engines such as final render, Brazil and mental ray. However, it quickly outranked its competitors to become the most popular rendering engine today.

Its current popularity is such that even Oscar-winning film studios such as ILM (Industry of Light & Magic) have also incorporated it into their rendering pipeline.

Recent reports suggest that 90% of companies/industries using rendering applications have at least one copy of V-Ray in their rendering pipeline.

V-Ray's meteoric rise is mostly attributed to its ease of use, support group, constant updates/improvements and its rendering speed.

Acknowledgments

I would like to take this opportunity to personally thank Sean Connelly and Taylor & Francis for the amazing opportunity and for being ever so patient with me throughout the entire process.

In addition, I would like to thank my family and friends, who have been my greatest supporters.

I would like to also thank everyone who contributed directly and indirectly to the production and completion of this book.

Special thanks to Shawn Lochman, Elitsa Dimitrova, Graham Macfarlane, James Goodman, Chaos Group, Teodora Mircheva, Ana Savova, Martin Minev, Nadeem Bhatti, George Podolski, Maher Zebian, Geoff Chilvers, Giacomo Arteconi, Andrew Gibbon, Jacob Adamiec, Mateusz Wawrzyniak and Mark Simpkin.

Finally, I would like to express my eternal gratitude for the continuous support from friends, family, esteemed colleagues, my book readers, my LinkedIn connections, followers, and my blog viewers: You rock!

Author

Jamie Cardoso is a renowned author, reviewer, computer artist and technologist with years of experience in creating state-of-the-art 3d photomontages, verified views, VR, AR, XR, MR, Stereos, photorealistic interior and exterior visualizations for architects and designers.

In collaboration with well-established marketing/design agencies and visualization companies, he has helped create iconic buildings and spaces such as the Gherkin, the Shard, the Welsh Assembly, 107 Cheapside, Heron Tower, Jaguar headquarters, Asos, Virgin cruise ship, One Hyde Park, Google and Battersea power station development.

Much of Jamie's work and contributions have been featured in books and magazines such as Area Autodesk, 3D World, CG Society, TutsPlus, CG Architect, Evermotion, Chaos Group and Udemy, to name but a few. Jamie also co-authored two successful books entitled *Realistic Architectural Visualization with 3ds Max and Mental Ray*, and most recently, a new book with Taylor & Francis, entitled *3D Photorealistic Rendering: Interiors and Exteriors with V-Ray & 3Ds Max*. In his spare time (whenever that is), he shares some of his knowledge with users, by posting free step-by-step tutorials on his blog, YouTube channel, Instagram, LinkedIn, Facebook and Twitter.

To connect with him, simply Google: Jamie Cardoso.

1

Using Resource Files

1 Using Resource Files

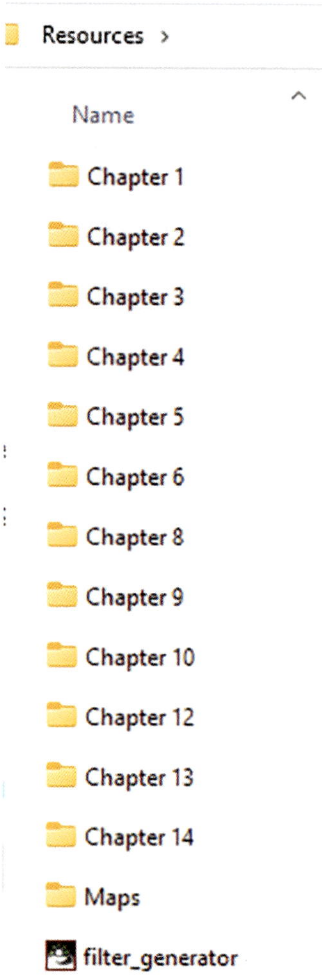

Resource Files folder with listed subfolders.

NOTE

Users need to install a WinRAR or WinZip program in order to be able to extract zip files.

This book comes with resources available for download from the link referred to earlier. Depending on how users choose to download the resources, they should appear in your computer drive as one zip file or multiple ones.

First, create a new folder dedicated to this book and rename it accordingly. Next, move the downloaded zip file/s into it, followed by selecting the zip file/s, right clicking and choosing the option to, Extract Here.

The final result should be, one main folder named, Resources, with additional subfolders (from chapter one to fourteen–) containing specific file types related to each of the chapters (3ds Max files, vfbl, LUT, IES, etc.).

Also, there should a subfolder named, Maps, containing textures and files associated with most 3ds Max scenes.

If/when users are required to open a specific 3ds Max file, missing files (if any) can be found in the folder named, Maps. Otherwise, in one of the other subfolders (1–14) associated with the chapter in question.

DOI: 10.1201/9781315770802-1

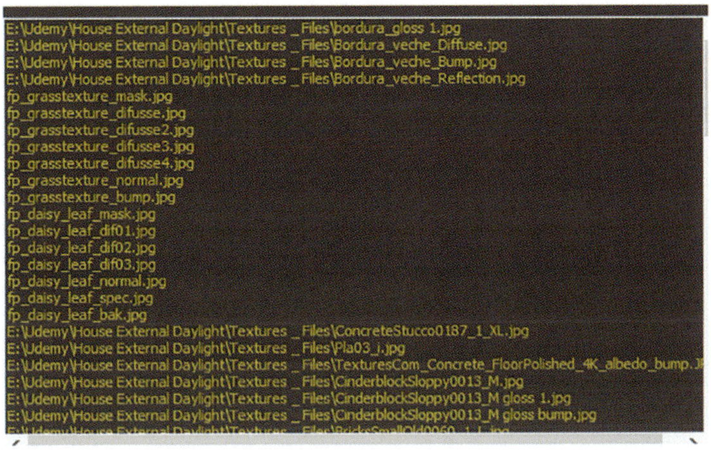

A dialog with a long list of missing files

To repath the missing files, simply click on the Browse button and find the folder named, Maps.

Folder named, Maps

Missing external files dialog with Browse Button highlighted

If there are still few missing files in the dialog list, simply ignore them and choose the option to, Continue. You can also choose the option to, Don't Display This Message at Render Time.

1 Using Resource Files

Clients, Projects, Pre-Production, Production and Post-Production Overview

This chapter introduces users to some of the best techniques to approach clients via emails, calls, meetings and social media.

In addition, it also provides valuable industry insights into handling projects, pricing, contracts, invoices, pre-production, production, rendering and post-production.

Approaching Clients

Emails

"Cold emails" are one of the best ways to fish for clients, when executed properly.

There's a higher chance of your emails being opened and read when you do the following:

- Ensure the subject of your email starts with "RE...."
  Email recipients are more likely to open such types of emails because the "RE" implies it is a reply of an existing conversation.
- As a sender, never use generic email addresses such as info@... and contact@....
  Email recipients are more inclined to open personalized email addresses such as jamiec@... and jamie.cardoso@..., because such email accounts do not come across as spams or as "mass emails".

Also, servers are less likely to automatically send your emails to the "junk" box.

- Prior to sending an email, ensure to send it to someone's personal email address; as opposed to general/public email addresses such as info@... and contact@....
  General/public email addresses tend to be ignored as they come across as unsolicited.
  However, it is worth noting that very small companies (1–5 employees) tend to open unsolicited emails.
  Otherwise, it is always best to address emails to specific individuals at companies. Especially those involved in marketing and communications (e.g., mary.eugene@arcthitects.com).

- Always start an email with "Dear" (e.g., Dear Jane), followed by a "Hi" emoji ().

This will also increase the chances of your email being opened. Especially on a mobile phone.

- Start by wishing the recipient well and in good health.
- Quickly introduce yourself and your firm's specialty.
- Embed compelling images (maximum of four) into your email, and include a link to your website and/or portfolio.

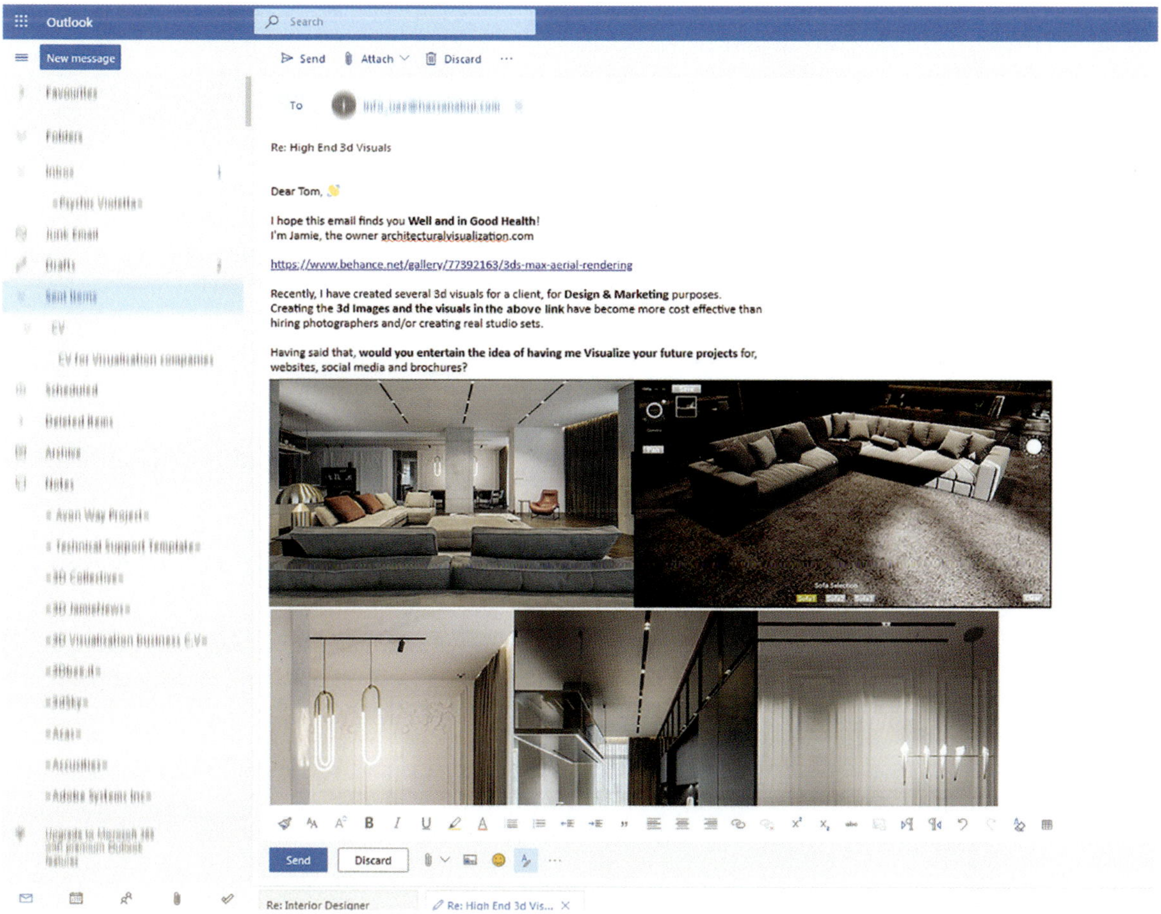

A sample email with text, a link and embedded images

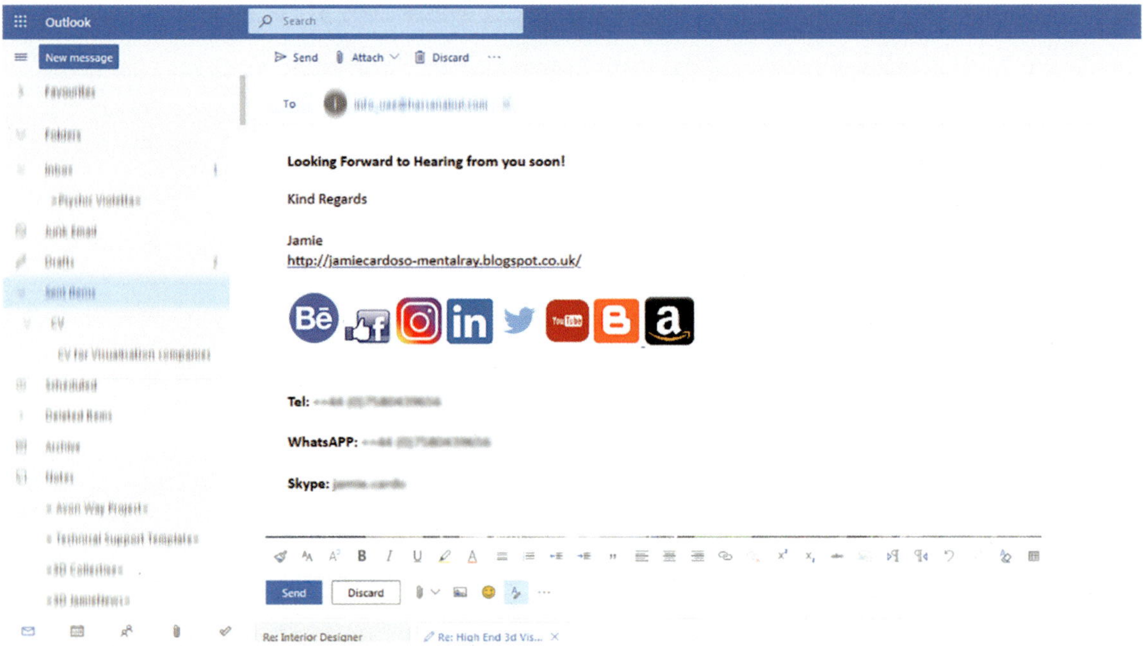

Email signature with a name, web link, telephone number, WhatsApp, Skype and social media logos

To find key email addresses at companies, first visit their websites.

It's often under, https://architect.com/people/

https://architect.com/aboutus/people

https://architect.com/studio/people

If perchance you cannot find any relevant email addresses from their website, simply use the website https://hunter.io/.

This service allows users to find personal email addresses of employees of a company by simply copying and pasting a website's URL into its search box (e.g., https://architect.com).

It also allows users to work out an individual's email address (if not publicly available) by seeing how a company's emails are formatted (e.g., jcardoso@ architects.co.uk).

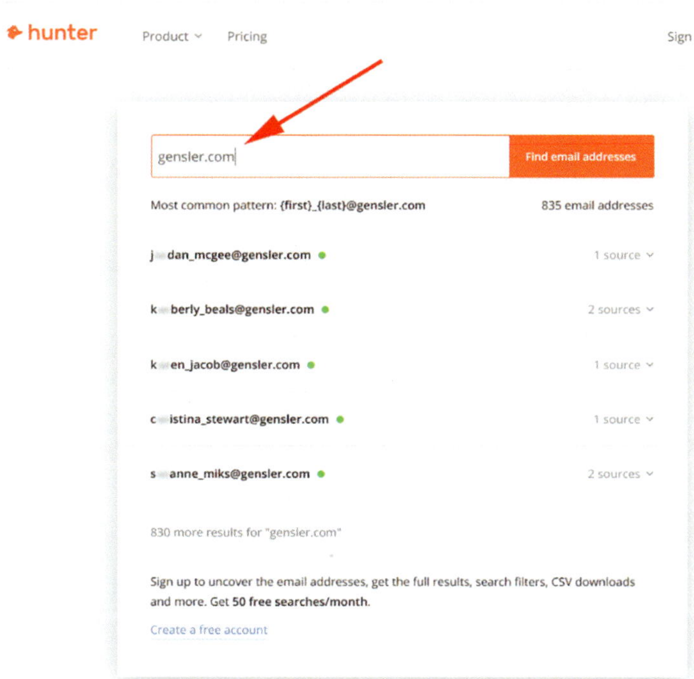

Email hunter web page

Calls

It is often best to communicate via email/messaging to keep a record of everything.

However, some clients also like to engage via phone calls using WhatsApp, Skype, Zoom or messenger.

Note book with written notes and a pen

Such clients find it quicker and easier to lay out their ideas using the above-mentioned mediums of communication.

Having said that, always keep a note of key instructions/requests during conversations.

1 Using Resource Files

Meeting the Client

There are times when you might be invited to meet a client at their office, or vice versa.

Depending on what you intend to showcase (e.g., images, animations), tablets are one of the most useful devices for meetings.

Google Chromecast devices can also be used in conjunction with your phone or tablet to cast content to a TV screen.

Three computer tablets

Chromecast electronic device

If it is VR content (virtual reality), then you need at least two headsets and a laptop to launch the content from.

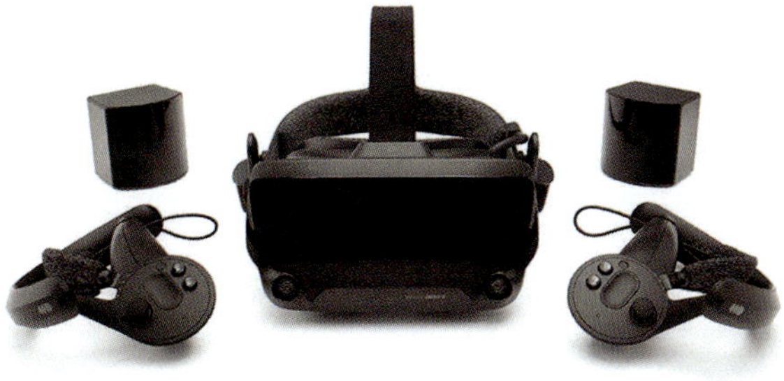

A virtual reality headset

In terms of dress codes, dressing casually smart works perfectly for most office environments.

Smart casual is a dress code that comprises well-fitting, neat, and appropriate pieces that are slightly less formal than a business casual or business professional dress code. However, smart casual is much more elevated than dressing for off-hours (casual or loose-fitting).

For more information about how to dress casually smart, simply Google: smart casual.

- First-time meetings are often set to evaluate personalities and to reassure expertise.
- When visiting a client, always turn up at least 10 minutes before the agreed time.
- Punctually convey respect toward the client and your organizational skills.
- Always start by introducing yourself with a smile and a handshake (if you are not social distancing).
- If offered a drink, always accept it by saying, "Yes, please; thank you". People often offer you a drink to be cordial and to make you feel comfortable on their premises.
- It is also a good opportunity to smile and engage in a quick conversation.
- Instead of delving into a work-related conversation immediately, start by saying something humorous about the weather or something humorous about your journey to their office. Or simply mention something complementary about your client's office.
- Most clients tend to remember/appreciate people that are respectfully humorous about themselves, and complementary toward the client.
- While discussing the project and receiving instructions from a client, always take notes throughout.

- Taking notes is a great way of showing you are listening and acknowledging them.
- While engaging in discussions, make humble suggestions when appropriate, to showcase your expertise and problem-solving skills.
- Furthermore, once the project discussions are over, try to leave the office in a similar way how you started; by saying something humorous (e.g., about the weather or your journey), followed by a handshake and stating how great it was to meet them.
- Finally, once you have repeated the above steps a few times (through trial and errors), you will gradually become better and better at it.

Emails/Newsletter

It is good practice to send your clients' newsletter emails periodically (once a month), about projects you have recently finished, and new Video/Blog posts.

Clients are easily persuaded and distracted by new competitors and recommendations by colleagues.

Your monthly emails will help remind your clients of your relationship with them and your expertise in the field.

Newsletter with a red banner and embedded images describing each project

Social Media and Forums

Having a strong social media presence will help remind your clients of your relevance and expose your work to potential new clients.

When it comes to social media, users and clients often have a very short attention span.

To stay on their radar, try to post relevant content as often as you possibly can (once or few times a week, if possible).

Some of the best social media platforms to showcase your work are:

LinkedIn

Instagram

Pinterest

https://archinect.com/forum

https://www.skyscrapercity.com/forums/architecture.4/

https://www.behance.net/

YouTube

When posting content, always use popular titles such as:

3d, 3d rendering, 3d visualization, 3d visualizer, 3ds max, architectural rendering, interior design rendering and 3d architectural visualization.

And hashtags such as:

#3dvisualization #3drendering #3d #architecturalvisualization #render #archviz #digitalart #illustration #rendering #illustrator #3dartist #3drender #renders #archdaily #architecturedesign #architecture #photoshop #architect #renderings #autodesk #autocad #rendered #design #scene #modelling #rendering3d #realestate

To have a better insight into the words your clients often search to find your type of services, use sophisticated tools such as Google ads keyword plan.

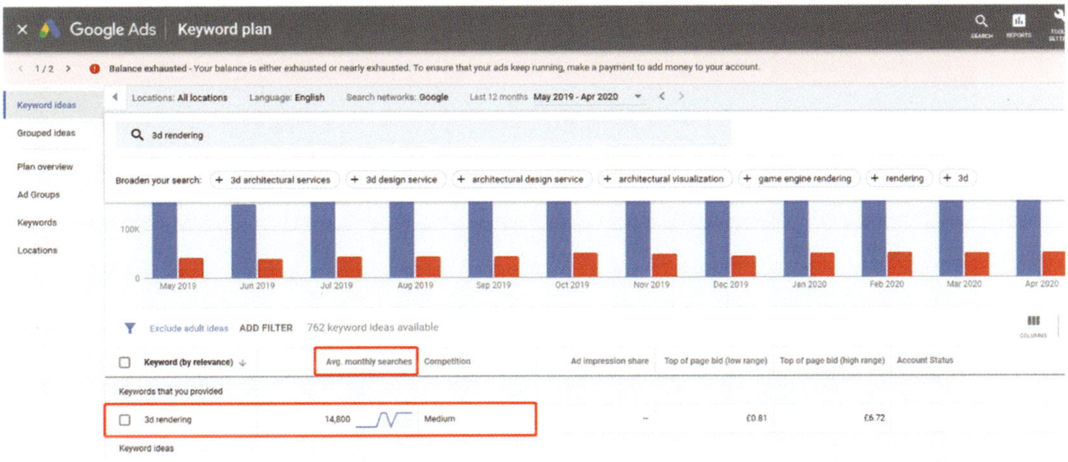

Google ads keyword plan with graphs and text

Finally, if you are looking to showcase your work to other visualization companies and 3d artists, you can post them on websites such as evermotion.org, cgarchitect.com and artstation.com.

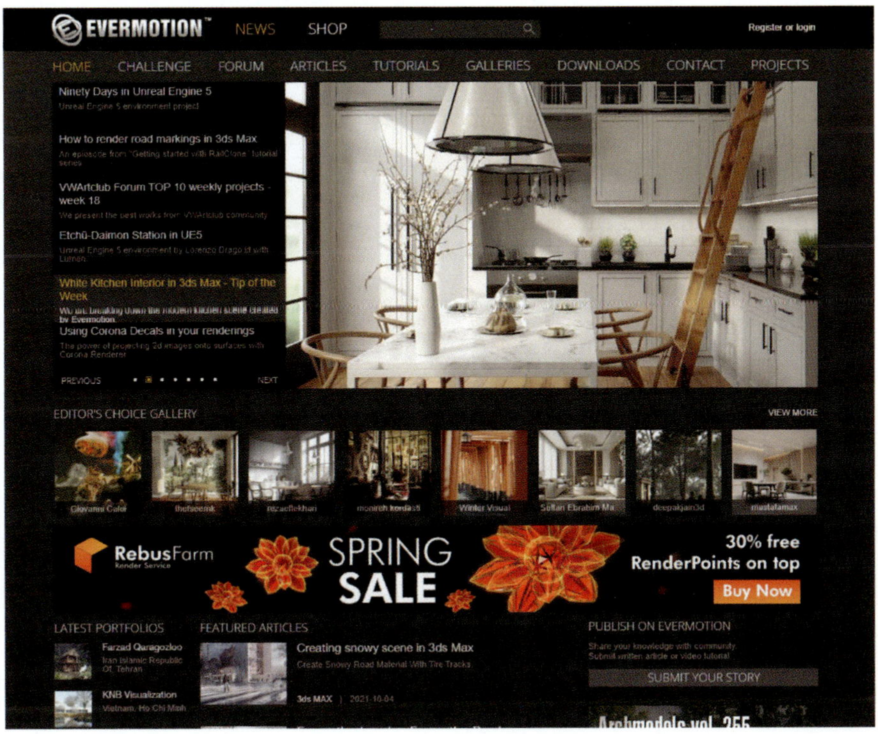

Evermotion website with images and text

1 Using Resource Files

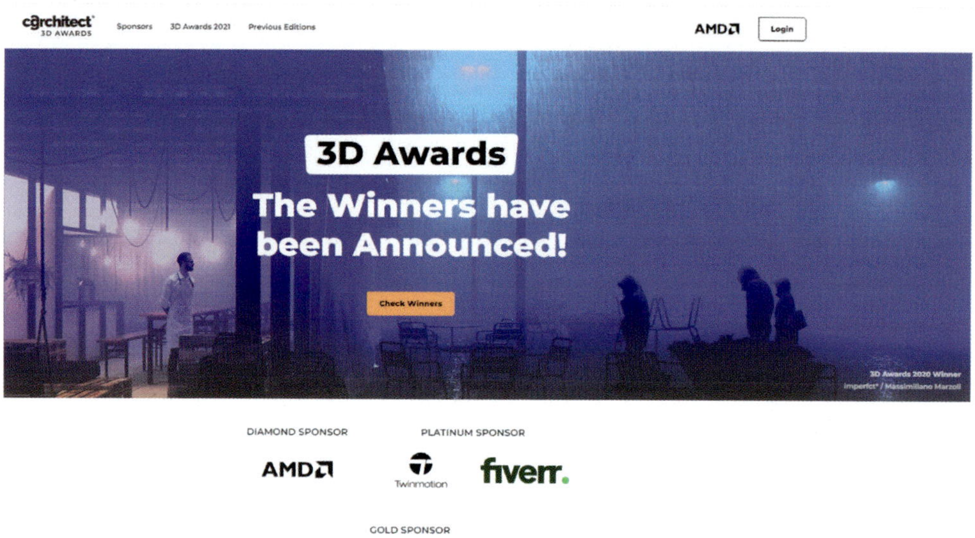

CG architect website with images and text

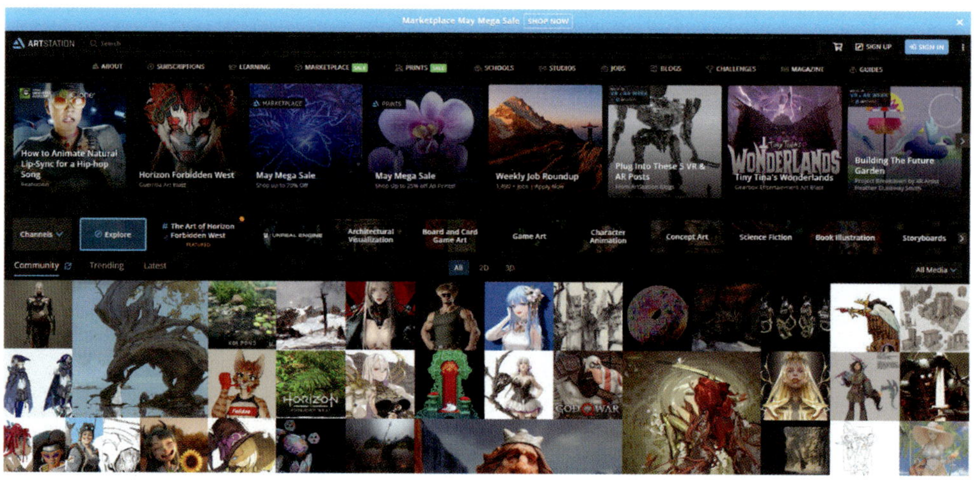

Artstation website with images and text

Projects

Most potential projects will start with a client sending you an email with the overall brief, drawings, mood boards, deliverables and deadlines.

In this first case scenario, you are expected to quickly go through the entire information pack provided, ask questions and come up with the final quotation.

There are also times when all you have are drawings/PDFs.

In such cases, you'll be left with the task of creating mood boards/art direction, ask questions, etc.

Before providing the final quotation, you should do the following:

- Check the drawings and/or the 3d models thoroughly prior to committing to the final budget and deadline.

AutoCAD with a dwg drawing

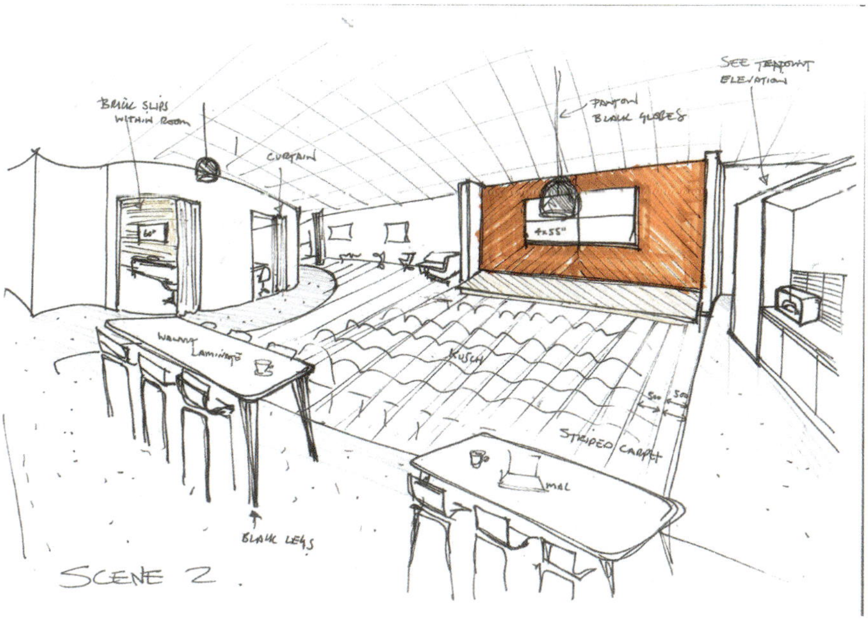

Hand-drawn sketches of an office space

1 Using Resource Files

Upon receiving the drawings/model from a client, it is utterly important to ensure assets are not riddled with artifacts or incomplete (e.g., missing textures, drawings).

Failing to do so may inevitably affect the original budget and the final deadline.

- With the client's help, mark up one or more camera positions that will help capture some of the most complementary parts of the space/design.

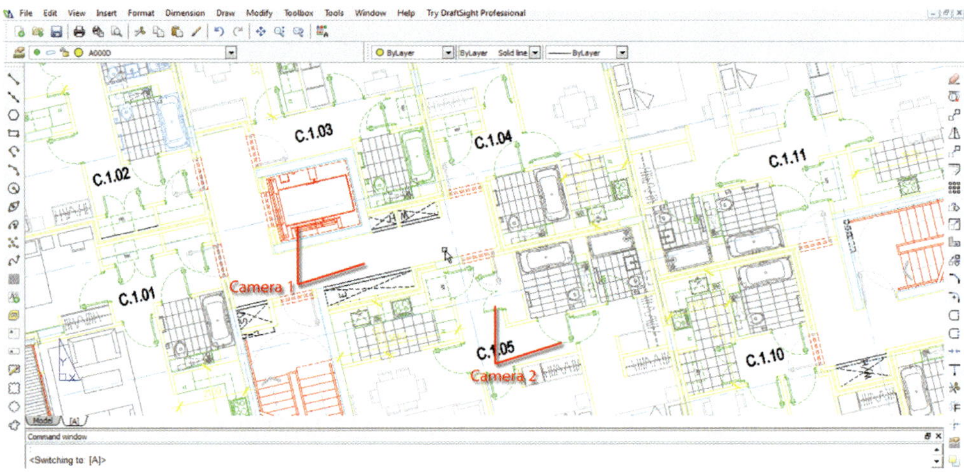

Dwg drawing with mark-ups of camera positions

During the process of marking up camera positions with the client, gather as much information as possible about furniture, mood boards, etc.

This will help you pre-visualize camera compositions, lighting, colors, 3d assets, etc.

Camera positions will help you forecast the amount of time involved in creating the space and its content.

- Once the above steps have been ironed out, the budget and the project deadline can be set.

The best way to manage clients' expectations is for artists/companies to be honest with themselves on matters of expertise, speed and available resources.

Nowadays, clients expect quicker turnarounds, higher quality and lower prices.

The lesser the time you spend on a project, the bigger the profit margins.

To help achieve this, only model the essentials such as drawings and bespoke furniture unavailable for download.

Otherwise, it is common practice to download ready-to-render 3d models/assets with shaders and textures from manufacturers' websites, evermotion, 3sky, TURBOSQUID, *anima*®, VIShopper, AccuCities, etc.

Some of these ready-to-render 3d assets are free, and most of them may cost as little as $6.00 each.

Convex Lighting Series

Made from London Plane and polished Copper Tube these bespoke light have great Utility chic! As featured in The Sunday Times. Designed to be used with an exposed antique bulb.

Dimensions

Mini 20 cm x 20 cm x 25 cm High

Small 20 cm x 20cm x 30 cm High

Large 20 cm x 20cm x 40 cm High

Available to buy from £100.00 each. This price is only available with London Plane base and Copper Arm. This item is Customisable.

Different timbers are available but will increase the price. Bulb not included.

INQUIRE NOW

How to order

You can order via contacting us directly. We have found it's easier for customers to contact us on a personalised basis due to bespoke nature of our orders. Contact us today via email or telephone if you are ready to order or have any questions. We are available to chat Monday to Friday 09:00 - 18:00

Customisable options

Colour:

We powder coat most of our furniture using the available RAL Classic Range colours, however, more specialist colours in the RAL Design range are available but can be expensive. Let us know what colour you have in mind and we can advise.

Material:

Most of our handmade furniture is made with Mild Steel tube which is powder coated. If you are after outside furniture we highly recommend using aluminum which is more expensive but weather resistant.

Explore our material library.

Dimensions:

Dimensions are as advertised but due to the nature of handmade products they can vary +/- 5 percent. If you want a higher stool to match a specific bar height we can accommodate this.

Lead times

We hold a small amount of stock of our best sellers which makes it quick to dispatch to customers but generally we ask for 3-4 weeks for orders to be fulfilled.

Delivery

Is charged extra we ship via courier and the price is worked out once your order has been placed. This allows us to account for creating or palletising the furniture for protection.

Web page depicting Convex Lighting Series

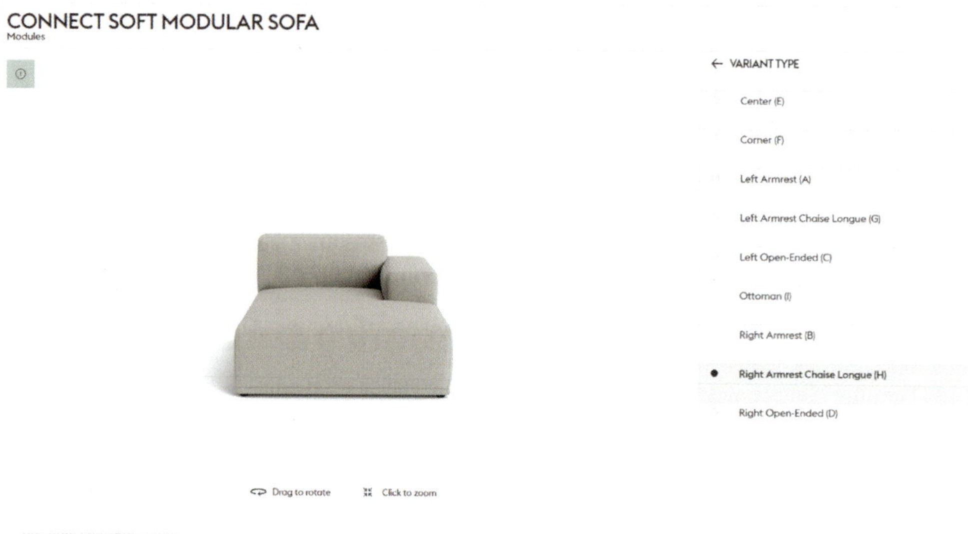

Web page depicting a modular sofa

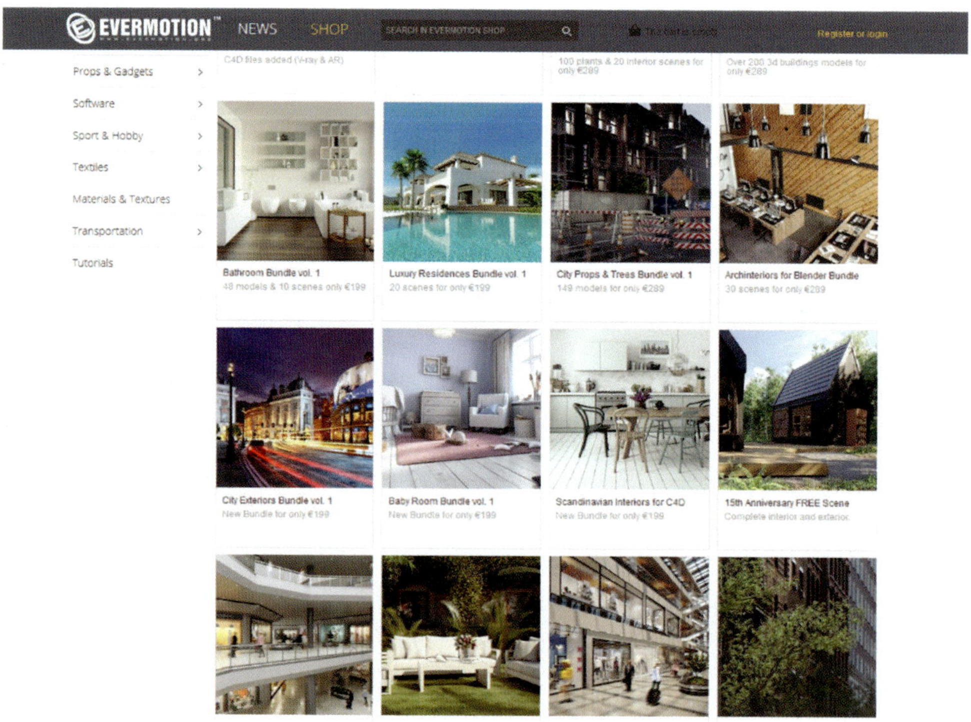

Evermotion website depicting a list of exquisite 3d scenes to purchase

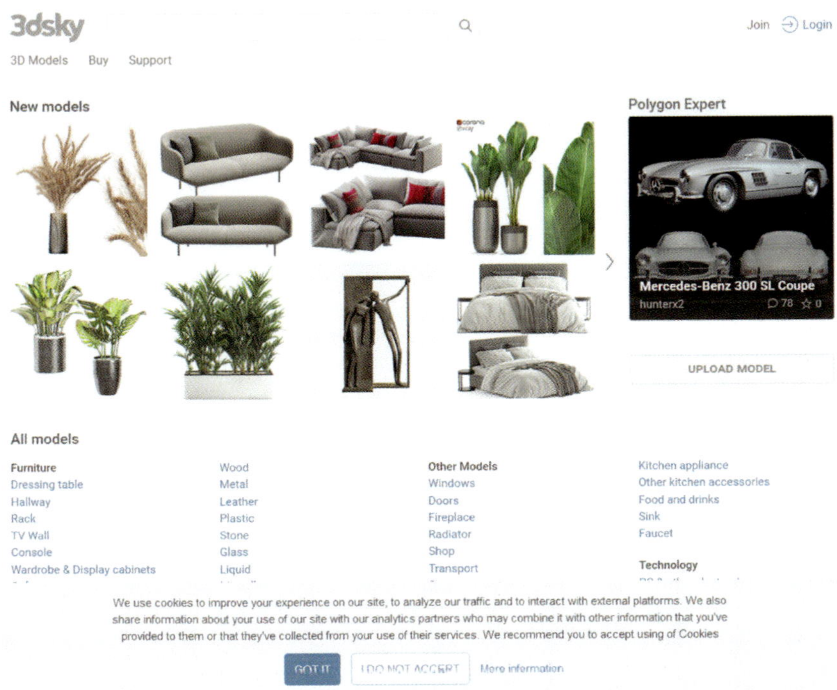

3dsky website depicting a list of detailed 3d models to purchase

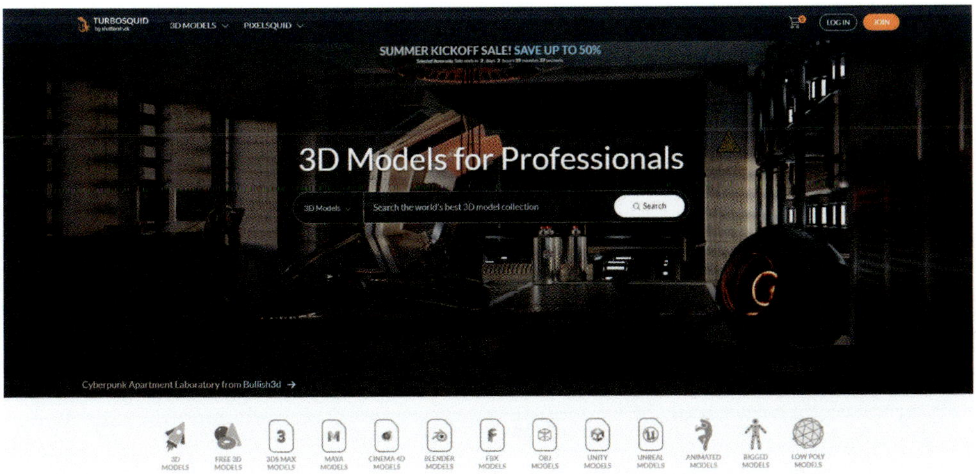

Turbosquid website showcasing 3d models to purchase

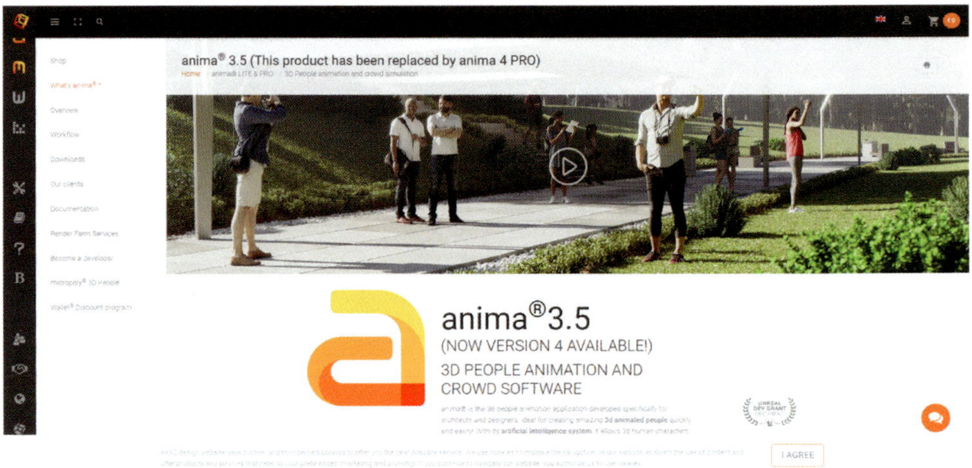

anima® website

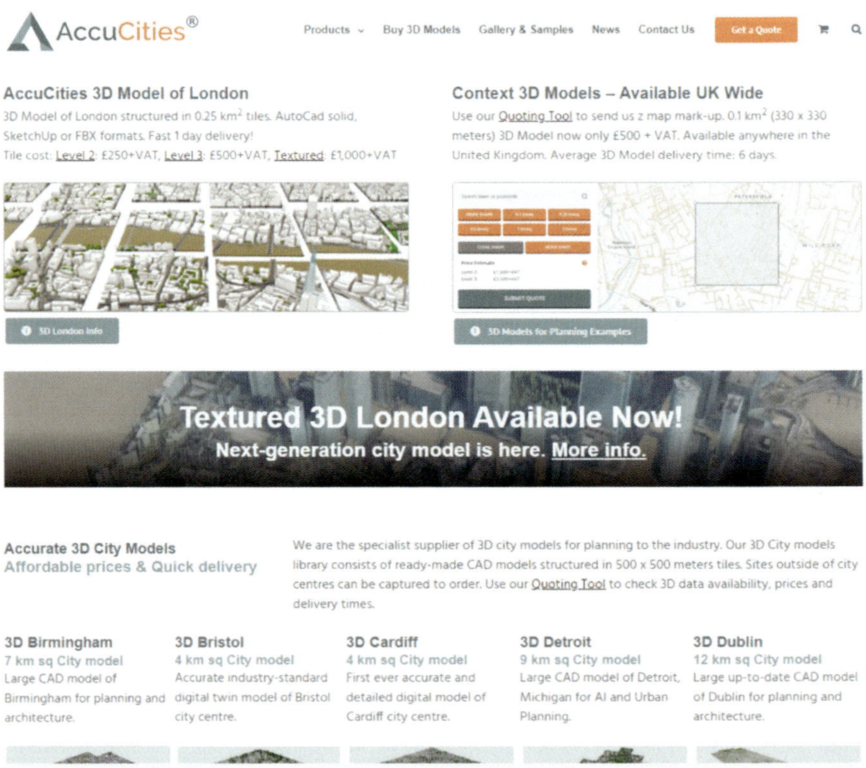

AccuCities website depicting their context city models services

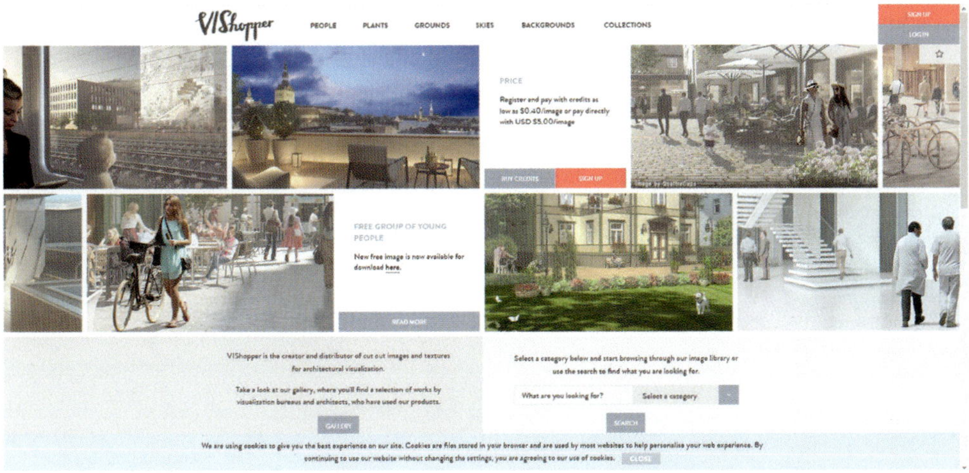

VIShopper website depicting 2d assets

Pricing Projects

The pricing of a project is always based on an hourly rate of one person or the number of days required to finish a project by one person (hence the term, man-days/hours).

Daily rates often start from as little as $150 to $700 (8 hours/day).

To avoid pricing yourself out of the market, simply visit a useful website called, Salary Expert:

https://www.salaryexpert.com/salary/browse/countries/3d-artist

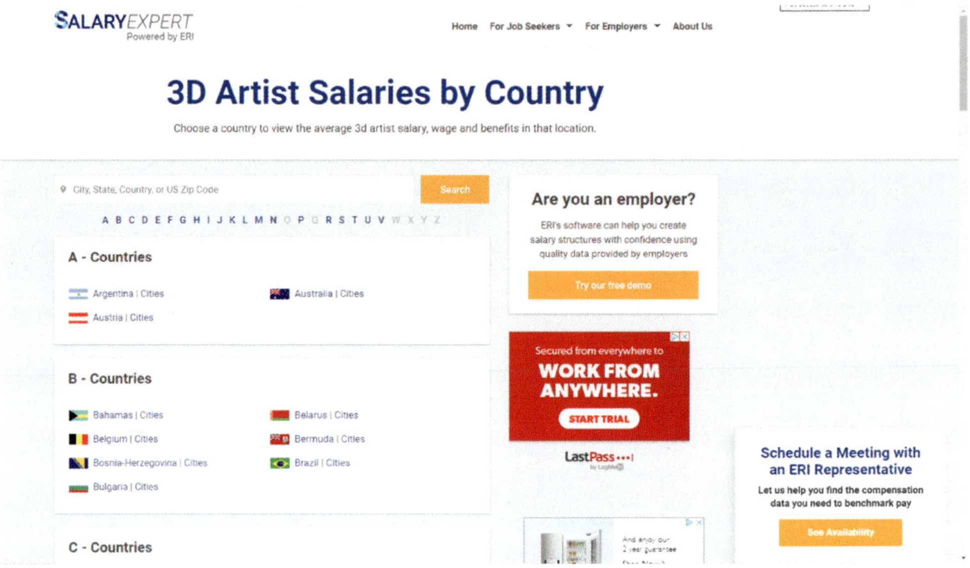

salaryexpert.com website depicting 3D Artist Salaries by Country

To quickly work out the day rate of an experienced freelancer, simply divide a 3d artist's annual salary by 52 (number of weeks in 1 year), followed by dividing the result by 5 (number of days in 1 week).

I.E: UK £50.000÷52=£961.00÷5=£192.00

So the average daily rate for experienced freelancers in the UK should be around £192.00. There are always exceptions where some freelancers may charge slightly more (£250.00–£700.00 per day).

If it is an ongoing contract with a company (longer than 5 days), some freelancers tend to reduce their prices down to £150.00 per day to make it feasible for clients to keep them for months at a time.

If you are approaching clients as a solid company with an office and overheads, then you need to always multiply your day rate by 2, at least.

Alternatively, as a company, to make it feasible to clients, set the project with a fixed price (e.g., normal day rate multiplied by 2 or more) based on the following guidelines:

- For instance, if it takes 6 months for one person to finish a project, but the client wants it delivered within 30 days, one would normally price it as if it were one person working for 6 months, followed by working out the number of people and resources necessary to finish the same project in 30 days.
- To work out the final budget, companies/artists also factor in the cost of hiring freelancers (if necessary), usage of render farms, and 2d and 3d assets.

chaos.com/cloud is currently the best, reliable and the cheapest render farm in the market.

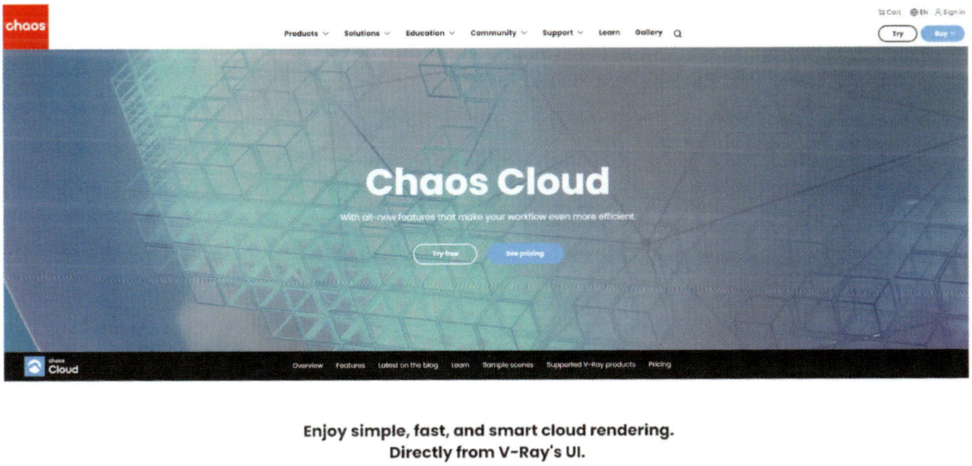

Chaos Cloud website

To display products on a standard web browser, many reputable companies use WebRotate 360 Product Viewer and its plugins. It is a standalone publishing software by WebRotate 360 for Windows and Mac that is capable of creating highly engaging 360-degree and multirow "3D" product presentations with interactive hotspots. Users can upload the media to optional web hosting provided by WebRotate 360 or their own servers, or even use it offline. For more information, please check their brochure in the book resources folders and their website at www.webrotate360.com.

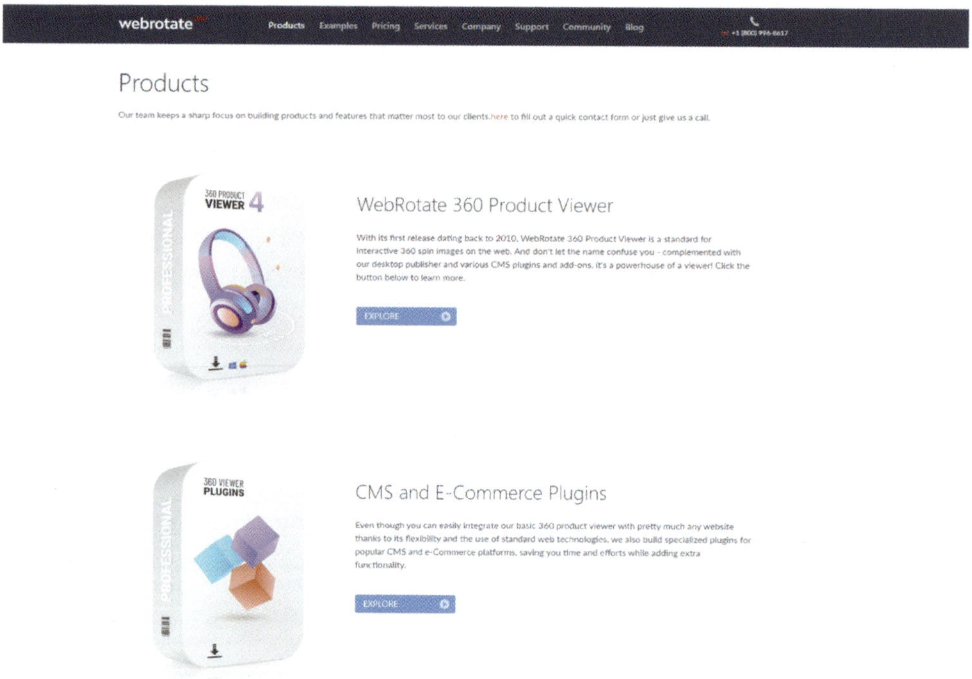

webrotate360

Since clients often insist on negotiating prices down, it is always best way to start with a higher price in order to be able to negotiate down to something more reasonable and sustainable for both parties.

Furthermore, the final deadline and budget should also reflect potential revisions throughout the project.

It is standard practise to accept two different sets of revisions per camera view, as long as they do not deviate from the original brief; otherwise, it is subject to additional costs (this should also be highlighted in the contract).

Finally, the user should always try to persuade the client (politely) to be more prompt and decisive with general comments and feedback in order to help meet the deadline and stay on budget.

There are instances when clients expect artists/companies to aid them with their design concepts and color decisions (mostly interior designers). In such exceptional cases, one should try not to have a fixed budget and deadline (if possible), as costs may rise exponentially!

Instead, try to work out a day rate.

Contracts

Contracts should always include the following terms and conditions:

1. Project description
2. Deliverables
3. Deadline
4. Comments
5. Fees
6. Acceptance
7. Application
8. Obligations
9. Definitions
10. Cost and expenses
11. Cancelations, weather, postponements
12. Intellectual property rights and release
13. Payment stages
14. Confidential information
15. Liabilities
16. General

The resource files should include an example of what a standard contract should look like.

Company Logo

QUOTE 145.5

Client Name

MOE RE-DEVELOPMENT

ANIMATION FILM

Standard contract cover with text, graphics and logo placeholder

QUOTE

Estimate Description: To create a high quality animation film capturing the essence and excitement surround construction and design.

Description	Quantity	Rate		Line Total
Animation Days	60	350		21000
Render Farm	1	3000		3000
Assets/Music/Software	1	1000		1000

Discount
Excl VAT 25000
20% VAT 5000
TOTAL 30000.00

Deliverables: A 2-2.5 minute animation rendered in HD, delivered in MP4 via Dropbox, Vimeo or ReviewStudio. With the following licensing to be conveyed to **your comapany**
Publicity, and Collateral for 1 film, in perpetuity.

Deadline: Film will be delivered by 31st May 2018 (4 weeks turnaround).

Comments: The entire project will be divided into three separate phases:

Phase 1: Create an animatic (a very draft screen preview) of the entire film, as described in your word document named " **Storyboard** ".
The sole purpose of the full animatic is to depict the pace of, 3d cameras/characters; storyline; and the full content/composition of the animation.
We will also provide you with up to 10 fully rendered frames (of your choice) along the animation path, to illustrate the final quality

Company Logo

3d Visual

Standard contract quote depicting project costs, deadline, etc.

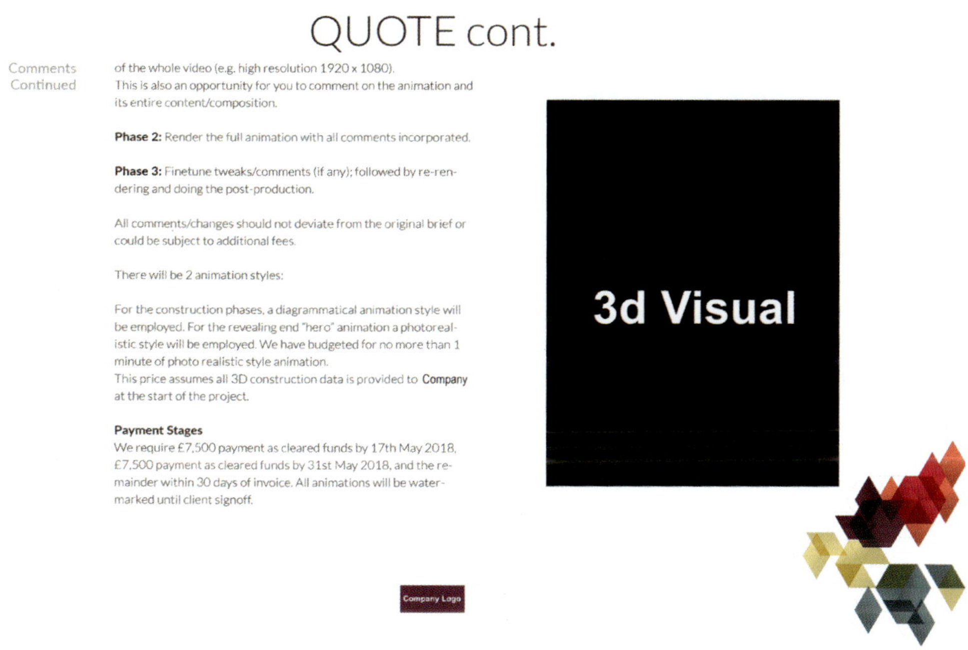

QUOTE cont.

Comments Continued

of the whole video (e.g. high resolution 1920 x 1080).
This is also an opportunity for you to comment on the animation and its entire content/composition.

Phase 2: Render the full animation with all comments incorporated.

Phase 3: Finetune tweaks/comments (if any); followed by re-rendering and doing the post-production.

All comments/changes should not deviate from the original brief or could be subject to additional fees.

There will be 2 animation styles:

For the construction phases, a diagrammatical animation style will be employed. For the revealing end "hero" animation a photorealistic style will be employed. We have budgeted for no more than 1 minute of photo realistic style animation.
This price assumes all 3D construction data is provided to **Company** at the start of the project.

Payment Stages
We require £7,500 payment as cleared funds by 17th May 2018, £7,500 payment as cleared funds by 31st May 2018, and the remainder within 30 days of invoice. All animations will be watermarked until client signoff.

Standard contract quote depicting continuation of the previous page

Invoices

Invoices should include the following details:

1. Project description
2. Days/rates
3. Total fee
4. Invoice number and date
5. Your company and client's name
6. Your company and client's address
7. Your company and client's Vat number
8. Your company's bank or PayPal details

The resource files should include an example of what a standard invoice should look like.

To be in good graces of the client, as a sign of good gesture, try to provide extra/complementary visuals (if possible), and be flexible with late payments.

Having said that, as mentioned in the contract, always have a watermark on your 3d visuals until the final payment is cleared.

The resource files should include an example of what a standard invoice should look like.

DESCRIPTION	DAYS	RATE
	10	$xxxx
Create three Interior 3d Visualisations for, **ArchViz ltd**		
		Total $5250.00

INVOICE 2020 No: 0001 Date: 25-May-2020

Company ltd	**Bill to:**
Company number: xxxxxxx Vat number: xxxxxxx	Client's Name Address Website Vat number
Paypal: xxxxxx@hotmail.com	
BANK: Name Account No: xxxxxxxx	
Sort Code: xxxxxx	
IBAN: xxxxxxxxxxxxxx	
BIC : xxxxxxxx	
BANK address: xxxxxxxx	

Standard Invoice depicting project days, description, company details, total costs, etc.

Pre-Production

The pre-production phase is often used as a stepping stone to all the subsequent steps such as production and post-production.

Once all of the above-mentioned options have been taken into consideration, and there is a mutual agreement on the time and budget, the user can begin discussing matters regarding the art direction, if not previously addressed.

During this process, the user and/or the client should begin creating digital mood boards depicting suggestions about the color of the artificial lights, natural light color, time of the day, light effects, camera angles, camera effects, overall color/feel, etc.

The images/photos should resemble the 3 render/s one is trying to create. These similarities should be in the composition, time of the day and colors.

Also, the proposed photo references should be striking enough to convince the client or/and the art director.

Camera & Lighting ideas

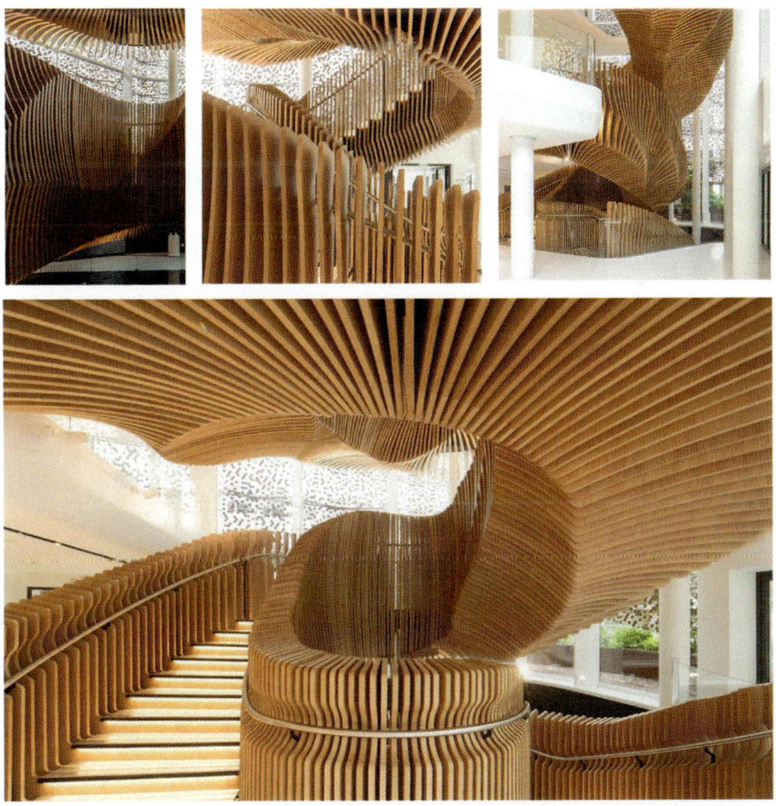

Mood board with composition ideas, lighting and camera angles

The 3d viewport scene composition depicting the parametric staircase

A final 3d render depicting the parametric staircase

A really good resource for online photo references is a website called:

https://www.behance.net/search?search=architecture

https://www.pinterest.com/

https://thecoolhunter.net/category/architecture/

https://www.archdaily.com/

https://www.dezeen.com/

https://www.architecturaldigest.com/

It is also common for clients to have their own set of photos as a guide and/or source of inspiration.

As mentioned earlier, this process usually takes few hours or days, depending on the client, budget or the project in question.

It is worth noting that most of the above-mentioned steps are usually adopted by companies/users commissioned to produce compelling "Hero shots" for marketing/campaign purposes.

However, if one is working in a fast-paced environment, whereby users are expected to model 3D scenes from scratch and create multiple camera renders on a daily basis, then some of the pre-production steps such as art direction might be impossible due to time constraints.

However, in such instances, users can still guide themselves through their own selection of private photo references/images while using their own artistic license and trained eyes to produce the expected images and "manage" the client's expectations.

NOTE

Most of the topics in this section and the next will be discussed in greater detail in later chapters.

Production Overview

The production process is typically the stage where the user begins modeling/ assembling the agreed 3d shots, followed by shading, texturing and rendering the views.

The process consists of the following steps:

1. Create the 3d model from the drawings supplied by the client.

   As mentioned earlier, focus the modeling solely on areas visible to the camera previously signed off.

   It is common practise to create and place cameras half way through the modeling process. Cameras are typically raised to 1.65 m in (average eye level).

   Alternatively, you can create cameras after modeling relevant areas of the scene.

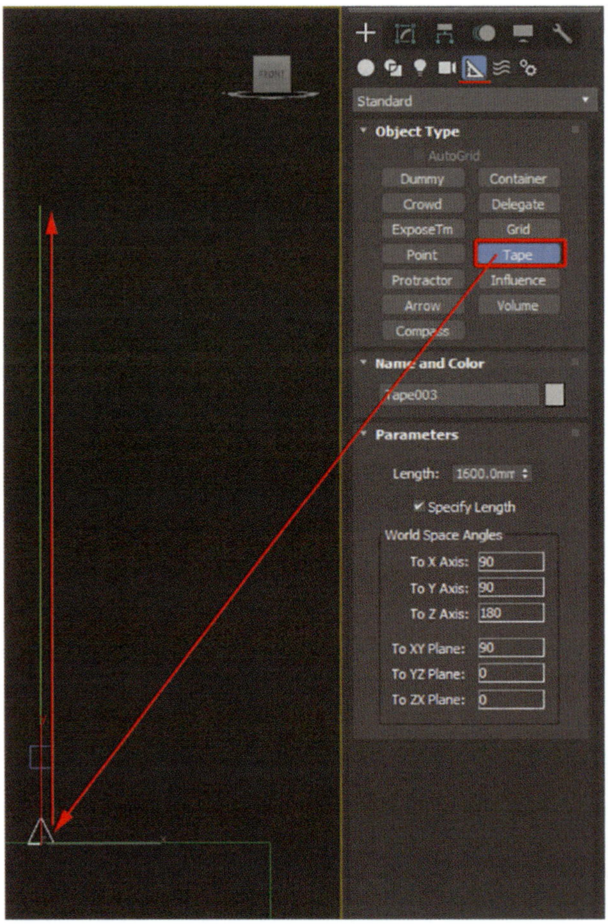

Tape tool being used to measure the height

2. Following that, one can adjust the camera and the composition to make the overall image more appealing.

As mentioned earlier, good photo references are useful guides to make the final renders more interesting.

Next, create/place artificial lights and/or sunlight in the scene to help sign off the camera composition and most of the 3d model.

During this stage, users can produce an appealing chalk render to help "sell/sign off" the chosen view.

Chalk renders consist of a basic white material/texture applied as an override render material.

To produce appealing chalk renders, users often insure that materials such as glass, water, transparent objects, window frames, picture frames, objects with glow, and bump/displacements are not part of the chalk override material/render.

A simple viewport IPR chalk render of the atrium with staircase

Also, the final chalk renders should look interesting in modeling details, well lit and with a good image sampler (antialiasing).

Lighting a scene realistically is one of the most important and crucial parts of the production.

When lighting, the prime focus should be on ensuring there's a clear definition between dark and bright areas in the scene (i.e., depth and contrast).

Most scenes consist of sunlight, ambient/diffused light and interior artificial lights.

The ambient/diffused light/s should always be present in most lit scenes. Sunlight can be recreated with a sunlight object.

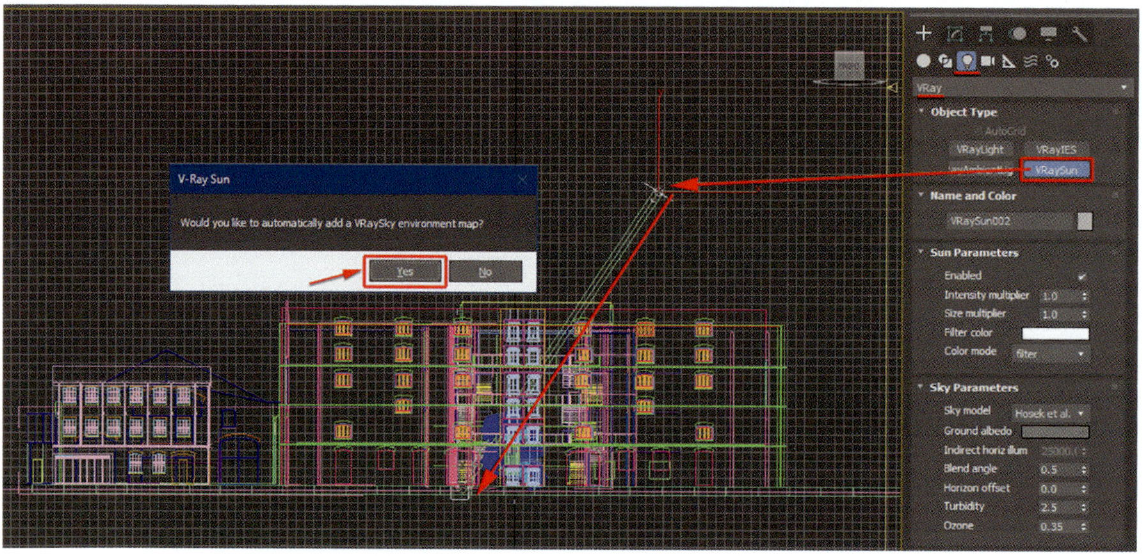

VRaySun object being created with a dialog to add VRaySky environment map

The ambient light is usually reproduced with a dome light and plane lights (for glass windows/openings).

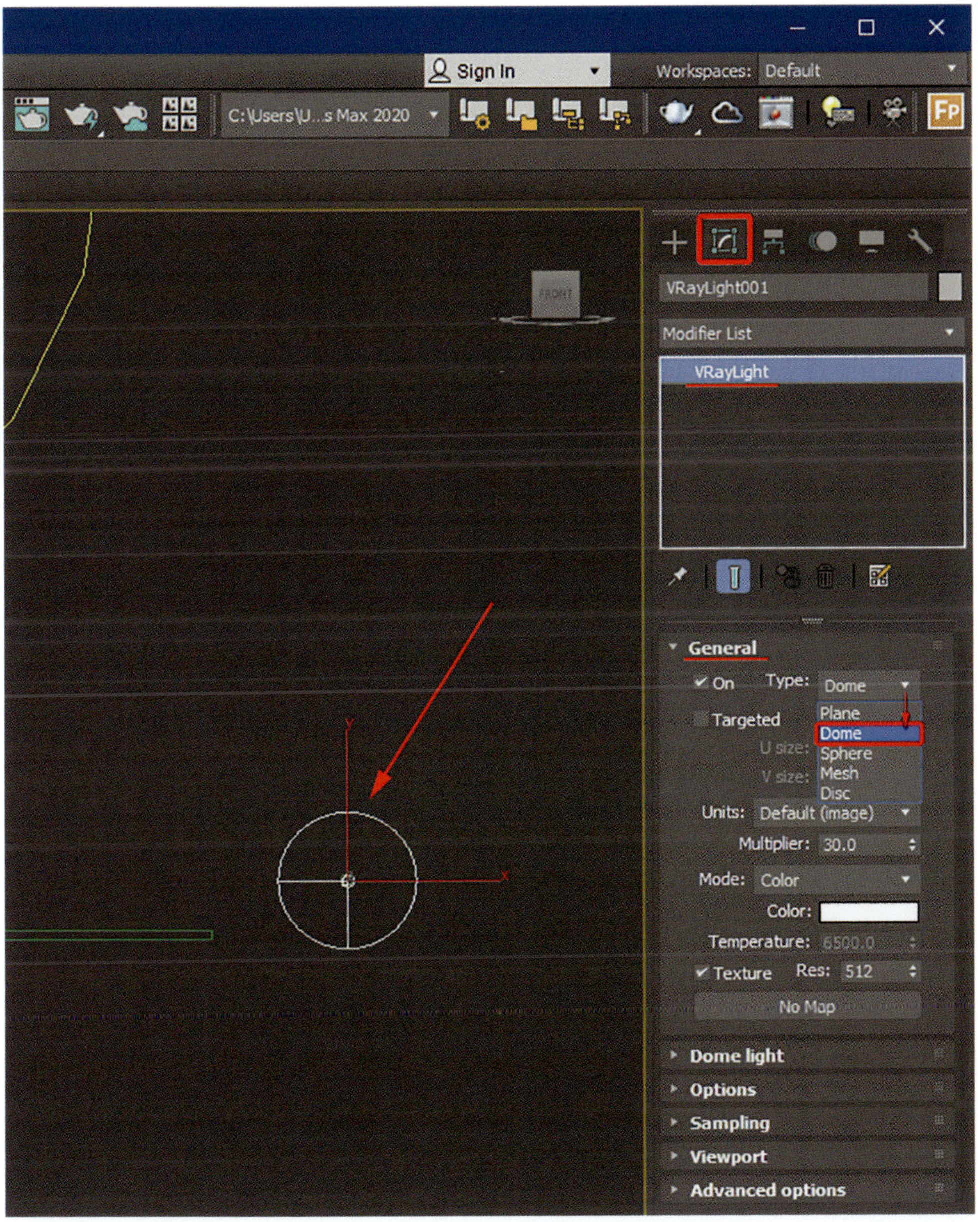

Modify panel with V-Ray dome light type chosen

Some users choose to simply apply a high dynamic range image (HDRI) to the dome texture toggle, to create both direct and indirect lights.

However, it will be challenging to later control these two separate elements in post-production and/or with the LightMix in the Frame Buffer.

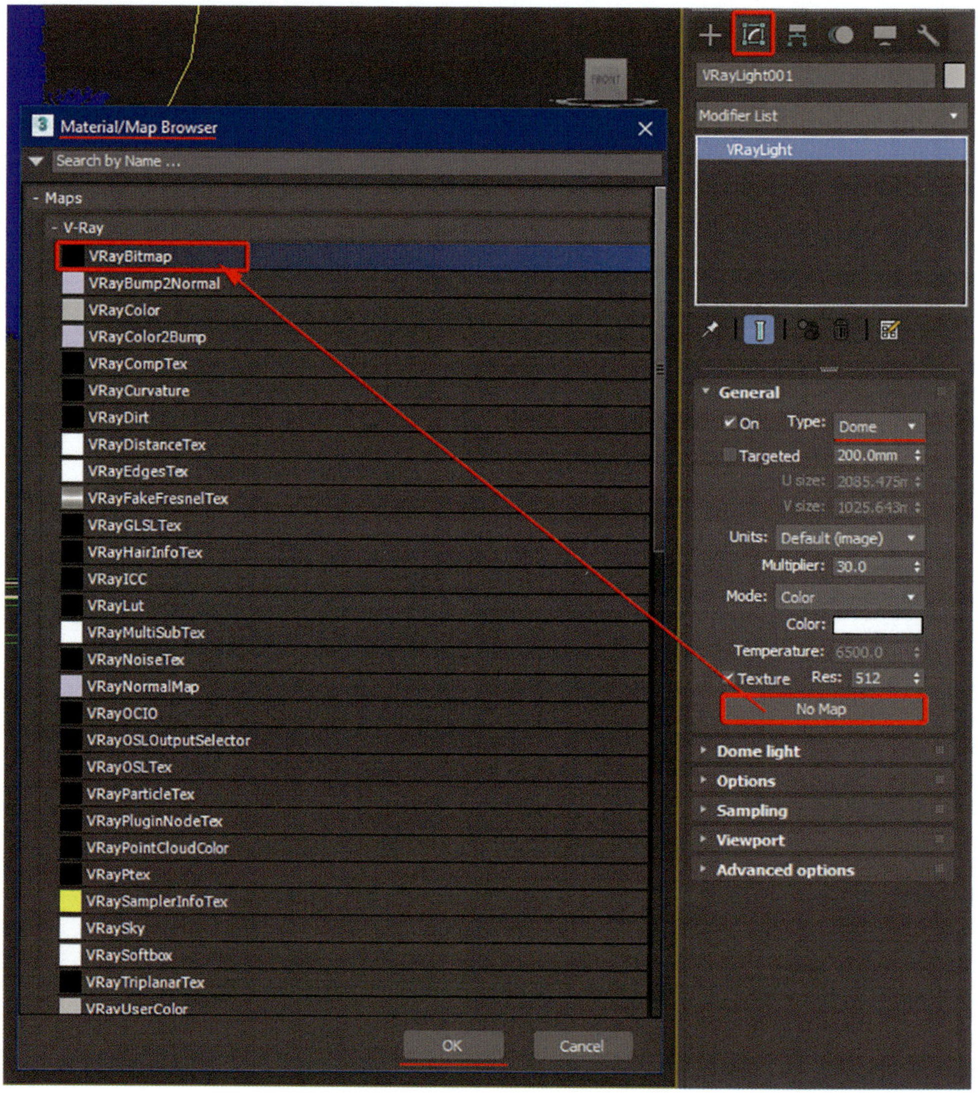

VRayBitmap added to the Texture toggle for HDRI

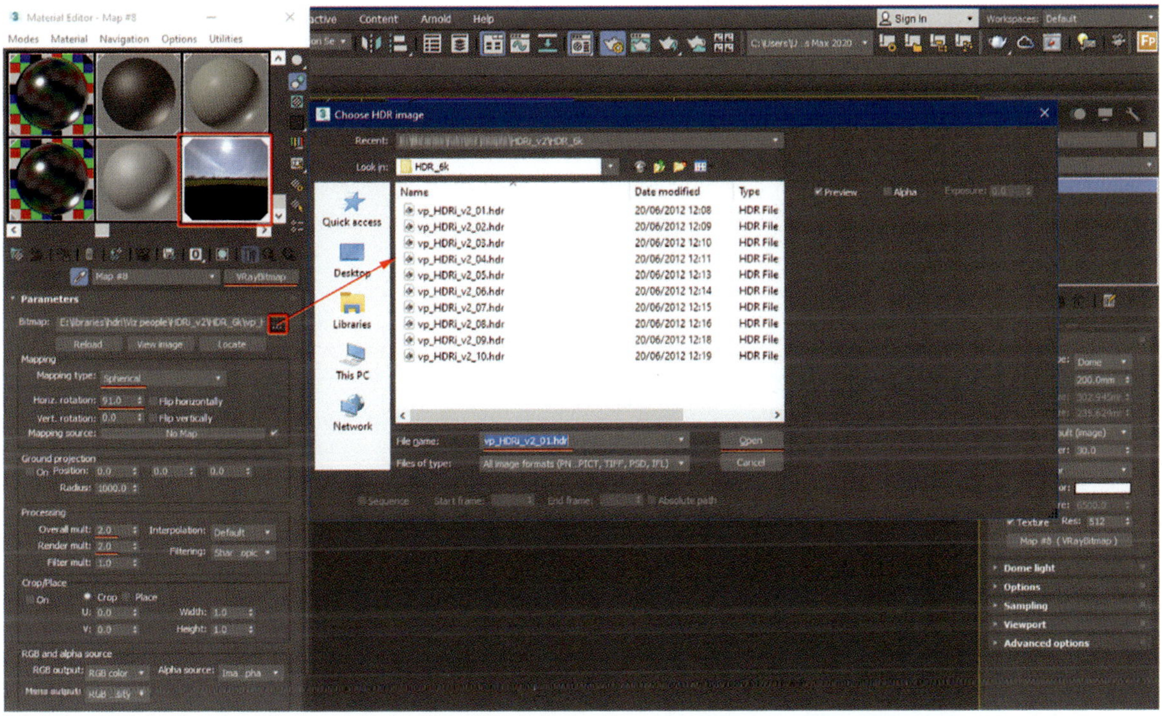

VRayBitmap parameters being used to load the HDRI

1 Using Resource Files

The artificial lights can be recreated with IES photometric lights.

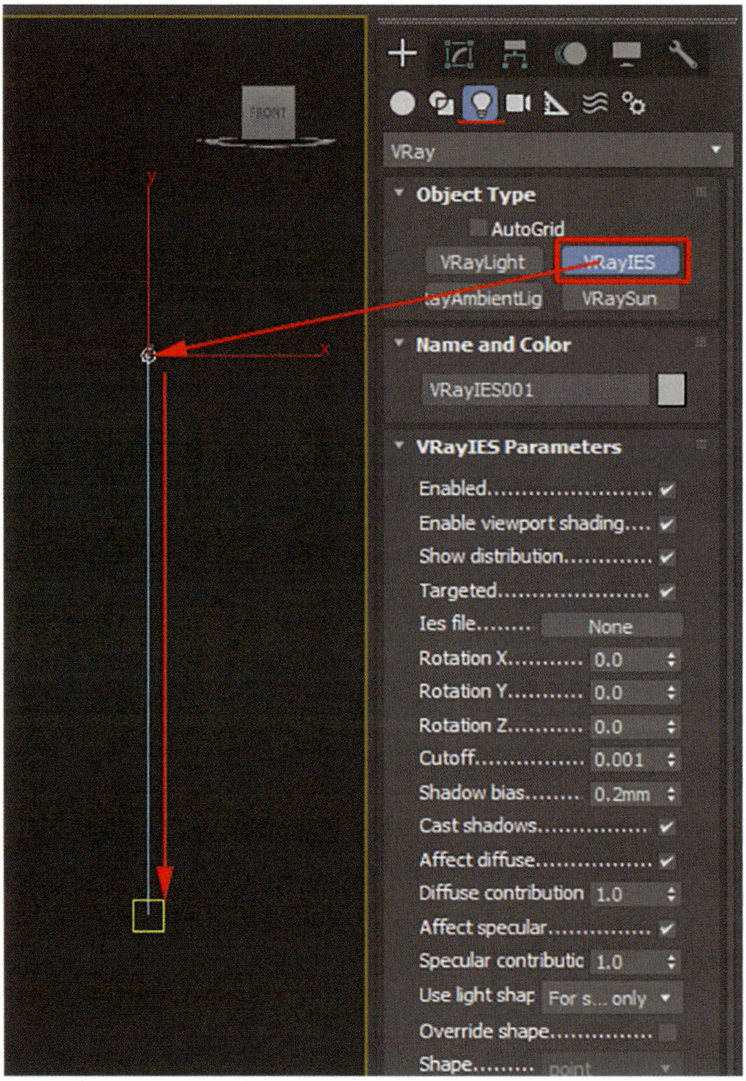

V-Ray IES light being created in the viewport with its target

Always choose Illuminating Engineering Society (IES) web files that cast pools of light, whenever possible.

The 14.IES is widely used to generate such effects and can be found in the book's resource files.

These pools of light will help create details, contrast and depth in the entire scene. In addition, ensure these pools of light don't overlap with each other. To prevent overexposed hot spots generated by the pools of light, simply space each light adequately, followed by test rendering periodically regions of the scene.

To add further light details in the scene, users usually position these lights close to the walls, so that their IES web patterns can be cast onto the walls.

To create more realistic patterns of light, position/rotate some of the lights so that the pools of light are projected in an oblique direction.

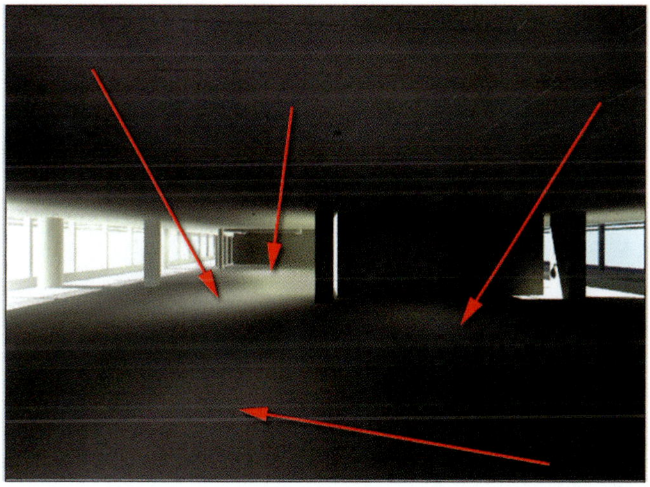

Interior chalk render depicting depth and pools of light

The light colors also play an important role in making a scene look more appealing. Blue and yellow tones are often seen in most striking images/photos.

The yellow light colors usually represent the artificial lights, and the blue colors represent the ambient/diffused light.

The sunlight color is usually white, unless it is sunset.

Before illuminating a scene, one should always determine where the main light source should be coming from.

This is often determined by the chosen camera view and the number of glass windows/openings close to the camera and/or visible in the shot.

The rule of thumb is to always choose the sunlight as the main light source in interior and exterior daylight scenes. In exterior daylight scenes, this choice is always a given.

In interior daylight scenes, one should choose the sunlight as the main light source, only when there are glass windows/openings visible and/or close to the camera view. In such cases, users should have a strong direct/angled sunlight cast onto surfaces, with hints of blue on areas indirectly lit by the ambient/diffused light.

Artificial lights caught in sun-lit areas should be dimmed or switched off, in order for the sunlight to have more prominence.

The indirectly lit areas can have the artificial lights switched on, with the ambient light in the mix.

Final 3d render of a bright interior daylight scene depicting the sun as the main source of light

3d render of an old road with doors and windows, where the bright sun being used as the main source of light

In all other interior daylight scenarios, users frequently choose artificial lights and ambient/diffused light as the main light sources.

When such happens, the sunlight should ideally be casting a direct light, in the distance, so the ambient and artificial lights can have more dominance in the scene.

3d render of a gym, where artificial lights are being used as the main source to light up the scene

In exterior night scenes, the main light sources should be the dome/ambient/diffused light and the artificial lights.

1 Using Resource Files

3d render of a night scene, where Dome and artificial lights are being used to light up the scene

Once the chalk render is signed off by the client, one can begin creating shaders and details in areas closer to the camera. These extra modeling details will help make the render appear more realistic.

For instance, details such as shadow gaps, general table contents, carpet, fur, chamfered edges, realistic plants/trees/grass, slight uneven surfaces/tiles, creases, subtle asymmetry and clutter always make a 3d scene look more appealing and realistic.

Close-up depicting detailed modeling of a ceiling

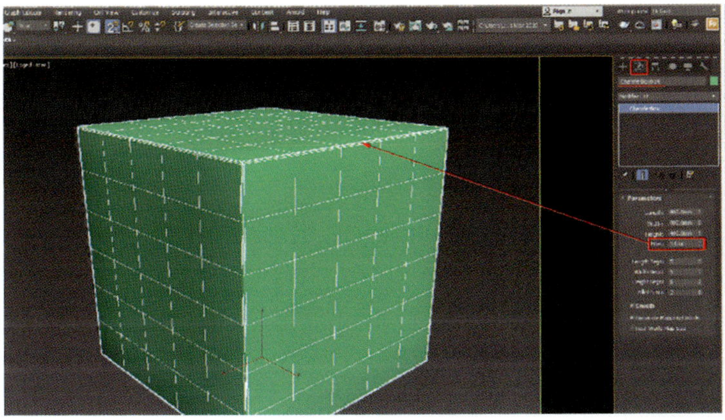

A box primitive in the viewport depicting the Chamfered edges

Having a vast library of pre-modeled assets from previous projects will help speed up the modeling process.

To really expedite the process of building your 3d scene with assets and materials in less than 1 day, simply use an amazing plug-in called Project Manager.

In Project Manager, models, materials, textures and other assets are neatly divided into five different tabs.

The "Models Tab" allows users to merge 3D files using a variety of options such as replace, export and render existing models.

This amazing plug-in also supports substance textures, interactive rendering previews for IES files and materials.

Furthermore, it is compatible with all 3DS Max image file formats (including PSD and Vrimg) and automatically attaches thumbnail views to image and file libraries.

Its amazing drag-and-drop interface features drastically reduce the time/effort involved in completing projects, while using groundbreaking intuitive workflows.

This book resource comes with a short video depicting some of its amazing functionalities.

https://3d-kstudio.com/product/project-manager/

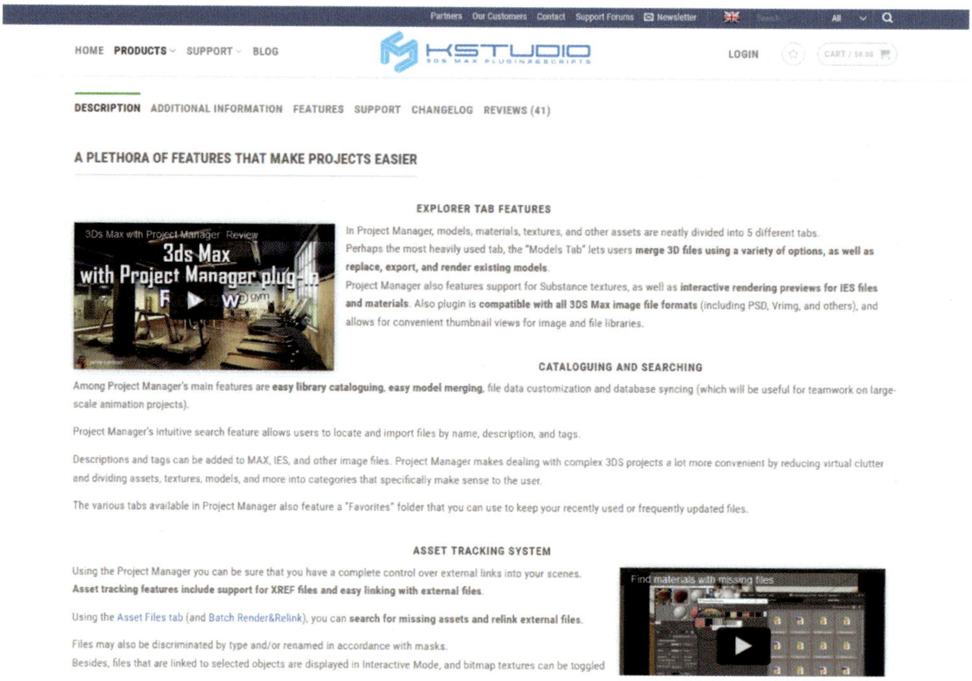

KSTUDIO website depicting a video and full description of the Project Manager plug-in

To quickly create trees, plants, ground, rocks, grass, gravel, hedges, ceiling details/services, etc., simply use IToo tools such as Forest Pack and Rail Clone.

With a click of a button, users can create and customize landscapes and environments with great ease.

IToo products can truly condense days/weeks of work into few hours.

For more information about IToo products, please visit: https://www.itoosoft.com/forestpack.

ITоo Software website depicting a video showcasing Forest Pack capabilities

Below are some of many guidelines one should keep an eye out for while shading and texturing the scene:

A. Ensure there is a photorealistic texture applied to most objects in the scene (even when the material is white).

3d render of an office space depicting realistic white walls

Having a realistic texture applied to a white wall often makes a surface appear more realistic than otherwise. In real life, even pristine surfaces come with subtle details that we usually take for granted.

When these subtle details are removed, our eyes may subsequently perceive the surface or the overall image to be unrealistic/CG.

These illusive details are generally captured in a photo of a texture.

Websites such as cgtextures.com have a range of realistic textures for walls and most surfaces. You may not find specific colors for all surfaces. However, one can use Photoshop to modify surface colors.

Alternatively, you may create your own textures by photographing them yourself.

B. Bump/displacement maps usually add more realism to a surface/texture.

To emulate and reinforce the appearance of a convincing bump/displacement surface, users frequently create and plug a grayscale version of the diffuse texture into the bump toggle.

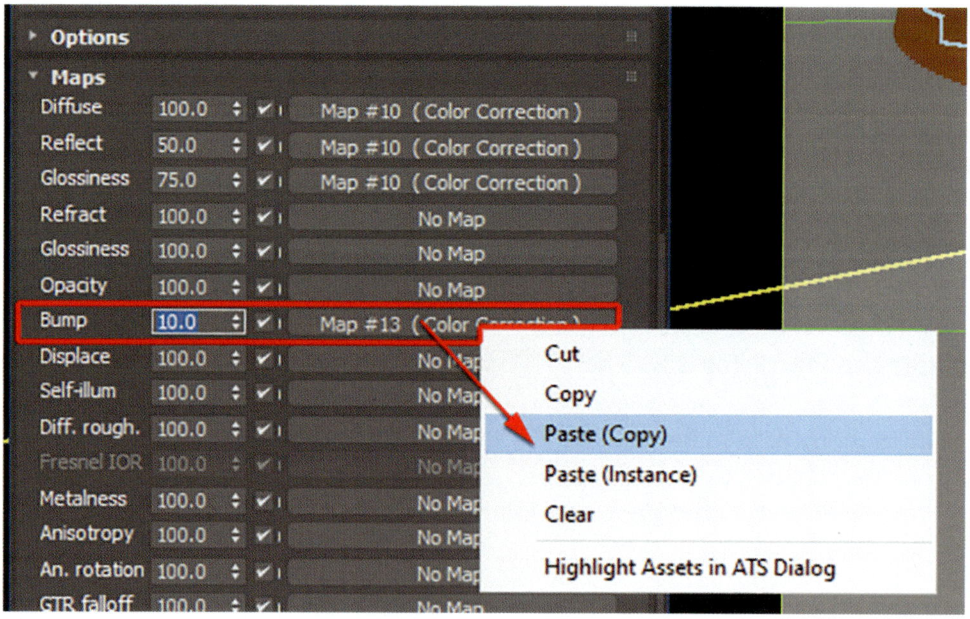

Bump toggle

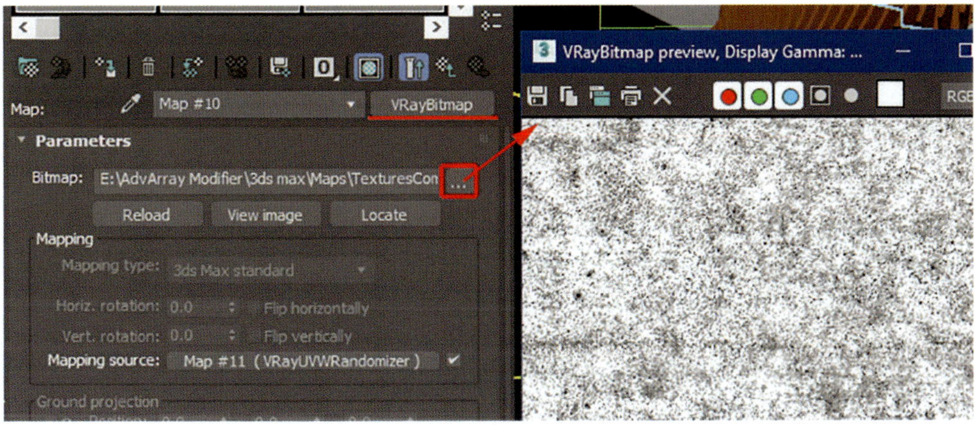

Inside Bump toggle with the grayscale texture being used

To create a grayscale version of the diffused map, simply open the texture in Photoshop first.

Next, desaturate and tweak with its contrast, followed by saving it in a separate file name.

The more the contrast between the black and white colors, the sharper the bump/displacement.

Close-up 3d render of a wall depicting the Bump effect on a surface

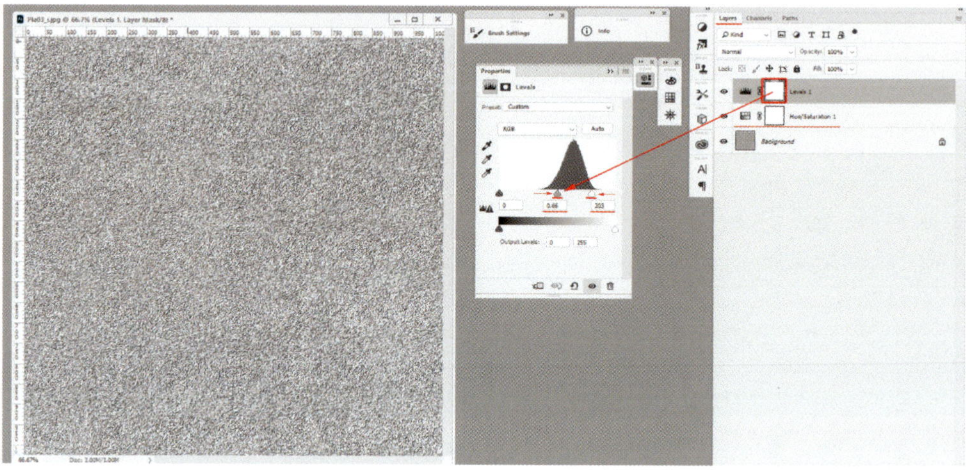

Photoshop Levels adjustment layer being used to create a grayscale image

While the bump effect adds more realism to a surface, the displacement will certainly increase its photorealism dramatically.

Displacing a 3d surface only adds value to a rendered image when the object/s in question is closer to the camera. Otherwise, the displacement details will go unnoticed on distant objects.

Close-up 3d render of a road and pavement depicting the effects of Displacement on surfaces

Add reflective/glossy surfaces whenever possible. Reflective/glossy surfaces generally make a scene more interesting and realistic.

HDRIs can also help add extrareflection/glossy details. If the HDRI is being used for reflection purposes only, ensure it is plugged to the environment reflection/refraction override toggle only. Otherwise, it will also contribute to the overall illumination.

Also, there will be times when HDRI reflection values such as position, rotation and intensity may require changing drastically in order to be visible in the scene.

3d render of an office front depicting HDRI effects on reflective surfaces

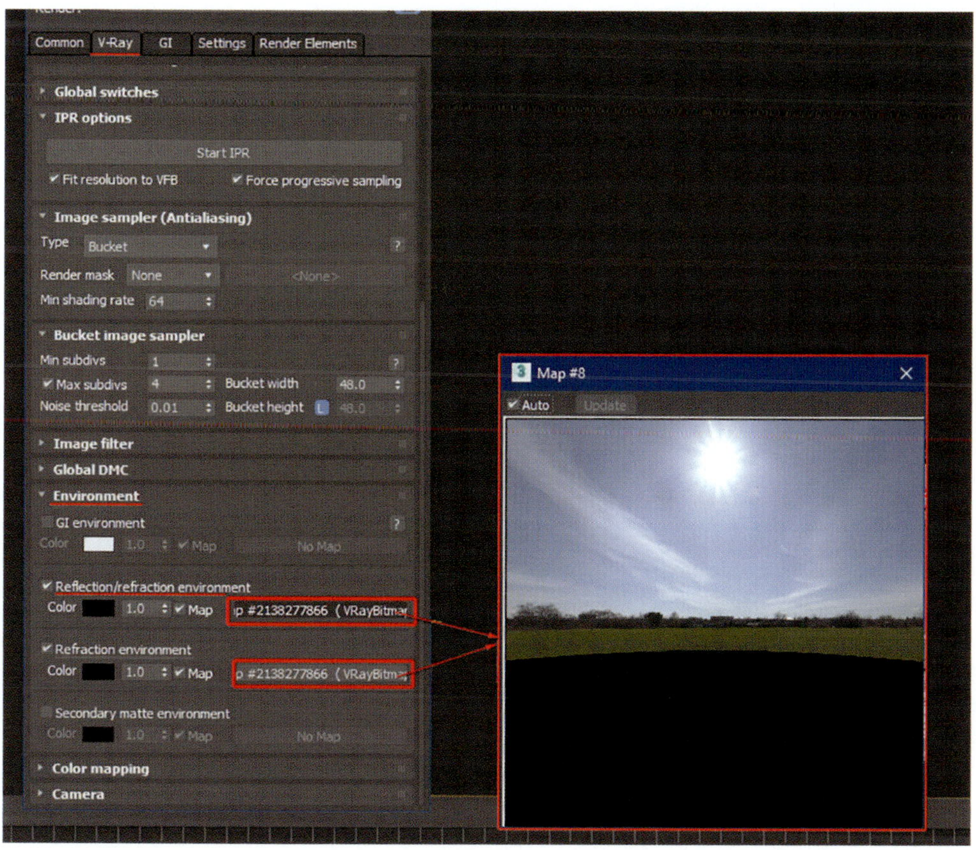

HDRI map being used in the V-Ray Reflection/Refraction environment toggles

Uneven reflectivity: Most surfaces in real life reflect light unevenly. To emulate this effect, simply plug a grayscale version of the diffuse map texture onto the reflectivity toggle.

As mentioned earlier, the grayscaling process can be achieved in Photoshop. The higher the grayscale contrast, the sharper the reflections.

Highlighted glossiness: Adding glossy highlights on surfaces frequently helps to make a scene more interesting and realistic.

3d render of a car depicting reflective surfaces with highlights and glossiness

Rendering

A variety of different test renders are carried out during the production stage. It is common practice to start with draft renders while setting up the lights and the chalk renders.

Users have an array of choices such as interactive production rendering (IPR), Progressive or Bucket rendering.

IPR (interactive production rendering) works in conjunction with progressive rendering settings to generate quick and draft renders while tweaking in real time.

Users simply need to click on the start IPR button.

Progressive renderings are quick renders that occur immediately after you update material settings, render settings, lighting, etc.

Unlike the IPR, it does not allow users to make changes while the renders are taking place.

If you happen to have a simple scene, it is a quick workflow.

Otherwise, it may hinder the progression of your work by automatically rendering your scene every time you make a slight change.

IPR is probably a better choice to continue the work while rendering.

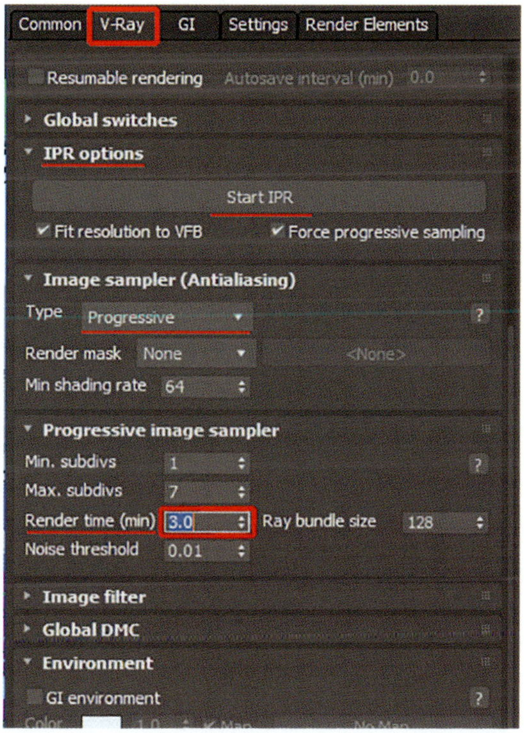

V-Ray tab depicting the IPR and Progressive rendering parameters

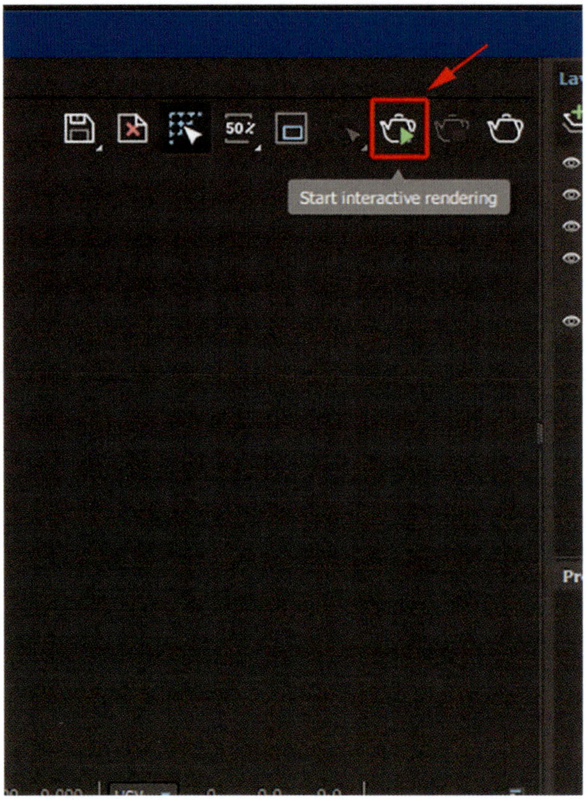

VFB dialog depicting the Start interactive rendering button

Main toolbar depicting last rendered VFB button

Alternatively, simply use the bucket rendering type with lower/draft settings.

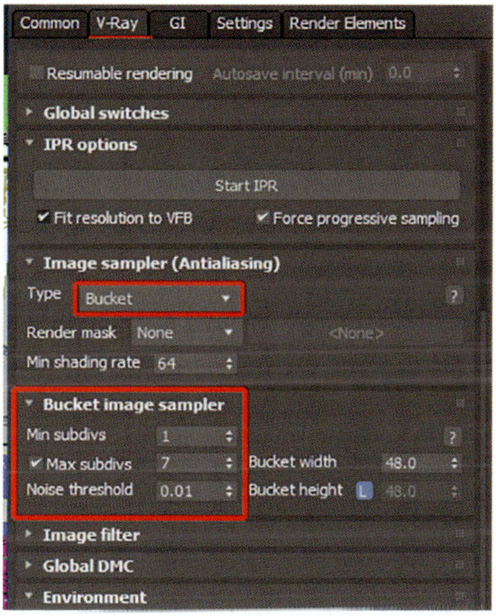

V-Ray tab depicting the Bucket Rendering type with draft Bucket image sampler values

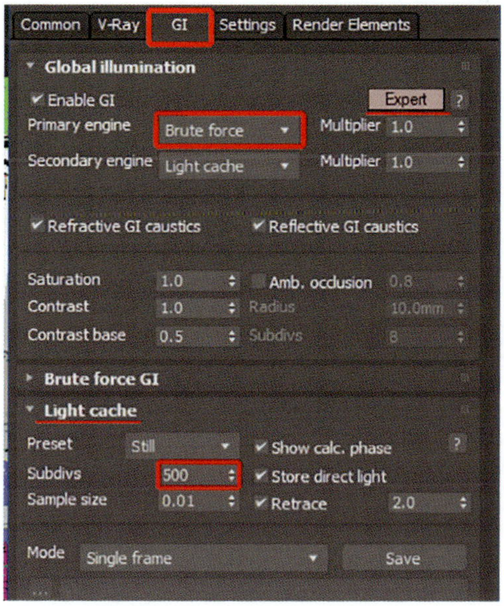

GI tab depicting Brute force and Light cache being used with low values

Once satisfied with the overall lighting and the scene, one can increase the light and render settings for the final high-resolution render (i.e., 3,000 pixels).

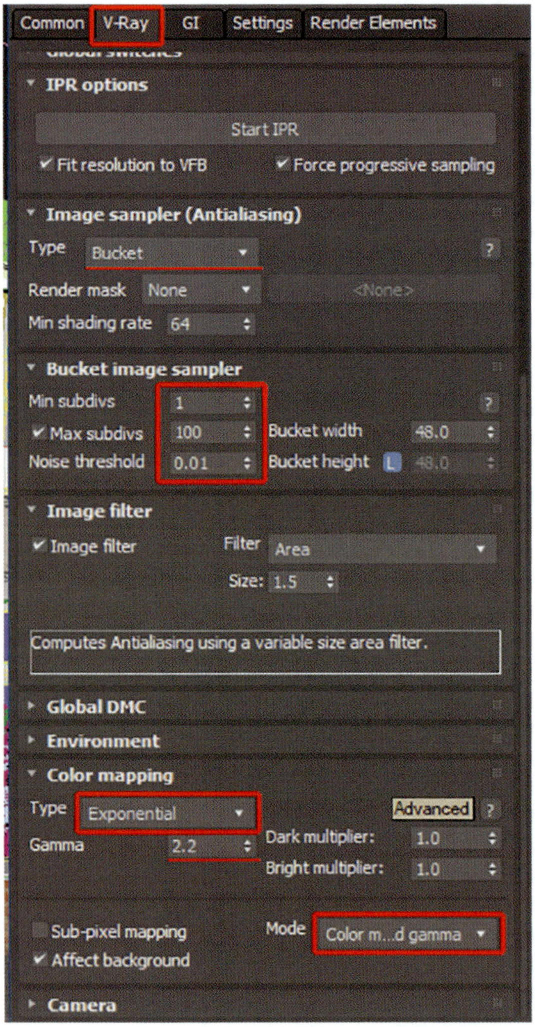

V-Ray tab depicting high values for bucket image sampler, color mapping and mode

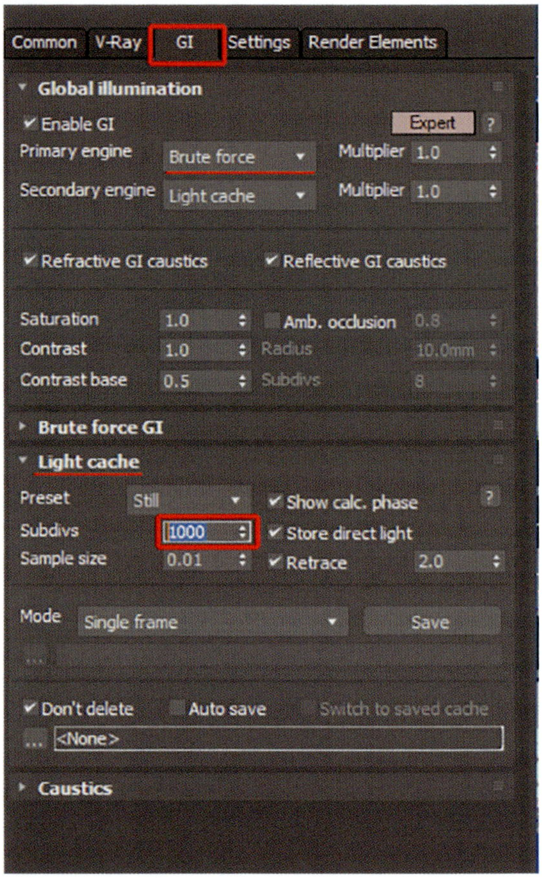

GI Tab depicting Brute force and Light cache being used with high values

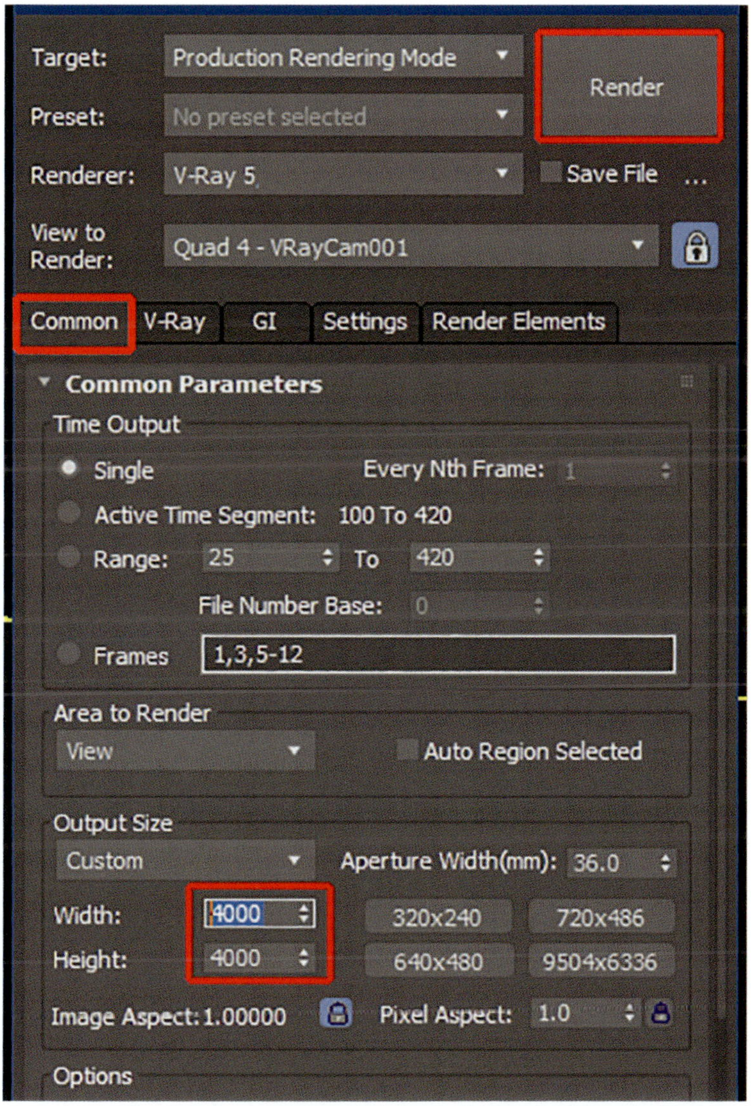

Render Setup dialog depicting the final output size values

Before sending the final render, it's common practise to do region renders, to ensure shaders/textures and the image quality are at the highest level.

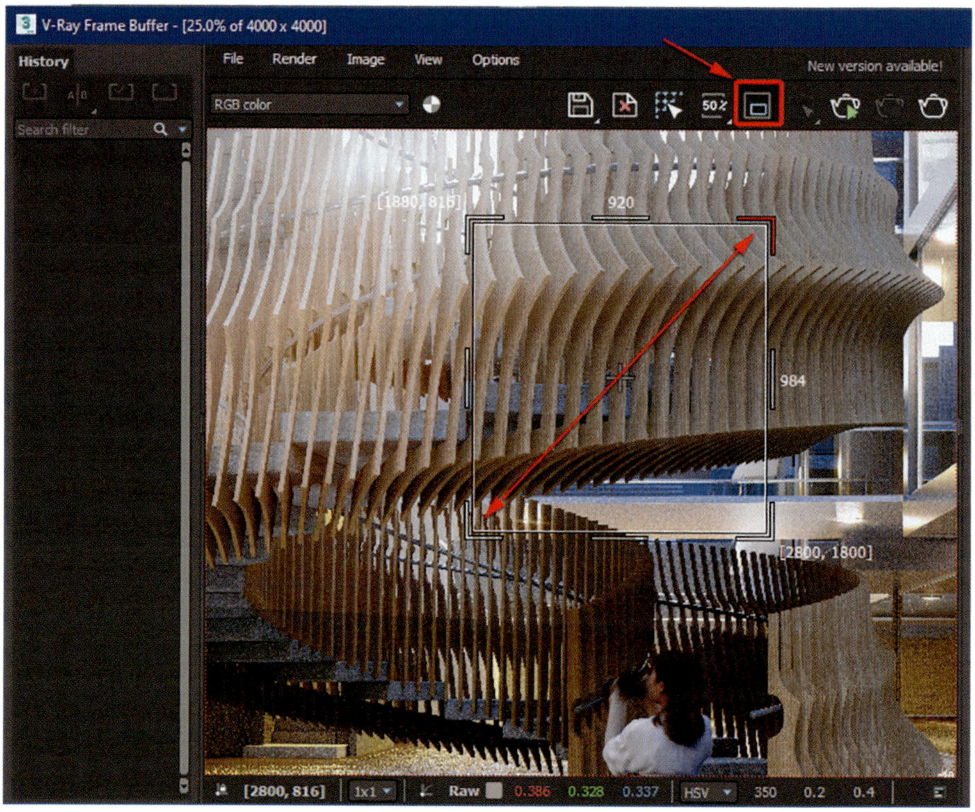

VFB depicting the Region render functionalities

With the lighting, shaders and textures fine-tuned, one can begin adding the render elements and test rendering them (without saving).

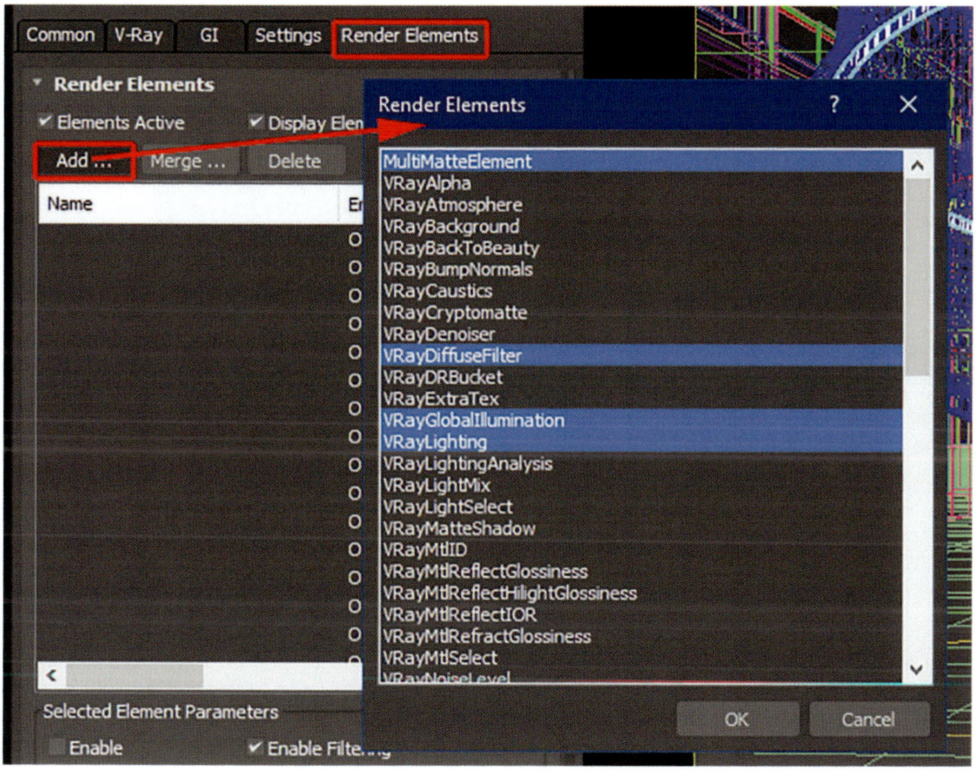

Render Elements tab depicting Render Elements being added in a dialog

The subsequent step is to name the final output file and render it.

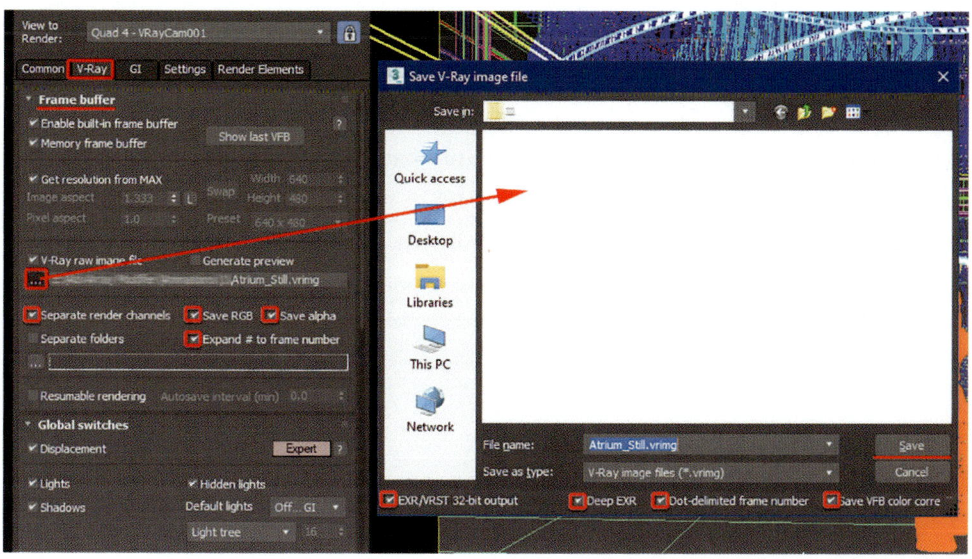

Name and Save to V-Ray image file

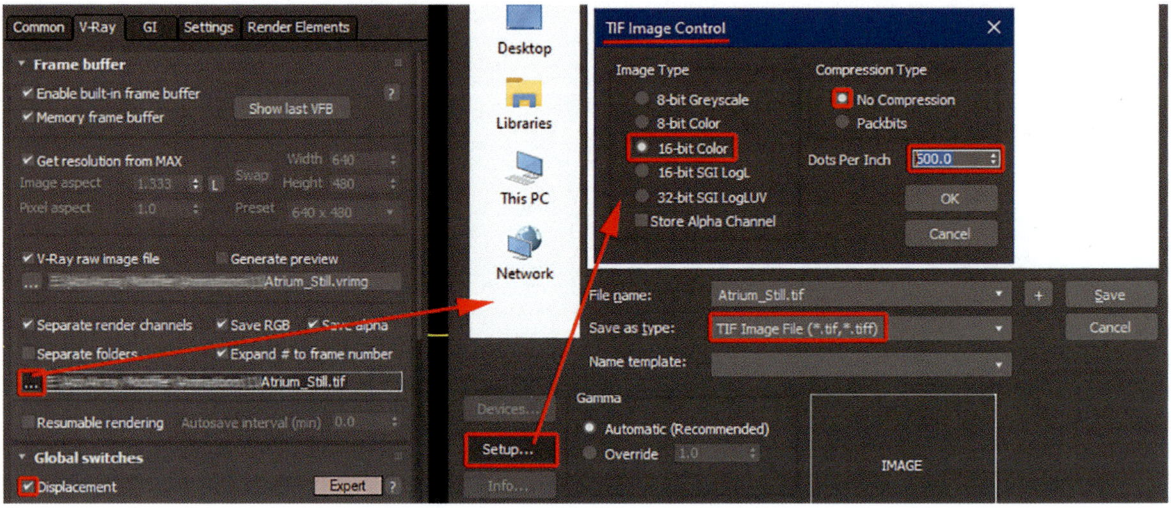

V-Ray tab depicting V-Ray raw image file being saved and resumable rendering enabled

Post-Production Overview

Post-production is often used to tweak specific materials, replace backgrounds and fine-tune the overall image.

While most users are recommended to get the raw renders looking as good as possible from 3ds Max, post work will always be necessary to take the final image to the next level.

More often than not, even in cases when the raw renders are already very good, adjusting render elements and the overall image in post will turn a good image into an excellent one.

To enhance materials in post, multiple render passes are frequently mixed with key Photoshop blending modes and adjustment layers.

Some of the most popular render passes for post-production are specular, reflection, lightselect, reflection filter, diffuse material, MultiMatteElement, Refraction, etc.

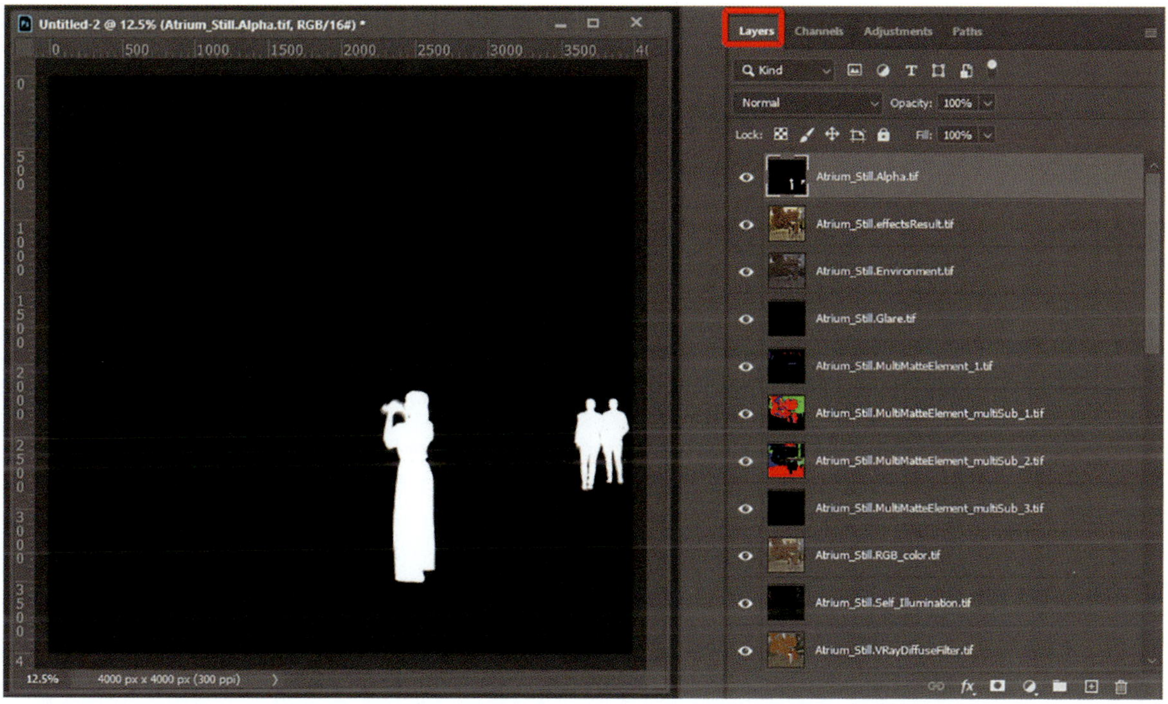

Render elements loaded in a Photoshop Layers stack

For better control of each material in post, some render passes are copied and moved into one specific group folder, with a mask attached to it.

To blend multiple render passes within each material group folder, users choose blending modes such as screen, multiply and overlay.

As mentioned earlier, adjustment layers are also used within the group folders to control the material contrast and its colors.

Some of the widely used adjustment layers are levels, curves, photo filter, exposure, color balance, hue/saturation and brightness/contrast.

These adjustment layers can also be used to grade and fine-tune the overall image.

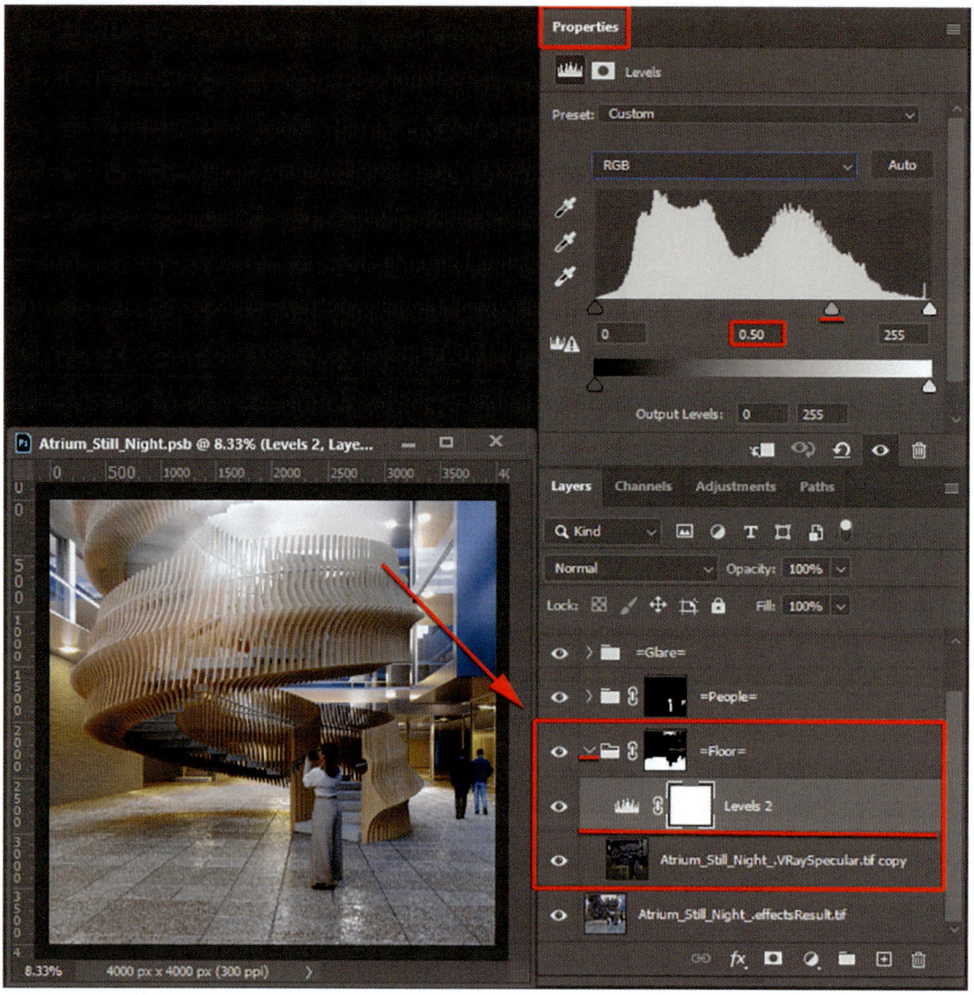

Render element being tweaked in Photoshop

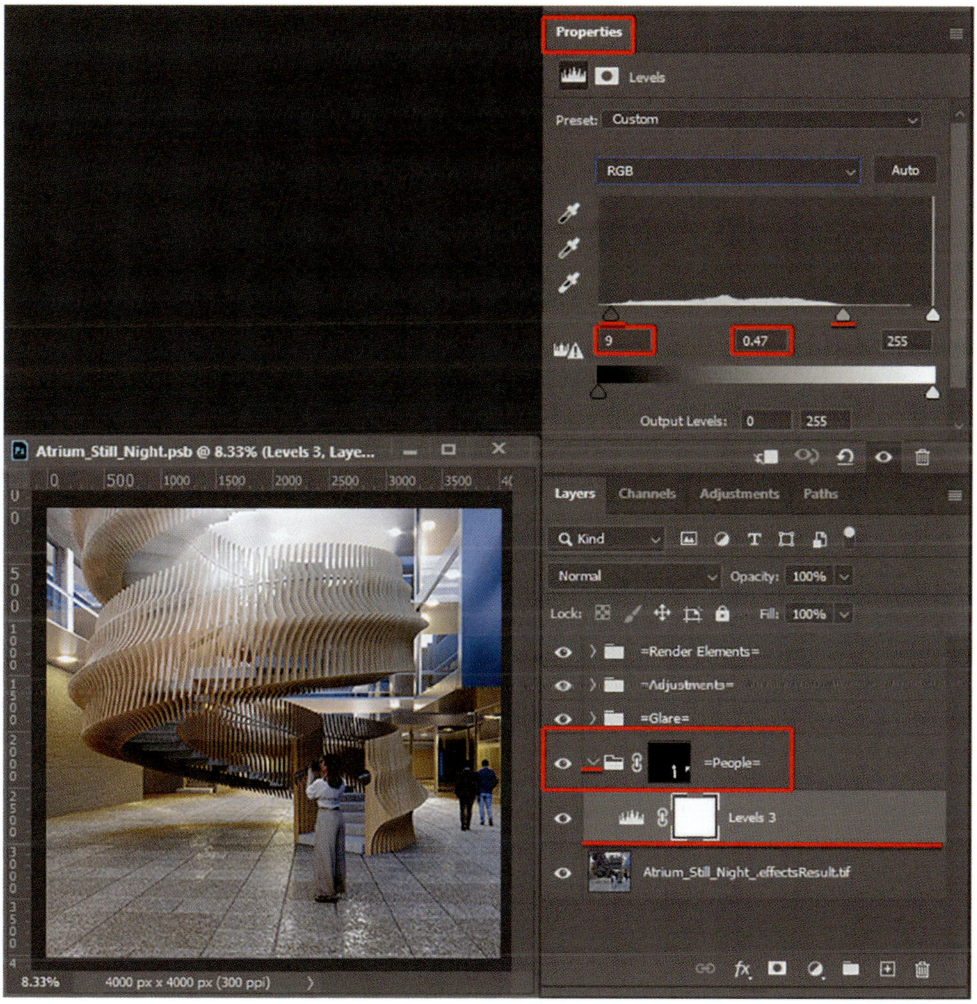

Levels adjustment layer being used to tweak the image

Alternatively, users and companies often use reputable companies to help expedite the post-production process in few hours.

Finally, vishopper.com offers some of the best and cheapest cut-out people library to be added in post-production.

For more information about, please visit, https://www.vishopper.com/

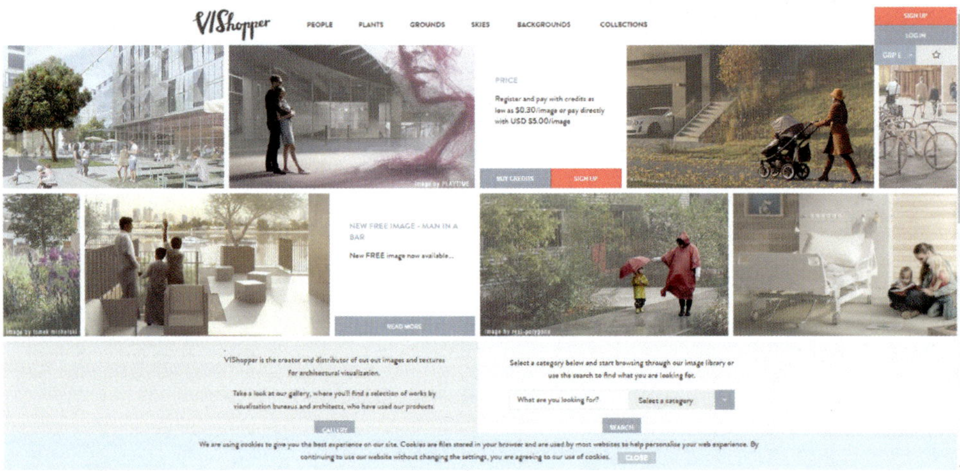

vishopper.com website

2

Creating Materials and Shaders in V-Ray 5

2 Creating Materials & Shaders

This chapter will start with a quick summary about the V-Ray 5 rendering engine, followed by taking users through the process of installing V-Ray 5 accordingly, and setting up the Custom UI and Default Switcher function.

Following that, users will be shown how to load and access the V-Ray Material Browser dialog.

Throughout this chapter, users will be taken through every single VRayMtl parameter and functionalities such as the Diffuse, Roughness, Reflect, Glossiness, Max depth, Fresnel reflections, Metalness, Refract, IOR, Abbe number, Fog color, Fog multiplier, Translucency, Affect shadows, Output, Falloff, BRDF, Coat, Sheen and Bump.

Finally, users will learn how to use procedural maps such as VRayBitmap, VRayTriplanarTex, Bitmaps, Bricks, Metals, Carpaint, VRayDisplacementMod, VRayUVWRandomizer, VRayMultiSubTex, VRayPointCloudColor, VRayDirt, VRayAerialPerspective, VRayLightMtl, VRayMtlWrapper, VRayOverrideMtl, VRay2SidedMtl, VRayBlendMtl, Mix and VRayEdgesTex.

V-Ray 5 is fully integrated with 3ds Max and comes equipped with a list of robust and powerful procedural maps and shaders to help achieve complex and striking results.

By default, most V-Ray 5 material presets are ready to render.

In the discussions that will follow, we will focus primarily on the VRayMtl parameters/presets and some of its most popular procedural maps.

In order to access the VRayMtl parameters, V-Ray 5 needs to be installed and loaded first.

To load V-Ray, press F10 to open the Render Setup dialog. Alternatively, simply click on its main toolbar button.

In the Render Setup dialog, go to the Common tab

DOI: 10.1201/9781315770802-2

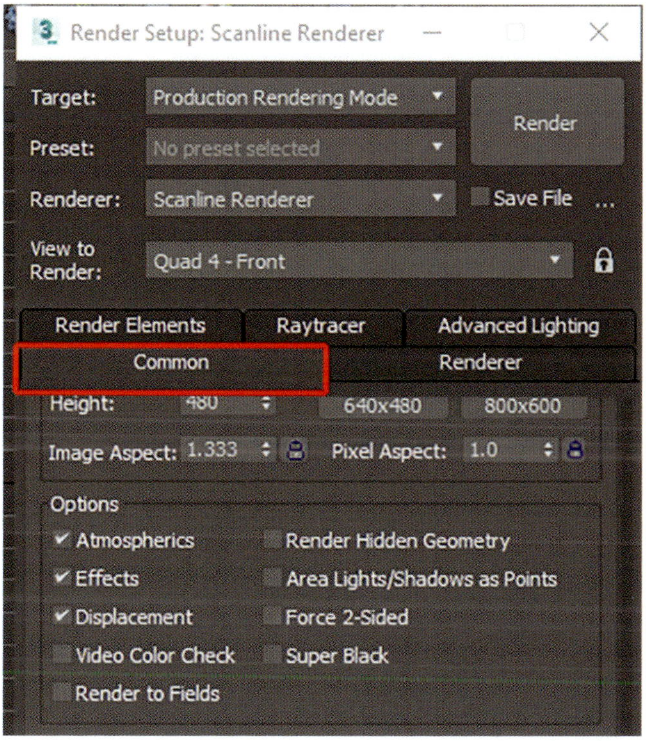

Common tab

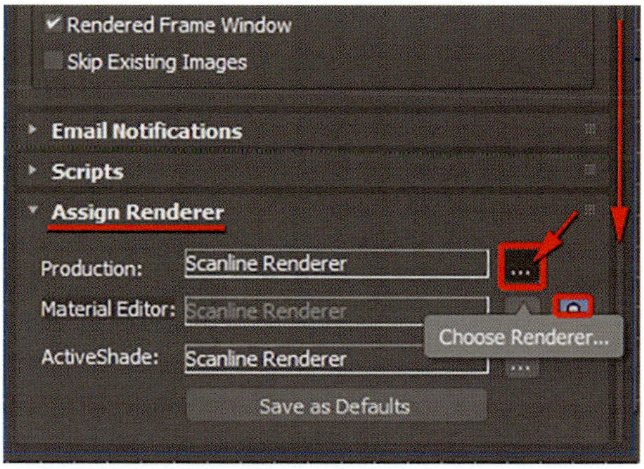

Assign Renderer rollout parameters and Production toggle

Pick the V-Ray 5 render, in the Choose Renderer dialog. The V-Ray renderer should load automatically.

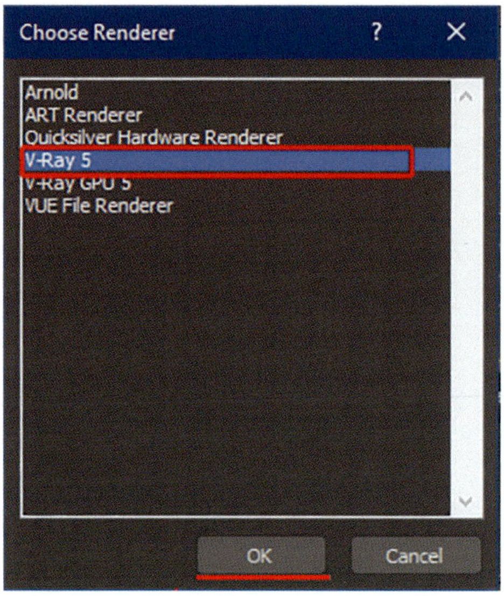

Choose Renderer dialog with V-Ray 5 highlighted

To begin using the VRayMtl, simply open the Material Editor (M).

For the purpose of this discussion, we will be using the Compact Material Editor version, as opposed to Slate (node base).

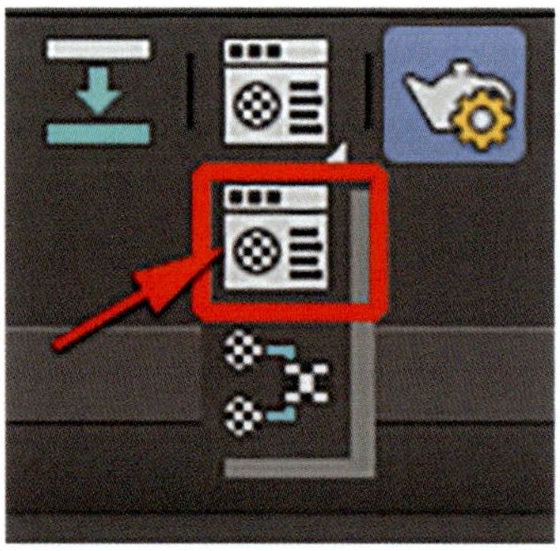

Compact Material Editor button on the main toolbar

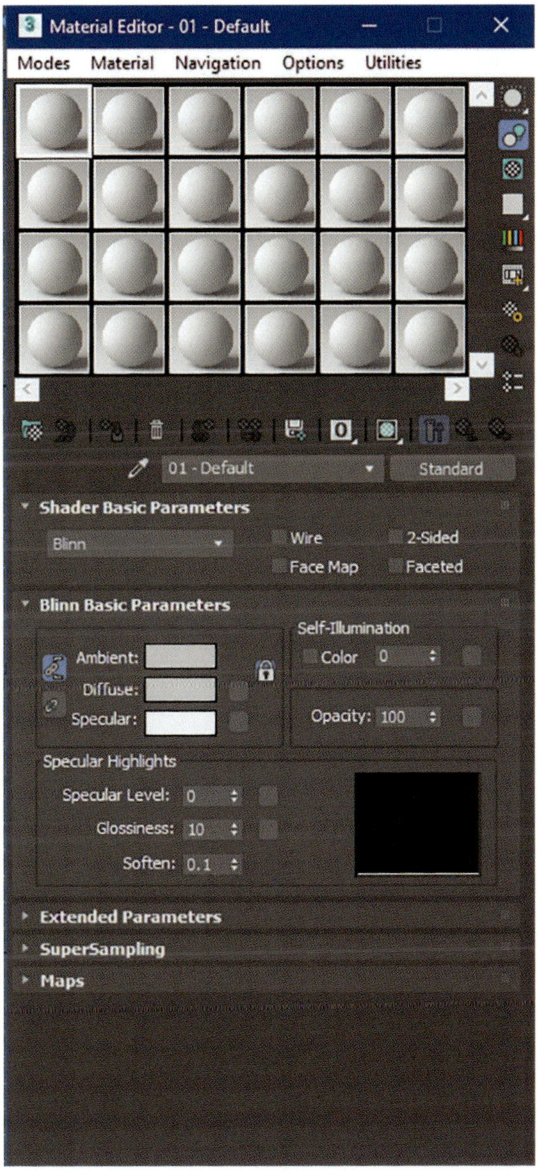

Material Editor dialog open

2 Creating Materials & Shaders

This chapter assumes the standard material was automatically loaded in the Material Editor dialog.

Otherwise, you should probably see the Physical Material instead.

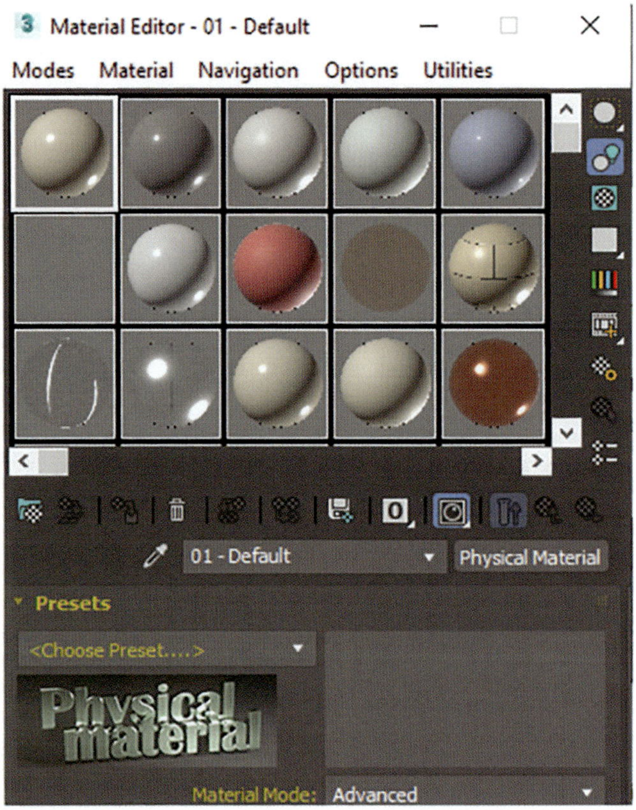

Physical Material dialog loaded

By default, 3ds Max has the Custom UI and Defaults Switcher set to, DesignVIZ. ART, which automatically loads the Physical Materials.

To change this, simply go to the Customize toolbar and choose the Custom UI and Defaults Switcher option.

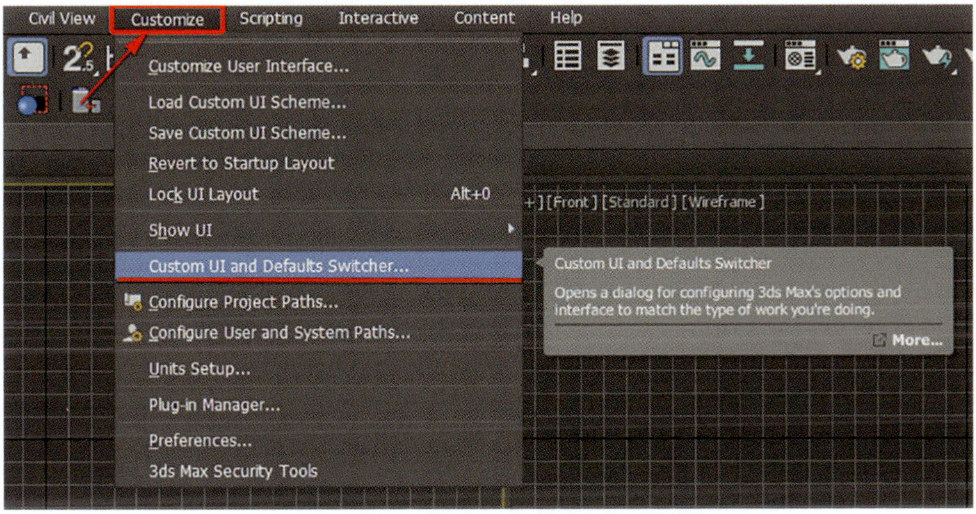

Custom UI and Defaults Switcher from the Customize main toolbar

Currently, you may have the DesignVIZ.ART loaded.

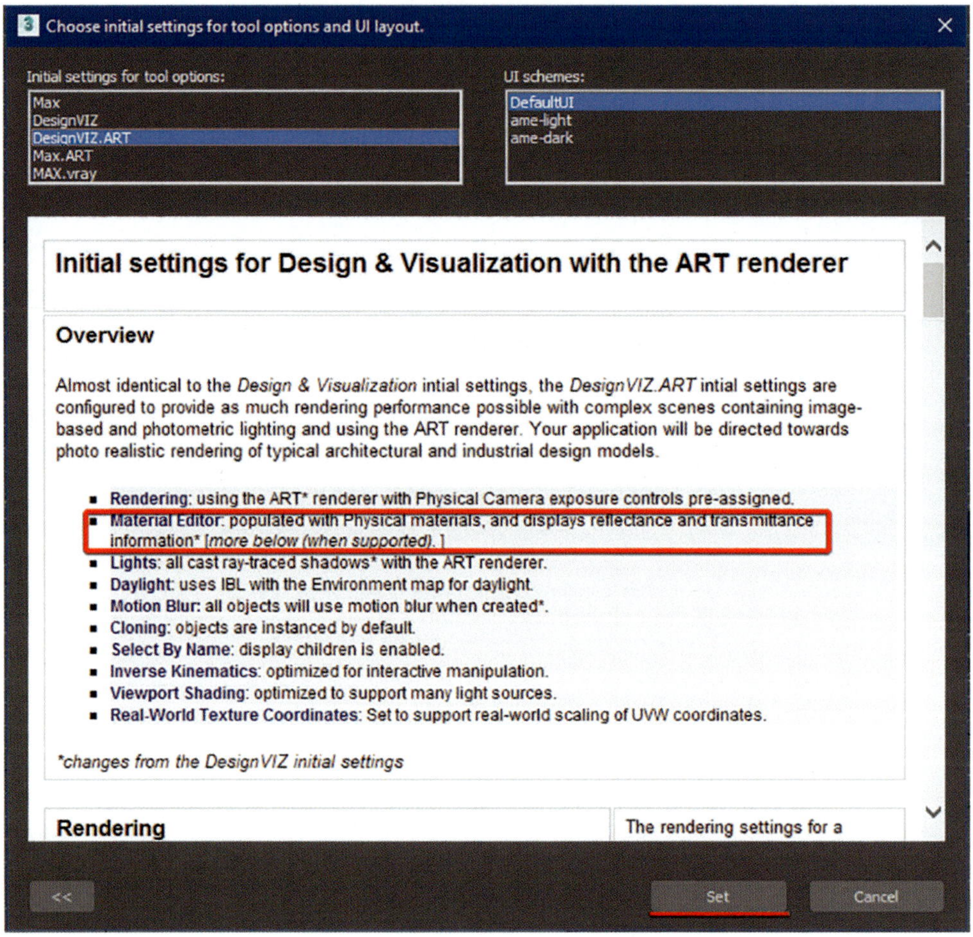

Dialog with DesignVIZ.ART loaded

To change it, simply select the Max.vray DefaultUI option, and click to Set.

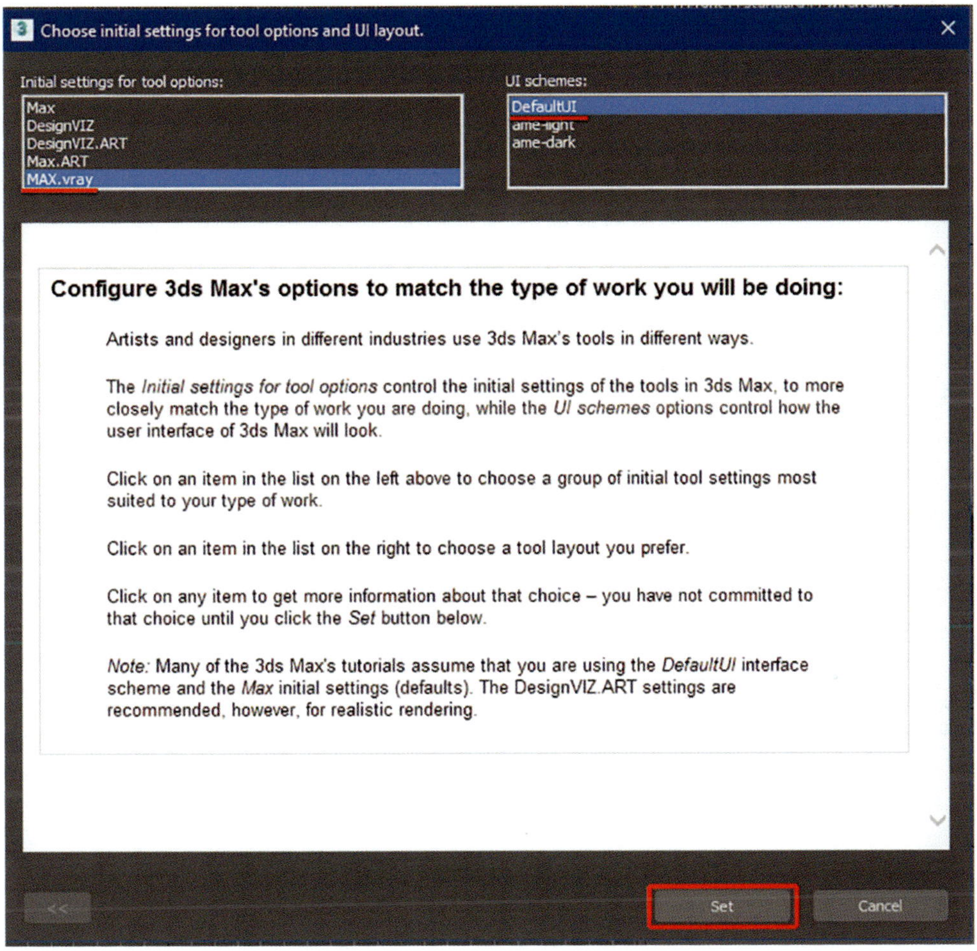

Dialog with Max.vray DefaultUI option Set

However, this action might remove the new V-Ray toolbar, along with the new Asset Browser.

New V-Ray toolbar with Asset Browser

Currently, there's no way to pull back the new V-Ray Asset Browser from the Customize User Interface.

For this reason alone, users will be required to close 3ds Max and uninstall V-Ray 5 first.

NOTE

Next time you open a brand new 3ds Max scene, the Material Editor should automatically load with V-Ray materials by default.

Next, open 3ds Max and set the Custom UI and Defaults Switcher to be Max.ray.

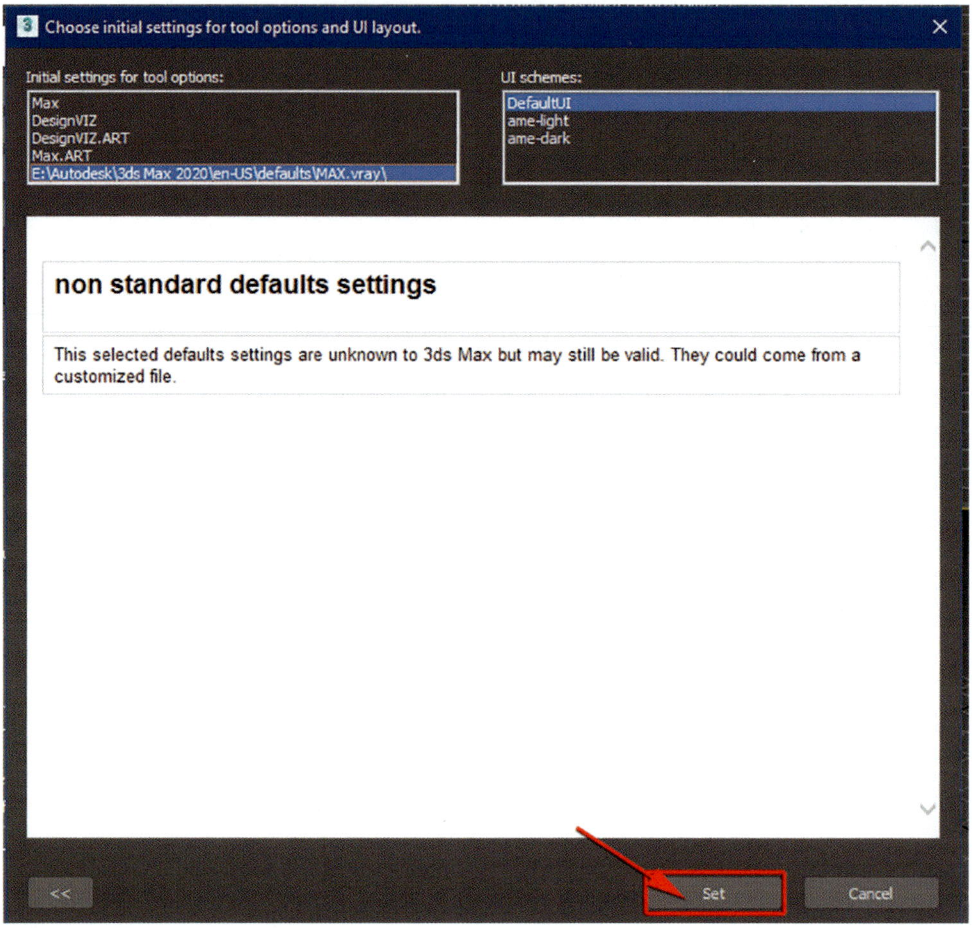

Dialog with Max.vray DefaultUI option

Close 3ds Max and reinstall V-Ray 5.

Next time you open 3ds Max, the new V-Ray toolbar should appear automatically, along with the V-Ray materials loaded in the Material Editor dialog.

To continue, let's assume most readers didn't reinstall V-Ray 5 and have the Standard Materials automatically loaded in the Material Editor.

To load the VRayMtl, simply click on the Standard toggle, and choose the VRayMtl from the Material/Map Browser list.

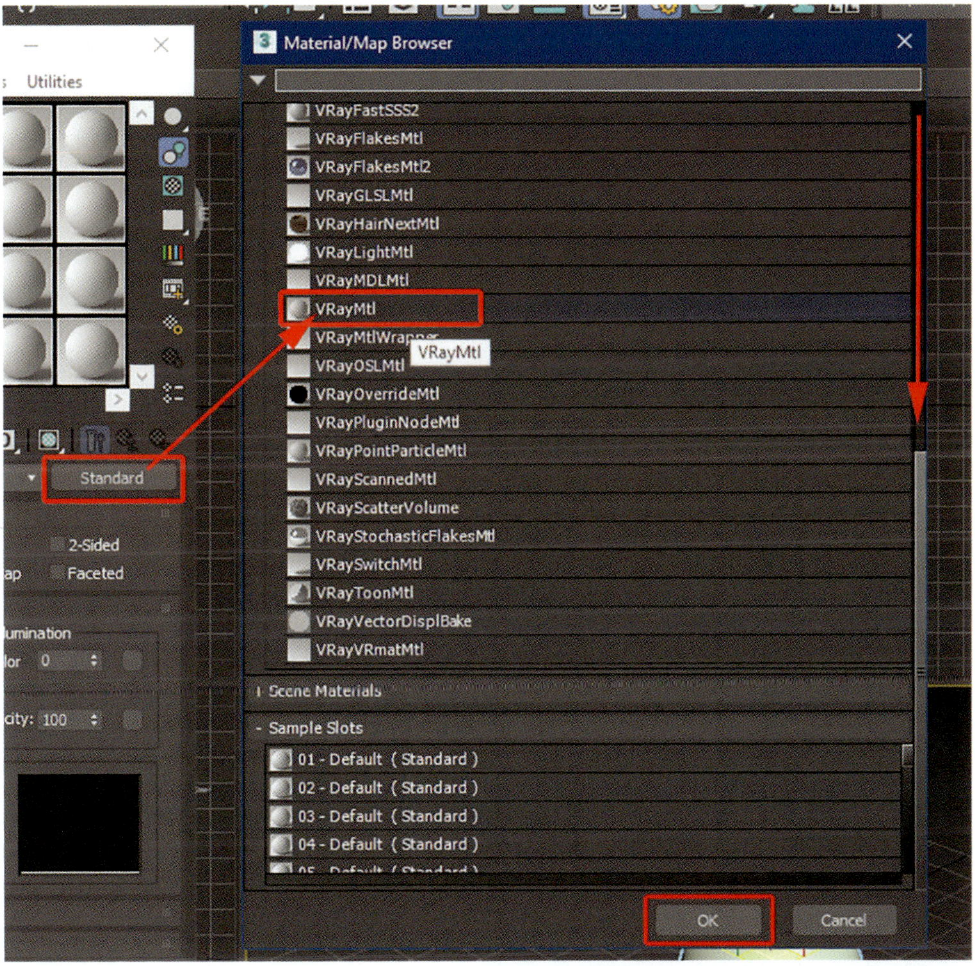

Standard toggle clicked to Load VRayMtl

If you happen to have the Physical Material loaded, simply click on its toggle to load the VRayMtl

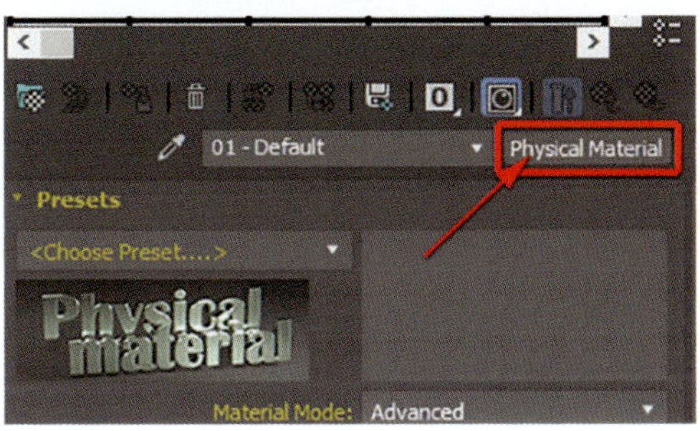

Physical Material toggle clicked to load VRayMtl

Because V-Ray 5 displays the shaders and lighting more accurately in the material slots, the shader preview may take slightly longer to update.

To avoid this, simply go to the Settings tab.

Under the System rollout parameters, enable the Native 3ds Max material swatches.

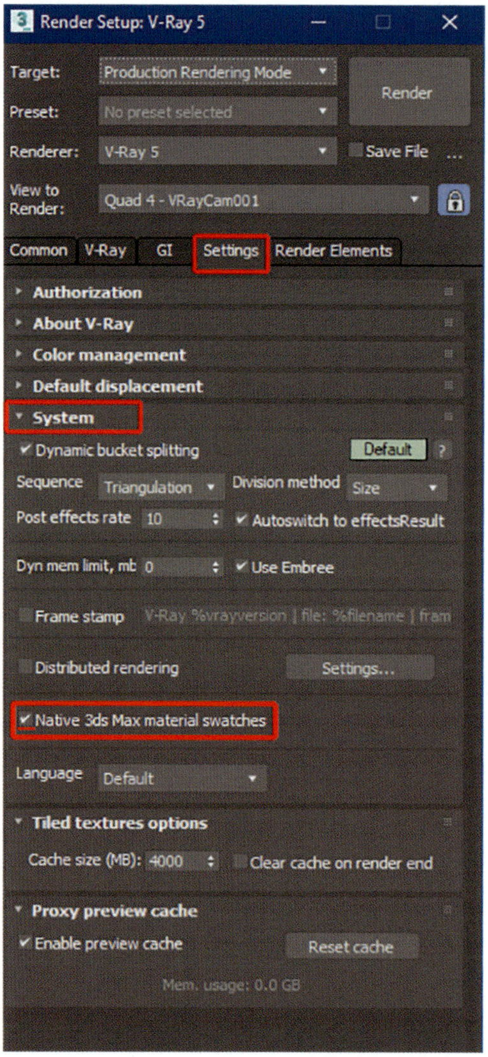

Settings tab with Native 3ds Max material swatches enabled under System rollout

For realistic material previews, users can still use the V-Ray Asset Browser toolbar.

This new V-Ray material library can also be found in: **C:\Users\User\Documents\V-Ray**.

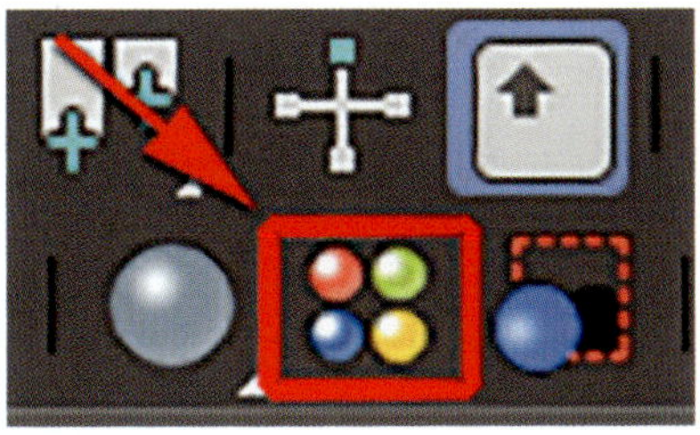

V-Ray Asset Browser toolbar

Material Library

Alternatively, simply visit the Chaos Group website to download it from there:

https://docs.chaosgroup.com/display/VMAX/V-Ray+Asset+Browser

V-Ray Asset Browser dialog comes with a huge range of ready-to-render Material Library presets which are fast to display, and provide a full preview of its physical properties.

Most of its physical properties derive from the VRayMtl parameters we will be discussing in this chapter.

The Material Library presets are a massive help to speed up users' workflow.

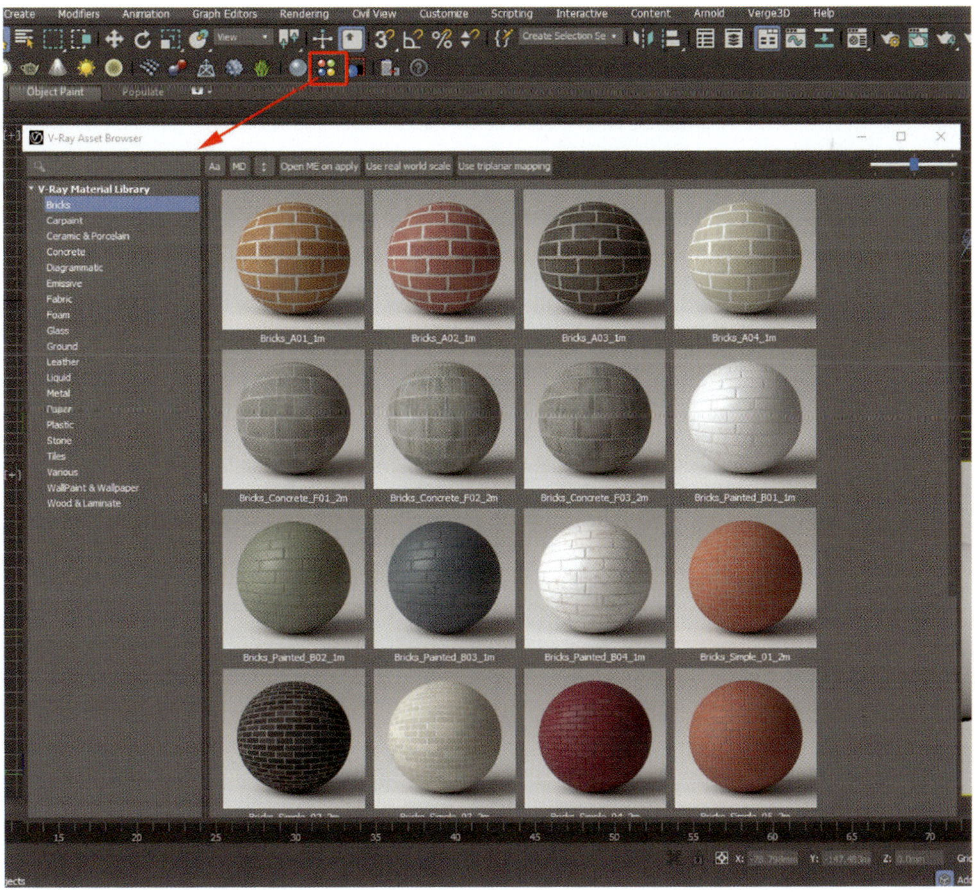

V-Ray Asset Browser dialog open

NOTE

This function can be found inside the coordinates rollout of textures applied. It may not work sometimes (bug), and users will be required to enable it manually.

V-Ray Asset Browser comes with the following functionalities:

Filter case sensitive: When enabled (it turns blue), this button takes into consideration the upper and lower cases of text typed in the search bar.

This text field is often used to quickly search for specific materials.

Filter by meta data: When enabled, it filters the searches by metadata.

Sort by name: When enabled, it sorts the materials displayed in the dialog alphabetically.

Open ME on apply: When enabled, the Material Editor dialog (M) opens automatically when materials are applied to object/s.

Users need to right click on a specific material slot and choose to, Apply to Selected objects.

Use real world scale: When enabled, it automatically enables the real-world scale function of selected VRayBitmaps, when applied via the V-ray Asset Browser dialog.

This function applies to the tiling and other material values.

Always enable this button prior to applying materials to selected objects, or adding materials to scene/material slot.

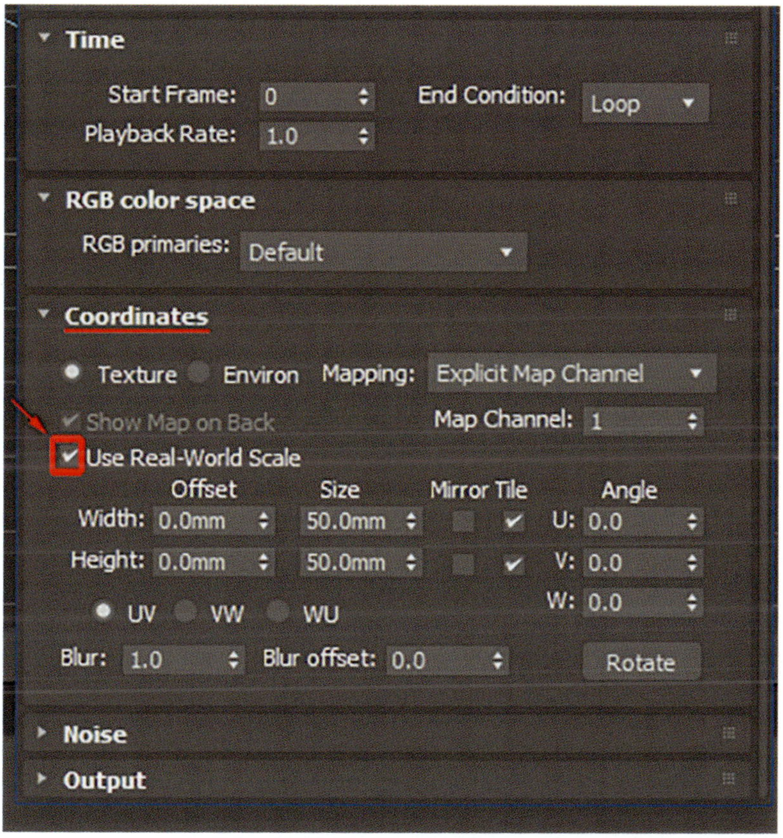

Coordinates rollout parameters with Use Real-World Scale enabled

Use triplanar mapping: When enabled, it adds the VRayTriplanarTex procedural map.

It serves as a substitute for UVW maps on objects. It's useful to apply it on objects without UVWs (merged 3d assets, etc.).

Always enable this button prior to applying materials to selected objects. Or prior to adding materials to scene/material slot.

As mentioned earlier, users can apply materials from the V-Ray Material Browser dialog, by simply right clicking on a specific material slot, and choosing to Apply to Selected object(s).

Users can also choose to, Preview the material, Add to scene and Add to favorites.

The option to Add to scene loads the selected material in the material slot.

Some of the V-Ray preset materials come with a VRayBitmap procedural map applied to its diffuse toggle and a TX file assigned to it.

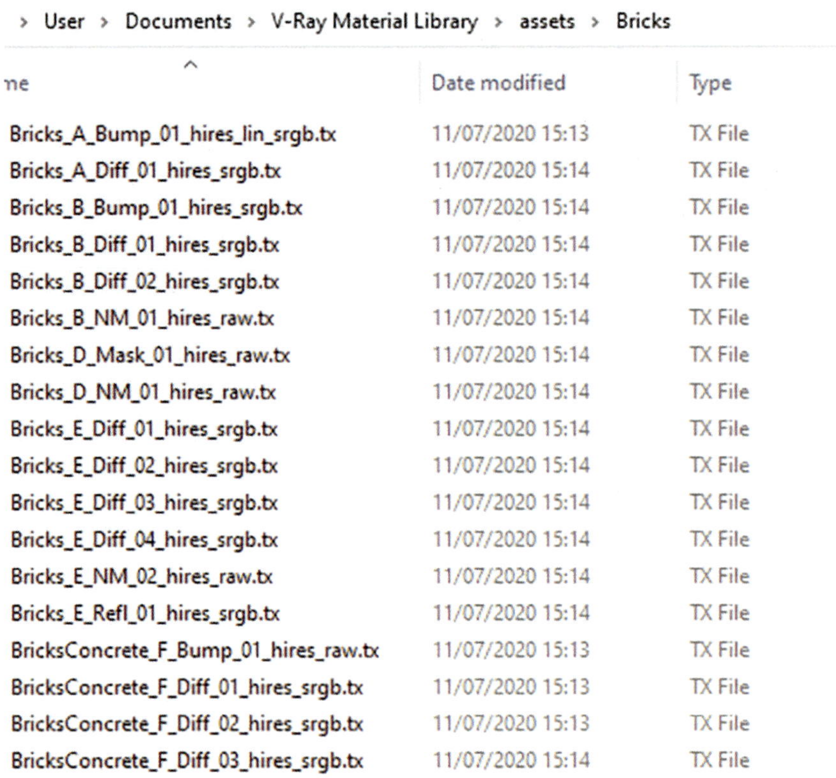

› User › Documents › V-Ray Material Library › assets › Bricks

ne	Date modified	Type
Bricks_A_Bump_01_hires_lin_srgb.tx	11/07/2020 15:13	TX File
Bricks_A_Diff_01_hires_srgb.tx	11/07/2020 15:14	TX File
Bricks_B_Bump_01_hires_srgb.tx	11/07/2020 15:14	TX File
Bricks_B_Diff_01_hires_srgb.tx	11/07/2020 15:14	TX File
Bricks_B_Diff_02_hires_srgb.tx	11/07/2020 15:14	TX File
Bricks_B_NM_01_hires_raw.tx	11/07/2020 15:14	TX File
Bricks_D_Mask_01_hires_raw.tx	11/07/2020 15:14	TX File
Bricks_D_NM_01_hires_raw.tx	11/07/2020 15:14	TX File
Bricks_E_Diff_01_hires_srgb.tx	11/07/2020 15:14	TX File
Bricks_E_Diff_02_hires_srgb.tx	11/07/2020 15:14	TX File
Bricks_E_Diff_03_hires_srgb.tx	11/07/2020 15:14	TX File
Bricks_E_Diff_04_hires_srgb.tx	11/07/2020 15:14	TX File
Bricks_E_NM_02_hires_raw.tx	11/07/2020 15:14	TX File
Bricks_E_Refl_01_hires_srgb.tx	11/07/2020 15:14	TX File
BricksConcrete_F_Bump_01_hires_raw.tx	11/07/2020 15:13	TX File
BricksConcrete_F_Diff_01_hires_srgb.tx	11/07/2020 15:13	TX File
BricksConcrete_F_Diff_02_hires_srgb.tx	11/07/2020 15:13	TX File
BricksConcrete_F_Diff_03_hires_srgb.tx	11/07/2020 15:14	TX File

TX file extensions in the folder list

TX file assigned and material slot maximized

TX file formats are extremely useful for memory cache efficiency, when rendering textures and reducing aliasing artifacts.

These file formats contain pre-filtered levels of detail of a texture (from low to high resolution).

Each level of detail is loaded according to their proximity to the camera/view.

The high-resolution version is automatically loaded for close-ups. And the low resolution when further away.

When the VRayTriplanarTex is applied, it automatically goes into the Mapping source toggle.

VRayTriplanarTex will be later discussed in more detail.

Material applied with Use triplanar mapping, and VRayBitmap with VRayTriplanarTex used in the Mapping source

To apply each V-Ray material from the Material Editor, users need to select a material slot and object/s in the scene, followed by clicking on the Assign Material to Selection button.

Click the Assign Material to Selection button

Basic Parameters

This chapter is an overview of V-Ray materials and parameters. Not step-by-step tutorials, as depicted from Chapter 6 and onwards.

However, to test some of the parameters described here, please open the 3ds Max file under the name, VRay Materials.max

This 3ds Max scene comes with a V-Ray Frame Buffer file format (vfbl) and a LUT file loaded in its V-Ray Frame Buffer dialog.

The LUT file associated with this chapter is under the name, 3DCollective_sRGB_Agfa_Futura_03Hard.cube

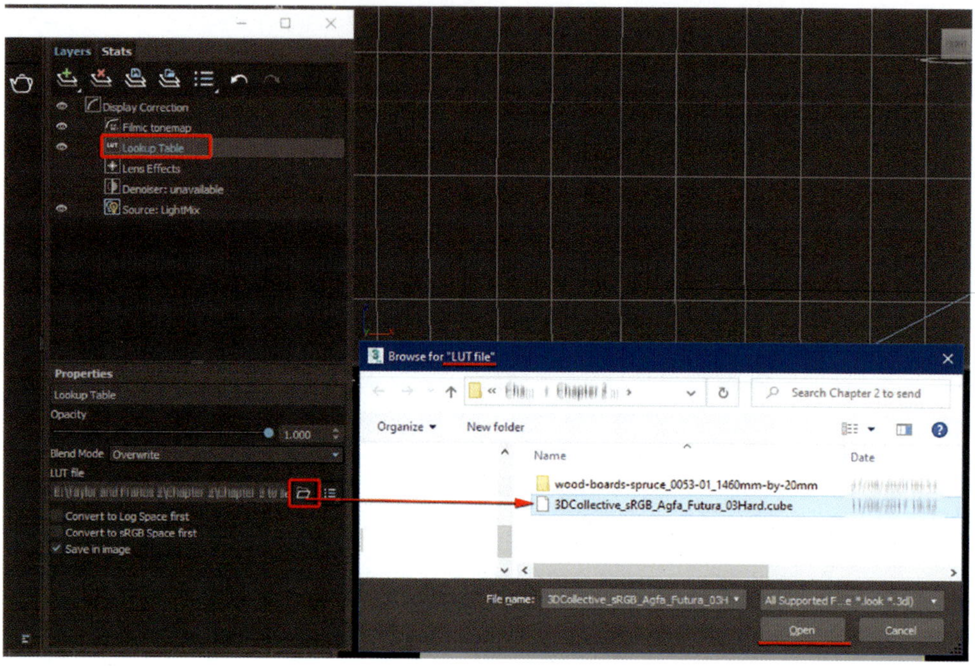

LUT file being loaded by clicking the Browse toggle

The VRay Frame Buffer file format associated with this chapter is under the name, VRay Materials.vfbl

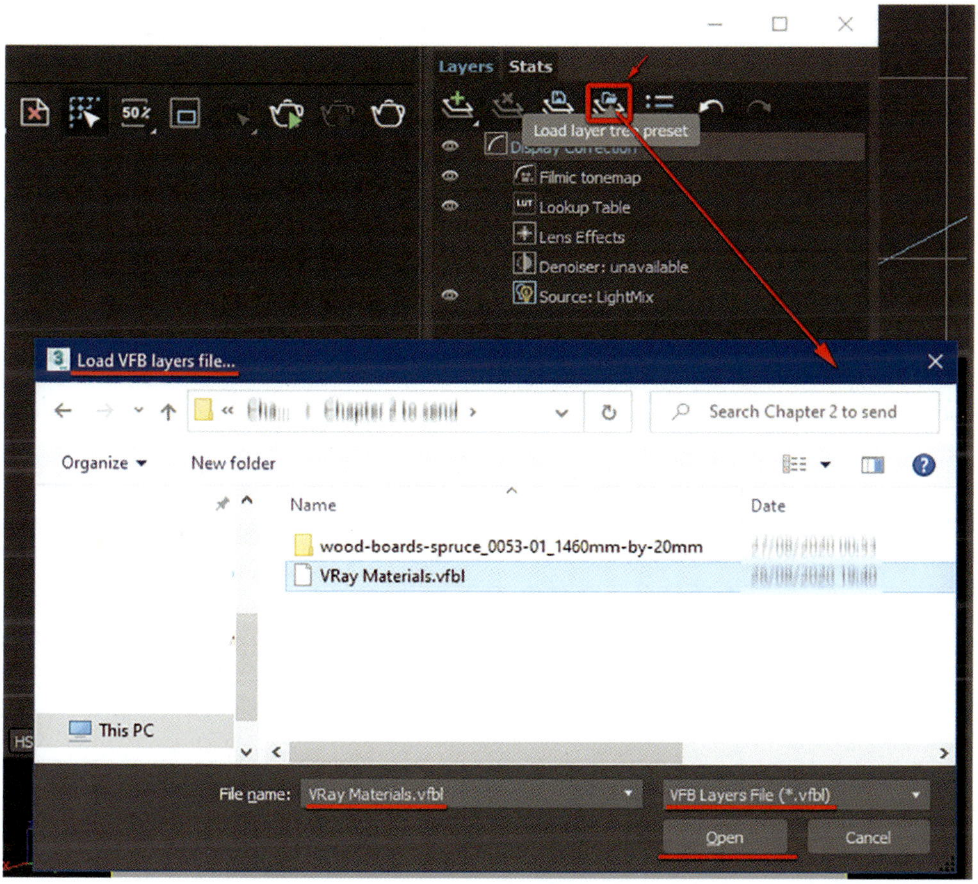

Load layer tree preset clicked to Load VRay Frame Buffer layers file

Diffuse

Diffuse color: This color swatch enables users to pick and choose a diffuse color, by using the Color Selector dialog.

To access the Color Selector dialog, simply left click on its color swatch and hold down. Once the Color Selector dialog appears, pick a color in the Hue section. Or type in a specific value and adjust its Whiteness slider.

Alternatively, one can sample colors by selecting the, Sample Screen Color picker, and picking a color inside, or outside 3ds Max.

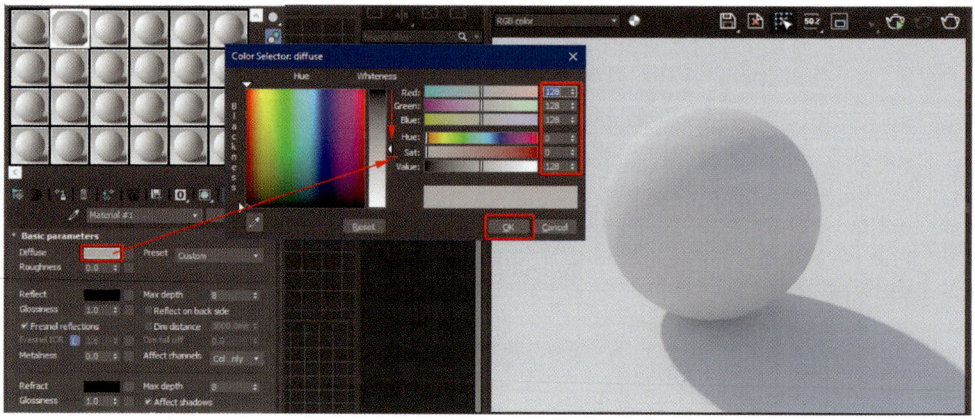

Diffuse color swatch dialog used to change colors

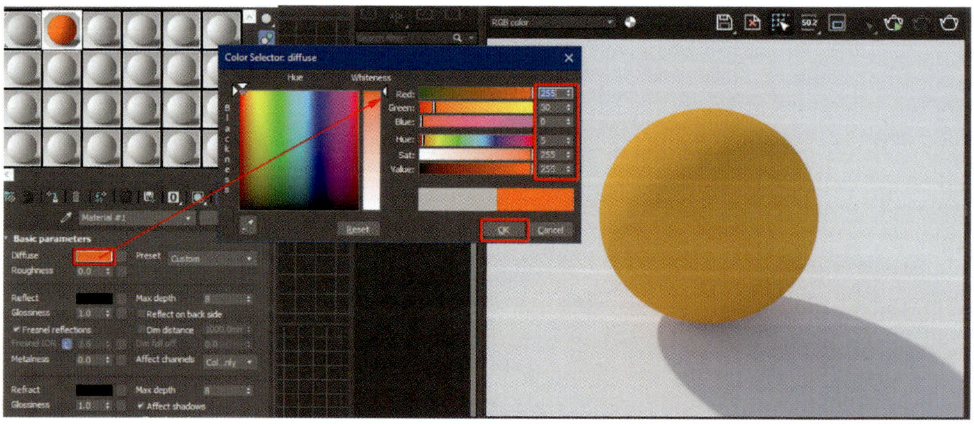

Color Selector dialog used to Diffuse color to orange

Sample Screen Color picker button

Diffuse toggle: The diffuse toggle allows users to plug a host of standard and V-Ray procedural maps listed in the Material/Map Browser.

The VRayBitmap procedural map is often used to apply textures to its Bitmap toggle, as previously shown. It's worth noting that reflective surfaces will affect the original diffuse color and/or its texture.

Users often increase the Metalness function value to darken materials, when materials lose too much of their original color because of reflectivity.

Some of the chapters ahead will show other ways to fix this problem.

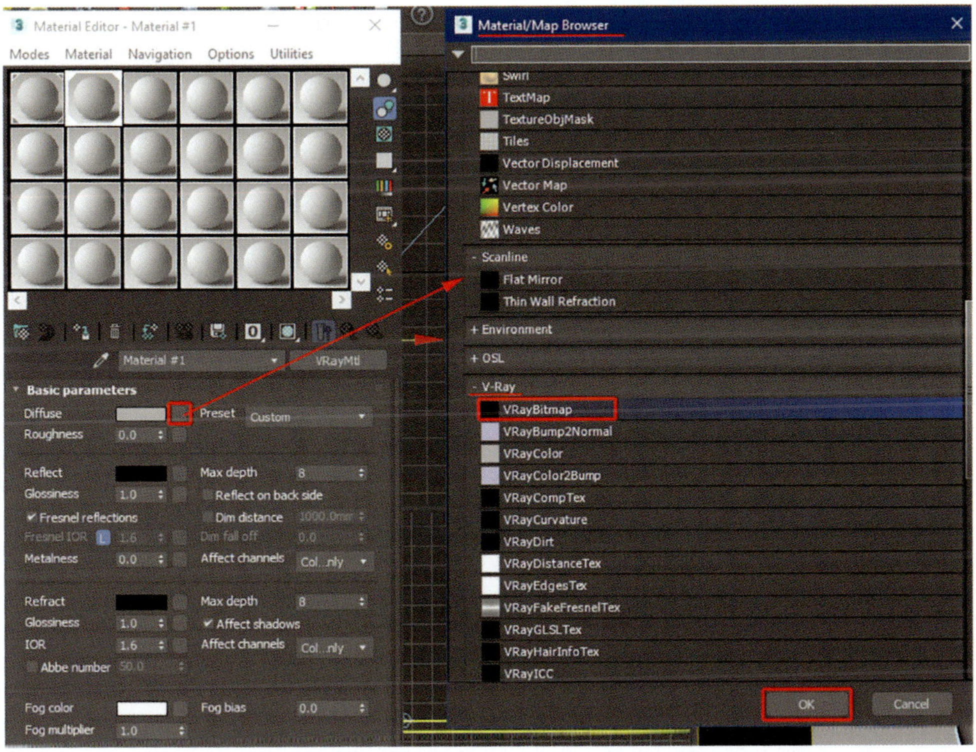

Diffuse toggle used to open a List of procedural maps in the Material/Map Browser

Roughness toggle: The toggle enables users to plug textures and other procedural maps from the Material/Map Browser list.

This toggle works best with black and white and grayscale textures/procedural maps. Once a texture is applied, it automatically overrides the numerical values.

Roughness value: This function determines how coarse a surface appears.

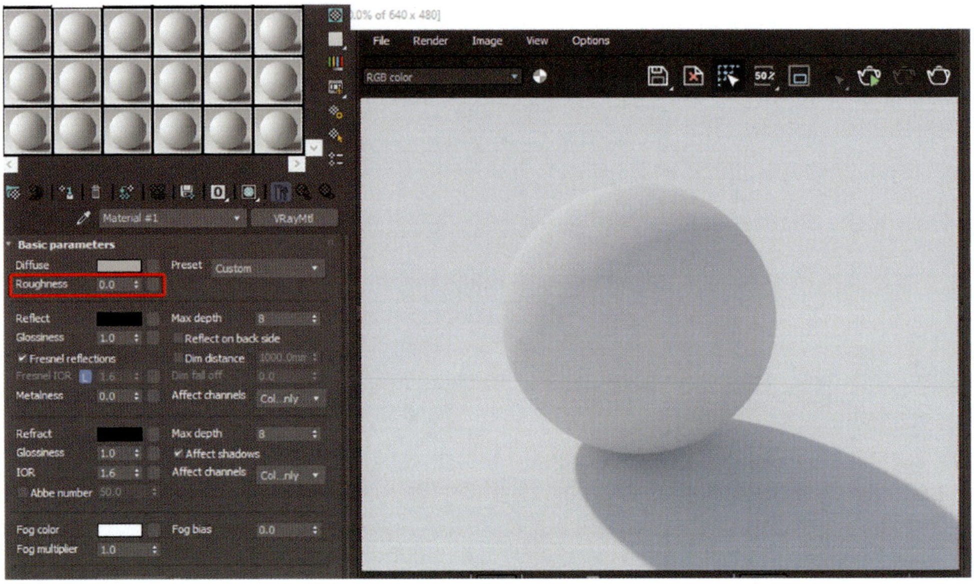

Roughness value set to 0.0

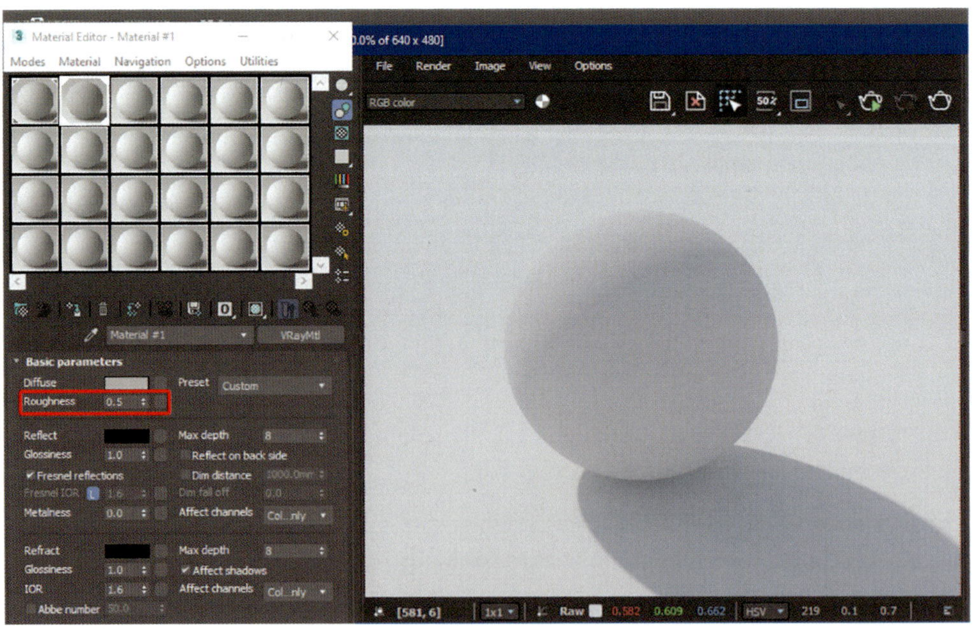

Roughness value set to 0.5

Preset rollout is a downsized version of the V-Ray Asset Browser dialog.

Unlike the V-Ray Asset Browser dialog, the Preset rollout allows users to choose a smaller number of material presets available from the dropdown list.

The preview for each material preset is available from the material slot.

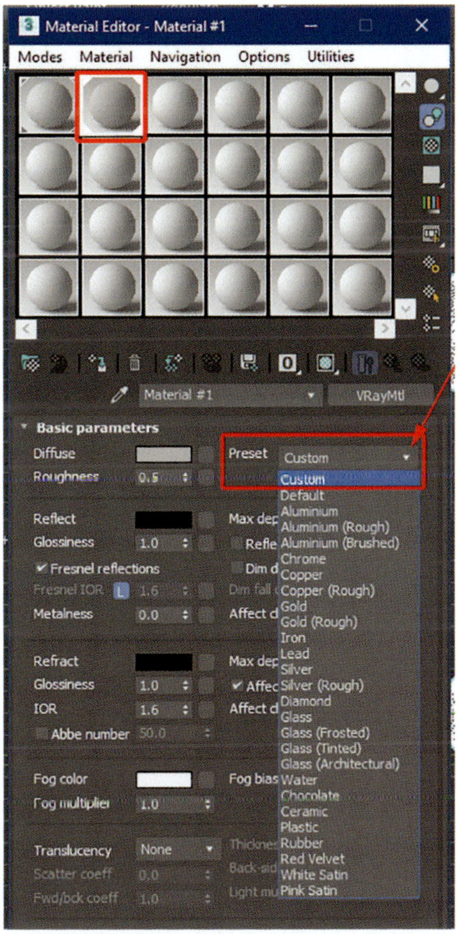

Material Editor dialog with V-Ray material Preset list

To maximize the material slot, simply double click on it.

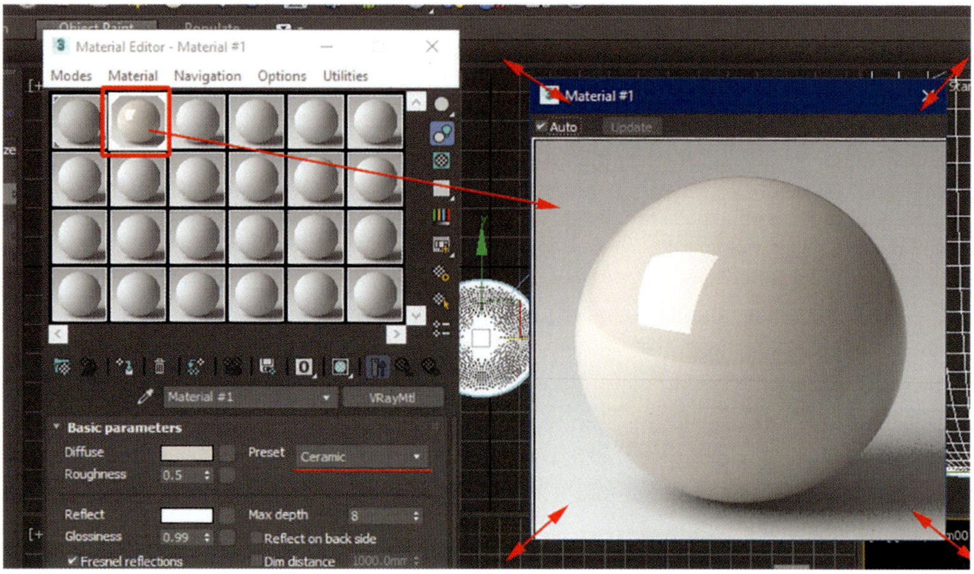

Material slot maximized

Reflect

Reflect Color: This color swatch allows users to pick and choose the Reflect intensity/color, by using the Color Selector dialog.

The default color is black, which's equivalent to no reflections.

Darker colors yield less reflections, and lighter colors (e.g., white) yield the opposite effect.

It's also common for users to set specific colors (e.g., orange/brass color), when creating metallic surfaces such as brass.

Reflect toggle: This toggle enables users to set the reflectivity of the surface, by plugging textures and other procedural maps from the Material/Map Browser list.

It works best with black and white and grayscale textures. Artists often plug a gray texture to this toggle, to realistically emulate a surface reflecting light unevenly.

Once a texture/procedural map is applied to the toggle, it automatically overrides the color swatch values.

Fresnel reflections: When enabled, the reflections and highlights are calculated automatically by the camera/viewing angle of the surface. This function is turned on by default.

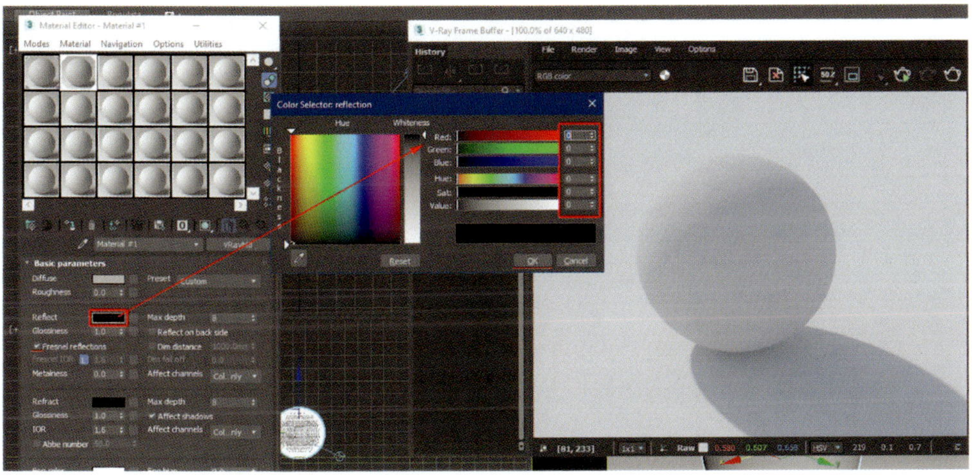

Reflect Color Selector dialog set to 0.0, with the Fresnel reflections enabled

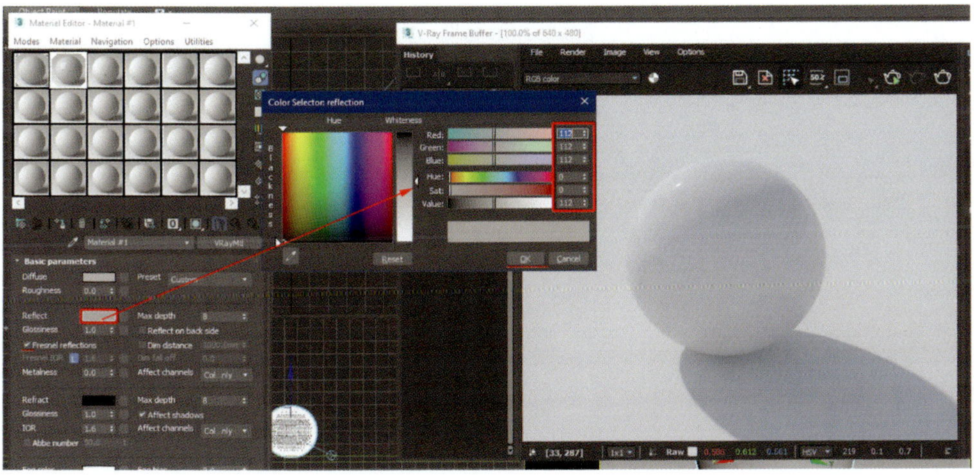

Reflect Color Selector dialog set to 112, with the Fresnel reflections enabled

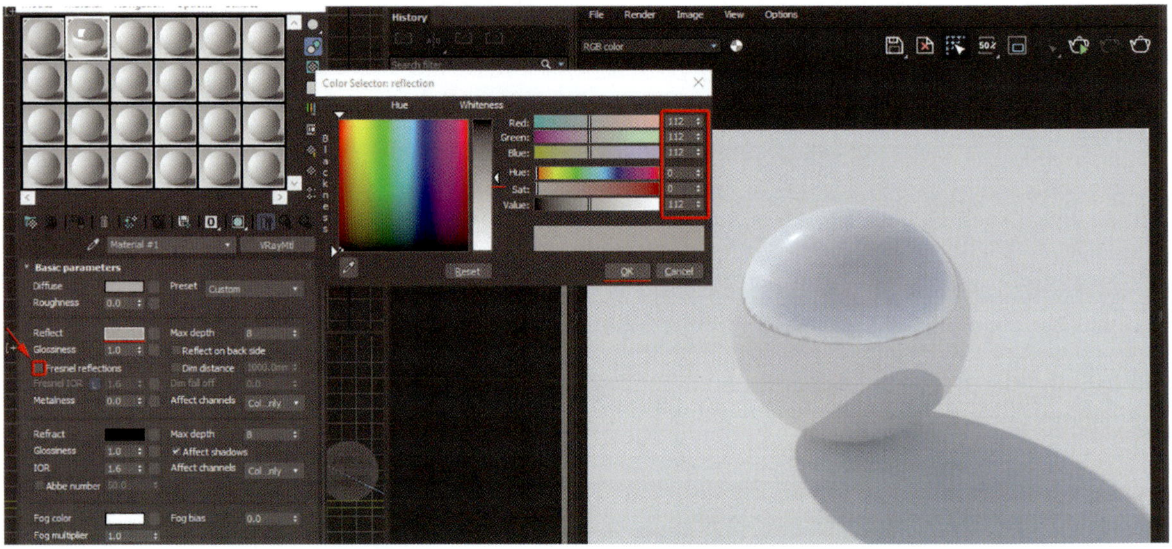

Reflect Color Selector dialog set to 112, with the Fresnel reflections disabled

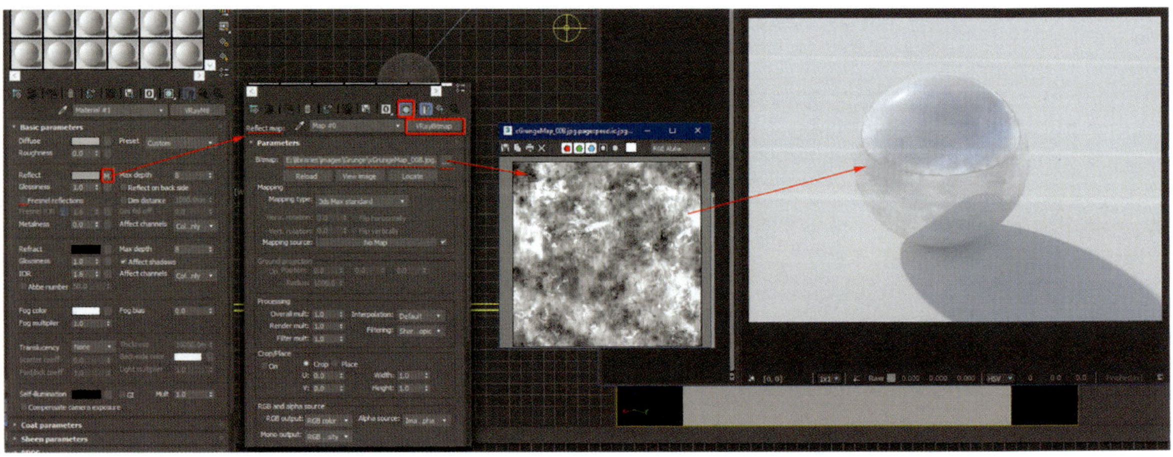

Reflect toggle, with gray texture applied via VRayBitmap and Fresnel reflections disabled

At times, having the Reflect toggle with a grayscale texture, in conjunction with, the Fresnel reflections enabled, can yield appealing results. It's just a matter of trying what works best (e.g., with or without Fresnel turned on).

The more contrast the grayscale texture has, the sharper the reflections/glossiness will be.

To achieve the opposite effect (e.g., more diffused results), the grayscale texture needs to have less contrast (e.g., more gray than black areas).

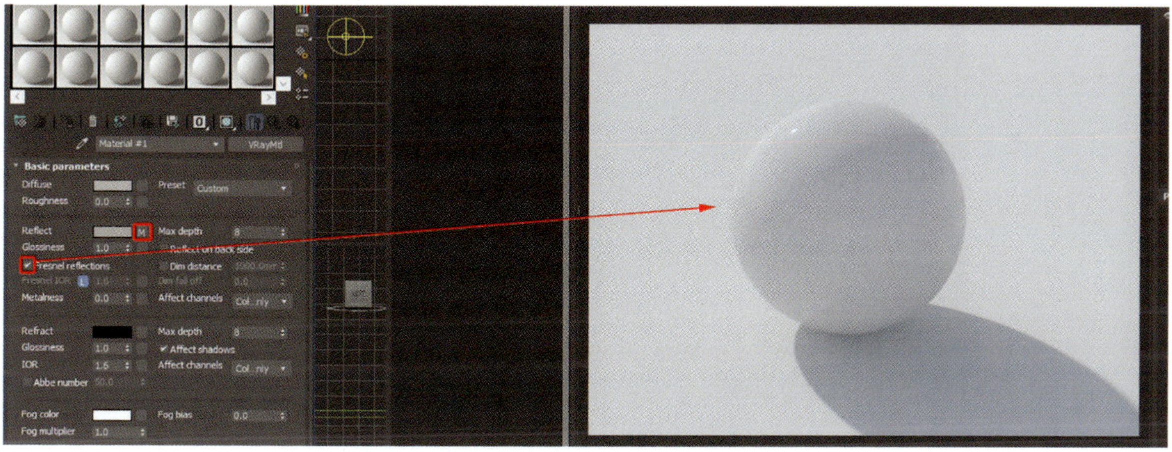

Reflect toggle, with gray texture and Fresnel reflections enabled

There are also instances when users might be required to invert the grayscale texture inside the Reflect toggle, in order to achieve specific results.

To do so, simply go inside the Reflect map Coordinates, and scroll down to the Output rollout.

In the Output rollout parameters, enable the Invert function. It works in the exact same way as the Invert tool in Photoshop (Ctrl+i)

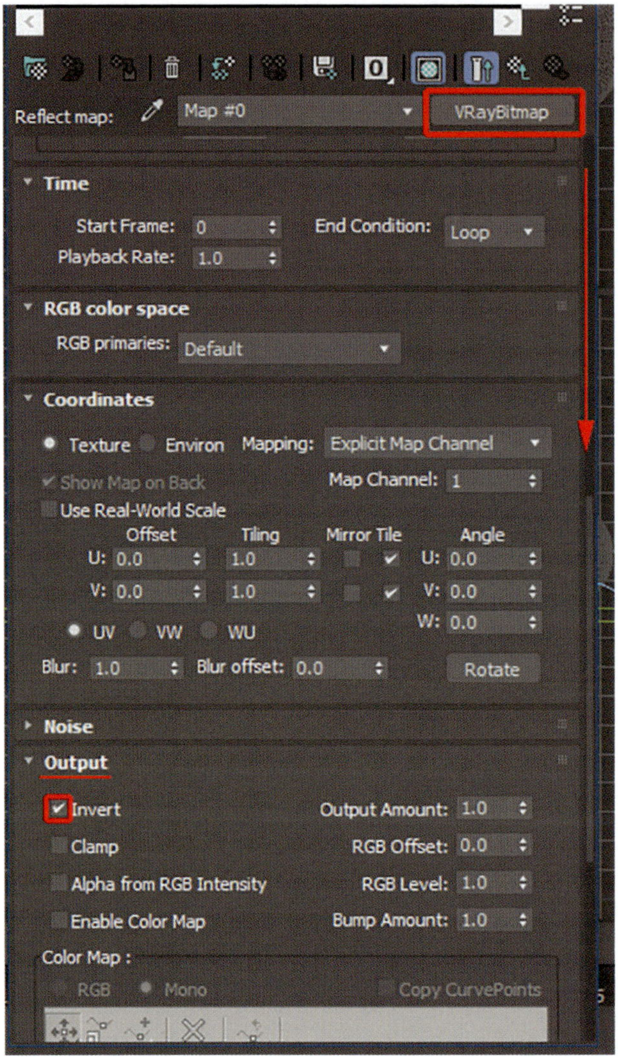

Reflect map grayscale texture inverted under the Output rollout

NOTE

This amazing technique can also be used with any function with a toggle.

The Reflect toggle texture can also be mixed/blended with its color swatch to produce specific results. To do so, simply scroll down to the Maps rollout, and reduce the Reflect toggle's numerical values.

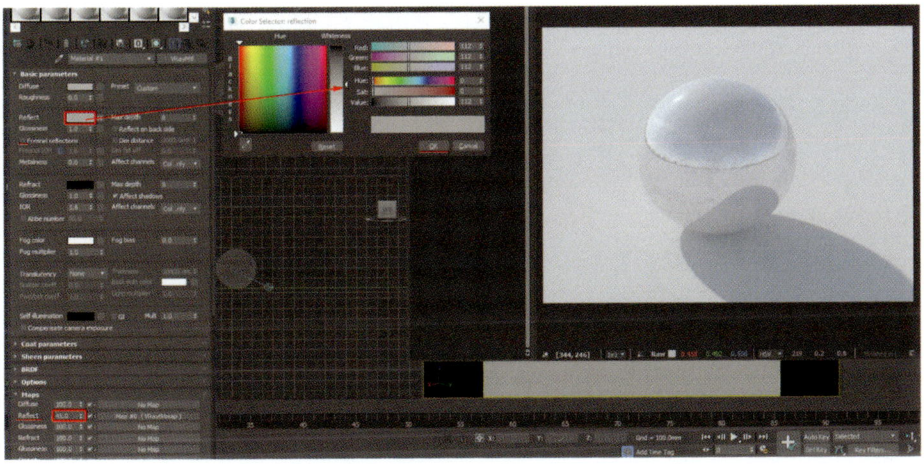

Reflect toggle value set to 45 and mixed with the Reflect color swatch

It is also common practice for users to apply the Falloff procedural map to help control the Fresnel effects, manually.

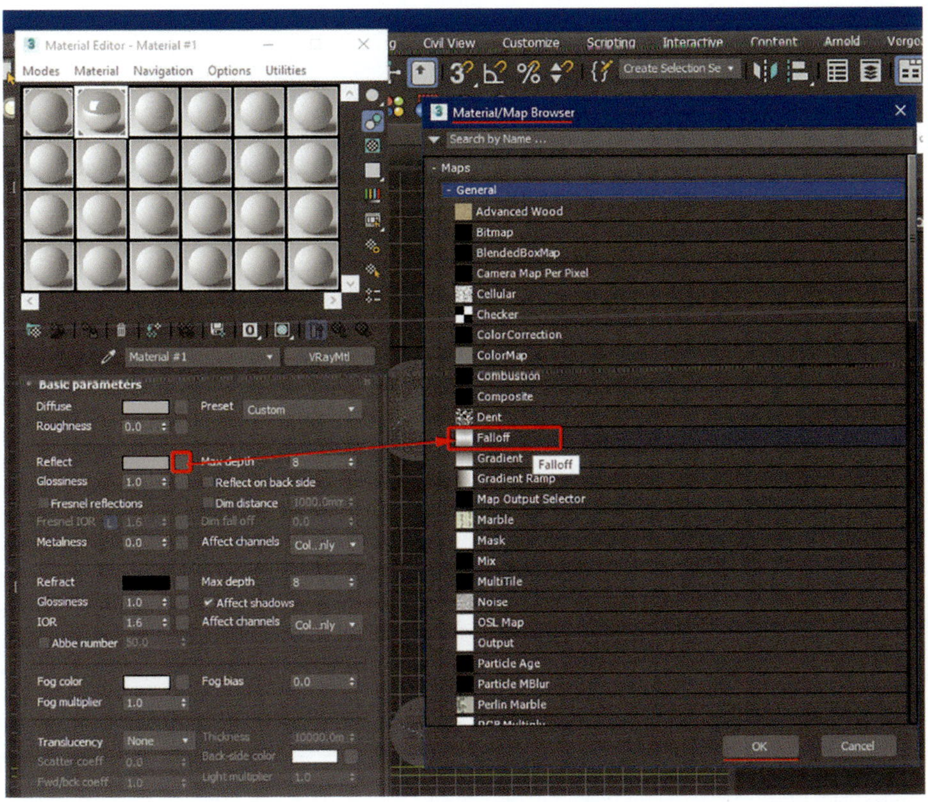

Falloff procedural map applied to the Reflect toggle

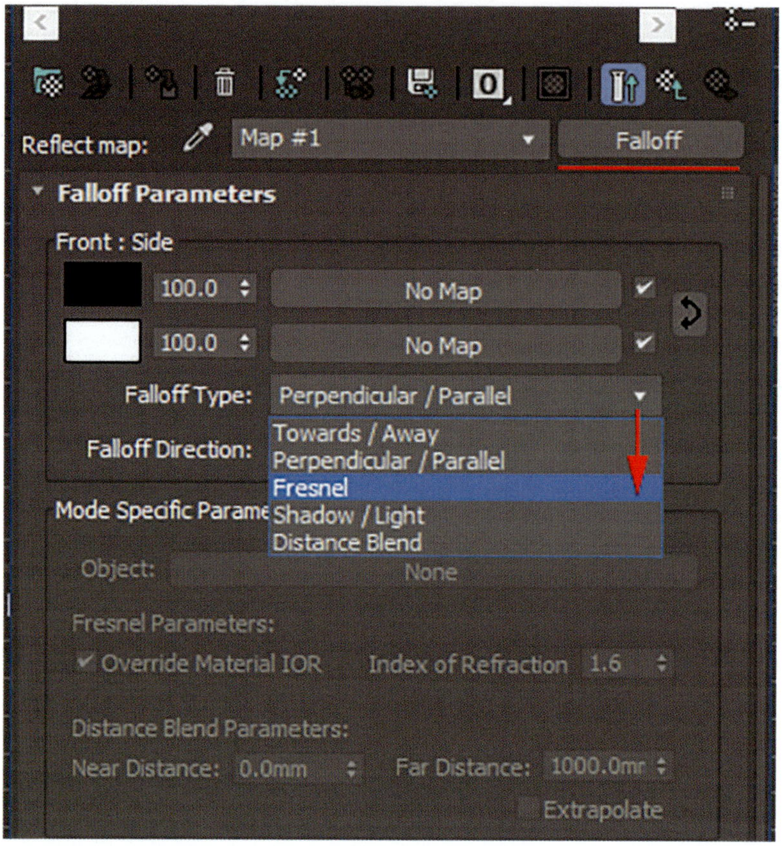

Fresnel Falloff Type

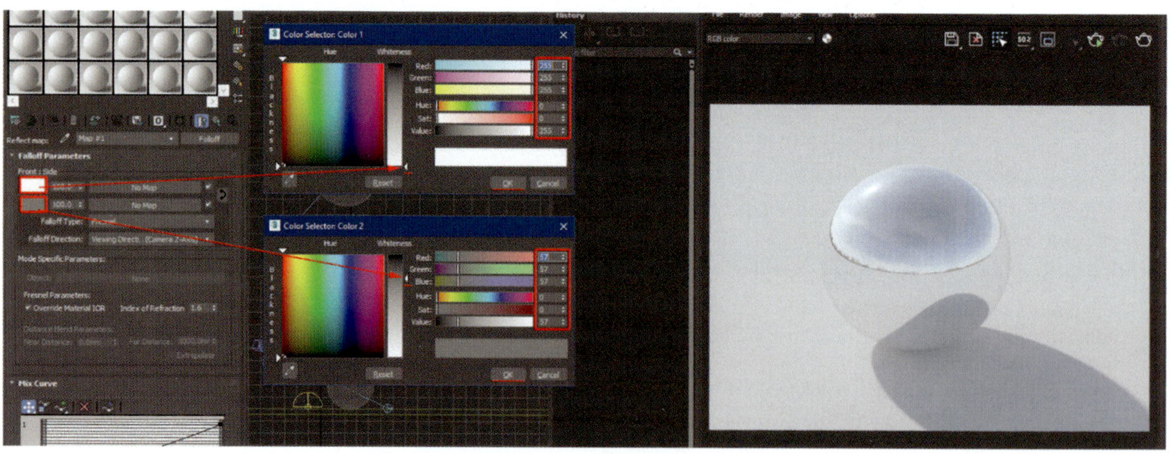

Front: Side color values tweaked to achieve different reflection map results

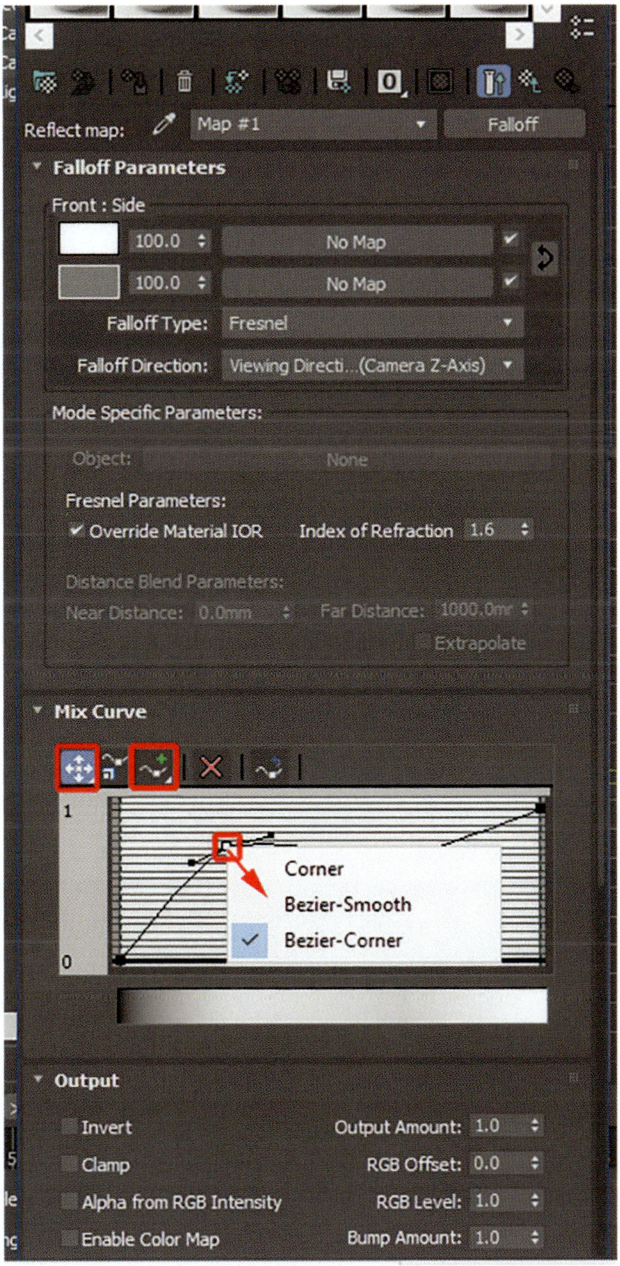

Mix Curve points tweaked to help control the reflections

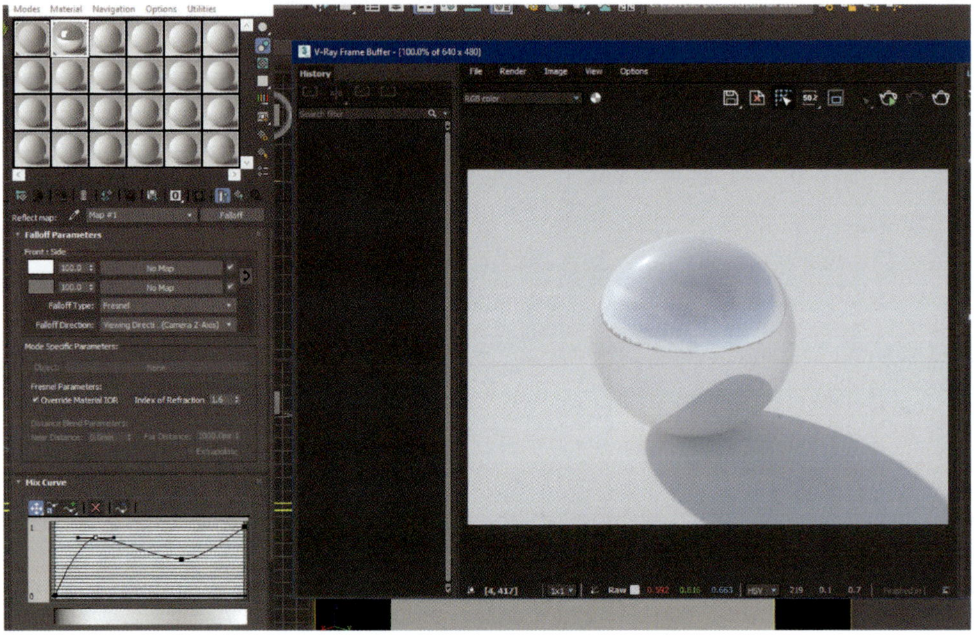

Final render result with Falloff Parameters tweaked

Fresnel reflections: This function is padlocked with Fresnel IOR, and it's set 1.6 by default. To manually change this, simply click on the L (padlock) button.

Its adjacent toggle allows users to plug bitmaps and/or procedural maps to it.

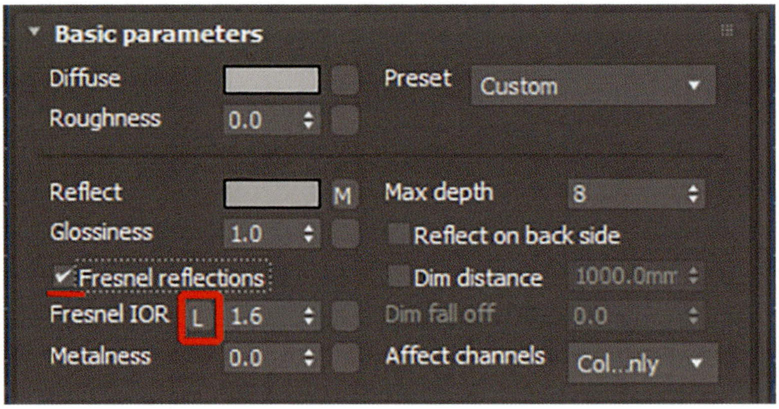

Reflect Fresnel IOR with the padlock(L) unlocked

Glossiness: This function determines the appearance of glossy highlights and the type of reflections on surfaces. Its value is set to 1.0 by default.

The value of 1.0 yields a sharp/linear highlight with sharp/linear reflections.

The appearance of highlights is only noticeable when there is reflectivity on the surface. Otherwise, the glossiness values will be redundant.

Lower values yield blurrier reflections and wider highlights.

For perfect highlight results, users should not reduce the Glossiness values below 0.5.

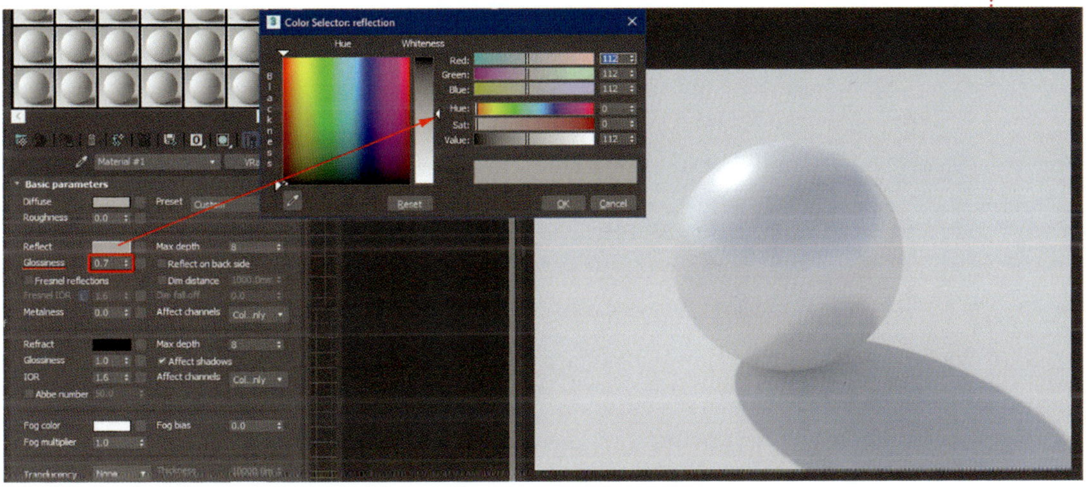

Reflect Glossiness value set to 0.7, with Color Selector dialog set to 112, and the Fresnel reflections turned off

Glossiness value set to 1.0, with the Fresnel reflections turned off

Glossiness toggle: This toggle allows users to plug a grayscale texture or/and a procedural map to it. Once applied, it automatically overrides its numerical values.

Once a texture/procedural map is applied to the toggle, it automatically overrides the Glossiness values.

Glossiness toggle with grayscale texture applied to VRayBitmap

Metalness: This function yields a metallic look to surfaces. Values range from 0.0 to 1.0.

The value of 1.0 darkens the surface and yields a more metallic look.

Users should only enter values 0.0 or 1.0, respectively. Values in-between yield physically inaccurate results.

The Metalness function works best when the Reflect color swatch is set to full white (255).

NOTE

When enabled, the Use roughness function will automatically switch the Glossiness function to Roughness.

To match PBR setups from external applications, users often plug the roughness texture to the Glossiness toggle, and enable the Use roughness function under the BRDF rollout parameters.

Metalness toggle: The toggle enables users to plug a grayscale texture or/and a procedural map to it. Once applied, it automatically overrides its numerical values.

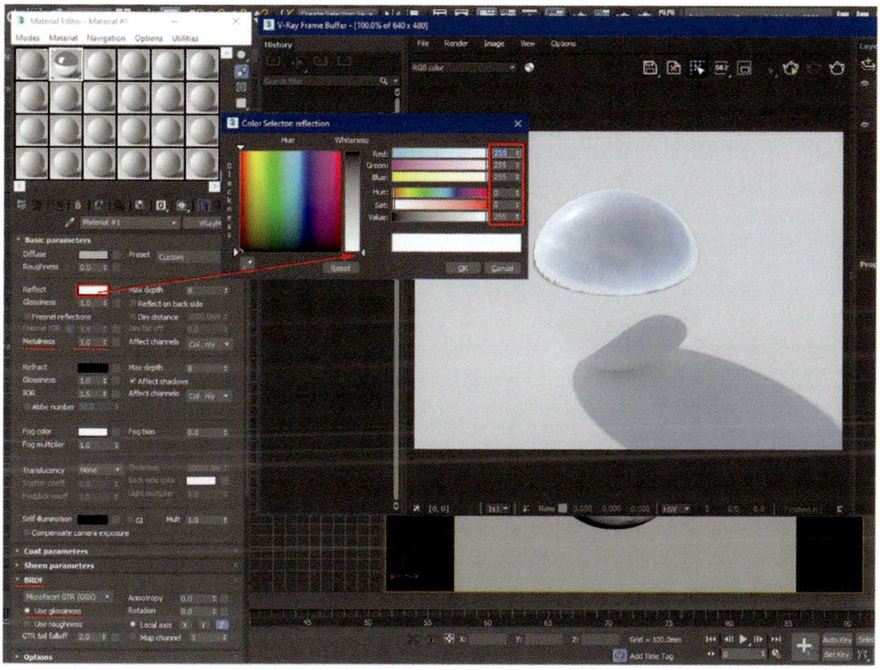

Reflect color swatch set to 255, Metalness value set 1.0 with BRDF Use glossiness function enabled

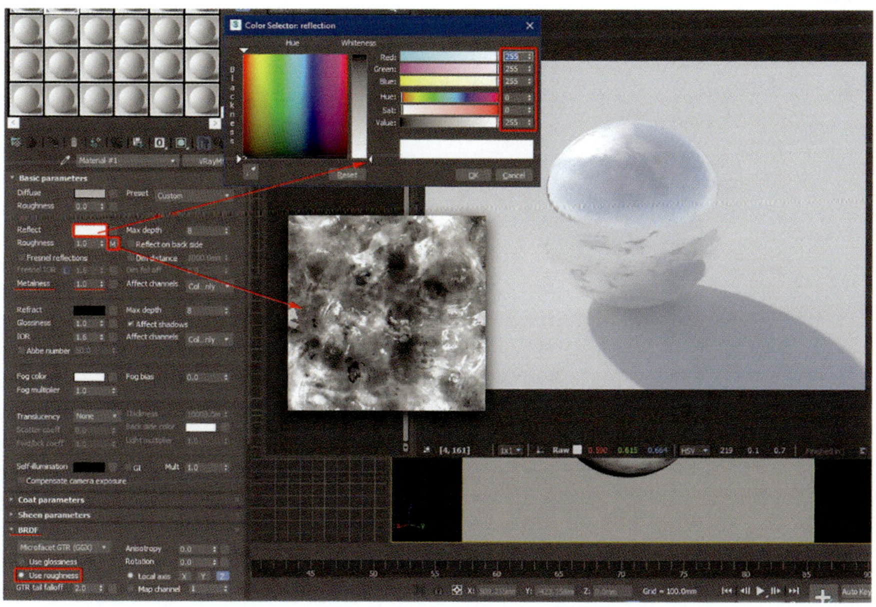

Reflect color swatch set to 255, Metalness set to 1.0 with BRDF Use roughness enabled and texture applied

Max depth: This function sets the number of times a ray can be reflected, before it stops, and begins using the Exit color.

This function is quite useful for scenes with numerous reflections/ refractions bouncing off each other. Increasing the Max depth value will eradicate any potential black areas (exit color) in the reflections/refractions.

However, it may increase the rendering times.

Max depth value is set to 5, by default.

Reflect on back side: This function works best on glass thickness.

The Refract color determines the opacity of a surface. A full white Refract color (255) makes a surface fully transparent.

To create a typical glass material, simply set its Diffuse color to Black 0, Reflect color 193, Refract color to 255 (white), and the Fog color to 109,57,220 (greenish tint).

Alternatively, simply load a Glass preset from V-Ray Asset Browser dialog.

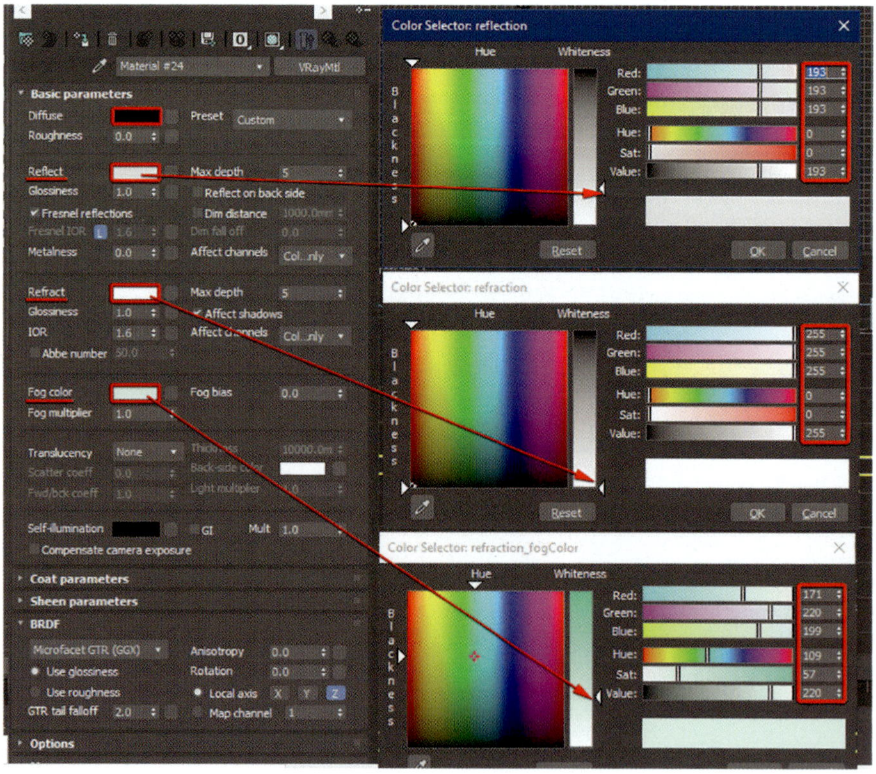

Glass material with Reflect Color Selector set to 193, Refract Color Selector set to 255, and Fog Color Selector set to 220

When the Reflect on back side function is turned on, V-Ray takes into consideration internal and back face reflections of an object, which will subsequently increase the rendering times (inevitably).

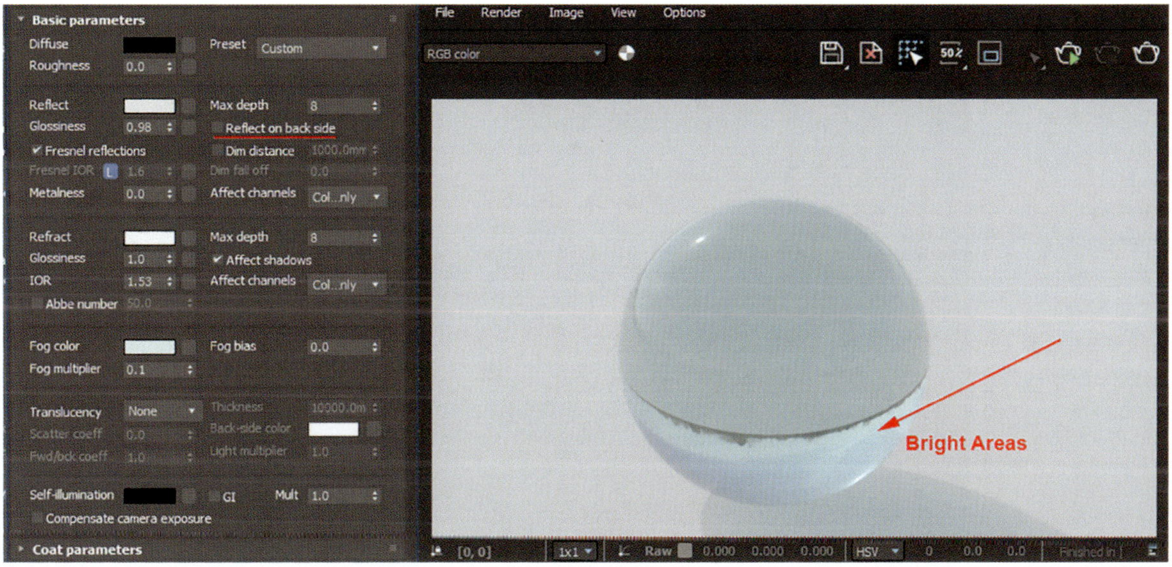

Reflect on back side function turned off

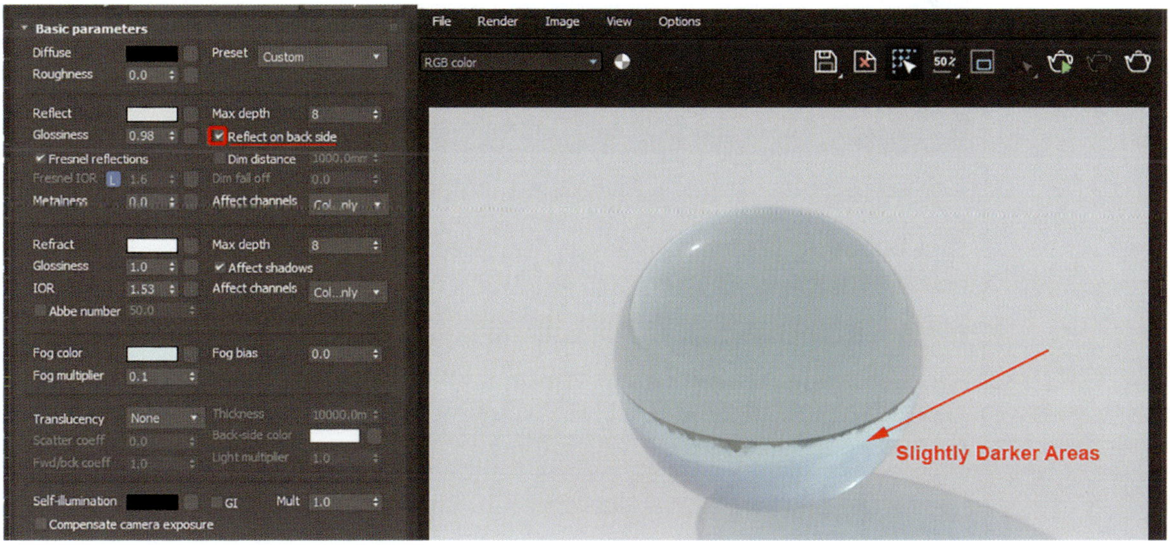

Reflect on back side function turned on

Dim distance: When enabled, it restricts the distance of traced rays, by entering the numerical radius. Disabled by default.

NOTE

For Multi Matte Element, if you wish to be able to select objects being reflected on this surface, the Affect channels need to be set to All Channels instead.

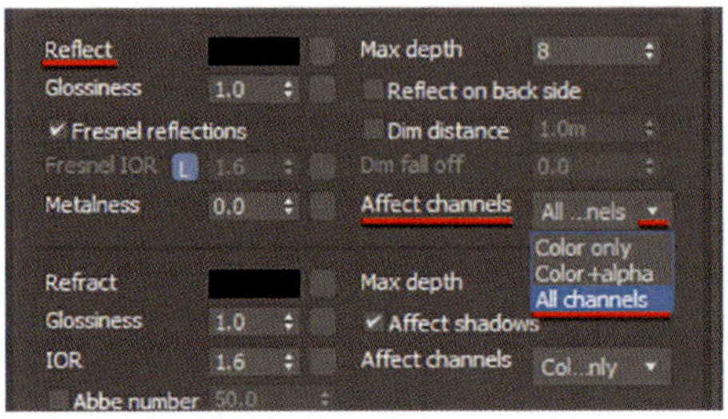

Reflect Affect All channels option selected

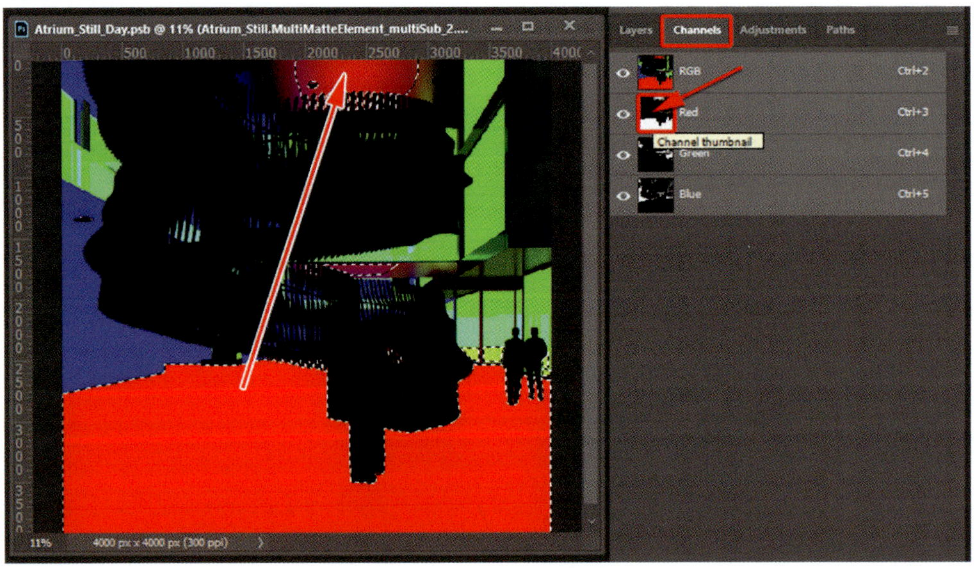

Reflect Affect All channels reflected in the Red MultiMatteElement

Dim fall off: When enabled, it sets the fall off radius of Dim distance. It is automatically enabled when the Dim distance is turned on.

It's grayed out by default.

Affect channels: This function controls how the render channels are being affected by the Reflection. It's set to Color only, by default.

Refract

Refract: The color swatch of this function controls the opacity of a surface. Black (e.g., 0.0) being completely opaque, and white (e.g., 255) being fully transparent.

Default color value is 0.0 (fully opaque). When the Refract color value is 0.0 (black), VRayMtl immediately uses the Diffuse base color instead.

NOTE

The main opacity of an object should always be controlled via refraction; as opposed to object properties (right click>object properties>Opacity).

Refract toggle: The refract toggle allows users to plug textures and/or procedural maps to it. Grayscale and/or black/white textures work best.

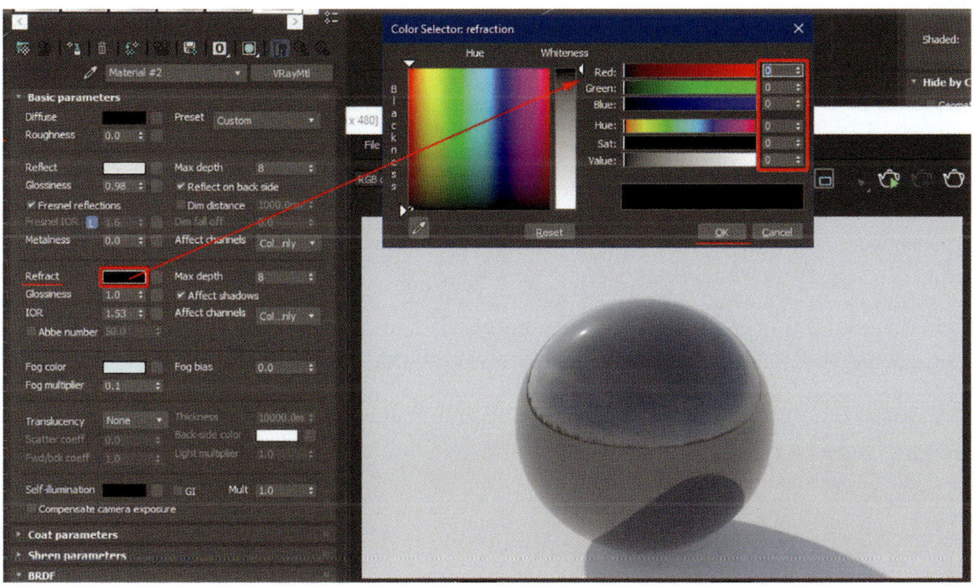

Refract color value set to 0.0 (black)

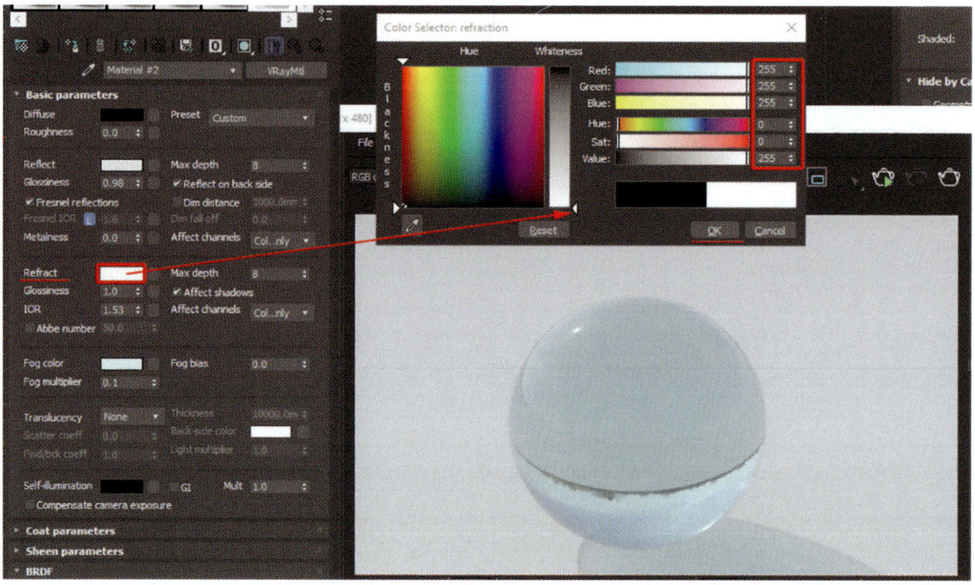

Refract color value set to 255 (white)

Glossiness: This function controls the sharpness of refractions. The value of 1.0 equals to sharp refractions.

The value of 0.0 is equivalent to completely diffused refractions. Users often reduce these values to emulate translucent surfaces.

It's worth noting that decreasing these values will subsequently increase the rendering times of this surface.

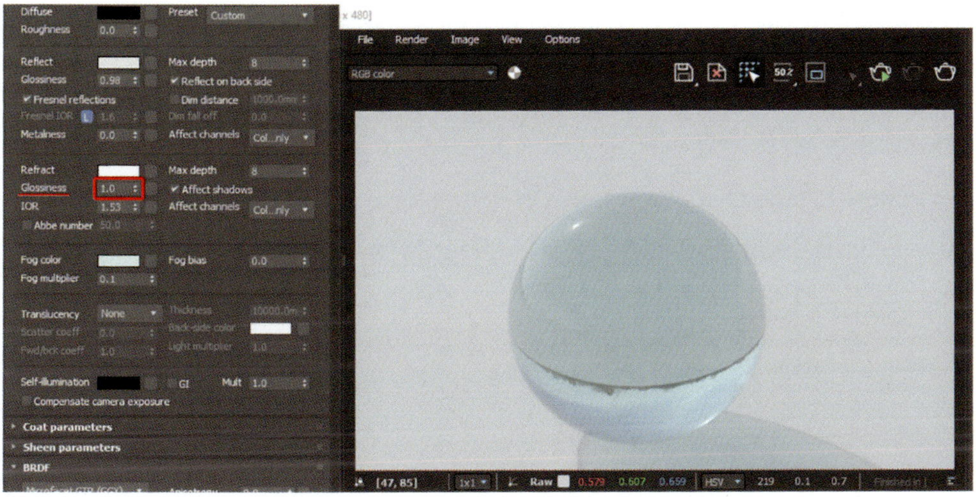

Refract Glossiness value of 1.0

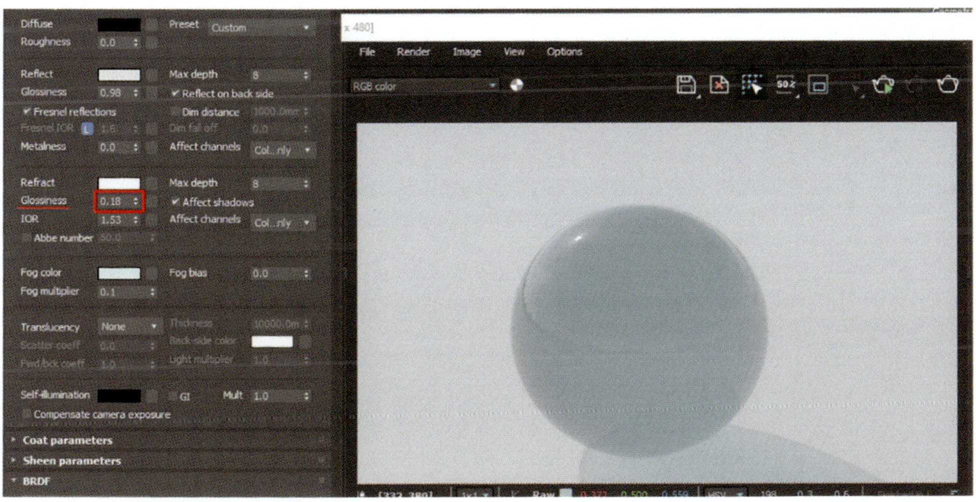

Refract Glossiness value of 0.18

IOR: The Index Of Refraction determines how a light interacts/bends through a transparent surface.

IOR effects are not visible on completely solid surfaces. Surfaces need to be partially or fully transparent.

An IOR value of 1.0 is equal to no refraction on a transparent surface. The default value is 1.6.

For a more detailed list of refractive indices, please visit the following website:

https://en.wikipedia.org/wiki/List_of_refractive_indices

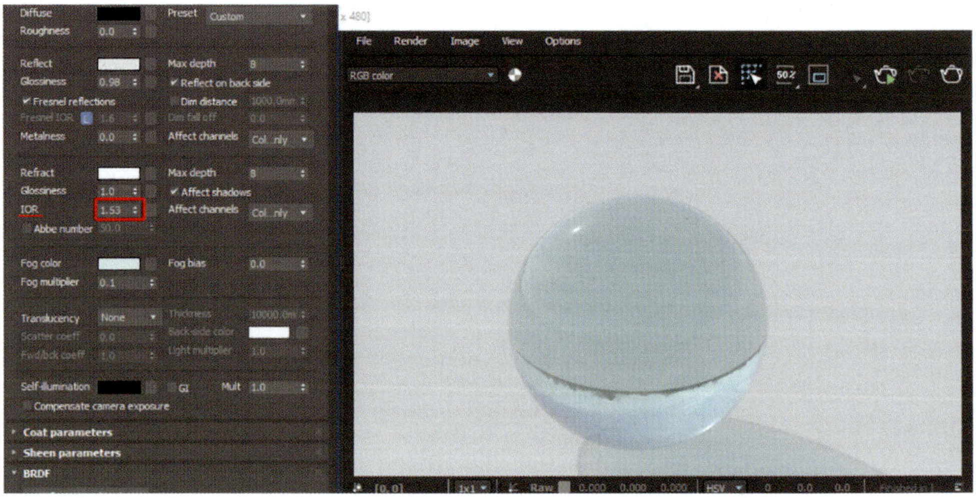

Refraction IOR value of 1.53

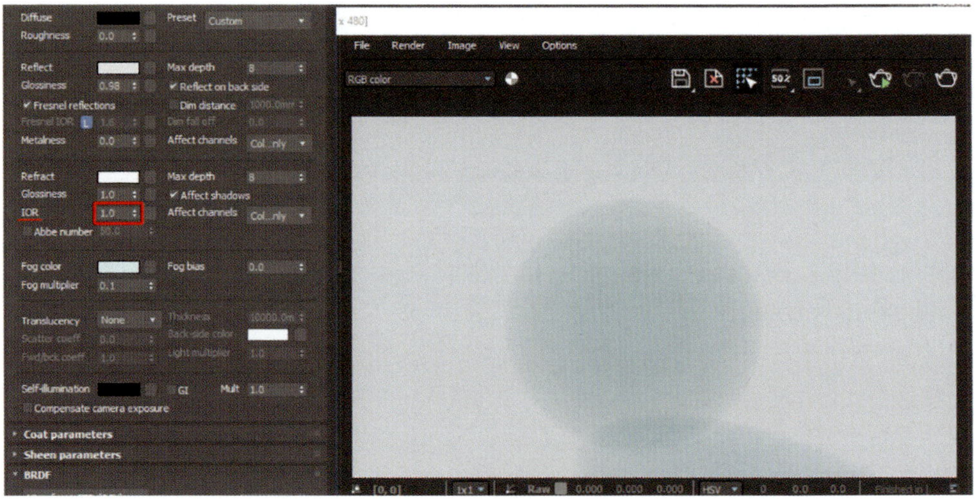

Refraction IOR value of 1.0

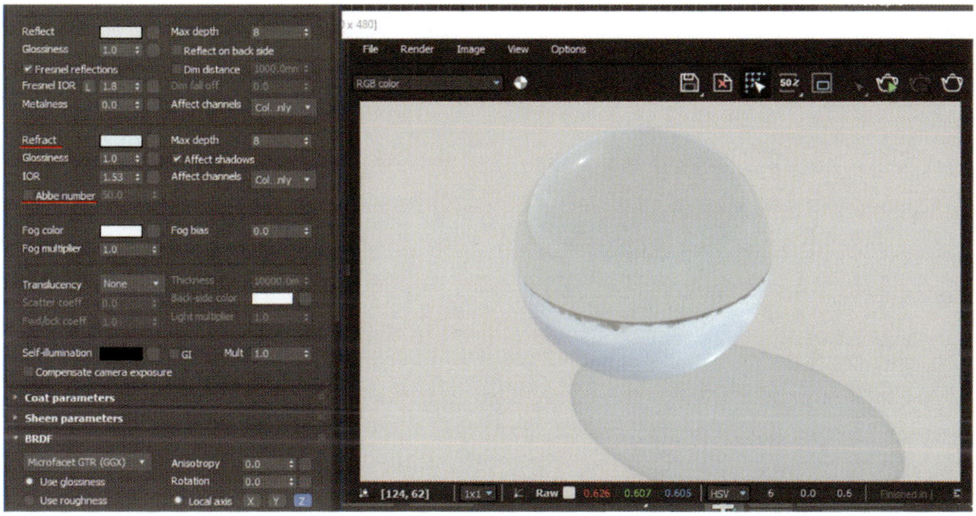

Refract Abbe number disabled

Abbe number: When enabled, it computes the light wavelength dispersion more accurately and photo realistically. However, the rendering times may skyrocket drastically.

The results are more noticeable when its value is set to a minimum of 10.

Also, abbe values help reinvigorate a spectrum of true light colors, which become apparent on the rim of objects, and on caustic effects (if enabled).

This function is more visible when there are physical lights interacting with an object. As opposed to HDRI being used as a light source.

Disabled, by default.

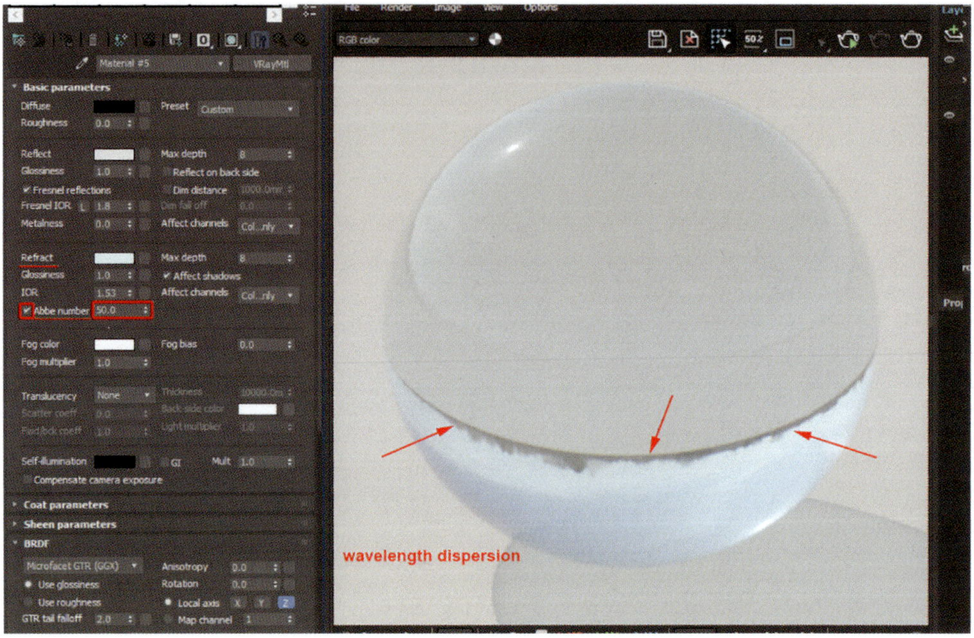

Refract Abbe number enabled with value set to 50.0

Max depth: This function determines the number of times a ray can be refracted, before it stops, and begins using the Exit color.

Max depth value is set to 8, by default. Increasing it will subsequently increase the rendering times of this surface.

Affect shadows: This function allows the light to pass through transparent surfaces (e.g., refractive objects) and cast its transparent shadows. The shadow colors may vary, depending on the surface.

This function is only noticeable on objects that are transparent (Refract color not completely black).

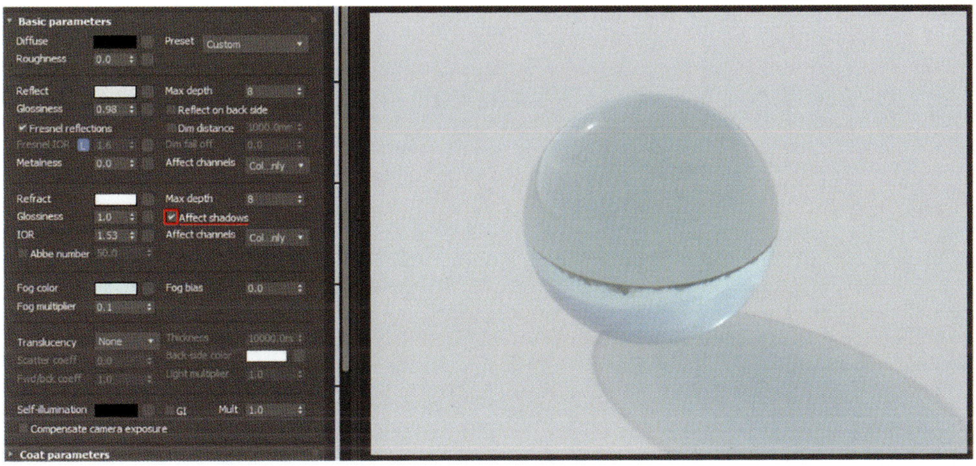

Refract Affect shadows enabled

Refract Affect shadows disabled

Refract Affect channels: When the surface is transparent, this specific function allows users to choose the channels to be affected by the refraction, in the rendering channels (e.g., Alpha, MultiMatteElement).

Professionals often choose the All channels option, as it helps to insert the background and other elements behind a refractive/transparent surface.

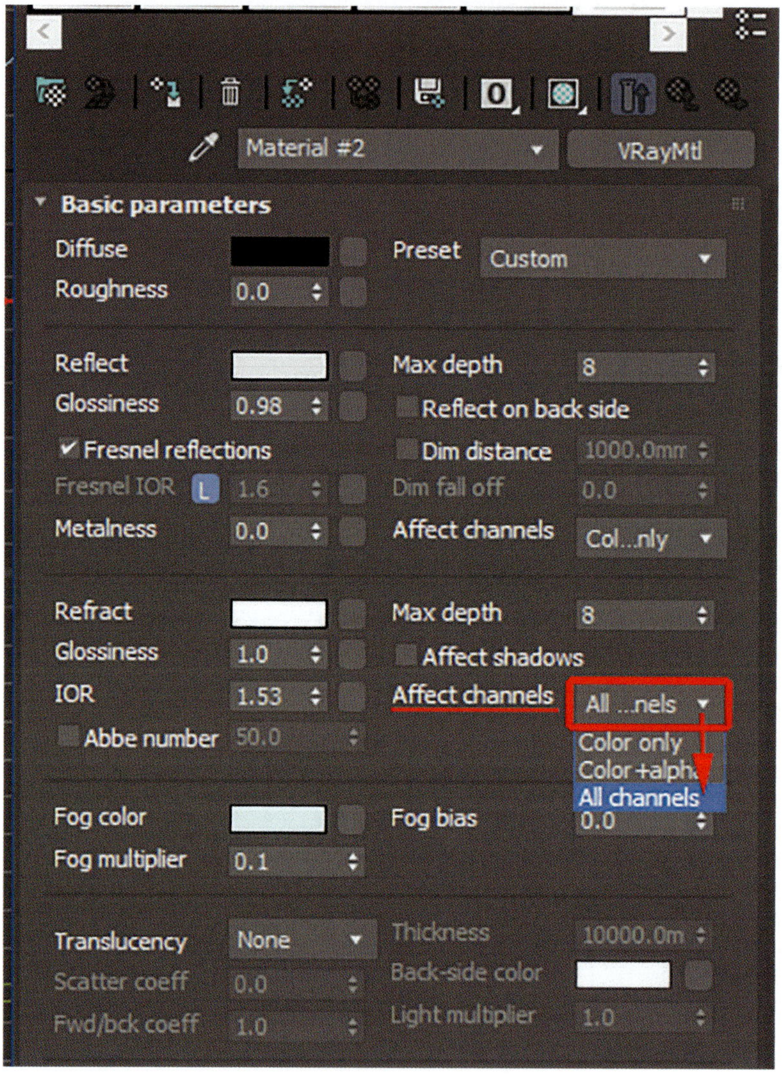

Refract Affect channels set to All channels

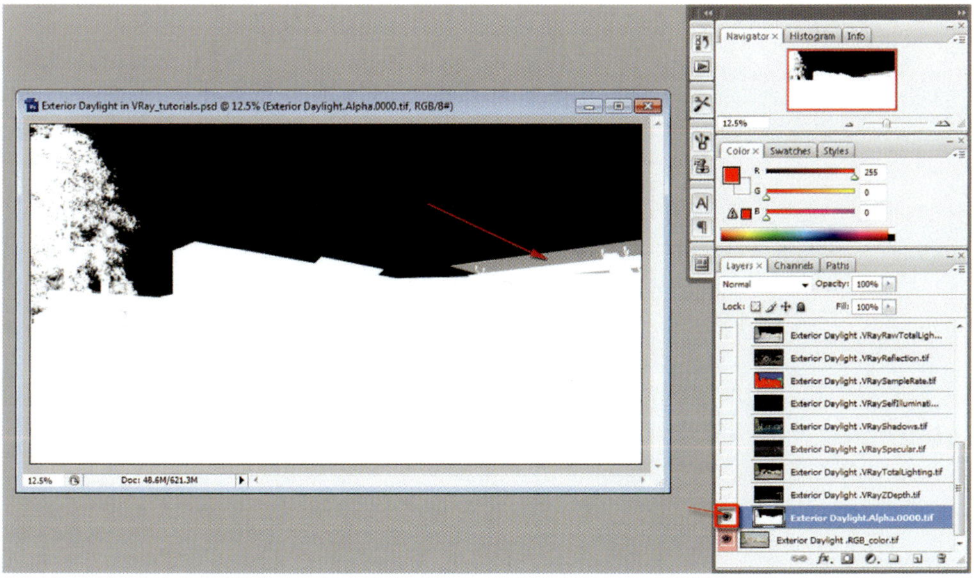

Alpha render element in Photoshop with Affect channels results

Final render with Background Sky inserted behind the glass

Fog

Fog color: This function enables users to change the color of refractive objects and/or emulate the effect of a more opaque object, depending on its size.

Darker colors make refractive objects look more opaque, and lighter colors yield the opposite effect.

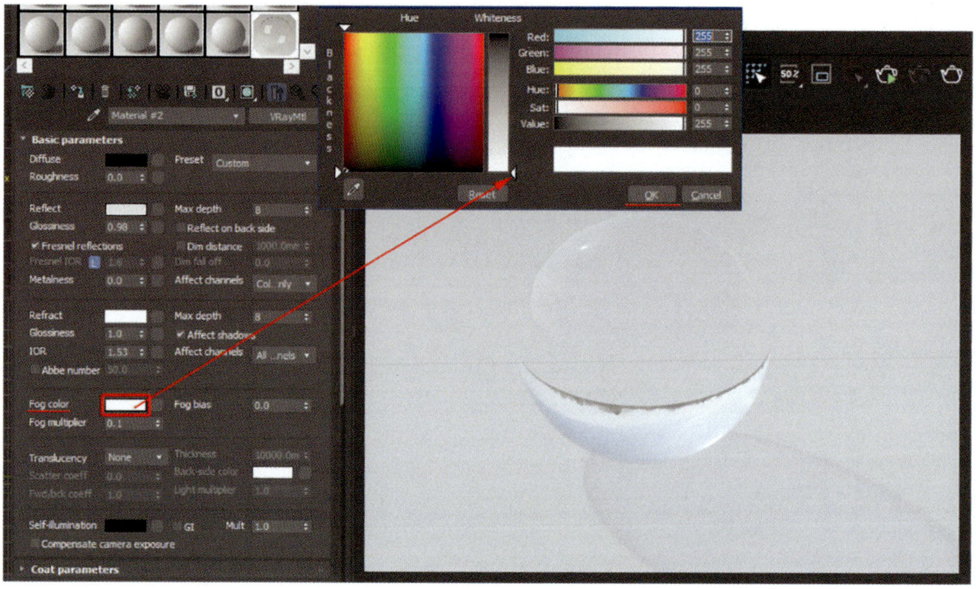

Fog color set to white

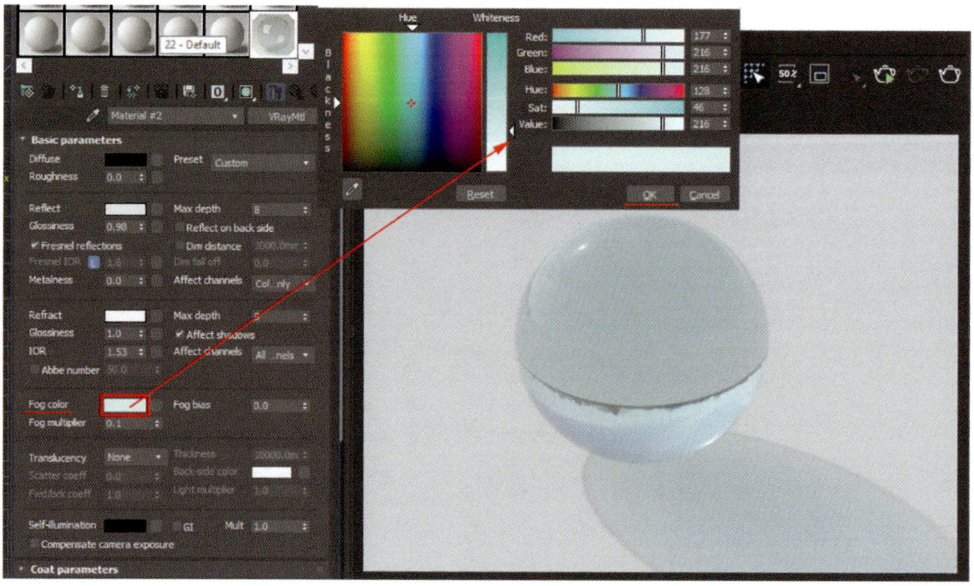

Fog color set to light green

Fog multiplier: This function determines the density/influence of the fog. Default value is 0.1.

Fog bias: The function allows users to control the density of objects (refractive surfaces mainly).

Default value is 0.0.

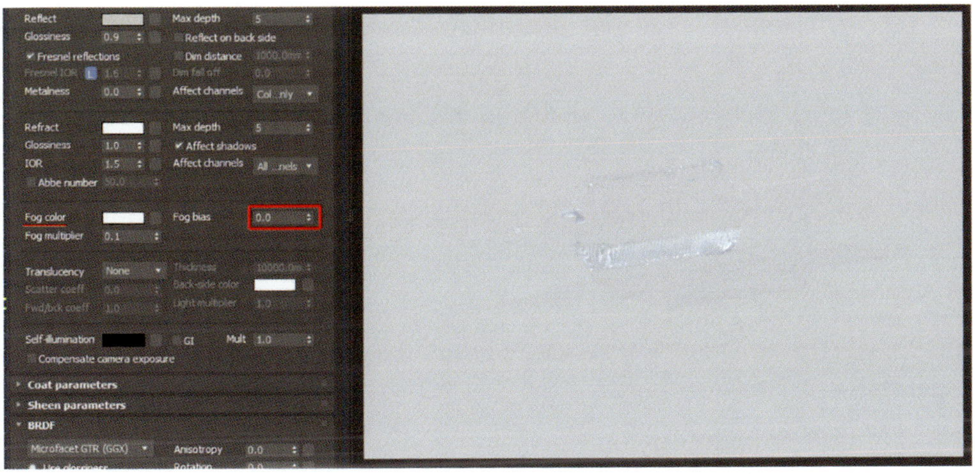

Fog bias set to 0.0

Fog bias set to –2.0

Translucency

Translucency: This function works in conjunction with refractions to calculate the amount of sub-surface scattering on a surface. It's set to None by default.

There are three types of translucent models: Hard wax model, Soft (water) model and Hybrid model

V-Ray Asset Browser comes with robust presets to emulate hard surfaces such as marble (Hard wax model), water and Hybrid models such as real translucent plastics, skin, milk and fruit juice.

Scatter coefficient: This function determines the amount of scattering inside a surface.

The value of 0.0 scatters rays in all directions. The value of 1.0 does the opposite.

It's set to 0.0 by default.

Forward/backward coefficient: This function controls the scattering direction. The value of 0.0 scatters the rays forward.

The value of 1.0 scatters the rays backward.

Thickness: This function is often used to limit the propagation of the rays traveling inside a surface.

It's set to 10.000 mm by default.

Back-side color: This function determines the color of the sub-surface scattering effect. It's set to white (255) by default.

Light multiplier: This function controls the strength of translucency.

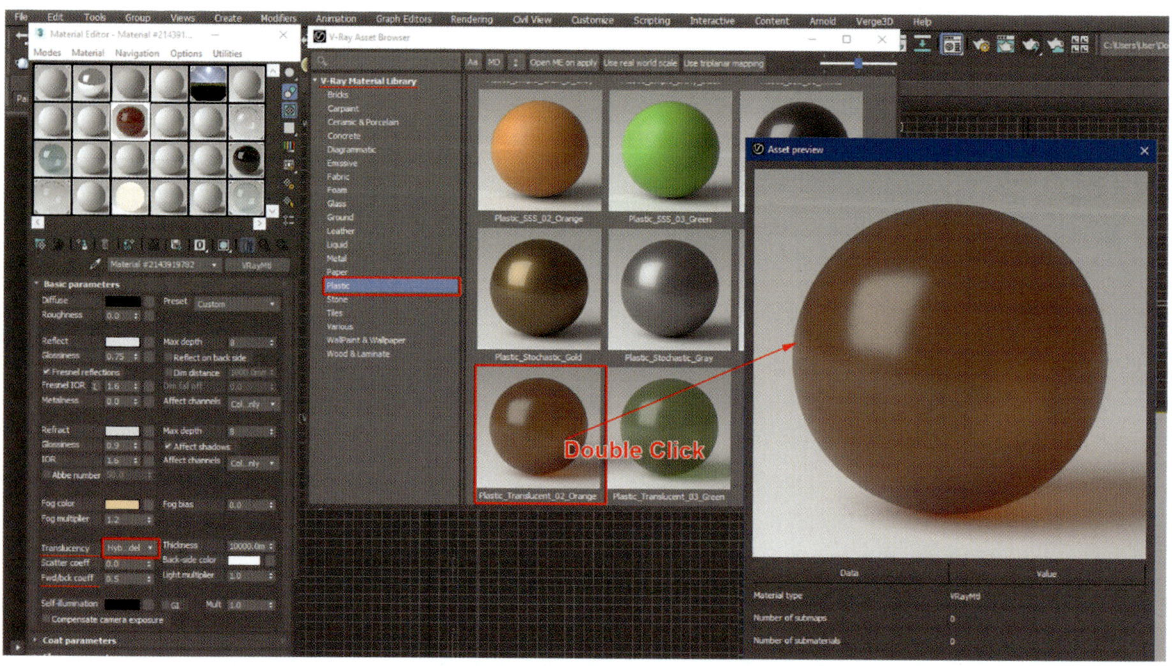

Plastic material with Translucency set as Hybrid model and Fwd/bck coeff set to 0.5

Self-Illumination

This function allows users to choose the Self-illumination color, from its color swatch, or plug a texture or/and a procedural map to its toggle.

To test this material, there's a scene named, Self-illumination.max

Self-illumination color: The self-illumination color swatch is set to black, by default.

Compensate camera exposure: When enabled, this function automatically adjusts the self-illumination intensity to compensate for the exposure of the scene.

GI: This function uses the Global Illumination settings to light up a scene. Otherwise, it will simply illuminate itself without contributing to the GI. Disabled by default.

Multiplier: This function controls the intensity of the self-illumination. Default value is set 1.0.

The self-illumination effect is more apparent in dark/dim scenes.

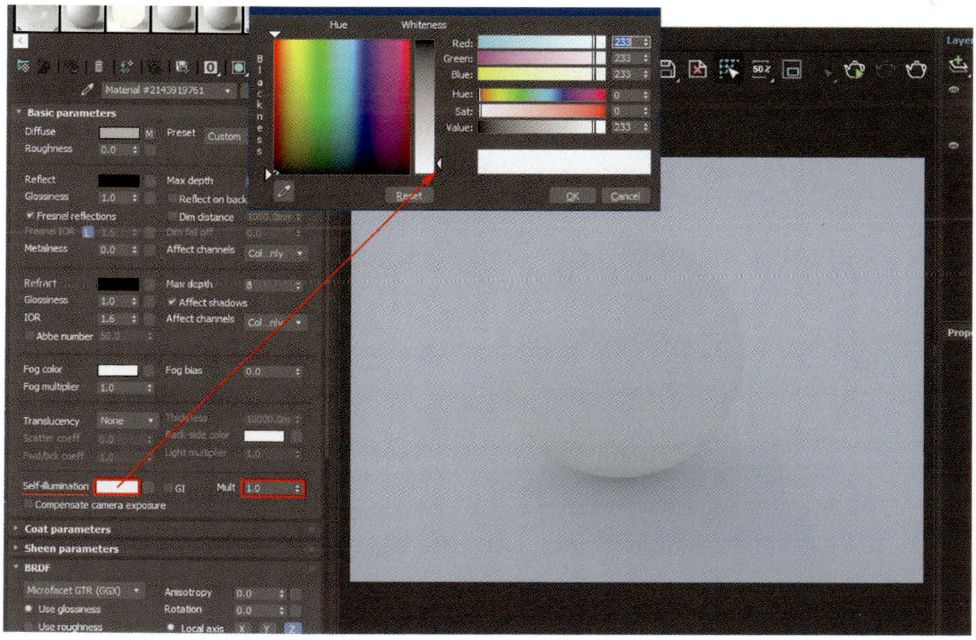

Self-illumination color set to white with Mult set to 1.0

NOTE

When using a bitmap/texture in the Self-illumination toggle, ensure its color swatch is black; otherwise, the texture will not be visible in the viewport.

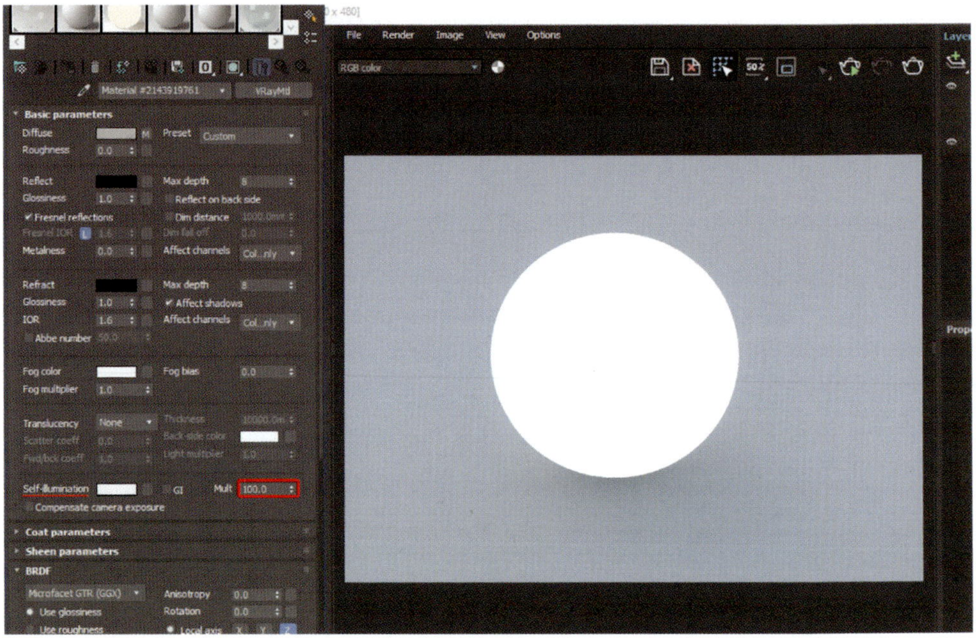

Self-illumination color set to white with Mult set to 100.0

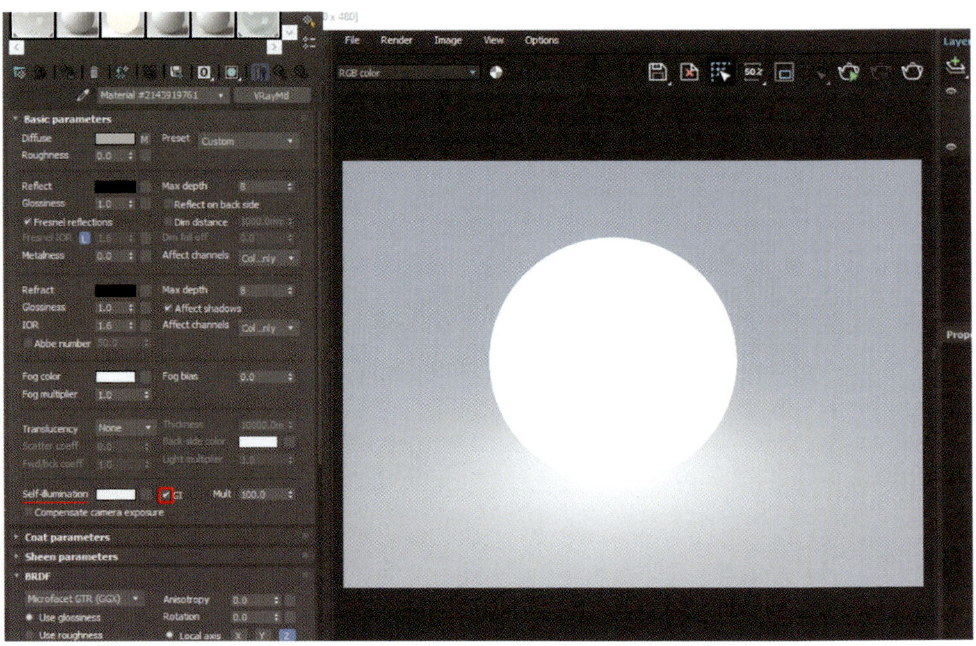

Self-illumination with GI function enabled

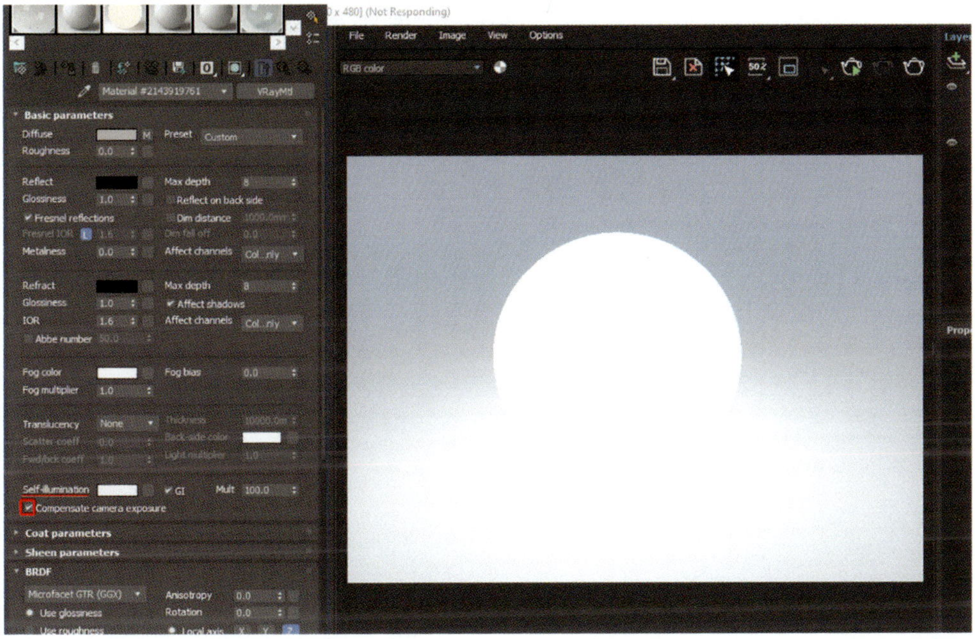

Self-illumination with compensate camera exposure enabled

Coat Parameters

To test this material parameter, there is a scene under the name, VRay Materials. max.

Coat amount: This function controls the blending amount (visibility) of the Coat color, Coat glossiness, Coat IOR, etc.

The value of 0.0 makes the Coat color or its map/layer in the toggle completely invisible.

The value of 1.0 makes the Coat color or its map/layer in the toggle completely visible and blending with the diffuse color or map/layer in the toggle.

Users can also use its adjacent toggle to plug materials or/and procedural maps.

The Coat amount is set to 0.0 by default.

Coat glossiness: This function sets the amount of glossiness and reflectivity of the coat.

Its toggle can be used to plug materials or/and procedural maps.

The default glossiness value is set to 1.0.

Coat IOR: This function sets the index of refraction of the Coat.

Users can plug materials or/and procedural maps to its adjacent toggle.

Its default IOR value is set to 1.6.

Coat color: This function controls the color of the coat.

Its adjacent toggle can be used to plug materials or/and procedural maps.

The default Coat color is set to white.

Lock coat bump to base bump: When enabled, it reinvigorates the base bump map over the coat bump map (if any).

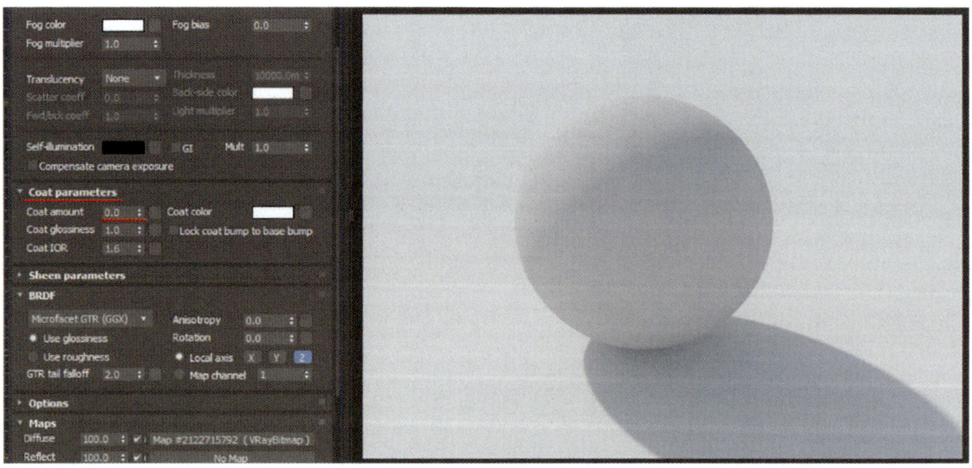

Coat amount set to 0.0

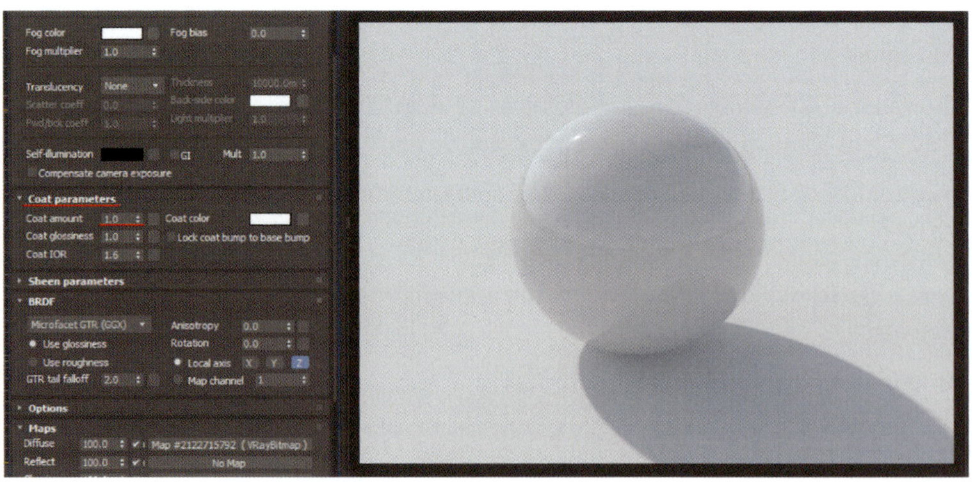

Coat amount set to 1.0

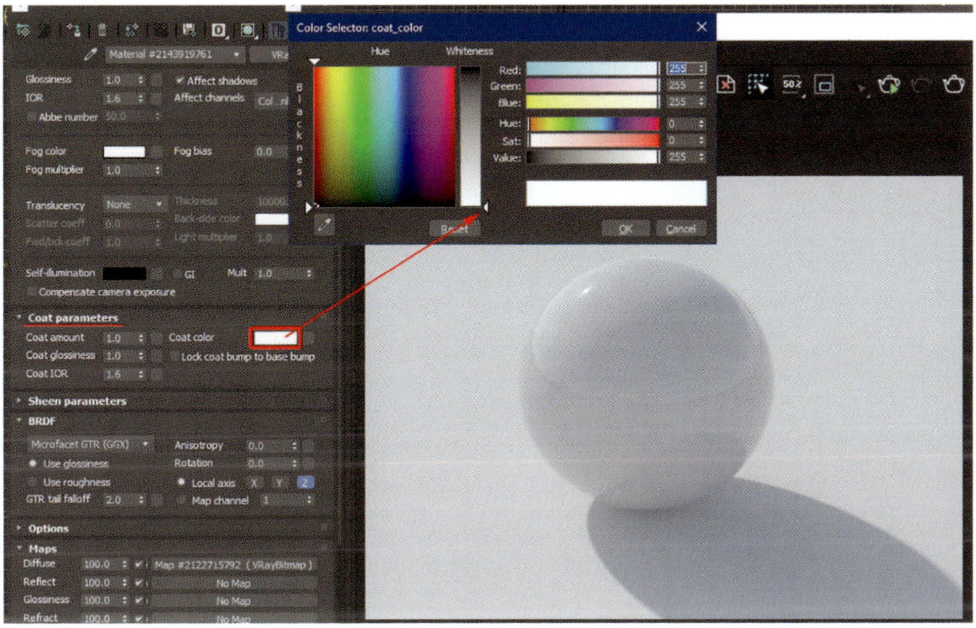

Coat color set to white

Coat color set to black

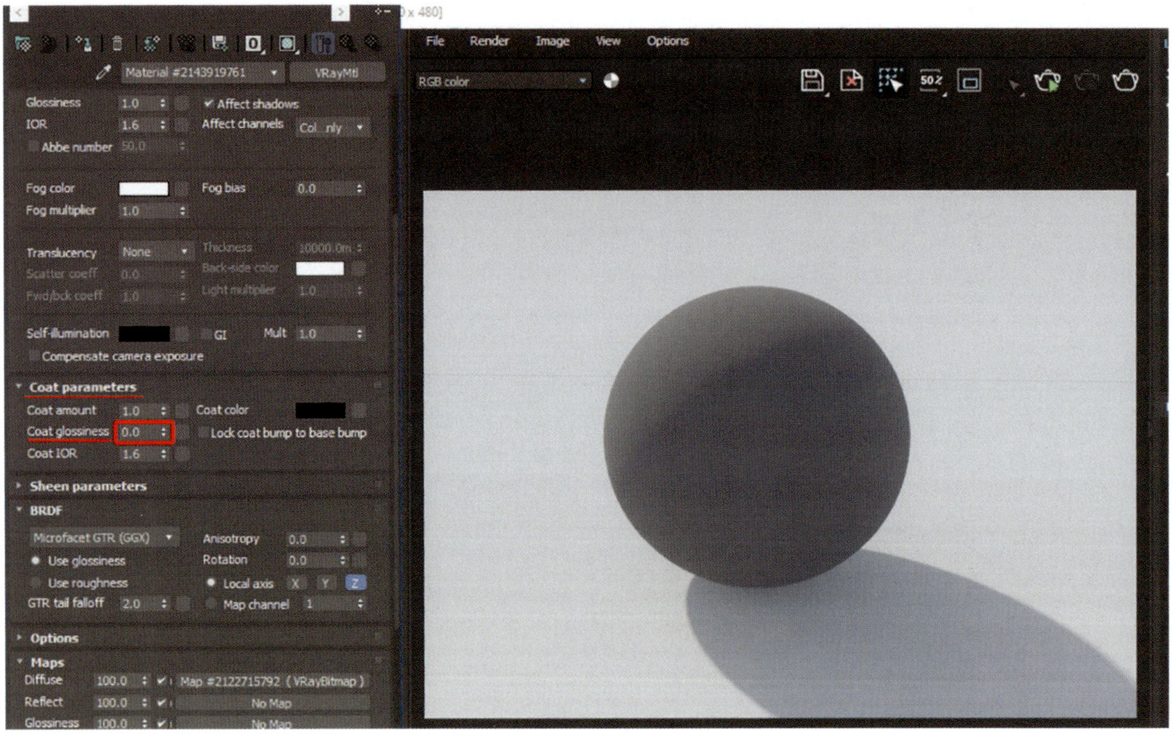

Coat color set to black with Coat glossiness/reflectivity set to 0.0

Sheen Parameters

This function helps to emulate surfaces such as velvet and satin.

Sheen color: This function determines the color of the sheen.

Its toggle can be used to plug materials or/and procedural maps.

The default color is black.

Sheen glossiness: This function controls the sharpness to the shine.

Lower values yield a more diffused shine (velvet look), and higher values have the opposite effect.

Default value is 0.8.

Its adjacent toggle can be used to plug materials or/and procedural maps.

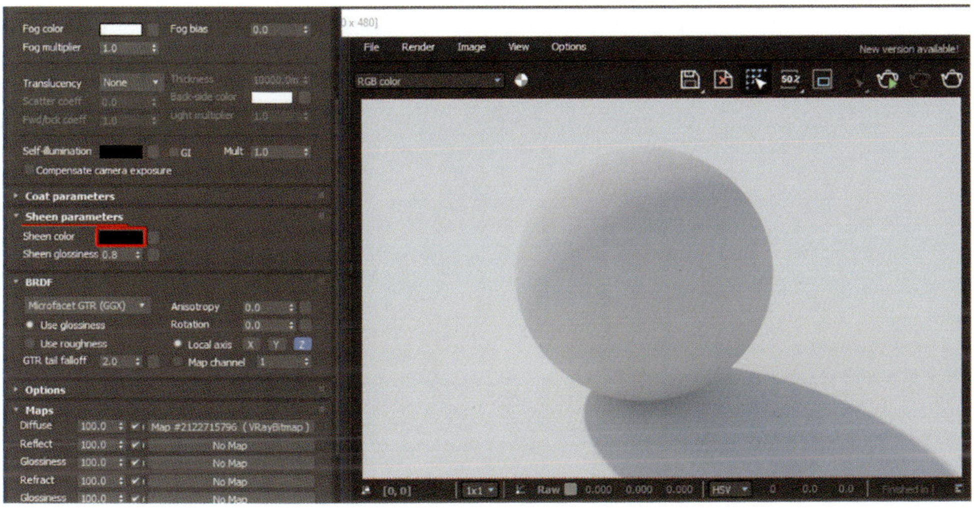

Sheen color set to black

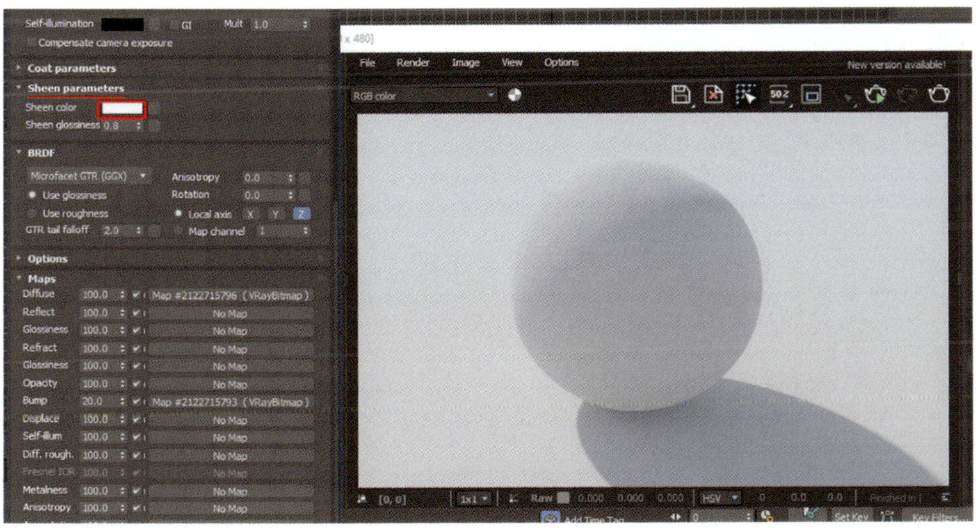

Sheen color set to white

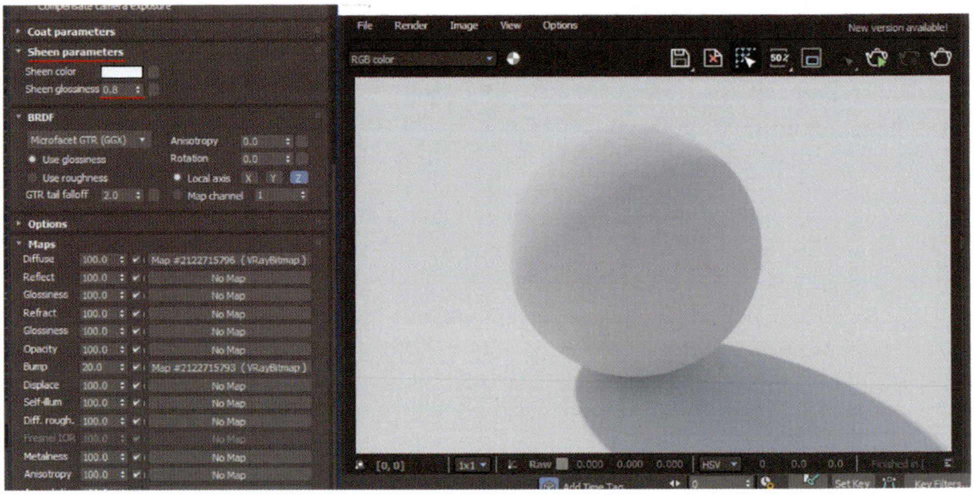

Coat color set to white with Sheen glossiness set to 0.8

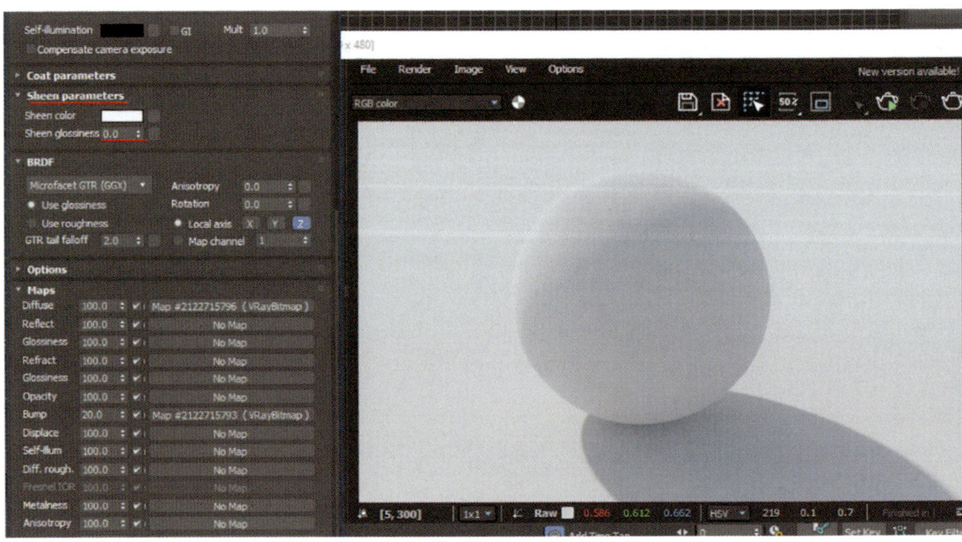

Coat color set to white with Sheen glossiness set to 0.0 (full velvet)

BRDF Rollout

For the purpose of illustrating this group of parameters, the Aluminium_Anodized_Bronze material was used.

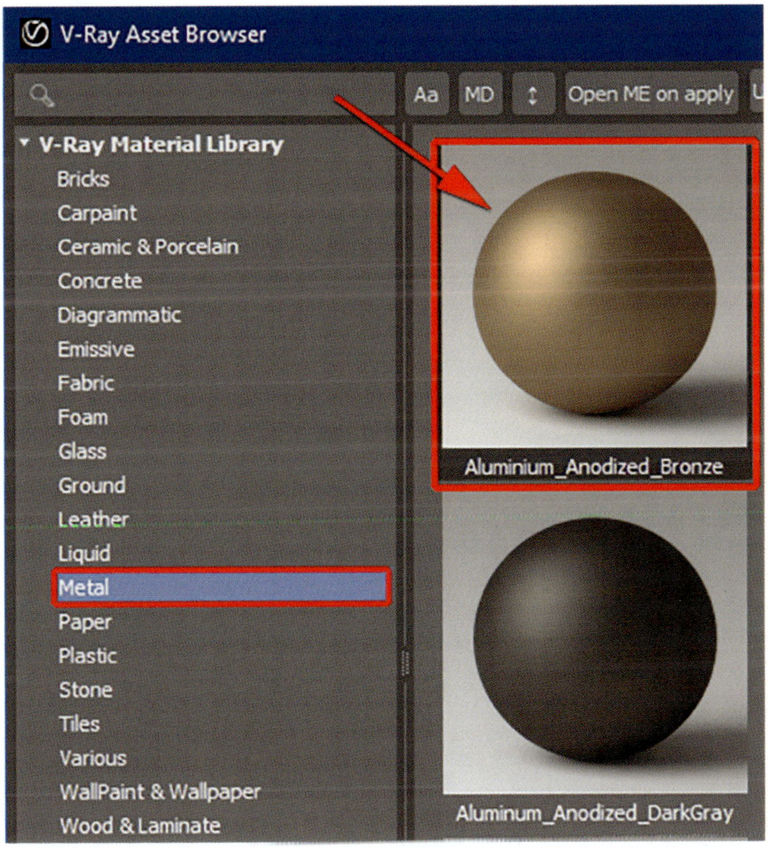

V-Ray Asset Browser dialog Metal with Aluminium_Anodized_Bronze material

Bidirectional reflectance distribution function (BRDF) parameters control the appearance of the glossy highlights and the reflections on a surface.

There are currently four types of BRDF.

Microfacet GTR (GGX): GGX is the most recent and flexible BRDF type, and yields a better representation of most materials due to its ability to control the shape of the specular lobe.

Phong: This type of BRDF yields a small/sharp glossy highlight.

Blinn: The glossy highlights of this type of BRDF are wider and less sharp.

BRDF Microfacet GTR (GGX) type with Use roughness option enabled

BRDF Microfacet GTR (GGX) type with Use glossiness option enabled

Ward: This BRDF produces even wider and more metallic glossy highlights.

BRDF Ward type with Use glossiness option enabled

Use glossiness: This function is enabled by default, and it uses the Reflect Glossiness parameters (in the Basic parameters) to yield the glossy highlights on a surface

Use roughness: When enabled, this function automatically switches the Reflect Glossiness function to Roughness type (in the Basic parameters), to emulate a more satin/matte glossy surface.

Anisotropy: This function dictates the direction of the glossy highlights. Users can also plug grayscale texture or/and a procedural map to its toggle. Default value is 0.0.

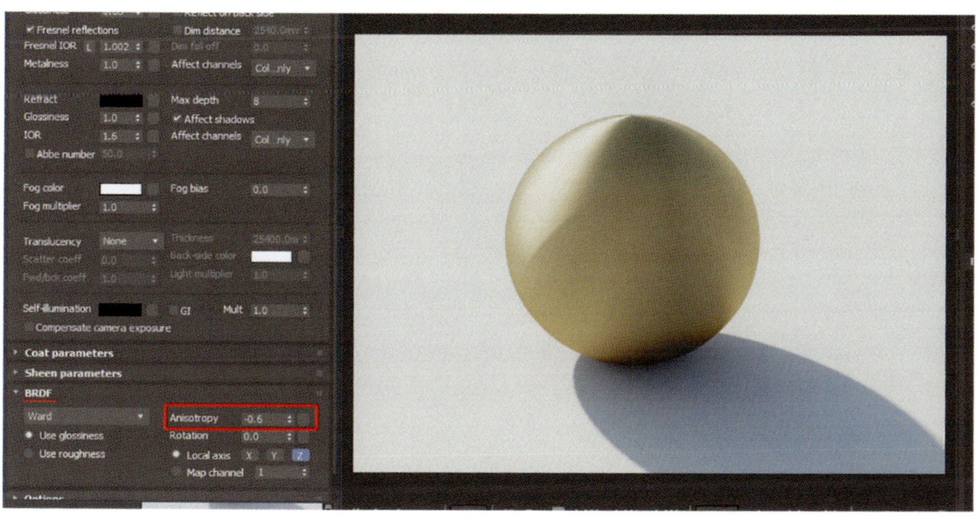

BRDF Ward Anisotropy value set to −0.6

Rotation: It allows users to manually set the direction (in degrees) of the reflections and highlights.

Users can apply a grayscale texture or/and a procedural map in its toggle. Default value is 0.0.

BRDF Ward Rotation value set to 90.0

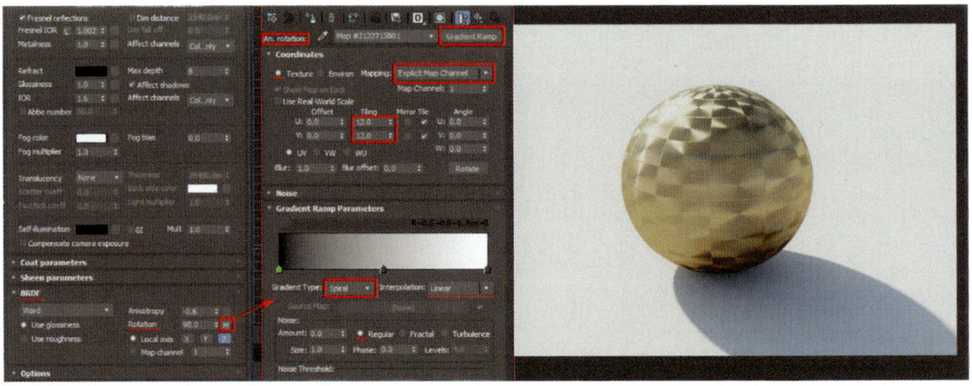

BRDF Ward Rotation toggle with Gradient Ramp procedural set to Spiral with U/V Tiling set to 12

Options Rollout

Trace reflections: This function enables reflections to be traced, when a surface is reflective. If reflections are not contributing much to a surface, this function can be disabled, to speed the rendering times.

Enabled by default.

Trace refractions: It allows refractions to be traced, when a surface is reflective/ refractive. Also, if refractions are not contributing much to a surface, this function can be disabled, to speed the rendering times of the surface.

Enabled by default.

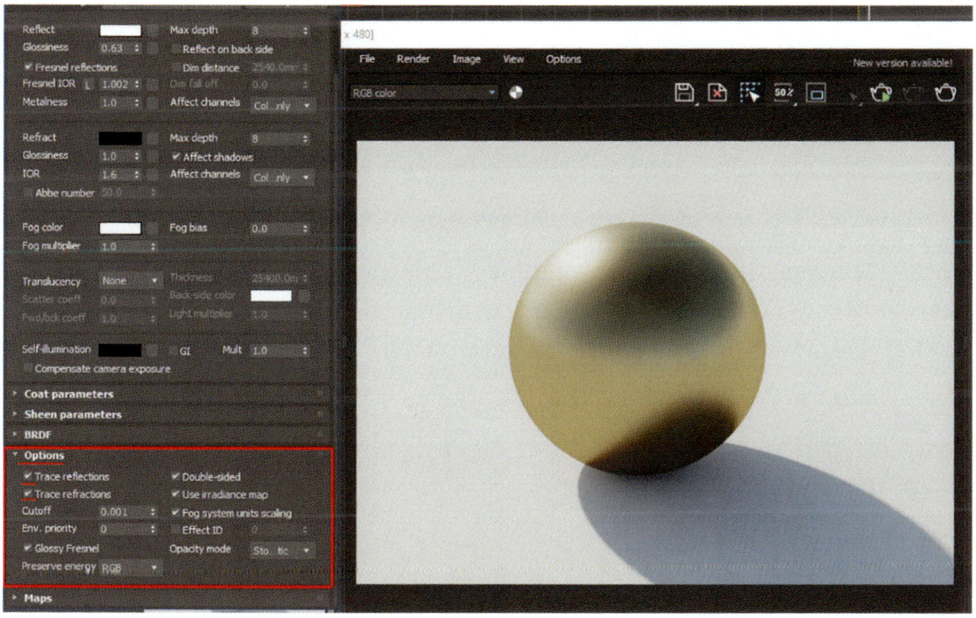

Material Options with Trace reflections and refractions enabled

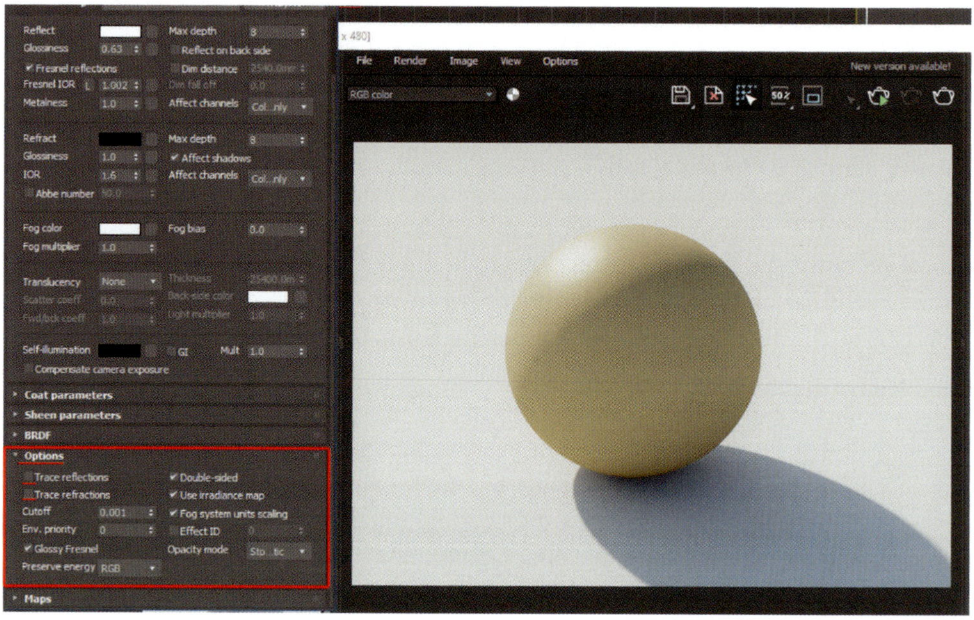

Material Options with Trace reflections and refractions disabled (faster rendering), but the shine remains.

Cutoff: This function sets the trace limit of reflections and refractions. High values reduce the tracing time (with a risk of artifacts), and low values increase the rendering times drastically (with more accuracy).

Default value is 0.01

Env.priority: This function prioritizes the environment being used for reflections and refractions.

Default value is 0.

Gloss Fresnel: When turned on, it takes into consideration the glossy Fresnel to interpolate the reflections and refractions.

Preserve energy: This function controls how the diffuse, reflections, and refractions affect each other.

Double-sided: This function is quite useful to correct surfaces with one side, or surfaces which one of its faces requires flipping the normals of (e.g., black/dark). Enabled by default.

Use Irradiance map: This function uses the irradiance map computation to calculate its surface, if enabled in the Global Illumination render settings.

Otherwise, it will automatically use the brute force (more accurate), if the GI is turned on. Enabled by default.

Fog system units scaling: When turned on, this function makes the fog color dependent of the systems units (it often darkens glass/transparent surfaces).

Effect ID: When turned on, this function allows the reflections/refractions to affect specific material ID numbers (which need to be specified/entered).

Default value is 0.

Opacity mode: This function determines how the opacity is sampled.

Maps Rollout

For the purpose of illustrating the functionalities of the rollout parameters, the Bricks_A01_m material was used.

NOTE

The Use real world scale function was not applied.

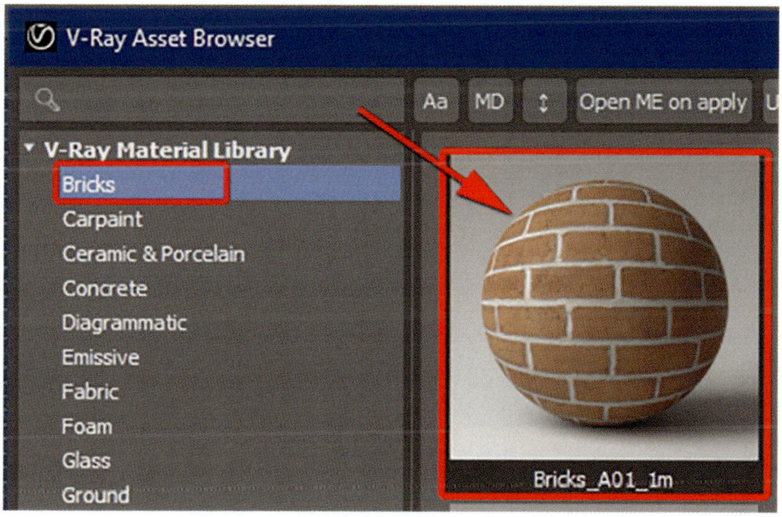

V-Ray Asset Browser dialog Bricks_A01_m material

Most Map toggles displayed under this rollout are directly connected to the textures/procedural maps being used in the V-Ray Basic Parameters.

When a texture/procedural map is being used in a toggle, it automatically overrides the colors and/or values displayed.

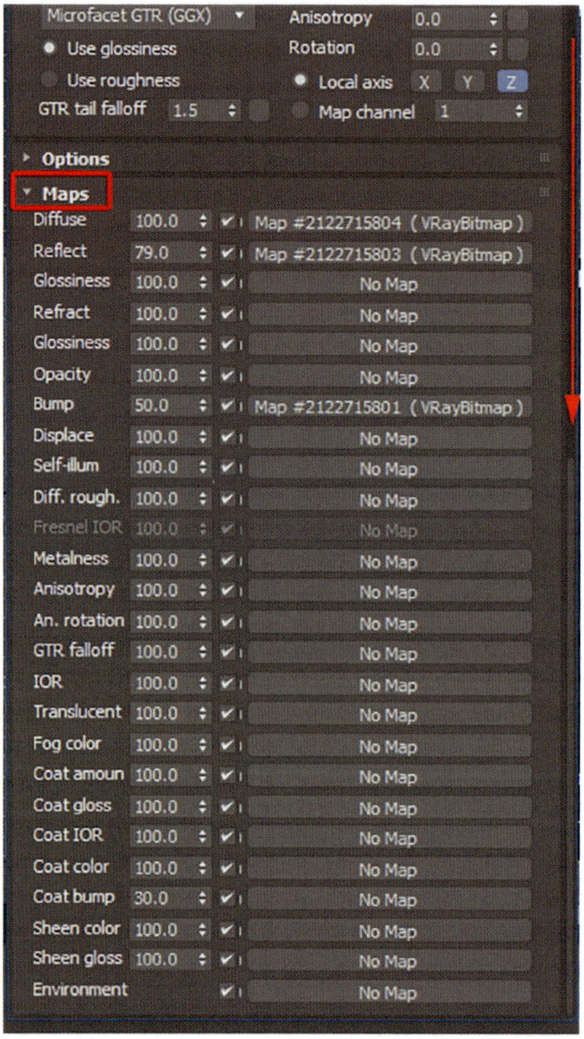

Maps rollout functions

The toggles being used have a capital letter M in them; and the toggles not being used are empty (e.g., none).

Users can increase or decrease the contribution of each toggle being used (in percentages) by typing in a value, or use its adjacent spinner.

The default value of each toggle is 100%.

In addition, users can completely disable any toggle being used, by simply disabling its adjacent tick box. When such happens, the toggle with the capital M will automatically become lowercase (e.g., m).

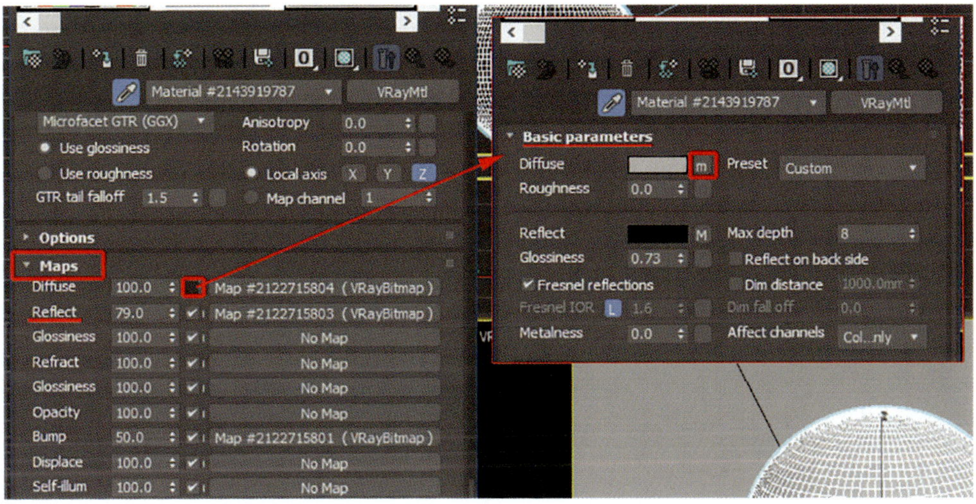

Maps rollout Diffuse Toggle disabled and Reflect percentage reduced to 79.0

Bump: It allows users to plug a texture and/or a procedural map to its toggle. It works best with grayscale and/or black and White bitmaps.

Maps rollout Bump map disabled

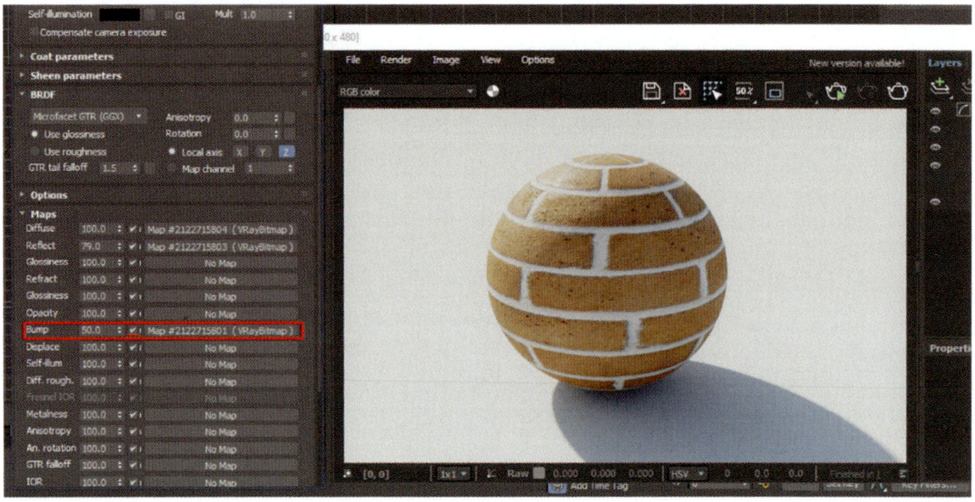

Maps rollout Bump map enabled

For the purpose of illustrating the Displace functionalities, a standard VRayMtl was loaded, as previously shown.

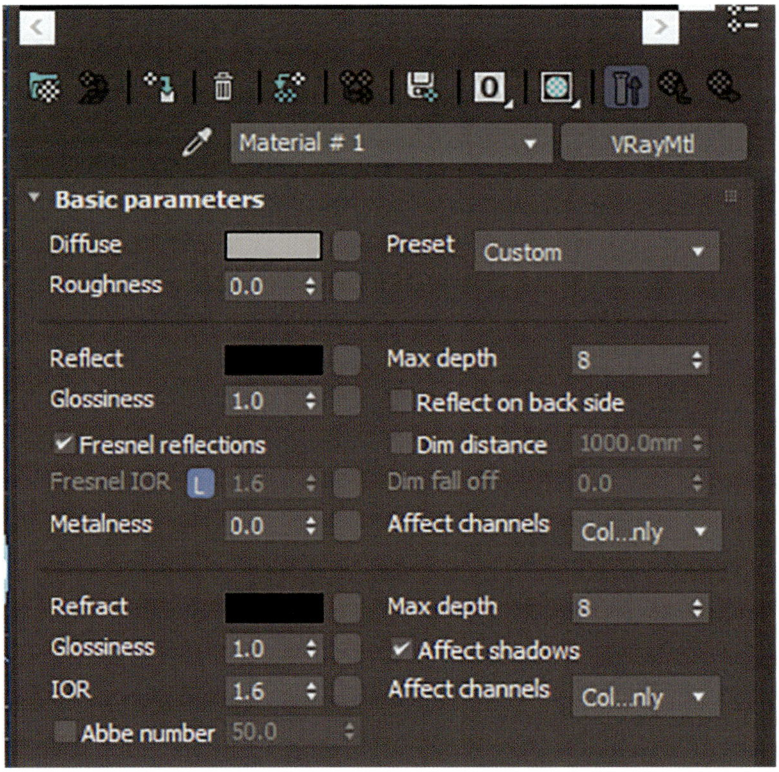

Standard VRayMtl loaded

Displace: This function physically modifies a geometry according to its mapping coordinates. For accurate results, users are recommended to have a detailed geometry (many segments).

Users can plug a texture and/or a procedural map to its toggle. Also, it works best with grayscale and/or black and white bitmaps.

It's worth noting that this type of displacement is very time-consuming to render.

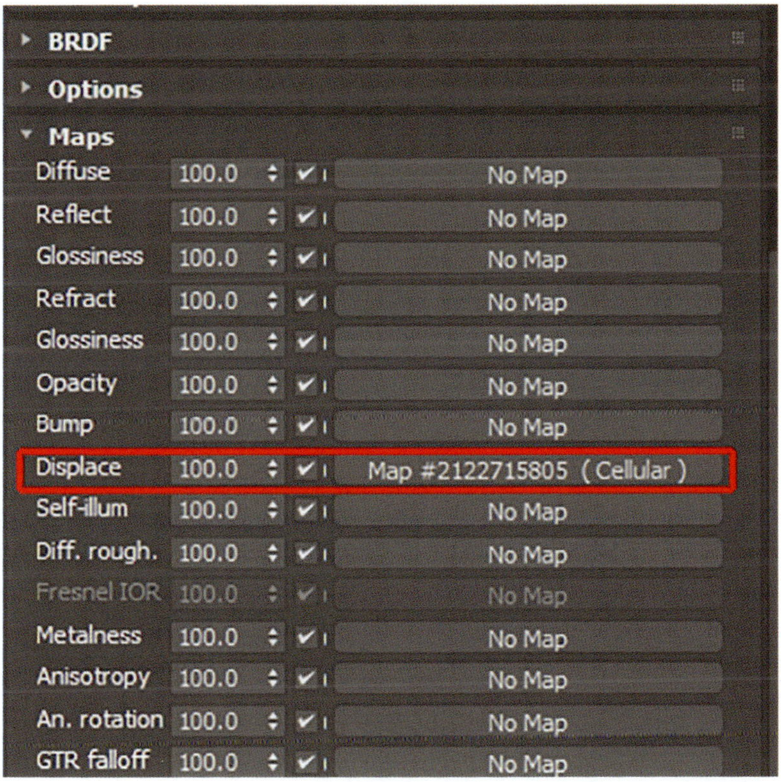

Maps rollout Displace function with Cellular procedural map

For relatively fast and accurate results, professionals tend to use the VRayDisplacementMod instead. When using this modifier, the Displace toggle needs to be disabled.

This VRay modifier can be accessed from the Modify list.

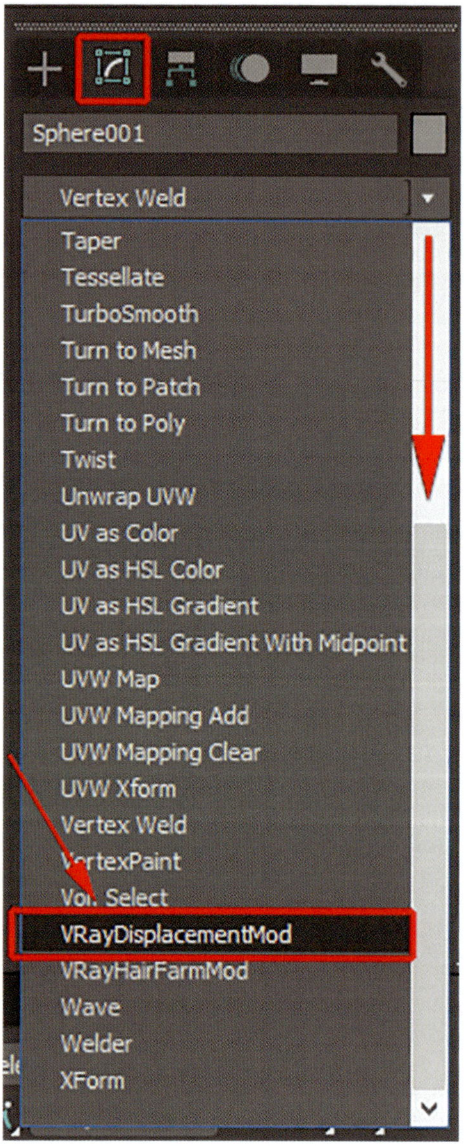

VRayDisplacementMod from the Modify list

NOTE

The VRayDisplacementMod works best when the UWM Map modifier is applied first. Otherwise, the procedural map/texture applied will not tile accordingly.

Also, the 2D mapping (landscape) option is the fastest to render from the three types.

To apply a grayscale texture or/and a procedural map, simply use the Texmap toggle.

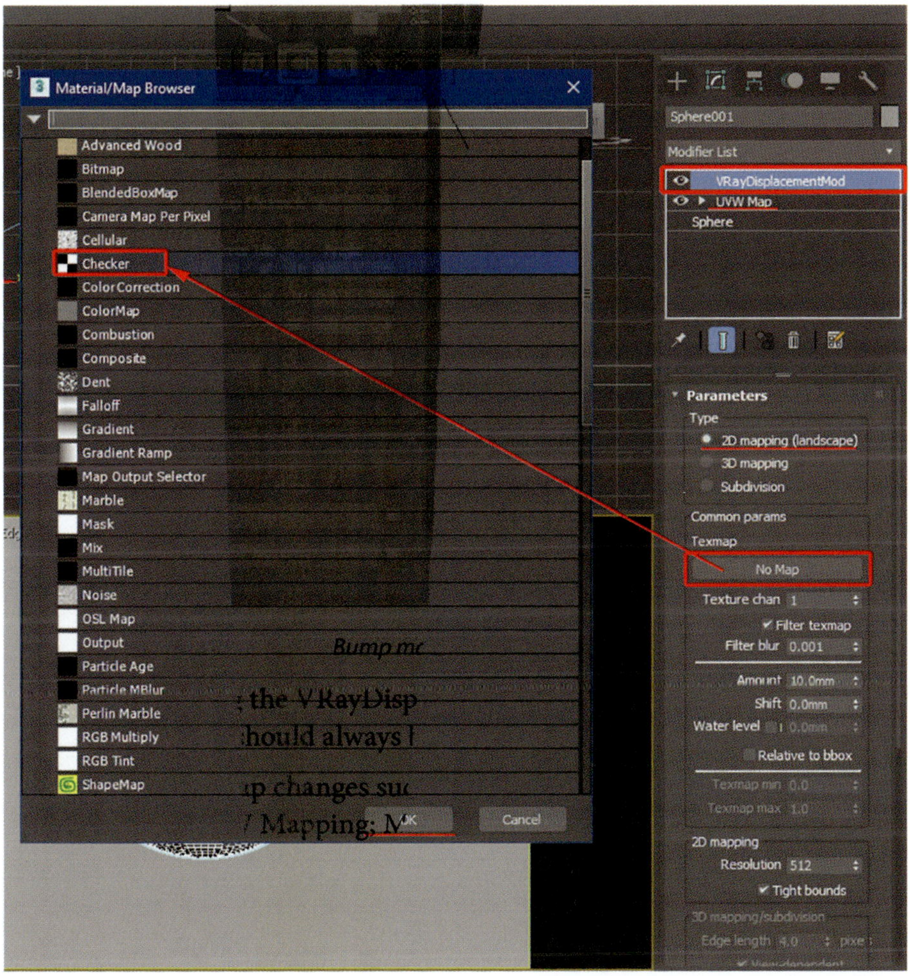

VRayDisplacementMod with 2D mapping Texmap toggle used to access the Material/Map Browser

To edit the texture or/and the procedural map, simply drag/drop it into a toggle, and to choose to instance it.

Also, ensure the toggle is disabled, to prevent doubling it up. Following that, enable the Show shaded Material in Viewport button.

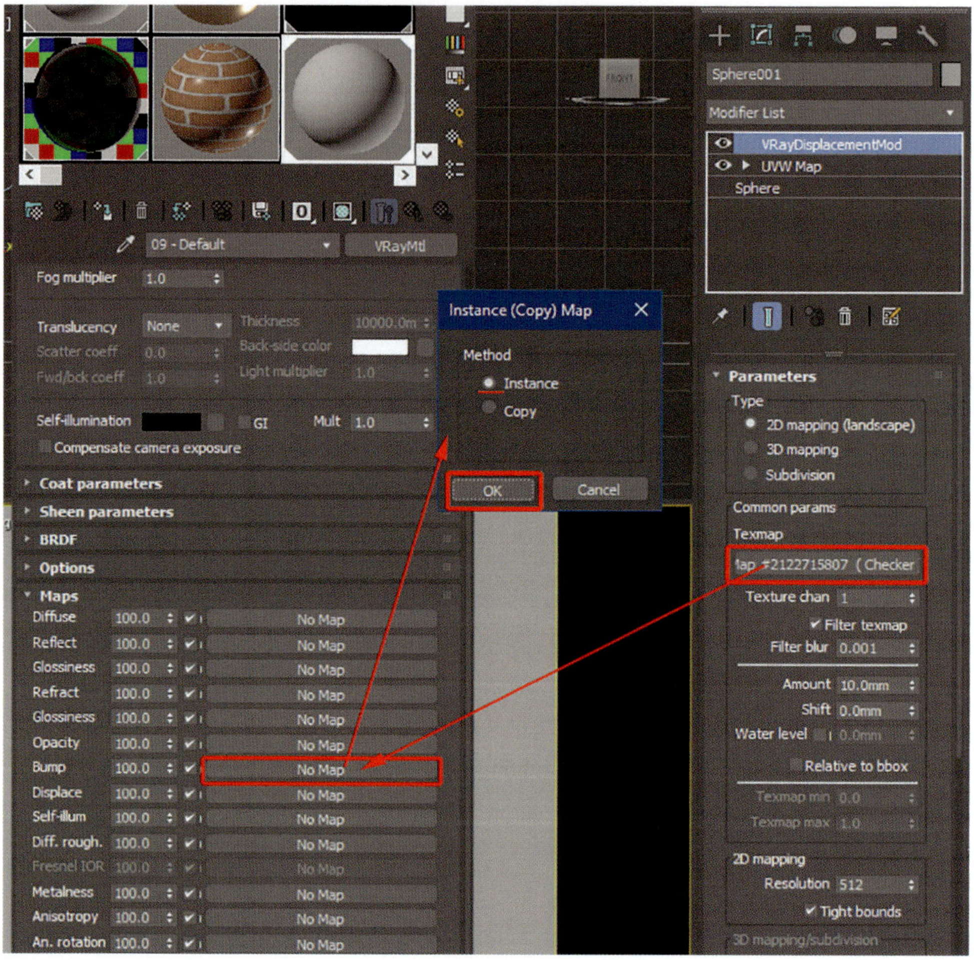

Texmap content dragged and dropped in the Bump function to copy instance

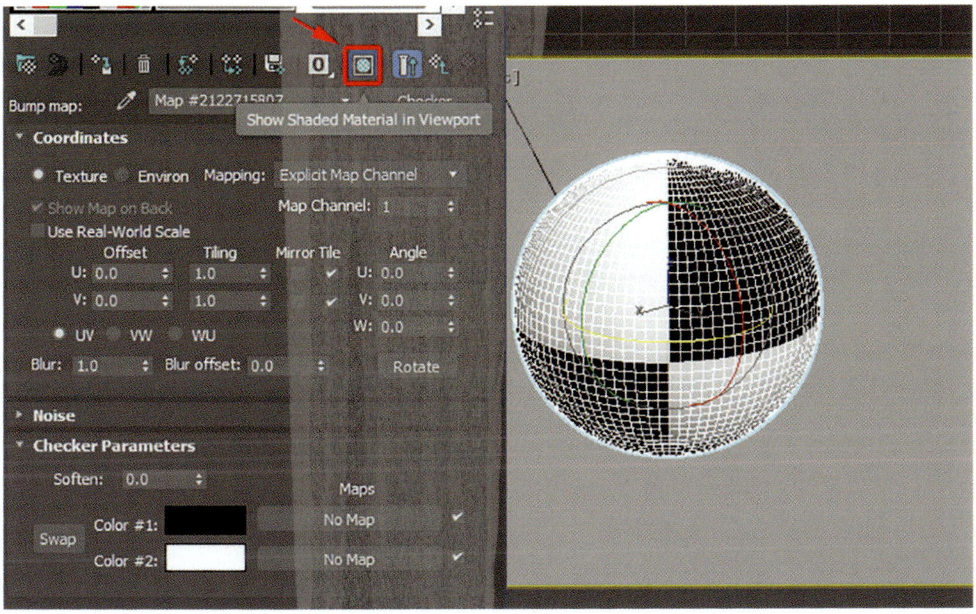

Bump map with Show shaded Material in Viewport enabled

Furthermore, when using the VRayDisplacementMod modifier, the texture/procedural map parameters should always be kept at 1.0, in the Material Editor.

All texture/procedural map changes such as tiling, should occur at the Modify level only (e.g., with UVW Mapping; MapScaler).

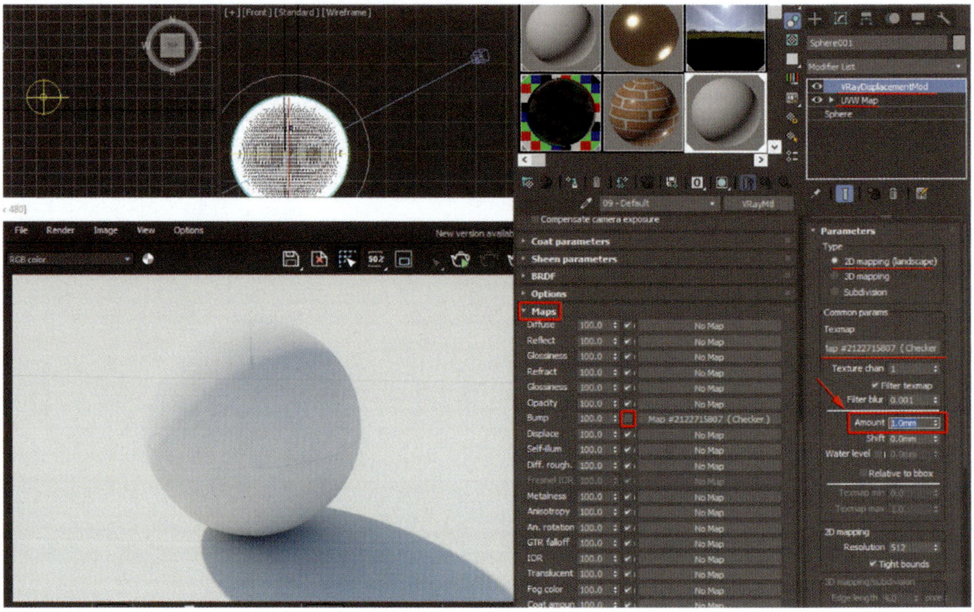

VRayDisplacementMod 2D mapping Amount set to 1.0mm with Bump function disabled

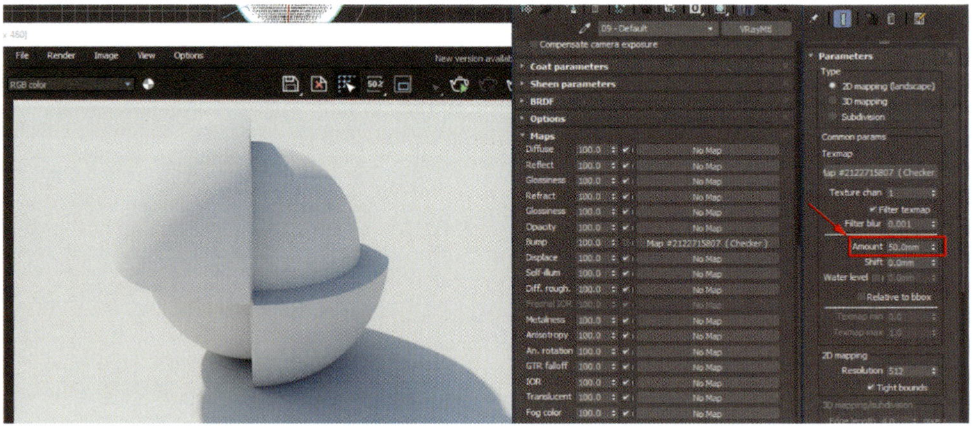

VRayDisplacementMod 2D mapping Amount set to 50.0 mm

Opacity: This function only works when textures and/or procedural maps are plugged to its toggle.

For the best results, use grayscale and/or black and white textures/procedural maps.

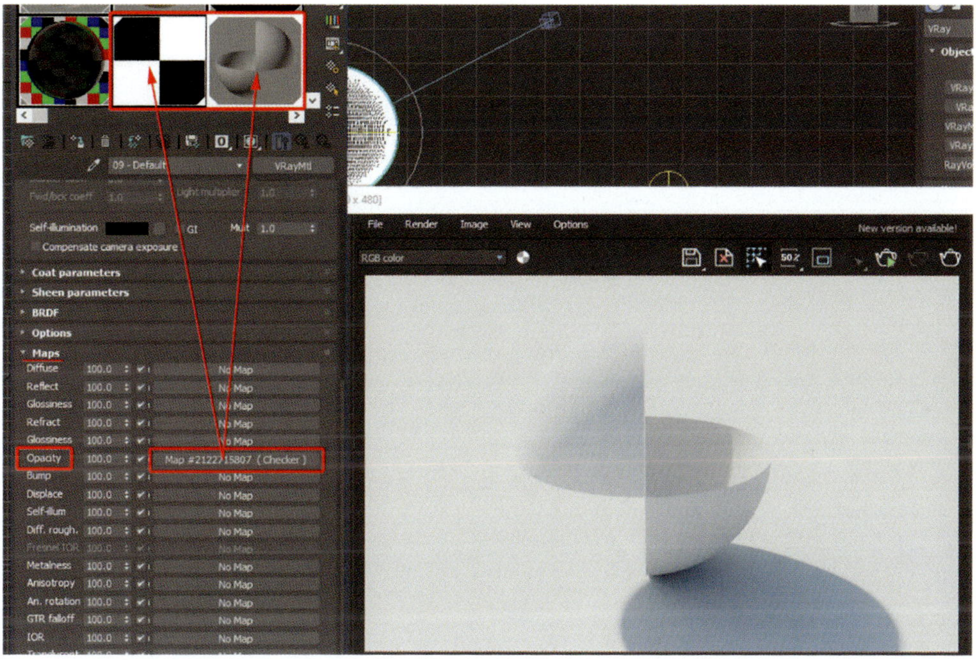

Checker procedural map applied to Opacity toggle and dragged to the material slots for preview

More VRay Shaders and Procedural Maps

While V-Ray has a host of shaders and procedural maps, the following discussion will focus mainly on the most used ones, by artists and industry professionals.

VRayBitmap

This procedural map is often used as the basis to plug Bitmaps and other procedural maps.

Its Bitmap toggle is often used to plug textures and file formats such as JPG, PNG, HDR, EXR, TIFF and TX.

Its Mapping source toggle allows users to plug amazing procedural maps such as VRayUVWRandomizer, VRayTriplanarTex and VRayMultiSubTex.

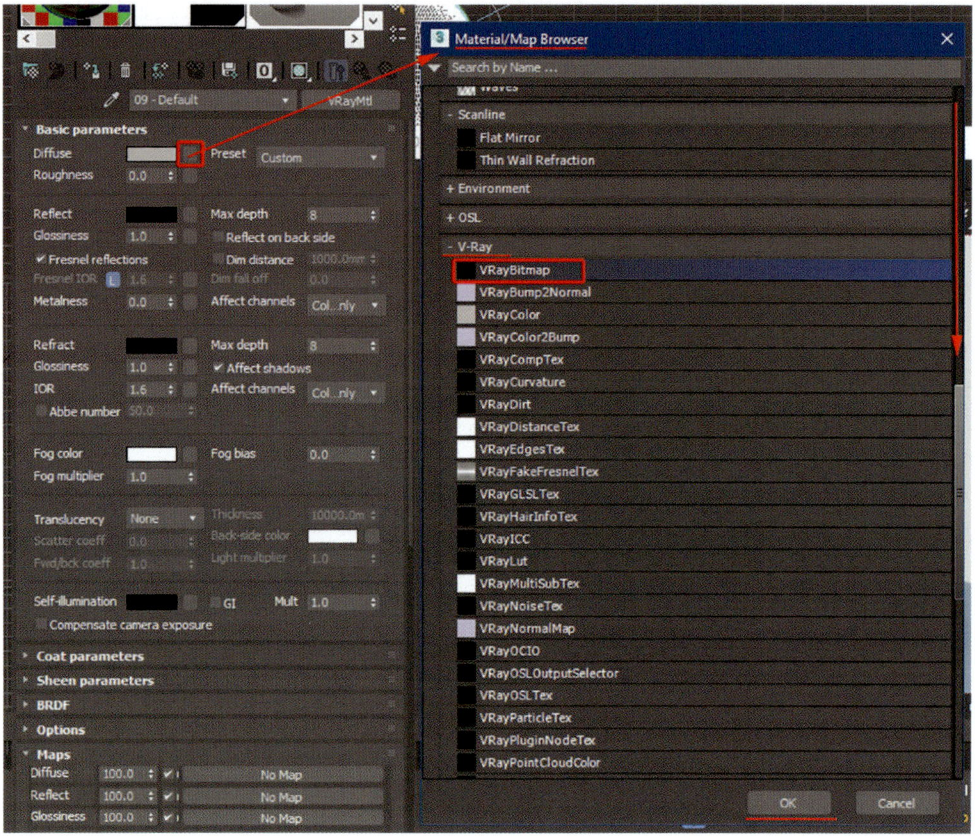

Diffuse toggle used to load VRayBitmap from the Material Browser dialog

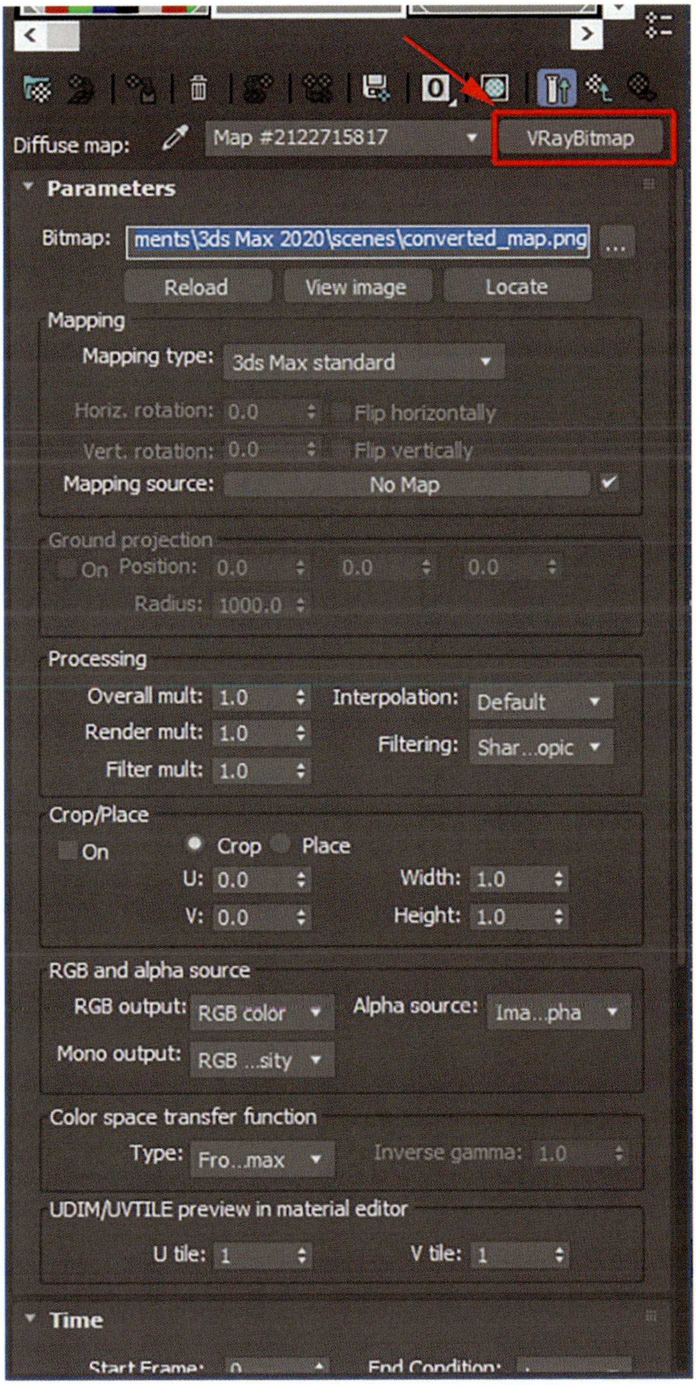

VRayBitmap loaded

NOTE

This button doesn't work with file formats such as TX.

Bitmap: This toggle allows users to locate and load file formats such as JPG, PNG, HDR, EXR, TIFF and TX.

Reload: When clicked, this button reloads the bitmap currently loaded.

View image: When clicked, this button opens the loaded bitmap inside 3ds Max.

Locate: When clicked, it locates the loaded bitmap, by opening it in a separate folder.

NOTE

This button doesn't work with file formats such as TX.

Mapping type: This function determines how the bitmaps are displayed.

The most commonly used mapping types are 3ds Max standard and Spherical.

3ds Max standard type uses the standard titling style often applied on surfaces.

When enabled, it automatically uses the Coordinates group to tile the loaded bitmap.

Spherical type is often used for HDR maps plugged in the Environment toggle.

Horizontal rotation: This function controls the horizontal rotation of a bitmap.

This function is only available when the mapping type is NOT set to 3ds Max standard.

Vertical rotation: This function controls the vertical rotation of a bitmap.

This function is only available when the mapping type is NOT set to 3ds Max standard.

Mapping source: This function allows users to plug useful procedural maps such as VRayUVWRandomizer, VRayTriplanarTex and VRayMultiSubTex.

Ground projection: This function only works when applied to the environments map toggle.

When enabled, it helps to ground the lower section of the environment map onto an imaginary plane that will receive shadows.

This function is particularly useful for 3d scenes with environment maps and floating objects without a physical ground (geometry) to cast shadows onto.

Position: This function controls the position coordinates of the projected environment map.

Overall mult: This function determines the overall intensity/brightness of the loaded material in the material editor preview and while rendering.

Render mult: This function determines the overall intensity/brightness of the loaded material, only while rendering.

Filter mult: This function controls the blurriness of the loaded image. Higher values yield blurrier results and faster rendering of the blurred image.

Interpolation: This function controls the rendering interpolation of textures (Bilinear, Bicubic and Biquadratic).

Filtering: This function controls the filtering method (isotropic, elliptical and sharp isotropic).

Crop/Place: When enabled, this function allows users to Crop or Place the loaded texture.

U and V: These two functions allow users to control the U/V tiling of the loaded material.

Width and Height: These two functions allow users to control the width/height of the loaded material.

The remaining parameters are self-explanatory, and can be found on: http://docs.chaosgroup.com/

VRayUVWRandomizer

This exquisite procedural map allows users to randomize the position, rotation and scale of bitmaps.

It can only be plugged from the Mapping source toggle of the VRayBitmap and VRayTriplanarTex texture nodes.

Once VRayUVWRandomizer is loaded, the bitmap tiling is overridden/controlled by its Coordinate parameters.

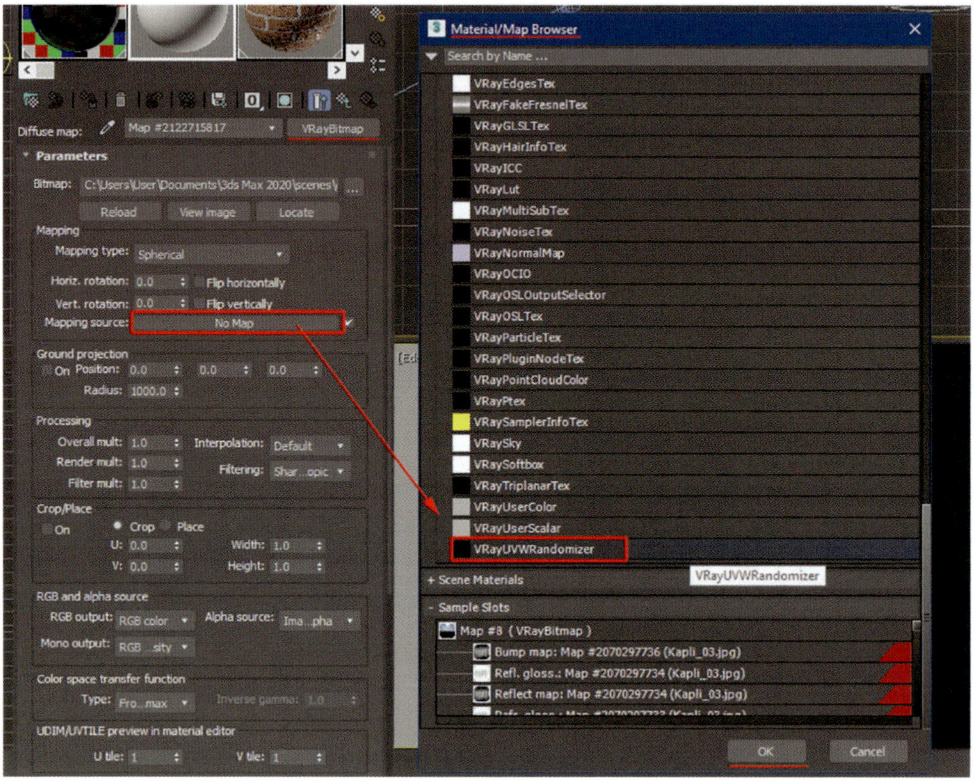

Mapping source used to load VRayUVWRandomizer in the Material Browser

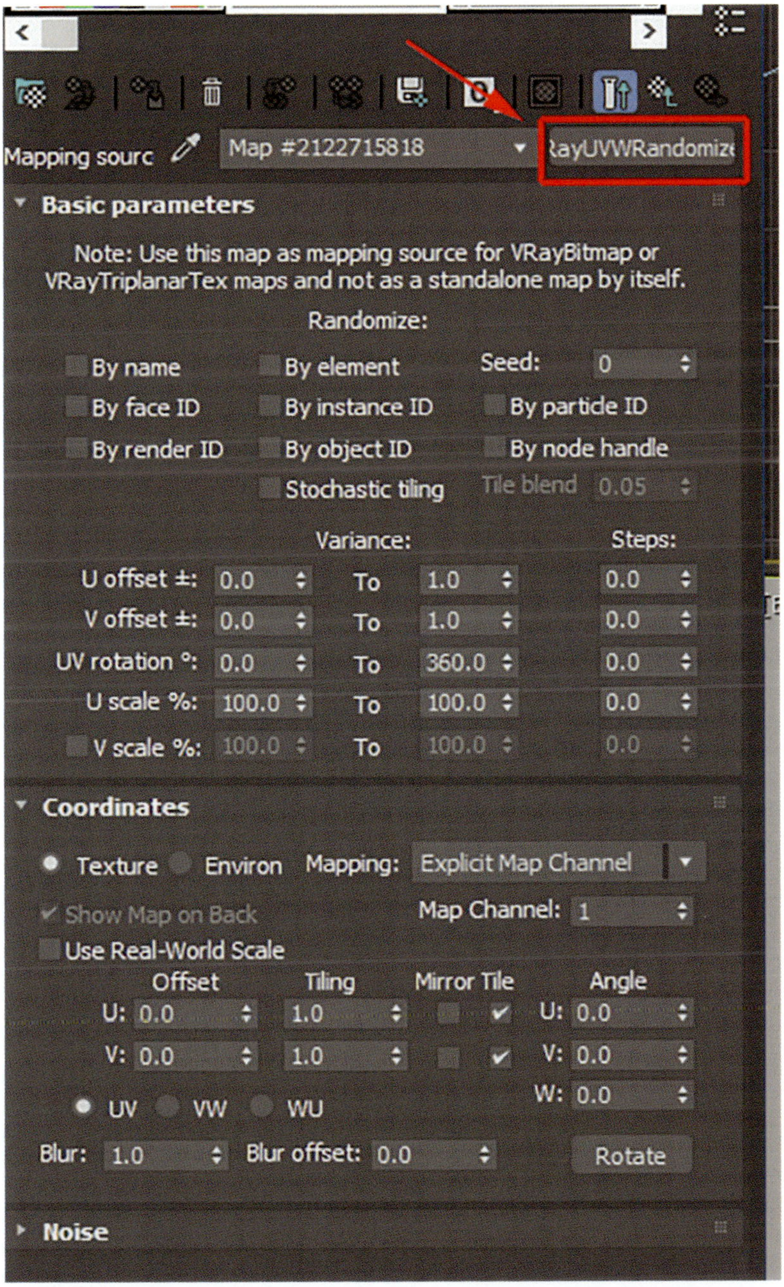

VRayUVWRandomizer loaded

To test the functionalities of this procedural map, please open the file under the name, VRayUVWRandomizer.max.

By name: When enabled, this function randomizes (color index) bitmaps by its name.

By face ID: When enabled, this function randomizes (color index) bitmaps by the face IDs of an object.

By render ID: When enabled, this function randomizes bitmaps (color index) of object's face ID.

By element: When enabled, this function randomizes bitmaps (color index) by the element IDs of an object.

By instance ID: When enabled, this function randomizes bitmaps (color index) by the face IDs of an object.

By object ID: When enabled, this function randomizes bitmaps (color index) by the face IDs of an object.

Stochastic tiling: When enabled, this function automatically changes the UV mapping tile.

Seed: This function allows users to change the pattern randomization by entering different values.

By particle ID: When enabled, this function randomizes bitmaps (color index) by the face IDs of particles.

By node handle: When enabled, this function randomizes bitmaps (color index) by the face IDs of an object.

Variance: This group controls the offset, rotation and scale variations.

U offset (horizontal): This function controls the horizontal position of your bitmap. Always enter values that are different from the V offset (vertical) values.

V offset (vertical): This function controls the vertical position of your bitmap. Always enter values that are different from the U offset (horizontal) values.

UV rotation: This function controls the rotation of your bitmap in U or V axis.

U scale % (horizontal): This function controls the horizontal scale of your bitmap.

V scale % (vertical): This function controls the vertical scale of your bitmap in percentages.

Steps: This function controls the variation intervals. Entering values higher than 1 can really make a difference on the overall look of a bitmap.

Always enter different step values in U and V directions.

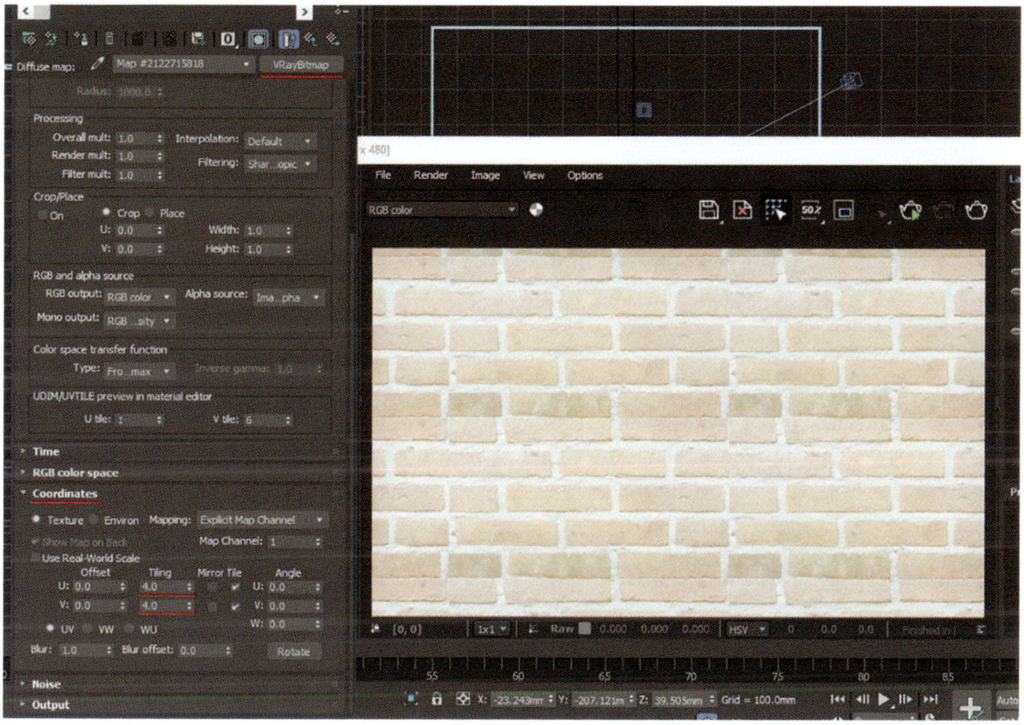

VRayBitmap Brick material Without VRayUVWRandomizer and Coordinates Tiling U/V tiling set to 4.0

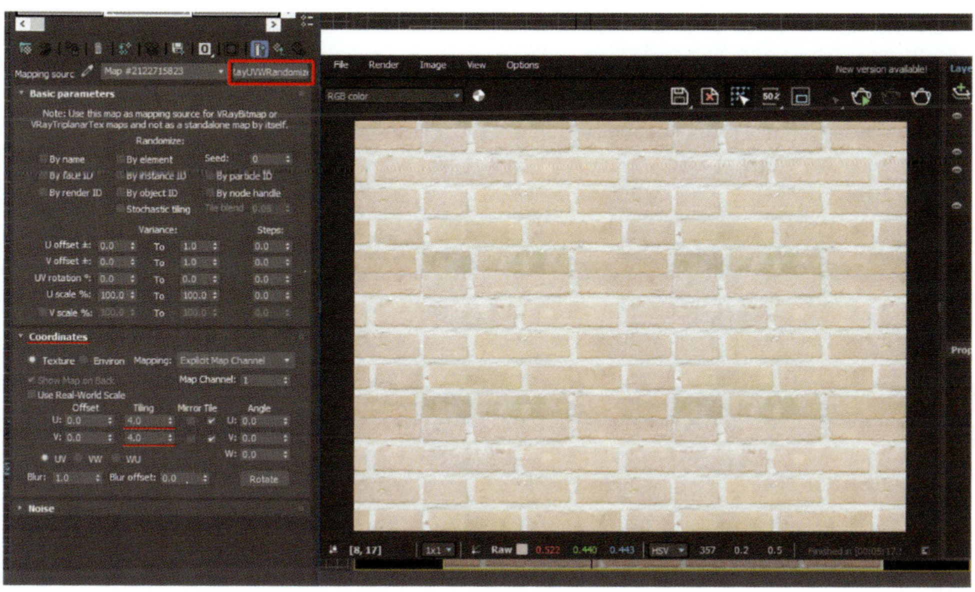

VRayBitmap Brick material With VRayUVWRandomizer via Mapping source

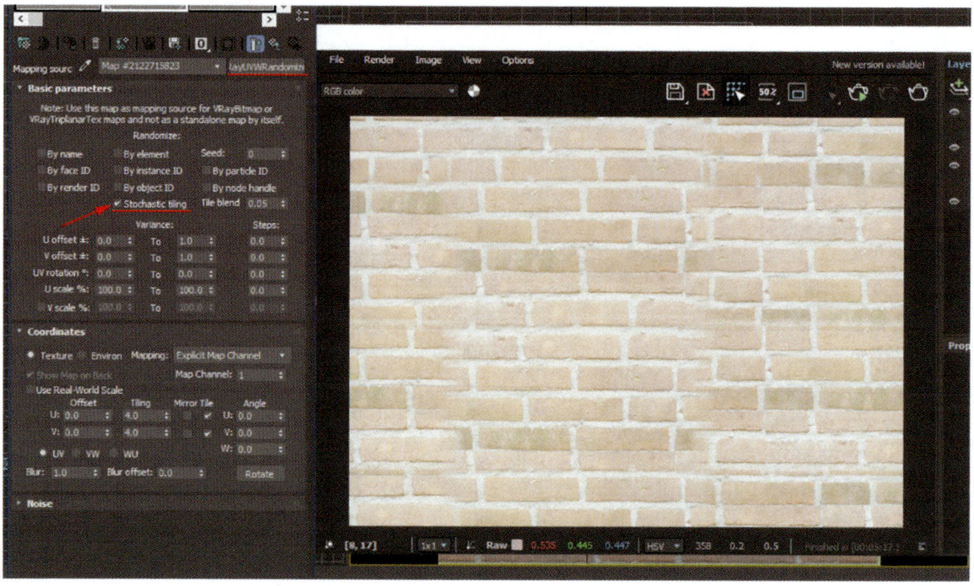

VRayUVWRandomizer with Stochastic tiling enabled

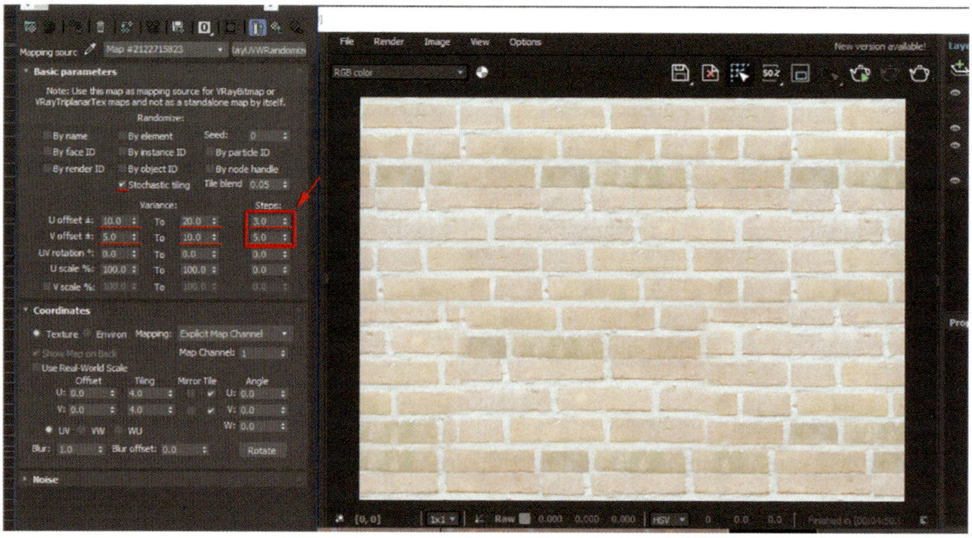

VRayUVWRandomizer with Stochastic enabled and U, V offset values set

VRayMultiSubTex

This unique procedural map allows users to randomize bitmaps and colors, based on material IDs, faces, elements, etc.

VRayMultiSubTex is best used with multiple bitmaps to emulate randomized materials across one surface.

> **NOTE**
>
> **VRayMultiSubTex colors are not visible in the viewport (only in the render).**

To apply it, simply click on the diffuse toggle and choose the VRayMultiSubTex from the Material/Map Browser dialog, under V-Ray rollout.

20 Total IDs are loaded by default. However, for the purpose of this exercise it was set for a Total of 15 IDs instead.

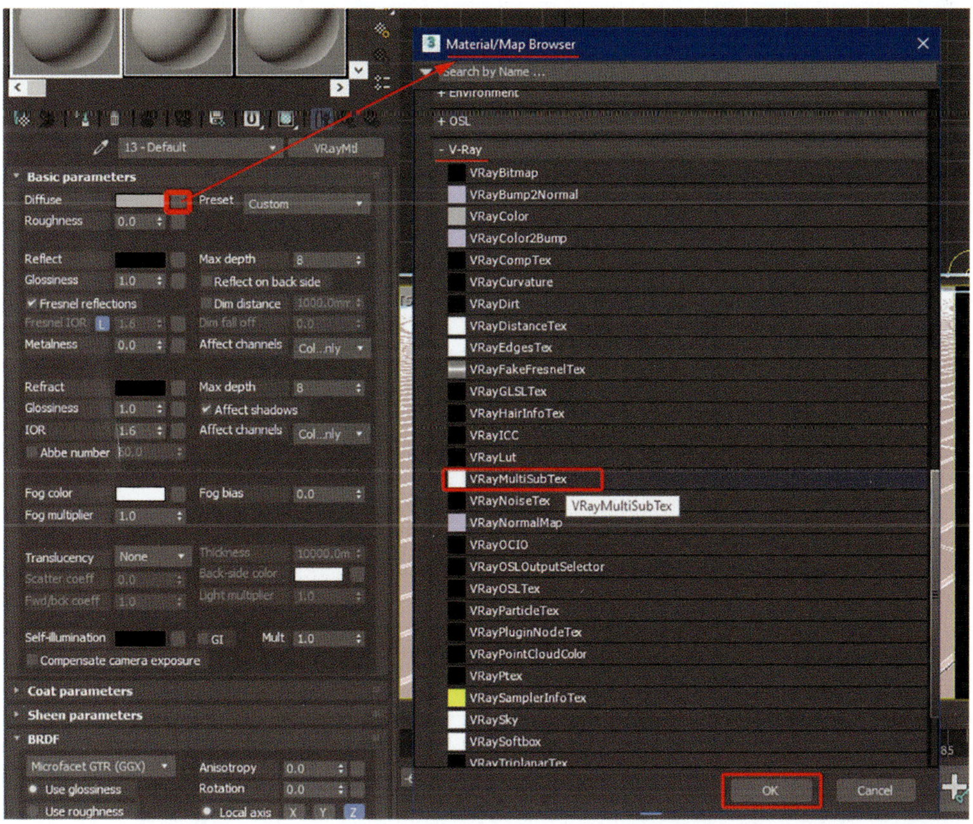

Diffuse toggle used to Load VRayMultiSubTex procedural map via Material/Map Browser

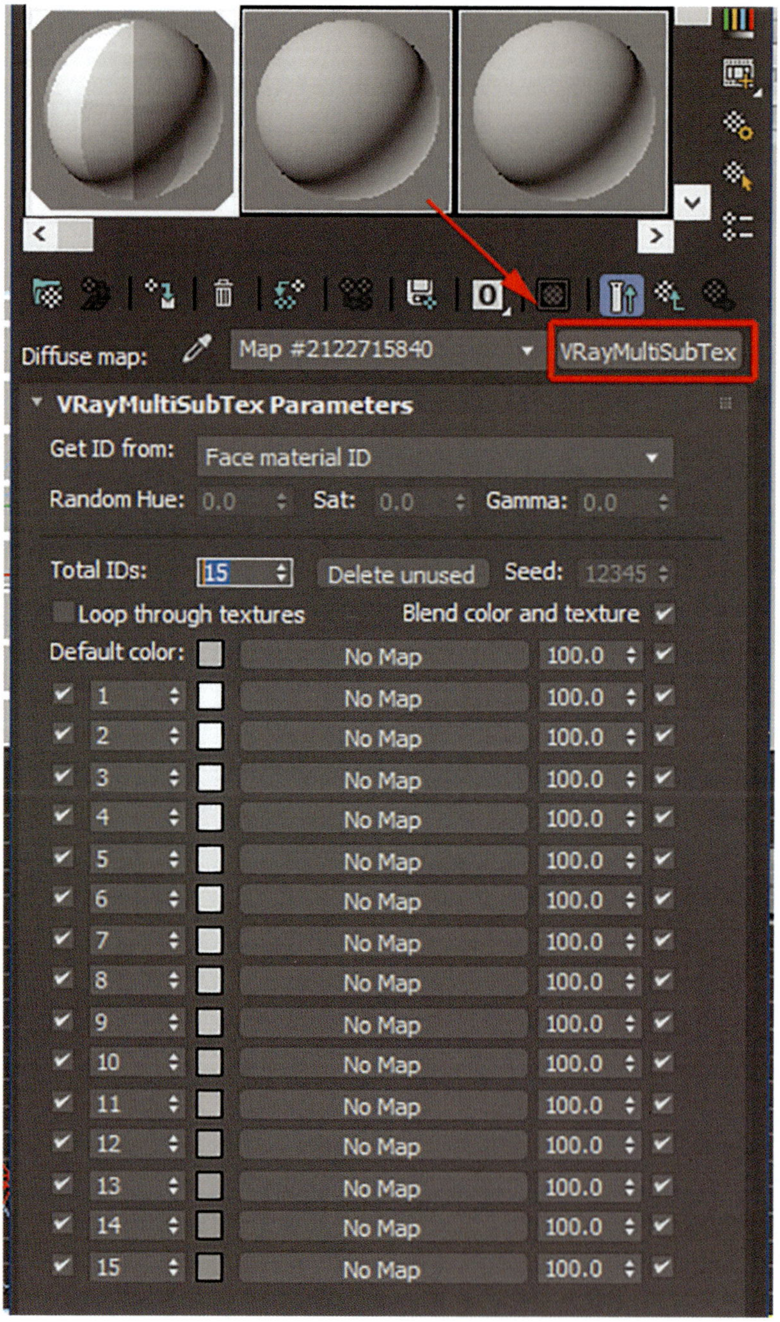

VRayMultiSubTex loaded

To test the functionalities of this procedural map, please open the file under the name, VRayMultiSubTex.max.

Get ID from: This function determines the type of ID to get from.

It is set to, Face material ID, by default.

Random by Face material ID is also quite popular to randomly distribute Bitmaps and/or colors across a one surface.

To set face and material IDs simply select a specific object with multiple faces, and add the Editable Poly modifier to it.

Under its Selection rollout, enable the Element type and select one element in the viewport.

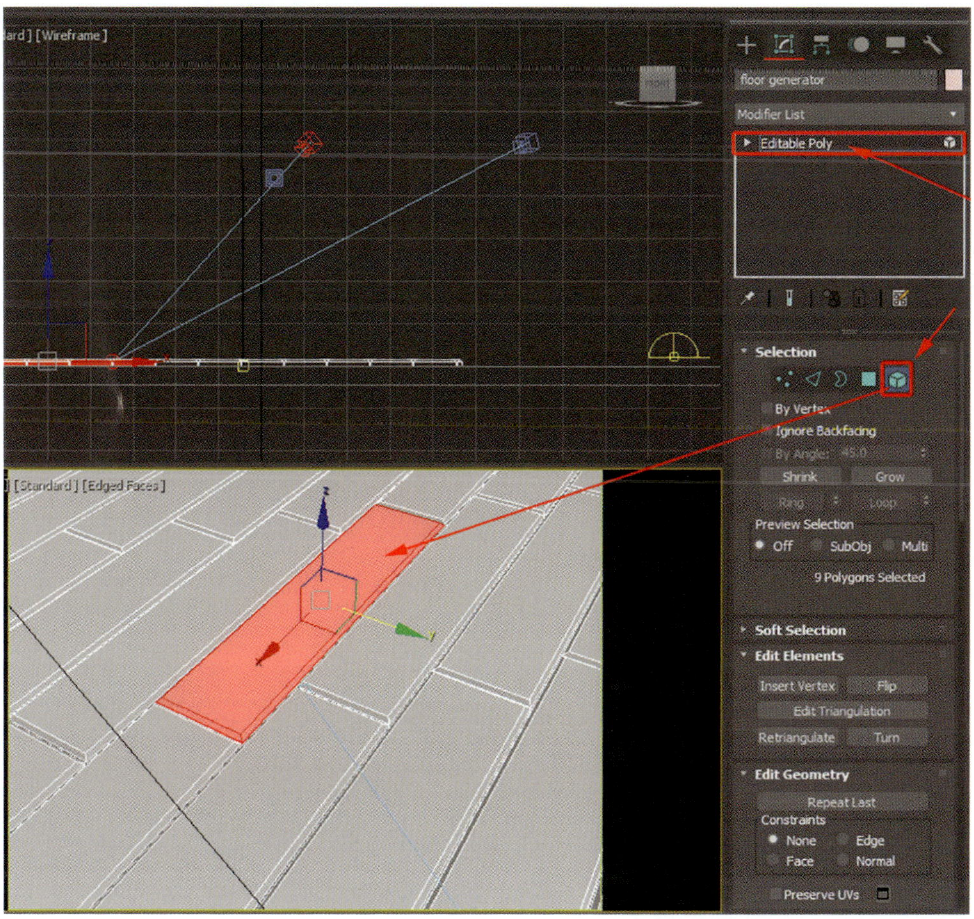

Editable Poly by Element enabled and selected in the viewport

Users can choose to manually enter a specific material ID number for each selected element, by scrolling down to its Polygon:Material IDs rollout parameters, and typing in any number in the Set ID name field.

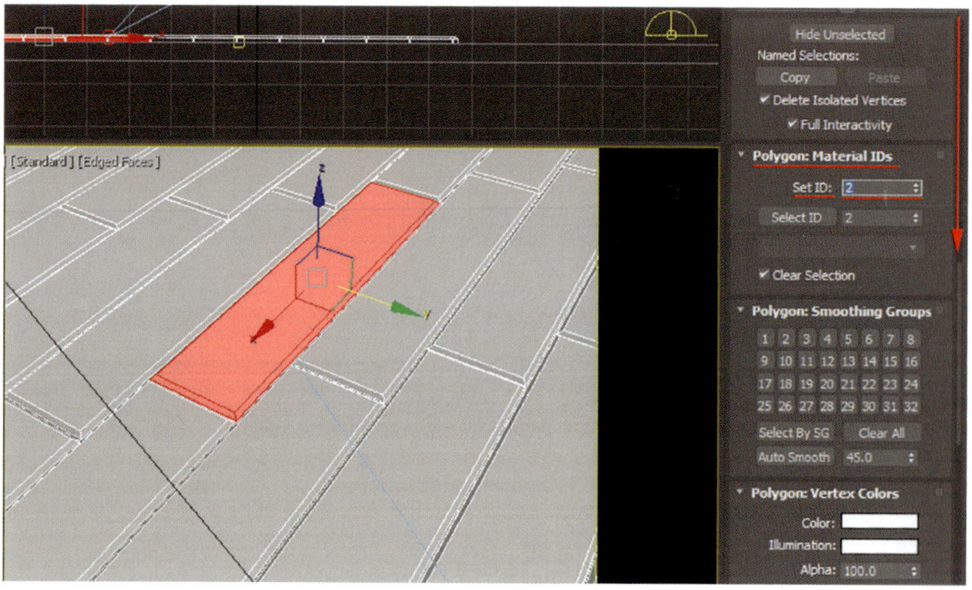

Element selected in the viewport and Material IDs number set manually

Alternatively, simply add the MaterialByElement modifier to automatically add ID numbers to each separate element randomly.

Users can also set the total count of ID numbers on the entire surface, by entering a number in the ID Count.

This ID Count number should always match with the Total IDs number in the VRayMultiSubTex.

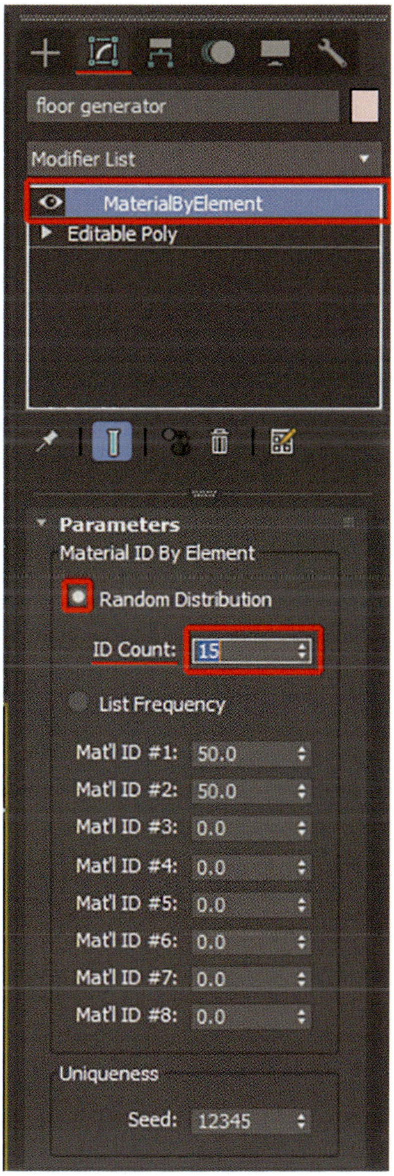

MaterialByElement modifier added with ID Count set to 15

To check which ID numbers were randomly assigned to each element, simply add another Editable Poly modifier on top of the MaterialByElement, and select each element to see the ID numbers randomly assigned (between 1 and 15).

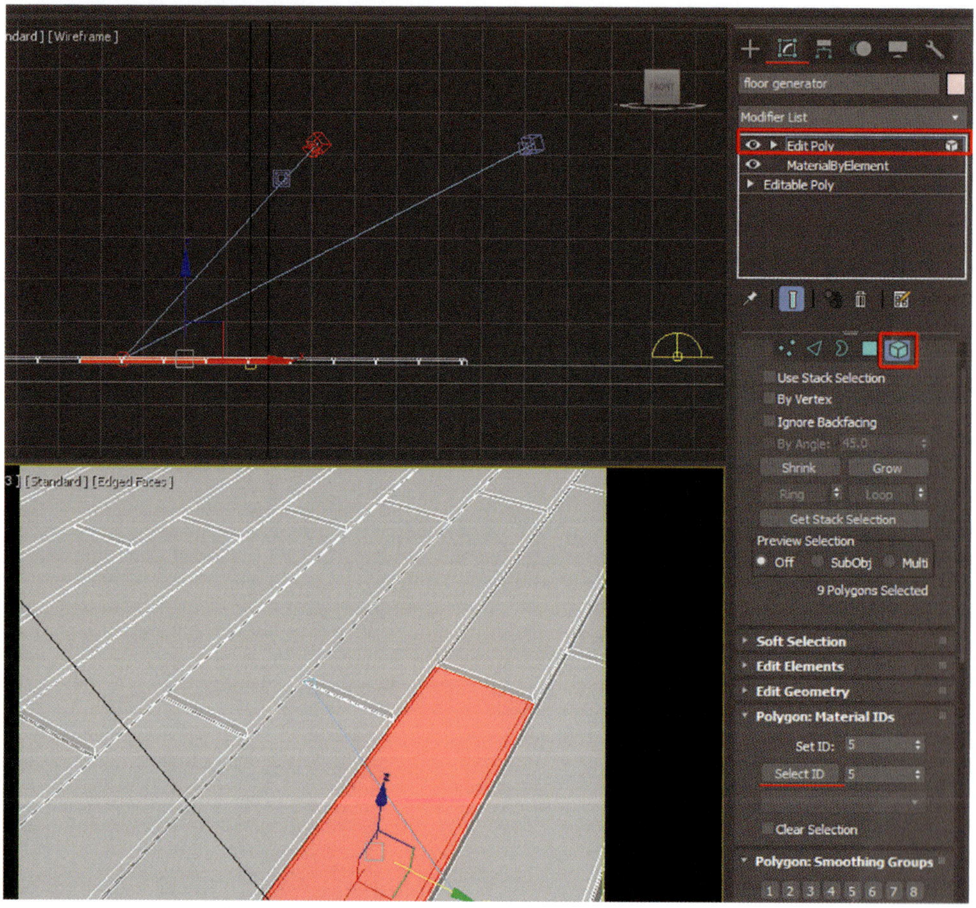

Editable Poly added on top of MaterialByElement

These ID numbers work in conjunction with the ID numbers displayed in the VRayMultiSubTex.

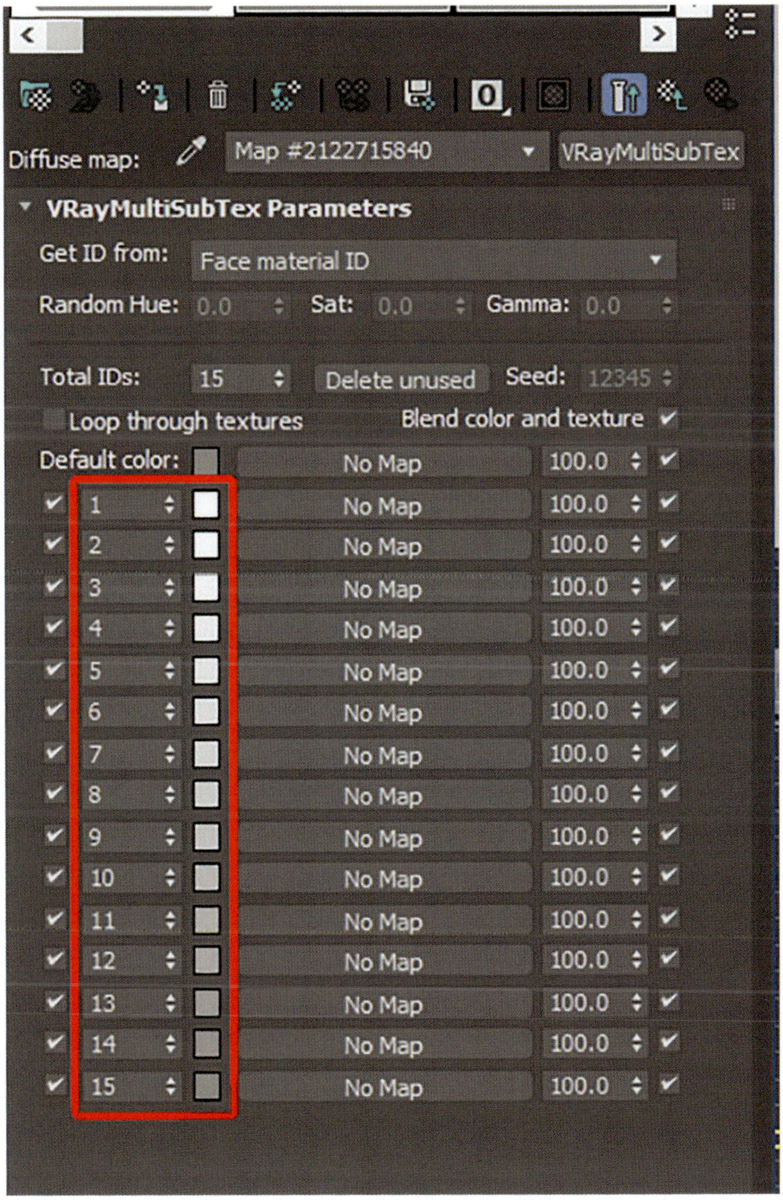

List of Material ID numbers from Total IDs

Or the bitmap/procedural map ID number being used in the toggle (if any).

To choose a material ID number, simply click and hold.

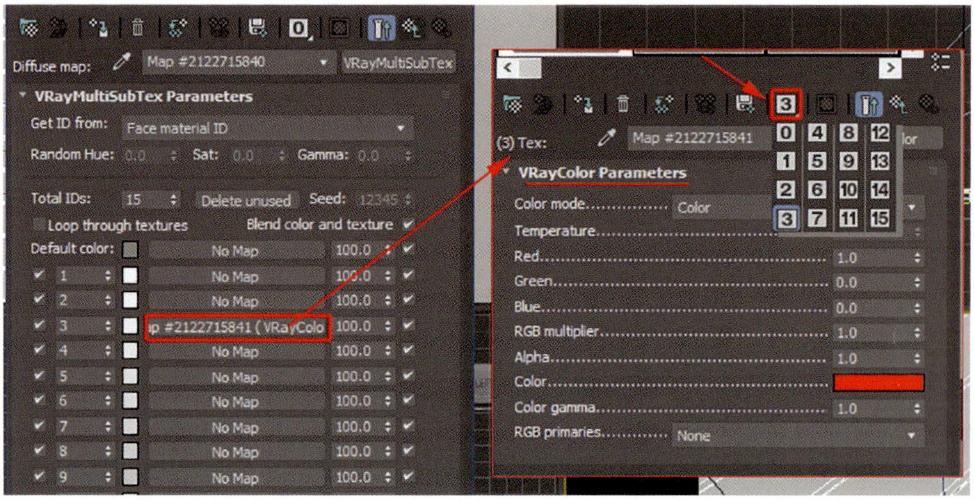

Material ID numbers set from Procedural Maps

To assign object IDs, simply select an object in the scene, and right click on it. Choose the Object Properties option in the quad menu.

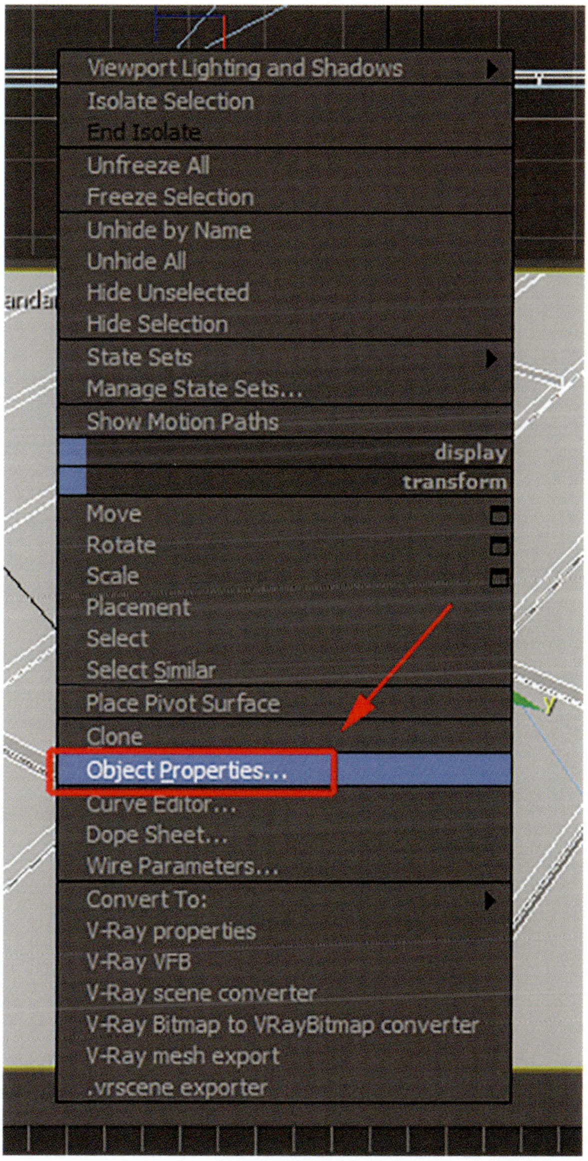

Object Properties in Quad menu list

In the General tab, under G-Buffer group, type in a specific number that matches one of the MaterialByElement object ID numbers (if the Object ID option is being used).

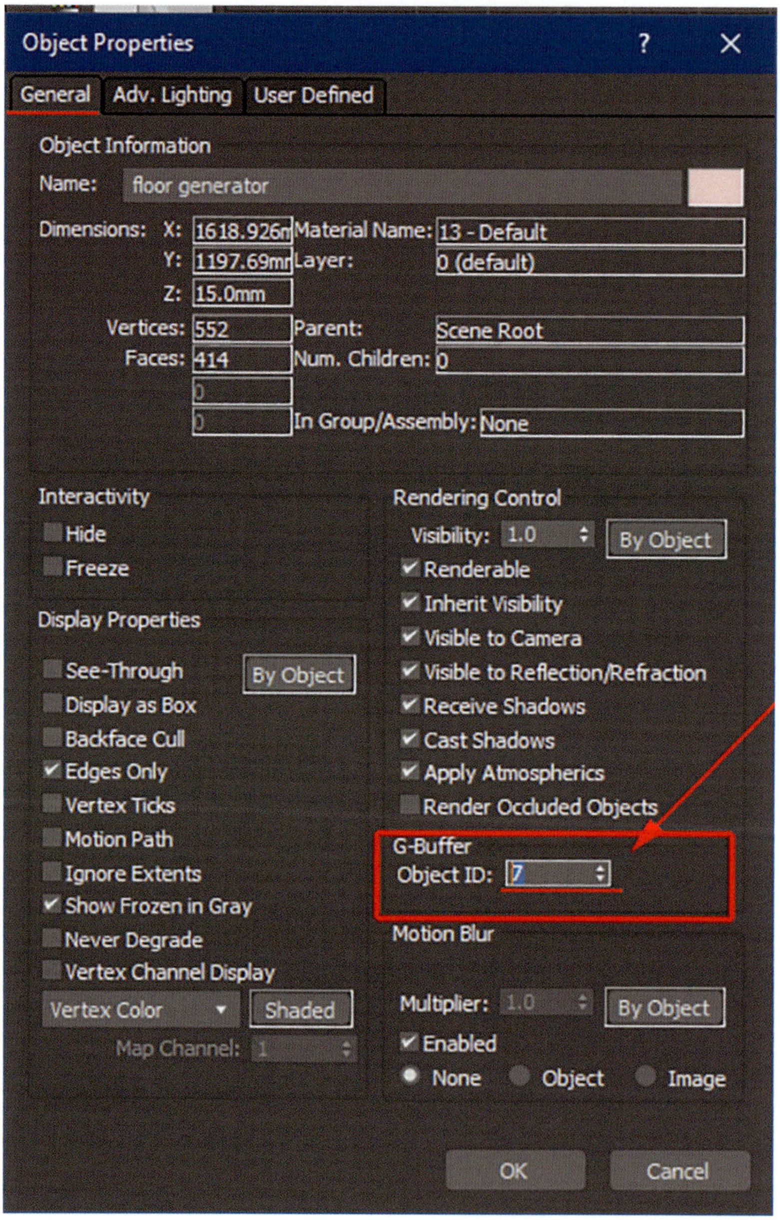

G-Buffer Object ID number under General Object Properties

Random Hue: This function only becomes available if any of the Radom ID modes are chosen from the list (Random by Node Handle, Random by Face material ID, Random by Object ID, etc.).

It randomizes the hue colors, procedural maps and bitmaps being used under Default color list.

Default value is 0.0.

Sat: Only available if any of the Radom ID modes are chosen from the list (Random by Node Handle, Random by Face material ID, Random by Object ID, etc.).

It randomizes the saturation colors, procedural maps and bitmaps being used under Default color list.

Default value is 0.0.

Gamma: It becomes available if any of the Radom ID modes are chosen from the list (Random by Node Handle, Random by Face material ID, Random by Object ID, etc.).

It randomizes the gamma colors, procedural maps and bitmaps being used under Default color list.

Default value is 0.0.

Total IDs: This function sets the total number of IDs being used/ displayed under the Default color list.

Default value is 20.

Delete unused: When clicked, it deletes disabled slots under the Default color list.

Seed: This function randomizes patterns, if the Random by name option is chosen from the list.

Entering different numbers will yield different pattern results.

Loop through textures: This function is useful when the number of Face material IDs or Object IDs in the scene exceeds the Total IDs number specified in the list.

It automatically applies one of the listed colors or/and textures specified in the list.

Blend color and texture: When enabled, this function automatically blends the current color displayed in the swatch with loaded bitmap/procedural map plugged in the toggle.

The default value of 100 uses 100% of the loaded bitmap/procedural map plugged in the toggle (if any is being used).

Otherwise, no blending will occur with default color swatch only.

NOTE

Different wood board textures from the folder, wood-boards-spruce_0053-01_1460mm-by-20mm, were used in each of the 15 toggles to achieve the final result.

The value of 50 uses 50% of the loaded bitmap/procedural map plugged in the toggle, and 50% of the color swatch.

Default color: This is the default base color or/and procedural map whose IDS are not matched. It works mainly with Object Id and Face material ID options.

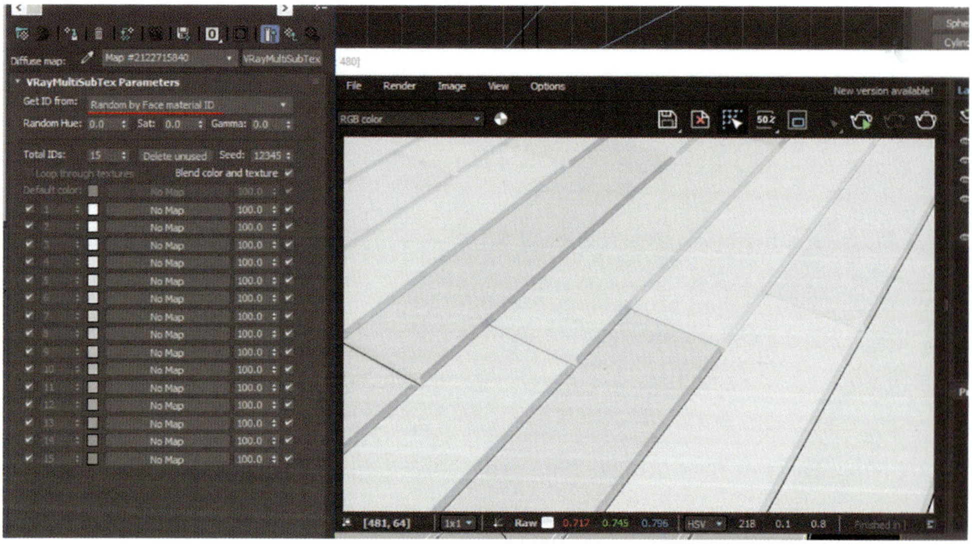

Random by Face material ID colors only option

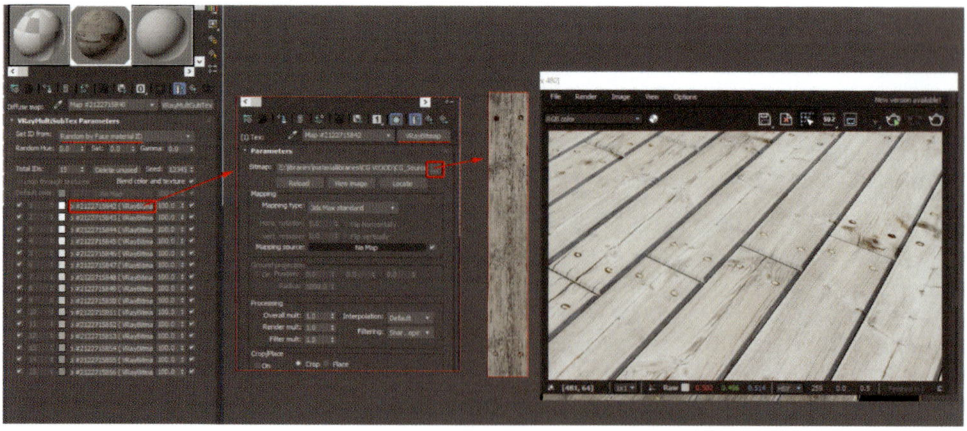

Random by Face material ID Bitmaps option

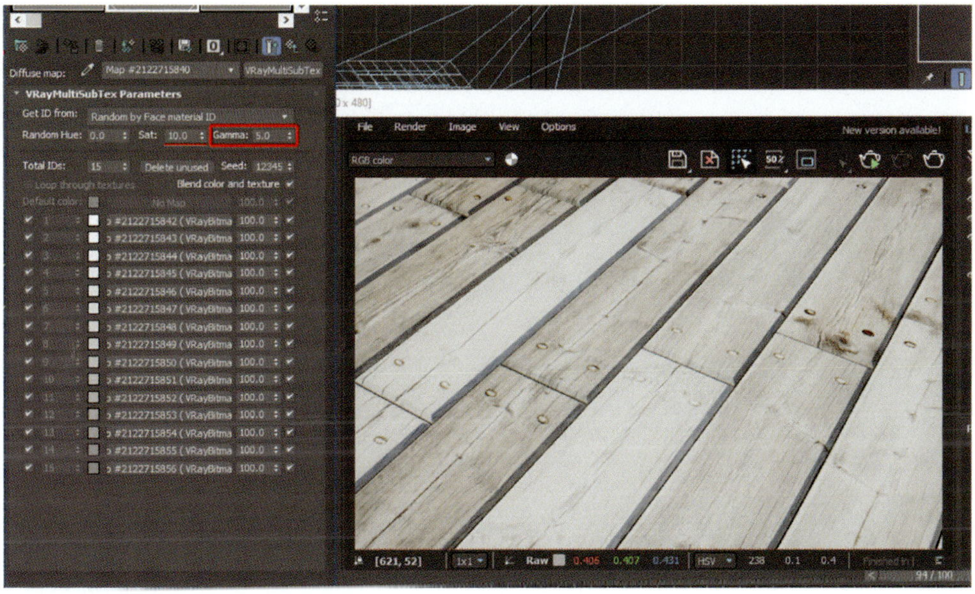

Random Gamma set to 5.0 and Saturation set to 10.0

VRayTriplanarTex

VRayTriplanarTex procedural map is extremely useful to apply on objects without the appropriate UVW Map.

It works by projecting one or more bitmaps along the axis of a surface.

To apply it, simply click on an existing VRayBitmap already being used.

In the material/Map Browser, choose the VRayTriplanarTex procedural map from the list.

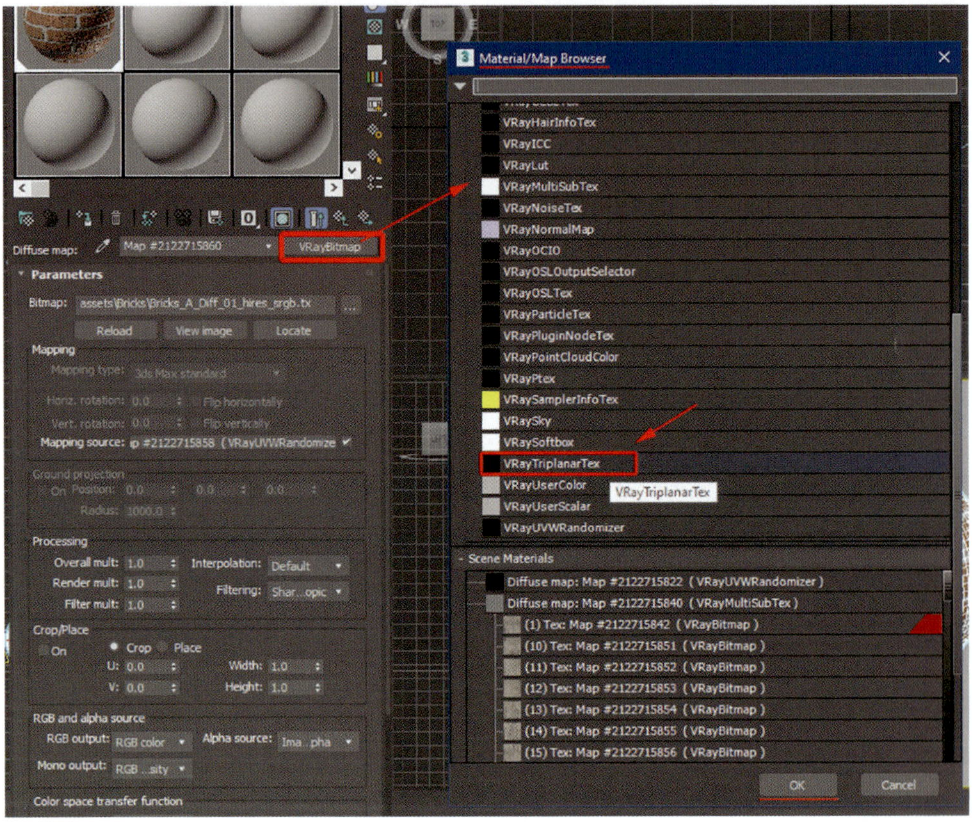

VRayBitmap used to load VRayTriplanarTex

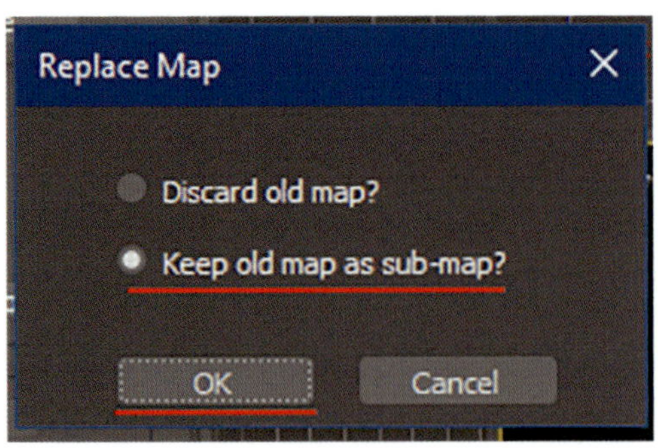

Keep old map as sub-map option

NOTE

Currently, VRayTriplanarTex procedural map is being used in the diffuse toggle.

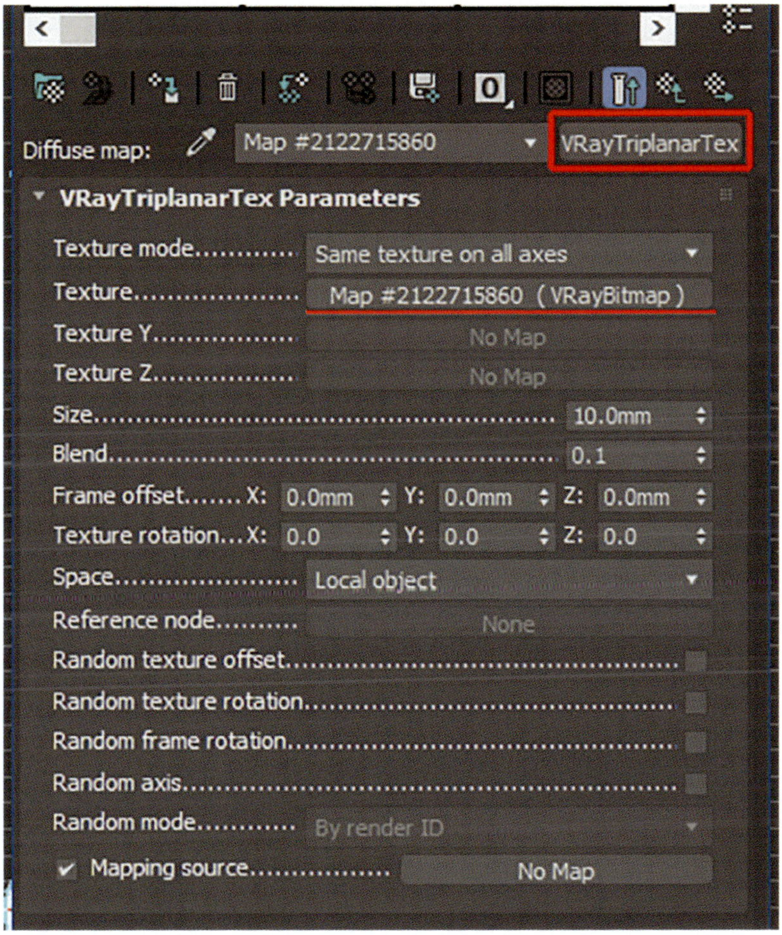

VRayTriplanarTex loaded

However, if other toggles are also being used (for reflections, bump, etc.), this procedural map needs to be applied to them also (with the same parameter values).

Texture mode: This function controls how the texture/s will be projected.

The option to use, Same texture on all axis, projects one texture (bitmap) on all axis of a surface.

The option to use, Different texture on each axis, projects different textures on each axis.

Texture: This toggle allows users to load textures and/or procedural maps.

Texture Y: This toggle only becomes available if the Texture mode is set to, Different texture on each axis.

It allows users to load textures and/or procedural maps on Y axis.

Texture Z: This toggle only becomes available if the Texture mode is set to, Different texture on each axis.

It allows users to load textures and/or procedural maps on Z axis.

Size: This function controls the size of the texture. Higher values tile the texture further.

Blend: This function is only useful when the Texture mode is set to, Different texture on each axis.

It allows users to set the amount of blend/blur between texture borders.

Frame offset: This function allows users to move the texture on X, Y, and Z axes.

Texture rotation: The function controls the rotation of textures.

Space: This function determines the projection space of the texture.

It's set to local object by default.

Users can also set the space type to, Reference to another node, and select a specific object in the scene. The selected object is often moved and/or rotated to see major changes the Material editor dialog.

The world space is used by default.

Frame offset values are more apparent in the render.

Random: Texture offset, rotation, frame rotation, axis and mode.

When enabled, this function randomly applies values to the parameters discussed earlier.

Mapping source: This function's toggle allows users to plug the VRayUVWRandomizer to it.

NOTE

These values are more noticeable when separate objects in the scene have the same VRayTriplanarTex applied (e.g., group of objects or different objects attached).

NOTE

When the Texture mode is set to, Different texture on each axis, the Size values need to be increased considerably in order for textures to be visible in the render.

NOTE

These values are more noticeable when separate objects in the scene have the same VRayTriplanarTex applied (e.g., group of objects or different objects attached).

NOTE

This function is more noticeable when separate objects have the same VRayTriplanarTex applied (e.g., group of objects or different objects attached).

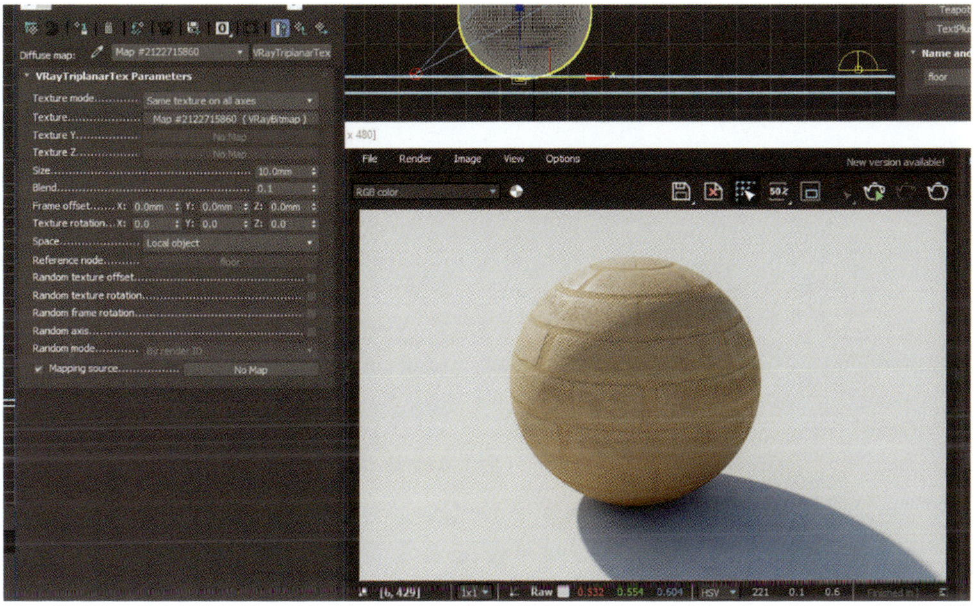

VRayTriplanarTex Size set to 10 mm

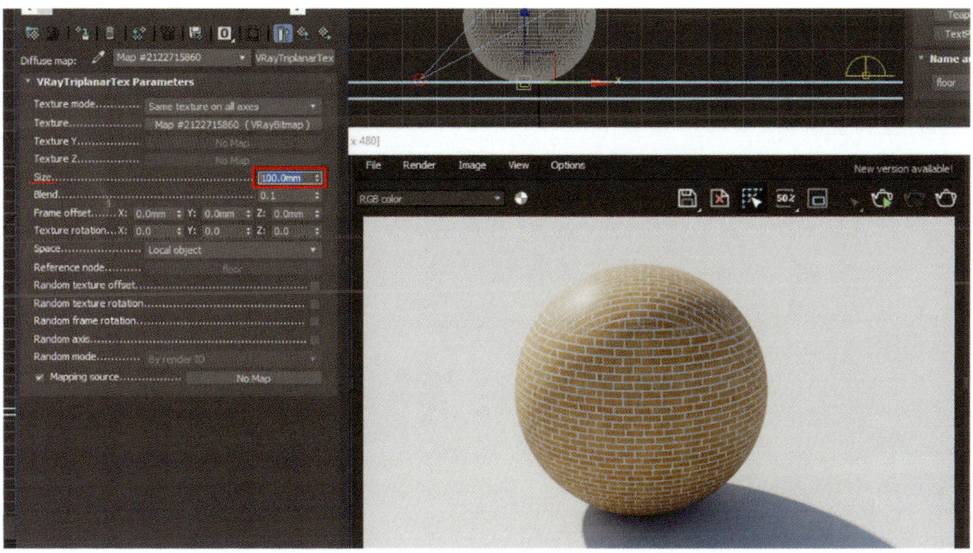

VRayTriplanarTex Size set to 100 mm

NOTE

A variety of different materials from V-Ray Asset Browser were used to achieve this result.

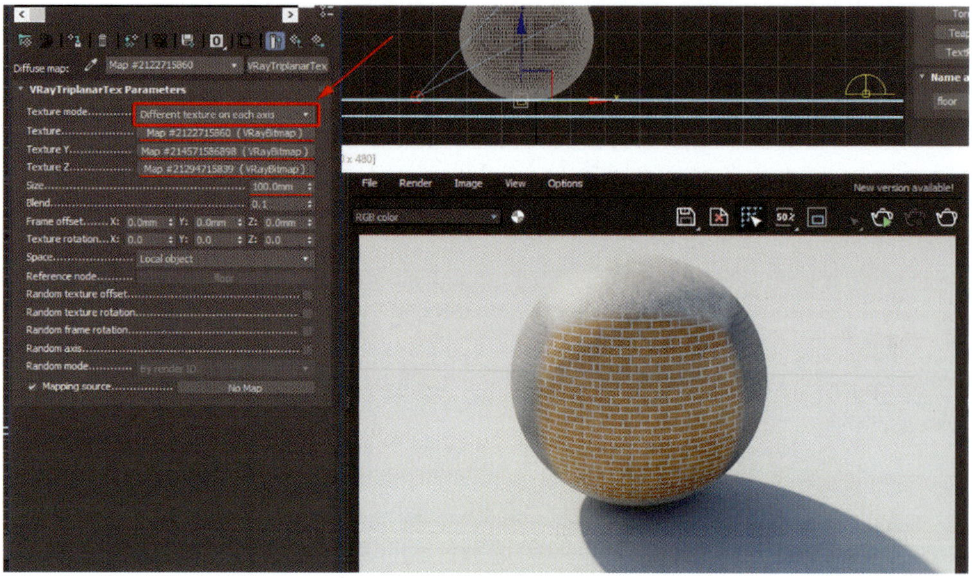

VRayTriplanarTex with different textures on each axis

To achieve similar results, simply use multiple materials/textures of your choice.

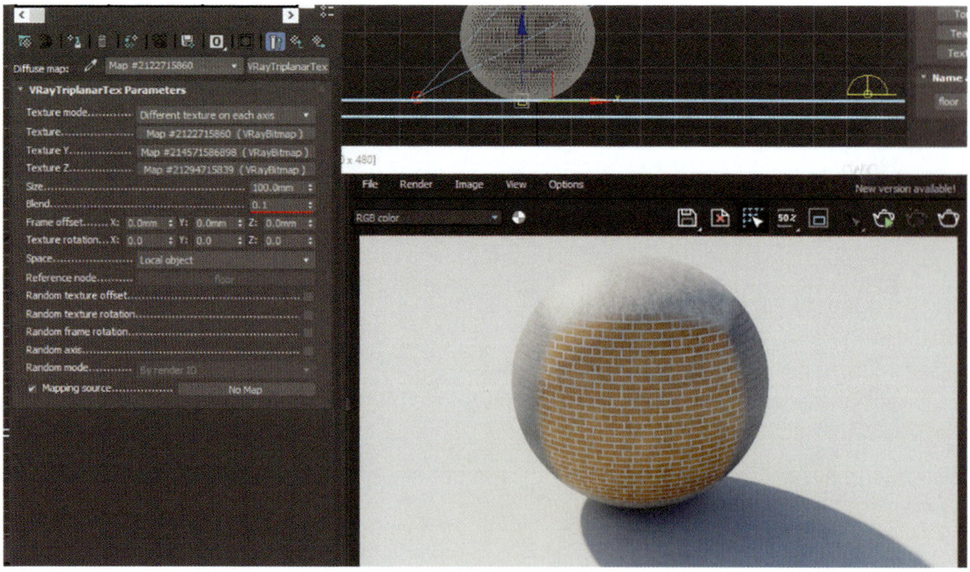

VRayTriplanarTex Blend value set to 0.1

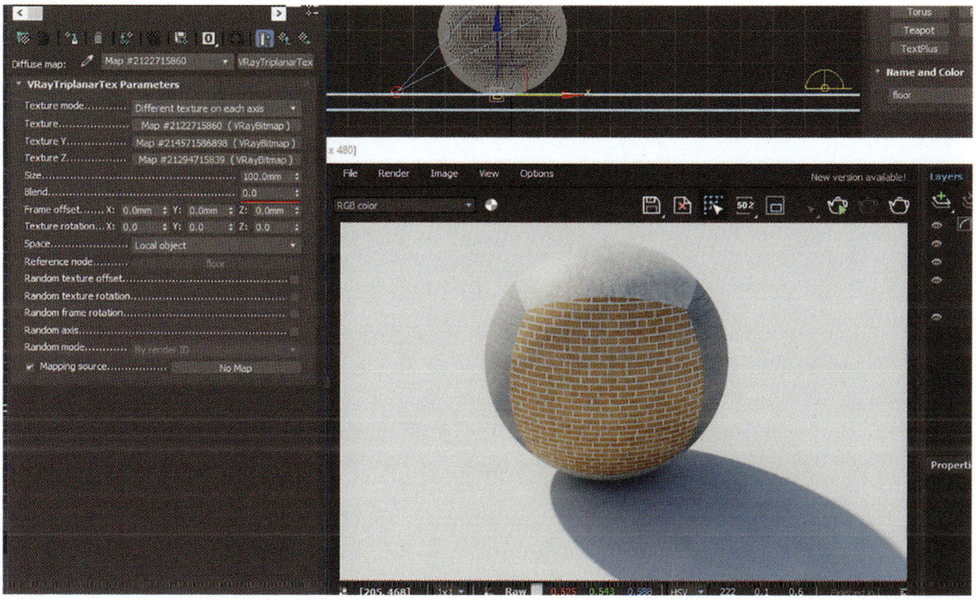

VRayTriplanarTex Blend value set to 0.0

NOTE

Objects with angled faces will yield undesirable results.

In the best-case scenario, only one of the angled faces will display a different material.

To correct this problem (bug), go to the Editable Poly or Mesh modifier, and specify the face/s ID numbers you want a different material applied to.

Use some of the steps shown previously.

Hold down the Ctrl key to select multiple faces, if required.

Do not use the MaterialByElement modifier.

Back in the Material Editor dialog (M), click on the Diffuse toggle and choose the VRayMultiSubTex procedural map.

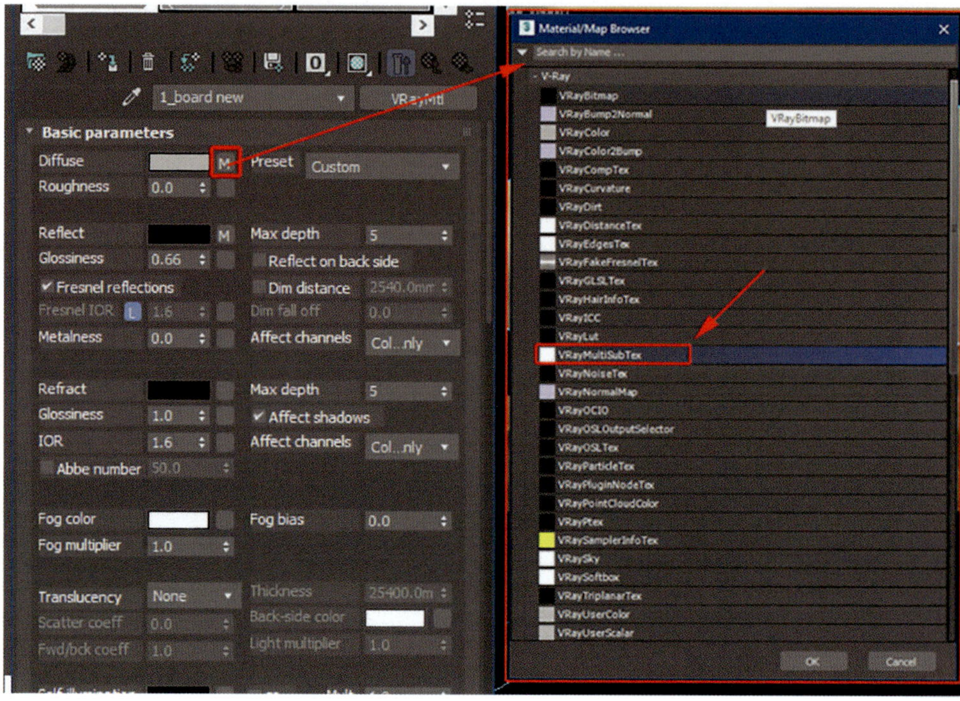

Diffuse toggle used to Apply the VRayMultiSubTex

In the VRayMultiSubTex Parameters, set the Get ID from as, Face material ID. This will recognize the ID faces previously numbered accordingly.

Under Total IDs, set the total number of IDs you want.

In the Default color toggle, apply the VRayColor2Bump to add detail to the surface.

Set its Material ID number to coincide with the face number previously set. And add the VRayTriplanarTex procedural map, as previously shown.

Under VRayTriplanar Parameters, set the Texture mode as, Different texture on each axis.

Copy the same texture or a different one into the X, Y and Z toggles.

Set its Size. And set the Space as, Local object.

Also, set its Material ID number to coincide with the face number previously set.

Repeat the same steps for the remaining Total IDs listed in the VRayMultiSubTex Parameters. Use different Id numbers, and set the Frame offset in X with deferent values.

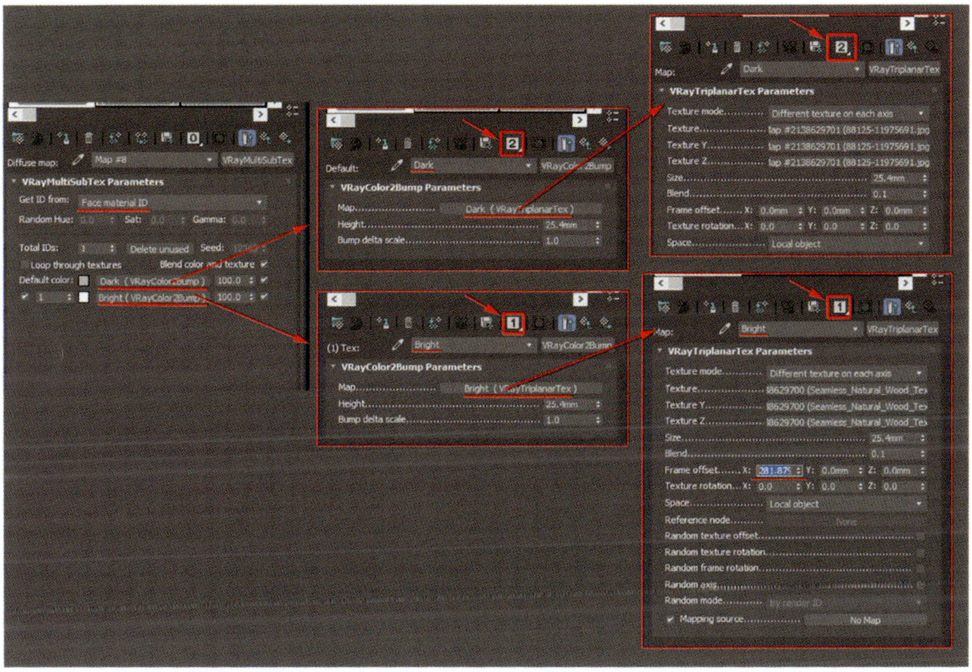

Diffuse map with VRayMultiSubTex, VRayColor2Bump and VRayTriplanarTex applied

VRayPointCloudColor

VRayPointCloudColor procedural map allows users to accurately render point cloud objects in 3ds Max without the renders having to look self-illuminated.

To use a specific bitmap, apply the VRayBitmap procedural map first, and load the VRayPointCloudColor via the Mapping source toggle.

VRayPointCloudColor doesn't have any parameters.

NOTE

This procedural map is only available via the Diffuse toggle.

NOTE

VRayDirt is less apparent on spherical surfaces.

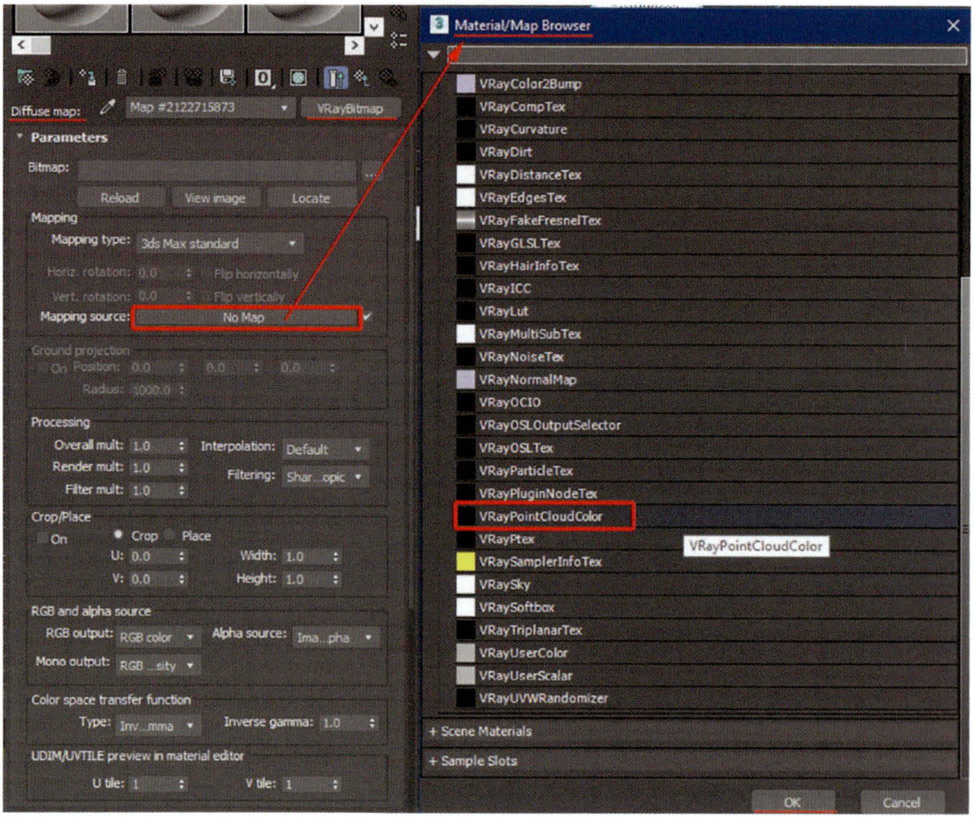

Diffuse map toggle with VRayBitmap and VRayPointCloudColor loaded via Mapping source

VRayDirt

This amazing procedural map allows users to emulate dirt or ambient occlusion effects around the crevices of objects.

Users can apply VRayDirt directly to the Diffuse toggle of a material.

Or Via the Render Elements (VRayExtraTex>VRayDirt).

Either way, VRayDirt increases the rendering times slightly.

To apply it via the Diffuse toggle of a material, simply click on the existing VRayBitmap or Bitmap, and choose VRayDirt from the Material Map/Browser dialog.

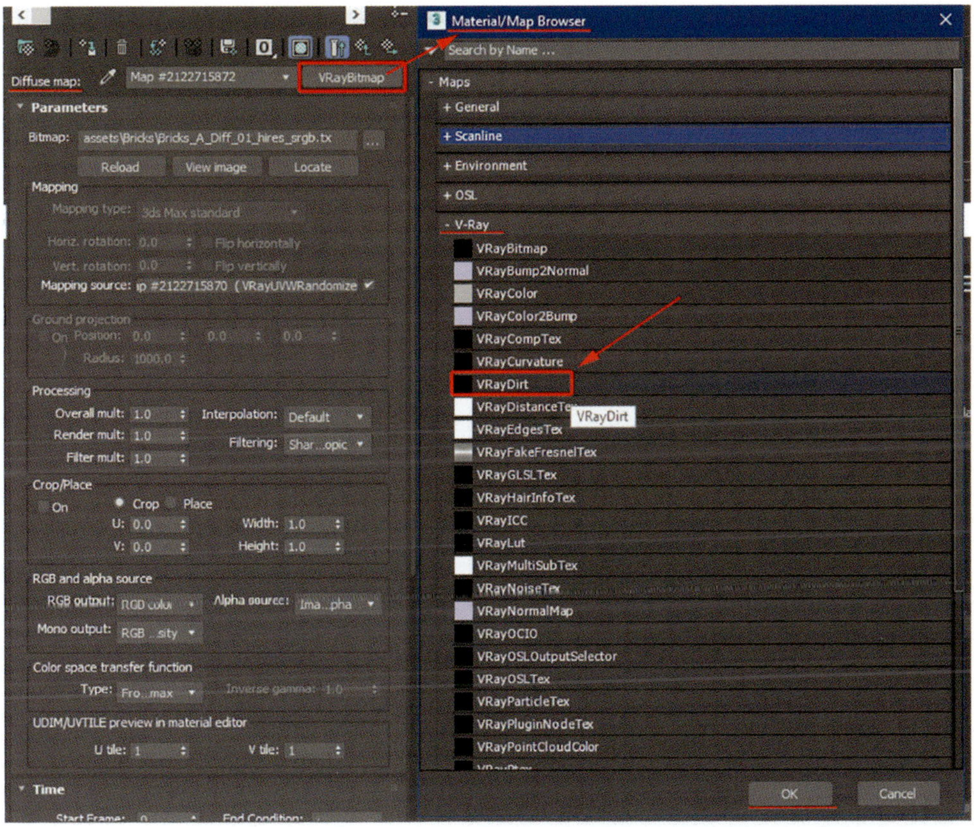

Diffuse toggle and VRayBitmap used to Load VRayDirt

Keep old map as sub-map option

VRayDirt loaded

To apply VRayDirt via render element, simply go to the Render Setup dialog, and open the Render Element Tab.

Under Render Elements group, click to Add, and choose the VRayExtraTex procedural map from its dialog.

Once loaded, click on its Texture toggle and load the VRayDirt from the Material/Map Browser dialog.

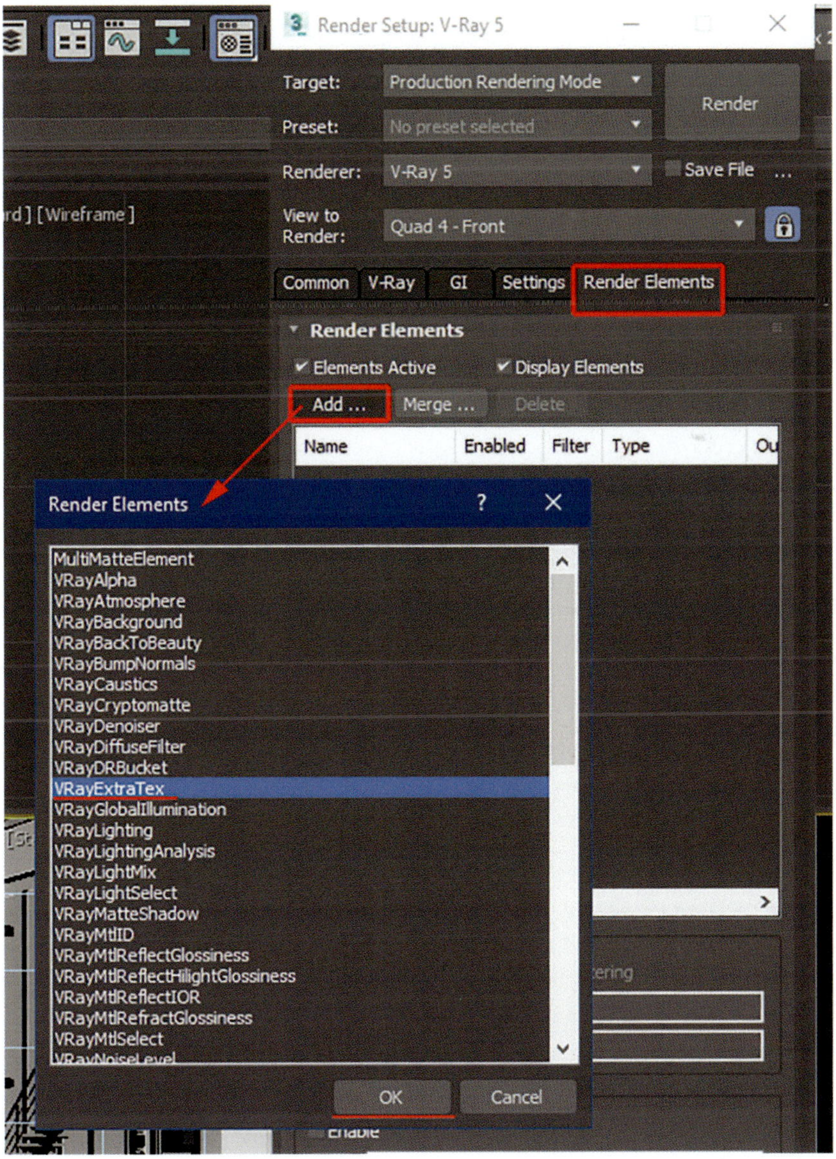

Render Elements tab used to Add VRayExtraTex Render Element

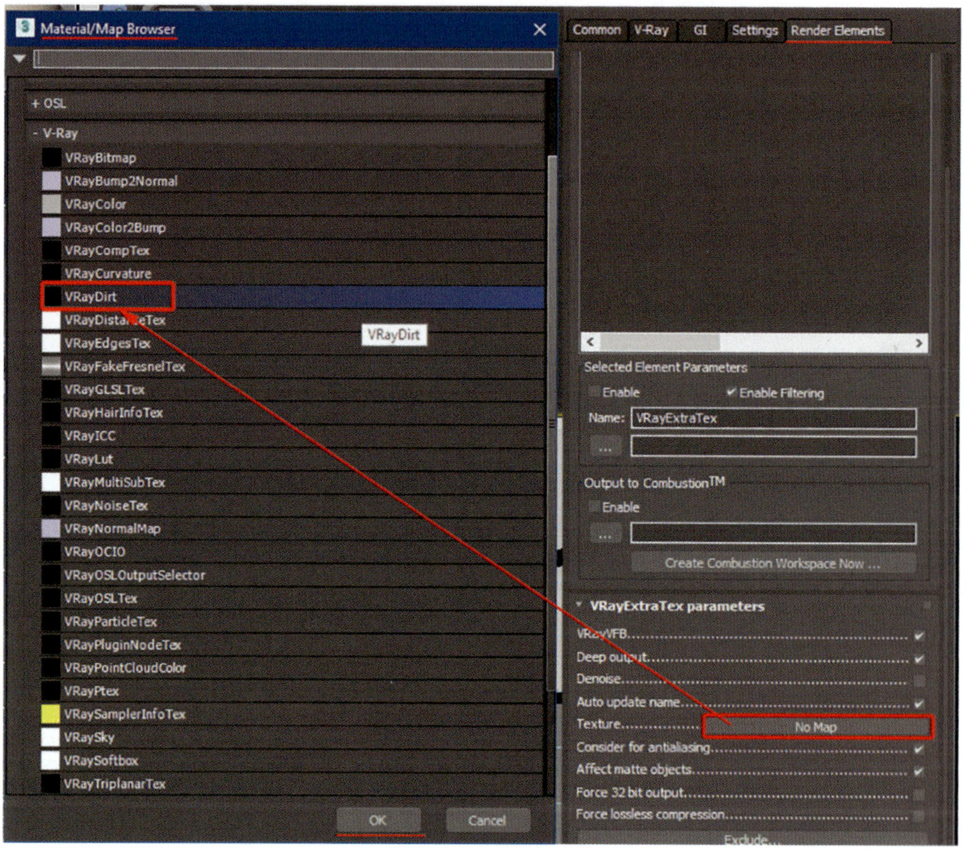

VRayExtraTex Texture toggle used to load Add VRayDirt

To edit its parameters, drag the VRayDirt from VRayExtraTex toggle onto an empty material slot.

Choose the Instance Method.

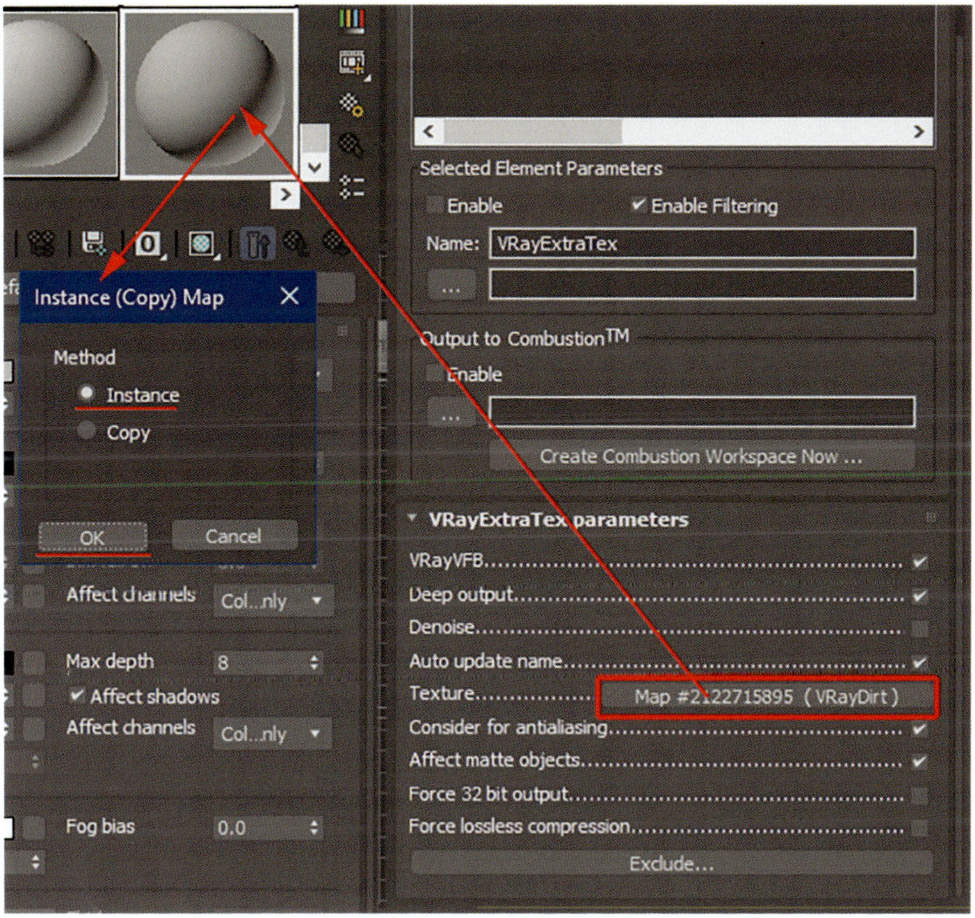

VRayDirt toggle dropped in the material slot to Copy Instance

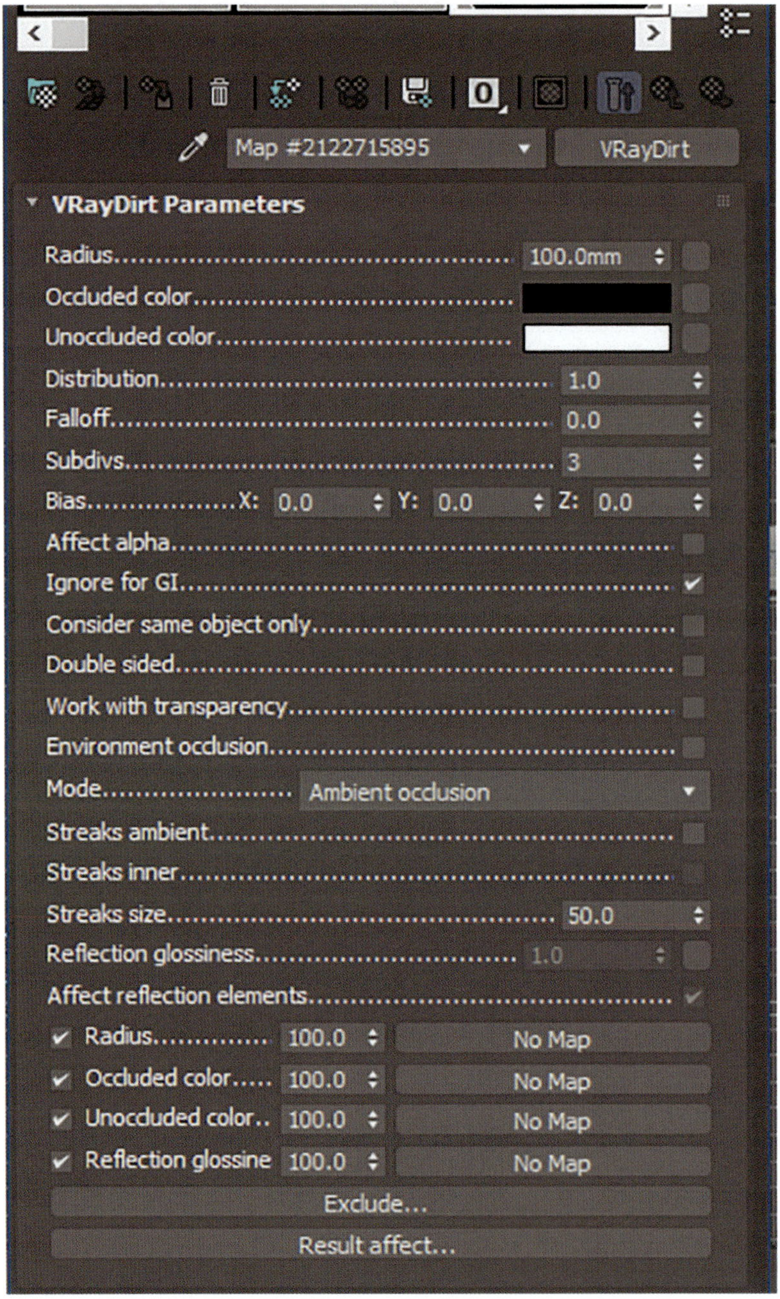

VRayDirt loaded

It's quicker to preview and adjust the VRayDirt parameters as a material override (under V-Ray global switches) tab.

Once satisfied with the results, you can copy/paste the final parameters onto the diffuse toggle, and disable the override.

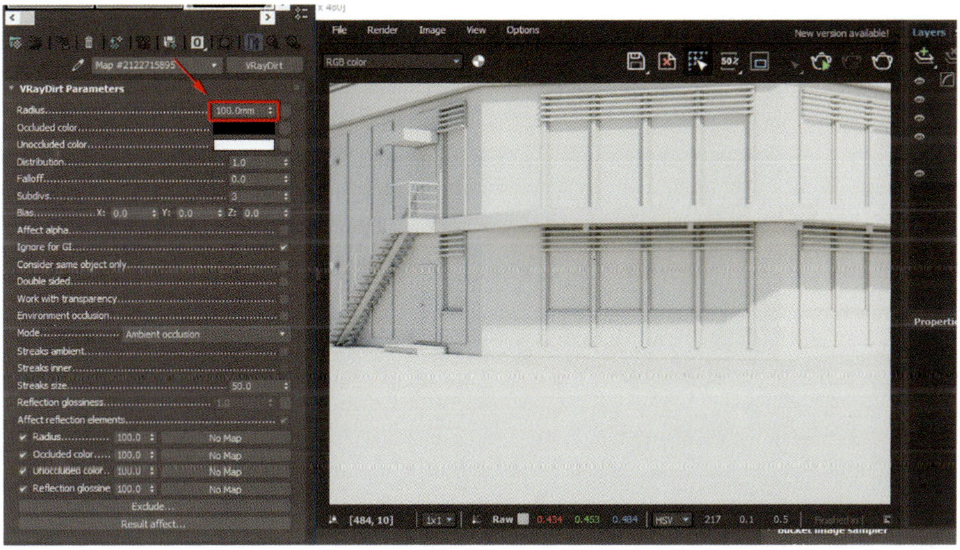

VRayDirt Radius set to 100 mm

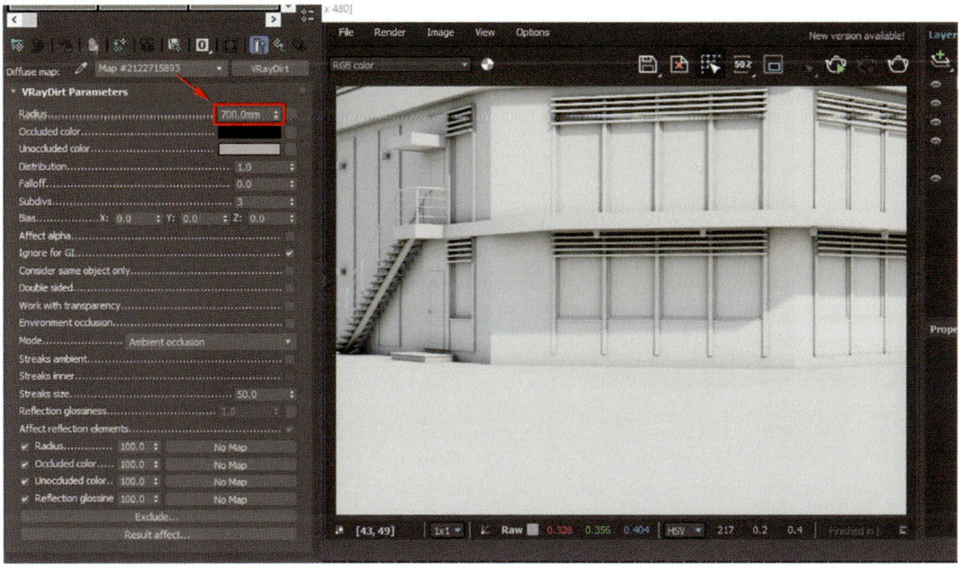

VRayDirt Radius set to 700 mm

NOTE

Enabling the Streaks ambient function will NOT yield streaks. One of the Bias axis needs to have a value applied (e.g., 30).

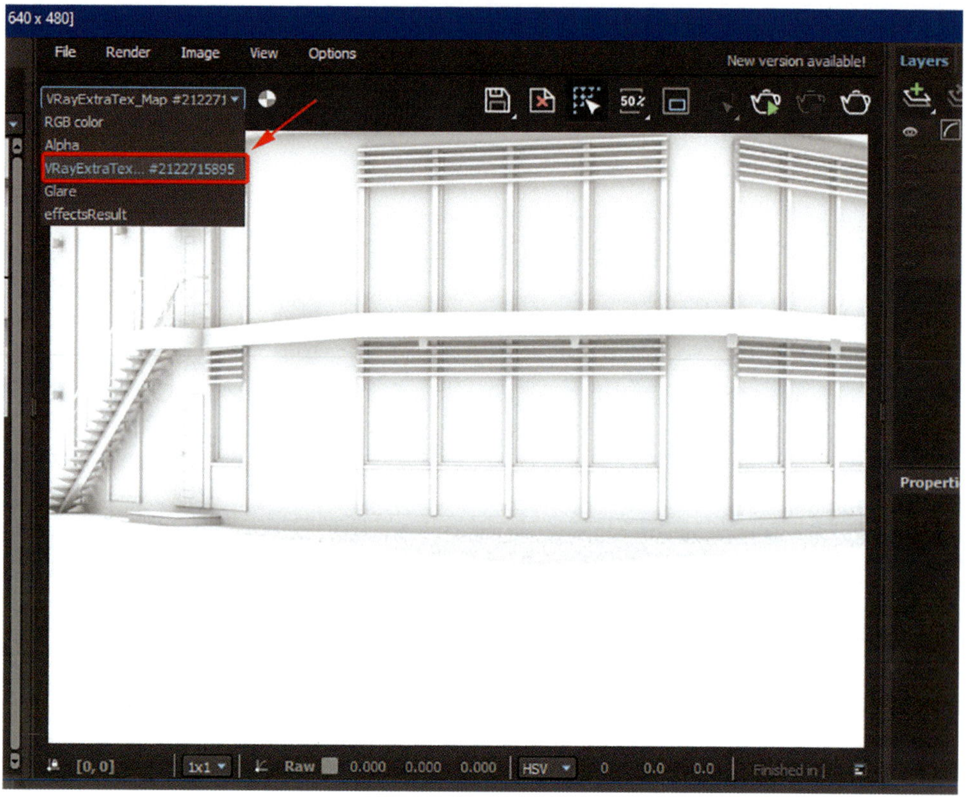

VRayDirt Radius set to 700 mm in Render Elements

It's common practice for users to focus mainly on the Z axis to create streaks in a vertical direction.

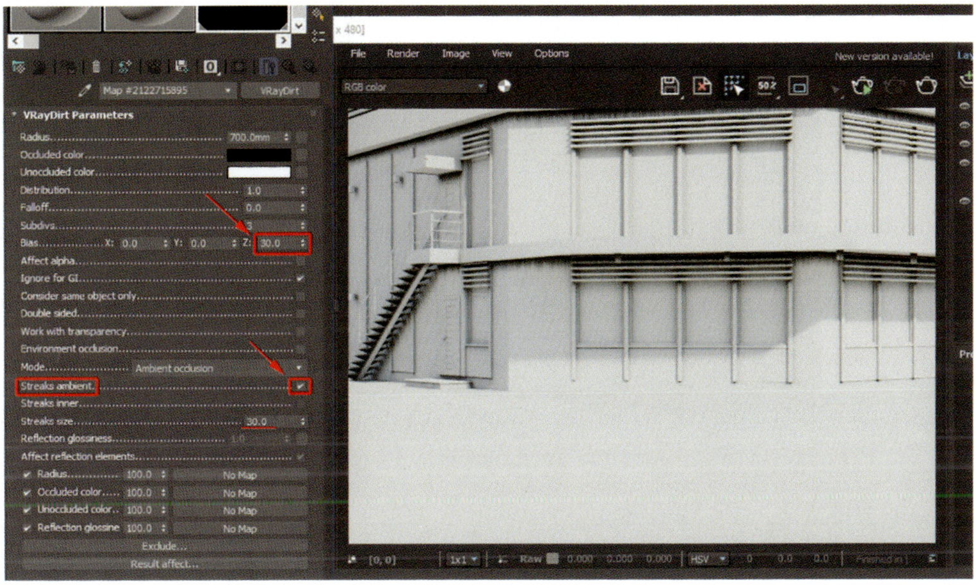

VRayDirt Streaks ambient with Z bias set to 30

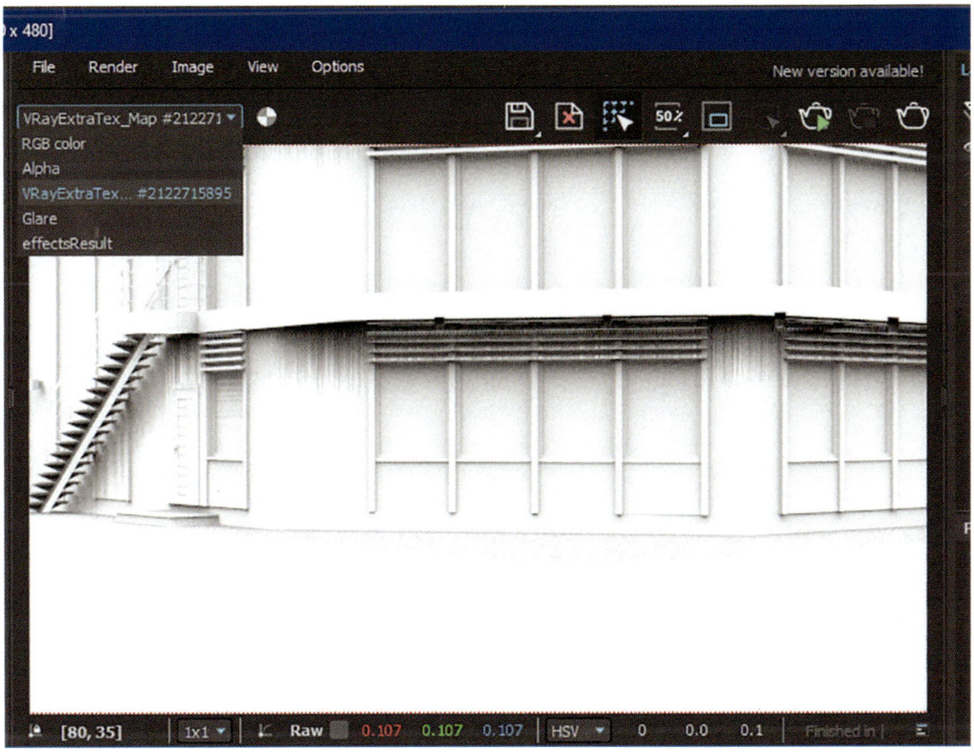

VRayDirt Streaks in VFB Render Elements list

Radius: This function sets the radius of the VRayDirt.

Default value is 100 mm.

Occluded color: This function controls the color of the VRayDirt.

Default color is black (0).

Unoccluded color: This function controls the main color/shade of objects.

When VRayDirt is used in the Diffuse toggle, users often have procedural maps plugged to this toggle (e.g., VRayMtl, VRayBitmap)

Distribution: This function narrows the spread of the VRayDirt.

The smaller the value, the wider the VRayDirt.

Default value is 1.0.

Falloff: This function controls the amount of gradient on the VRayDirt.

High values reduce the spread of the gradient. Keep the default value (0.0) to have a wide gradient.

Default value is 0.0.

Subdivs: This function controls the quality of the VRayDirt. High values yield smother results (less grainy) at a cost of longer rendering times.

The default value is often OK.

Default value is 3.

Bias: This function sets the direction of the VRayDirt. Z axis sets the direction of the VRayDirt vertically.

The default value of 0.0 (in X, Y and Z) sets the ambient occlusion in all directions.

Affect alpha: When turned on, the alpha values of the Occluded and Unoccluded colors/toggles are applied.

Enabling this function doubles the rendering times.

Disabled by default.

Ignore for GI: When enabled (by default), this function omits the VRayDirt preview during the pre-calculation process of the render.

By default, VRayDirt is only visible during the rendering time. Not pre-calculation.

Enabled by default.

Consider same object only: By default (disabled), VRayDirt is spread to nearby objects.

When this function is enabled, the ambient occlusion will no longer affect adjacent objects.

Disabled by default.

Double-sided: When turned on, this function affects crevices and edges of objects.

It often creates undesirable results.

Disabled by default.

Work with transparency: When turned on, this function takes into consideration transparent objects in the scene, including mapped opacity.

Disabled by default.

Environment occlusion: This function takes into consideration the Environment contribution on unoccluded areas.

Disabled by default.

Mode: This function controls how the VRayDirt will be used (Ambient Occlusion, Reflection occlusion, Inner occlusion, ambient + inner occlusion).

Set to Ambient Occlusion mode by default.

Streaks ambient: When enabled, this function adds streaks to the ambient occlusion.

Streaks are only visible when the bias value is set in one direction (positive values) or the other (negative values).

VRayDirt will be projected in both directions without streaks, if the Bias values are set to 0.0 (in X, Y, Z).

It's common practice for users to focus mainly on Z axis to create streaks in one direction.

The value of 30 seems to work well in most scenes.

Disabled by default.

Streaks inner: This function only becomes available when the Inner occlusion mode is set.

When enabled, it adds streaks to crevices.

Disabled by default.

NOTE

When sending the final high-resolution renders, it's best Not to use VRayDirt as render element in your main scene.

Streak size: This function controls the width of each streak. The bigger the value, the more the streaks will overlap horizontally.

Default value is 50.0.

This will reduce the rendering times substantially.

Instead, create a separate scene with a basic VRayMtl as an override material, and use multiple passes of VRayDirt as render elements (e.g., with streaks, without streaks).

These VRayDirt render passes/elements can be later used in post-production by overlaying them (Multiply blending mode) against the main render, in Photoshop, AfterEffects, Nuke, etc.

Reflection glossiness: This function becomes available if the Mode is set to, Reflection occlusion (Phong, Blinn, Ward).

It controls the direction of the rays traced for Reflection Occlusion.

Affect reflection elements: This function becomes available if the Mode is set to, Reflection occlusion (Phong, Blinn, Ward).

When turned on, the ambient reflection affects the reflection in the render element.

Exclude: This toggle allows users to choose object/s to exclude from VRayDirt.

VRayAerialPerspective

This truly amazing procedural map works in conjunction with the VRaySun and VRaySky to emulate perspective atmospheric effects such as fog or haze.

Unlike the VRayEnvironmentFog, it's much faster to render and does not cast volumetric shadows.

To apply it, simply open the environment dialog by pressing eight on your keyboard, or by going to the Rendering toolbar and choosing the Environment option from the list.

Next, in the Environment and Effects dialog, under Atmosphere group, click the Add toggle and choose the VRayAerialPerspective.

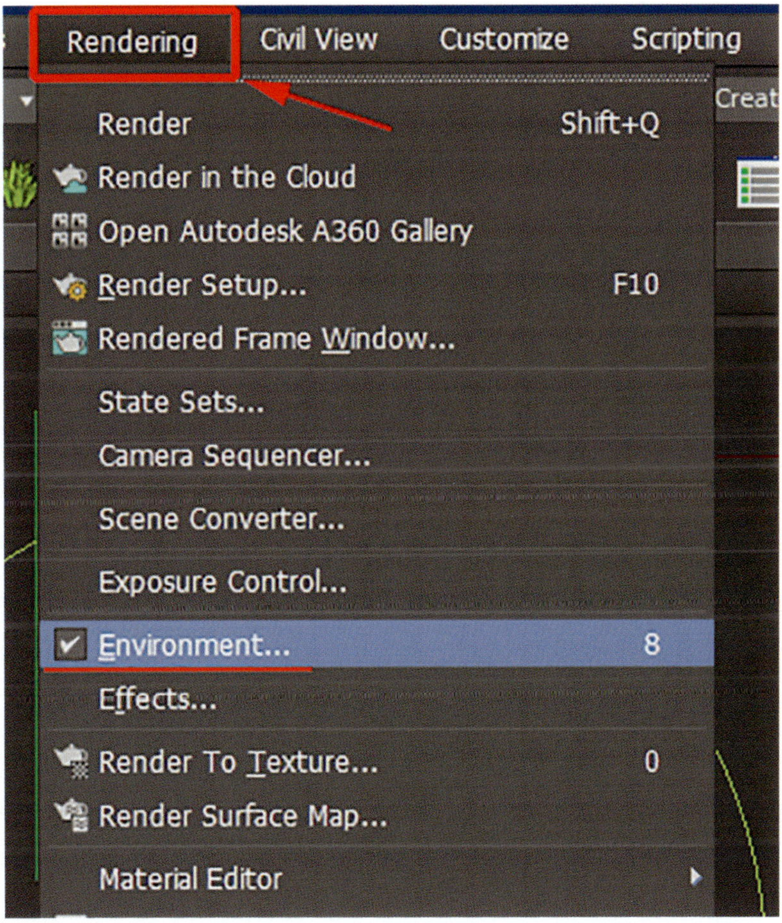

Click the Rendering toolbar and choose the Environment option

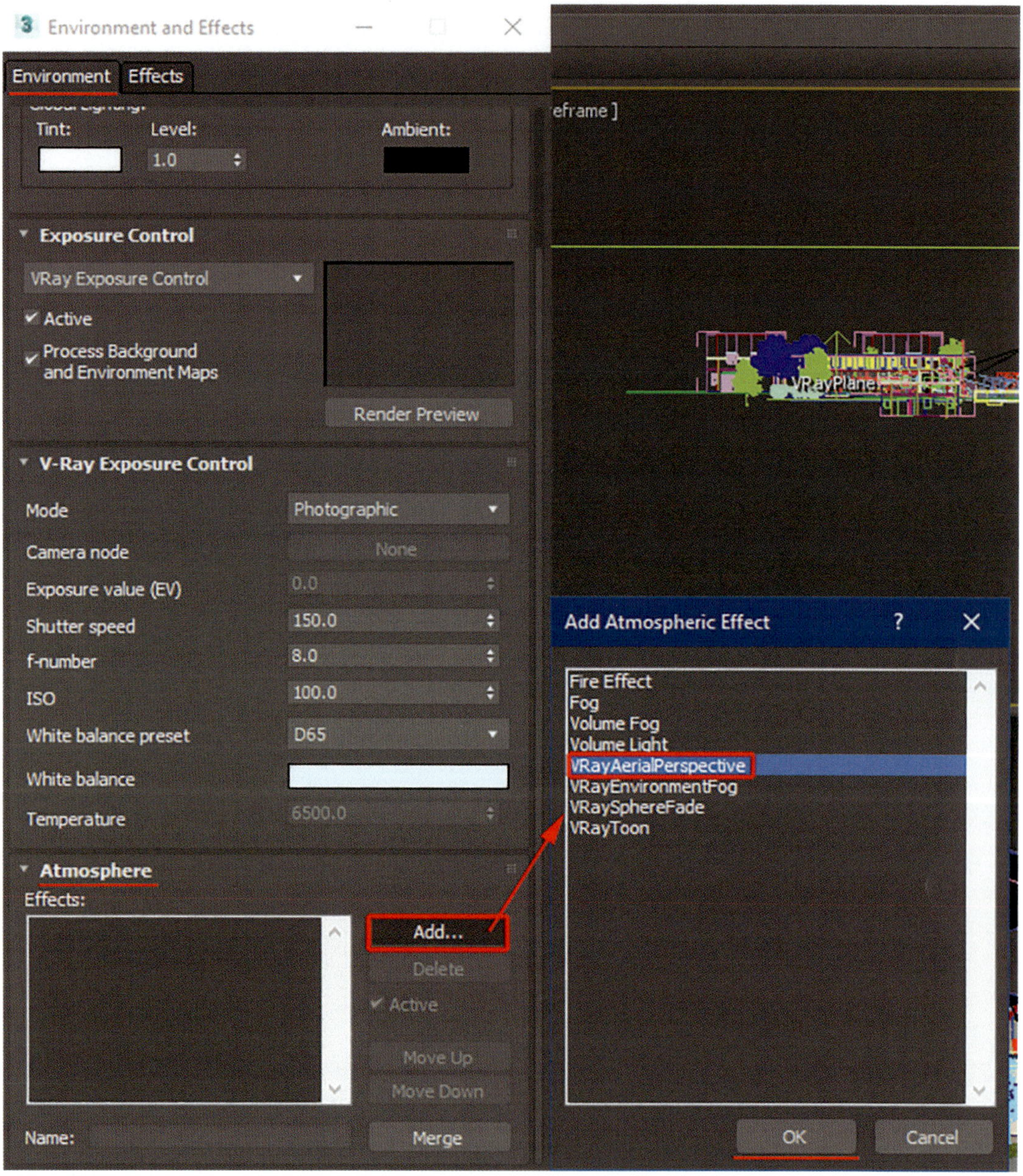

In the Environment tab, under Atmosphere Effects click to add VRayAerialPerspective

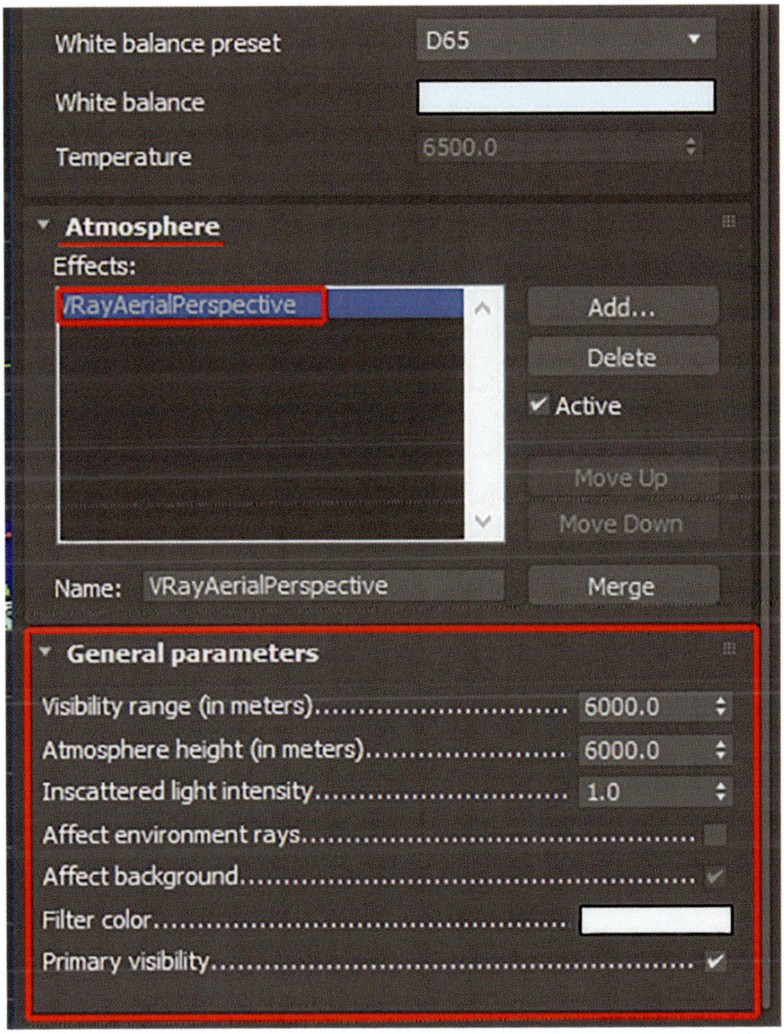

VRayAerialPerspective Loaded with default parameters

Visibility range (in meters): This function controls the fog/haze proximity to the camera.

Low values bring the fog/haze closer to the camera. And High Values do the opposite.

Default value, 6000.0 (far away).

VRayAerialPerspective Visibility range 6000.0

VRayAerialPerspective Visibility range 600.0

Atmosphere height (in meters): This function controls the height of the fog/haze.

Low values reduce the height of the fog/haze. And high values do the opposite.

Default value is 6000.0.

VRayAerialPerspective Atmosphere height 6000.0

VRayAerialPerspective Atmosphere height 100.0

Inscattered light intensity: This function controls how much light passes through the fog/haze.

Values lower than 1.0 reduce the brightness/shadows in the scene. Values higher than 1.0 yield the opposite effect.

Default value is 1.0.

Affect Environment rays: When enabled, this function blends the fog/haze with the horizon (sky).

Disabled by default.

VRayAerialPerspective Affect Environment rays disabled

VRayAerialPerspective Affect Environment rays enabled

Affect background: This function adds the fog/haze to the background. When disabled the background is darker (assuming the Filter color is white). Enabled by default.

VRayAerialPerspective Affect background enabled

VRayAerialPerspective Affect background disabled

Filter color: This function controls the color of the fog/haze.

Default color is white.

Primary visibility: This function enables the visibility of the fog/haze.

Enabled by default.

VRayAerialPerspective Primary visibility enabled

VRayAerialPerspective Primary visibility disabled

VRayLightMtl

This shader is primarily used to add self-illumination to objects. And can easily be accessed through the Material/Map Browser dialog, under the V-Ray rollout list.

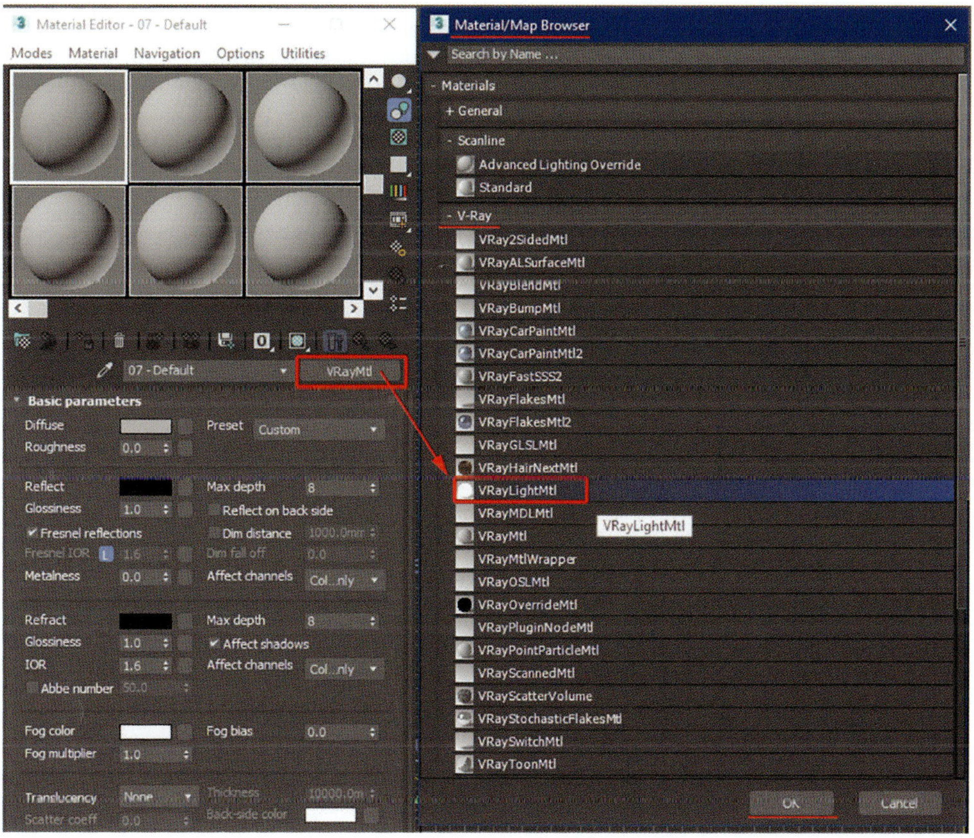

VRayMtl used to load VRayLightMtl from Material/Map Browser dialog

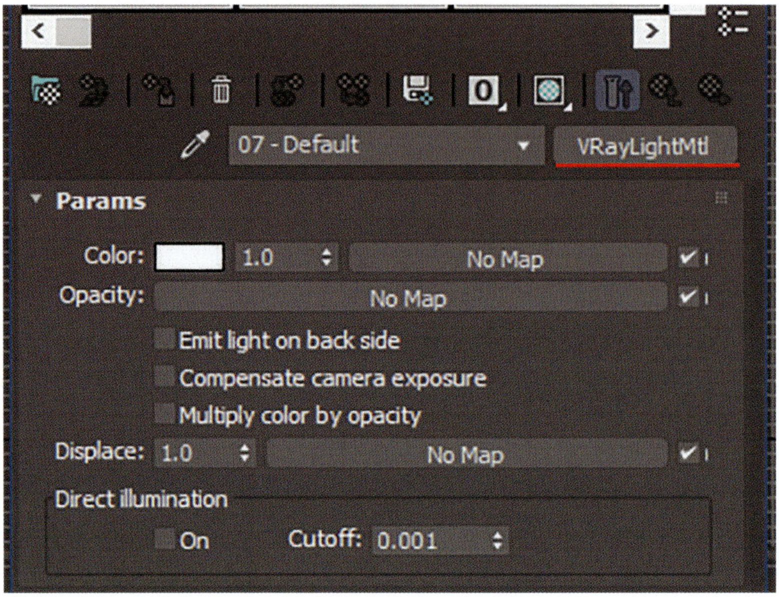

VRayLightMtl parameters

VRayLightMtl works in exact same way as the VRay Self-Illumination function. In addition, it comes with features such as:

Opacity: This function allows users to plug textures and/or procedural maps to its toggle.

As with most opacity toggles, it works best when a grayscale and/or black and white texture/procedural map is used.

Emit light on back side: This function allows the light to be emitted from a side of an object that isn't emitting light.

Disabled, by default.

Compensate camera exposure: This function is quite useful for scenes where the exposure controls are causing the self-illumination to be slightly dimmed. Turning this function on, will essentially make the self-illumination more visible, by compensating for the exposure.

Disabled, by default.

Multiply color by opacity: When turned on, it increases the color of the light material, based on the texture/procedural map applied to the Opacity toggle.

Disabled, by default.

Displace: This function is only available when the Direct illumination is disabled. Users can plug a texture/procedural map to it.

Displacement works best with grayscale and black and white materials.

Direct illumination: When turned on, it emits light in the same manner as a VRay Mesh light. As such, it can be time-consuming to render.

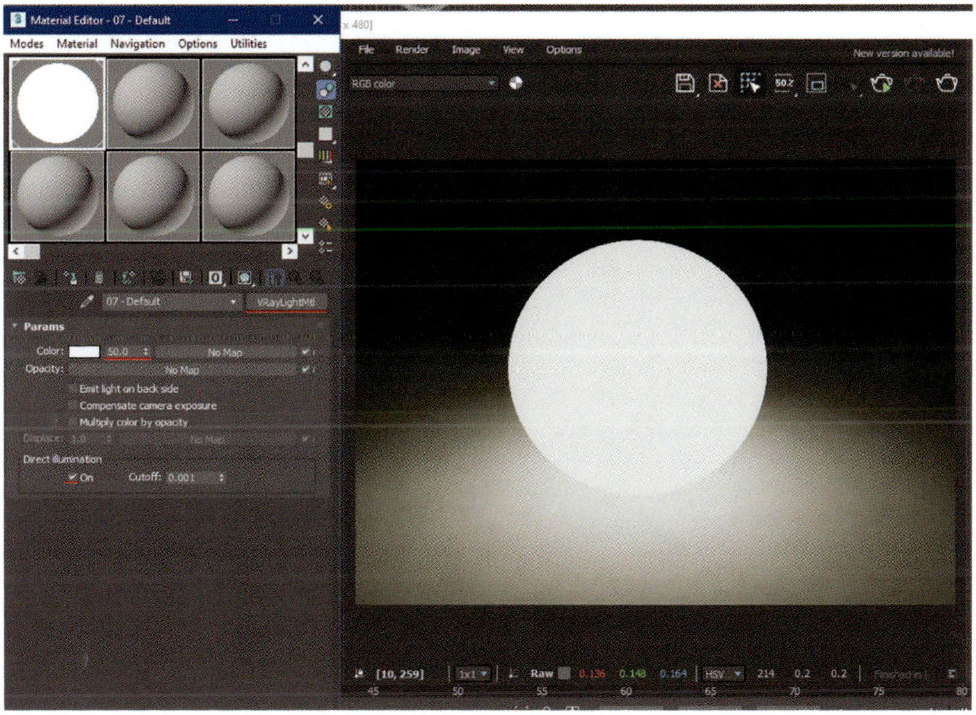

VRayLightMtl Color value set to 50 with the Direct Illumination enabled

VRayMtlWrapper

This shader only works if the Global Illumination (GI) and/or the Caustics are enabled in rendering parameters.

It's mainly used to allow certain materials to receive or generate GI and Caustics.

To access it, simply select an existing material slot and click on the main shader toggle, followed by choosing the VRMtlWrapper shader from the Material/Map Browser list.

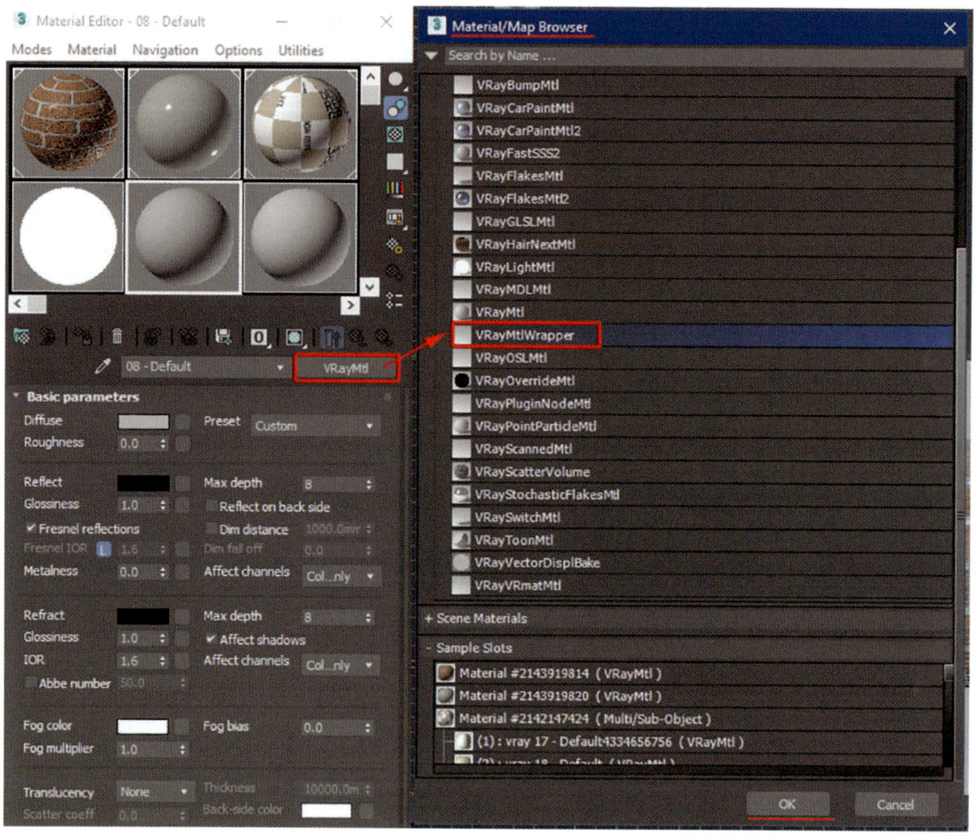

VRayMtl used to load VRMtlWrapper shader from the Material/Map Browser dialog

The Replace Material dialog should be prompted. Choose to keep old material as sub-material.

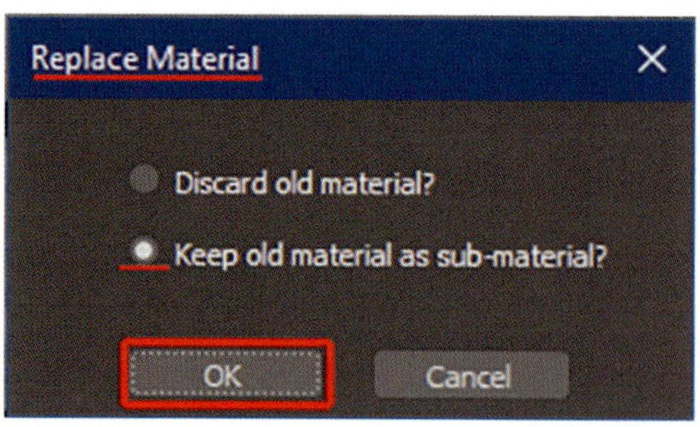

Keep old material as sub-material option

It's parameters should load up automatically.

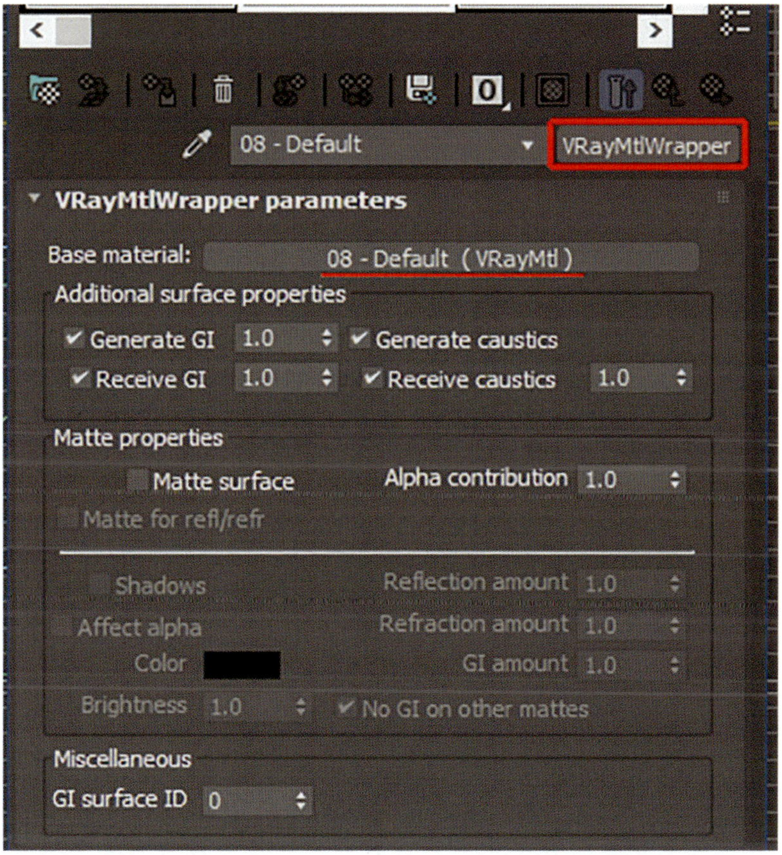

VRMtlWrapper parameters

Base material: The sub-material is kept in this toggle.

Generate GI: This function enables users to increase or decrease the quantity of GI being generated by the Base material.

Receive GI: The function allows users to increase or decrease the amount of GI being received by the Base material. Its value is set 1.0, by default.

This feature is widely used to make shadows/indirectly lit areas darker or brighter.

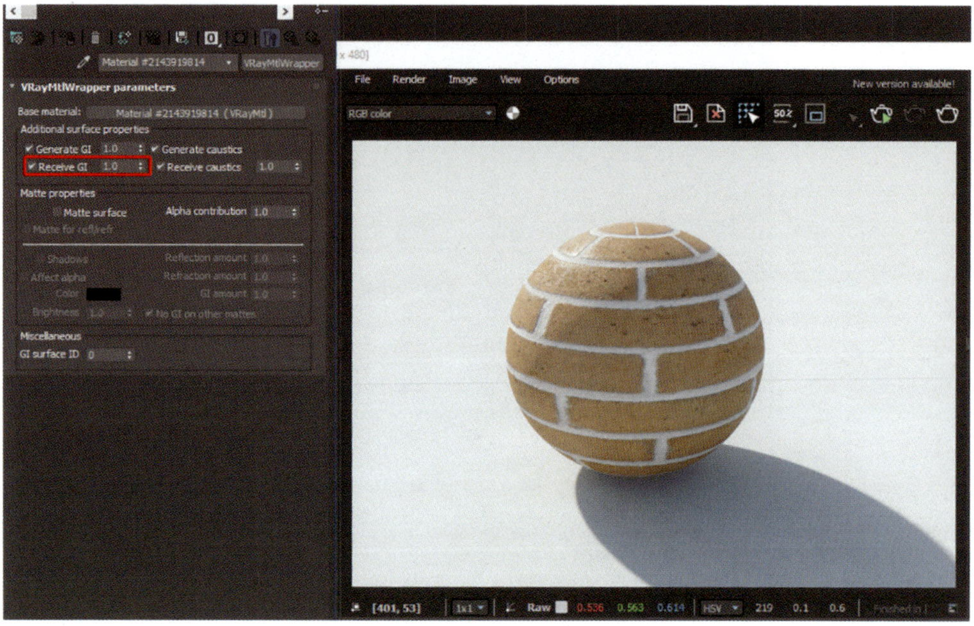

VRMtlWrapper function to Receive GI set to 1.0

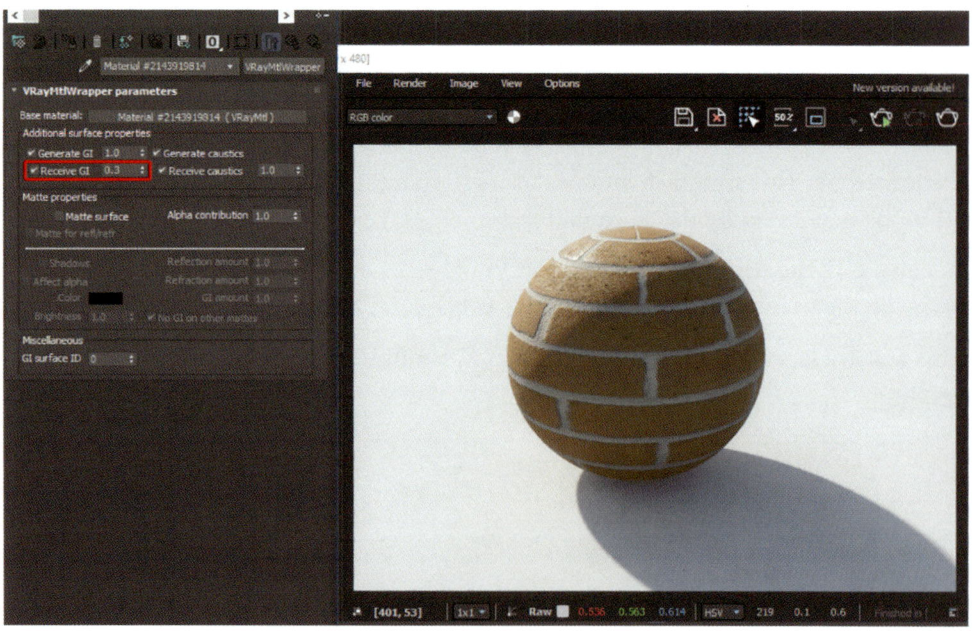

VRMtlWrapper function to Receive GI set to 0.3

Generate caustics: When turned on, it allows caustics to be generated. Enabled by default.

Receive caustics: Users can increase or decrease the amount of caustics being received by the object. Its value is set 1.0, by default.

VRayOverrideMtl

This shader is mostly used as an override, to correct GI "color bleeding" artifacts, reflections, refractions and shadows.

It can easily be accessed by clicking on the main shader toggle, followed by choosing the, VRayOverrideMtl, from the Material/Map Browser dialog.

Following that, in the Replace Material dialog, choose to, Keep old material as sub-material.

The VRayOverrideMtl should load up automatically thereafter.

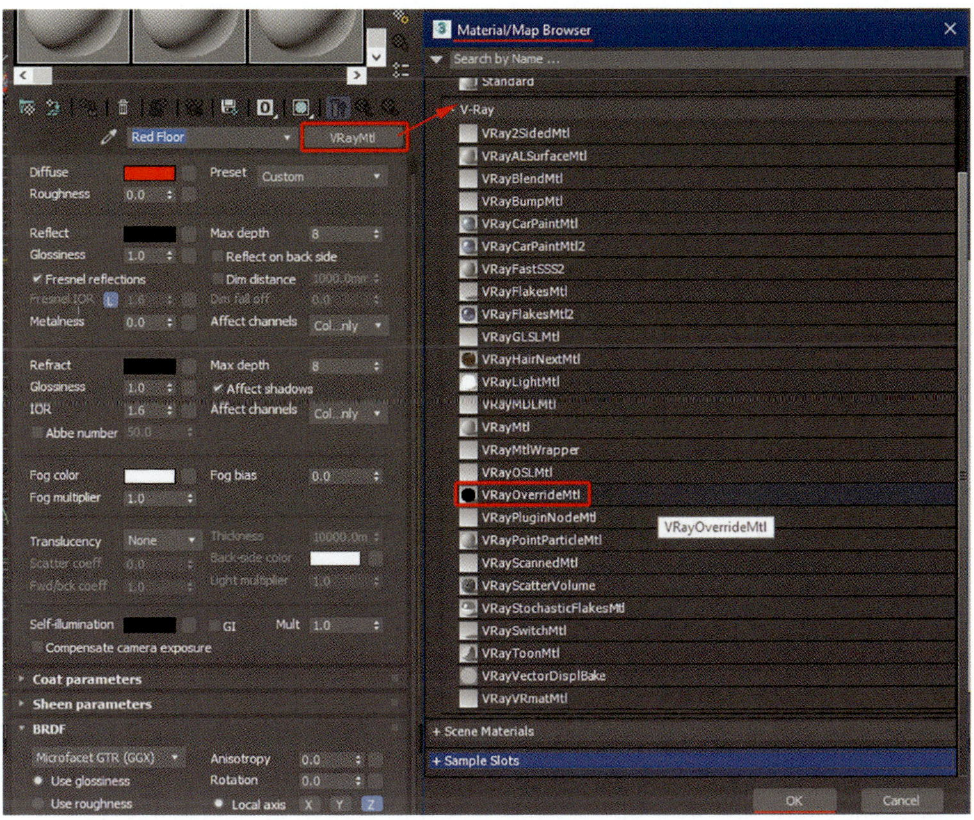

VRayMtl used to load the VRayOverrideMtl shader

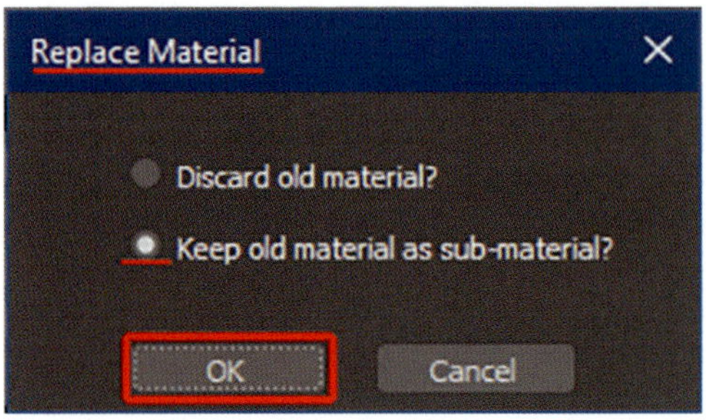

Keep old material as sub-material option

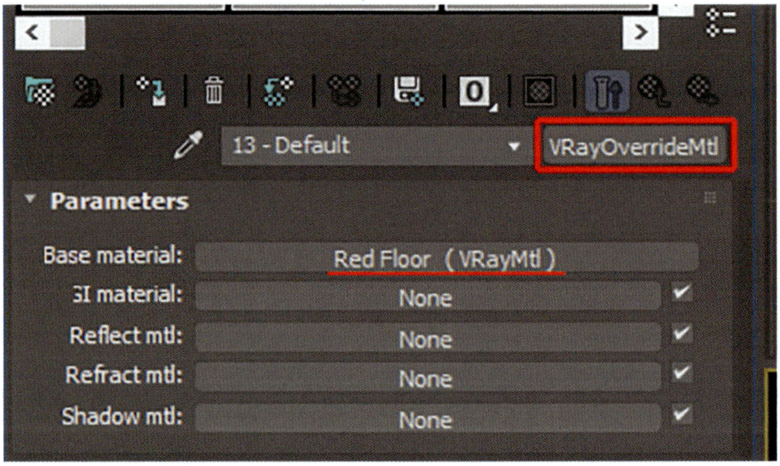

VRayOverrideMtl shader loaded

Base material: This is the toggle where the base *sub-material* is kept in.

GI: The toggle allows users to plug a material, to be used as a new source of GI reflectance. This toggle is very useful to override GI "color bleeding" effects on nearby objects.

Reflect mtl: This function can be used to override its material appearance, when "seen" on other reflective objects.

Refract mtl: This toggle works in a similar way to Reflect mtl. It can be used to change how the refractions are seen by other reflective surfaces.

Shadow myl: The toggle allows users to override the shadow appearance when cast onto its surface.

The examples below depict how the "color bleeding" and the reflection colors were easily changed/corrected, by simply plugging different shaders (white VRayMtl) in both, GI and Reflect mtl toggles.

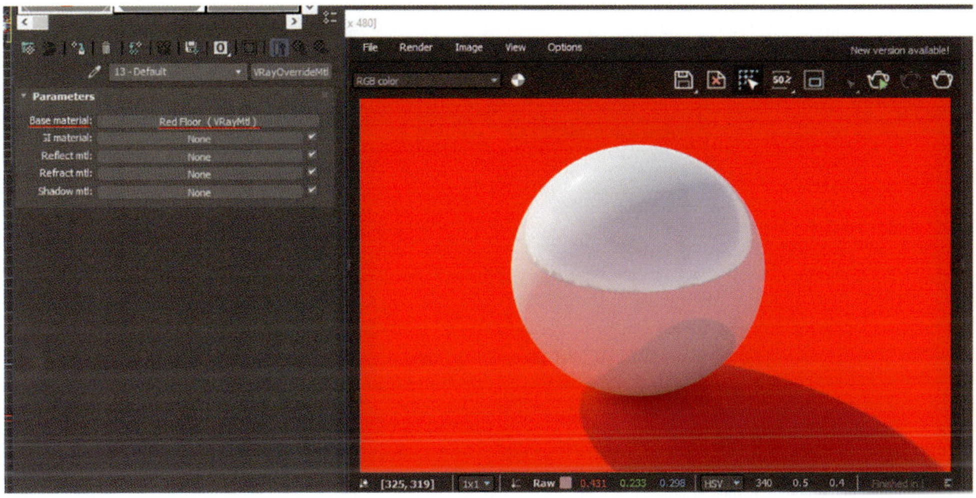

Color reflected and spilling from the Red floor in the Base material

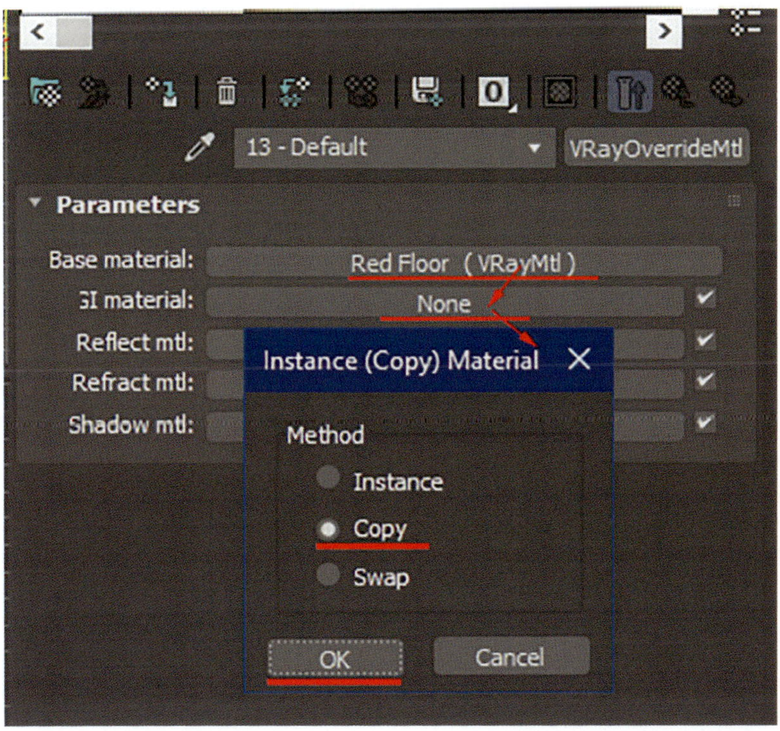

Copy Base material to GI material

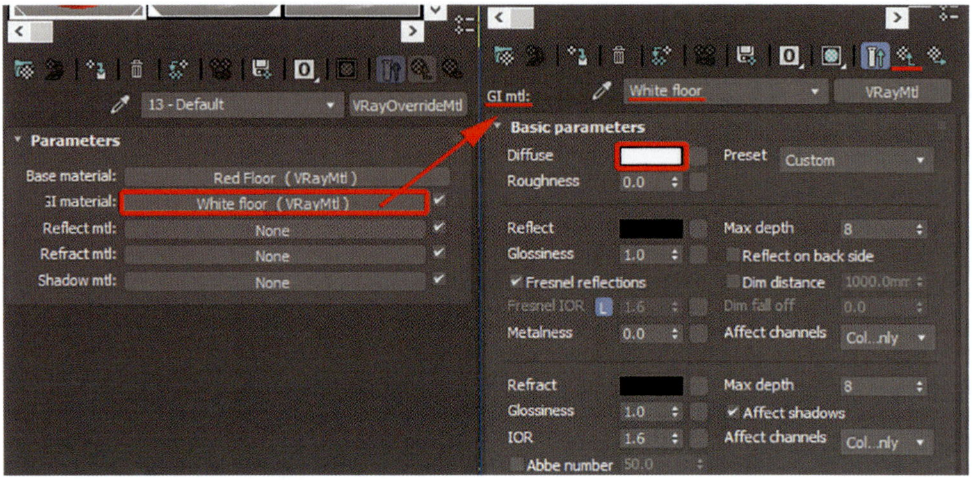

GI mtl color changed to white, and renamed

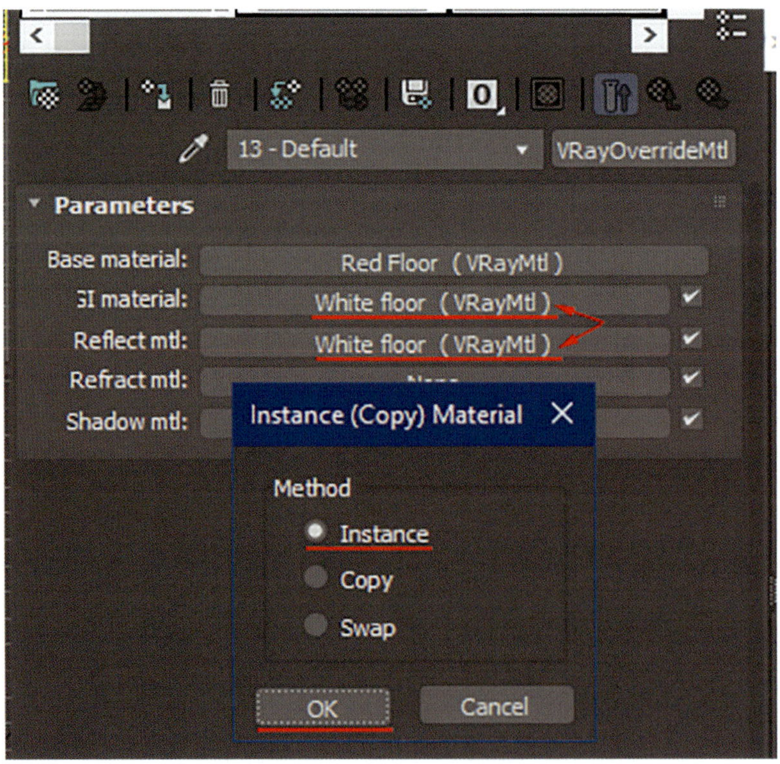

Copy instance the GI toggle

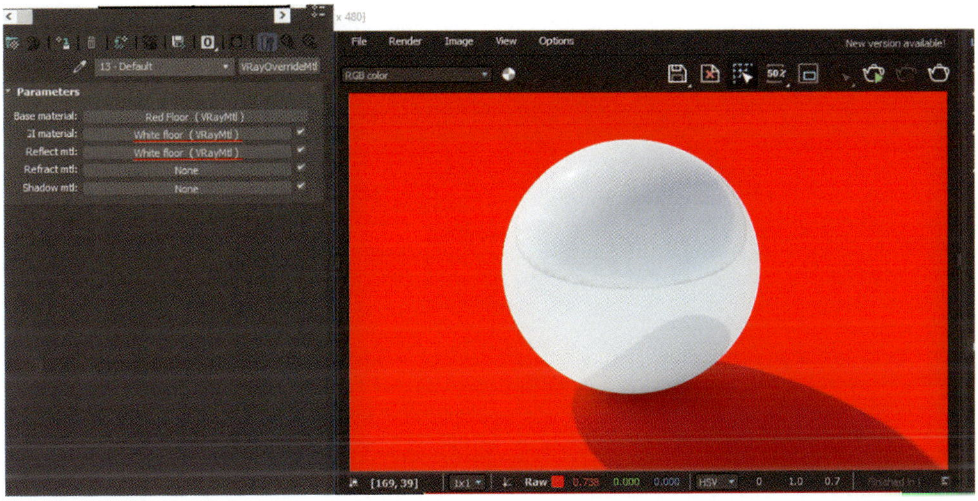

Final result, no color spills or red reflections

VRay2SidedMtl

This material is mostly used to emulate translucent objects. Its properties are more apparent when there's a strong light hitting its surface internally or/and externally (lamp shades or plant leaves).

To access this shader, simply click on the main VRayMtl toggle and choose the VRay2SidedMtl shader, from the Material/Map Browser list.

Following that, choose to keep old material as sub-material, in the Replace Material dialog.

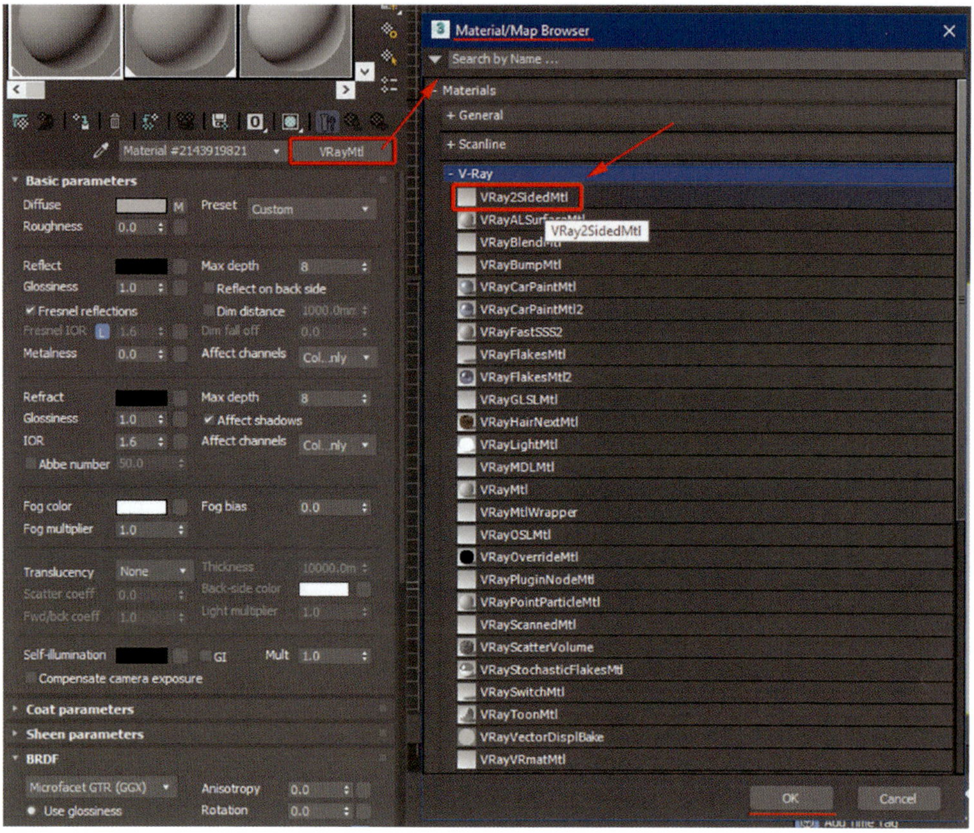

VRayMtl used to load the VRay2SidedMtl shader

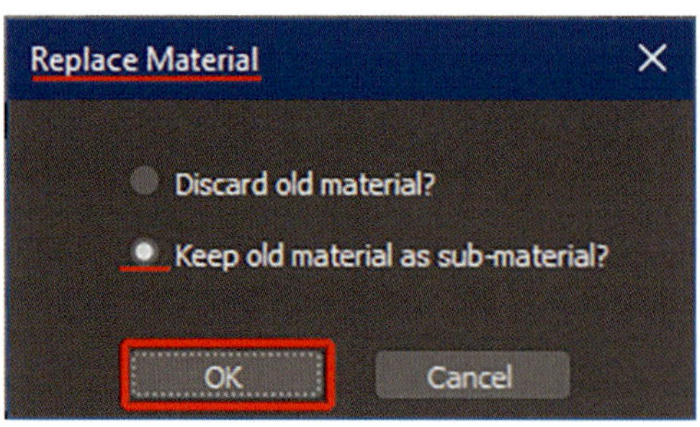

Keep old material as sub-material option

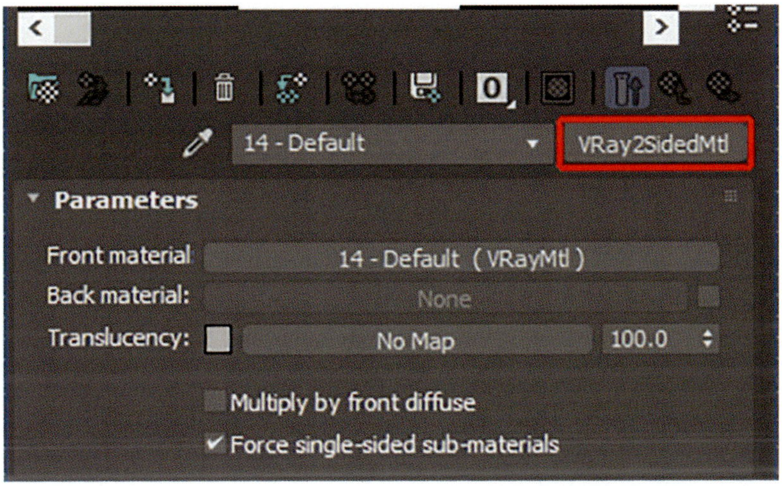

VRay2SidedMtl shader loaded

Front: This toggle allows users to set up the Front material surface. Often more opaque and with a slight difference in color (preferably).

Back material: The material for this toggle is frequently set up to be less opaque (e.g., more refractive/transparent) and with a slight difference in color (generally light yellowish color).

In addition, being a more refractive material, users normally enable its refraction to, Affect shadows.

Translucency: This function allows users to control the transition between the two surfaces (Front and Back material) with the Color Selector, or a procedural map through its toggle.

If the toggle is being used, the numerical values allow users blend the toggle content, with the color selector values.

To create a translucent lamp shade, simply go inside the Front material toggle and make it more transparent, in the Refract color swatch.

Also, rename it as White Material

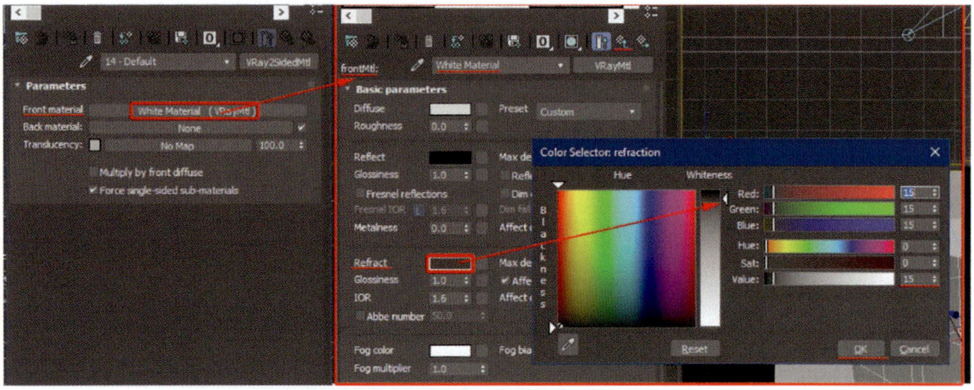

VRay2SidedMtl Front material Refract color swatch changed to 15

Next, copy (drag and drop) the Front material toggle into the Back material toggle.

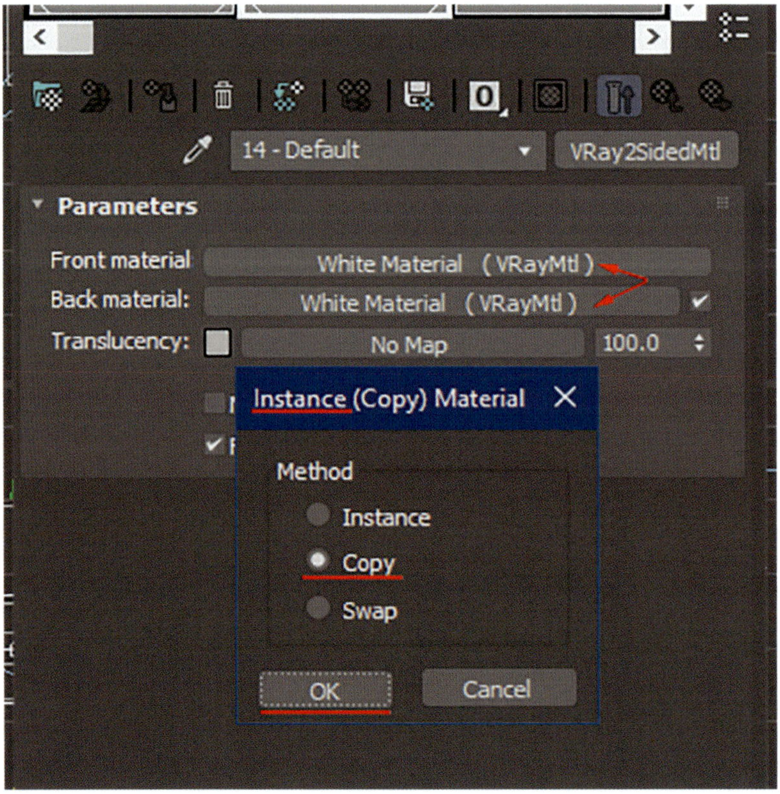

Copy the Front material toggle into the Back material

Rename the Back material as Yellow Material and change its diffuse color swatch.

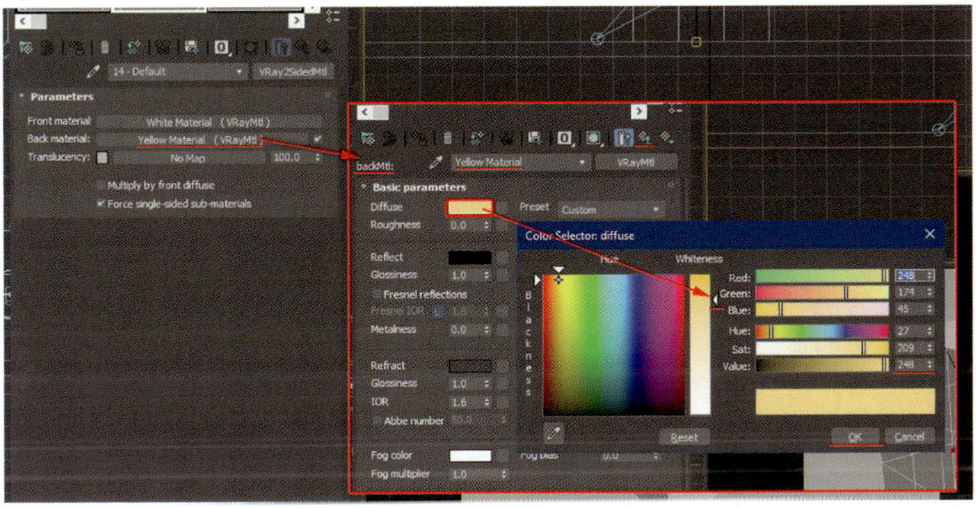

Rename the Back material and change its diffuse color to yellow (248)

NOTE

In order to see the light through a translucent object, ensure its Multiplier is high enough, invisible to the camera and set it to cast shadows.

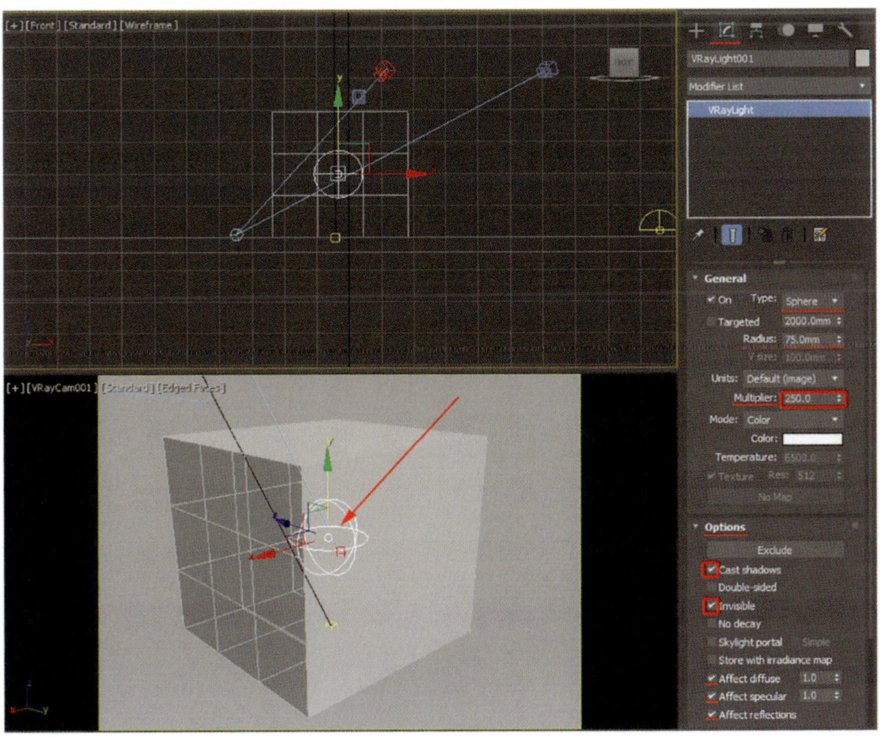

Sphere Light parameters with Radius set to 250, Invisible, Affect diffuse, Affect specular, Affect reflections

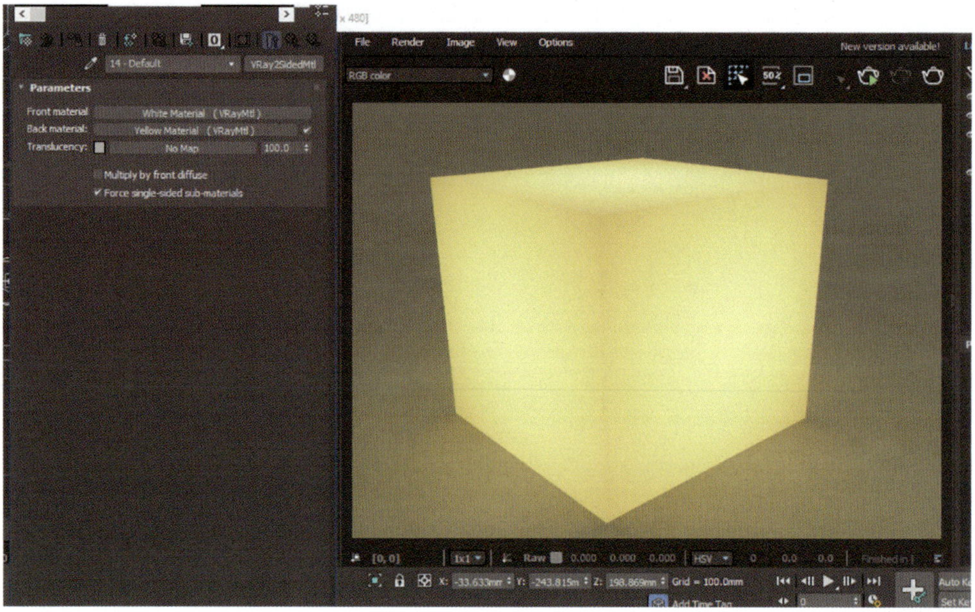

An box primitive with a VRay2SidedMtl shader applied, and a physical light inside

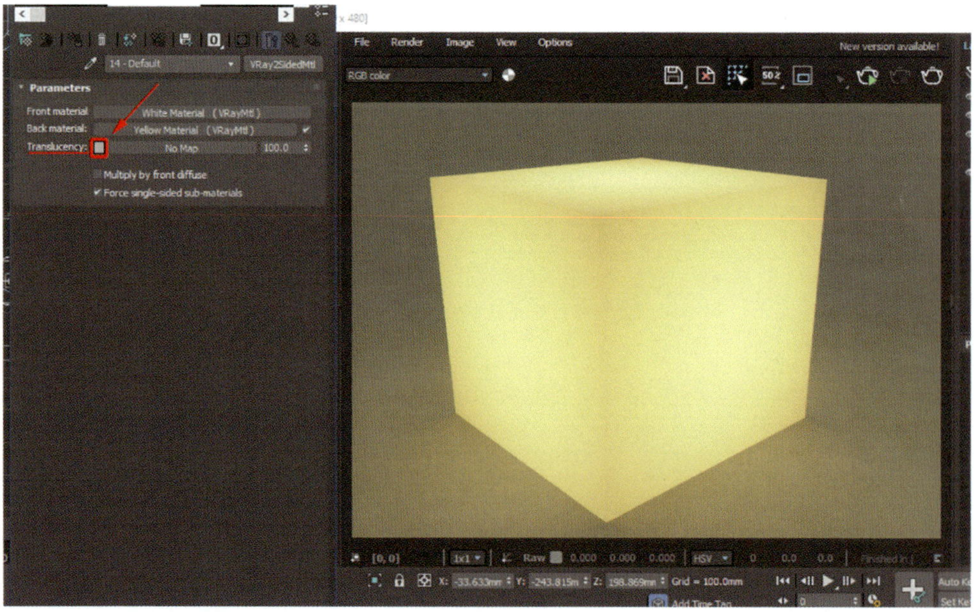

Translucency set to gray

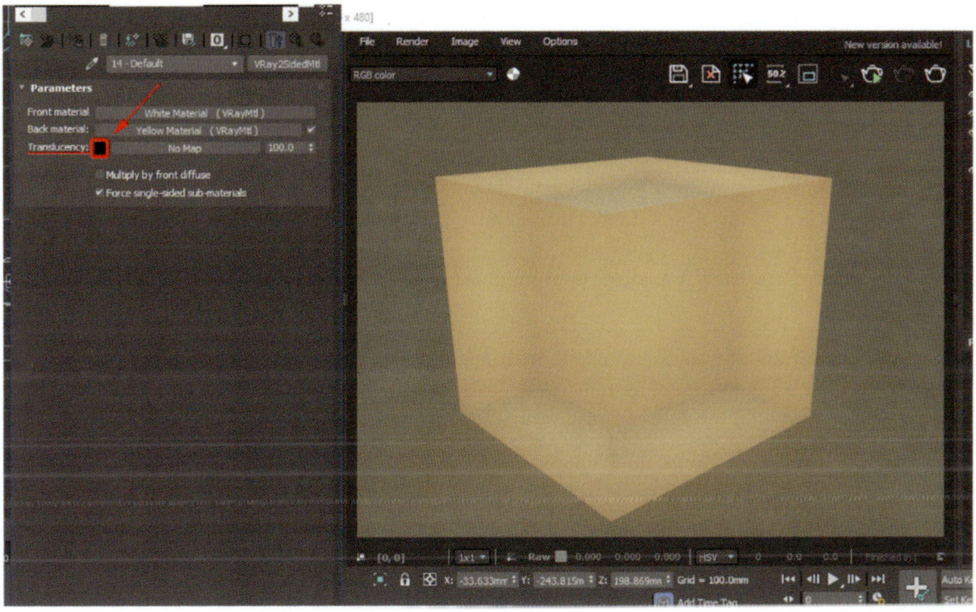

Translucency set to black

There are times when you may want the physical light to be visible in the camera. The results may not be desirable, by default.

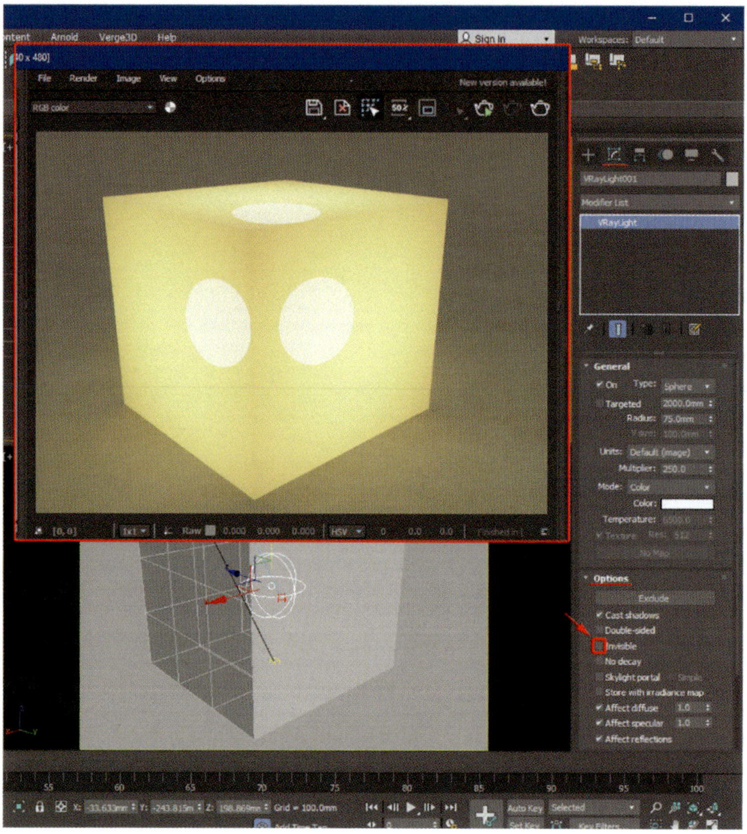

VRayLight Option set to be visible in the render

To correct this, always go the Front material toggle, and change its Refract Glossiness value to 0.5.

These settings have already been discussed in detail.

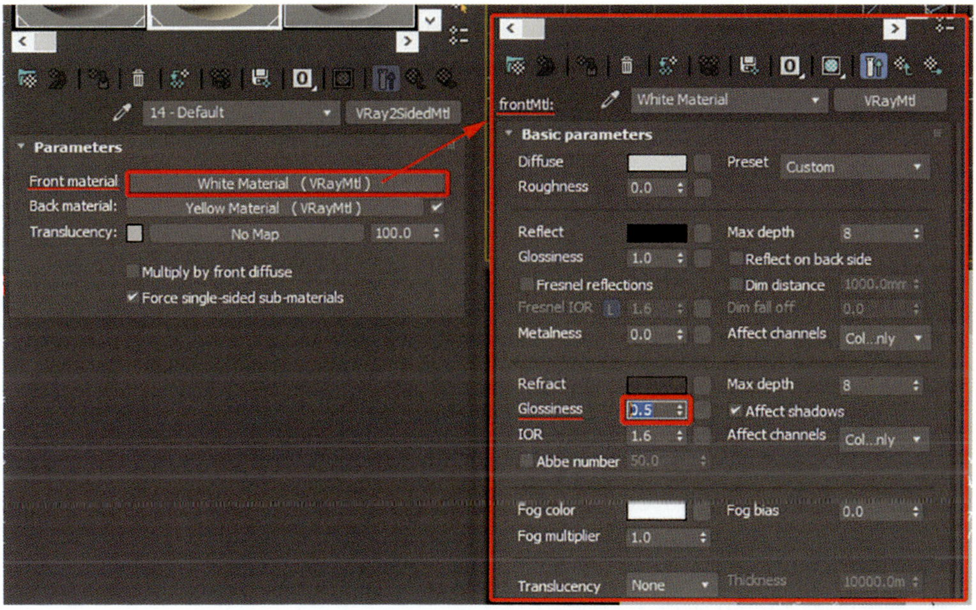

Front material Refract Glossiness changed to 0.5

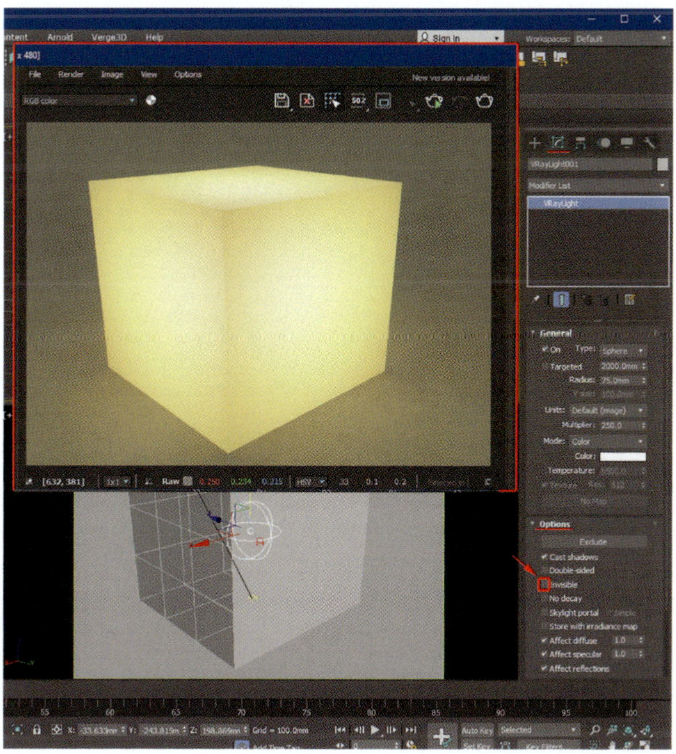

Final result with Refract Glossiness set to 0.5 and VRayLight Option set to be visible in the render

VRayBlendMtl

To help highlight the functionalities of this shader, the Aluminium_Anodized_Bronze material was used as the base material.

This material was previously loaded from the V-Ray Asset Browser dialog.

VRayBlendMtl is very useful to create unique and exquisite materials, by blending multiple shaders together.

However, because of its complexity, it may take slightly longer to compute.

Materials can be blended through a toggle, or the color selector dialog.

To load it, simply click on the main shader toggle and pick the VRayBlendMtl, from the Material/Map Browser dialog list. And choose to keep old material as sub-material, in the Replace Material dialog.

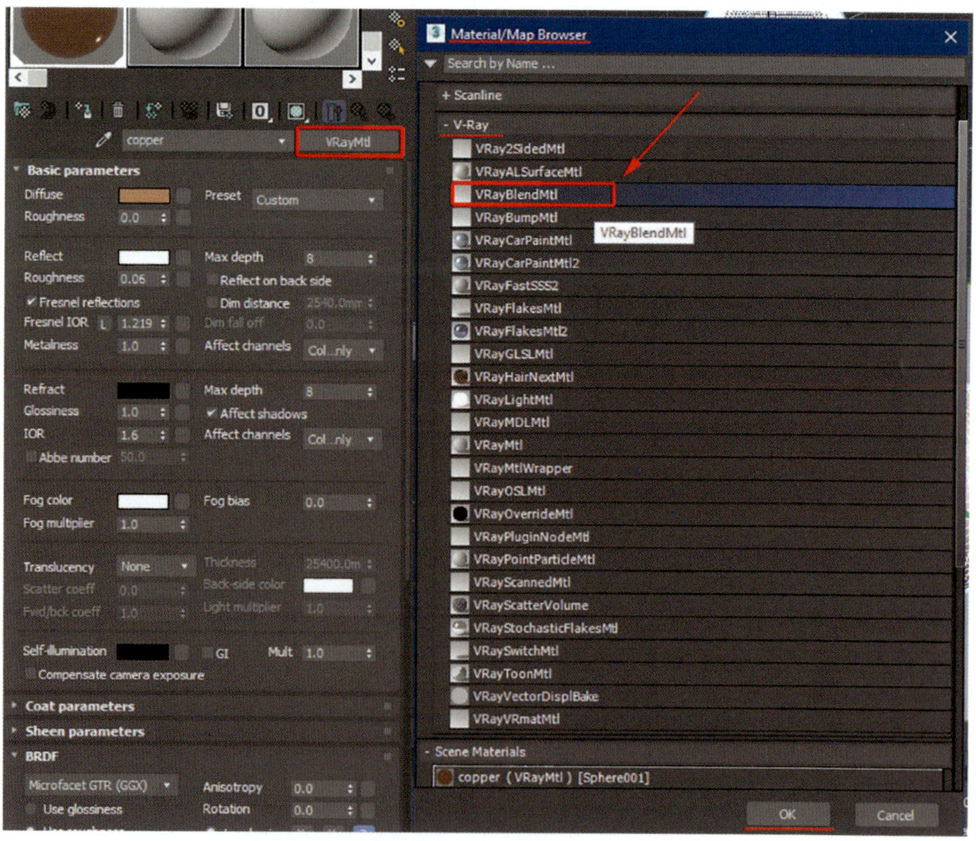

VRayMtl used to load the VRayBlendMtl

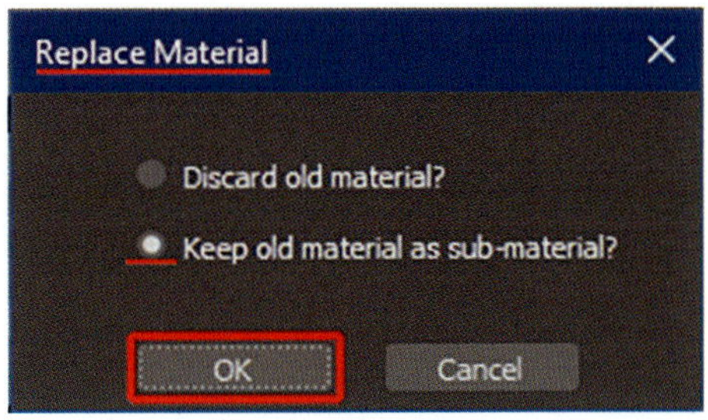

Keep old material as sub-material option

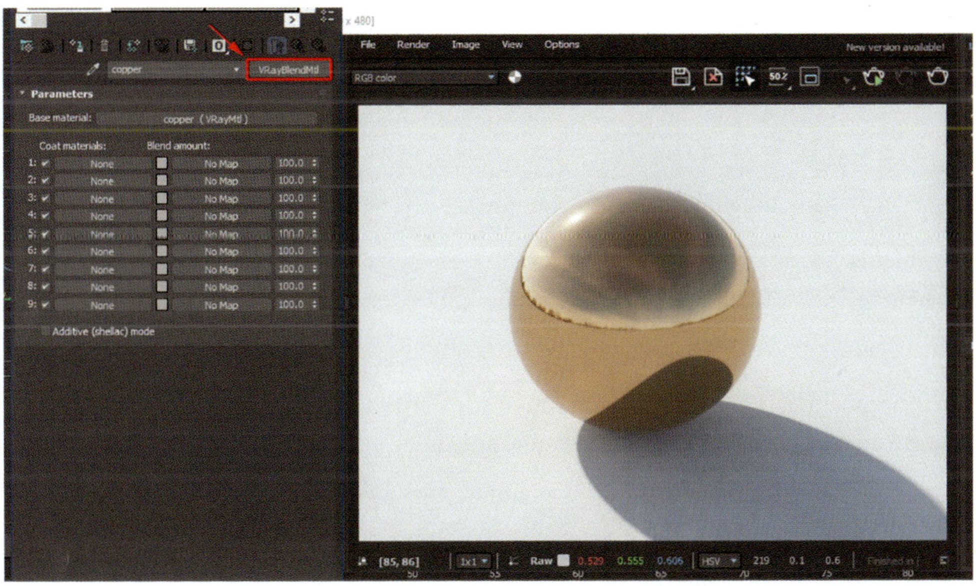

VRayBlendMtl loaded with copper as the Base Material

Base material: This toggle is used as a the base sub-material.

Coat materials: This function has nine listed toggles that can be used to mix shaders with the Blend amount.

To demonstrate this functionality, the material Metal_Pattern_K_bmp_5cm was loaded from the V-Ray Asset Browser dialog.

When a VRayMaterial is loaded in its toggle it automatically blends with the Base material.

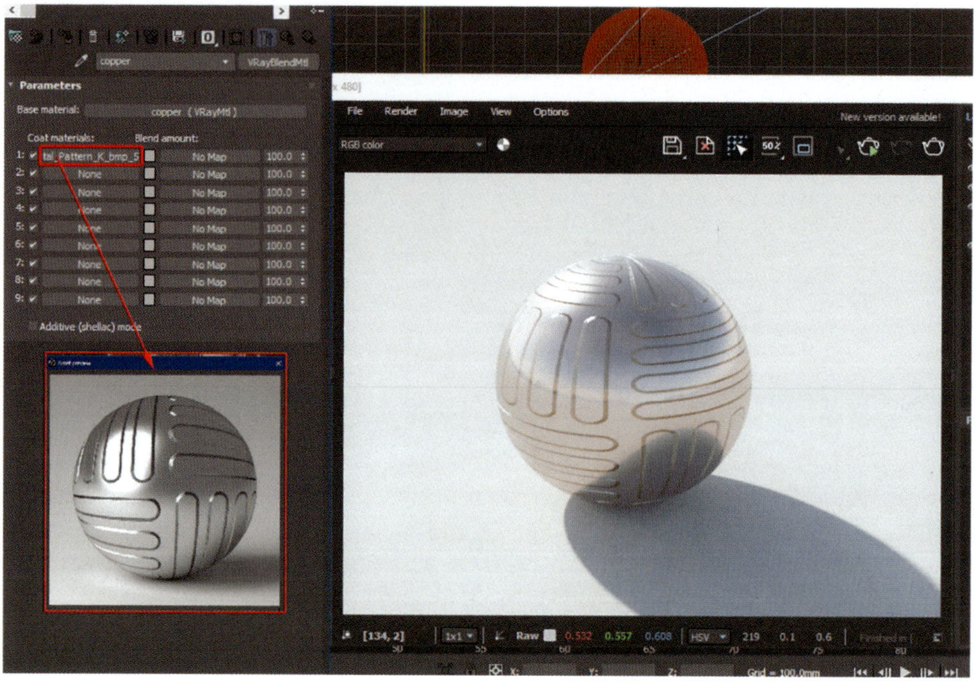

Coat materials with a toggle loaded

Blend amount: The function consists of nine listed toggles, with color swatches and numerical values to set the blend amount.

When a procedural map/bitmap is plugged into its toggle, it automatically overrides the color swatch.

Black and white or grayscale bitmaps work best.

The adjacent numerical values only work when there's a procedural map/bitmap inside the toggle.

Blend amount set to 128

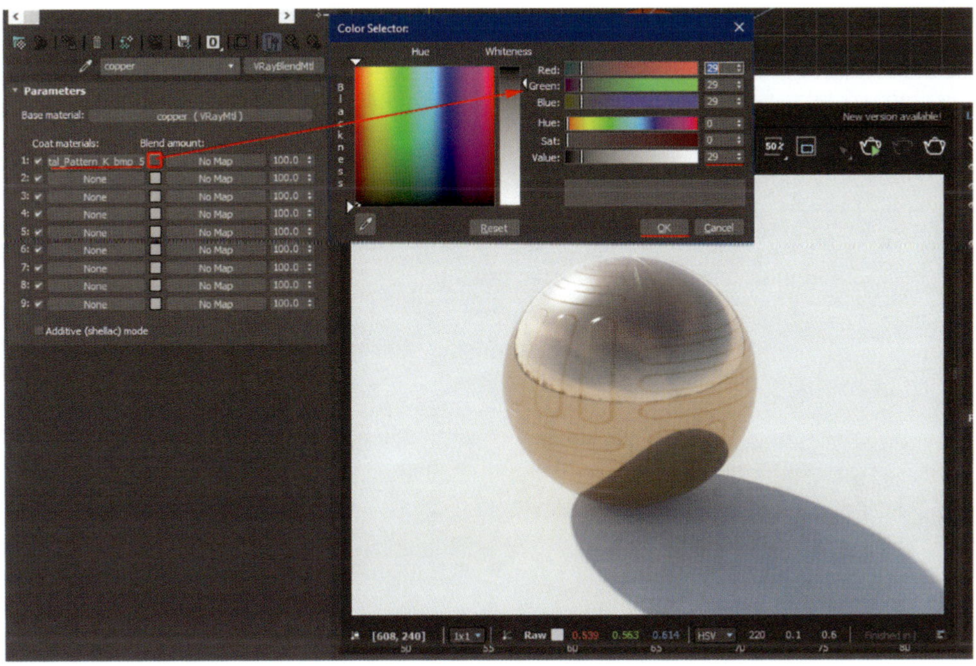

Blend amount set to 29

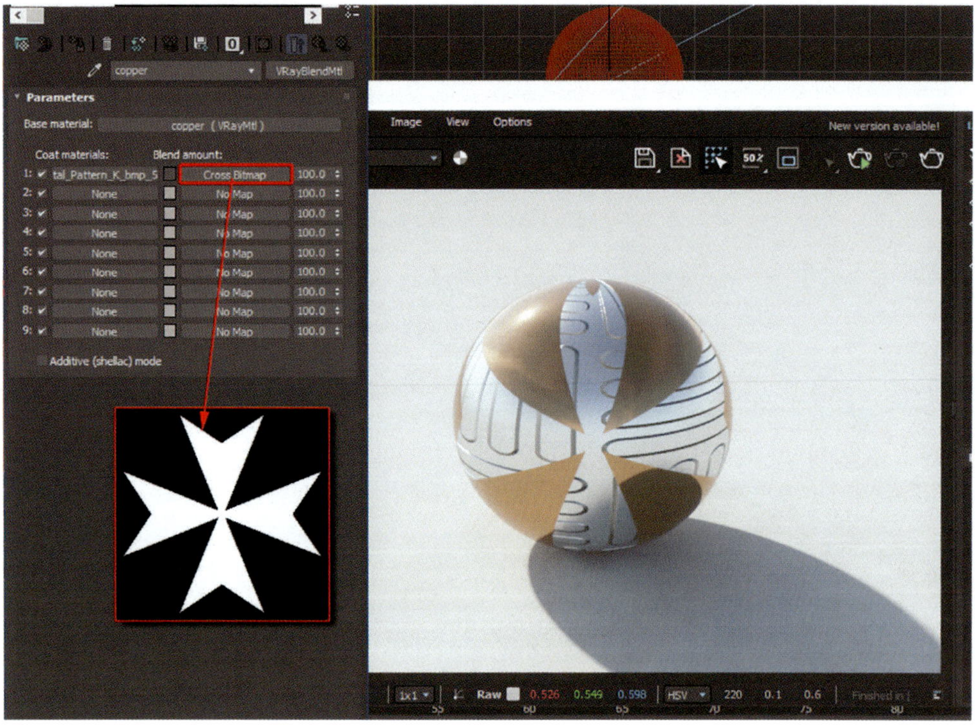

Grayscale bitmap applied to the Blend amount toggle

This bitmap is available in the resource files

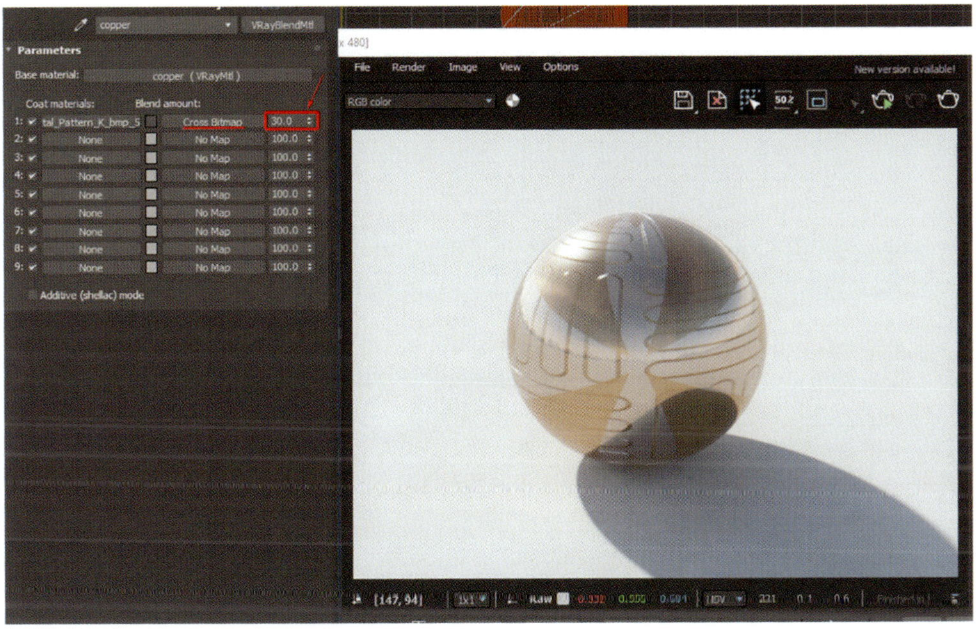

Blend amount Bitmap set to 30.0

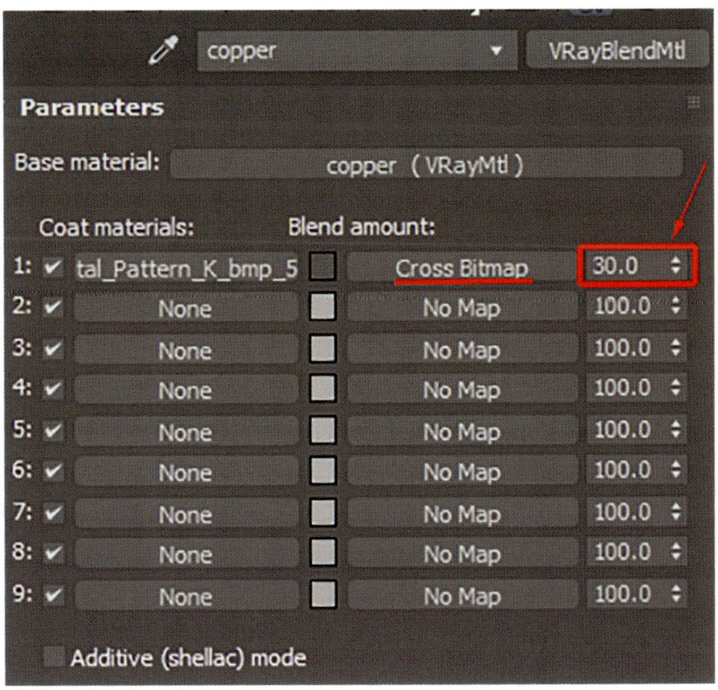

Blend amount Bitmap set to 30

Blend amount Bitmap set to 30 result

VRayCarPaintMtl

As the name suggests, this shader emulates the physical properties of a metallic car pain finish.

Depending on System Unit Setup being used, a UVW Map modifier might be required in order for the flake layer to be visible.

To access it, simply click on the main shader toggle and choose the VRayCarPaintMtl from the Material/Map Browser dialog.

The shader should load up automatically.

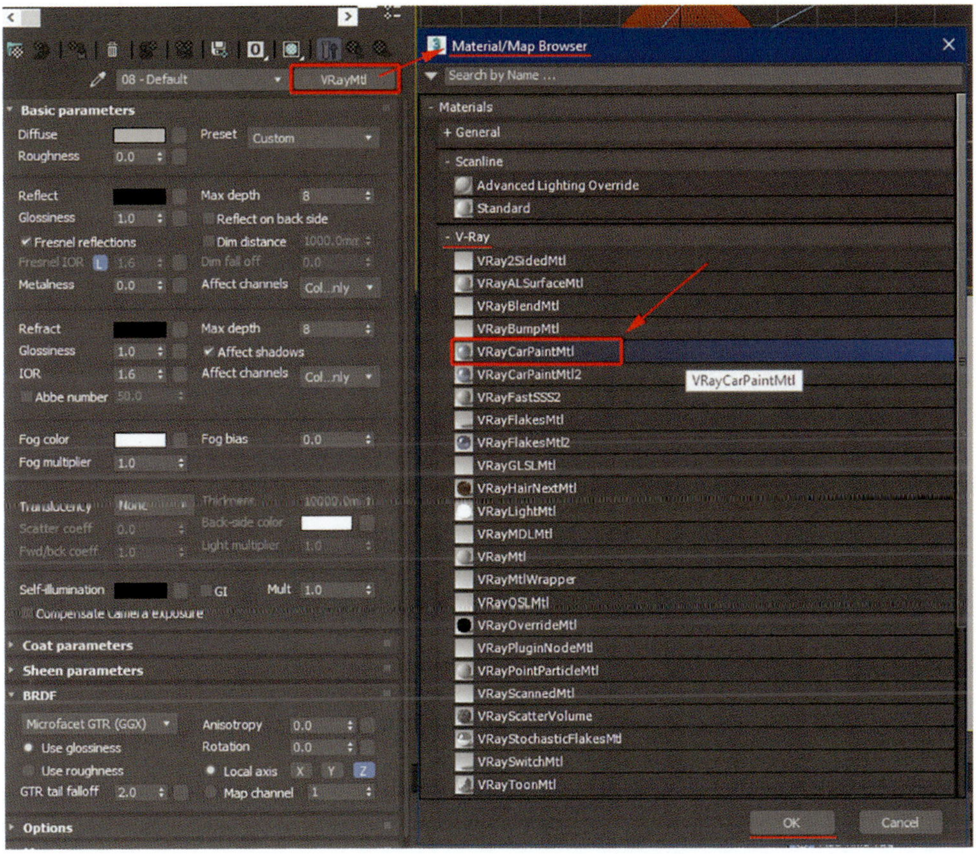

VRayMtl used to load VRayCarPaintMtl shader

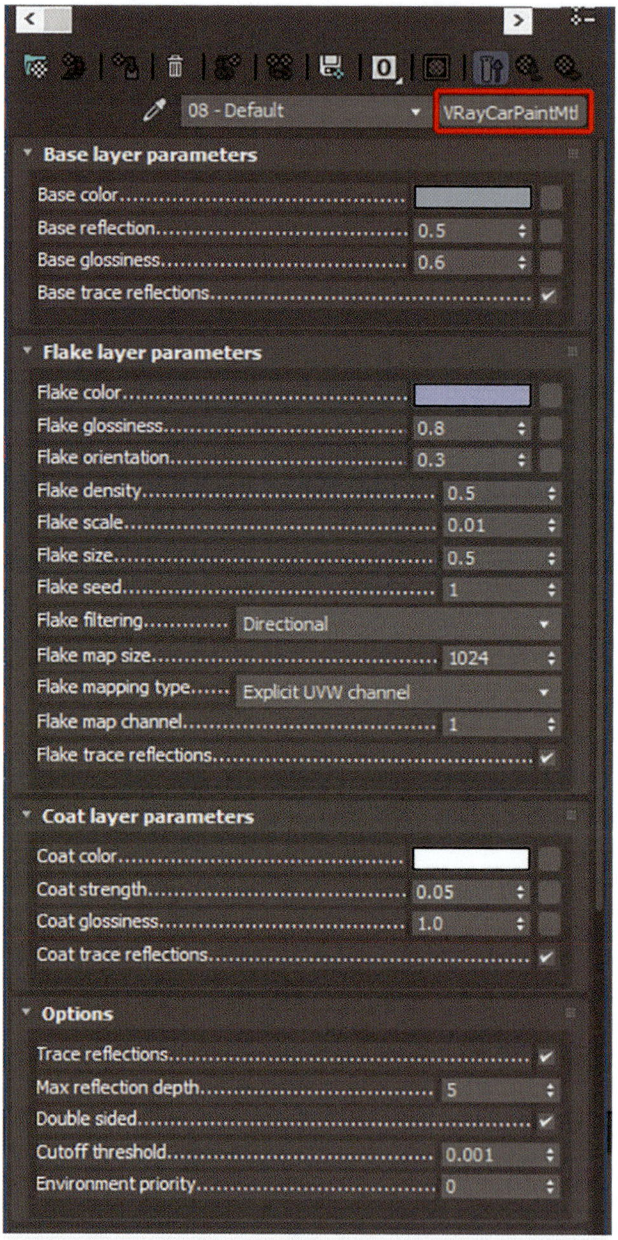

VRayCarPaintMtl shader loaded

Base color: This function determines the main color of VRayCarPaintMtl.

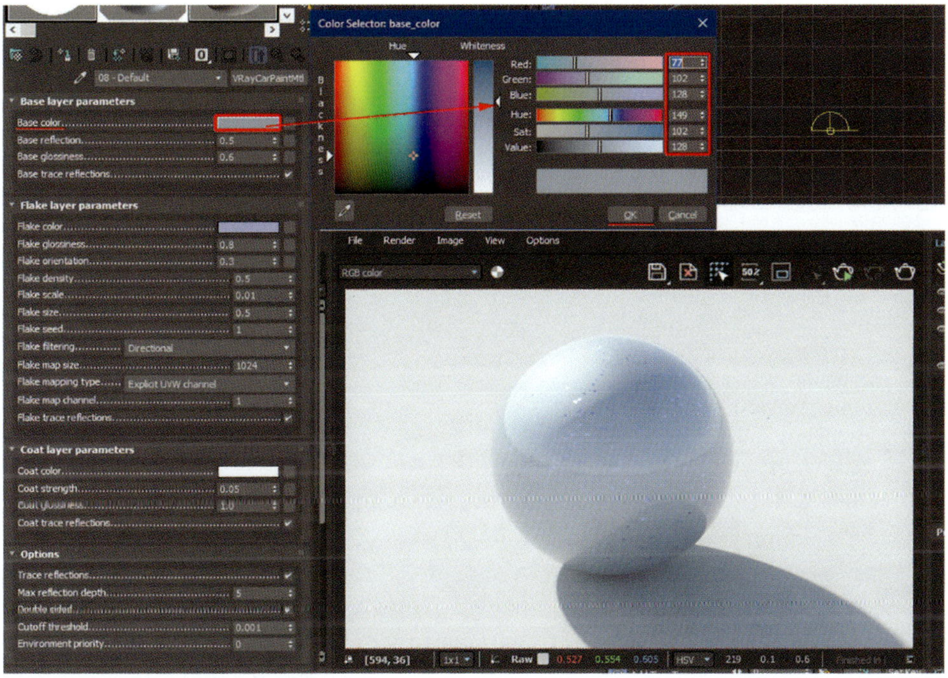

VRayCarPaintMtl base color: blue

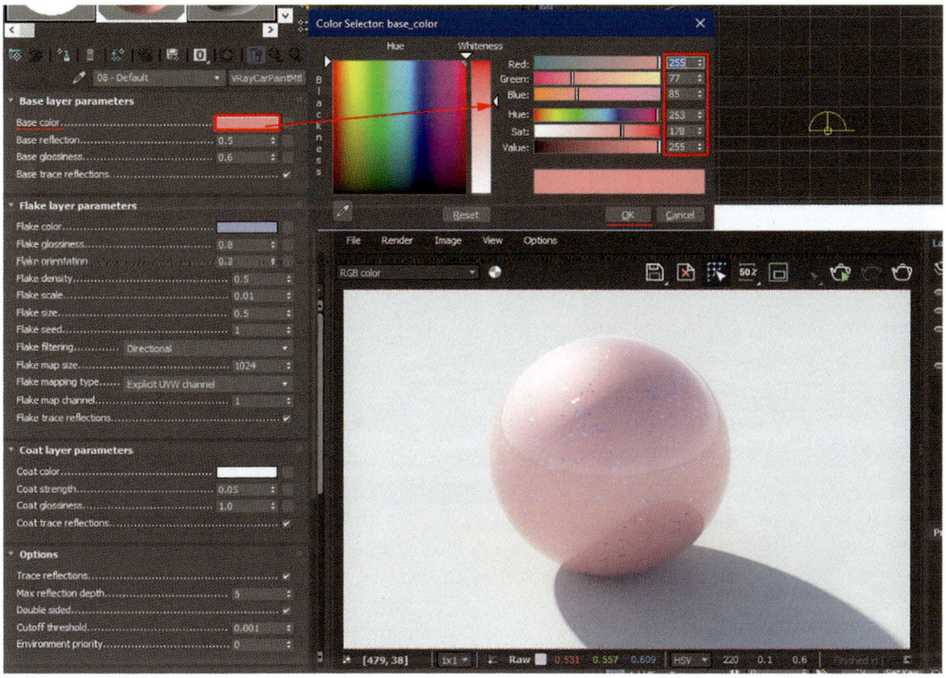

VRayCarPaintMtl base color: red

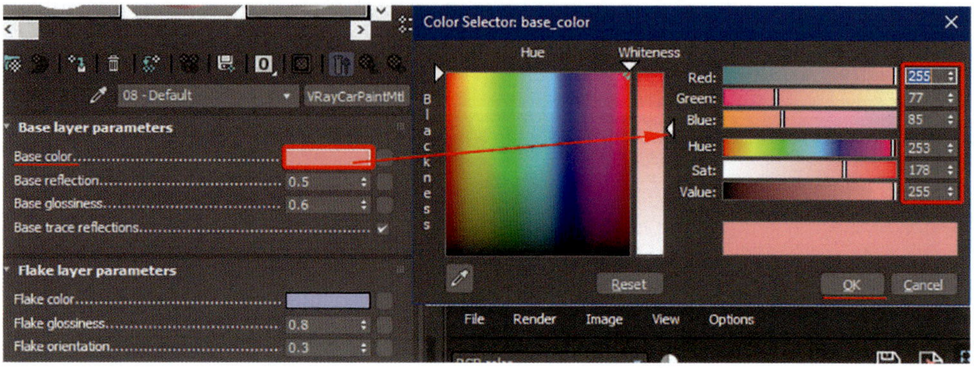

VRayCarPaintMtl base color red

Base reflection: This function controls the amount of reflectivity, with its numerical values. Default value is 0.5.

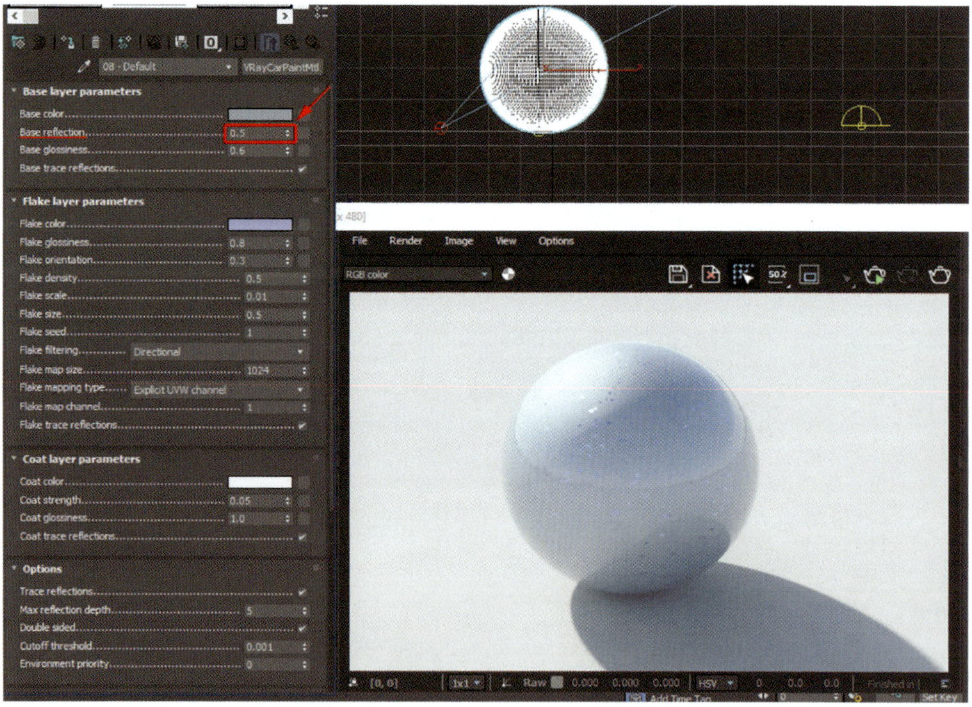

VRayCarPaintMtl base reflection: 0.5

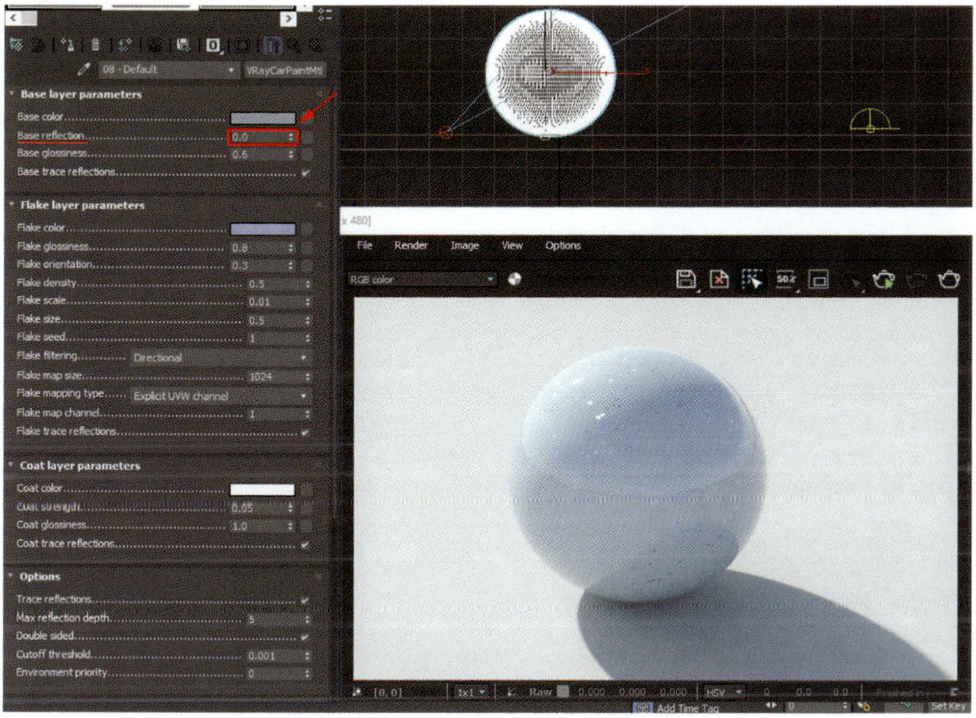

VRayCarPaintMtl base reflection: 0.0

Base glossiness: This function's numerical values determine the amount of glossiness on the surface. Default value is 0.6.

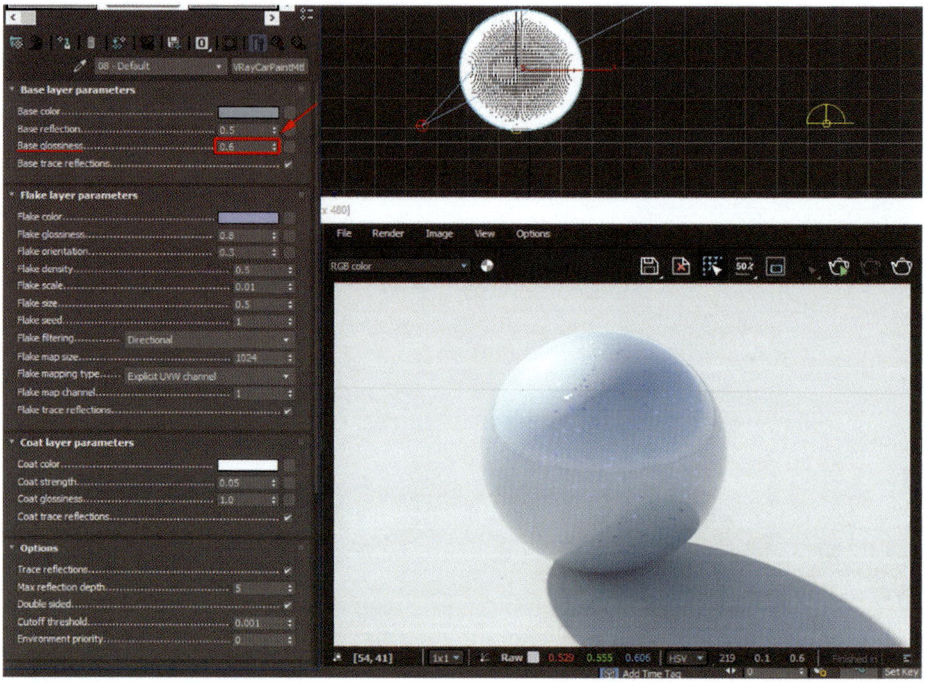

VRayCarPaintMtl base glossiness: 0.6

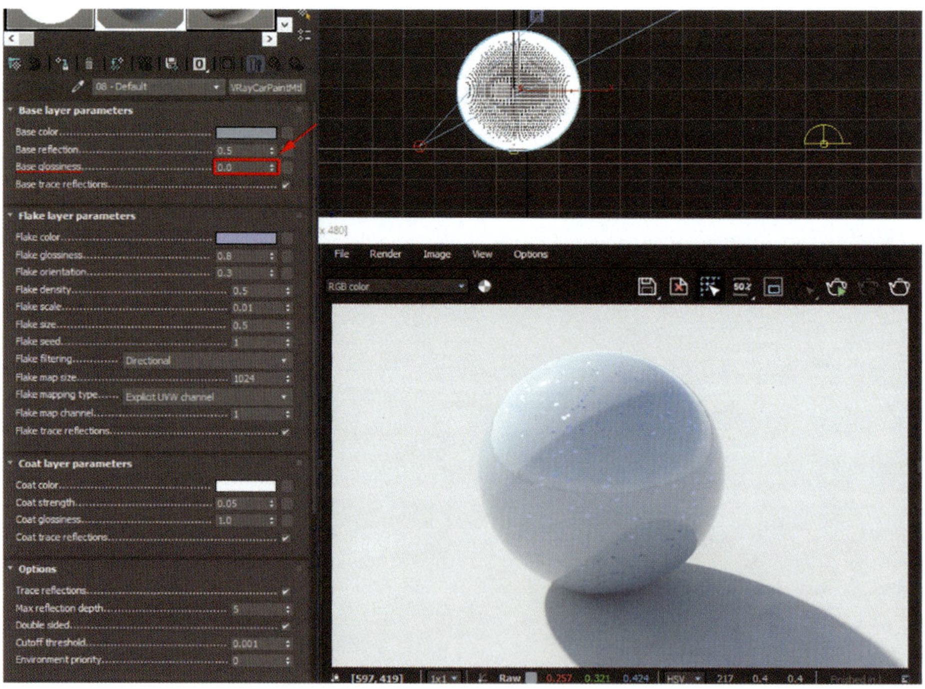

VRayCarPaintMtl base glossiness: 0.0

Base trace reflections: If enabled, this option allows the reflections to be traced. Enabled by default.

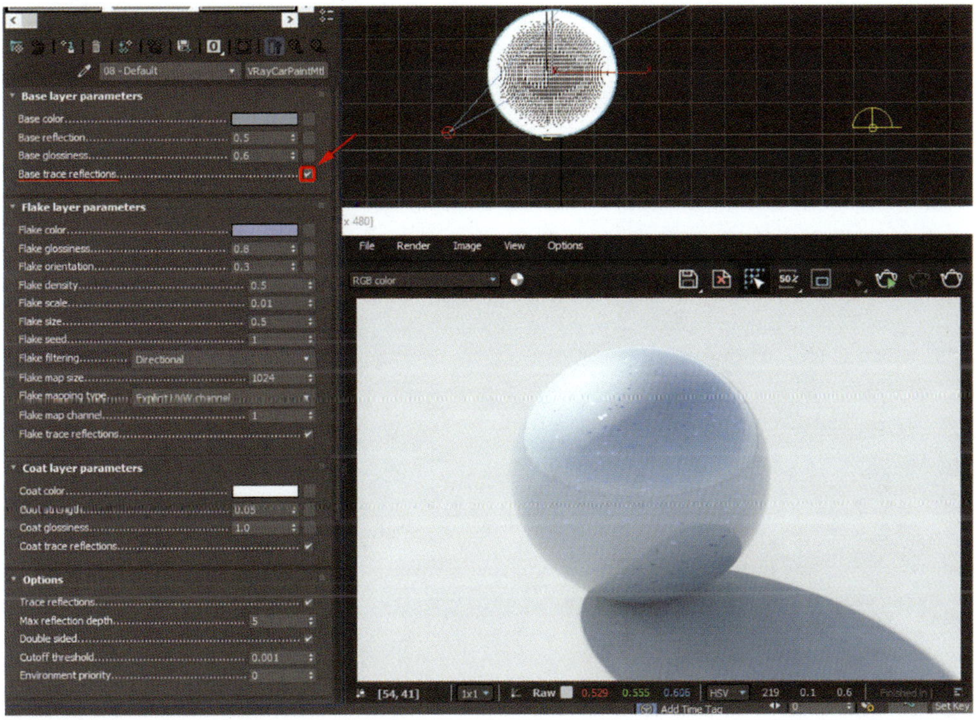

VRayCarPaintMtl base trace reflections: enabled

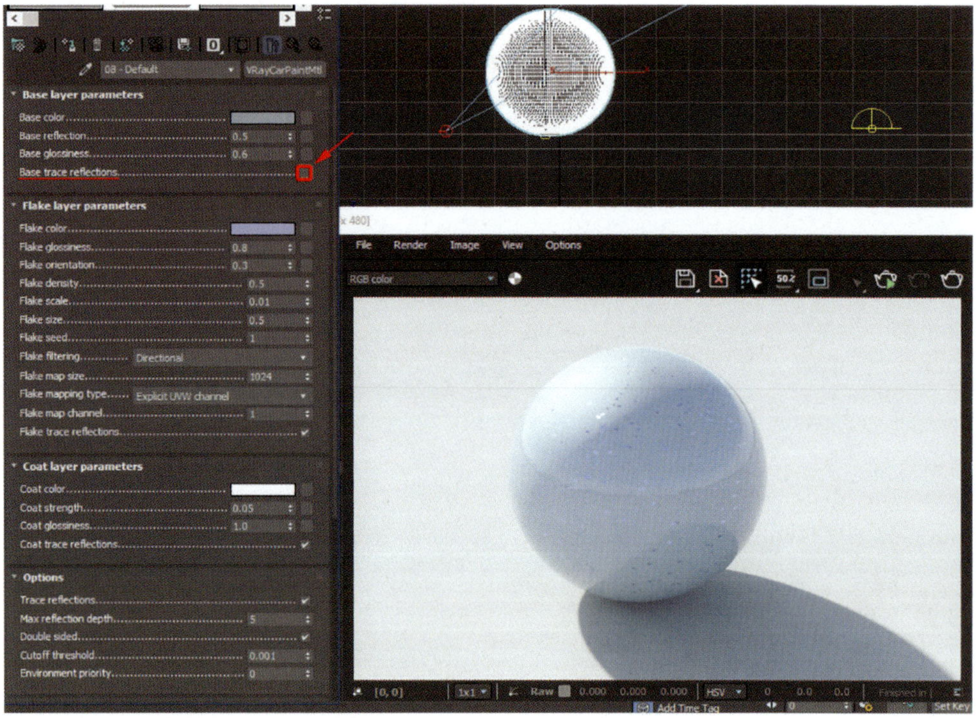

VRayCarPaintMtl base trace reflections: disabled

Flake color: This color swatch enables users to choose the flake color, through the Color Selector dialog.

Default color, blue.

Flake glossiness: Its numerical values allow the users to control the amount of glossiness on the flake. Default value is 0.8.

Flake orientation: This function's numerical values control the orientation of the flake. This option is widely used to randomize the flake rotation.

Default value is 0.3.

Flake density: This function controls the density/number of flakes seen on the surface. Default value is 0.5.

Flake scale: This option controls the structure of the flakes. Default value is 0.01.

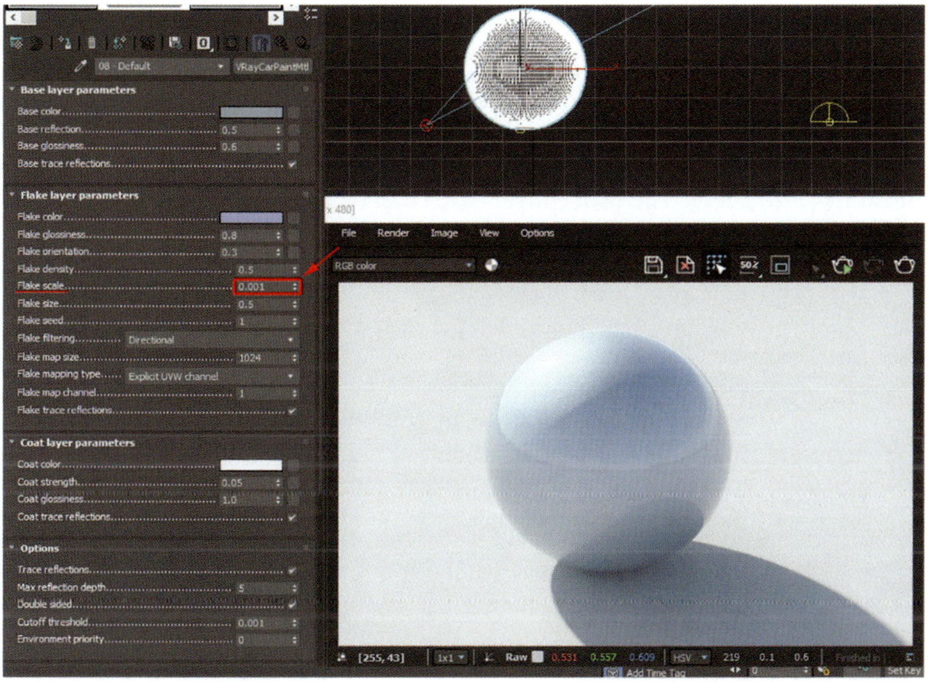

Flake scale set to 0.001

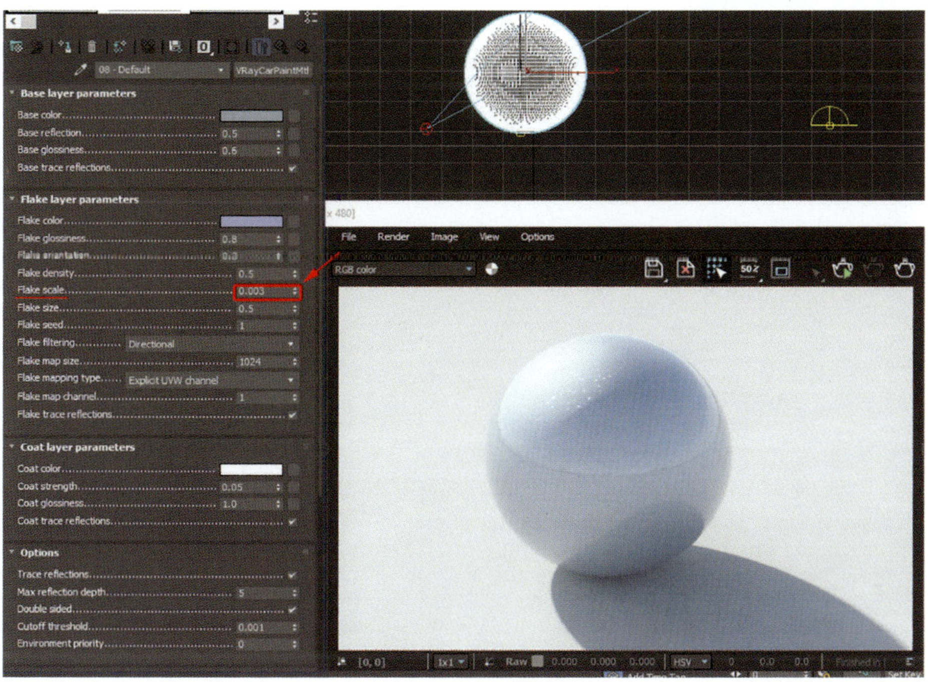

Flake scale set to 0.003

Flake size: This function determines the distance and size of the flakes. Default value is 0.5.

Flake seed: This option enables users to change the flake pattern. Default value is 1.

Maps: The list of toggles seen under the Maps rollout allows users to plug procedural maps in them. The procedural maps can be used at 100% value, or blended, by reducing the numerical values.

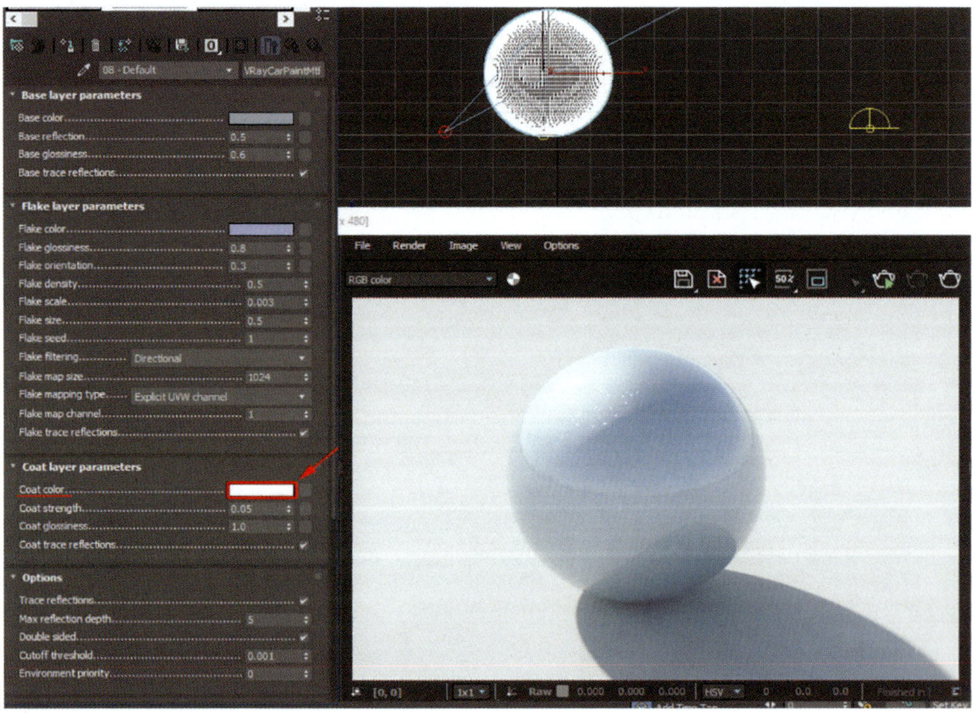

Coat color set to white

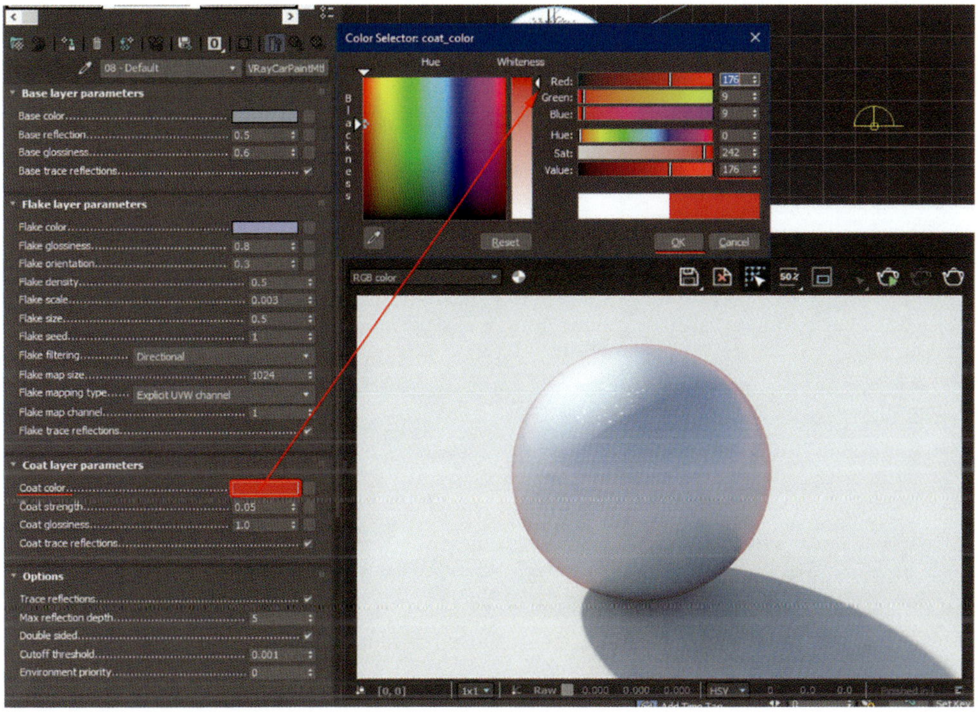

Coat color set to red

VRayEdgesTex

To test the functionality of this procedural map, please open the file under the name of VRayEdgesTex.max.

This procedural map is widely used on top of a material or color, to create edges/wirelines around the surface. It can be plugged through the diffuse toggle, or as a render element, to be composed in post.

Also, it can also be used to emulate chamfered edges on corners/edges of surfaces through the Bump toggle.

The render below depicts a metal box prior to using the VRayEdgesTex in its Bump toggle.

NOTE

The following steps assume you already have an existing bitmap/procedural map plugged into the Bump toggle.

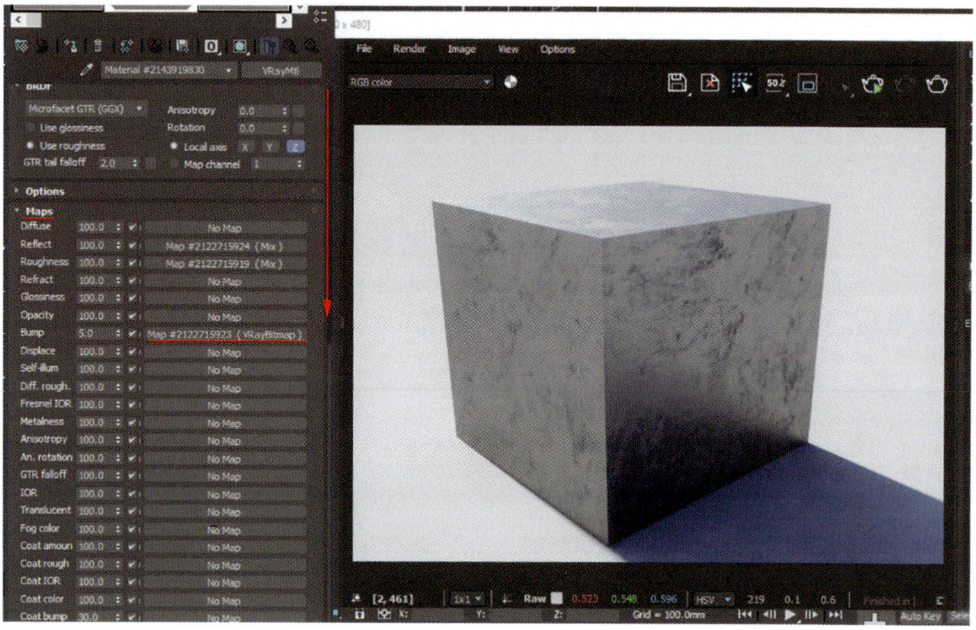

Metal box without VRayEdgesTex in its Bump toggle

To add the VRayEdgesTex procedural map to the Bump toggle, simply scroll down to the Maps rollout and click on the Bump toggle.

Inside the Bump toggle, click on the VRayBitmap toggle to open the Material/Map Browser dialog.

In the Material/Map Browser dialog, under the V-Ray rollout, choose the Mix procedural map from its list.

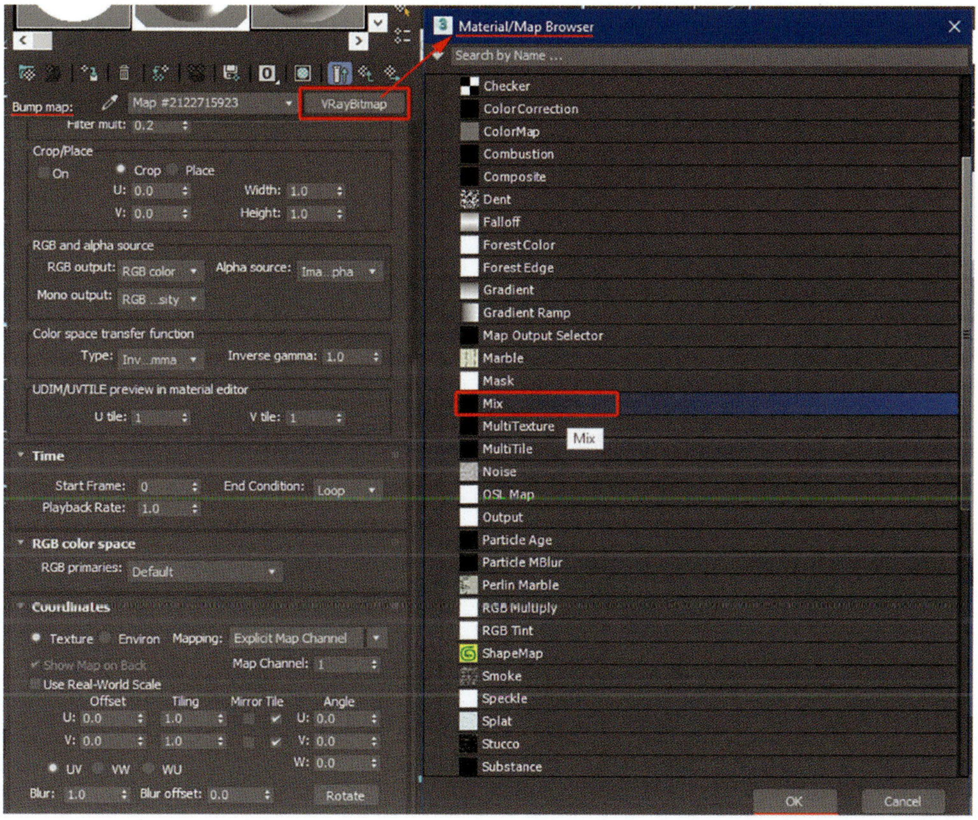

Bump map with VRayBitmap used to load the Mix procedural map

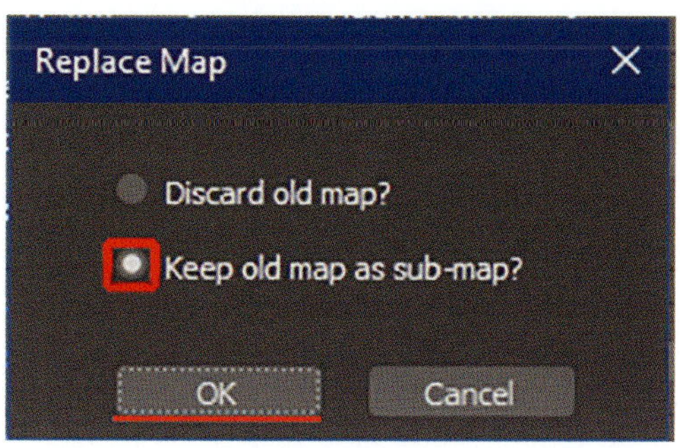

Keep old map as sub-map option

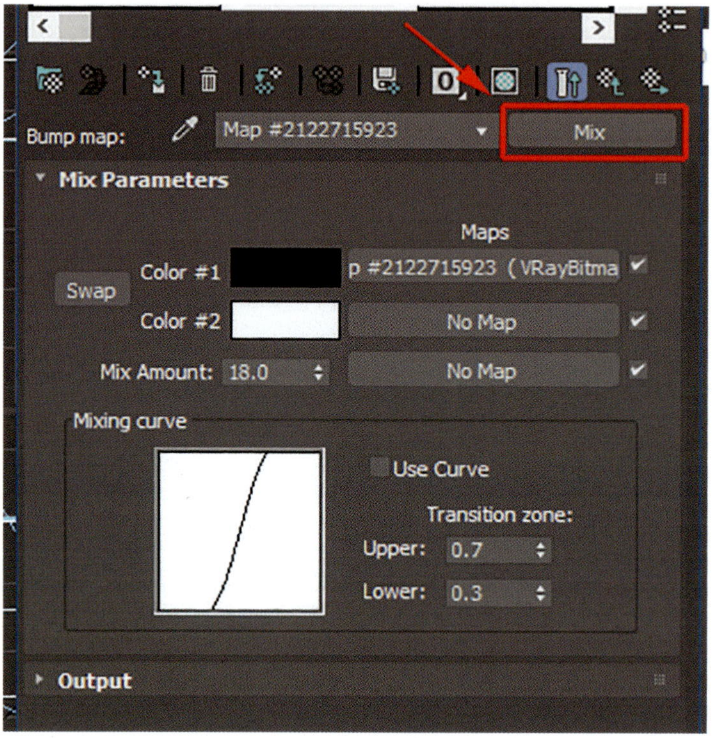

Mix procedural map loaded

The Mix procedural map will help keep the prominence of both, VRayEdgesTex and the original bump bitmap (Color #1).

Color # and #2: These toggles allow users to plug procedural maps and/or Bitmaps to it.

Alternatively, users can simply use their color swatches.

Mix Amount: This function controls the amount of blend between Color #1 and Color #2.

With the default value set to 0.0, Color #1 will be 100% visible.

Users can also plug procedural maps and/or bitmaps to control the Mix Amount.

Grayscale and black and white bitmaps work best in the Mix Amount toggle.

Mixing curve: This group overrides the Mix Amount values when the Use Curve function is enabled.

The Upper and Lower values control the Transition zone/gradient.

To load the VRayEdgesTex, click on the Color #2 toggle, and choose the VRayEdgesTex procedural map from the Material/Map Browser dialog.

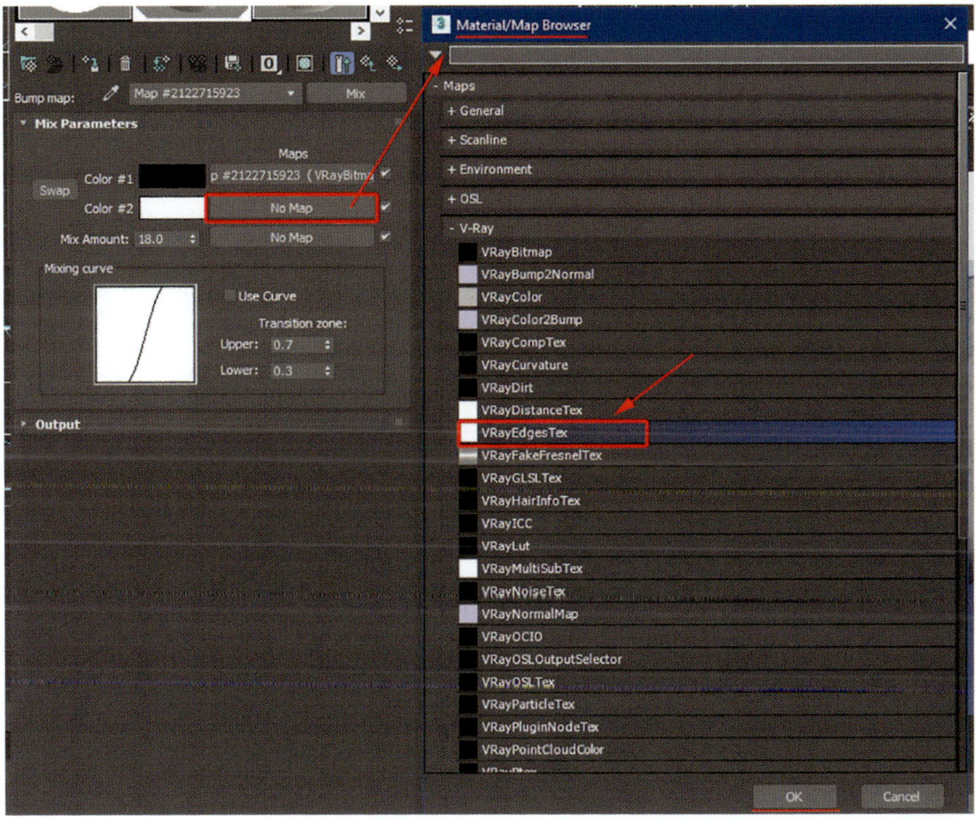

Color 2 toggle used to Load VRayEdgesTex

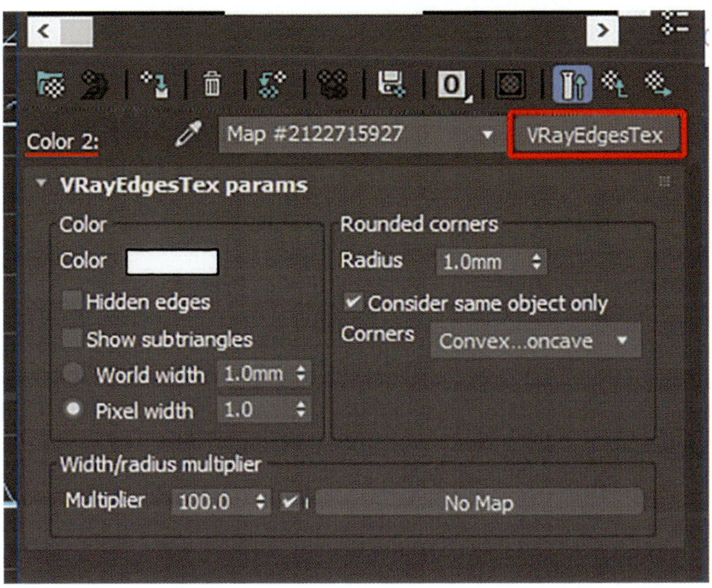

Color: This color swatch sets the direction of the Bump, when used in the bump toggle.

White color produces an outward bump.

Black color produces an inward bump.

When applied in the diffuse toggle, it serves as the wireframe color (white) wrapped around the geometry.

Hidden edges: When enabled in the diffuse toggle, this function displays hidden wireframe edges of a geometry.

Disabled, by default.

Show subtriangles: When enabled in the Diffuse toggle, this function displays the subtriangles of a geometry (in wireframe mode).

Disabled, by default.

World width: When enabled in the Diffuse toggle, it displays the wireframe thickness based on your scene's system units.

Disabled, by default.

Pixel width: When applied to the Diffuse toggle, this function controls the wireframe thickness, in pixel units.

Enabled and set to 1.0, by default.

Round corners: This group controls the bevel/chamfer size on objects, when applied to the Bump toggle.

Radius: This function controls the size of the bevel/chamfer.

Set to 1 mm, by default.

Consider same object only: When enabled, this function will apply the bevel/chamfer effect on the objects applied only.

Enabled, by default.

Corners: This function allows users to choose the type of corners to apply the Rounded corners to.

It is set to affect convex and concave, by default.

Depending on the size of the object or the scenes' Unit Setup, one can set up appropriate Radius value.

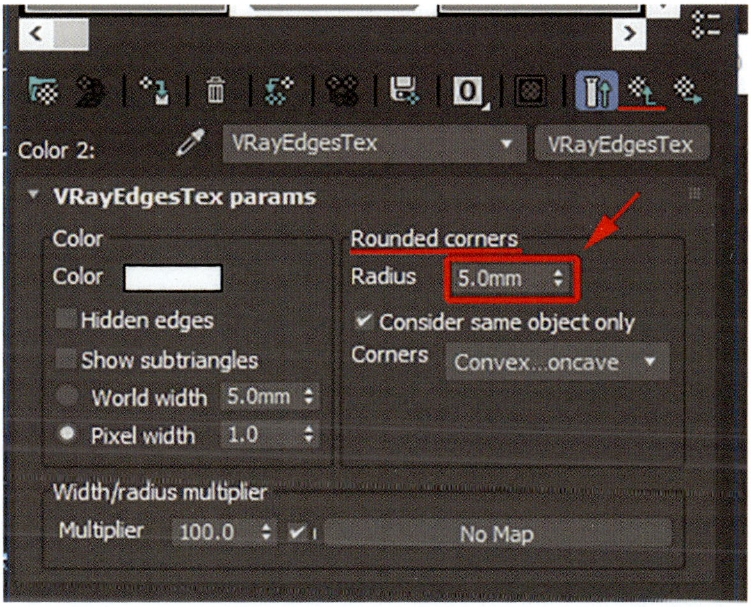

VRayEdgesTex Round corners Radius value set to 5 mm.

Because we are currently using the VRayEdgesTex mixed with the main Bump bitmap, we need to increase the Mix Amount value, in order for the Round corners to be visible in the render.

To do so, click on the Go to Parent button, to go back to the Mix main parameters.

Increase the Mix Amount value to about 18.0.

These values were achieved after few region renders to see what worked best.

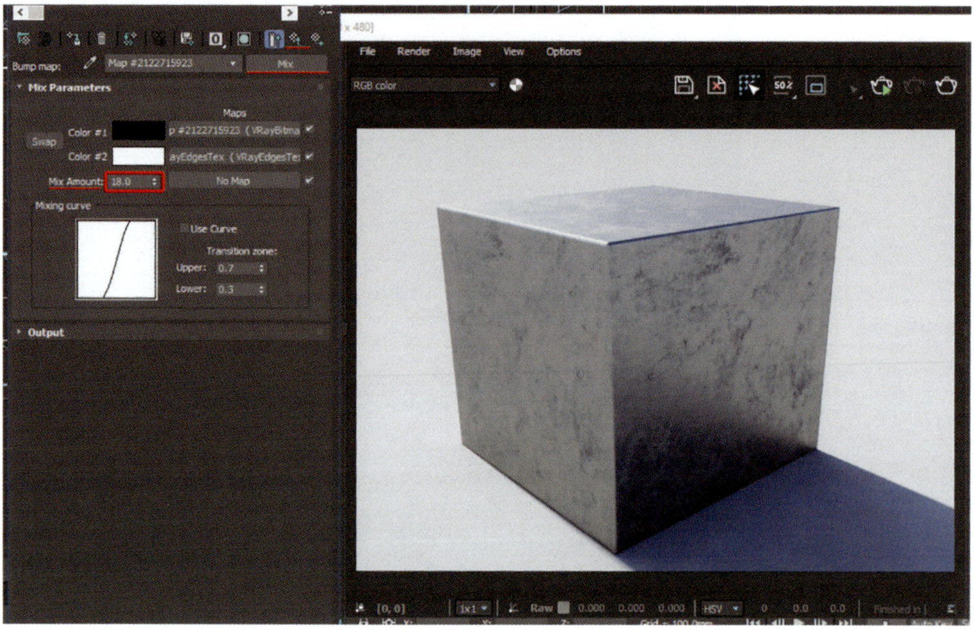

Mix Amount value set to 18.0

Conclusion

This chapter has introduced users to some of the most popular V-Ray shaders and procedural maps, followed by guiding users through the process of accessing and using them.

Some functionalities and parameters were discussed in more detail than others, by relevance.

Finally, new procedural maps will be introduced and discussed in more detail throughout the book.

For more information about other V-Ray shaders and procedural maps, please visit:

http://docs.chaosgroup.com/

3

Cameras and Lighting in V-Ray

3 Cameras and Lighting in V-Ray

NOTE

As referred to earlier, the V-Ray renderer needs to be loaded into the scene first, prior to using some of the tools and techniques covered in this chapter.

Camera and lights are the building blocks of any 3d scene.

As such, users will be taken through the parameters and functionalities of a V-Ray camera and all its light objects.

This chapter will start by depicting how to create and set up a V-Ray camera, followed by going through key functions such as Still cameras, Movie cameras, Video Cameras, Show horizon line, Film gate, Field of view, Focal length, zoom factor, Film speed, F-Number, Shutter speed, Exposure, Vignetting, White balance, Custom balance, Temperature, Tilt and Shift, Distortion, and Clipping and Environment.

Also, it will depict how to create and use VRay light objects such as the VRaySun, VRayIES and the VRayLight type.

Finally, in the VRayLight general parameters, users will learn all the functionalities associated with, Plane lights, Dome, Sphere, Mesh and Disc light.

To test some of the topics covered here, please open the 3ds max file, VRay Cameras.max.

If you are ever prompted with the message, File Load: Units Mismatch dialog, simply choose to, Adopt the File's Unit Scale. And OK to open it.

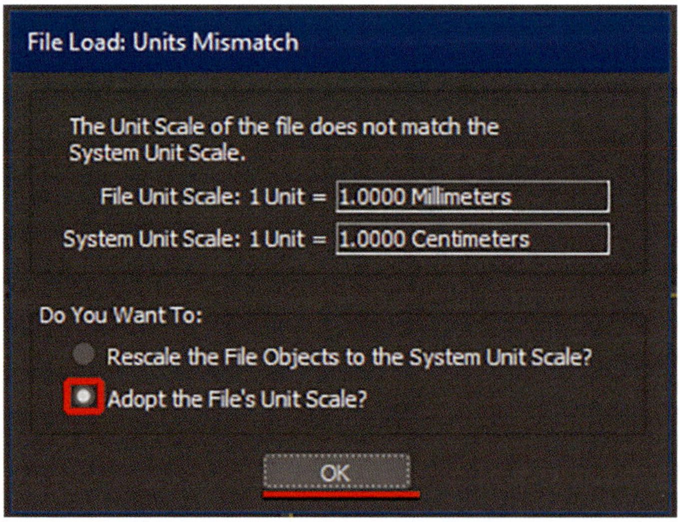

File Load: Units Mismatch dialog with the option to Adopt the File's Unit Scale enabled

Also, use the Load layer tree preset named, VRay Cameras.vfbl, with the Lookup Table file named, 3DCollective_sRGB_Agfa_Futura_03Hard.cube.

DOI: 10.1201/9781315770802-3

Cameras: VRayPhysicalCamera

This type of camera is the more popular of the two, and it emulates the physical properties of a real camera.

To create a VRayPhysicalCamera, go to the Create command panel and click on the Cameras button.

Under the Cameras group, select the Standard menu and choose VRay from the list.

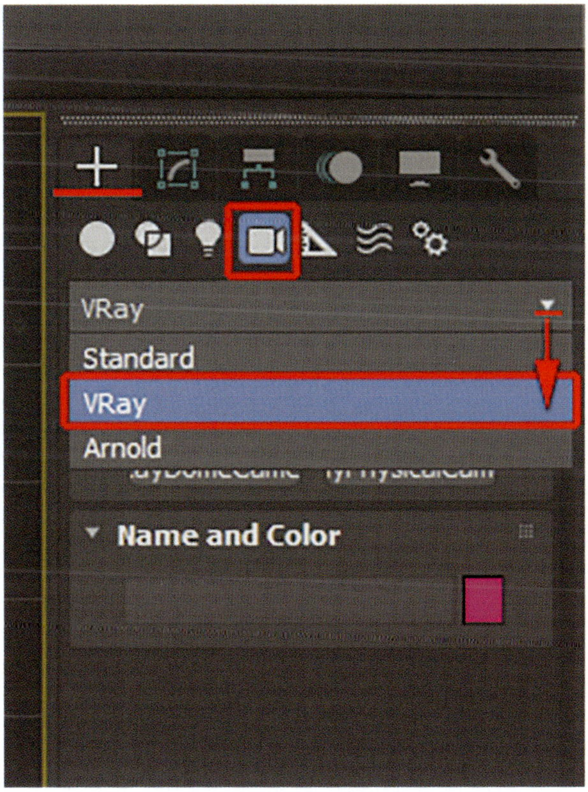

V-Ray menu chosen from the Cameras group

In the VRay Object Type group, select the VRayPhysicalCamera button, followed by clicking its cursor in the top viewport and dragging it across the screen to create the camera target.

Right click after the camera creation to exit, and go to the Modify command panel thereafter.

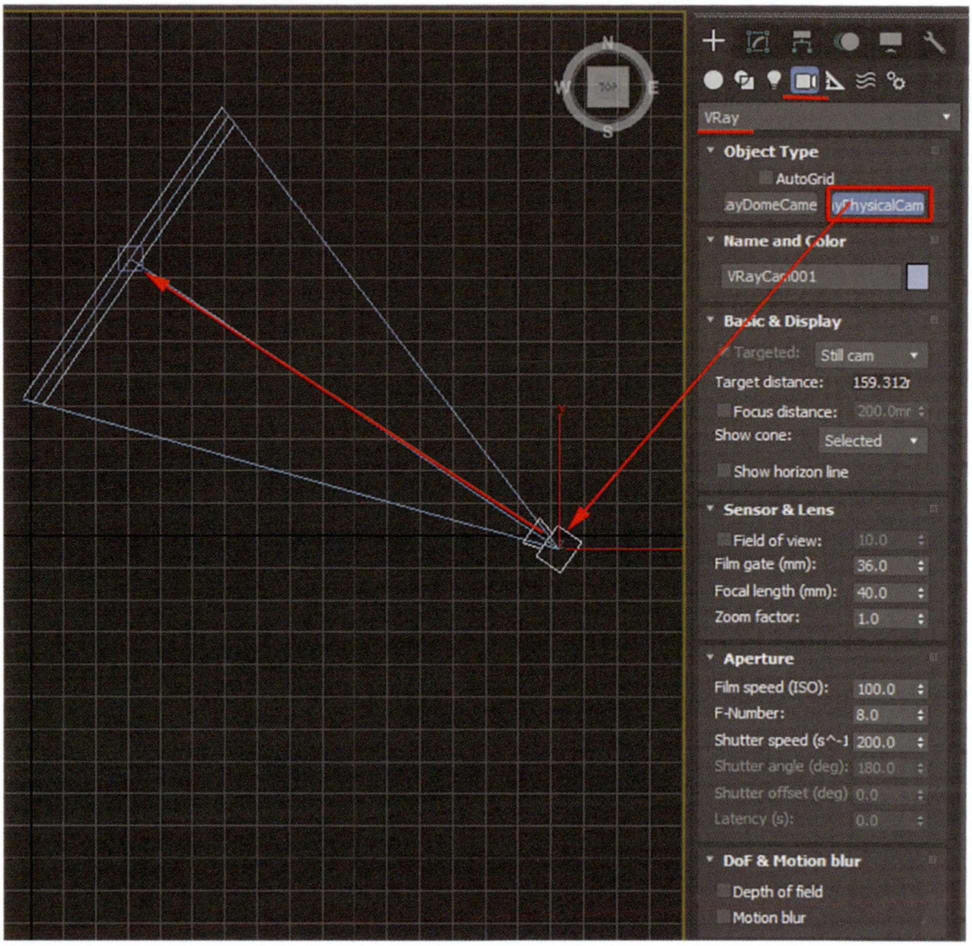

VRayPhysicalCamera being created in the Top Viewport

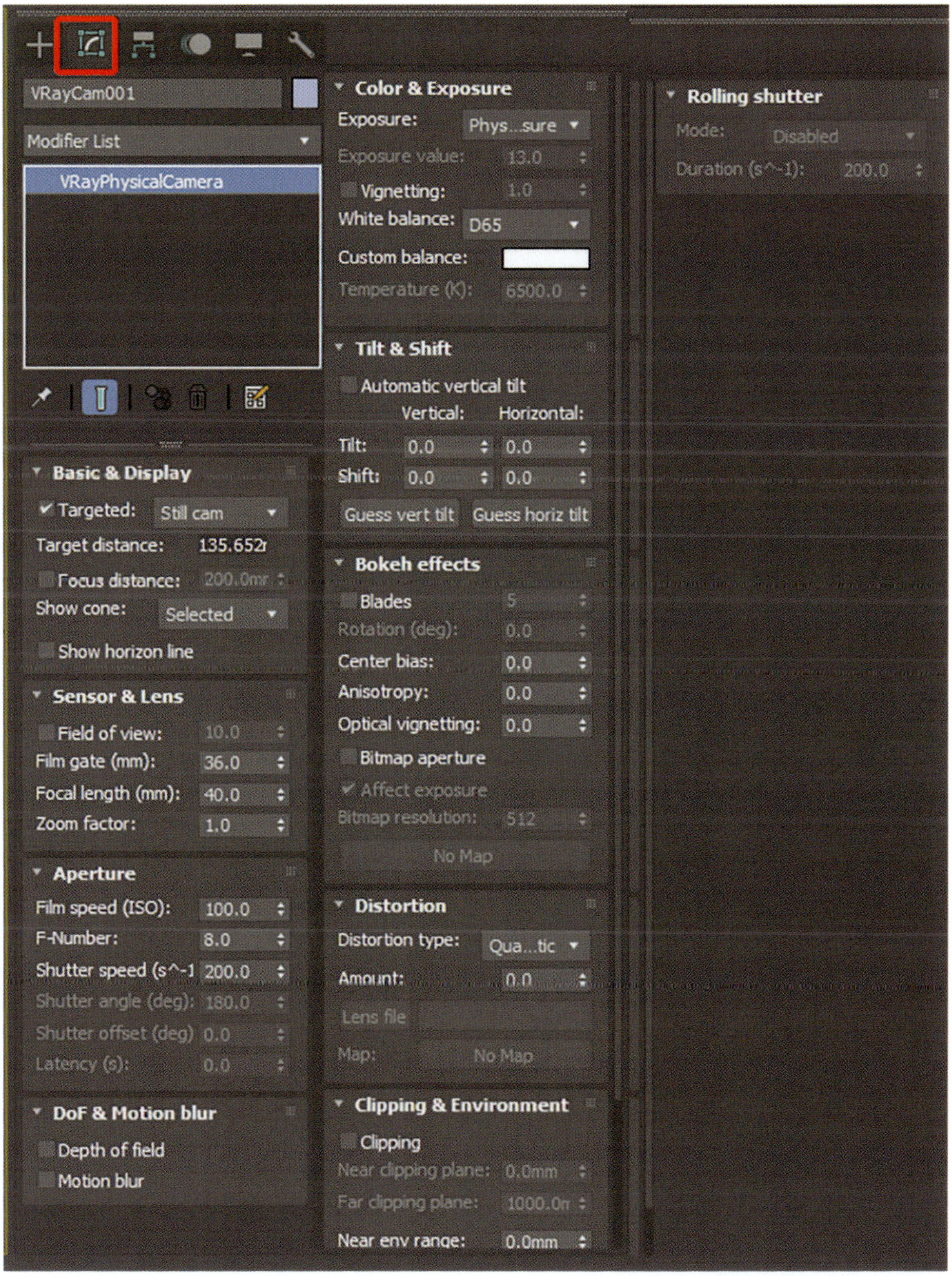

VRayPhysicalCamera parameters

Targeted: When enabled, this function adds a target to the physical camera. The target can be moved by the user to set the direction of the camera.

To move the camera itself, one has to either select both, the camera and its target. Or simply disable the Target function.

Enabled, by default.

Type: This camera function allows users to choose from three types of cameras available:

Still cam: This camera comes with a host of typical parameters to emulate a still camera.

Default shutter speed set to 200.0

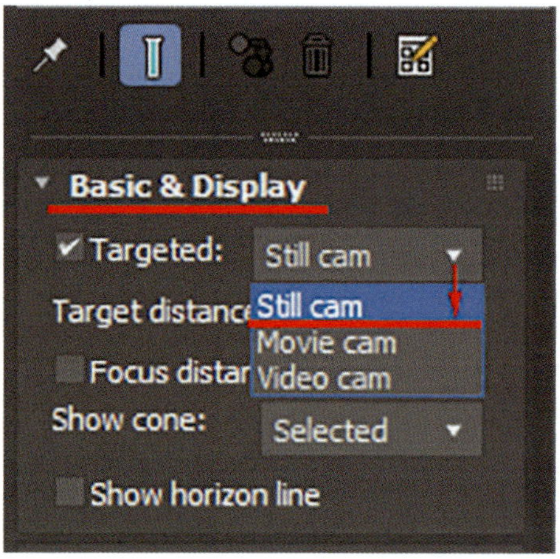

Physical camera options from the basic and display group

Movie cam: This type of camera emulates a movie camera from motion pictures, using a standard shutter angle set to 180.

Video cam: This camera type emulates a standard video camera without a shutter and with a Charge-Coupled-Device (CCD) matrix.

Latency set to 0.0, by default.

Target distance: The function sets the distance of the target camera.

Focus distance: Its function value sets a new camera distance.

Disabled by default.

Horizon line: When turned on, it displays the exact position of horizon line in the camera viewport.

This tool is quite useful for matching camera views in photomontages or verified views.

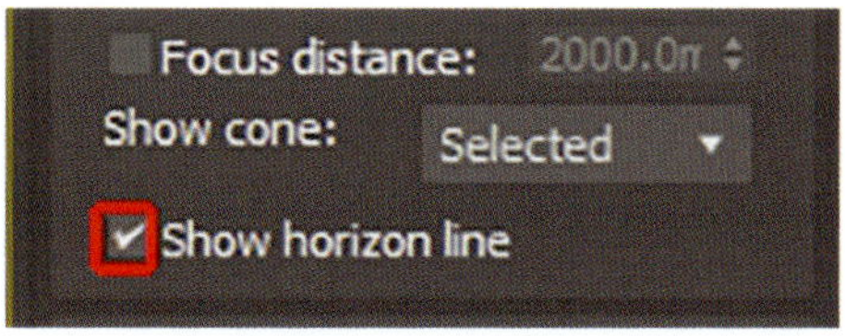

Show horizon line function enabled

Horizon line visible in the camera viewport

Sensors and Lens

Field of View: When enabled, this function is an alternative to using the Film gate and Focal length functions.

High values have the effect of a camera zooming in.

Lower values have the opposite effect.

Disabled by default.

Film gate (mm): This function determines the horizontal size of the film gate, in millimeters. It is worth noting that the values displayed here are directly connected to the Units Setup dialog.

High values have the effect of a camera zooming in.

Lower values have the opposite effect.

Default value, 36.0.

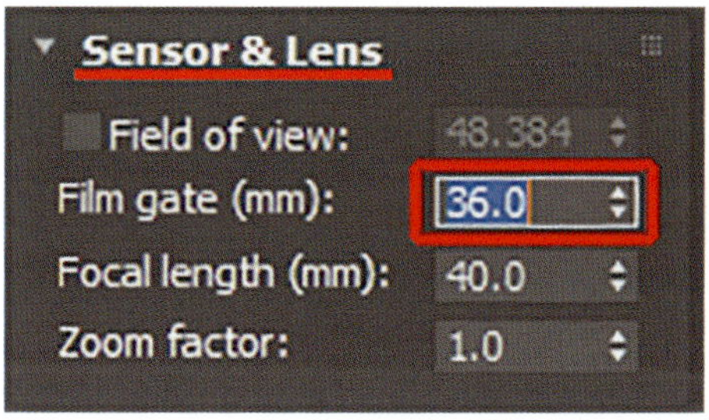

Film gate value set to 36.0

Render result of Film gate value set to 36.0

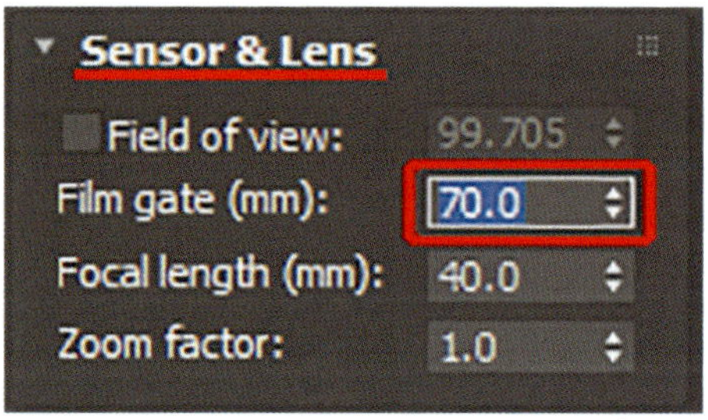

Film gate value set to 70.0

Render result of Film gate value set to 70.0

Focal length (mm): This function emulates the Focal length of a real camera lens.

High values have the effect of a camera zooming in.

Lower values have the opposite effect.

Default value, 40.0.

Zoom factor: This function allows the camera to zoom in and out of the scene.

Default value, 1.0.

Aperture

Film speed (ISO): It controls the camera sensitivity. Lower values darken the render.

Higher values produce opposite results.

Default value, 200.0.

F-number: This function is often used to increase or decrease the render brightness when the exposure function is turned on.

High values decrease the render brightness. Low values yield opposite results.

Default value, 8.0.

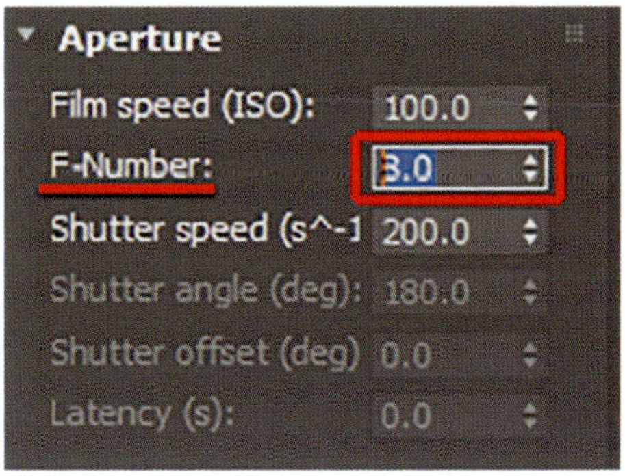

F-Number value set to 8.0

Render result of F-number value set to 8.0

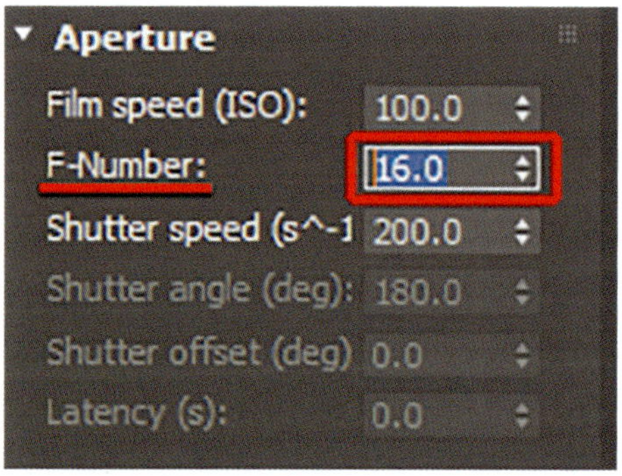

F-number value set to 16.0

Render result of F-number value set to 16.0

Shutter speed: This function controls the overall exposure time of the camera and the motion blur prominence (if there are moving objects in the scene). Lower numerical values yield brighter results and more accentuated motion results. Higher values have the opposite effect.

Default value, 200.00.

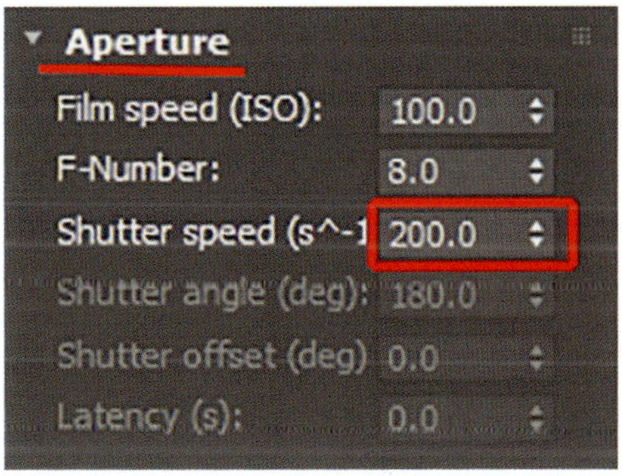

Shutter speed set to 200.0

Render result of Shutter speed set to 200.0

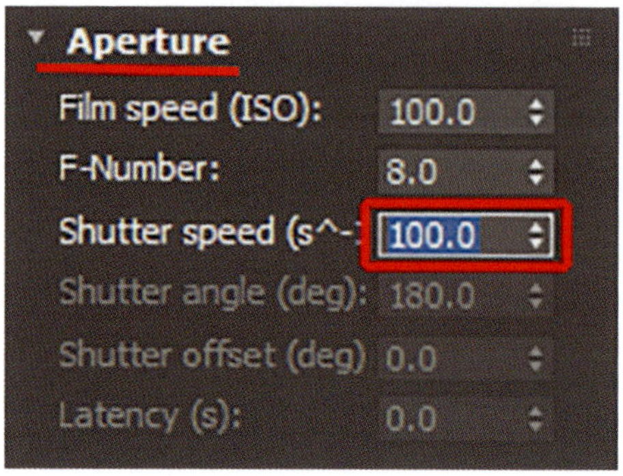

Shutter Speed set to 100.0

Render result of Shutter speed set to 100.0

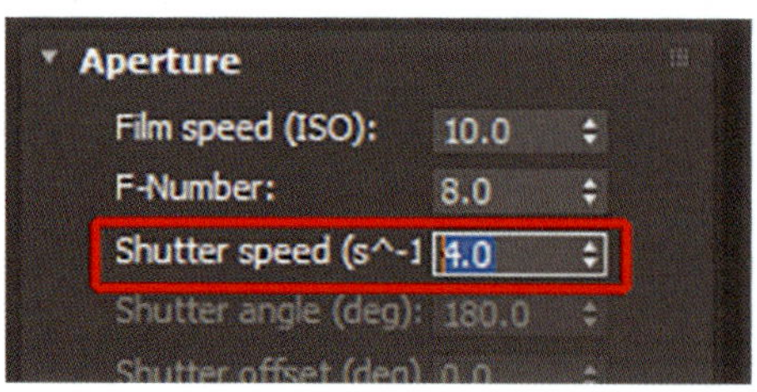

Shutter Speed set to 4.0

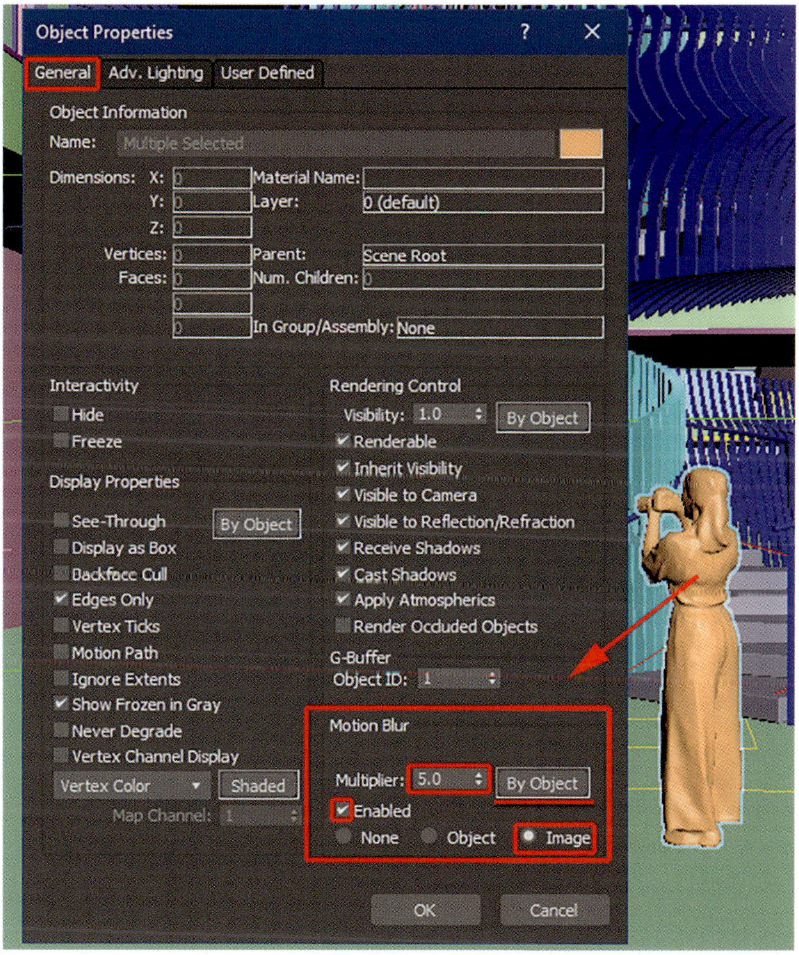

Object Properties Motion Blur enabled and Multiplier set to 5.0

Render of shutter Speed set to 4.0 (motion blur on moving hands)

Shutter angle (deg): This option determines the shutter angle of the camera, in degrees.

Disabled, by default.

It becomes live (180.0) when the camera type is set to a Movie cam.

Shutter offset (deg): It becomes live simultaneously with the shutter angle when the camera type is set to a Movie cam.

Its numerical values determine the shutter offset of the Movie Cam type.

Latency (s): This function is only available when the Cam type is set to, Video cam. It controls the CCD latency of a Video cam.

Default value, 0.0.

NOTE

The DoF effect increases the rendering time drastically. It is often best to add the DoF effect in post-production, using the VRayZdepth render element.

Depth of Field and Motion Blur

Depth of field (DoF): When enabled, it adds the DoF effect to the camera.

For stronger results, it is imperative to enable the focus distance function and decrease the F-Number value.

Low Focus distance values add the DoF effect in areas closer to the camera.

High Focus distance values add the DoF effect in areas further away from the camera.

We will cover this process in more detail in the chapters ahead.

Disabled by default.

NOTE

The motion blur effect increases the rendering time substantially.

Motion blur: When enabled, it adds the motion blur effect to a moving object.

For strong results, ensure the Shutter speed value is low (20.0) and the object is moving or/and rotating in the rendered frame (animated). The motion blur effect will never be visible at the beginning or end of a frame (only in the frames in-between).

Disabled by default.

Color and Exposure

Exposure parameters control the overall brightness of the render, in conjunction with other functions such as f-number, ISO and shutter speed.

Enabled, by default.

Physical Exposure: This exposure type is controlled by the F-Number and Shutter speed values.

Exposure Value (EV): When loaded this type of exposure is controlled by the Exposure values entered, the Shutter speed and the F-number.

Disabled by default.

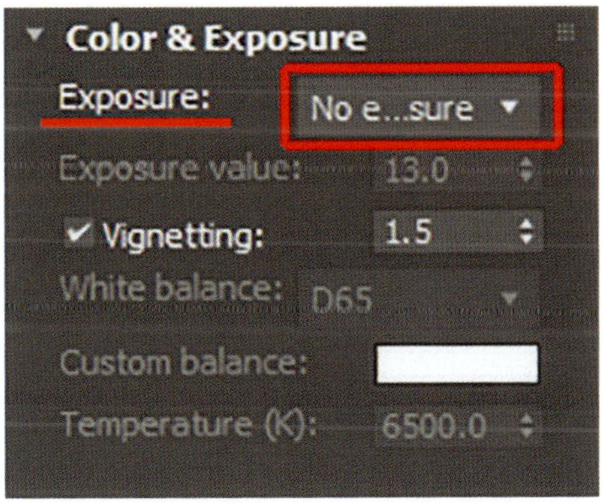

Exposure function disabled

Render result of the Exposure function disabled

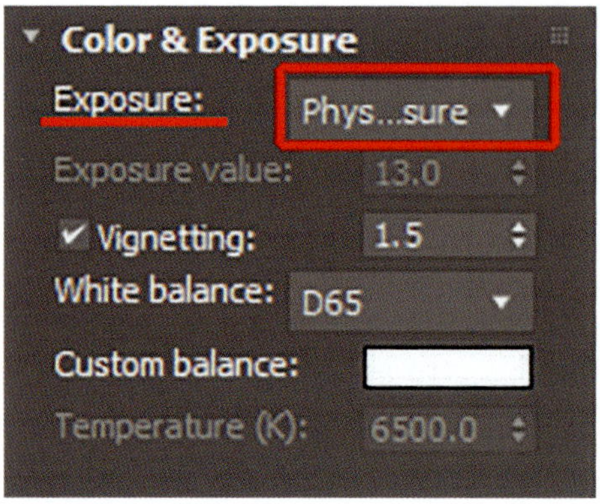

Exposure function enabled

Render result of Exposure function enabled

Vignetting: When enabled, it creates a slightly more contrasting image by darkening the four corners of the render. This real camera effect is known as vignetting.

The higher the values, the more apparent and darker the vignetting effect will be.

Disabled, by default.

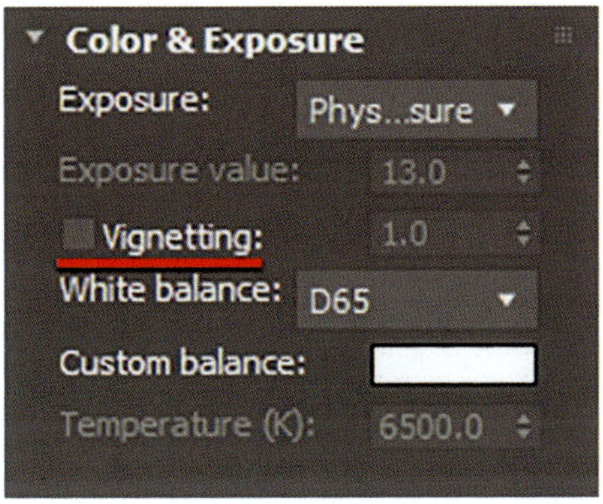

Vignetting function disabled

Render result of Vignetting disabled

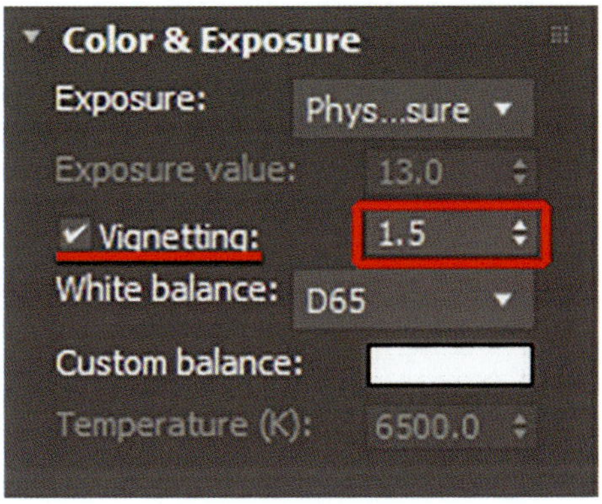

Vignetting enabled, value 1.5

Render result of Vignetting enabled, value 1.5

White Balance: As the name suggests, its parameters control the colors that will appear white, or whiter in the render.

It is widely used to balance out overpowering colors in the scene.

The pull-down menu comes with numerous presets such as Custom, Neutral, Daylight, D75, D65, D55, D50 and Temperature.

Default preset, D65.

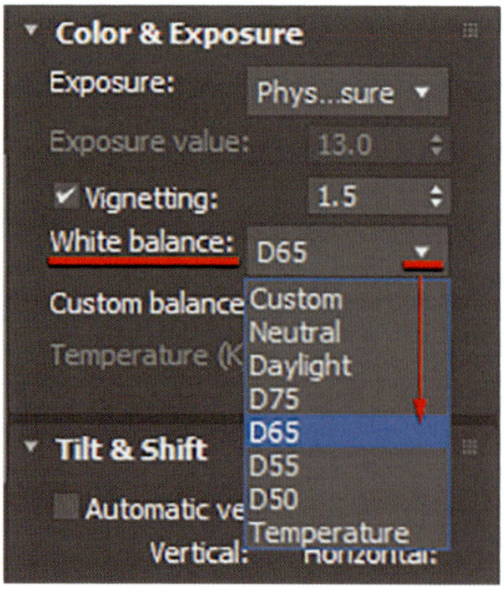

White balance pulled down menu

Custom balance: This color swatch allows users to pick or sample a custom color from the Color Selector dialog. The color displayed here will look more toward white in the render.

Default color, white (255).

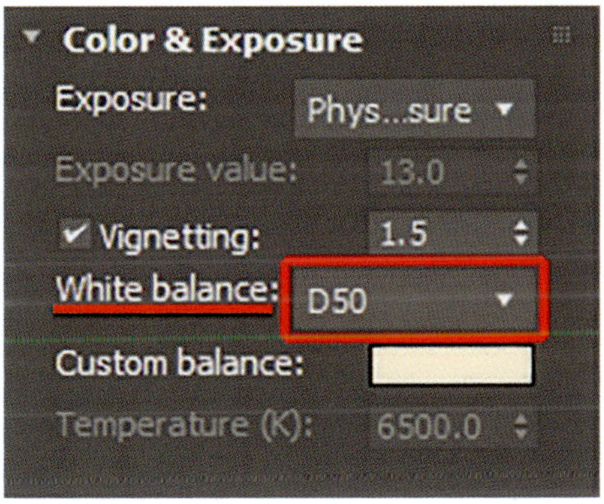

White balance set to D50

Render result of White balance set to D50

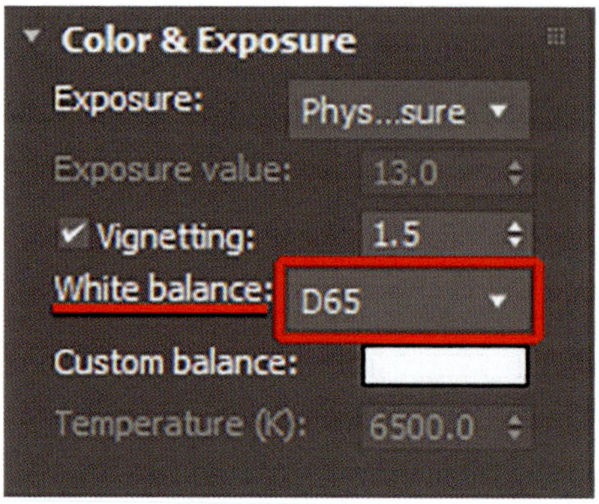

White balance set to D65

Render result of White balance set to D65

Temperature: This option becomes live when the Temperature preset is chosen from the default White Balance dropdown menu.

It allows users to type in a numerical color temperature value, if selected. For information about color temperature values, simply Google: kelvin color chart

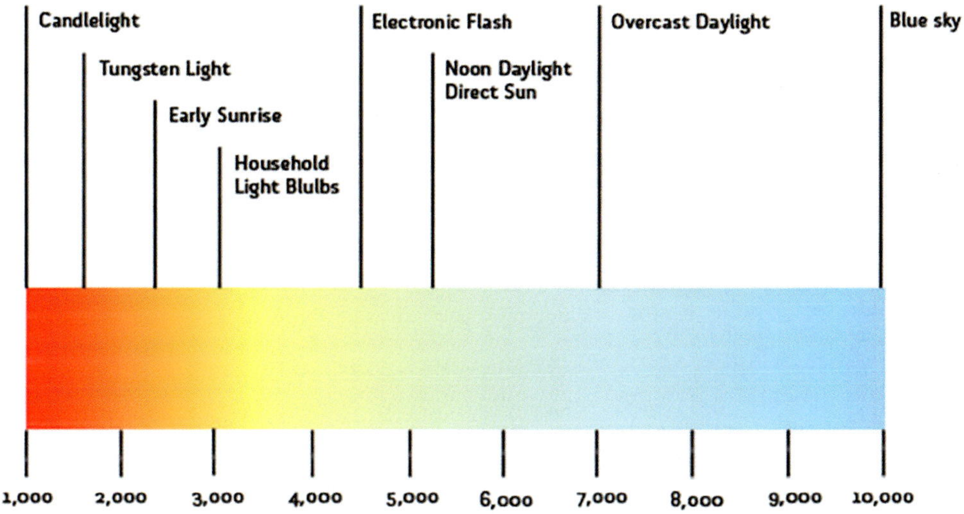

Kelvin color chart

Tilt and Shift

Automatic vertical tilt: When enabled, this function automatically corrects vertical tilt.

In addition, the Guess vertical tilt and Tilt functions become automatically unavailable (grayed out).

Disabled by default.

Tilt

Vertical: This function is used to correct the verticals of distorted cameras, by entering a value.

Default value, 0.0.

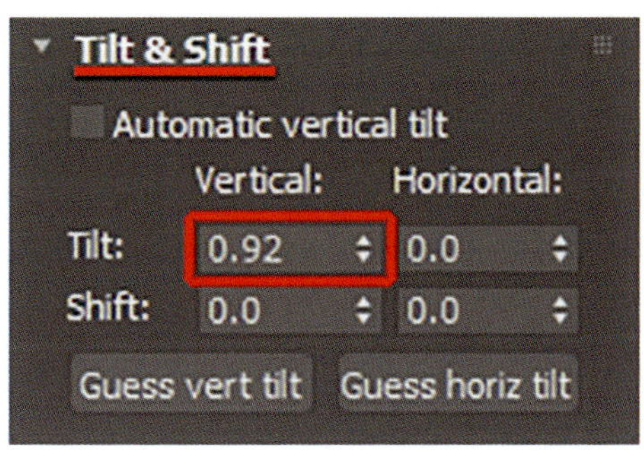

Vertical tilt value set to 0.92

Render result of Vertical tilt value set to 0.92

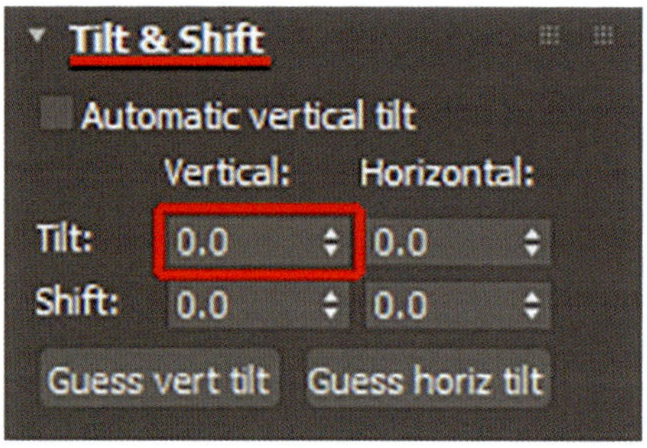

Vertical tilt value set to 0.0

Render result of Vertical tilt value set to 0.0

Horizontal: This function allows users to correct the camera distortion/tilt horizontally, by entering a value.

Default value, 0.0.

Shift

Vertical: This function enables users to offset/move (shift) the camera target vertically.

Positive values shift the camera up. Negative values shift the camera in the opposite direction.

Default value, 0.0.

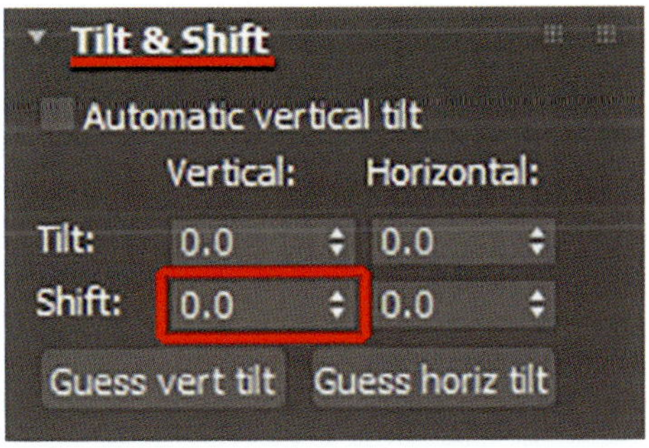

Vertical Shift value set to 0.0

Render result of Vertical Shift value set to 0.0

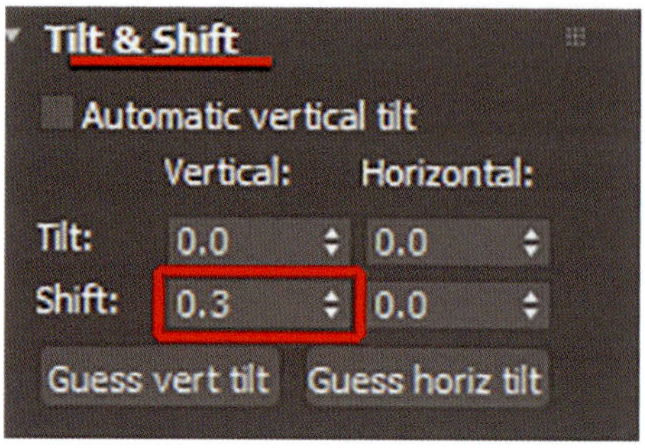

Vertical Shift value set to 0.3

Render result of Vertical Shift value set to 0.3

Horizontal: The function offsets/moves (shifts) the camera target horizontally. High values shift the camera to the right and low values shift the camera in the opposite direction.

Default value, 0.0.

Guess vertical tilt: When clicked, the button automatically guesses the vertical tilt values.

Guess horizontal tilt: When clicked, the button automatically guesses the camera distortion tilt, horizontally.

Bokeh Effects

In a real production environment, the DOF, bokeh effects, etc. are often applied in post-production.

It is done so, due to these effects being extremely time-consuming to fine-tune/render in 3ds max. Especially when there's a need for quick turnarounds.

In the VRayPhysicalCamera, the bokeh effect is only visible if/when the DoF function is enabled.

The bokeh effect is mostly visible in overly bright areas of an image (overexposed).

Through the camera lenses, the bokeh effect is depicted in a circular or polygonal shape.

Disabled by default.

Blades: This function controls the shape of the bokeh effect. The higher the number of blades, the more circular the bokeh effect will be.

When disabled, the bokeh effect is totally circular.

Default value, 5.

Disabled by default.

Rotation (deg): This function controls the rotation of the blades (bokeh).

Default value, 0.0.

Disabled by default.

Center bias: This function controls the brightness of the bokeh. Negative values brighten the center of the bokeh effect.

Positive values brighten the outer edge of the bokeh effect.

Default value, 0.0.

Anisotropy: This function stretches the bokeh effect horizontally or vertically to emulate anamorphic lenses.

Default value, 0.0.

Optical vignetting: This function determines the strength of the optical vignetting.

Default value, 0.0.

NOTE

This function is extremely slow to calculate, and yields noise effects.

Bitmap aperture: This function allows users to load a bitmap to control the shape (and scratches) of the bokeh effect.

Black and white bitmaps work best. White areas of a bitmap are interpreted as transparent.

Disabled by default.

Affect exposure: This function affects the overall exposure of the render.

Disabled by default.

Bitmap resolution: this function controls the sampled resolution of the loaded bitmap.

Disabled by default.

Distortion

Distortion type: This function controls the type of camera distortion (Quadratic, Cubic, Lens file, Texture).

Default distortion, Quadratic.

Popular camera tracking applications, such as Boujou, use the Cubic distortion camera type.

Amount: This function controls the amount of distortion.

Default value, 0.0.

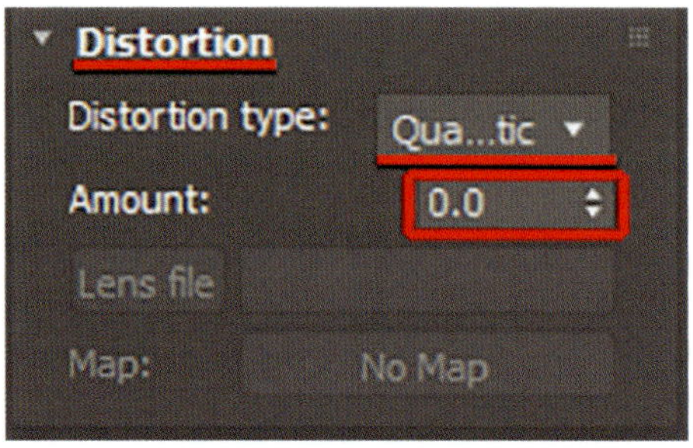

Quadratic distortion set to 0.0

Render result of Quadratic distortion set to 0.0

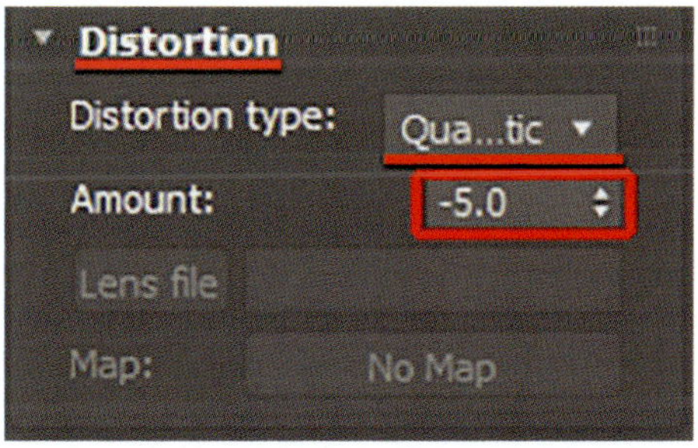

Quadratic distortion set to −5.0

Render result of Quadratic distortion set to −5.0

Lens file: This distortion type allows users to load a lens file type, often generated by the VRay Lens Analysis tool.

Texture: This distortion type allows users to load a Map from third-party applications such as Nuke, to set the camera distortion.

Clipping and Environment

Clipping: When enabled, it allows the selected camera to clip/slice objects within a specified distance, using the near clipping plane and the far clipping plane options.

The clipping option is widely used in tight/close shots, where objects such as doors and walls are obstructing the camera composition.

Near clipping plane: This function controls where the nearest clipping plane starts from.

Far clipping plane: This option determines where the far clipping plane starts from.

Clipping function disabled

Render result of the Clipping function disabled

Clipping function enabled, with far clipping set to 2178

Clipping enabled, with far clipping to 2178 render

Near env range: This function controls the near environment range of atmospheric effects in 3ds max.

Far env range: This function controls the far environment range of atmospheric effects in 3ds max.

Rolling shutter: This function controls/stabilizes the direction of the motion blur.

Disabled by default.

When enabled, it controls the amount of motion blur.

There are four types of rolling shutters to choose from: Top to bottom, bottom to top, left to right, and right to left.

Duration (s^-1): This function controls the time the shutter passes an image in 1/ seconds.

The Rolling shutter function only becomes live when the Motion blur function is enabled.

NOTE

To test some of the VRayLight parameters discussed here, simply open the 3ds max scene named, VRayLights.max. Also, use the Load layer tree preset named, VRayLights.vfbl, with the Lookup Table file named, 3DCollective_sRGB_Agfa_Futura_03Hard.cube.

Lighting in V-Ray

In the discussion that will follow, we will begin by introducing some of the most popular V-Ray lights and take users through the process of using them to light a scene.

It is worth noting that it is common practice to copy/instance lights whenever possible, as they are faster to compute.

VRayLight

To create a VRayLight, go to the Create command panel and click on the Lights button.

Under the lights group, select the Photometric menu and choose VRay from its dropdown list.

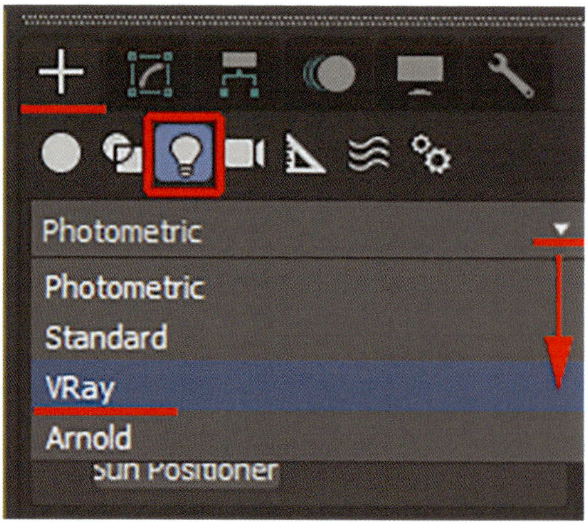

V-Ray menu chosen from the Lights group

Under the VRay Object Type group, select the VRayLight button, followed by clicking and dragging the cursor across the viewport to create it.

To exit creation, simply right click.

Next, go to the Modify command panel to see its parameters.

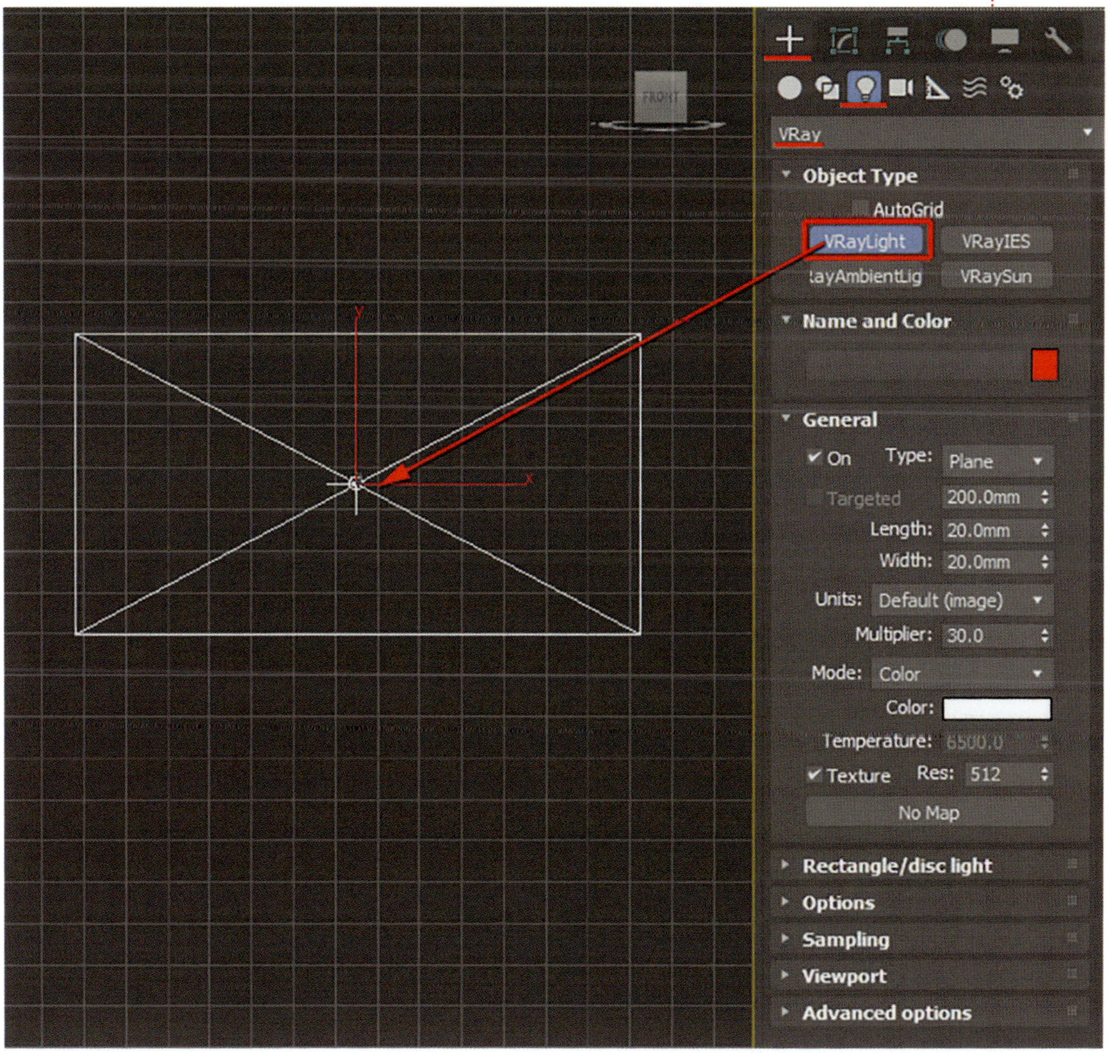

Creating a VRayLight object in the viewport

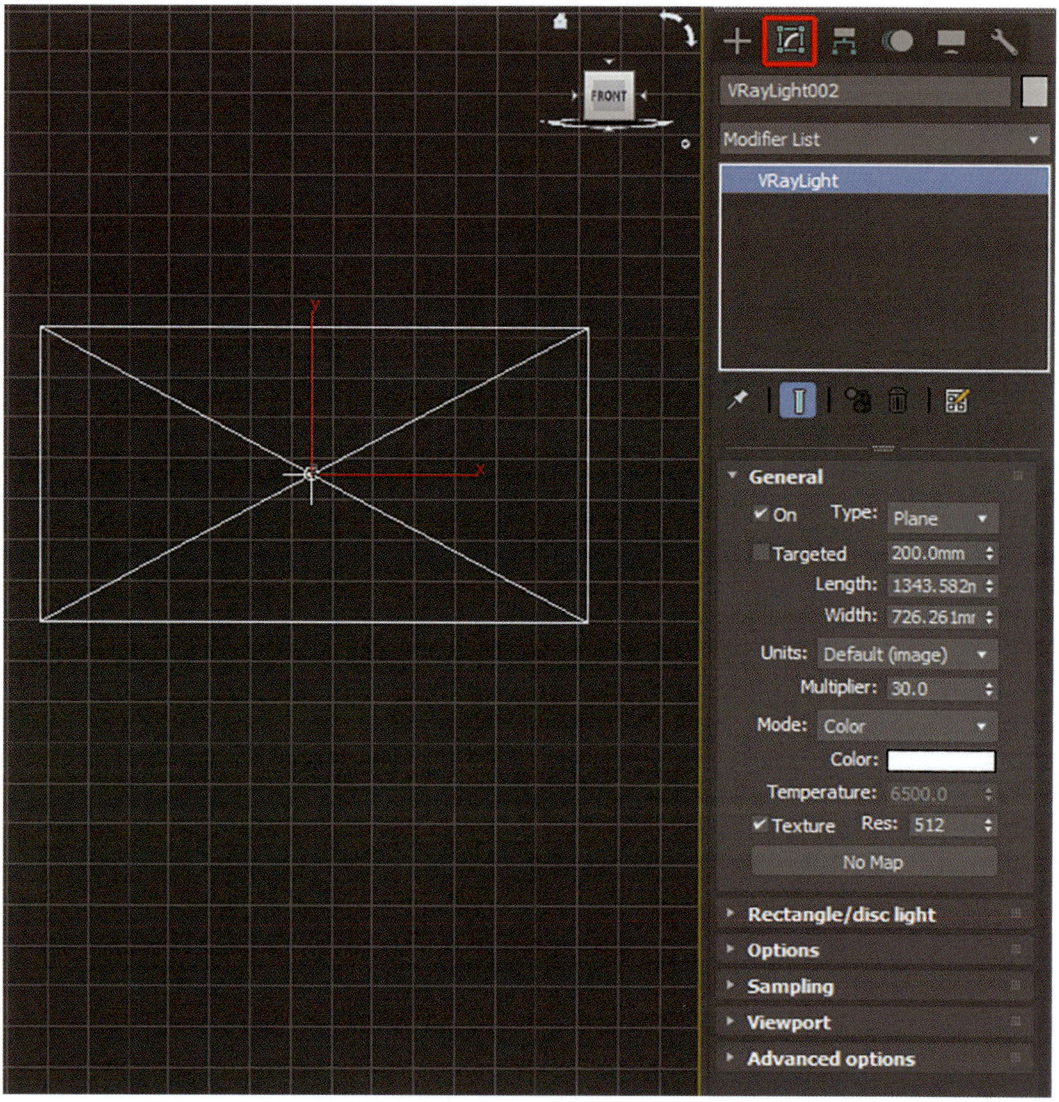

VRayLight parameters in the Modify panel

Plane Light

On: This function allows the light to be turned on, and off.

Enabled, by default.

Type: This function allows users to choose from a list of light types such as Plane, Dome, Sphere, Mesh and Disc.

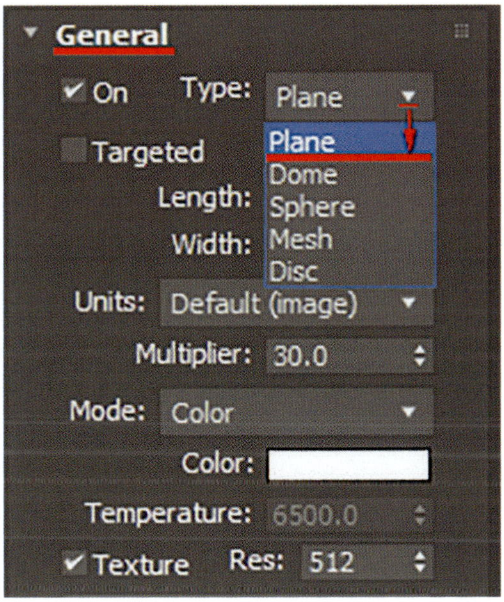

General VRayLight Types

Targeted: When enabled, it automatically creates a target direction of the light (only seen in the viewport).

The light target helps the user to see and change the direction of the light, if required.

Length: This value determines the length of the light object.

Width: This function controls the width of the light object.

The bigger the light size, the softer the shadows will be. This feature is coherent with most V-Ray lights.

It is worth noting that plane lights can be scaled independently with the Select and Uniform Scale toolbar, without affecting the size of other instanced lights in the scene.

As mentioned earlier, instanced lights are substantially quicker to render than copied lights.

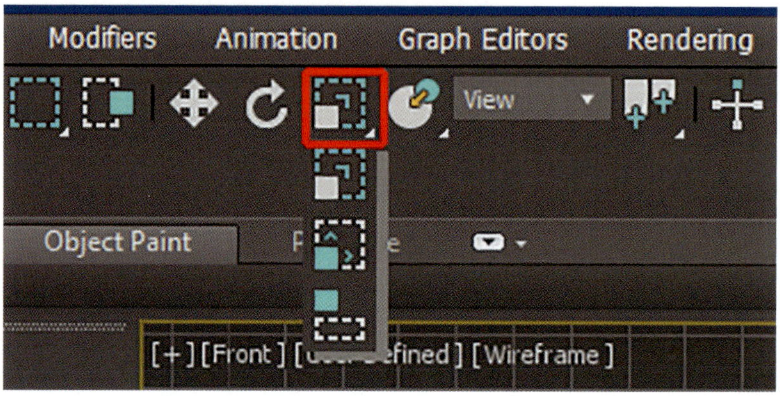

Select and Uniform Scale toolbar

Units: This function allows users to choose from a list of well-known light units, to light a scene.

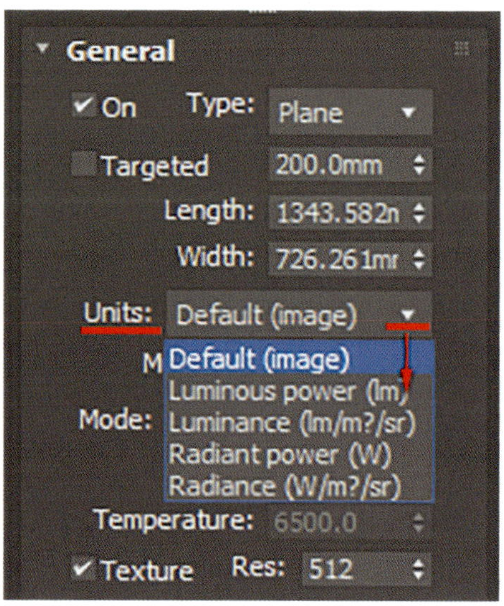

List of different light Units

Default (image): This intensity unit is based on the Color Mode and the Multiplier value (30.0 by default). The overall intensity is also dependent on the physical scale/size of the light object.

Luminous power (lm): It determines the light power in lumens. This unit acts independently from the physical size of the light object.

Luminance (lm/m²/sr): This intensity is measured in lumens square meters per steradian.

Radiant power (W): This numerical intensity unit is measured in watts. Also, this unit acts independently from the physical size of the light object.

Radiance (W/m²/sr): This unit of intensity is measured in watts in square meter per steradian. The overall intensity of this unit is dependent on the physical scale/size of the light object.

Multiplier: The default numerical value is based on the type of Units chosen.

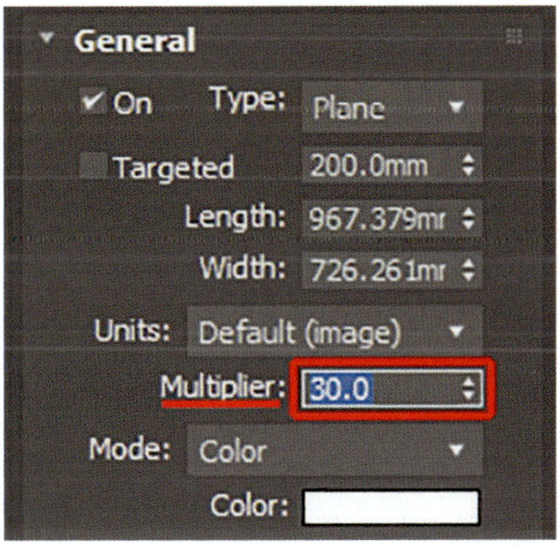

Multiplier value set to 30.0

Multiplier value set to 30.0 render

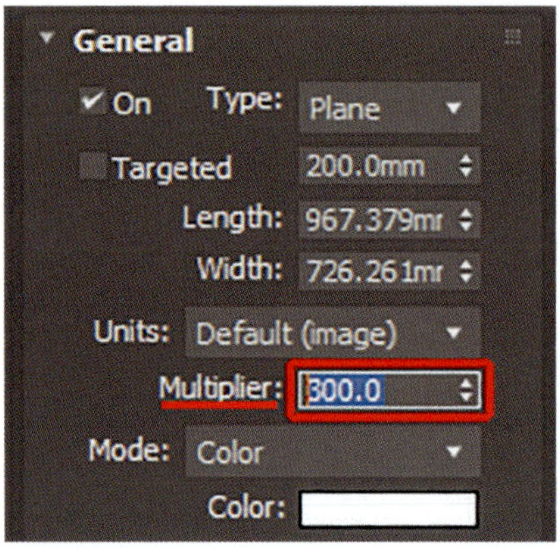

Multiplier value set to 300.0

Render result of Multiplier value set to 300.0

Mode: This function controls the color of the light source. Users have the option between Color and Temperature mode.

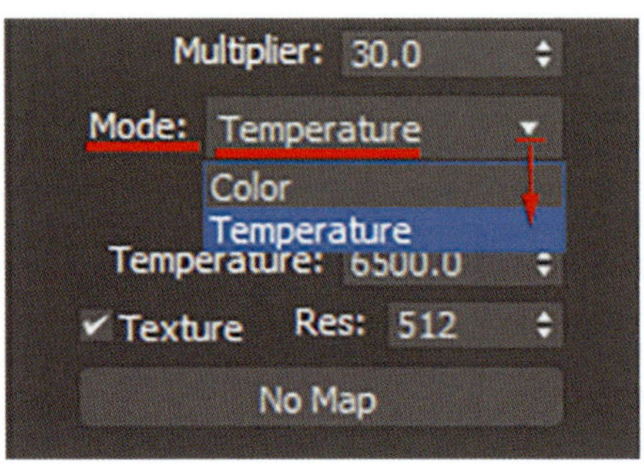

Color Modes

Color: This mode allows users to click on the color swatch to choose/sample a color from the Color Selector dialog.

Temperature: If this mode is chosen, users are able to type in a color temperature value.

For more information about color temperature values, simply refer to the color chart depicted earlier, or Google: **kelvin color chart**.

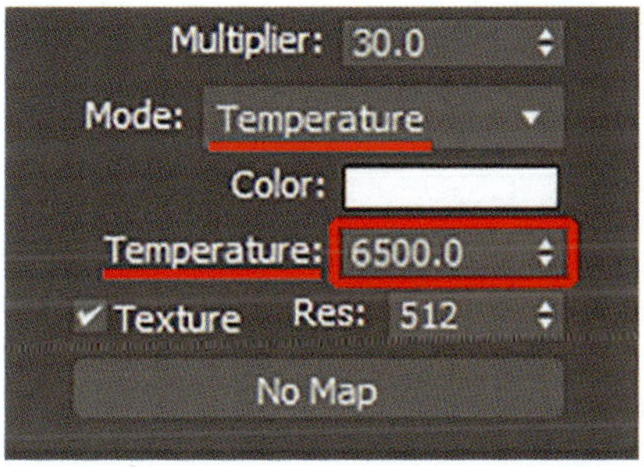

Color Temperature set to 6500.0

Render result of Color Temperature set to 6500.0

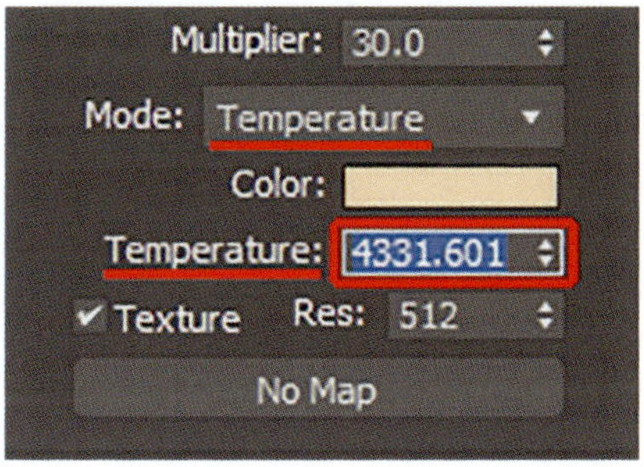

Color Temperature set to 4331.601

Render result of Color Temperature set to 4331.601

NOTE

HDRI works best in open spaces.

Texture: When enabled, this toggle allows users to plug a Bitmap or an HDRI via the VRayBitmap procedural map.

High Dynamic Range Images have a greater dynamic range of luminosity than normal images.

As such, they can be used to illuminate a scene accurately.

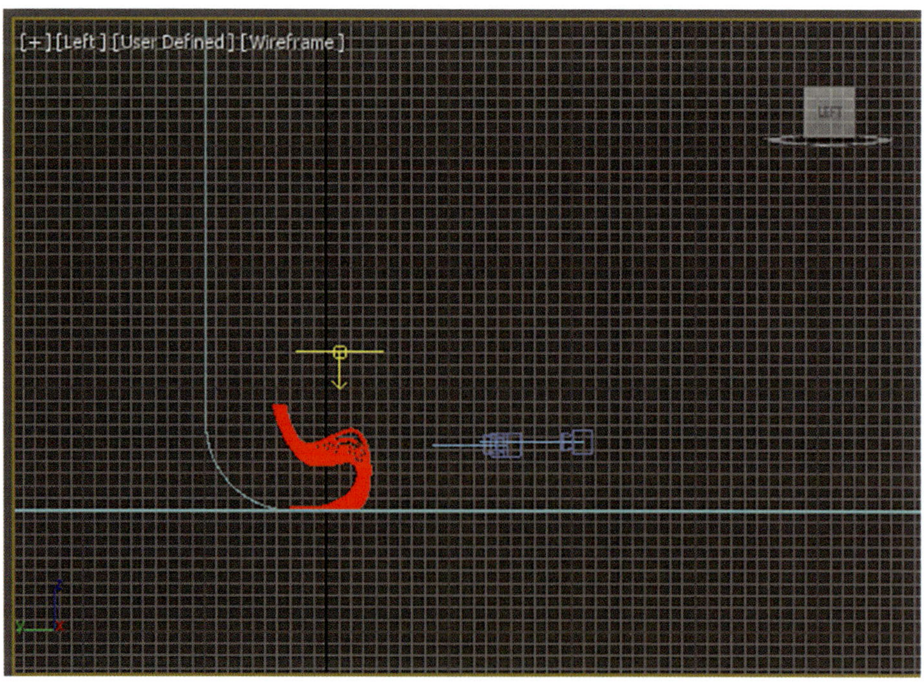

Viewport depicting an open space studio without ceilings or surrounding walls

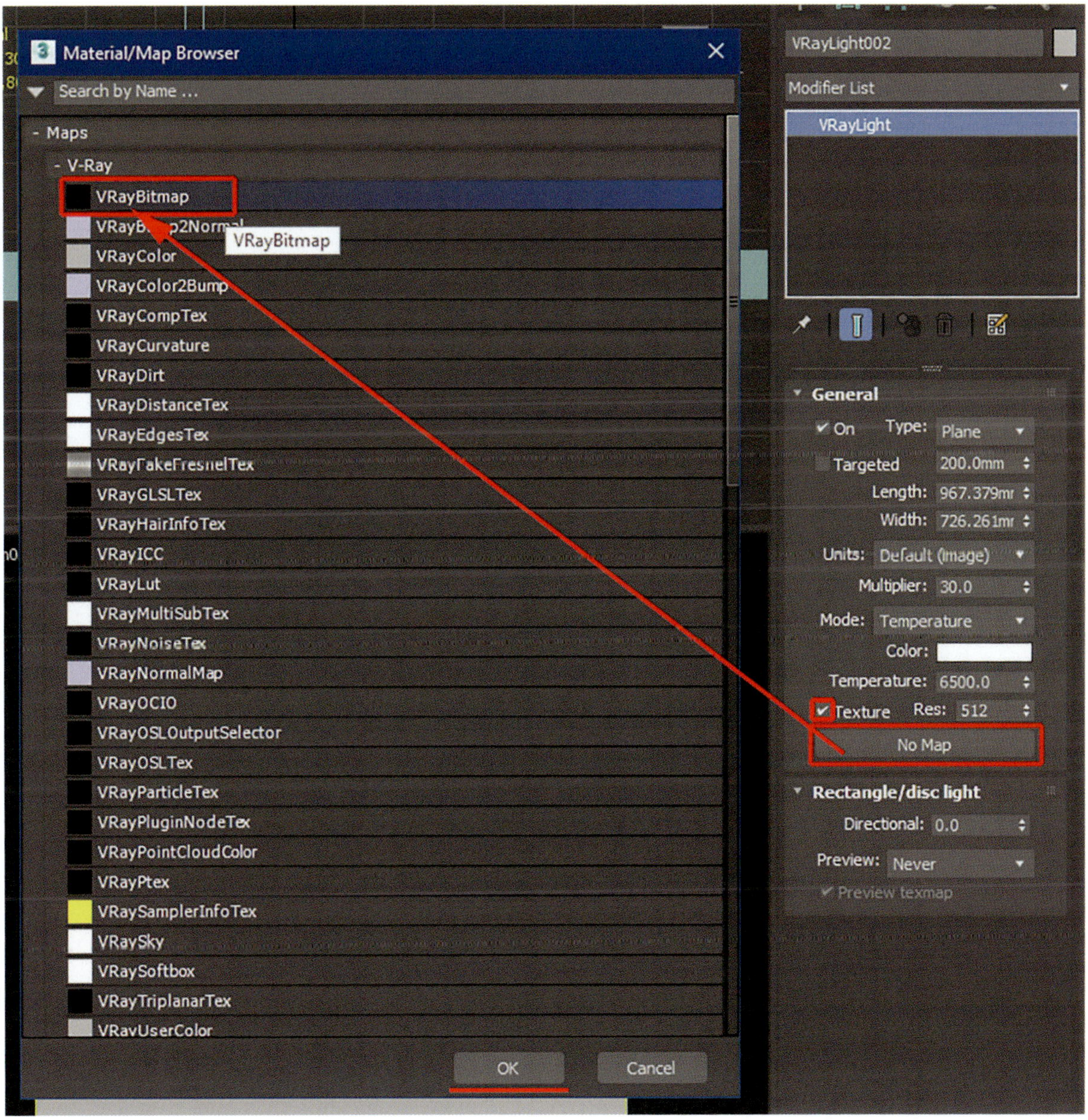

VRayLight Texture toggle being used to load the VRayBitmap procedural map

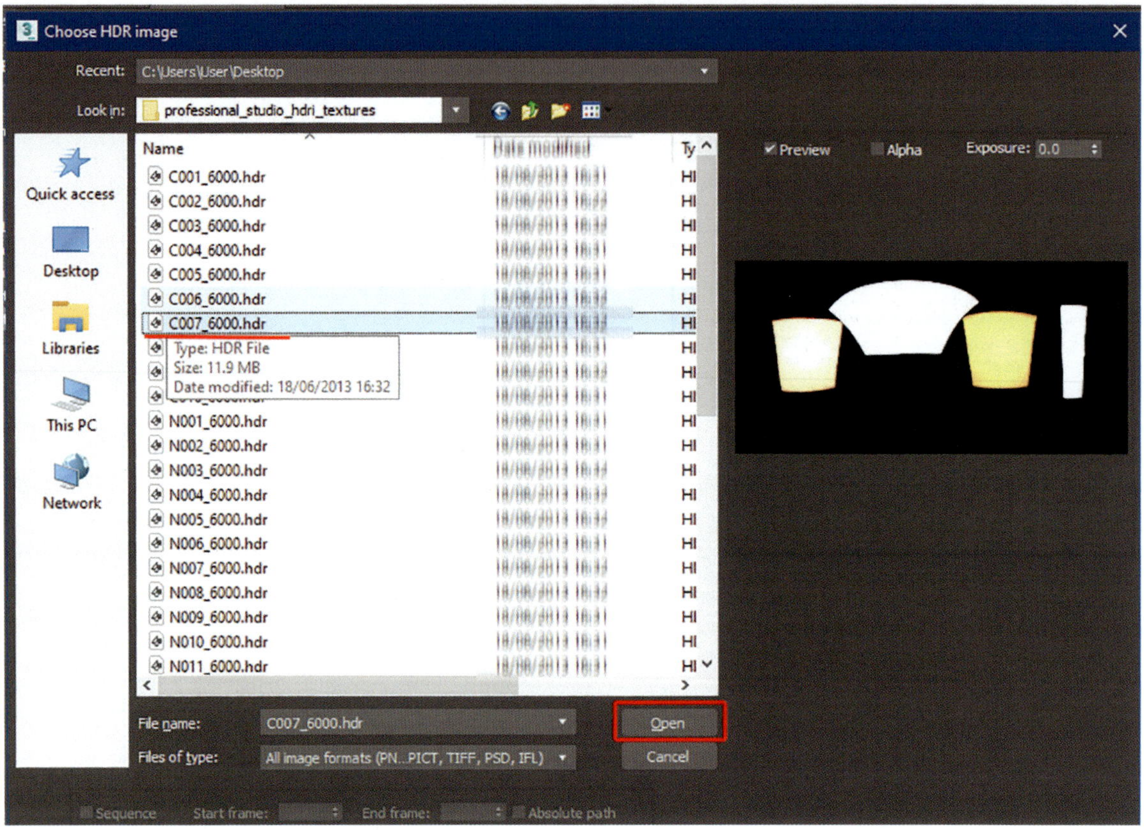

Choose HDRI image dialog with HDRI files

Once applied, users can edit it, by simply dragging and dropping it into the Material Editor slot.

Choose the Instance option, from the Instance Copy Map dialog.

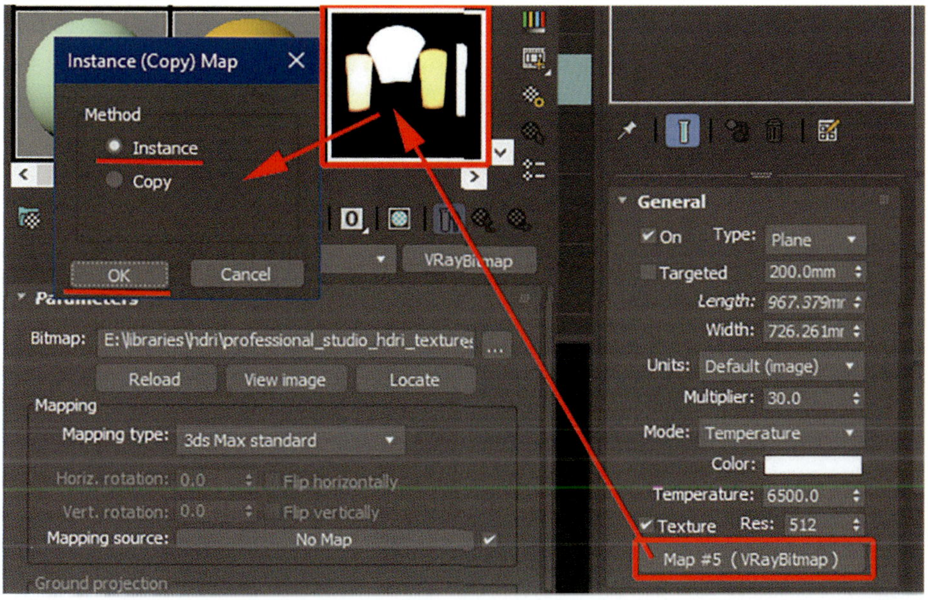

Texture toggle dropped into the Material slot to Copy Instance and edit the VRayBitmap

In the VRayBitmap parameters, set the Mapping type to, Spherical.

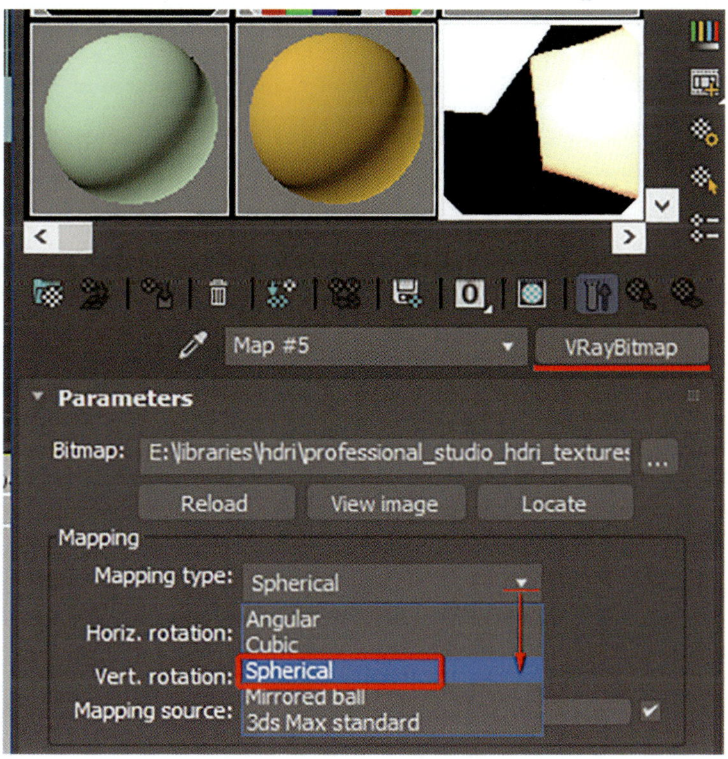

VRayBitmap with HDRI Mapping type set to Spherical

Use the Horiz.rotation, Vert.rotation, Flip, and Crop/Place tools to move, rotate, and/or crop the HDRI accordingly to fit a specific area.

Plane lights can also be used to plug light procedural maps such as VRaySoftbox.

This light procedural map is often used to emulate a studio softbox light, by creating gradients around the edges of the plane light.

This is also a good technique to remove hard edges from the plane lights.

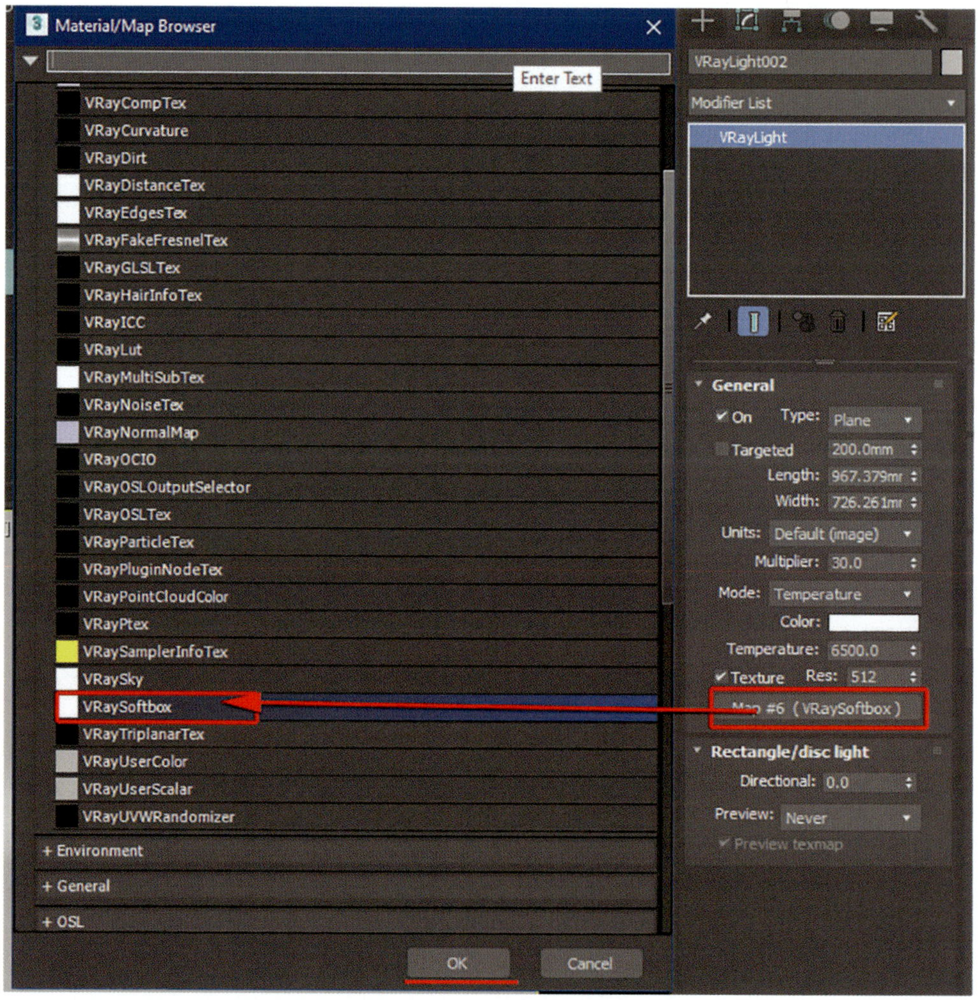

Texture toggle being used to load the VRaySoftbox procedural map

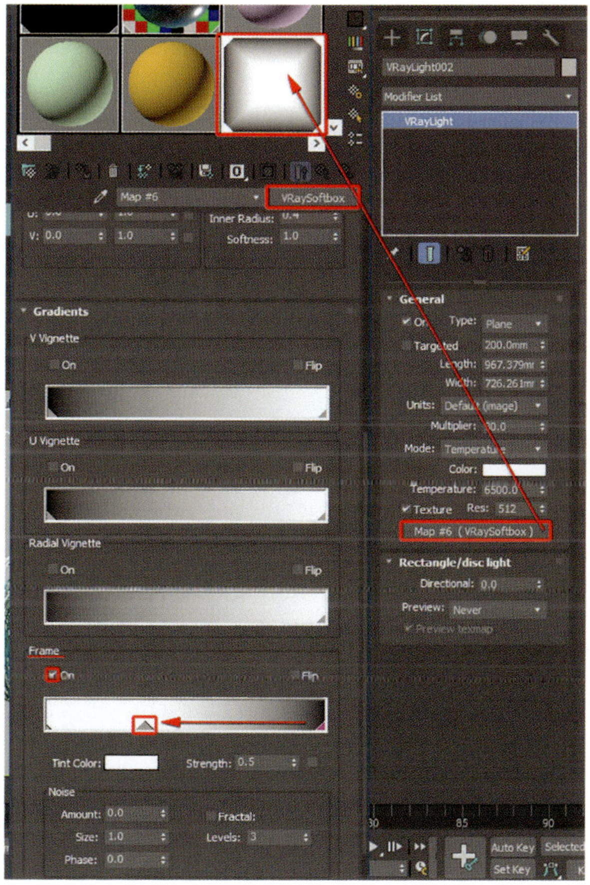

VRaySoftbox dropped/copied in the Material slot with Frame function enabled and soft edges created

Also, users can apply, black and white bitmaps on its Base parameters to emulate dust/scratches effects.

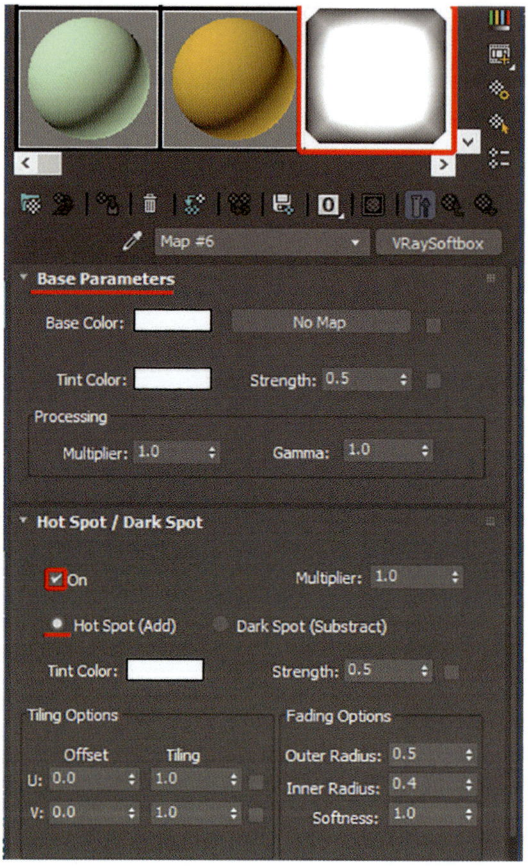

Hot Spot function enabled

Render result of Hot Spot function enabled

Rectangle/Disc Light

This option is only available when the light type is Plane or Disc.

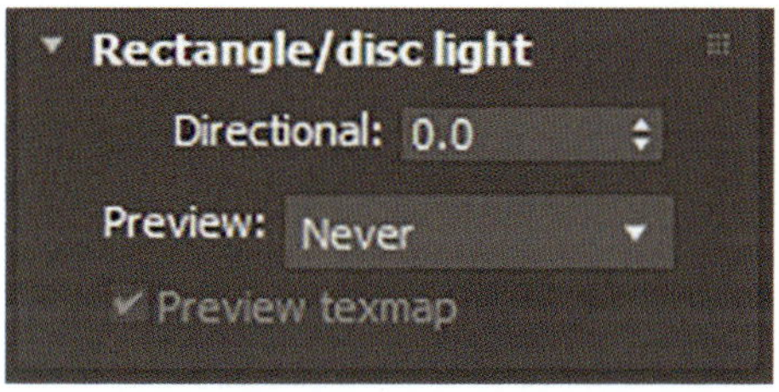

Rectangle/disk light group parameters

Directional: This function controls the direction of the light. With the default value set 0.0, the light is spread.

When the directional value is increased toward the value 1.0, the light emission is less spread and more localized/directional.

Default value, 0.0.

Preview: This function provides users with the option to preview the light in the viewport.

Never: This option will never preview the light in the viewport.

Always: This option will always preview the light in the viewport.

Selected: This option will only preview the selected light in the viewport.

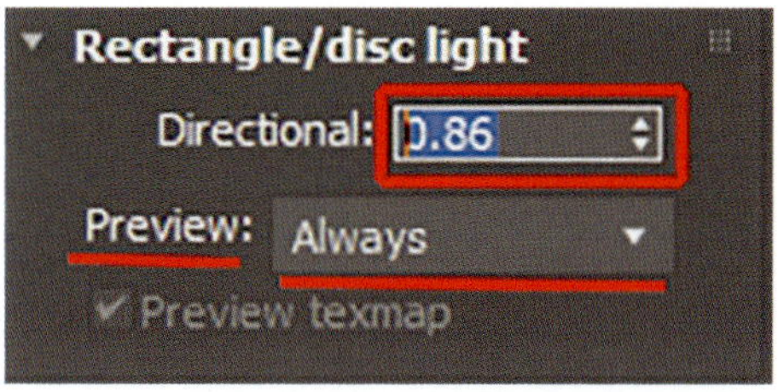

Directional value set to 0.86

Directional value preview in the viewport

Render result of Directional value set to 0.86

Options

Exclude: This toggle allows users to pick and choose scene objects to be excluded from the effects of this light.

The left and right arrows in the middle allow users to add or remove listed scene objects.

To add objects, simply select them from the Scene Objects list, and click on the button with an arrow point toward the right.

To remove objects, select them from the Include or Exclude list, followed by clicking on the button with an arrow pointing toward the left.

By default, the dialog is set to Exclude Both, Illumination and Shadow Casting.

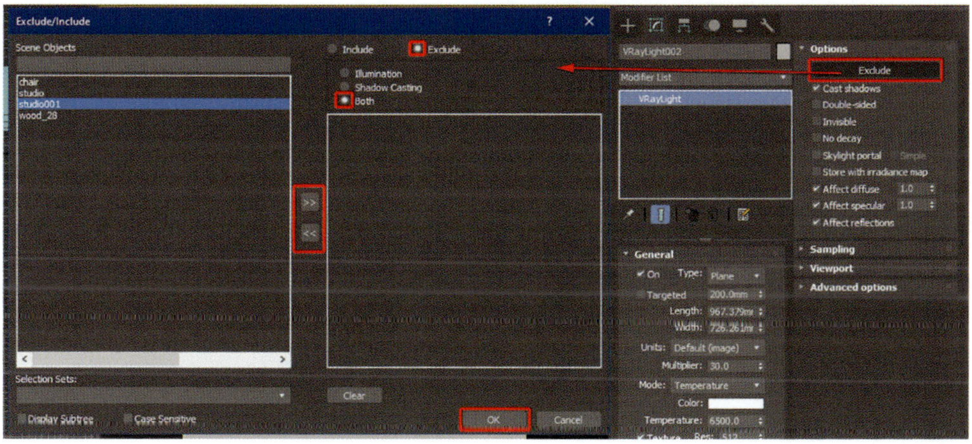

Options group with Exclude toggle clicked to open the Exclude/Include dialog

Cast shadows: This function enables the light to cast shadows in the scene.

Enabled, by default.

Double-sided: If enabled, it allows both sides of the plane light to cast light and shadows (if turned on). Disabled, by default.

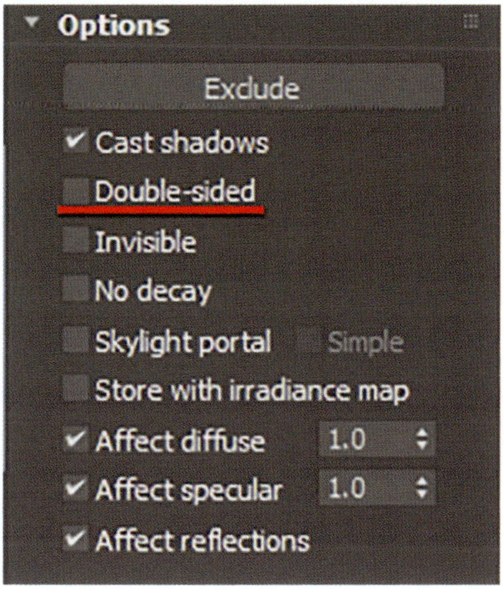

Options group with Double-sided option disabled

Render result of Double-sided option disabled

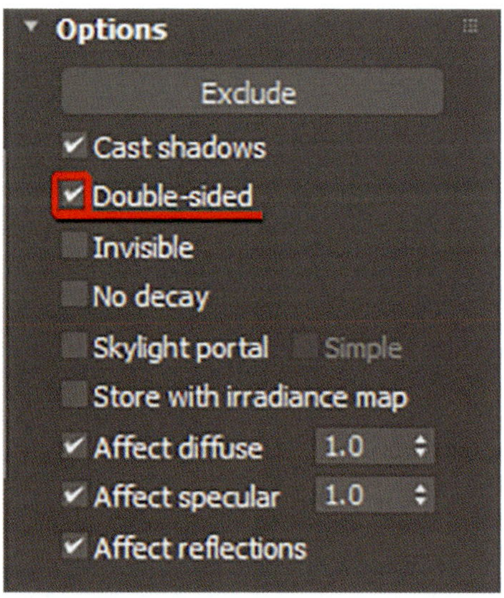

Double-sided option enabled

Render result of Double-sided option enabled

Invisible: This function allows the light object to be invisible in the render. Disabled, by default.

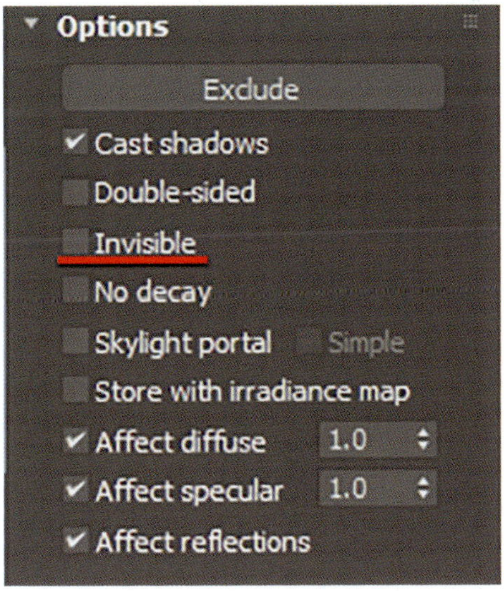

Invisible option disabled

Render result of Invisible option disabled

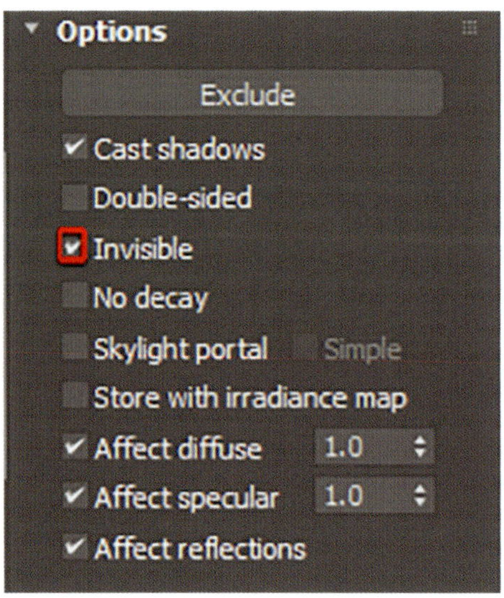

Invisible option enabled

Render result of Invisible option enabled

No decay: When turned on, this function allows the light to travel infinitely without decaying/dimming, from its emitter/source.

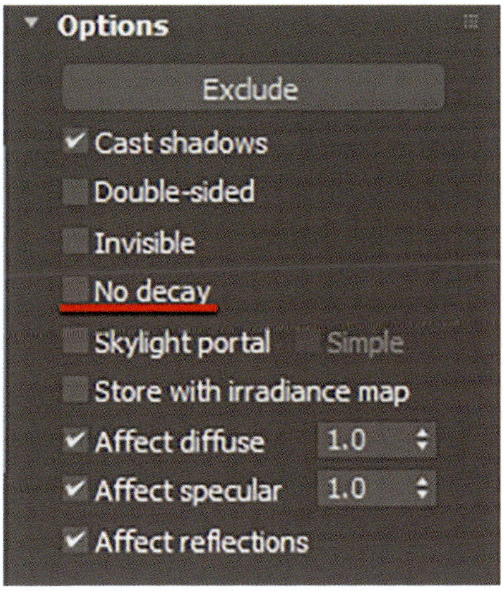

No decay option disabled

Render result of No decay option disabled

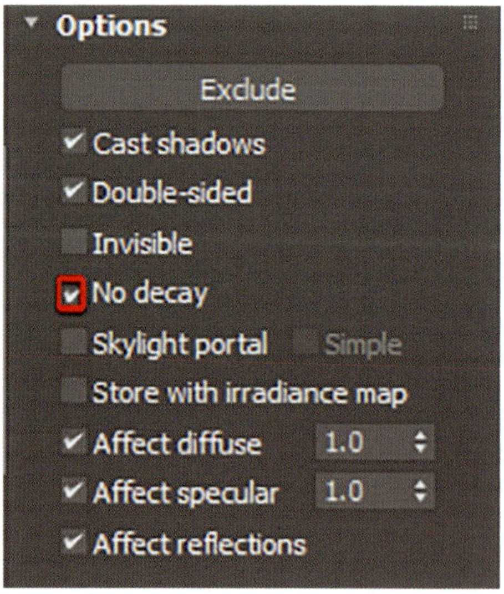

No decay option enabled

Render result of No decay option enabled

Skylight portal: When on, this function uses the environment intensity, to cast light and shadows. Disabled, by default.

Simple: It livens up when the Sky portal option is enabled. When on, it computes the sky portal lighting much quicker.

Store with irradiance map: When enabled, this function caches these light effects and stores them in the irradiance map (if enabled).

While this process saves the pre-calculation time, the shadows will be less accurate.

This option is widely used to correct light artifacts from Dome light or VRay mesh light (e.g., graininess and/or splotches).

Disabled, by default.

- **Affect diffuse**: This function allows this light source to affect the diffuse object. Enabled, by default.
- **Affect specular**: It enables this light source to affect the specular/glossiness of objects. Enabled, by default.
- **Affect reflections**: This option allows the light object/shape to be visible on reflections. Enabled, by default.

Sampling

Shadow bias: This function controls the position of the shadows. Low values bring shadows close to the object/s. High values do the opposite.

Default value, 0.02 mm.

Cutoff: This function controls the light distance/reach (and therefore its intensity). The lower the light distance, the quicker its render computation.

Default value, 0.001.

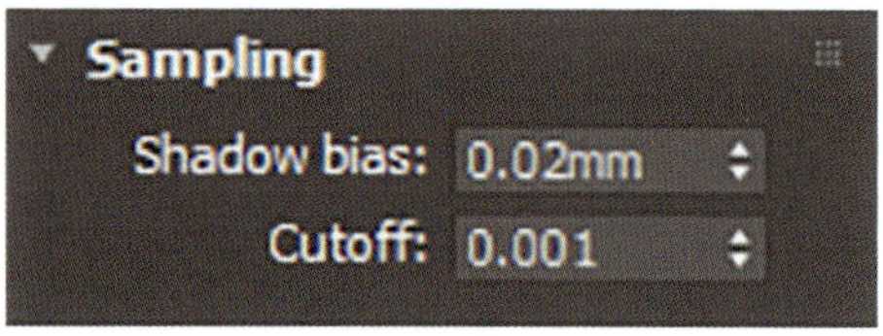

Sampling group parameters

Viewport

Enable viewport shading: When turned on, the light effects will be seen in the shaded viewport (Not wireframe).

Enabled, by default.

Viewport wire color: If enabled, it allows users to choose a wire color for the light object.

To change the default color, simply click on its color swatch to bring up the Color Selector dialog.

Default color, yellow.

Disabled, by default.

Icon text: This function enables the light name (text) in the viewport.

Disabled, by default.

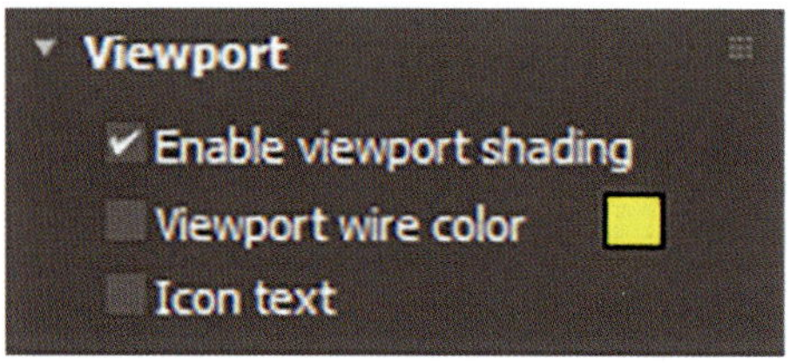

Viewport group parameters

Advanced Options

Use MIS: This function (Multiple Importance Sampling) uses direct and indirect lighting to compute its contribution.

Enabled, by default.

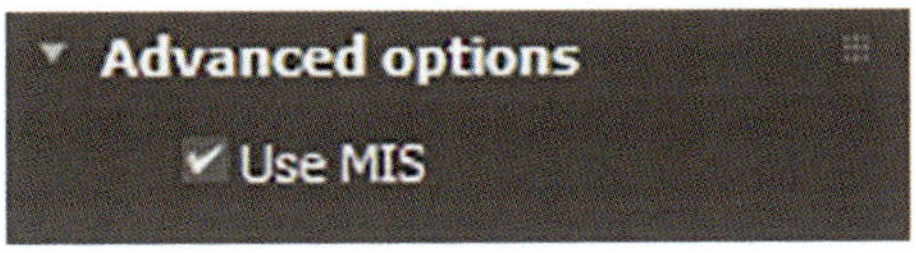

Advanced options group parameters

Dome Light

When chosen, it automatically emulates the effect of diffused environment light and shadows. This effect is independent from the dome light location in the scene.

It is worth noting that VRaySky has a similar effect.

For this reason, when a Dome light is chosen, the environment light is doubled up, if the VRaySky is being used.

NOTE

Dome light works best in open spaces.

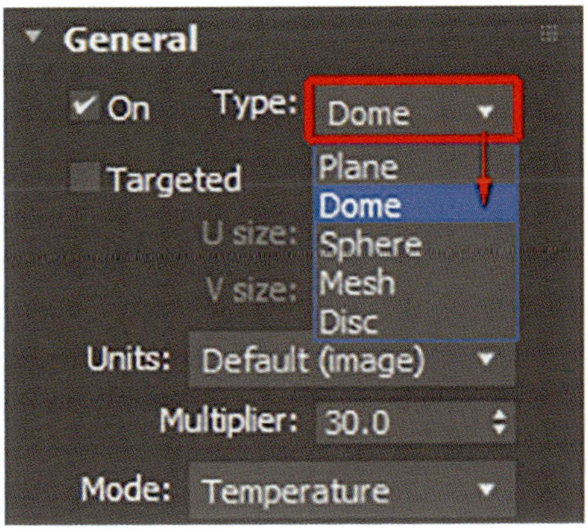

Dome light chosen from General group Type

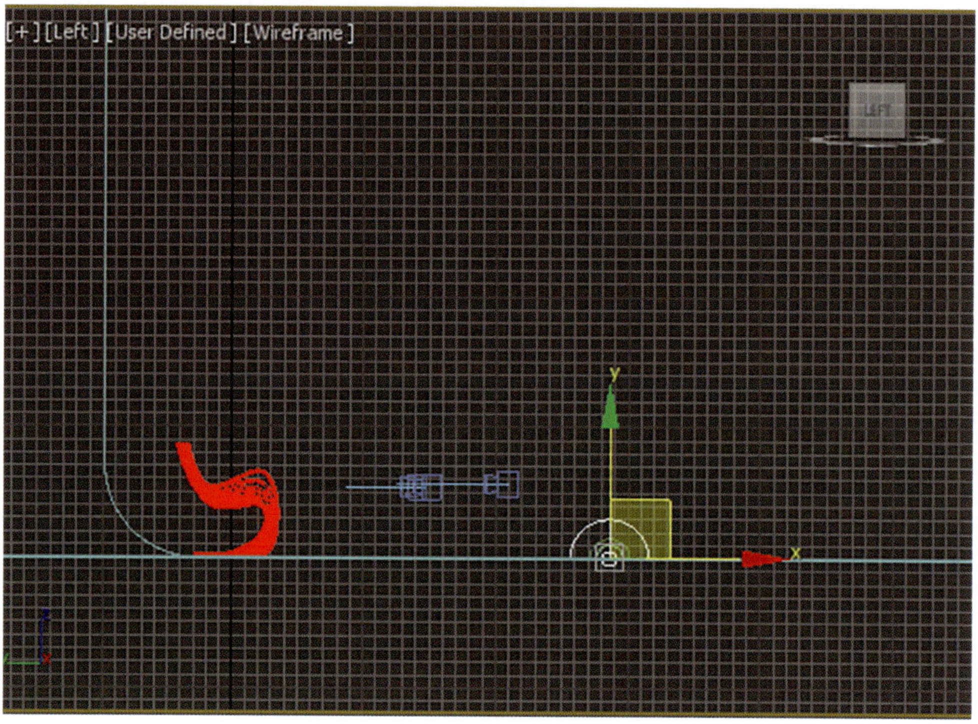

Dome light object in the viewport

Texture: This toggle is used to plug an HDRI via VRayBitmap, as previously shown.

Users often plug HDRI of a sky with sunlight to emulate both direct and indirect lighting.

HDRI only casts direct shadows if the image is sharp; as opposed to blurred.

Also, to cast direct shadows, the HDRI needs to have a very bright spot (sun-lit exterior HDRI).

Or bright spots emulating artificial lights.

NOTE

The Texture function needs to be enabled.

HDRI with sky and the sun

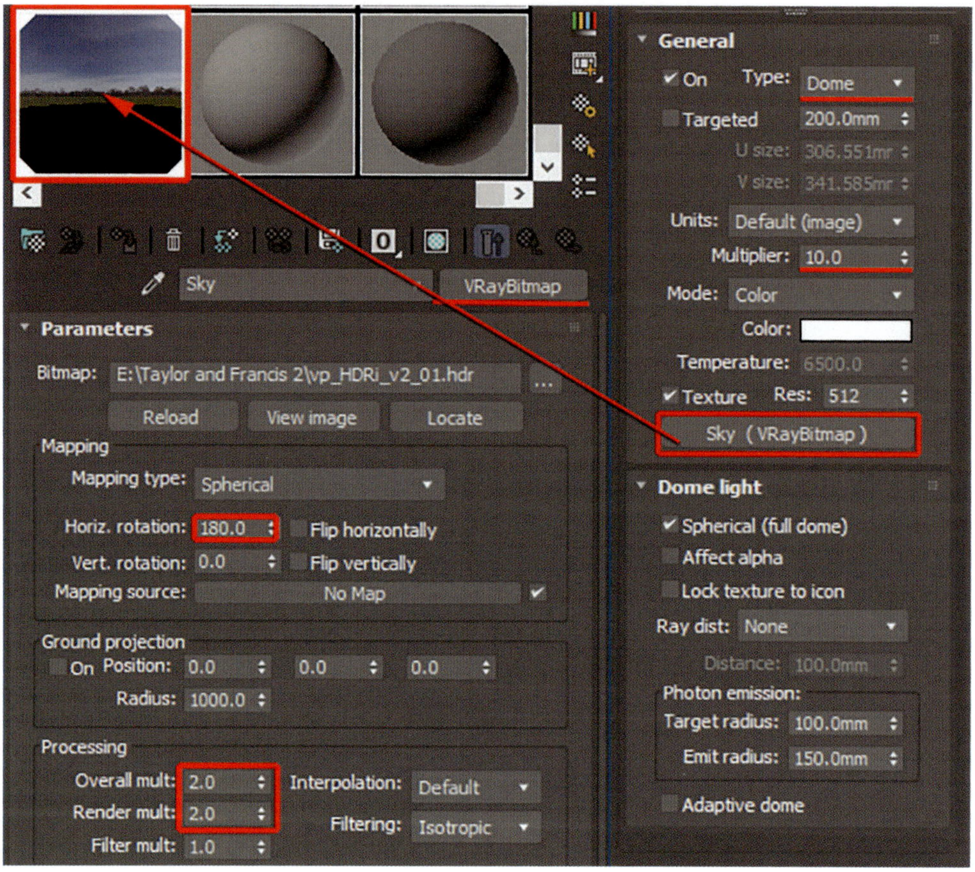

VRayBitmap parameters with an HDRI sky/ sun opened in the Material slot

Render result of HDRI with sky and the sun render

Alternatively, users can plug HDRI of a cloudy sky to emulate diffused shadows. And create a separate VRaySun object for the direct light.

This will provide users with the flexibility to control both light sources separately.

When lighting a scene with an HDRI, it is recommended that users disable the VRaySky in the Environment Map toggle (8).

VRaySky has a similar dynamic range to HDRI. In addition, the dome light Multiplier value shouldn't be set too high, to prevent overexposing the scene.

Dome Light

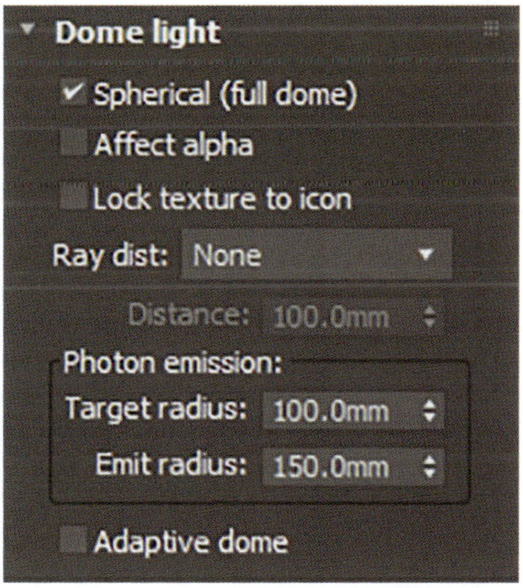

Dome light group parameters

Spherical (full dome): This function applies the lighting spherically (full dome). Otherwise hemispherical (if the spherical function is disabled).

Enabled, by default.

Affect alpha: When enabled, the dome color or image (HDR) wrapped around the dome will be displayed as a solid render element (White). As opposed to Alpha (Black).

Disabled, by default.

Render elements such as alpha channels will be covered in more detail in the chapters ahead.

Lock texture to icon: When enabled, it locks/links the dome color/HDRI to the dome object in the scene.

So when the dome object is rotated in the scene, the color/HDRI will also be rotated automatically.

Disabled, by default.

The Invisible function needs to be disabled in order for the Lock texture to work.

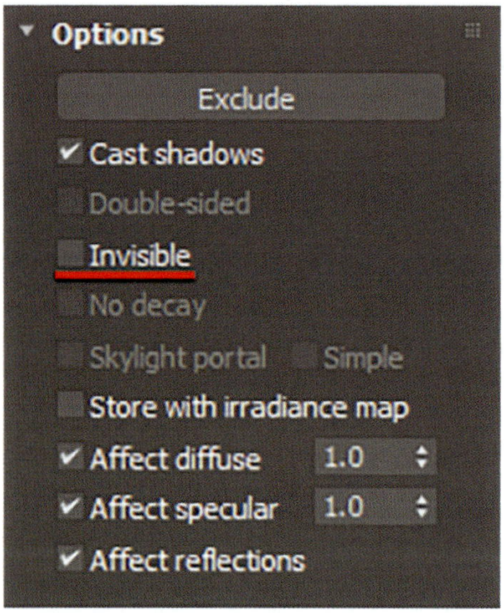

Invisible option disabled

Ray dist: It allows users to specify the maximum distance V-Ray will trace the shadows to.

None, by default.

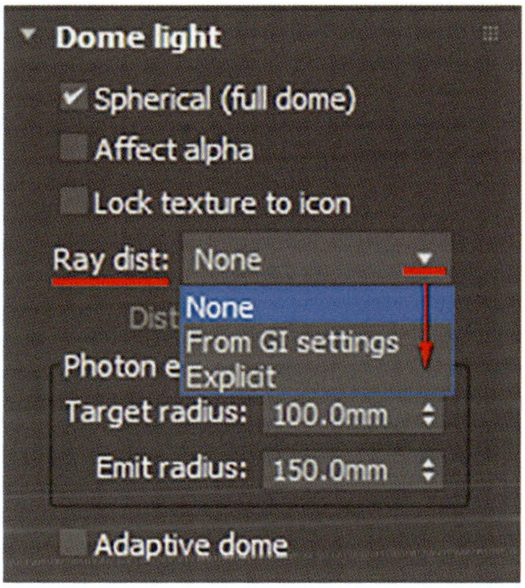

Ray distance options

From GI Settings: This option uses the Global illumination parameters to trace the shadows.

Explicit: This option allows users to specify the distance.

Default value, 100 mm.

Target radius: This function controls the photon emission radius. This icon is displayed in the viewport.

Default value, 100 mm

Emit radius: This function controls the photon emission radius. This icon is displayed in the viewport.

Default value, 150 mm

Adapt dome: When enabled, this function helps to reduce/eliminate the noise/grain often generated by the dome light.

Disabled, by default.

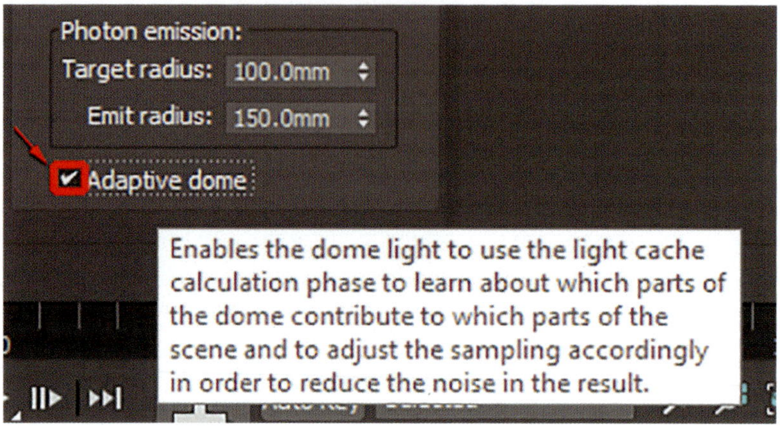

Adapt dome function enabled

VRay Sphere Light

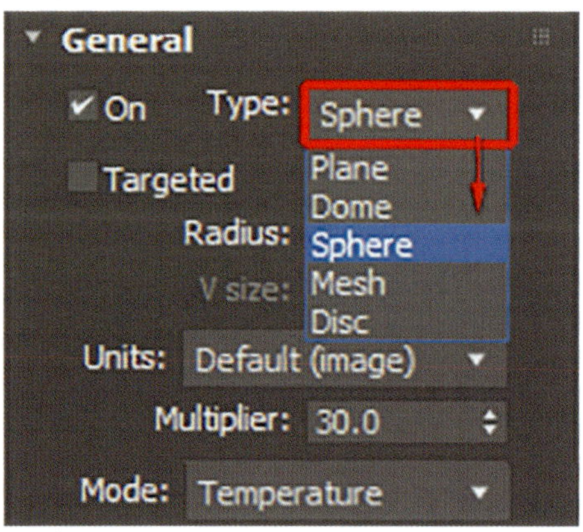

Sphere light chosen from General Type

This type of light becomes spherical when chosen. The light is emitted from all sides (spherically).

The intensity is based on the size of sphere Radius.

A bigger sphere Radius results in softer shadows.

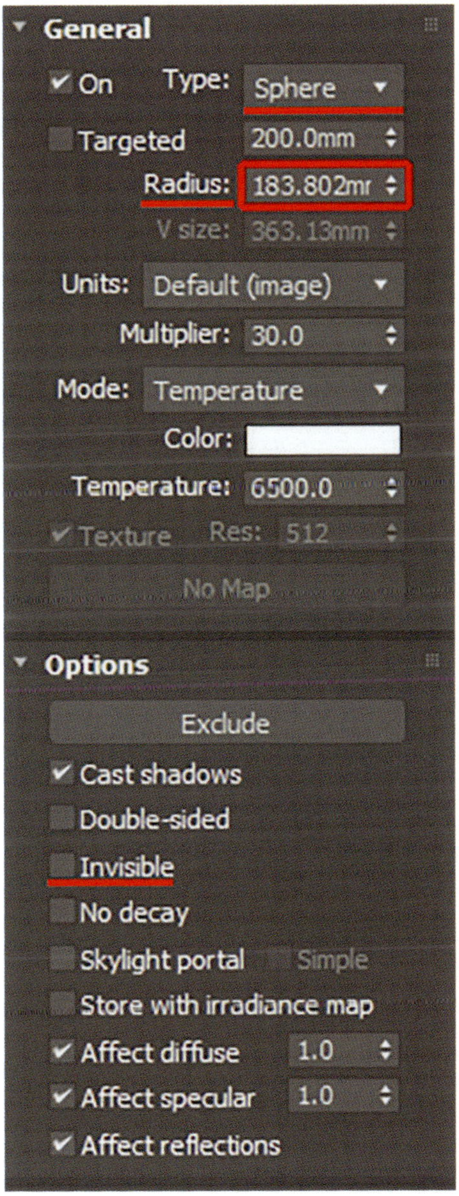

Sphere light Options parameters

Sphere light options render

VRay Mesh Light

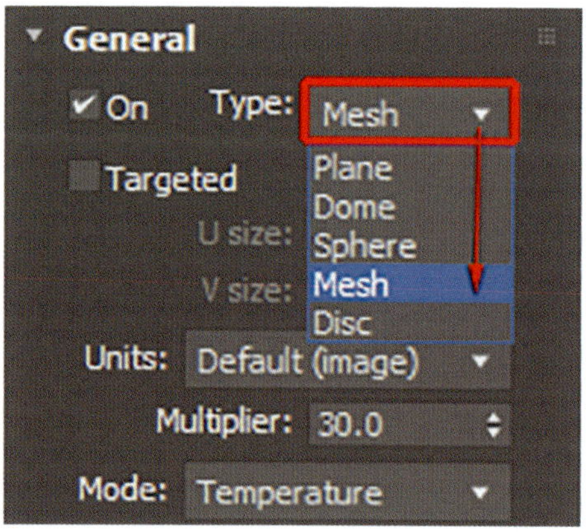

Mesh light chosen

NOTE

To pick a mesh, simply unhide the geometry named, Torus Knot001.

When a Mesh light type is chosen, the mesh light options group becomes available.

The Pick mesh toggle allows users to pick any mesh/geometry in the scene, to be used as a light emitter.

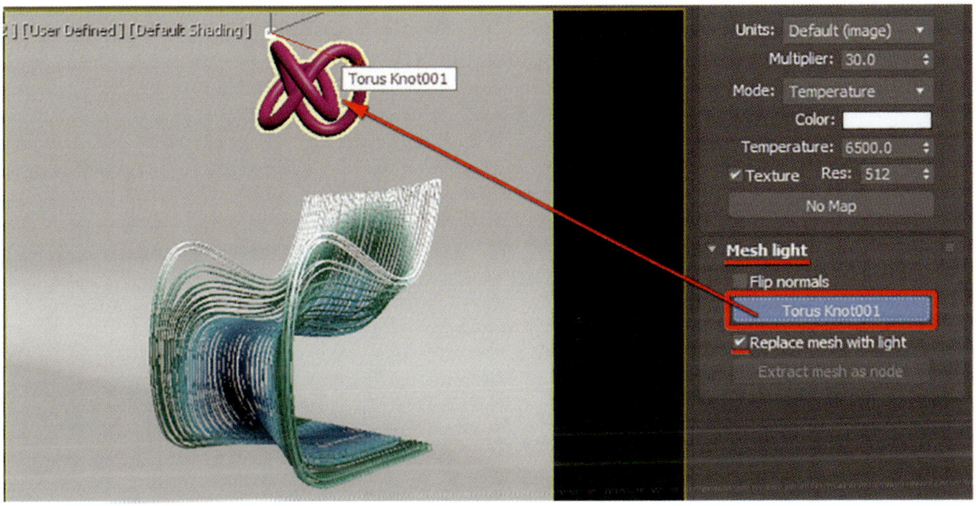

Pick a mesh/geometry in the scene

Once the mesh/geometry is picked, it is automatically transformed into a physical light source (if the Replace mesh with light option is enabled).

Also, the geometry/mesh is automatically added to the Modify stack.

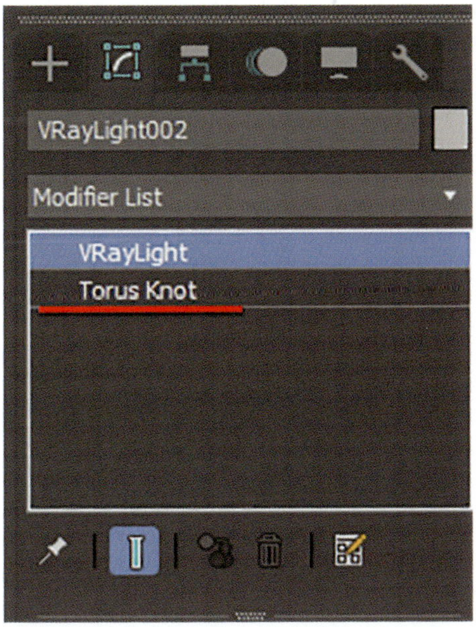

geometry/mesh automatically added to the Modify stack

Scene lit with a Mesh light render

Rendering a scene lit with a Mesh light can be time-consuming to render.

Also, it may yield grainy results, unless the Image Sampler Noise threshold value is low (0.07 or lower).

Extract mesh as node: This option allows users to extract the original mesh from the mesh light, by clicking on its button.

VRay Disc Light

When the Disc light type is chosen, the rectangle/disc light parameters group becomes available, along with the radius values.

The wider the radius, the softer the shadows.

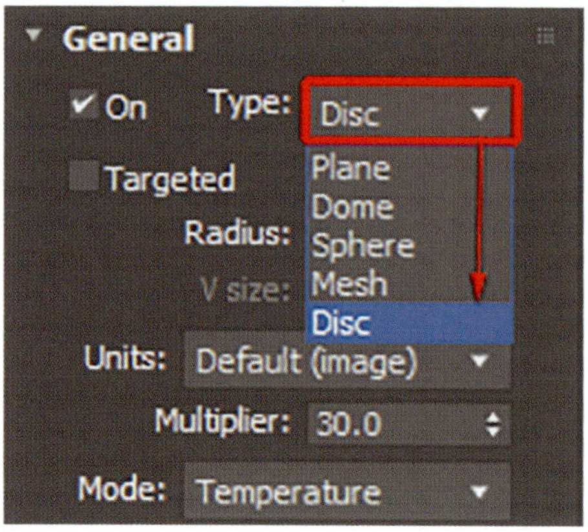

Disc light chosen

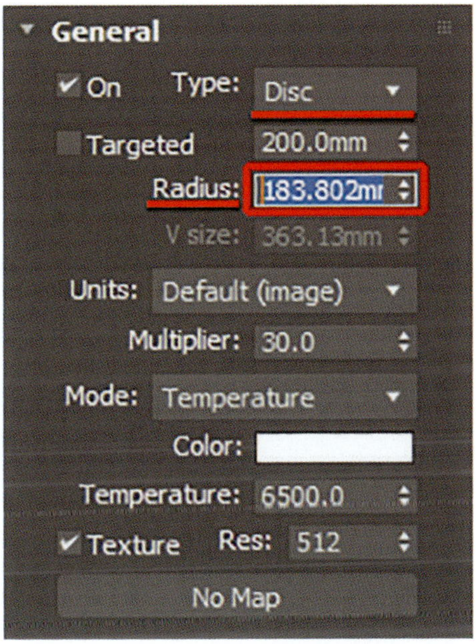

Disc light parameters

Disc light render

VRayIES

VRayIES lights are often used to recreate existing artificial light profile distributions, for interior scenes.

Companies such as ERCO and Color Kinetics have a host of exiting IES light profiles ready for download:

https://www.erco.com/download/en/

https://www.colorkinetics.com/global/support/ies

To create a VRayIES light, use some of the steps described earlier, followed by selecting the VRayIES button, clicking the cursor in the Front/Left viewport, and dragging it down to create it.

Right click to exit light creation

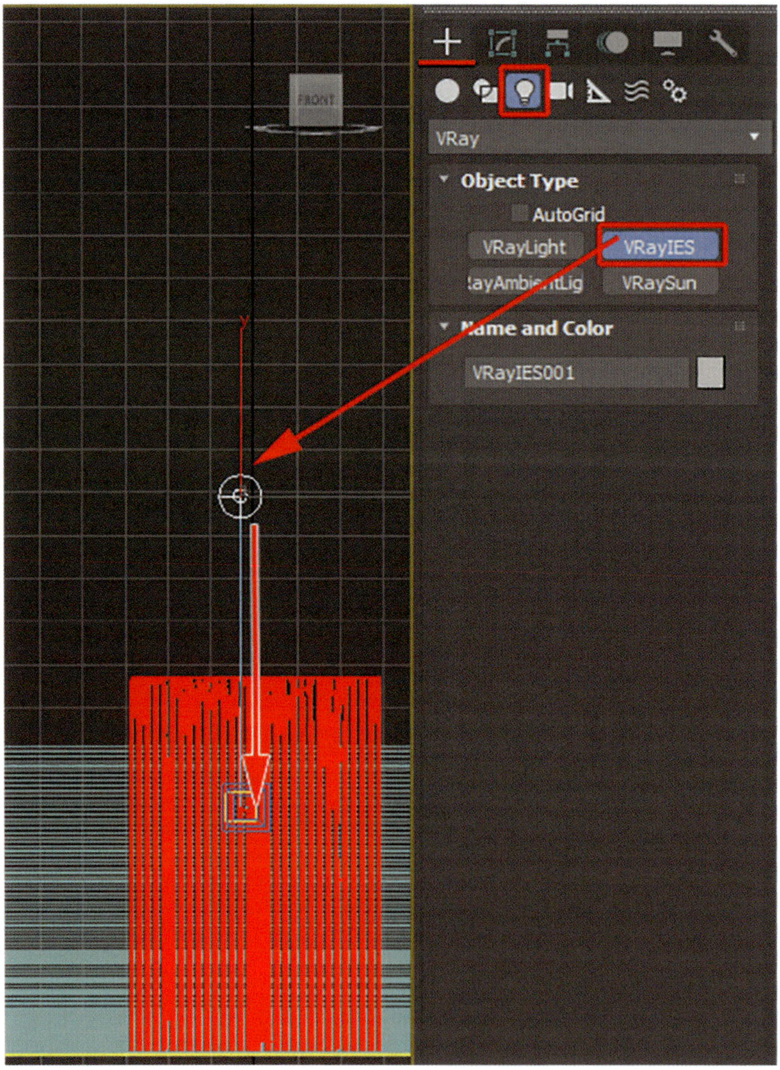

Creating a VRayIES light in the viewport

Once the VRayIES light has been created (with its target facing downwards), users can disable the Targeted function, to move the VRayIES light.

Most of the VRayIES parameters are self-explanatory. The following discussion will focus mainly on the most important ones.

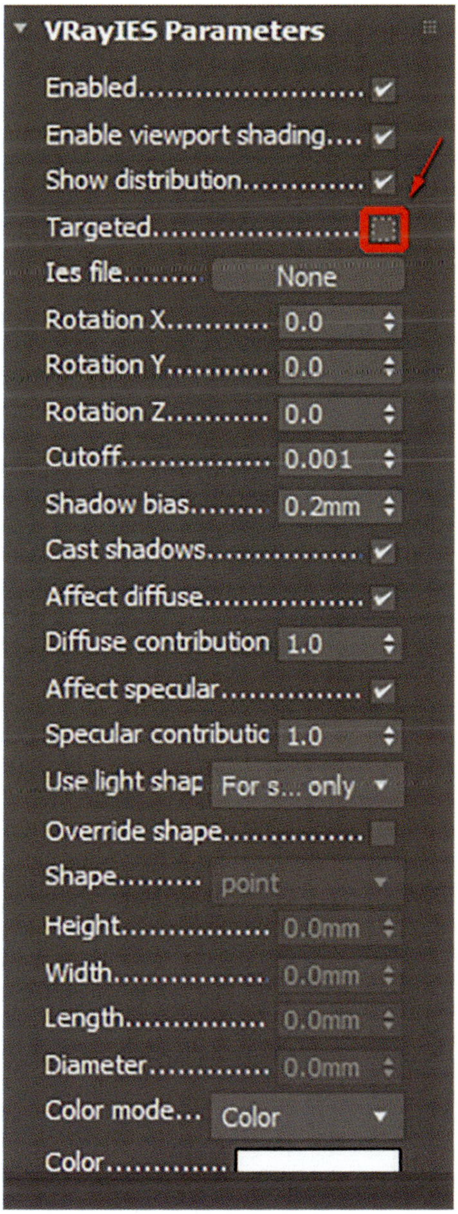

VRayIES light parameters

NOTE

IES 14 is included in the book resources.

Enable: It enables the light to be turned On or Off.

Show distribution: It shows the distribution of the IES light in the viewport.

IES file: This toggle allows users to locate and plug IES light profile.

IES web profiles are based on a real-world light distribution. IES 14 is one of the most popular light profiles used to create patterns of pools of light on the floor and walls.

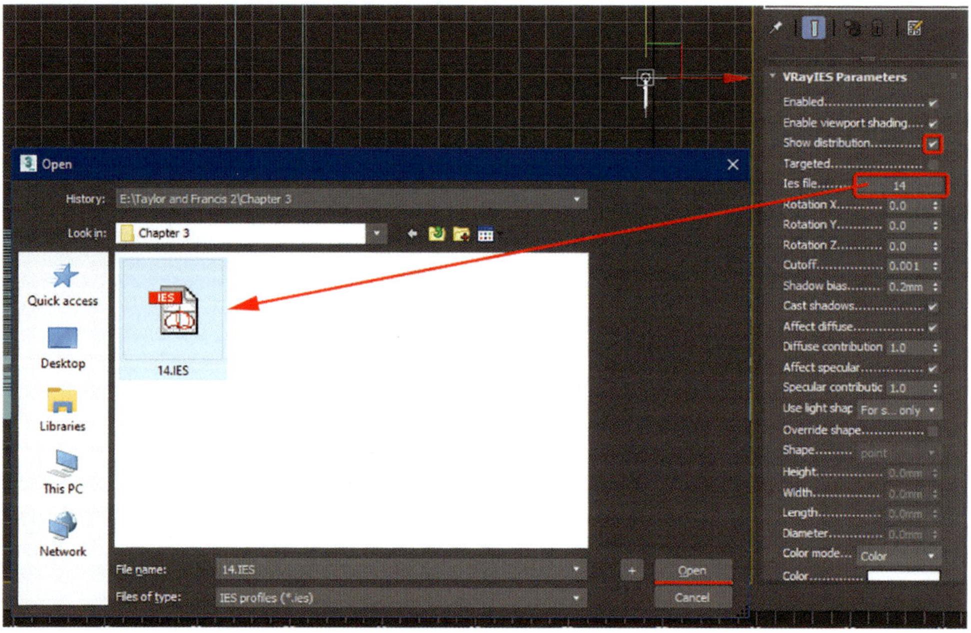

IES web file 14 loaded from dialog

To preview the IES distribution in the shaded viewport, simply click on the User Defined text, and choose the Light and Shadows option, followed by choosing to, Illuminate with scene Lights.

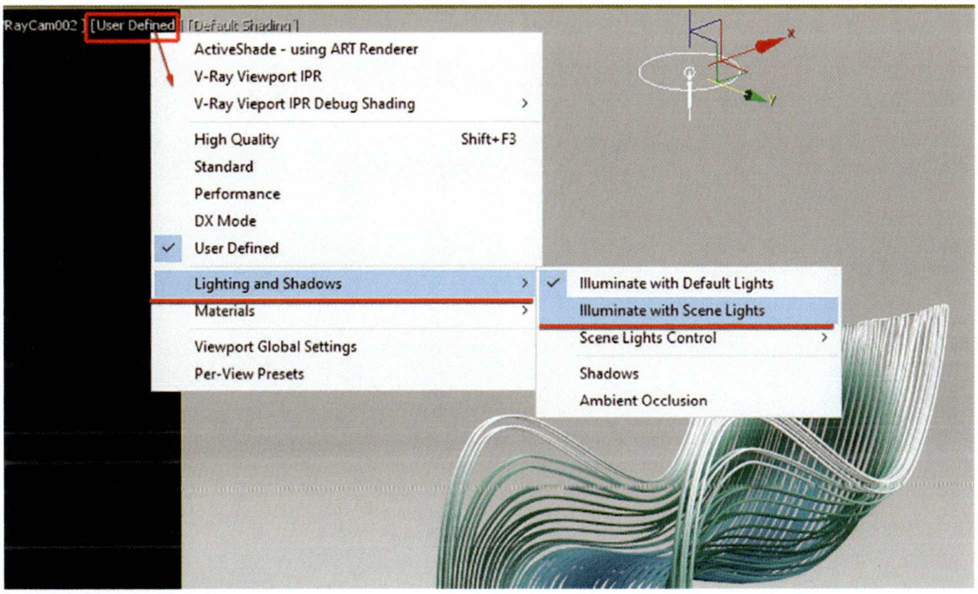

User viewport option to Illuminate with scene Lights

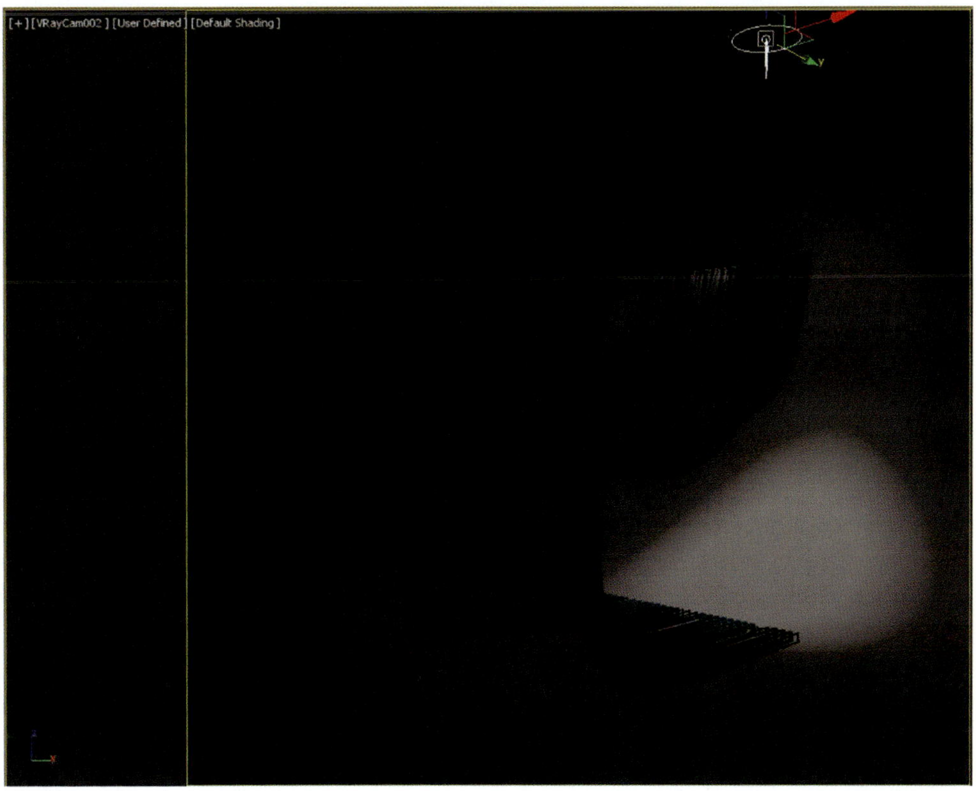

Results of Illuminate with scene Lights in the viewport

If you happen to have a good graphics card, enable the V-Ray Viewport IPR (Interactive Production Rendering) to display a fast and accurate preview of the final render in the viewport.

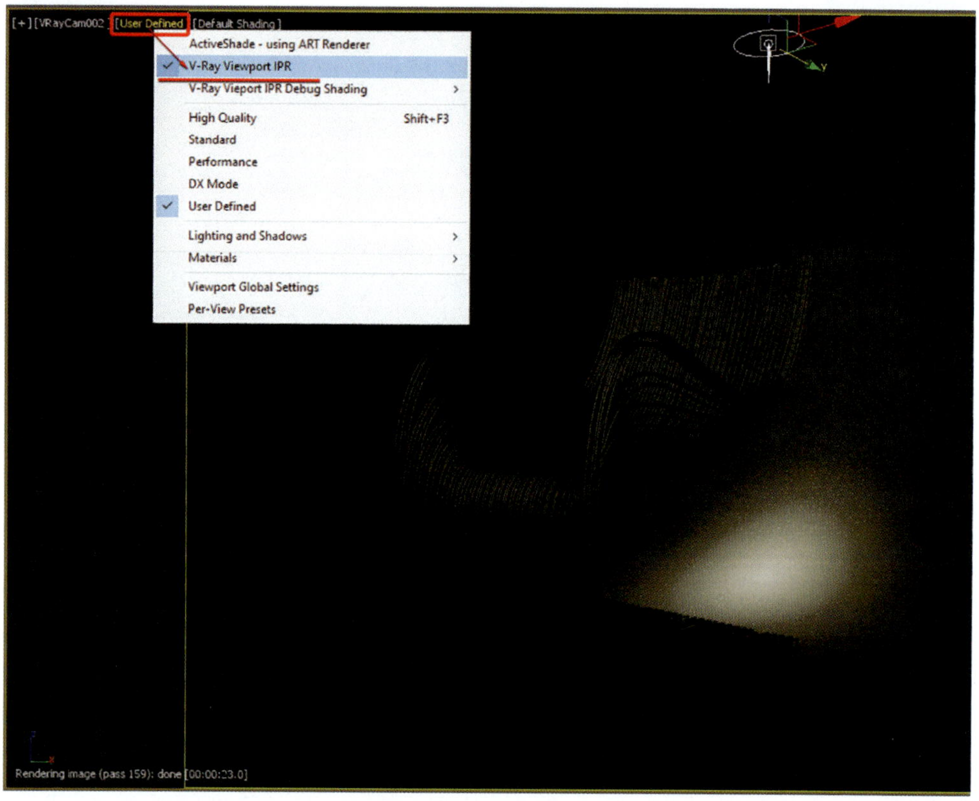

User viewport option to choose the V-Ray Viewport IPR

Affect diffuse: This function determines whether the IES light will affect the diffuse color of objects, or not.

Enabled, by default.

Diffuse contribution: This function controls the intensity of the lights on the diffuse color of objects.

Default value, 1.0

Affect specular: This function determines whether the IES light will affect the specular/glossiness of objects, or not.

Enabled, by default.

Specular contribution: This function controls how much the IES light will affect the specular/glossiness of objects.

Default value, 1.0

Use light shape: This function controls how the shape of the light will be factored in to process the shadows and the illumination.

For shadows only, is used by default.

Override shape: If chosen, it disables the IES profile shape and enables functions such as Shape, Height, Width, Length and Diameter.

Override Intensity: This function controls how the IES light intensity will be used.

Rescale: This function matches the light intensity defined by the user.

Replace: This function recalculates (multiplies) the intensity based on the IES distribution.

Intensity type: This function determines the units of light intensity.

Intensity value: This function controls the intensity of the IES light.

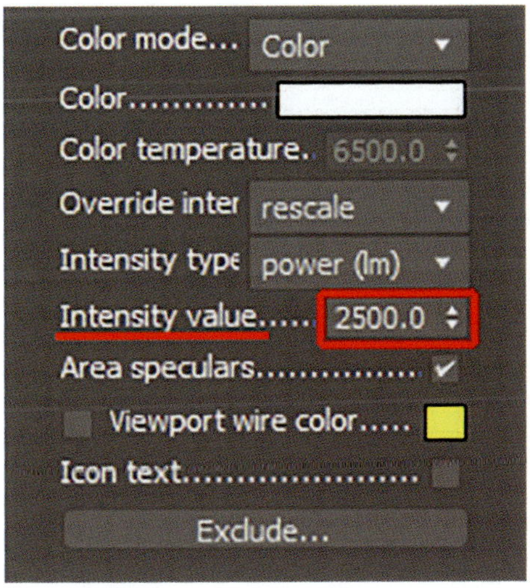

VRayIES light Intensity value set to 2500.0

Render result of Intensity value set to 2500.0

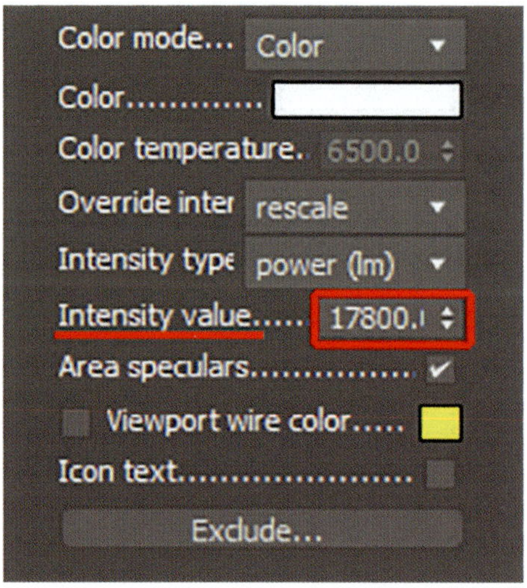

Intensity value IES power set to 17800.0

Render result of Intensity value set to 17800.0

VRaySun

The VRaySun emulates the physical properties of real sunlight.

It is always best to have all four viewports in display (Top, Right, Left, Camera/ Perspective) before creating the VRaySun object.

This will help control its position and placement in the scene.

When the VRaySun is created, a dialog to automatically add a VRaySky in the environment map is prompted.

If there's already a Bitmap, you'll be asked to Replace it, if desired.

The VRaySky works like an HDRI for diffused lighting and shadows.

The intensity of the VRaySky and VRaySun vary, depending on the sun's position.

NOTE

To test some of the VRaySun parameters discussed here, simply open the 3ds max scene named, VRay Sun. max.

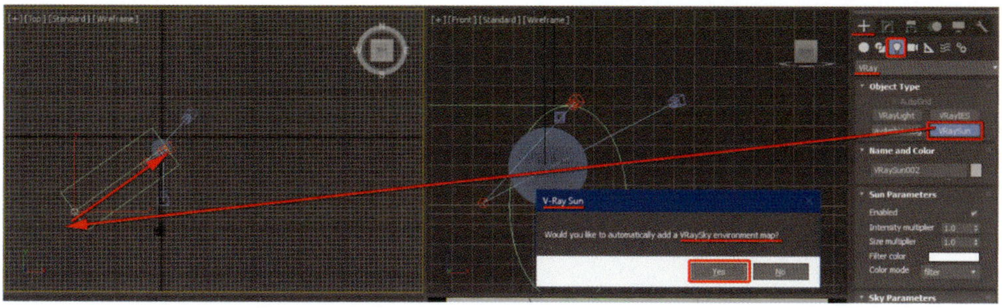

Creating the VRaySun in the viewport with dialog to add VRaySky environment map

Also, use the Load layer tree preset named, VRay Sun.vfbl, with the Lookup Table file named, 3DCollective_sRGB_Agfa_Futura_03Hard.cube.

Move the VRaySun object up to a position where shadows are cast across the camera.

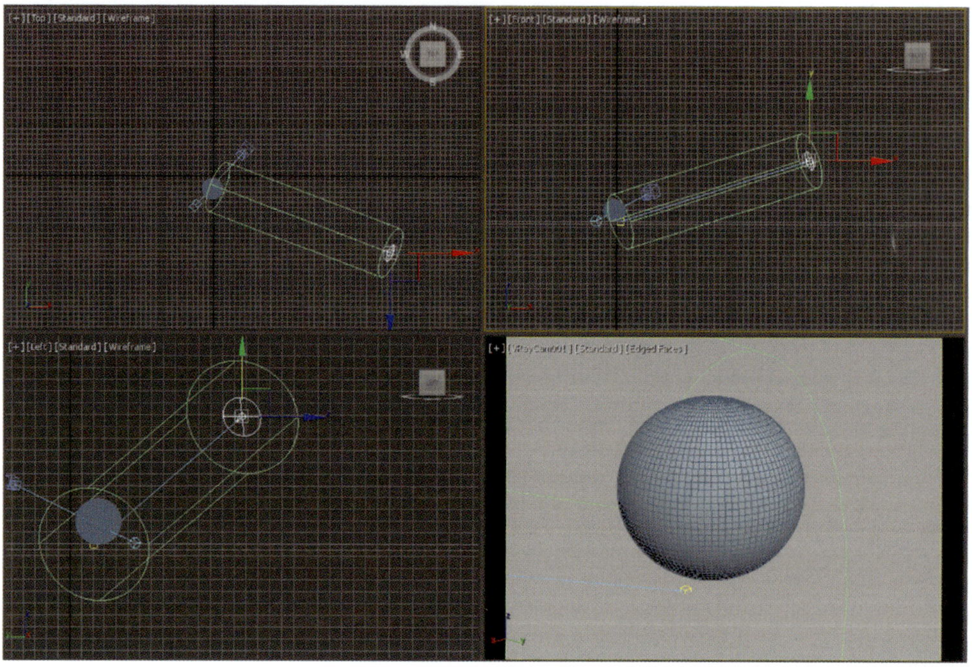

Position the VRaySun object in the viewport

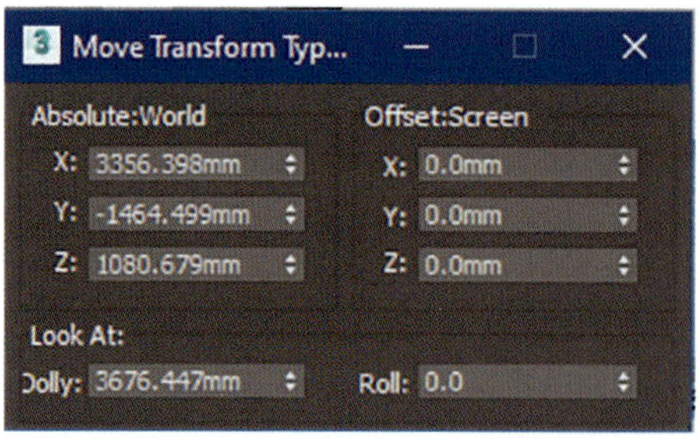

VRaySun Move dialog position values in the viewport

VRaySun Modify parameters

VRaySun rendered

Sun Parameters

Enabled: This function turns the VRaySun On or Off

Intensity multiplier: This function controls the intensity of the sun.

Default value, 1.0.

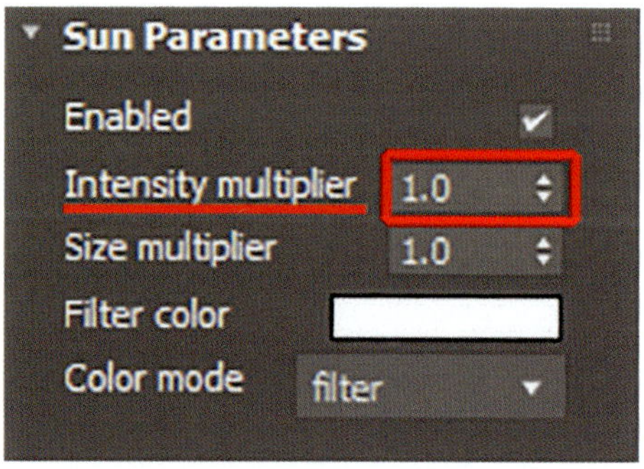

Intensity multiplier set to 1.0

Render result of Intensity multiplier set to 1.0

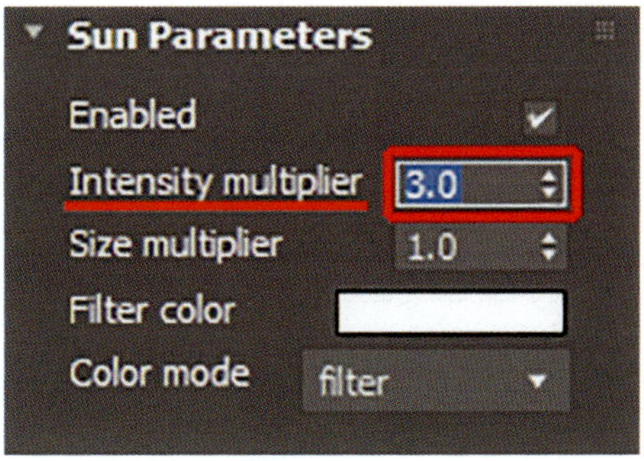

Intensity multiplier set to 3.0

Render result of Intensity multiplier set to 3.0

Size multiplier: This option controls the size of the sun in the VRaySky (it is visible on reflections).

The bigger the Size multiplier, the softer the shadows will be.

Filter color: This function controls the color of the VRaySun.

As the VRaySun object is moved downward, the default color changes automatically.

White, by default.

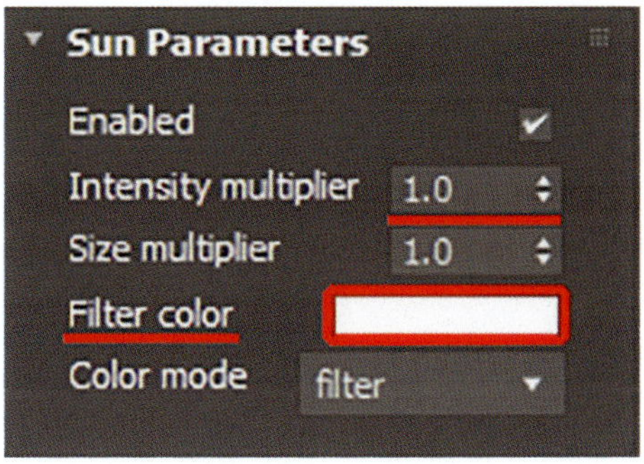

VRaySun default Filter color white

Render result of VRaySun default Filter color white

Filter color automatically changed with the sun sunset moved down

Color mode: This function controls how the VRaySun is affected by Filter color.

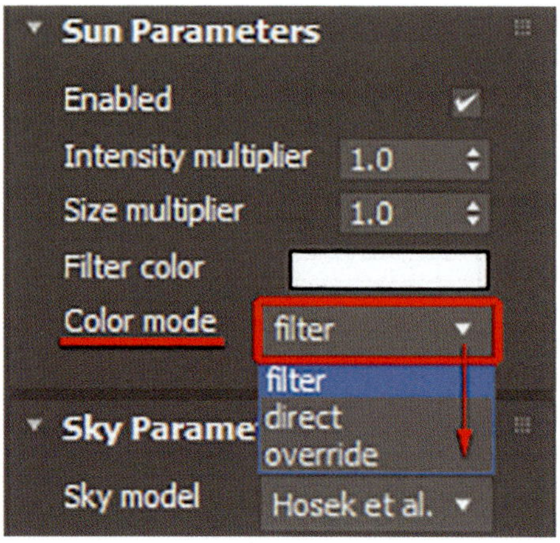

Color mode options

Filter: This option uses the color specified in the Filter color function.

Direct: This option uses the VRaySun color to coincide with the filter color. The intensity of the VRaySun is automatically controlled by the Intensity multiplier function.

Override: This option uses the VRaySun to coincide with the filter color. The intensity of the VRaySun is controlled by its position

Sky Parameters

Sky model: This function allows users to choose a specific sky model, from its dropdown menu. This sky model is directly connected to the VRaySky.

Note: Always use the Improved Sky model type, as it uses a more photorealistic and sophisticated Sky.

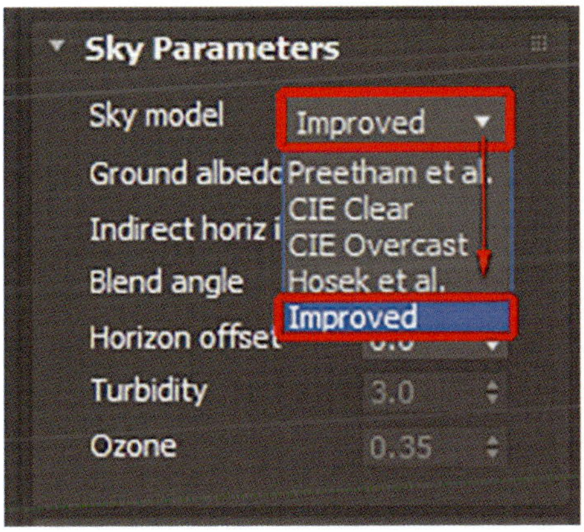

Sky model options

Ground albedo: This function controls the color of the ground (below the horizon line).

Indirect horiz illum: This function controls the indirect illumination on horizontal surfaces, generated by the sky VRaySky.

Blend angle: This function controls the size of the gradient seen in the VRaySky.

Horizon offset: This function allows users to offset the default horizon position.

Turbidity: It controls the color of the sky and the sun. Lower values yield bluer/clear skies; while higher values produce yellowy/orangey skies.

Ozone: This function controls mainly the color of the sunlight. Higher values yield bluer tones and lower values produce more yellowy hues.

Options

Exclude: This toggle allows users to choose specific objects in the scene to exclude from the effects of the VRaySun.

Invisible: This option controls the visibility of the VRaySun in the sky.

Visible, by default.

Affect diffuse: Allows the VRaySun to affect the diffuse color of objects in the scene.

Enabled, by default.

Affect specular: It enables the VRaySun to affect the specular/glossiness of objects in the scene.

Enabled, by default.

Cast atmospheric shadows: When enabled, atmospheric shadows will affect the scene.

Enabled, by default.

Sampling

Shadow bias: This function controls the position of the shadows. Lower values bring the shadows closer to object/s.

High values yield the opposite effect.

Default value, 2.0 mm.

Values higher than 5 mm may result in shadow artifacts.

Photon emit radius: It sets the radius/perimeter of the photon areas (seen in the viewport).

Users often increase it big enough to encapsulate the area seen by the camera.

V-Ray Light Lister

This amazing function (dialog) allows users to control the functionality of all V-Ray lights in the scene.

Some of these functionalities include the ability to rename lights, select lights, change light Multiplier, Color, Temperature, Type, Units, etc.

To open its dialog, simply click on the Tools toolbar and choose the V-Ray Light Lister from the dropdown menu.

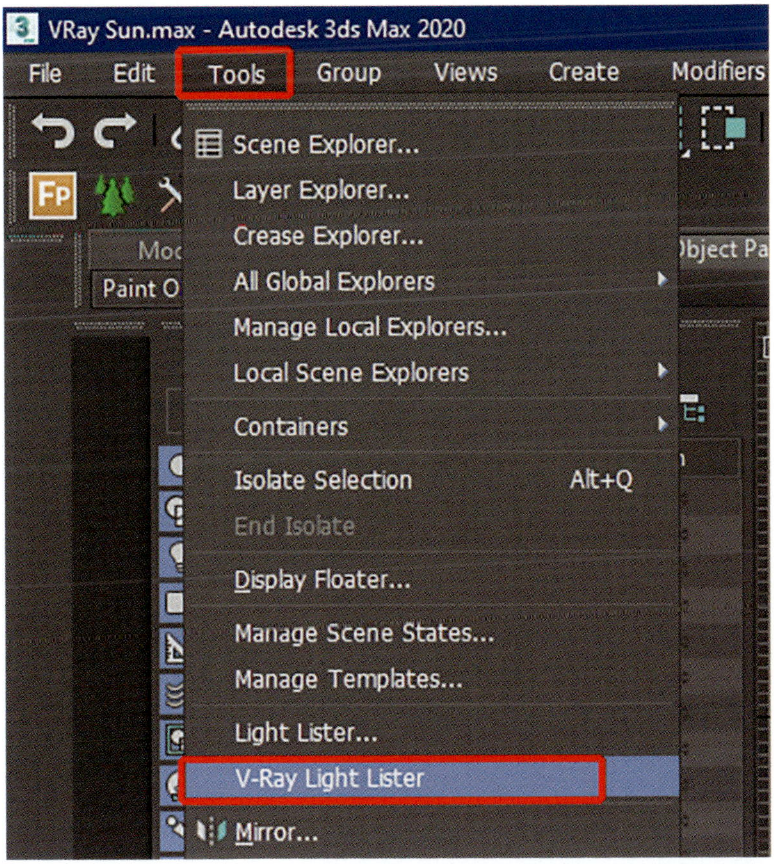

Tools clicked to open the Choose V-Ray Light Lister

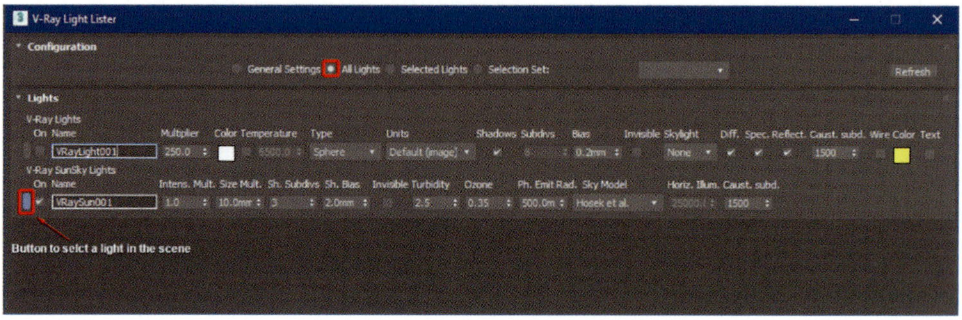

V-Ray Light Lister dialog

Daylight System

> **NOTE**
>
> To test some of the VRaySun parameters discussed here, simply open the 3ds max scene named, Daylight system.max.

The daylight system object allows users to accurately pick and choose the geographical location, movement, and angle of the sun around the earth.

Also, use the Load layer tree preset named, VRay Sun.vfbl, with the Lookup Table file named, 3DCollective_sRGB_Agfa_Futura_03Hard.cube.

To create it, ensure to have all four viewports on the display.

Open the Create main toolbar and choose the Standard mode, followed by selecting the Systems button.

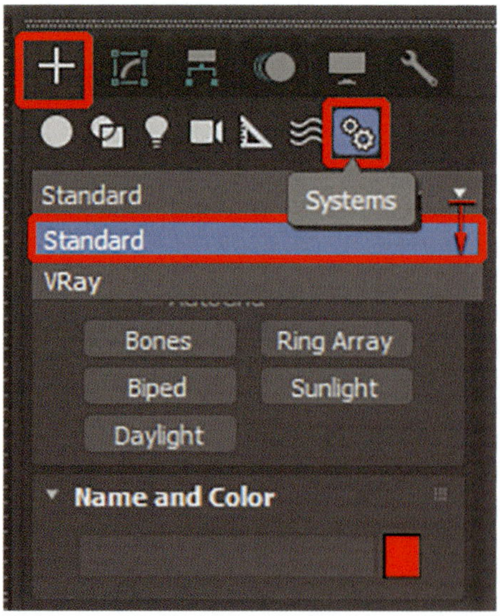

Standard System option chosen

Under the Systems Object type, select the Daylight button, followed by clicking and dragging its cursor in the Top viewport to create the compass and the sun object.

Release the left click and drag the mouse to begin setting the distance of the sun's head from the ground. Right click to exit creation.

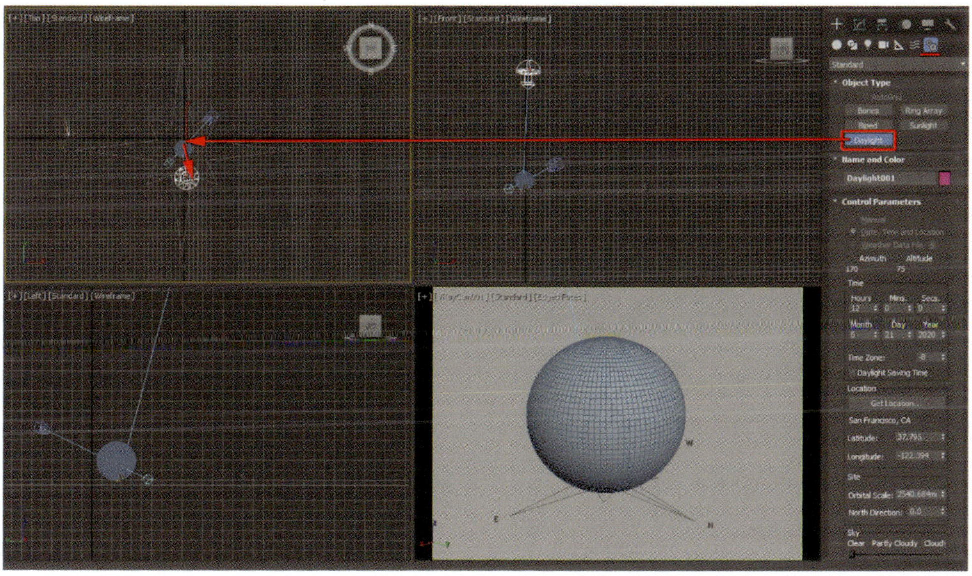

Creating the Daylight System object in the viewport

To load the VRaySun, simply open the Modify command panel.

In the Sunlight option, pick the VRaySun from its dropdown menu.

A dialog should be prompted, to automatically add a VRaySky in the Environment Map. Choose the Yes option.

VRaySun option chosen from Modify panel

Under Skylight, choose the No Skylight option.

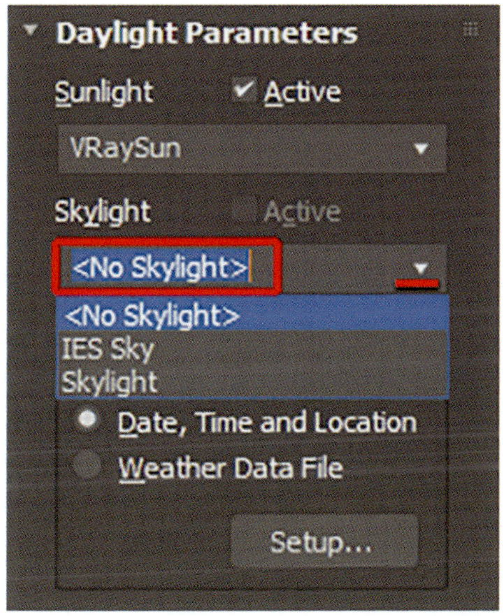

No Skylight option chosen

VRaySun already has the Skylight parameters discussed earlier.

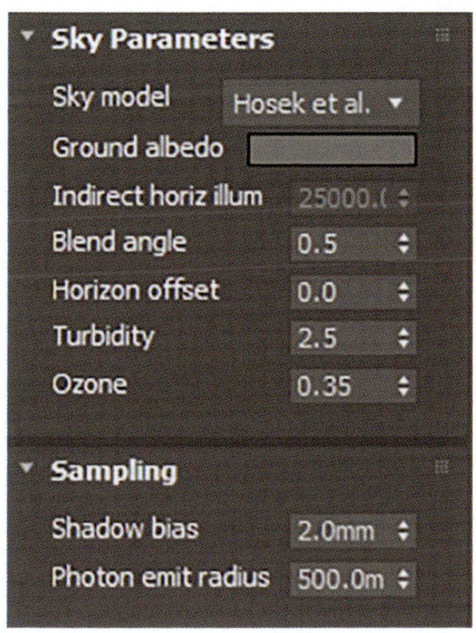

VRaySun Sky Parameters

To pick a location and set up the Time, simply click on the Setup button.

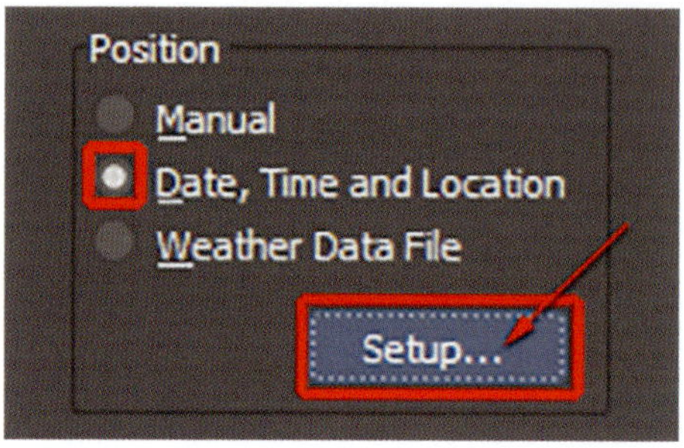

Date, Time, and Location Position Setup button

The Motion command panel should open automatically.

The Control Parameters allow users to set up the Year, Month, day, Hours, Minutes and Seconds, by typing in the relevant numerical values.

To find a location, simply click on the Get Location toggle, to bring up its dialog.

The Map area allows users to pick a location by clicking on it. Or by selecting a continent from the Map dropdown menu, and choosing a City from its list.

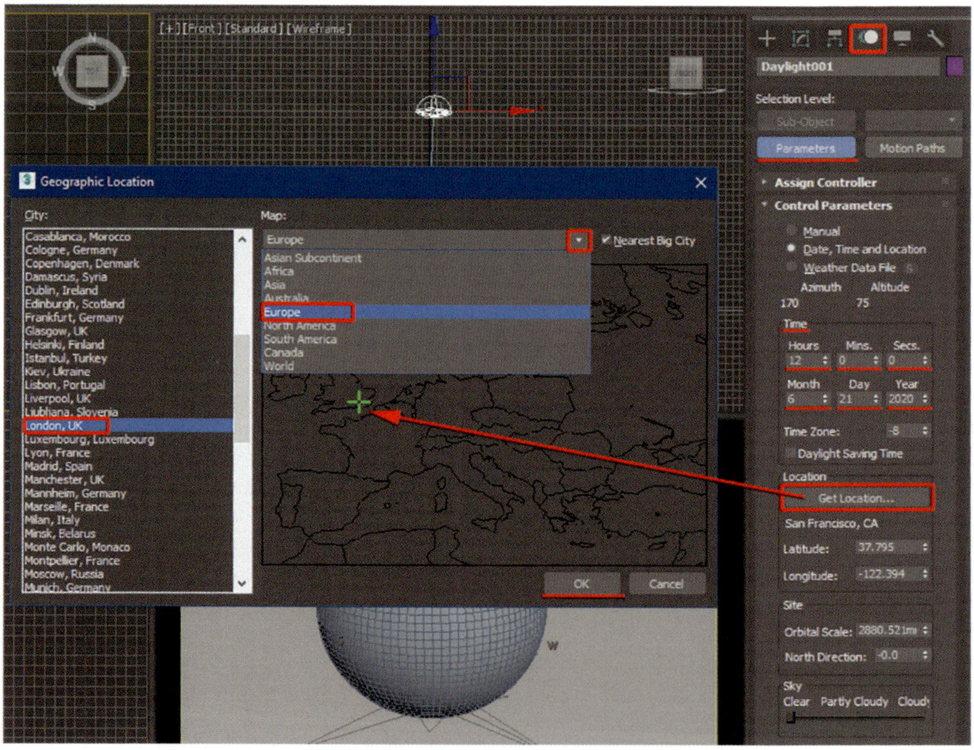

Location toggle clicked to choose a Geographic Location (City and Map)

The other parameters should NEVER be tweaked/adjusted when using the Daylight System for accuracy.

Geographic Location render

Conclusion

This chapter has taken users through the process of accessing and using V-Ray camera parameters, along with some of the most popular V-Ray lights.

Users were also introduced to the Daylight System, and shown how to fine-tune some its common parameters.

For more detailed information about V-Ray lights, Cameras, and other topics discussed here, please visit the Chaos group official website:

http://docs.chaosgroup.com/

4

Rendering in V-Ray

4 Rendering in V-Ray

In this chapter, users will be taken through key V-Ray render setup parameters such as Frame buffer, Global switches, Interactive Production Rendering (IPR) options, Image sampler (Antialiasing), Bucket image sampler, Progressive image sampler, Image filter, Global DMC, Environment, Color mapping, Global Illumination, Brute force GI, Light cache, Color management, Distributed rendering, System and Render elements.

In the V-Ray Frame Buffer section, users will have a full understanding of how the VFB new parameters work. A lot of emphasis will be put into functionalities such as Load image, Save all image channels to single file, Save all image channels to separate files, Save current channel, V-Ray image file format, Start interactive rendering, IPR Debug Shading, Render, Isolate Selected, Render History settings, Region Controls, Layers, Lens Effects, LightMix, Film tonemap, Hue/Saturation, Lookup Table and Stats.

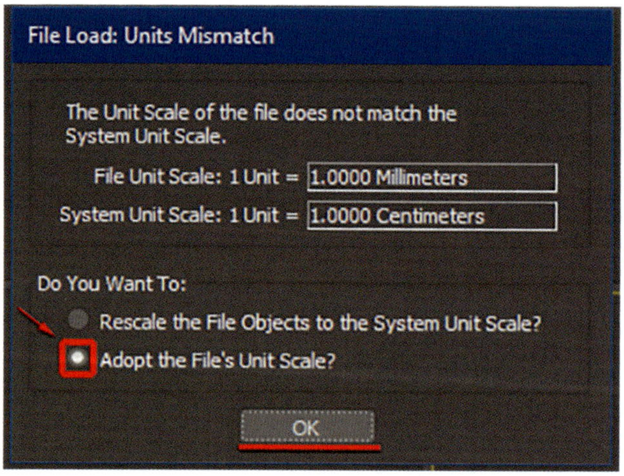

File Load dialog with Adopt the File's Unit Scale option chosen

To test some of the parameters being discussed in this chapter, please open the file under the name, Rendering in VRay.max.

If there's a File Load Mismatch, choose to Adopt the File's Unit Scale.

Render Setup: V-Ray

To open the Render Setup dialog, simply press F10 or click on its icon from the main toolbar.

Render Setup button

DOI: 10.1201/9781315770802-4

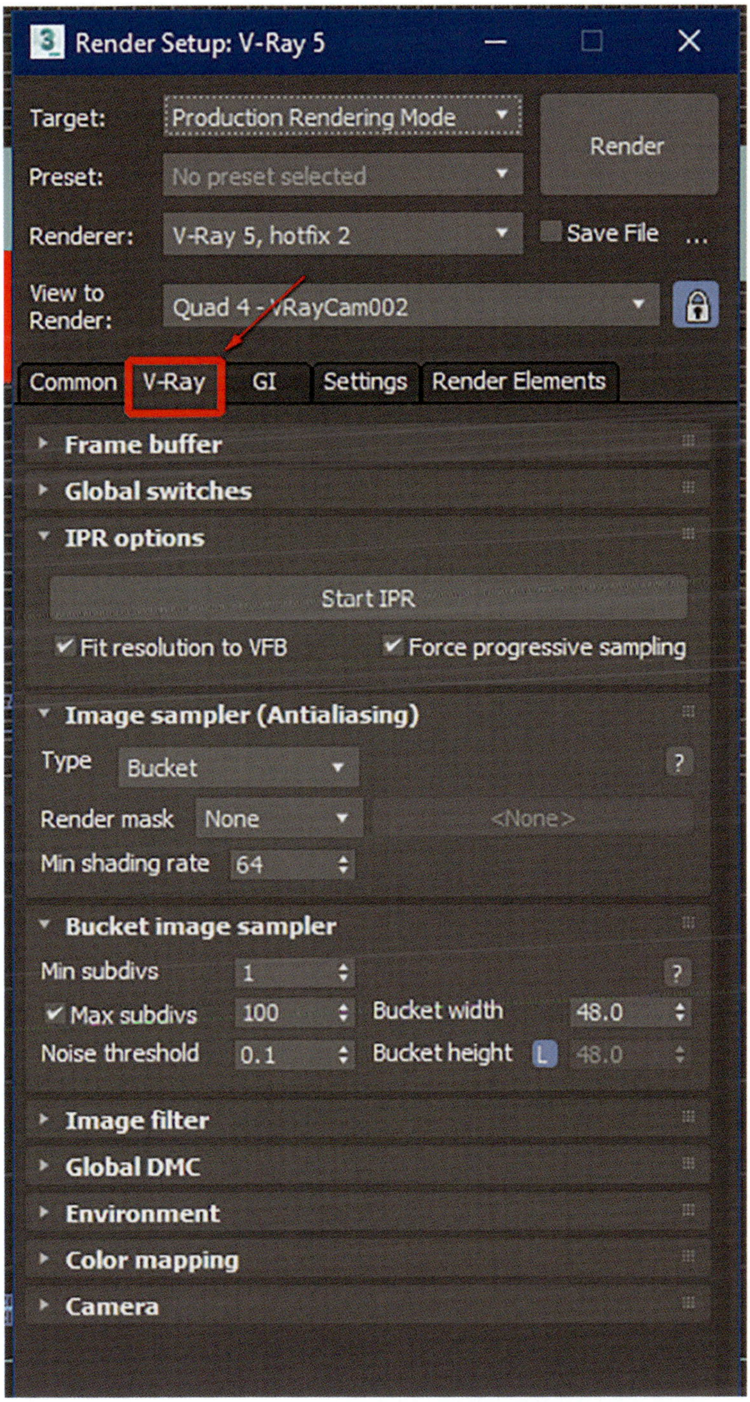

Render Setup dialog with V-Ray tab open

Under V-Ray tab, extend the Frame buffer rollout parameters.

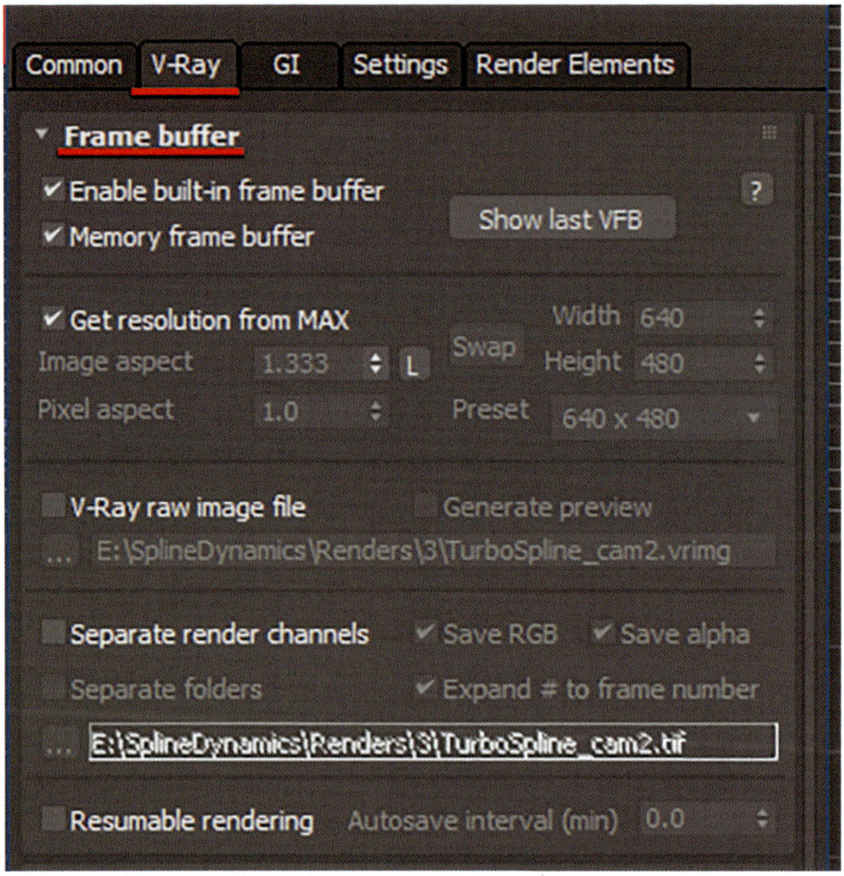

Frame buffer rollout parameters

Enable built-in frame buffer: This function uses the V-Ray frame buffer to render the scene. Enabled, by default.

Memory frame buffer: When enabled, this option saves/displays all the rendering data into the memory of the Frame buffer. The rendering data is what's viewed in the VRF (e.g., RGB, Alpha) while the rendering is taking place, and after the rendering is finished.

Enabled, by default.

Show last VFB: This toggle opens up the V-Ray frame buffer, by clicking on its button.

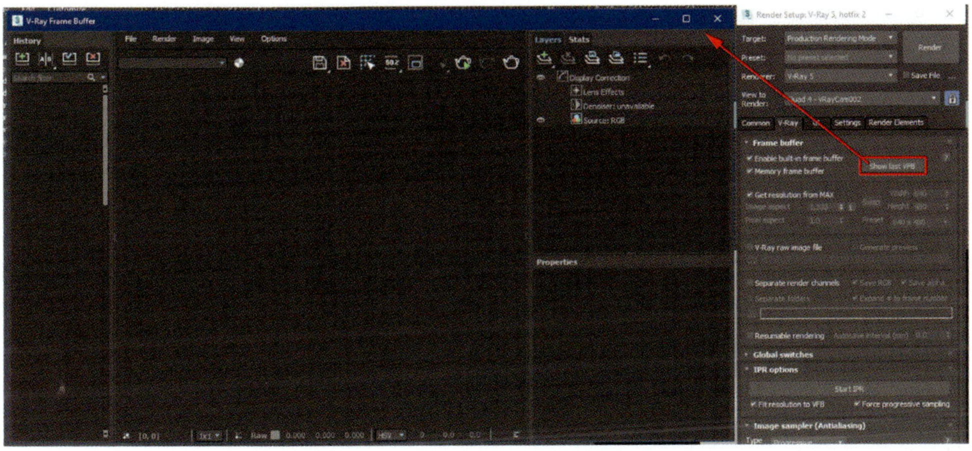

Show last VFB toggle clicked to open the V-Ray Frame Buffer dialog

The V-Ray frame buffer button can also be accessed from the main toolbar.

Show last VFB toolbar button

V-Ray Frame Buffer Parameters

File: Load Image: This button allows users to locate and load files into the VFB. Users can choose to load from any of the listed file types.

V-Ray image file (*.vrimg) is the most commonly used file.

V-Ray image file (*.vrimg) format is specific to V-Ray and typically big in size. It' is mainly because it contains key render data such as, render passes and render logs.

NOTE

For the purpose of this chapter, please load the V-Ray image file under the name, Rendering in VRay.0000.vrimg

4 Rendering in V-Ray

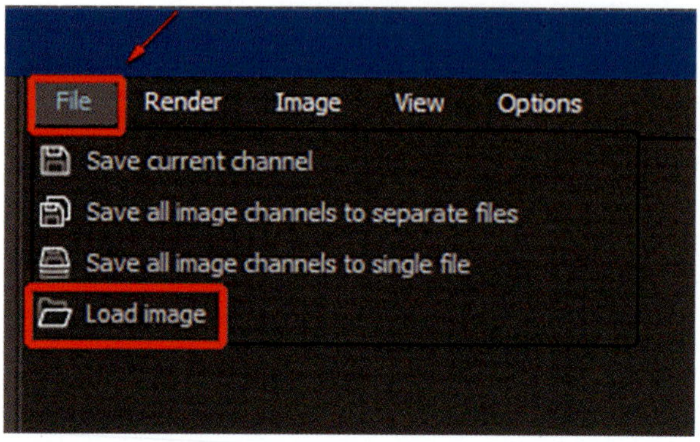

VFB File tab with Load Image option

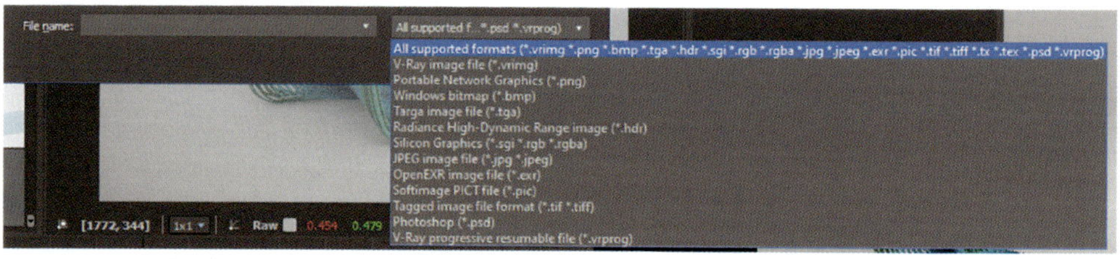

Load Image dialog with a list of all supported file formats

Once the V-Ray image file (*.vrimg) is loaded in the frame buffer, it allows users to save them out in a variety of file formats such as, exe and tiff.

Users can also utilize the V-Ray image file (*.vrimg) to continue rendering previously crashed files, region renders, render selected objects in the scene, and use Frame Buffer functionalities such as Lens Effects, LUT files, VFB L and Layers.

To create/generate V-Ray image files (*.vrimg), simply open the Render Setup dialog (F10).

In the V-Ray tab, under Frame buffer, enable and name the V-Ray raw image file function before rendering the final scene.

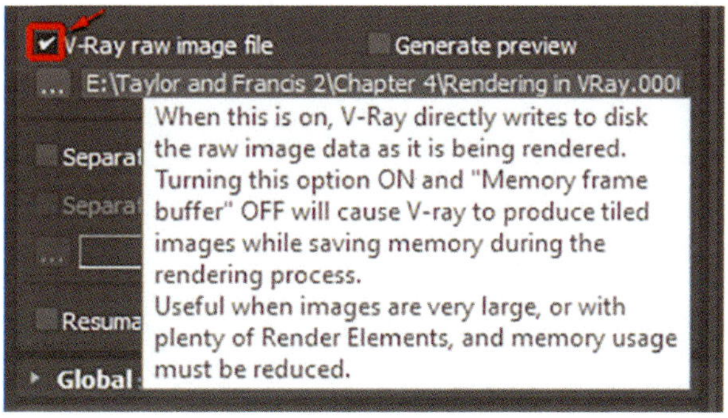

V-Ray raw image file function enabled

File: Save all image channels to a single file: This function automatically saves all image channels/render elements listed in the frame buffer into a single file (OpenEXR image file).

VFB dialog with a list of rendered channels/elements

VFB dialog File tab with the option to Save all image channels to a single file

Clicking this function will prompt a dialog, for users to type in the file name, choose a location to save files into, and the file extension (OpenEXR image file).

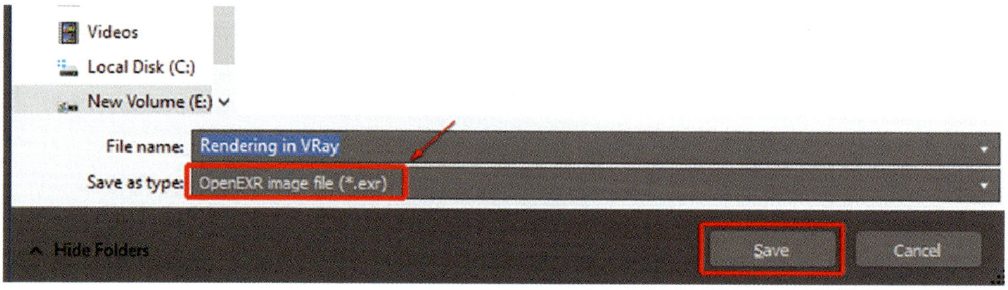

File name and OpenEXR image file type chosen in the Save dialog

Users can also Save all image channels to a single file by clicking and holding down the button on the V-Ray Frame Buffer, followed by choosing it from the dropdown list.

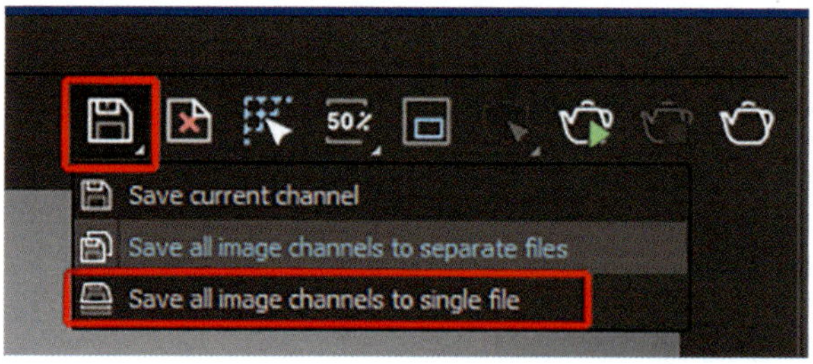

VFB dialog with Save all image channels to single file button

File: Save all image channels to separate files: This function is the most used one.

It automatically saves all image channels/render elements listed in the frame buffer into separate individual render elements/channels, each named accordingly.

Clicking this function will prompt a dialog, for users to type in the file name, choose a location to save the files into, and the file extension. Users often choose TIF Image File formats.

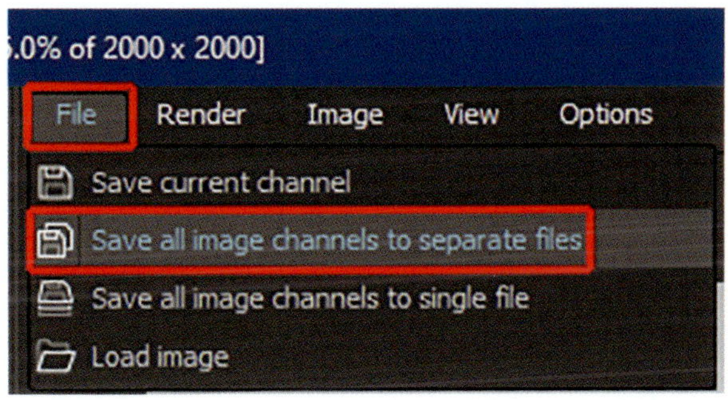

VFB dialog with Save all image channels to separate file buttons

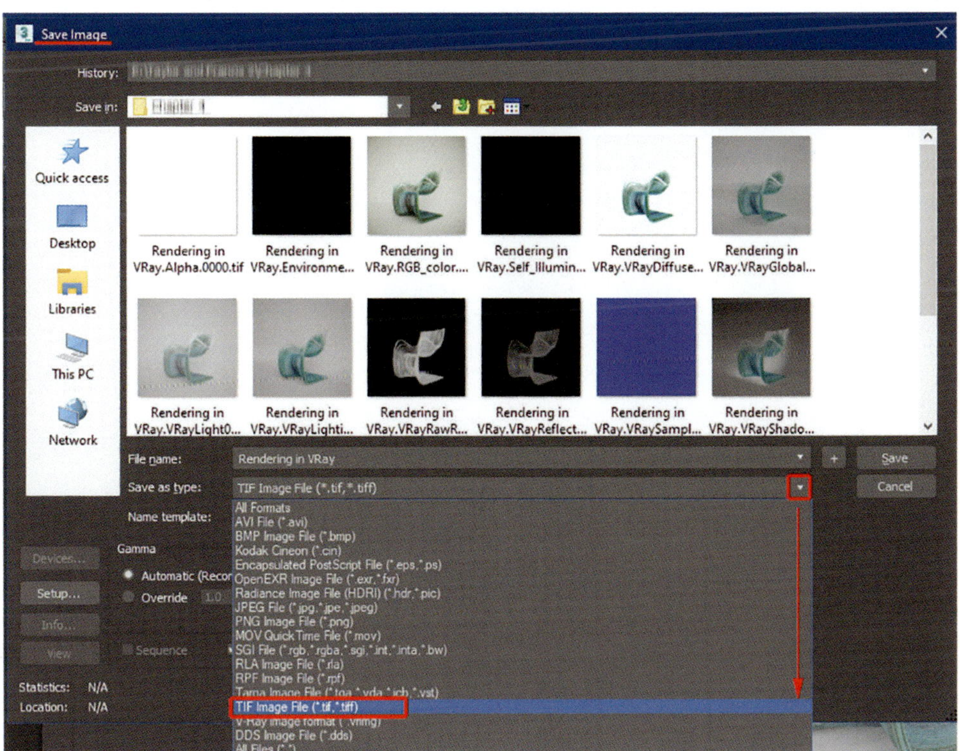

Save Image dialog with TIF Image File chosen to be saved in separate files

Users can also Save all image channels to separate files by clicking and holding down the button on the V-Ray Frame Buffer, followed by choosing it from the dropdown list.

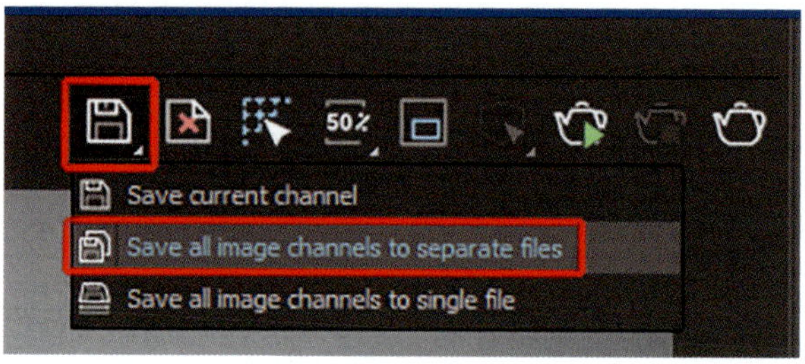

VFB dialog with Save all image channels to separate files button

File: Save current channel: This button enables users to save the image currently being displayed in the frame buffer. Clicking this button will prompt the Save Image dialog, for users to choose a path location, the file extension type and the name of the file.

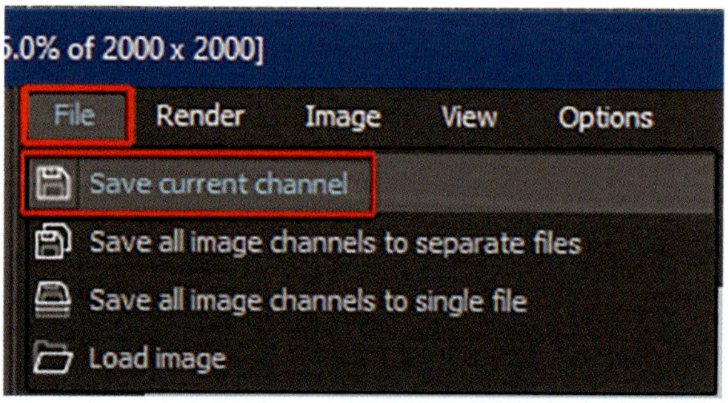

VFB dialog with Save current channel button

Users can also Save current channel by clicking its button on the V-Ray Frame Buffer.

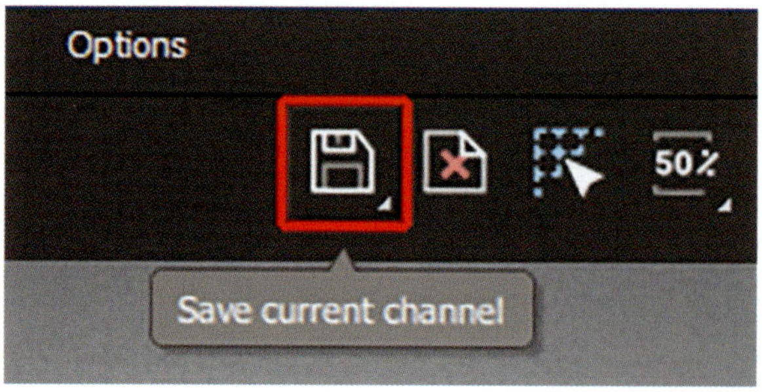

Save current channel button

Render: Start interactive rendering: When enabled, this function starts the interactive rendering. Interactive rendering works in conjunction with the IPR.

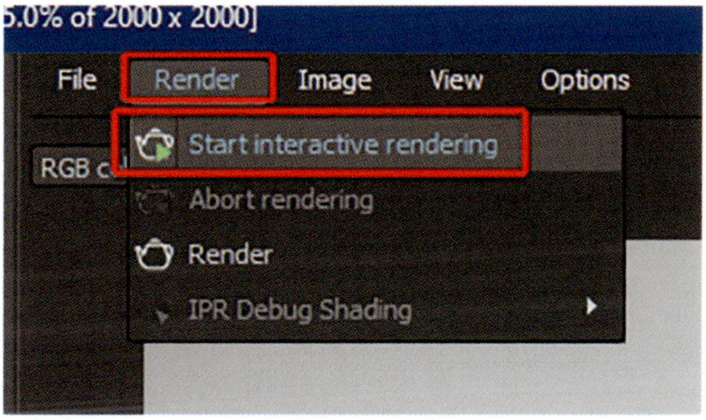

Start interactive rendering option

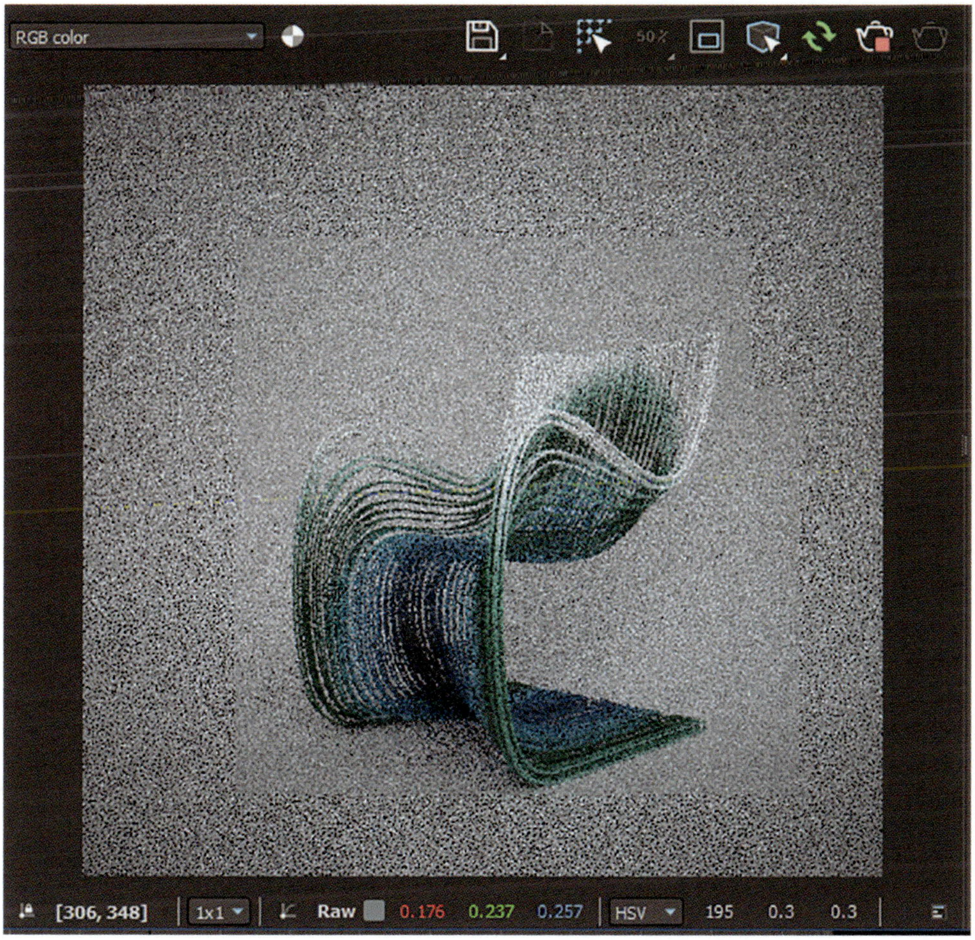

Interactive rendering process in the VFB dialog

The interactive rendering function automatically uses the Progressive image sampler settings to quickly render the final results.

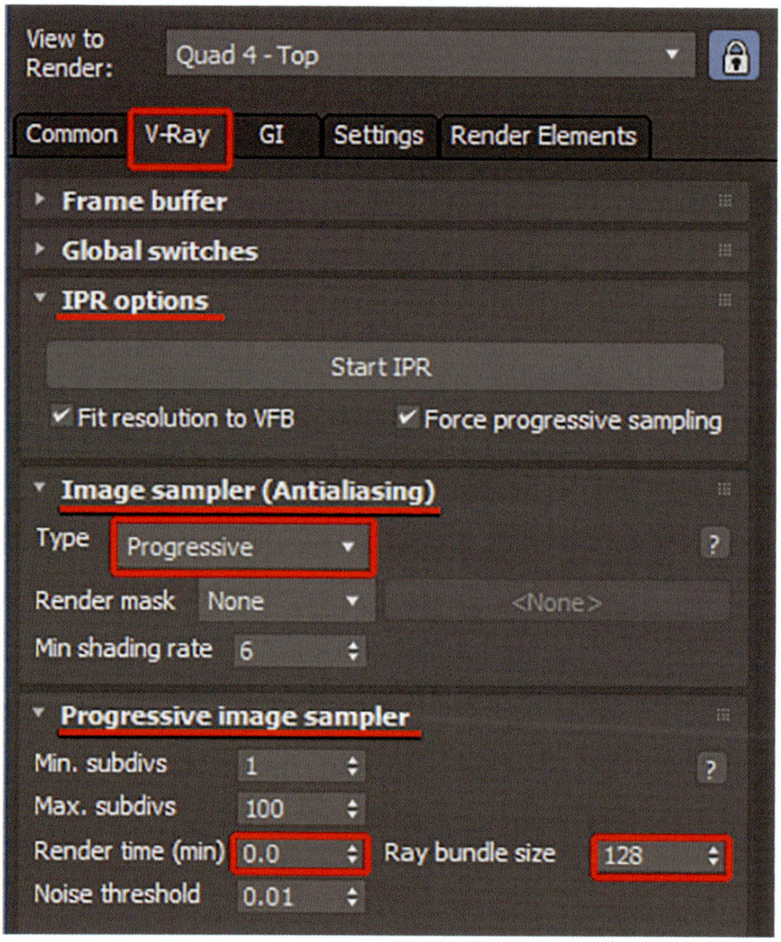

V-Ray tab with IPR option and Progressive image sampler parameters

This function can also be used by clicking its button on V-Ray Frame Buffer

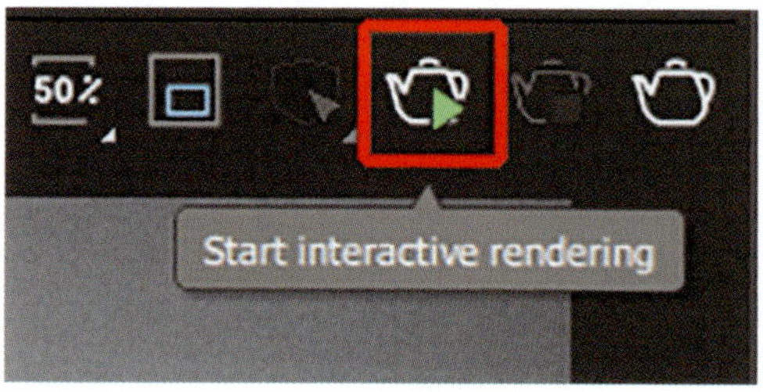

Start the interactive rendering button

By clicking the button twice, it will automatically switch to Refresh interactive rendering.

This button will automatically render interactively every time a camera is moved and/or parameters are changed. Users can input new changes while the render is taking place, interactively.

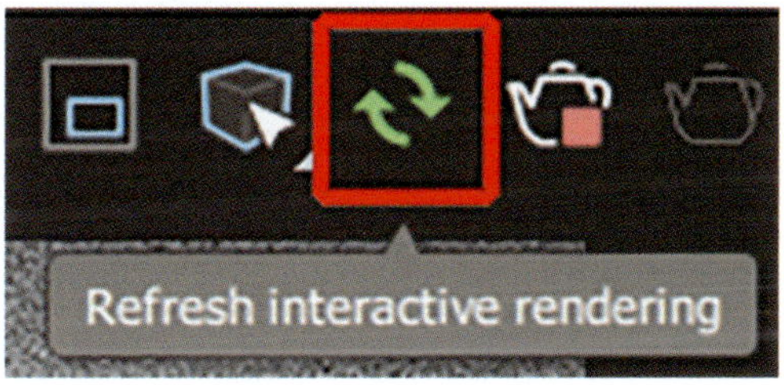

Refresh interactive rendering button

To stop interactive rendering simply click the button to Abort rendering. This button only becomes available while interactive rendering is taking place.

Grayed out, by default.

Abort rendering button

Users can also Abort rendering through the Render tool dropdown list.

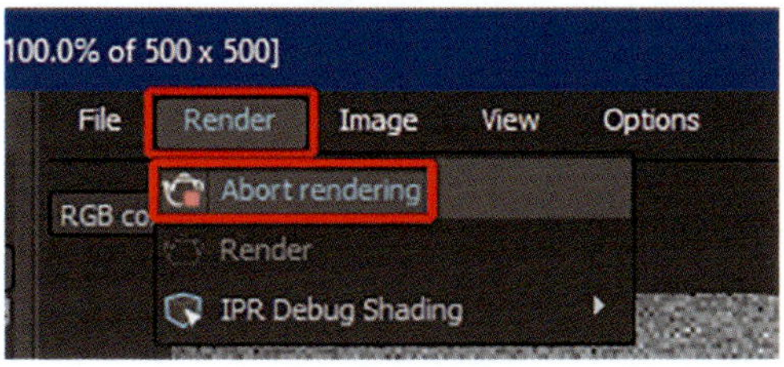

Abort rendering via Render dropdown list

Render: When clicked, it renders the current camera or viewport.

Render function

This function can also be enabled via its button on the V-Ray Frame Buffer.

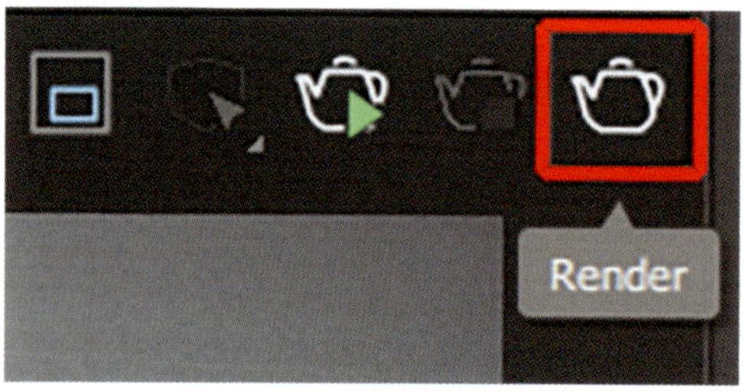

Render button

Render: IPR Debug Shading: This function only becomes available when the Start interactive rendering is chosen, or the IPR button is clicked, under V-Ray IPR options. Also, the IPR button is available from the main toolbar (click and hold to choose from the list).

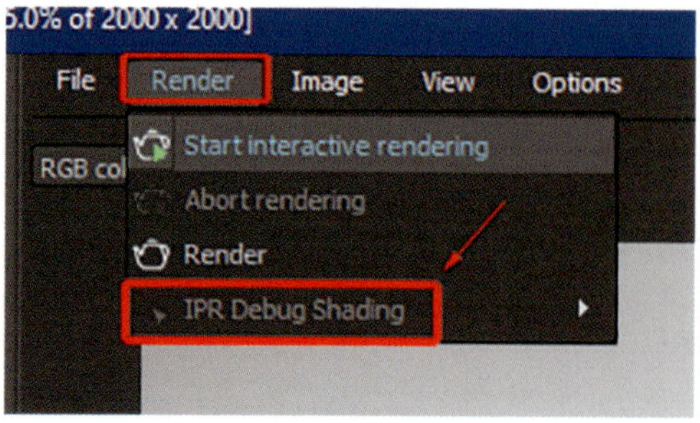

IPR Debug Shading option

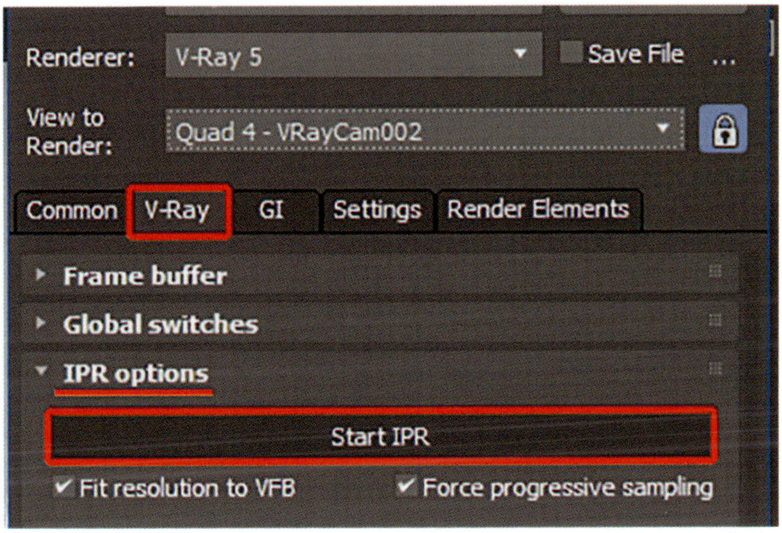

Start IPR options under V-Ray tab in the Render Setup dialog

IPR Mode button from the main toolbar

Once enabled, the IPR Debug Shading becomes available with options to Isolate Selected, Isolate locked selection, Lighting, Ambient Occlusion, Wireframe, Normals and UVs.

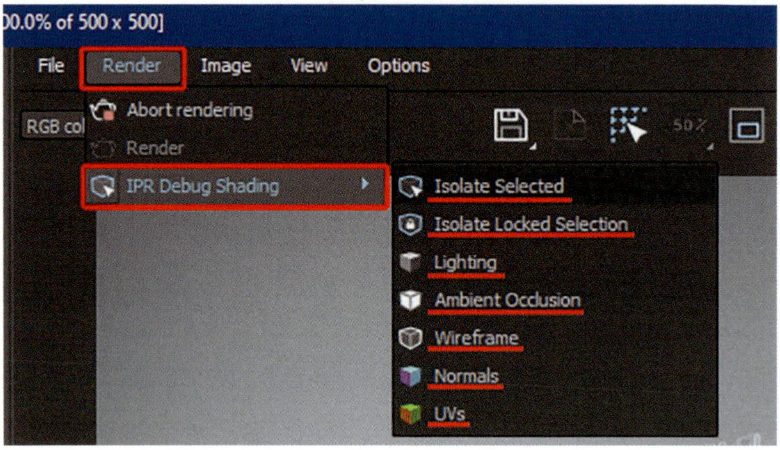

IPR Debug Shading available options

Once the IPR or Interactive rendering is enabled, the IPR options can also be accessed via the V-Ray Frame Buffer button.

Grayed out, by default.

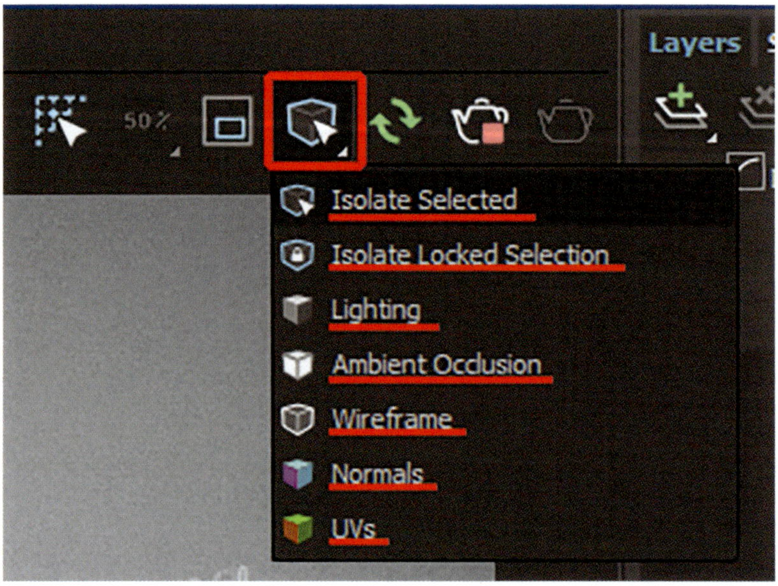

IPR Debug Shading available buttons

The IPR can also be activated via the viewport.

To do so, simply click on the User Defined text, and choose the V-Ray Viewport IPR option.

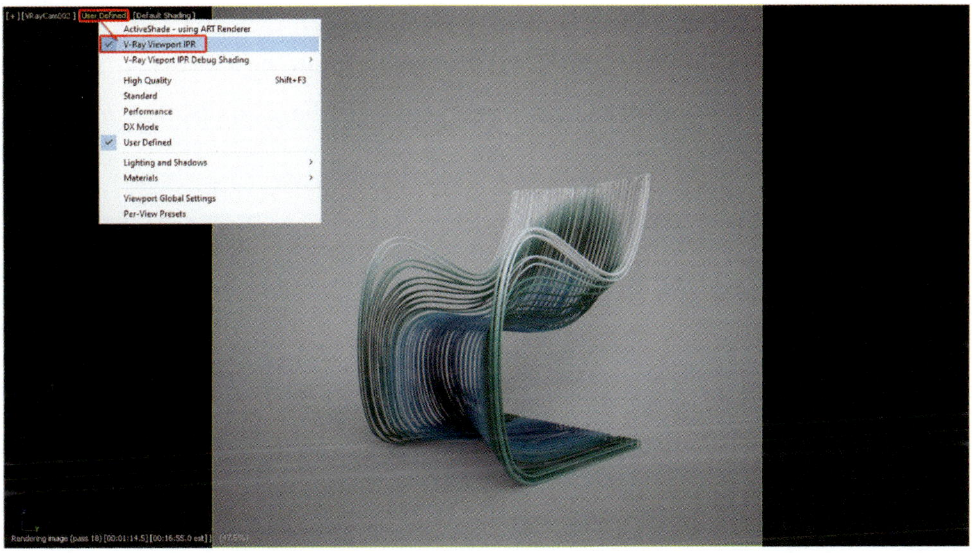

V-Ray Viewport IPR option rendered

IPR can use the CPU (default) or the V-Ray GPU to carry out the IPRs.

To do so, simply go to the Render Setup dialog, and load V-Ray GPU 5 from the Renderer dropdown list.

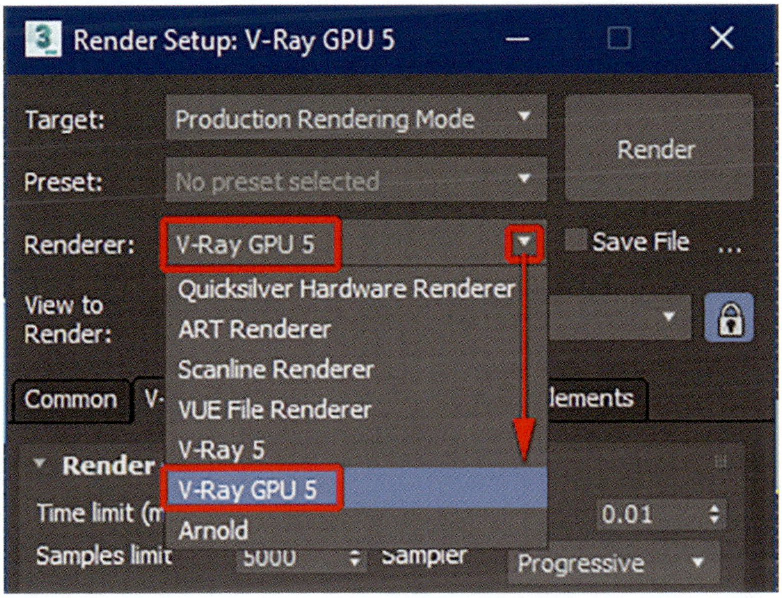

V-Ray GPU 5 loaded in the Render Setup dialog

Image: Follow mouse: If buckets are still rendering, when enabled, V-Ray automatically renders buckets where the mouse is hovering over in the V-Ray Frame Buffer.

If the area the mouse is hovering has already been rendered, no buckets will appear.

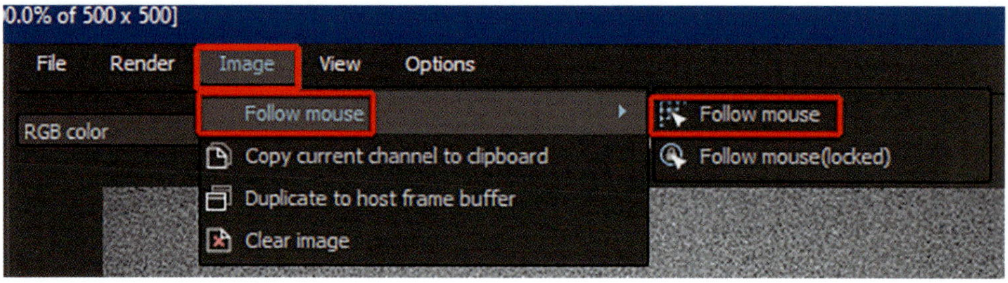

Follow the mouse function option in the VFB dialog

This function only works if the Image sampler type is set to Bucket.

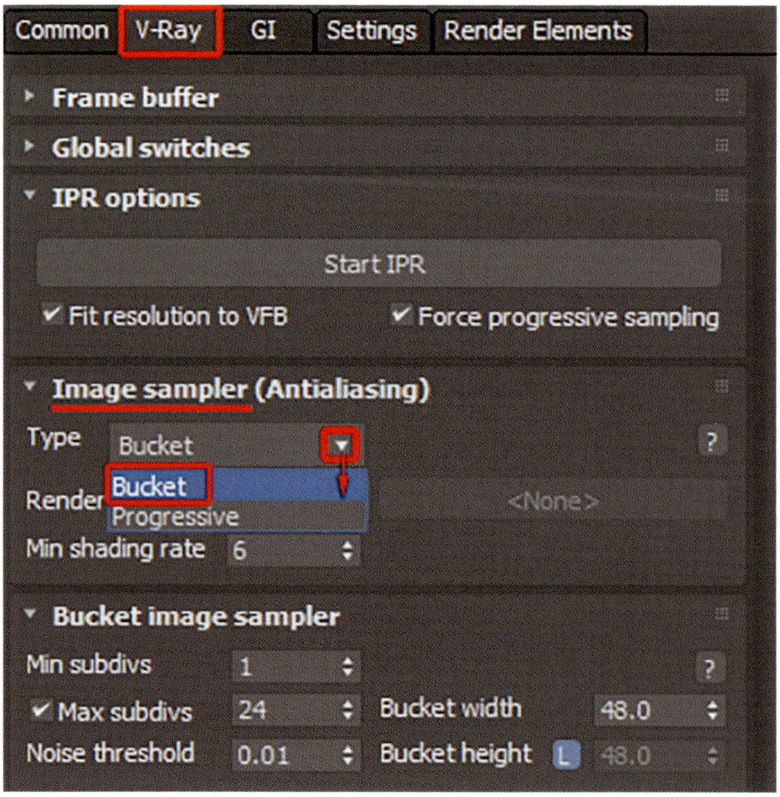

Bucket Image sampler under V-Ray tab in Render Setup dialog

This function can also be enabled by clicking its button on the V-Ray Frame Buffer.

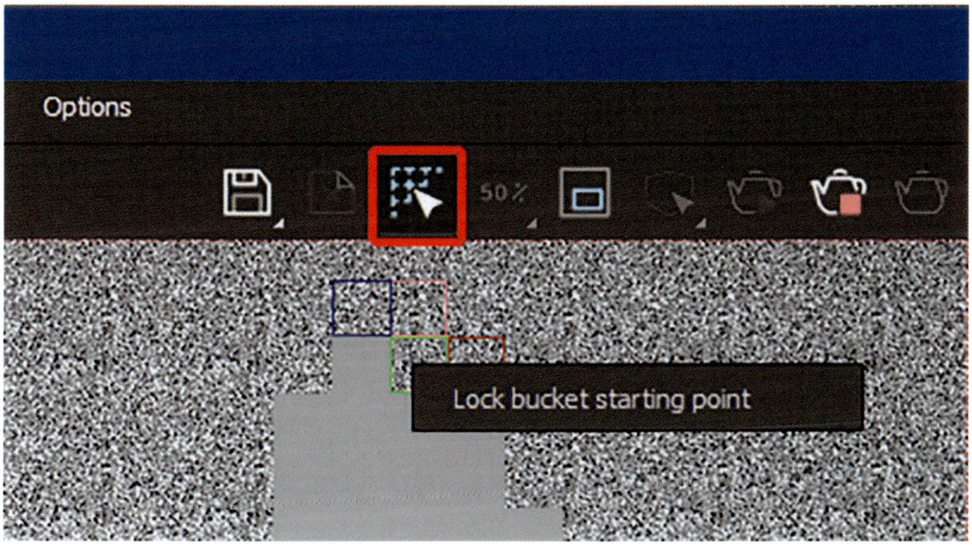

Follow the mouse button in VFB dialog

Image: Follow mouse/Lock bucket starting point: This function locks the bucket starting point on the V-Ray Frame Buffer, and no longer follows the mouse.

Users can enable it via the Image dropdown list, or by right clicking on the V-Ray Frame Buffer and clicking it.

Image: Copy current channel to clipboard: When selected, this function copies the image/channel to the clipboard.

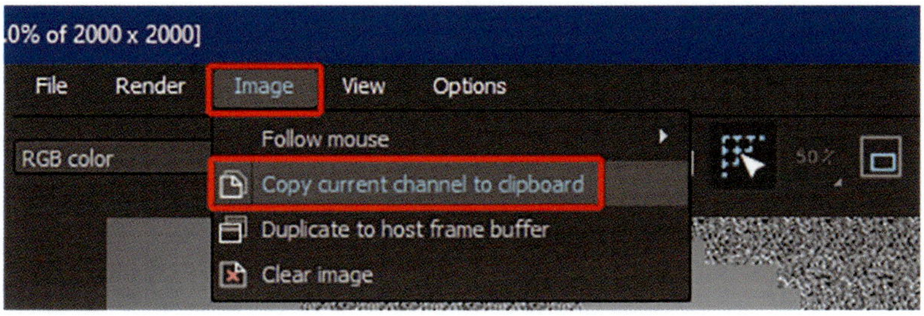

Copy current channel to clipboard function in VFB dialog

Image: Duplicate to host frame buffer: When chosen, this function duplicates the image/render displayed in the frame buffer, into a new dialog.

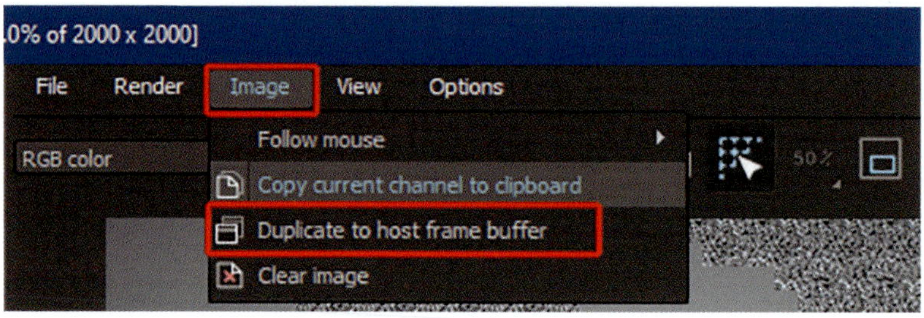

Duplicate to host frame buffer function

Image: Clear image: Clicking this button clears (removes) the channel/render being displayed in the V-Ray Frame Buffer.

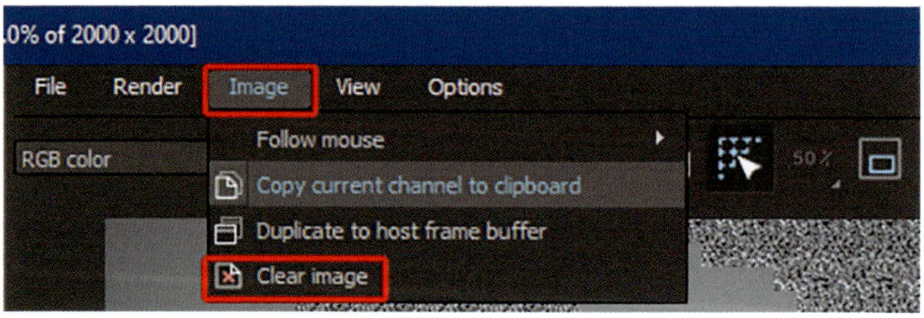

Clear image function in the VFB dialog

This function can also be accessed from the V-Ray Frame Buffer

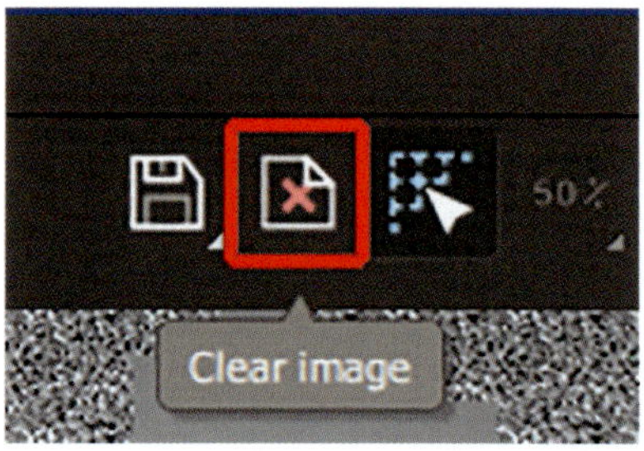

Clear image function button in the VFB dialog

View: Display color space: This function controls the color balance of your renders in the V-Ray Frame Buffer.

Users have the option to choose from color spaces such as sRGB, OCIO, ICC, Gamma 2.2 or None.

Default color space, sRGB.

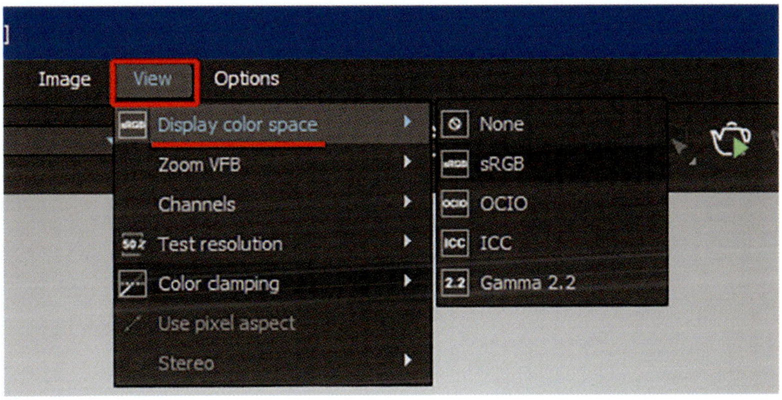

Display color space options

View: Zoom VFB: This function allows users to zoom in from a variety of zoom percentages (50%, 100% and 150%).

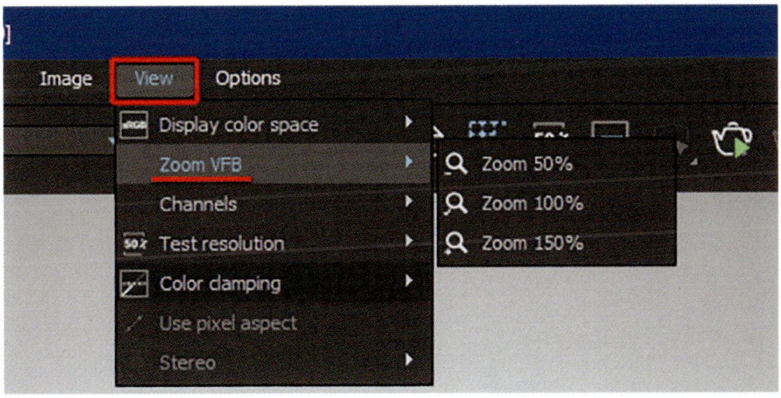

Zoom VFB options

NOTE

A dotted red line will always be present around the VFB, if the zoom exceeds 100% of the original image/render.

View: Channels: This function allows users to view the render in a variety of different channels such as red, green, blue, alpha channel and monochromatic.

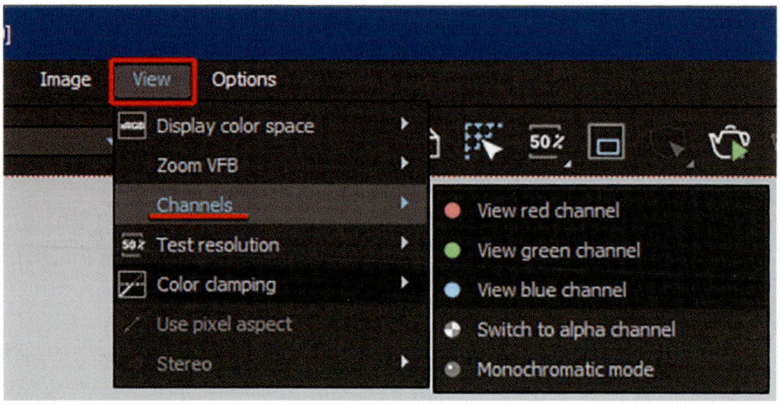

View channels options

View in Monochromatic mode

View: Test resolution: This function allows users to test the resolution in the VFB.

Default value, 50%.

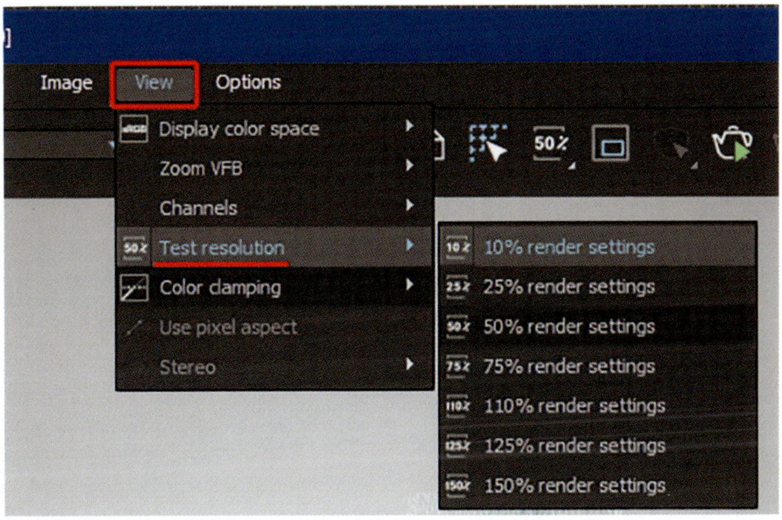

Test resolution options

This function can also be accessed via the VFB button.

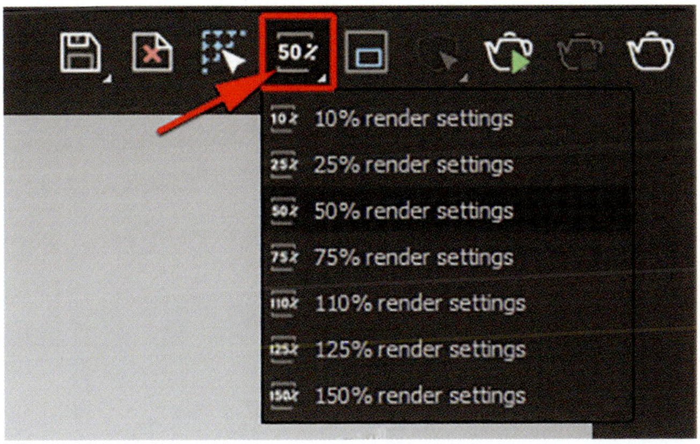

Test resolution options button

View: Color clamping: This function allows users to Force color clamping or View clamped colors in the VFB.

Default, Force color clamping.

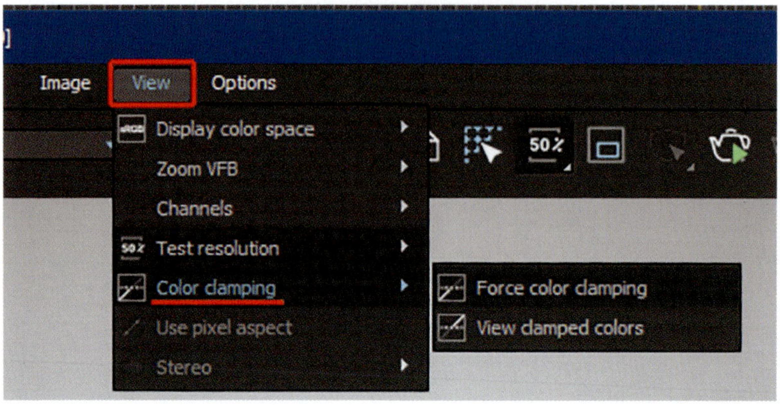

Color clamping options

View: Use pixel aspect: This function allows the visualization of the pixel aspect ratio.

Grayed out by default.

View: Stereo: This function previews the stereoscopic render in the VFB.

This function only becomes available if a stereoscopic render is being executed (split screens).

Grayed out by default.

Options: VFB settings: This function allows users to open the VFB Settings dialog and set up keep parameters such as Render view, Render Region controls, History and Layers.

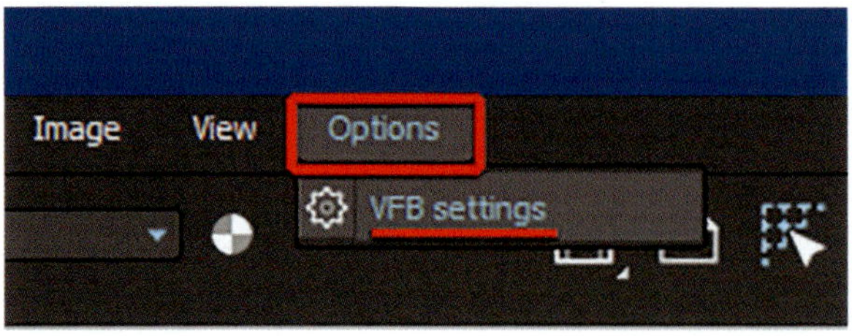

Options tab

Render View: This tab allows users to set the Zoom Multiplier values and the Bucket outlines colors (Different colors by bucket, White, Black and None).

The Show Advanced Settings (when enabled) provides users with additional and more complex functionalities.

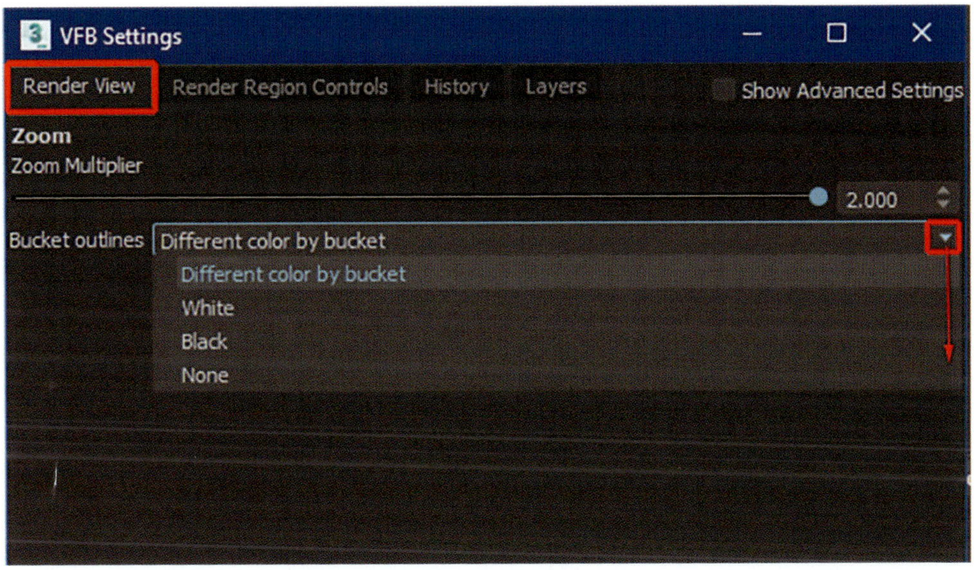

Render View tab

Render Region Controls: This tab controls the Region Render settings, with functionalities to Show controls on hover only and Show region sizes.

The Show Advanced Settings (when enabled) provides users with additional and more complex functionalities.

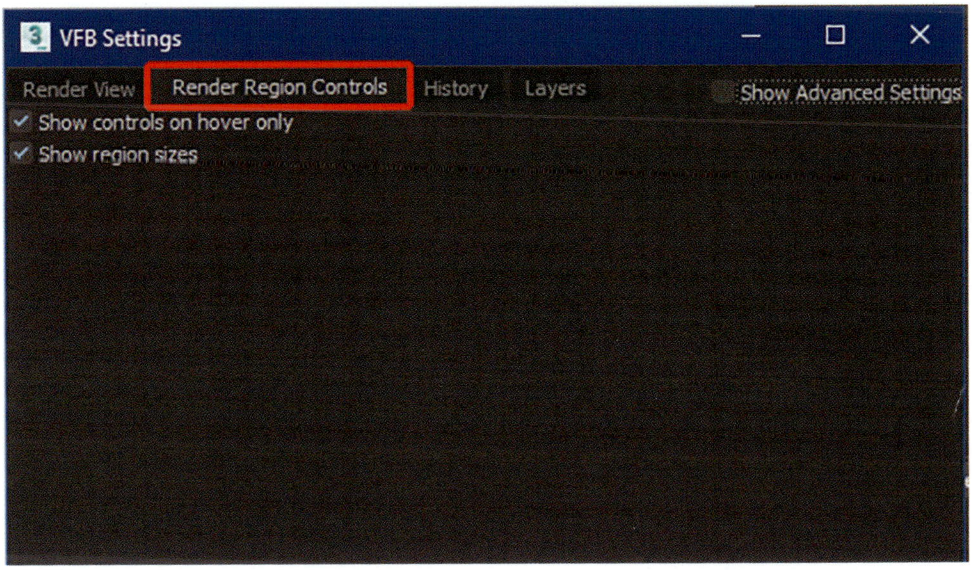

Render Region Controls tab

History: This unique tab allows users to Enable the History of rendered frames in the VFB History list.

If disabled and the Location is not set, no renders will appear in the VFB History section.

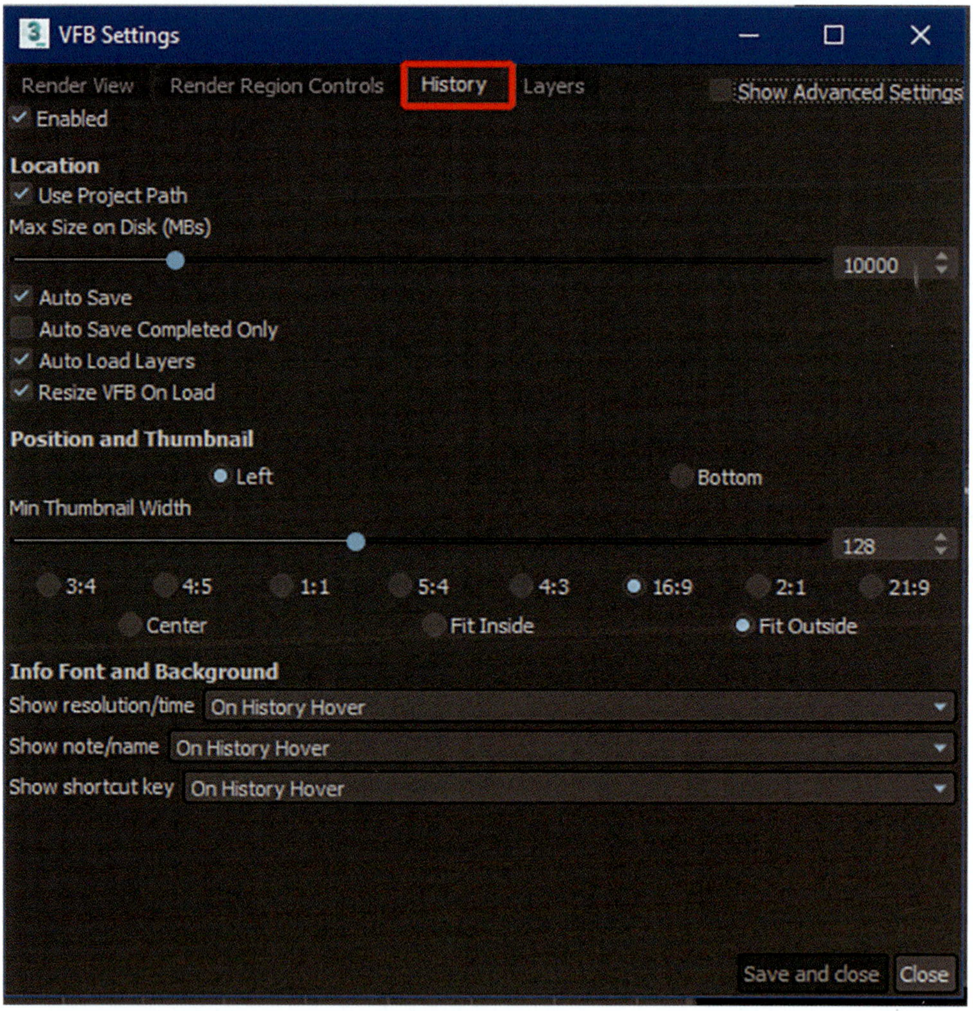

History functionalities tab

History in VFB Disabled

When the History location is set, every time a frame is rendered it will automatically appear in the History list.

Similarly, when you click on its thumbnail in the History list, it will immediately appear in the VFB.

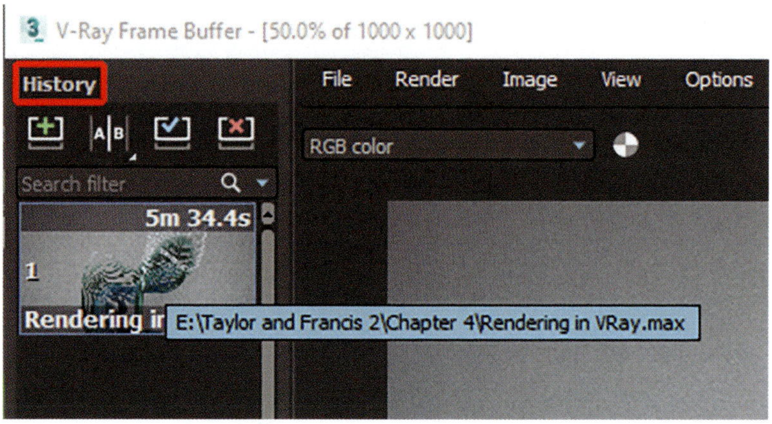

History in VFB Set to a location

Save to history button: Clicking this button automatically adds the current render in the VFB to the History list.

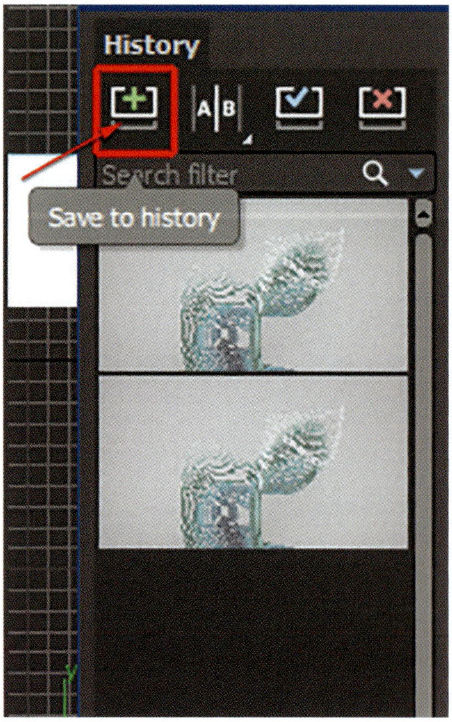

Save to history button

A/B horizontal: This button allows users to compare two or more renders in the VFB History horizontally (A/B), vertically (A/B) or (A/B/C/D). To enable this button simply click on it.

When the option is A/B horizontal, a vertical white line should appear promptly in the middle of the VFB dividing two renders listed in the History list.

The vertical white line can be moved across horizontally.

To choose from one of the three options available, simply click and hold the button.

Once there is more than one render saved in the VFB History list, users can select and right click to choose to, Edit note, Set A, Set B, Load to VFB, Delete, Load layers, Load V-Ray settings, Open scene or Reload history.

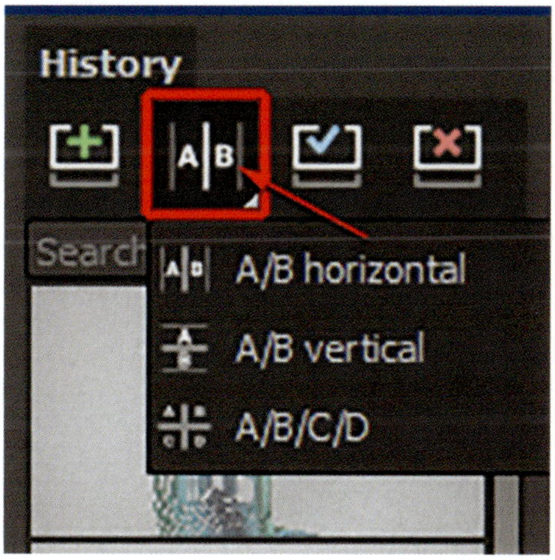

A/B button

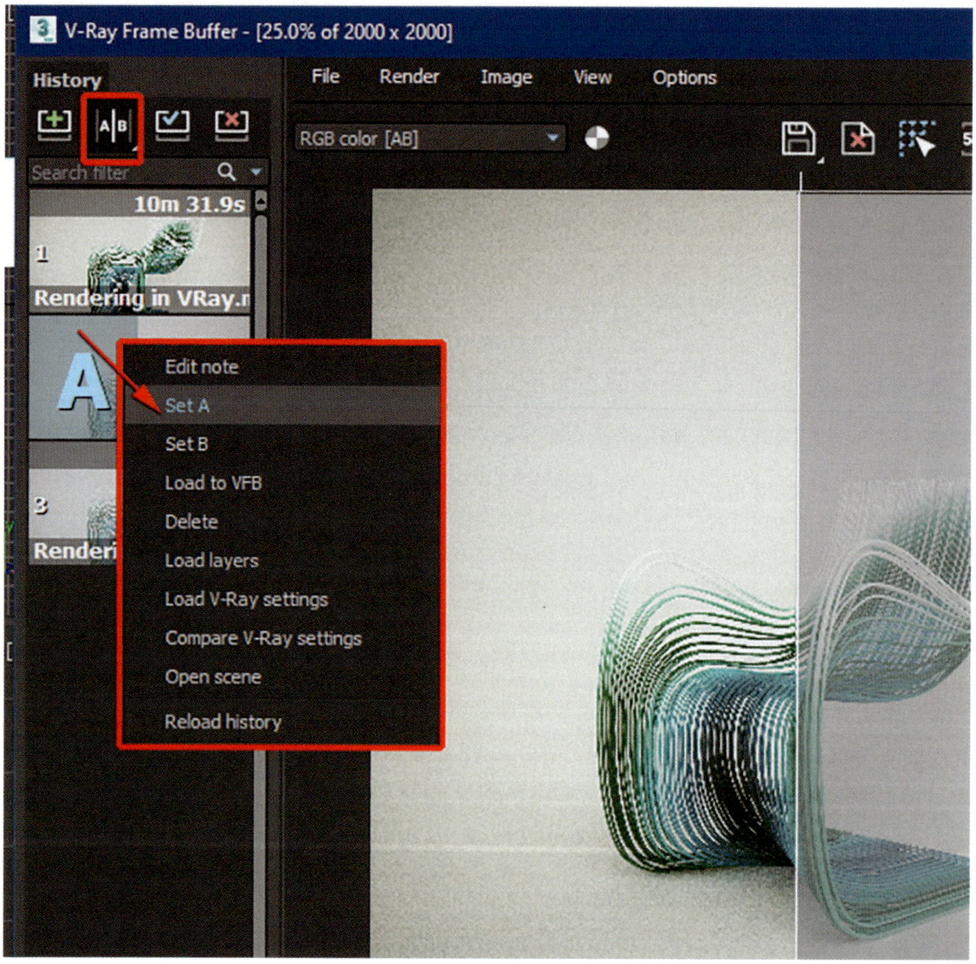

VFB history options

Load to VFB button: This button allows users to load to VFB

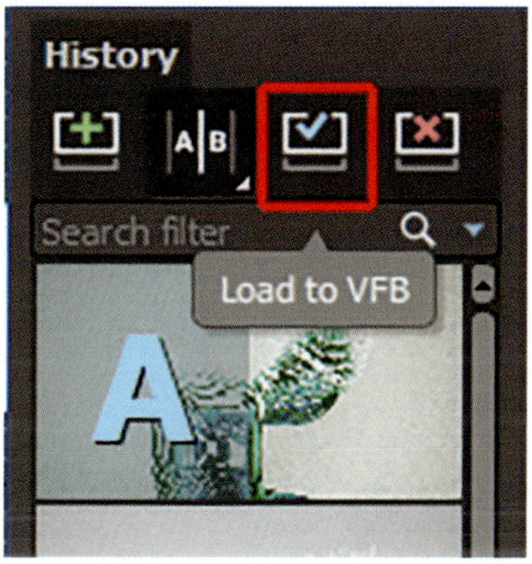

Load to VFB button

Delete button: This button allows users to delete any selected render in the VFB History list.

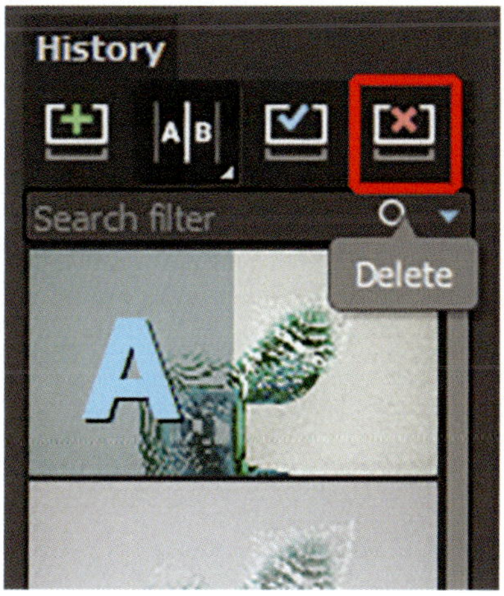

Delete button

Search filter: This text field allows users to type in and search for specific saved renders in the VFB History list.

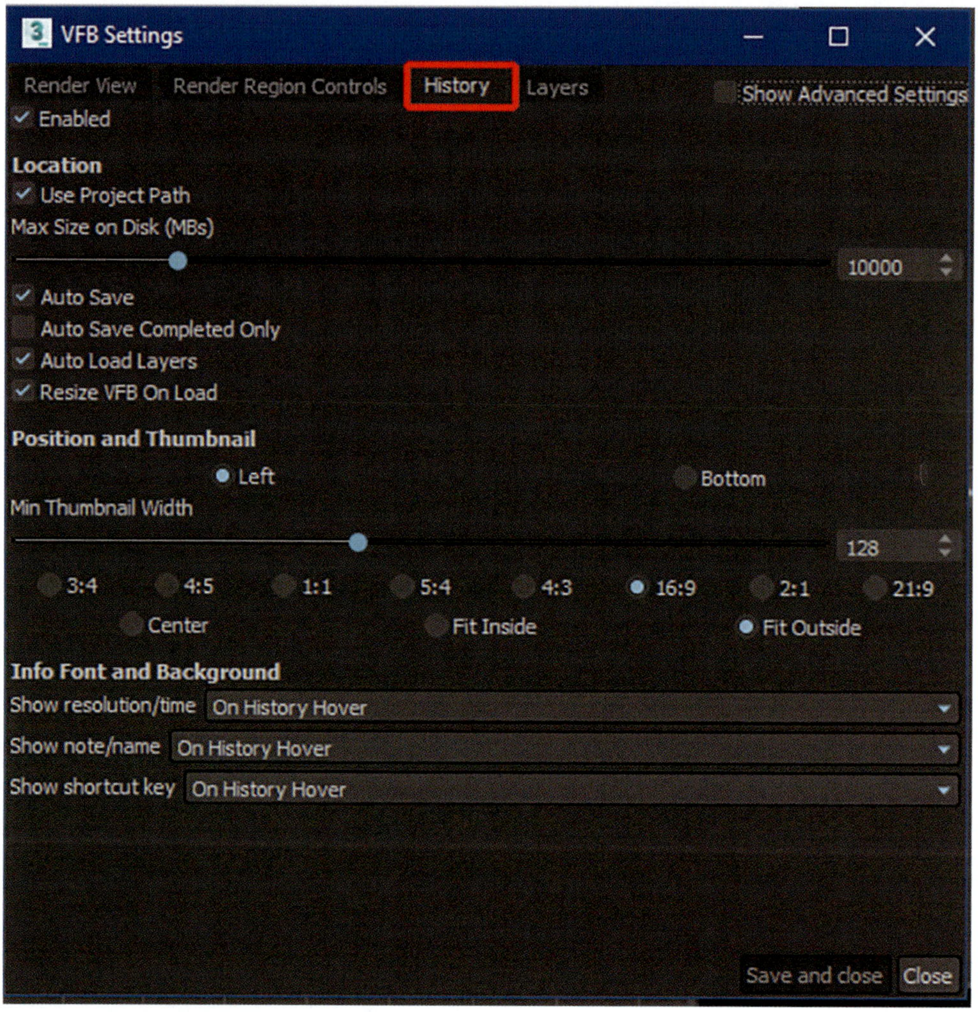

History functionalities tab

Location: Use Project Path: When enabled, it automatically uses the default location of where the current 3ds Max file is saved.

This location is depicted when hovering over the saved render in the history section/list of the VFB.

Max Size on Disk (MBs): This function controls the maximum size of each of the renders saved in the history list displayed in the VFB.

Users can utilize the slider or simply type in a specific value.

Auto Save: If enabled, it automatically saves the recent render into the VFB history list/location.

Auto Save Completed Only: When enabled, it only saves the completed renders into the VFB history list/location.

Auto Load Layers: When enabled, every time a thumbnail in the VFB history is clicked, it automatically appears in the main VFB with all its render elements/passes loaded (if any).

Resize VFB on Load: If enabled, every time a thumbnail in VFB history is clicked, it automatically resizes the VFB to fit the original render.

Position and Thumbnail: These parameters control the position and size of thumbnails displayed in the VFB history list.

Info Font and Background: These parameters control the font (text) and background information displayed on history thumbnails.

Users have the option to change functionalities such as Show resolution/time, Show note/name and Show shortcut key.

Layers: This tab allows users to set, save and load recent preset paths.

Layers tab

Save and close: When clicked, this button saves and closes the dialog.

Close: When clicked, this button closes the dialog.

Region render button: This button allows users to enable it (by clicking it), followed by clicking and dragging it in the VFB to draw a region to render.

Layers tab

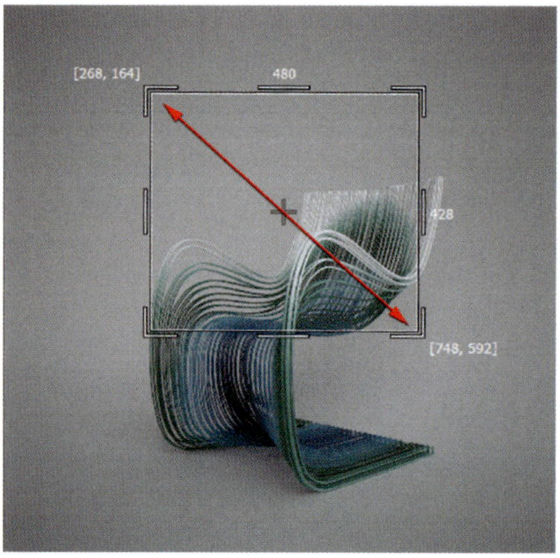

Click & drag in VFB to draw a region

The cross in the middle allows users to click and move the region anywhere in the VFB.

The eight handles around the drawn region allows users to click/select on any of them individually, followed by stretching them in any direction (X & Y axis), to draw a specific region.

To disable the region render, simply deselect its button.

VFB Layers: This tab allows users to view all available layers from its list by clicking on its button first, followed by choosing a specific adjustment layer to add to the list.

By default, there are two adjustment layers loaded and enabled: Display correction, and the Sources: RGB.

Lens Effects and the Denoiser are loaded but not enabled.

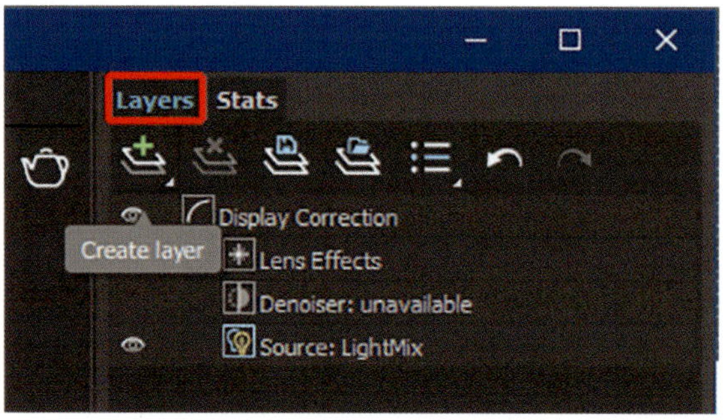

Default Adjustment layers

By selecting and right clicking any of the listed layers, users have the option to Reset, Save, Load Delete, New Layer, Duplicate and Blend Modes.

The grayed-out options are not available to the default layers.

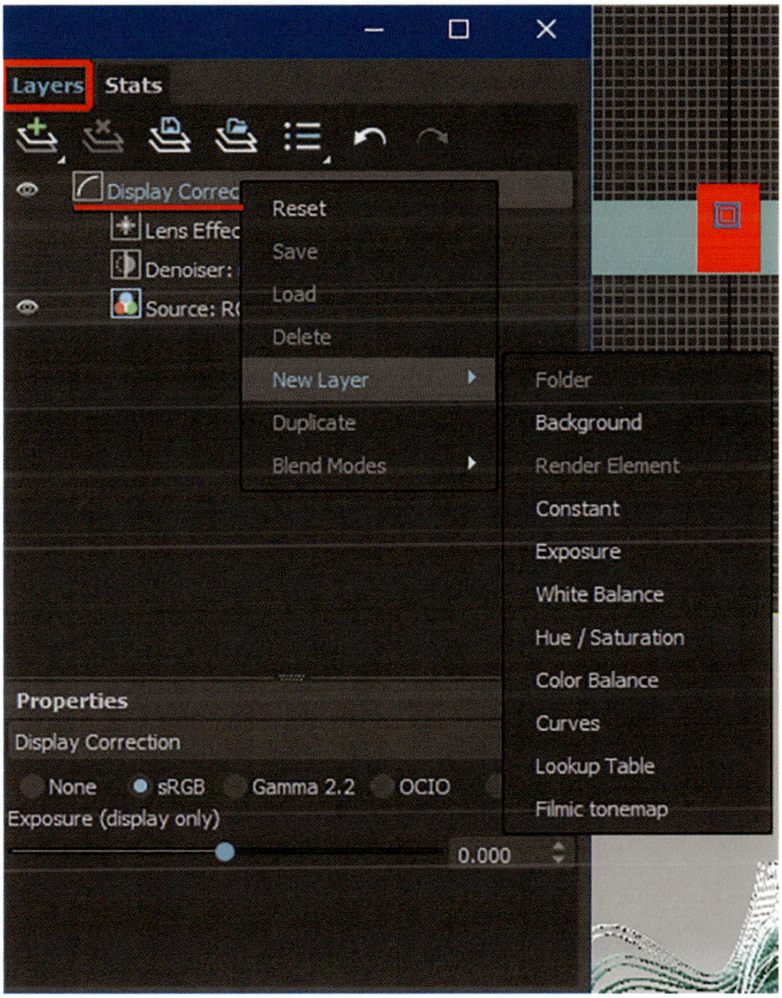

Right click options available

Each adjustment layer selected/ chosen comes with its unique adjustable properties.

To make any layer visible (and saved in VFB), simply select its layer first.

Next, enable its function under Properties and click on the empty section where the eye icon should be.

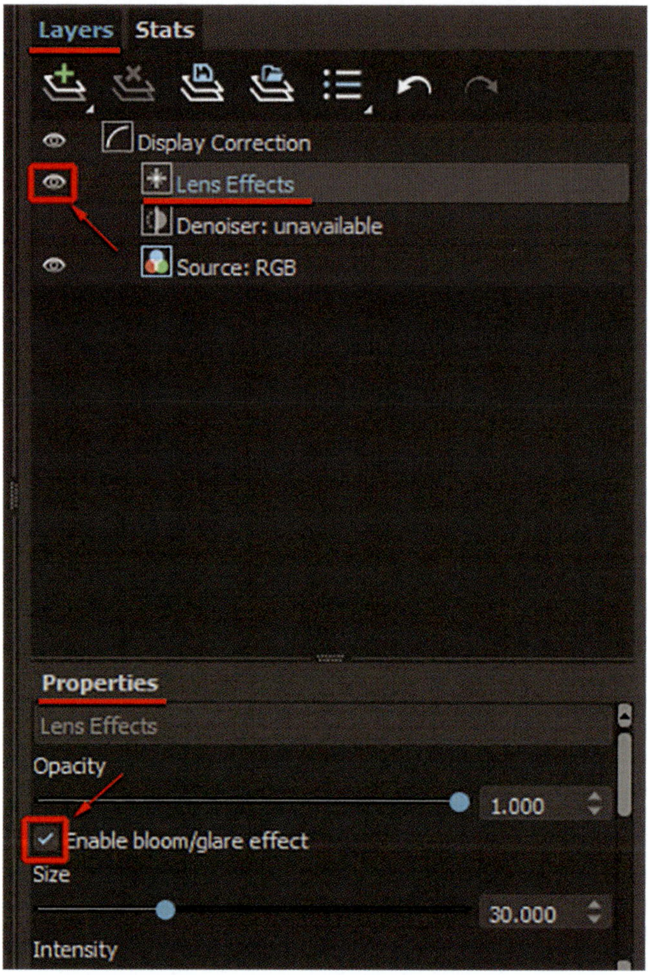

Enable Adjustment layers

The Denoiser and Light Mix only become available under Layers once added in the Render Elements and rendered.

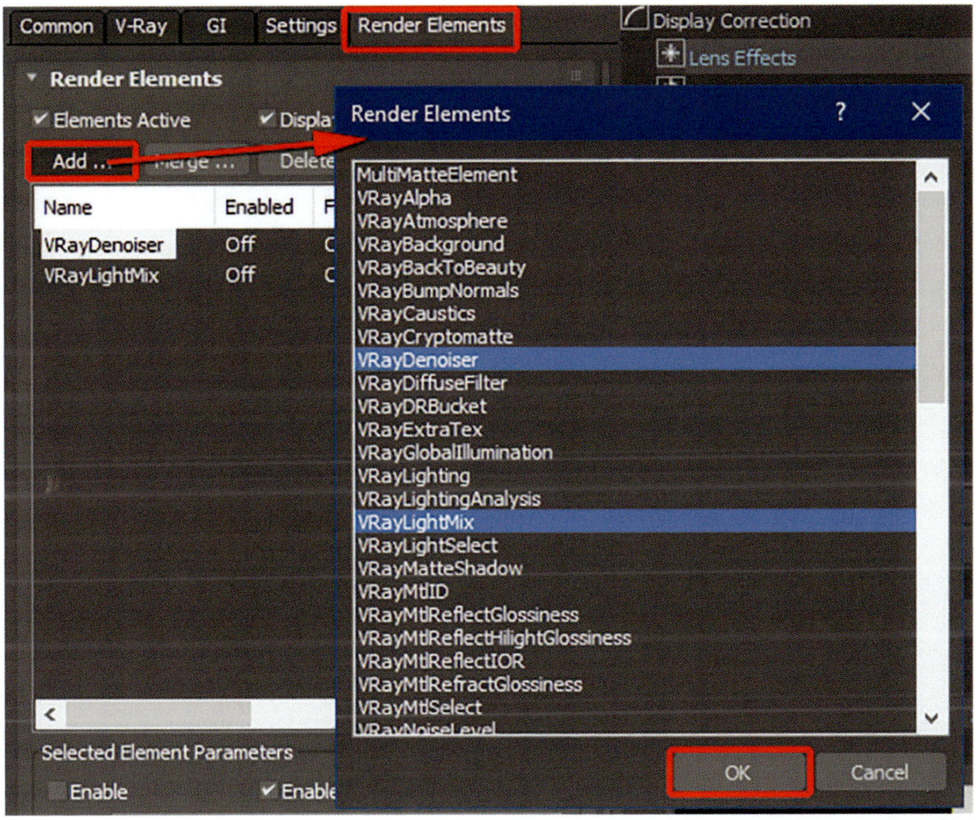

Enable Adjustment layers

Finally, before rendering, the GI primary engine needs to be set to Brute force in order for LightMix to work.

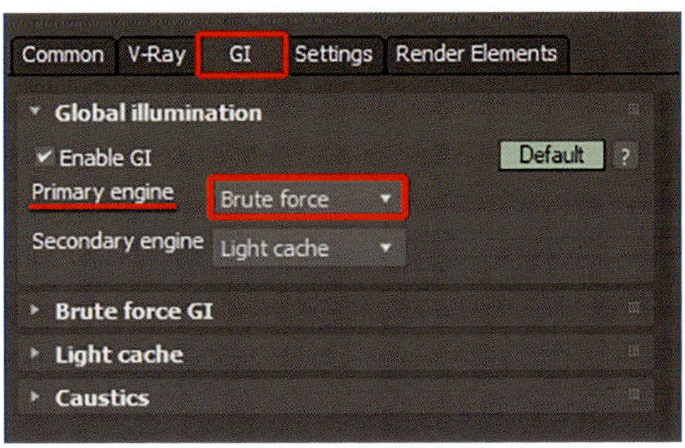

Primary engine set to Brute force

NOTE

Because Denoiser often "smears" shadows/parts of a render and adds additional rendering time, it's common practice for some users to disable/remove it, sometimes.

Once a render is carried out with the LightMix added, users are prompted with Properties such as All, VRayLight, Environment, Self-Illumination and Rest.

Each of the listed functions has the default value of 1.000, with a white color swatch (255).

Every physical light in the scene is listed by its original name. Instanced lights are listed as one (same).

If you intend to control lights separately via LightMix, you need to copy them instead.

Reset/Refresh: This button resets any added changes.

Save: This button allows users to Save the current settings as LightMix file (*.lightmix).

Load: This toggle allows users to load any presaved LightMix file (*.lightmix).

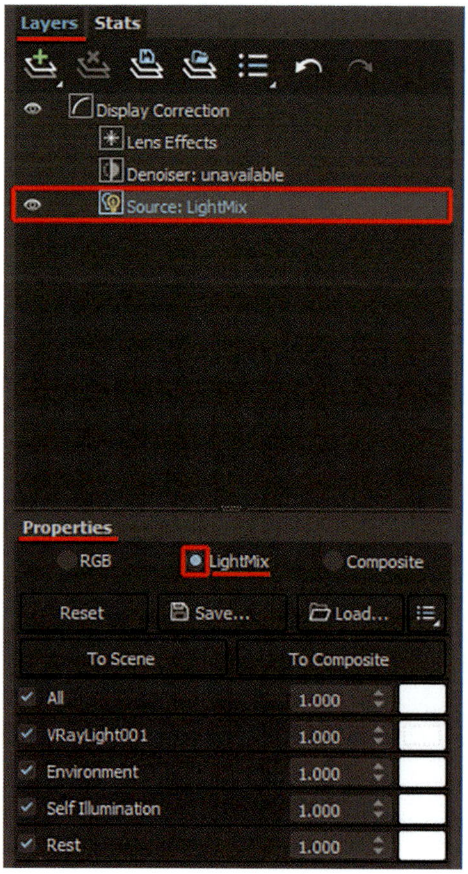

LightMix Properties

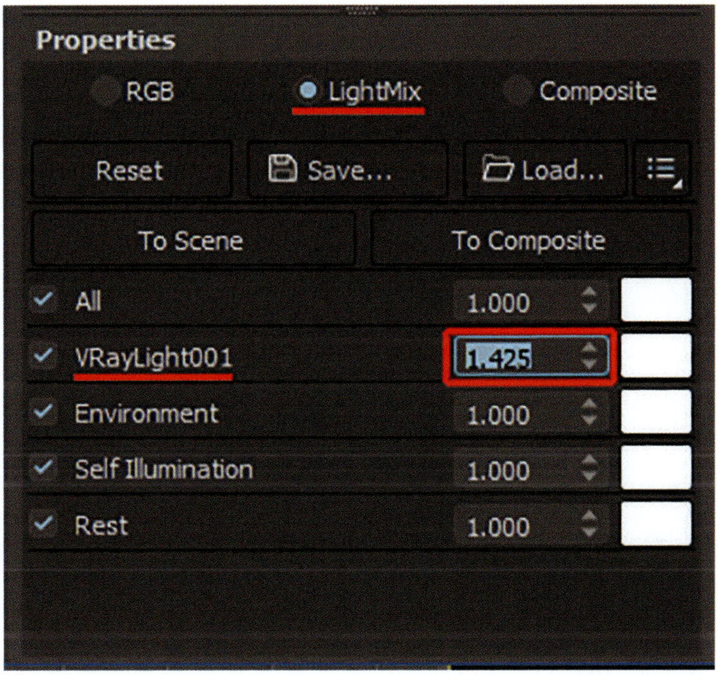

VRayLight set to 1.425

VRayLight set to 1.425 rendered

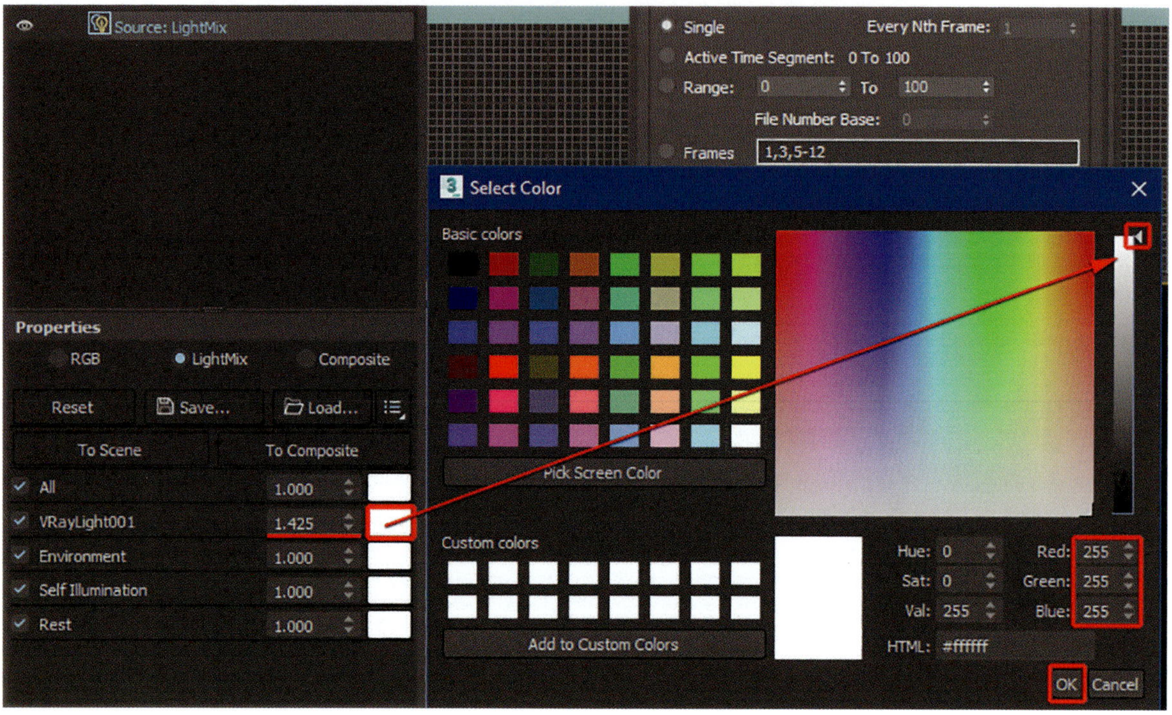

VRayLight color set to white (255)

VRayLight color set to white (255) rendered

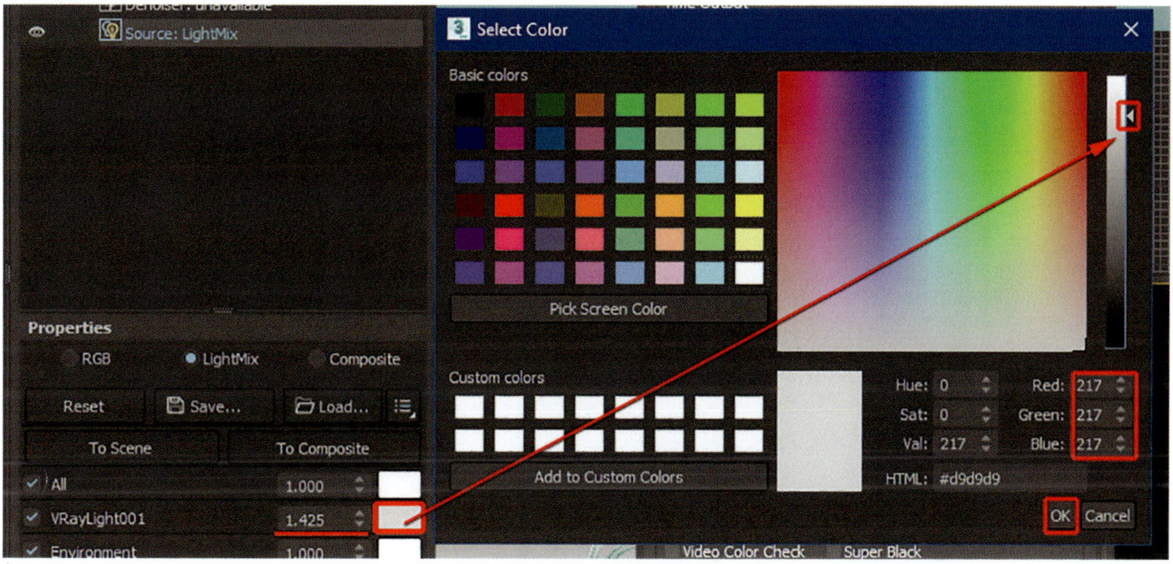

VRayLight color set to gray (217)

VRayLight color set to gray (217) rendered

Most adjustment layers listed are similar to those commonly used in Adobe Photoshop and other postproduction applications such as Adobe After Effects and Nuke.

For the purpose of this exercise, we are going to focus on adjustment layers such as Filmic tonemap, Lookup Table, Hue/Saturation and lens Effects.

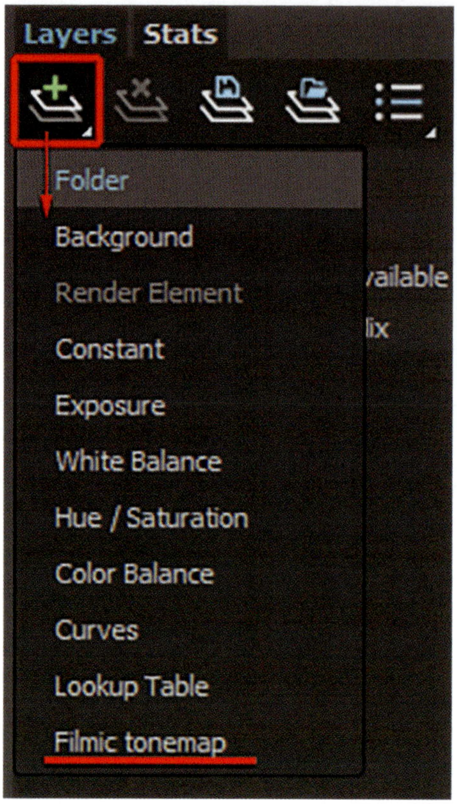

Layers Tab and Button

Filmic tonemap: This adjustment layer allows users to accurately control the overall contrast of a render, by fine-tuning functions such as Blend Mode, Tone mapping space, Type, Log space, Shoulder strength, Linear strength, Linear angle, Toe strength and White point.

For this scene, the functions that really made a difference were the shoulder strength and toe strength.

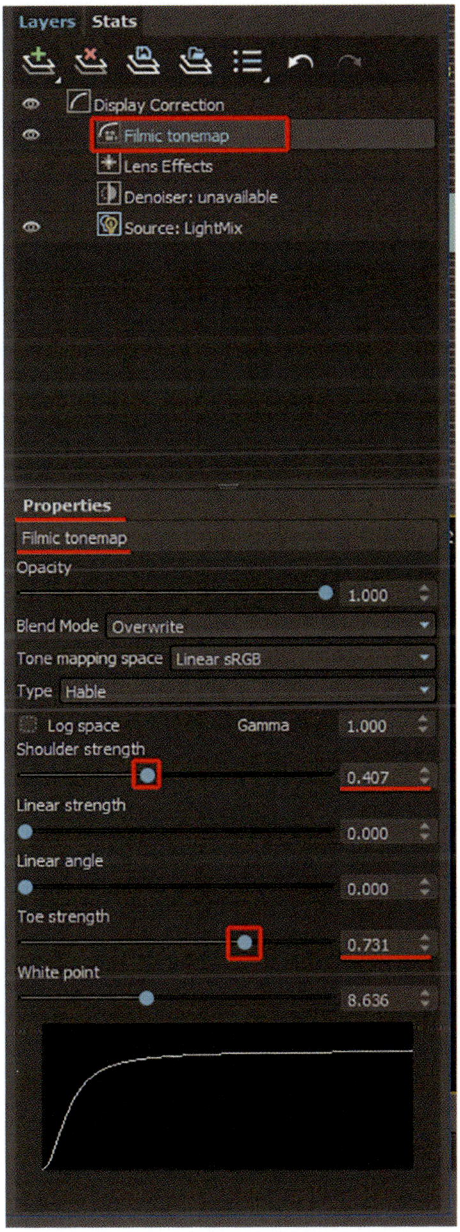

Filmic tonemap settings

Hue/Saturation: This adjustment layer is mostly used to saturate and/or desaturate renders.

For this scene, the function that really made a difference was the saturation.

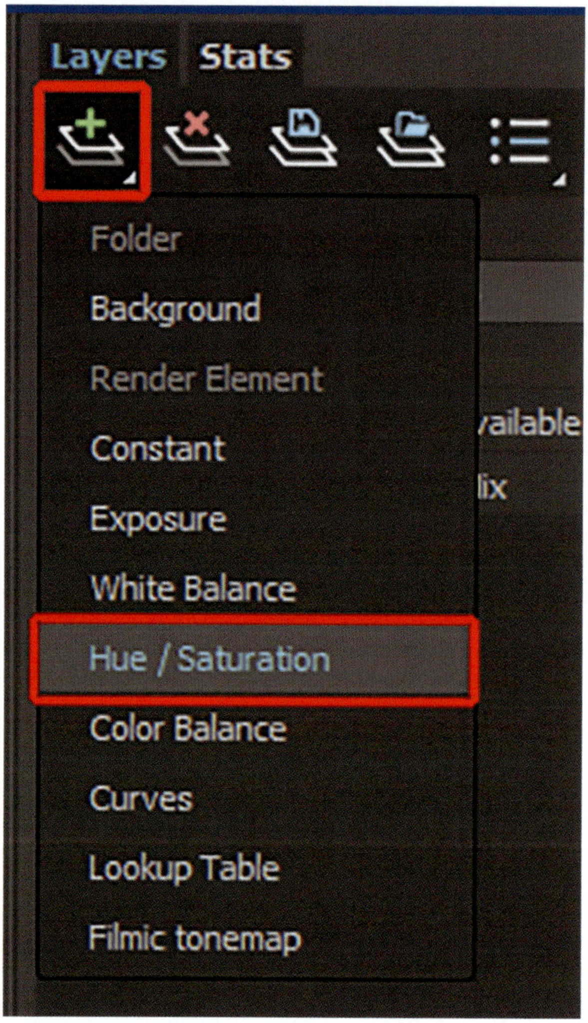

Add Hue/Saturation layer

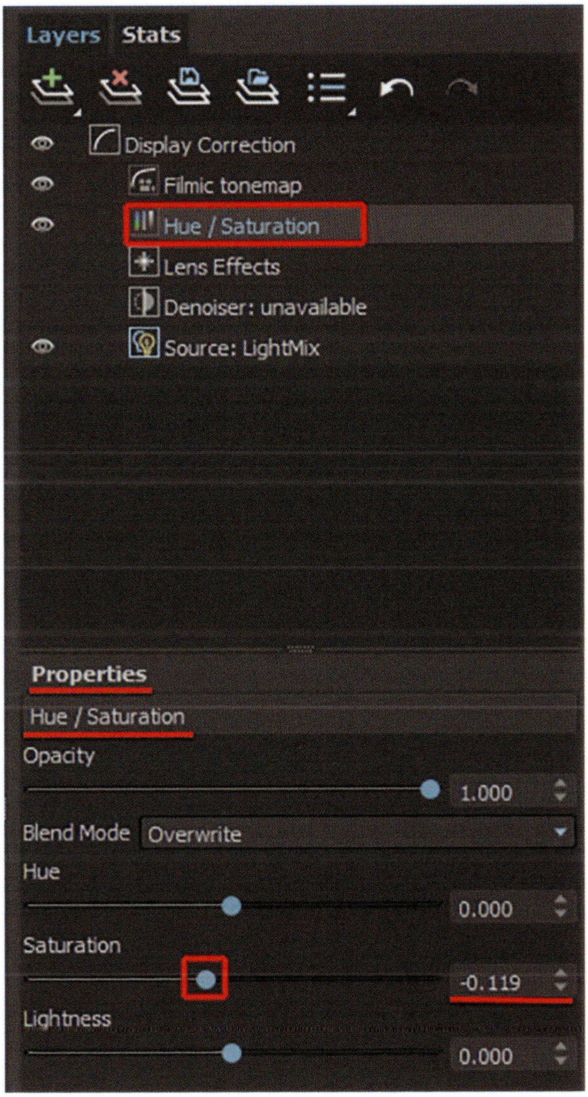

Hue/Saturation settings

Lookup Table: This adjustment layer allows users to load presaved LUT files to color grade your final renders.

To bake/save the LUT file with the final render, simply enable the function to, Save in image.

For this scene, I have used a LUT file under the name of 3DCollective_sRGB_Agfa_Futura_03Hard.cube

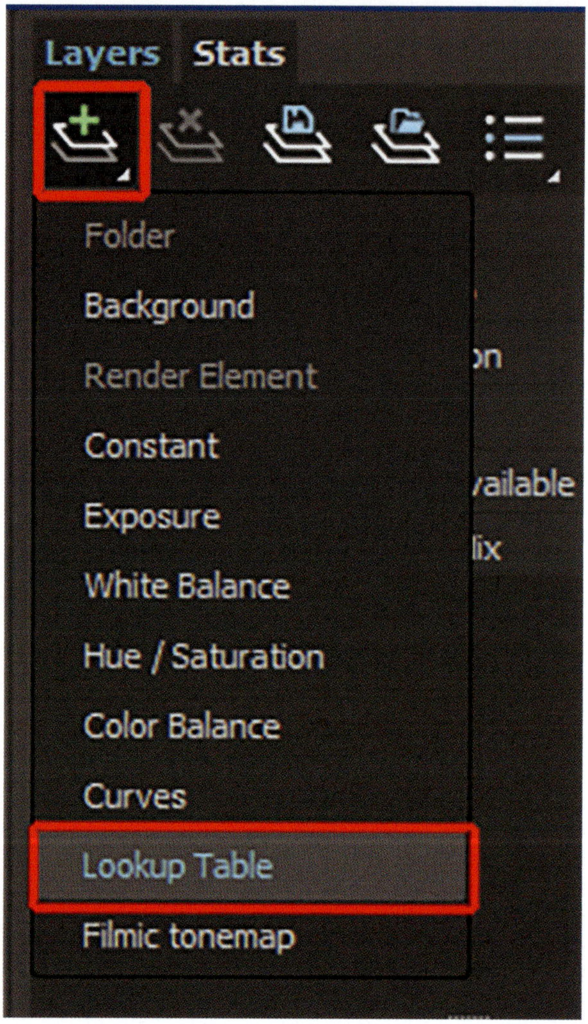

Add Lookup Table layer

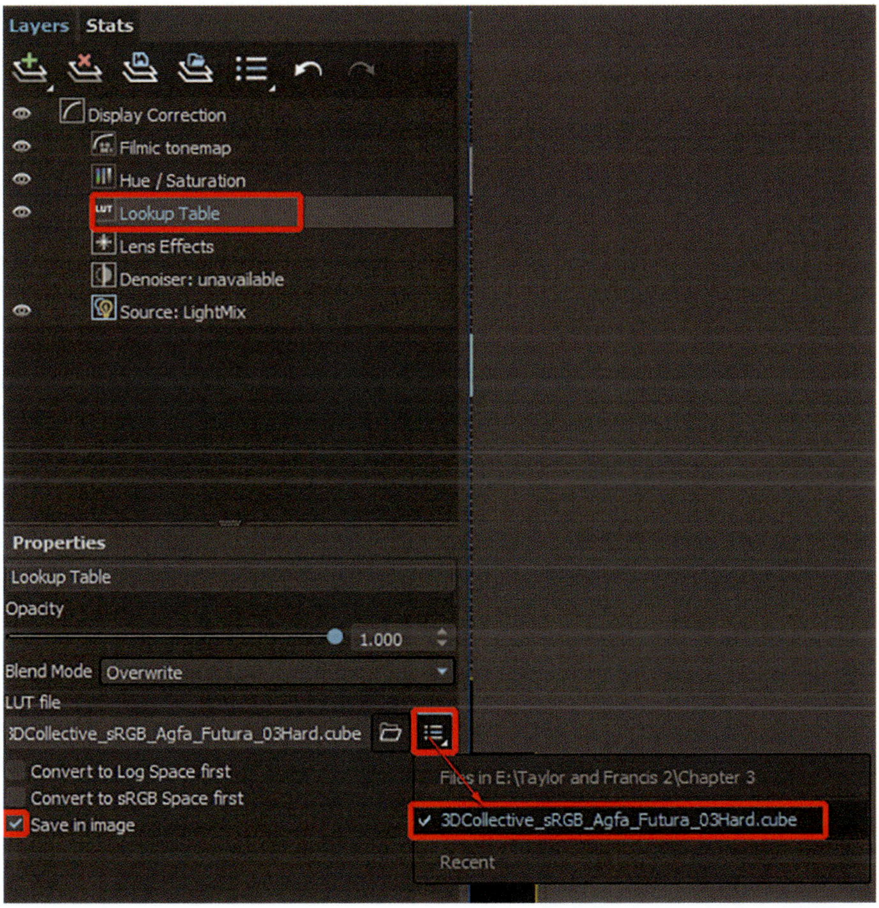

Lookup Table settings

Lookup Table final result

This LUT file was downloaded from the website 3dcollective.es

However, LUT files can also be created in Photoshop.

To do so, simply add your own adjustment layers first.

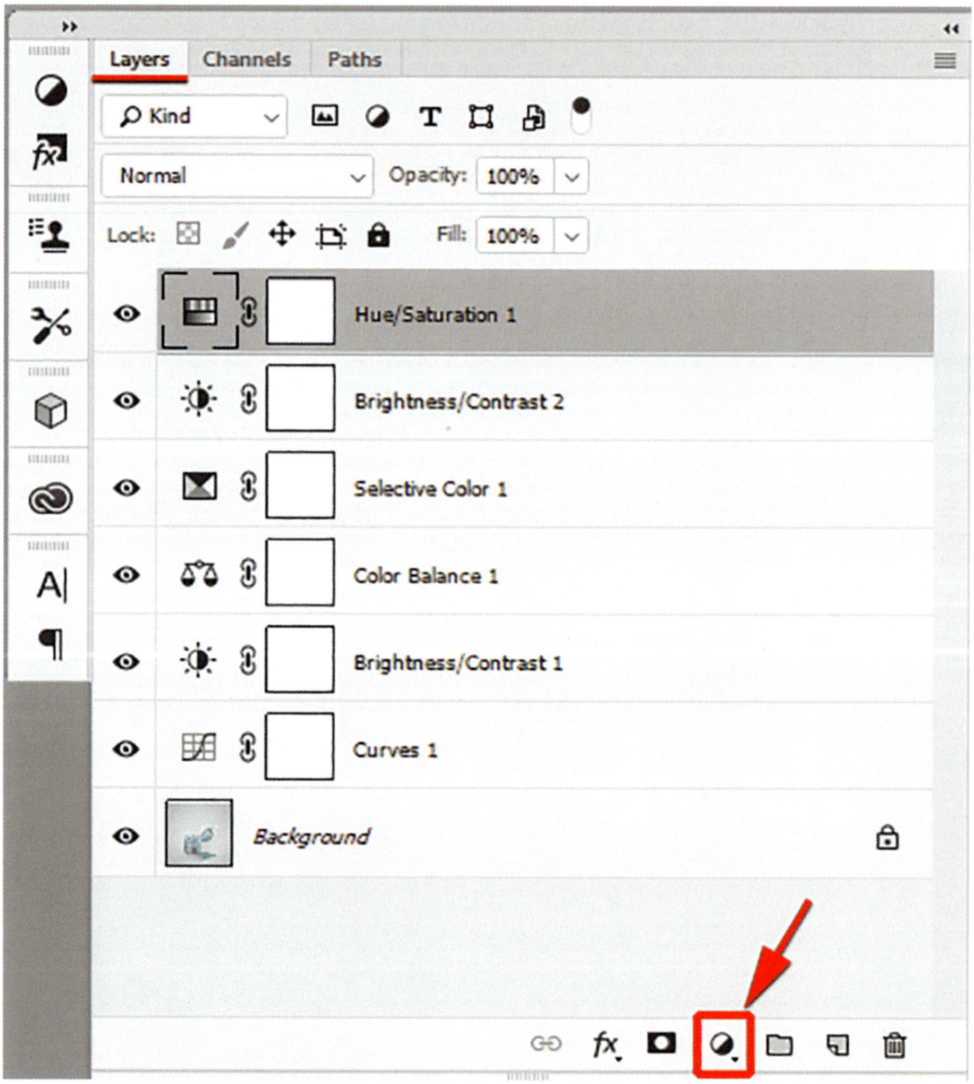

Add adjustment layers in Photoshop

Next, go to File, Export, and choose the Color Lookup Tables option.

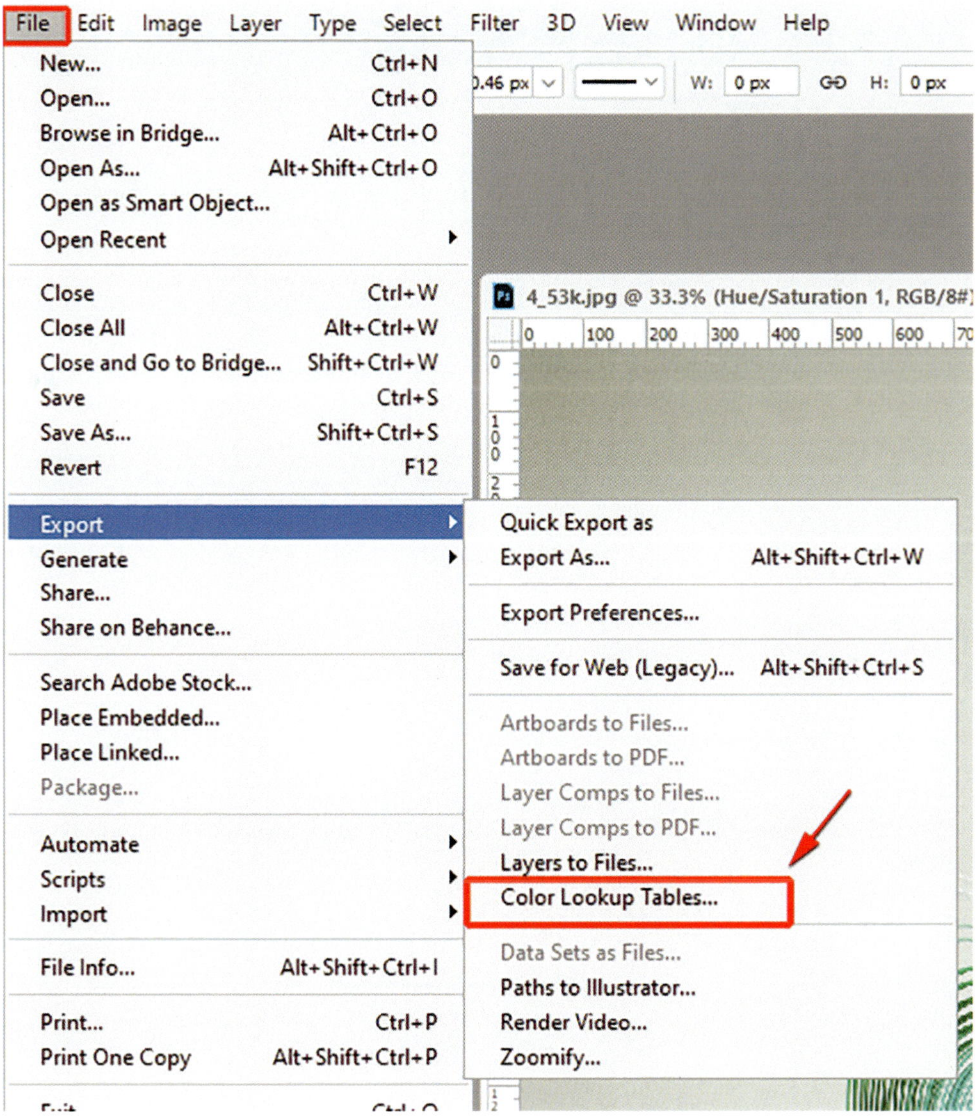

Add Color Lookup Tables option

Adjust and OK to close the dialog.

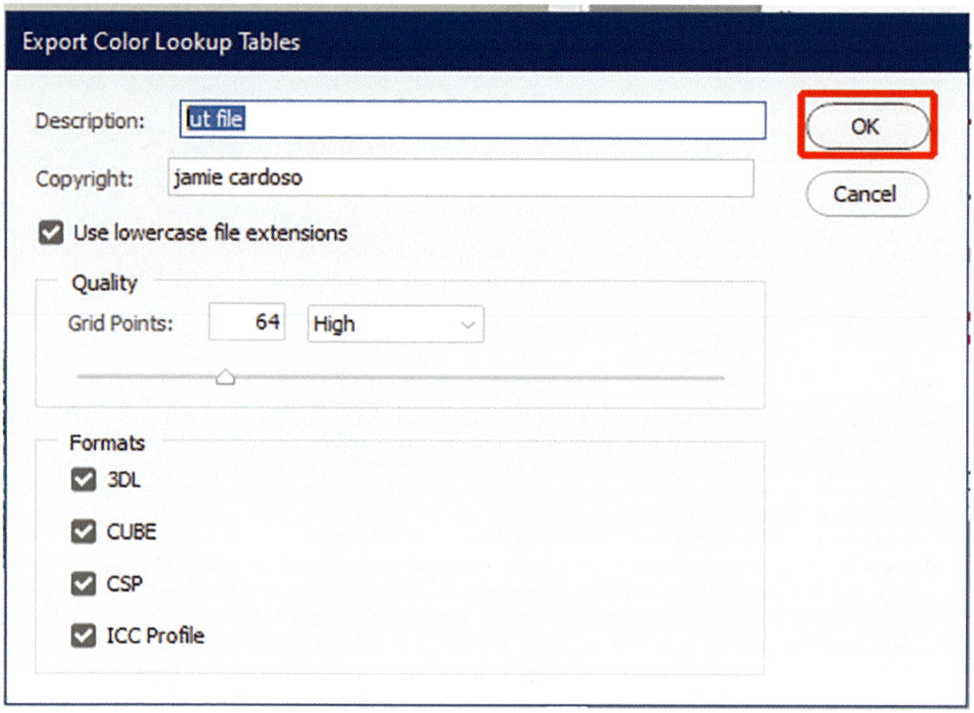

Export Color Lookup Tables dialog

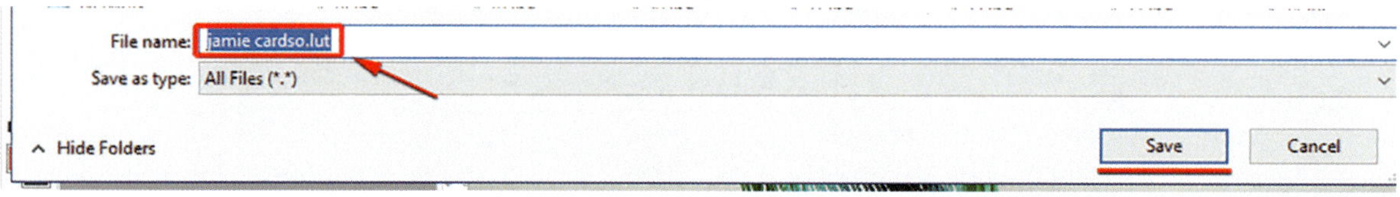

Save the LUT file

In 3ds Max, after loading it, you might need to enable the function to, Convert to Log Space first.

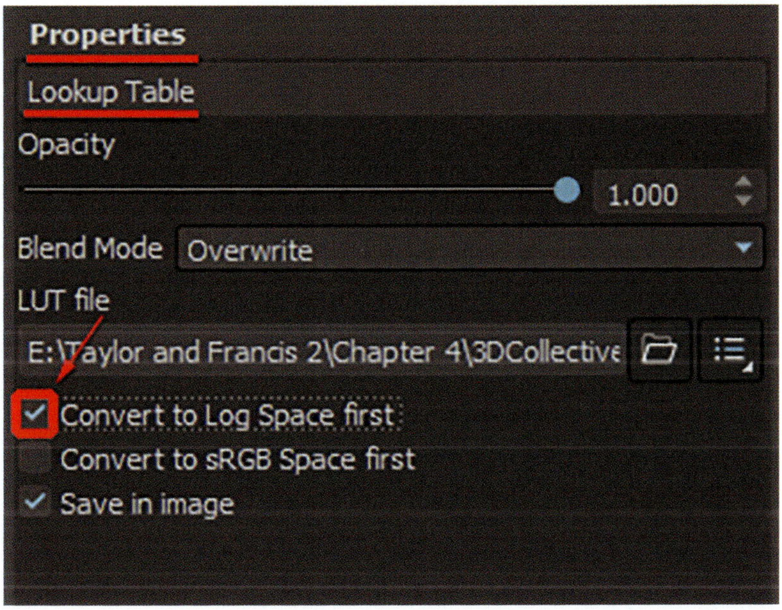

Convert to Log Space first

Lens Effects: To enable this default layer, users need to select it first, and turn on the function to, Enabled the bloom/glare effect.

This effect is only visible in finished rendered scenes with high contrast (bright & dark areas). And scenes with extreme highlight/bright spots, such as the sun and visible light sources. Users can set its Bloom Size, Intensity, Rotation, Threshold, Saturation, Aperture, etc.

NOTE

When you enable the Lens Effects in a fresh/new 3d scene, it will not show in VFB until the render is completed. Subsequent Lens Effects values can be adjusted while the render is taking place.

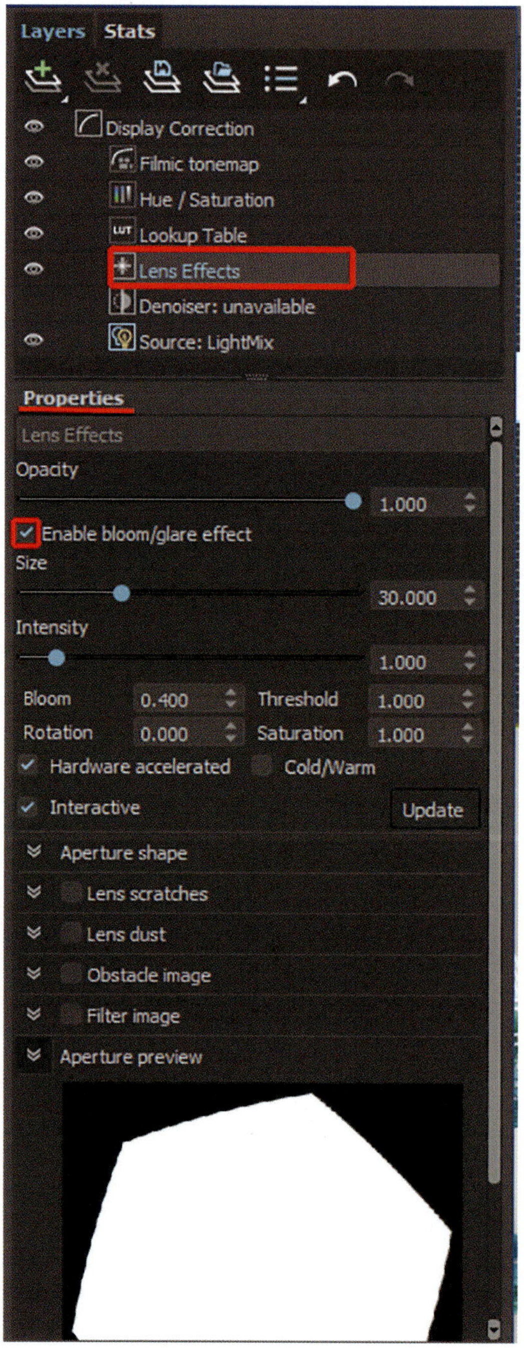

Lens Effects Properties

NOTE

There are times when you will need to right click and Reset the Lens Effects and increase values in order to appear in VFB. Also, click to Update.

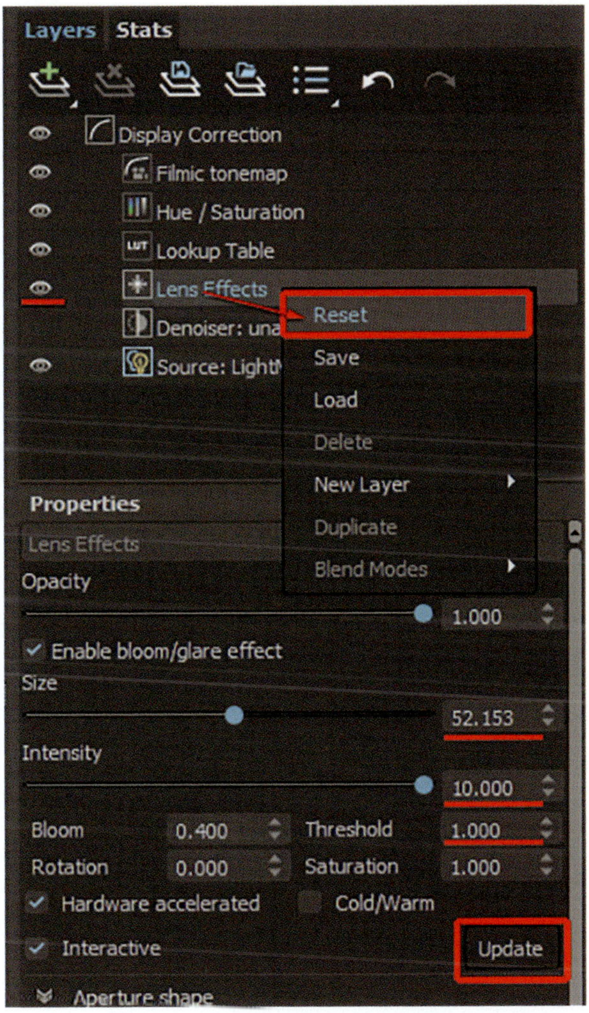

Lens Effects Reset and re-adjusted

The LightMix value might also need increasing at times.

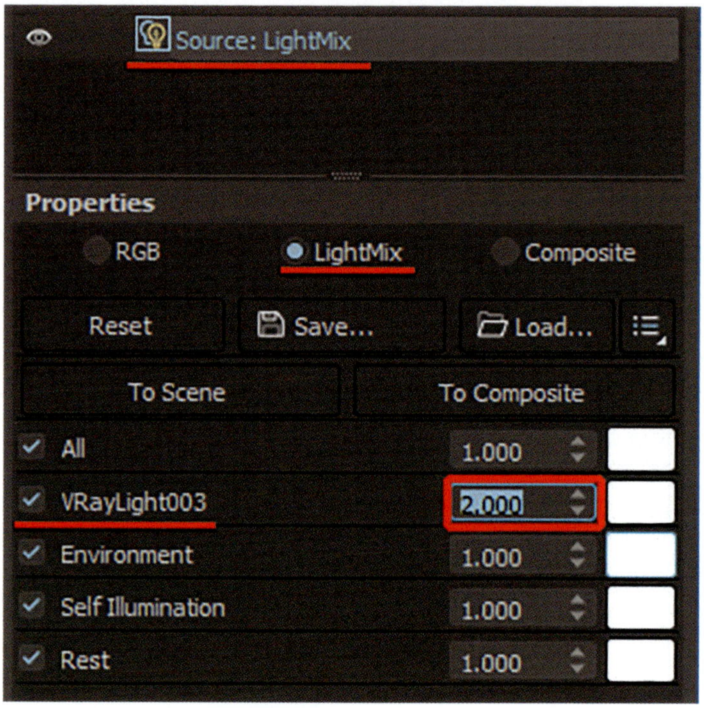

LightMix value increase to 2.000

Lens Effects final result in the VFB

NOTE

This button is grayed out (not available) when any of the default layers are selected (Display Correction, Lens Effects and Denoiser).

Delete selected layers button: This button allows users to delete a selected layer from this.

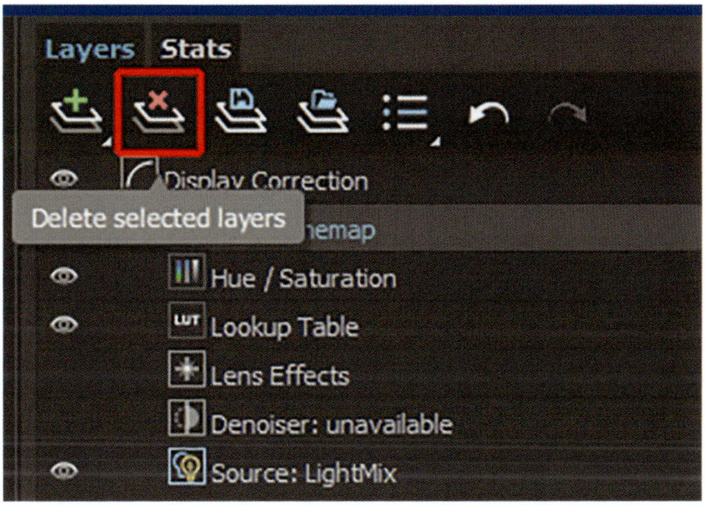

Delete selected layers button

Save layer tree preset button: This button allows users to save the list of layers added as a *.vfbl file format.

This file format can later be added in another 3ds Max scene.

For the purpose of this exercise, a file under the name of, Rendering in VRay.vfbl was saved. It can be loaded using the Load layer tree preset.

NOTE

The LightMix might not load with the original settings, if the VRayLight names and types differ (might require re-rendering with scene lights).

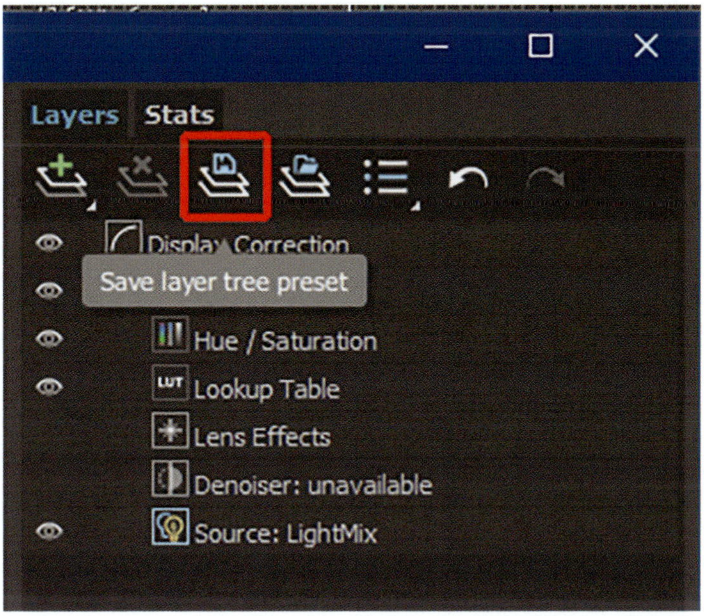

Save layer tree preset button

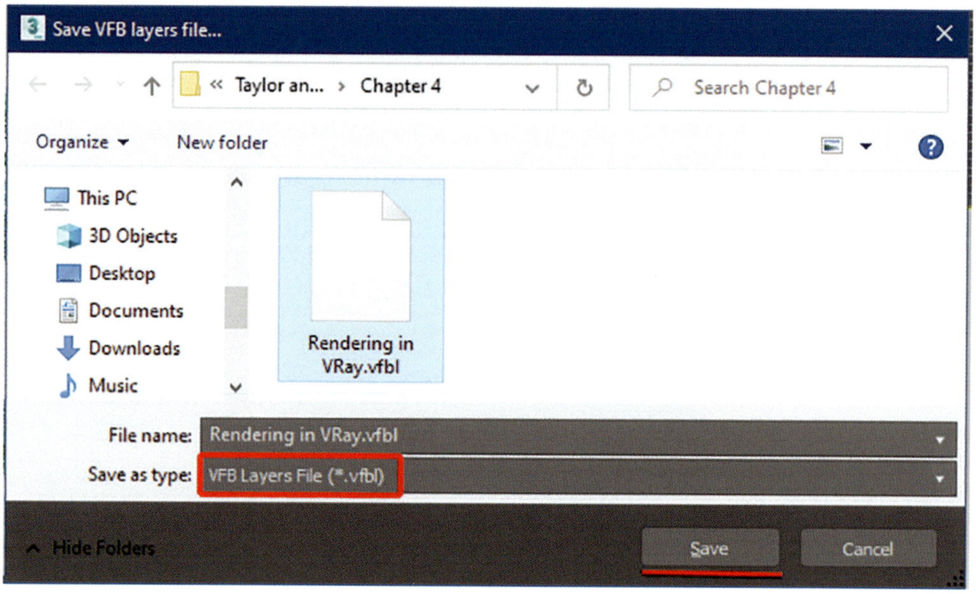

vfbl file saved

Load layer tree preset button: This button allows users to load and presaved vfbl file formats. For the purpose of this exercise, a file under the name of, Rendering in VRay.vfbl was loaded.

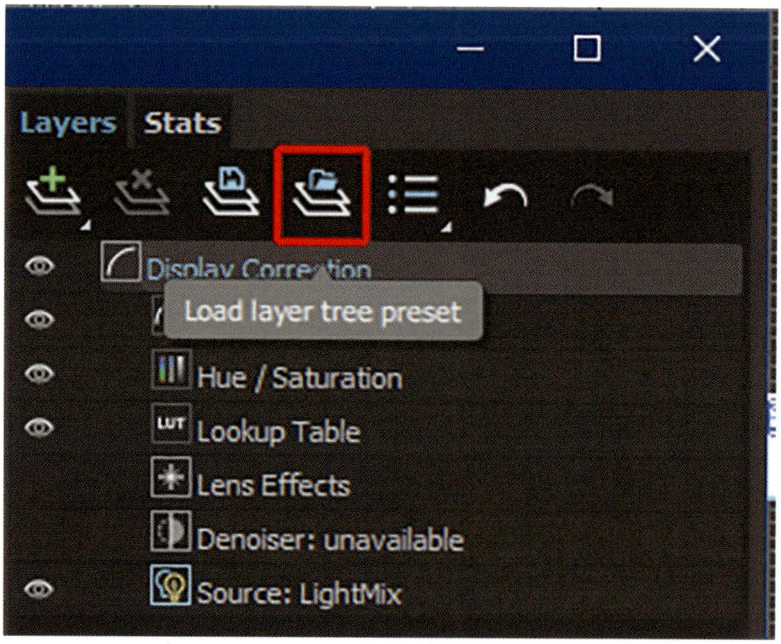

Load layer tree preset button

Undo/Redo Loading layers from file: These buttons allow users to Undo or Redo actions in the Layers tab.

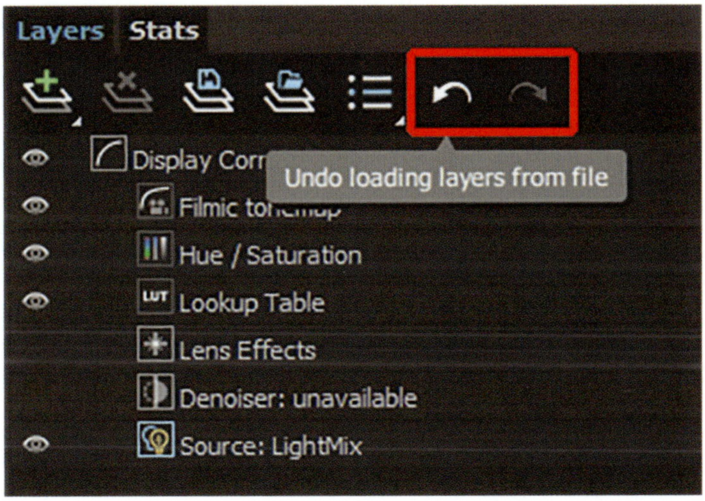

Undo/Redo Layers' actions

Show log button: Clicking this button unhides or hides the V-Ray messages dialog.

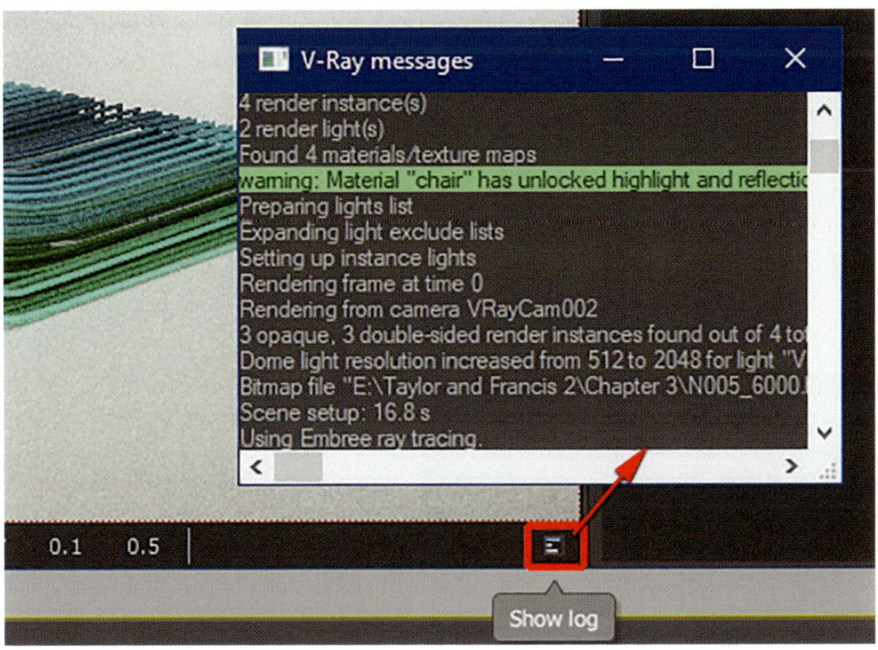

Show log button

HSV: Displays the colors in Hue, Saturation and Value under where the current mouse is on VFB.

Web: Displays colors in HEX of the pixel under where the current mouse is on VFB.

8bit: It displays the colors in 8 bit palette under where the current mouse is on VFB.

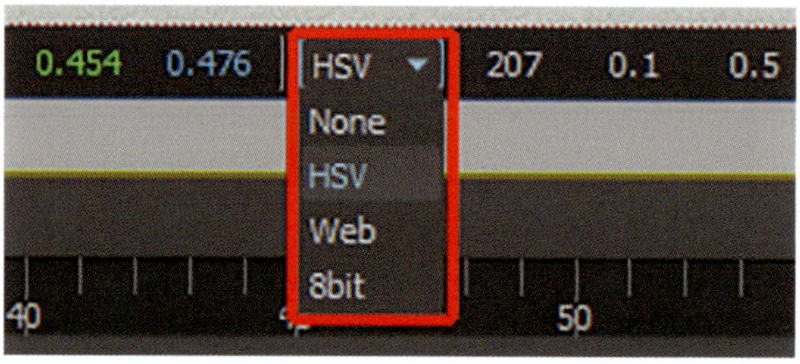

Color displays under the mouse

Show corrected colors button: It displays the corrected colors in the VFB. Enabled by default.

Show corrected colors button

Lock pixel info coordinates button: When enabled, it locks the mouse pointer coordinates and displays the pixel information. Unlocked by default.

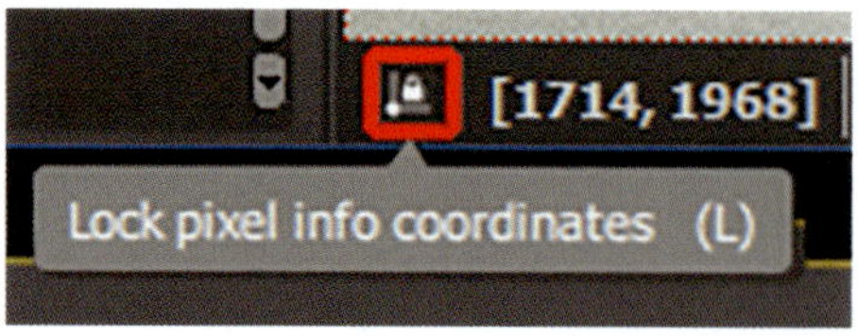

Lock pixel info coordinates button

V-Ray Raw Image File

V-Ray raw image file

V-Ray raw image file: When enabled, it renders the raw image format directly into the disk (bucket by bucket as the render progresses). This feature is quite useful when rendering extremely high-resolution images that may cause the VFB to crash during the rendering process.

Disabling the Memory frame buffer function while using this option will still render your high-resolution images into the *.vrimg file.

The function to generate a preview allows users to have a small preview of the render in progress.

The toggle to save the V-Ray image file allows users to find a location to save the *.vrimg file. Users can also enable functions such as EXR and Deep EXR.

V-Ray image file formats are often massive in size because of key render data stored in them.

As mentioned earlier, the *.vrimg file can be loaded into the VFB and saved out in any specific file format.

NOTE

Only enable this function prior to sending the final renders.

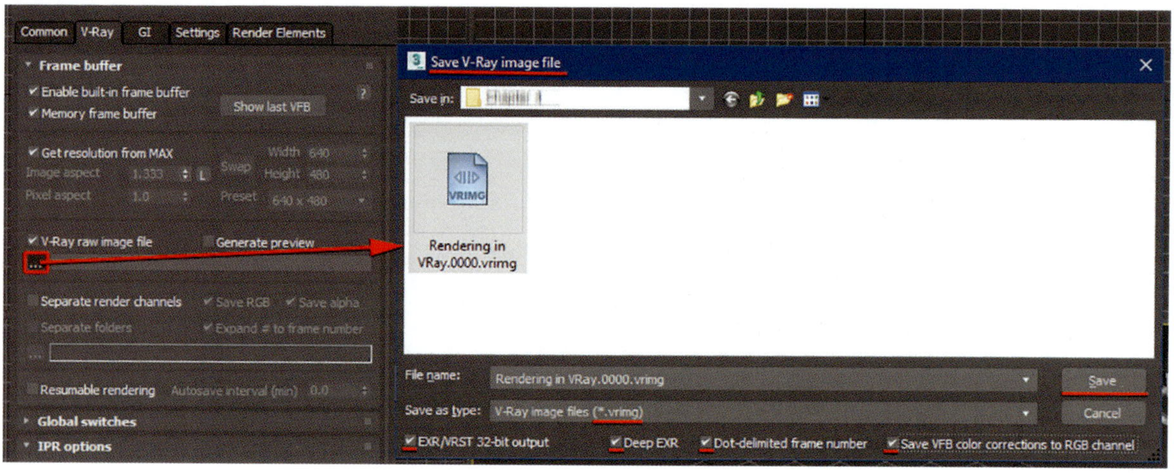

Save V-Ray image file toggle

Separate render channels: When enabled, it saves the render elements/channels (if added) into separate/individual files when rendered.

Also, when enabled, functions such as Save RGB, Save alpha and Expand # to frame number are automatically enabled.

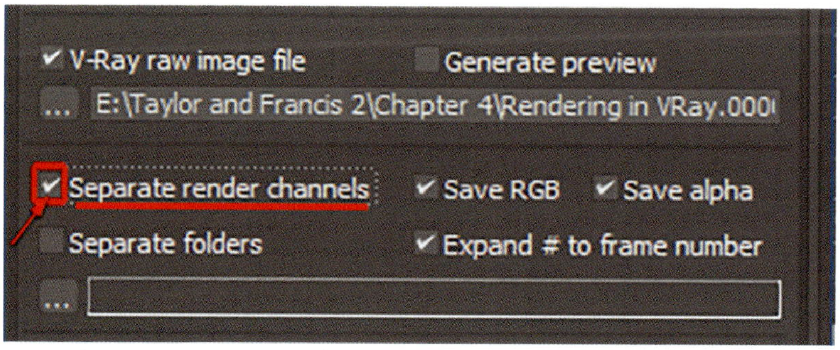

Separate render channels

NOTE

Only use this toggle prior to sending the final renders.

Separate folders: When enabled, it renders each element/channel into a separate folder. Disabled by default.

Browse toggle: This toggle allows users to name the file to be rendered and specify its folder destination and file format.

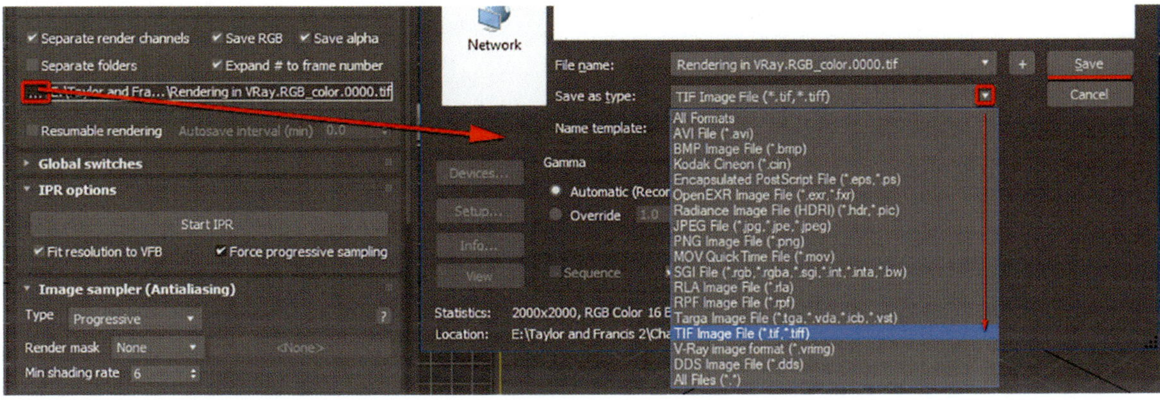

Browse toggle

Resumable rendering: When enabled, it only works in conjunction with the V-Ray raw image file (*.vrimg) to save the rendering progress. If per chance the computer shuts down abruptly, users can continue the render from where the last bucket finished before crashing.

No precalculation will be computed, for as long as users don't change any of the original settings/parameters.

NOTE

Only use this function prior to sending the final renders. And remember to disable it after the render is completed. Otherwise, it might render black.

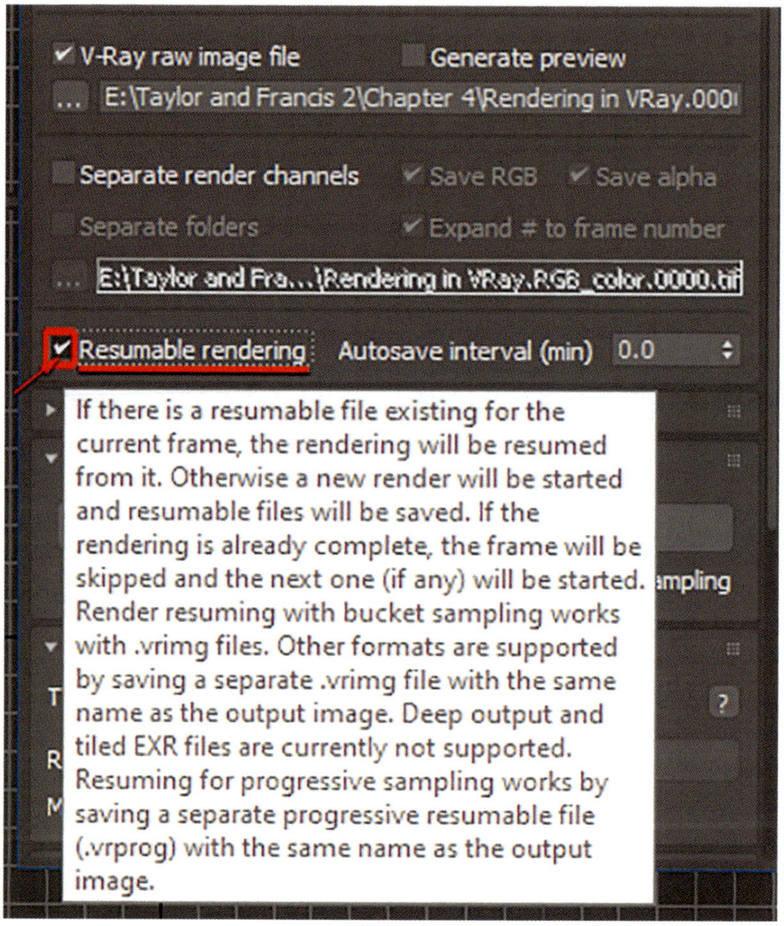

Resumable rendering function

Autosave interval (min): This function only works in conjunction with Resumable rendering and V-Ray raw image file. The value of 0.0 only saves when the render is completed.

Otherwise, it will save every minute specified/typed in.

Global Switches

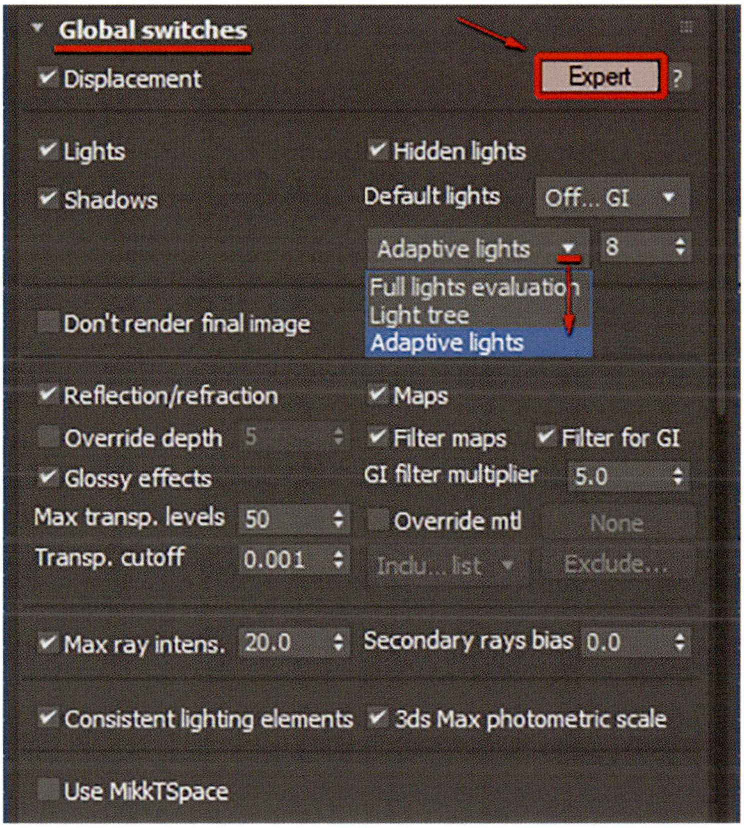

Global switches Expert options

To see more of the Global switches functions, simply click on the Basic button twice to get to the Expert mode.

Displacement: When on, it renders the displacement effects applied on materials. Enabled, by default.

Lights: When on, it renders the light effects in the scene. Enabled, by default.

Shadows: If turned on, it renders the shadows. Enabled, by default.

Hidden lights: When on, it renders the effects of hidden/isolated lights. Enabled by default.

Adaptive lights: Controls how many lights are sampled in the scene, based on the light cache points. It's best used in scenes with many lights.

Light tree: This mode is the fastest to compute, as it only calculates lights based on their proximity to the camera.

Full lights evaluation: This option calculates all lights in the scene (time-consuming).

Don't render final image: When enabled, it computes the pre-pass without rendering it. It's quite useful for saving the GI precalculation.
Disabled, by default.

Reflection/refraction: It computes the refraction of objects in the scene, if enabled.

Enabled, by default.

Override depth: If enabled, it overrides the depth value of all materials in the scene with a specified value entered.

This function is only used when there are merged objects/materials with extremely high depth values that are causing the renders to slow down.

Disabled, by default.

Glossy effects: It calculates the glossy effects on reflections and refractions. Otherwise, glossy effects on reflections will be mirror like (nondiffused). Enabled, by default.

Override mtl: This toggle allows users to plug a material/shader to override all materials in the scene.

This function is quite useful for quick chalk renders or light studies. Whereby the entire scene has one basic white/gray material, with lights turned on.

The Include/Exclude toggles allow users to pick and choose which objects in the scene to exclude from the override material.

IPR Options

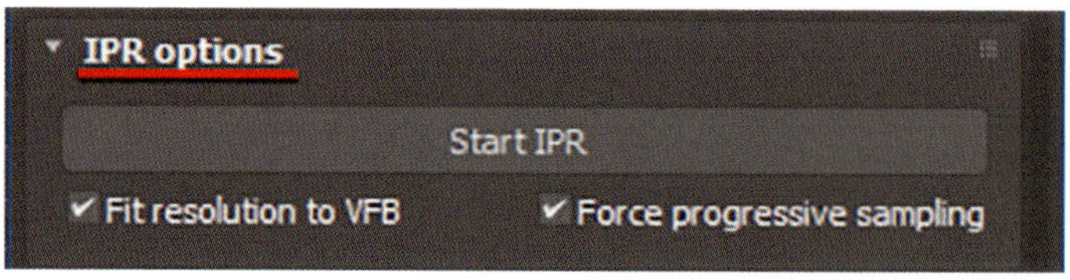

IPR options

Interactive Production Render options allow users to execute quick and interactive renders using the Progressive image sampler parameters.

As mentioned earlier, this function can also be accessed via the main toolbar or the Viewport.

Start IPR: This button starts the IPR rendering in the VFB, when clicked.

Fit resolution to VFB: This function forces the original render size to fit the VFB size. Enabled by default.

Force progressive sampling: When enabled, this function uses the Progressive image sampler parameters to compute the renders. Enabled, by default.

While the IPR is taking place in the VFB, users can right click and choose to, Real Zoom, View Navigation, Re-initialize, Select object (Ctrl + Click), Get object material (Shift + Click) and Set focus distance (Alt + Click).

Every time one of the functions is chosen, the IPR updates the render in the VFB.

NOTE

IPR works with both Bucket and Progressive image samplers.

NOTE

This function is for display purposes in the VFB only.

VFB IPR options

Image Sampler (Antialiasing)

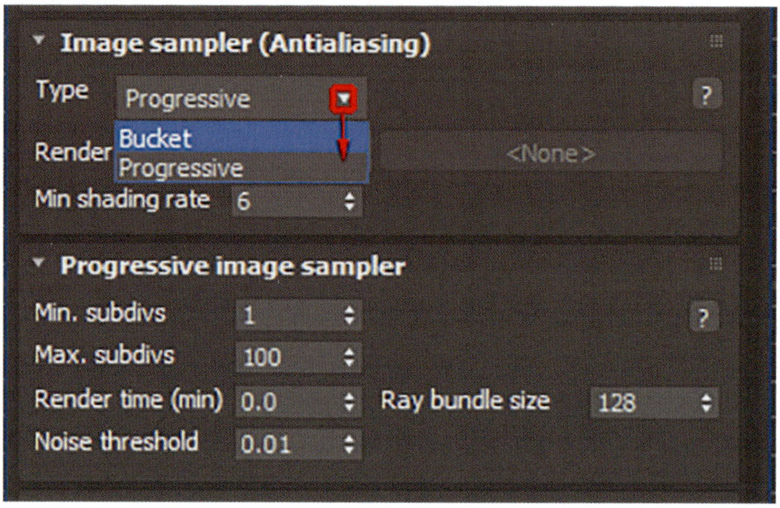

Image sampler types

This rollout controls the final quality of the renders.

Type: This function allows users to choose Progressive (default) or Bucket type from its dropdown list.

Render mask: This function doesn't work well with region renders. It allows users to choose from a list of different types of areas/masks to render such as Texture, Selected, Include/Exclude list and Layers.

This tool is quite useful for final renders that require one or two object surfaces to be changed. Instead of having to re-render the entire scene, users can select the object/s in question and re-render them.

Default, none.

Min shading rate: This amazing function allows users to increase the render quality without affecting the rendering times. The higher the value, the better the shading quality.

Default value, 6

NOTE

I often set it to 64 for final renders.

Progressive Image Sampler

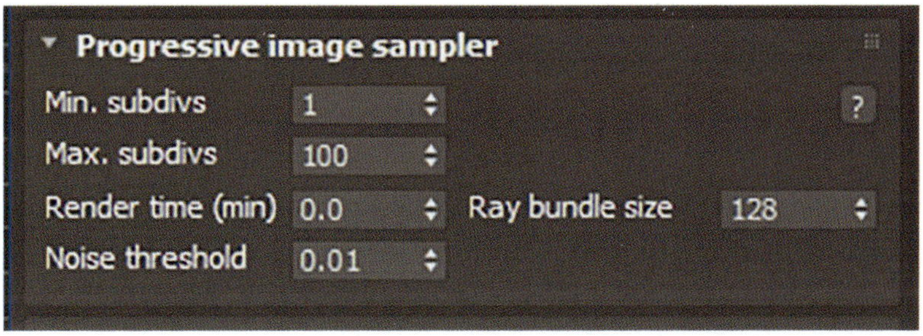

Progressive image sampler options

This image sampler type is often used for test renders while building the scene. It cannot be used for strip network renders, etc.

Min. subdivs: This function controls the minimum number of samples required to process the antialiasing. The higher the value the slower the rendering times.

Default value, 1

NOTE

For optimal results, this value should always be kept at 1.

Max. subdivs: The function controls the maximum number of samples required to process the antialiasing.

Default value, 100.

NOTE

For optimal results, this value should always be kept at 100.

Render time (min): The values entered here specify the total number of minutes a render should take, regardless of its final quality. The default value of 0.0 sets the rendering time to progressively unlimited, until the final quality is achieved.

If the renders are set to Interactive (IPR), users can continue making changes to the scene and materials while rendering interactively in the viewport or VFB simultaneously.

Ray bundle size: This function controls the number of rays calculated on each machine (if many) when the render is set to distribute.

Default value, 128.

Noise threshold: This function is the main parameter to control the overall quality of renders. The smaller the value the better the quality.

However, rendering times will increase.

For draft renders, the value of 0.1 should be sufficient.

For high-resolution progressive renders, values between 0.007 and 0.01 often work perfectly.

Default value, 0.01.

Progressive Noise threshold set to 0.01

Progressive Noise threshold set to 0.007

Bucket Image Sampler

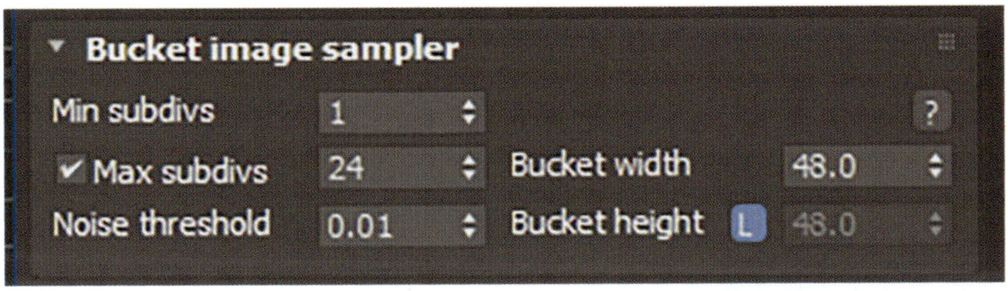

Bucket image sampler options

This image sampler type is often used for final renders and animations via network rendering using strips, etc.

Min subdivs: It controls the minimum number of samples necessary to compute each rendered pixel.

Default value, 1.

Max subdivs: It controls the maximum number of samples necessary to compute each rendered pixel.

Default value, 24.

Noise threshold: This function is the main parameter that controls the overall quality of a render. The smaller the value the better the quality.

However, rendering times will increase.

For draft renders, the value of 0.1 should be sufficient.

For final high-resolution renders, values between 0.007 and 0.01 often work perfectly.

NOTE

For optimal results, this value should always be kept at 1.

NOTE

For optimal "universal workflow" settings, this value should be set to 100.

Bucket Noise threshold set to 0.1

Bucket Noise threshold set to 0.007

NOTE

Uncloaking the padlock allows the user to set the bucket's width and height sizes individually.

Bucket width and height: The default value of 48 pixels sets the size of each bucket rendered on VFB.

Image Filter

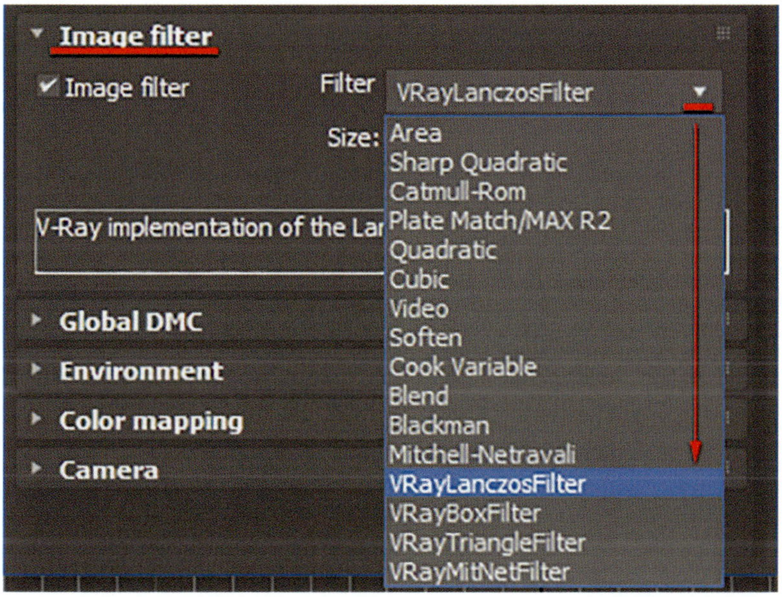

Image filter options

This section controls the filter applied to the renders.

Image filters such as Mitchell-Netravali, yield sharp results, and increase the rendering times slightly.

Default filter, VRayLanczosFilter.

I often use the Area filter.

Global DMC

This section controls how the noise is processed.

Lock noise pattern: When enabled, it forces similar noise patterns to be locked.

It's mainly used for animations.

Disabled, by default.

Blue noise sampling: When enabled, it optimizes the noise pattern uniformly across a render.

Enabled, by default.

Global DMC group

Environment

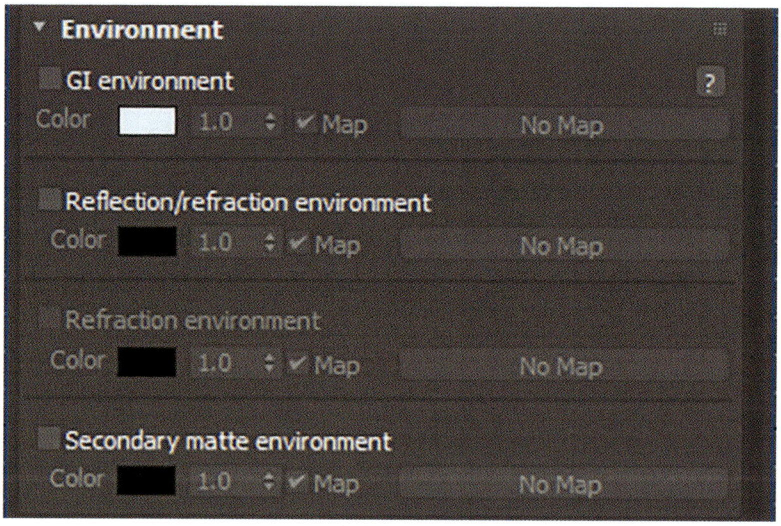

Environment rollout parameters

When used, the environment parameters will override the Environment map toggle.

GI environment: If turned on, it controls the environment/background Global Illumination parameters.

Color: This function allows users to pick a color from its color swatch dialog and control the intensity with its values.

Map: Users often plug a VRayBitmap with an HDRI in this toggle to produce accurate environment lighting.

Reflection/refraction environment: If turned on, it controls the global reflection/refraction of the environment.

Map: VRayBitmap with an HDRI is often used in this toggle to produce the environment's reflection/refraction.

Color Mapping

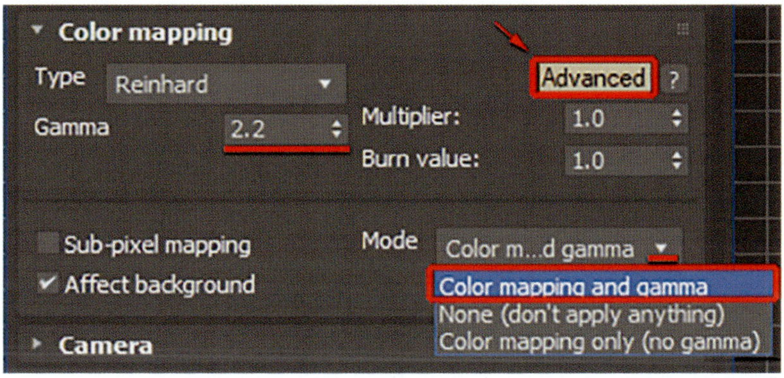

Color mapping rollout parameters

These parameters control how the overall render is processed and saved on your computer.

Type: This function allows users to choose the Color mapping type, from its dropdown list. One of the most popular ones in the Linear multiply.

I personally prefer the Exponential type, because of its overall photographic look and the ability to balance overexposed renders.

Default type, Reinhard.

Gamma: This function controls the gamma value. The value of 2.2 is the most accurate one.

Users should also set the gamma from Preference Settings to 2.2.

NOTE

Ensure to click on the Default button to bring up the Advanced parameters.

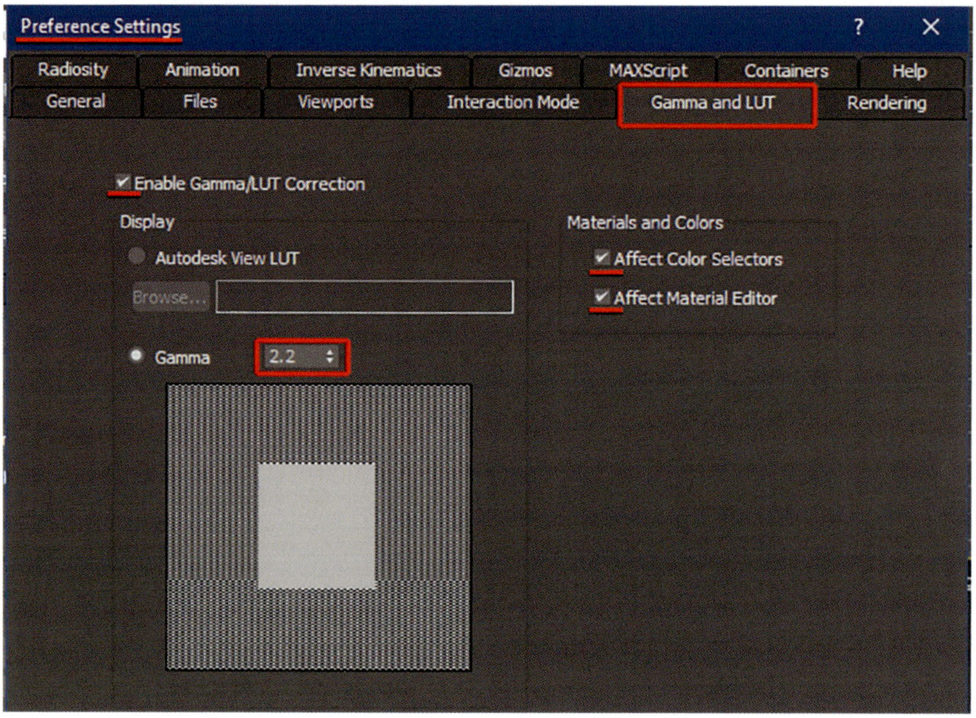

Gamma Preference Settings to 2.2

Multiplier: This function controls the intensity of the multiplier in the render. Default value, 1.0.

Burn value: This option controls the intensity of exposed/burnt areas in the render. Default value, 1.0.

This function is quite useful to help integrate Photomontages or Verified views. In addition, it can be used to help reduce overly bright areas.

Sub-pixel mapping: This function applies the color mapping to individual sub-pixel samples.

Also, it helps to remove artifacts such as bright pixel dots on a render. It often increases the rendering time slightly, when enabled.

Disabled, by default.

Affect background: When on, the color mapping is applied to the environment map.

For photomontages, users often disable this option to avoid doubling the gamma. Enabled, by default.

Mode: This option controls how the VFB renders are saved into your hard drive.

Scenes from earlier versions of 3ds Max should be merged in a scene setup with Color mapping and gamma mode. Otherwise saved images/renders may differ from what is seen in the VFB.

Default mode, Color mapping only (no gamma).

> **NOTE**
>
> Color mapping and gamma mode are the best, because it saves the renders exactly as seen in the VFB. Ensure to always setup your scene in this manner prior to beginning a project.

Global Illumination

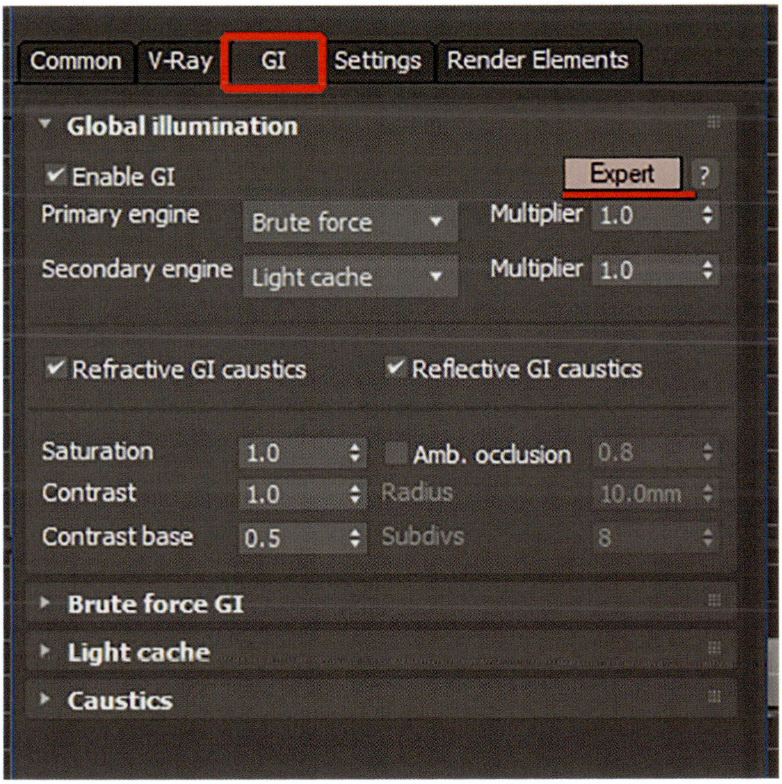

Global Illumination parameters

Enable GI: This function activates the Global Illumination.

Enabled, by default.

Primary engine: This option computes the GI primary bounces. Its dropdown menu allows users to choose other prime engines such as Irradiance or Light cache.

> **NOTE**
>
> Ensure to click on the Default button twice to bring up the Expert parameters.

NOTE

Brute force is the most accurate Primary engine. Its parameters are grayed out because it's physically accurate (unbiased).

Furthermore, in V-Ray 5, lights, render elements and most parameters only work with Brute force.

Default, Brute force.

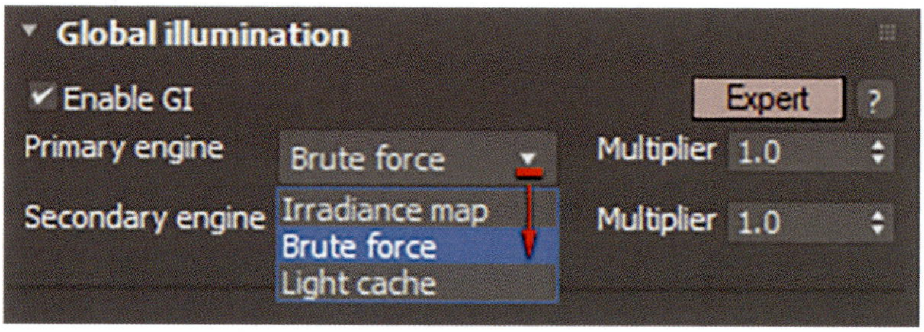

Brute force primary engine

Secondary engine: This option computes the GI secondary bounces. The light cache is the default secondary engine.

Multiplier: For both, Primary and secondary engines, this function helps to reinvigorate or diminish their influence in the GI calculation.

Default value, 1.0.

NOTE

They only work when the Caustics rollout parameters are enabled.

Refractive/Reflective GI caustics: When enabled, these functions allow the GI caustics to be computed on refractive and/or reflective (transparent) surfaces.

Enabled, by default.

Caustics parameters are disabled, by default.

Saturation: This option controls the color saturation of the GI effect. Higher values cause the GI to produce more saturated colors.

Default value, 1.0.

NOTE

Ambient occlusion works in a similar way to VRayDirt (previously covered).

Contrast: This function determines the overall contrast of the GI. Higher values increase the GI contrast.

Default value, 1.0.

Contrast base: This option controls the base contrast values. Default value, 0.5.

Amb. Occlusion: When on, it adds connecting shadows on indirectly lit areas globally. Disabled, by default.

Radius: This option controls the propagation of the connecting shadows from its starting point. Default value, 10 mm.

Subdivs: This option controls the smoothness of the connecting shadows. Higher values yield smoother results.

Default value, 8

Light Cache

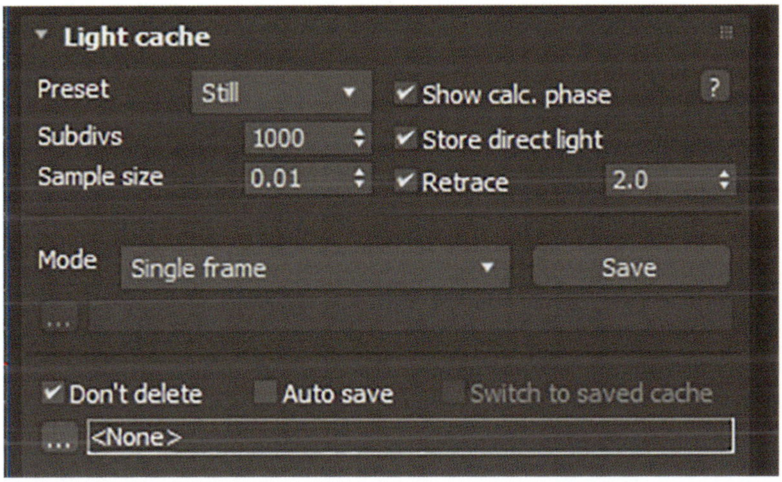

Light cache parameters

This secondary GI engine is an approximation (biased). It's ideal for most high-resolution still renders and animations,

Preset: This function allows users to choose between Still and Animation presets.

The Still preset comes with the default Subdivs value set to 1000.

The Animation preset comes with the default Subdivs value set to 3000.

Subdivs: This function determines the accuracy of the light cache calculation. Extremely high values produce results closer to Brute force (unbiased).

Values between 1000 and 3000 work well for most scenes. Default value, 1000.

Sample size: This function controls the spatial detail of the light cache. The default value of 0.01 works well for most scenes and animations.

Default value, 0.01

Show calc. phase: This function displays the precalculation of the light cache in the VFB, prior to rendering.

Enabled, by default.

NOTE

The value of 8.0 is ideal for animations.

Store direct light: This function caches the direct light (if any) in the light cache calculation.

Enabled, by default.

Retrace: This function retraces the light in tight areas such as corners. Having this option turned on prevents light leaks and flickering.

Default value, 2.0. Higher values increase the light cache precalculation time.

Mode: This option allows users to choose between, Single Frame or From file mode.

Default Mode, Single frame.

Save: This toggle allows users to name and save a Light cache file (*.vrlmap)

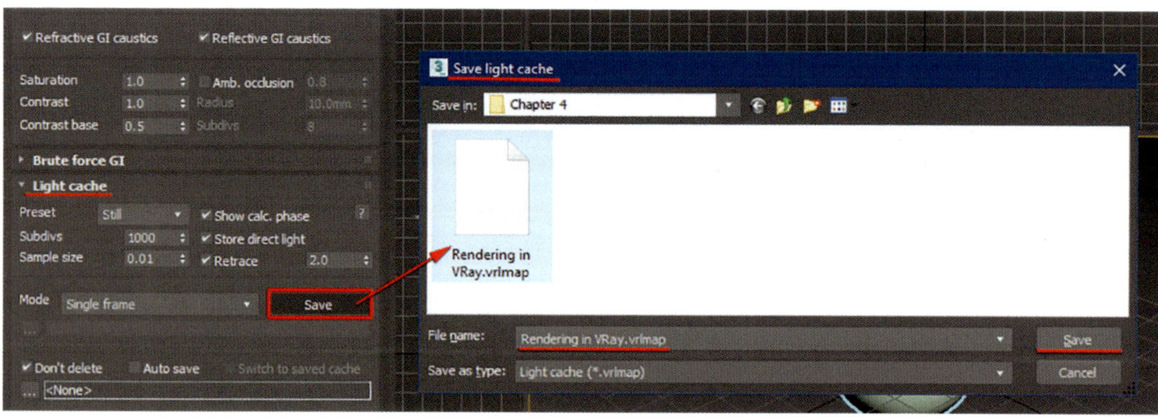

Save Light cache dialog

Don't delete: When turned on, it keeps the light cache in memory after rendering. It's faster for subsequent renders.

However, it uses up computer memory.

Enabled, by default.

Auto save: When enabled, it automatically saves the light cache file entered in the toggle below (<None>).

Disabled, by default.

Switch to saved cache: This function only becomes available if the Auto save option is enabled.

It automatically uploads the saved light cache file in the toggle below (<none>), after being saved previously.

Users tend to enable the Don't render final image option while saving the light cache file. Having this function enabled will allow users to save the light cache precalculation file without having to render the image.

Also, ensure to disable the Don't render final image option, prior to sending the final render.

Settings

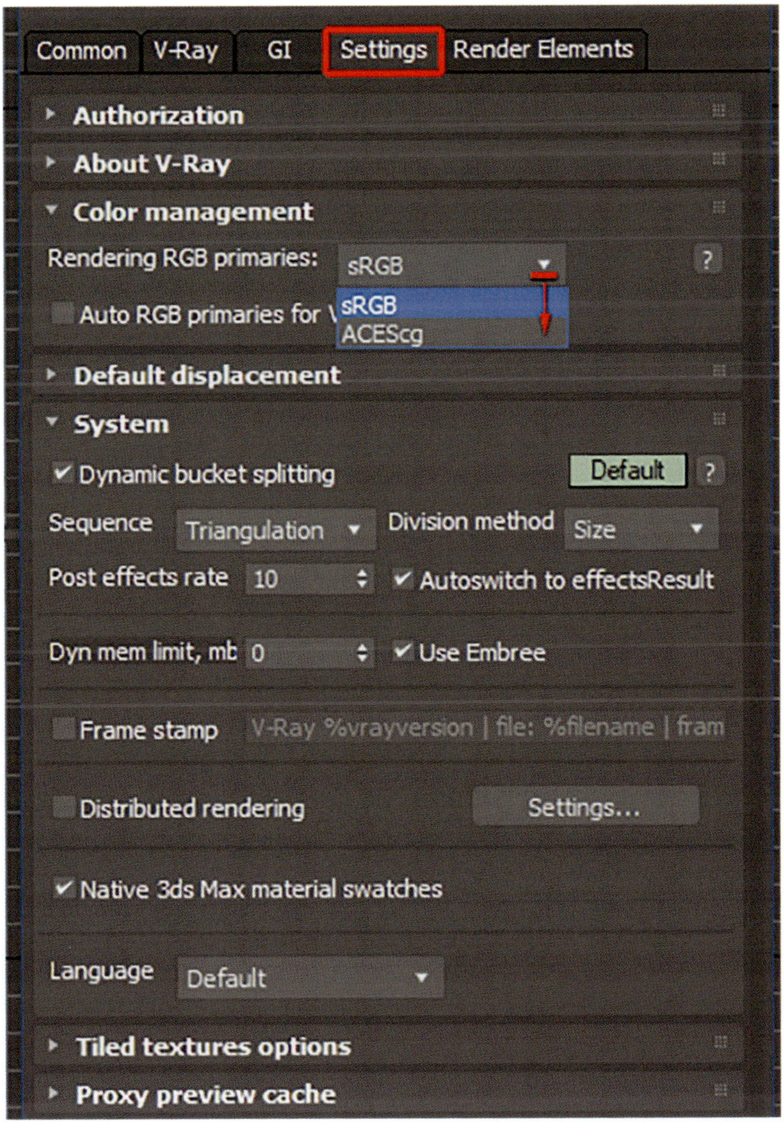

Settings parameters

Color Management

Rendering RGB primaries: This option allows users to choose between sRGB and ACEScg color display spaces.

sRGB is the default color space for most monitors.

Auto RGB primaries for VRayBitmap textures: When enabled, this function forces the RGB primaries for VRayBitmap textures.

Disabled, by default.

Default Displacement

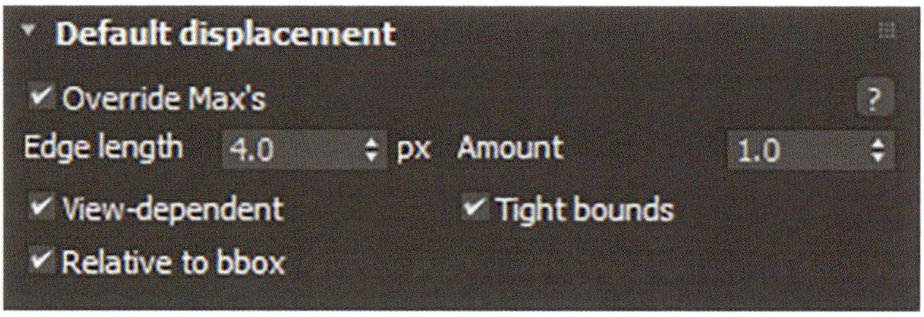

Default displacement parameters

Override Max's: When enabled, it uses V-Ray's micro triangulation system to calculate displacement values. Enabled, by default.

Edge length: This function controls the edge length of the displacement, in pixels (if view-dependent). Default value, 4.0.

Amount: This option controls the default scaling amount of the displacement. Default value, 1.0.

View-dependent: When enabled, the Edge length is in pixels. Otherwise world units. Enabled, by default.

Relative to bbox: This function forces the displacement to be relative to the bounding box. Enabled, by default.

Tight bounds: When enabled, it computes the displacement as closely as possible to the original mesh (preserves the integrity of the original mesh). Enabled, by default.

System

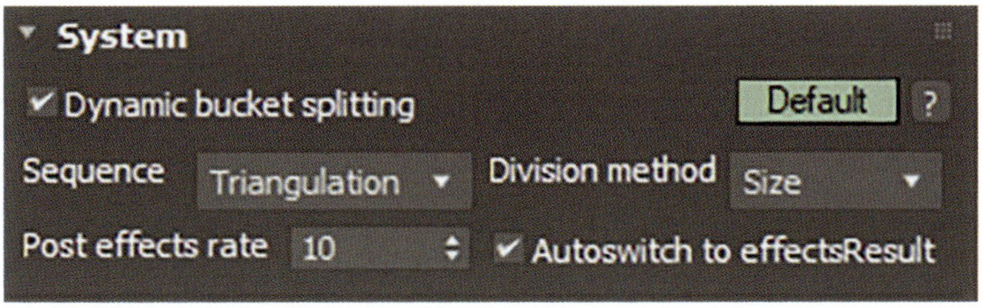

System parameters

Dynamic bucket splitting: It automatically splits the bucket rendering size according to the bucket width value. In addition, it automatically decides whether to reduce or increase the bucket size depending on the areas of the VFB being rendered.

Enabled by default.

Sequence: It determines the sequence/movement of the bucket rendering in the VFB. Default sequence, Triangulation.

Posteffects rate: This function determines the frequency of progressive rendering updates on the VFB. The value of 0 disables render updates during progressive rendering.

High values updates progressive renders more frequently. The default value of 10 is often sufficient.

Division method: This function controls how the render is divided in buckets when rendering in VFB. Users can choose between Size and Count division methods.

Both methods use pixels to measure the buckets. The Image sampler type needs to be set to Bucket.

Autoswitch to effectsResult: This function uses the effectsResult channel/ render element to display the final render result. It's mostly useful when effects are being used under the VFB Layers tab.

Enabled, by default.

Dyn mem limit, mb: This option sets the memory limit to compute a render. This function is quite useful to increase or decrease the rendering power, depending on one's resources.

The default value of 0 uses as much memory as possible to compute the final render.

Use Embree: This function uses the Intel Embree raycaster. Enabled by default.

Dyn mem limit, mb parameters

Frame stamp: When enabled, the bottom part of the V-Ray Frame buffer will display key render information such as V-Ray Version (V-Ray %vrayversion) and File name (file: %filename).

Disabled, by default.

Frame stamp parameters

Distributed rendering: When enabled, it uses the distributed rendering system to allocate assigned computers to the rendering calculation.

Computers are assigned/allocated through the Settings toggle.

The more computers are assigned, the faster the renders will be. Distributed rendering only works in conjunction with V-Ray Spawner.

For more information about V-Ray Spawner, please visit http://docs.chaosgroup.com/

Distributed rendering is disabled, by default.

Settings: This toggle allows users to add/allocated computers to the distributed rendering process.

V-Ray distributed rendering settings dialog has the following functionalities:

Add server: This function allows users to type in the machine/server name or IP address

Edit server: It allows users to edit an existing machine/server name or IP address. To do so, simply select the listed Host name, followed by clicking on the Edit server function.

Remove server: It enables users to select and remove existing servers from the list.

Resolve servers: This function allows V-Ray to automatically resolve incorrect server names/IP addresses listed in the dialog.

NOTE

Always enable the functions to, Restart servers on the render end and Transfer missing assets. This will prevent numerous problems associated with remote servers.

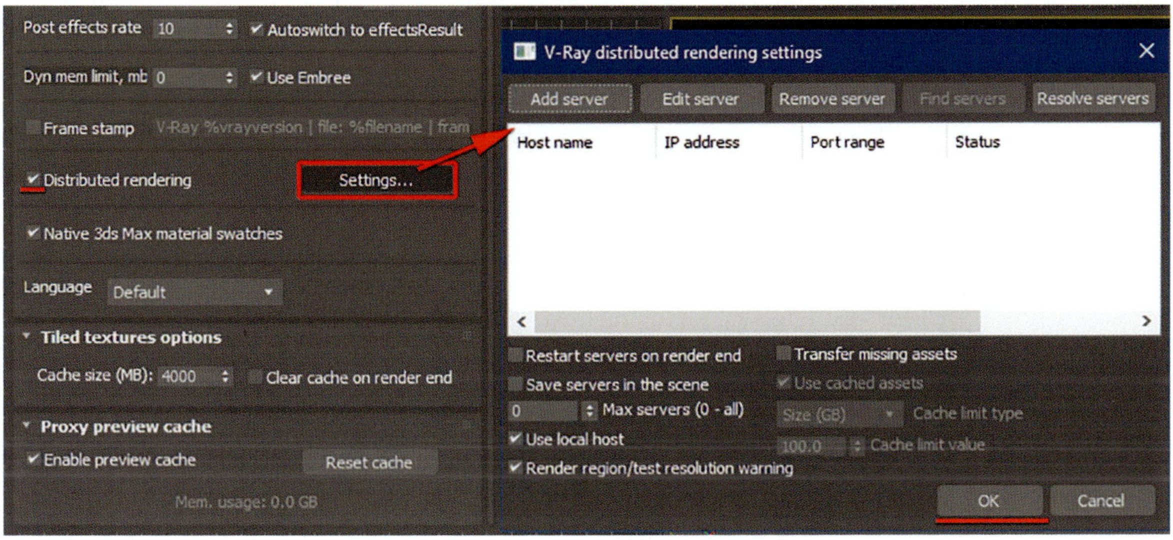

Settings dialog

Native 3ds Max material swatches: This function allows users to enable the Native 3ds Max material editor.

As mentioned earlier, this function should be enabled for quick previews of materials in the Material Editor slots. Otherwise, material previews will be more realistic, at a cost of slower performance.

Disabled, by default.

Native 3ds Max material swatches function

Language: This function allows users to choose a preferred language to translate the V-Ray tooltips to.

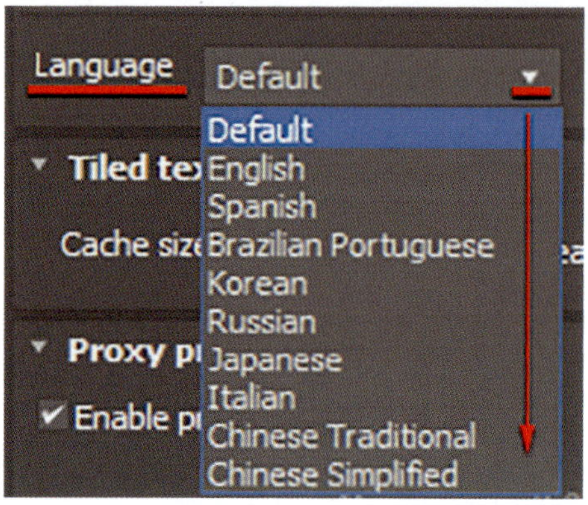

Language options

Tiled Textures Options

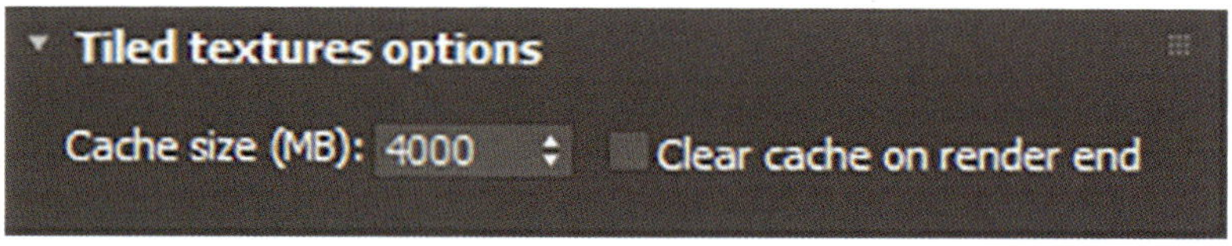

Tiled textures options

Cache size (MB): This function allows users to specify the maximum amount of memory (MB) to be used to cache tiled textures (OpenEXR and TIFF files). If set to 0, V-Ray will use as much memory as required.

Default value, 4000.

Clear cache on render end: When enabled, it clears the texture cached after a render is completed.

Proxy Preview Cache

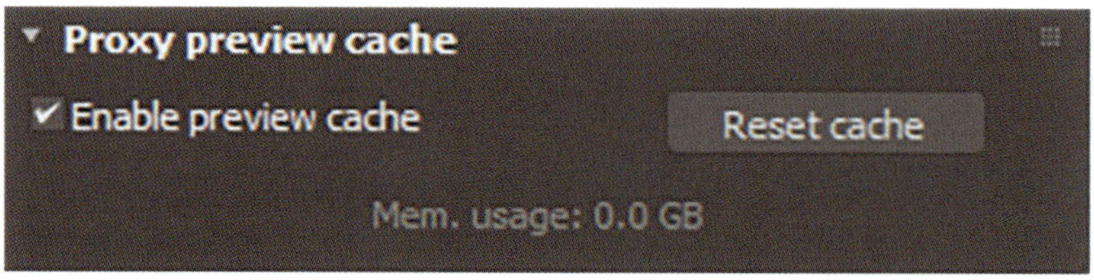

Proxy preview cache parameters

Enable preview cache: This function allows the viewport to preview all VRayProxy objects in the scene, which speeds up the viewport performance. Enabled, by default.

Chapter 5 will showcase how to create VRayProxies.

Reset cache: Clicking this button clears up the cached information.

Render Elements

Render Elements are often used to help enhance the overall render, key physical properties of materials and lights in postproduction.

Most render elements can only be used if/when the function to Separate render channels is enabled (except for VRayLightMix and VRayDenoiser).

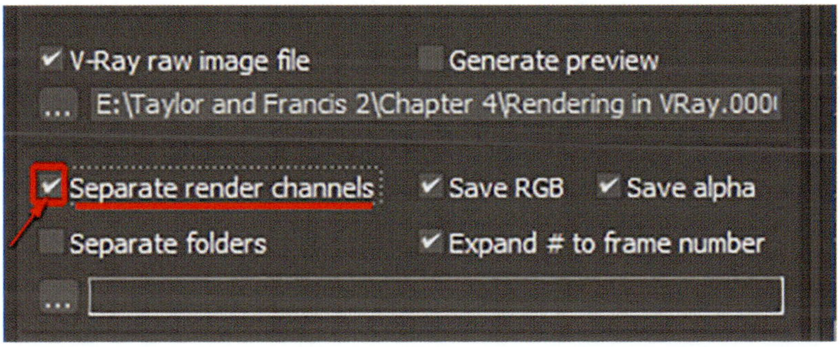

Separate render channels

To add a render element, go to the Render Elements tab first.

Under Render Elements, click on the Add button, followed by selecting one or more of the listed elements in the dialog. And clicking OK.

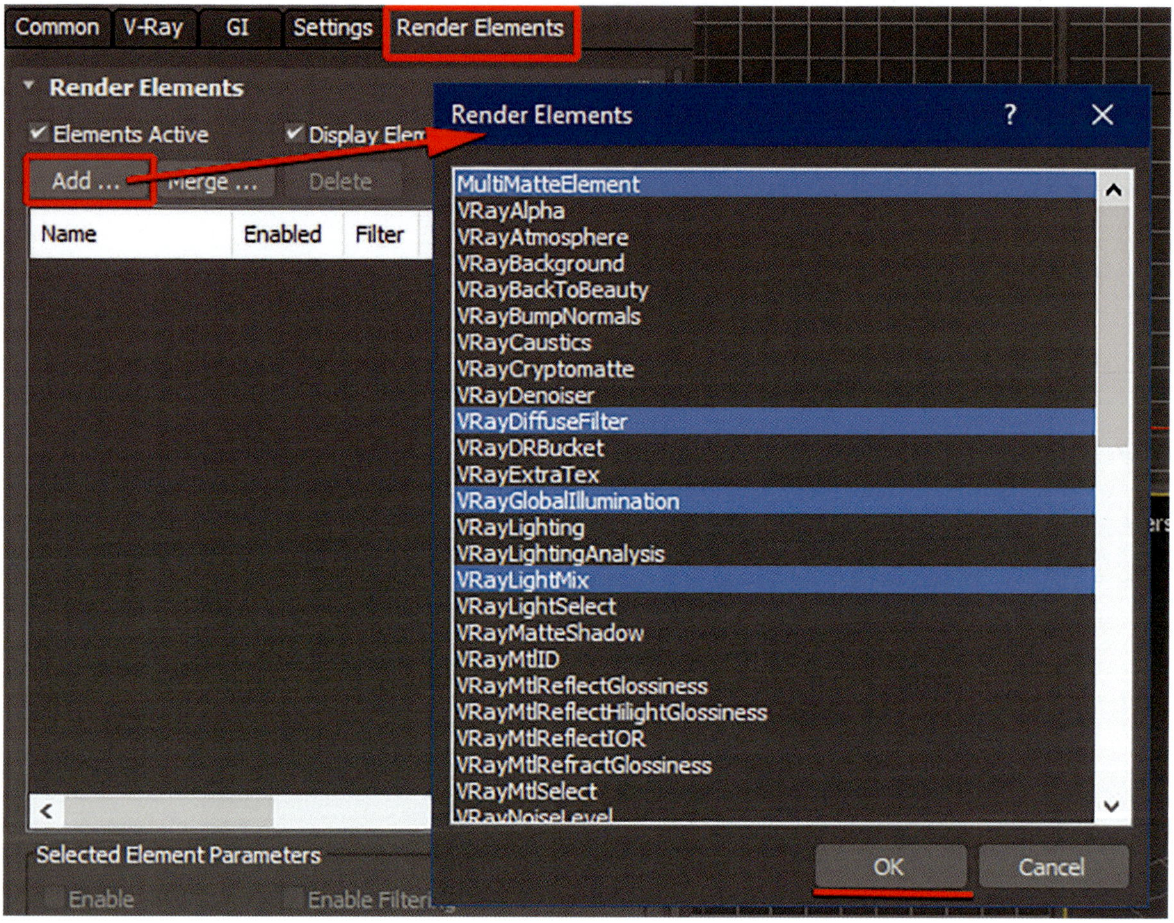

Add Render Elements

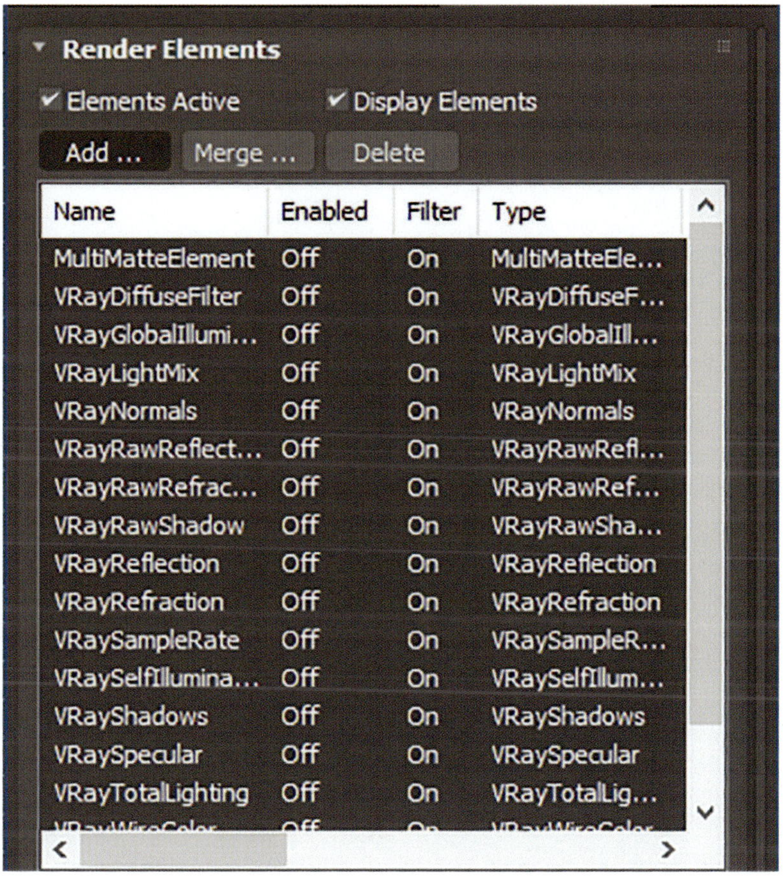

Add Render Elements added

When selected individually, each render element comes with its own set of parameters.

Some of the most useful render elements are:

VRayLightMix: This render element allows users to control the intensity and color of all lights in the scene, via the VFB.

By default, it is set to Group by Instanced lights. This option displays all instanced lights in the scene as one Layer in the VFB.

If you want the flexibility to manipulate the instanced lights individually, simply choose the option to Group by Individual lights.

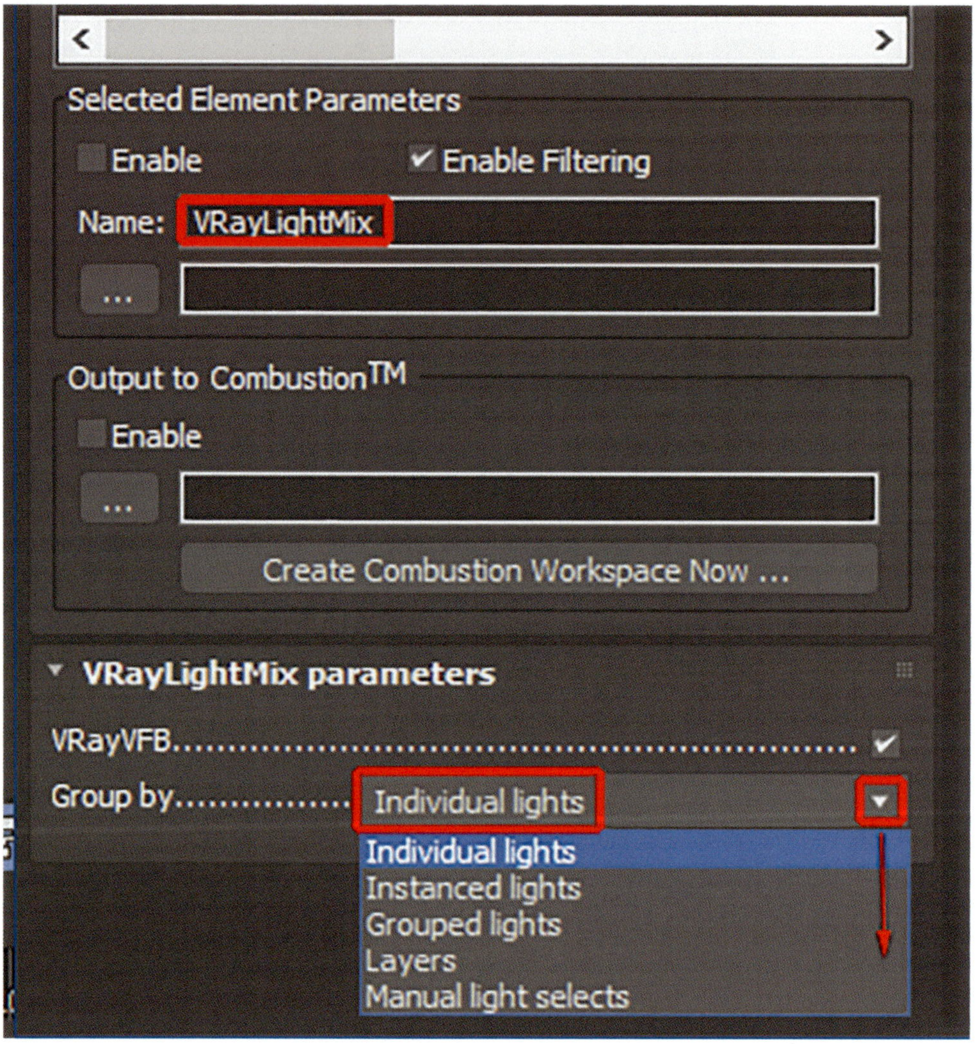

VRayLightMix parameters

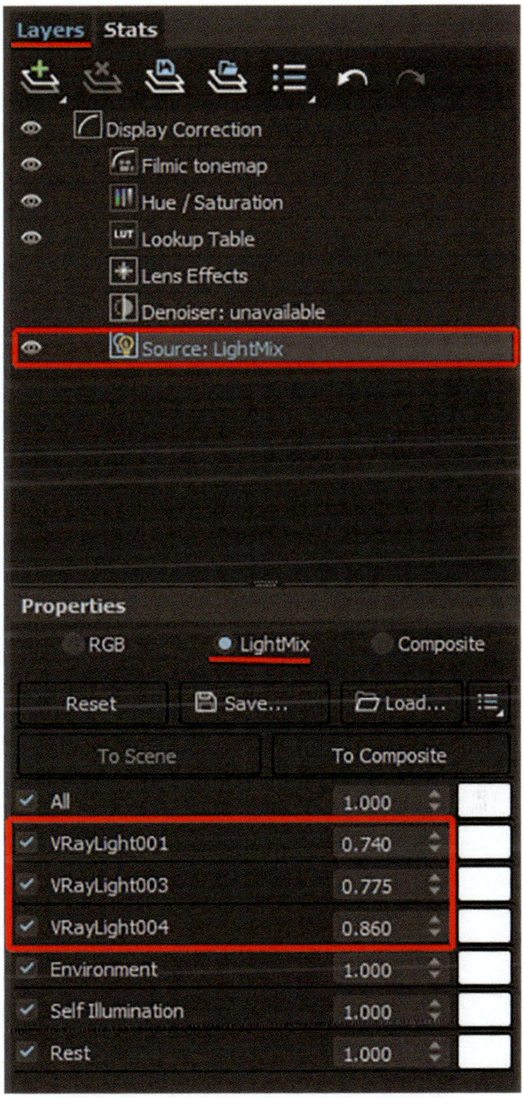

LightMix with instanced lights displayed individually

MultiMatteElement

MultiMatteElement

This render element represents the true R (red) G (green) and B (blue) colors, which are extremely accurate to select in postproduction (they don't yield jagged edges).

The RBuf, GBuf and BBuf IDs allow users to specify numbers associated with each color. By default, the RBuf ID (red) is associated with id number 1.

The GBuf ID (green) is associated with id number 2, and the BBuf ID (blue) is associated with id number 3.

The IsMATID function determines whether the id numbers are related to materials or object ids.

If disabled (default), the numbers are related to object ids.

Each object id number needs to coincide with one of the numbers specified here.

To create object id numbers, simply select any object in the scene and right click to bring up the quad menu.

Choose the Object Properties option.

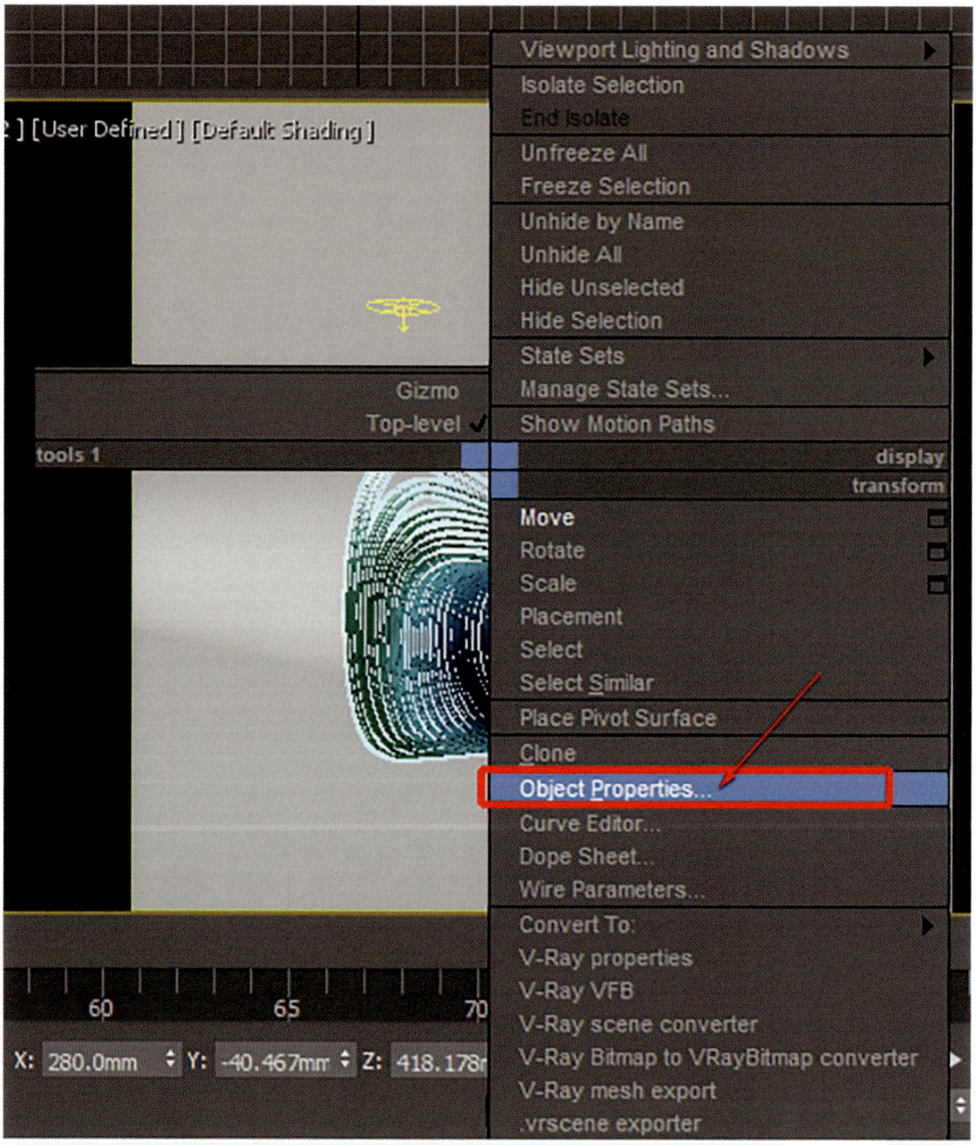

Choose the Object Properties option

In the Object Properties dialog, under G-Buffer Object ID, enter a number to coincide with any of the ID numbers listed in the MultiMatteElement parameters.

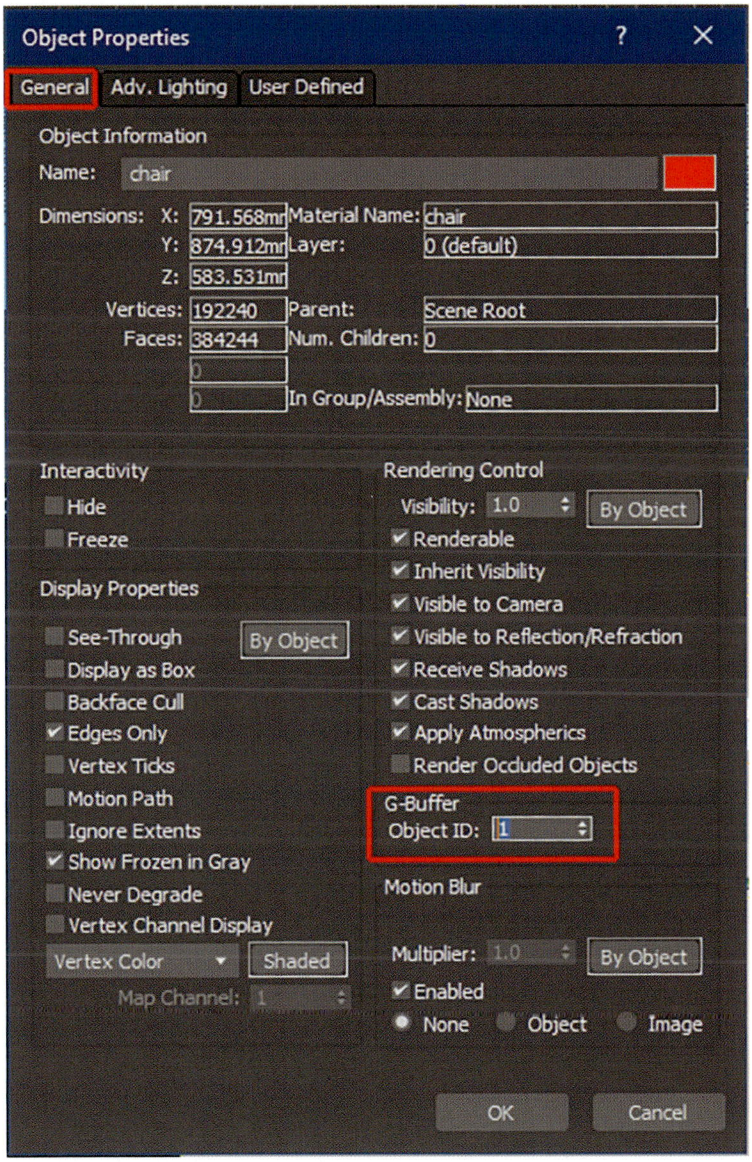

G-Buffer Object ID number

Repeat the same actions to other objects in the scene, entering ID numbers 2 and 3 to coincide with the MultiMatteElement numbers.

The final result (when rendered) should look similar to the image below.

MultiMatteElement with RGB colors rendered

If you have more objects in the scene you want to add different object id numbers to, you need to add a second MultiMatteElement to the list, and name it differently (MultiMatteElement 2).

Also, the RGB id numbers need to differ from the previous ones (4, 5, 6). The new objects in the scene need to have id numbers to coincide with the new MultiMatteElement 2.

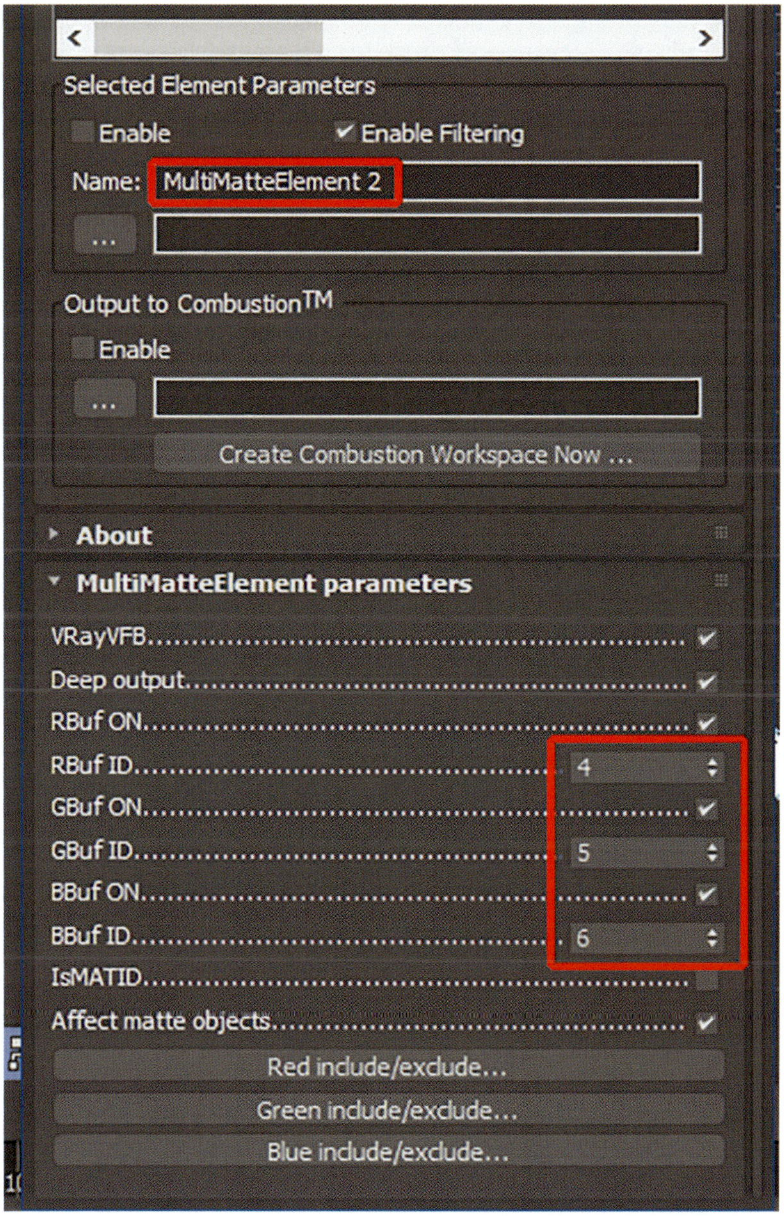

MultiMatteElement 2 with different id numbers

Second MultiMatteElement with RGB colors rendered

If you want to have a new MultiMatteElement with ids associated with materials instead, simply enable the IsMATID function.

Also, name the new render element differently (MultiMatteElement_sub 1).

IsMATID function enabled

In the Material Editor, change the material number to coincide with one of the MultiMatteElement _sub 1 ids (select and hold).

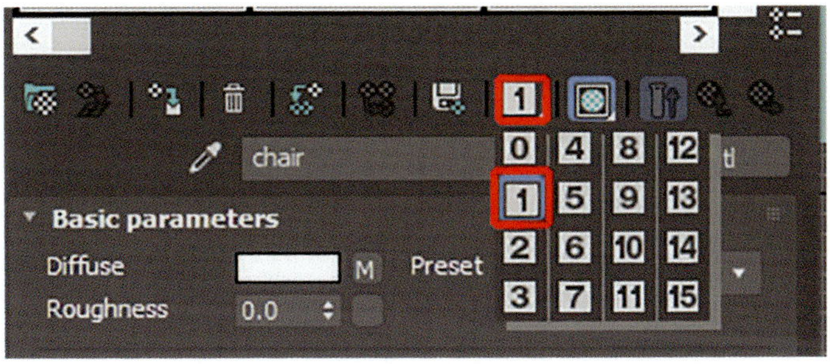

Change the material id number

Repeat the same action to other materials in the scene.

In the end, users often end up with a long list of different MultiMatteElements: Some of the render elements affecting the object ids, and others affecting the material ids.

To select the colors in the post, simply go to the Channels tab, hold down the Ctrl key and select one of the three listed colors.

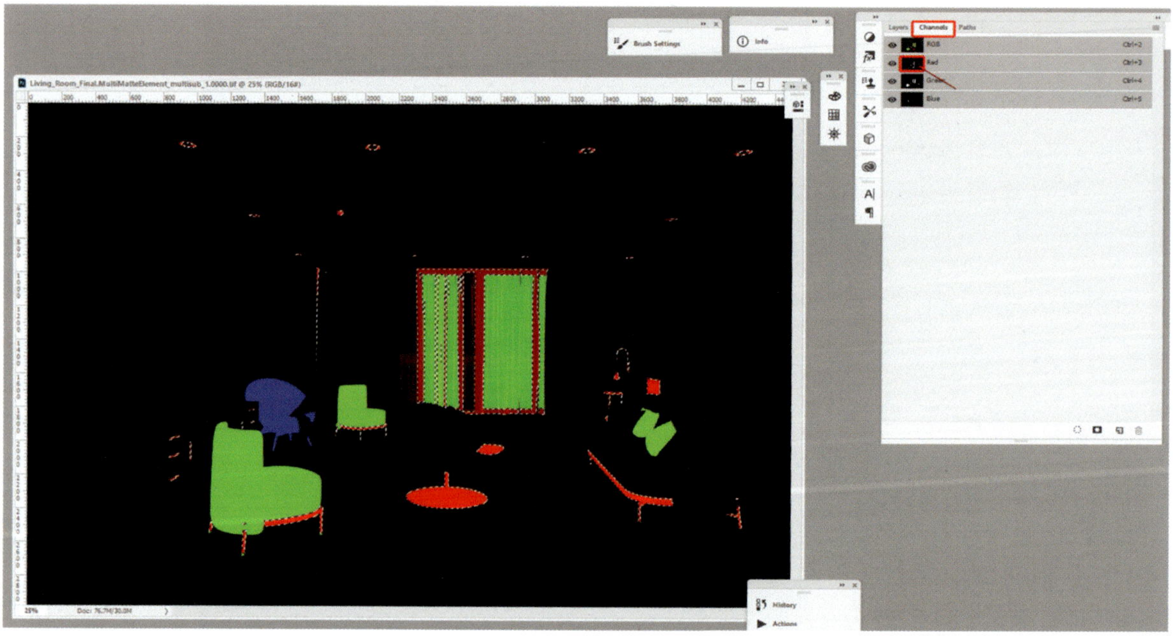

Select colors in postproduction

Next, select the Layers tab and create a new group, clicking its button.

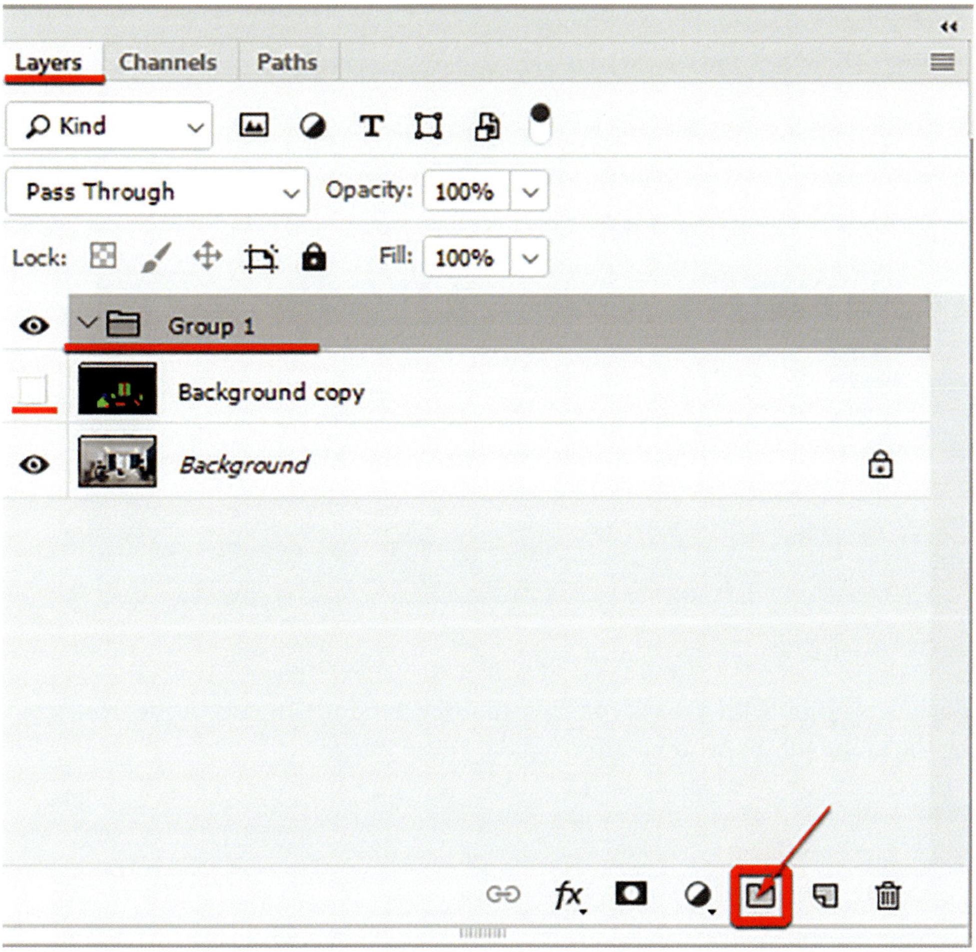

Create a new Group

While the selection is still on, click on the mask button to create a group mask.

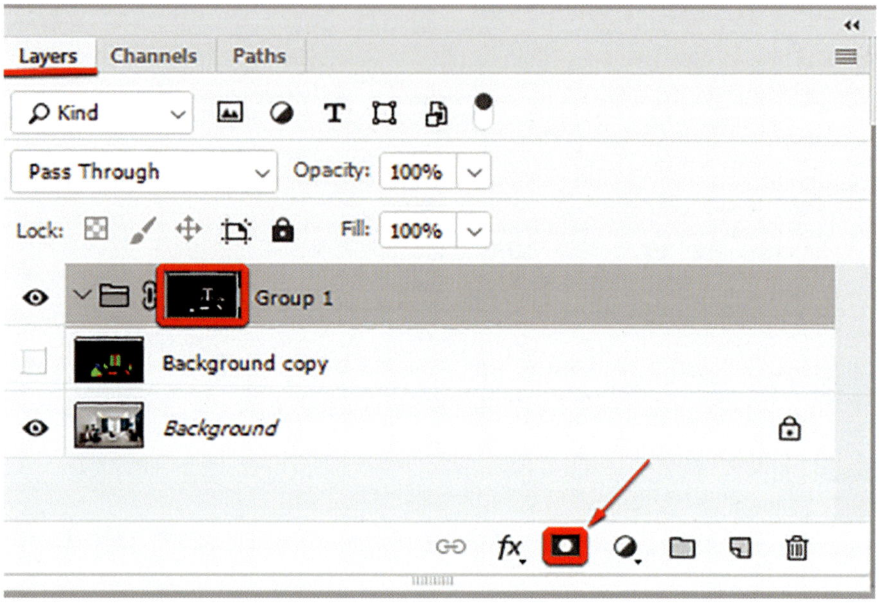

Create a Group mask

Each new group with a mask can have multiple render elements inside (restricted by the group mask), without affecting the entire image.

VRayReflection/VRayRawReflection

VRayReflection render element

VRayRawReflection render element

These two render elements are quite useful to extra the reflections from materials. If there are no reflections in the scene, these elements will render black.

In postproduction, VRayReflection works best with Screen blending mode.

VRayRawReflection works best with Normal blending mode, and the opacity is reduced accordingly.

VRaySampleRate: This render element is quite useful to see areas of the scene that are problematic to render (green and red). Green areas are slightly problematic to render, but red areas are the most severe.

NOTE

In 3ds Max, when enabling reflections on materials, it's best to always disable the Fresnel reflections function, in order to see reflections in the render element.

VRaySampleRate render element

VRayBackToBeauty: This render element allows V-Ray to save the V-Ray Frame Buffer layers applied (beauty) and without it (raw render).

This render element also adds automatically the VRaySSS2 pass (only seen while rendering).

VRaySpecular

VRaySpecular render element

This render element is amazing to add/control specular/glossy highlights in post-production. If there are no specular/glossy highlights in the scene, this element will render black.

In postproduction, VRaySpecular works best with Screen blending mode.

NOTE

In 3ds Max, when enabling reflections/highlights on materials, it's best to always disable the Fresnel reflections function, in order to see specular/highlights in the render element.

VRayRefraction/VRayRawRefraction

VRayRefraction render element

VRayRawRefraction render element

These render elements help to control the refractions/transparency in postproduction. If there is no refraction/transparency in the scene, these elements will render black.

In postproduction, VRayRefraction works best with Screen blending mode.

VRayRawRefraction works best with Normal blending mode in postproduction.

VRayDiffuseFilter

VRayDiffuseFilter render element

This element renders mainly colors, shades and textures, without GI, lighting or shadows. It's quite useful to help control the colors and textures of objects in postproduction (reducing its layer opacity slightly).

In postproduction, it works best with Normal blending mode.

VRayWireColor

VRayWireColor render element

This render element is an alternative to the MultiMatteElement. Unlike MultiMatteElement, it automatically creates colors based on objects' wire color in 3ds Max.

Users often use the Magic wand tool to select VRayWireColors in postproduction. This method of selection is not accurate and often leaves selection edges jagged.

VRayZDepth

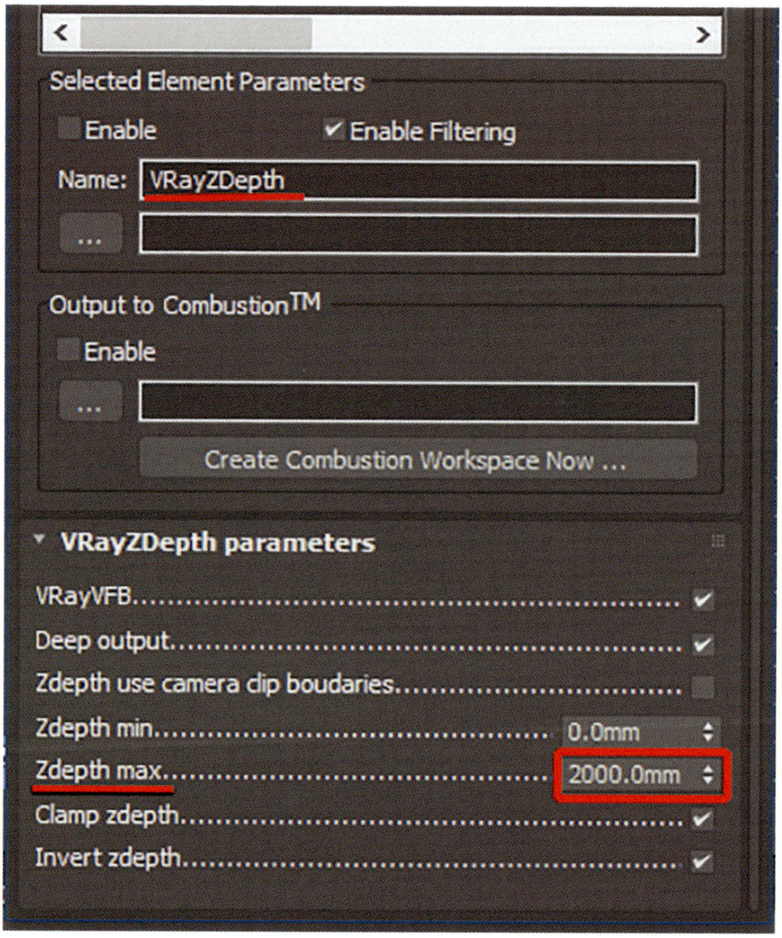

VRayZDepth render element

This render element is often used to create effects such as fog and depth of field in postproduction.

To set its distance in 3ds Max, simply enter a value in Zdepth max function.

Set the Zdepth max value

To create the depth of field effect in postproduction, go to its Channels tab. Hold down the Ctrl key and select its RGB or Red channel.

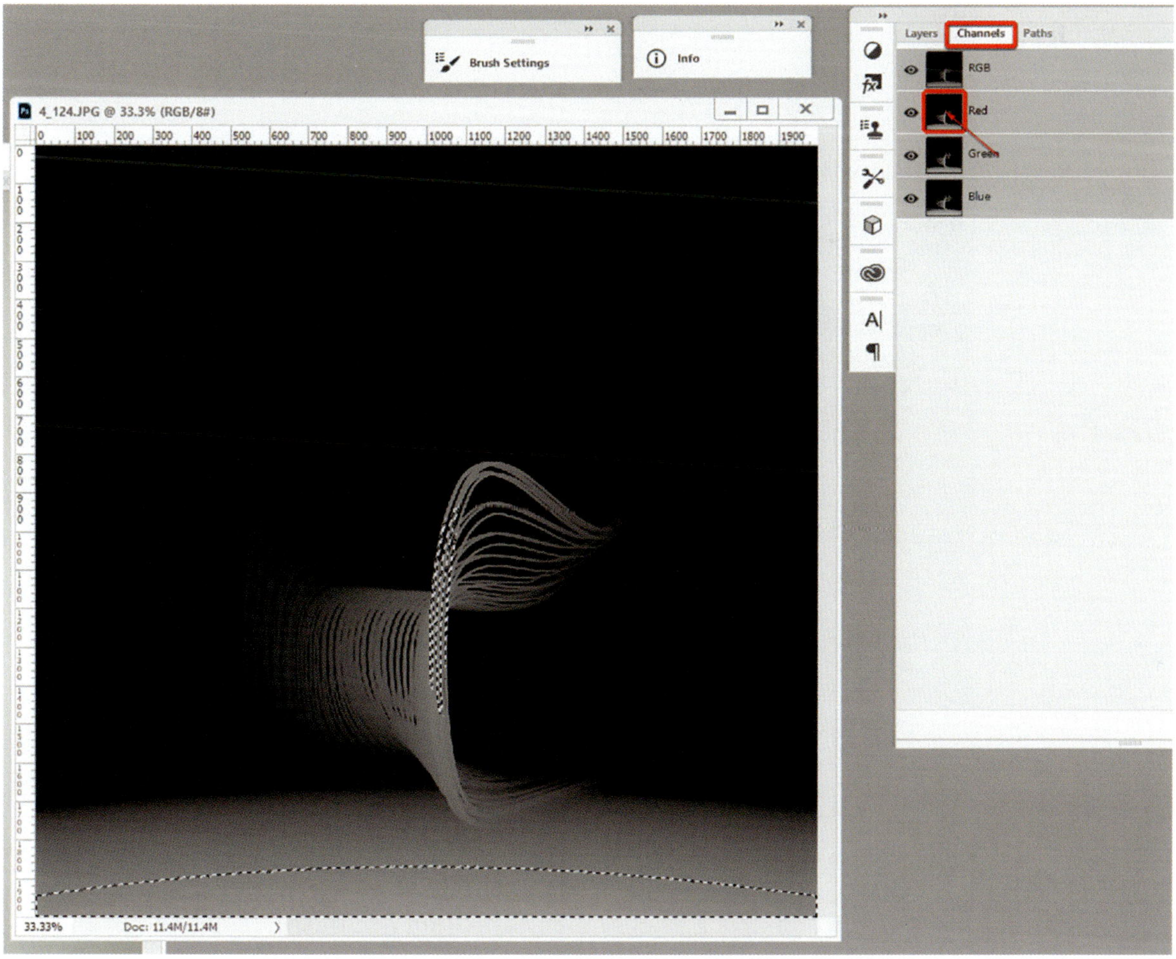

Red channel selected

While the selection is still on, click on the Select tool and choose to Save selection. The document you wish to add the depth of field to.

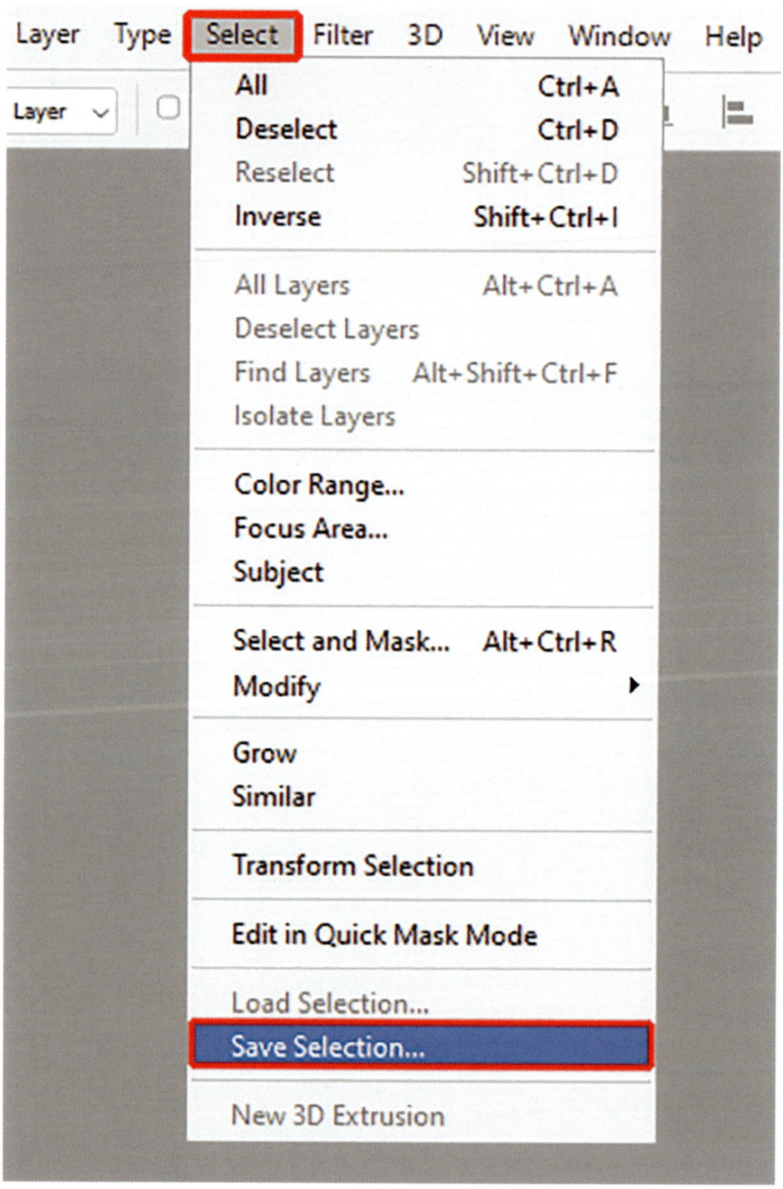

Choose to Save selection

In Save Selection dialog, choose the Destination document (main render) and Name the new selection accordingly.

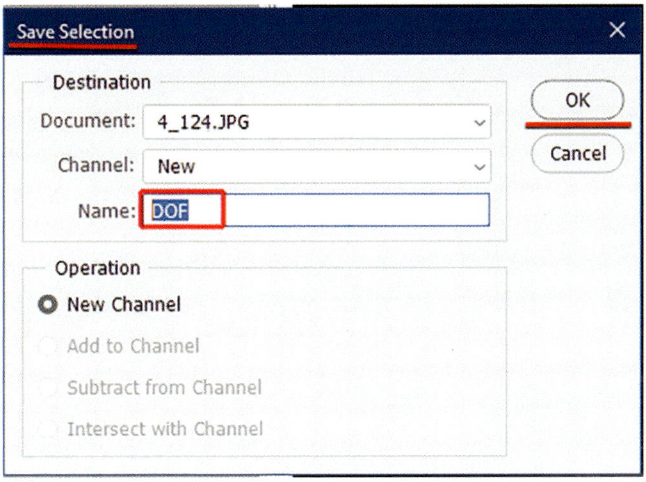

Name selection

Select the main render. Right click and choose to Duplicate Layer.

It's always good practice to work on a Duplicated layer. Not the original one.

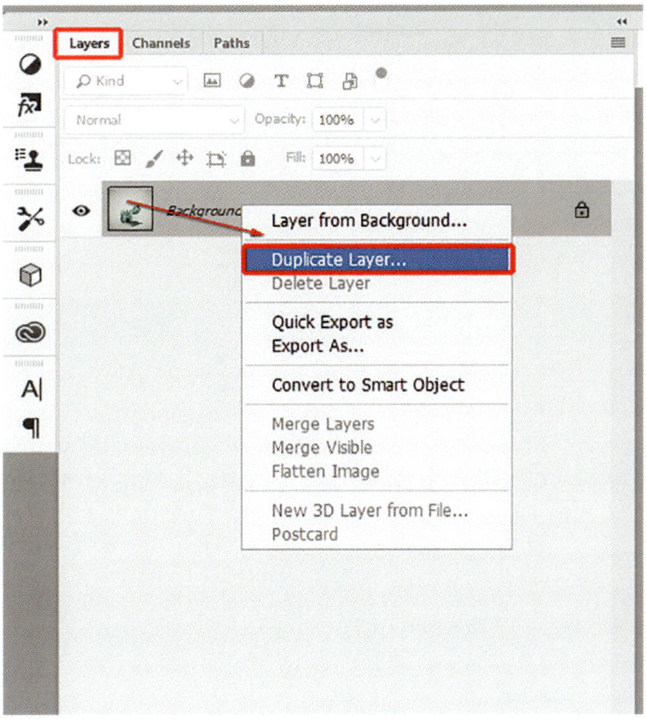

Duplicate Layer

Next, go to the Filter tab. Under Blur, choose the Lens Blur option.

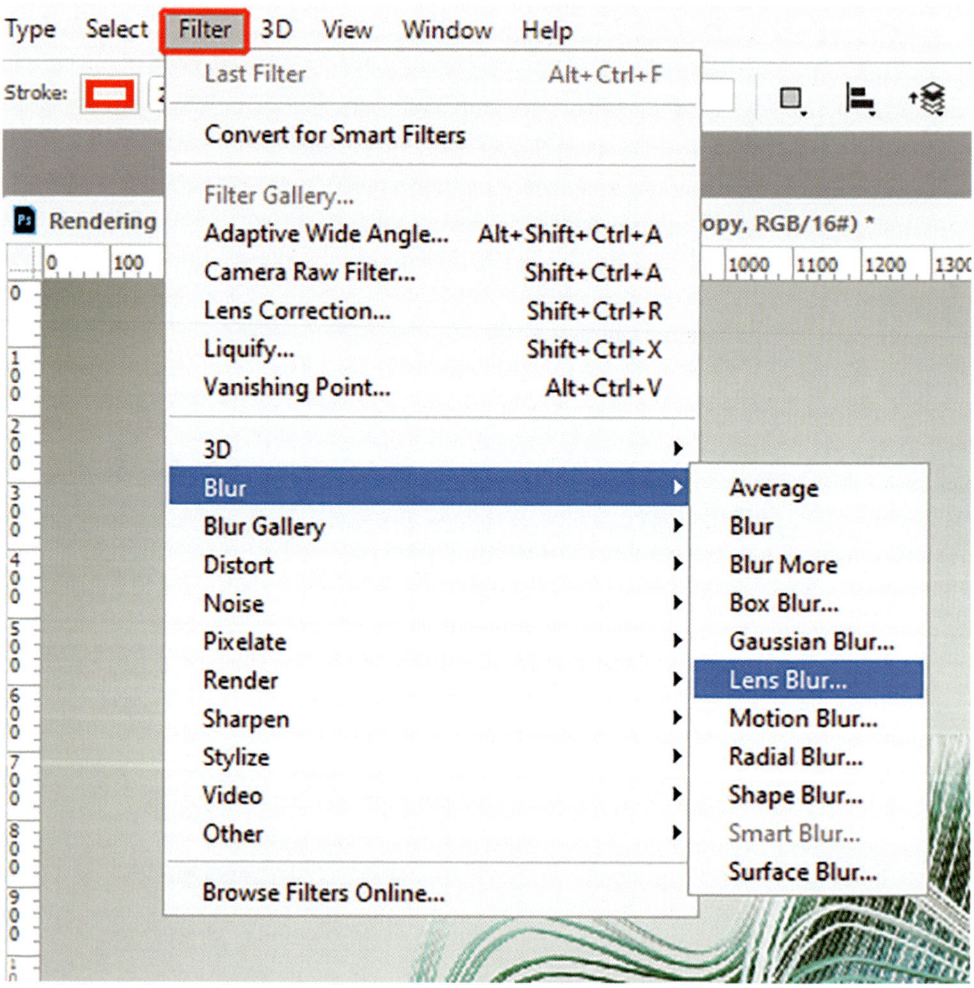

Choose the Lens Blur option

In the Lens Blur dialog, load the Depth Map previously saved (DOF) and adjust the Blur Focal Distance and Radius functions.

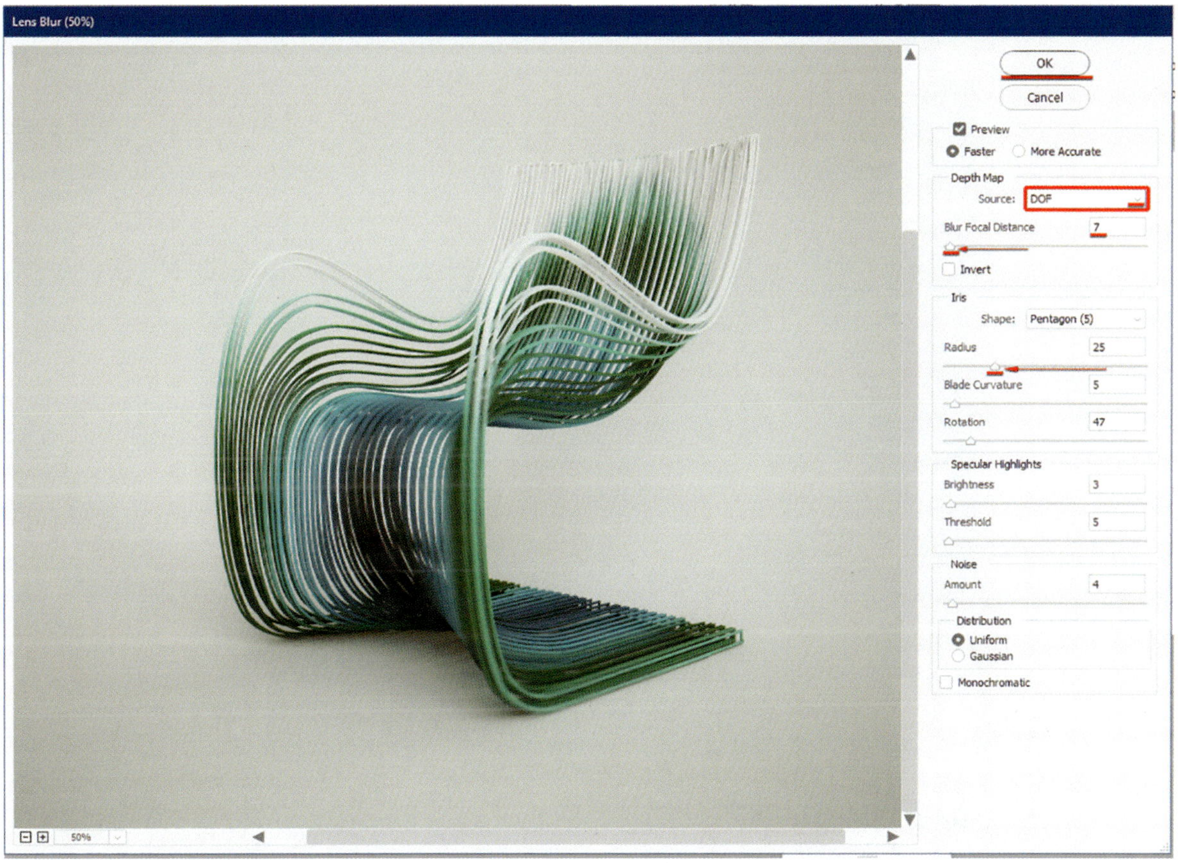

Choose and adjust the Lens Blur option

VRayNormals

VRayNormals render element

This amazing render element is often used as a final step to add extra highlights to the overall render.

To do so, place the VRayNormals render element on top of your final postprocessed image. And add the Levels adjustment layer.

Add the Levels Adjustment layer

To increase the contrast between the colors displayed, move the Levels midpoint to the far right (0.09).

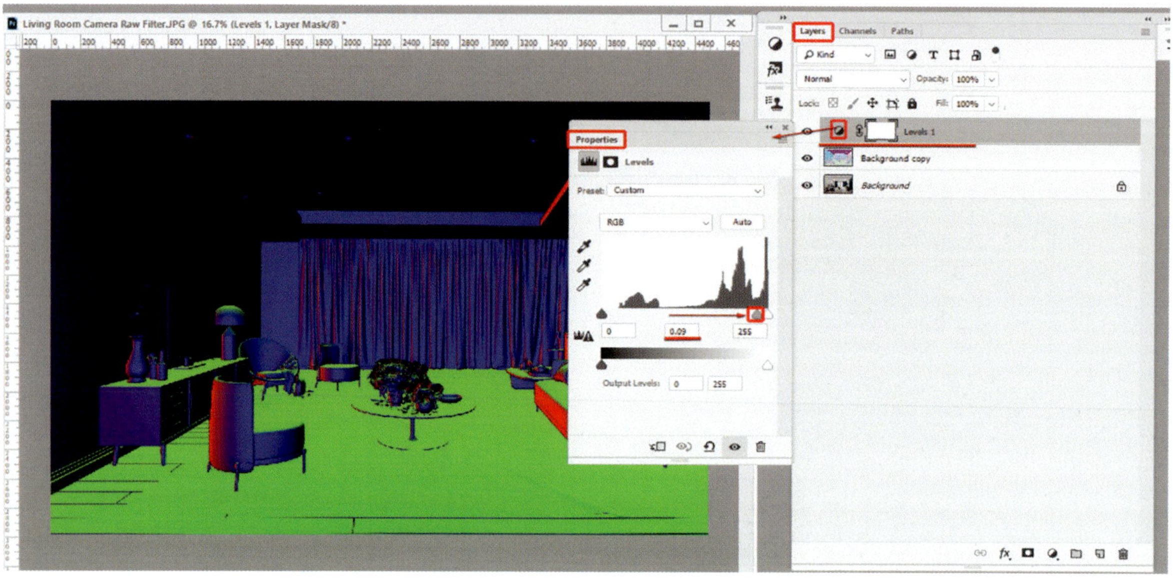

Increase Levels contrast

To restrict the Levels effects to the layer directly below it (VRayNormals), simply hold down the Alt key and hover over the Levels adjustment layer until you see the clipping mask sign.

While holding down the Alt key, click to clip it to the layer directly below it. The Levels adjustment layer is now only affecting the VRayNormals layer.

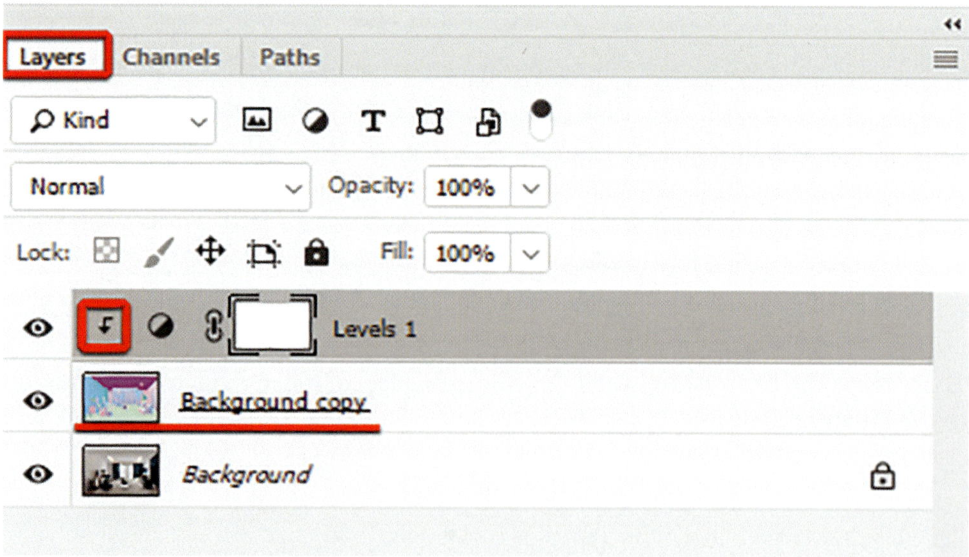

Levels clipped to the VRayNormals layers

Next, Add the Hue/Saturation, Channel Mixer and another Hue/Saturation adjustment layer on top. Ensure to clipping all to the layers below.

All Adjustment layers are now connected to the VRayNormals layer below.

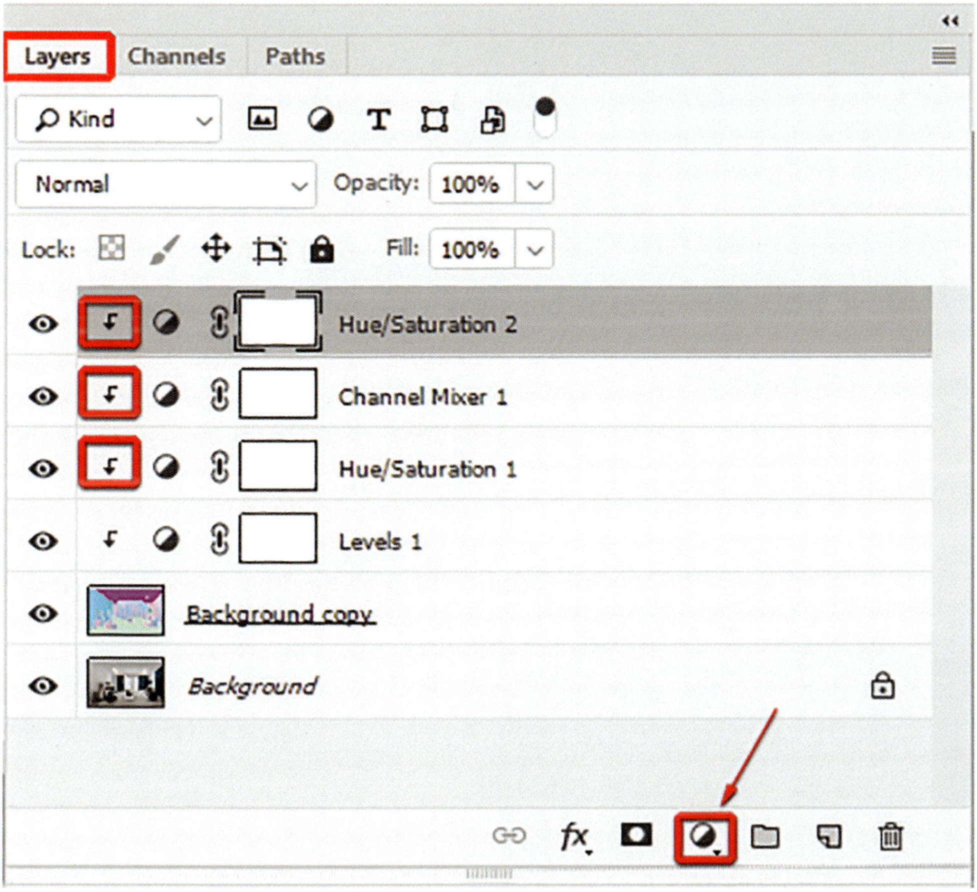

New adjustment layers added

Next, select the Channel Mixer layer and enable the Monochrome function.

To adjust the highlighted areas of the image, begin moving the sliders for Red, Green and Blue.

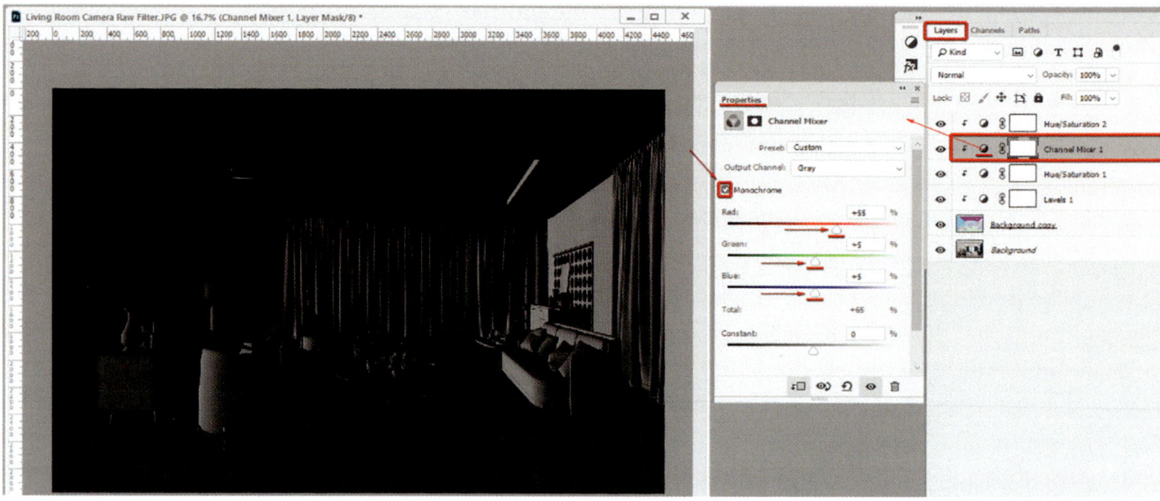

Adjust the Monochrome sliders of Channel Mixer

Use the first Hue/Saturation layer to control the direction of the highlights. Users often move the Hue slider to control the highlight direction.

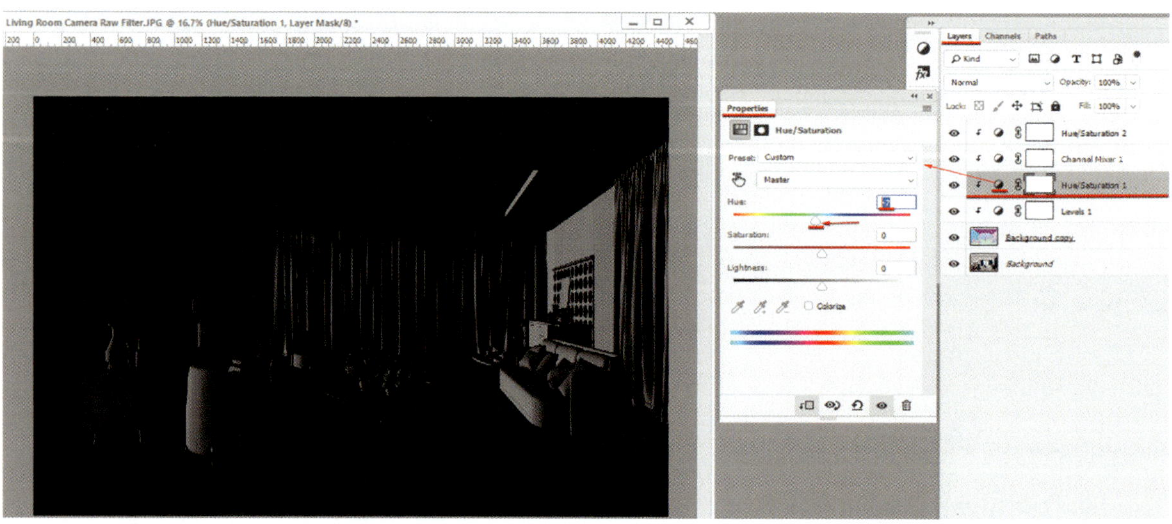

Control the highlights with Hue/Saturation slider

Next, select the VRayNormals layer and change its blending mode to Screen. Also, reduce its opacity to about 50%.

Turn the VRayNormals layer on and off see the amazing difference it makes to the overall final render.

Change the VRayNormals layer blending mode to a Screen type

Furthermore, you can add a layer mask to the VRayNormals layer, and brush away highlights on unwanted areas.

To do so, while the VRayNormals layer is still selected, click on the layer mask button to add it to the selected layer.

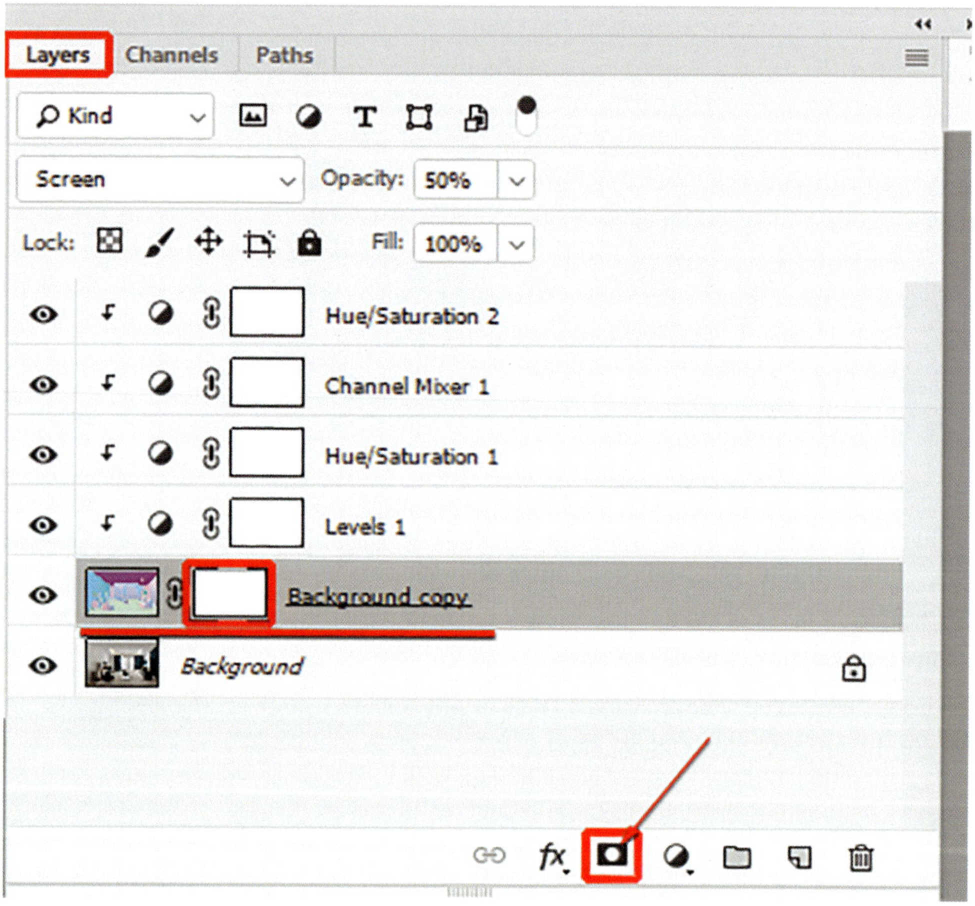

Added Layer Mask

Layer masks work best with black and white colors in the background toolbar(X). With a brush tool enabled (B), black/dark colors take away pixels with each brush stroke.

White/brighter colors do the opposite.

Before you begin brushing away pixels (B), ensure the layer mask is selected and the brush opacity is set. The lower the brush opacity value, the slower the pixels will be taken away.

A brush opacity set to 100% immediately takes away pixels.

User Layer mask to brush away pixels

Finally, if you wish to colorize the highlights, simply select the top Hue/Saturation layer and enable the Colorize function.

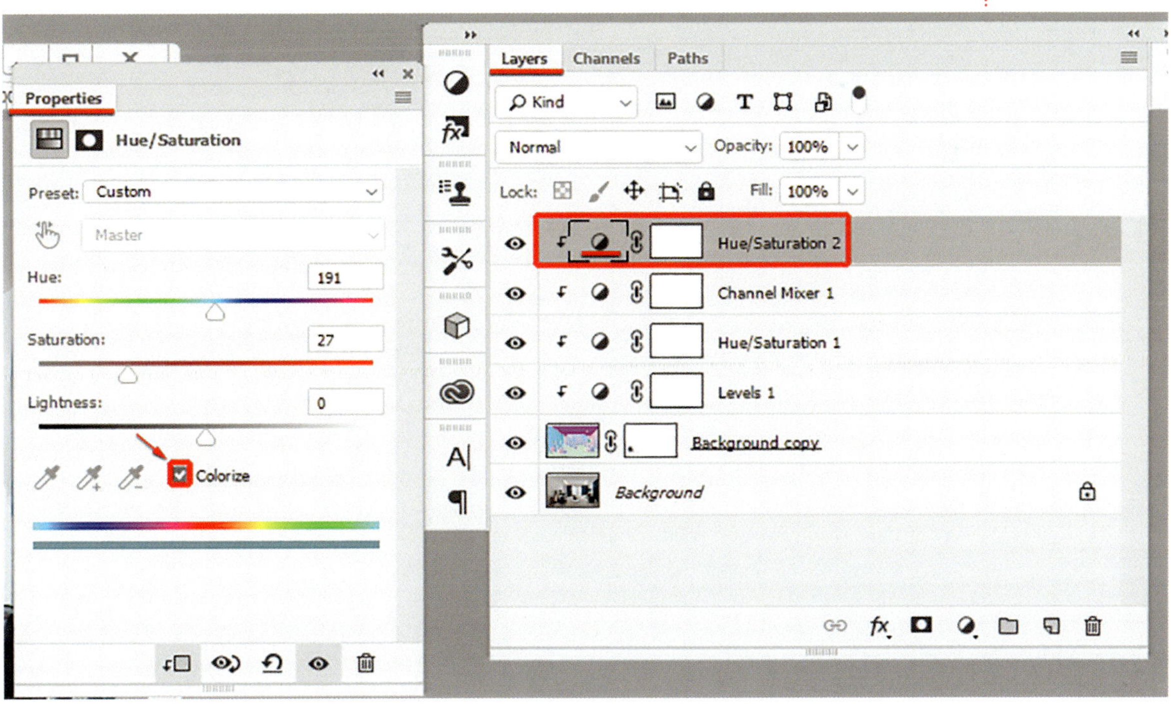

Colorize the highlights with Hue/Saturation

Chapters 8, 9 and 12 will take users through the process of using some of these render elements.

Conclusion

This chapter has introduced and navigated users through some of the key V-Ray rendering parameters and render elements.

For more detailed information about V-Ray rendering parameters, please visit the following V-Ray official website:

http://docs.chaosgroup.com/

5

Tips and Tricks

5 Tips and Tricks

Create Interactive and Immersive Apps with Verge 3d

Verge3D is a powerful and intuitive toolkit that allows Blender, 3ds Max or Maya artists to create immersive web-based experiences. Verge3D can be used to build interactive animations, product configurators, engaging presentations of any kind, online stores, explainers, e-learning content, portfolios and browser games.

The following tutorial will take users through the process of creating, eye-catching interactive apps, using this amazing plug-in. A video tutorial of this tutorial is also available in the book resource files.

Verge3D is compatible with 3ds Max 2018 and above.

Let's start by googling the name, Verge3D, and clicking on its link.

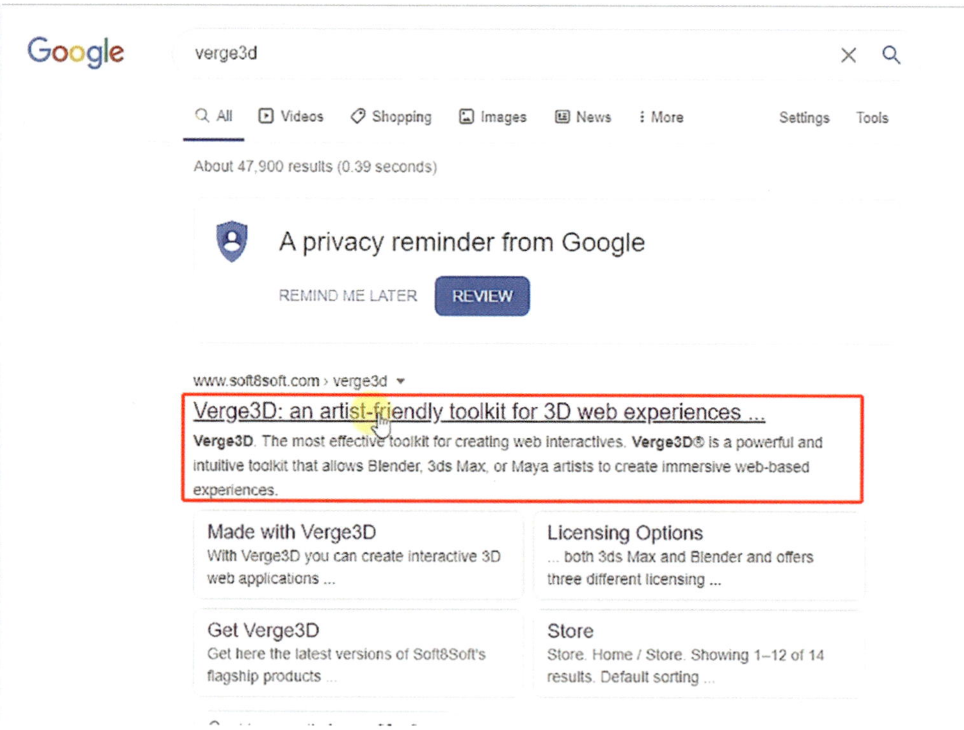

Google verge3d and click on the main link

DOI: 10.1201/9781315770802-5

Once on the website, scroll down and choose the tab, verge3d for 3ds Max. To download it, simply click on the button to Get Verge3D.

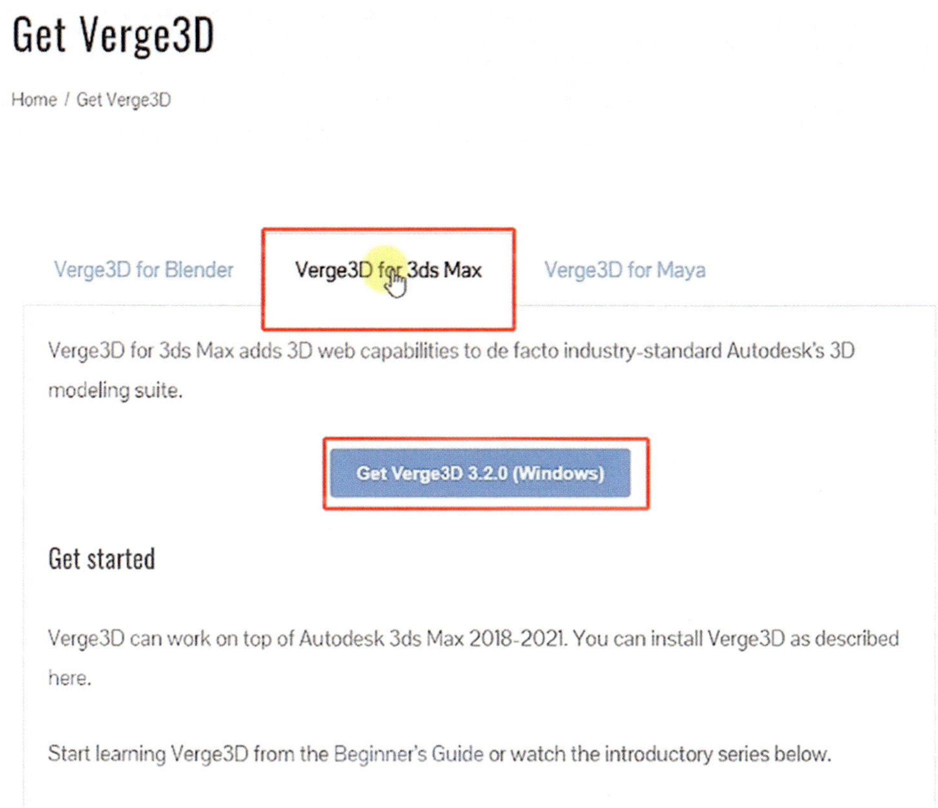

Open the verge3d for 3ds Max tab and click the button to Get Verge3D

It's worth noting that the website has numerous step-by-step video tutorials on how to use it. Also, the book resource files contain a video tutorial on how to use it.

Once the software is downloaded, simply install it. Once installed, restart 3ds Max and open the file named Car Start.max.

Verge3D should appear on your toolbar.

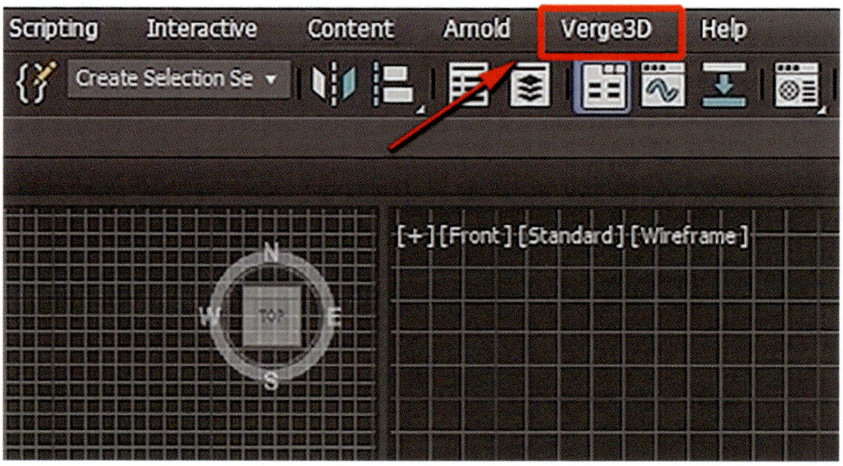

Verge3D on the toolbar

Currently, Verge3D is only compatible with 3ds Max physical materials and standard lighting. To start, open the Material Editor (M) by clicking on its button.

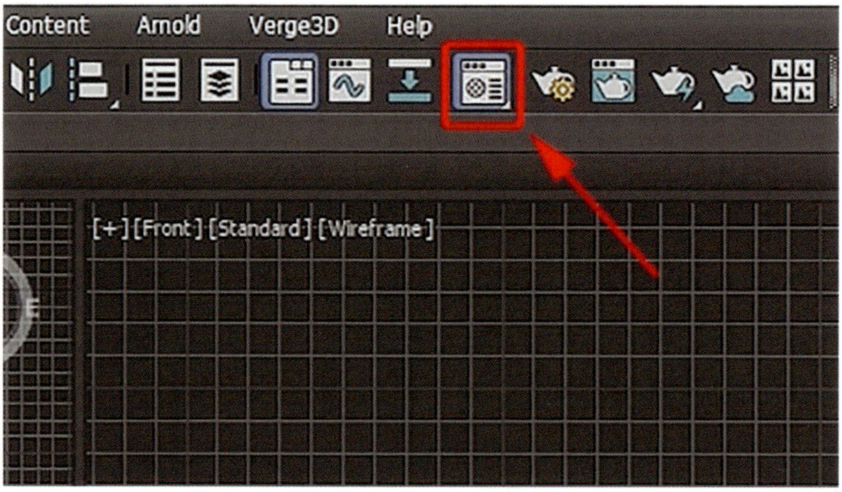

Click on Material Editor toolbar

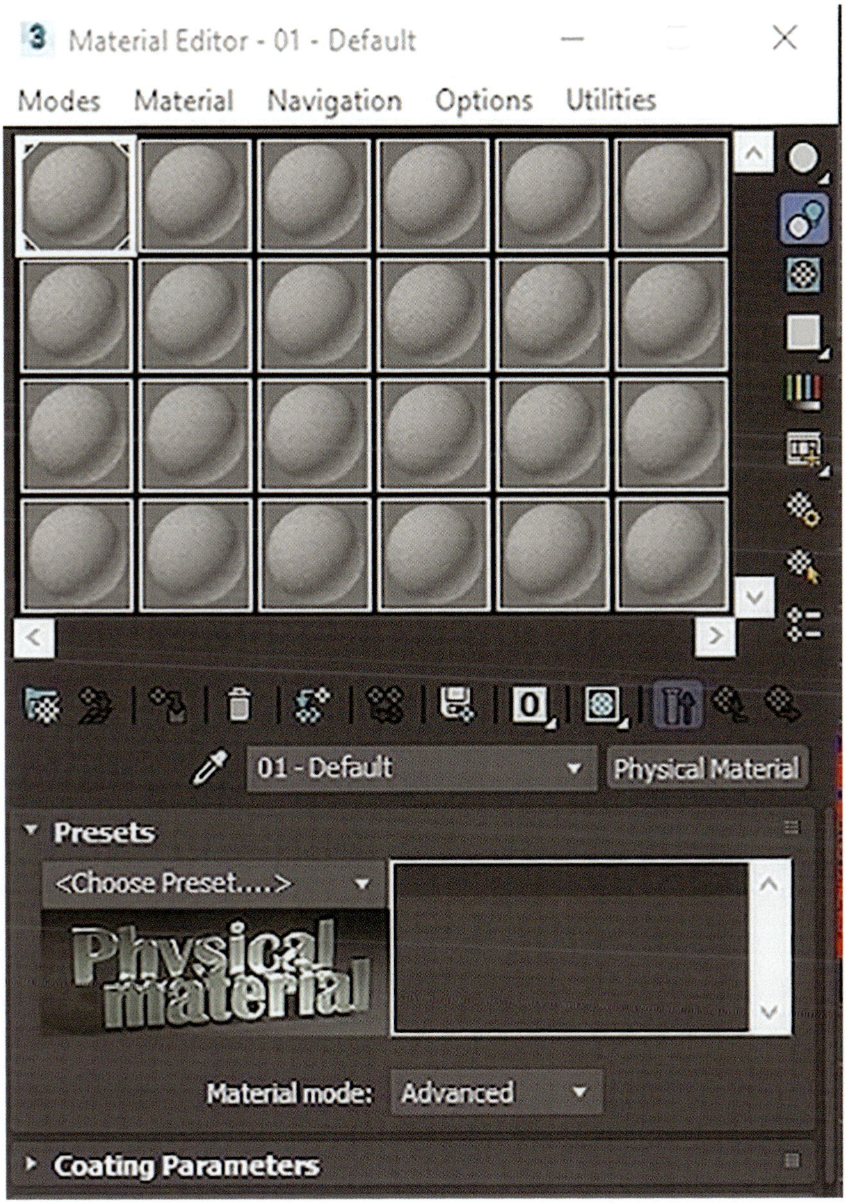

Material Editor dialog open

To load up the physical material shader, simply click on its toggle. And choose the shader, from the Material Browser dialog.

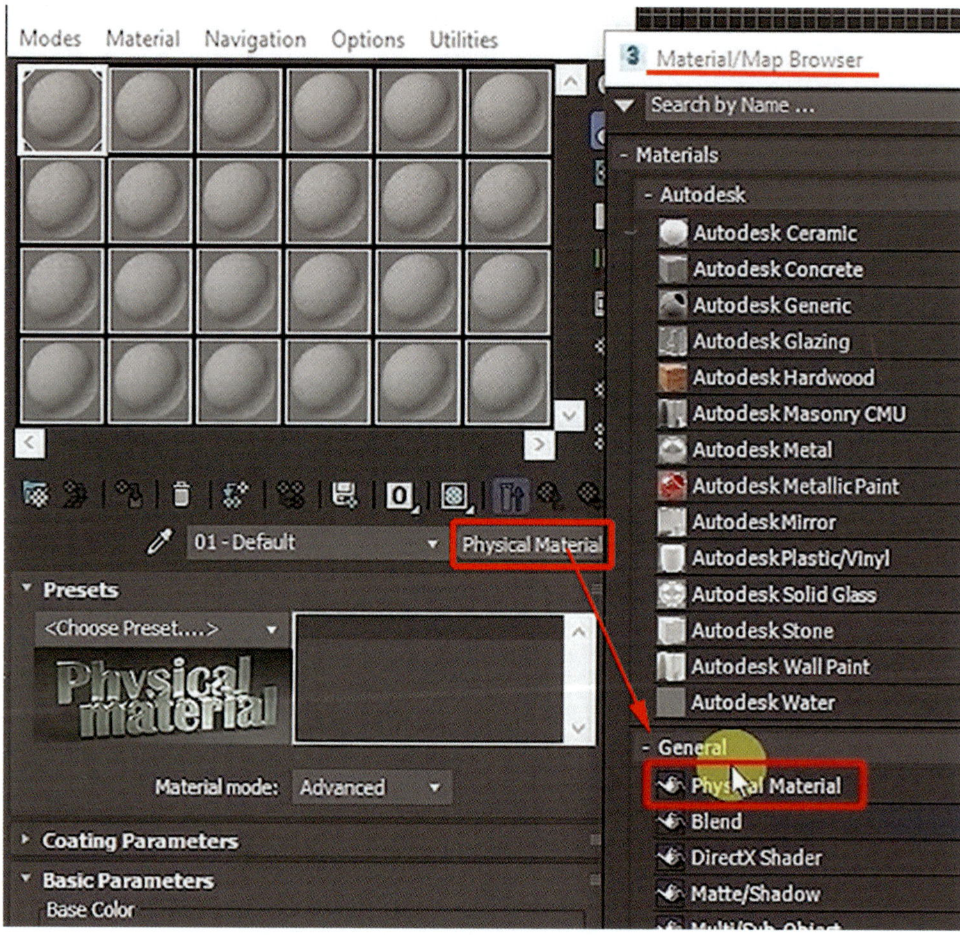

Physical material shader loaded from the Material Browser dialog

Next, choose a material preset by clicking on its icon, and choosing the red sports car paint from the list.

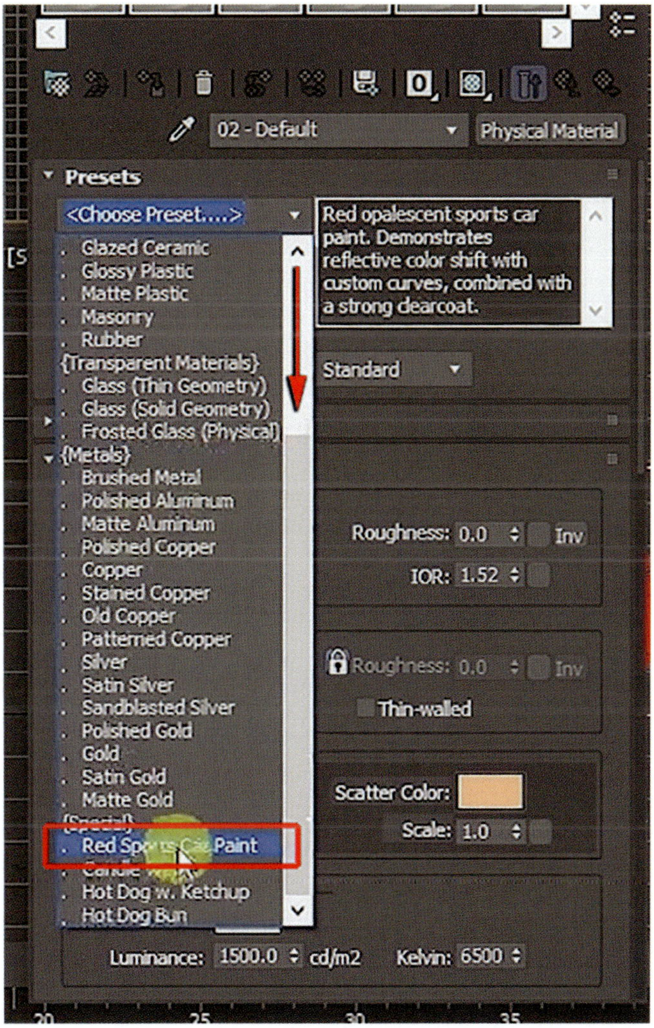

Red sports car paint material chosen from the material preset list

To name the material slot, select the preset name; right click and choose to copy the text. And paste it into the name field.

Material name edited in the Material Editor dialog

By default, the material mode is sometimes set to Standard; as opposed to Advanced.

Always set it to Advanced in order to have access to the Reflections group and other important functions.

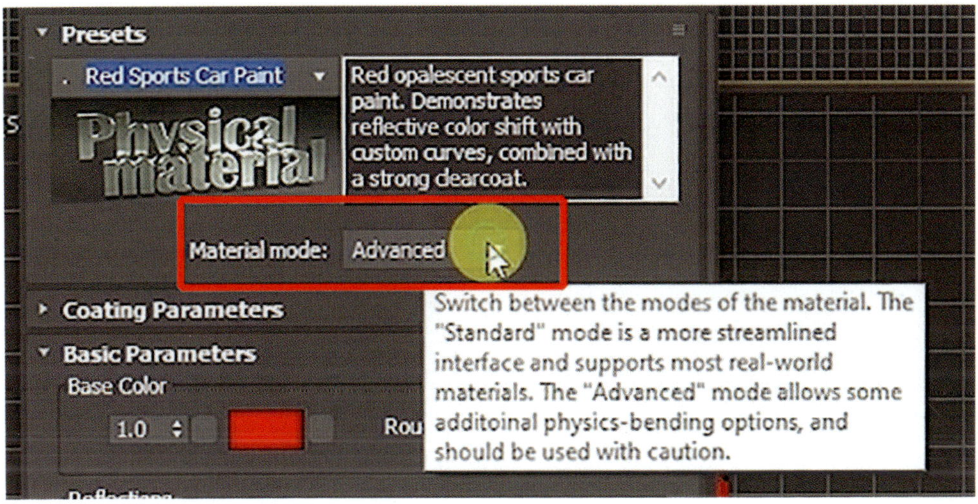

Material mode set to Advanced

Copy the Base color swatch and paste it onto the reflections. Make it slightly darker, by clicking and holding its color swatch.

In the Color Selector dialog, enter the following values: Red 0.23, Green 0.0, Blue 0.0, Alpha 1.0, Hue 1.0, Sat 1.0 and Value 0.23.

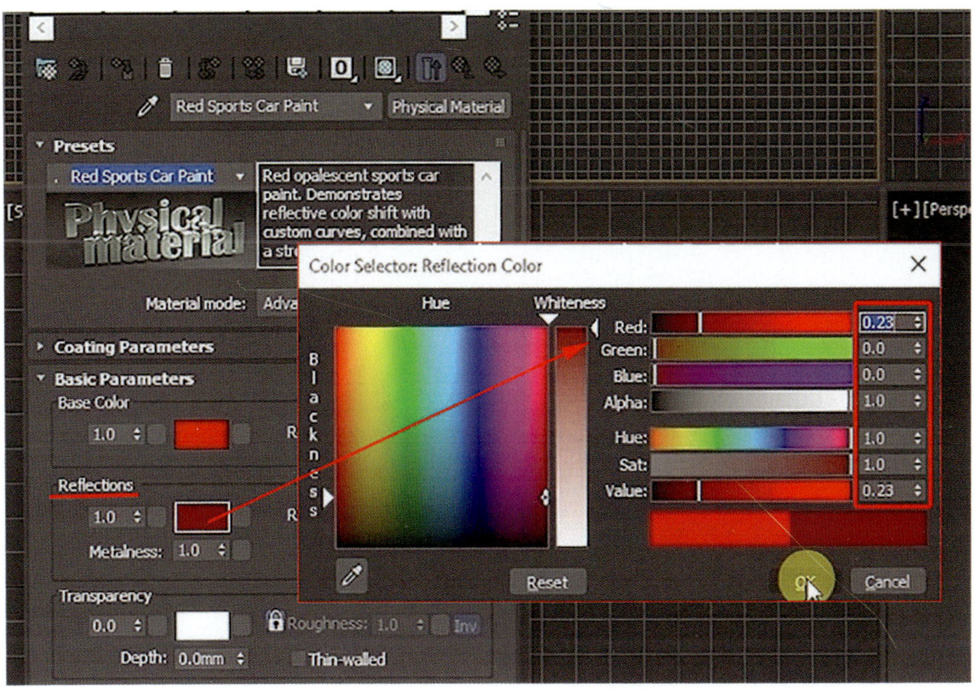

Reflections color swatch made dark red

Select the car body in the viewport, and assign this material to it.

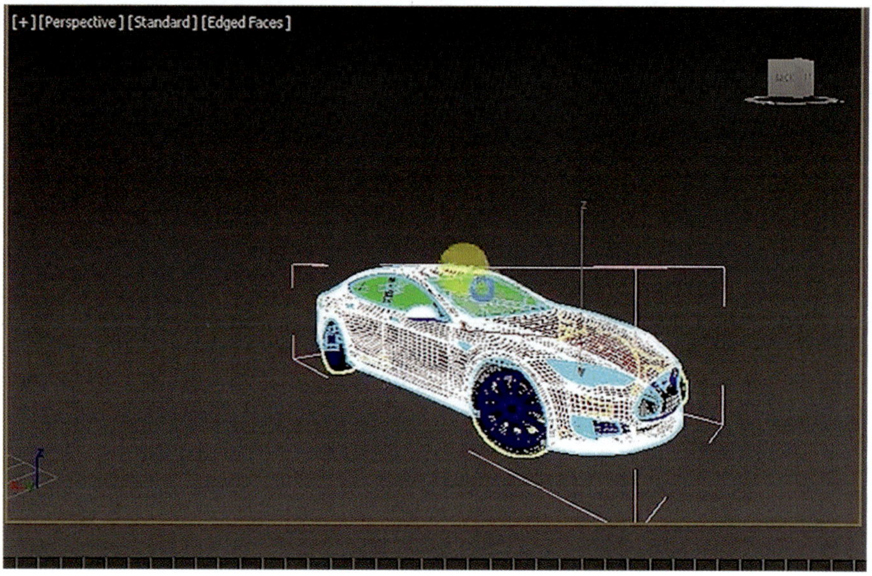

Car body selected in the viewport

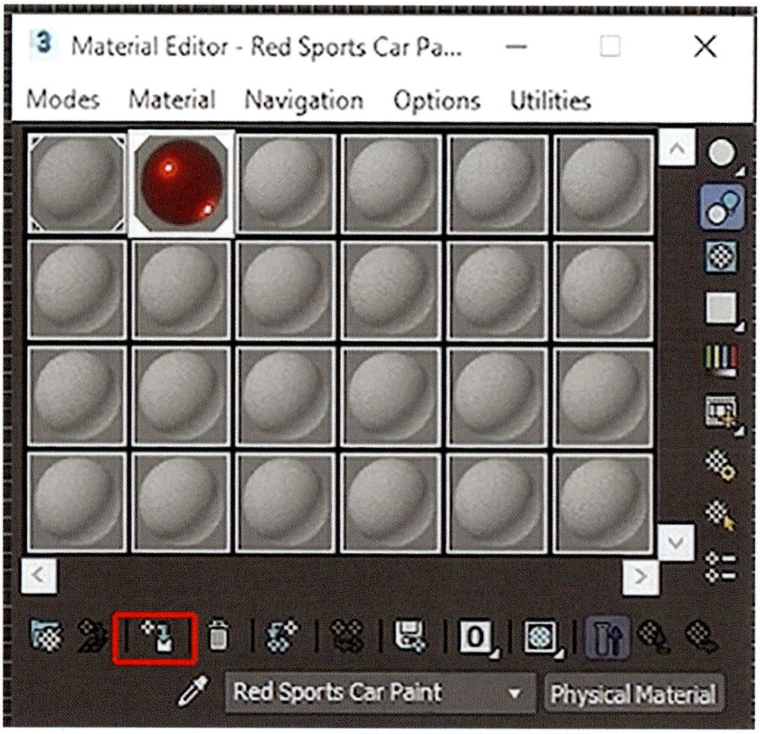

Red Sports Car Paint assigned in the Material Editor

Next, select the car glass in the scene. It's currently grouped.

Go to the groups toolbar and choose to open the group. Select the glass object in the scene.

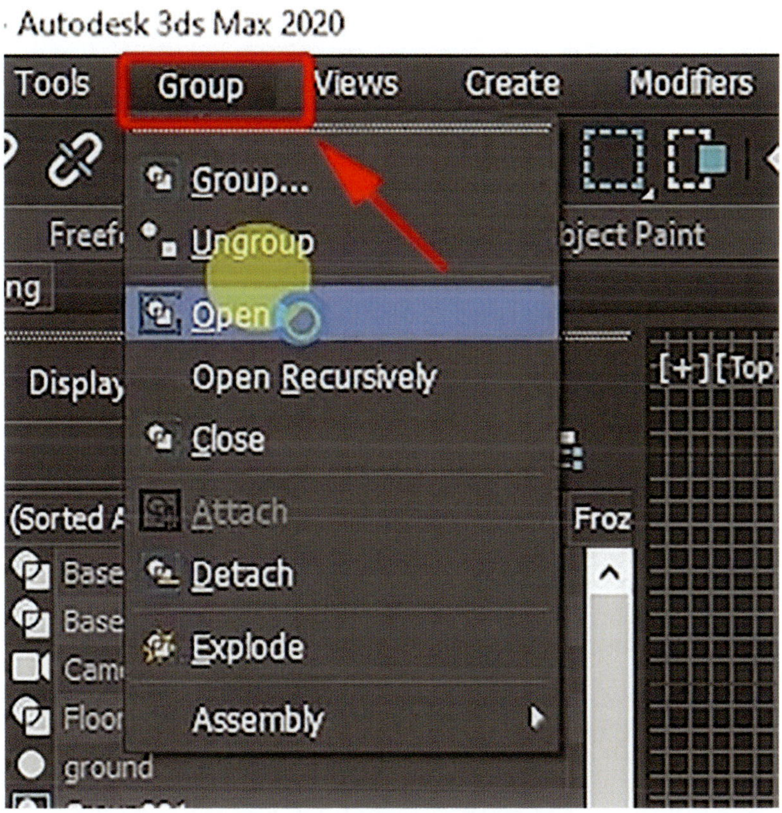

Car glass Group Open on the main toolbar

Select a new material slot, and load a new physical material, as previously done. Choose the glass solid geometry preset, as opposed to glass thin geometry.

Glass thin geometry is mostly applied to glass surfaces such as window glass and tables.

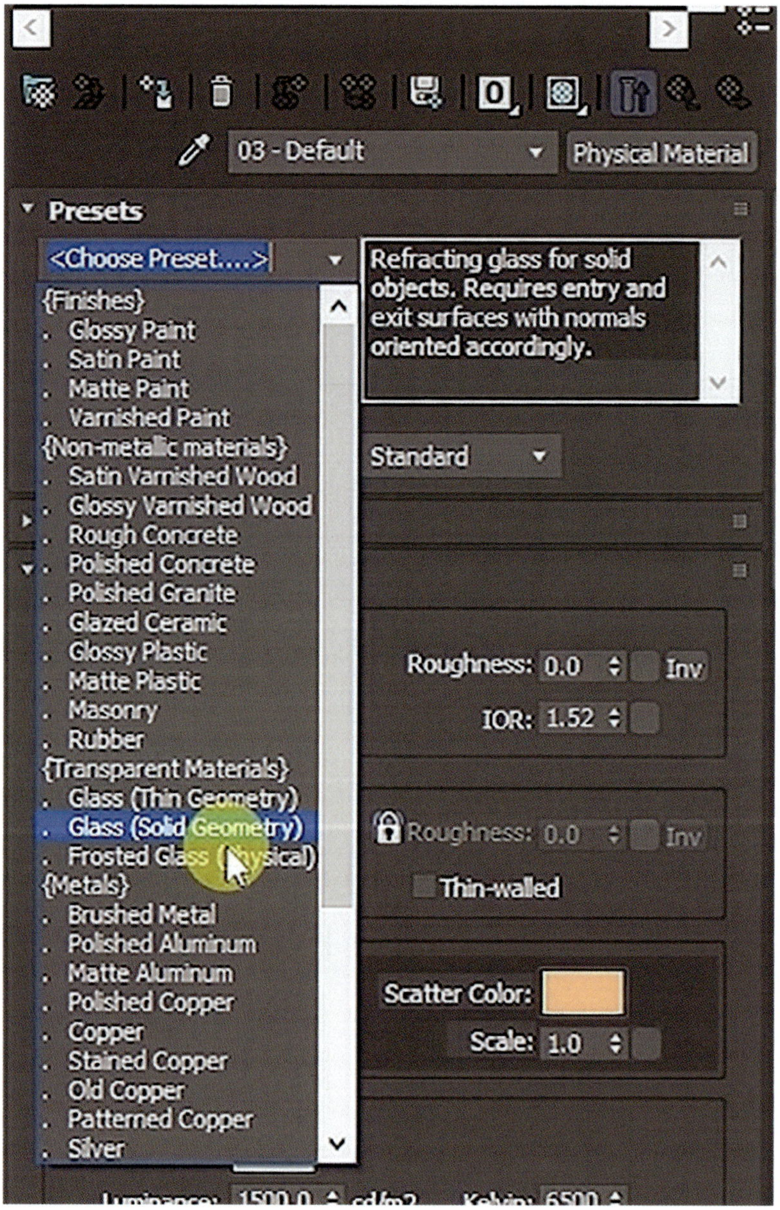

Choose the glass solid geometry preset from the material Presets list

As previously done, copy the text, and paste it onto the material slot. Name and assign it to the car glass.

Pasted text and assigned Glass material in the Material Editor dialog

To create the car headlights, copy the glass material, by dragging it to the next slot, and renaming it. Change the material mode to, Advanced.

Because we want the headlight to be self-illuminated, increase the emission value to about 0.19.

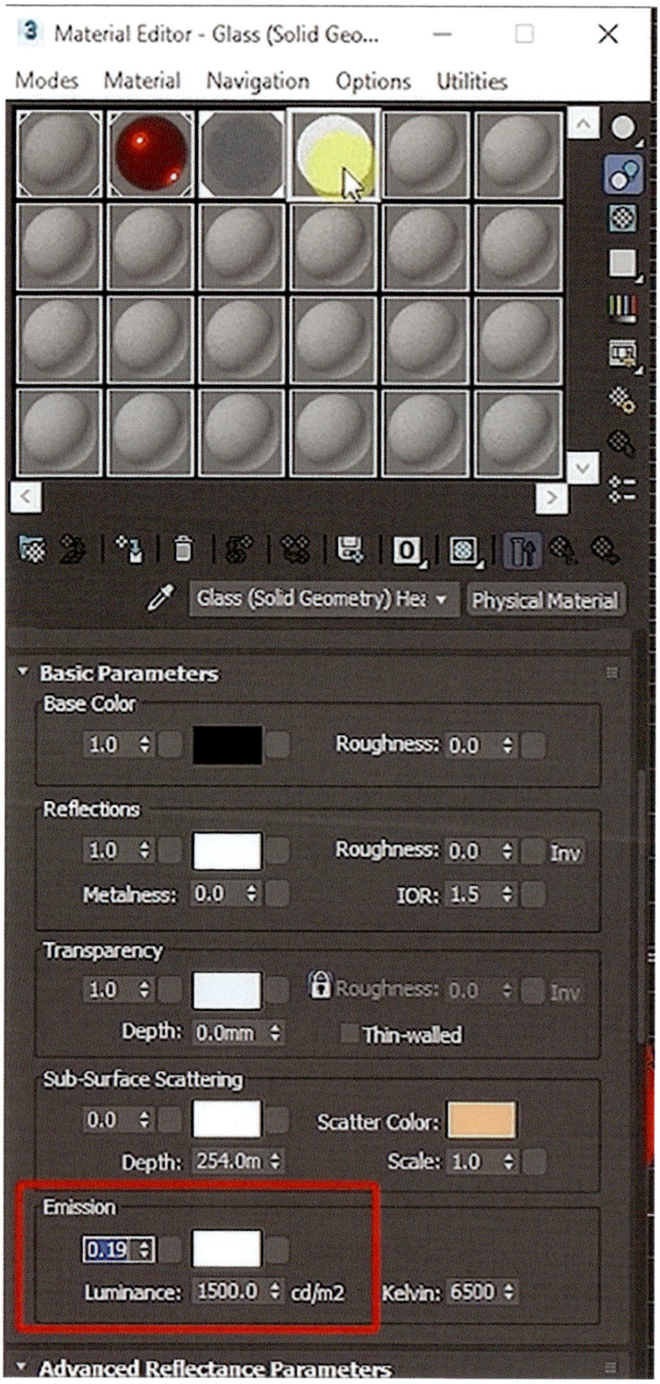

Emission Value increased to 0.19

The glass material should be slightly brighter now. Assign it to the headlight object in the scene.

Next, select the rim objects in the scene. Followed by selecting a new material slot, and loading a new physical material, as previously done.

In the material preset, choose the Gold material. Change its Base color swatch to dark gray, and change the material mode to Advanced.

Assign it to the car wheels and rename the material as, chrome.

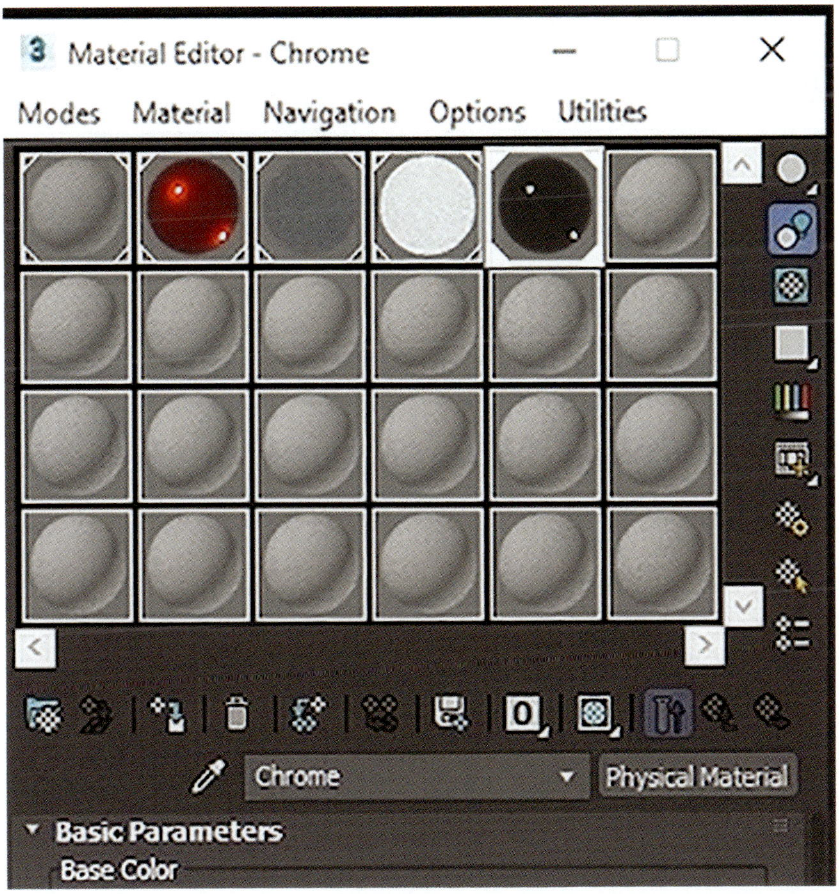

Chrome material created, renamed and assigned in the Material Editor dialog

The next material to create is plastic material. In the viewport, select the front part of the car and maximize the viewport.

In a new material slot, load the physical material, as previously done, and choose the rubber material preset from the list. Copy and paste the preset name on the material slot.

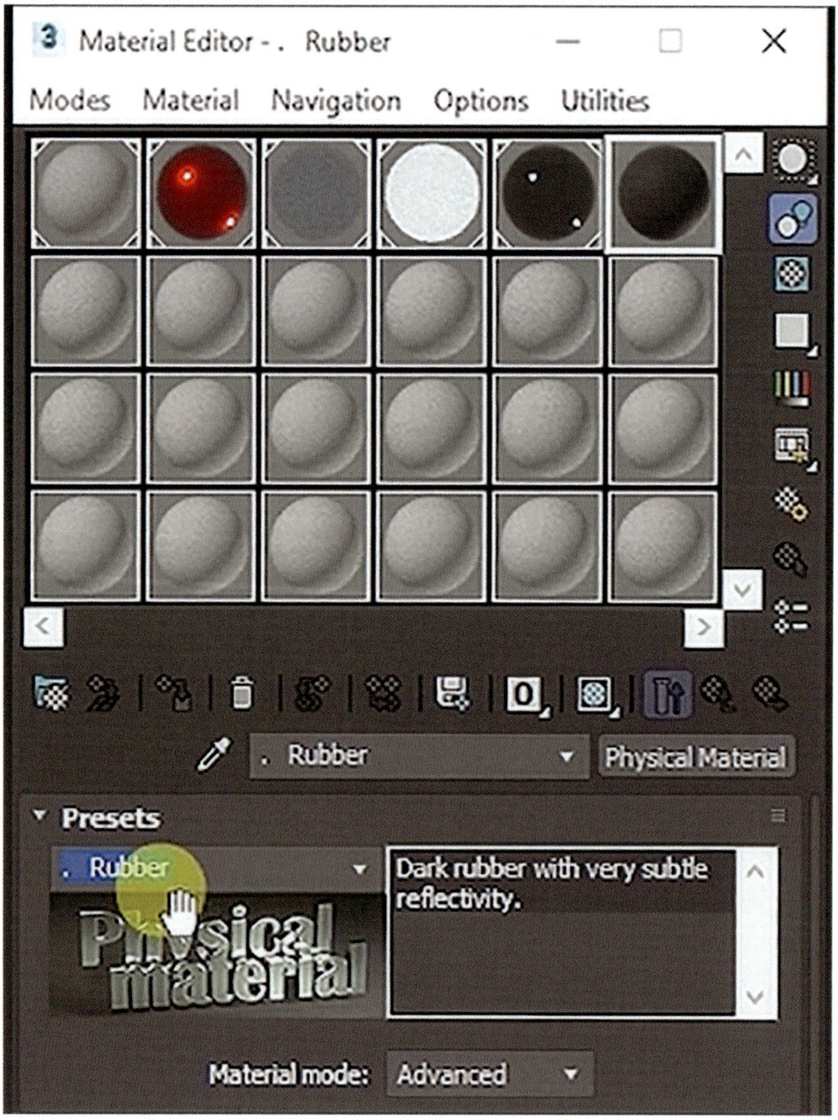

Rubber material preset added and material text renamed

Because we want the plastic material to be really dark, let's click on its reflections color swatch, and change it to a darker color, to reduce reflectivity.

Double click on the material editor to maximize it. Next, decrease the roughness values, until we see the shine coming through the surface.

Also, let's make the base color completely dark. Select the car fenders and tires, and assign the rubber material to them.

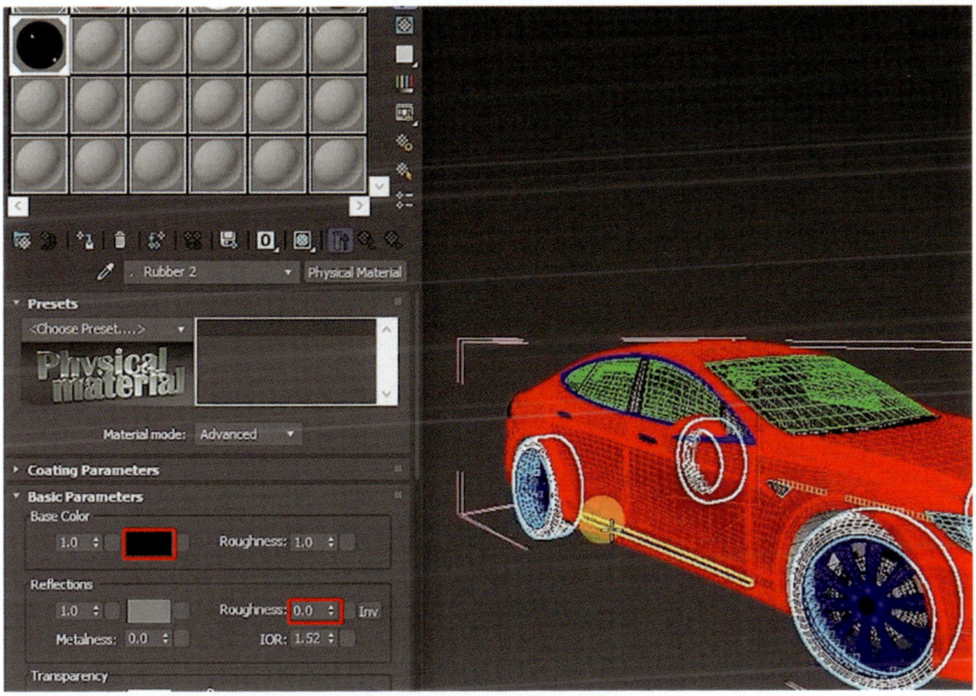

New Rubber material created and assigned to the car fenders and tires

Next, let's create a camera by clicking on its command icon. Select the camera button. Followed by clicking and dragging it in the top viewport. Right click to exit creation.

Right click and choose the move tool. Move and adjust the camera accordingly.

Open the modifier panel and change it to a free camera. This will give you the flexibility to move the camera freely, without the target constraint.

Zoom out the viewport and move the camera up, to eye level, or 1.64 m. In the perspective viewport, change the view, to the selected camera.

Please refer to the final scene, Car Final.max, to see the position of the final camera.

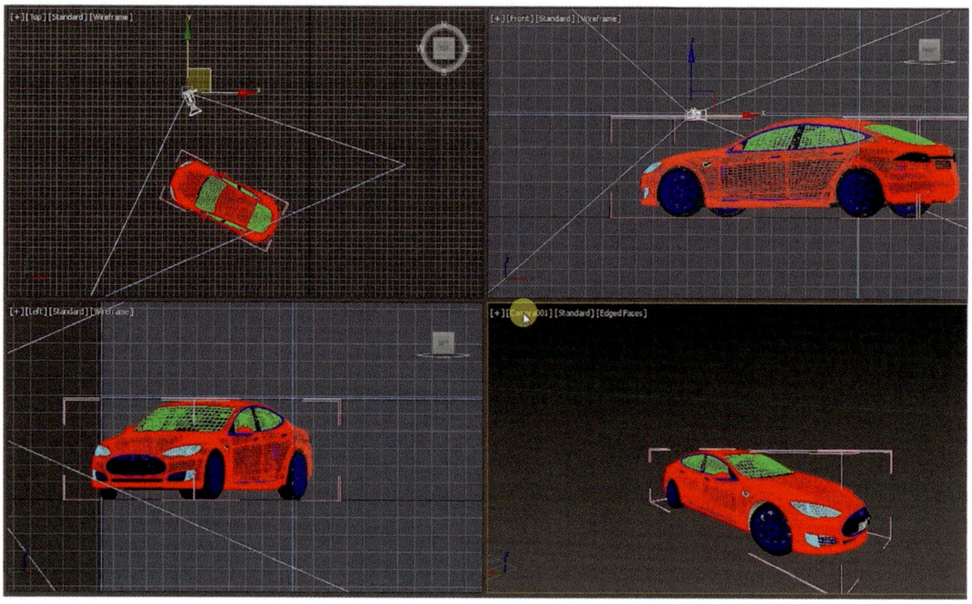

New camera created in the viewport

The next step is to load an HDRI map to the environment map. Before we do so, click on the plus text, and choose to configure viewports.

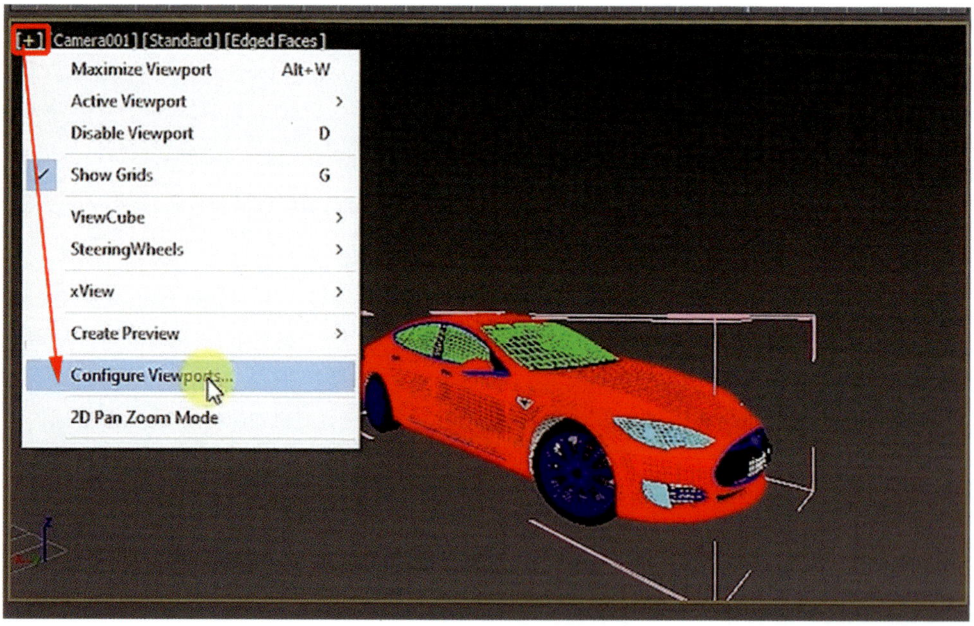

Configure viewports option enabled

Under the Display Performance tab, change the viewport background to 1,500 pixels, if it's not set to that size already. Higher values will be sharper.

However, it may slow down your computer.

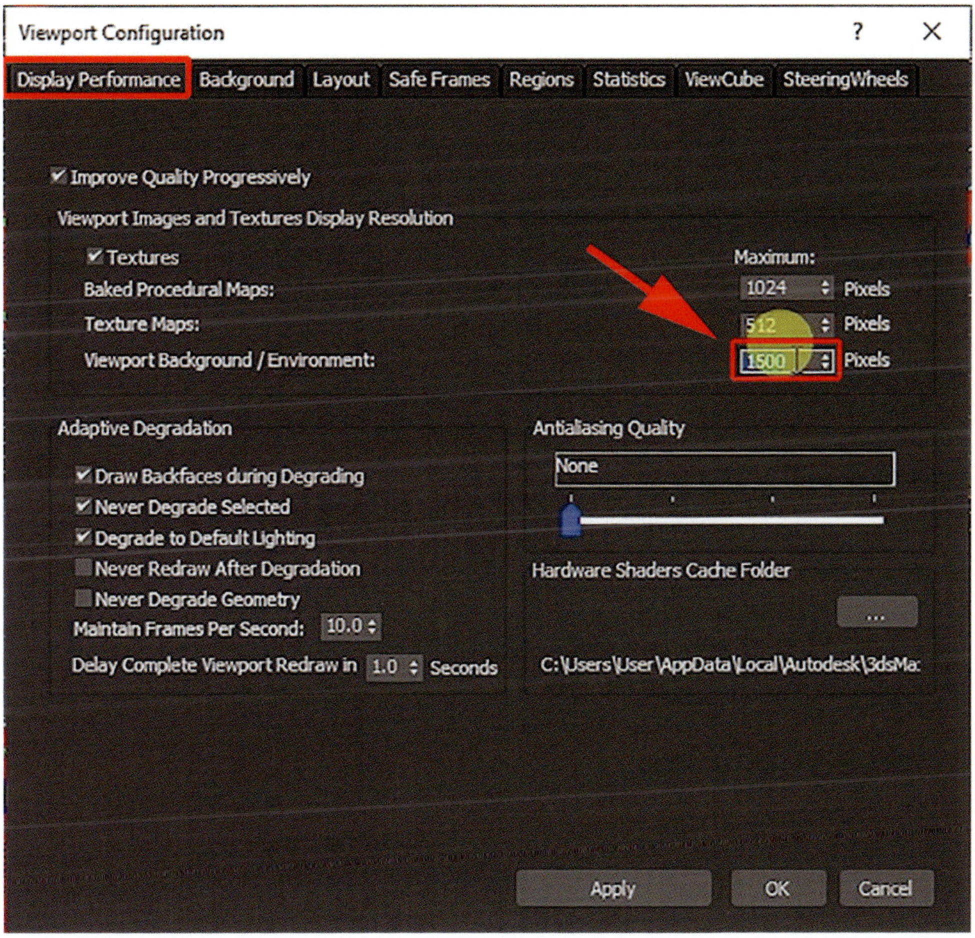

Under the Display Performance tab, Change the viewport background to 1,500 pixels.

Under the Background tab, change its current function to, use environment background.

And click to apply to the active view.

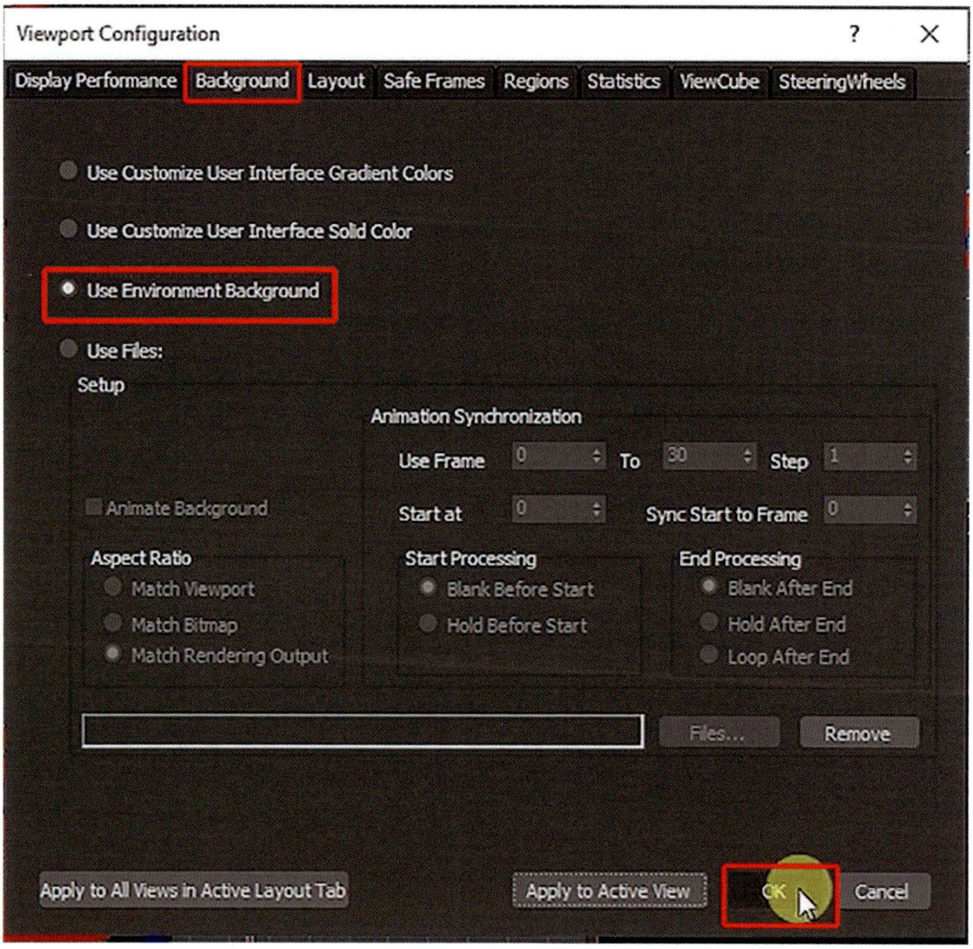

Change function to use environment background

Next, click on the Rendering toolbar and choose the Environment option from the list.

Alternatively, simply press 8 on your keyboard.

Change function to, use environment background

Followed by clicking on the environment map toggle.

In the material browser, click on the bitmap and choose the HDR image named, WinterGardens_Night.hdr

NOTE

If this HDRI slows down your computer, use the image named, WinterGardens_Night smaller 2.JPG, instead.

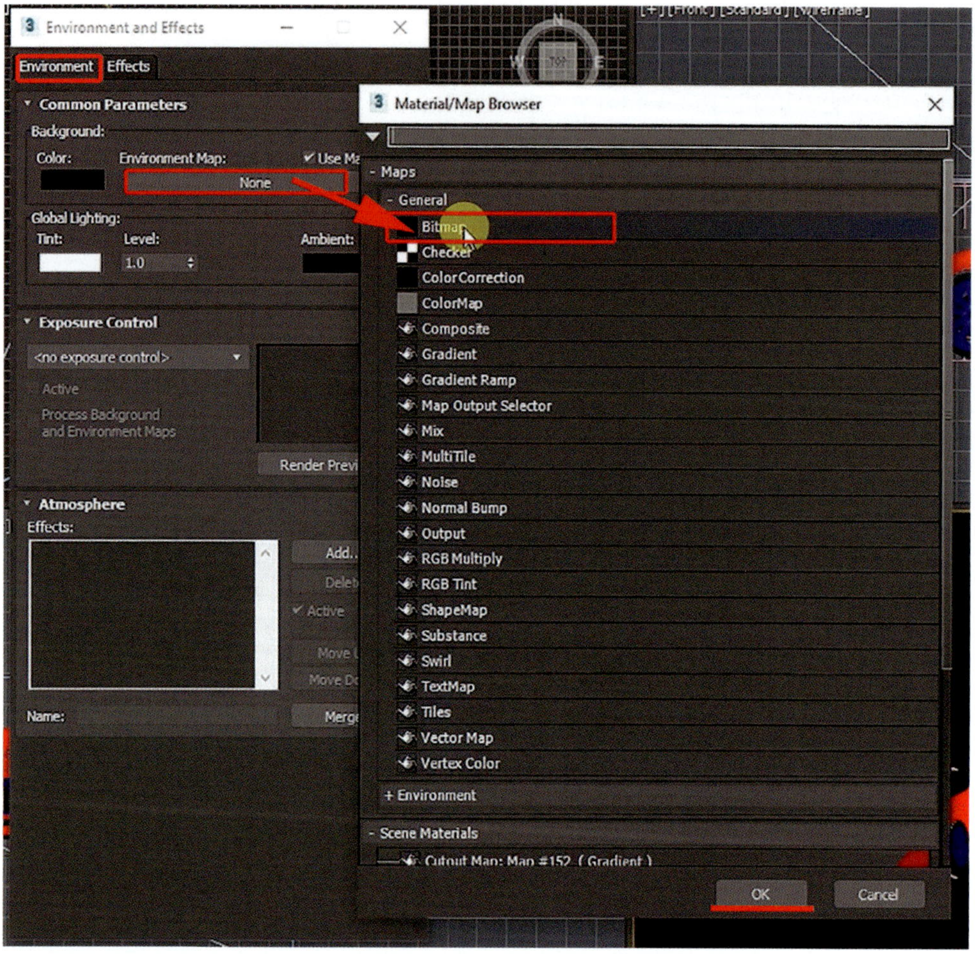

Click on the environment map toggle to bring up the Material/Map Browser dialog

Unlock the Display scaled colors by, padlock, and set its display scaled colors to 10. This value worked OK for this exercise.

However, feel free to enter different values, if desired.

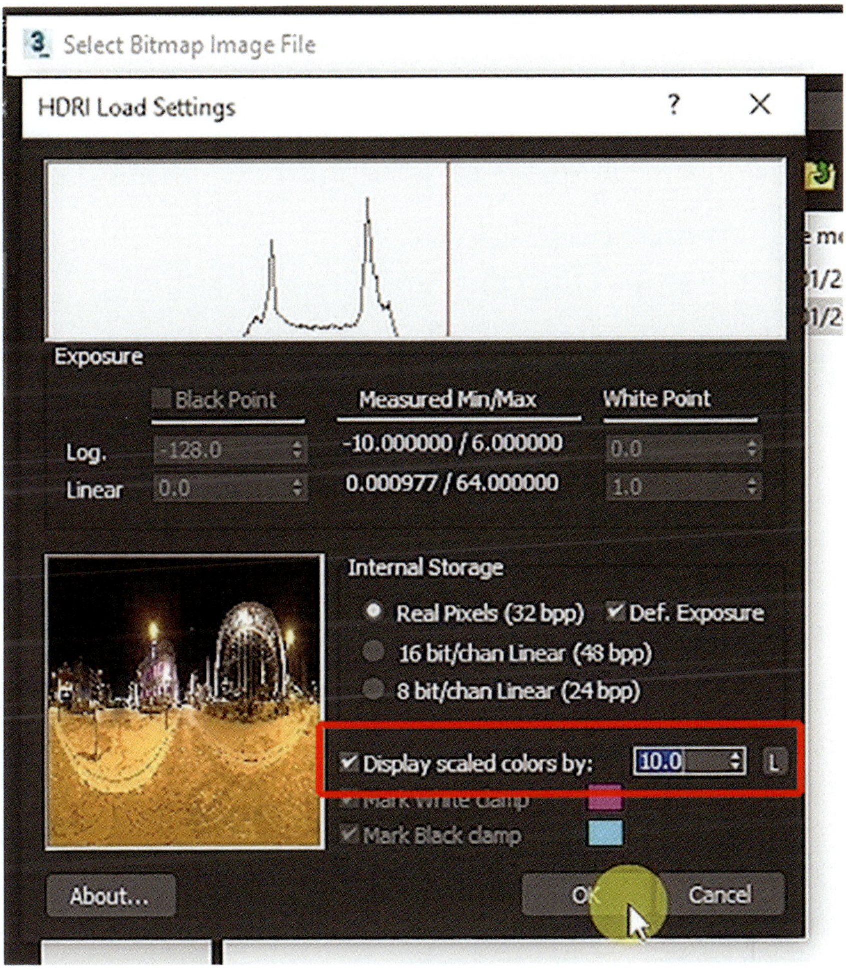

Set the display scaled colors function to 10

Next, drag and drop its toggle into an empty material slot.

And choose the instance method.

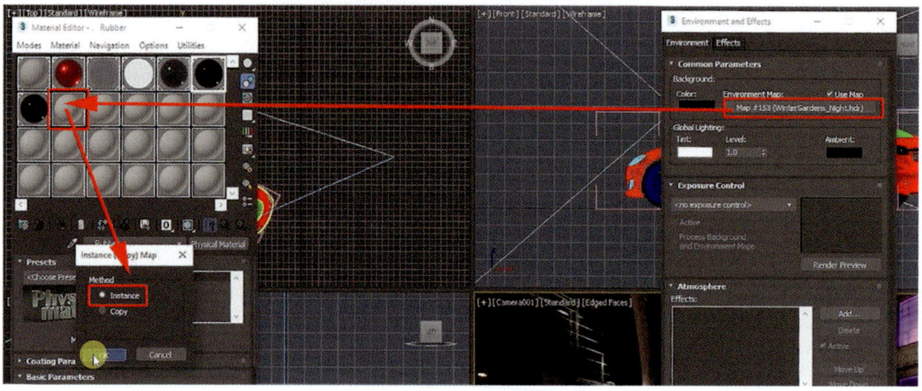

Drag/drop its toggle into an empty material slot, and choose the instance method

To create lights, click on the lights command button.

Verge3D works mainly with standard lights, such as target spot, free spot, target direct, free direct and Omni lights.

For the purpose of this exercise, select the Omni light and create it in the scene.

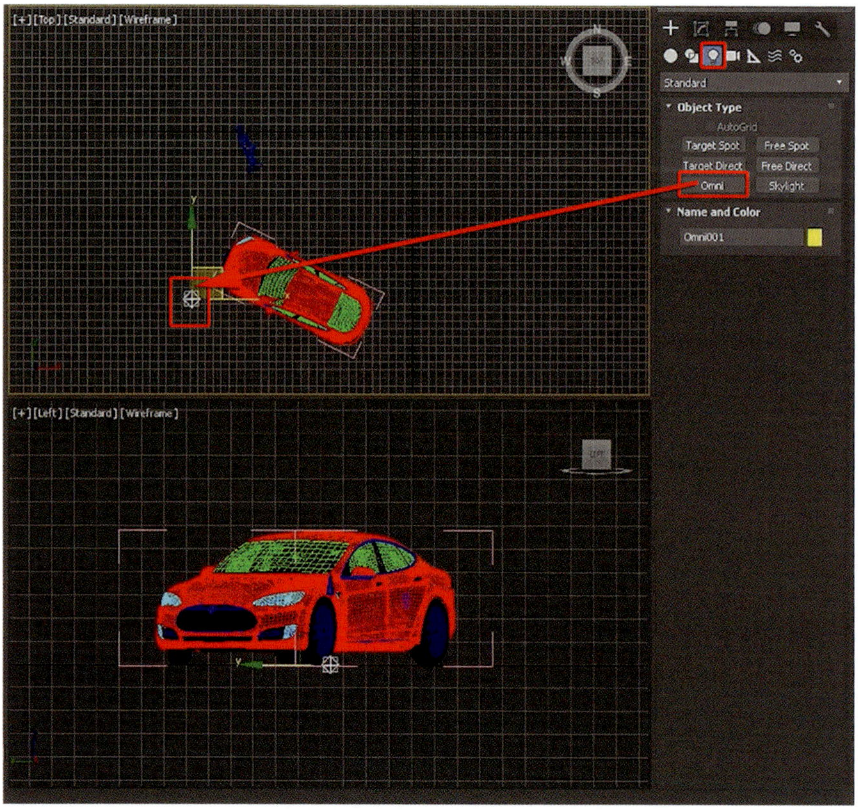

Select the Omni light, and create it in the scene

Move and adjust the light.

Followed by going to the modify panel.

To enable the shadows, simply check its function.

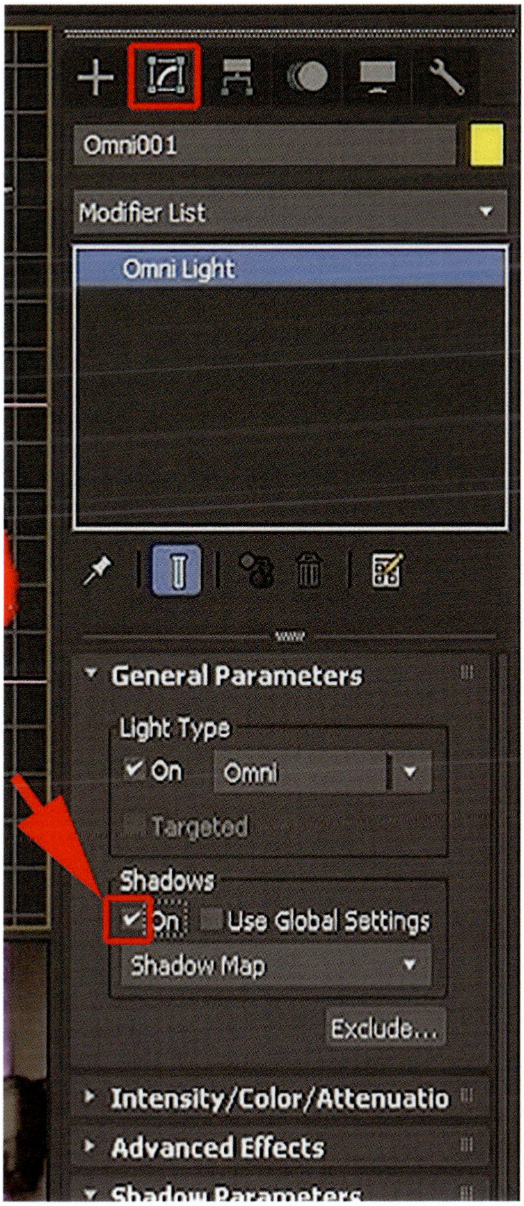

Enable the shadows function in the Modify panel

The remaining light parameters work well by default.

However, when a scene is exported to Verge3d, the shadows may look darker than usual.

To rectify this, simply increase the emission values of specific materials slightly.

Because we want this scene to be interactive, we are going to create buttons, to be later used to change the material of the car body.

To create the first button, let's go to the shapes commands and choose the circle.

In the front viewport, click and drag to create the circle.

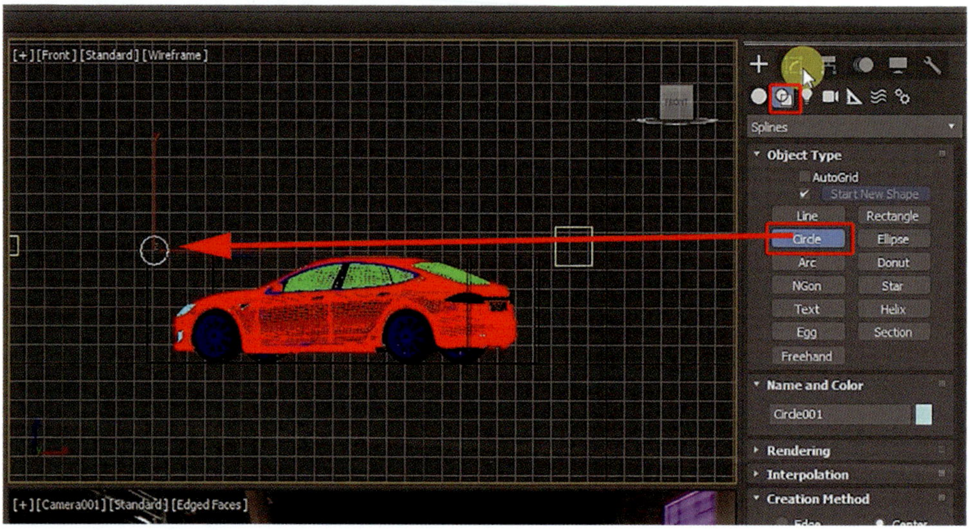

Click and drag to create the circle

Go to the modify panel.

Increase its interpolation to make the circle smoother.

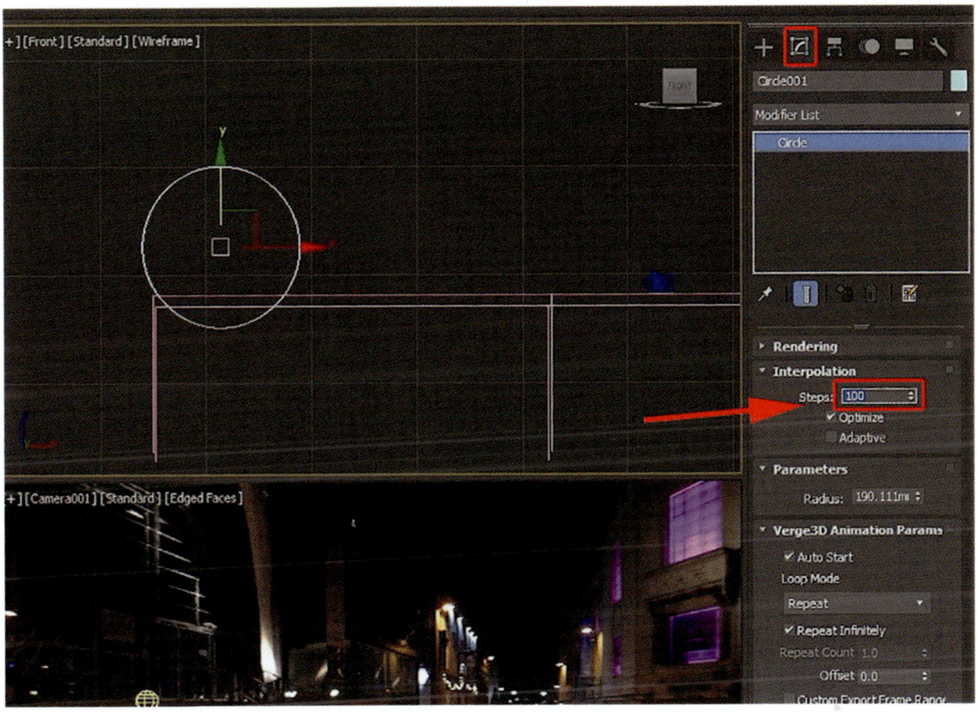

Increase the interpolation of the shape to make the circle smoother

Move and position the circle so it's in front of the camera.

Expand the parameters and reduce its radius to make it smaller.

Next, open the material editor.

Select the red car paint material, and copy the text name.

Followed by pasting it, in the circle object name field.

Add the text object in front of it.

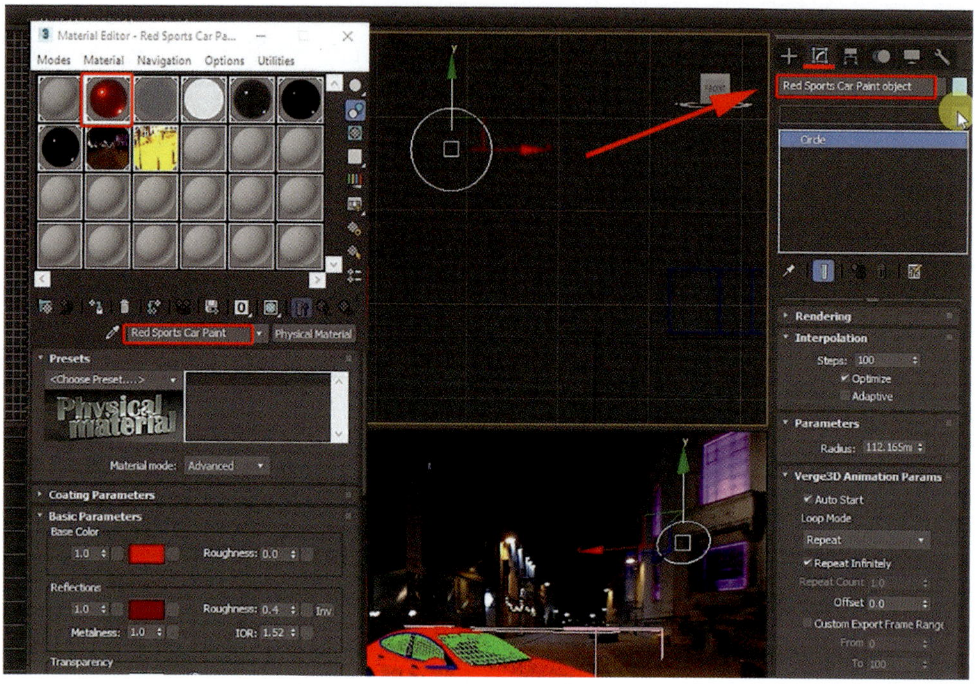

Rename the material name

As mentioned earlier, it's crucial to name materials and objects accordingly, to later pick them in Verge3d.

Add the extrude modifier and increase the amount to 5 mm.

To copy it, while selected, hold down the shift key, and move the circle down.

Name the object as, blue and text object in front.

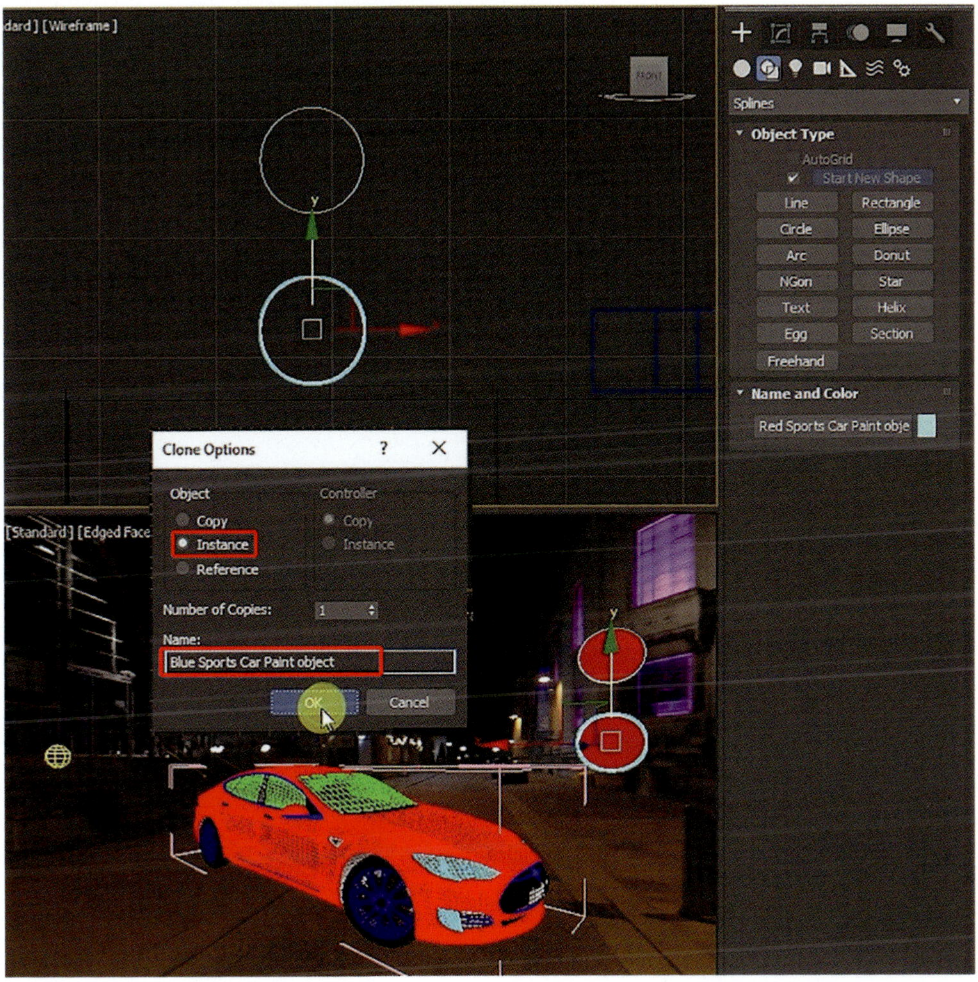

Copy and rename the new object

Change its object color to blue by clicking in its color swatch, and changing its color.

Also, change the color of the first circle to red.

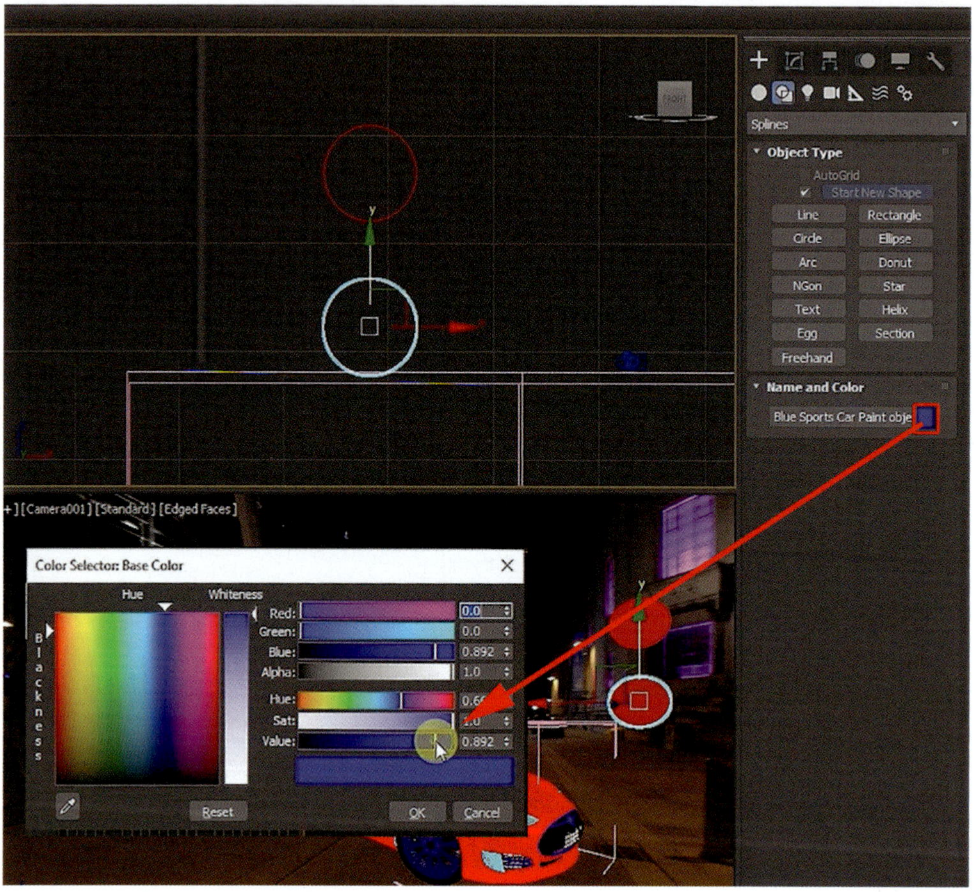

Change the object color to blue

Next, let's create a new material slot, by dragging and dropping this red material. Add the name blue in front of it. And change its colors to blue.

Assign this material to the blue circle object.

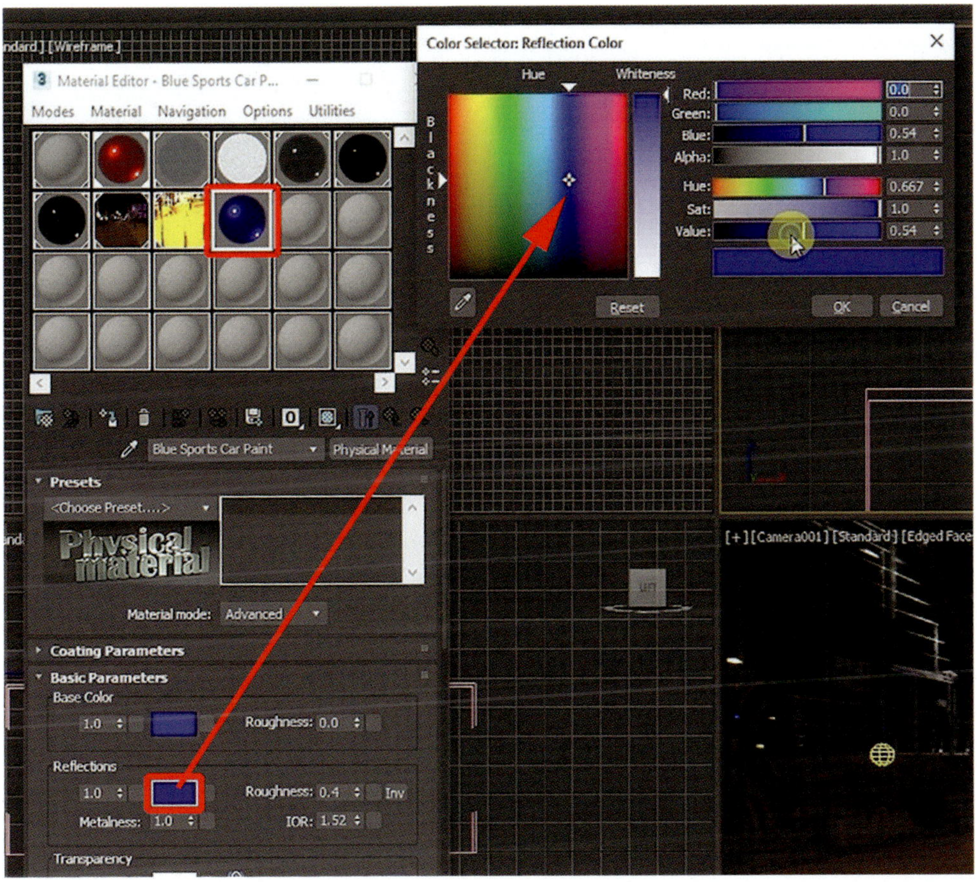

Change the material color to blue

Copy the last circle, and name it yellow object.

Change its color as previously done.

Create a new yellow material using the same approach as before.

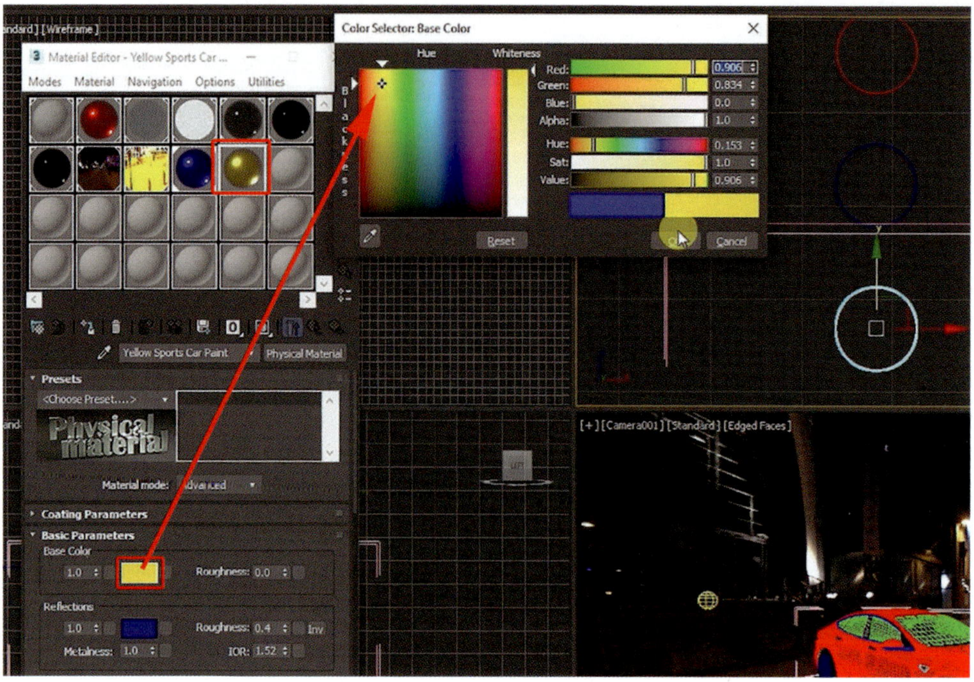

Change the material color to yellow

Before exporting this scene to Verge3d, click on the Verge3D toolbar, and choose the option to Sneak Peak.

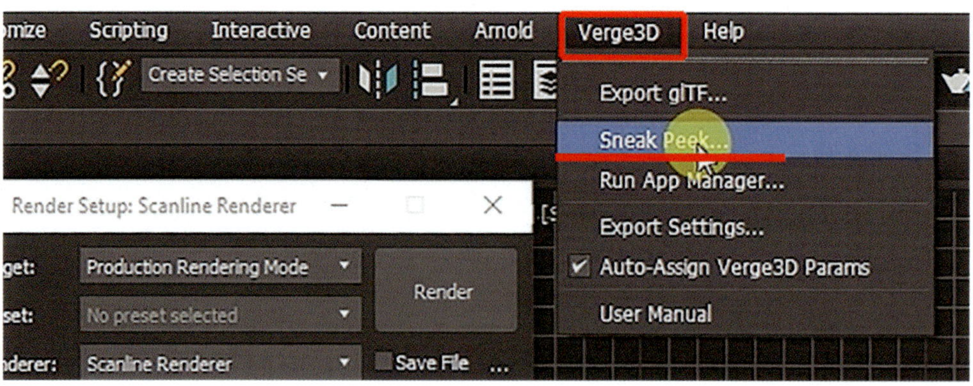

Click on the Verge3D toolbar, and choose the option to Sneak Peak

Sneak Peak result

Next, go to the Verge3d toolbar and choose the option to run app manager.

Go to the Verge3D toolbar and choose the option to run app manager

To create a new app, click on its icon, name it accordingly, Accept the default settings and click to Create App.

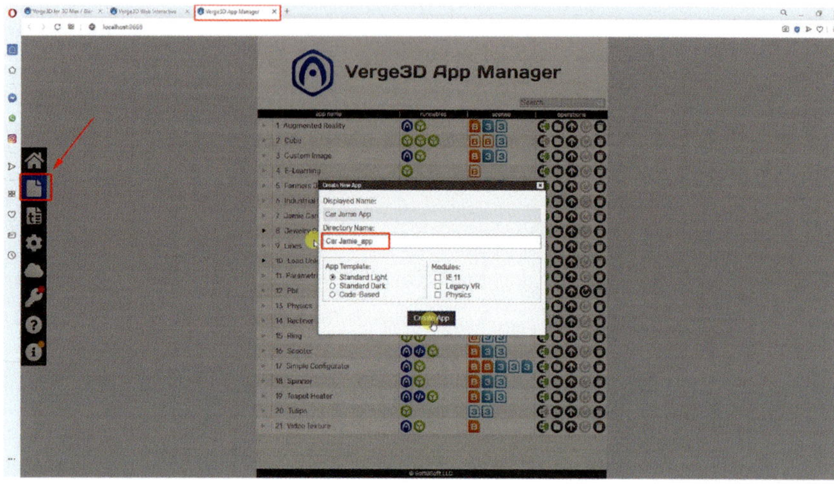

Click the App icon, name it accordingly, Accept the default settings and click to Create App

Every time an app is created, it goes into a specific folder. It's often under your local C drive, users, users, verge3d and applications,

Inside the applications folder, one can see all the apps created.

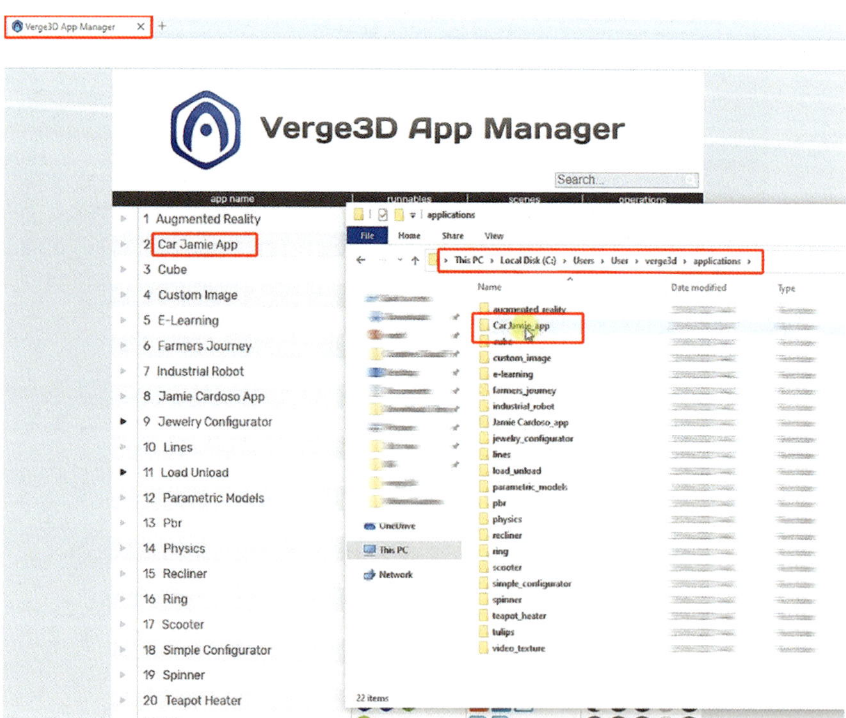

Location of the apps created

A temporary GLTF and a 3ds Max file were automatically created under the name of the app.

They need to be overridden with our own 3ds Max and GLTF file.

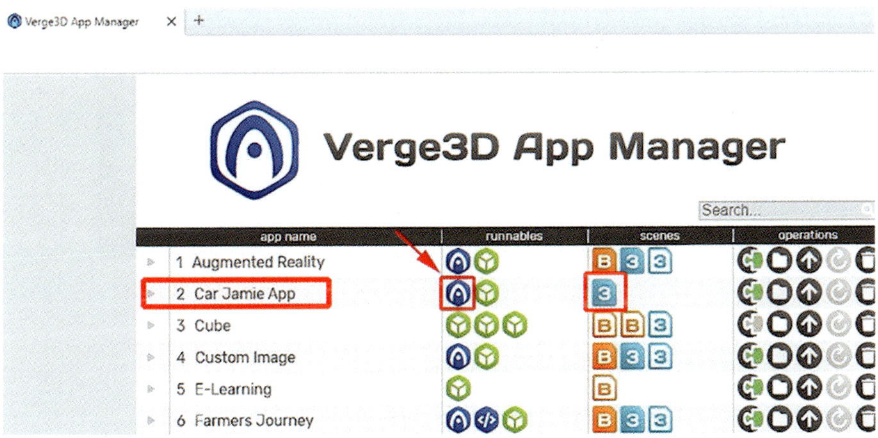

Temporary GLTF and a 3ds Max file automatically created

To create Puzzles coding for this new app, click on its button.

Puzzles coding button

Before we start creating puzzle codes, we need to first export the current 3ds Max scene as a GLTF file format.

Back in 3ds Max, go to the Verge3D toolbar, and choose to export to GLTF.

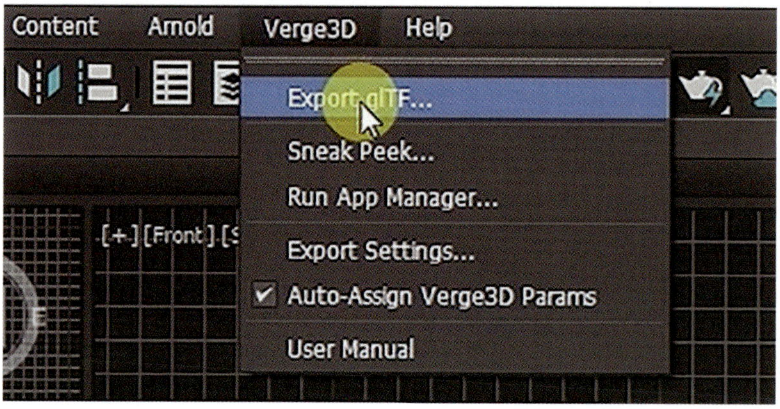

Choose to export to GLTF

In the export dialog, make sure to override the placeholder file automatically created under the name of the car Jamie app.

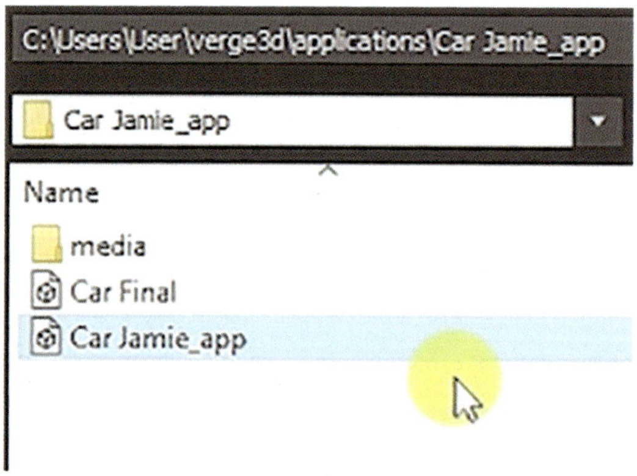

Override the GLTF named, Car Jamie_app

Back in the App manager, click on the puzzles button to load up the recently exported file.

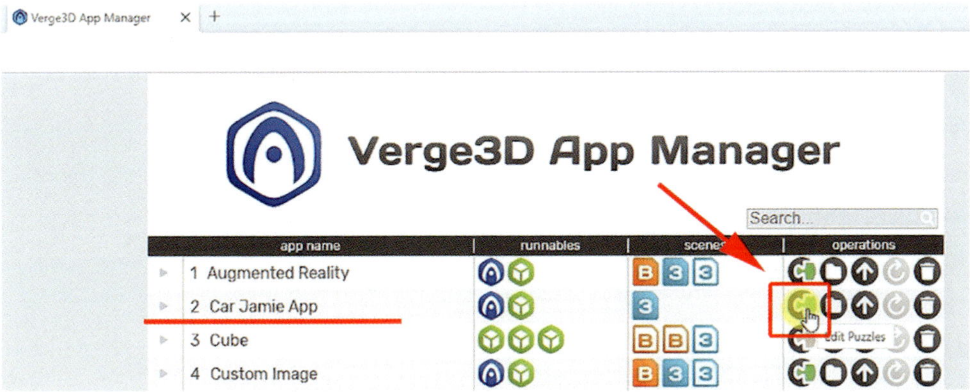

Click on the puzzles button to load up the recently exported file

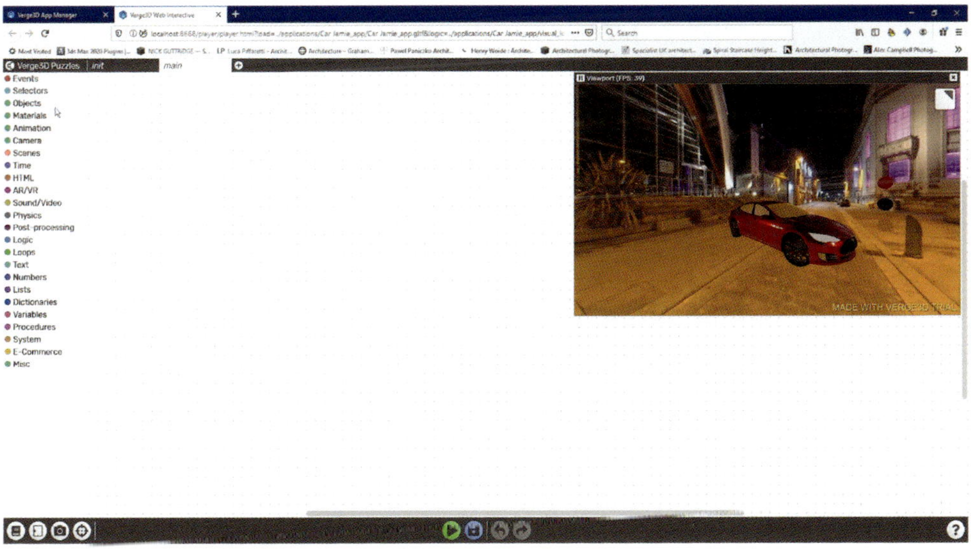

Puzzles App page

This puzzles page is unique, and truly groundbreaking, as users don't need any experience in coding, to create amazing interactive and immersive applications

The puzzles list is broken down into Events, Selectors, Objects, materials, Animations, Cameras, Scenes, Time, HTML, AR VR, Sound Video, Physics, Post-processing to add bloom and other effects, Logic, Loops and many more.

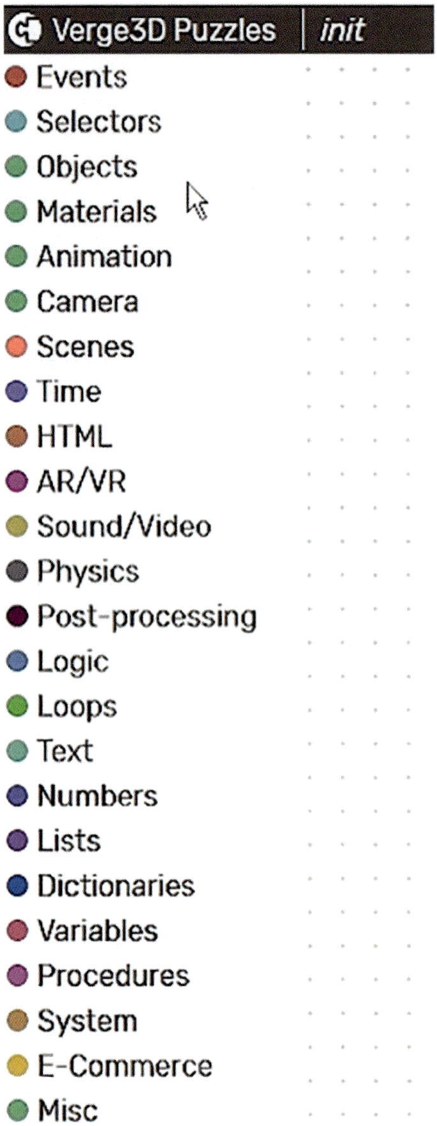

Puzzles list

Let's start by clicking on the Events Puzzles. Double click on its button to select it.

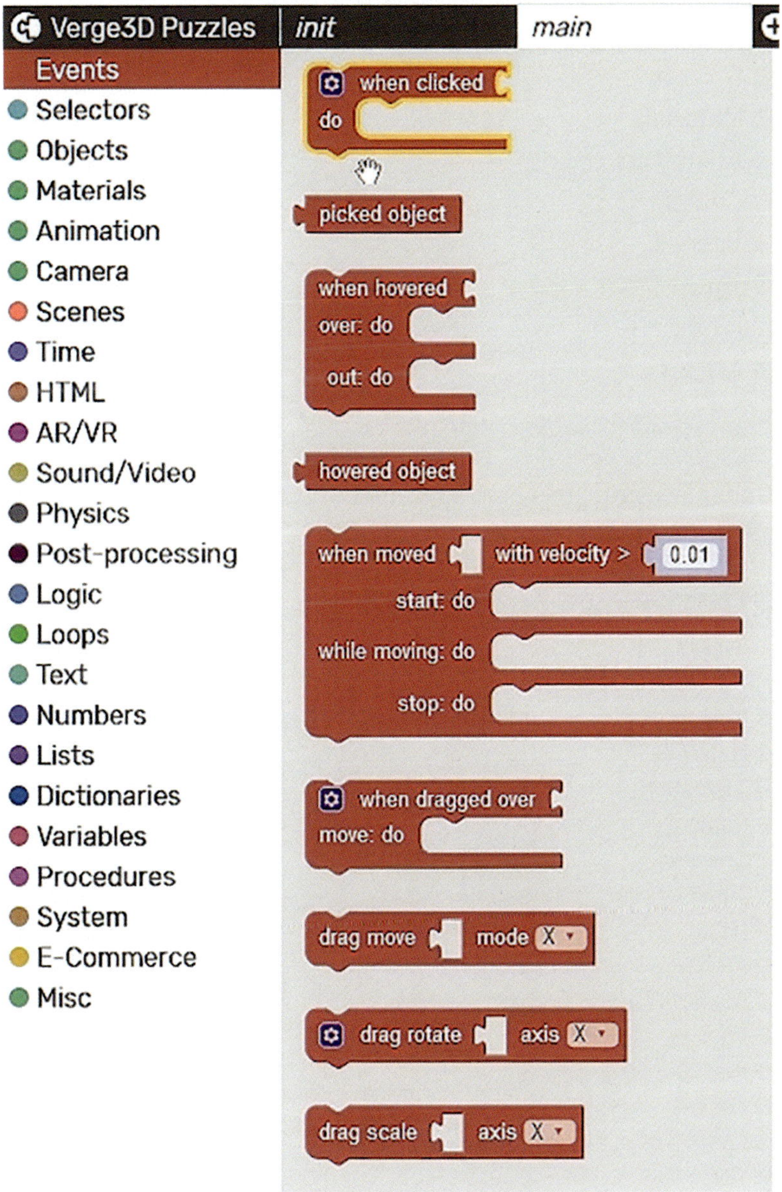

Events Puzzles open

For the purpose of this exercise, we want, when clicked, to go to the selectors puzzles.

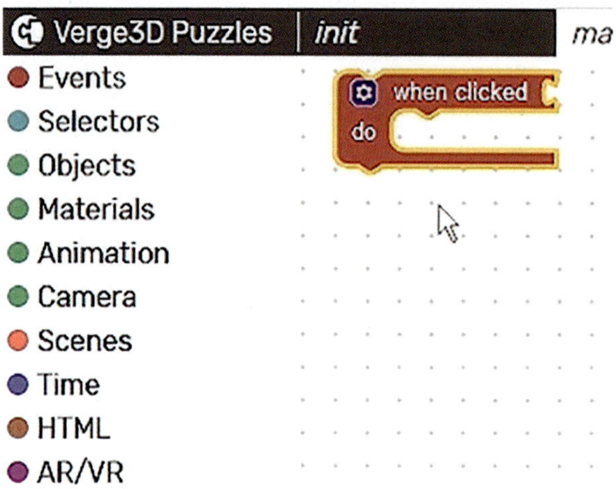

When clicked, to go to the selectors puzzles

Under Selectors, there are a number of functions. Let's double click on, Select an object function.

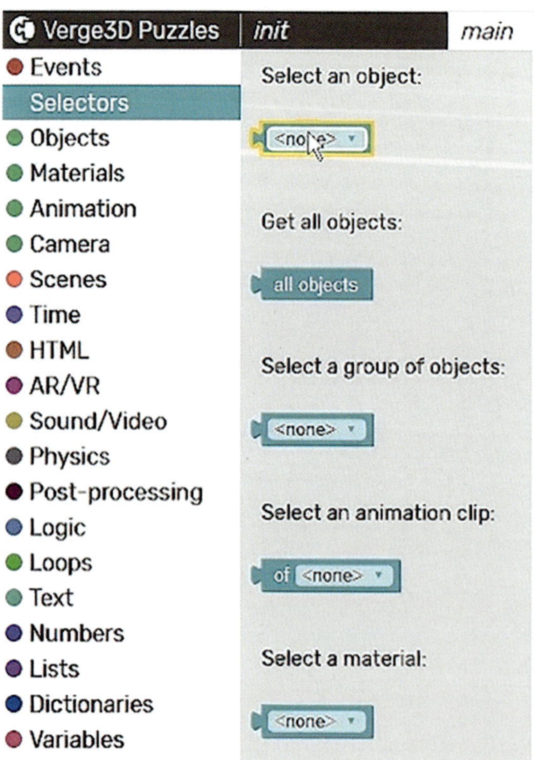

Selectors functions

Drag and fit it to, when clicked puzzle. Click on none, to pick the object from the max scene.

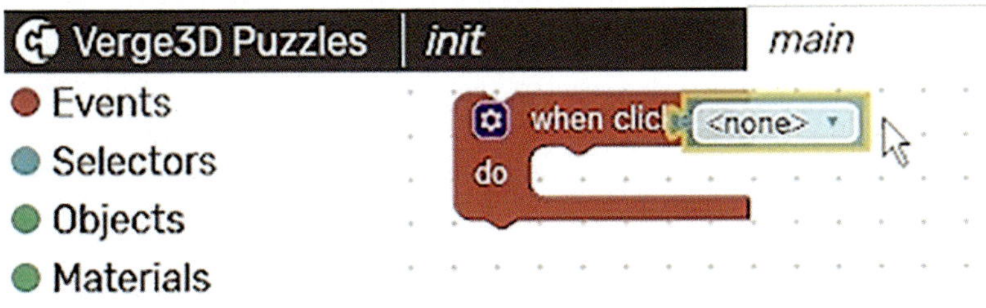

Drag and fit it to, when clicked puzzle

Pick the brushed metal Red object from the list. This is why it's utterly important to name objects and materials accordingly in your 3ds Max scene.

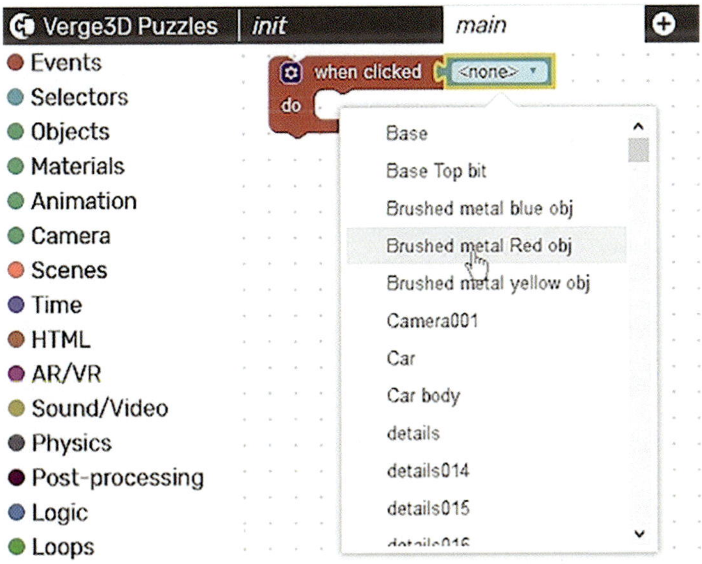

Click on none, to pick the object from the max scene

Brushed metal Red object picked

So when clicked on, the brushed metal Red object, we want to do something.

Click on, Materials puzzles, and choose to assign a material puzzle.

There are also other puzzles to, replace texture, set color and much more.

For the purpose of this exercise, we are choosing the, assign material puzzle.

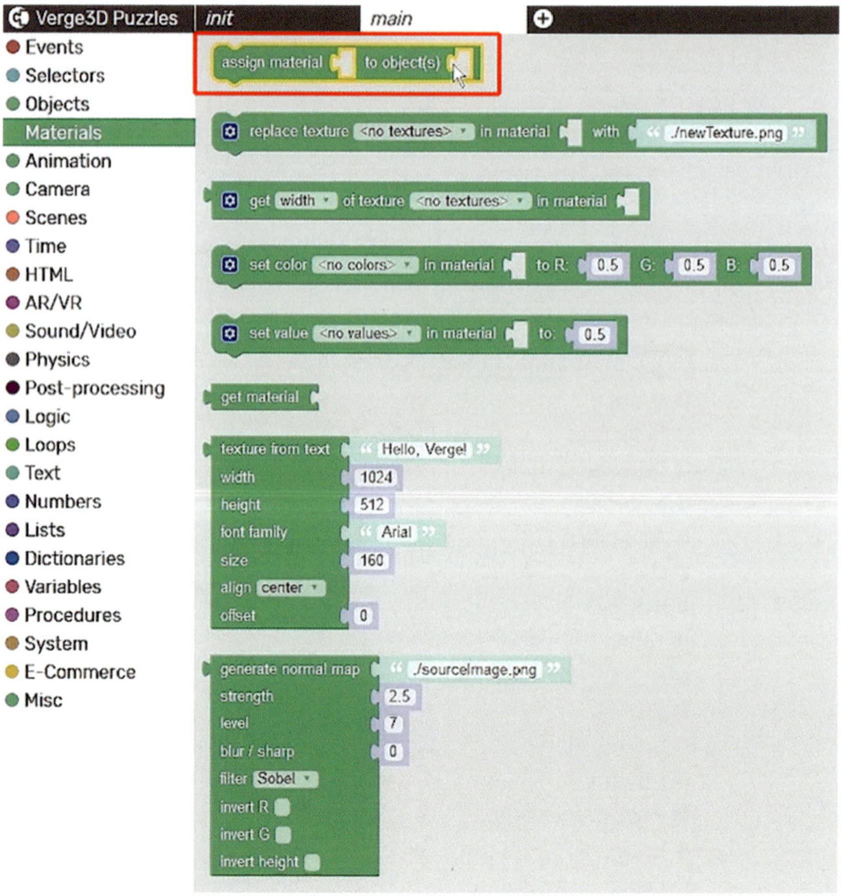

Assign material to objects picked

Let's drag and fit it to the main puzzle.

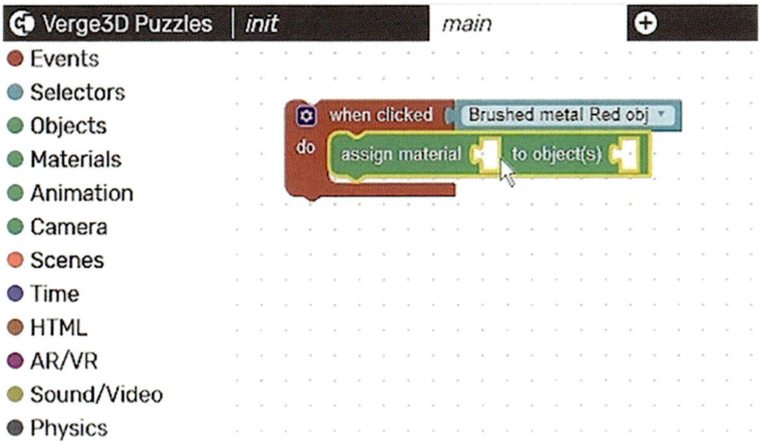

Assign material fitted to the main puzzle

In the assign material, let's choose another selector puzzle. Under Select a material, choose this puzzle.

Drag and fit it to the assign material puzzle. Click and choose the, Red Sports Car Paint, from the list.

Again, this is why it's utterly important to name objects and materials accordingly, in your 3ds Max scene.

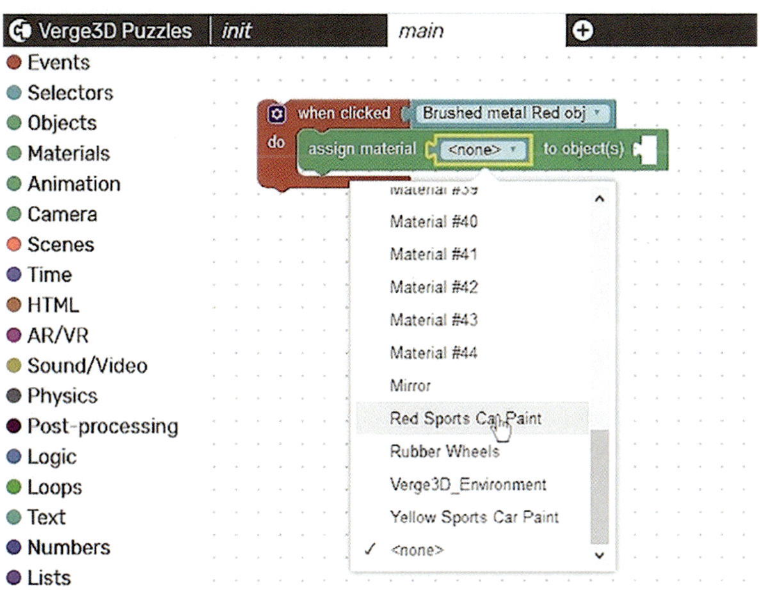

Red Sports Car Paint assigned

In the section "to objects", we are going to find the right puzzle to fit into it.

To do so, click the Selectors puzzle. Under the Select and object, choose its puzzle (<none>), and fit it to the objects puzzle.

If this puzzle wasn't correct, it wouldn't fit and click. Sometimes users need to go through the list of puzzles to see what fits.

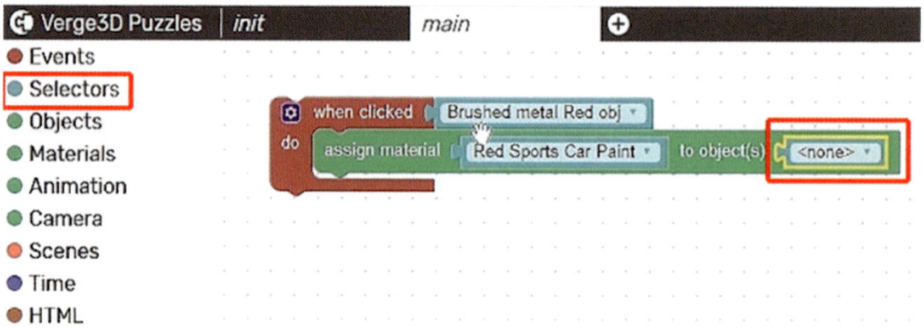

Select and object function selected

Click on the (<none>) puzzle, and choose the car body object from the list.

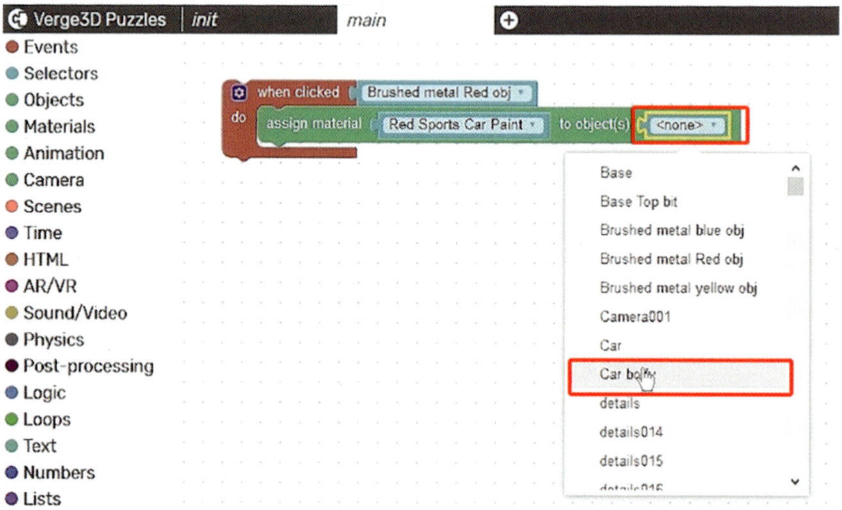

Choose the Car body object from the list

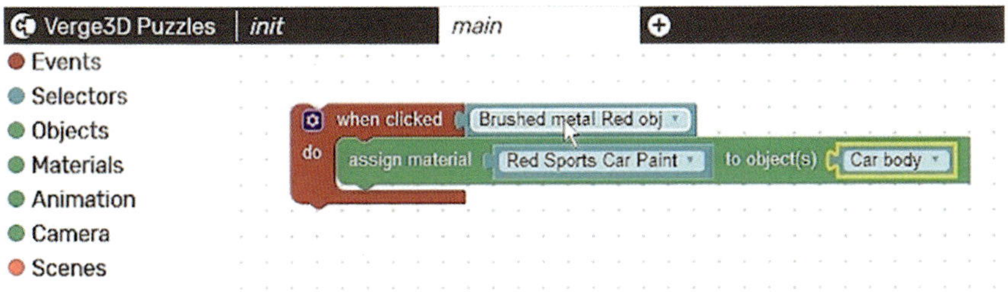

Car body object chosen

In summary, when users click on the Brushed metal Red object, the assign material to a Red Sports Car Paint links to the object Car body.

These functionalities were applied to the red button.

The following step is to duplicate these puzzles and apply them to the blue and the yellow buttons.

To duplicate the entire set of puzzles, simply right click on the back side of the set, and choose to Duplicate.

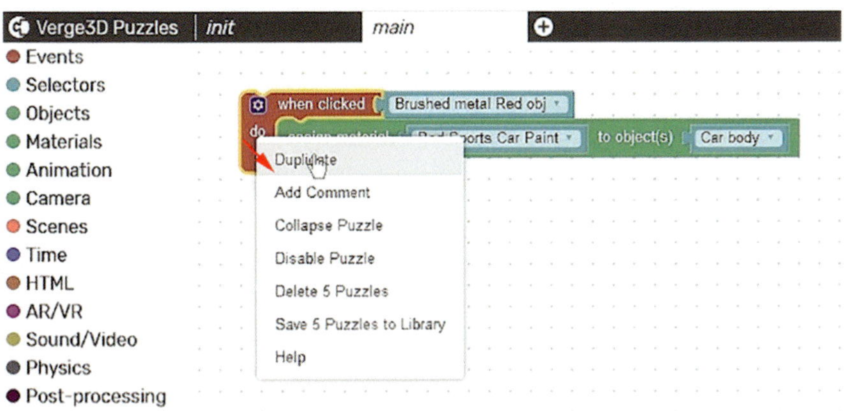

Right click on the back side of the set, and choose to Duplicate

The entire set of puzzles should duplicate.

Next, simply replace the name of objects and materials accordingly as previously done, and repeat the process for the remaining button.

Save the coding created, by clicking on the Save button. Once saved, the button will turn gray.

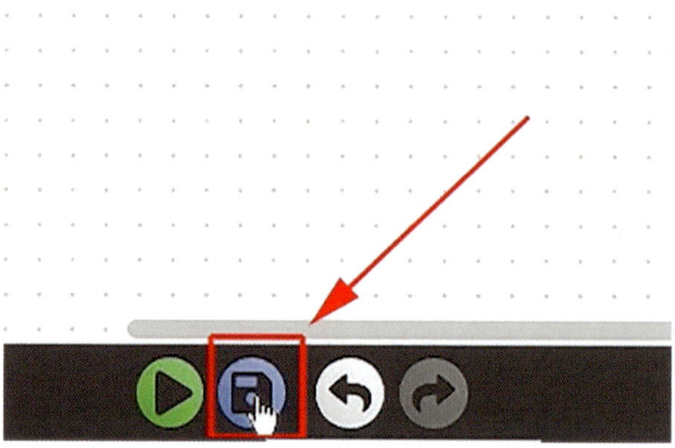

Saving the coding created, by clicking its button

Test the buttons to see how the coding is working, and navigate around the scene.

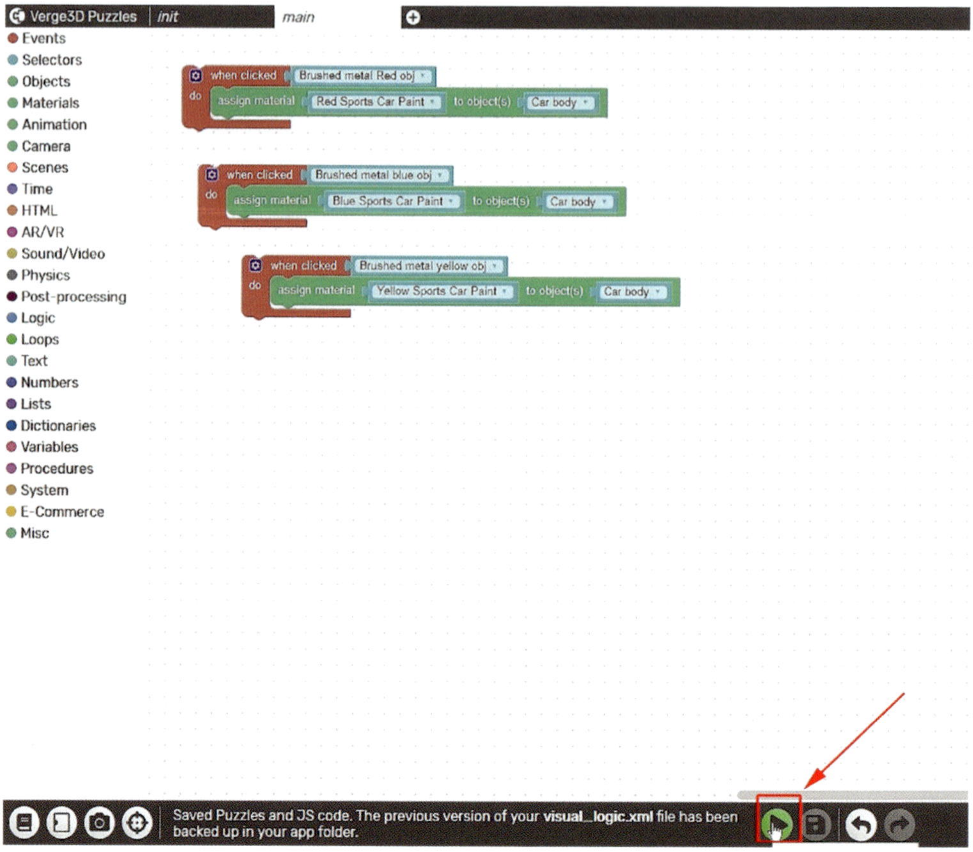

Clicking the Play button to test the file

As mentioned earlier, we can use the same approach for textures, lighting, animation, e-commerce and much more, without having to be programmer.

These apps can go on a website or be sent as links to clients.

Adopt the File's Unit Scale

Always enable the function to, Adopt the File's Unit Scale, when opening a new file. This will prevent scenes from being rescaled and looking inaccurate.

However, there are only a handful of exceptions when one might be required to choose to, Rescale the File Objects to the System Unit Scale.

It only happens when the incoming file is not accurate and requires rescaling.

One should also use the same approach for incoming gamma settings.

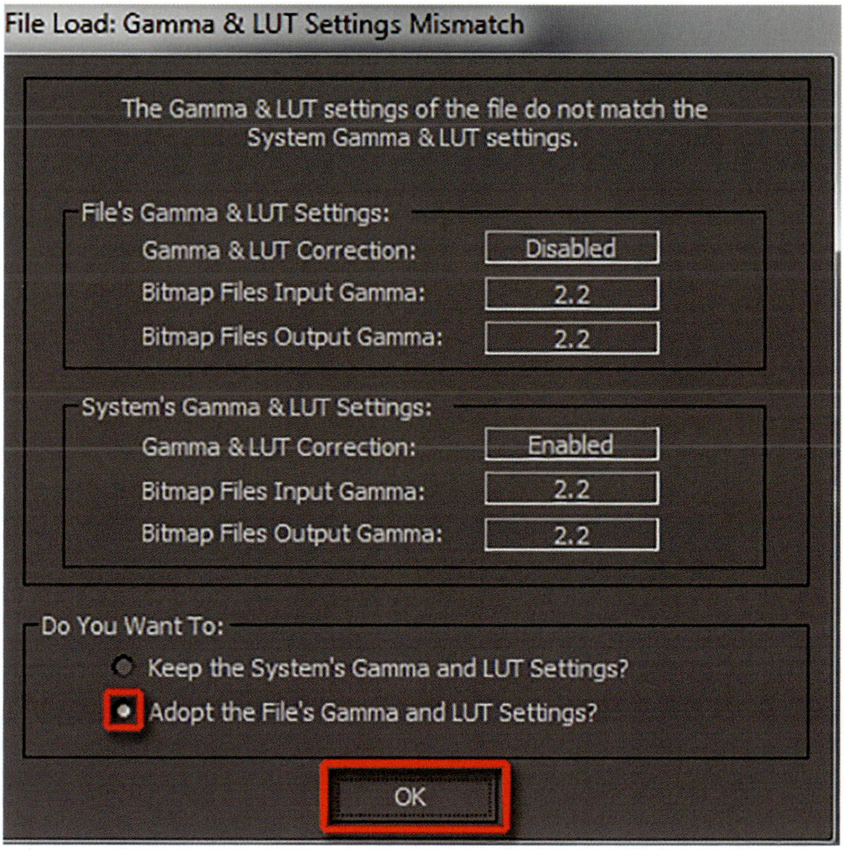

Dialog with the function to, Adopt the File's Gamma and LUT Settings enabled

5 Tips and Tricks

Creating Named Selection Sets

To select multiple objects that are difficult to find in a 3d scene, users often create, Named Selection Sets.

This toolbar allows users to create named selection sets to add as many objects as desired in its list, for bulk selections.

To create named selection sets, click on its main toolbar button to open the dialog.

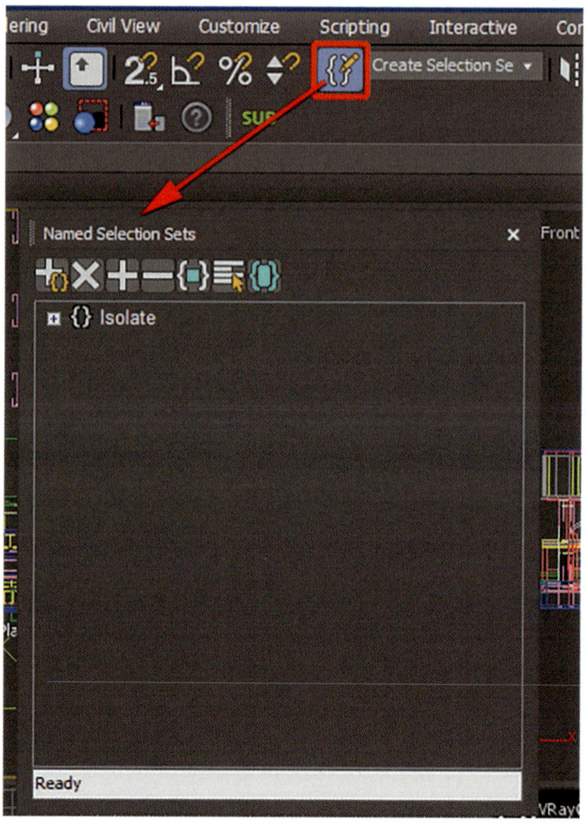

Selection set toolbar clicked and Named Selection Sets dialog open

To create a new selection set, click the button to, Create New Set, and name it accordingly. After naming it, click outside the text field to close the creation.

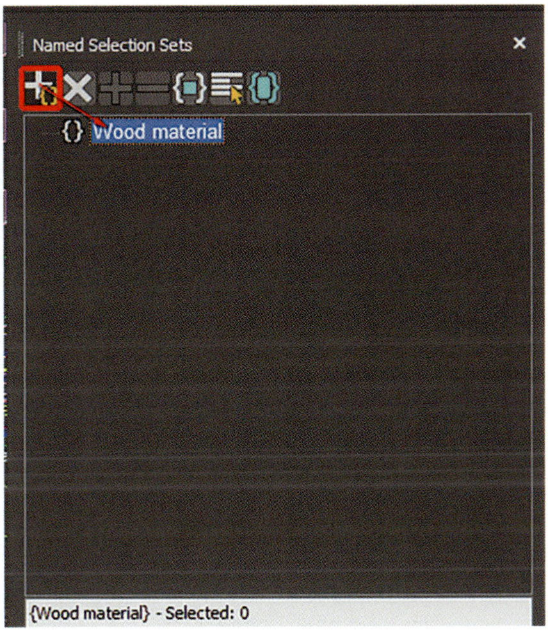

Create New Set button clicked and a Named Selection Set created

While the new selection set is selected, in the scene explorer, select an object and click the button to, Add selected objects.

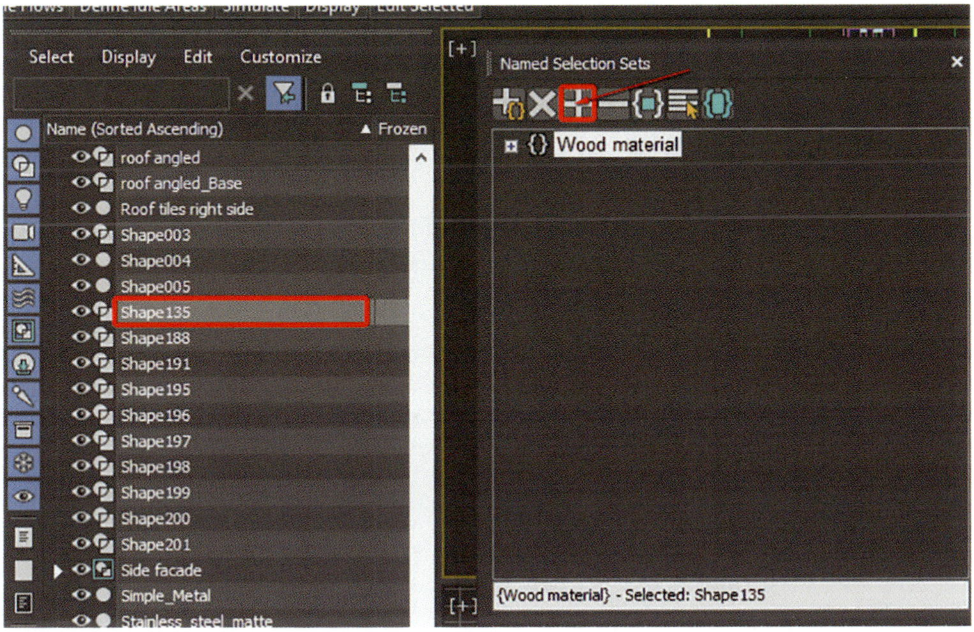

Shape135 selected in the scene explorer and Add selected objects button clicked

Select another object in the scene explorer and click the button to, Add selected objects. You can click on the small adjacent plus (+) or minus (–) button to see the added objects to the set.

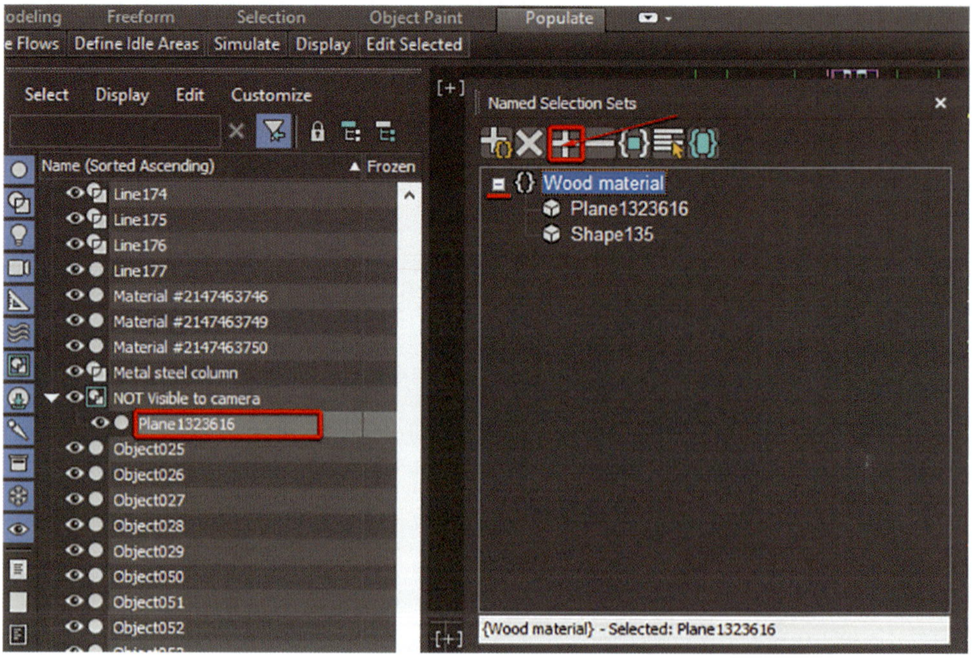

Plane1323616 selected in the scene explorer and Add selected objects button clicked

To select the set, simply go to the main toolbar and select it from the list.

Selection Sets text field clicked from the Main toolbar to see the Named Selection Set list

Importing DWG Drawings

Before importing 2D drawings (DWGs) into 3Ds Max, it's important to do the following:

- Ensure to have the original 2D drawing completely "cleaned/stripped" from AutoCAD or microstation (e.g., omit unnecessary text and other layers). This action will reduce the incoming file size, when imported into Max.
- Drawings are often created far away from the 0.0.0 point, therefore 3Ds Max and most 3D applications will have difficulty in displaying/representing lines or objects accurately at such distances.
  Therefore, it's imperative to reposition the drawings as close to 0.0.0 point as possible, prior to importing them into 3Ds Max.
- One of the most popular techniques to reposition the drawings is to first create a dummy/point/line at 0.0.0 point.
  Select the drawing layers from the file, and move/snap them onto the previously created dummy/point/line (i.e., at 0.0.0 point).
- Once the drawings are close/or at the 0.0.0 point, it's important to save the file out under a different name, to prevent overwriting the original file.

Prior to importing the Cad file into Max, ensure to bind all files in AutoCAD.

To bind Xreferenced files, simply type in Xref to enable its dialog box.

Next, in the dialog box, select the relevant file/s and right click to enable its pop-up list. The pop-up list should give the user the option to click on the bind function, or not.

In some cases, one may be required to explode objects in AutoCAD in order to ensure that specific objects/lines are imported, and without artifacts.

5 Tips and Tricks

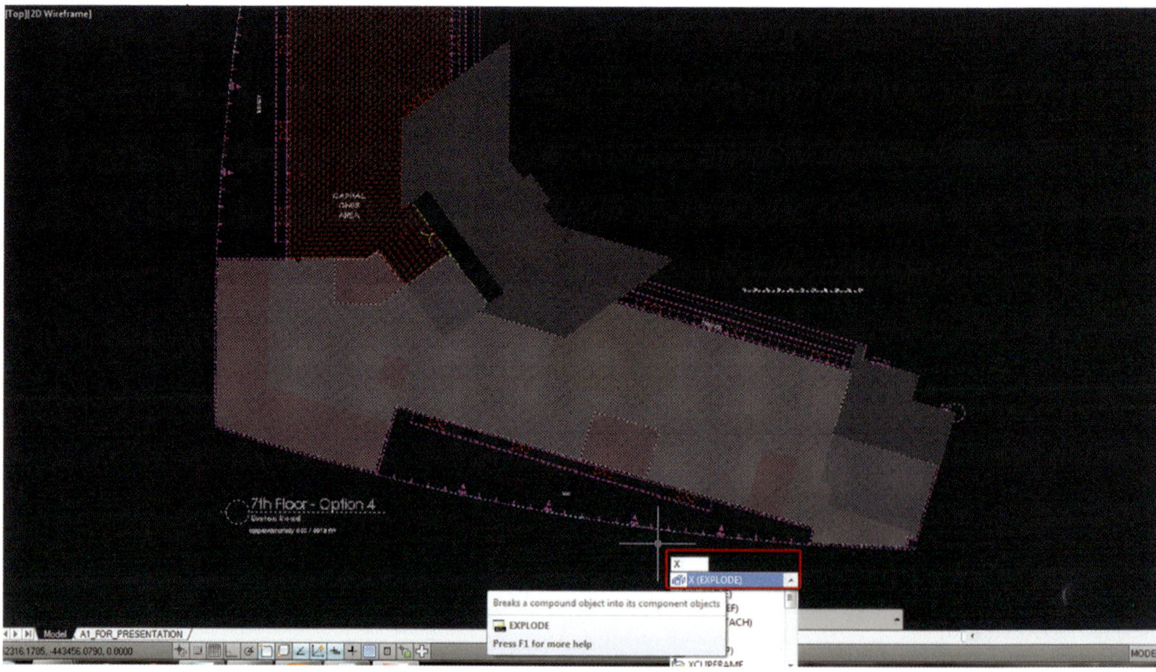

Function to Explode objects in AutoCAD typed in

There are occasions when drawings will come with multiple elevations and sections; therefore unwise to be imported as a whole in 3ds Max.

The common approach is to first use the rectangular selection (click and drag to region select a specific area); followed by typing the "Ctrl + C" to copy the selection; create a new document by typing the "Ctrl + N", and paste the previously copied drawing to its original position in the new document by typing "Paste + O" + "Enter" button + double click the "middle mouse button" anywhere in the viewport.

- In MicroStation, professionals often to select the "fence" tool; draw around the desired area, and type in the "FF=", to save out the drawing under a different name.

  Note that, by default MicroStation is set to automatically save the file every time a change is made to the drawing. For this reason, one is required to "fence save" first, prior to moving/snapping the drawings to the dummy line/point/object.

  It's worth mentioning that, the DGN (i.e., Microstation) file has to be saved as DWG first, prior to being imported into 3Ds Max.
- It's also important to have the metric system setup (e.g., millimeters, meters); as opposed to keeping the default system to "Generic Units".

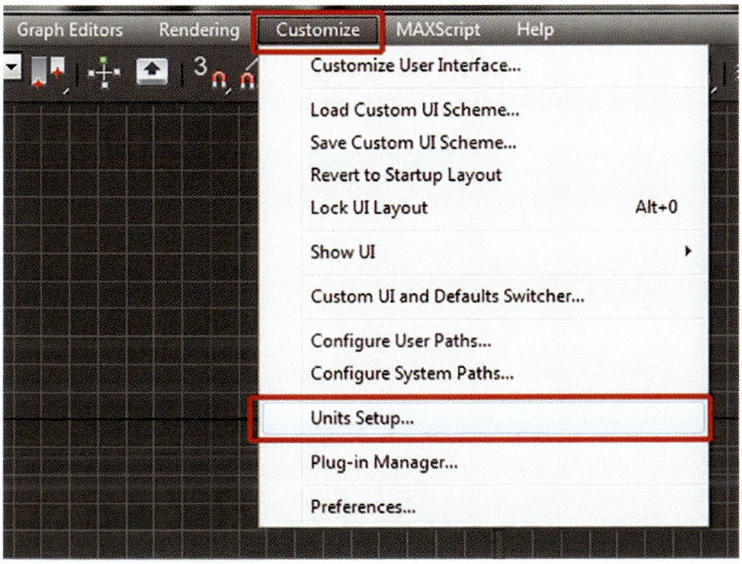

Customize toolbar clicked and Units Setup option chosen

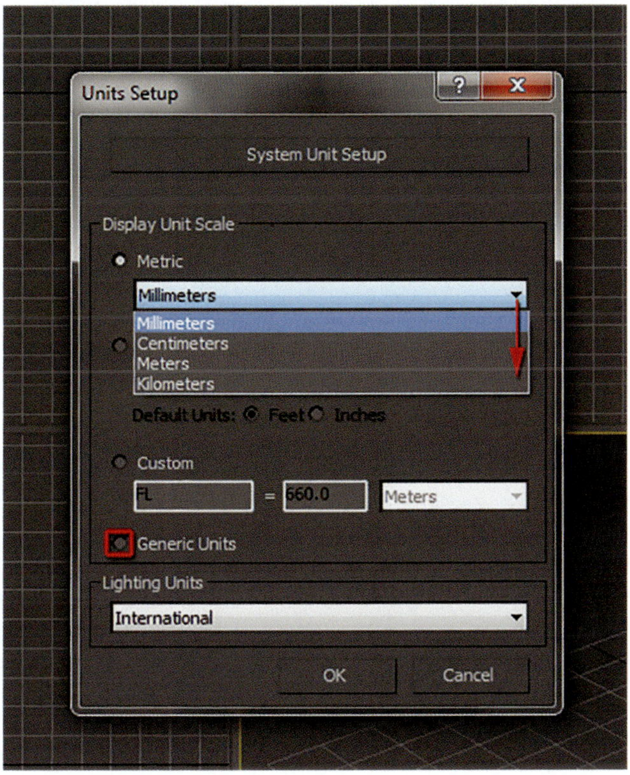

Units Setup dialog with the Metric Unit Scale chosen in millimeters and Generic Units disabled

Also one needs to set the system to "Respect System Units in Files". These two functions will prove vital in ensuring that incoming files are not disproportionate in size and/or automatically rescaled.

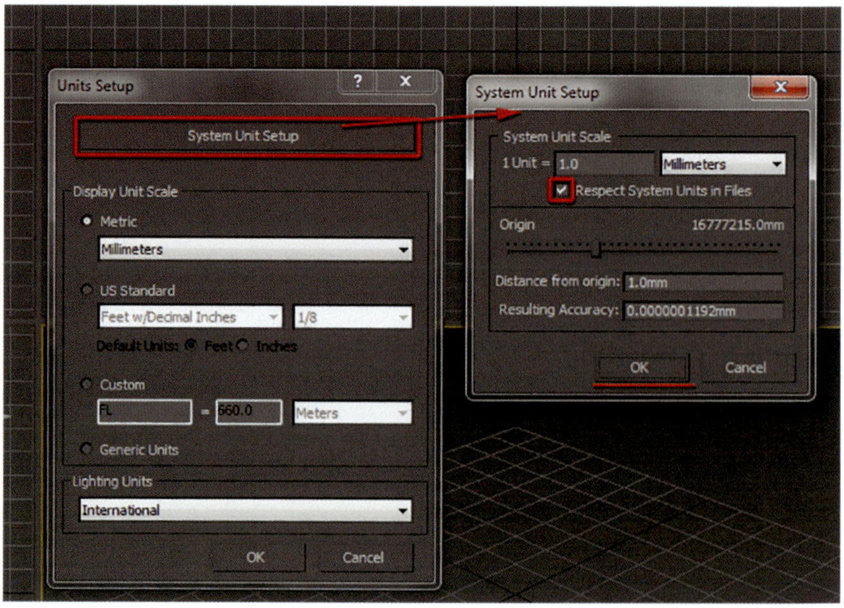

Units Setup dialog with System Unit Setup open and the option to Choose to Respect System Units in Files enabled

Furthermore, one should pay extra attention to the "model scale" group, in the "AutoCAD DWG/DFX Import Options" dialog box.

The "Incoming file units" function should be left untouched.

Simply enable or disable the "Rescale" function, depending on the total value of the "Resulting model size" function.

The rule of thumb is to always choose the smaller metric value displayed on the "Resulting model size" text field.

Also, the "Curve steps" values should be increased if the smooth curves of the incoming drawings are not accurate in the main 3D software. This function will essentially increase the number of vertices in such areas.

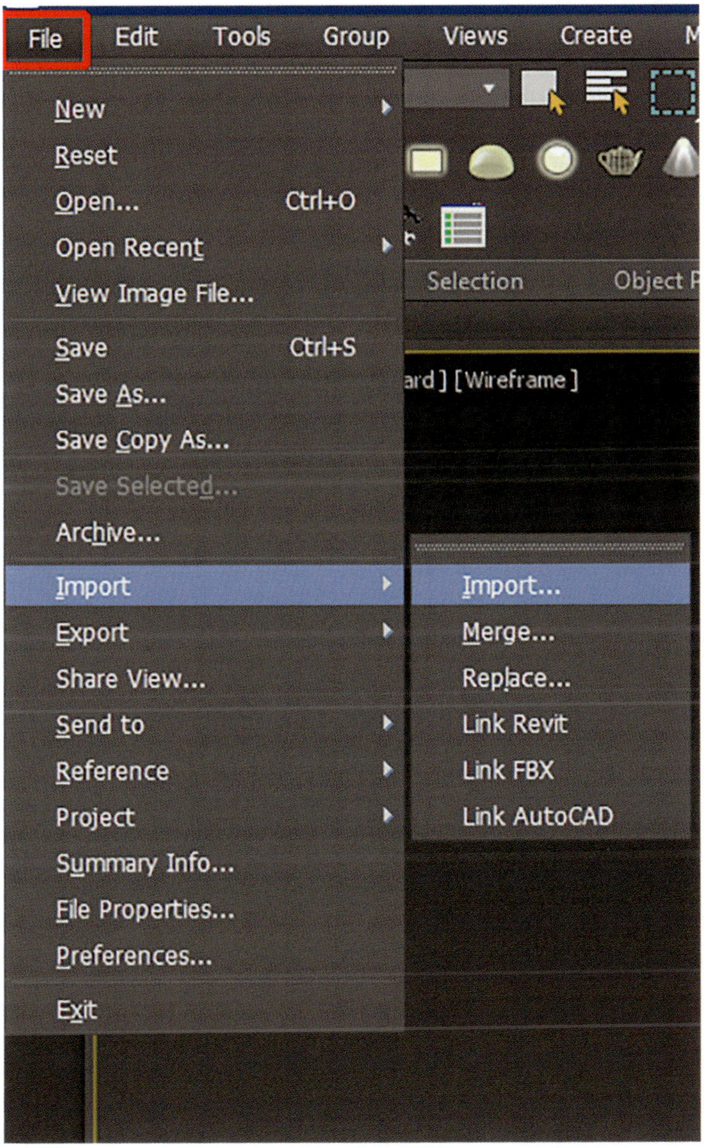

File Import function

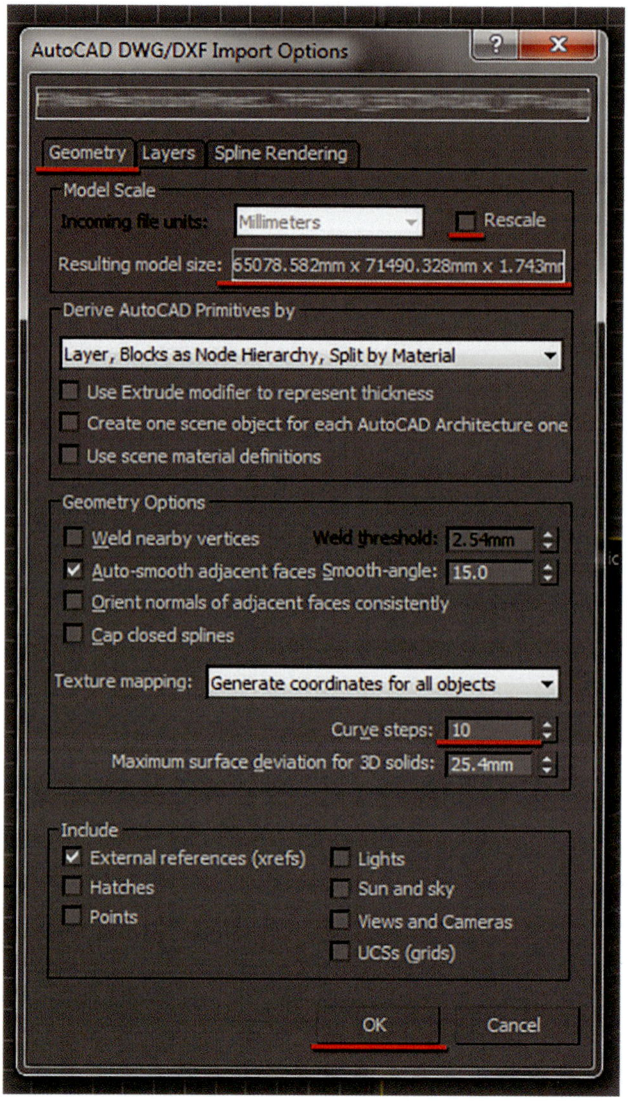

AutoCAD DWG/DXF Import Options

Once the drawing is imported into the scene, it's common practice to quickly check the dimensions of walls, stairs, chairs, etc. with the "Tape" helper. This precautionary measure is to ensure that the scale of the imported file is correct.

Doors are often 2.2 m in height; chairs 400/600 mm in width, etc. Some professionals find it easier to continuously switch the metric "Display Unit Scale" between meters, millimeters, centimeters, etc. depending on the amount of value required to input (e.g., small values = millimeters; large values = meters).

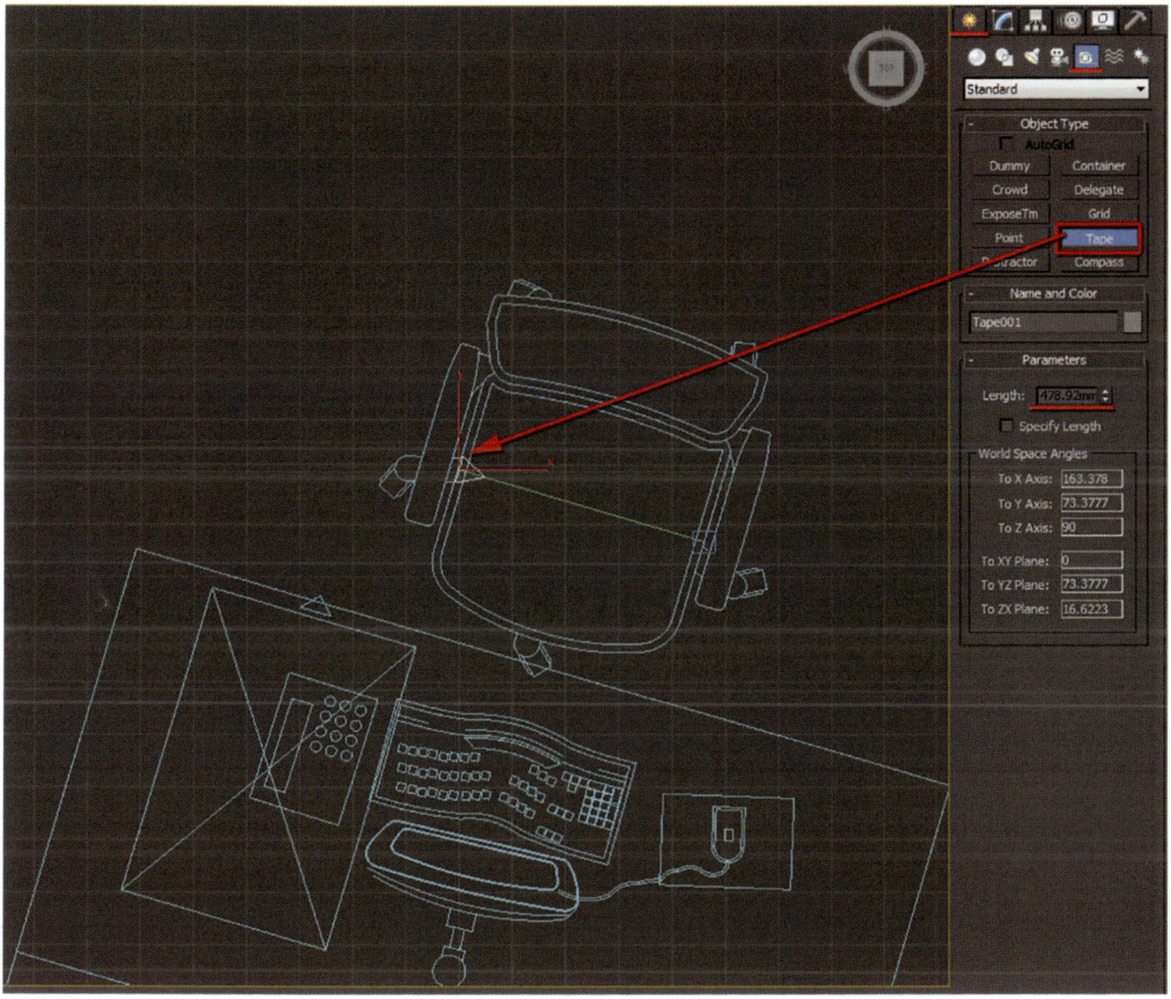

Tape tool used to measure scene elements

Once the drawing is in the scene, select it in its entirety by first pressing the H to open the Select From Scene dialog, followed by clicking on the Select All button and OK to close the dialog.

With all objects in the scene selected, one can then group it.

It is common practice to name the group in accordance to its original name (e.g., 2D_DWG_Level 1).

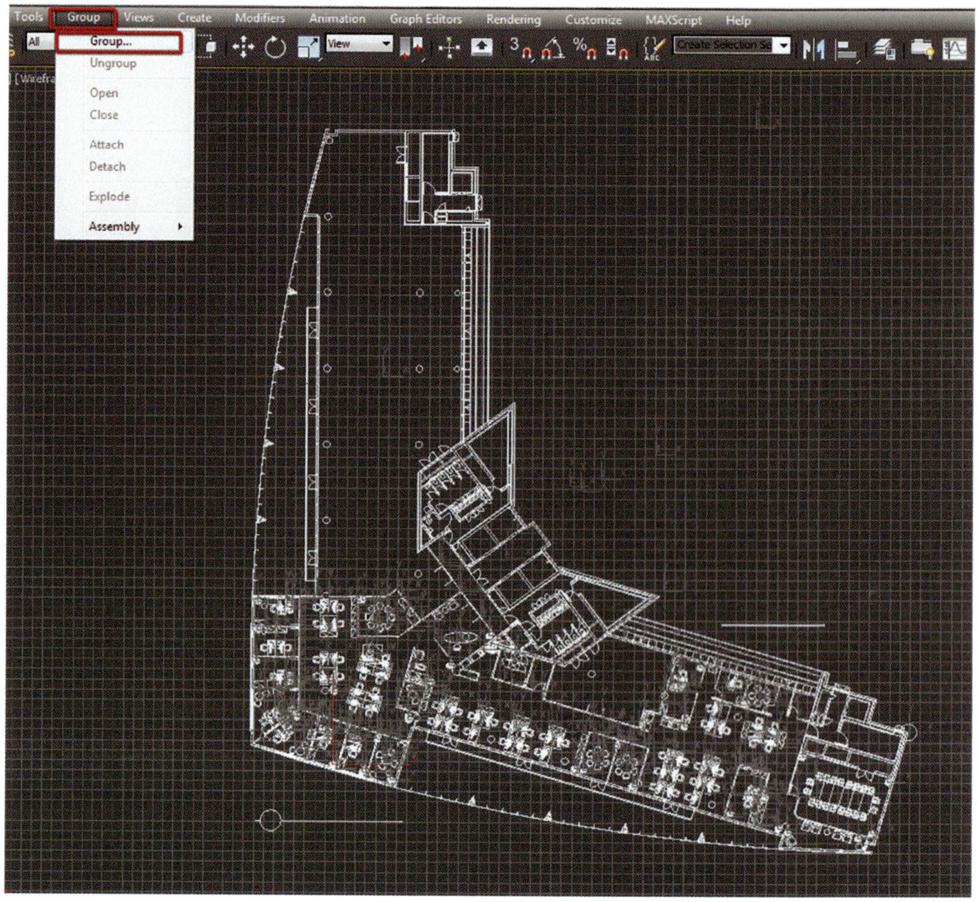

Group DWGs

Some users also choose to create a layer under a similar name. However, the only drawback is the fact that all the drawing content will be culminated into one single color.

To prevent this artifact, simply place the script under the name of, color layer, in the following folder:

C:\Program Files\Autodesk\3ds Max 2014\scripts\Startup

To create new layer, simply select the relevant objects in the scene; followed by opening the layer dialog; clicking the Create New Layer button and renaming it, if necessary.

When renaming the layer/s of objects, one should create names such as "#3D_DWG_Ceiling...".

This is to ensure layers of relevance always stay on top of the list, as it can easily be overlooked/lost among the other named layers.

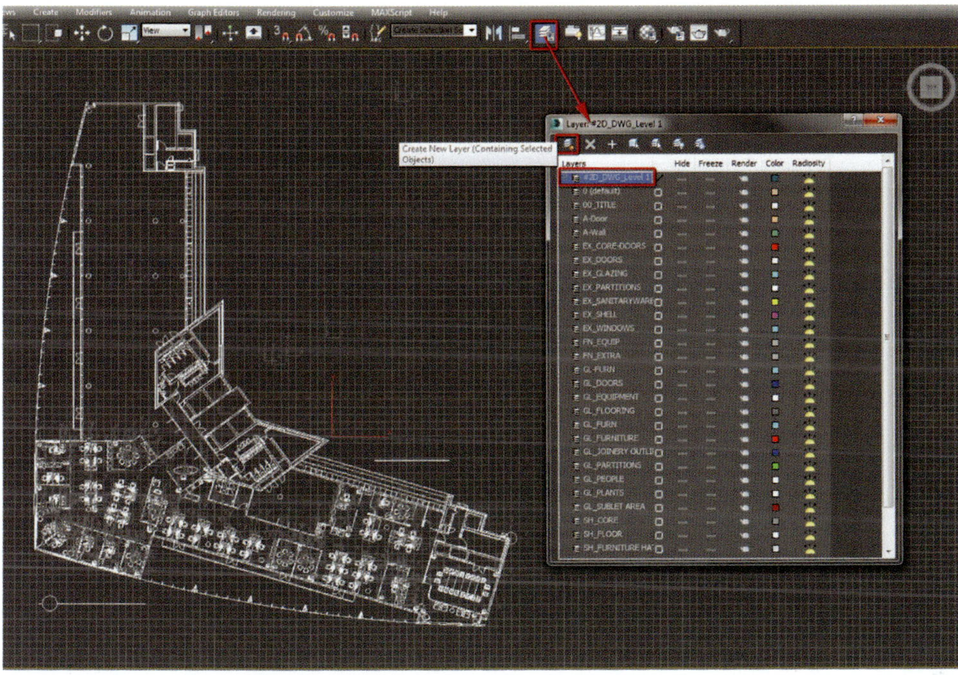

Create New Layer dialog

To edit, move or delete layers/folders, one has to select it/them from the dialog list first (e.g., highlighted).

To rename a layer/folder from the list, one is required to double click it, followed by typing in the name.

Some studios find it easier to work with layers mainly, due to its ease of use and its flexibility to provide control over the contents in the scene.

While selecting an object in the scene and creating a new layer, the dialog box adds/moves the selected object of the list into the newly created layer.

It works almost like a folder that one can choose to select as a group or to select individual objects from its content list, to turn on/off, to freeze, etc.

When a layer/folder is created, and the objects are automatically moved into this newly created layer/folder; the main "layer" dialog box list will still retain the unused copies of the object's name/s in the list.

These unused names/layers can be found at the root of the dialog box, or inside another layer/folder.

It is also common practice to delete all unused layers/objects from the list, in order to clean/tidy up the dialog box.

The layer under the name of "0(default)" is the default layer created automatically, and Can NOT/should NOT be deleted.

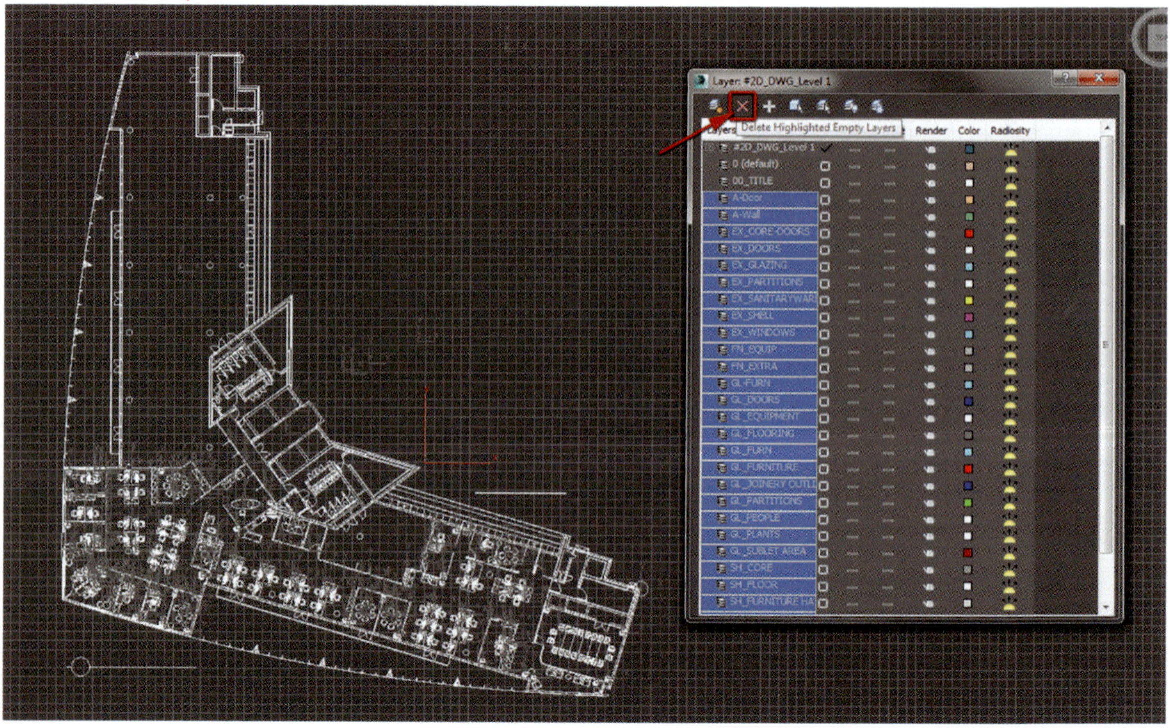

Delete unused layers

If the user doesn't manually create a new layer/folder, most objects created in the scene will be automatically added/moved into this default layer/folder.

Although one can select and move the contents of this default layer/folder, users are unable to delete it (e.g., "0(default)"), even when empty.

As with all new layers/folders created by the user, one is able to select and move its content into a different layer/folder, and delete the empty layer/folder thereafter.

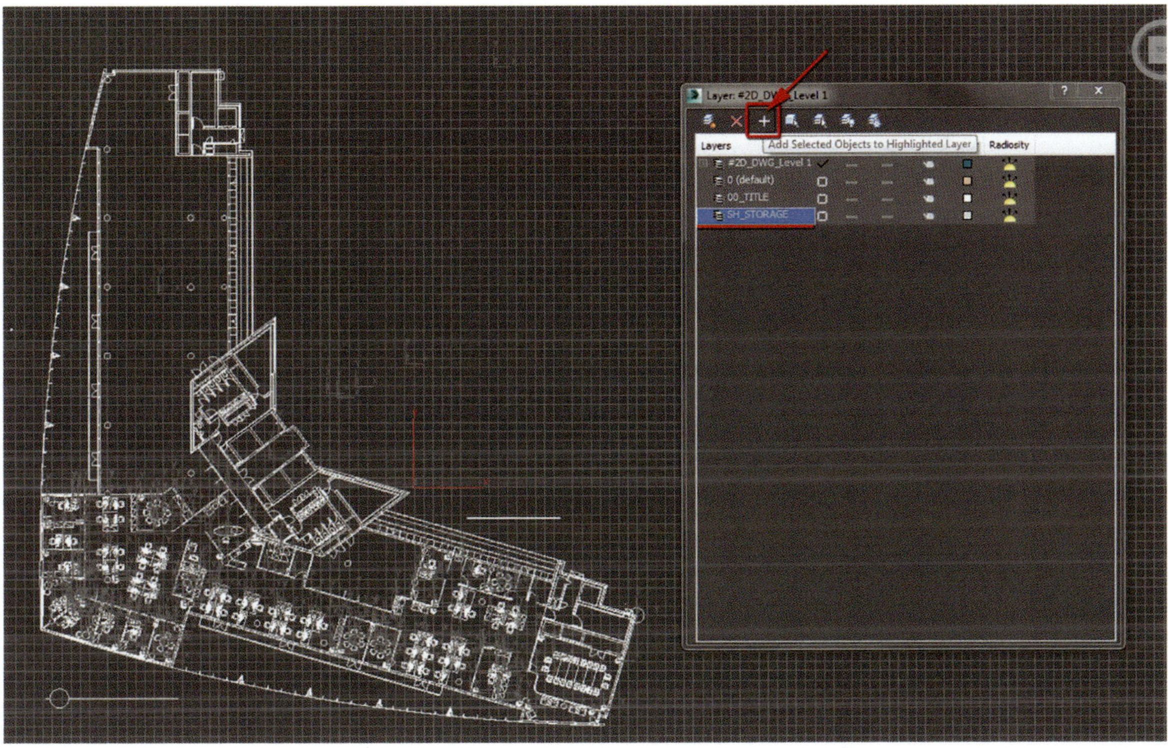

Adding selected objects in the scene into the highlighted layer

Before beginning to trace the drawing to create 3d objects, it is imperative to do the following:

Set up the snap tools parameters and the toggle to 2.5(2d).

Since the drawings are in 2d (e.g., splines), professionals usually change the "snaps toggle" from the default "3" to "2.5", by simply left clicking and holding down on the tools' icon, from the "main toolbar".

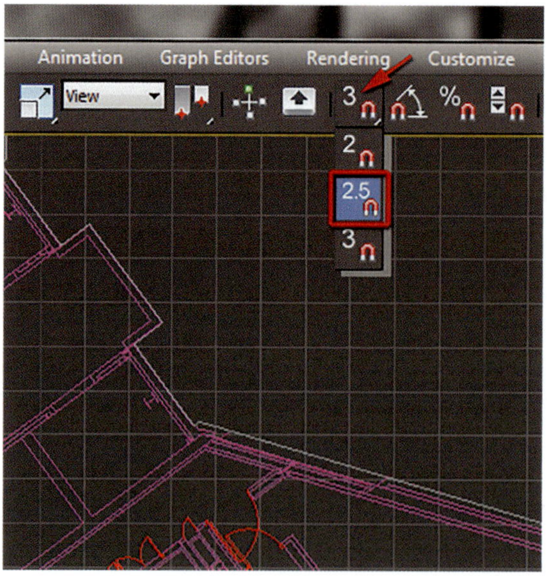

Choose the 2.5 toggle

To quickly snap the splines while tracing the drawing, one is required to change some key parameters:

Right click on the "snaps toggle" icon from the "main toolbar". Its dialog box should pop up.

Enable the "vertex" and "endpoint" functions.

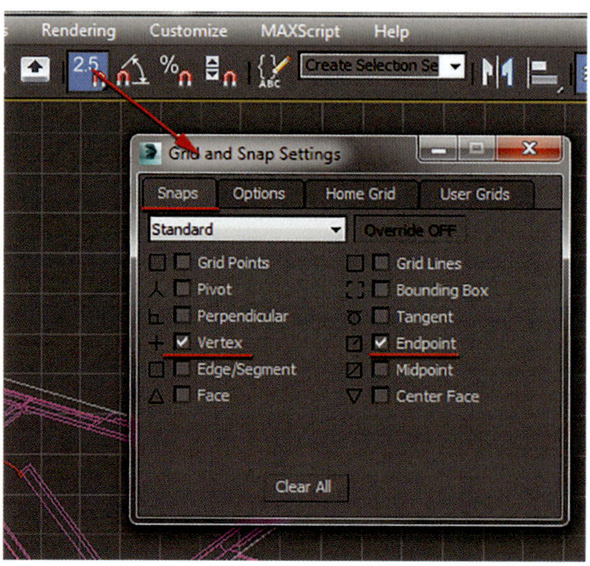

Right click to open its Grid and Snap Settings dialog

Also, in the “options” tab, enable the “snap to frozen objects” function. This will ensure that even frozen drawings/splines can be traced and snapped onto.

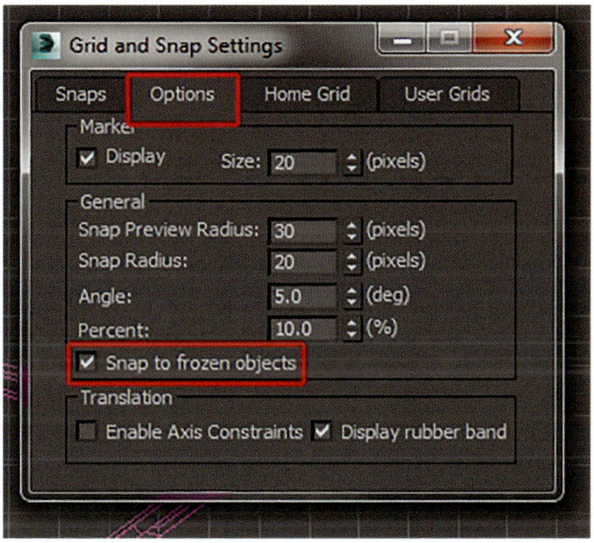

Enable the snap to frozen objects function

Some Users may be wondering why not simply extrude the 2d drawing lines in 3ds Max?

Most drawings’ vertices are not welded (e.g., opened), and often NOT drawn on the same plane/level therefore difficult to extrude as a whole. Even when welding vertices globally with a target distance value.

Welding the drawings manually often takes much longer than tracing them.

DWG plans are always more accurate than the elevations or sections.

To ensure the elevations and sections line up with the plan/s, one should trace/draw the simplest area of the drawing plan that is relevant to the section or elevation first. Extrude it thereafter.

Next, position the elevation or section to match this newly created object. One should use the same procedure to position the following elevations and sections.

There are times when it’s difficult to trace and create objects from rotated DWG drawings.

To make this process easier, users are often required to create a grid helper from the rotated DWG drawing and use it as the basis to trace and create objects from a specific angle.

The following step is to use the, Auto grid pivot point, script to automatically create and align a grid to any particular spline or object angle.

One should start by selecting the relevant spline in the viewport, followed by clicking on the MAXScript main toolbar, and choosing the Run Script option.

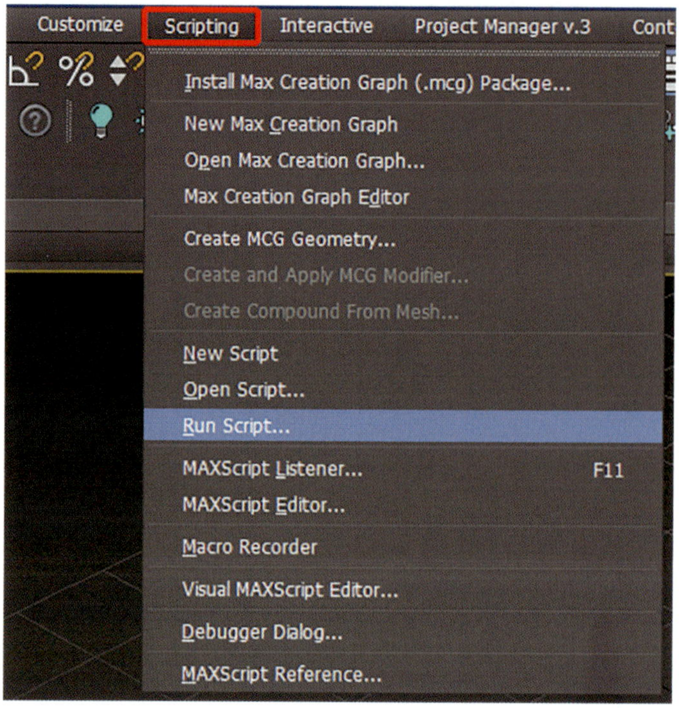

Choose the Run Script option

Next, locate and open the, Auto grid pivot point, script.

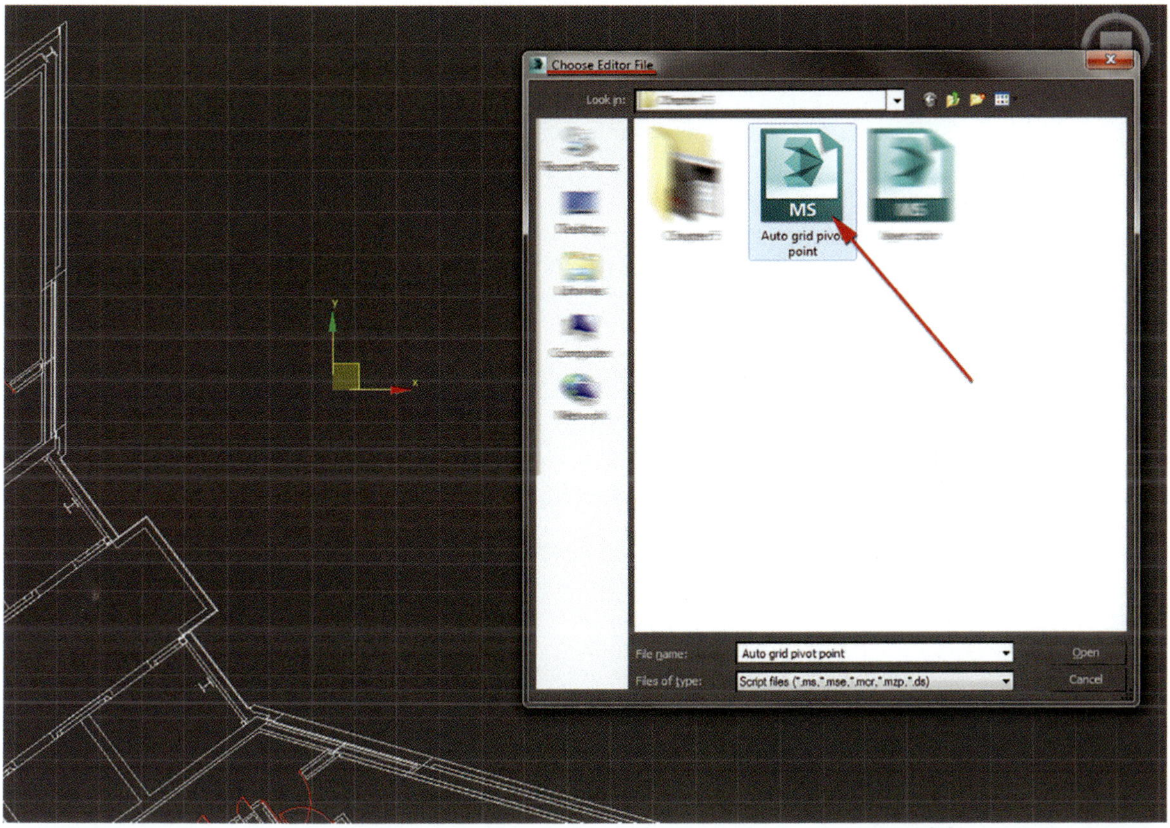

Open the Auto grid pivot point script

The grid should appear and activate itself automatically.

If the grid is too small, one can use its Modify parameters to increase it.

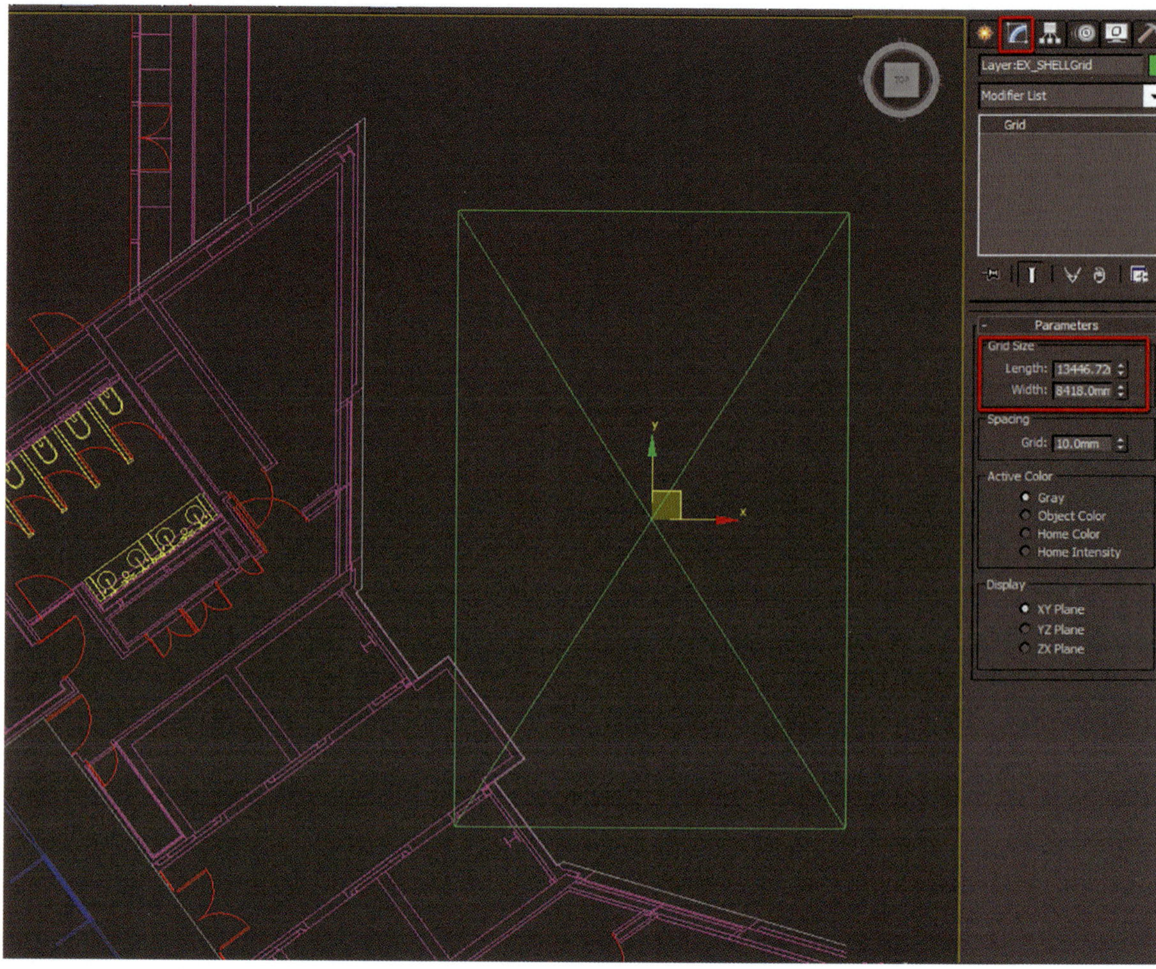

Modify the grid parameters, if necessary

From this point, one can begin tracing and creating shapes and geometry from the grid angle/position.

To view the rotated drawing plan in a straight angle, simply do the following:

Right click on the top viewport text and select the "Extended Viewports" function.

Next, choose the "Grid" option, followed by choosing the "top" view.

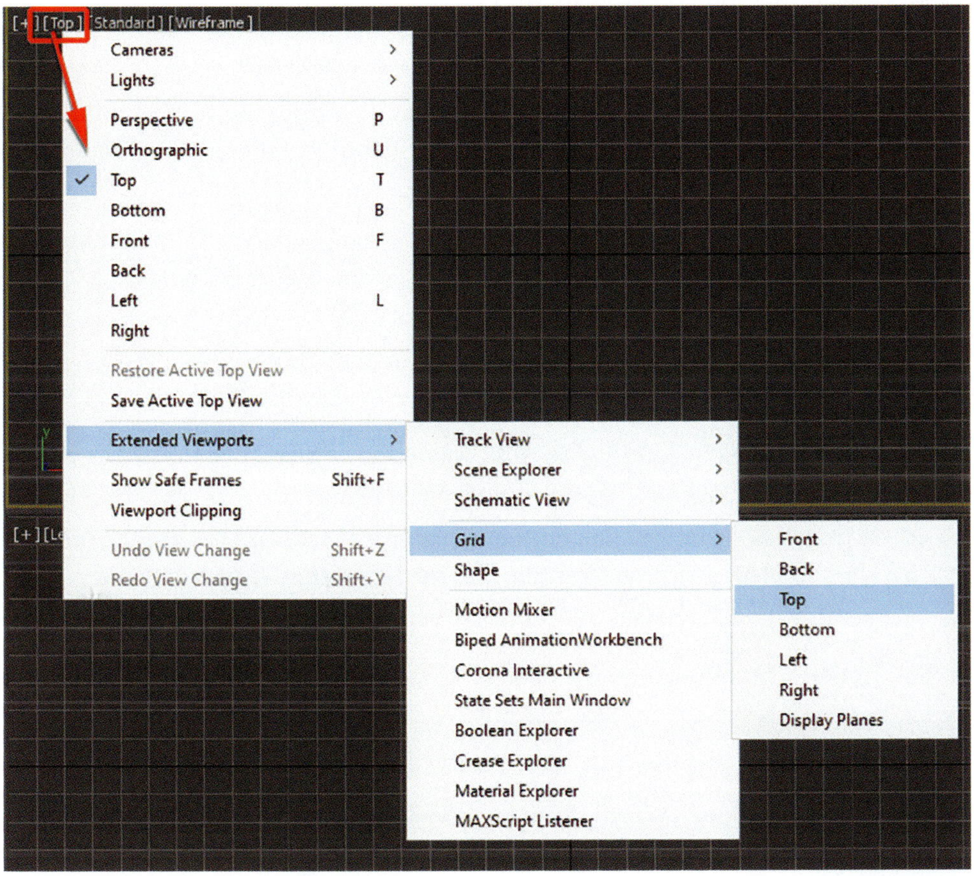

Change the viewport to grid top

The drawing should automatically rotate and position itself correctly. The grid tool is the ideal solution when working with rotated drawings.

This way one is NOT required to rotate the drawing/s individually.

The grid helper can also be very useful when setting Max to automatically create objects at a certain height level (i.e., 2.5 m) without having to manually move the objects from the 0.0.0 point.

To do so, simply move the grid to the desired height level on the left or right viewport.

Before moving/rotating the grid, ensure to **deactivate** it, and set the view to normal viewport first (e.g., NOT grid view).

Once finished moving and rotating the grid helper, simply activate it again.

If you desire to start tracing lines in the "front" viewport, simply create a grid in the front viewport.

As drawings are produced in plans, elevations and sections; professionals often have to work with a variety of grid helpers, at different height levels, and in different viewports.

One good technique to trace and create a spline continuously without having to exit creation is occasionally press the "I" and "Z" keys on the keyboard.

It is also important to set a key shortcut to freeze selected objects. This is to ensure that even objects from opened groups can be frozen, without the need to close the group first.

Professionals often resort to this key shortcut to have better selection control of objects, when working in dense and complex scenes.

To access this dialog simply click on the "Customize" tab, and choose the "customize User Interface" option from the list. Its dialog should open.

In the "Action" list, scroll down to select the "freeze selection" option.

In the "hotkey" function, type in "Ctrl+F" keys and click "assign" to apply it.

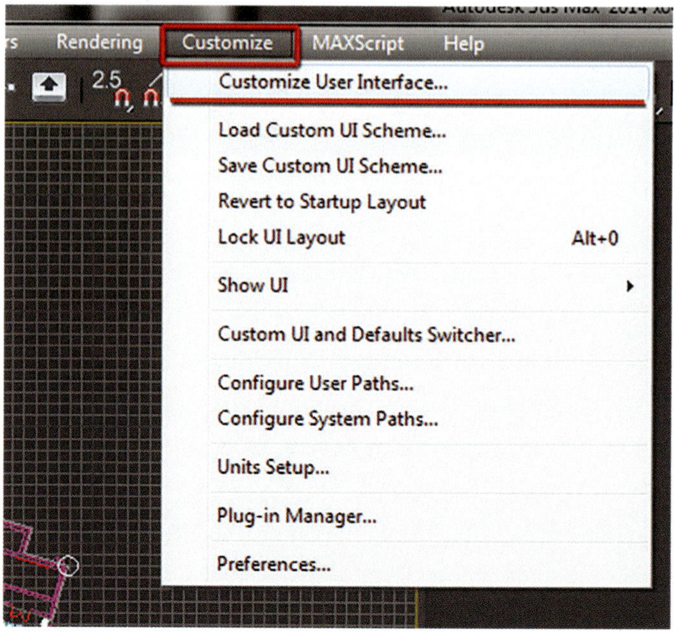

Choose the Customize User Interface option

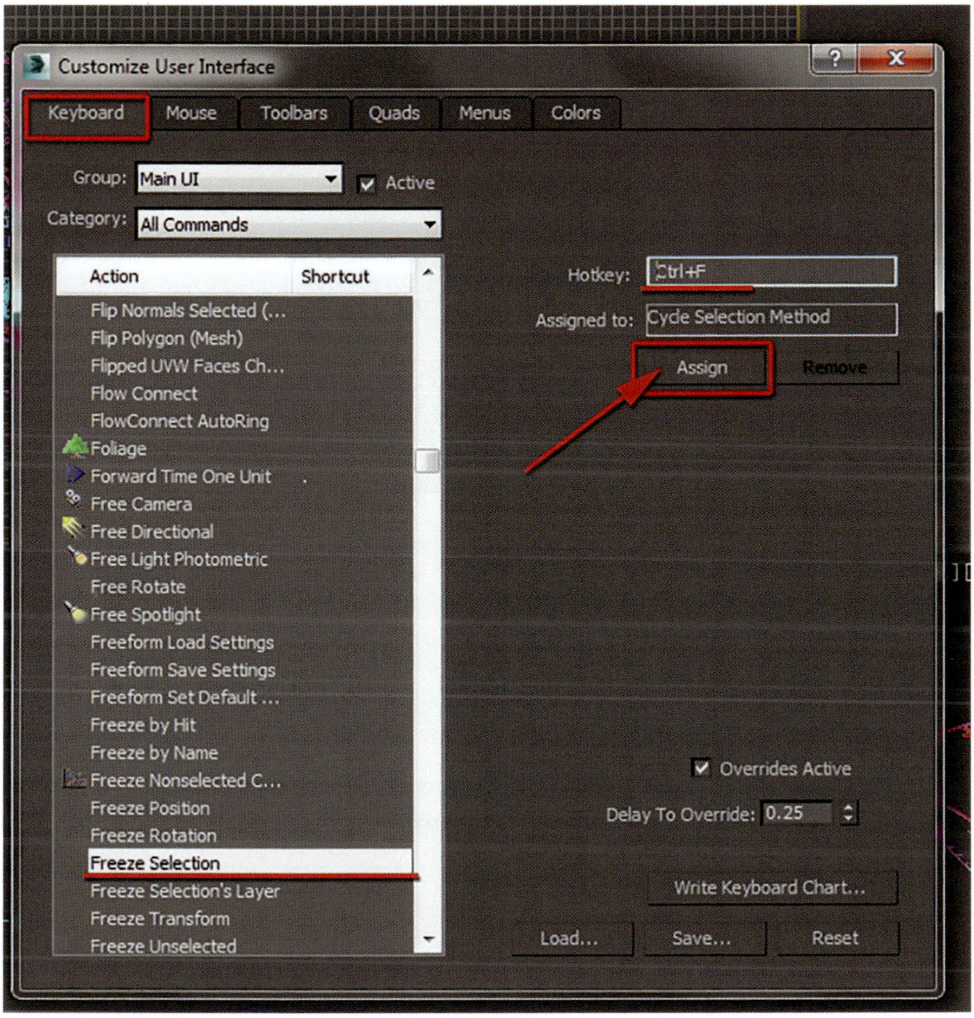

Assign a Hotkey

Orbit Selected Tool

It's also important to set the viewport "orbit selected" tool to rotate around the selected object. This function enables users to rotate the viewport around the axis of the selected object.

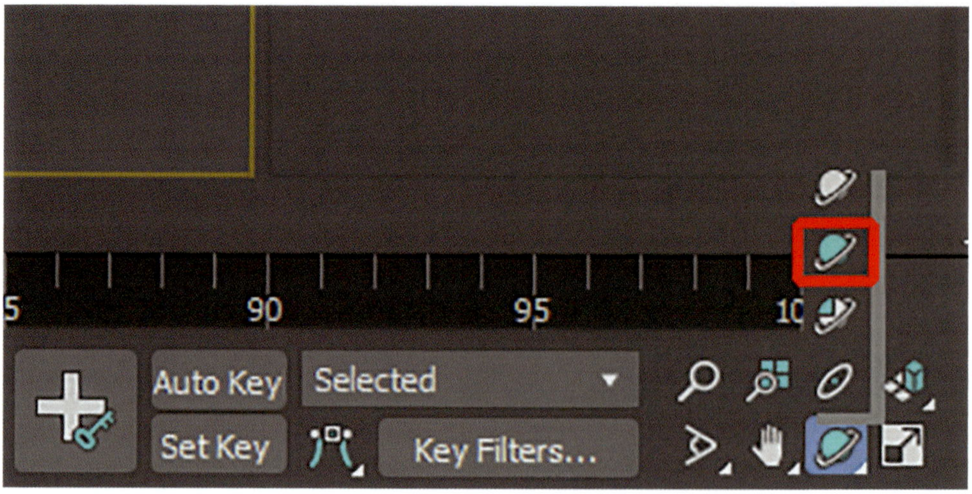

Orbit selected tool

Furthermore, set Max to show the most commonly used "modify" buttons such as extrude and UVW map.

Doing this will save users time, by NOT having to constantly search and pick for commonly used modifiers from the dropdown list menu.

To customize and display the modifier buttons, simply click and hold the "configure modifier sets" button, and choose the same from the pop-up list.

Choose to configure Modifier Sets

In its dialog, drag and drop your commonly used modifiers from the list, onto the "modifiers" group buttons (e.g., add and replace). Also, scroll down the list to pick other useful modifiers.

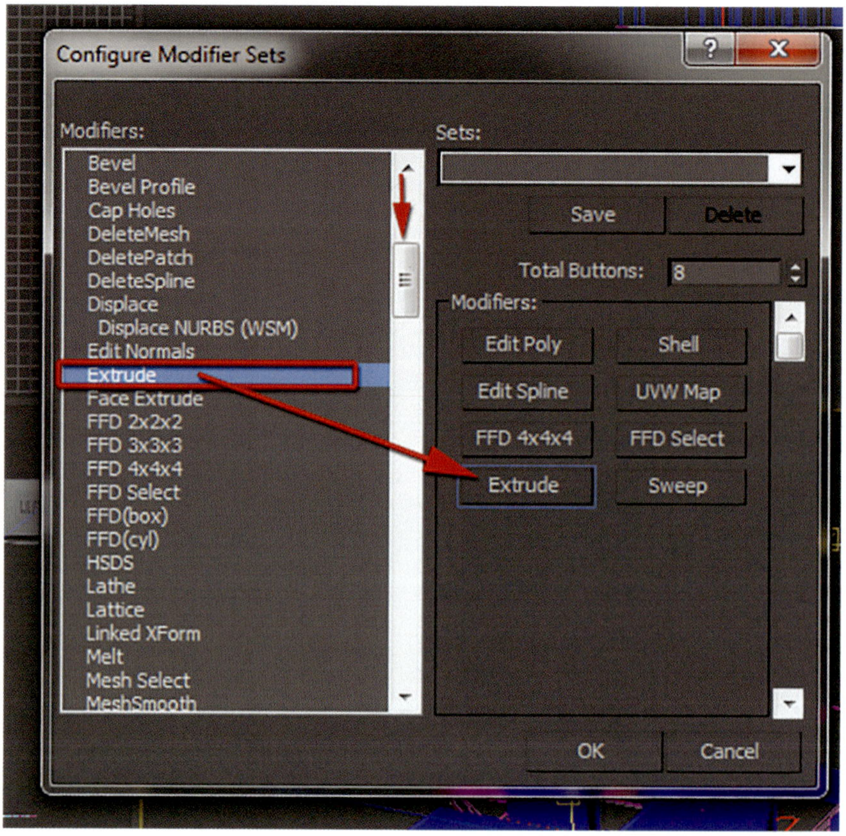

Drag and drop Modifiers

Once finished, close the dialog and set the "configure modifier sets" to "show buttons".

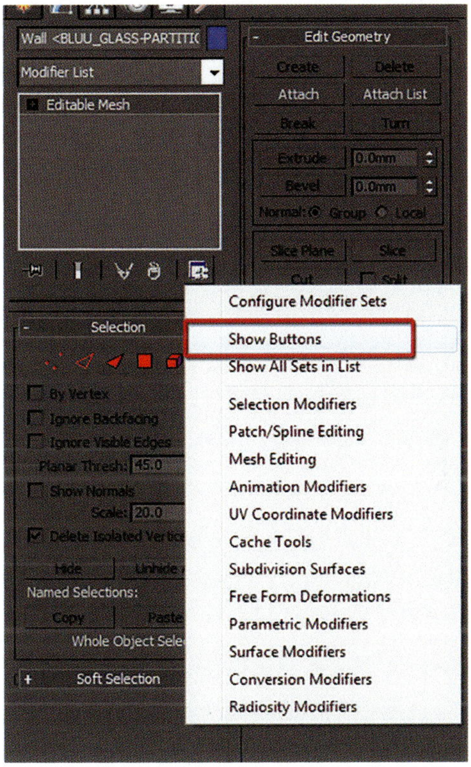

Choose to Show Buttons

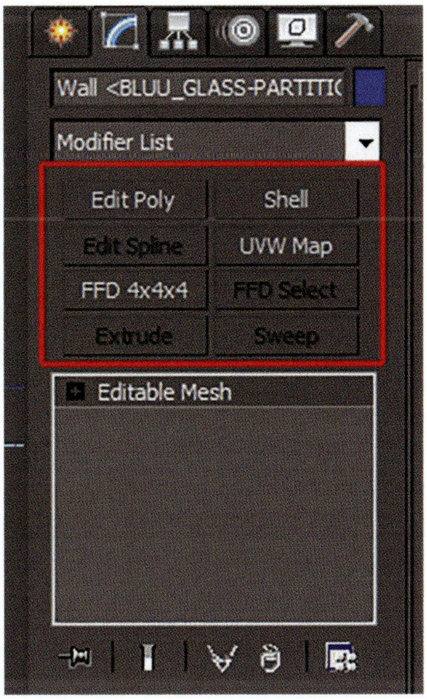

Buttons displayed

5 Tips and Tricks

While it's important to use photo references and drawings to help create convincing 3D models, one should concentrate mainly on detailing objects that are closer to the camera.

Objects in the distance often look acceptable with a realistic texture and a good shader applied.

Furthermore, it is also crucial to pay extra attention to scale relationships between objects by using 2D drawings, photos, and around you as reference points, as our eyes can inexplicably pinpoint scale discrepancies, when apparent!

Finally, when creating and detailing models, it is worth finding an efficient way of navigating in the viewport, by occasionally displaying the less relevant objects as boxes (i.e., box display mode) and/or hiding them when necessary.

This technique will help speed up the viewport performance while navigating and creating geometry the 3D scene.

Although not always necessary, creating proxies is also a great technique of working and rendering efficiently.

VRay proxies can reduce the Max file size and rendering times astronomically.

To create a proxy, simply select the object in question and right click to bring up the quad menu.

Choose the V-Ray mesh export option to open its dialog.

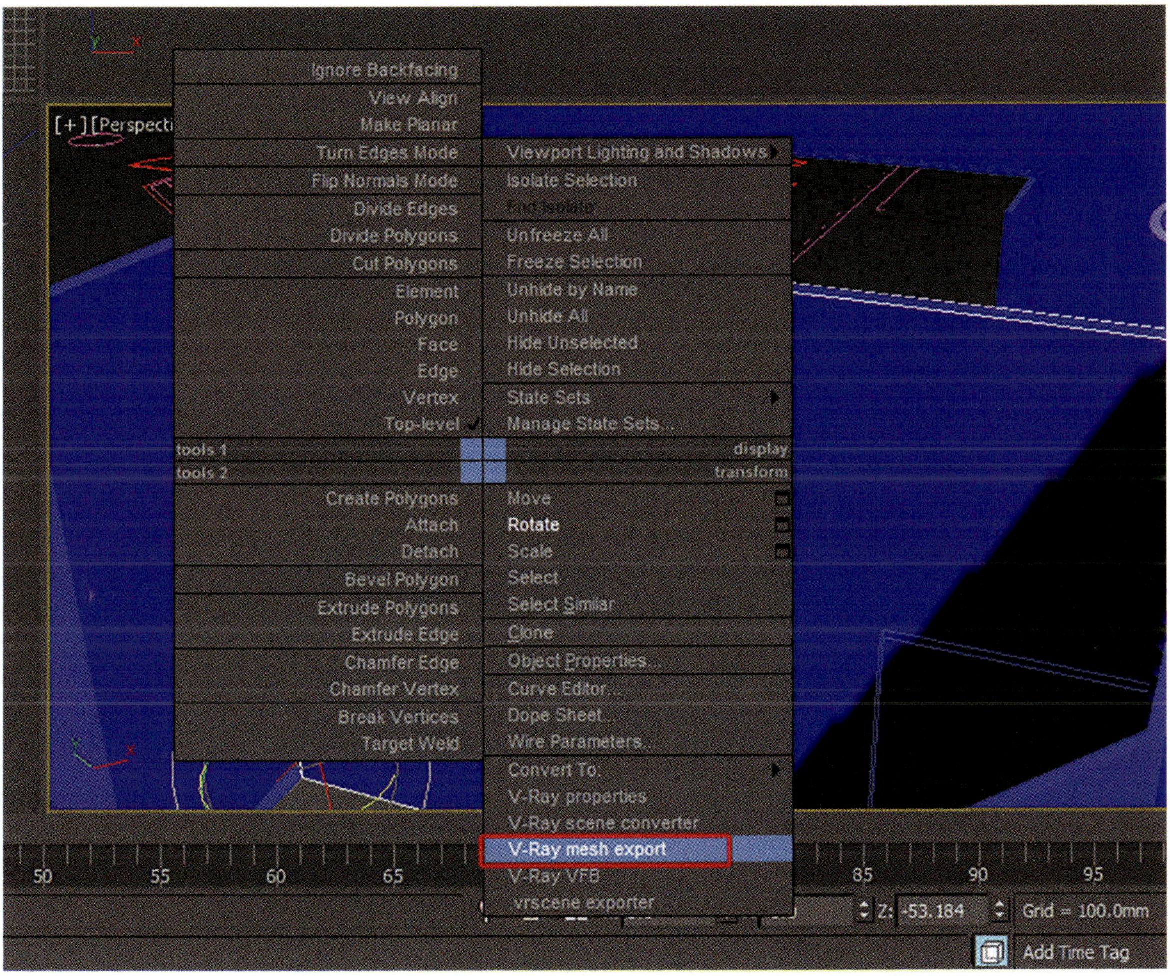

Choose the V-Ray mesh export option

The Folder toggle allows users to choose the location where the proxy mesh will be saved into.

The File name field allows users to name/rename the vrmesh file.

The file name should be kept as simple as possible (e.g., sphere.vrmesh).

To prevent unexpected proxy artifacts, always choose the option to, Export each selected object in a separate file.

Finally, always choose the Automatically create proxies option.

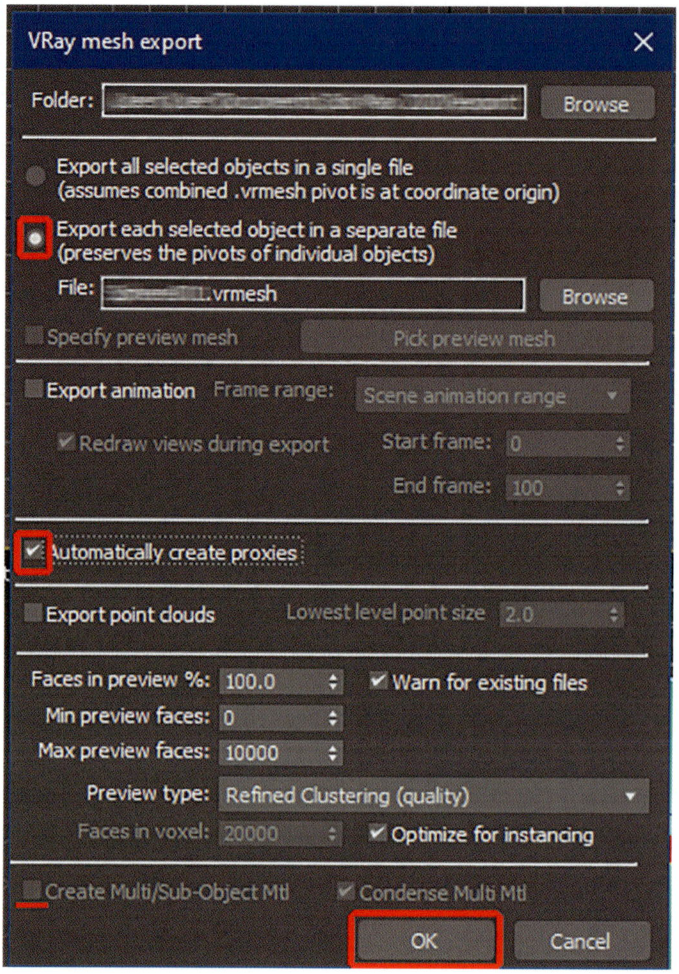

VRay mesh export dialog

To control the display and other aspects of the VRayProxy, simply open the Modify panel.

The Scale function allows users to control the size of the proxy in the scene. The value of 1.0 is often correspondent to the original size of the object.

The Display group controls the preview of the proxy object in the viewport. Users often choose the Bounding box display type for very dense objects such as trees, grass and hairs.

The Import as mesh function allows users to retrieve the original mesh. Complex geometry may take a considerable amount of time to retrieve. In some cases, it may even crash the system.

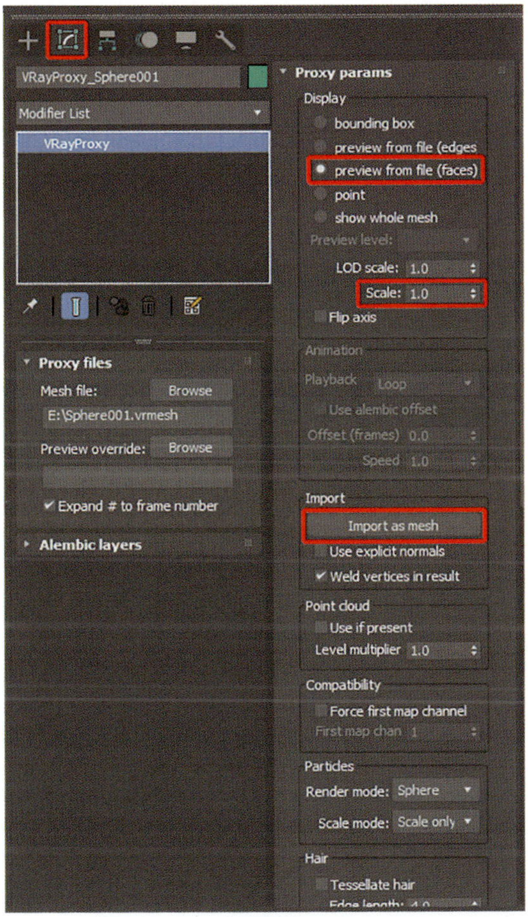

VRayProxy Modify parameters

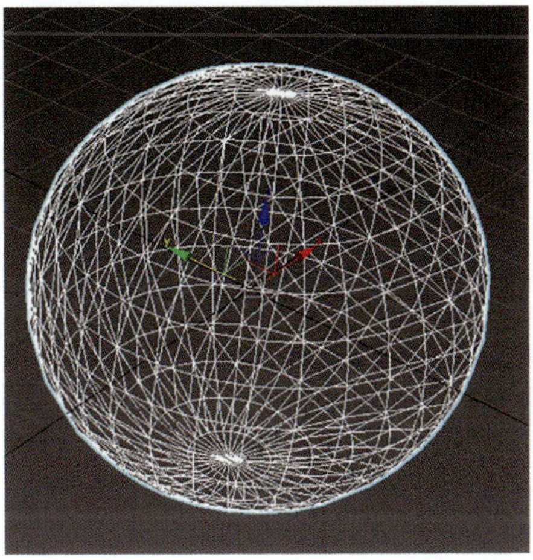

VRayProxy Mesh

5 Tips and Tricks

Camera Matching without a Survey Data

Before beginning the process of camera matching a photo, it's imperative to be aware of the following:

1. Have an almost accurate dimension of a relevant object in the photo (e.g., at least one object in the photo).
2. Be aware that photos are usually taken at eye level (e.g., 1.65 m); unless stated otherwise.
3. The average height of most people in photos is between 1.70/1.75 m; unless there's an exception.
4. The average door height is around 2.2 m; unless there's an exception.
5. The average height of a chair is about 0.4 m; unless there's an exception.

Start by setting up the Output size to match the incoming background photo to be camera matched.

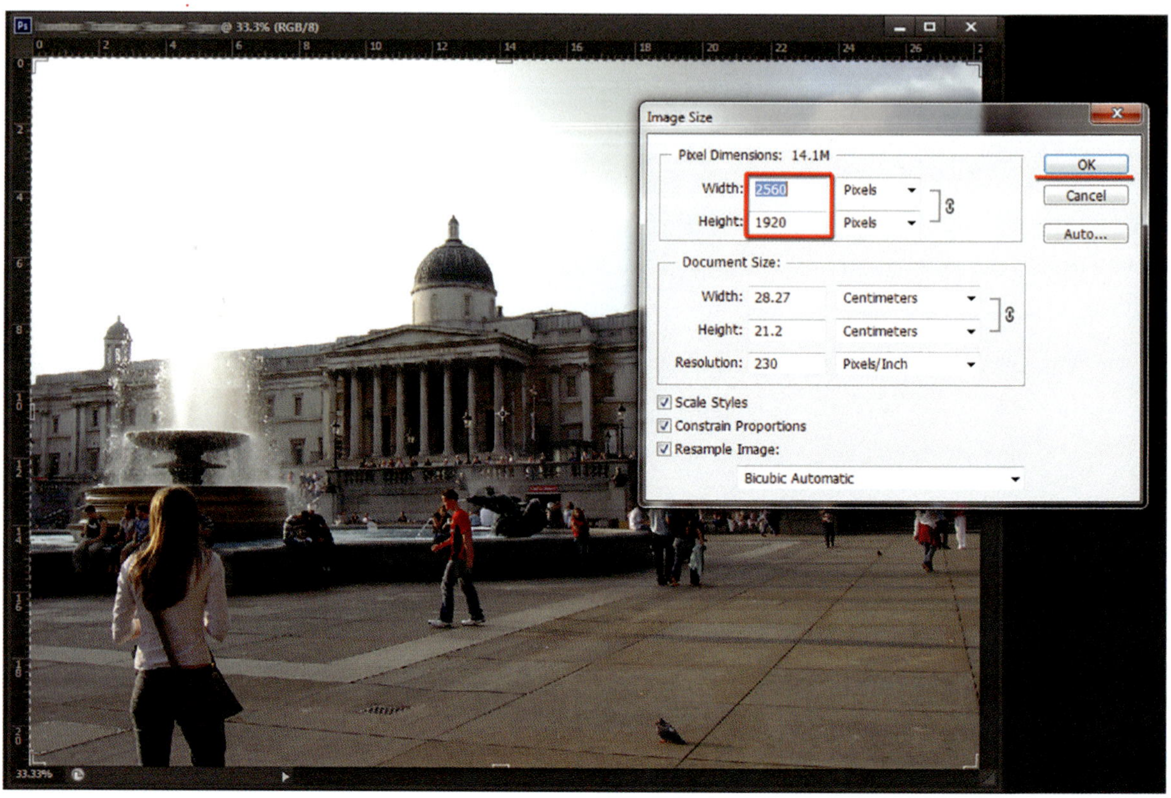

Background photo Image Size

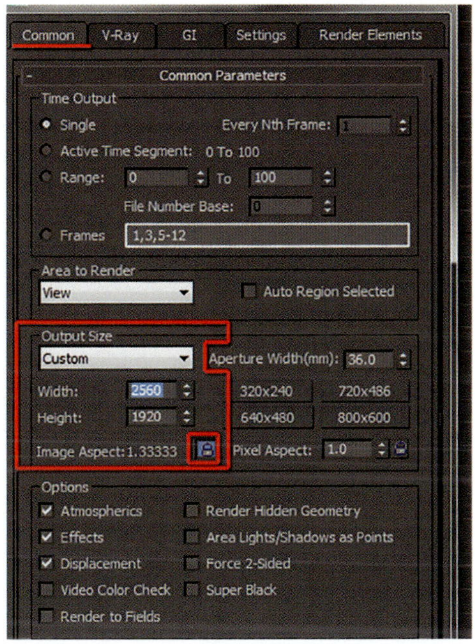

Output Size in 3ds Max

Next, load up the background photo in the perspective viewport using the Configure Viewport Background (Alt+B), and use the Shift+F to enable the Show Safe Frames option.

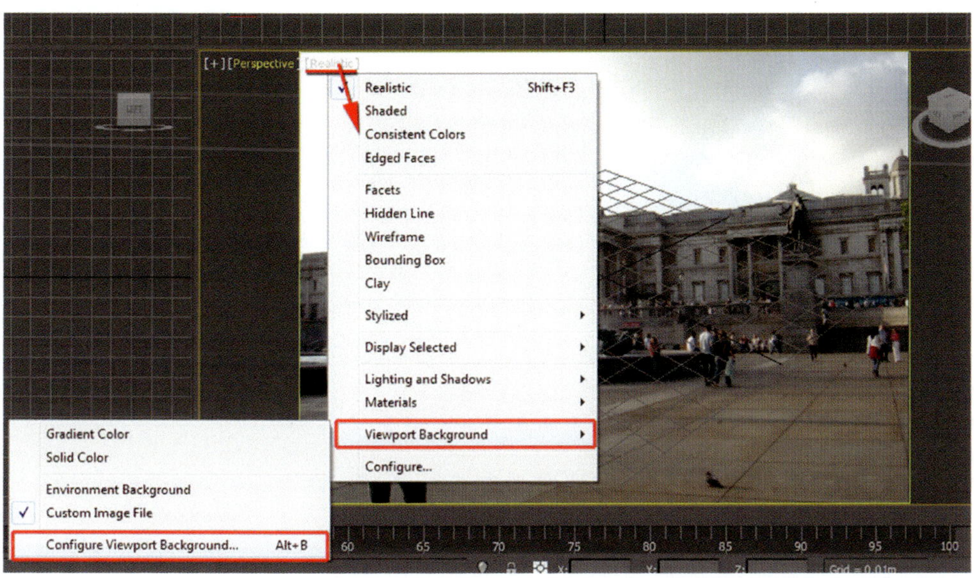

Choose to Configure Viewport Background

While the perspective viewport is still selected, click on the Tools from the main toolbar, followed by choosing the Perspective Match option.

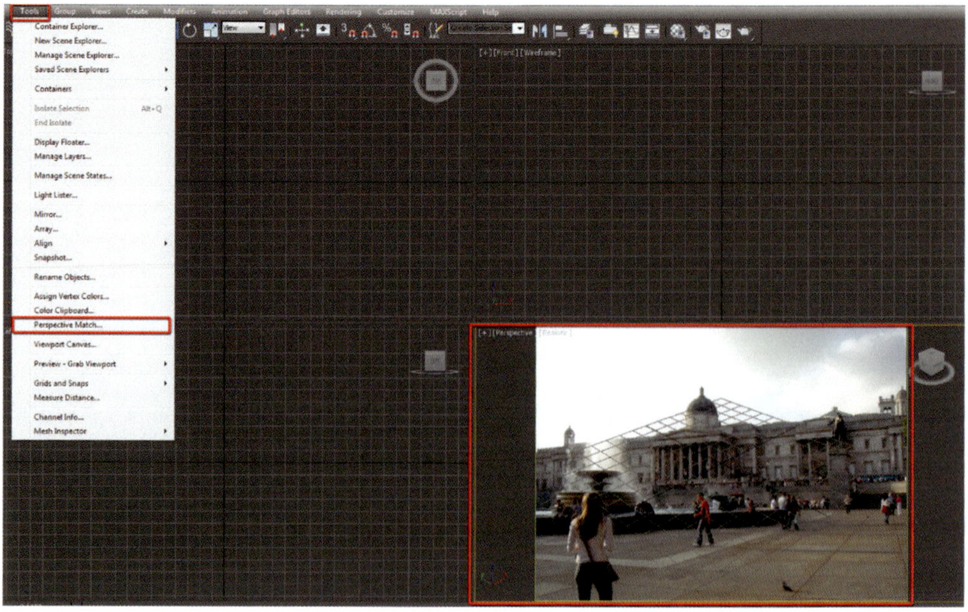

Choose the Perspective Match tool

The Perspective Match from the Utilities command panel should be prompted automatically. Click on the Hide Vanishing Lines button to turn it to, Show Vanishing Lines.

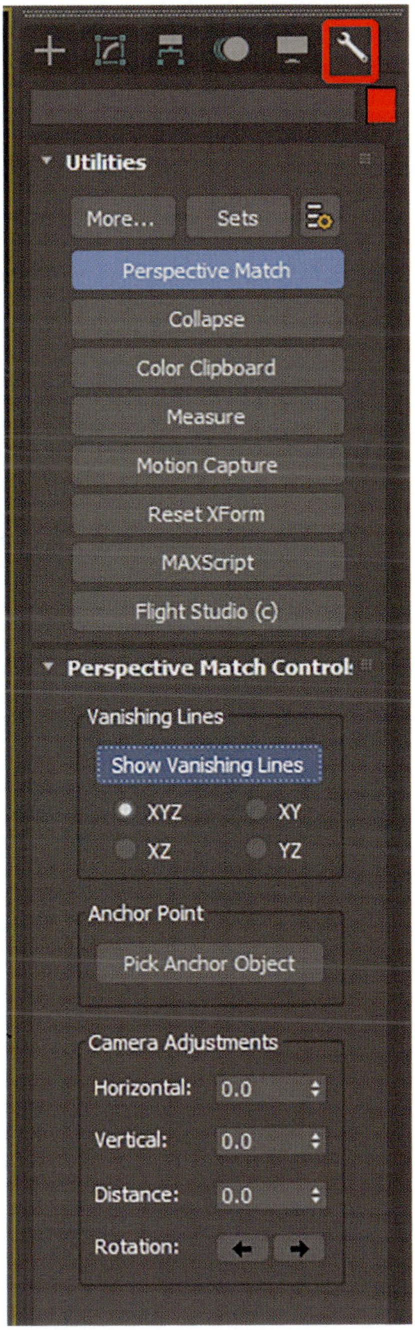

Click on Hide Vanishing Lines button to turn it to, Show Vanishing Lines

The two Blue Vanishing lines are usually moved to line up closely to two key horizontal lines of the photo.

The two Green vanishing lines are often moved to line up closely to two key perspective lines of the photo (e.g., bottom/foreground and a top perspective line).

The two Red vanishing lines are often moved to line up closely to two key horizontal lines of the photo.

Vanishing lines lined up

To move a vanishing line as a whole, simply left click on its middle point, followed by moving it.

To move parts of the vanishing line, simply click on one of its handles and move it accordingly.

The rule of thumb is to keep the top vanishing lines (e.g., red and green) on upper areas of the photo; and the lower vanishing lines (e.g., red and green) on the lower areas of the photo.

After much pulling and moving the vanishing lines around, the result should look similar to the figure depicted below.

Vanishing lines lined up

Once satisfied with the position of the vanishing lines, simply Create Camera From View (Ctrl+C).

Create Camera From View

As mentioned earlier, since cameras are often at eye level (e.g., 1.65 m), one can create a surface (e.g., Box- geometry standard primitive) 1.65 m below the camera, and increase its width and length to fit the dimensions of the photo reference.

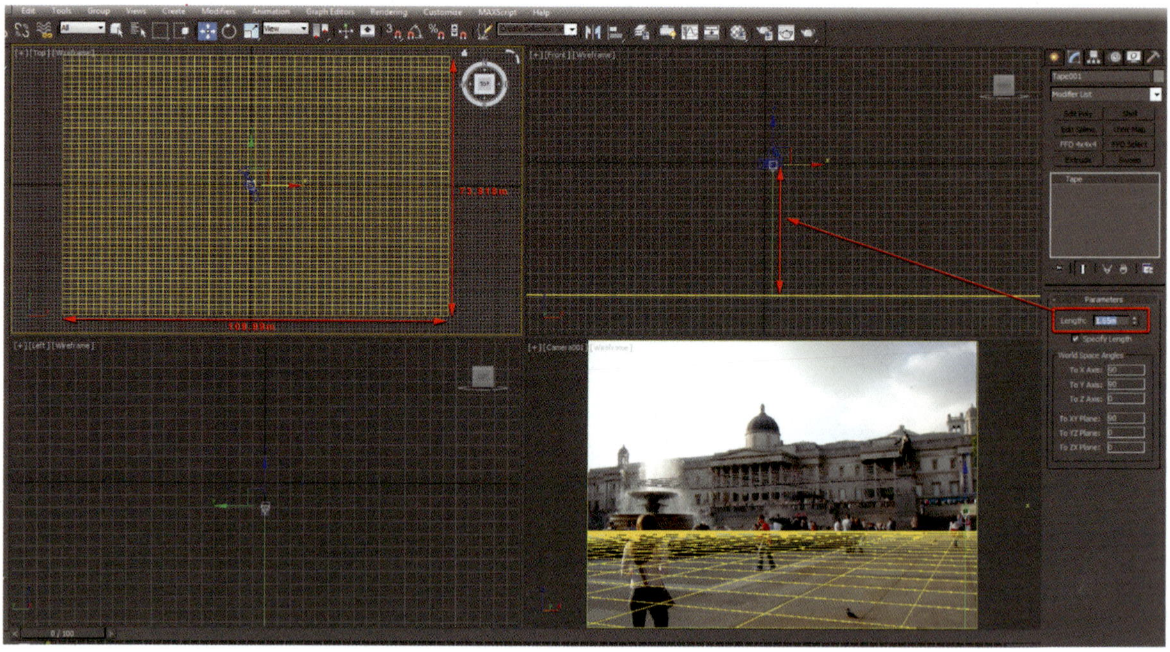

Create a surface 1.65 m below the camera

From this point onwards, one can create other reference points such as people and other objects in the scene.

Since a standard 3ds Max camera is currently being used in the scene, one can recreate a similar VRayPhysicalCamera manually or via a script camera converter.

Alternatively, simply keep the current standard 3ds Max camera, and open the Environment and Effects dialog (8).

In the Exposure Control rollout parameters, load the VRay Exposure Control option from its dropdown list.

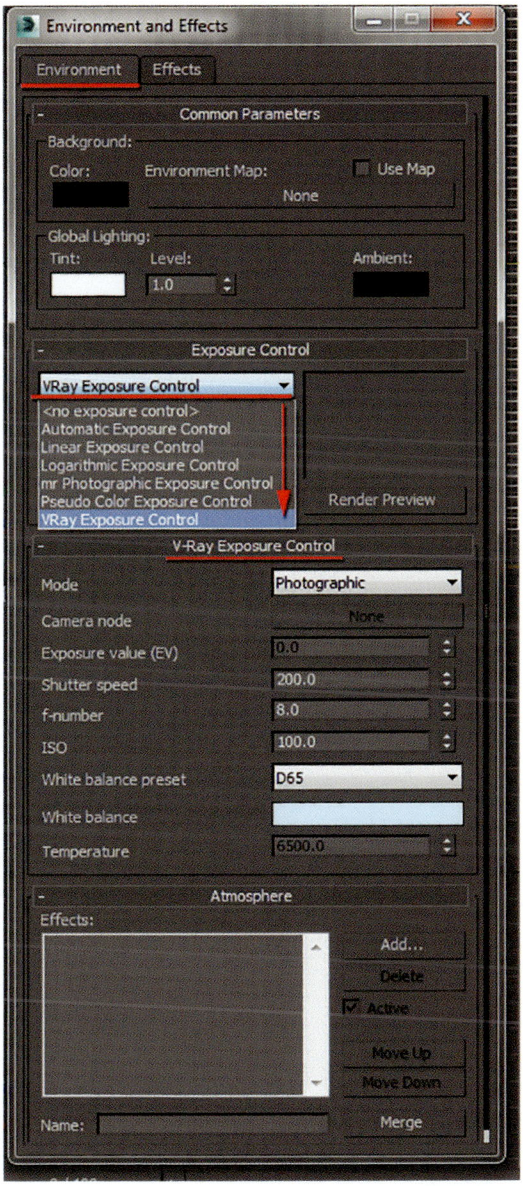

Load the VRay Exposure Control

Use the background photo Properties Details to enter more accurate camera detail parameters such as Focal Length, F-stop and ISO speed.

The Origin info from the Properties Details can be used in the Daylight System parameters (Chapter 3) to enter the time, day and location of the photo taken.

Also, refer to Chapters 9, 12, 16 and 19 to match in post, the overall color and feel of the render with the background photo.

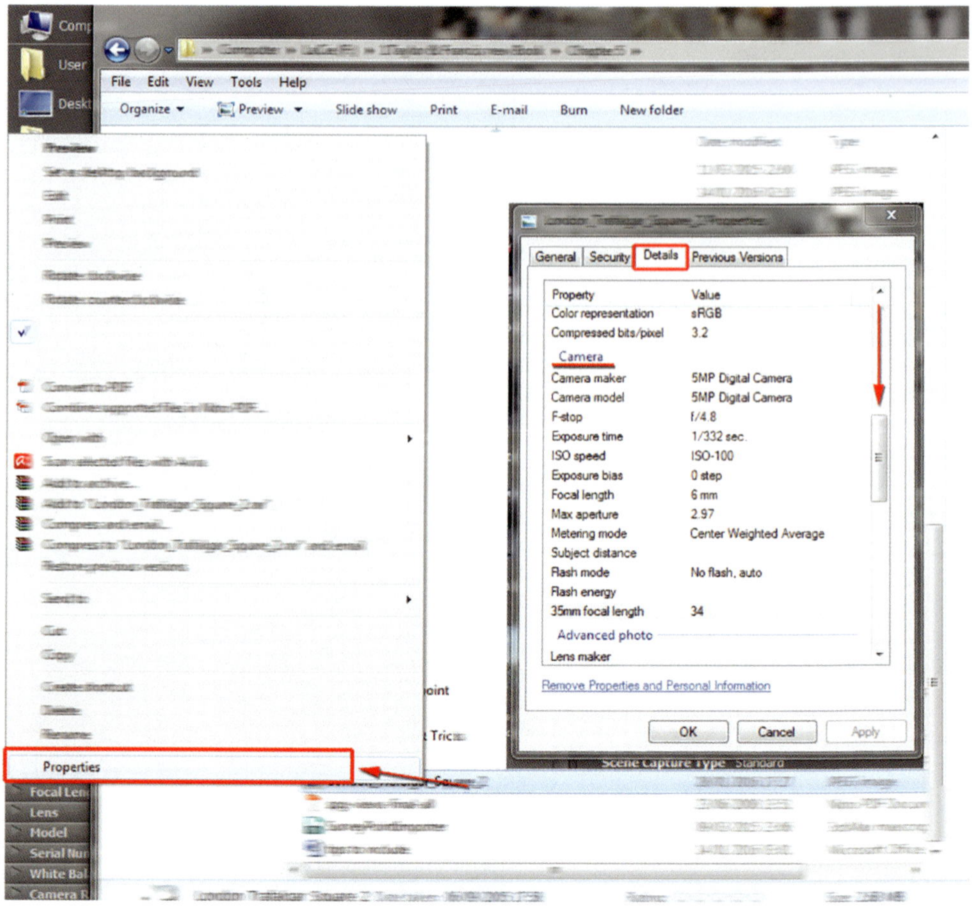

Background photo Properties Details

For aerial shots looking down; the previously described methodology might not work. Instead, users might have to eyeball the correct camera perspective, by constantly rotating, moving and tilting the camera accordingly.

It often takes a bit of practice to camera match aerial shots accurately.

Integrating Shots in 3ds Max

Prior to starting, ensure the background photo is plugged into the Environment Map toggle, and that its mapping coordinates are set to Screen type.

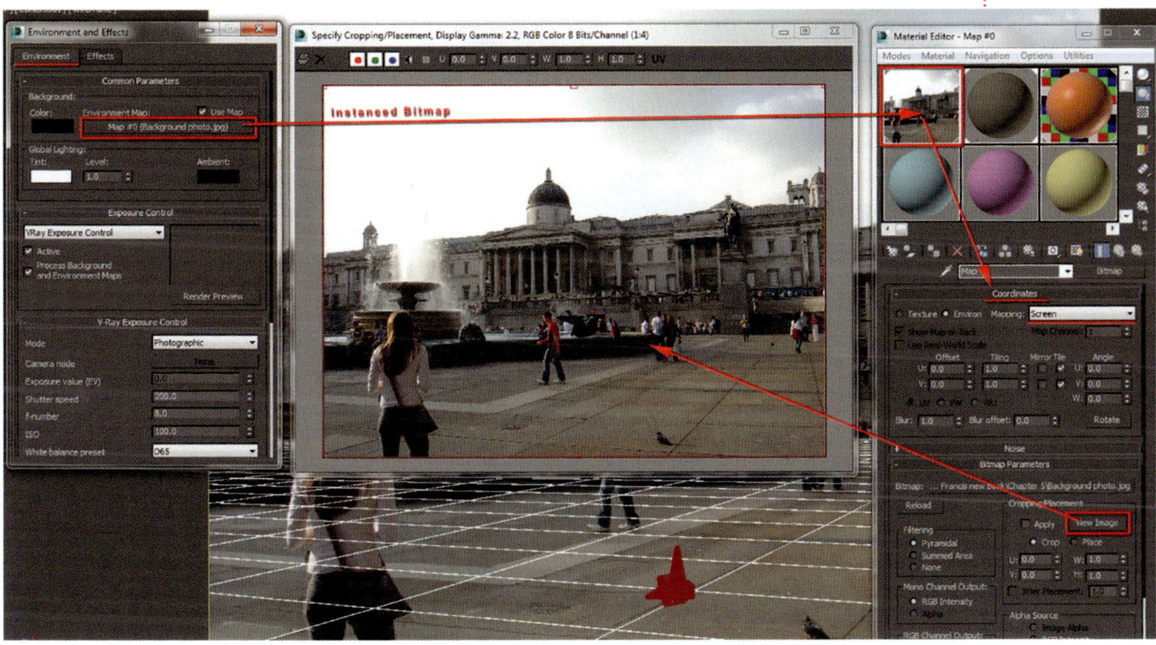

Background photo plugged in the Environment Map toggle

In the Color mapping rollout parameters, ensure the Affect background function is disabled.

This function will prevent the environment background photo from being affected by the GI and the VRayPhysicalCamera settings (e.g., prevent it from being washed out, overexposed).

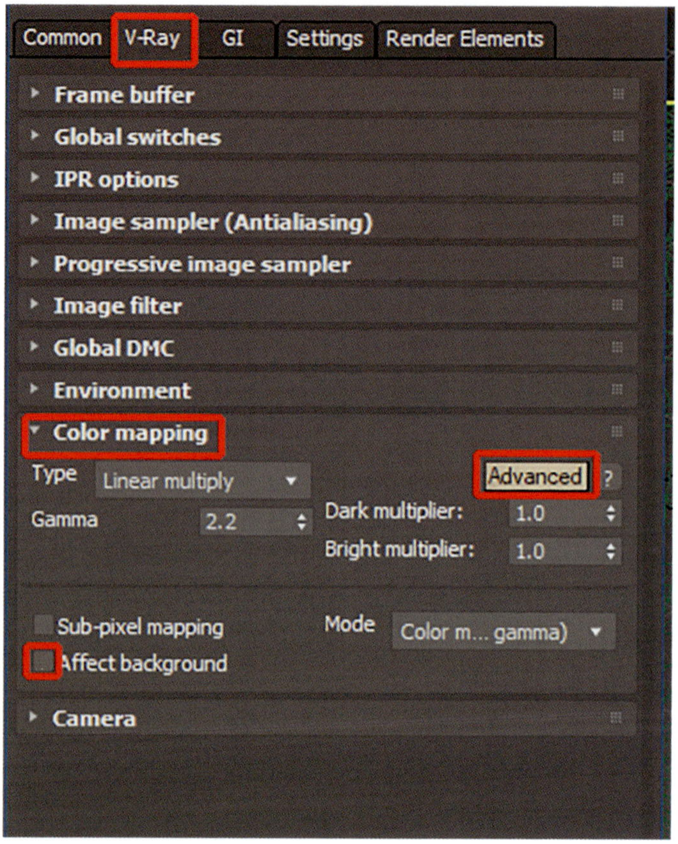

Affect background disabled

Next, ensure the Enable GI option is turned on.

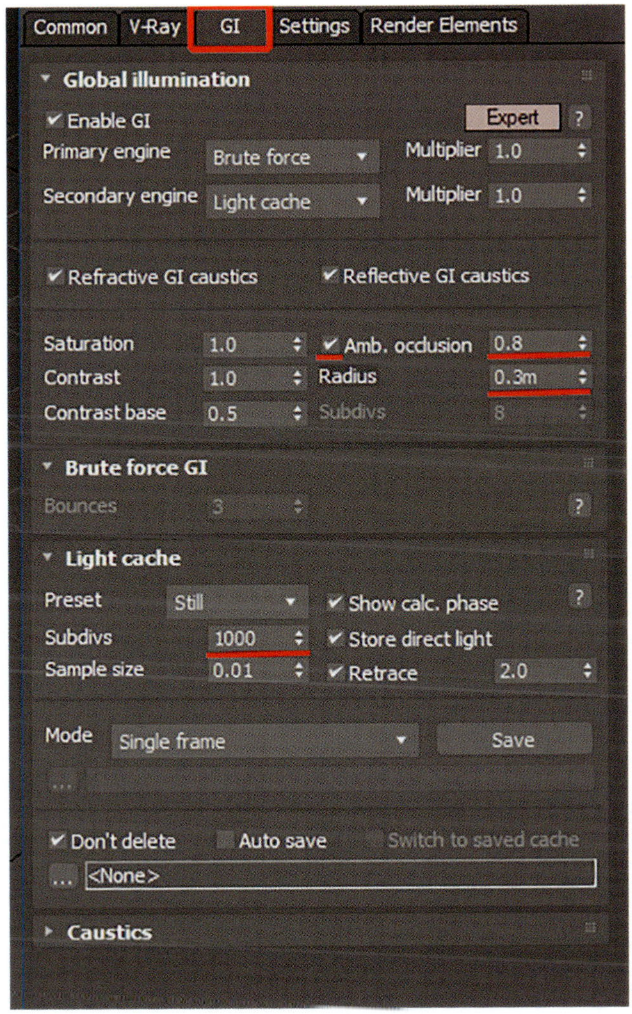

Enable GI option is turned on

If the 3d surface/ground in the scene is to be used as a Matte object to cast shadows; simply do the following:

Select the surface in the scene and right click on it to bring up its quad menu. Select the V-Ray properties option, to open its dialog.

In the Matte properties group, enable the Matte object option and set the Alpha contribution to –1.0.

The value of –1.0 will ensure the 3d surface is not included in the alpha channel.

To have shadows cast onto its matte surface, simply enable the Shadows option in the Direct light group, and Close the dialog.

After closing the dialog, apply a VRay material similar to the ground surface seen in the background photo.

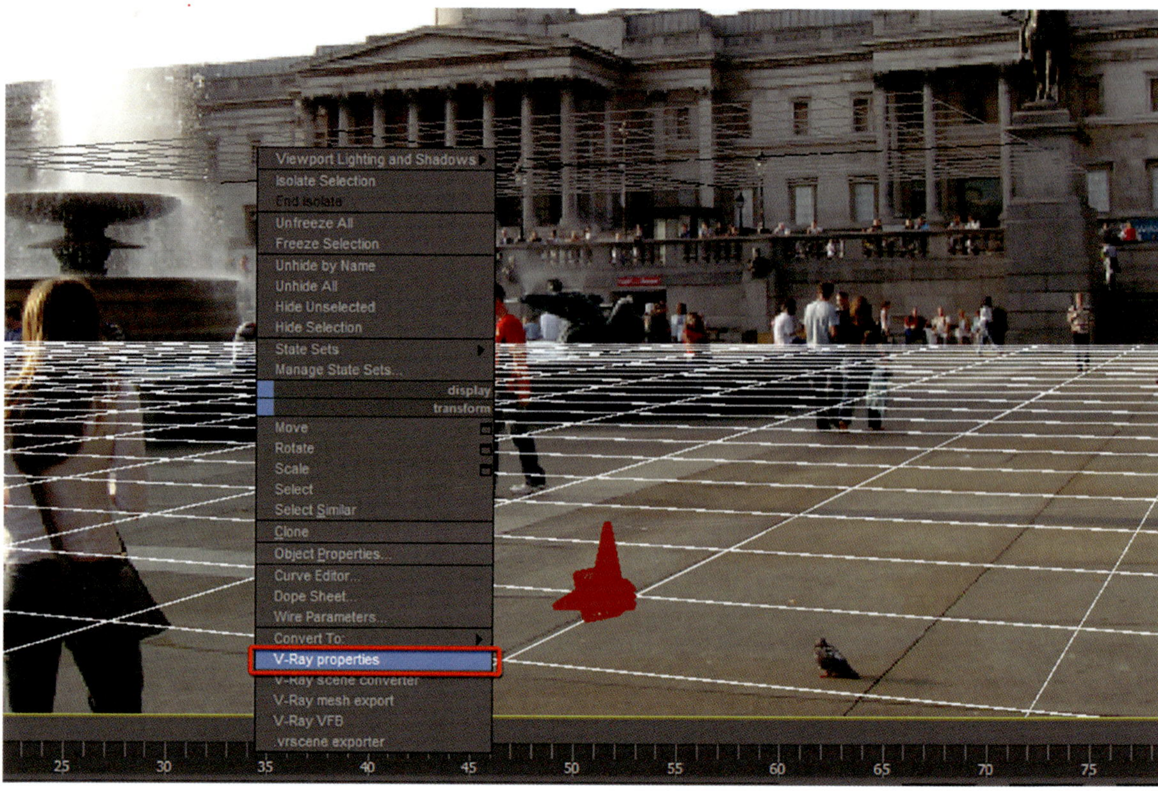

Select the V-Ray properties option

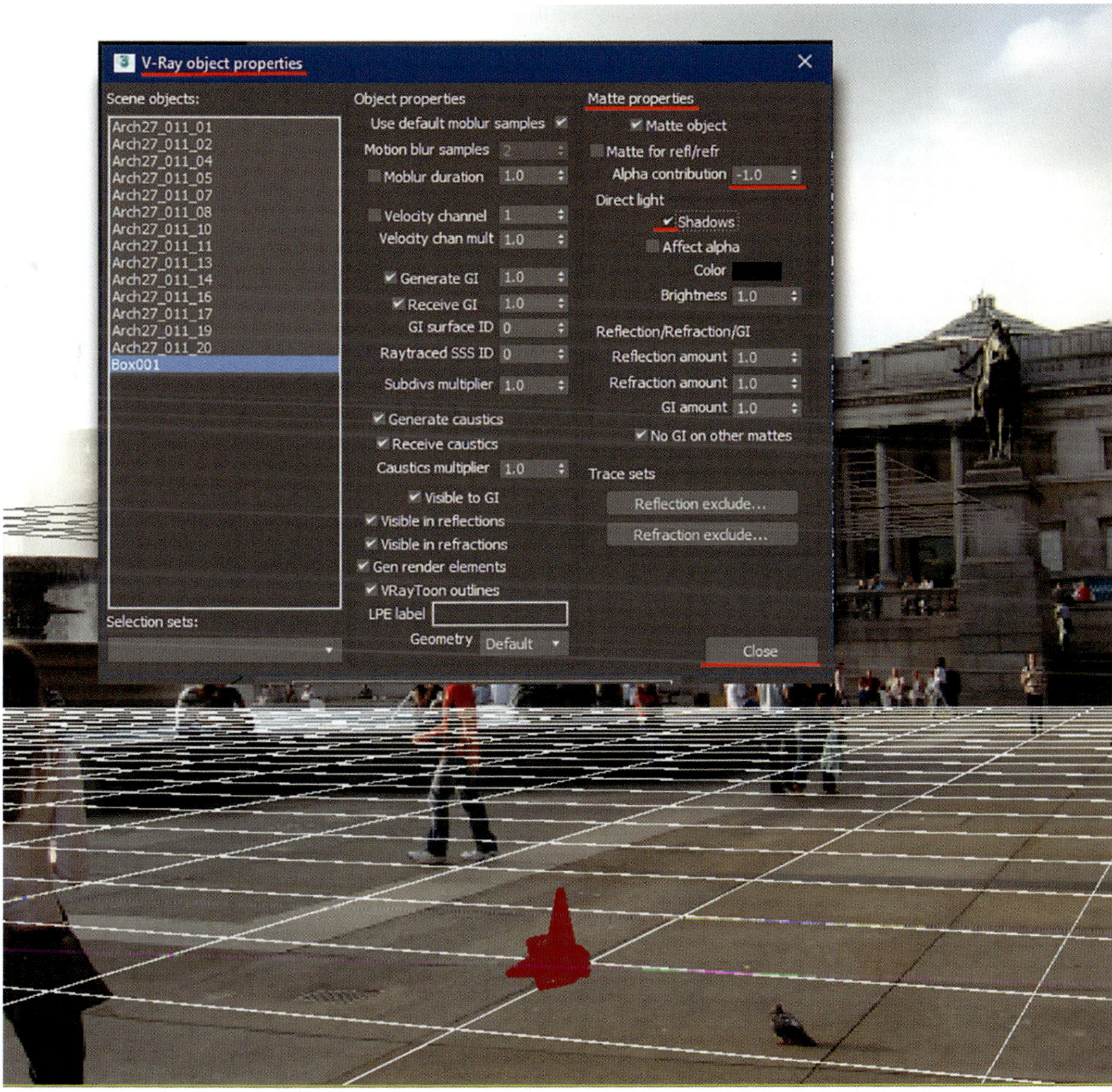

VRay object properties dialog

If it's a daylight shot, ensure a daylight system object is created and the date and time information is accurately entered in its parameters.

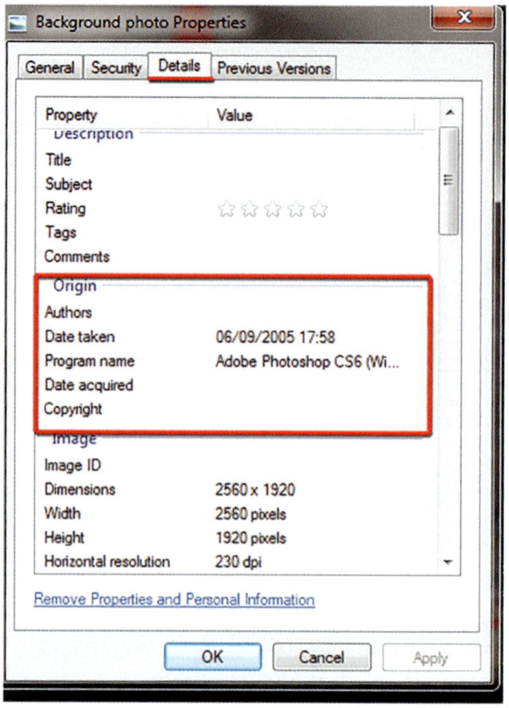

Origin Properties Details from image properties

It's utterly imperative to enable the Daylight Saving Time option.

Also, the daylight compass should be placed on the same level as the ground.

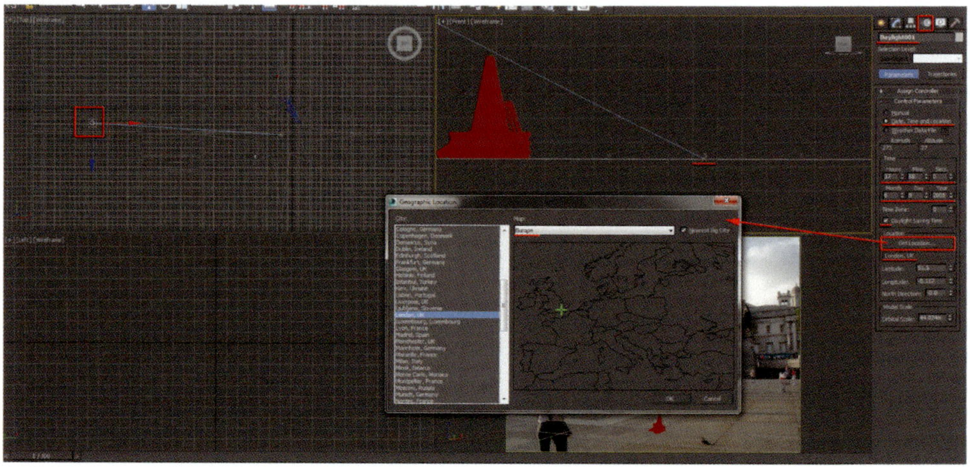

Daylight System position and parameters

To prevent the 3d orange cone in the scene from color bleeding onto the Matte object surface, a VRayOverrideMtl needs to be applied onto the original material.

A VRay black material (or similar) should be plugged into its GI toggle. For more information about this procedural map, refer to Chapter 2.

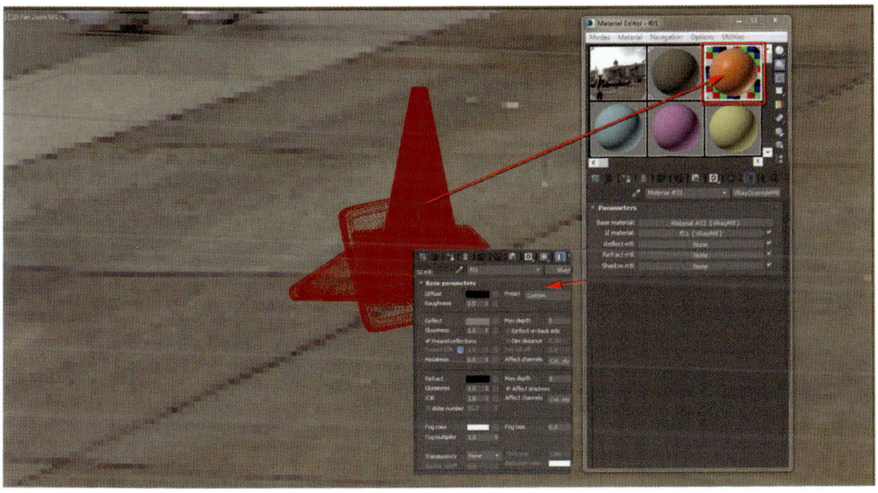

VRayOverrideMtl applied

Also, to make its indirectly lit areas slightly darker; simply open its VRay object properties dialog and set its Receive GI value to about 0.1.

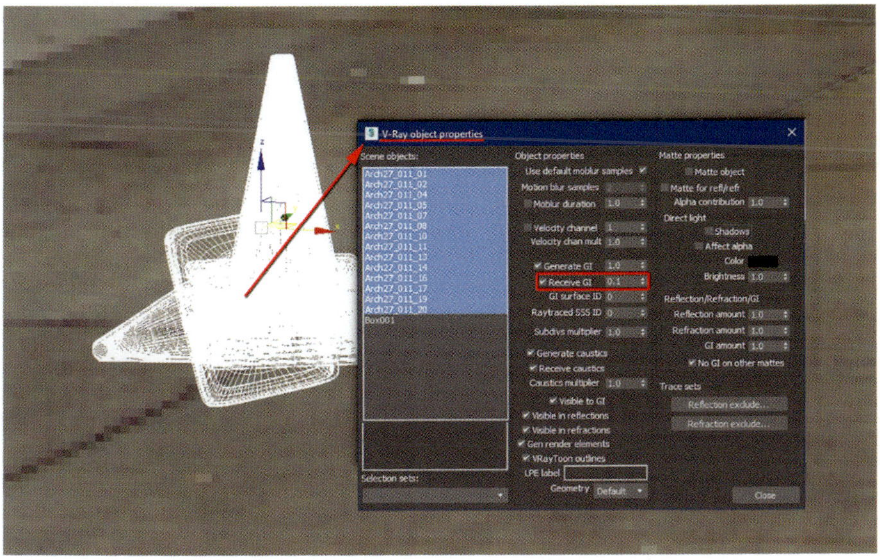

Receive GI value set to 0.1

Next, create a VRay dome light and increase its Intensity value until the shadow color is matched with the background photo.

Tweak with its Color temperature; or simply sample it from the background photo in the viewport.

Alternatively, plug an HDRI into the dome light as depicted in Chapter 3.

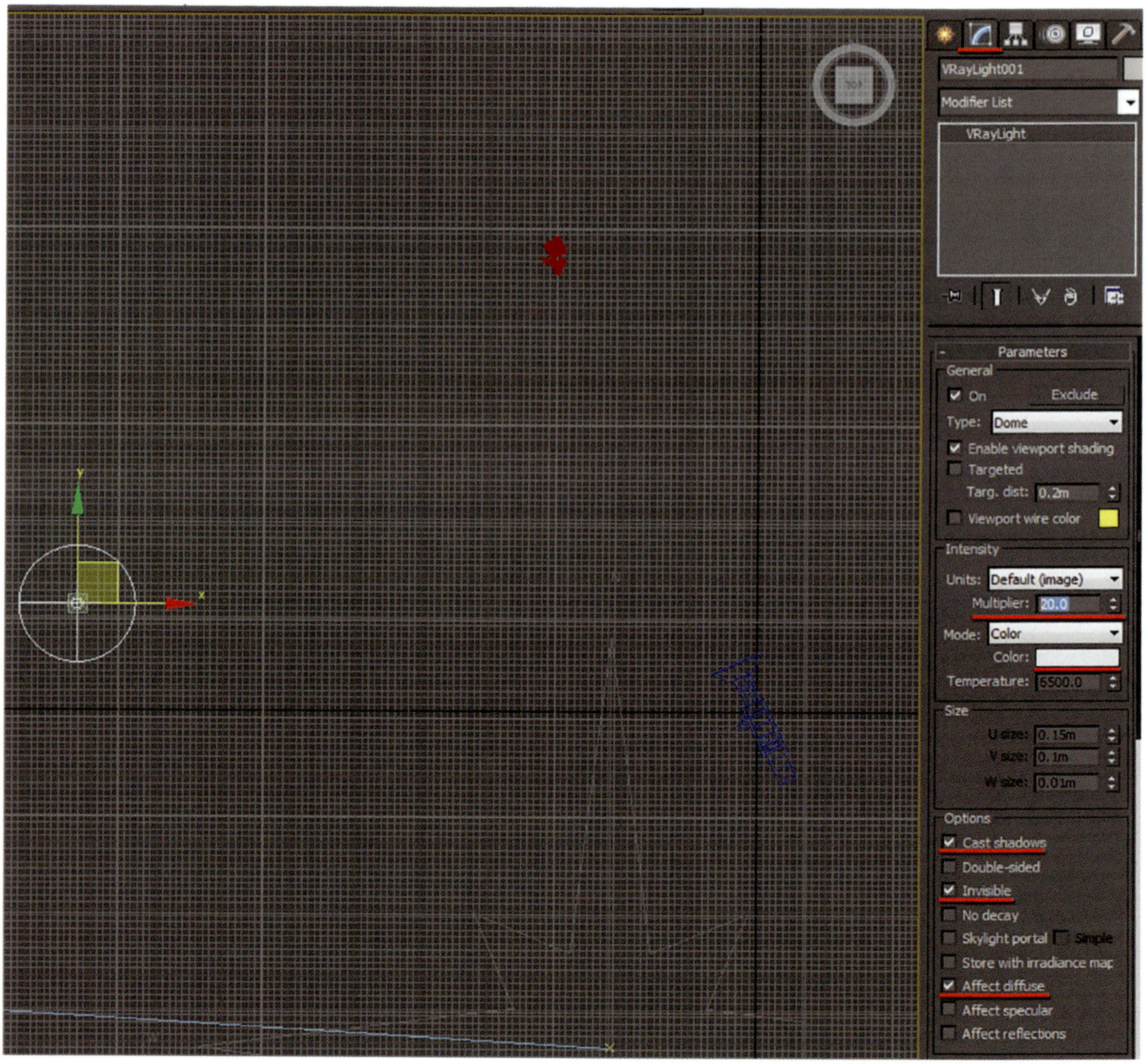

VRay dome light parameters

Shadow brightness matched, by increasing the VRay dome light Intensity Multiplier

If it's a Night shot, the daylight system object needs to be deleted or disabled.

By default, the 2d reflections/refractions in the scene come from the Environment Map toggle.

To override this, simply open the Environment rollout from the Render Setup dialog and enable the Reflection/refraction environment option.

Following that, simply plug a different bitmap or an HDRI (spherical mapping coordinates type) into its toggle. Refer to Chapter 3 to see how an HDRI can be used.

To seamlessly match the bright highlights of the render with the background photo, simply go to the Color mapping rollout parameters and increase the Bright multiplier to about 1.8 or higher.

Bright multiplier value increased to about 1.8

Final render

AdvArray Modifier

AdvArray render

AdvArray is an advanced parametric array modifier for Autodesk® 3ds Max®, and does not ship with standard 3ds Max®. This parametric array modifier has a number of advanced arrays features not found in 3ds Max, or in other third-party modifiers/plug-ins.

To find it simply Google: AdvArray

To download it, please go to apps.autodesk.com, and search for, AdvArray: https://apps.autodesk.com/3DSMAX/en/Detail/Index?id=7221085778557027350&appLang=en&os=Win64

Or, simply contact: tim_catalano@hotmail.com

Before running its installation, first, ensure to disable the Windows Defender Firewall.

After double clicking the exe file to install it, if prompted with a protection dialog, go to more information, and choose to Run Anyway.

Choose the installation type.

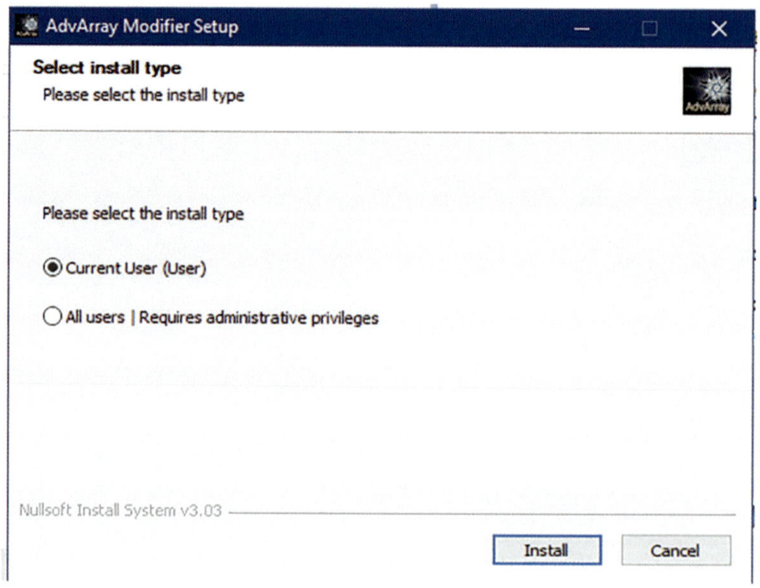

Choose the installation type

Once the installation is completed, click Next, followed by clicking to Finish.

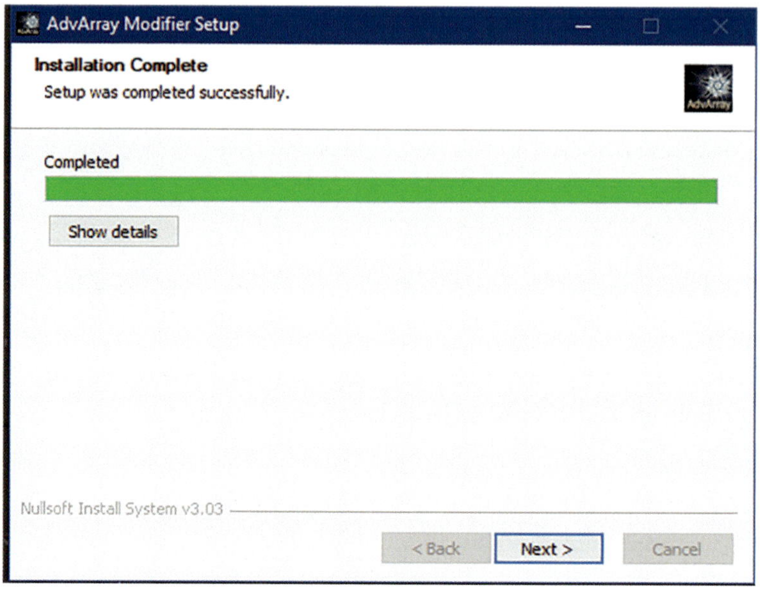

Click Next once the installation is complete

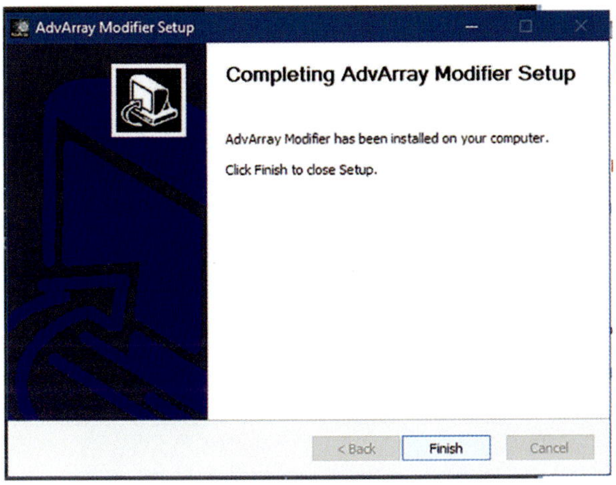

Click Finish to complete installation

To start building the spiral staircase, let's go to the Create panel and click on the Geometry button. Under Standard Primitives, select the Stairs from its list.

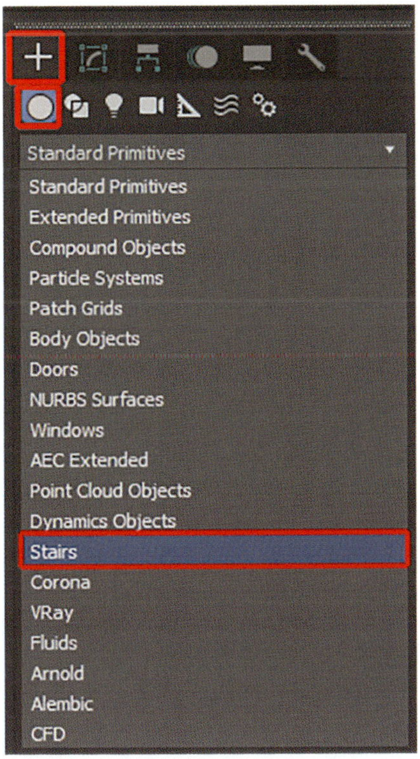

Select the Stairs from the Standard Primitives list

Next, select the Spiral Stair type.

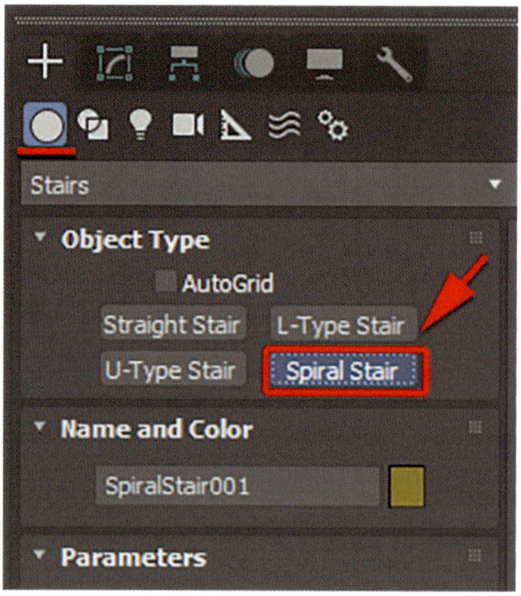

Select the Spiral Stair type

Left click and hold the mouse in the Top viewport, followed by dragging the mouse to set its width first.

Release the left click and begin moving the mouse upwards to set its height.

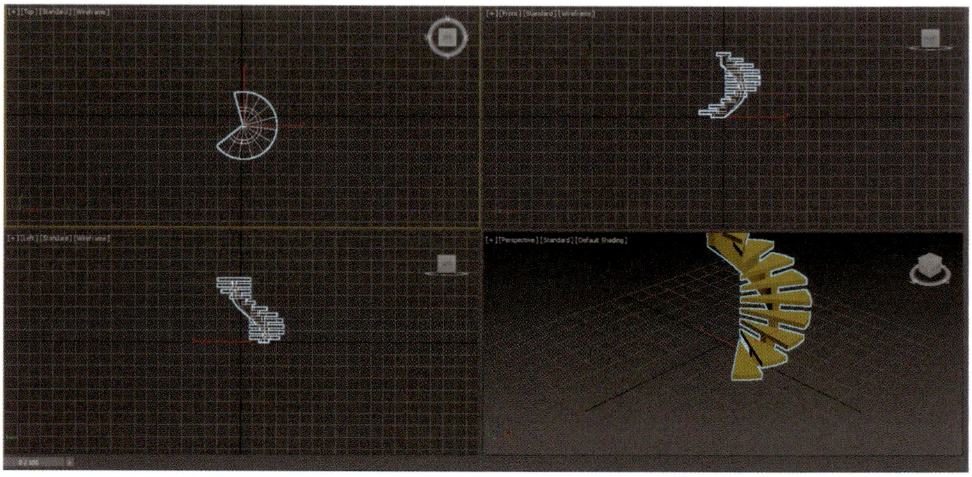

Create the Spiral Staircase in the Top viewport

To create any staircase, a client would have already provided you with the dimensions to refer to. Otherwise, simply Google: staircase dimensions in meters (or millimeters), to find out the generic staircase dimensions.

While the Spiral Staircase is still selected, open the Modify panel. Under Parameters, enabled the Closed option.

Under Layout CCW, set the Radius to 3.404 m, the Revs to 1.96 m and Width to 1.728 m. Simply type the letter "M" after typing the values, if the display unit is set to millimeters.

Under Rise group, set the Overall value to 6.997 m and Riser HT to 0.179 m. To edit the Riser Ct values (Gray), click the Overall toggle to gray it out. And change the Riser Ct value to 39.

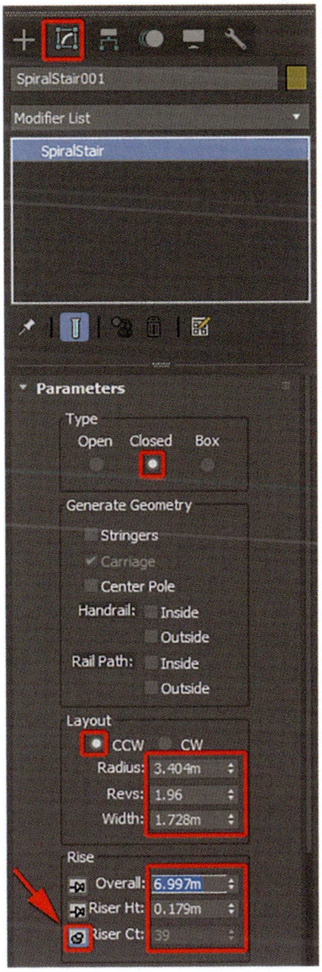

Spiral Staircase new parameters

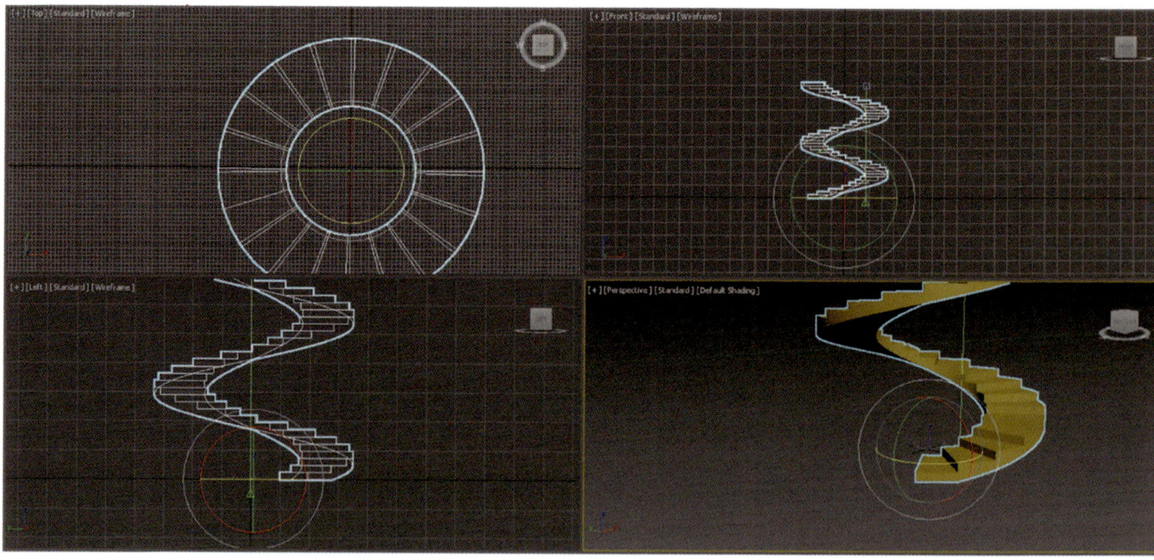

Spiral Staircase final result in the viewport

Under Generate Geometry group, enable the option to add Rail Path Inside and Outside. These two rail paths will be later used to generate the parametric slats along them, and the handrails.

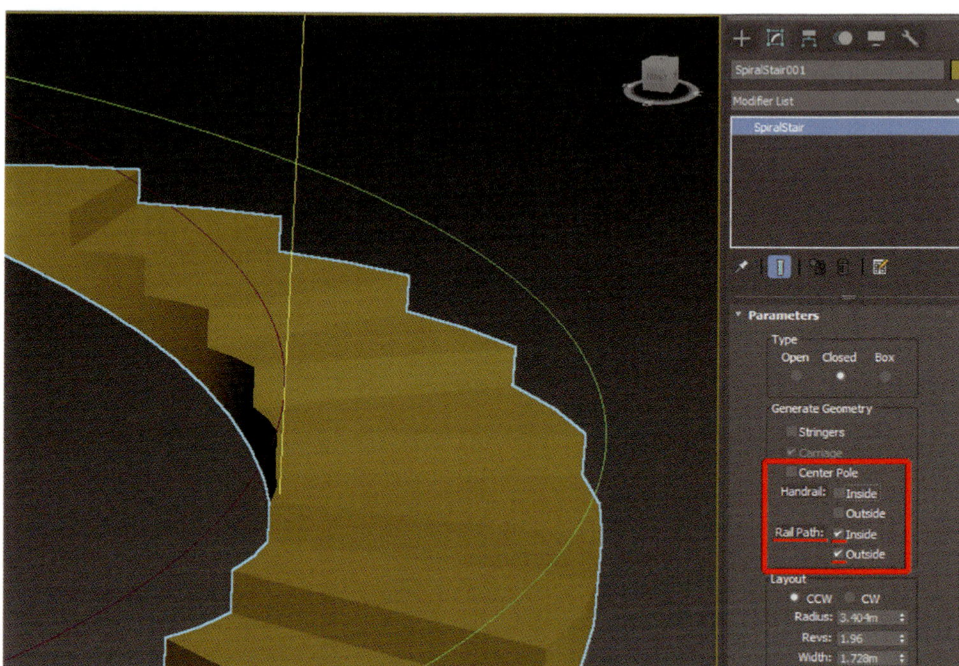

Enable the option to create Rail Path Inside and Outside

The following step is to create the shape of one of the slats to run along the staircase. To do so, go to the Create panel and select the Shape button.

Next, select the Line button and begin creating the slat profile, in the Left Viewport.

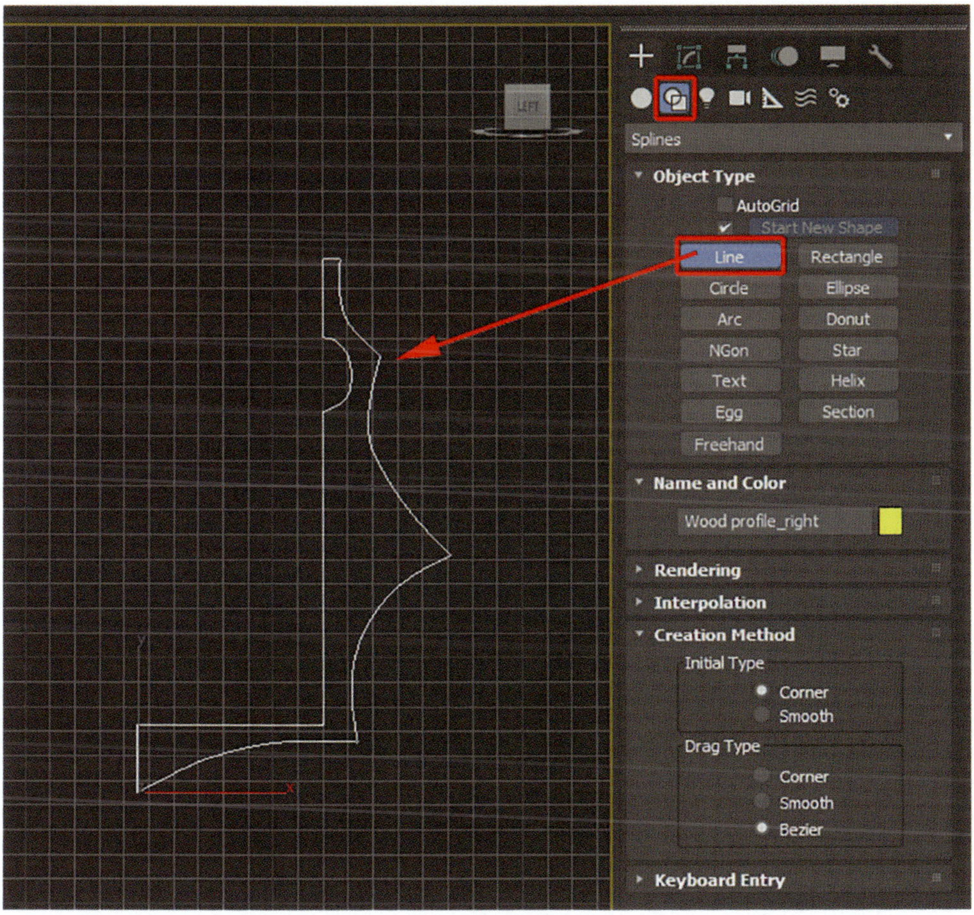

Select the Line button and begin creating the slat profile

Also, use the Modify panel to edit the profile accordingly. Refer to the 3ds Max file named, Wood profile_Right.max, to see the final result.

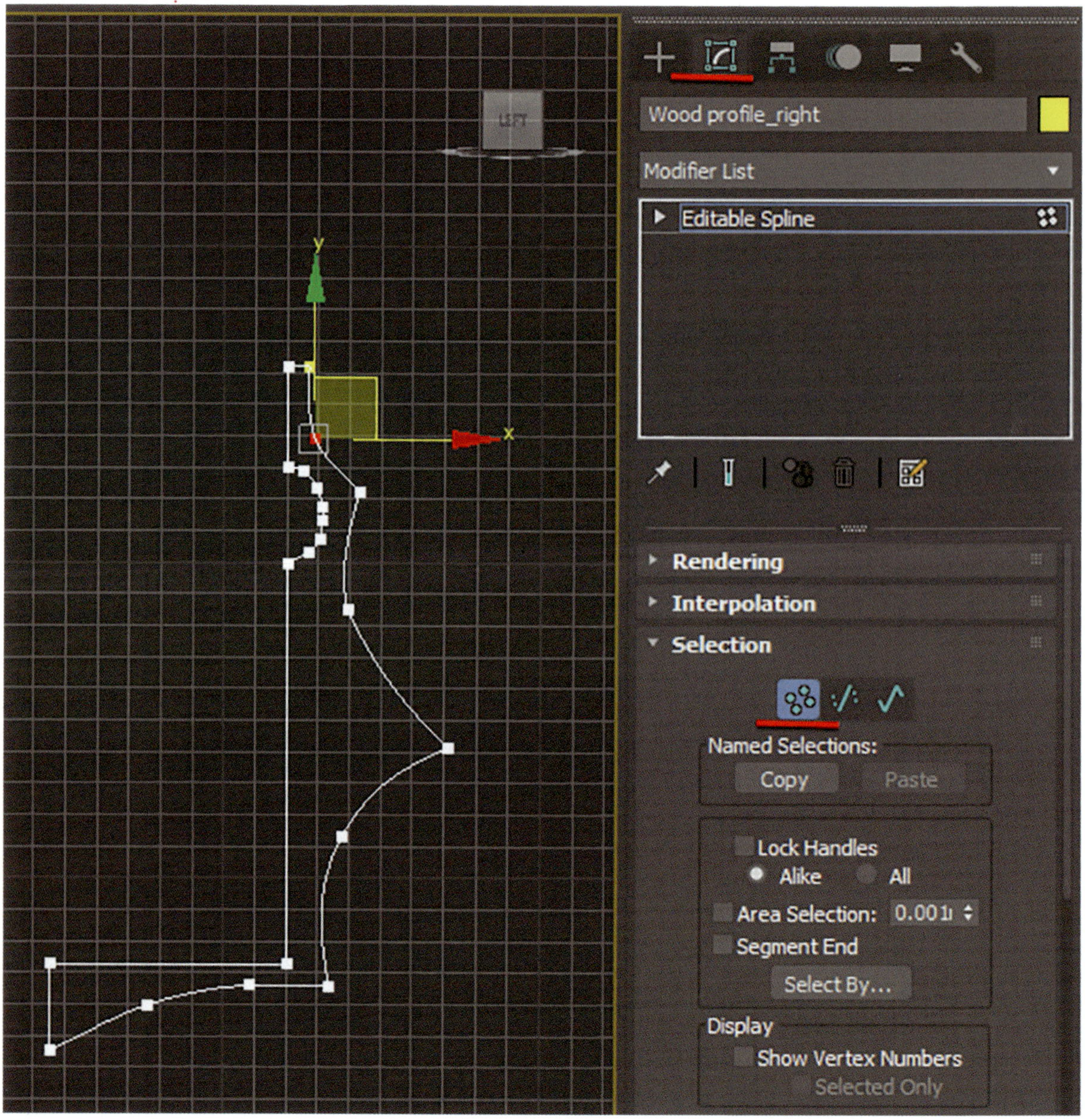

Use the Modify panel to edit the profile accordingly

To add a bit of depth to the slat, add the Extrude modifier and set the amount to about 0.03 m (30 mm).

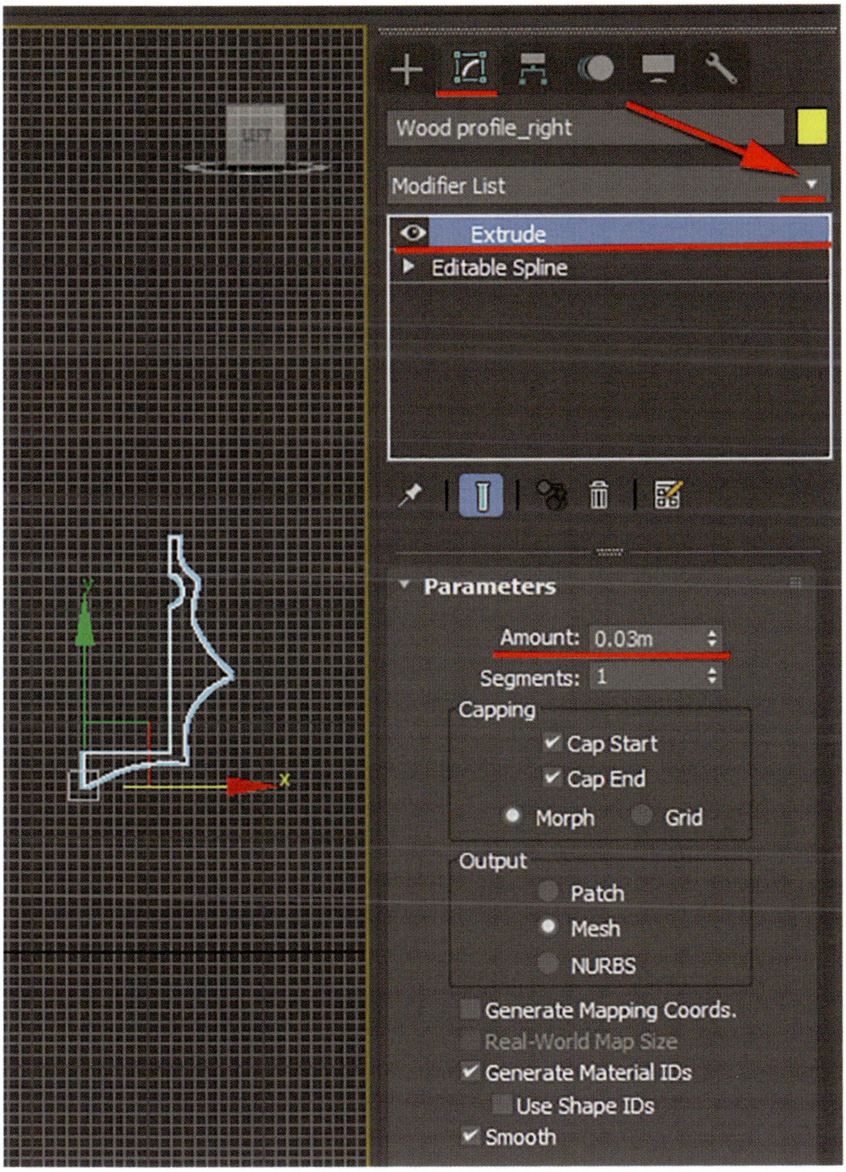

Add the Extrude Modifier and set its amount to 0.03 m

Also, ensure the Pivot point is set to be at the base of the slat object in order to follow along the path properly. Click the Affect Pivot Only button and use the Move tool to move the Pivot gizmo.

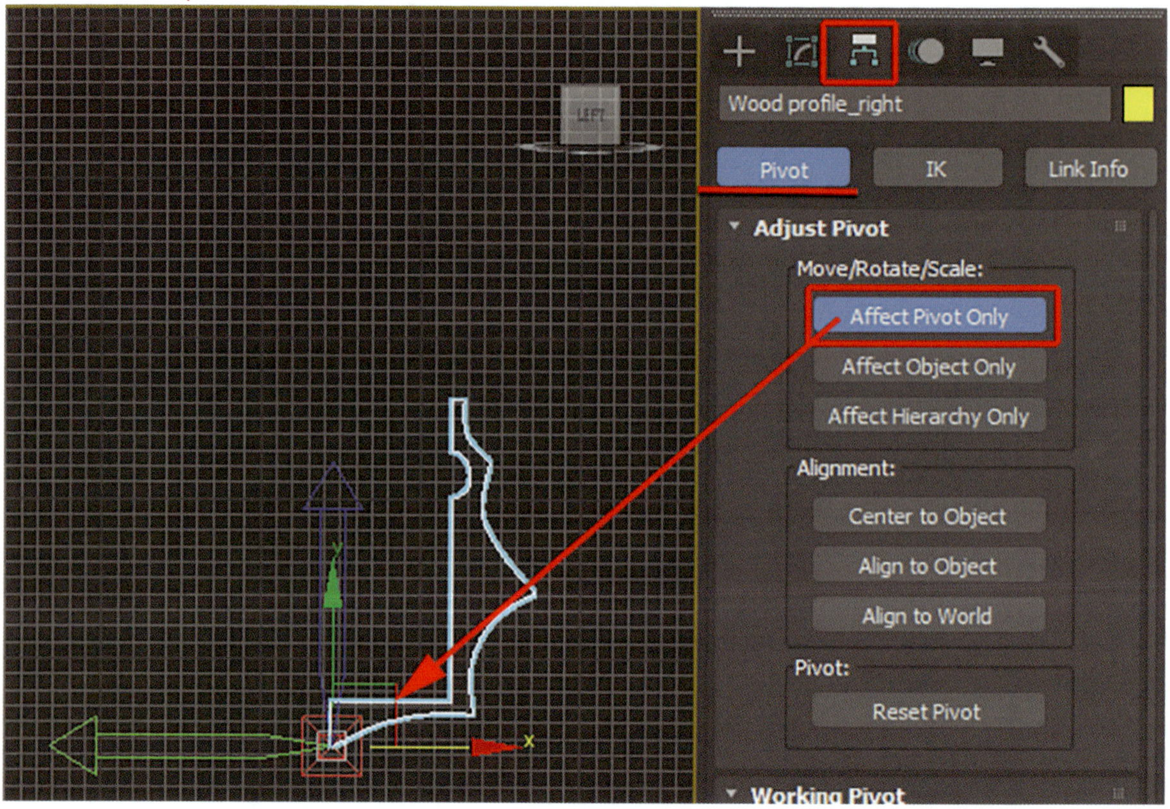

Pivot point placed at the base of the slat object

To ensure there are no problems with the way the slats will be aligned along the path, go to the Utilities panel and select the Reset XForm. Followed by clicking the button to Reset Selected.

NOTE

If the Reset XForm Utility is not available from the list, click on the Configure Button Sets to add it to the list.

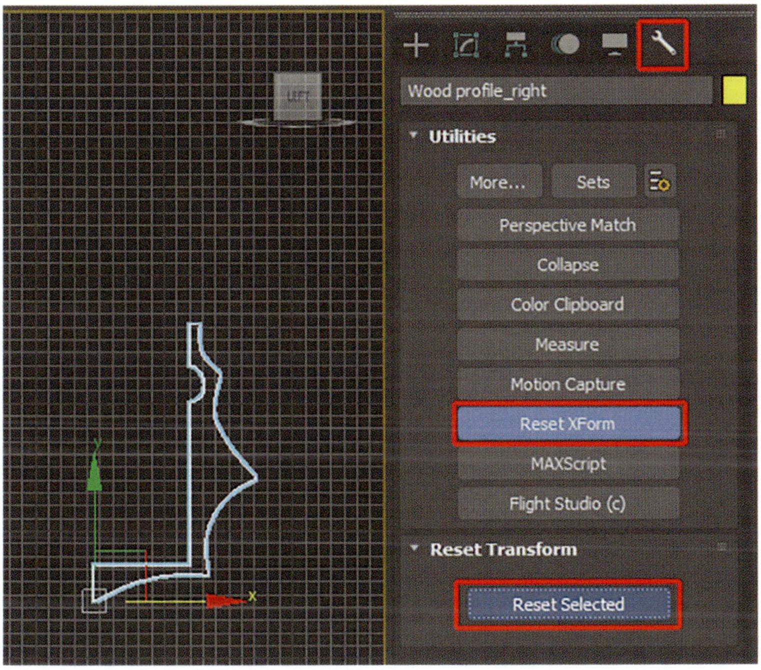

Select the Reset XForm and click the button to Reset Selected

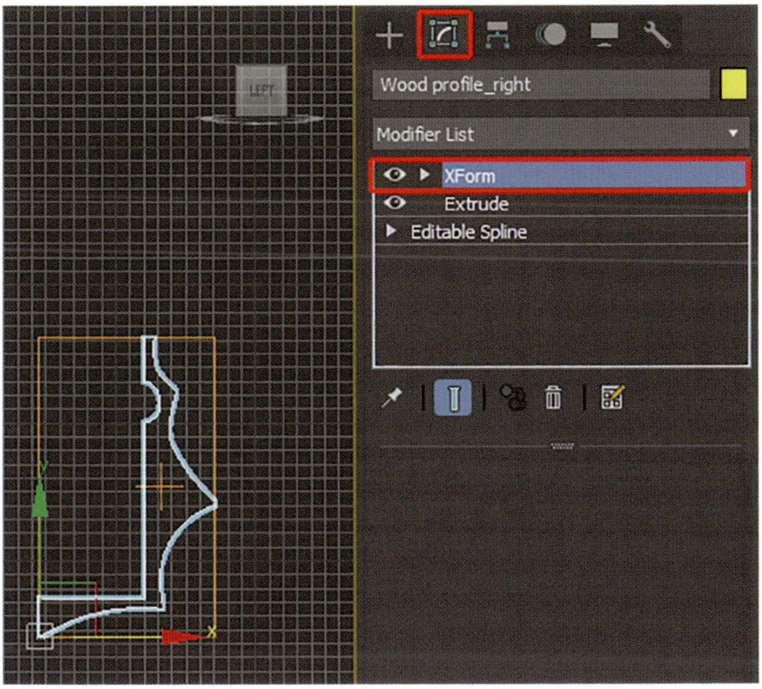

Reset XForm under the Modifier list

Next, Copy/Clone the slat (Shift+Move), to ensure the original model stays intact, in case you need to refer back to it.

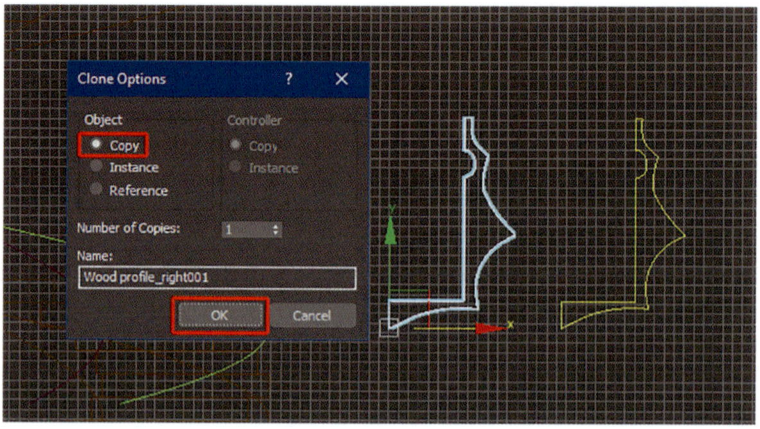

Copy/Clone the slat (Shift+Move)

The following step is to add the AdvArray modifier from its dropdown list.

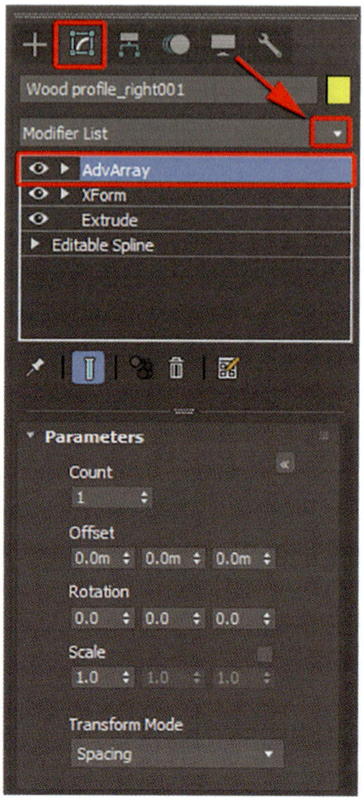

AdvArray modifier added from its dropdown list

To get the slat to follow along the staircase path, under AdvArray Path group, click on the button to Pick path and select one of the paths/splines along the staircase.

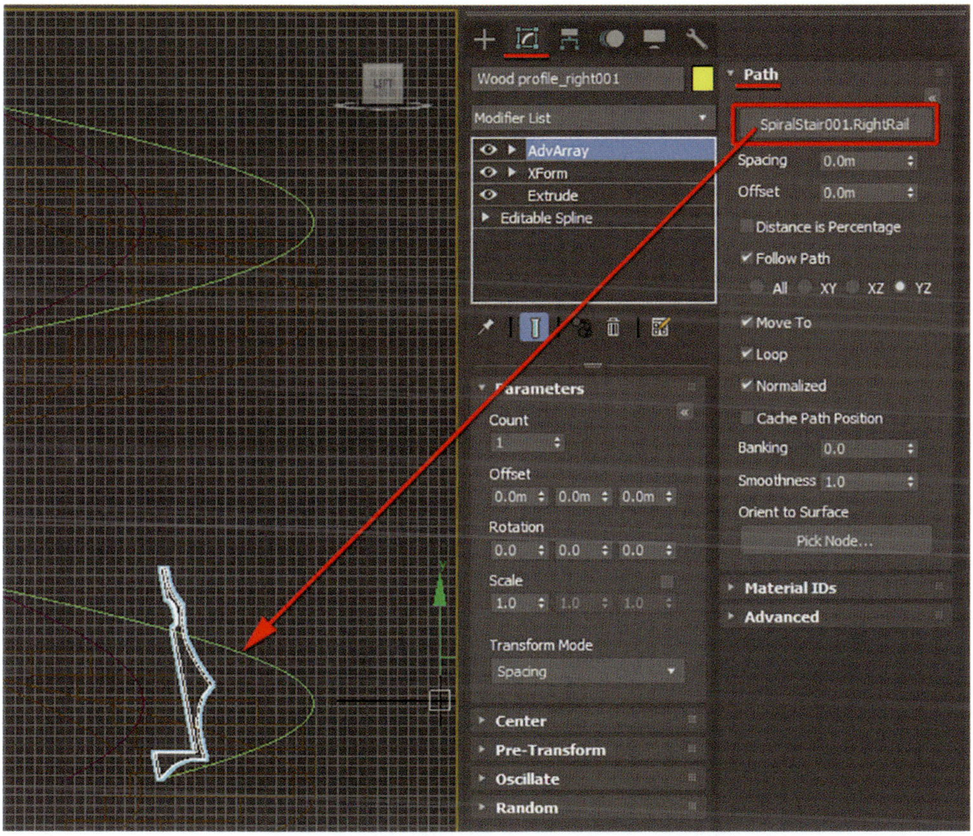

Click to Pick path and select one of the paths/splines along the staircase

To align the slats properly along the staircase, change the Transform Mode to, Final Transform, and enable the option to, Distance is Percentage. The Slat may seem to have disappeared from the viewport.

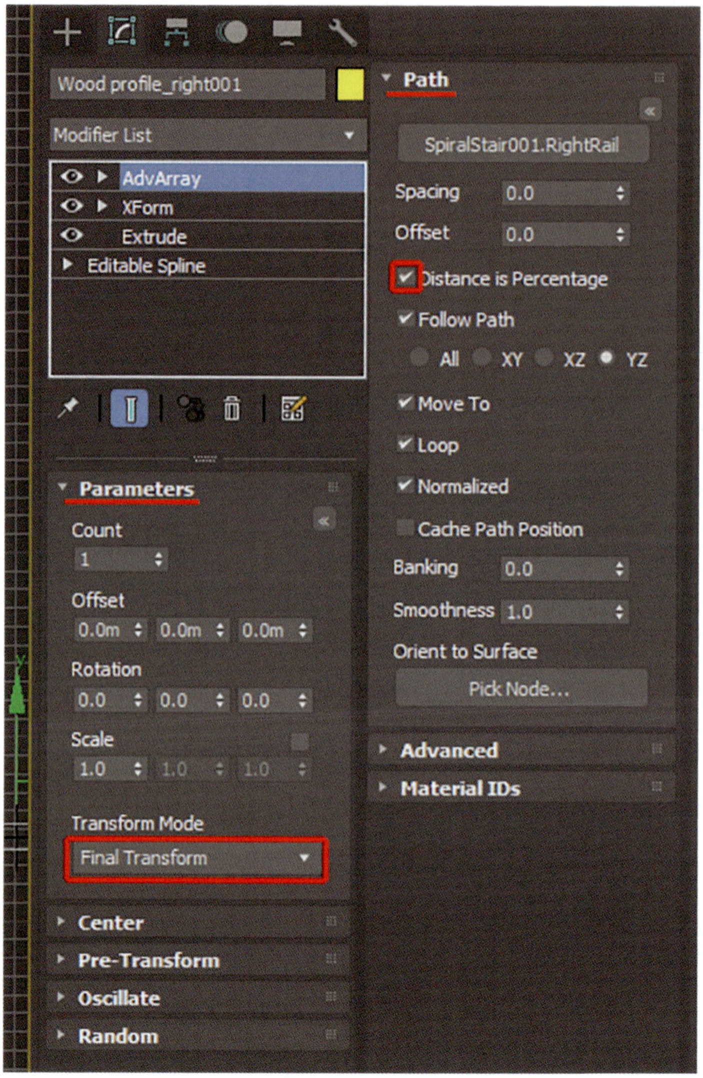

Change to Final Transform, and Distance is Percentage

Start by increasing the Count number by 300, and the Spacing to value 1.0. Also, disable the Loop function to avoid having additional slats at both ends of the path.

To straighten the slat rotation along the path, under Pre-Transform parameters, set the X Rotation to –6.0 and the Y Rotation to 12.0.

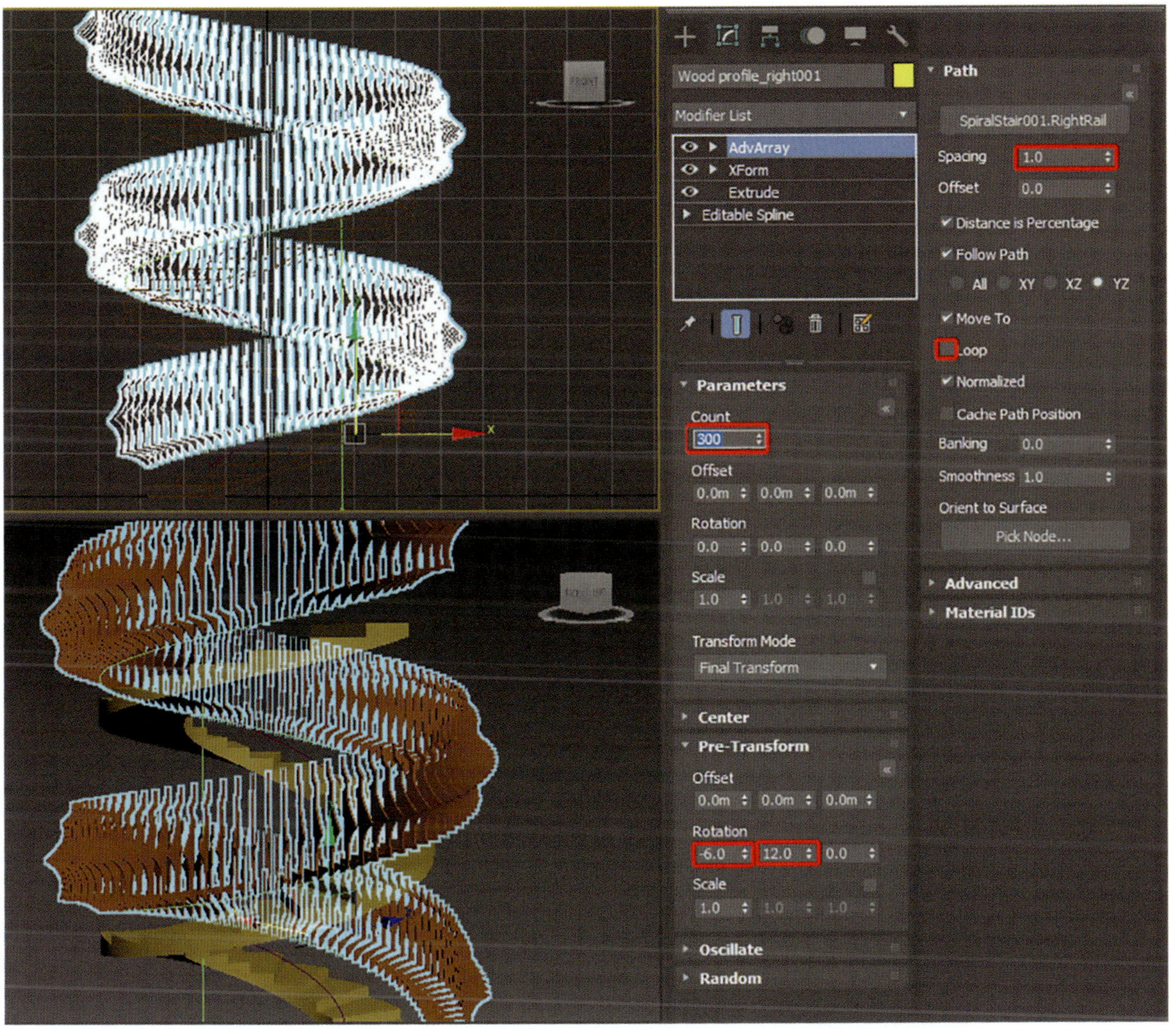

Adjust the AdvArray parameters to follow along the path accordingly

To move the slats down to start from the floor, simply select both handrail paths and move them down simultaneously.

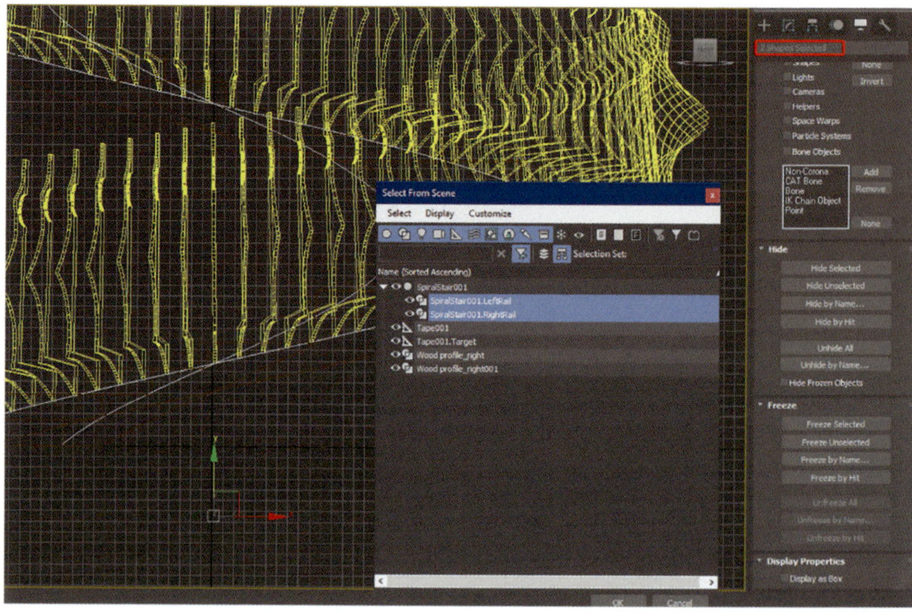

Select and move both handrail paths down simultaneously to move the slats

To create the left profile of the slat, use some of the steps covered earlier. The final 3ds Max file is under the name of, Wood profile_Left.max.

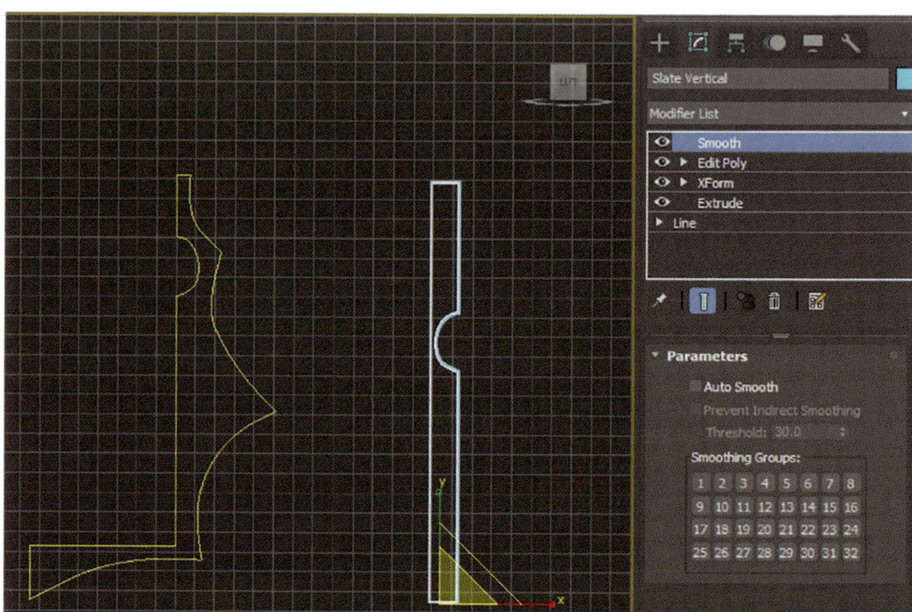

New Wood profile for the left path along the staircase

Next, add the AdvArray modifier to create the slats along the left path following the staircase. Use some of the parameters entered previously.

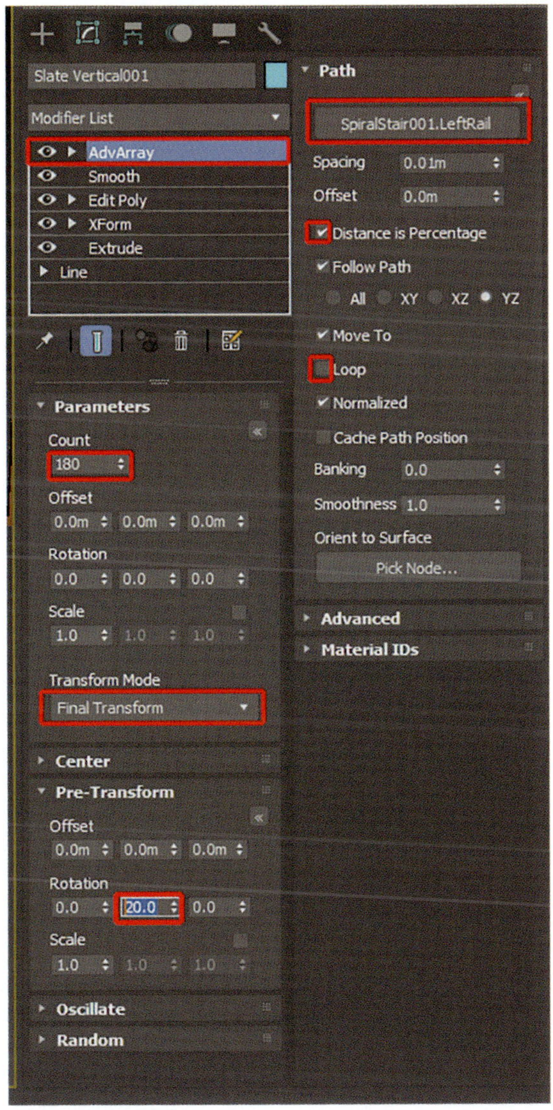

Add the AdvArray modifier to create the slats along the left path

To create handrails, simply copy one of the staircase paths and add the Sweep modifier to it. Set its Radius to about 0.025 m.

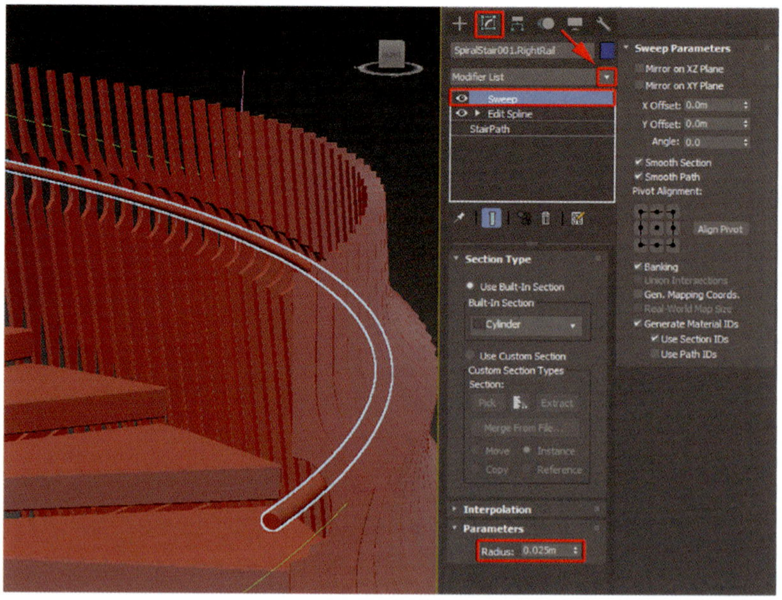

Create handrails with Sweep modifier

Finally, add the Chamfer modifier to the slats to increase detail on its edges. Set the Amount Type to Legacy and Amount to 0.003 m.

The final 3ds Max file containing the staircase with slats and handrails is under the name of, Staircase Atrium_Start.max (Chapter 8 and later chapters).

Chamfer modifier added to the slats to increase detail on its edges

For more information about AdvArray parameters and settings, please check the documentation file named (AdvArray Documentation.pdf) in the Resources folder for Chapter 5.

6

anima® from AXYZ design®

6 anima® from AXYZ design®

Final render by, narrativ., using anima® from AXYZ design®

Introduction

This tutorial will focus mainly on the step-by-step process of integrating 3d static and animated people in a real project, to help add realism and a sense of scale with few simple clicks. anima® from AXYZ design® is currently the best and most advanced solution to populate scenes with people.

To help expedite the process of populating and setting up scenes, anima® uses a state of art application named anima® from AXYZ design®. anima® application is used as a direct link between 3Ds Max and anima®, with unprecedented ease.

To follow this tutorial, it's best to install anima.exe file available in the book recourses. Once installed and registered, double click on its icon to launch it.

DOI: 10.1201/9781315770802-6

Launching anima® software

Open the default generic scene. To ensure anima® is directly linked with your live 3d project, open your main 3DSMax file.

For the purpose of this exercise, open the file named, Staircase Atrium_Start_Matte.max. Select a group named, Staircase, and isolate it (Alt+Q). Due to the size of the file, it's best to keep geometry to a minimum prior to linking it to anima®.

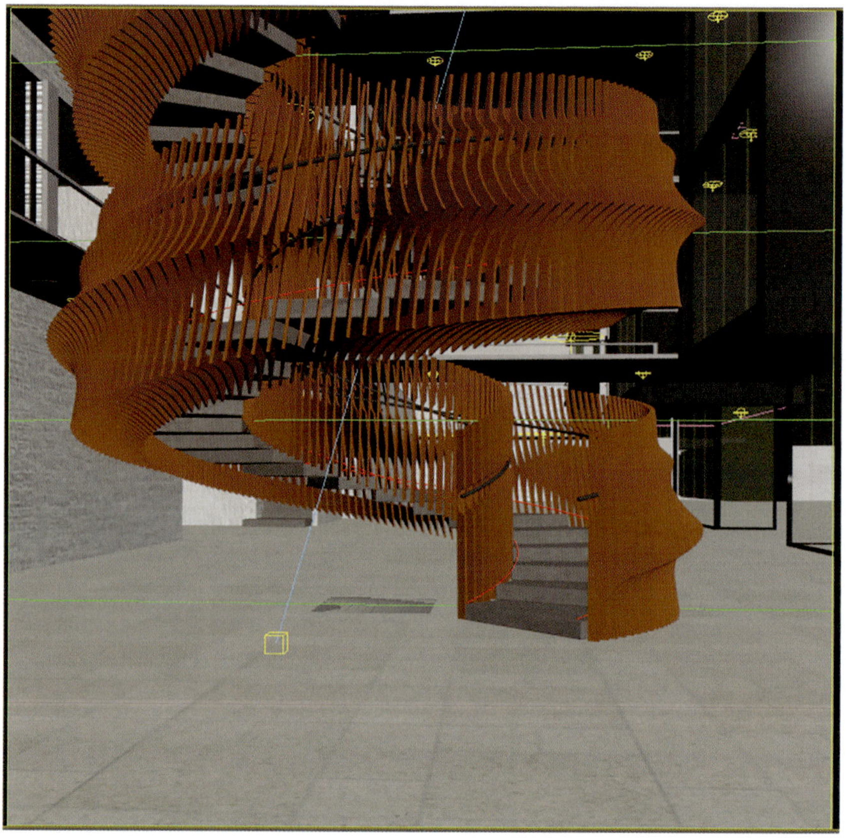

Staircase Atrium_Start_Matte.max scene

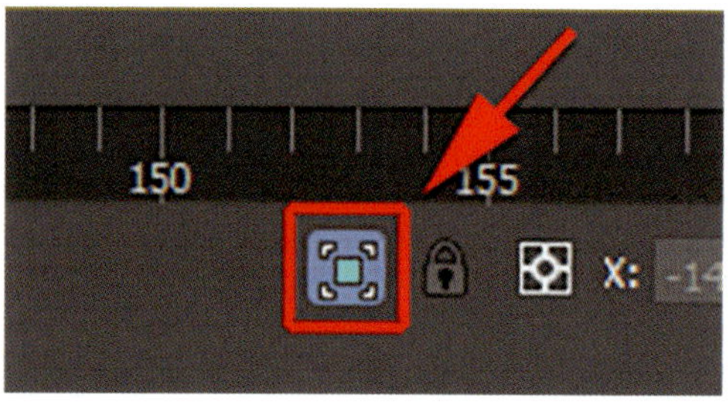

Select the group named, staircase (Alt+Q)

Back in the anima® application, select all default objects in the scene and press Delete on your keyboard.

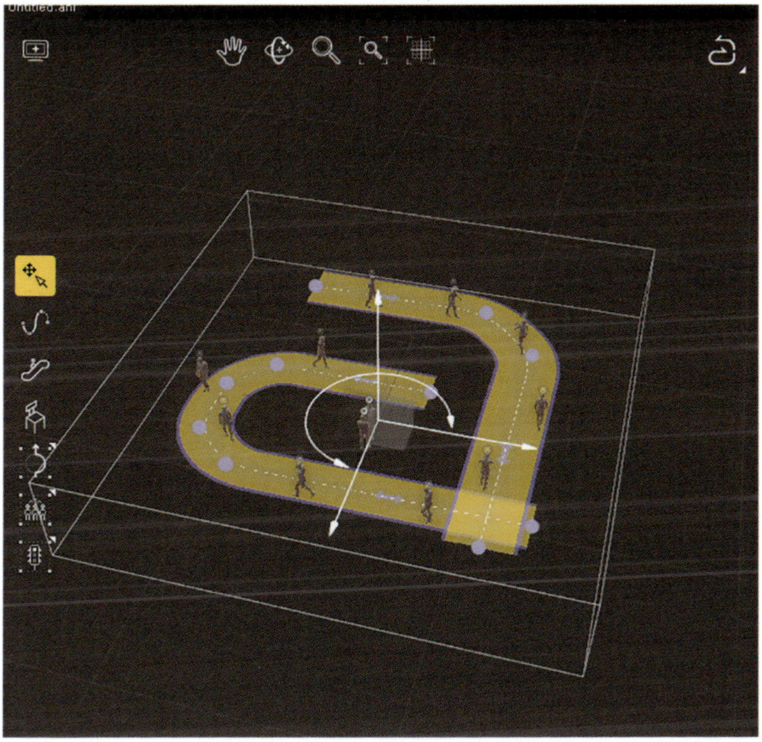

Select all default objects in the scene

Next, choose to save the anima® project (Ctrl+S).

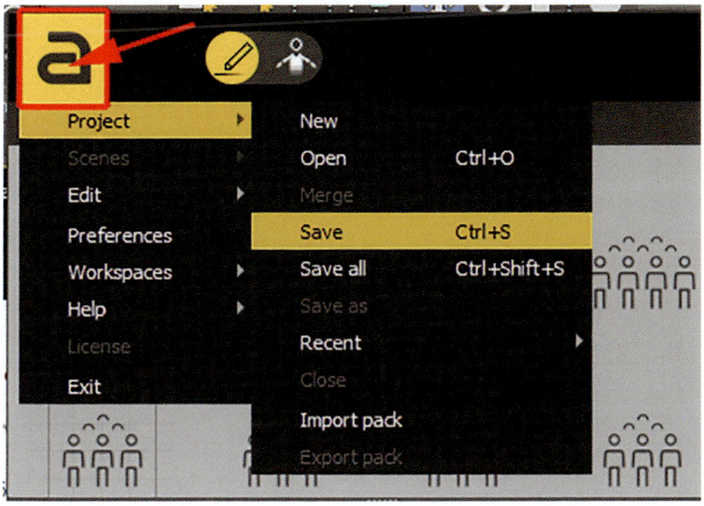

Save the anima® project (Ctrl+S)

You should be prompted to name the project first.

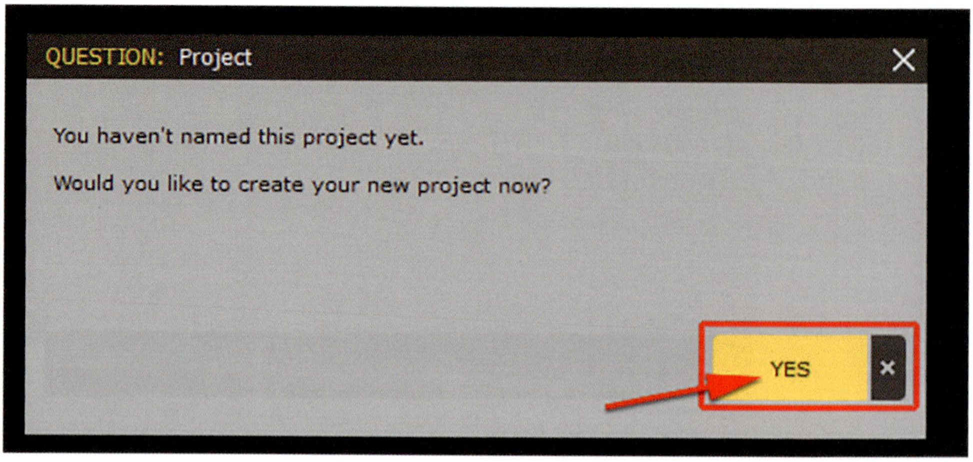

Name the project question

Click YES. Name the project and find its location accordingly, followed by naming the file.

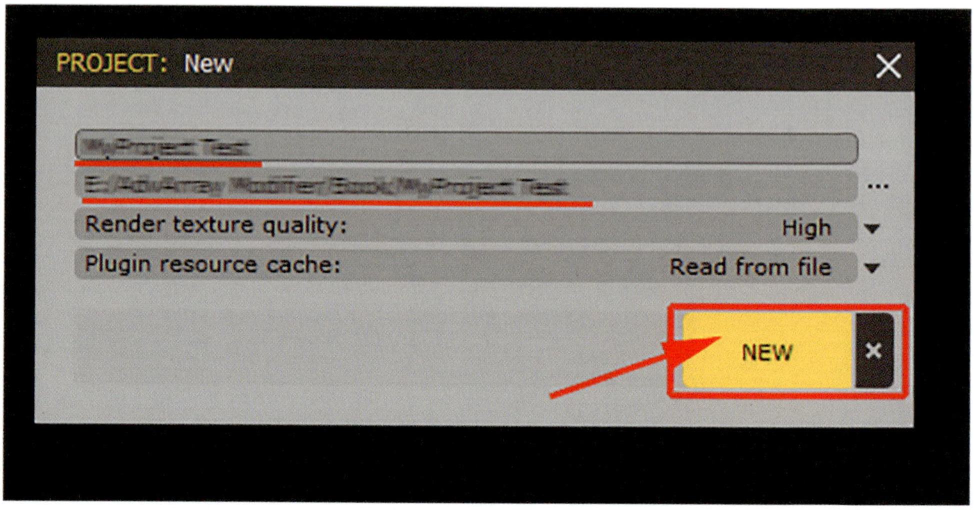

Name the project and find its location accordingly

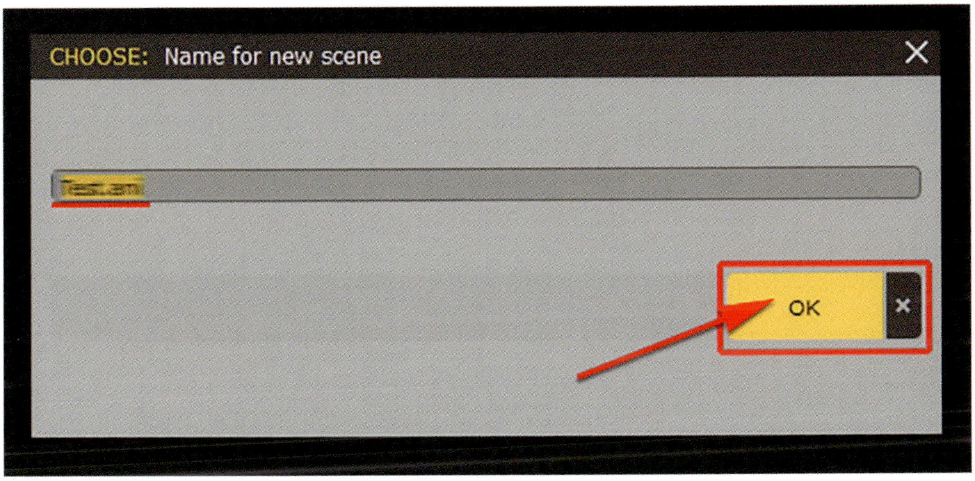

Name the file

To begin synchronizing anima® with your open 3DS Max file, click on its alive™ button.

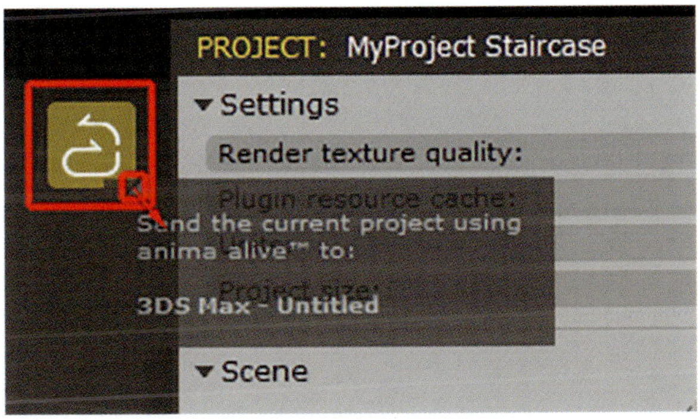

Click on anima® alive™ button to synchronize/send the project

Click YES to send the project to 3DS Max.

NOTE

If per chance anima® is not synchronizing to the correct file name, simply close and reopen the same anima® project again to refresh it. Followed by clicking the anima® alive™ button to turn it to yellow.

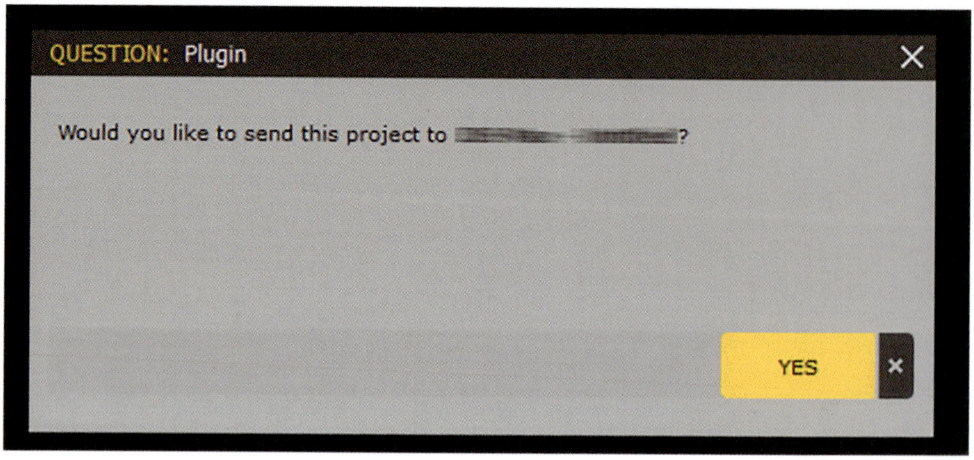

Question:Plugin

anima® alive™ button enabled (yellow)

The synchronized file may look empty at first, because users need to go into 3ds Max file and send specific geometry into anima®.

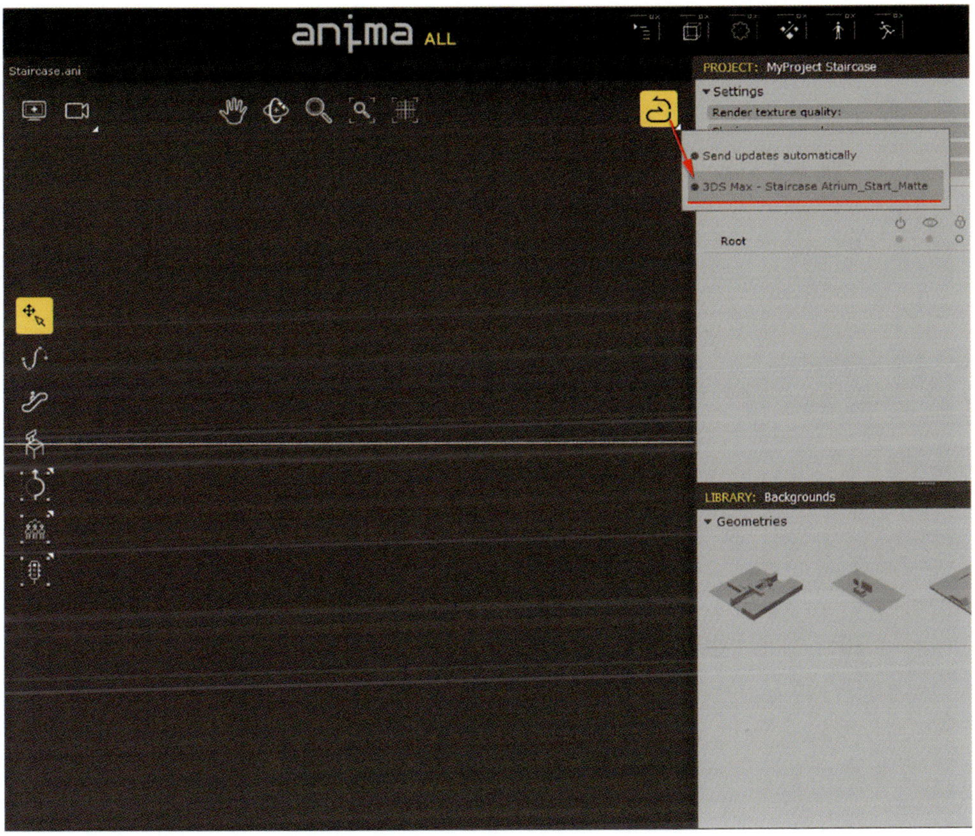

Synchronized file

As result, an animaScene001 icon (Helper) should appear in your synchronized 3DS Max file.

NOTE

Every time you open a compatible 3D application while anima® is open, your file will immediately start blinking. It is an indication that anima® has automatically detected an open 3DS Max file, and it is ready to be synched.

animaScene001 icon (Helper) in 3DS Max file

Next, select the animaScene001 icon (Helper) in the viewport and open the Modify panel

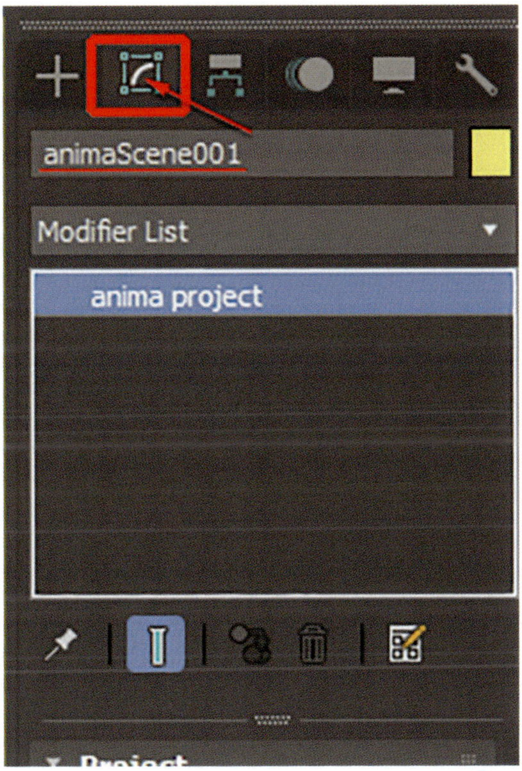

Select the animaScene001 icon (Helper) in the viewport and open the Modify panel

Under Geometry backgrounds parameters, click on the Add button and select the Staircase group in the scene. All objects encompassing the Staircase group should appear added to the list.

The following step is to click on the Sync project and then send to anima® button.

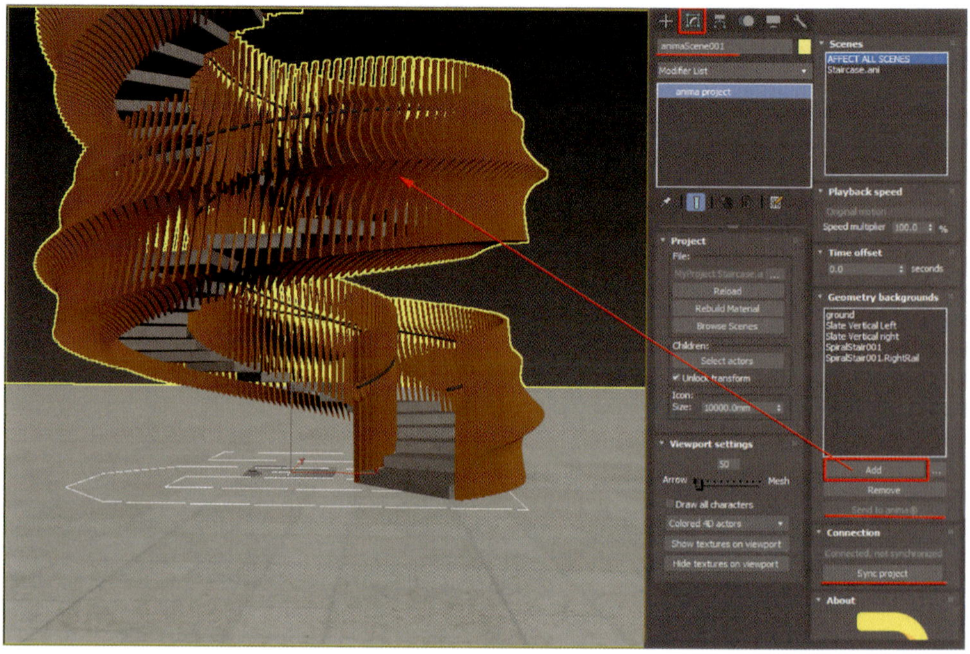

Staircase group added to the Geometry backgrounds list and Synched to anima®

Back in anima®, you should get the updated scene sent from 3DS Max. If not, simply click on the anima® alive™ button to update it.

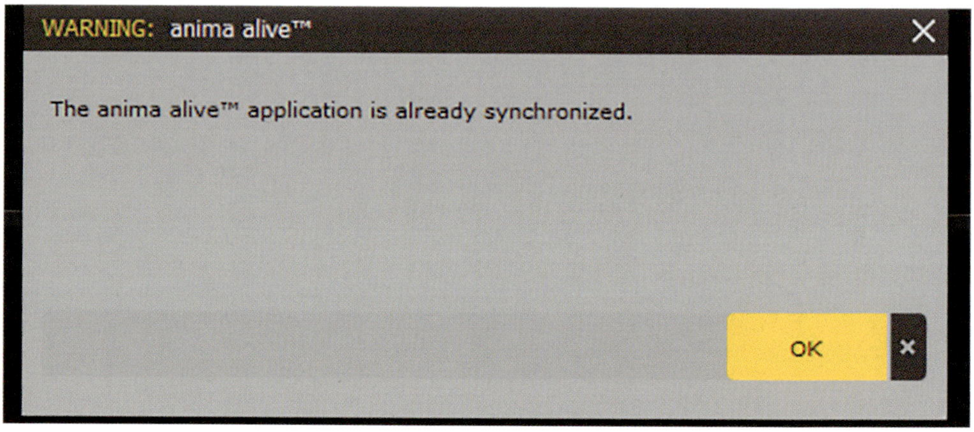

anima® alive™ dialog prompted

Next, click C on your keyboard to enable the camera view directly synched from the 3DS Max application (if any). Or, simply click on its camera icon to enable it (yellow).

If there's more than one camera in the scene, click on its small arrow to select one of the cameras from its dropdown list.

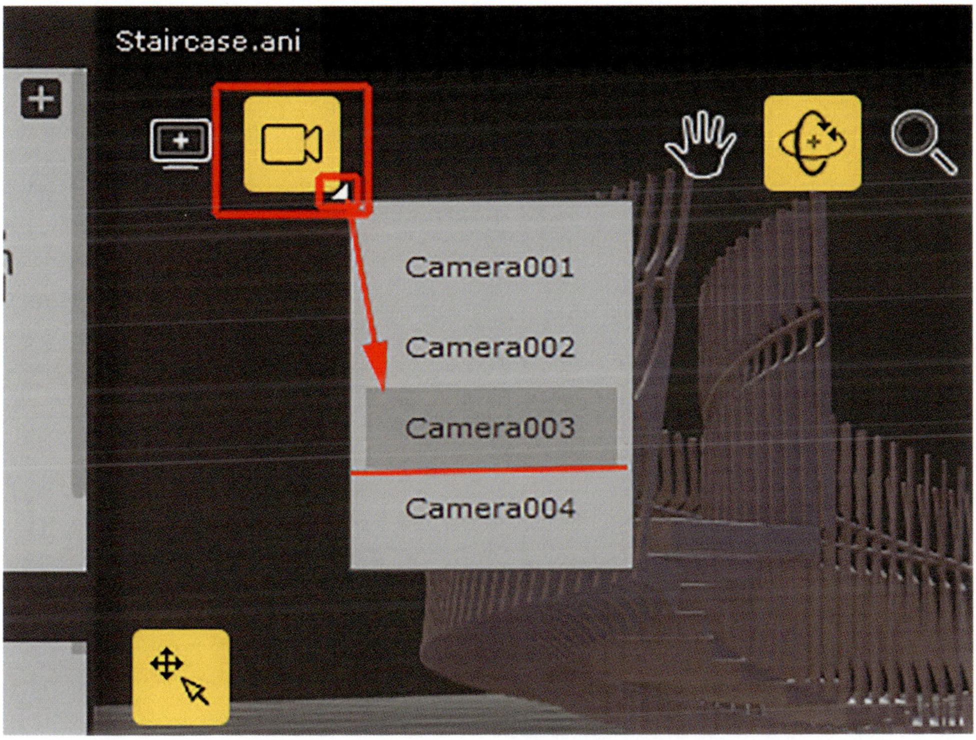

Select one of the cameras from its dropdown list

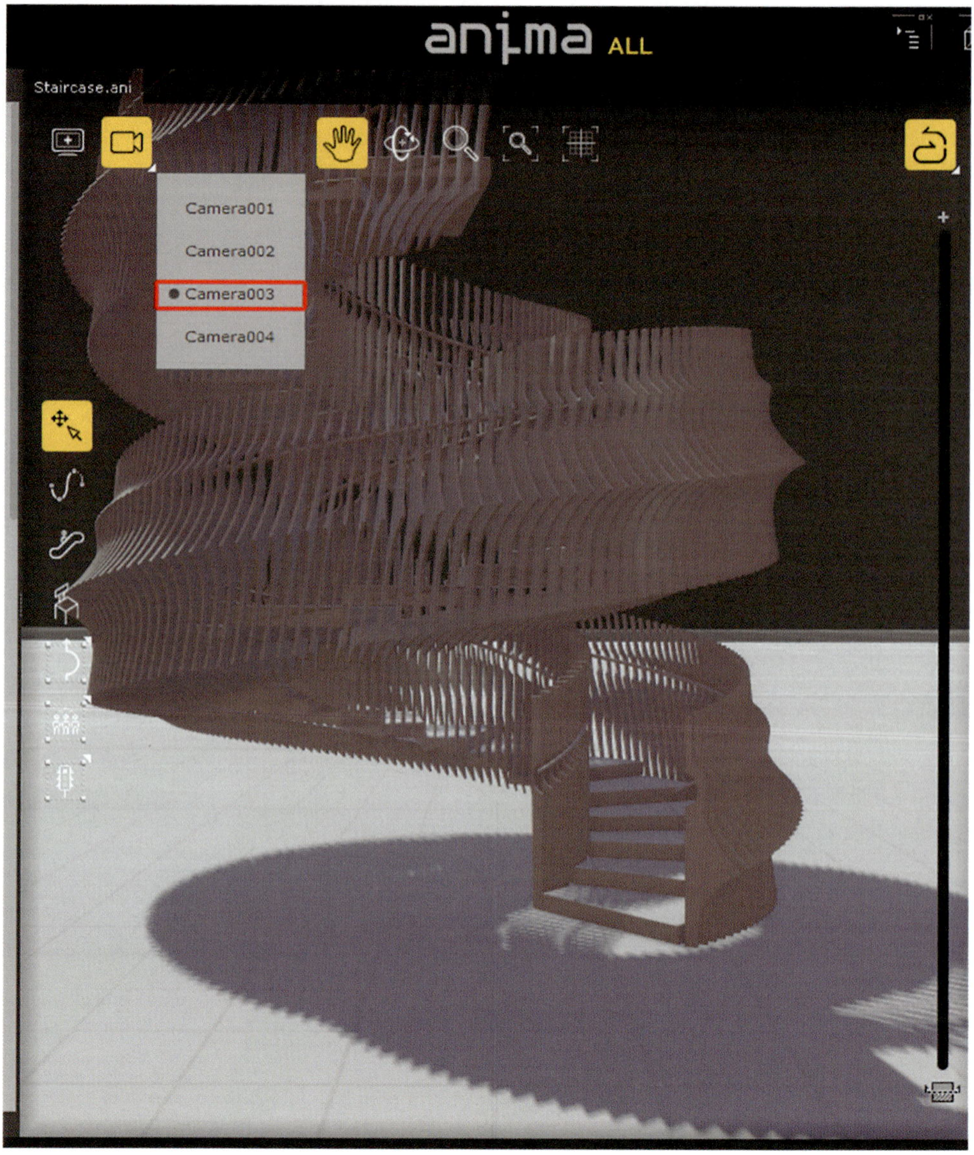

Camera003 enabled in anima® viewport

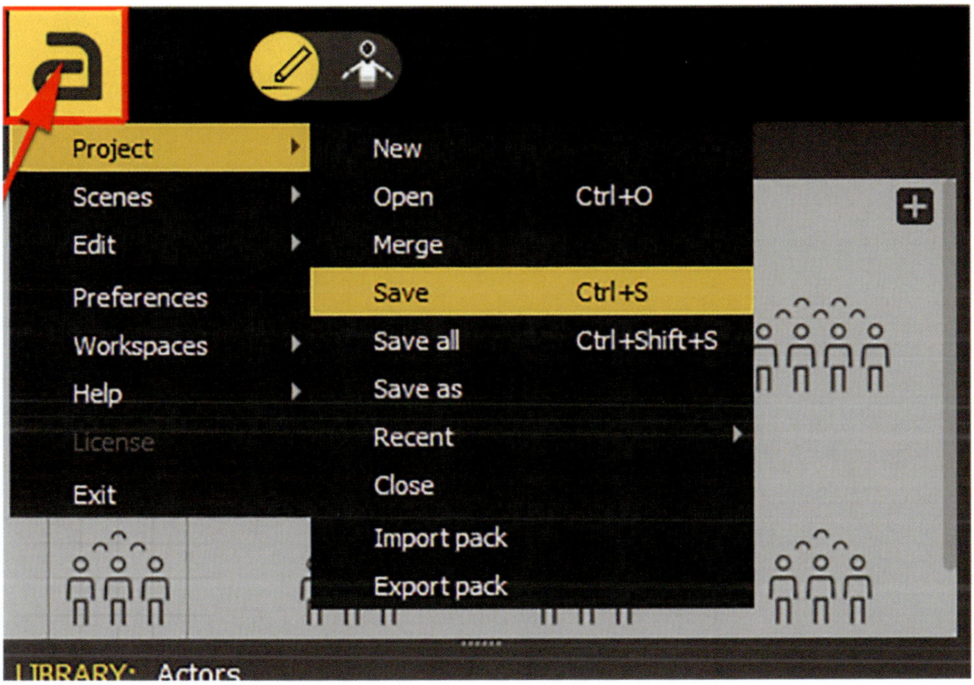

Save the project

Next, go to the Library search box and type in, 4d people. The 4D People I Animated option should appear in the search box dropdown list. Click to open it.

Due to its hyperrealism, 4D people are mostly used for close-up shots. 4D people come as static models or pre-animated. However, users are not able to drag and drop custom animated clips into them.

Standard rigged 3d models are slightly less photorealistic. However, users are able to drag and drop custom animated clips onto them.

NOTE

If per chance anima® viewport is not switching to the camera view, save the project/ scene (Ctrl+S), followed by closing and re-opening the project.

NOTE

Every time you use the Pan, Zoom and/ or the Orbit navigation tools in the anima® viewport, the live camera (in yellow) will turn back to gray. To turn the live camera back on to yellow, simply click C on your keyboard again.

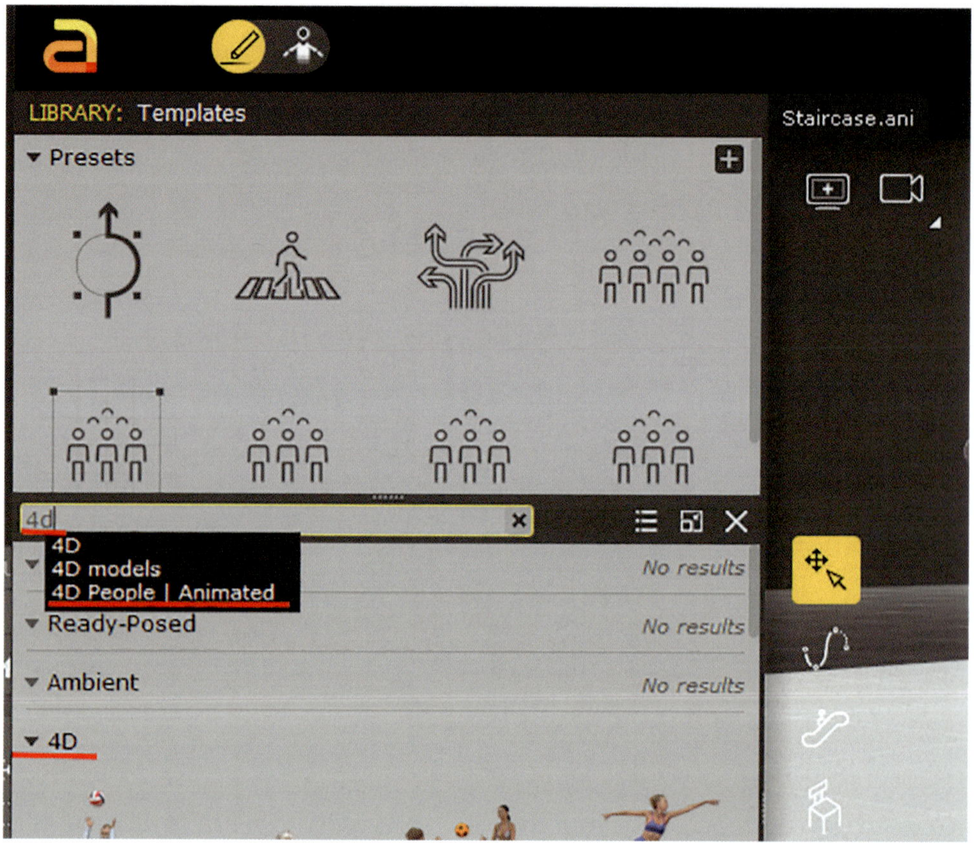

Type in 4d people, in the Library search box

For the purpose of this exercise, scroll down the 4D Library, select the model, cwom0012a4d_photographer, followed by dragging and dropping her into the anima® scene. Left click once to drop it, release the left click to move it anywhere in the scene, and left click once more to exit creation.

The 4D model should detect the surface to be dropped automatically. Save the project updates (Ctrl+S).

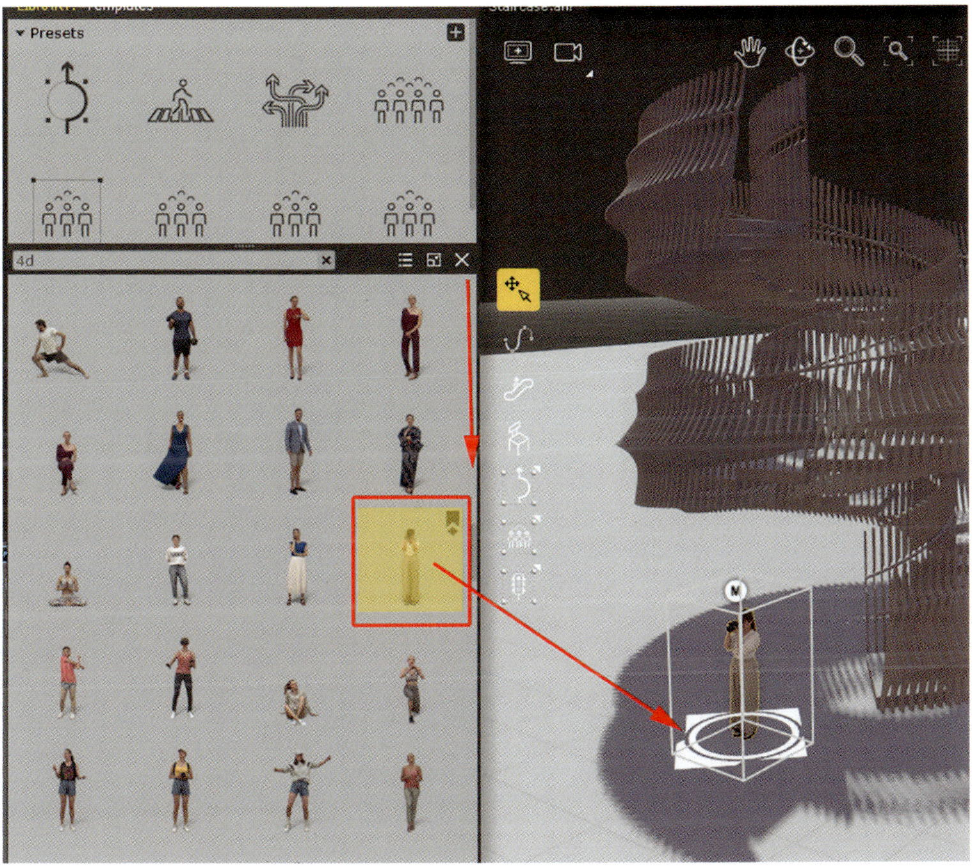

Drag and drop the 4d model in the scene to create it

To rotate or move the 4D character, simply hover over its Move/Rotate icon at its base. If/when either of the tools is highlighted, left click and move it.

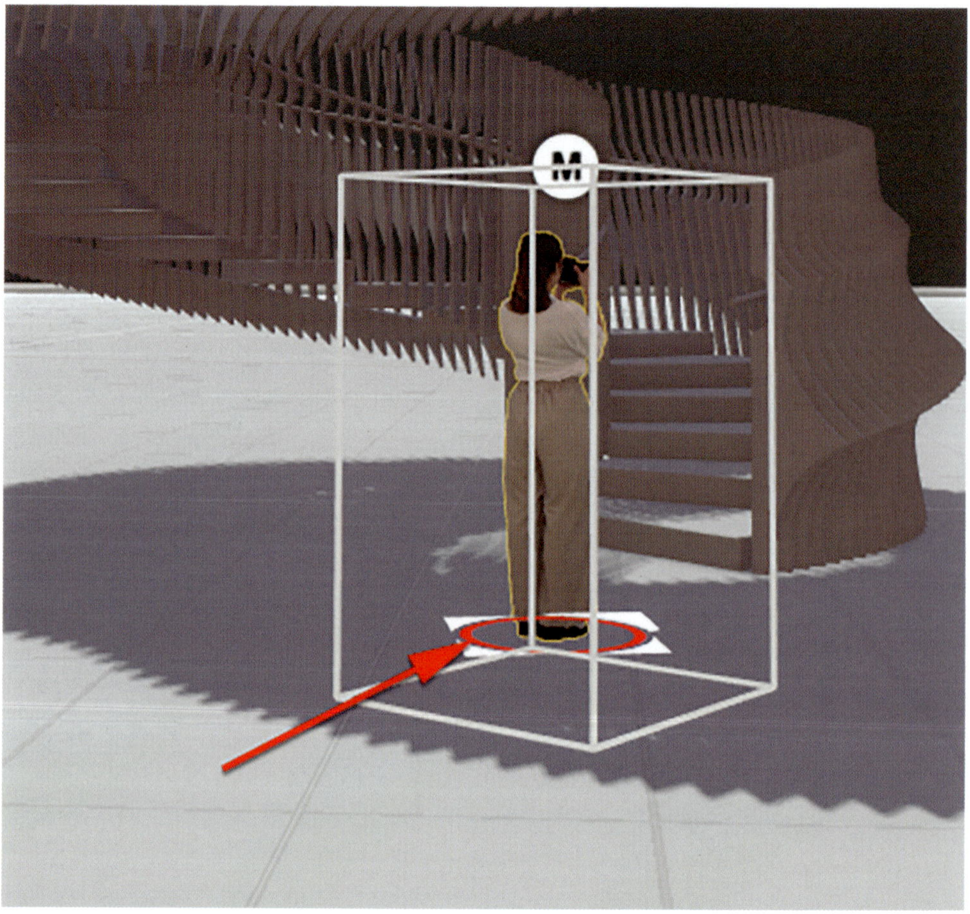

Rotate icon highlighted in red

Users can also play the clip icon to check the 4D animated character and/or capture a specific frame of the animation.

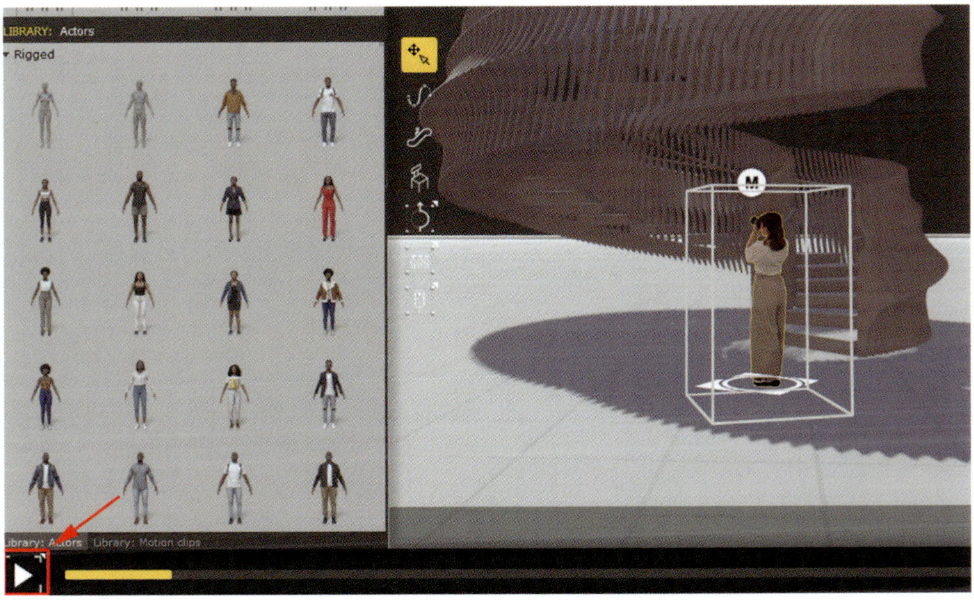

Users can play the clip icon to check a specific frame

The following step is to begin adding rigged people in the distance, motion clips and Walkway tool. To start, type in, Rigged, in the Library search box. The entire library of rigged people should appear. As mentioned earlier, rigged people are best to be used in the middle ground or background (in the distant). Not close to the camera, due to its lack of hyperrealism. 4D people are best for close-up shots.

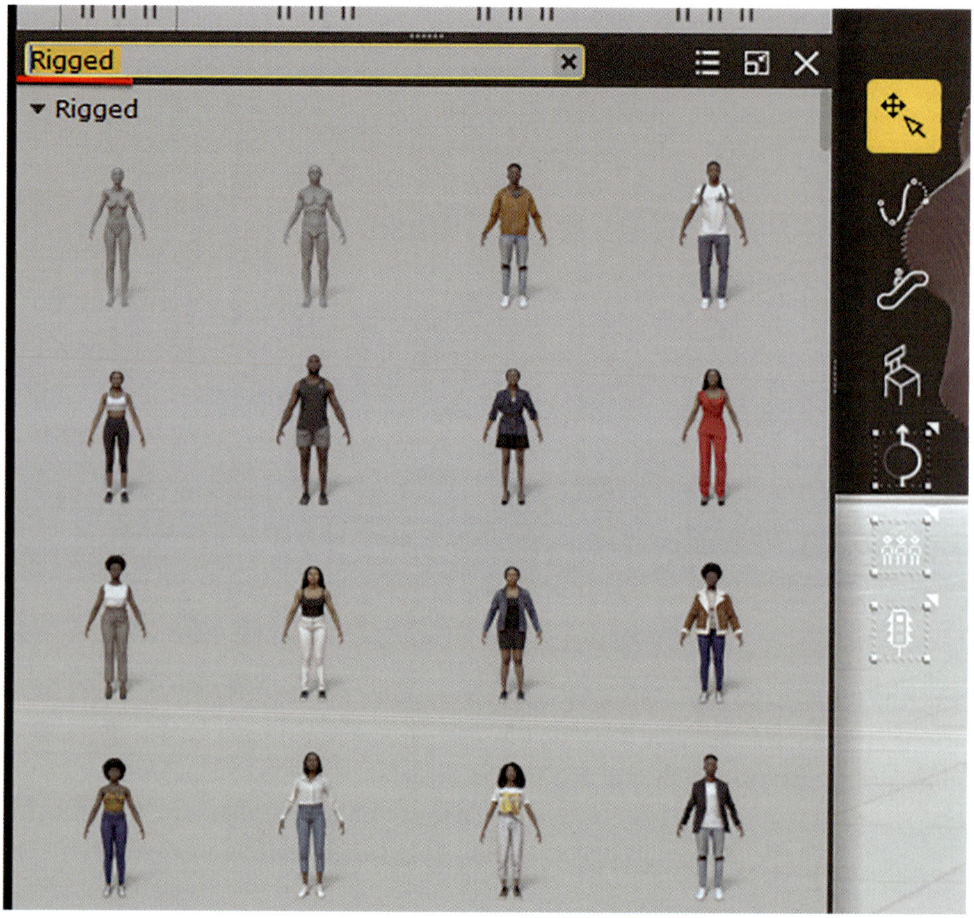

Type in, Rigged, in the Library search box

As previously done, drag and drop one of the rigged characters into the scene to create it.

Drag and drop one of the rigged characters into the scene to create it

The following step is to create a path for this 3d rigged character to walk on. To do so, select the Walkway tool and left click on the floor surface to create the first point.

Move the arrow further in to extend the path (move the mouse) and left again to create the second. A pathway should be created. Right click to exit creation.

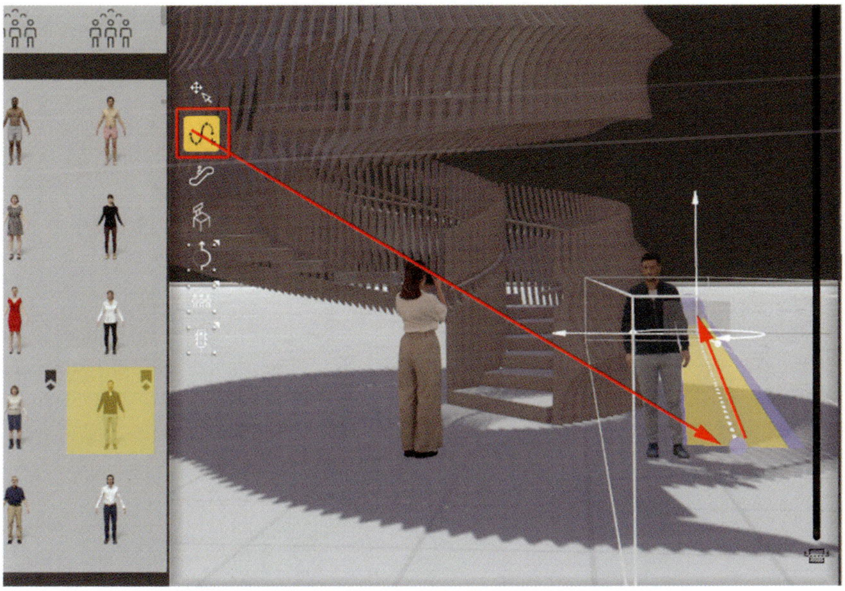

Use the walkway tool to create a path

NOTE

To add vertices to the pathway, select it and enable the Walkway tool again. An additional path should appear attached to the first one. After exiting the creation of the extended path (right click), use the mouse to select a specific vertex and move/edit it accordingly.

Next, select the rigged character and manually move it to the middle of the pathway, to automatically reposition the character to a walking position. The Character should automatically start walking, if the play button is clicked.

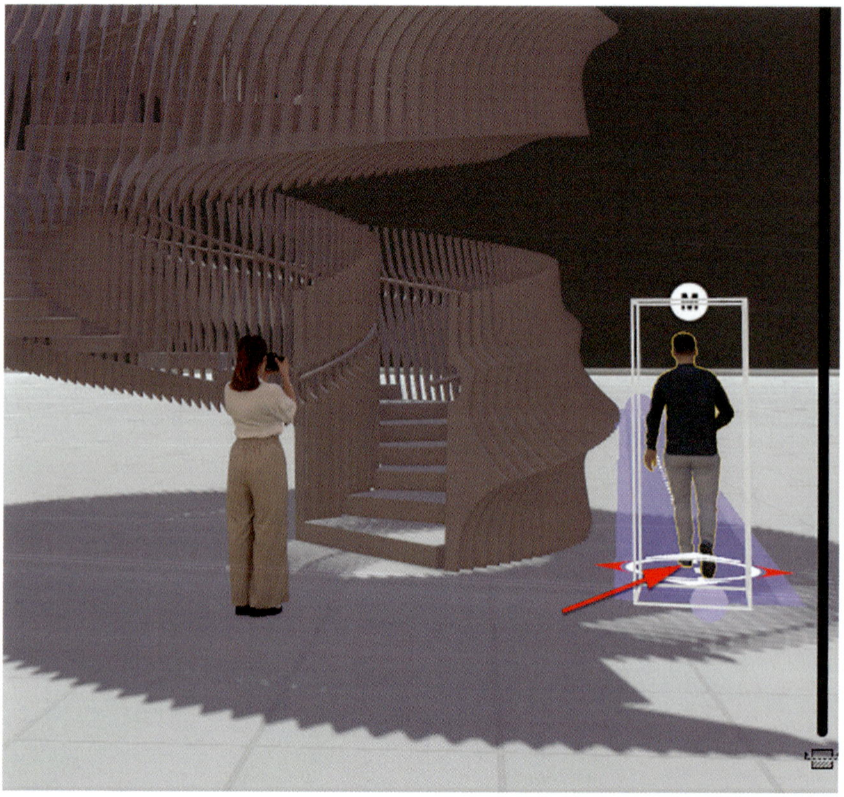

Rigged character moved to the walkway to automatically adjust to a walking position

Select a new rigged character from the library and drag and drop it in the scene to create it.

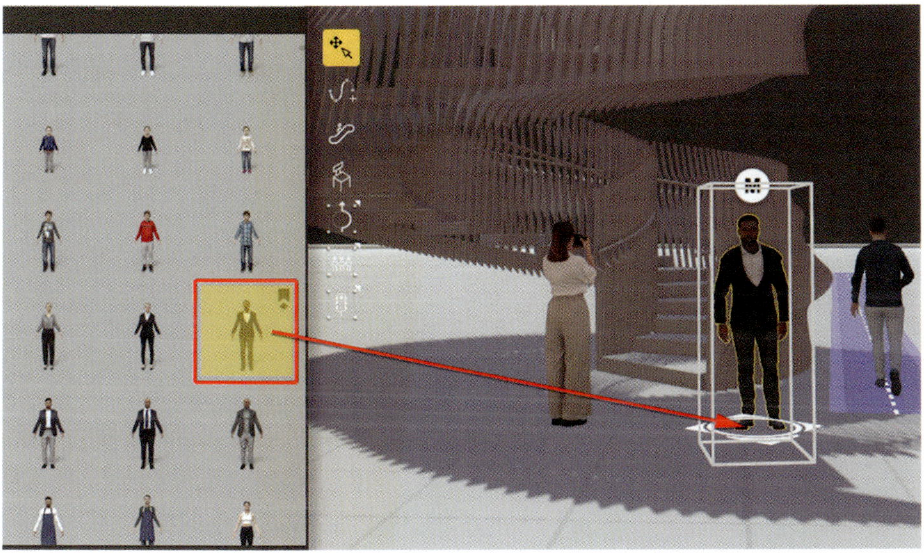

New rigged character created

Users can also drag and drop Motion clips into the rigged characters. Ensure the motion clip is dragged in precisely into the middle of the gizmo/character in order for the motion clip to work. Otherwise, users might be prompted with the Incompatible Category warning clip.

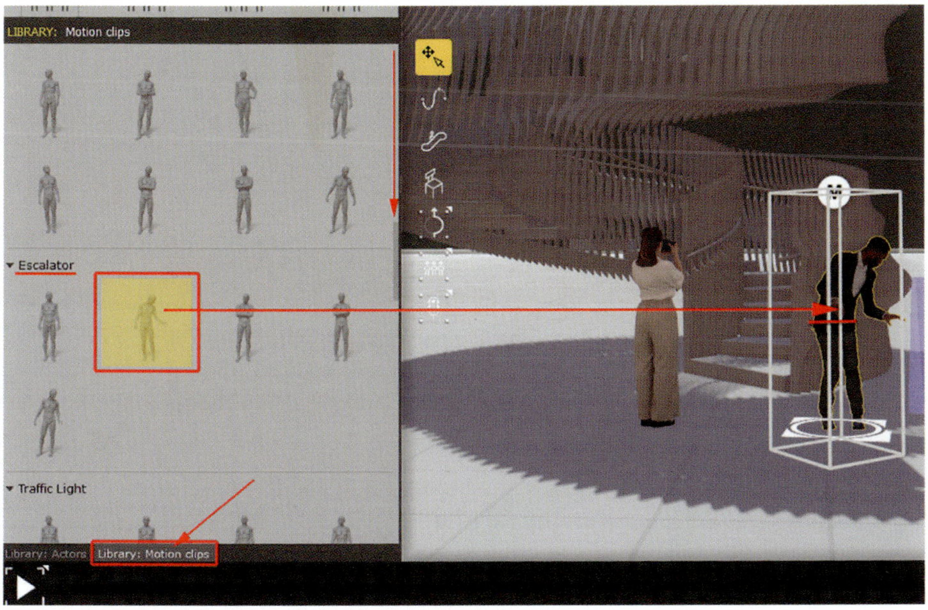

Drag and drop Motion clips into the rigged characters

NOTE

Locomotion Walk and Locomotion Run only work for characters linked to a walkway (Walkway tool). Otherwise, users will be prompted with the Incompatible Category warning clip.

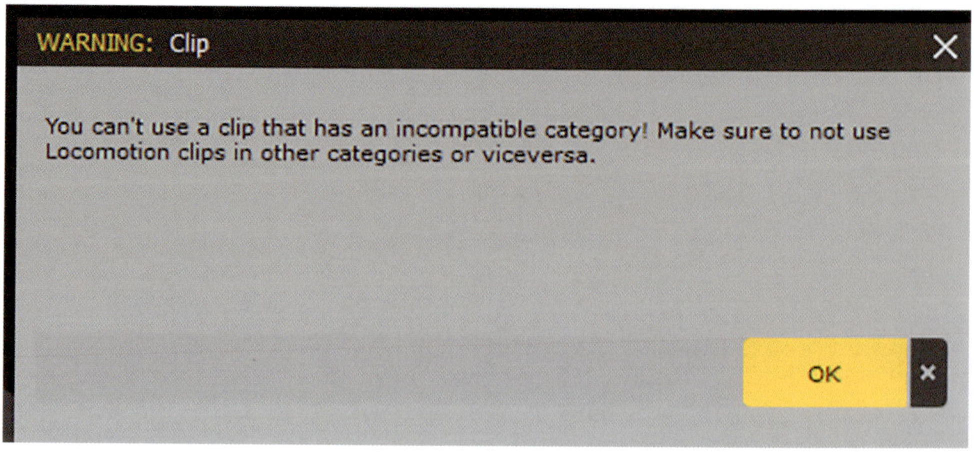

WARNING: Clip

While a rigged character linked to a walkway is automatically walking, users can still add clips from Locomotion Walk and Locomotion Run library into them. In addition, moving rigged characters can automatically detect and avoid collisions with other characters.

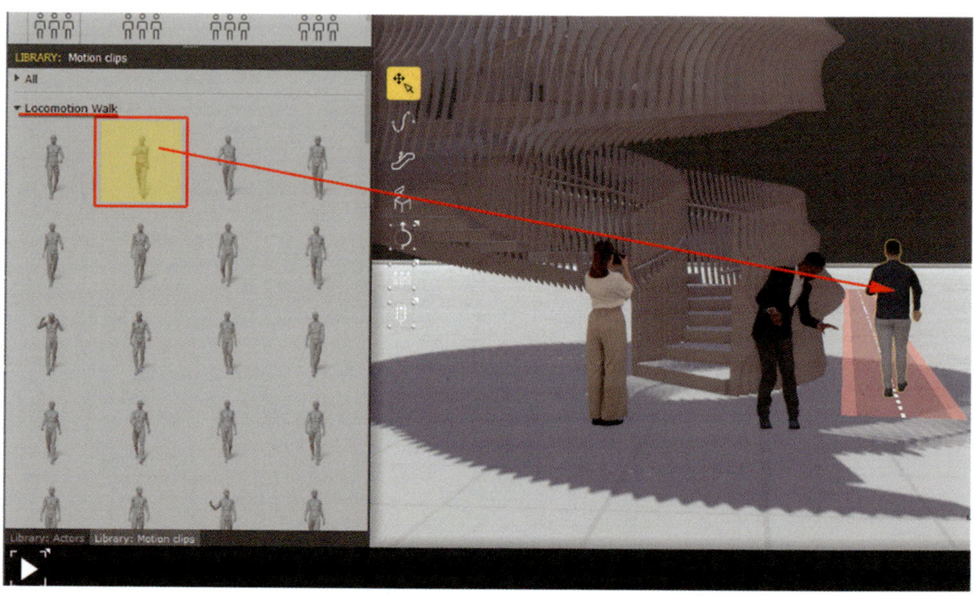

Add a Locomotion Walk clip to a walking rigged character

Also, to fit two or more characters on the same pathway, simply hover over either side of the pathway edges and begin expanding it once you see the tool to expand it.

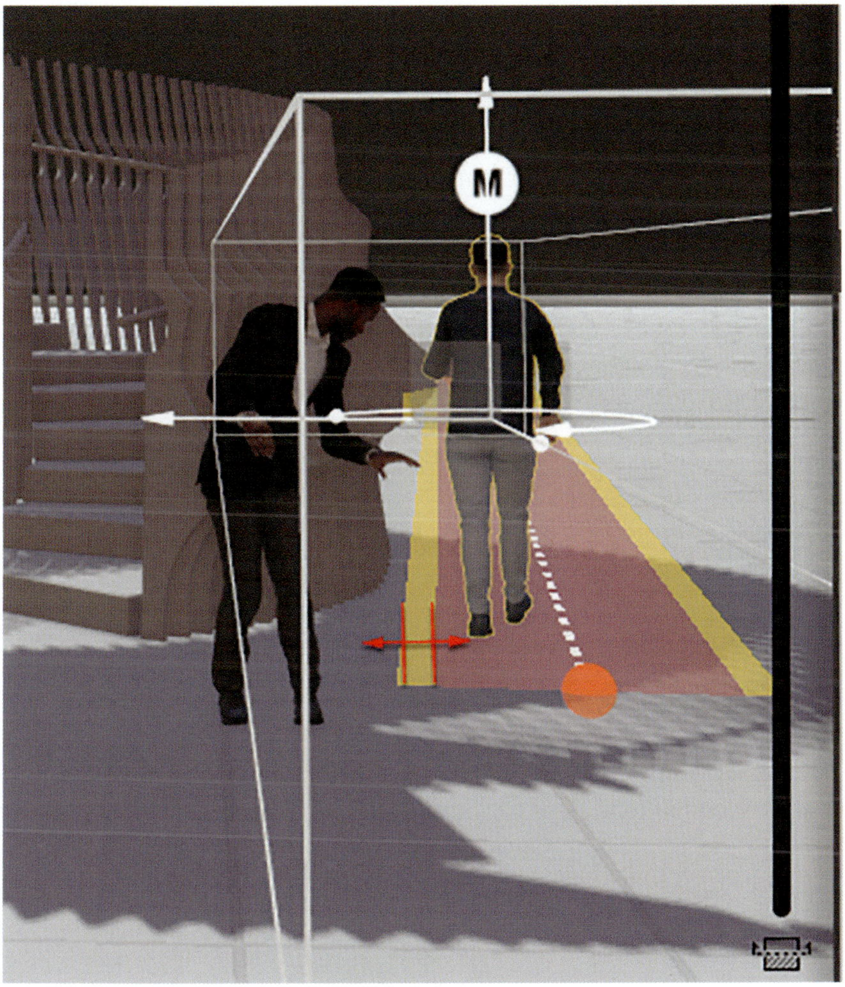

Expand the walkway edges to fit more rigged characters

Move and adjust both rigged characters to fit the newly extended walkway.

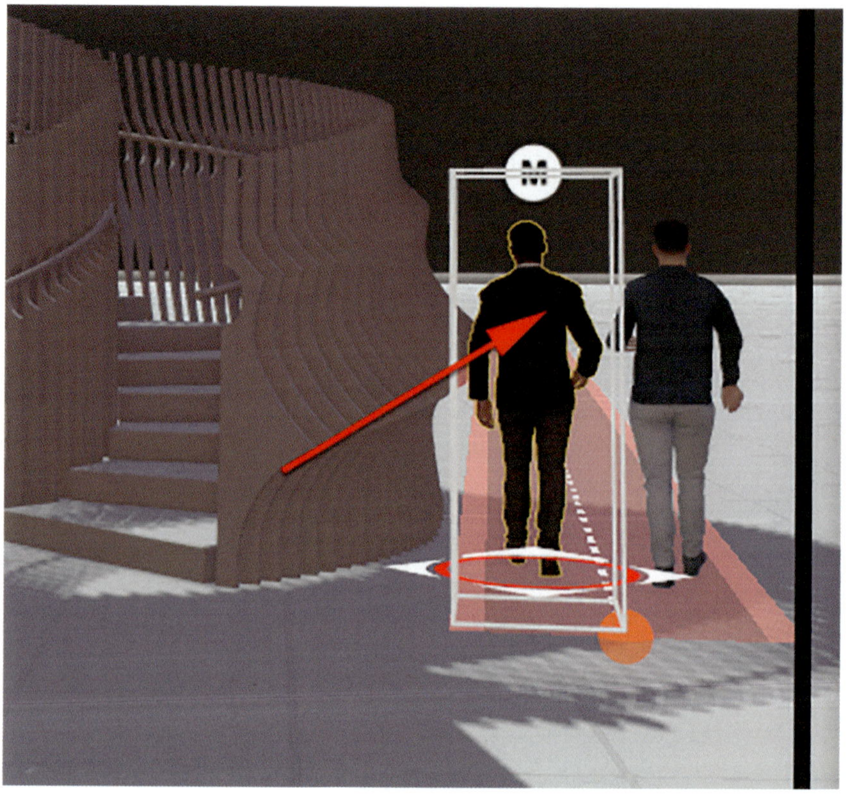

Newly extended walkway with both rigged characters

Similar techniques can be used to quickly implement the Escalator tool, Table tool, Avoid area tool, Area tool and Traffic light tool.

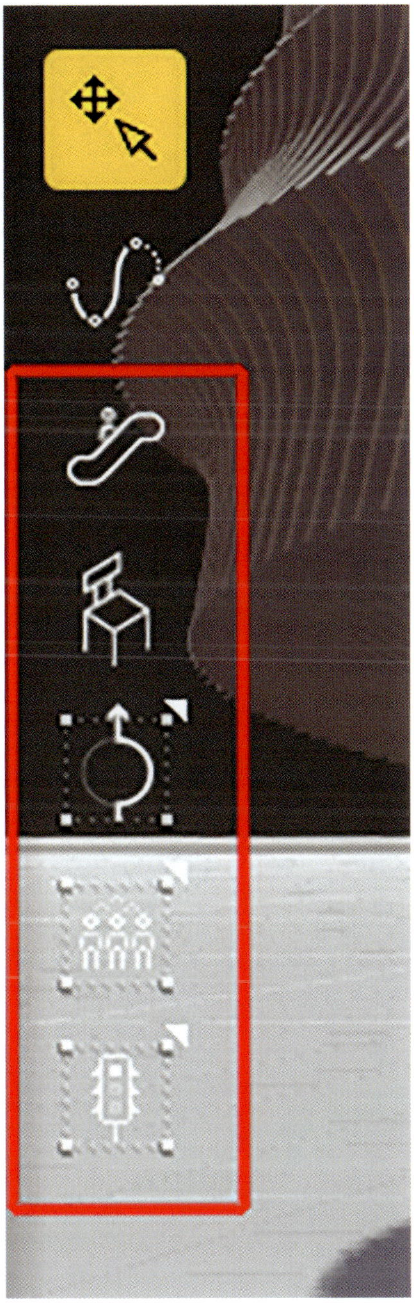

Escalator, Table, Avoid area, Area and Traffic light tool

In addition, users also have the Preset Templates, to quickly help set up the tools previously mentioned. Users can set up, create and add new templates to this library.

Preset Templates

The remaining tools are self-explanatory, especially when there's a description for every toolset when users hover over them. Save the latest updates (Ctrl+S).

Tool description

In addition, please visit https://docs.axyz-design.com/ for more details about workflows.

The following step is to switch to 3DS Max while the file is still open to check the live updates.

Once in 3DS Max, if the anima® files are not updating properly, simply go back to anima, File>Projects>Save. In addition, go to File>Scenes>Save.

The 3DS Max file should immediately start blinking and updating live.

File>Projects>Save

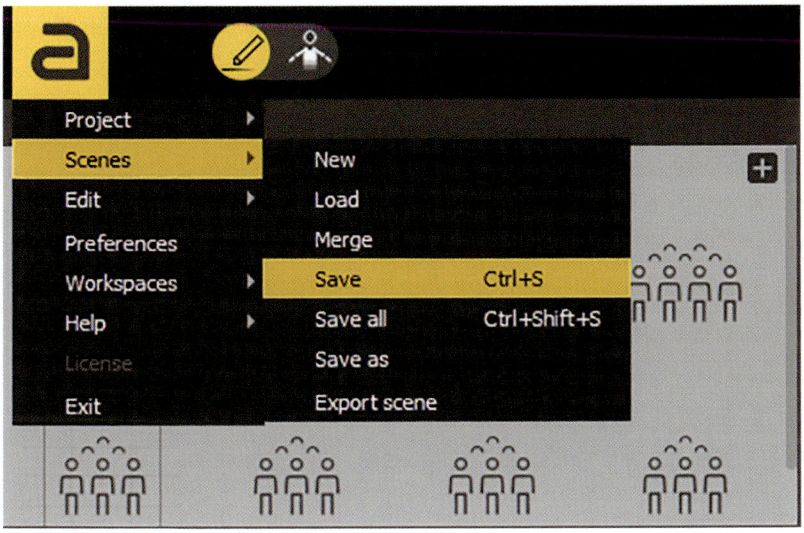

File>Scenes>Save

The newly added anima® people should be updated in 3DS Max. Select the animaScene001 icon (Helper) again and open the Modify panel.

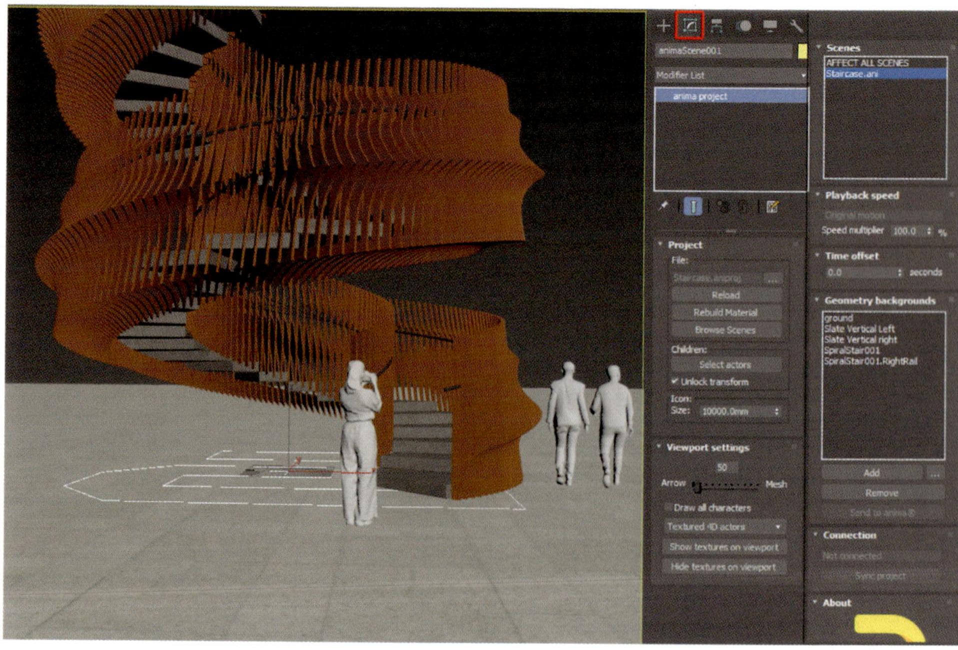

anima® Scene001 icon Modify parameters

Most of its parameters are self-explanatory. However, let's go through some of its main functionalities and toggles:

File: This toggle allows users to locate and load an anima® scene project, by clicking on its toggle.

Reload: This function allows the user to Reload/update the anima® scene project loaded in the File toggle, by clicking on its button.

Rebuild material: This function allows users to automatically convert the anima® materials and shaders into the rendering engine being used, if incompatible. To do so, first change the rendering engine and click on this button to quickly/automatically rebuild the material to reflect the loaded rendering engine.

Browse scenes: This function allows users to click, browse and open any pre-saved anima® project scenes.

Unlock transform: If disabled, this function allows users to move/rotate the animaScene001 icon.

Textured 4D actors: This function allows users to choose between Textured 4D actors or Colored 4D actors to be displayed in the viewport. Textured 4D actors option is chosen by default.

Show textures on viewport: This function allows textures to be displayed in the viewport, by clicking on its button.

Hide textures on viewport: This function allows textures to be hidden in the viewport, by clicking on its button.

Speed multiplier: This function allows users to increase or decrease its default speed, by typing in values. Default value, 100%.

Geometry backgrounds: This section allows the user to Add, Remove and send to anima® new 3DS Max geometry. This tool is quite useful to update new 3DS Max geometry interacting with anima® models.

Add: This button allows users to click and select objects to be added to the Geometry background list. To use it, simply click on its button and select objects in the scene.

Remove: This button allows users to select any of the listed objects in the Geometry background list and remove it, by clicking this button.

Send to anima®: This button only becomes live (Not grayed out) when new objects are added to the Geometry background. When live, this button is used to send new Geometry to anima®, by clicking on it.

Sync project: This button allows users to sync 3DS Max with anima®, by clicking on its button.

Click on the Show textures on viewport button to make the textures visible in the viewport.

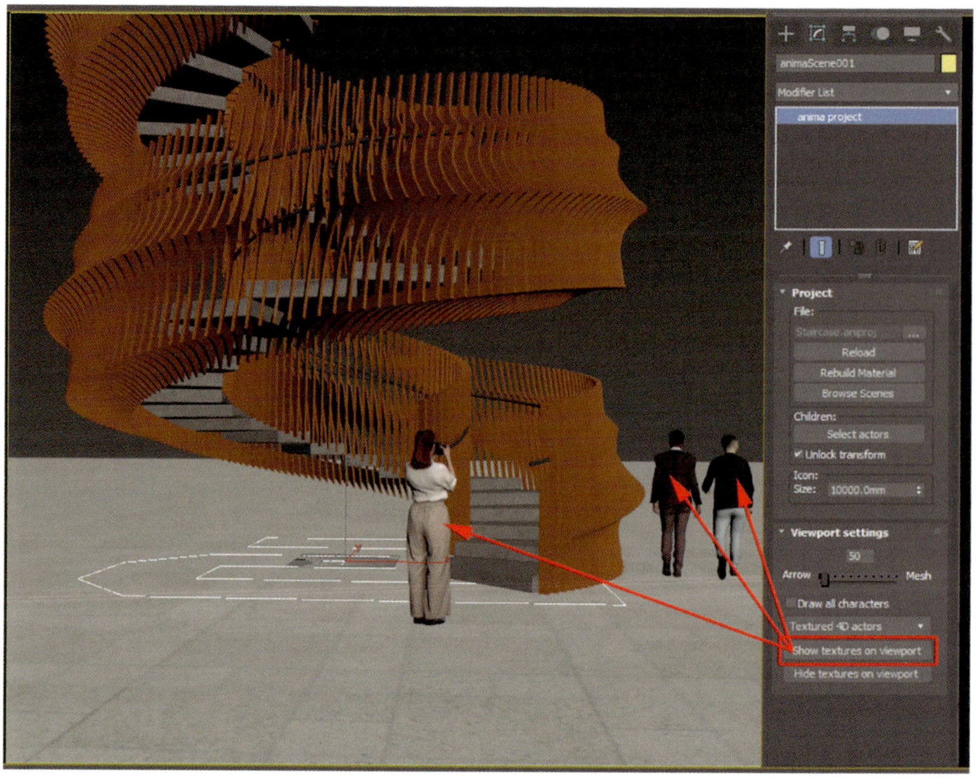

Show textures on viewport function enabled

To capture a specific frame, click on the Time Configuration toggle and increase the End Time to 200.

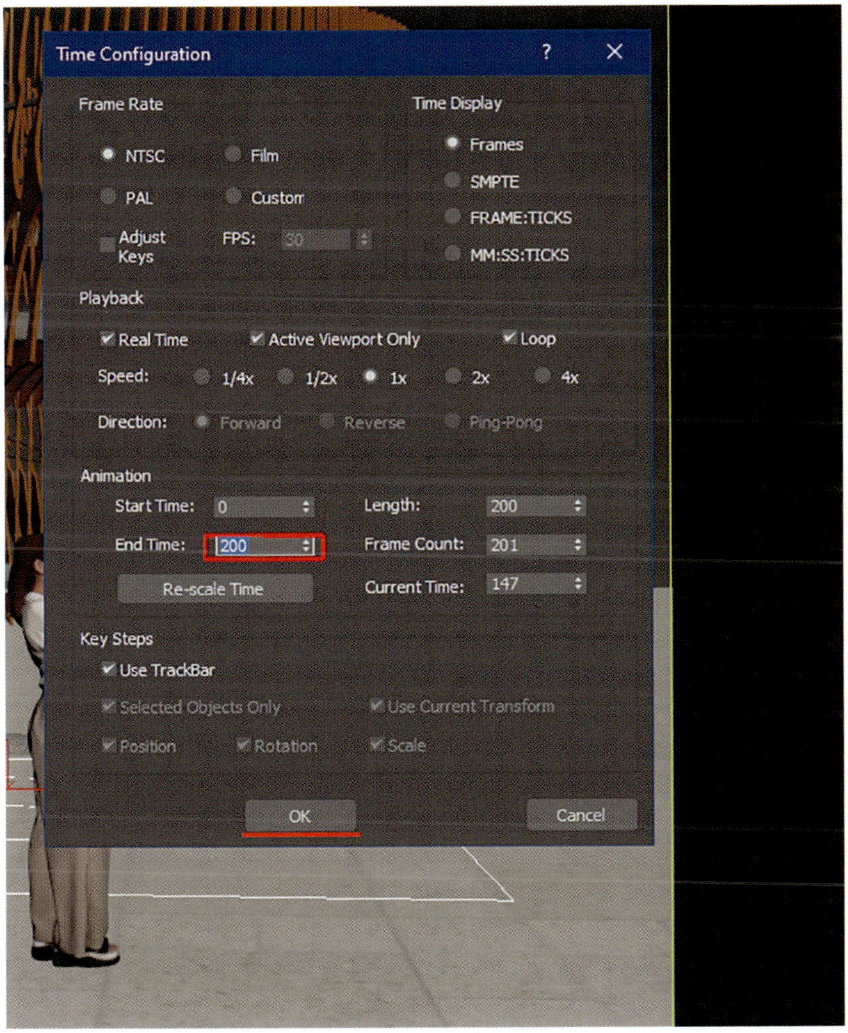

Click on the Time Configuration toggle and increase the End Time to 200

Frame 98 seems to work the best. However, feel free to try different frames. Next, disable the Unlock transform function and move the anima® characters close to the camera.

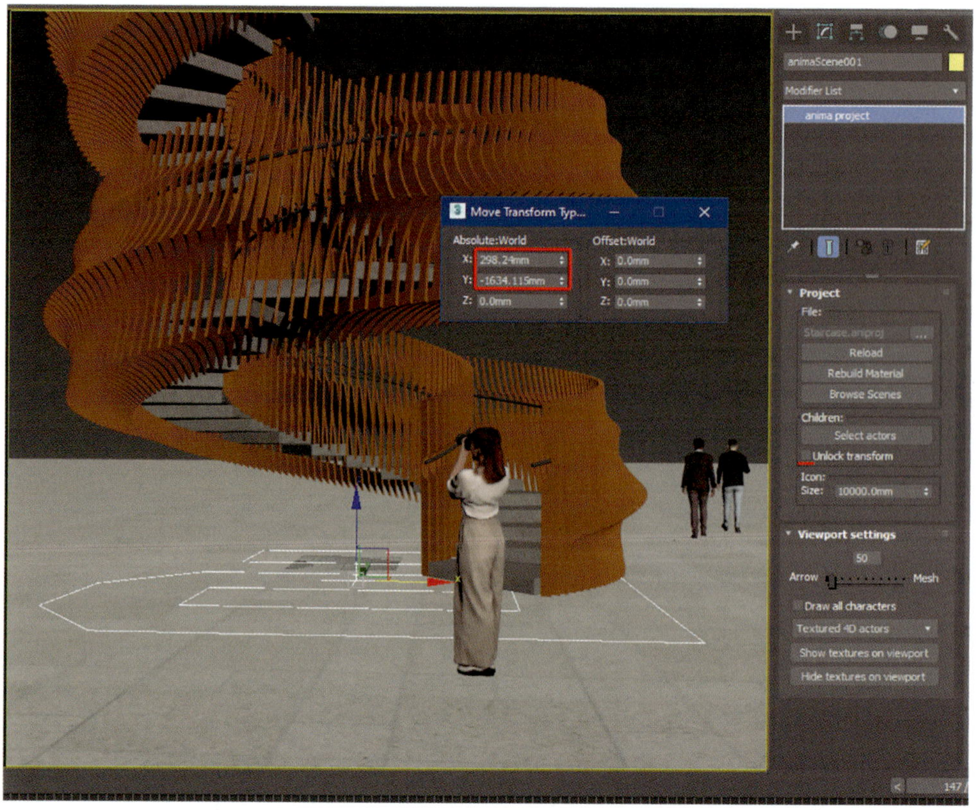

Disable the Unlock transform function and move the anima characters close to the camera

To set up a realistic motion blur, first, select the anima® characters in the scene, right click and choose the Object Properties.

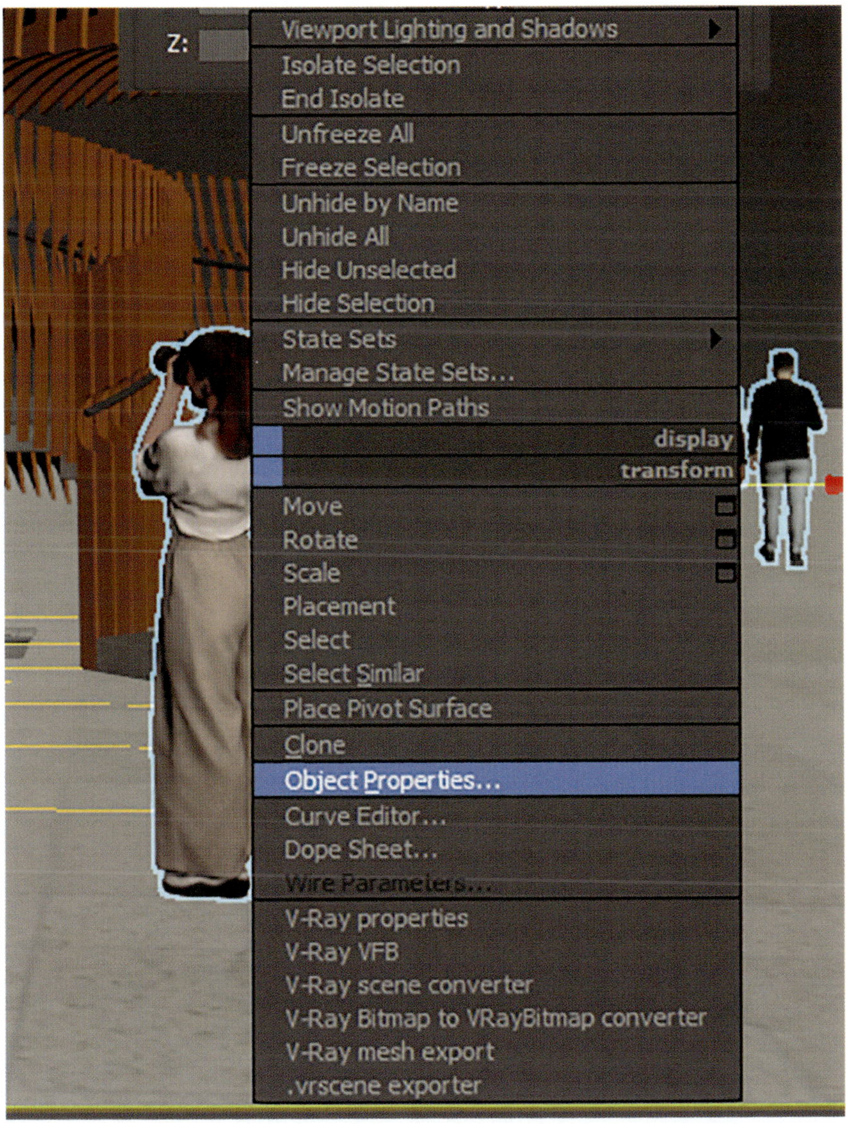

Select anima® characters, right click and choose the Object Properties

Under Motion Blur group, choose the Image type, and set the Multiplier to 5.0.

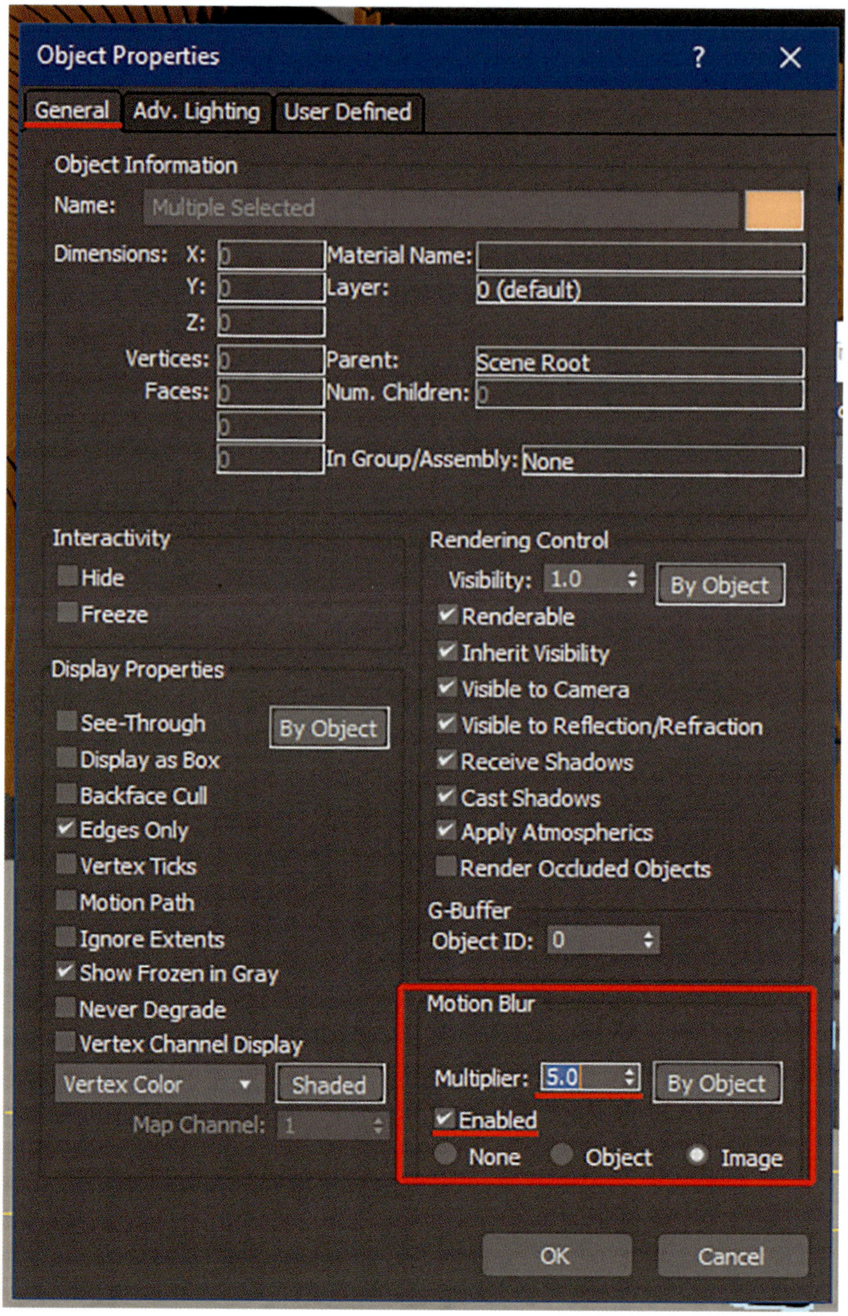

Choose the Motion Blur Image type, and set the Multiplier to 5.0

To set up motion blur globally, open the Render Setup dialog (F10). In the V-Ray tab, under Camera parameters, enable the Motion blur function and set the Duration (frames) to 4.0.

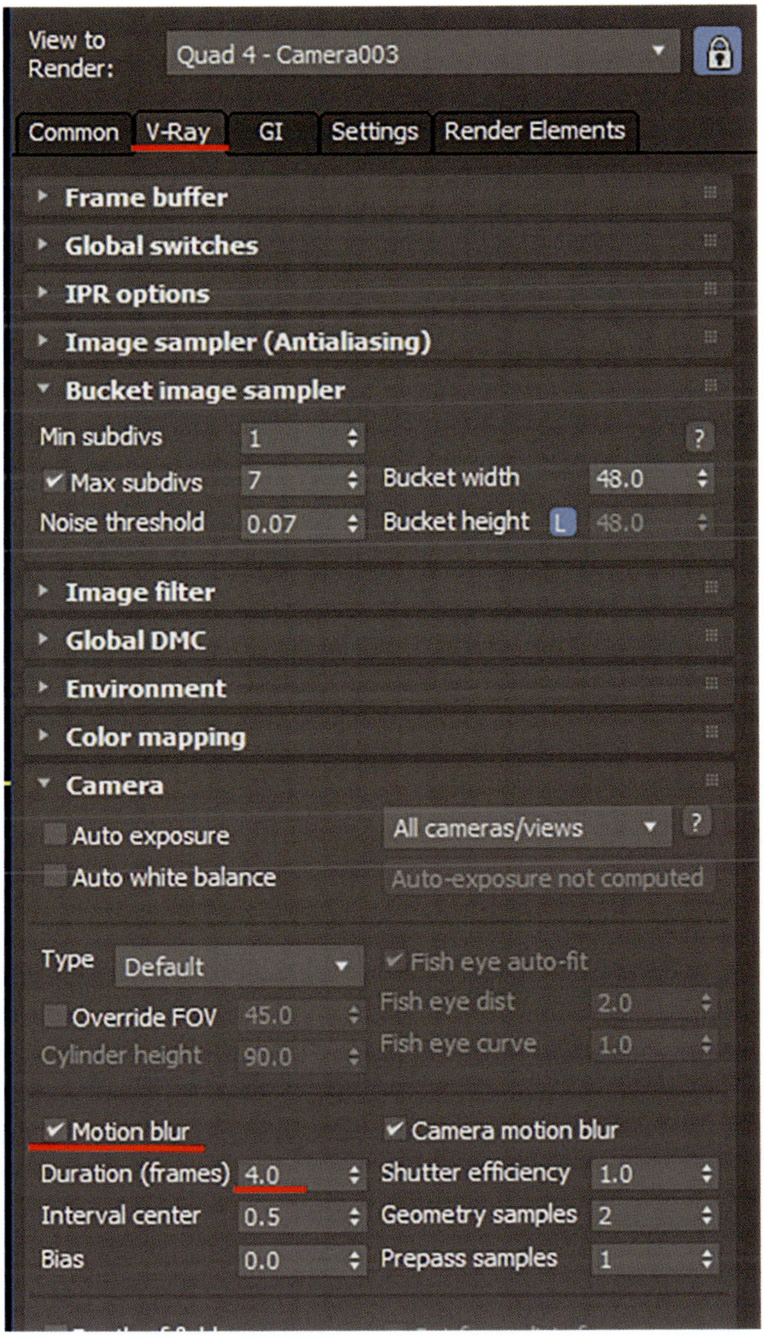

Enable the Motion blur function and set the Duration (frames) to 4.0

If you prefer to control the motion blur via a V-Ray Camera, simply decrease the Shutter speed value under Aperture parameters, until you're happy with the motion blur results.

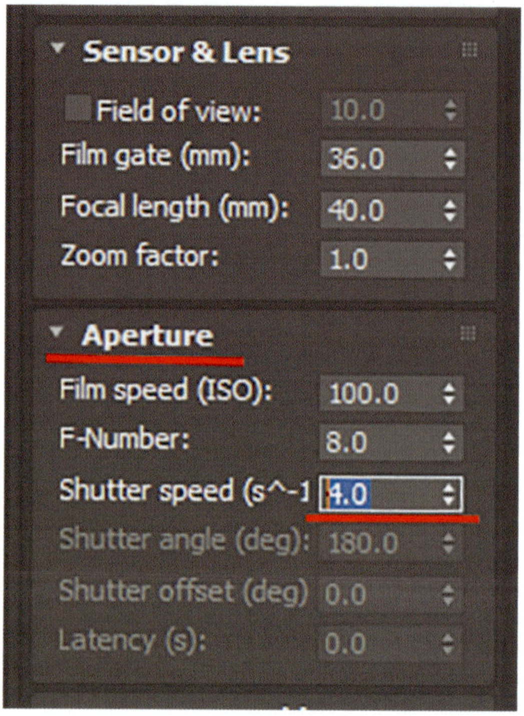

Decrease the Shutter speed Aperture If you prefer to control the motion blur via V-Ray Camera

Final render with anima people and realistic motion blur

AXYZ design panel also allows users to quickly drag and drop anima® models directly from 3DS Max. To do so, simply click on the AXYZ design toolbar and choose to Quick Drop.

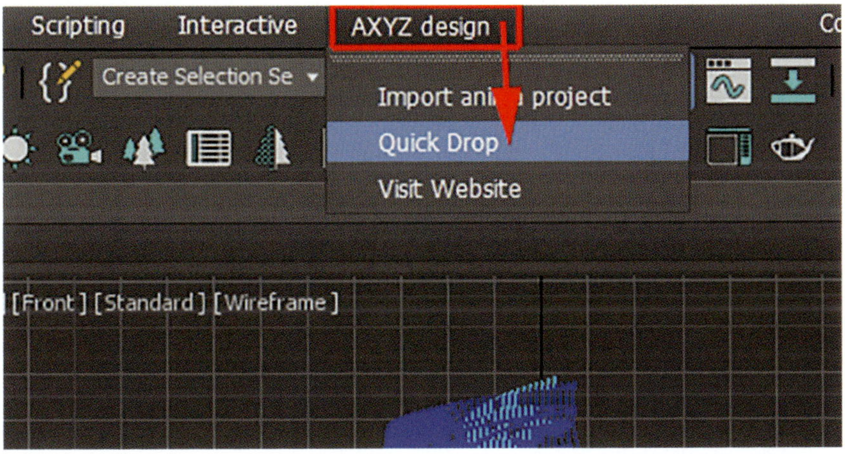

Click on the AXYZ design toolbar and choose to Quick Drop

To create a model, simply select one from the AXYZ design library, followed by dragging and dropping it in the viewport. The first left click in the viewport is to automatically detect a surface and place the model in the scene. The second click is to move the character anywhere in the scene.

Right click to exit creation.

6 anima® from AXYZ design®

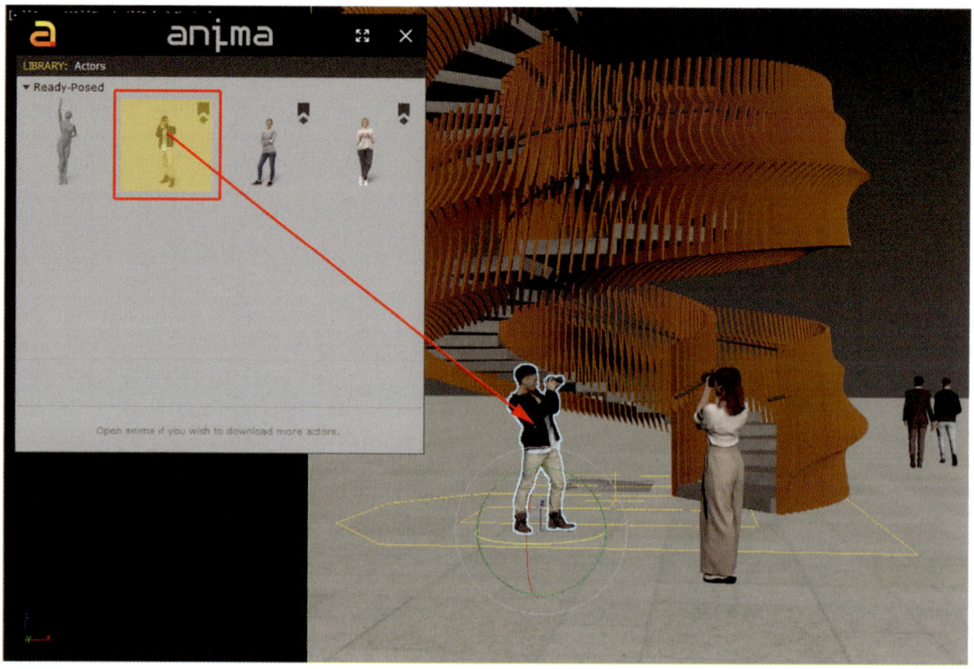

anima® model created directly in 3DS Max viewport

Upcoming anima® 5 new features:

The new animation engine is solely based on A.I. (Artificial Intelligence). This new feature will correlate to better and more natural interactions between characters. Some of these interactions will include, climbing stairs, crowded places, running and much more.

anima® 5 will also introduce new 4D Walking models, in both anima® software and AXYZ design library panel inside 3D applications.

Animation clips will now include Closed loops in paths.

In the plug-ins, there will be new per-scene gizmos, to enable users to link animated objects from 3D applications such as 3DS Max, Maya and Cinema4D, and create groups of animated people inside vehicles such as trains, cars, boats and buses.

The updated Quick Drop panel inside 3d applications will now have a vaster library, and enable users to directly download 4D animated and ambient models.

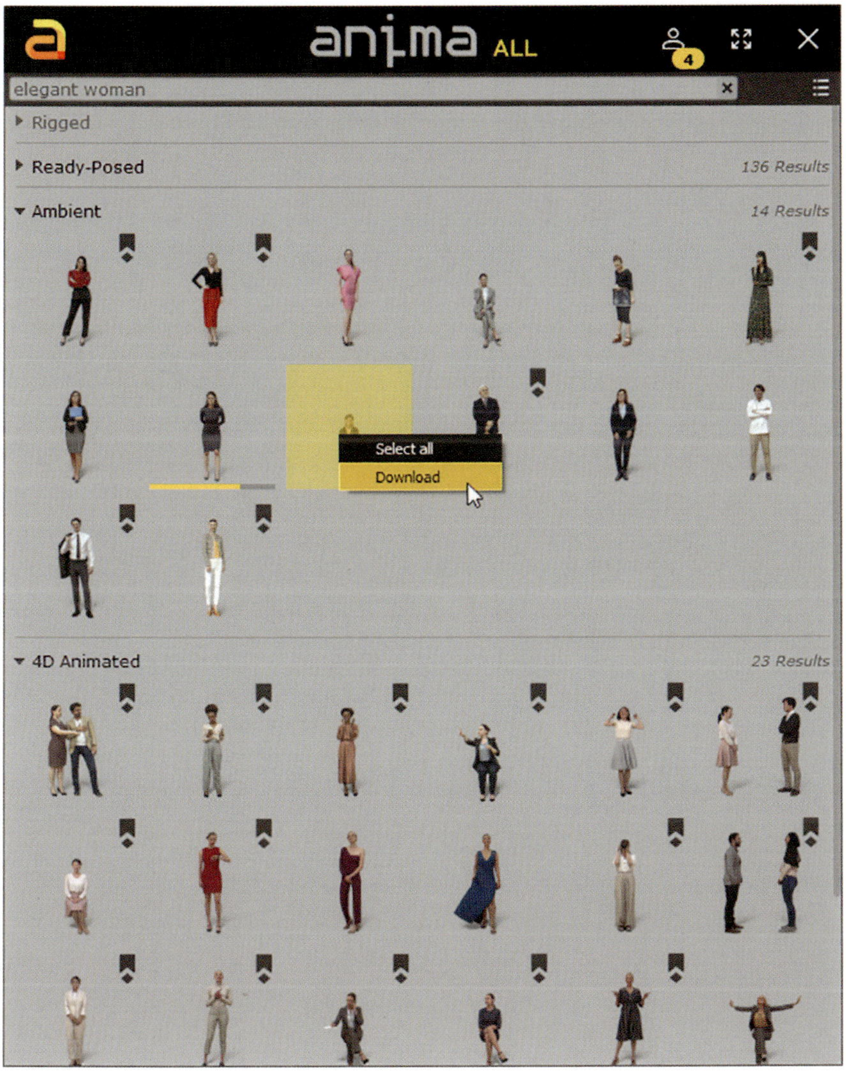

Quick Drop new panel in anima® 5

7

Daylight Scene Pre-Production

7 Daylight Scene Pre-Production

Client Brief

For this project, the main brief was to create a daylight shot of the atrium, with the main camera focused on its main feature, the staircase.

Finally, the overall lighting should help highlight the main staircase.

Photo References and/or Mood Board

To help convey ideas and aspirations, designers and architects often provide users with reference images.

In addition, the studio/artists choose specific photo references to help conceptualize the overall lighting and "mood" of the final render.

It's worth noting that most designers and architects supply the studio/artists with their own design mood board/s depicting their furniture, landscape and material samples.

Some of the chosen furniture can be found on the manufacturer's website, or, from websites such as ever motion and 3d sky.

Alternatively, if/when required, users will create bespoke 3d models.

DOI: 10.1201/9781315770802-7

Camera & Lighting ideas

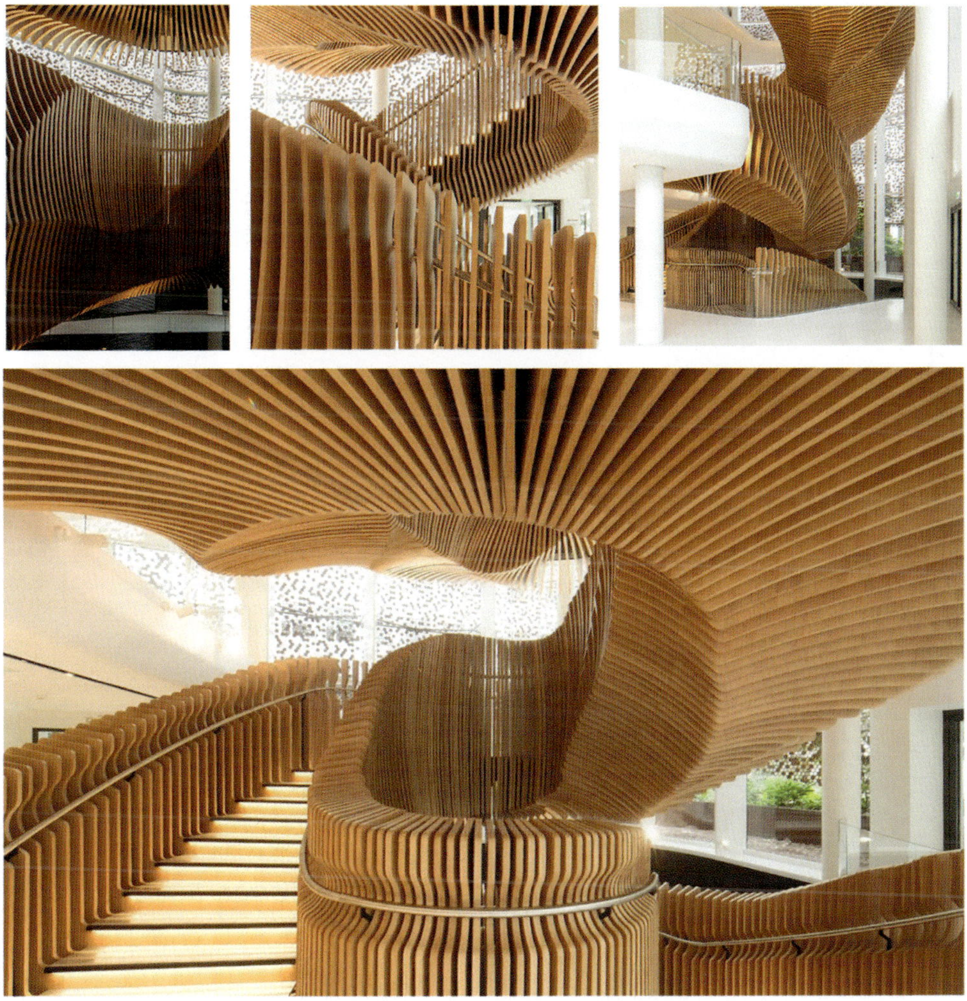

Photo references for camera, lighting and color depicting a daylight interior scene with a staircase

Photo reference of wood material

Photo reference of concrete material

Photo reference of metal material

Photo reference of floor material

Photo reference of glass material

Conclusion

The pre-production process is vital to sign off key camera angles and the scene composition as a whole. Also, the studio/artist often uses this process to iron out the art direction, materials, colors and much more prior to entering the production phase.

8

Scene, Camera and Lights

8 Scene, Camera and Lights

Introduction

This chapter will take users through the standard process of setting up the overall scene diligently, along with the camera composition and the overall lighting.

The initial steps described here will be vital in ensuring the subsequent steps are successful.

The chapter will start by adopting the file's unit scale, Show Safe Frame, Edge Faces, Units Setup, Preferences, Gamma and LUT, Files, Configure Viewports, V-Ray Image filter, Color mapping and other important settings.

It will continue by creating and setting the VRay camera accordingly, setting the Render Output Size, the VRaySun object, VRaySky, Improved Sky parameters, V-Ray Viewport IPR, setting up the VRaySun direction, VRayLightMix render element, Lookup Table parameters, V-Ray disc lights and much more.

Setting Up the Scene

This chapter assumes that the Custom UI and Defaults Switcher are already set to Max.vray as previously suggested in Chapter 2.

As such, the assigned renderer and materials loaded should be V-Ray 5 by default.

Let's start by opening the file under the name of Staircase Atrium_Start.max

If prompted with the Units Mismatch dialog, choose to Adopt the File's Unit Scale

DOI: 10.1201/9781315770802-8

File Load: Units Mismatch with Adopt the File's Unit Scale enabled

To ensure the framing in the viewport is coherent with what is rendered, click on the Perspective text, and choose the option to Show Safe Frames (Shift+F).

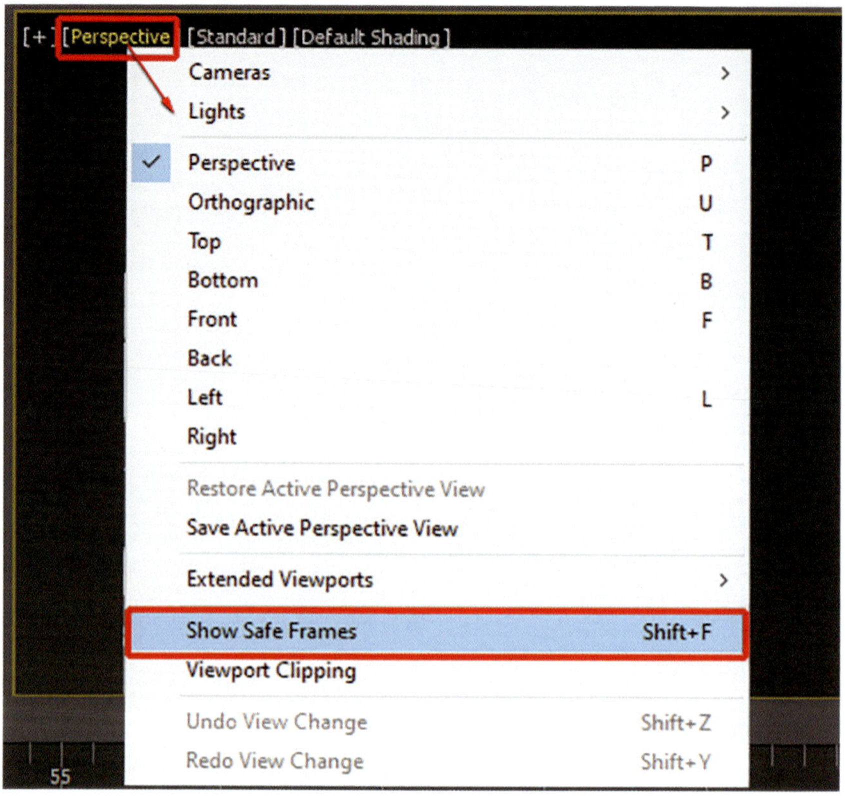

Perspective viewport with the option to Show Safe Frames

Also, to help distinguish different objects in the shaded viewport, simply click on the Default Shading text, and choose the Edged Faces option from the list.

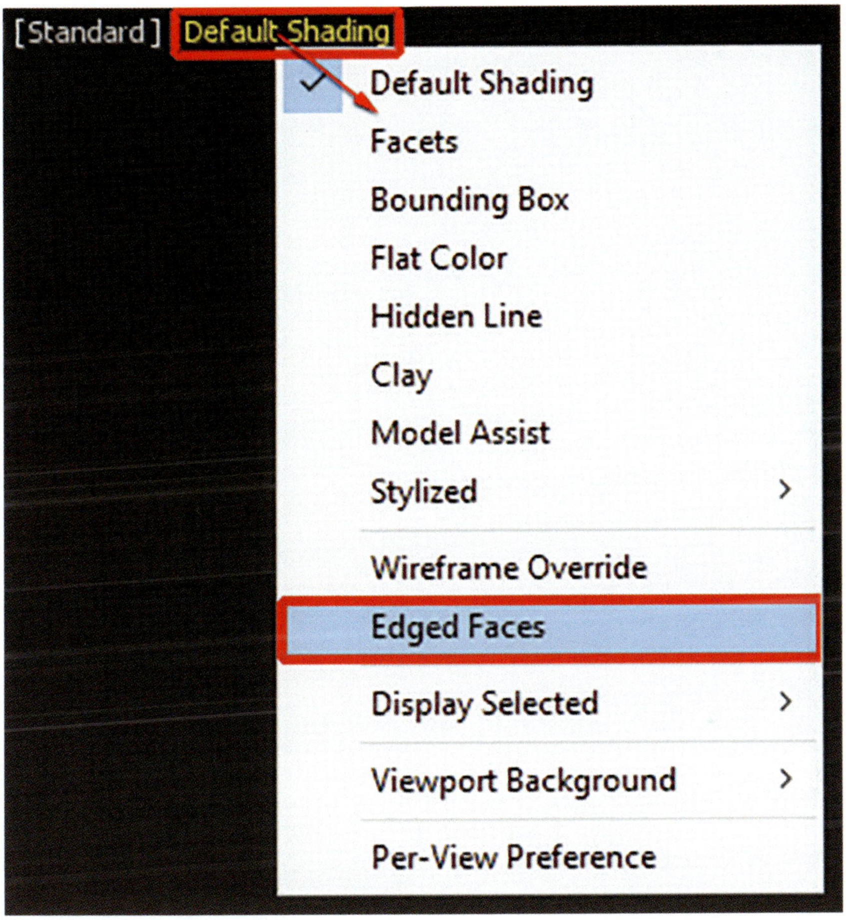

Viewport Default Shading with the Edged Faces option chosen

The Display Unit Scale of this scene was set to Metric/millimeters. And the System Unit Setup was set for 1 Unit to be equal to 1 cm.

The Display Unit Scale doesn't affect the scene but only displays the file's metric system in the viewport.

The System Unit Setup is utterly important, and controls the size of objects in scene.

Before starting to model and/or create lights in a scene, ensure to have these parameters set up properly and accordingly.

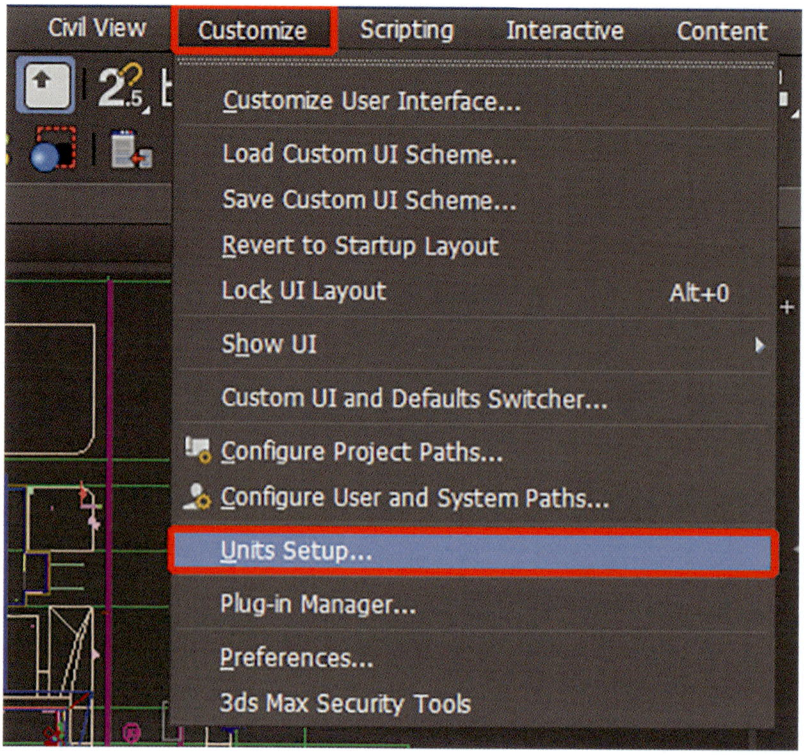

Customize toolbar clicked with Units Setup chosen

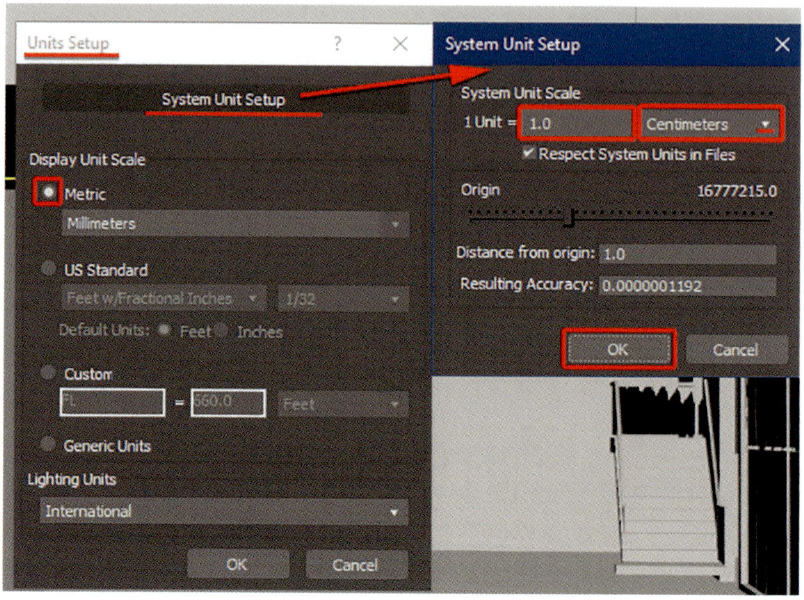

Units Setup dialog with System Unit Setup set to Centimeters

Also, go to the Customize toolbar and choose the Preferences option.

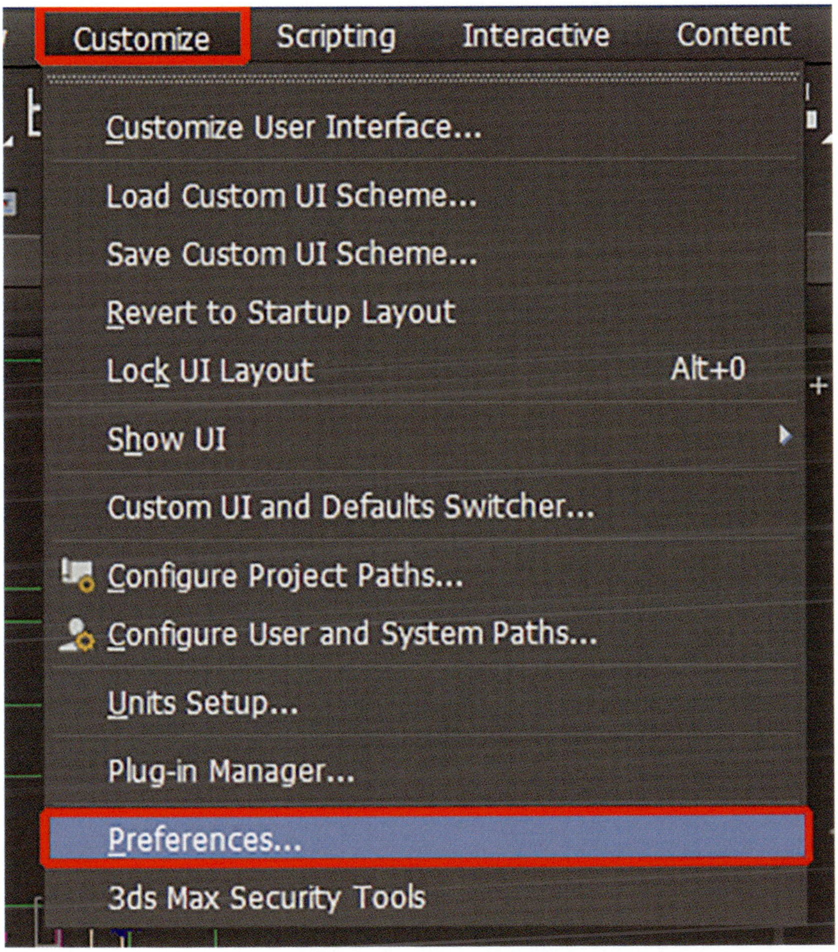

Customize toolbar clicked with Preferences option chosen

Under Gamma and LUT tab, turn on the Enable Gamma/LUT Correction, and set it to 2.2.

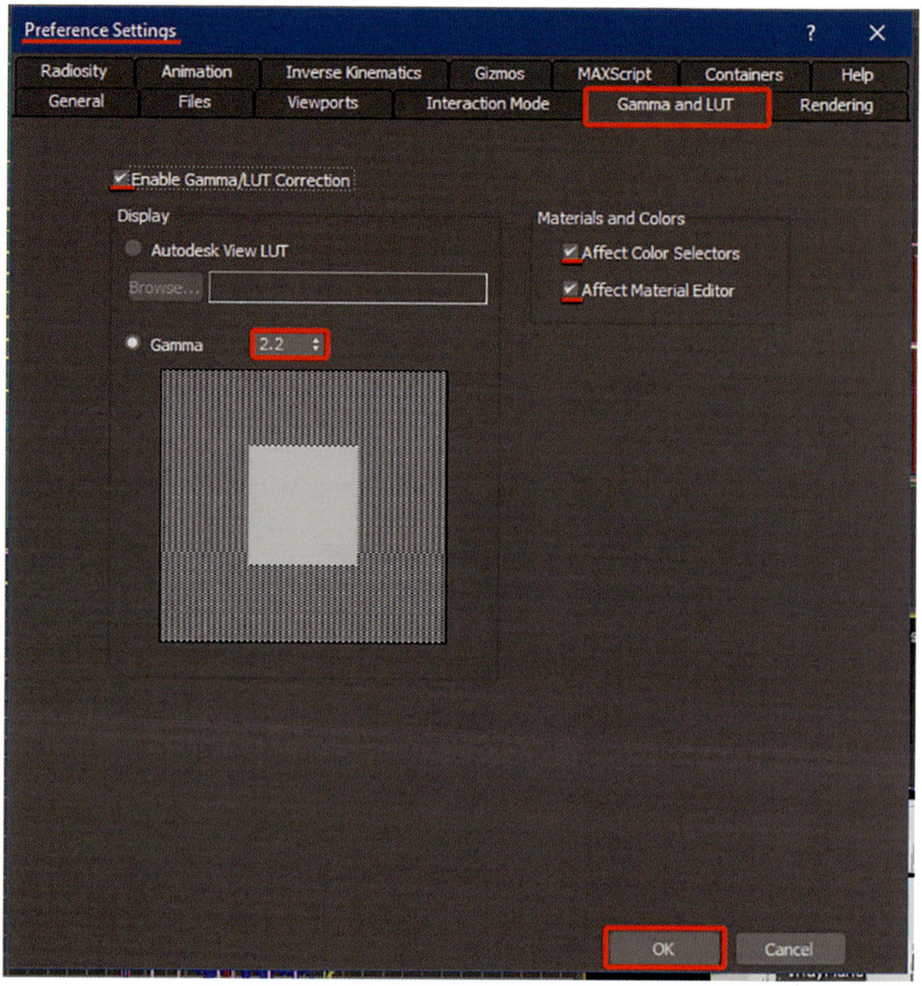

Preferences dialog with Gamma and LUT tab set to 2.2

Under Files tab, if you happen to be working on a large file that's taking too long to save, you can increase the Backup Interval (minutes) to 30 or higher and choose to Compress on Save.

Compressed Max files are automatically reduced to half or less of their original size when saved.

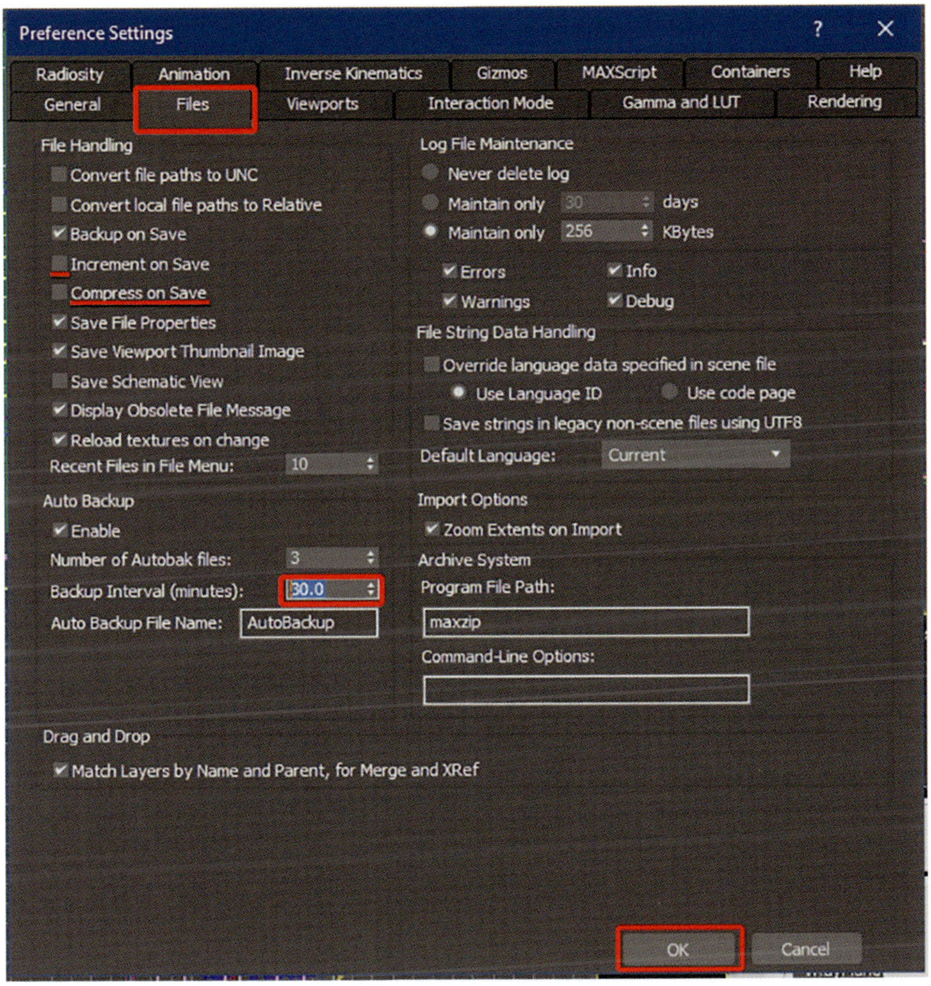

Preferences dialog with Files Tab set for 30 minutes Backup Interval

Under General tab, increase the Scene Undo Levels to about 500. This will give you the flexibility to undo (Ctrl+Z) up to 500 levels, if required.

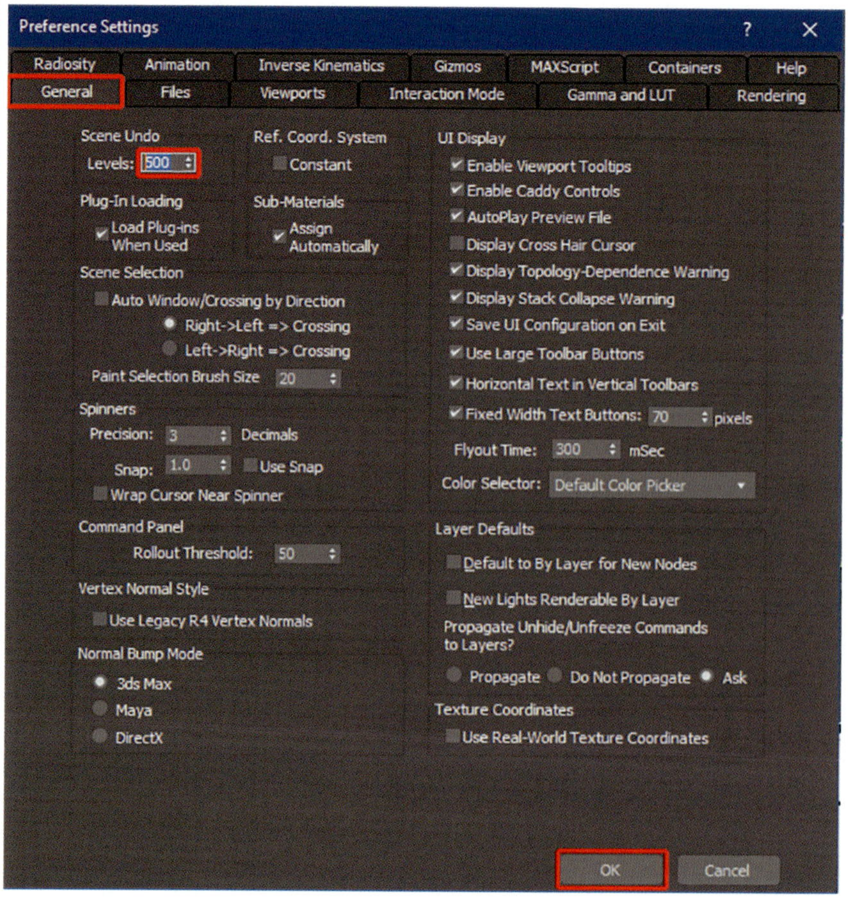

Preferences dialog with General tab set to Undo 500 Levels

To configure the viewports, simply click on the + text and choose to Configure Viewports.

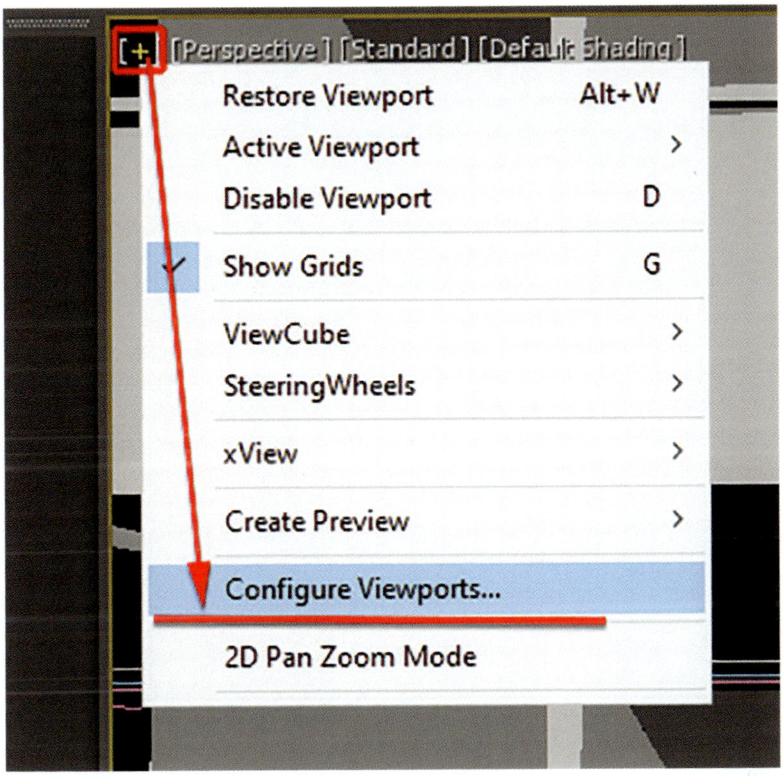

Perspective viewport with Configure Viewports option chosen

Under the Layout tab, select a suitable viewport layout. Users can also right click on a specific layout and choose the viewport..

NOTE

When creating the sunlight object, it's best to choose a four-viewport layout

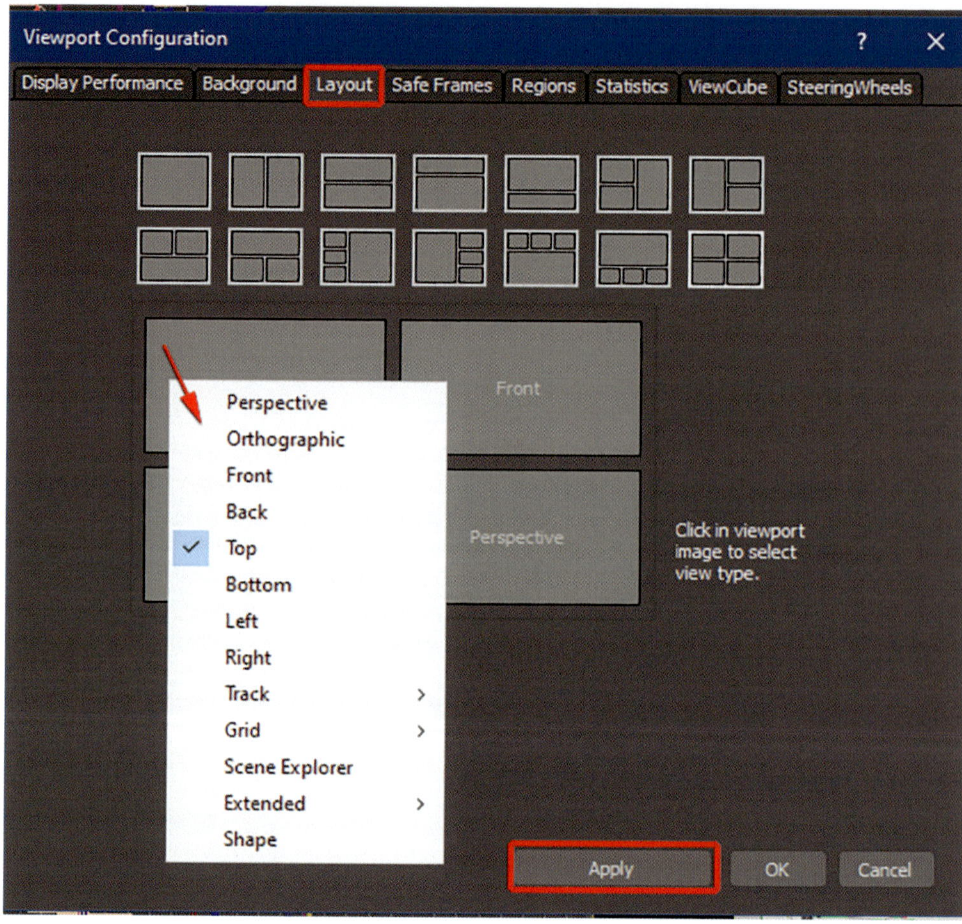

Viewport Configuration dialog with Layout tab set to Top

The Display Performance is frequently used to set the display quality of Textures in the viewport, etc.

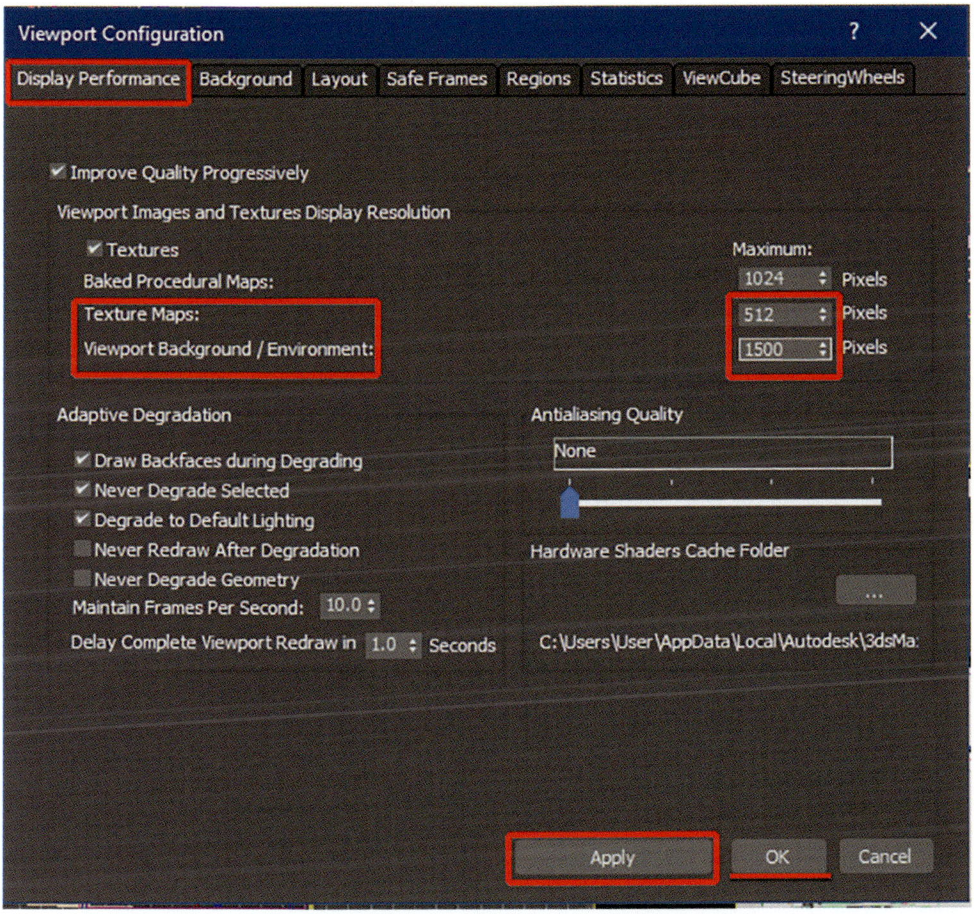

Viewport Configuration dialog with Display Performance tab parameters

Next, open the Render Setup dialog (F10). Under V-Ray tab, set the Image filter as VRayLanczosFilter.

Under Color mapping parameters, set its Type to Exponential. This will reduce overly burnt areas in the image, and give a more realistic look to the render.

Set, the Gamma value to 2.2.

Under Mode, set it to, Color mapping and gamma.

This will ensure what is seen in the VFB is consistent with what is saved on your hard drive.

NOTE

If you choose another Color Mode type, your saved renders will look either darker or brighter from what is seen in your VFB.

Scenes saved in earlier versions of 3ds Max may require merging in a completely new 3ds Max scene with the above Color Mode type, in order to override the problem.

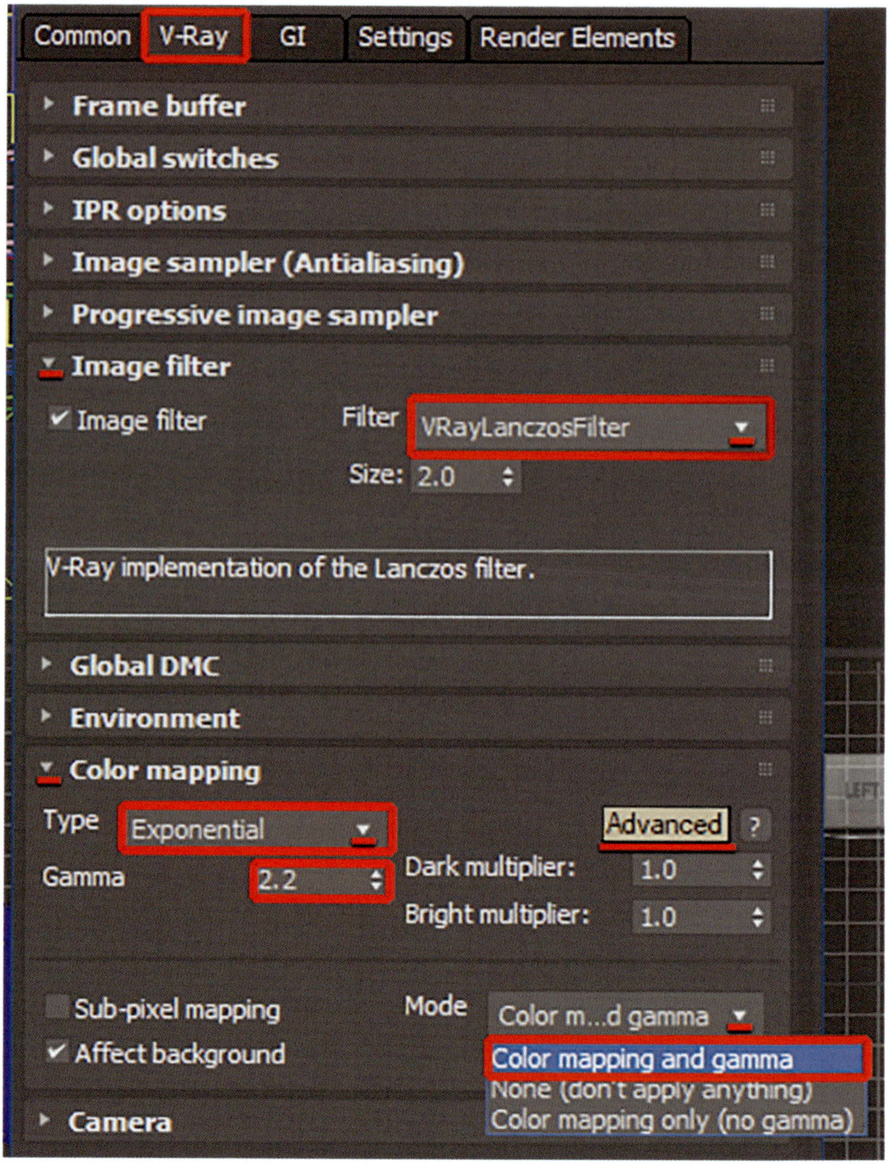

Render Setup dialog with V-Ray tab, Image filter and Color mapping parameters

Camera Composition

Under Create panel, select the Camera button and choose a VRay type from its list.

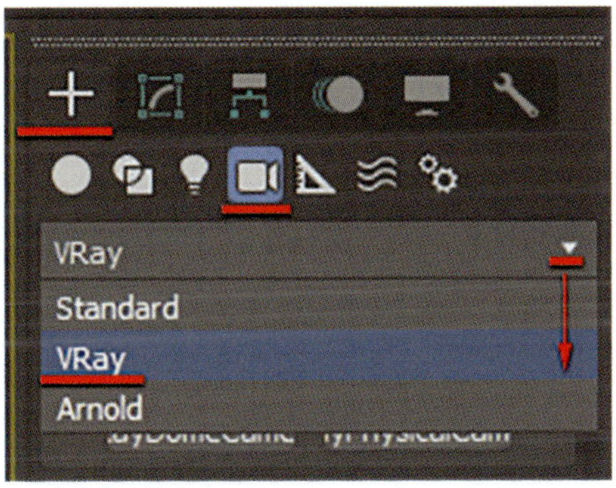

VRay camera type chosen from Create panel

Under Object Type group, choose the VRayPhysicalCamera.

In the Top Viewport, click and drag to create the camera and its view direction.

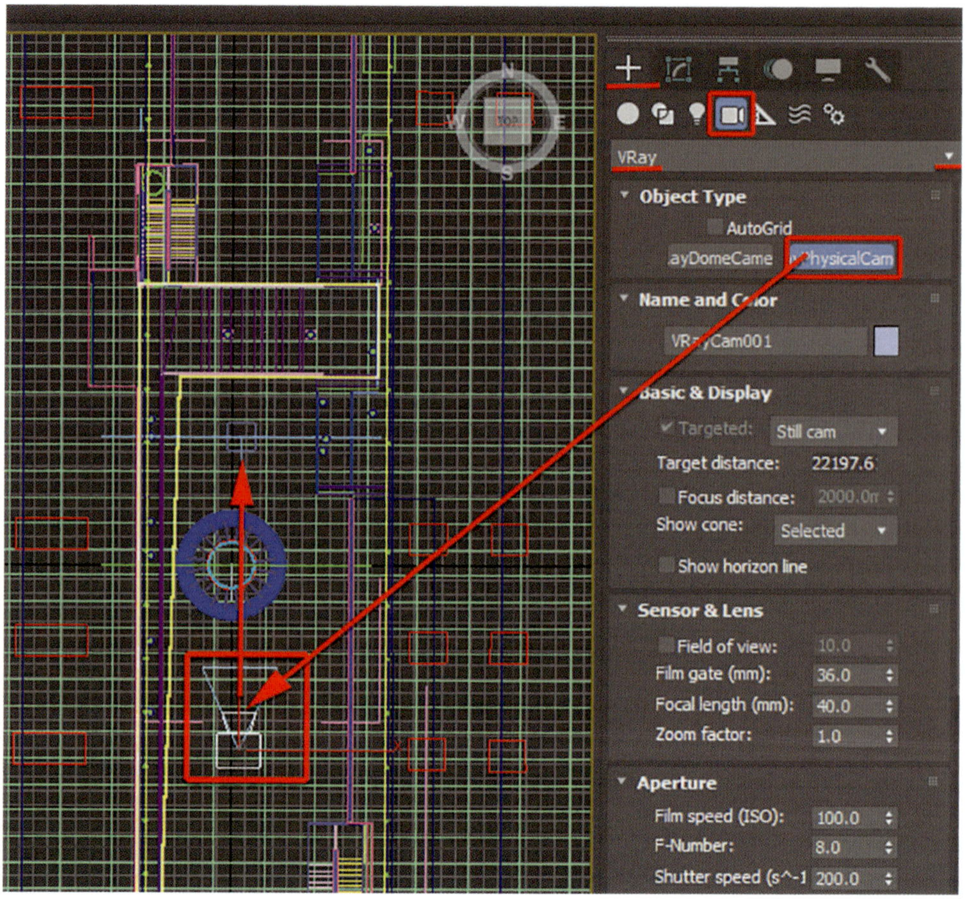

Create the VRayPhysicalCamera in the Top viewport by clicking and dragging it

Next, select the Perspective viewport and click on the Perspective text. Choose the Cameras option and select the VRayCam001.

Alternatively, simply select the Perspective viewport and press C on your keyboard.

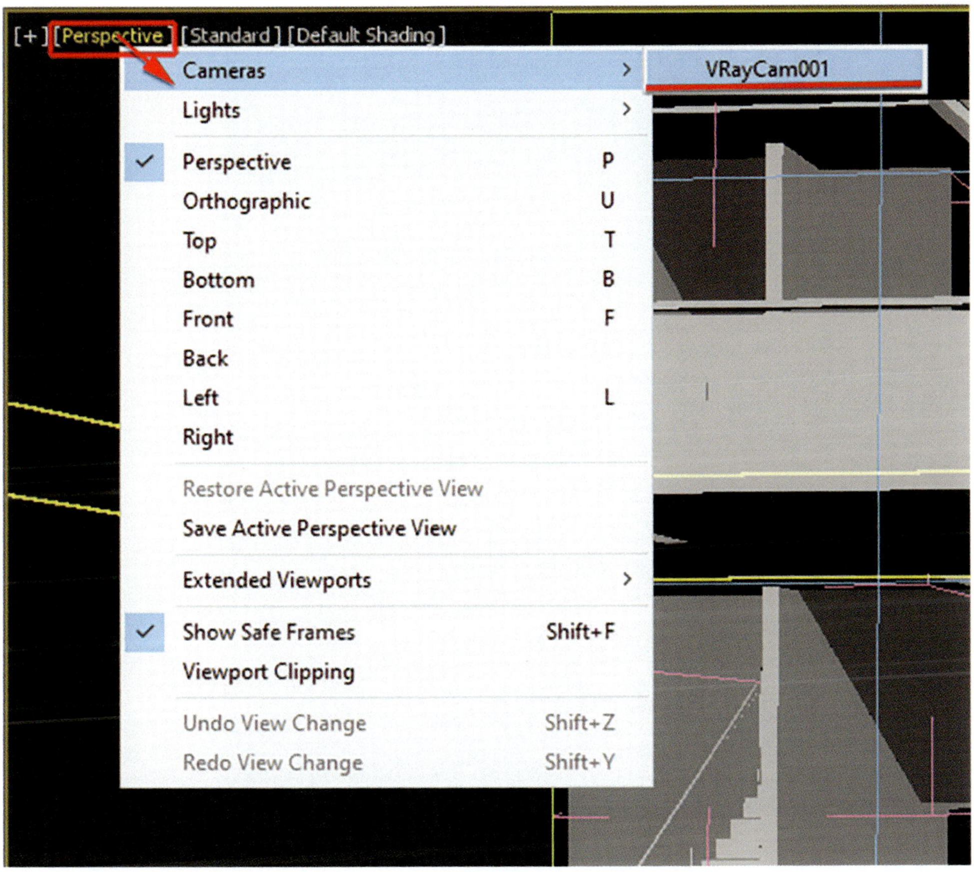

Choose the VRayCam001 from the Perspective viewport

For more flexibility to move and rotate the camera, let's open its Modify panel and disable the Targeted option.

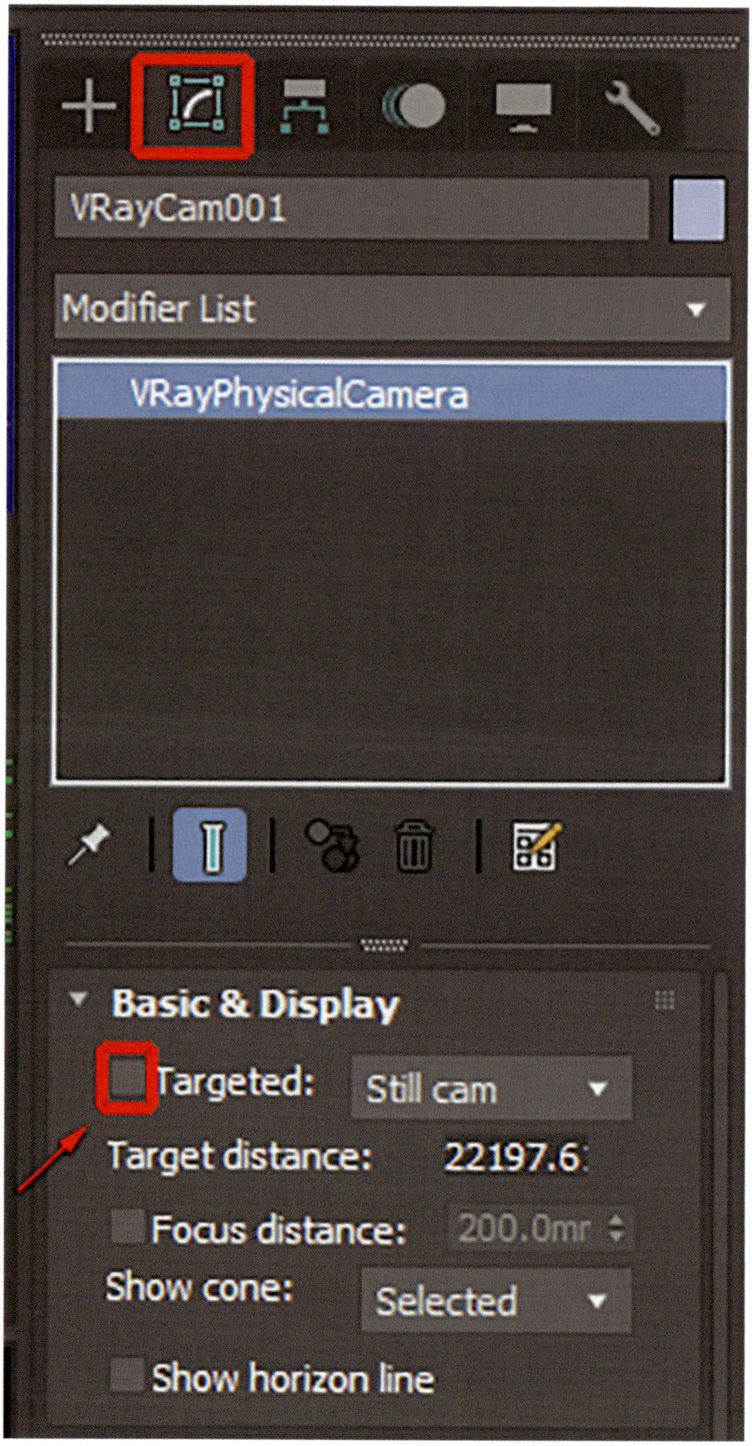

Disable the Targeted option in the Modify panel

To ensure you don't accidently select objects while moving and rotating the camera, go to the main toolbar. Under filter options, select the Cameras from it dropdown list.

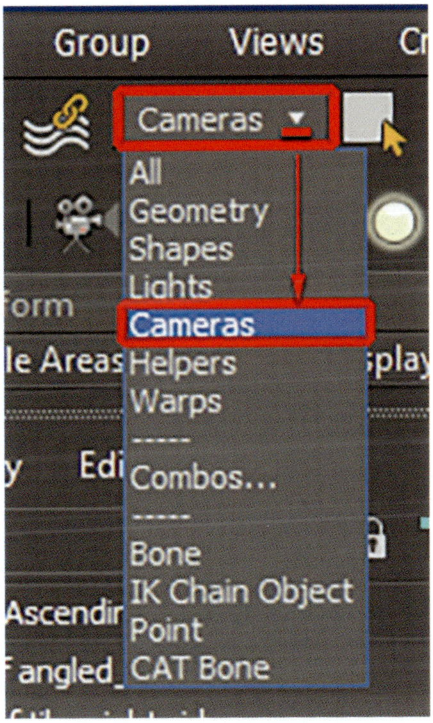

Select Cameras filter options from the main toolbar

Begin moving and rotating the camera to capture the main staircase. Always use photo references to see how similar buildings are framed.

The final Move values of the camera ended up being X: 1440.97 mm, Y: −12246.605 mm, and Z: 1554.238.

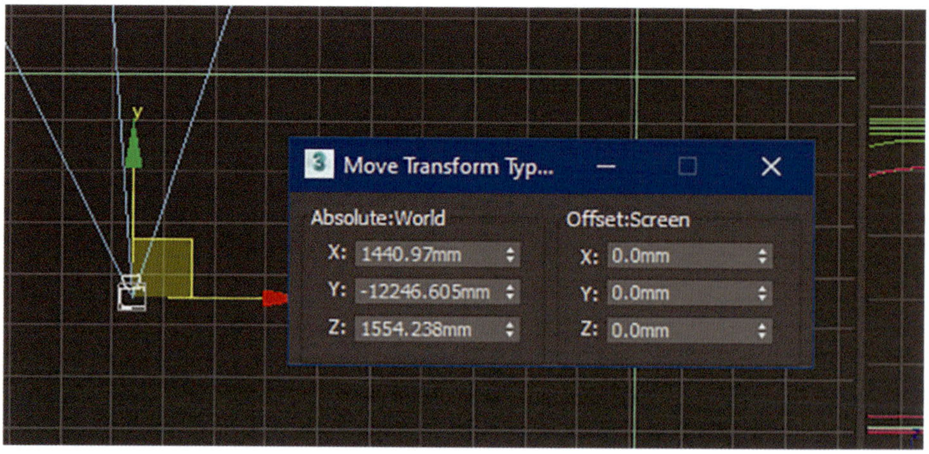

Camera Move values in the dialog

And the Rotation values were X: 93.617, Y: –0.0, and Z: 4.297.

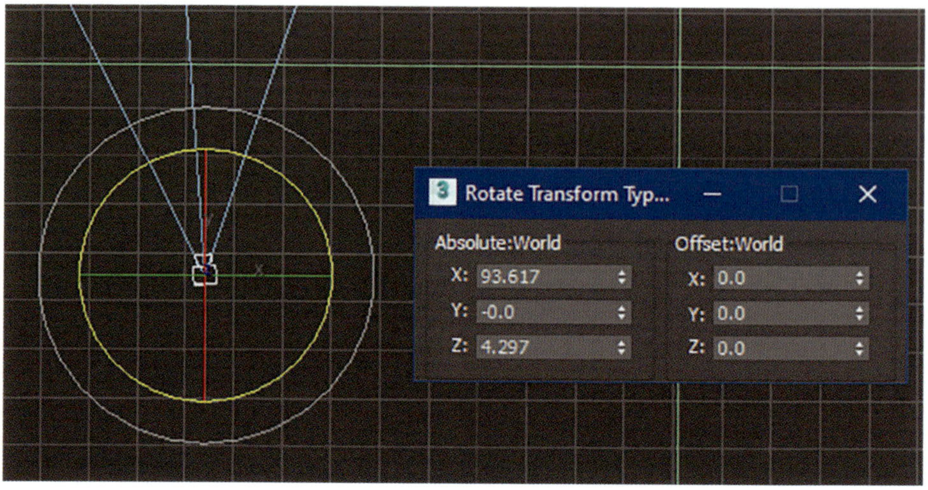

Camera Rotation values in the dialog

To help frame the main staircase, go back to the camera's Modify tab. Under Sensor & Lens rollout parameters, change its Film gate (mm) value to about 33.3

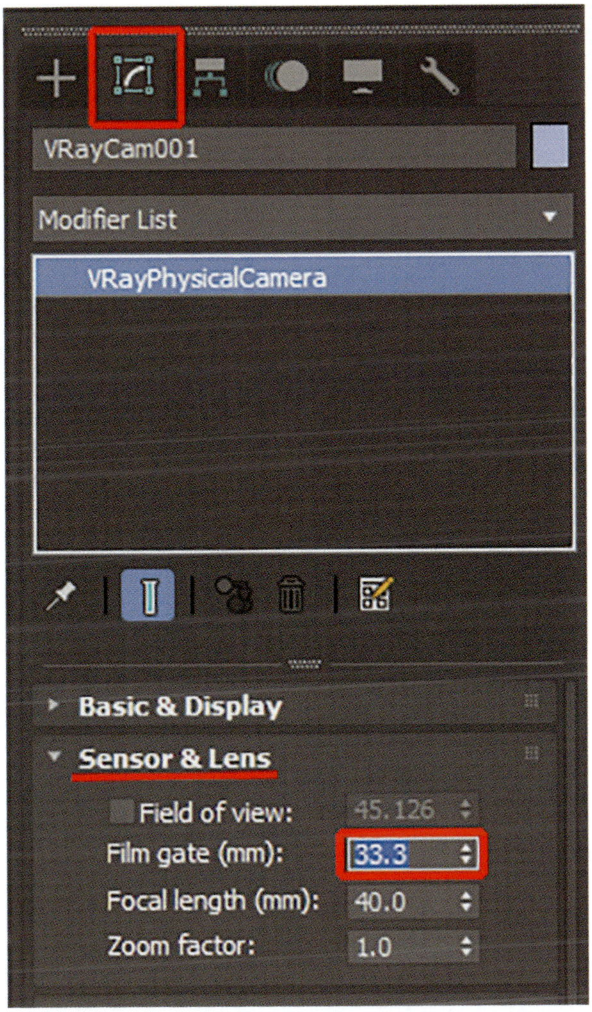

Camera Sensor and lens Film gate set to 33.3

To correct the camera tilt slightly, under Tilt and Shift parameters, enable the Automatic vertical tilt option.

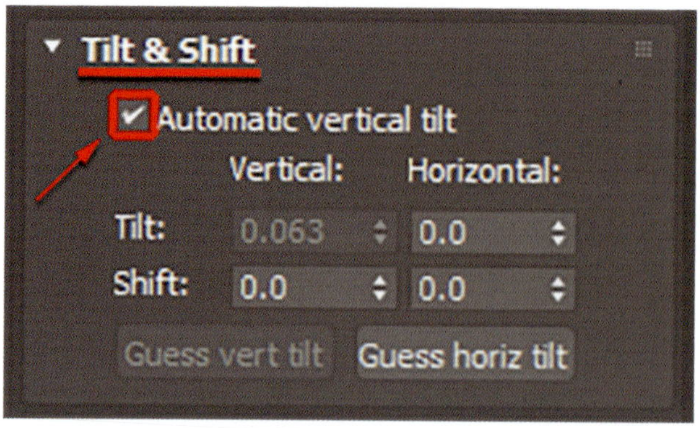

Automatic vertical tilt enabled

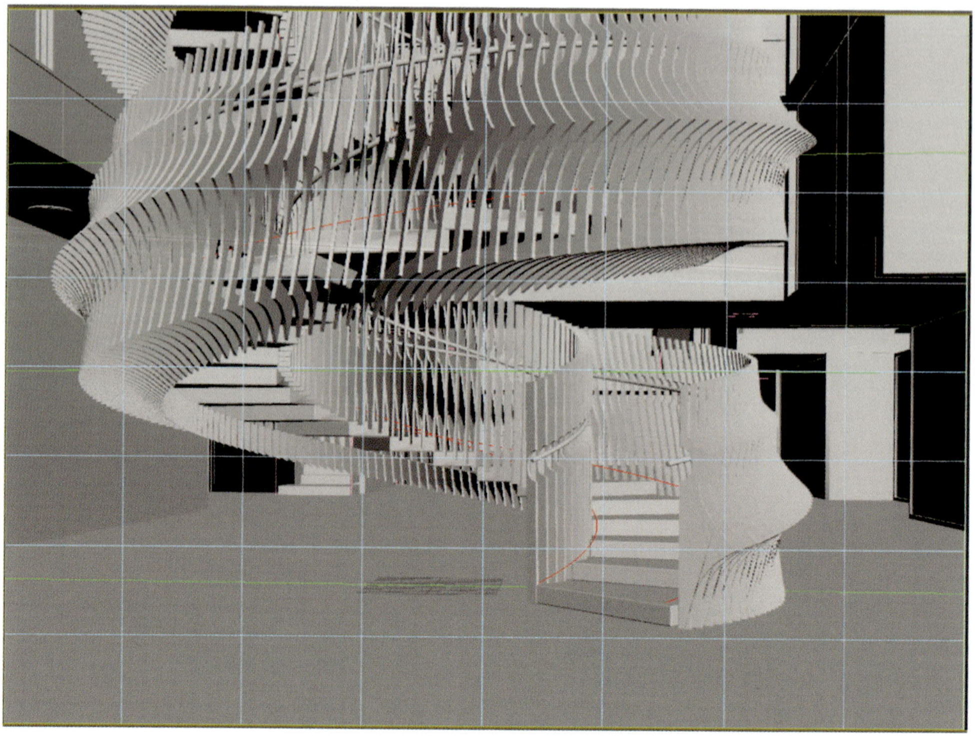

Camera view in the Viewport

To frame the camera slightly better, let's go to the Render Setup dialog (F10). Under Common tab, set the Width Output Size to 1,000 pixels and the Height to 1,000 pixels.

Also, enable the padlock button to lock the Image Aspect ratio.

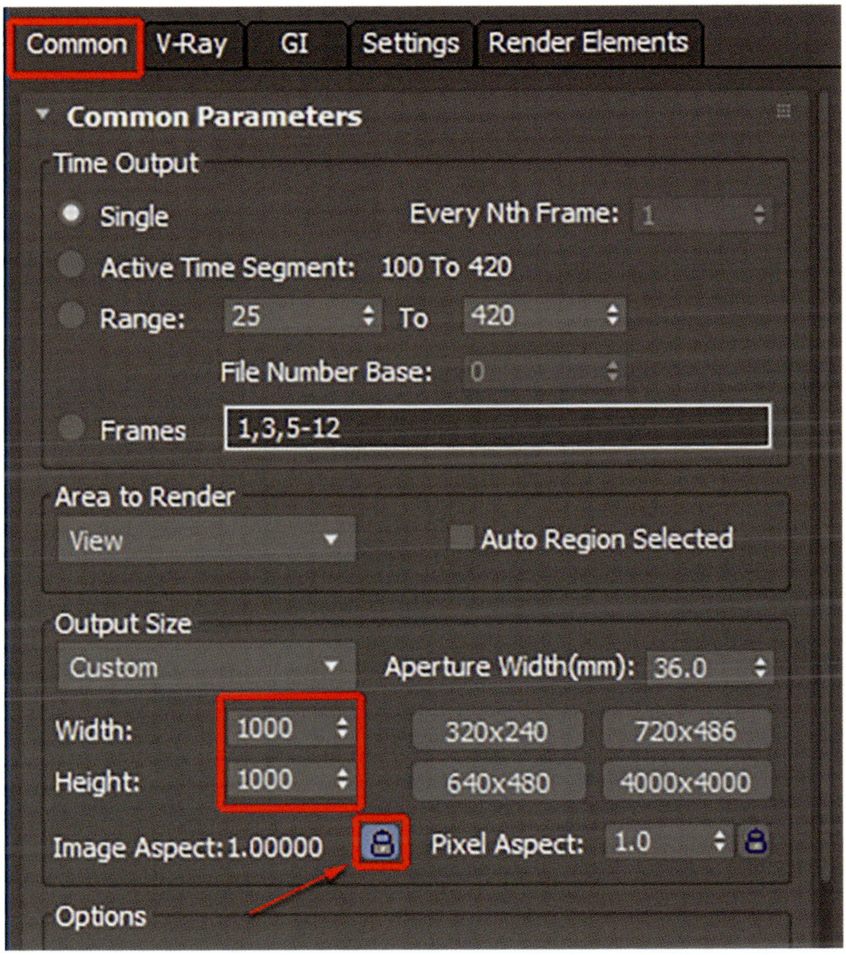

Render Setup dialog, common tab with new Output Size locked

Lights

To create the sunlight, ensure to have all four viewports on display (zoomed out).

Go to the Create panel and select the Lights button.

Under Photometric list, choose the VRay type.

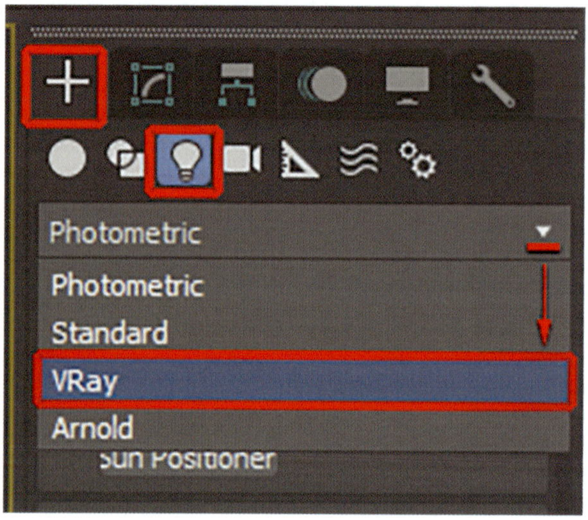

VRay light chosen from Create panel

Next, select the VRaySun button, followed by clicking and dragging it in the Front viewport to create it.

If prompted with the dialog to automatically add a VRaySky environment map, click Yes to accept it.

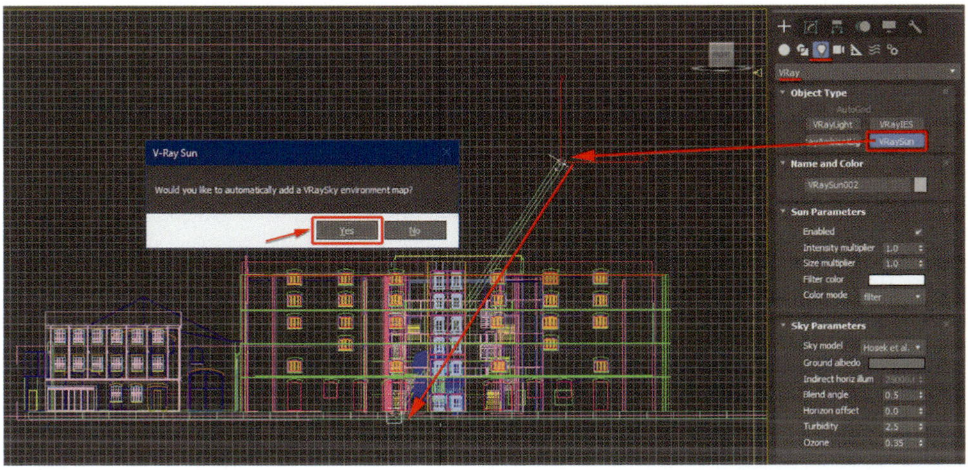

VRaySun object being created in the Front viewport

Also, go to the Modify panel and change the default Sky model to Improved.

Sky model type chosen as Improved

Next, enable the V-Ray Viewport IPR option in the camera viewport.

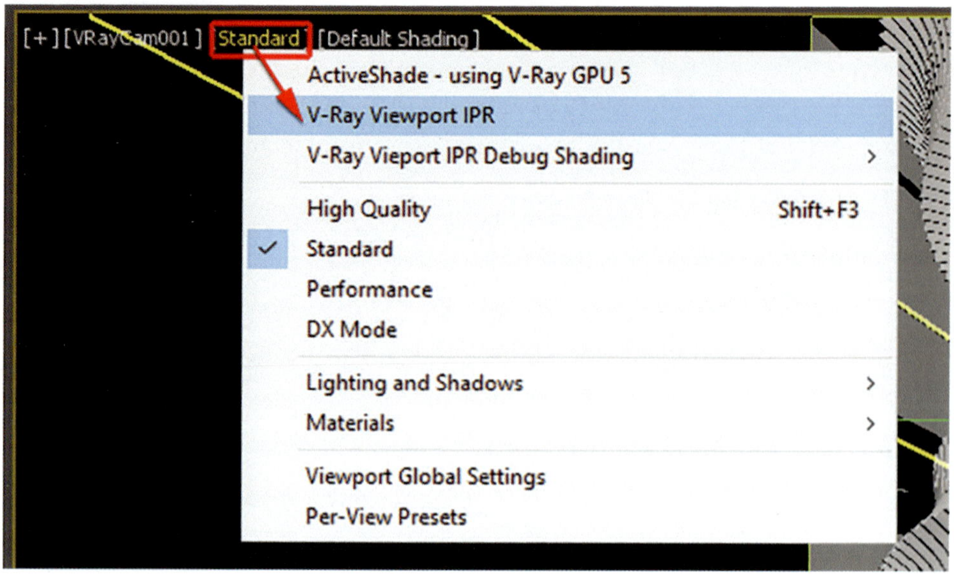

V-Ray Viewport IPR option enabled in the camera viewport

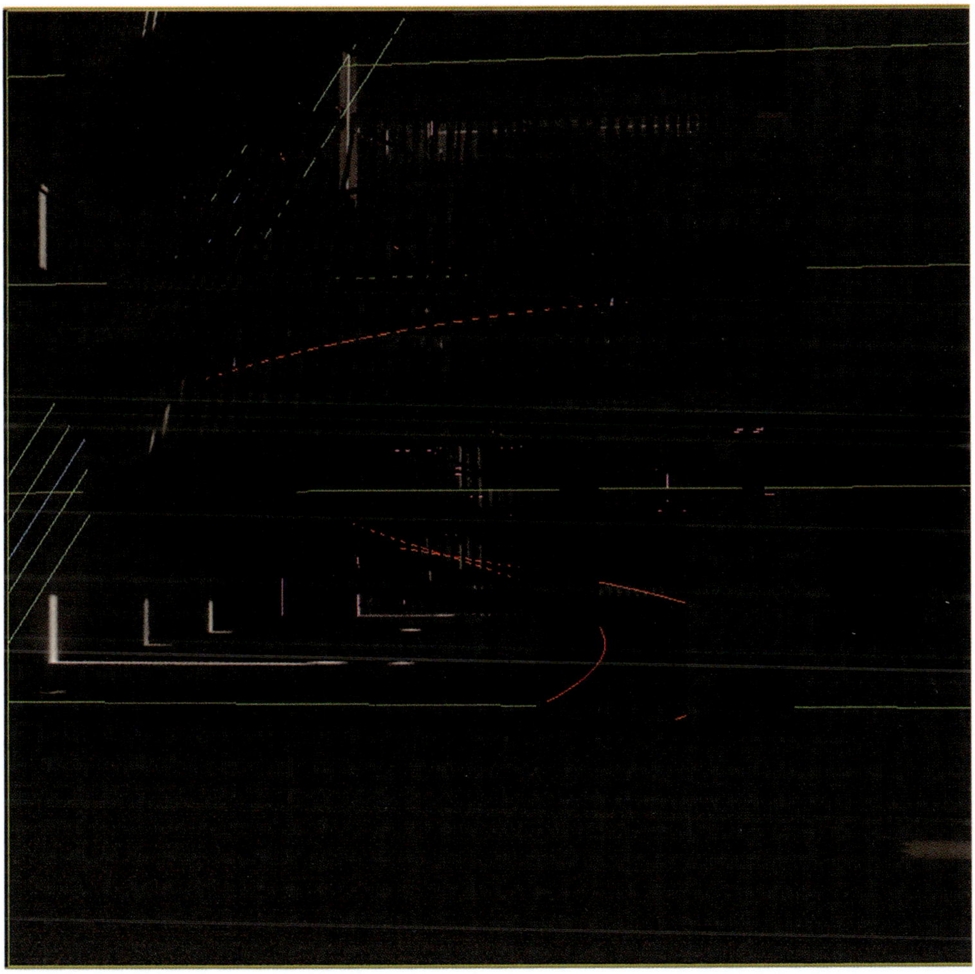

IPR rendered in the viewport

The camera viewport seems a bit dark due to the roof light blocking the sun from coming through.

To rectify this, in the scene, select the object named, etfe cushon roof. Right click on it and choose its Object Properties option from the quad menu.

In Object Properties dialog, under General, uncheck the function to Cast Shadows, and OK to close its dialog.

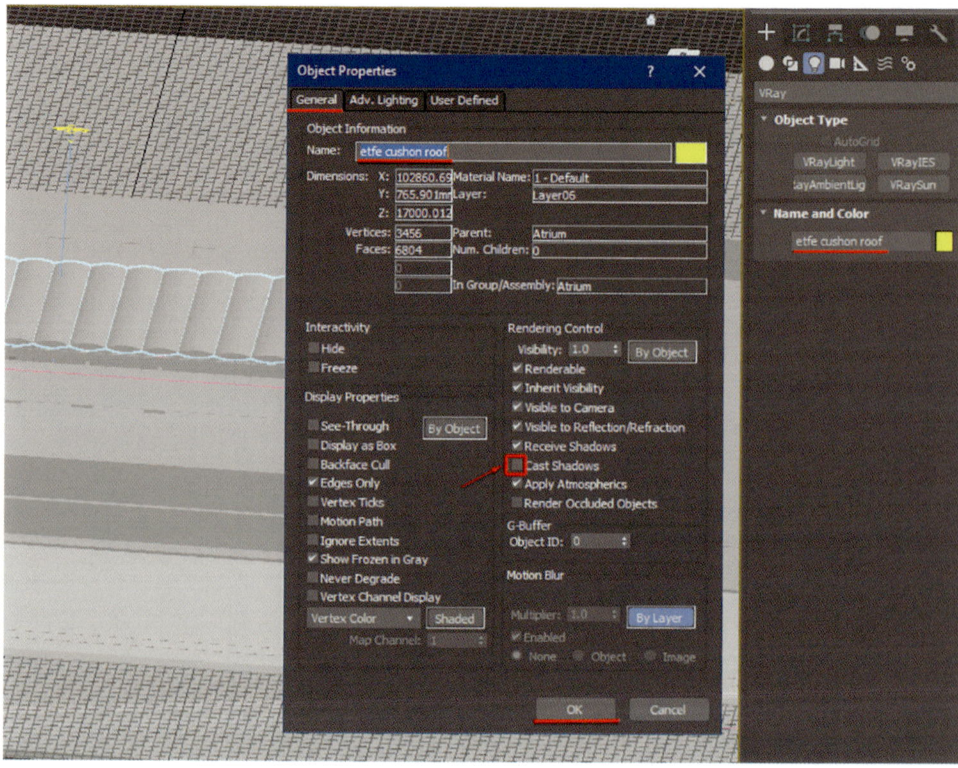

Object Properties dialog with Cast Shadows function disabled

Sunlight coming through the roof light

Begin moving the VRaySun object and its target, until an appealing sun direction with shadows is achieved.

The final sun head position was X: 7602.166 mm, Y: 74590.894 mm and Z: 73616.338 mm.

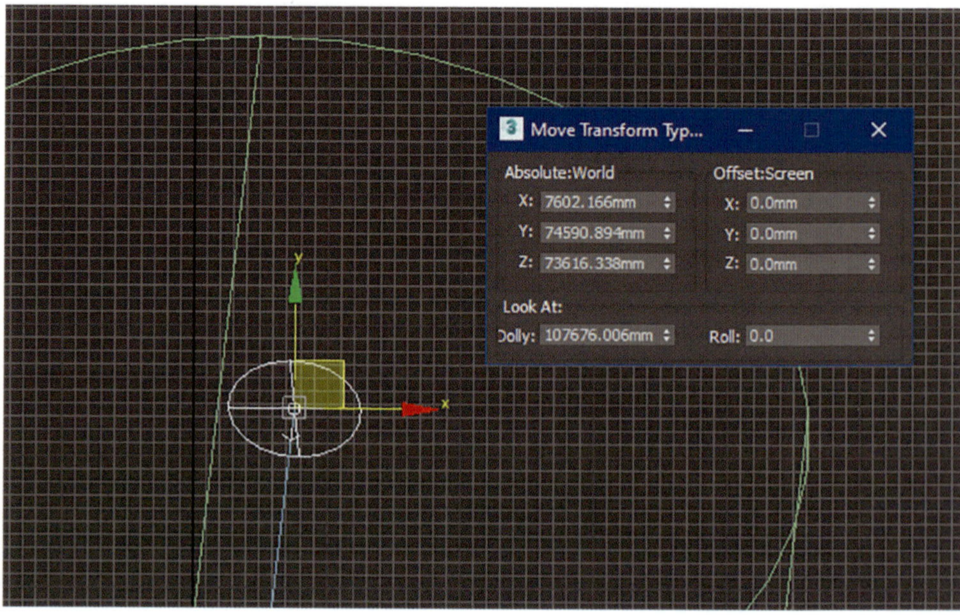

VRaySun head position values in dialog

Its final target position was X: –444.927 mm, Y: –3690.811 mm and Z: 122.511 mm.

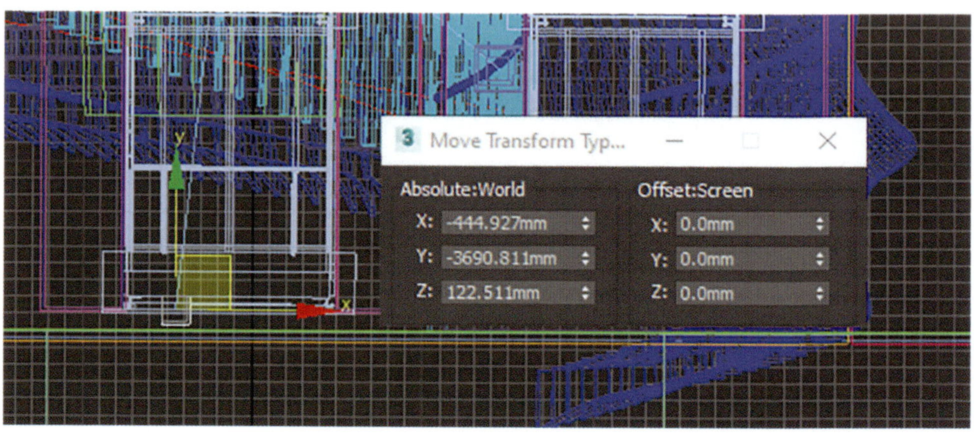

VRaySun target position values in the dialog

For quick V-Ray Viewport IPR results, open the Render Setup dialog (F10). Under V-Ray tab, scroll down to Progressive image sampler parameters.

Set the Max. subdivs to 10 and the Render time to 5.0.

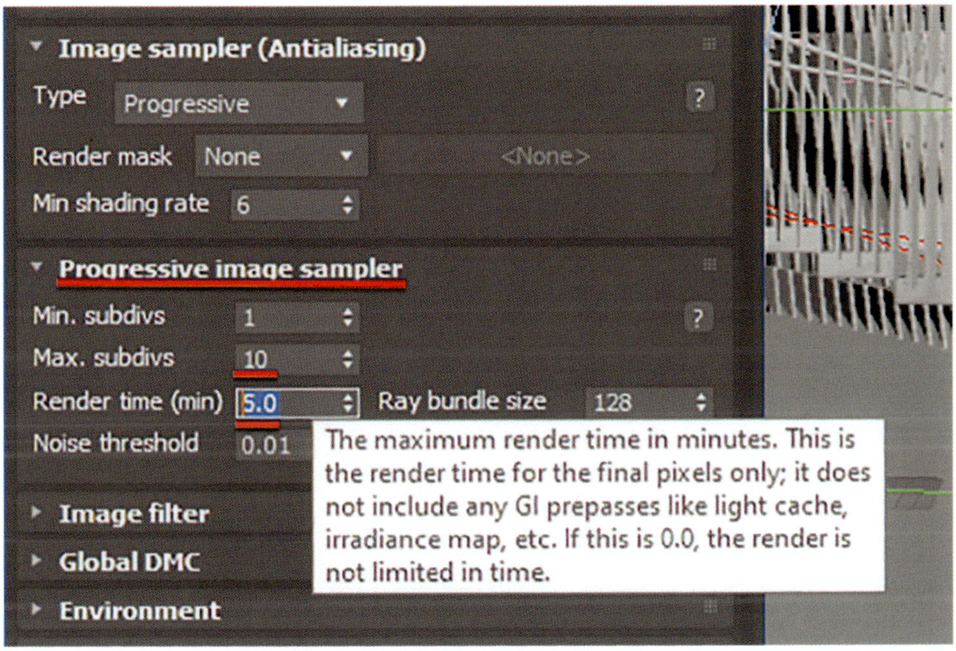

Progressive image sampler new values

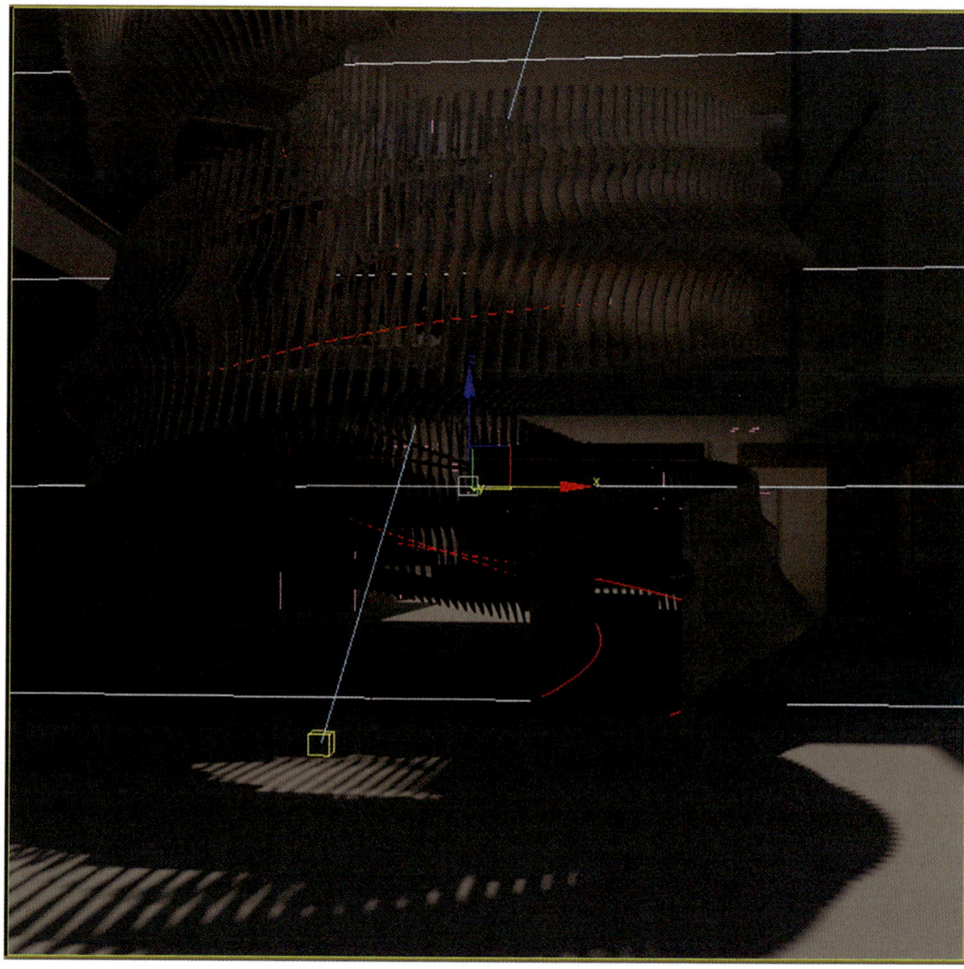

Final image of the VRaySun position in the V-Ray Viewport IPR

Next, Under Render Elements tab, click to Add the VRayLightMix element.

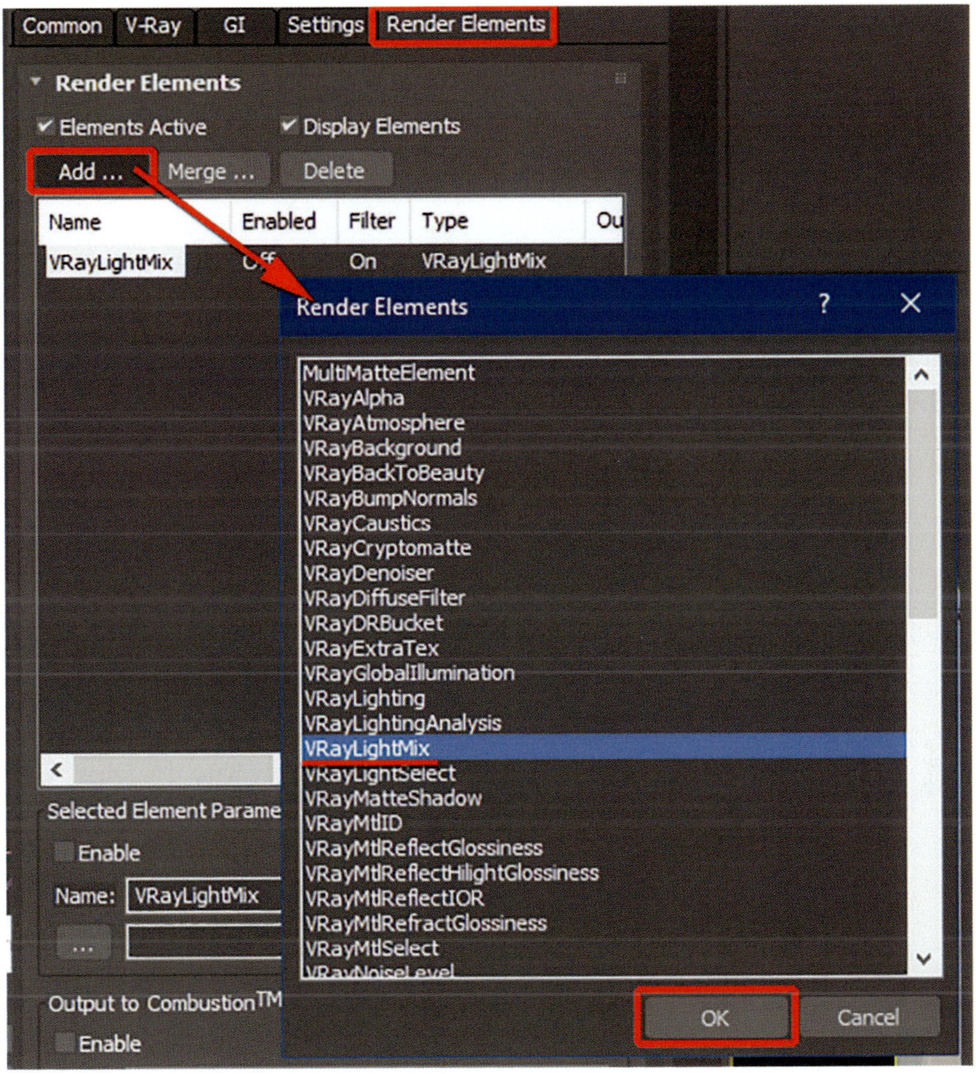

Add VRayLightMix element from Render Elements tab

If you want the flexibility to manipulate the instanced lights individually, simply choose the option to Group by Individual lights.

NOTE

By default, it is set to Group by Instanced lights. This option displays all instanced lights in the scene as one Layer in the VFB LightMix parameters.

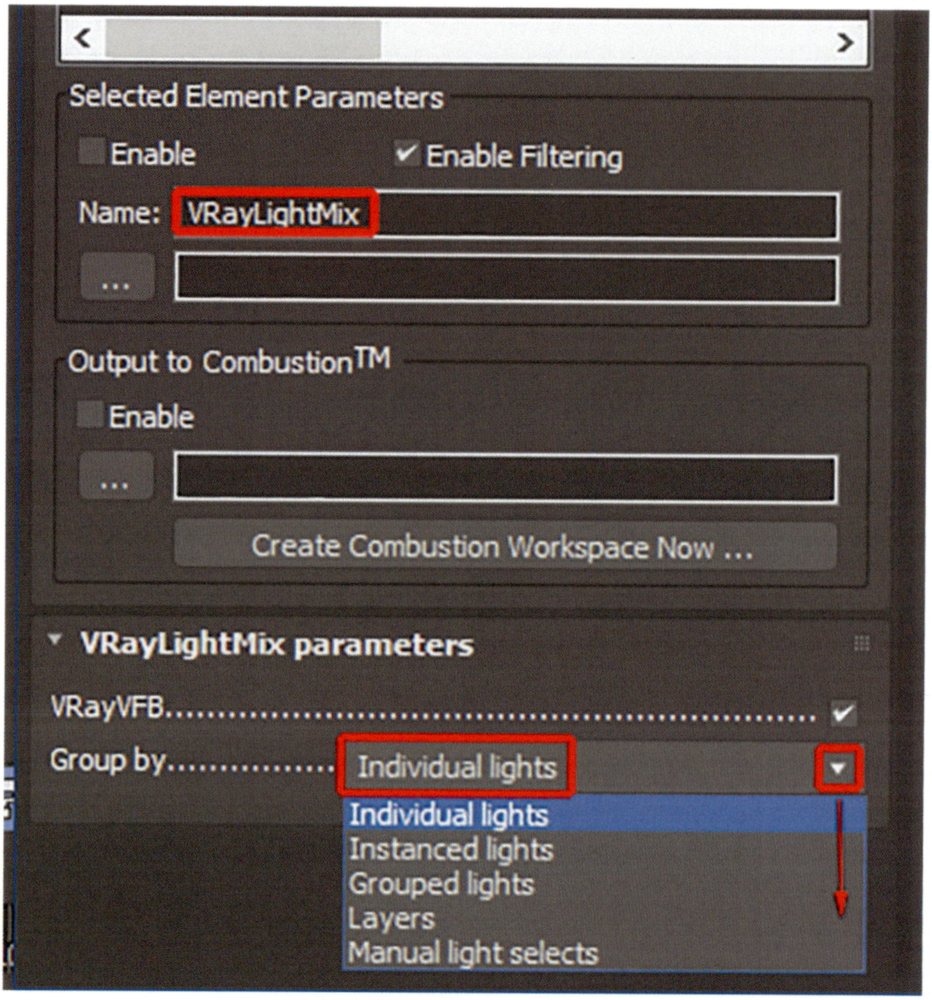

LightMix element with the option to process instanced lights as individual lights

Open the V-Ray Frame Buffer dialog and add the Lookup Table Layer from the list.

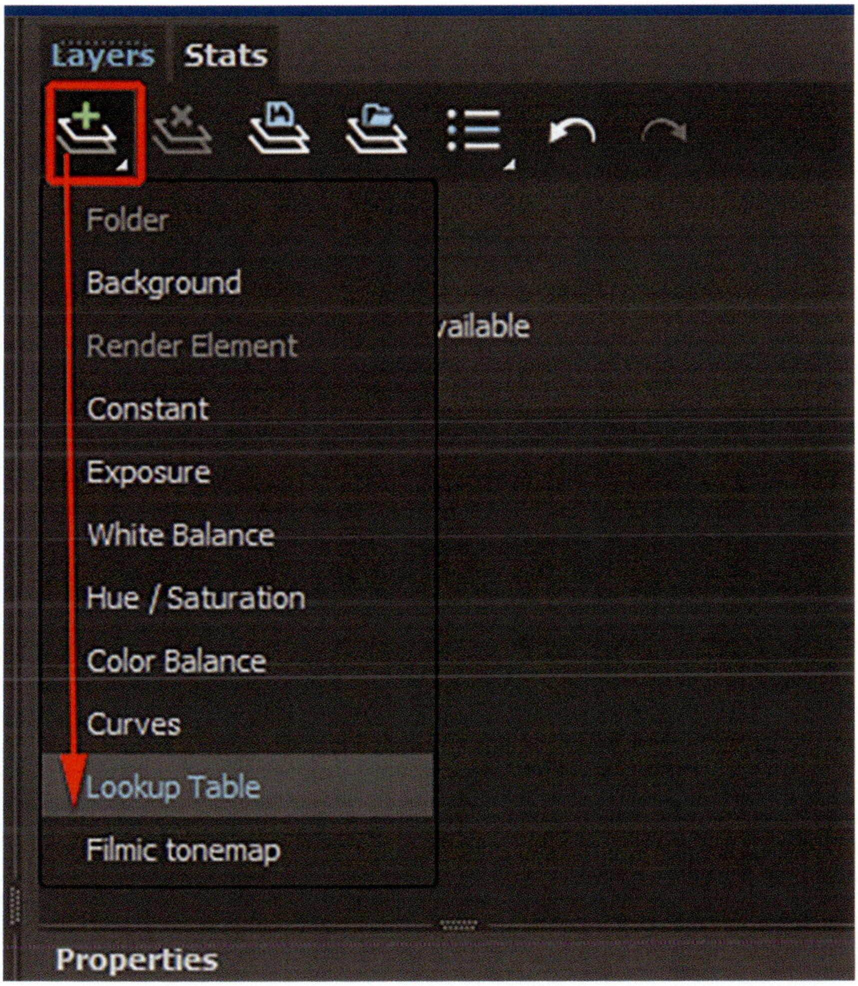

Lookup Table Layer added in the VFB dialog

Under Lookup Table Properties, click on its folder toggle and load the file named, 3DCollective_sRGB_Agfa_Futura_03Hard.cube.

NOTE

This LUT file worked well for this scene. However, feel free to use another LUT file, if desired.

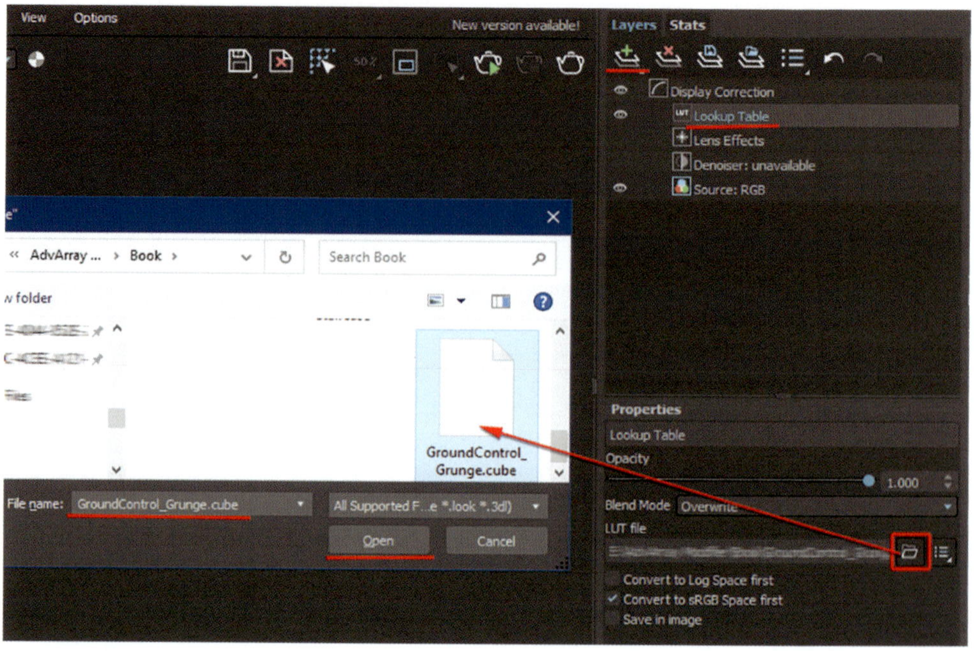

Lookup Table file loaded

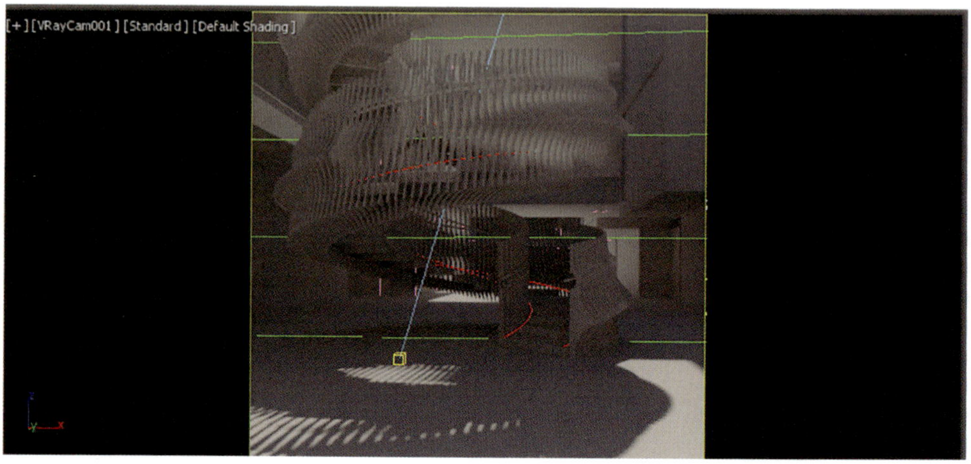

Lookup Table file effect in the V-Ray Viewport IPR

The following step is to begin adding VRay artificial lights in the scene. To do so, go to the Create panel and select the Lights button.

Under Photometric list, choose the VRay type, followed by selecting the VRayLight button, changing its Type to Disc, and clicking on the Top viewport to create it.

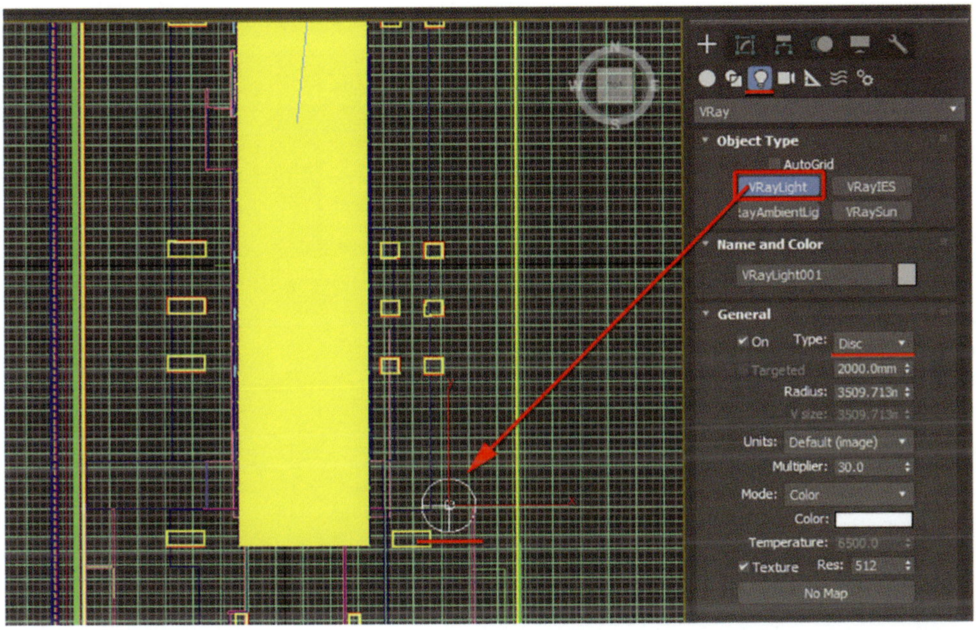

V-Ray Disc light created in the Top Viewport

While the disc light is still selected, open the Modify panel. Under the Light Color, change it to yellow, by clicking on its swatch and choosing it (R: 243, G: 158, B: 10, H: 27, sat: 245 and Value: 243).

Also, set its Multiplier value to 1,000 and its Radius to 225.338 mm. Under Option, enable the options to Cast shadows, Invisible, Affect diffuse, and Affect specular.

Finally, move the disc light object to almost flush with the recessed light fixtures.

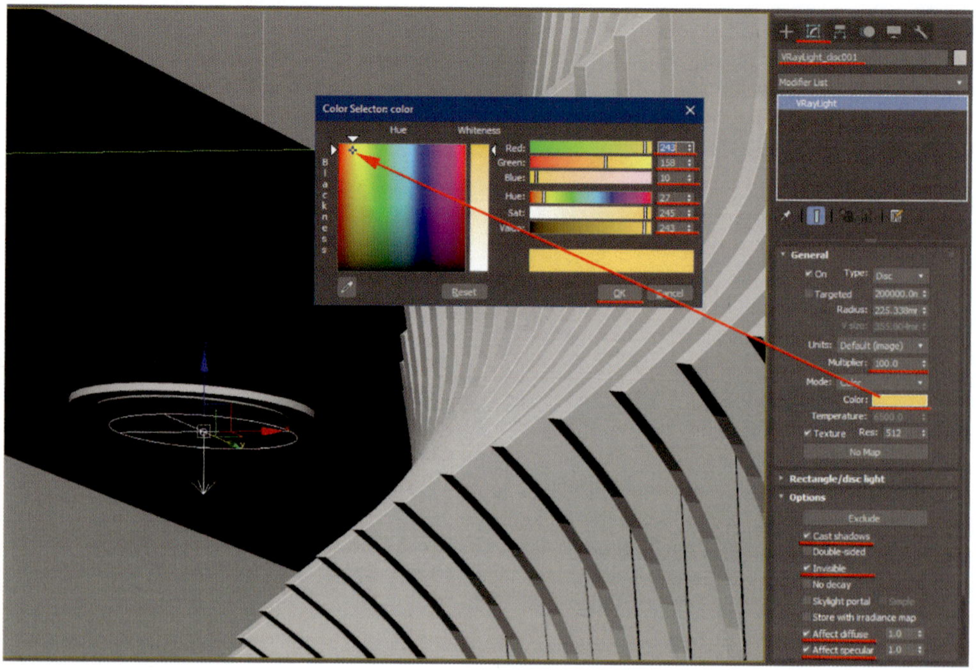

Move the V-Ray Disc light, change its Color swatch, and Options

Next, Clone Instance this disc light across all the recessed light fixtures in the scene (Hold down Shift+Move to copy instance lights).

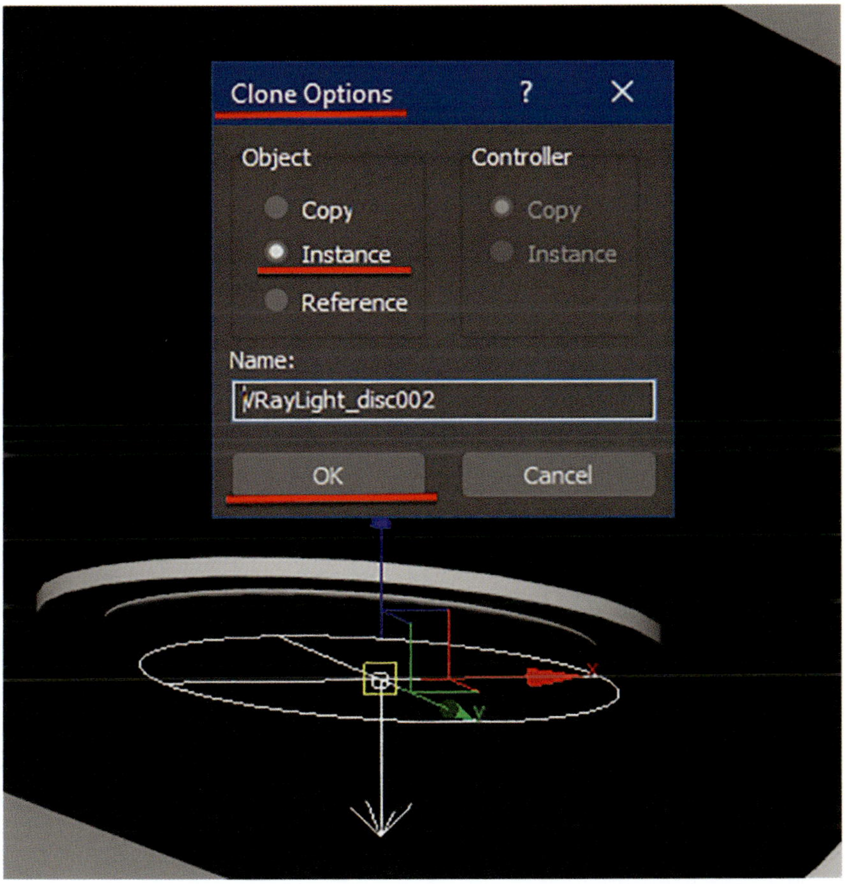

Clone Instance the disc light across the scene

To randomize the scale of each disc light individually without affecting the other instances, use the Scale toolbar Offset:World values.

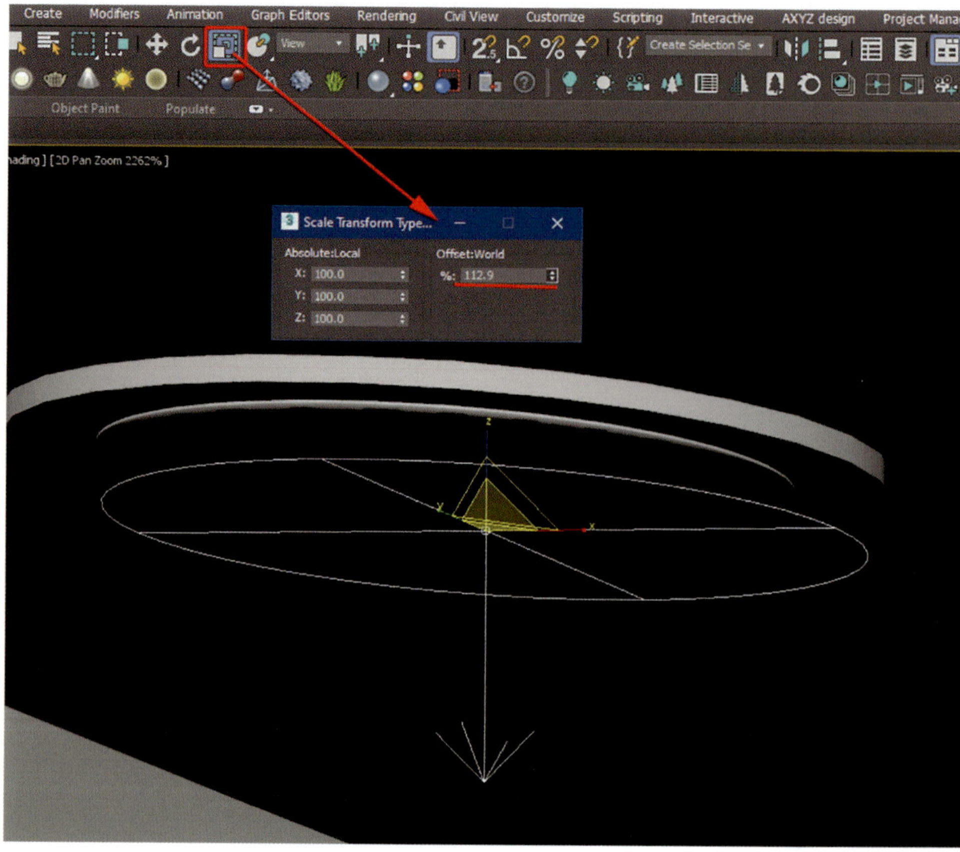

Randomize the scale of each disc with the Scale toolbar

Alternatively, to see the final position of the artificial lights, merge them in your scene from a 3ds max scene named Artificial Disc Lights.max, or simply open the 3Ds Max file named Staircase Atrium_Night_Start_001.max.

The final result in the V-Ray Viewport IPR

Conclusion

It's vital to start your 3d scene by setting the System Units Scale accordingly in order for objects and lights to work accurately.

Similarly, the Color mapping and scene Preference Settings will play a crucial role in the input/output render results.

Finally, after lighting a scene, VFB layers will be indispensable to help achieve the final "look and feel" of the final render output.

9

Materials and Final Render

9 Materials and Final Render

Introduction

Creating materials and rendering the final scene are one of the most crucial parts of the entire production process.

As such, the following tutorial will take users through the intricacies of creating materials, setting up the final scene, and rendering the final image realistically.

This chapter will take users through the process of creating materials and rendering the final scene.

It will start by taking users through the steps of creating materials, setting up the scene for final rendering, and rendering the final image realistically.

The V-Ray procedural map and its Asset Browser will be used to create materials such as wood, concrete, glass, metal and the tiled floor. Followed by using Modifiers, other procedural maps and functionalities such as UVW Map, ColorCorrection, VRayDisplacementMod, Material IDs, Refraction and Reflection to achieve photorealistic results.

Finally, users will be shown how to set up the Image sampler, Render Elements, and the final high-resolution renders for printing.

NOTE

This chapter is a continuation of the previous one. Hence, the scene, camera, lighting and LUT files have already been created and set up.

Creating Materials

Let's start by opening the file under the name of Staircase Atrium_Materials_Start.max.

DOI: 10.1201/9781315770802-9

Wood Material

Wood material

Before we begin working on the wood material, it's worth paying close attention to physical properties such as color, texture, grain, hardness and how it interacts/reflects light, as depicted on the photo directly above.

In the scene, select the object named, Slate Vertical right, and isolate it (Alt+Q).

Also, maximize the camera viewport (Alt+W).

Open the Material Editor dialog (M) and select an empty material slot. Name the empty material slot as, wood (1). The (1) was added to later coincide with the Material ID number to be changed to 1.

If a V-Ray material is not automatically loaded in the Material Editor, click on the Standard toggle, and choose the VRayMtl procedural map from the Material/Map Browser dialog list.

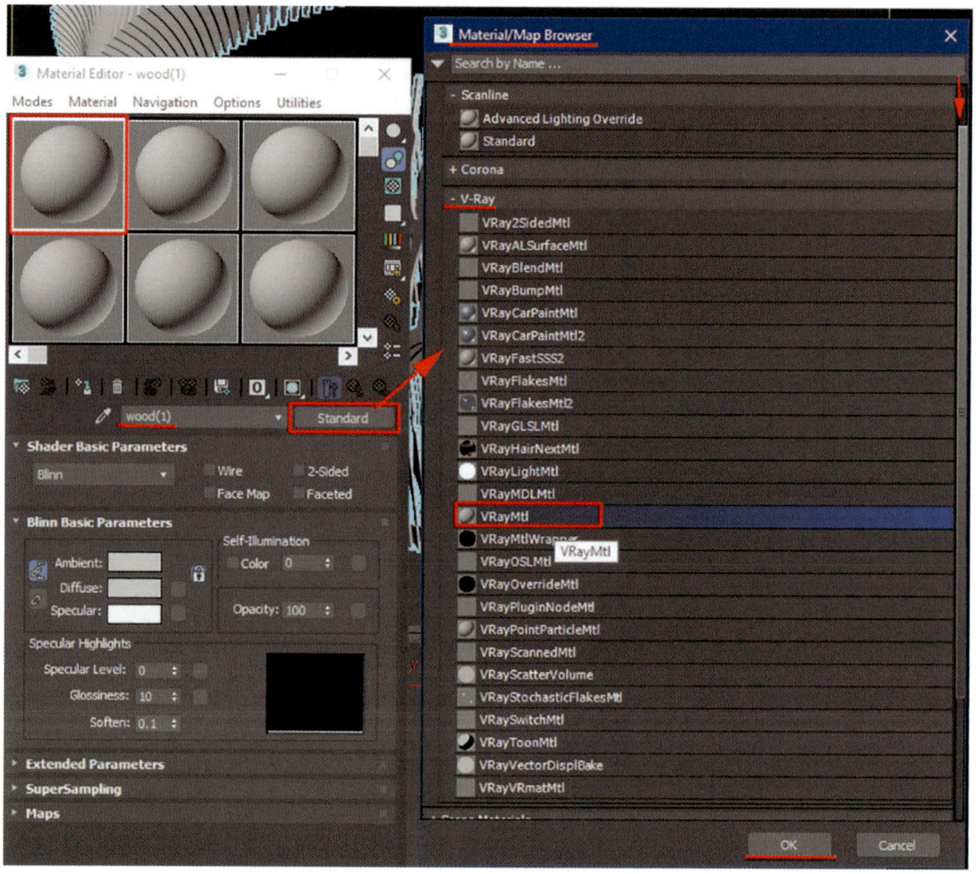

Material slot named and VRayMtl procedural map loaded

Next, while the Slate Vertical right object is still selected, click on its Diffuse toggle and add the VRayBitmap procedural map to it.

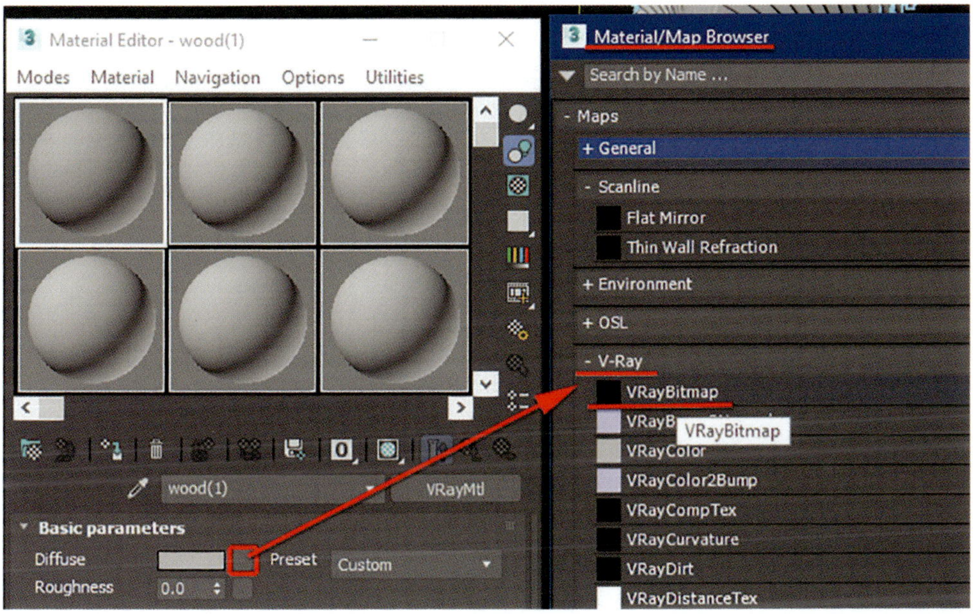

Add the VRayBitmap procedural map to the Diffuse toggle

Once the VRayBitmap is loaded, click on its Bitmap toggle to load the texture named, wood-048_afzelia-1_d.JPG.

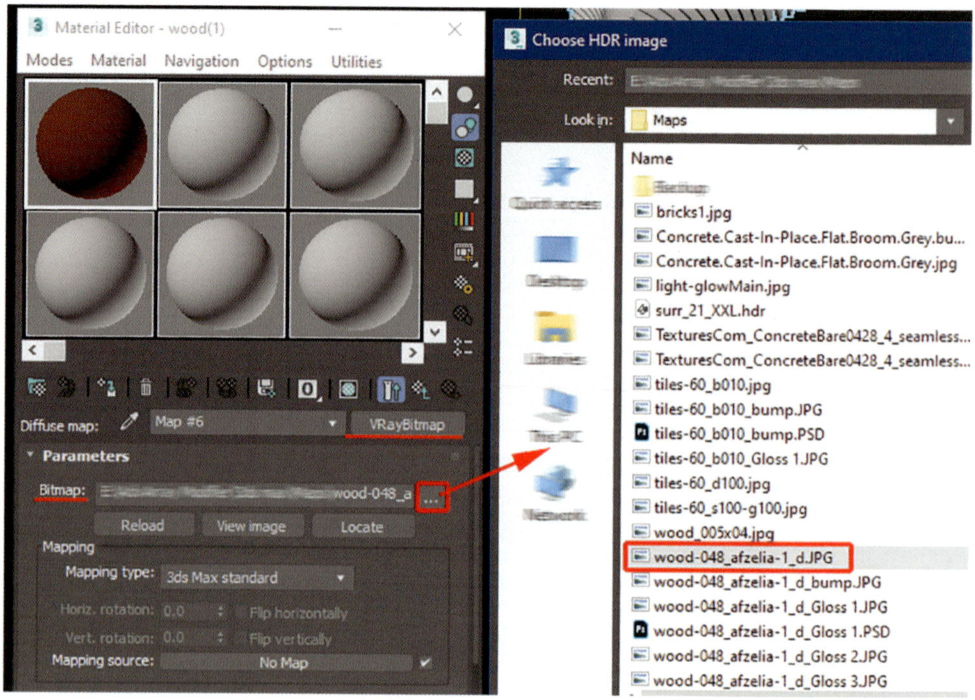

wood-048_afzelia-1_d.JPG texture loaded in the VRayBitmap

Choose to Assign Material to Selection and Show Shaded Material in Viewport.

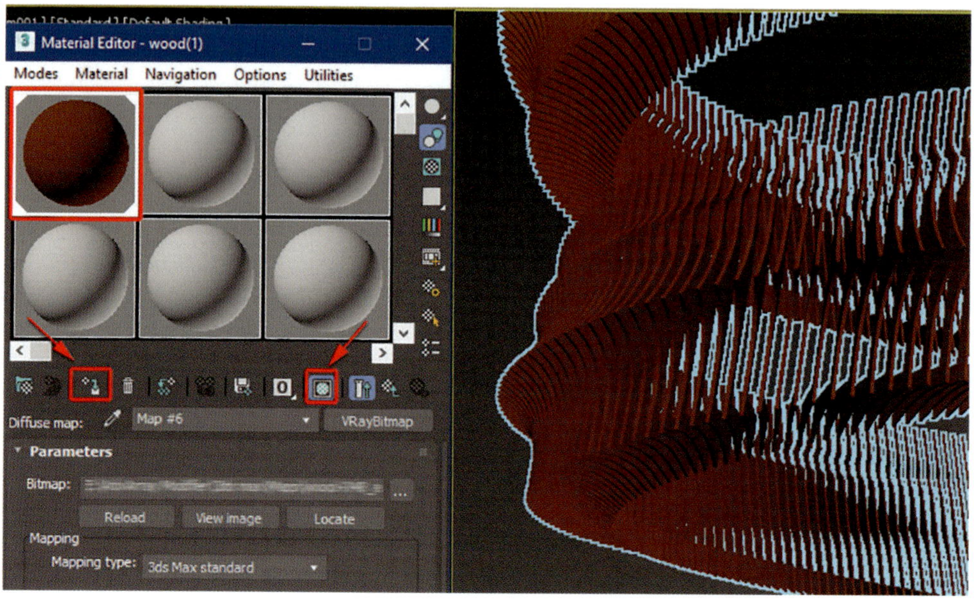

Assign Material to Selection and Show Shaded Material in Viewport

To automatically randomize the texture, click on Mapping source toggle to load the VRayUVWRandomizer.

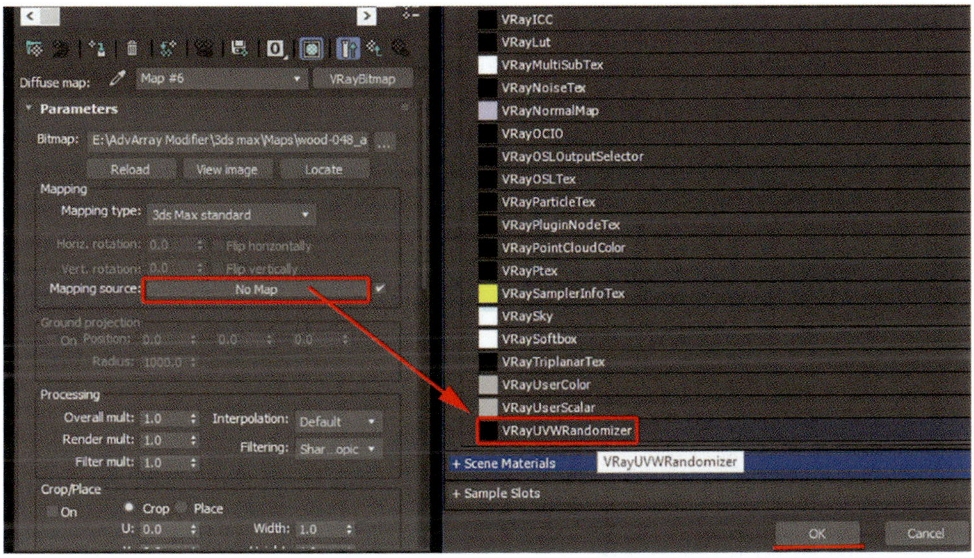

Click on Mapping source toggle to load the VRayUVWRandomizer

In the VRayUVWRandomizer parameters, enable the Stochastic function. Set the U offset value to 0.07, the UV rotation Variance to 0.0 and U offset Steps to 0.1.

NOTE

These values worked well. However, feel free to try different values, if desired.

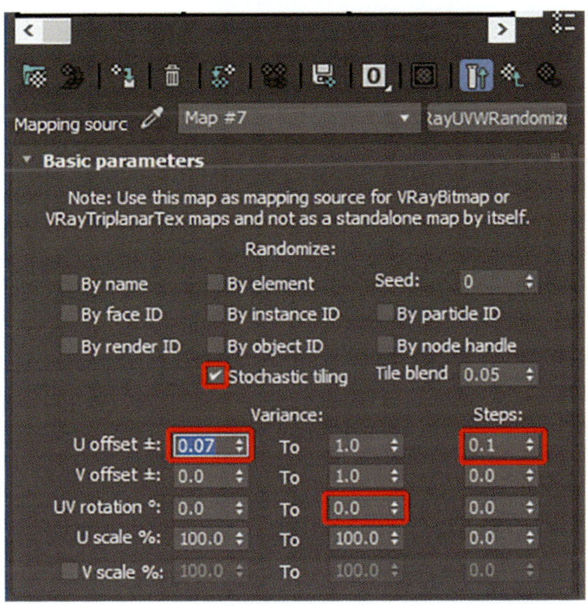

VRayUVWRandomizer parameters changed

The following step is to open the Modify panel and add the UVW Map modifier from its dropdown list.

Change its Mapping type to Box, and set the Length, Width, and Height values to 7758.104 mm. Under Alignment, set it to X. The V-Ray Viewport IPR should update the results.

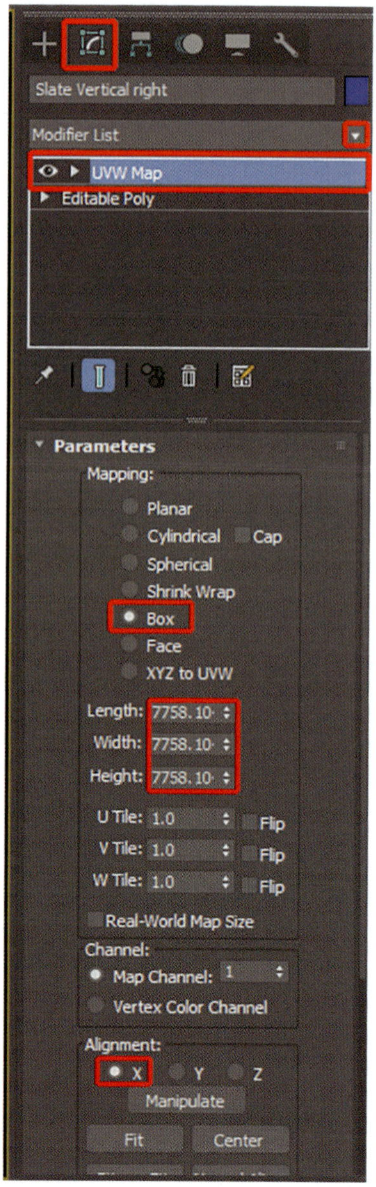

Mapping set to Box, Length, Width and Height values set to 7758.104 mm with X Alignment

To increase the brightness of the wood finish slightly, click on the Go to Parent button and add the Color Correction procedural map. Choose to Keep old map as sub-map.

Click on the Go to Parent button

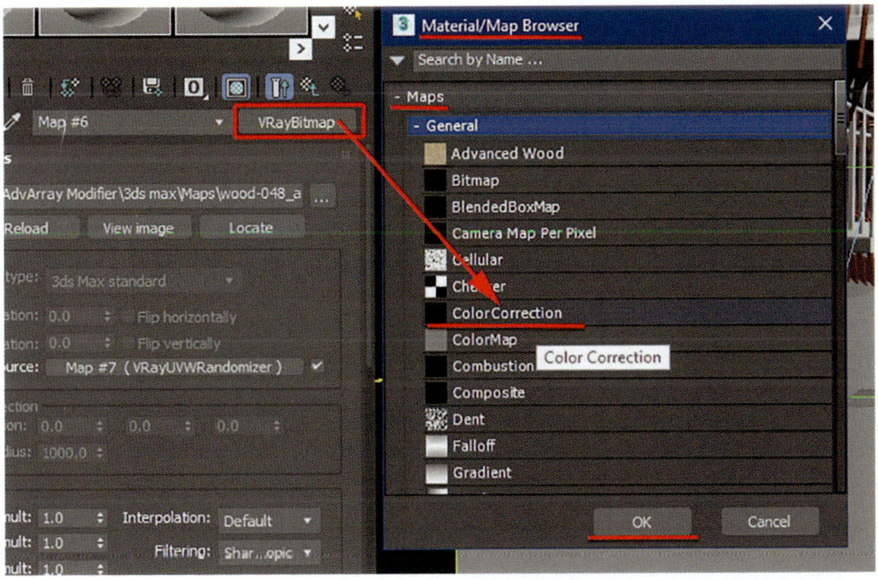

Add the Color Correction procedural

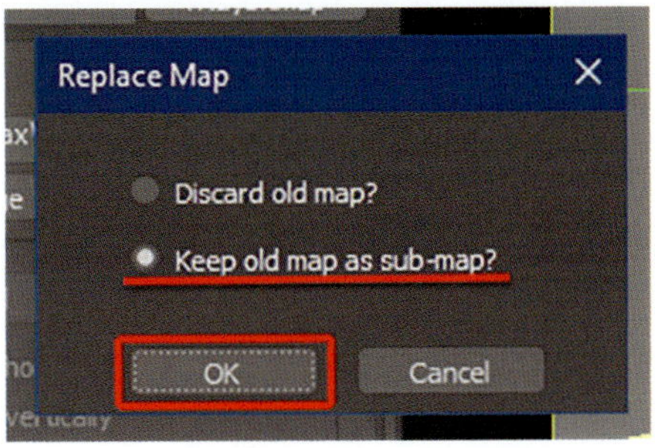

Choose to Keep old map as sub-map

NOTE

These values worked well. However, feel free to try different values and settings, if desired.

In the Color Correction parameters, enable the Show Shaded Material in Viewport button. Under Saturation, increase it to about 1.661.

Under Lightness, enable the Advanced function and increase the Gamma/ Contrast value to 1.39.

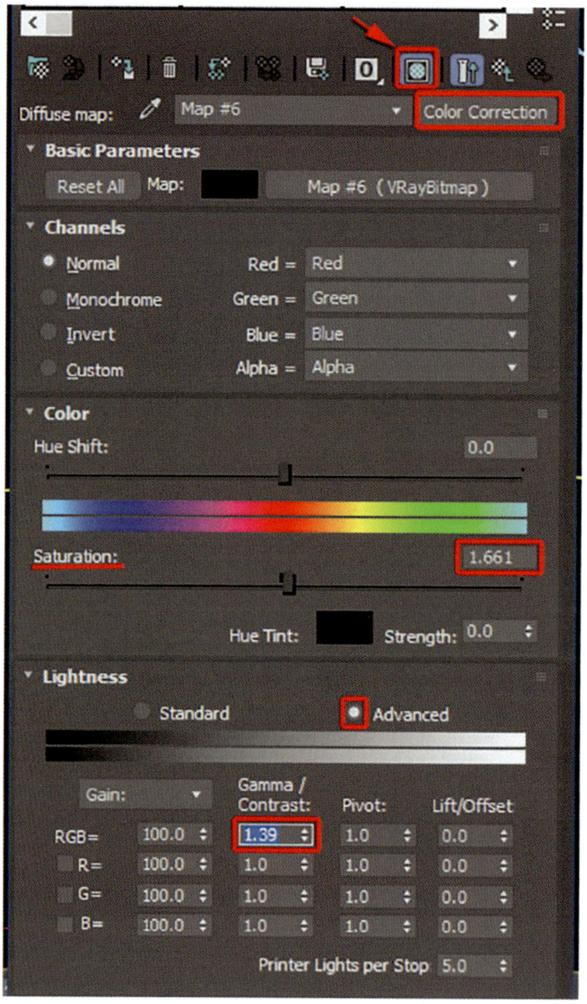

Color Correction parameters changed

Click on the Go to Parent button to go back to the main parameters, and change the Material ID number from 0 to 1 (click+hold+select), to coincide with the label (1).

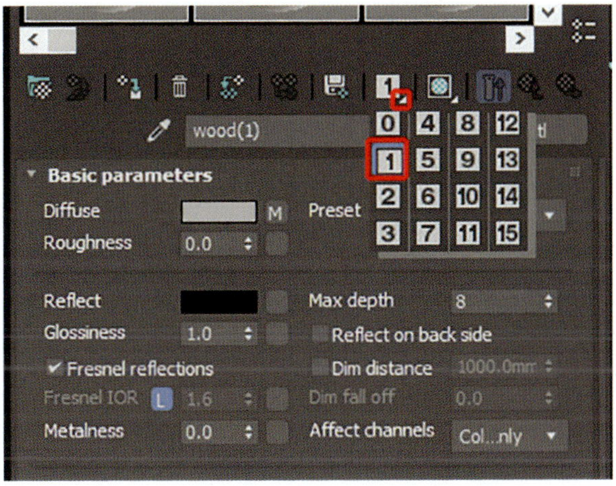

Material ID number changed from 0 to 1

Next, disable the Fresnel reflections function to control the Reflect parameters. To increase its reflectivity slightly, change its Whiteness Value to about 12.

To add a bit of glossiness, decrease its value to about 0.84

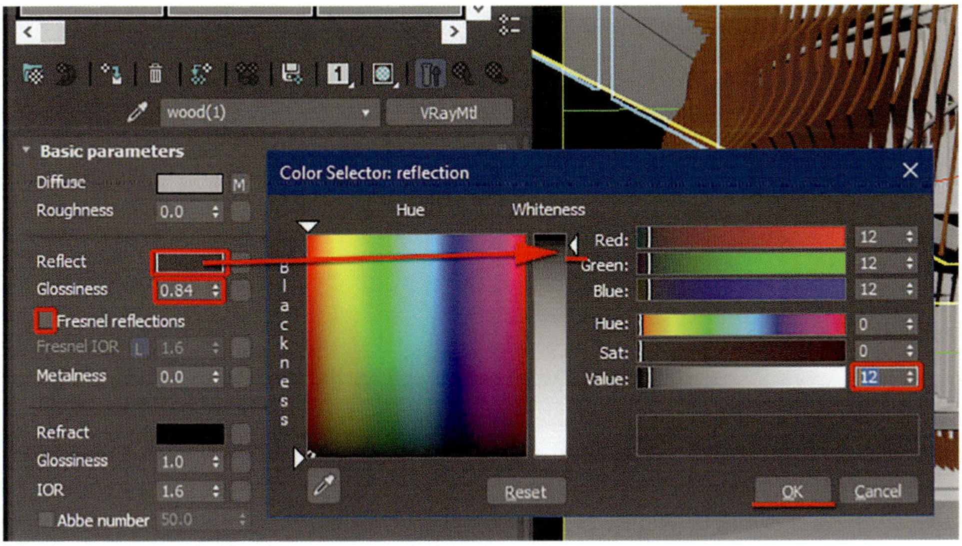

Fresnel reflections disabled and Reflect parameters changed

To have the surface reflect light unevenly, drag and drop the Diffuse toggle into the Reflect toggle. Choose the Copy Method.

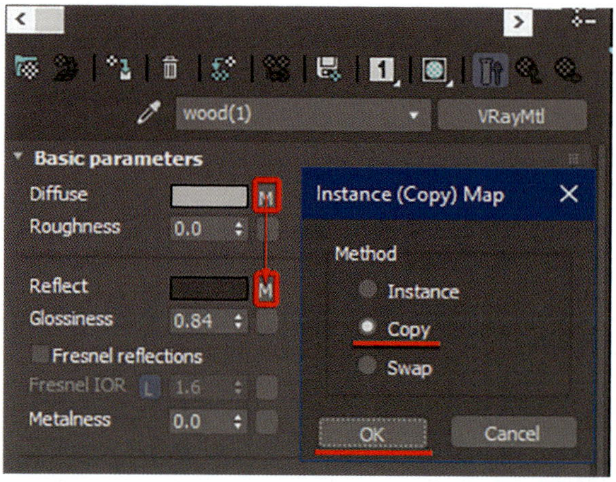

Drag/drop the Diffuse toggle into the Reflect toggle, and choose the Copy Method

Go inside the Reflect toggle to its VRayBitmap level. Change the current Bitmap to, wood-048_afzelia-1_d_Gloss 3.JPG.This is a grayscale version of the diffuse texture.

As mentioned earlier, grayscale bitmaps work best for reflections, glossiness, bumps and displacements.

This can easily be achieved by adding the Hue/Saturation adjustment in Photoshop, and decreasing the Saturation value to –100.

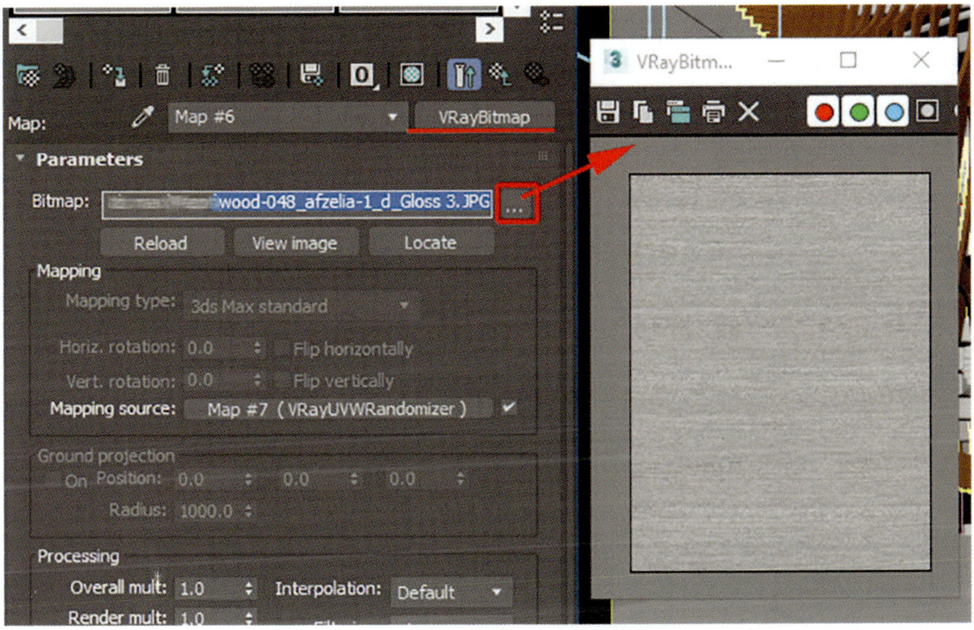

Reflect toggle Bitmap changed to, wood-048_afzelia-1_d_Gloss 3.JPG

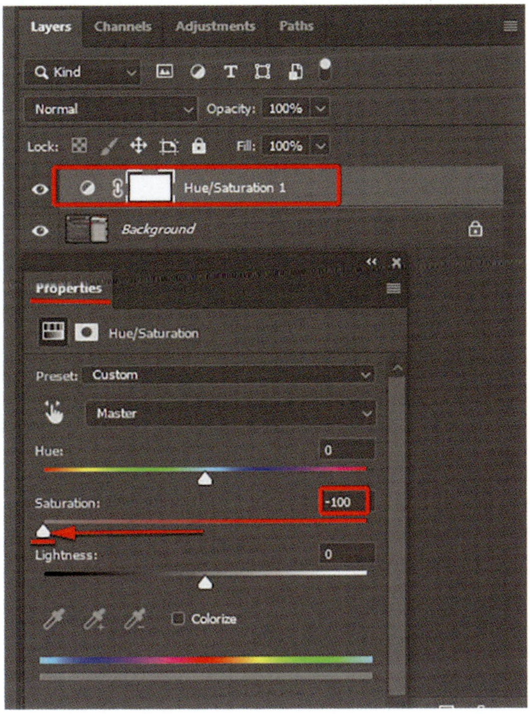

Hue/Saturation adjustment in Photoshop

Click on the Go to Parent button to go to the Color Correction parameters. Reduce its Saturation to –100.

To add a bit of contrast between the bright and darker areas of the grayscale texture, under Lightness, change it to Standard, followed by reducing the Brightness to –39.535 and the Contrast to –14.95.

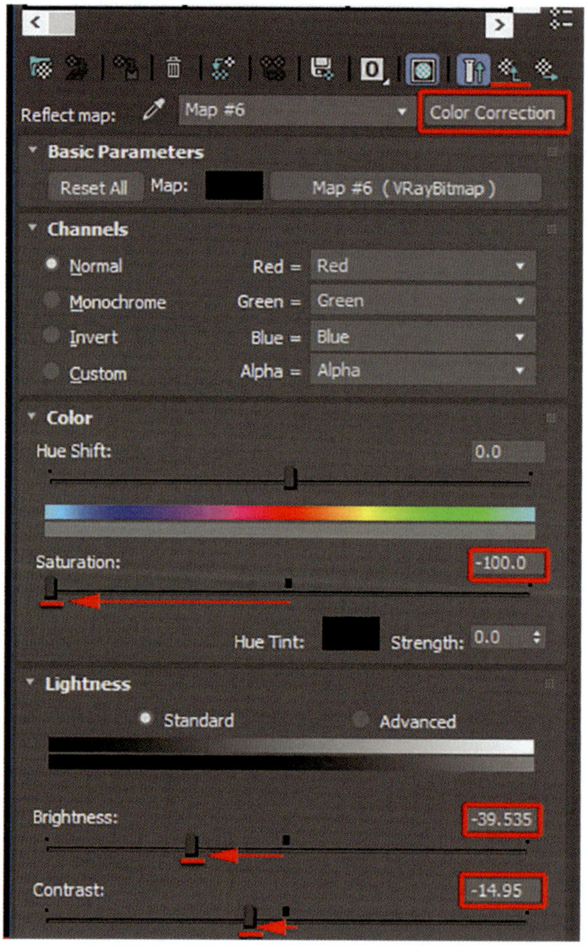

Color Correction new adjustments

Next, go back to the main parameters. Drag/drop the Reflect toggle into the Glossiness toggle, and choose to Copy it.

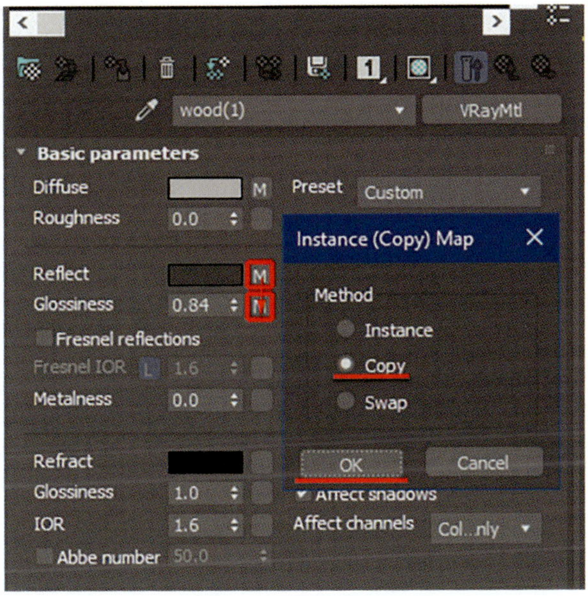

Copy the Reflect toggle to Glossiness toggle

Inside the Refl. gloss toggle, under Color Correction Lightness, decrease the Brightness to –30.897 and the Contrast to –54.817.

NOTE

These values worked well. However, feel free to try different values, if desired.

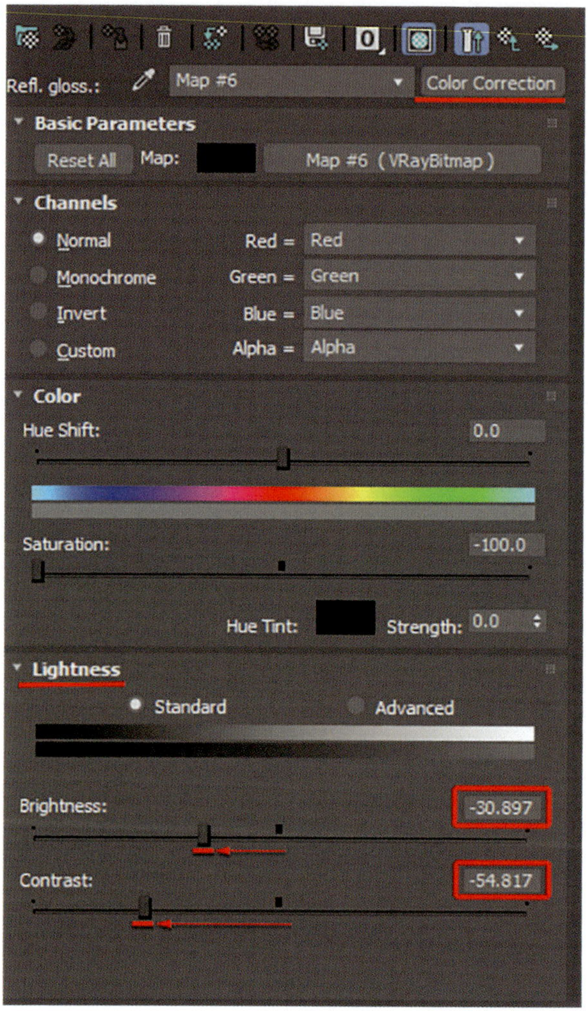

Color Correction Lightness values decrease

To mix between the Reflect color values and its material toggle, scroll down to the Maps rollout and reduce the Reflect values to 64.0.

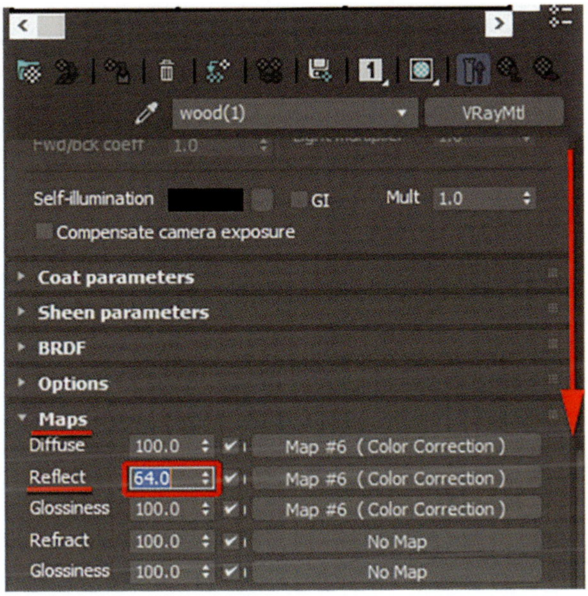

Maps rollout Reflect values reduced to 64.0

NOTE

The Acquire function only works on other objects with UVW Map modifier applied to. Otherwise, no objects will be picked.

Also, in the scene, assign this material to the object named, Slate Vertical Left. Open its Modify panel and apply the UVW Map modifier to it, as previously done.

Next, under Alignment group, click on the Acquire button and pick the object named, Slate Vertical right, which already has a similar UVW Map modifier applied to, in order to acquire its UVW Map modifier.

Once the Slate Vertical right object is picked, the Acquire UVW Mapping dialog should be prompted. Choose the option to Acquire Relative. Unlike the option to Acquire Absolute, the Acquire Relative acquires other object's UVW coordinates according to its dimensions.

Finally, test render the material using the V-Ray Viewport IPR.

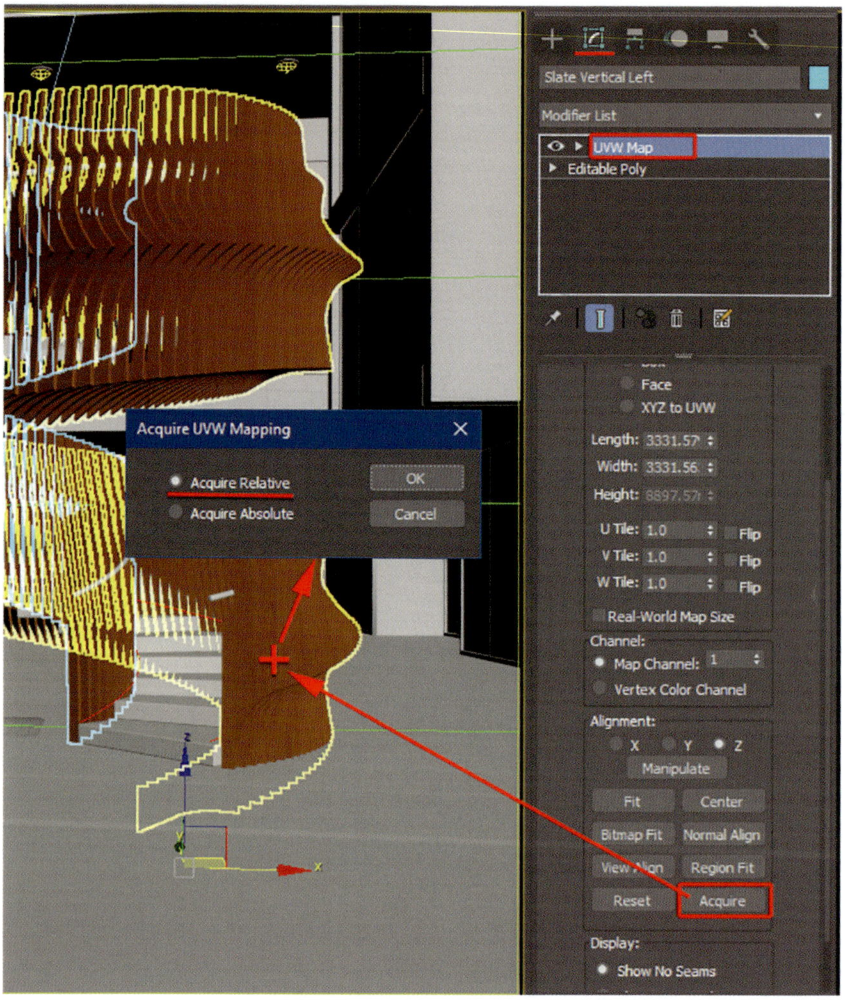

Click on the Acquire button and pick the Slate Vertical right object in the scene

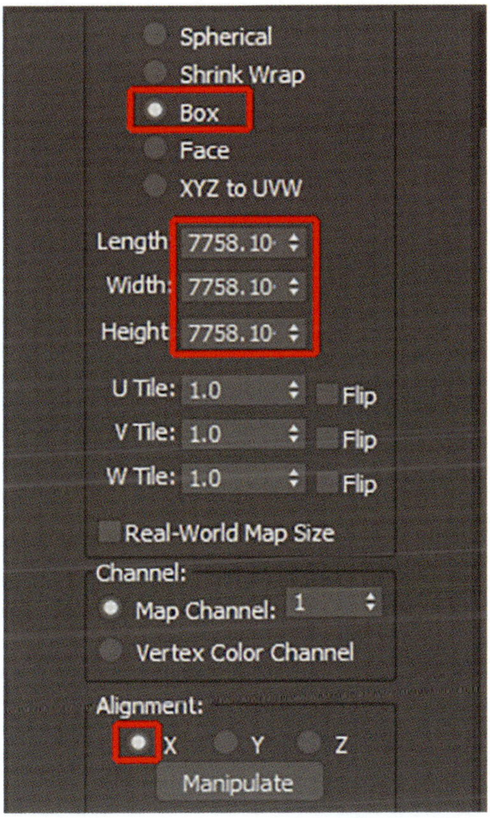

Acquire final result

Concrete Material

Concrete finish

Concrete material's main physical attributes are its color, coarse finish and the manner in which it interacts/reflects light.

In the scene, select the object named, SpiralStair001. Choose an empty material slot and assign it to the selected object.

Next, change its Material ID number to 3, and rename it as, Concrete (3).

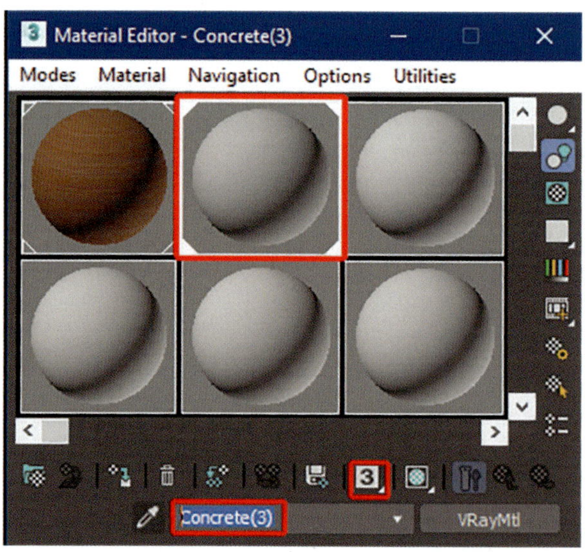

Change the Material ID number to 6, and rename it

As previously done, in the Diffuse toggle, use the VRayBitmap and apply the texture named, TexturesCom_ConcreteBare0428_4_seamless_L.

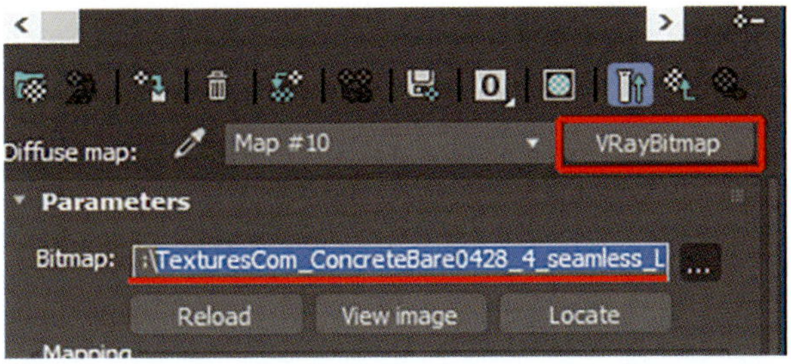

Apply a texture to the Diffuse/VRayBitmap toggle

To randomize the texture, apply the VRayUVWRandomizer to the Mapping source toggle. Enable the Stochastic tiling function and increase the Seed to 1.

Next, change the U offset and V offset to 0.01. Also, change the U offset Steps to 0.2 and V offset Steps to 0.01.

And set the UV rotation To 0.0.

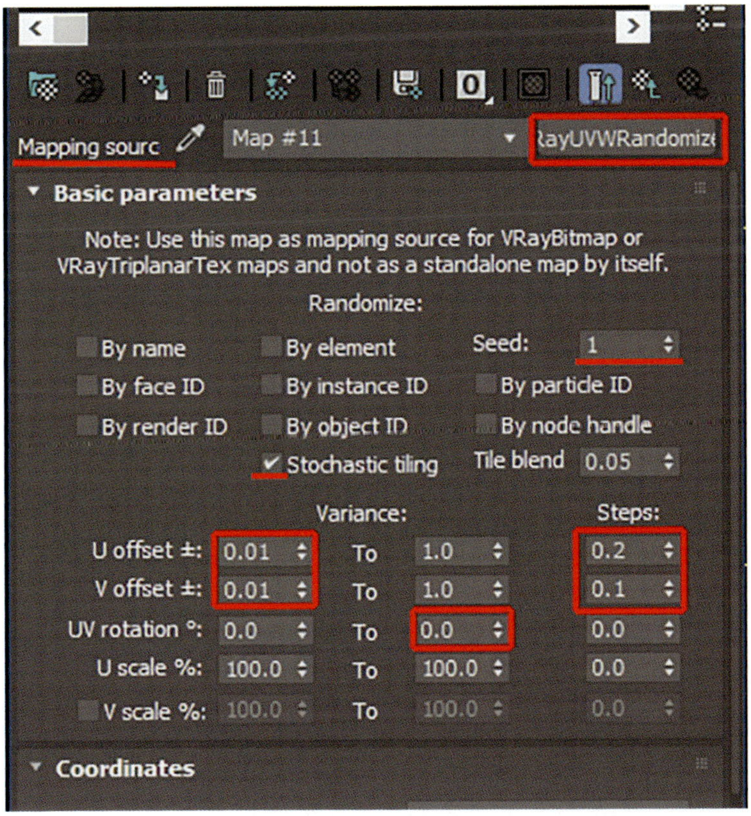

Apply the VRayUVWRandomizer to the Mapping source toggle

To control its brightness, Go to Parent, click on the VRayBitmap toggle and choose the Color Correction from the Material/Map Browser dialog.

Choose to keep old map as sub-map.

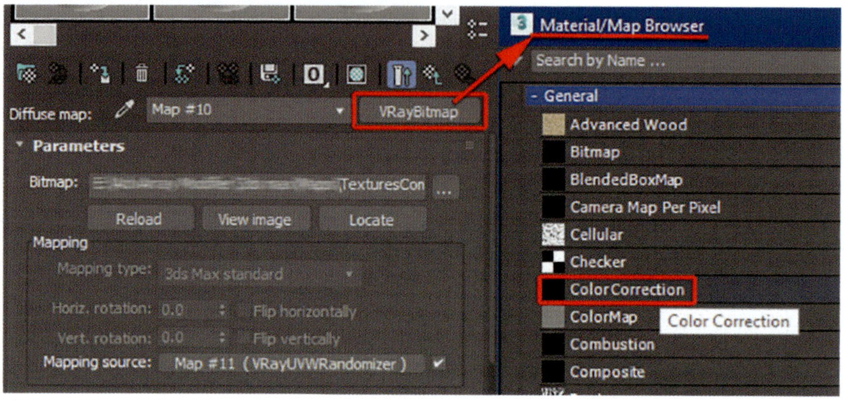

Pick the Color Correction from the Material/Map Browser dialog

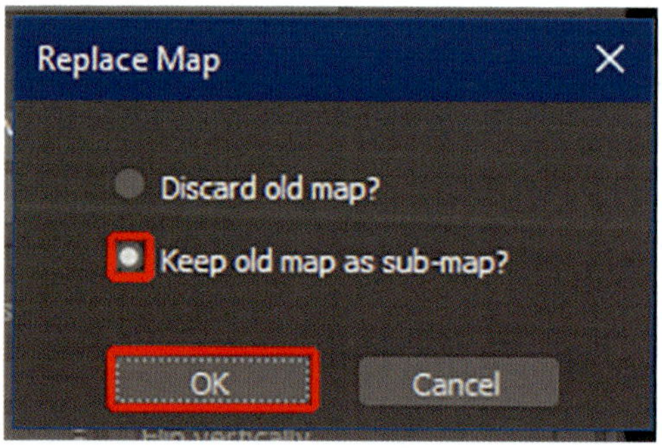

Choose to Keep old map as sub-map

Under Lightness, enable the Advanced option and increase the RGB Gamma/ Contrast to 0.5.

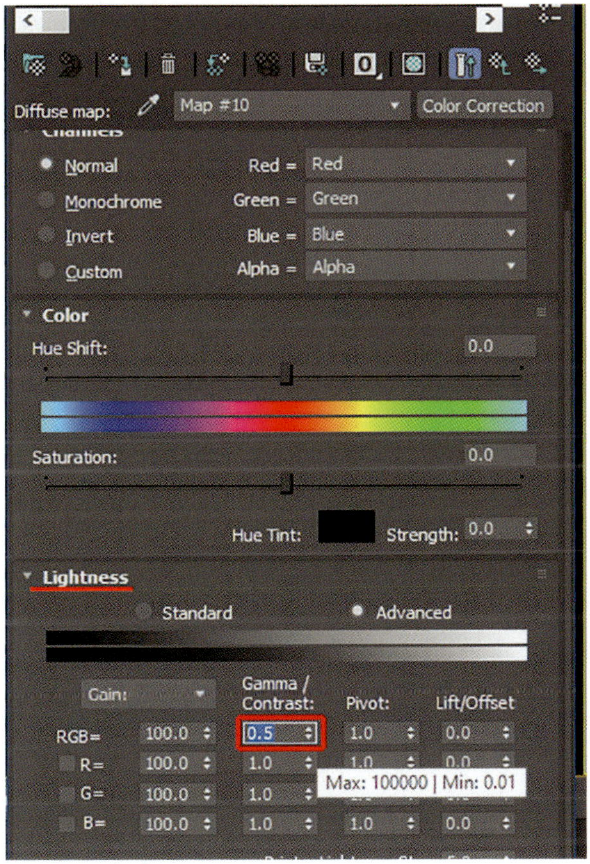

Enable the Advanced option and increase the RGB Gamma/Contrast to 0.5

To emulate the concrete surface reflecting light unevenly, go back to the main Basic parameters, and copy the Diffuse toggle into the Reflect toggle.

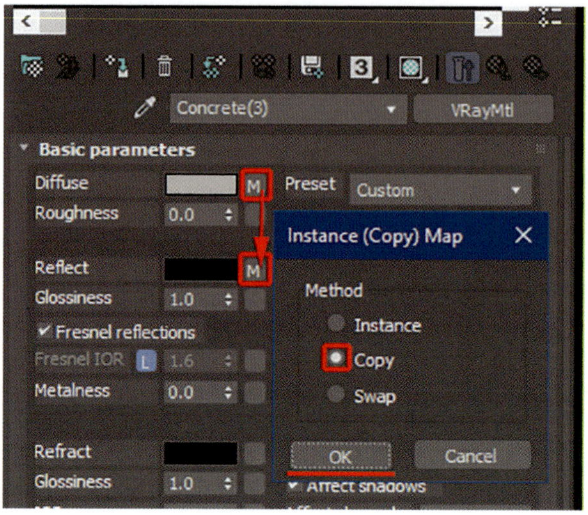

Copy the Diffuse toggle into the Reflect toggle

In the Reflect map, decrease the Saturation to –100. Under Lightness, enable the Standard option.

Decrease the Brightness to, –24.917 and increase the Contrast to 35.548.

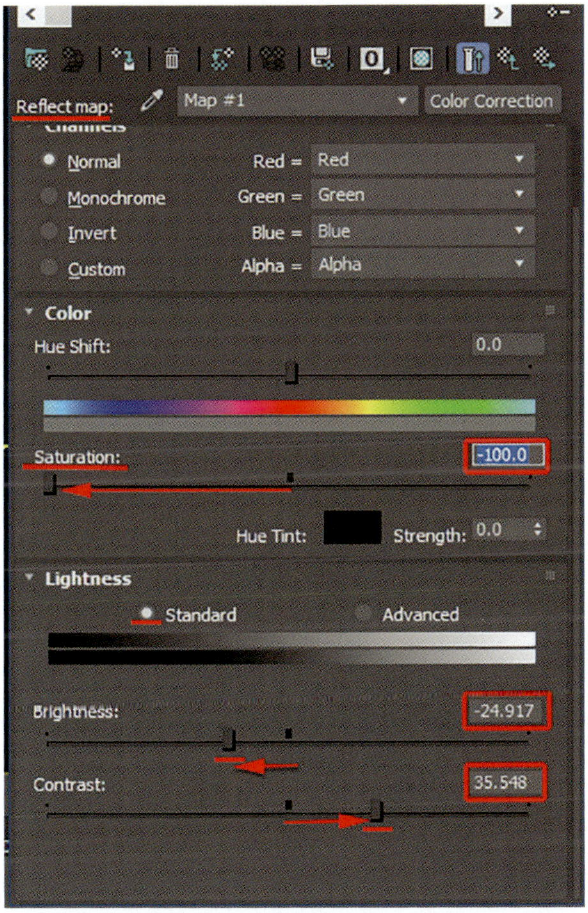

Decrease the Saturation to –100 and tweak with the Lightness values

Back in the main Basic parameters, disable the Fresnel reflections and increase the Reflect color by 12. Also, decrease the Glossiness value to 0.84.

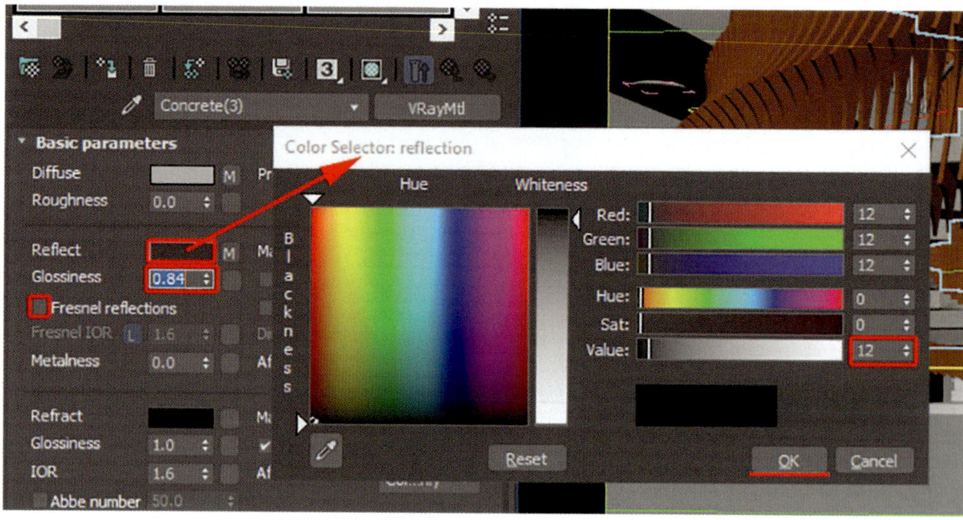

Disable the Fresnel reflections, tweak the Reflect color and Glossiness value

To control the Glossiness effects via a grayscale map, copy the Reflect toggle into the Glossiness toggle.

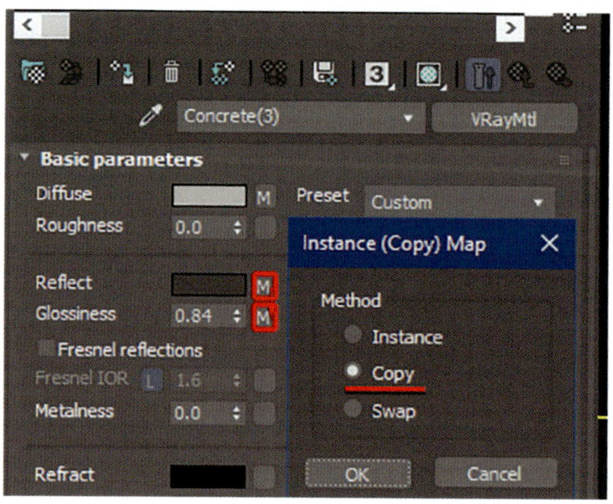

Copy the Reflect toggle into the Glossiness toggle

Inside the Refl. gloss toggle, under lightness, set the Brightness value to 8.306, and the Contrast to −64.784.

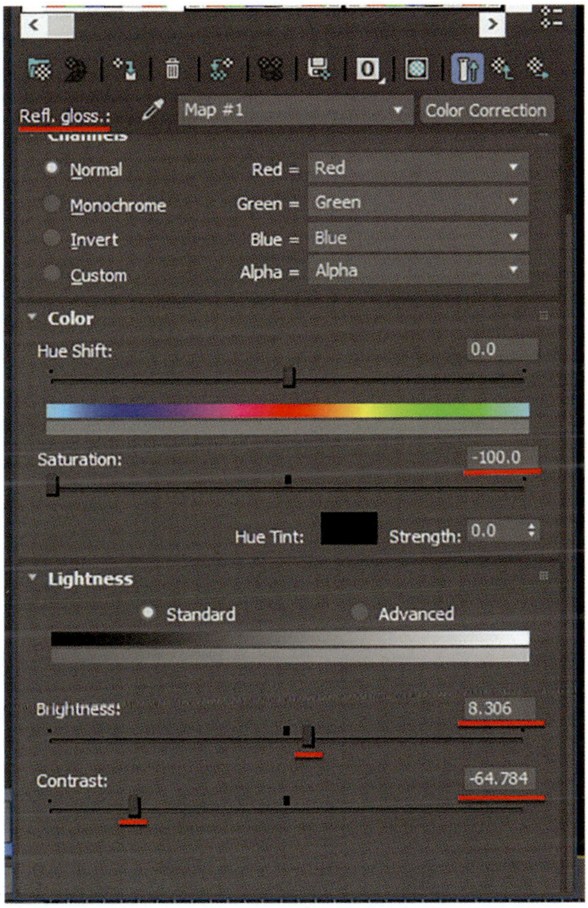

Set the Brightness value to 8.306, and the Contrast to −64.784

NOTE

These values worked well. However, feel free to try different settings and values.

To mix between the numerical values and the toggle grayscale contrast, scroll down to the Maps rollout parameters. Decrease the Reflect value to 50, and Glossiness to 75.

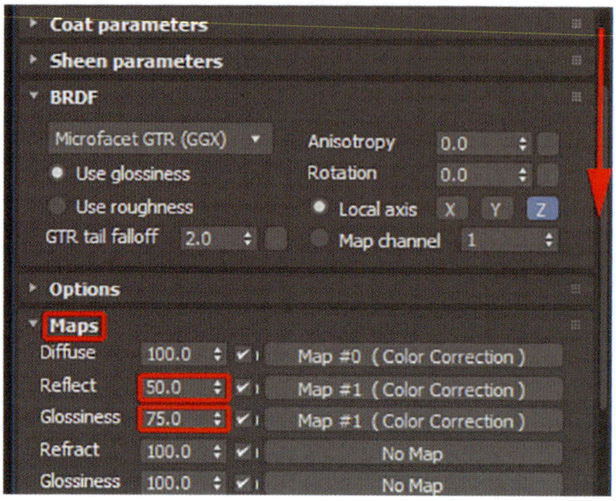

Decrease the Reflect value to 50, and Glossiness to 75

To add a bit of bump to the concrete surface, right click on the Diffuse toggle and choose to Copy it.

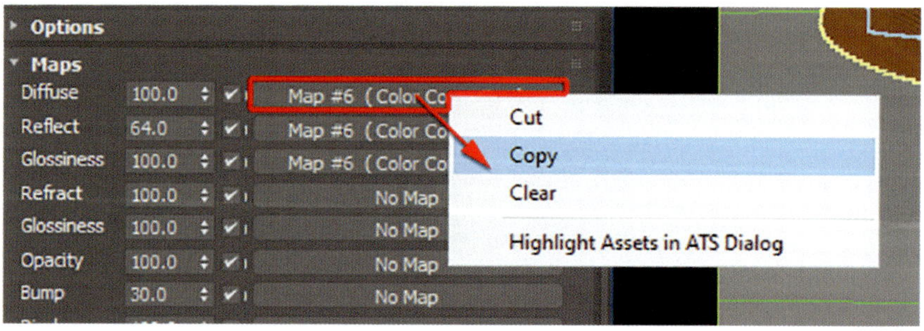

Right click on the Diffuse toggle and choose to Copy it

Under the Bump toggle, right click and choose to paste (Copy)

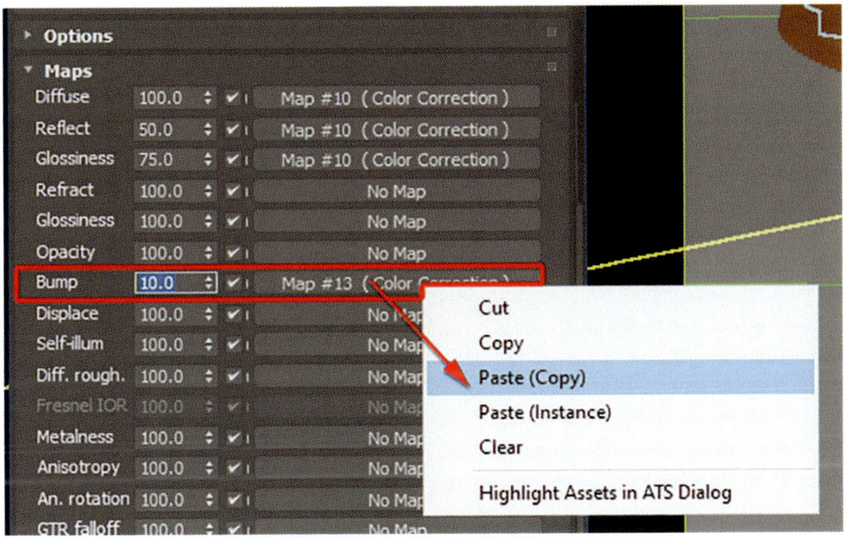

Right click and choose to paste (Copy) to the Bump toggle

To change the current Bump texture into a grayscale one, go inside its toggle and switch its current VRayBitmap texture to, TexturesCom_ConcreteBare0428_4_seamless_L_bump.JPG.

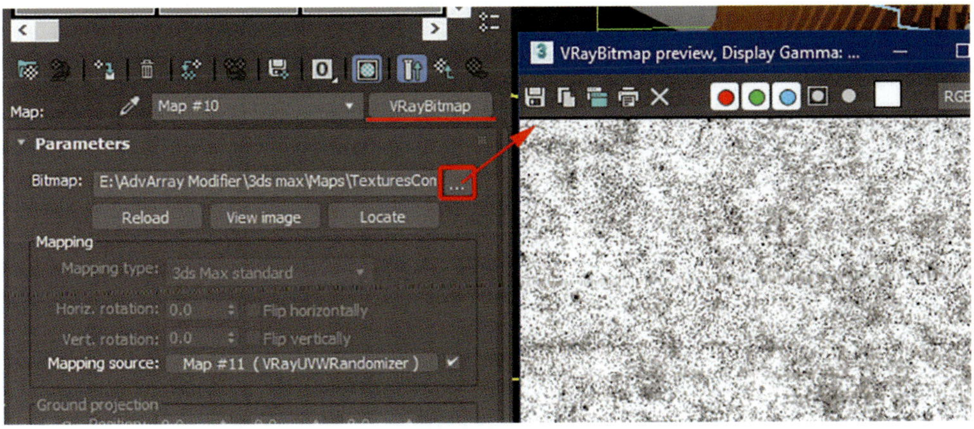

Change the Bump VRayBitmap texture to a grayscale one

Next, while the SpliralStair001 object is still selected, open the Modify panel and apply the UVW Map modifier to it.

Set its Mapping to Box type and the Length, Width, and Height values to, 2450.413mm. Also, set its U Tile, V Tile, and W tile to 2.0

NOTE

These values/settings worked well. However, feel free to try different settings and values.

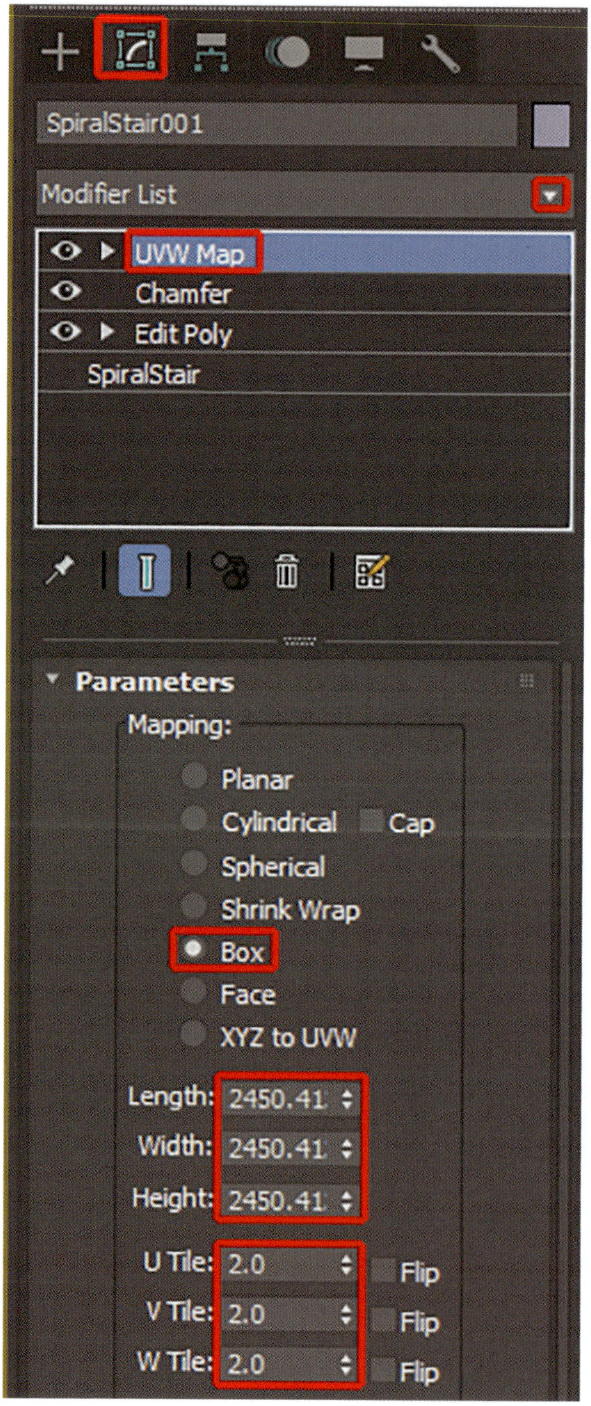

Apply the UVW Map modifier and change its parameters accordingly

The following step is to add the VRayDisplacementMod. Next, drag/drop its Bump toggle from the Material Editor into the Texmap toggle, and choose the Instance Method.

Set its Type to 2d mapping (landscape) and the amount to 2 mm. Finally, use the V-Ray Viewport IPR to preview the results.

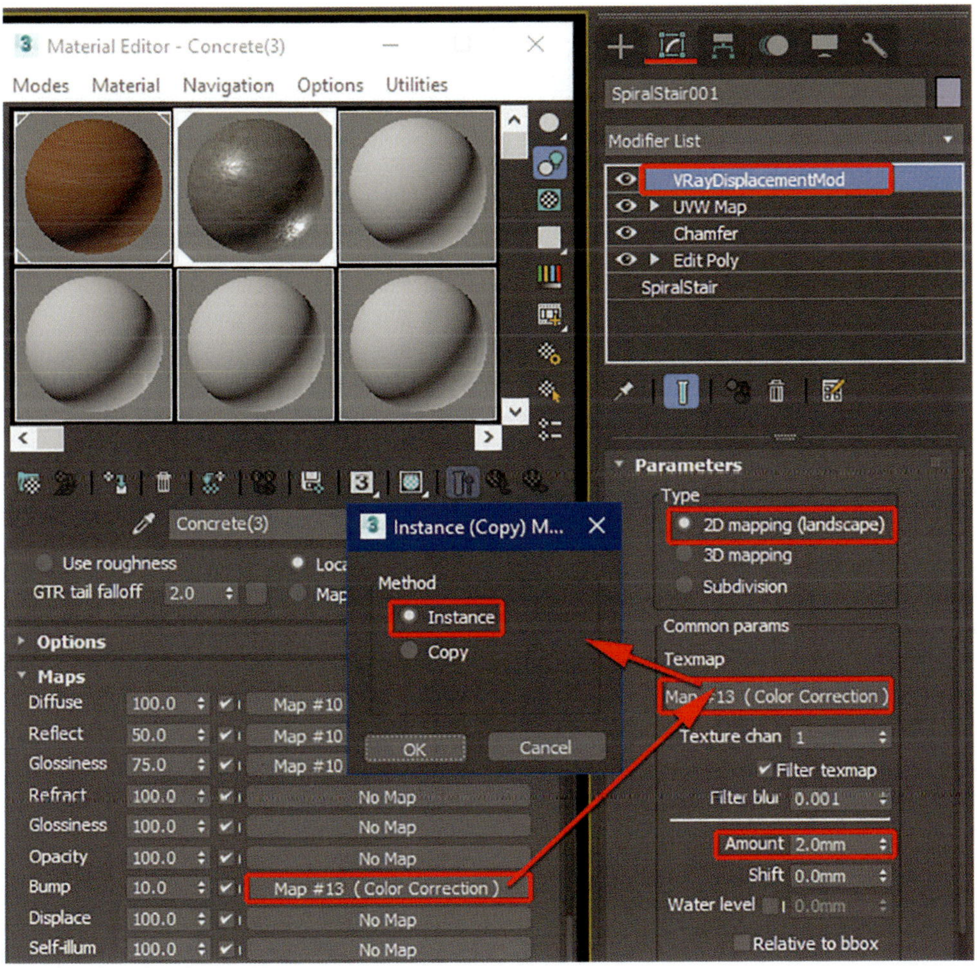

Add the VRayDisplacementMod, drag/drop the Bump toggle into the Texmap toggle, and choose the Instance Method

NOTE

These settings/values worked well. However, feel free to try different settings and values, if desired.

9 Materials and Final Render

Tiled Floor

Tiled Floor

The tiled floor to be created for this space will have similar physical properties to the one depicted in the photo reference. At first glance, its overall appearance looks slightly coarse, and substantially diffused, when viewed from an angle.

However, for the purpose of this exercise, we will be adding a bit of gloss and reflectivity to make it more appealing.

In the scene, let's start by selecting the object named, ground. In the Material Editor, select an empty slot and assign it to the selected object.

Rename the material as, ground (4) and change the Material ID to 4.

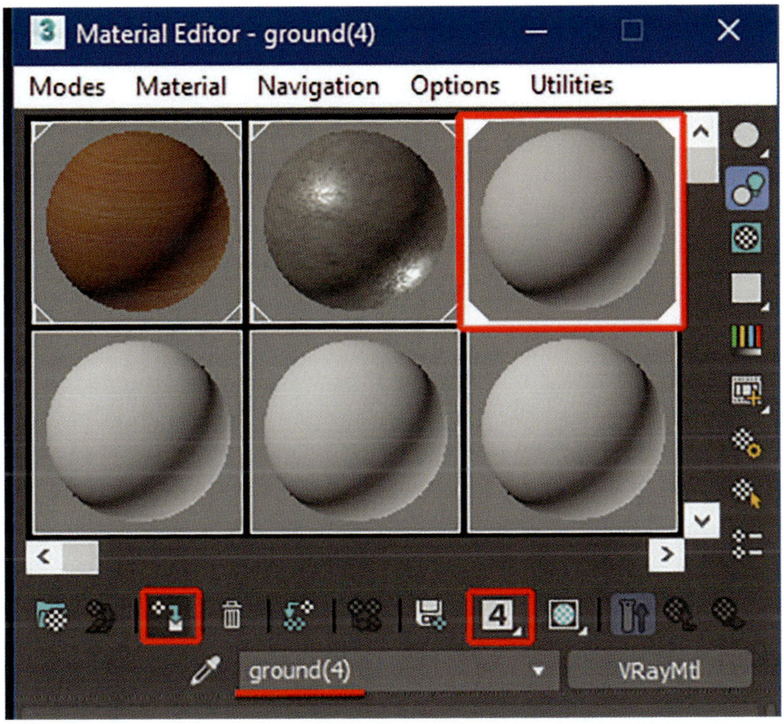

Rename the material, change the Material ID to 4 and assign it

Next, go to its Diffuse toggle, apply the VRayBitmap and choose the texture named, tiles-60_d100.jpg.

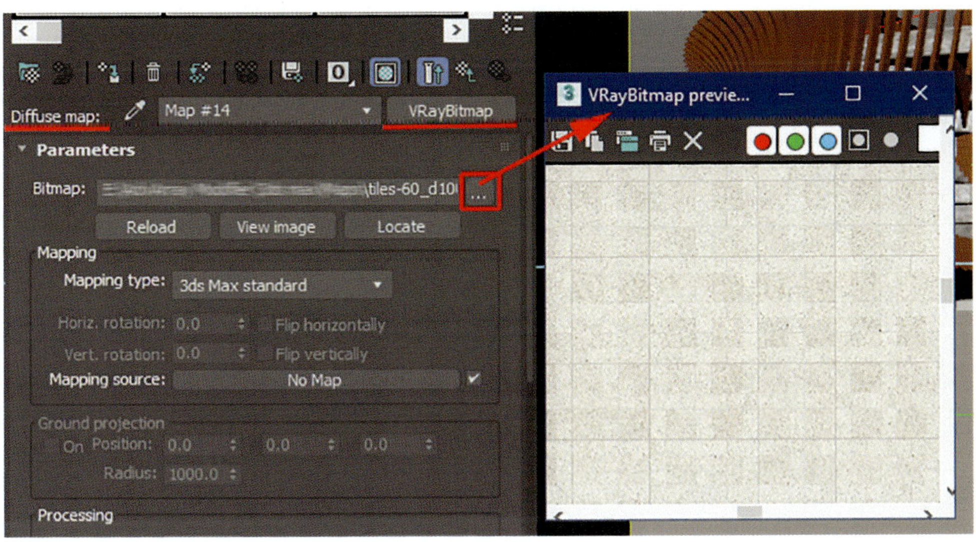

Apply the VRayBitmap and choose a texture in the Diffuse toggle

To color correct the texture, click on the VRayBitmap toggle and choose the Color Correction from the Material/Map Browser dialog.

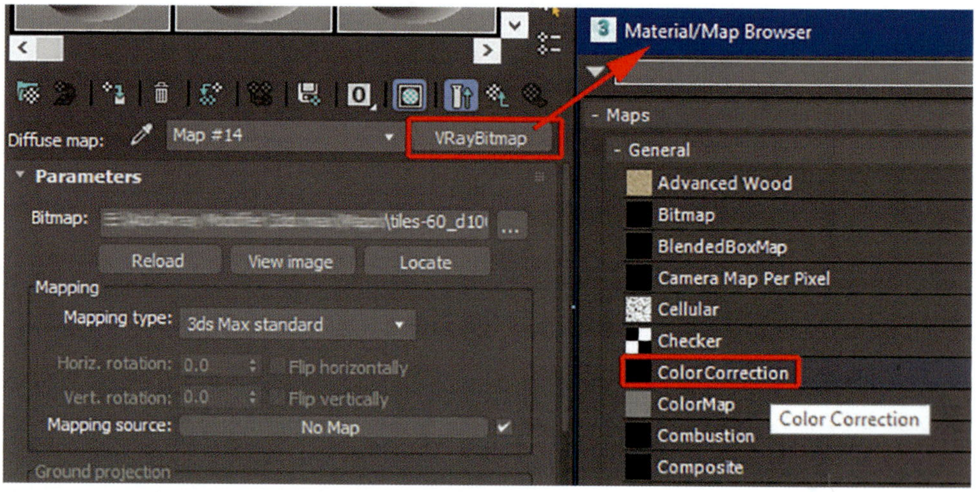

Click on the VRayBitmap toggle and choose the Color Correction

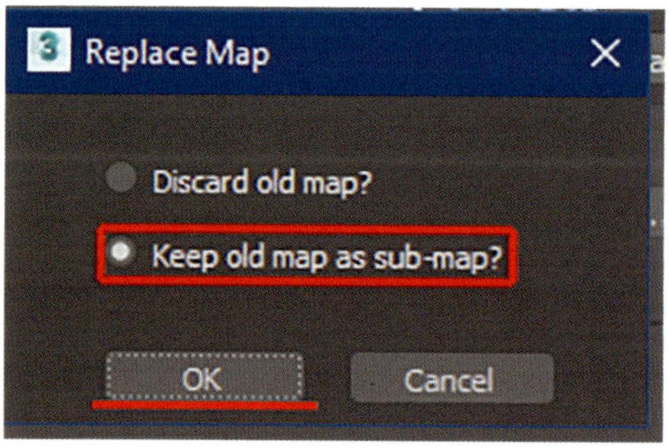

Choose to Keep old map as sub-map

In the Color Correction parameters, increase its Saturation to about 2.0. Under Lightness, choose the Advanced method and decrease the RGB Gamma/Contrast to 0.2.

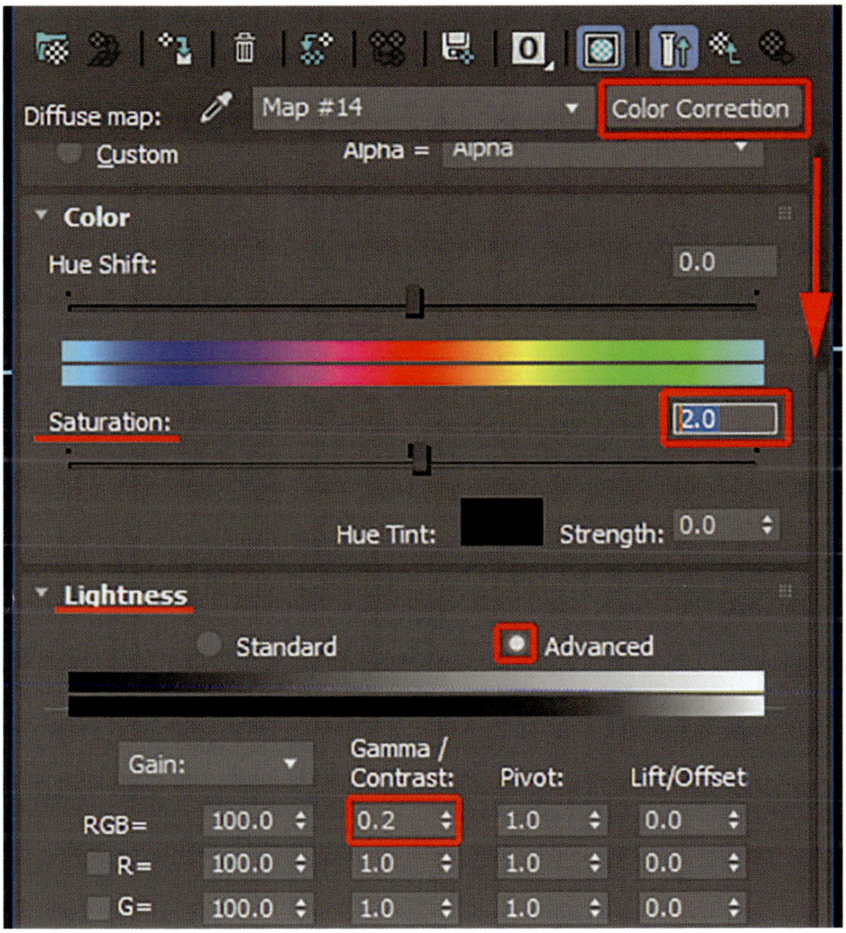

Tweak the Color Correction parameters

Back in the main Basic parameters, drag/drop the Diffuse toggle into the Reflect toggle. Choose the Copy Method.

NOTE

While these settings/values worked well, feel free to try different settings and values, if desired.

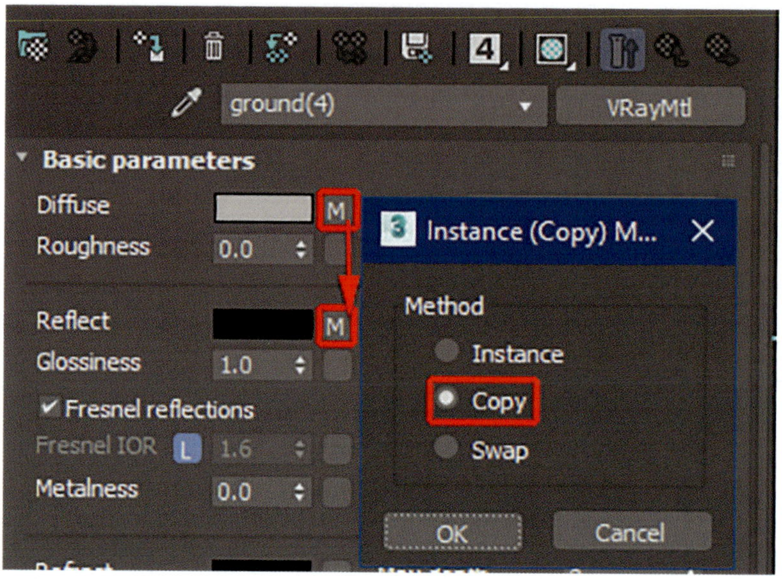

Drag/drop the Diffuse toggle into the Reflect toggle

In the Reflect map Color Correction, change the Saturation to 0.0. Under Lightness, change it to Standard.

Decrease the Brightness to –30.897 and Contrast to –3.654.

Tweak the Color Correction Reflect map

Back in the main Basic parameters, disable the Fresnel reflections function. Increase the Reflect color to 129 and the Glossiness value to 0.95.

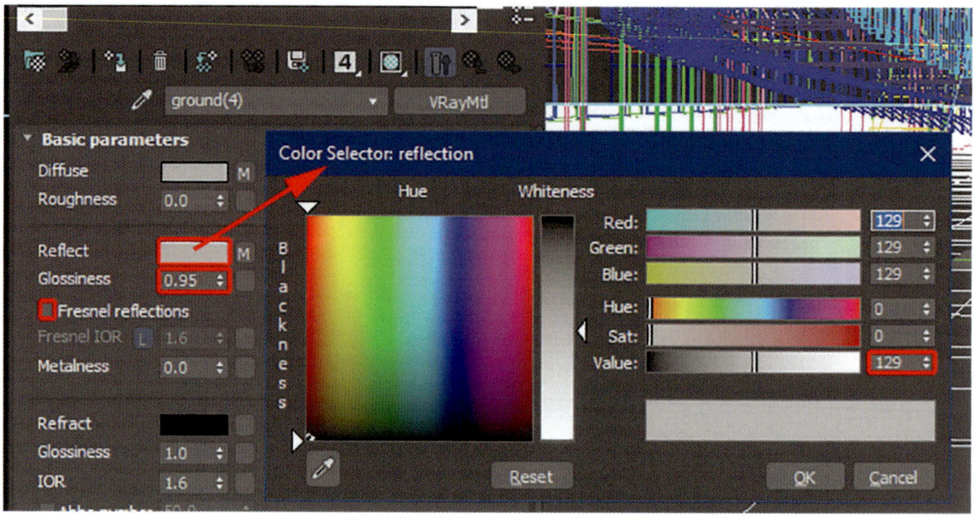

Disable the Fresnel reflections and tweak with the Reflect and Glossiness values

Next, drag/drop the Reflect toggle into the Glossiness toggle. Choose the Copy Method.

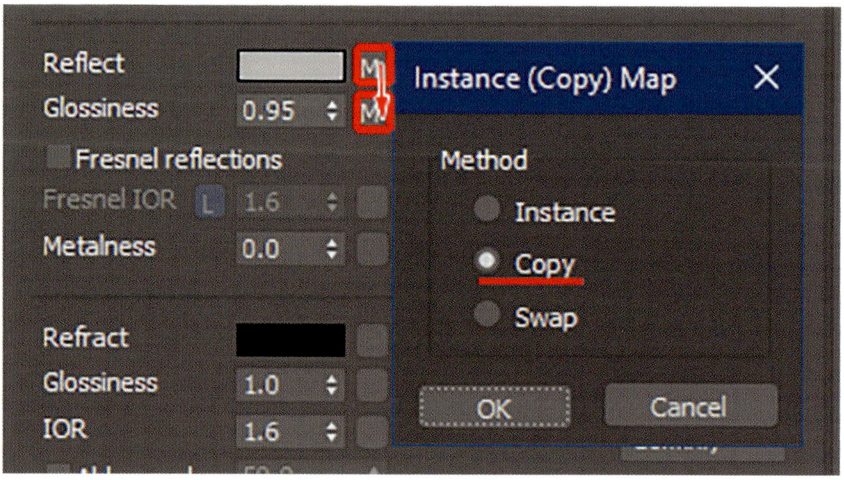

Copy the Reflect toggle into the Glossiness toggle

Inside Ref. gloss Color Correction parameters, under Lightness, enable the Standard option. Increase the Brightness value to 21.595 and the Contrast to –44.85.

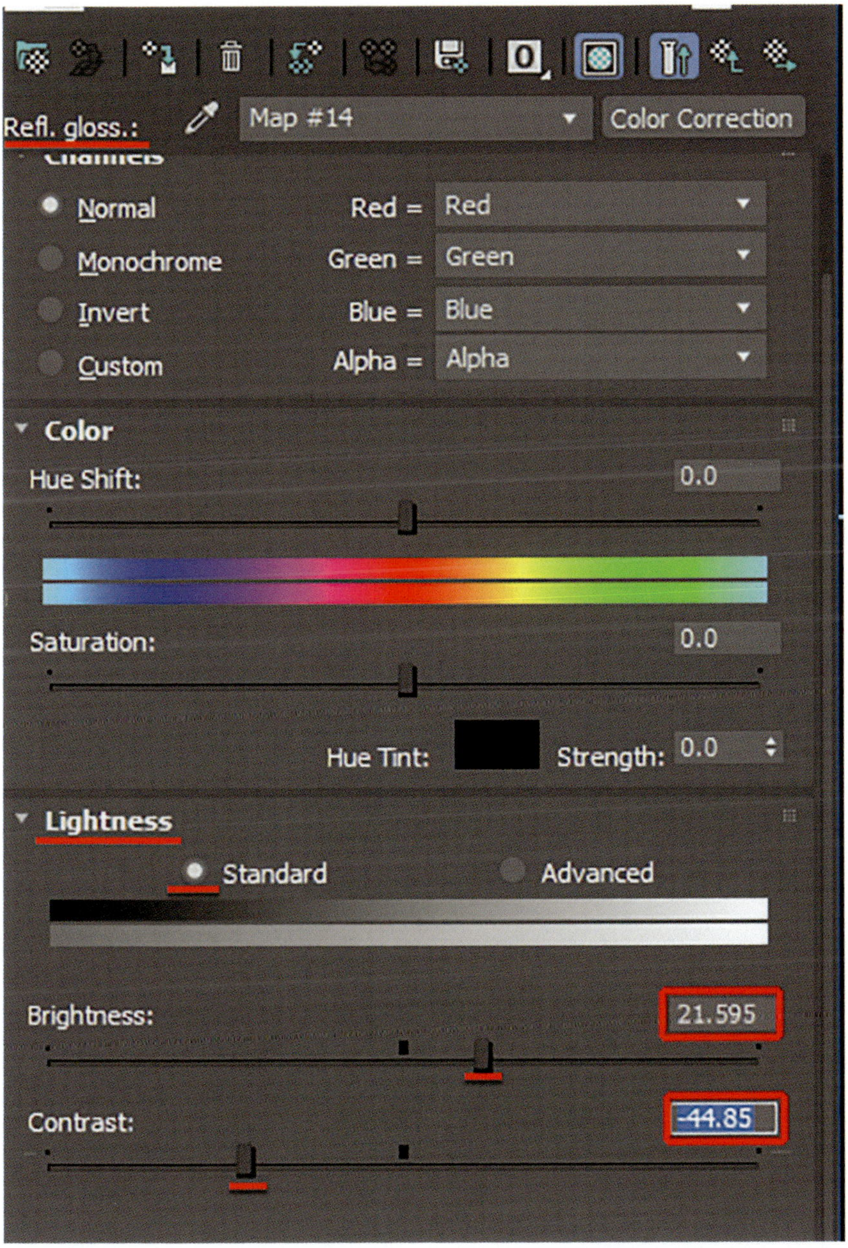

Under Lightness parameters, Increase the Brightness value to 21.595 and the Contrast to −44.85

To mix the Reflect and Glossiness toggle materials with their values, under Maps rollout parameters, decrease the Reflect value to 30 and the Glossiness to 7.0

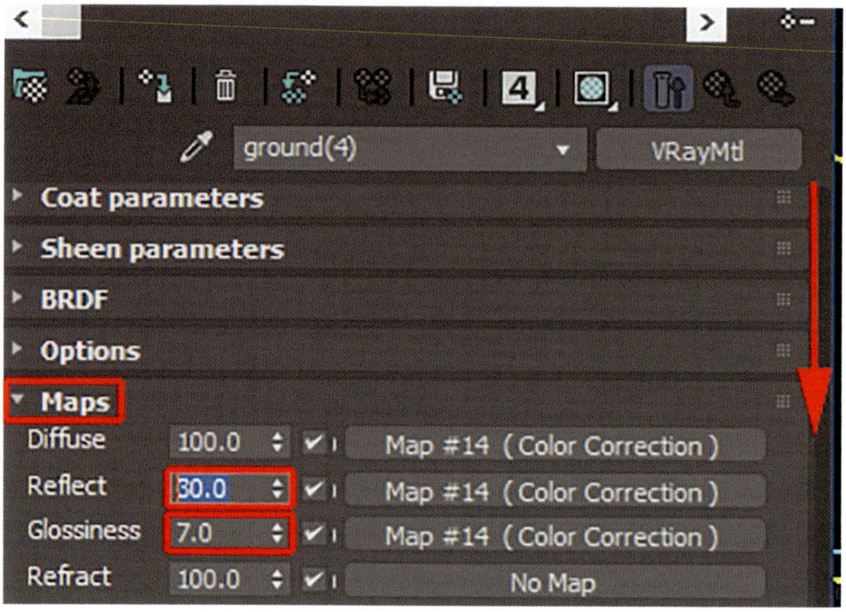

Under Maps rollout parameters, decrease the Reflect value to 30 and the Glossiness to 7.0

To add a bit of bump to the tiled surface, drag/drop the Diffuse toggle into the Bump toggle. Choose the Copy Method and set the Bump value to about 15.

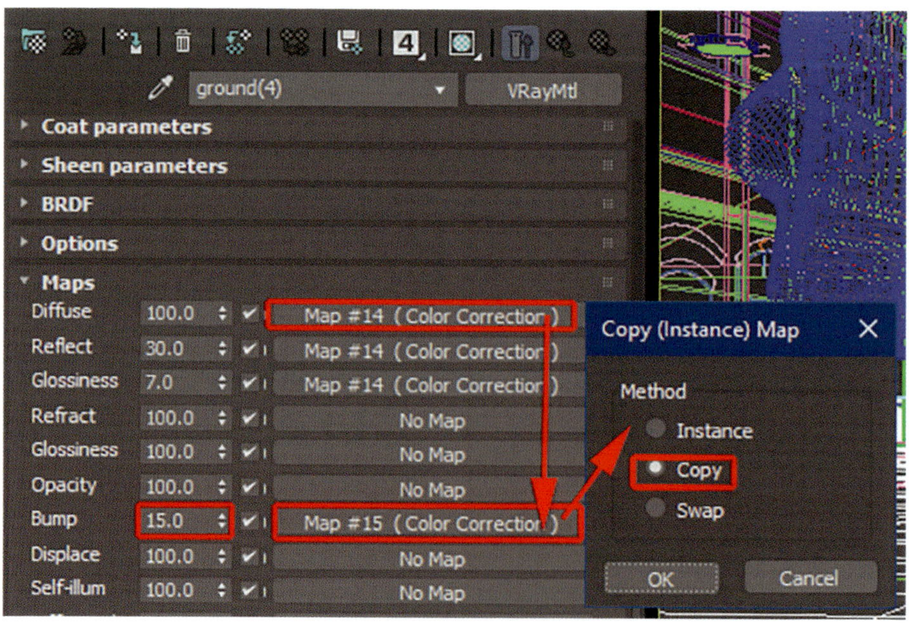

Copy the Diffuse toggle into the Bump toggle and set the Bump value to about 15

Inside the Bump toggle, go to the VRayBitmap and change the texture to, tiles-60_b010_bump.JPG.

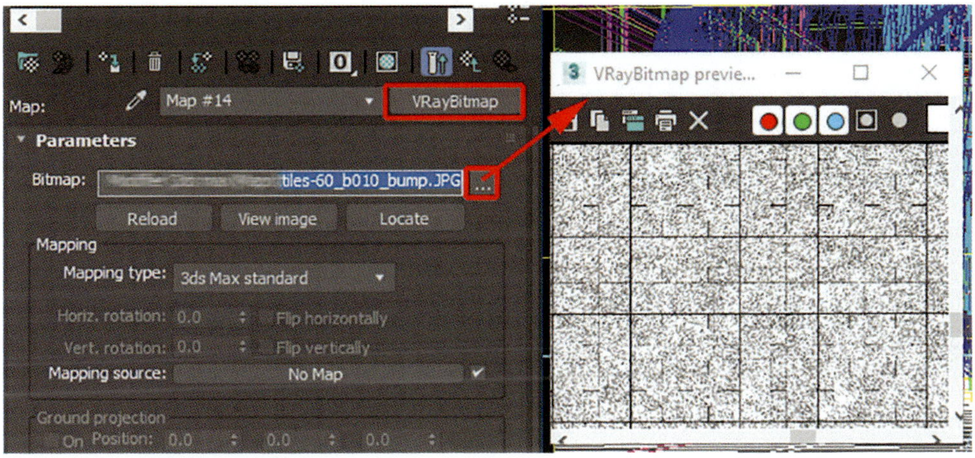

Inside the Bump toggle, change the VRayBitmap texture to a grayscale version of the same

Back in the Bump map Color Correction, decrease the Saturation to –100 and enable, the Standard option, under Lightness.

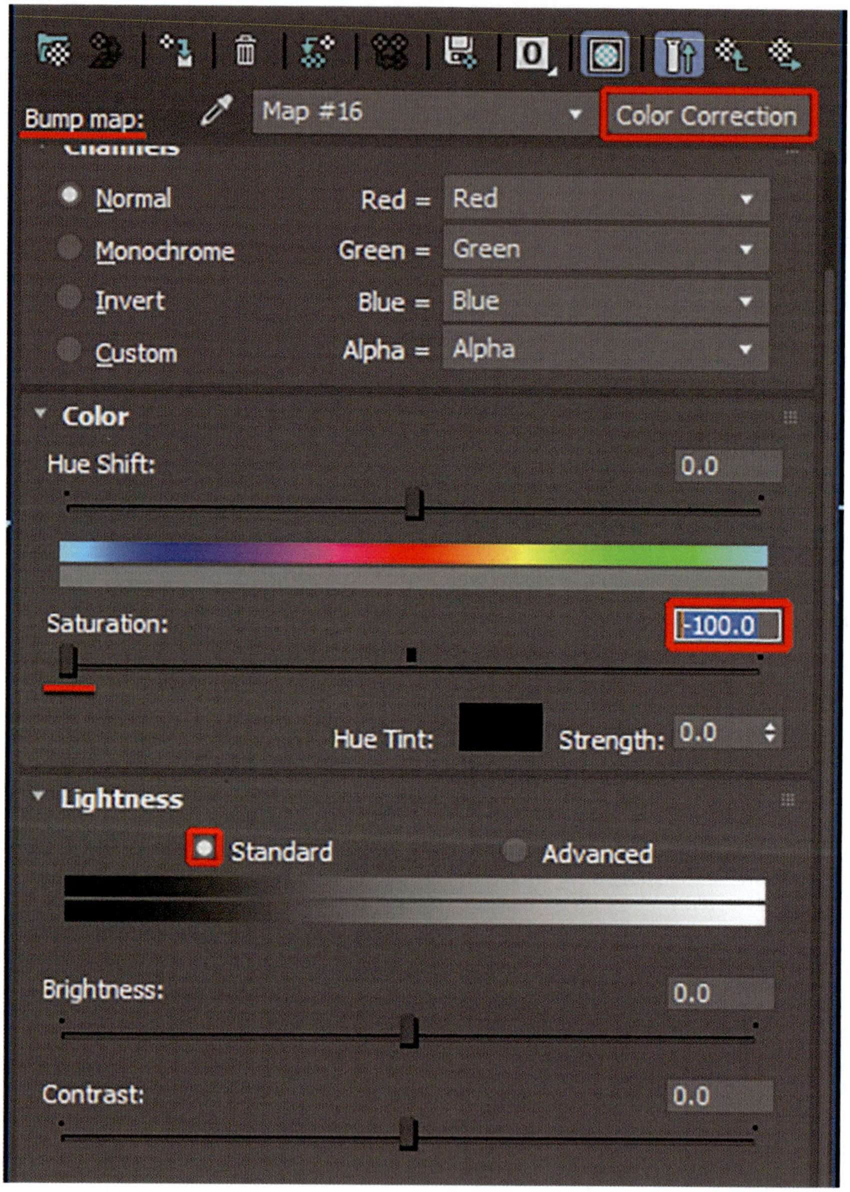

Decrease the Bump map Color Correction Saturation to –100 and enable the Standard option

While the "ground" object is still selected, open the Modify panel and apply the UVW Map modifier to it.

Enable the Box Mapping type. Set the Length, Width, and Height values to 188651.758 mm.

Also, the U and V Tile values to 9.0 and W to 11.0.

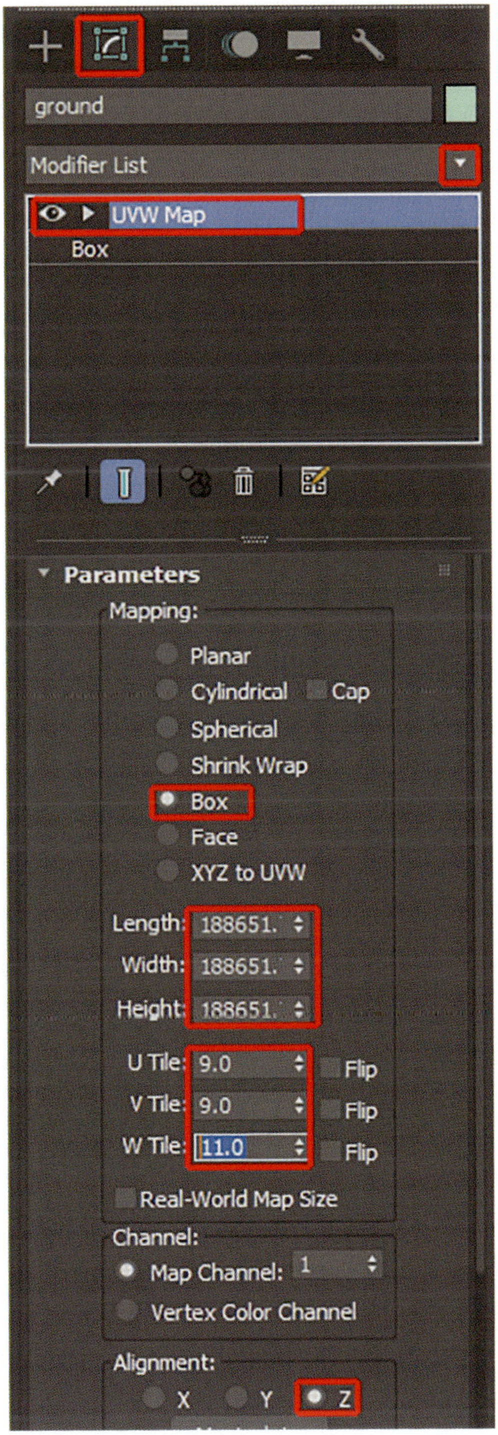

Apply the UVW Map modifier to the "ground" object and set its values accordingly

Next, to add more detail to the surface, apply the VRayDisplacementMod and enable the 2d mapping type (landscape).

In its Material Editor Maps rollout, drag/drop the Bump toggle into the Texmap and choose the Instance Method. Set the amount to 1.5 mm.

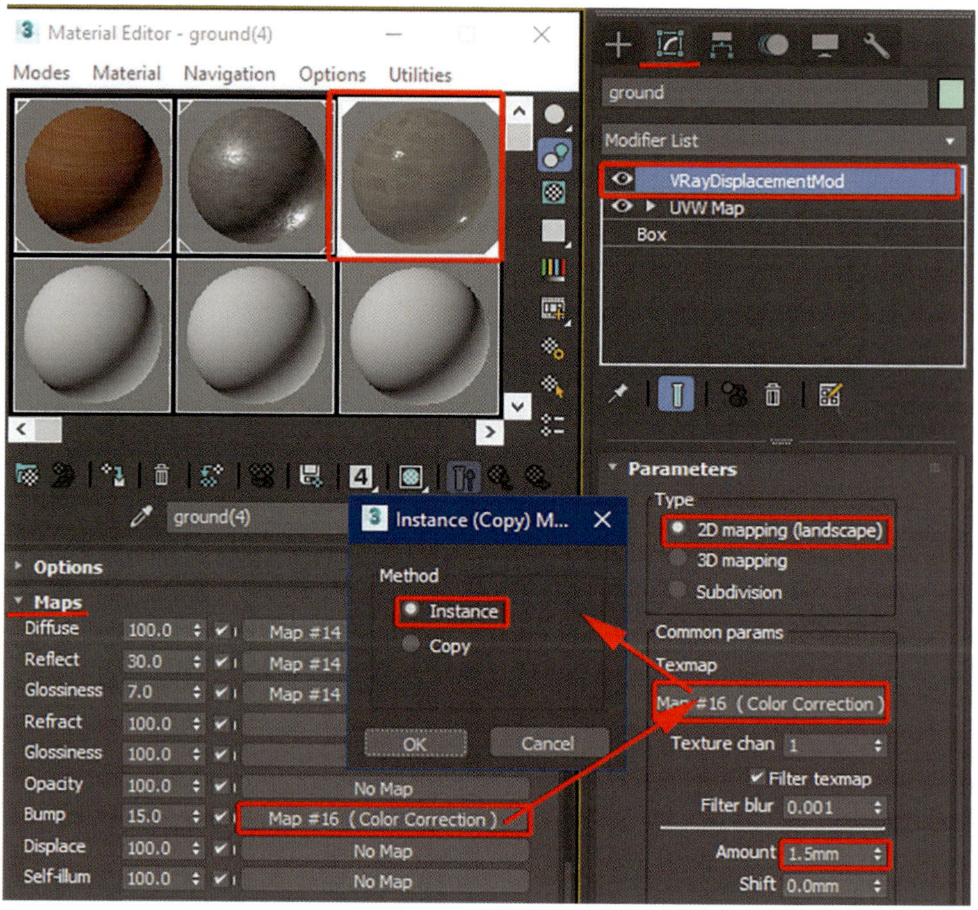

VRayDisplacementMod applied, Bump toggle instanced, and set to 1.5 mm

In terms of aesthetics, it looks better when the tiles are lining up with the main subject (the spiral staircase). To do so, go to the UVW Map Gizmo level and highlight it (in blue).

Next, move the Gizmo in the X direction, to about, 21477.405 mm. The vertical tiles should now line up with the staircase.

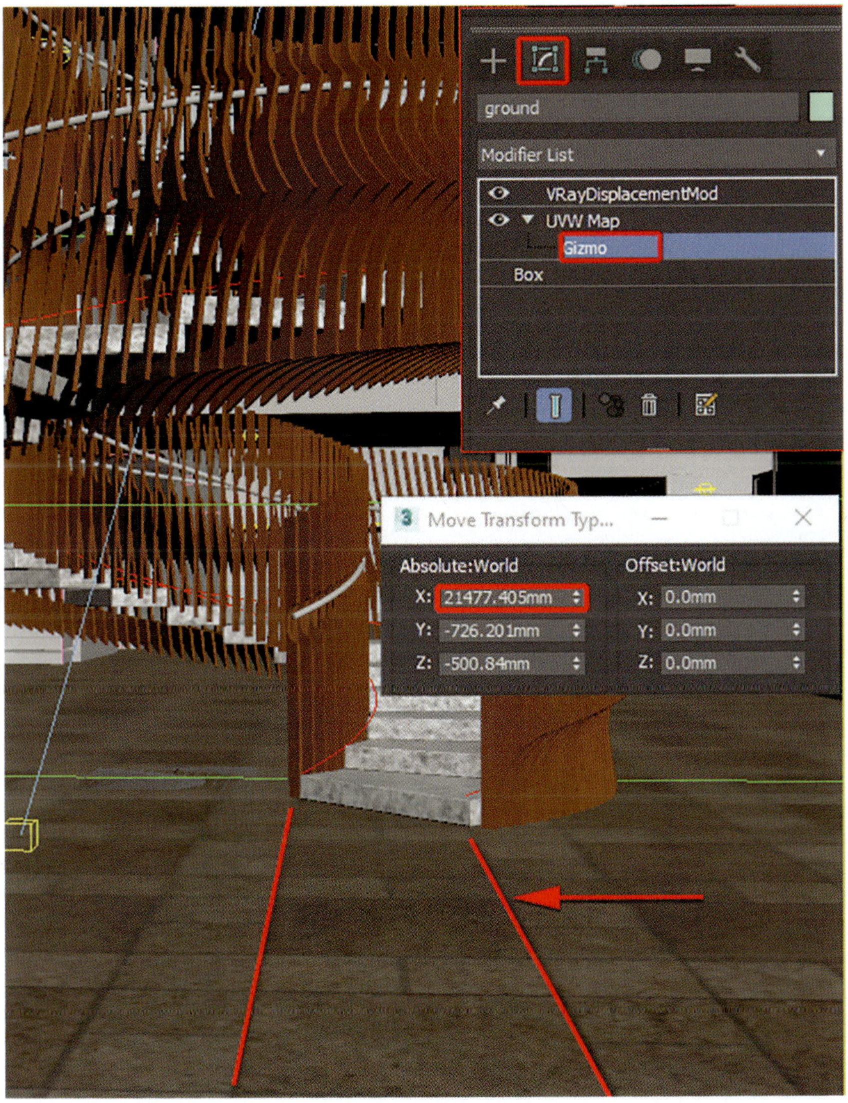

Move the UVW Map Gizmo in the X direction, to about, 21477.405 mm

Use the V-Ray viewport IPR to preview the results. As mentioned earlier, these values worked well. However, feel free to try different values, if desired.

Glass Material

Glass window

The window glass material needs no introduction. It's a slightly reflective sheet of glass, with a tint sometimes.

In the viewport, select the object named, Doubled glazed curtain walling, followed by opening the V-Ray Asset Browser dialog and choosing the Glass Window_cement_Gray material from the list.

In the Material Editor, select an empty material slot, right click on the Glass_ Window_Cement Gray material and choose to Add to scene.

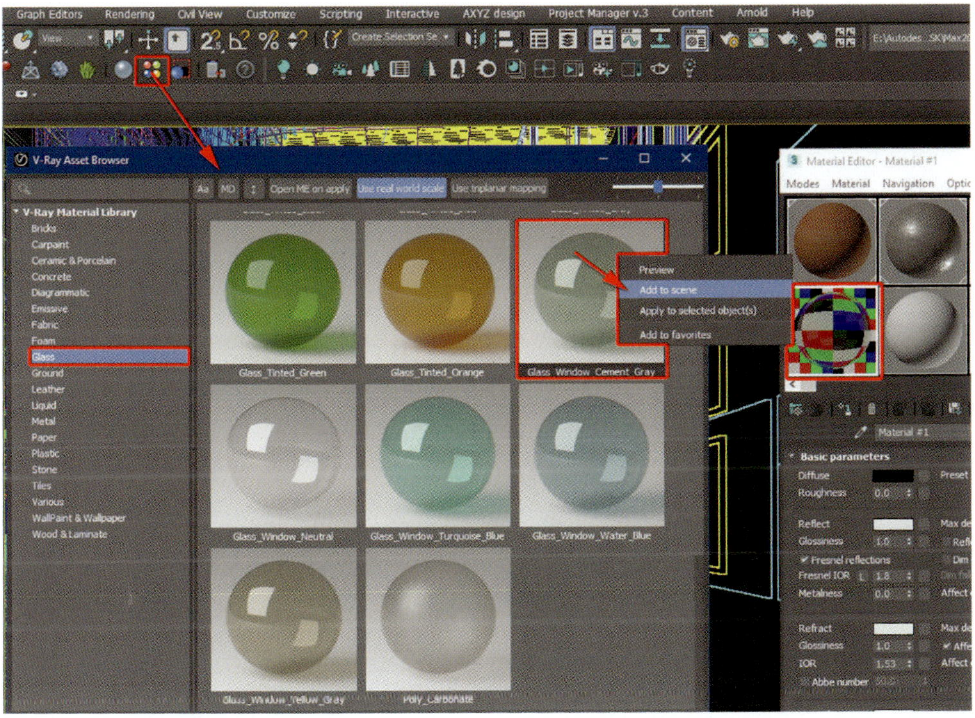

Right click on the Glass_Window_Cement Gray material and choose to Add to scene

Select the new added material into the Material Editor and assign it to the selected object, followed by renaming it as, Glass_Window_Cement_Gray (5) and changing the Material ID to 5.

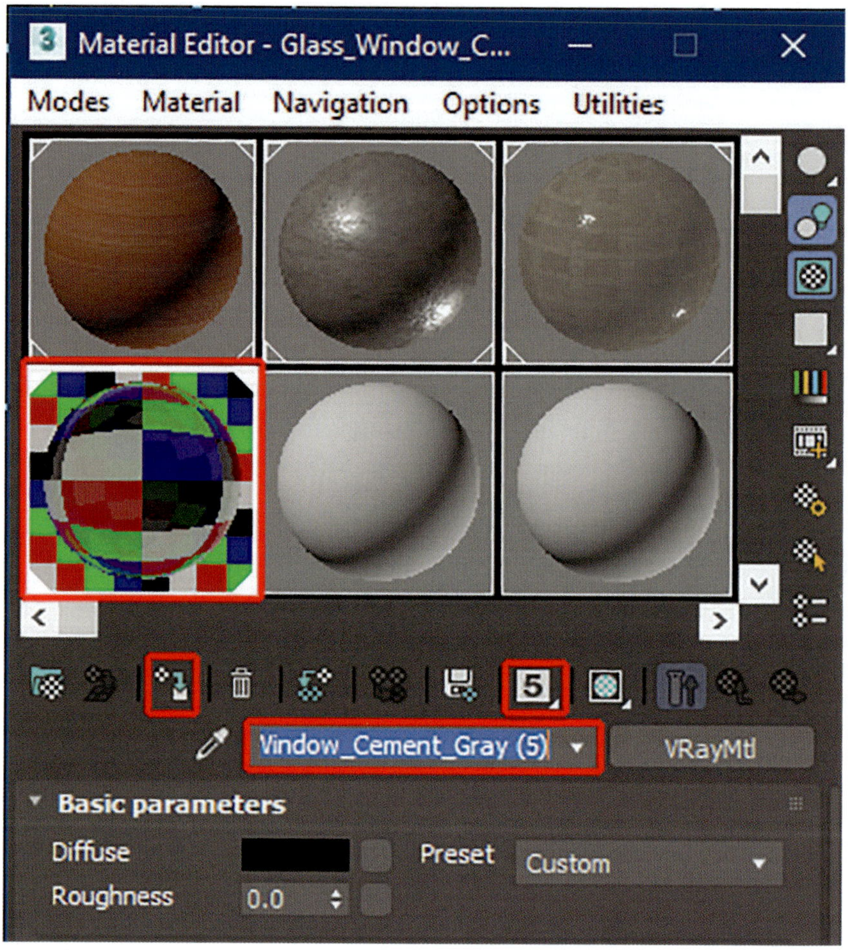

Assign the new material, rename it, and change the Material ID to 5

To be able to select objects being reflected on this surface in post-production, under Reflect group Affect channels, choose the All channels option from the list.

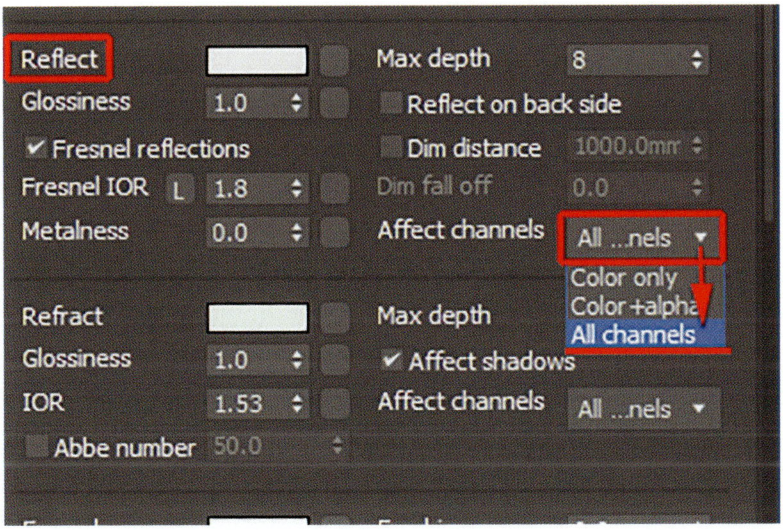

In the Reflect group, choose the All channels option from the Affect channels list

Finally, assign this material to other objects in the scene such as double glazed curtain wall, double glazed curtain wall01, double glazed northlight, Doubled glazed curtain walling, etfe cushon roof and glass.

Use the scene explorer to quickly navigate and select objects in the scene (Alt+Ctrl+O).

You can also create new variations of this glass (name them differently), with different refraction and reflection values, if desired.

Previously, the object named, etfe cushon roof, had its Object Properties to Cast Shadows disabled. With the new glass material assigned to it, the Cast Shadows function can be enabled back again.

Please check the final scene named, External daylight scene_Final.max, to see how materials were applied.

9 Materials and Final Render

Metal Material

Metal material

The type of metal surface we will be emulating in this scene will be reflective, grayish, and with glossy shine.

To start, select the object named, Metal Panel. Open the V-Ray Asset Browser dialog, and select the Metal Library.

Next, select the material, Aluminium_Blurry, and choose a new empty slot in the Material Editor. Right click and Add to scene, Aluminium_Blurry.

To be able to select objects being reflected on this surface in post-production, under Reflect group Affect channels, choose the All channels option from the list.

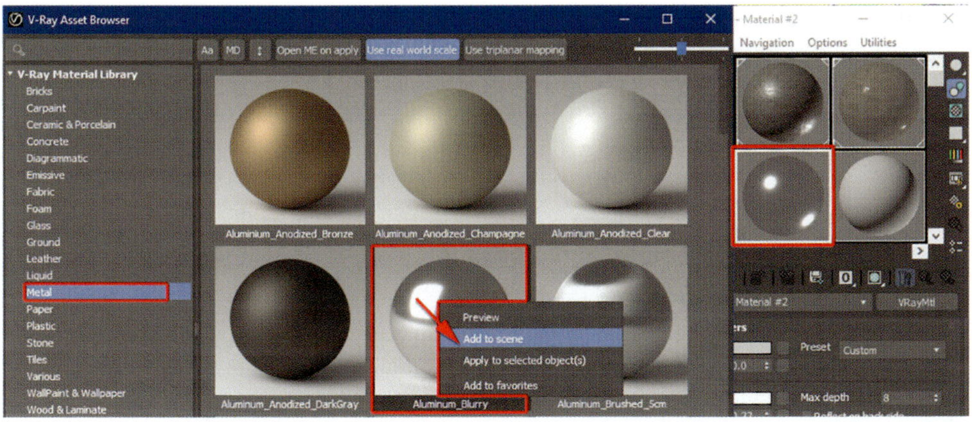

Right click and Add to the scene, Aluminium_Blurry

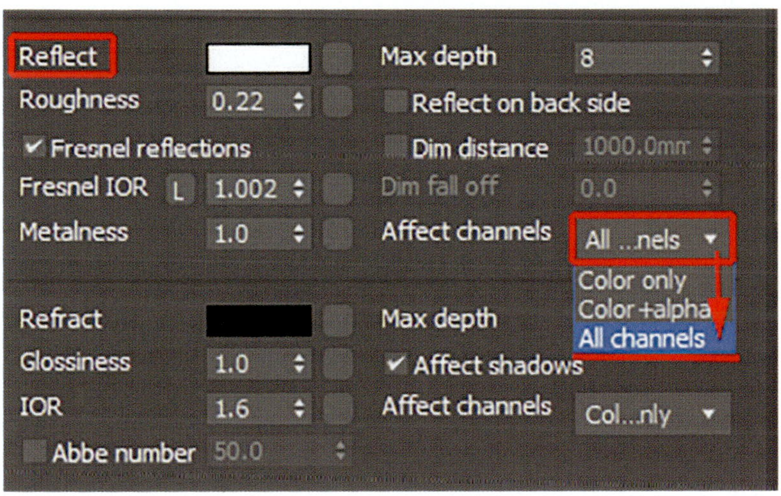

In the Reflect group, choose the All channels option from the Affect channels list

Assign it to the selected object and rename it as, Aluminium_Blurry (2). Also, change its Material ID number to 2.

NOTE

The final scene has animated 3d people from anima®/ AXYZ design®. If per chance you don't have it installed, please discard the errors and continue without them.

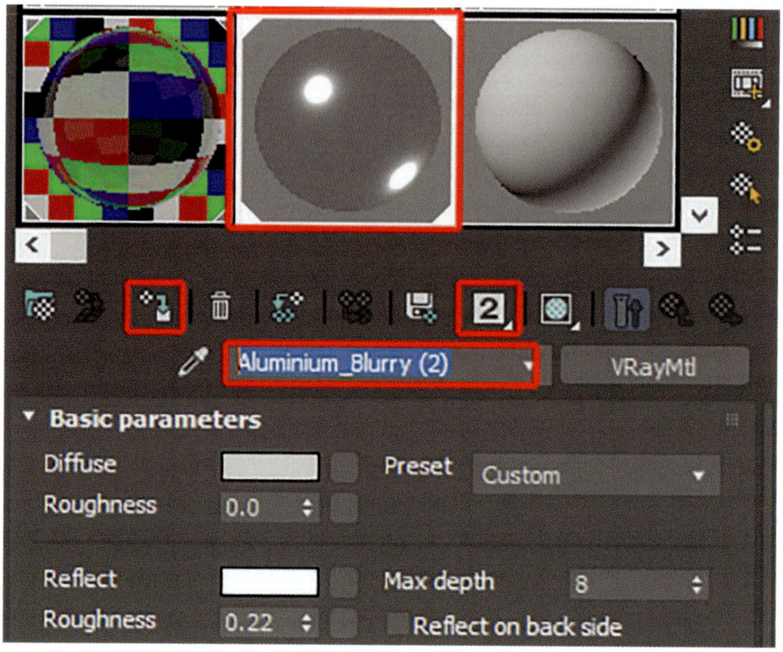

Assign material to object, rename it and change its Material ID number 2.

Assign this material objects such as Frame_doubled glazed curtain walling, ppc metal balustrades, _metal frame_Doubled glazed curtain walling, Acoustic absorbent metal panel, frame, Frame glass door, Frame glass door_otherside, Frame_double glazed curtain wall, Frame_double glazed curtain wall01, Frame_doubled glazed curtain walling and louvers.

As mentioned earlier, create few variations of this material (name them differently), using different parameters and/or other Metal sets from the Asset Browser dialog.

Finally, please check the final scene named, Staircase Atrium_Final.max, to see how materials were applied.

Also, because a VRay camera is being used, if you want to see the motion blur being generated by the 3d moving people, the Shutter speed value needs to be reduced to about by 4.0. Reducing the Shutter speed value makes the motion blur more visible. However, it will also brighten the scene.

To counterbalance the brightness, reduce the Film speed (ISO) value to about ten. Finally, ensure the Motion blur function is enabled, and the Properties of the moving 3d objects are enabled.

While these values worked well, feel free to try different values, if desired.

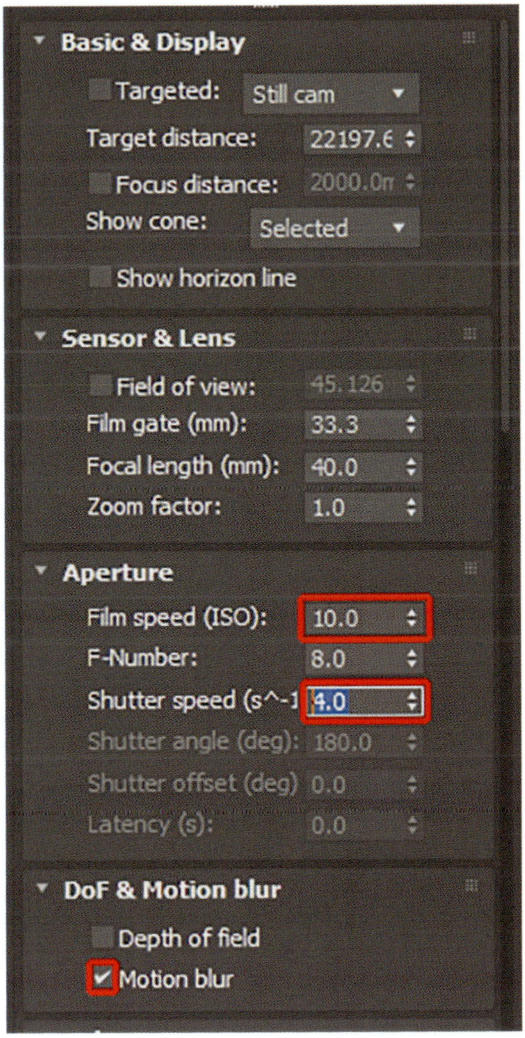

VRay camera Shutter speed set to 4.0, Film speed set to 10, and Motion blur enabled

9 Materials and Final Render

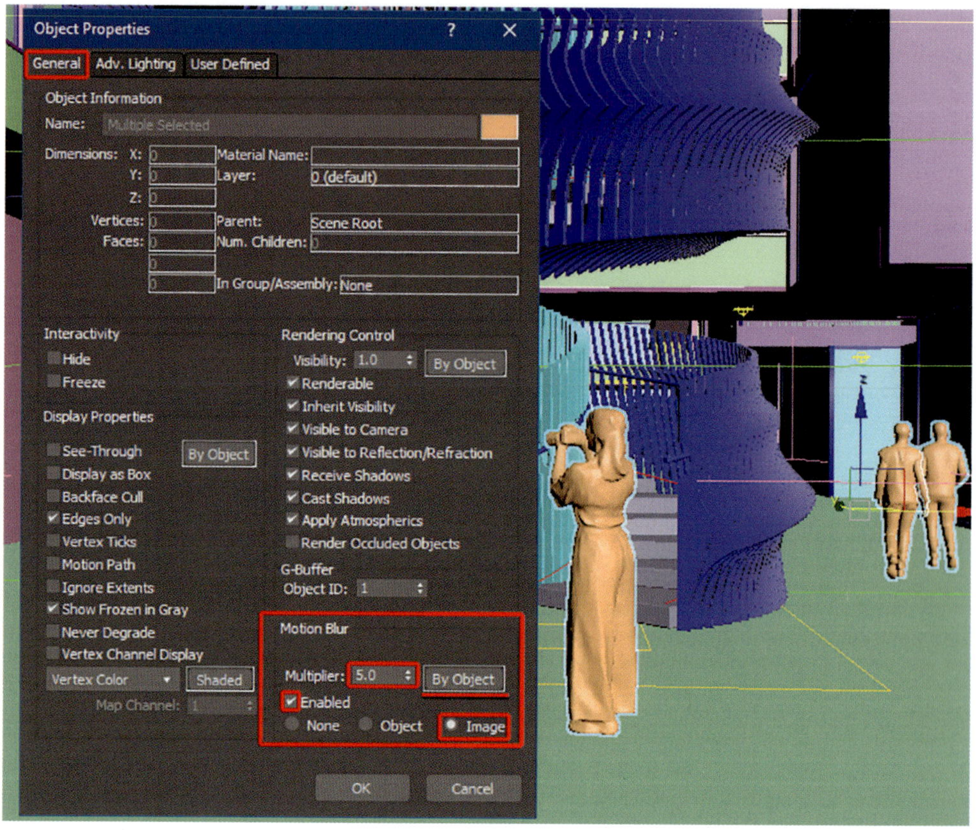

3d people from anima®/ AXYZ design® Properties Motion blur enabled

Setting Up for Final Render

This final step will take users through the process of tweaking the render settings to achieve high enough resolution renders for 600 DPI printing purposes.

To do so, let's start by opening the V-Ray tab. Under Image sampler (Antialiasing), change its Type to Bucket.

Under Bucket image sampler, change the Max subdivs to ten and decrease the Noise threshold to 0.007.

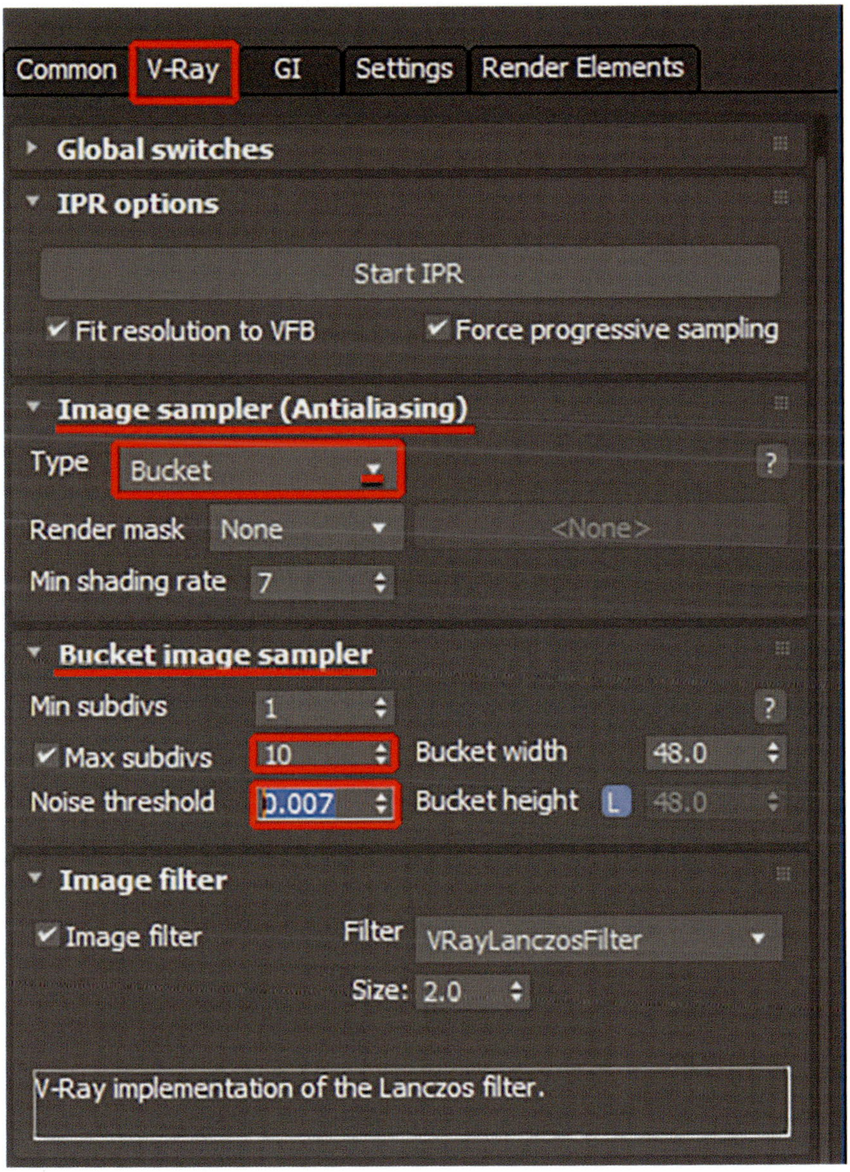

Change the Image sampler Type to Bucket, Max subdivs to 10, and Noise threshold to 0.007

NOTE

While these parameters/values worked well. However, feel free to try different settings and values, if desired.

Next, go to the Render Elements tab and add the render elements discussed in Chapter 4.

In addition to VRayLightMix (previously added), ensure to add many elements of MultiMatteElement to cover most important materials in the shot.

Again, use the techniques covered in Chapter 4 to set them up properly.

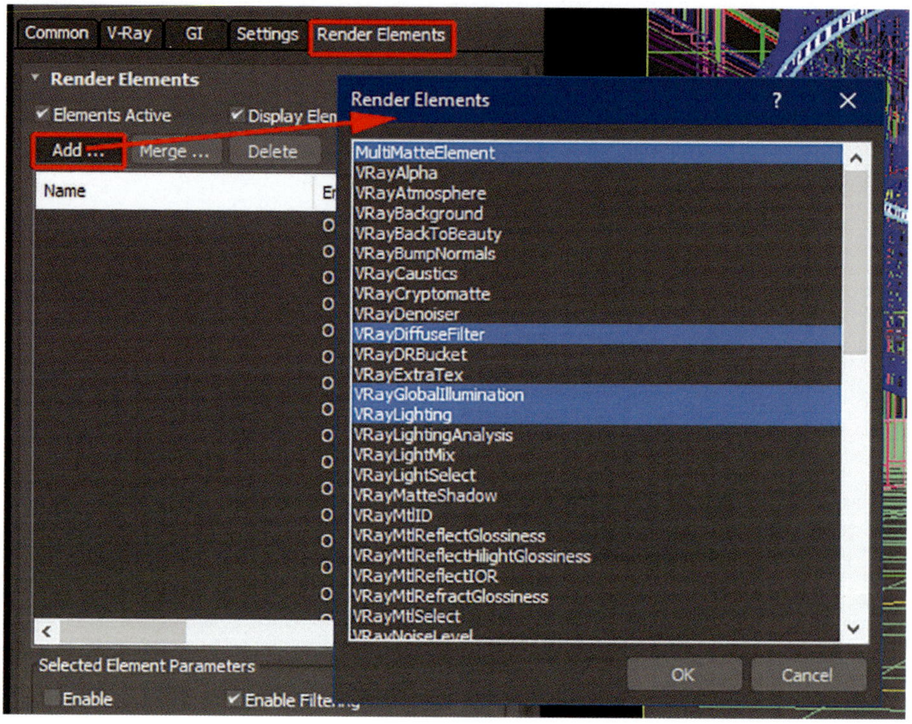

Add the render elements

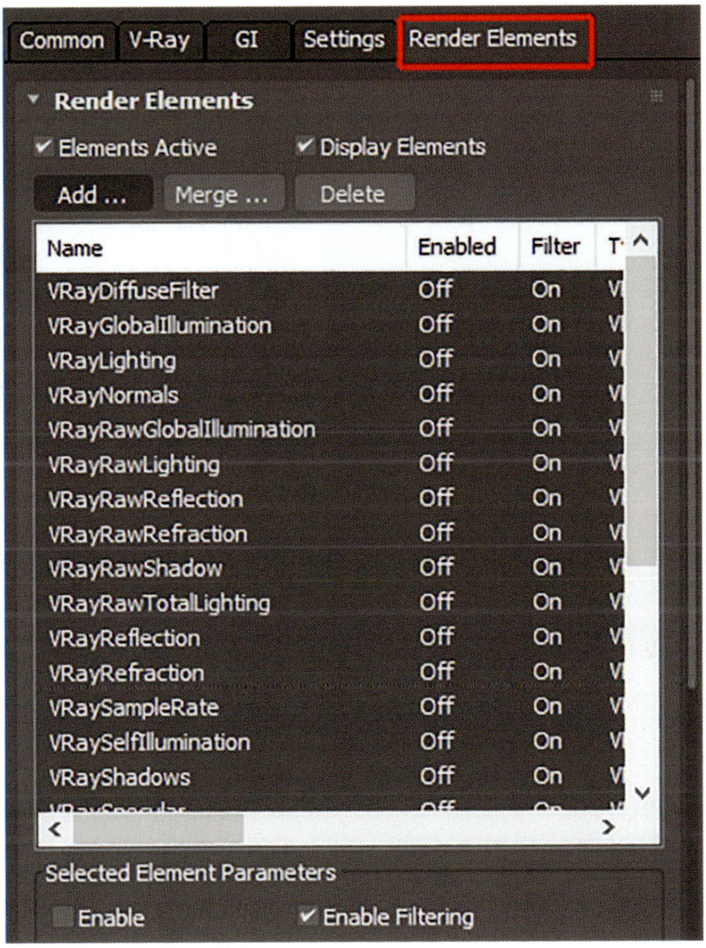

Render elements tab with passes added

Also, add render elements such as VRayGlobalIllumination, VRayDiffuseFilter, VRayNormals, VRayRawReflection, VRayRawRefraction, VRayReflection, VRayRefraction and VRaySampleRate – this render element is quite useful to see areas of the scene that are problematic to render (green and red). VRaySpecular, VRayWireColor, and VRayZDepth –for this scene, the zdepth max value was set to 13000.0 mm. VRayLighting, VRayTotalLighting, VRayRawTotalLighting, VRaySelfIllumination, VRayShadows, VRayRawShadow.

Back in the V-Ray tab, under Frame buffer, click on the V-Ray raw image file toggle to name and save the file.

In its dialog, keep the file type as *.vrimg and name it as Atrium_Still. Also, enable the following options, EXE/VRST 32-bit output, Deep EXR, Dot-delimited frame number, and Save VFB color correction.

In addition, enable the option to, Separate render channels, Save RGB, Save alpha, and Expand # to frame number.

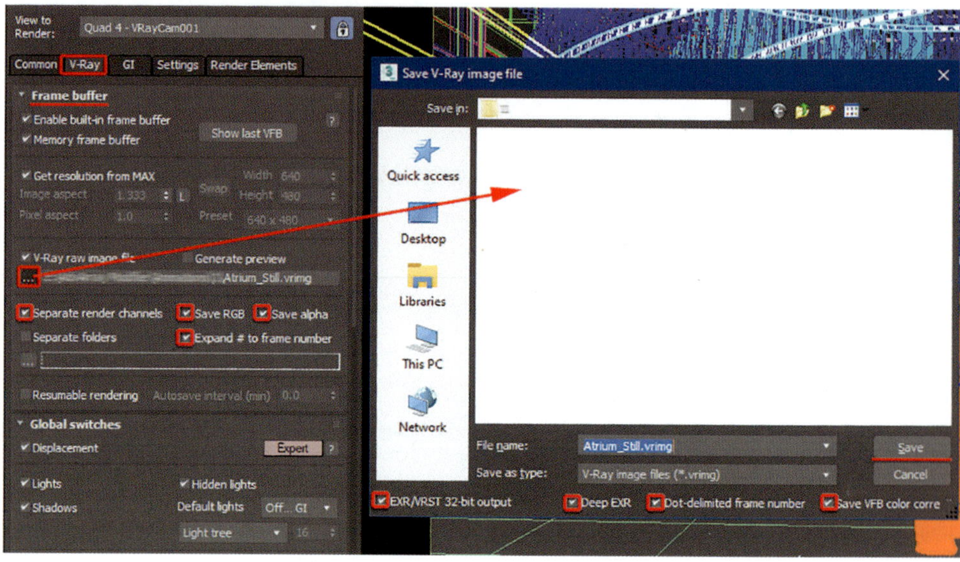

Enable the Frame buffer settings and save the V-ray raw image file

To set the file name and format of the render channels, click on its toggle and set the file type as TIF Image file format. Next, click on the Setup toggle to open the TIF Image Control dialog.

Under Image Type, choose the 16-bit Color, No compression, and 600 Dots Per Inch. Finally, name the TIF as, Atrium_Still, to coincide with the vrimg name.

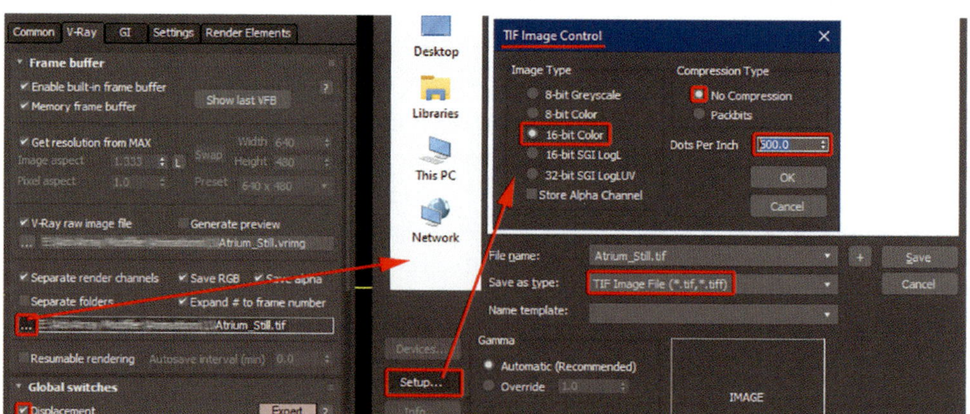

Set the file name and format of the render channels

Before sending the final render, open the Common tab. Under Output Size, set the Width and Height size to 4,000 pixels and click to Render.

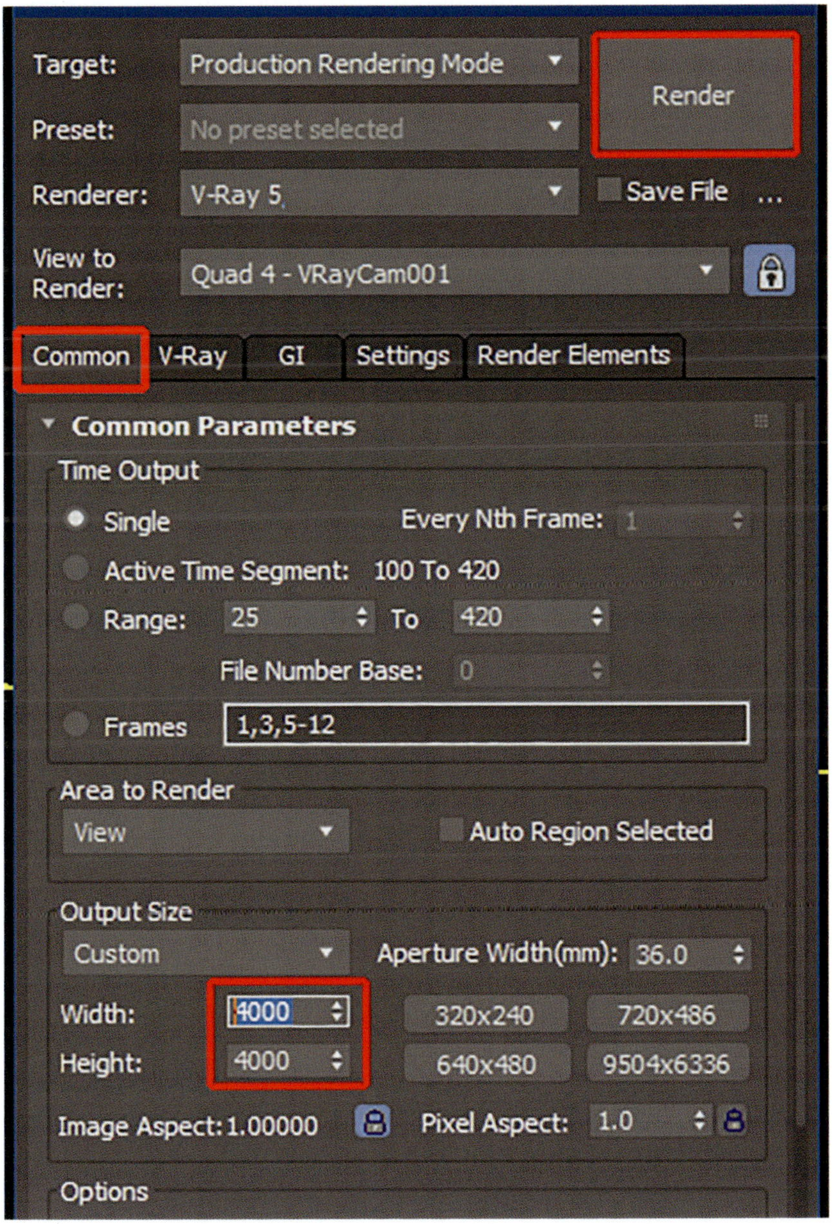

Set the Width and Height size to 4,000 pixels and click to Render

As mentioned earlier, please check the final scene named, Staircase Atrium_Final.max, to see the final scene.

Conclusion

This chapter guided users through the methodical steps of creating V-Ray materials realistically and setting up the scene for final rendering.

Throughout the process, users were shown how to use the V-Ray procedural map and the Asset Browser.

Following that users were guided through the detailed step-by-step methodology of creating specific materials realistically, set up the final scene, carry out final adjustments, and finalizing the renders in 3ds Max.

Finally, the next chapter will take users through the fascinating process of using seasoned post-production techniques to take the render to the next level.

10

Daylight Scene Post-Production

10 Daylight Scene Post-Production

Introduction

Post-production is one of the most important steps toward enhancing and finalizing the renders. As such, in this chapter, users will be shown the importance of the V-Ray Frame Buffer (VFB) to tweak the lights using tools such as LightMix parameters, Lookup table (LUT), V-Ray Lens Effects Filter Generator and Lens Effects.

Finally, in Photoshop, users will learn the importance of loading files into a stack, organize, and name them into groups with masks, how to use Adjustment Layers, glare effects, render elements and much more.

DOI: 10.1201/9781315770802-10

V-Ray Frame Buffer (VFB)

Once your final high-resolution image is finished rendering, the following step is to use the VFB to tweak the lights and Lens effects.

If you have just re-opened 3DS Max and the final renders are currently not in your VFB, simply go to VFB File and choose to Load image named, Atrium_Still.vrimg.

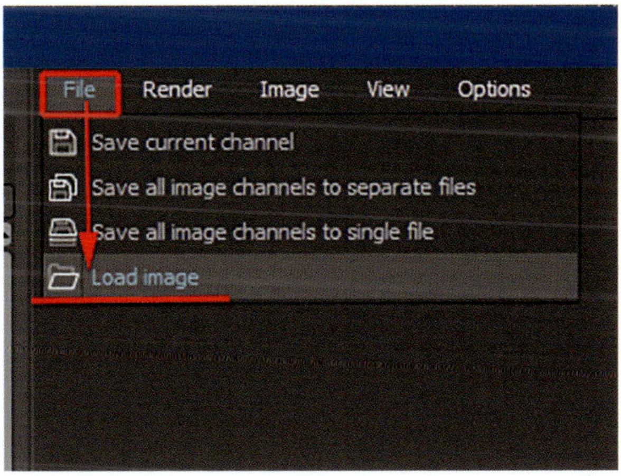

Go to VFB File and choose to Load image named, Atrium_Still.vrimg

In the VFB Layers tab, select the Lookup Table and choose the LUT file named, Kim_Amland_Photographic_01.cube.

Also, ensure the option to Save in image is enabled.

NOTE

This LUT file worked well. However, feel free to choose other LUT files you may prefer.

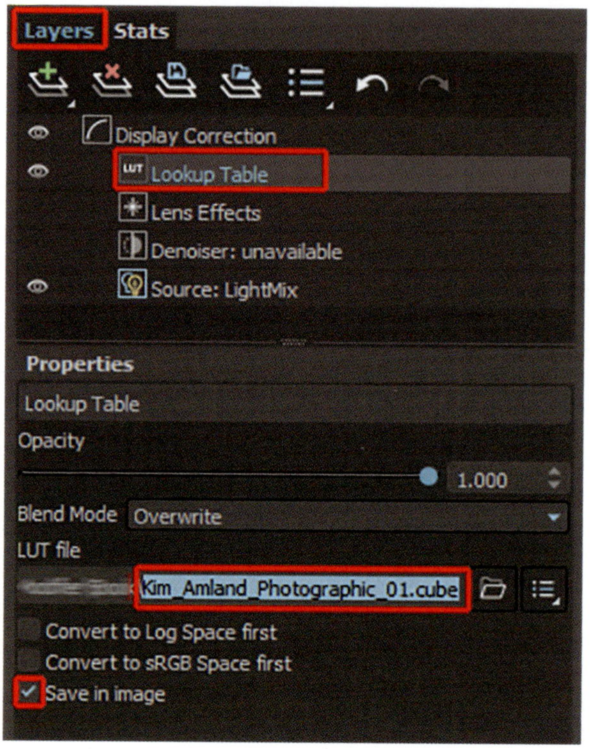

Select the Lookup Table and choose the LUT file named, Kim_Amland_Photographic_01.cube

To tweak the lights a bit further, select the Source: LightMix Layer. Under LightMix, increase the VRayLight_disc022 value to about 1.500 and the Self Illumination to 2.000.

NOTE

While these values and settings worked well, feel free to try different values and settings, if desired.

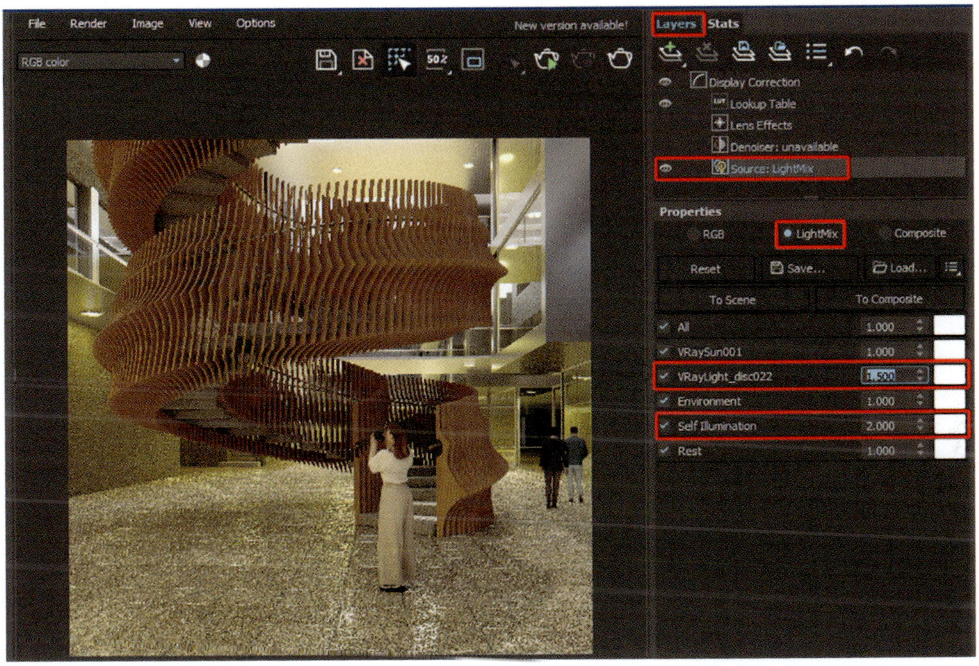

Increase the VRayLight_disc and Self Illumination values

To add a custom glare effect filter, open the V-Ray Lens Effects Filter Generator. This exe file can be found in, C > Program Files > Chaos Group > V-Ray > 3ds Max 2020 > bin.

Or, Start Menu>Programs>V-Ray for 3ds Max>Tools>Files> Filter Generator Tool.

Once open, under Corona Flare Lines Pattern, increase its Radius to 100 and Number of Lines to 20.

NOTE

While these values and settings worked well, feel free to try different values and settings, if desired.

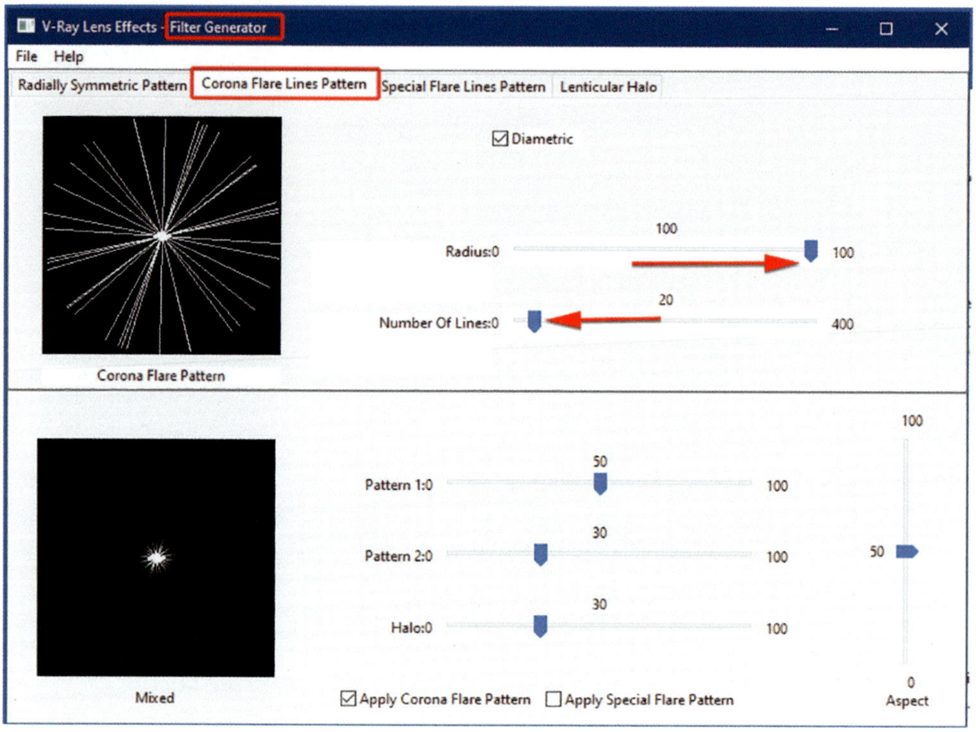

Increase the Filter Generator Radius to 100 and Number of Lines to 20

Next, click File and choose to Export HDR (Ctrl+E). Accept its default Image Size settings and name it, glare.

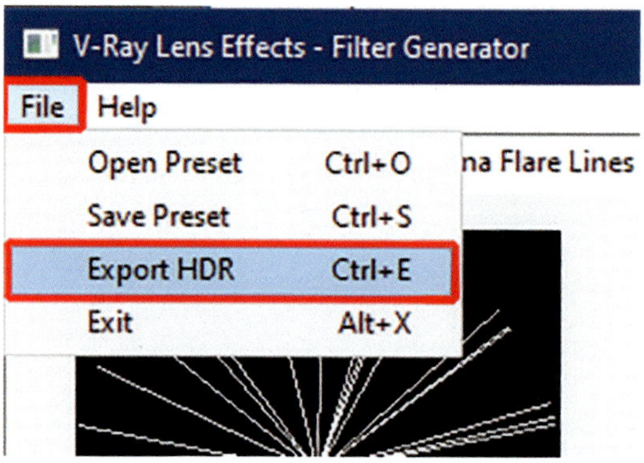

Click File and choose to Export HDR (Ctrl+E)

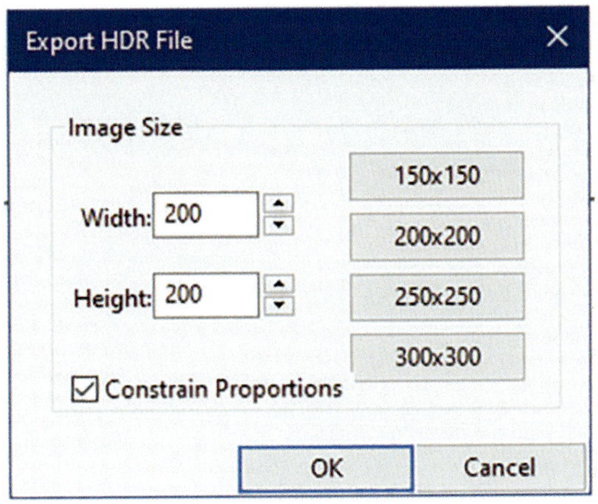

Export HDR File Image Size

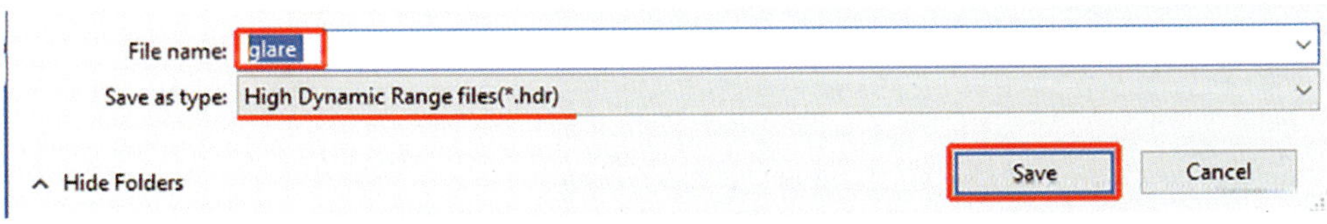

Name the HDR file as, glare

Back in VFB, under Layers, enable the Lens Effects layer, by clicking on its eye icon (the icon is gray initially). Under its Properties, enable the bloom/glare effect and load the glare.hdr filter image file previously created.

Also, set its Size to about 10.550 and the Intensity to about 7.982. Ensure the Hardware accelerated and Interactive options are enabled.

NOTE

As mentioned earlier, these parameters and values worked well. However, feel free to try different ones, if desired.

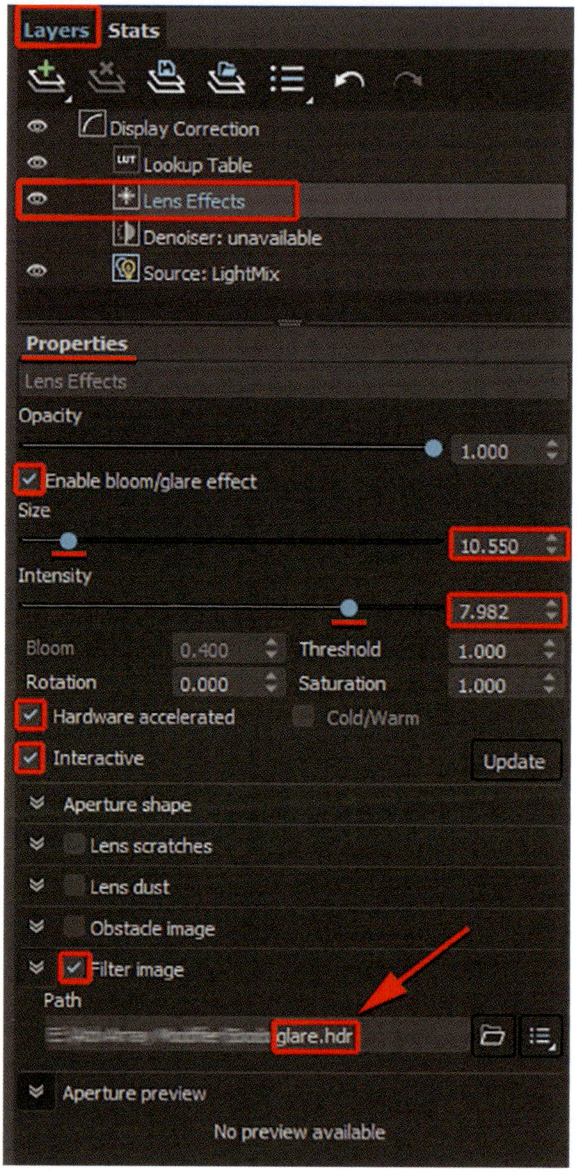

Lens Effects layer parameters

Lens Effects final result

Once happy with the results, in the VFB, click on the File and choose to Save all image channels to separate files.

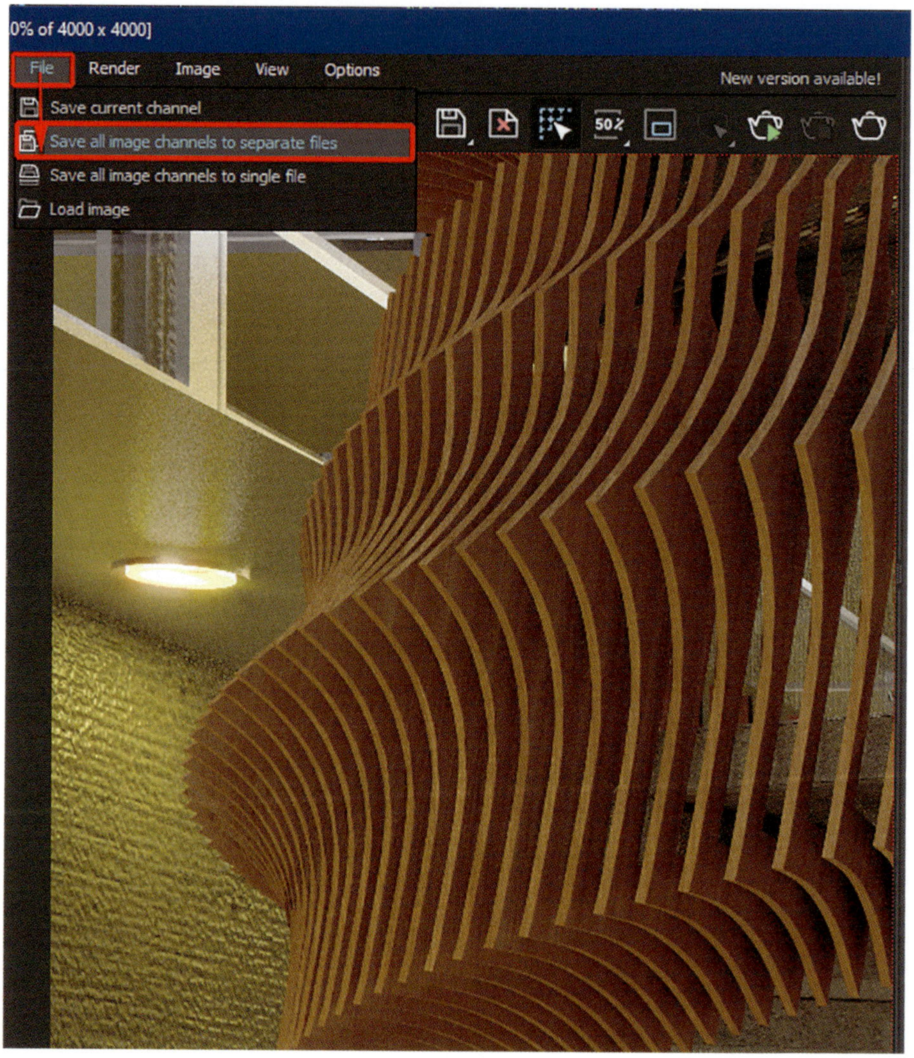

Click on the File and choose to Save all image channels to separate files

Create a new folder and save the channels as a TIF file, using the same parameters previously discussed.

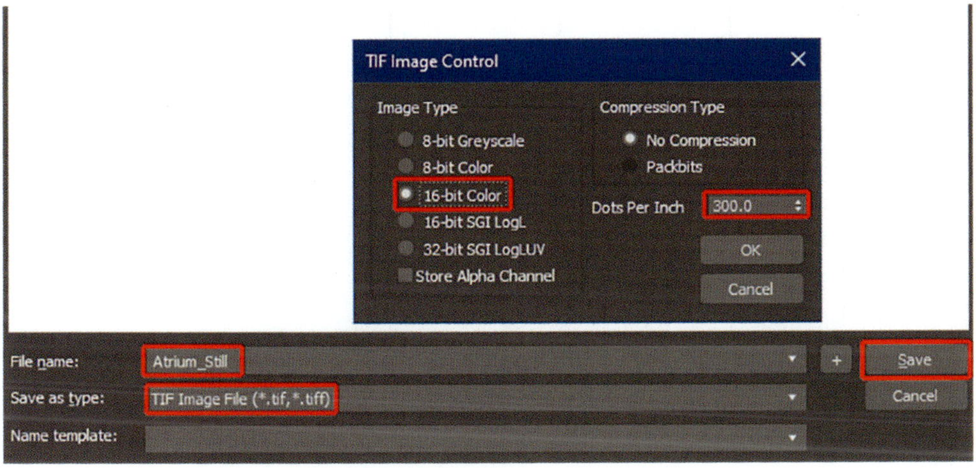

Save the channels as a TIF file, using the same parameters previously entered

Photoshop

To bring all the previously saved layers into a stack, in Photoshop, go to File>Scripts>Load Files into Stack.

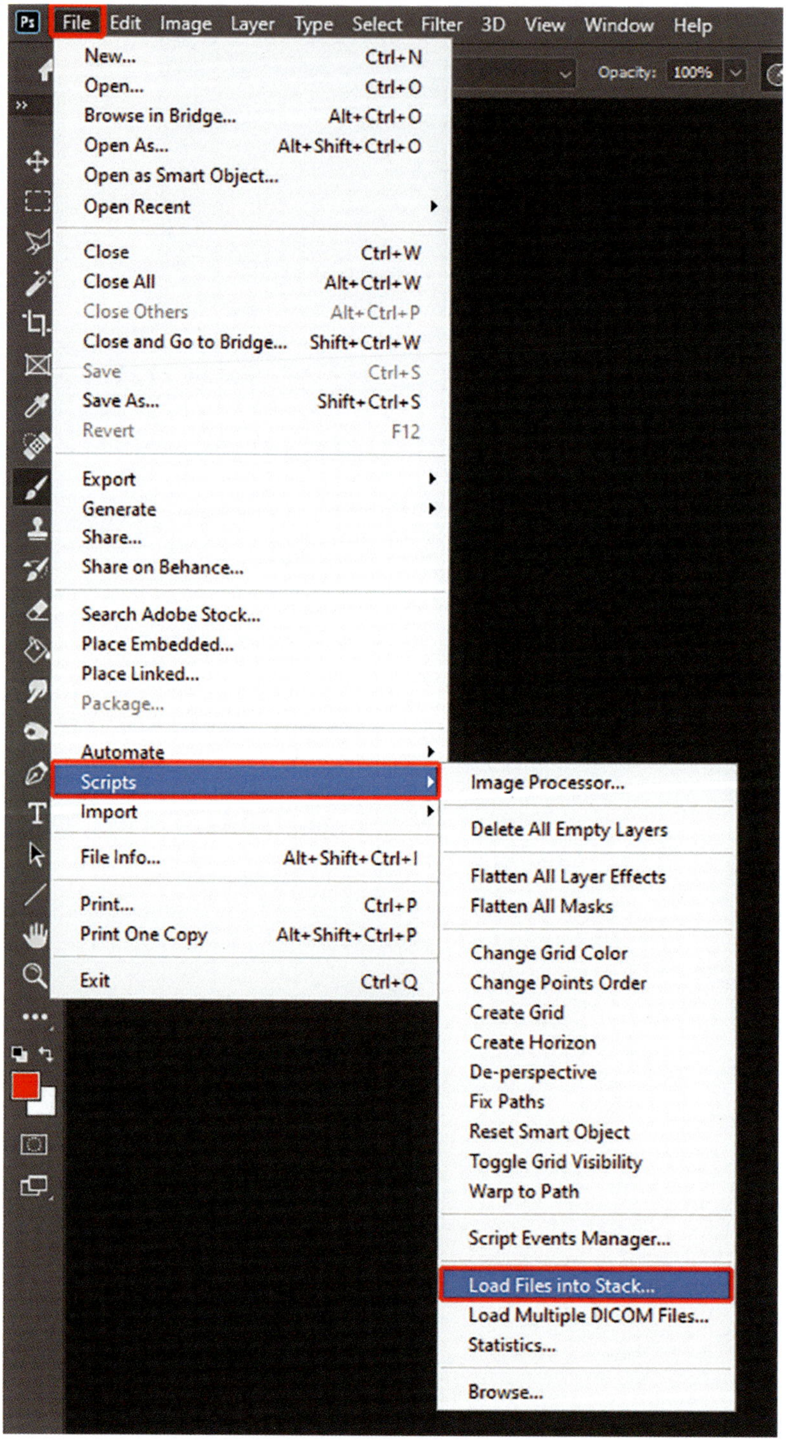

go to File>Scripts>Load Files into Stack

In the Load Layers dialog, click on the Browse button to locate the TIF files. Select all TIF using Ctrl+Click, or Select+Shift+Select.

Once all TIF files are selected, click OK to Open and Load them into a stack.

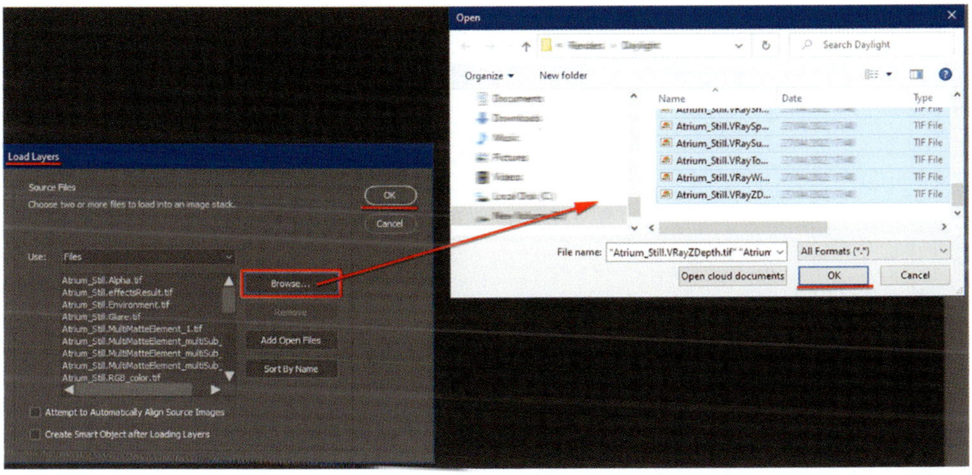

Use the Load Layers dialog to Select the TIF files

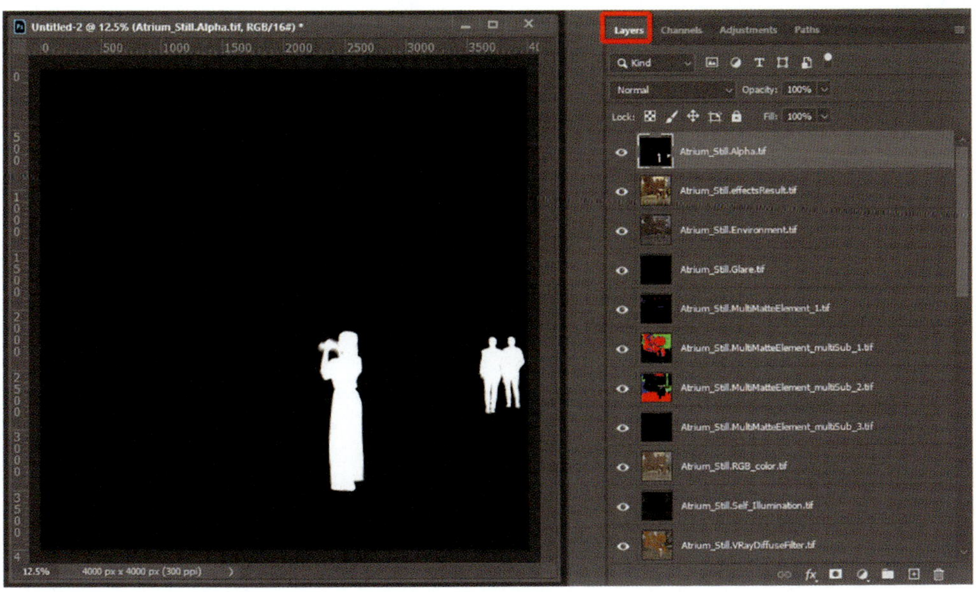

Loaded layers in a stack

Choose to Save the document as a PSB file format (Ctrl+S). Name it as Atrium_Still_day. Disable the option to Save As a Copy and enable the Layers function to keep layers.

PSB file format allows users to save Photoshop files bigger than 2GB in size.

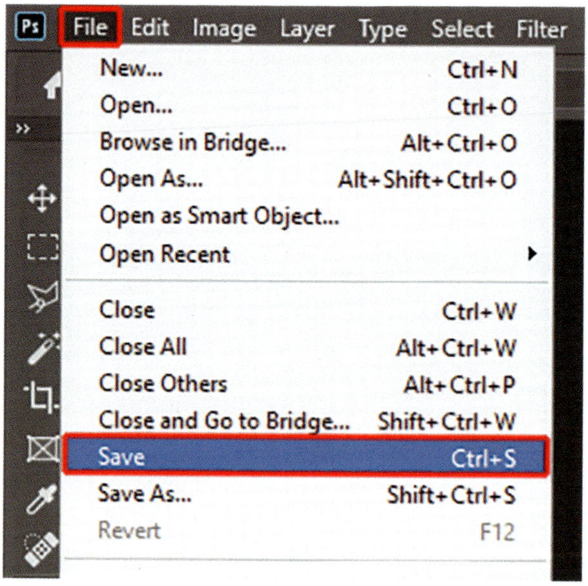

Save the Files as

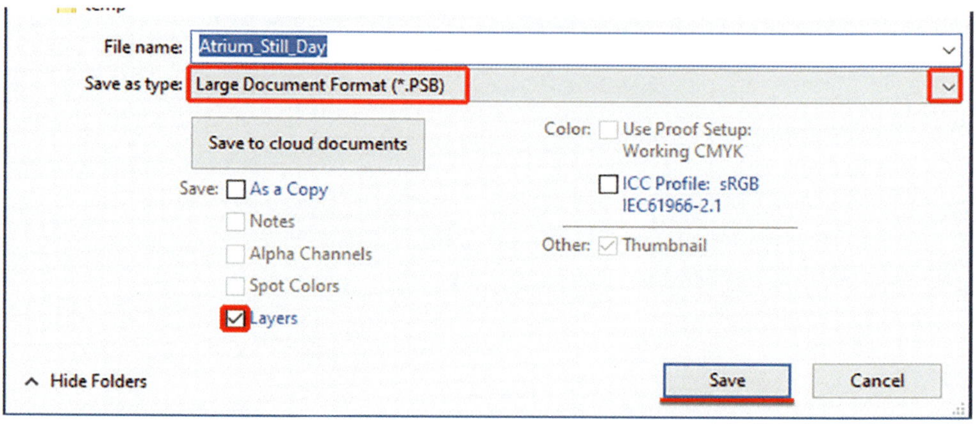

Save the document as a PSB file format

To begin organizing the layers, let's start by holding down the Alt key and clicking on the eye icon of the layer named, Atrium_Still.effectsResult.tif.

All remaining layers should automatically become turned off as result.

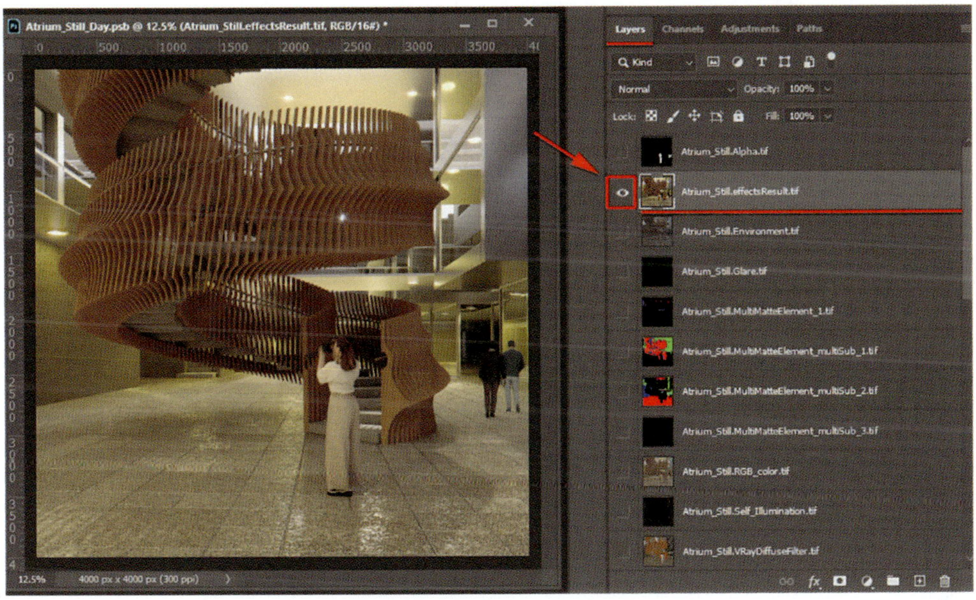

All layers but Atrium_Still.effectsResult.tif turned off automatically

Following that, select and move the layer named, Atrium_Still.effectsResult.tif to the bottom of the list. It's common practice to have the main layer at the bottom of the list before starting to add any subsequent layers on top.

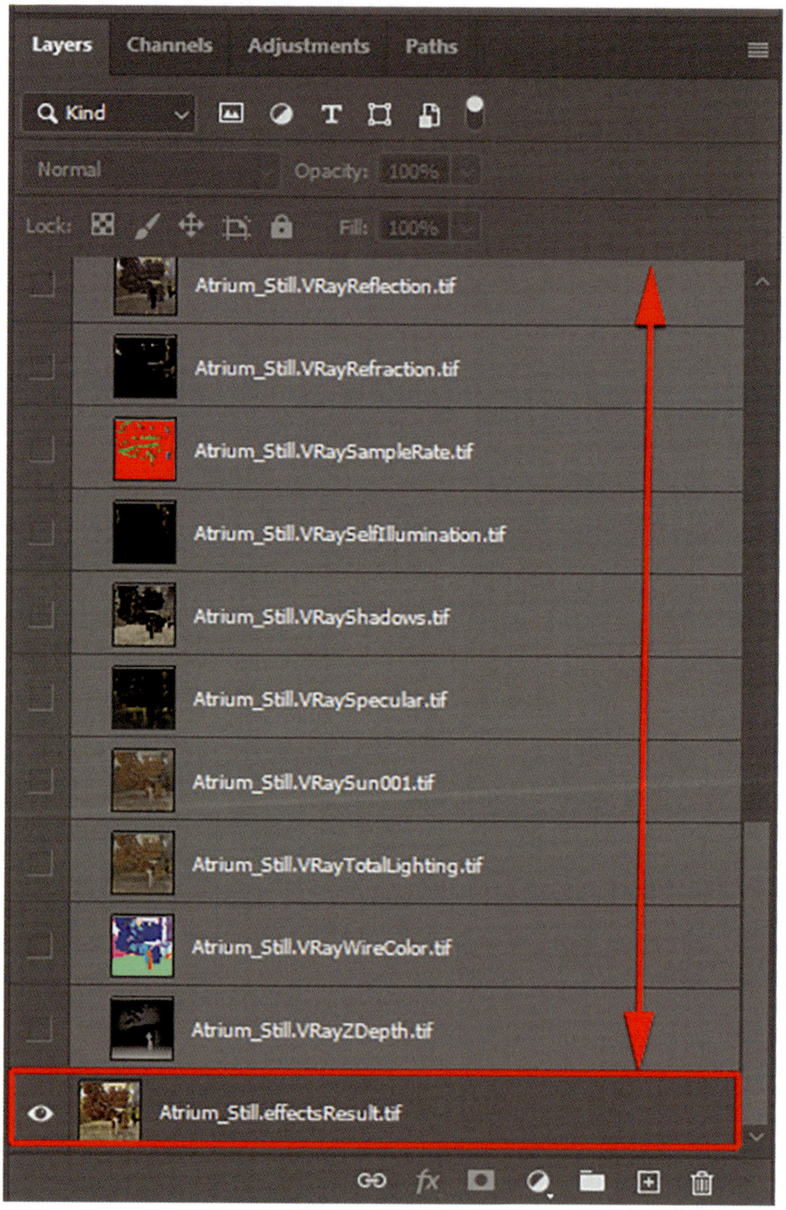

Move the layer to the bottom of the list

Select all the layers turned off using Select+Shift. Next, click the button to Create a new group, followed by naming the new group as, =Render Elements=, and moving all the layers turned off inside the group. It's always good practice to organize layers in a document.

New group created and named with layers inside

The "=" is being added before and after the name, to make it easier to select a specific layer inside the group (visible layers only) when users right click on the document to.

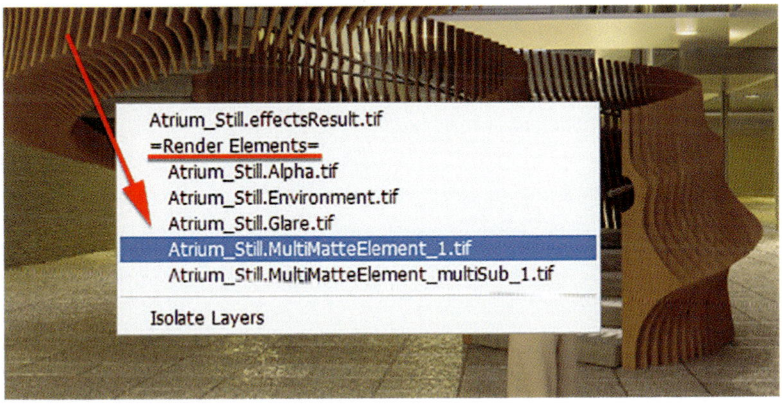

Right click on the document to select visible layers

The following step is to create a new group and name it, =Adjustments=. This is the group where the global effects and adjustments will be added into.

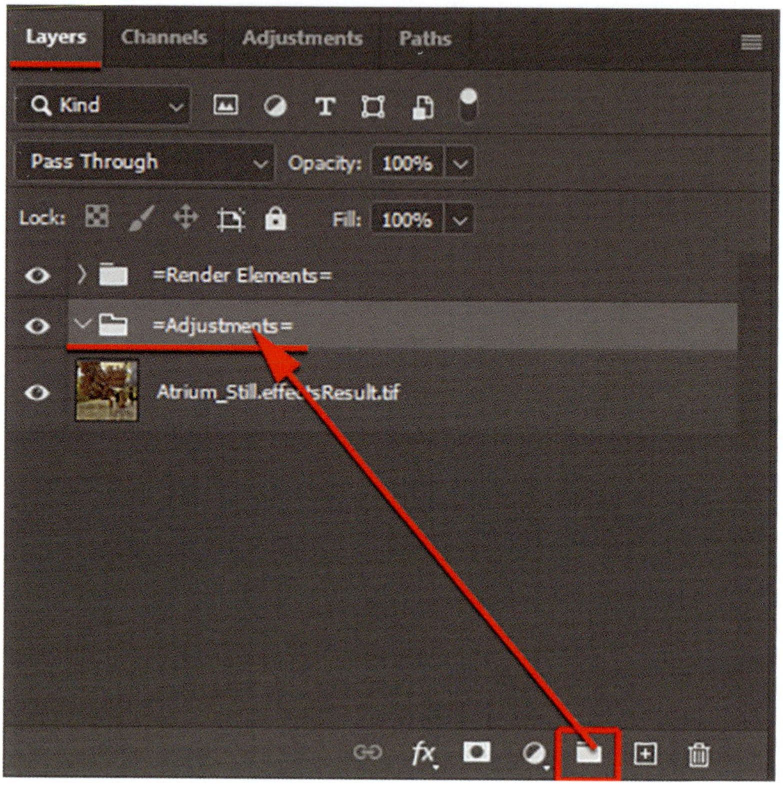

Right click on the document to select visible layers

While the Adjustments group is still selected, click on the adjustment layers button and choose the Color Lookup option from the list.

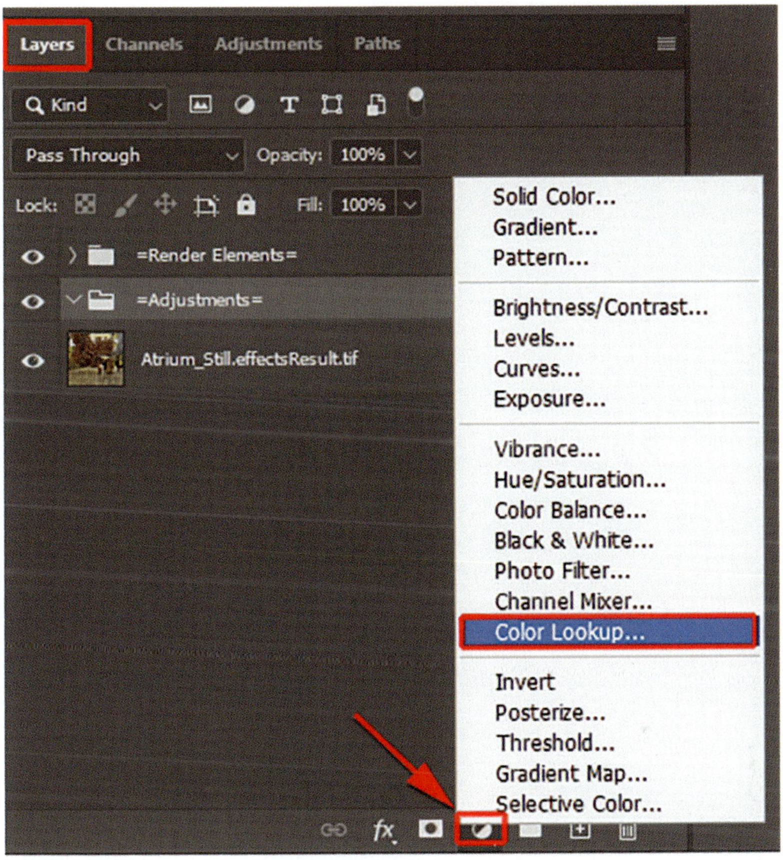

Color Lookup option chosen from the adjustment layers list

To locate and load a LUT file, while selected, go to its Properties tab and click on the Load 3D LUT function.

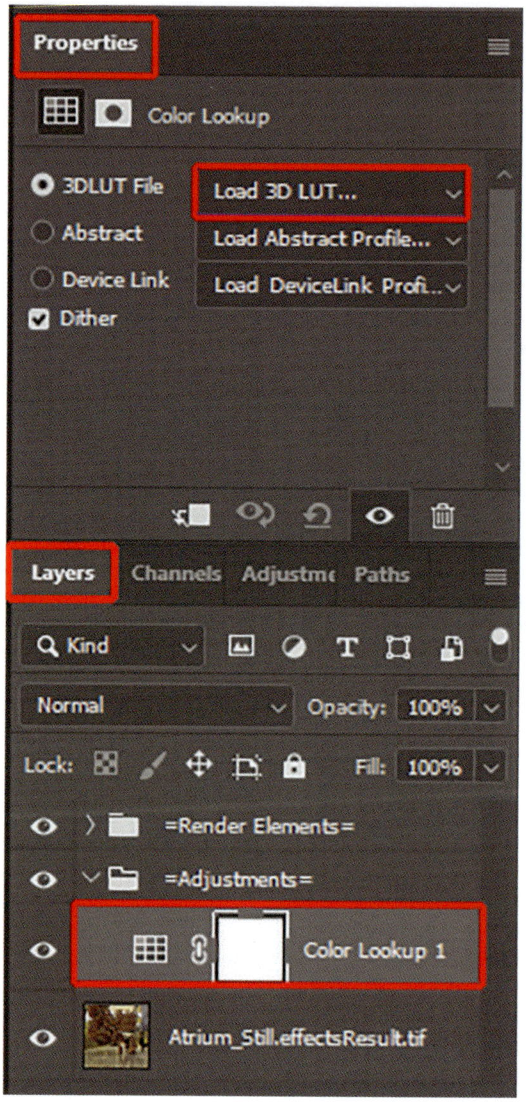

Go to LUT's Properties tab and click on the Load 3D LUT function

Locate and load the LUT file under the name, F-9180-STD.cube. Also, rename the LUT file accordingly.

Or under, C:\Program Files\Adobe\Adobe Photoshop 2020\Presets\3DLUTs

NOTE

This LUT file worked well. However, feel free to experiment with LUT files, if desired. Photoshop 2020 has a host LUT files available, under, C:\Program Files\Chaos Group\V-Ray\3ds Max 2020\bin.

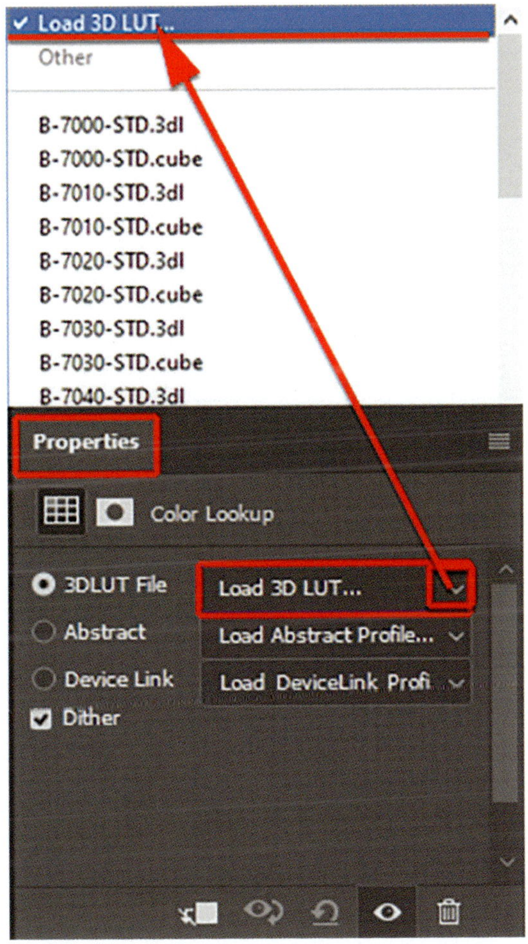

Locate and load the LUT file under the name, F-9180-STD.cube

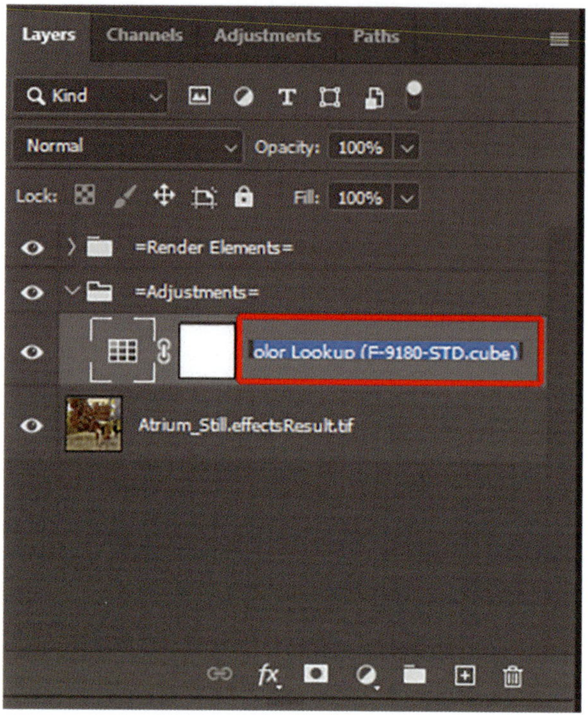

Rename the LUT file accordingly

LUT result

To reinvigorate the shadows, go to the render elements group and select the VRayLighting render element from the list. Next, hold down the Alt key and move it down into the Adjustments group to copy the VRayLighting element.

Also, enable the layer visibility and change its layer blending mode to a Screen type.

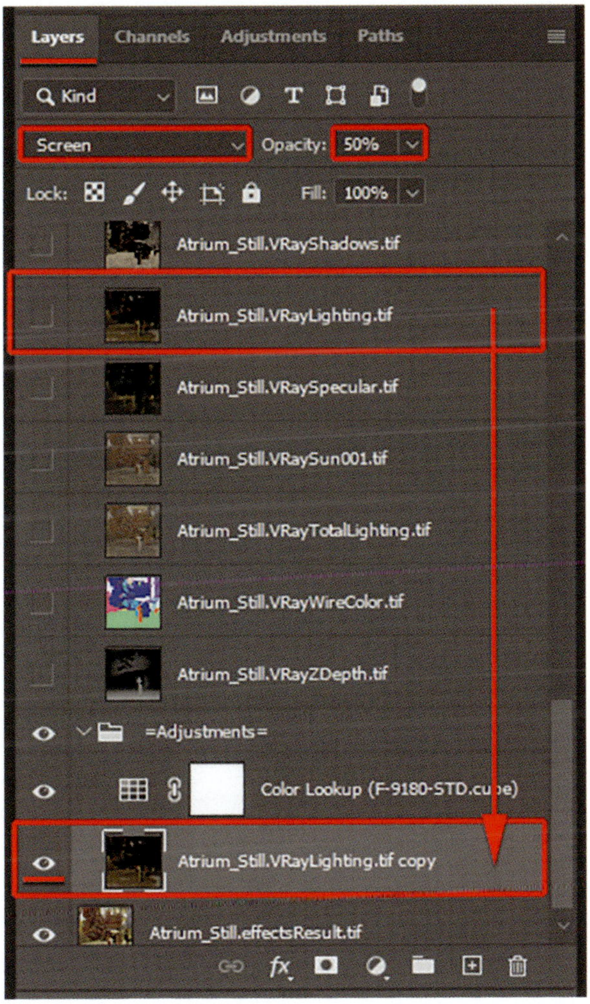

Copy the VRayLighting element into the =Adjustments= group

The following step is to create a new group and name it as, =Glare=. This group will be used to overlay glare layers.

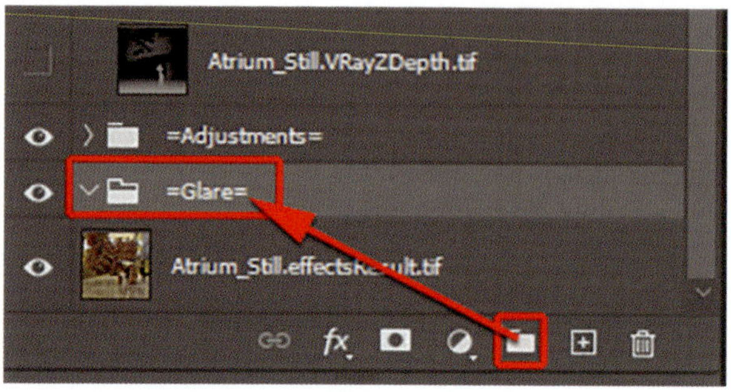

Create a new group and name it as, =Glare=

Open the document named, Glare.psd, followed by dragging and dropping it into the main document.

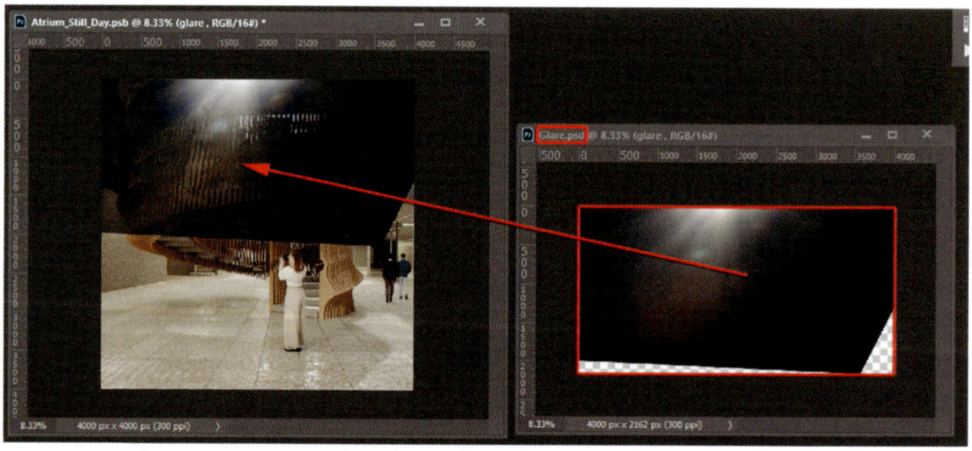

Drag and drop the glare layer into the main document

Once in the main document, ensure to move the glare layer inside the =Glare= group, and change its layer blending mode from Normal to a Screen a type.

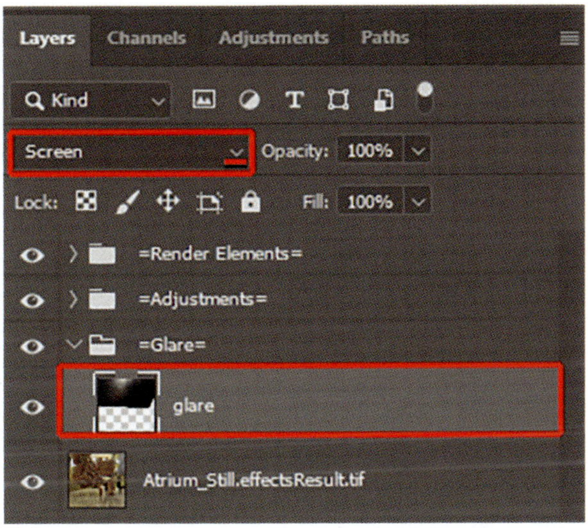

Change the glare layer blending mode to a Screen type

To reinforce its effect, duplicate the layer by holding down the Alt key and moving the layer to copy it.

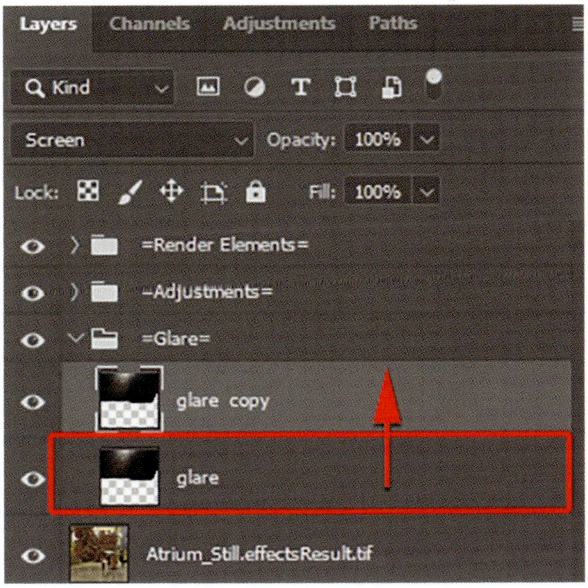

Duplicate the layer by holding down the Alt key and moving it

Final result with two glare layer

Currently, the edges of the glare layers are very prominent. To make them less prominent and more realistic, we will be using a brush and layer masks.

To start, enable the Brush tool by pressing B on your keyboard or clicking on its tool (B).

Enable the Brush tool

While the brush tool is enabled, increase its Size to about 385 px and decrease its Hardness value to about 0% to be very soft.

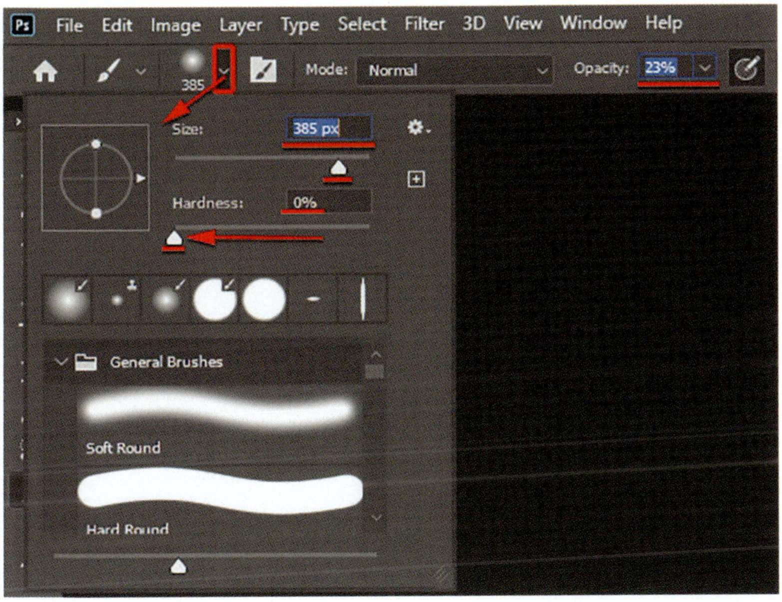

Adjust the brush settings

Next, create a layer mask by clicking on its button, followed by switching (X) the background color to black and brushing away pixels around the edges.

When a layer mask is selected while using the Brush tool, a black background color brushes pixels away, and a white background color does the opposite. Use the X key to switch between colors and always ensure a layer mask is selected before brushing away pixels…otherwise, you will paint a layer instead.

Use the Brush tool and layer mask to brush away pixels

To edit the floor material, let's start by enabling the layer under the name, Atrium_Still.MultiMatteElement_multiSub_2.tif.

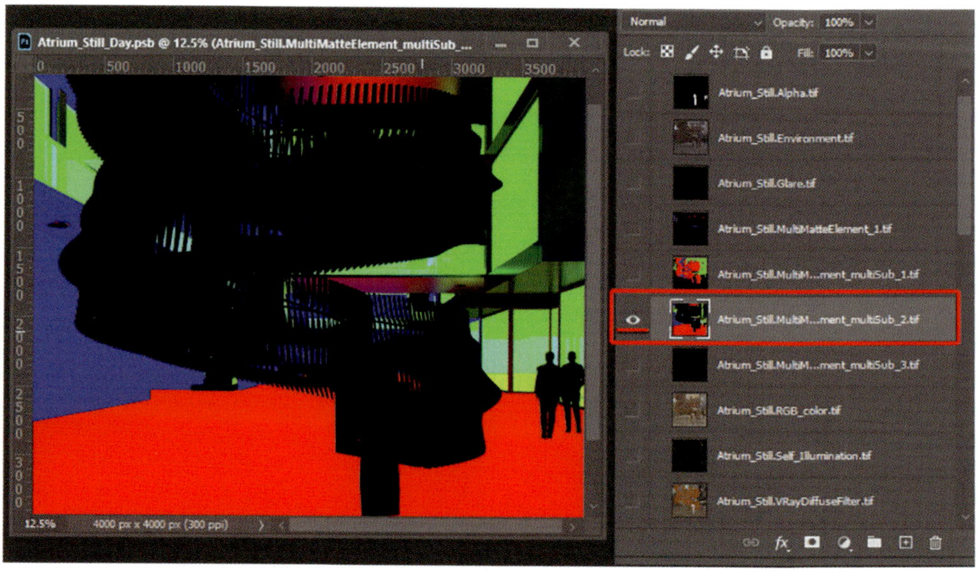

Enable the layer visibility

Next, select the channels tab. Hold down the Ctrl key and select the Red channel to enable its selection.

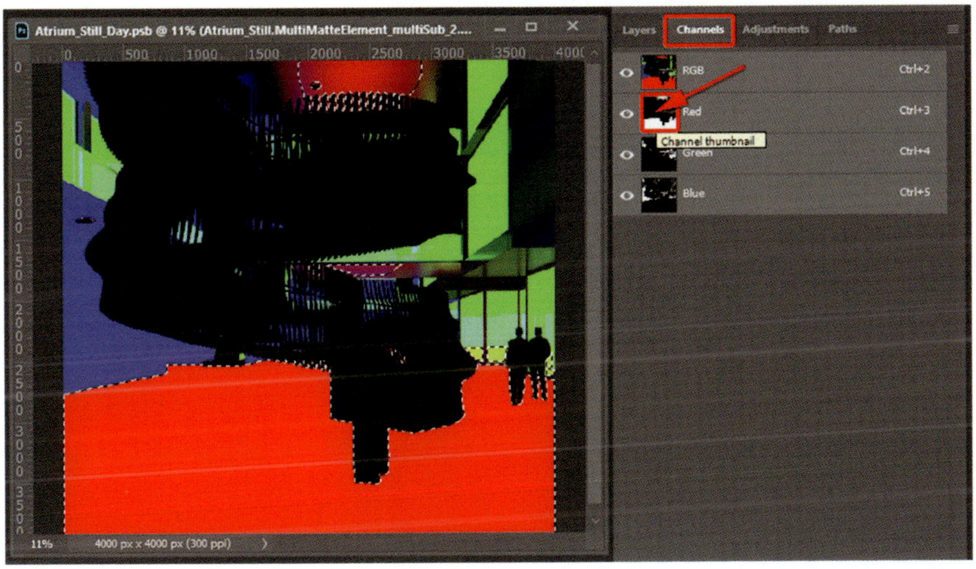

Enable the Red channel

Back in the Layers tab, disable its visibility.

Under Layers tab, disable the layer visibility

While the floor selection is still on, create a new group and click on the group mask button to create one.

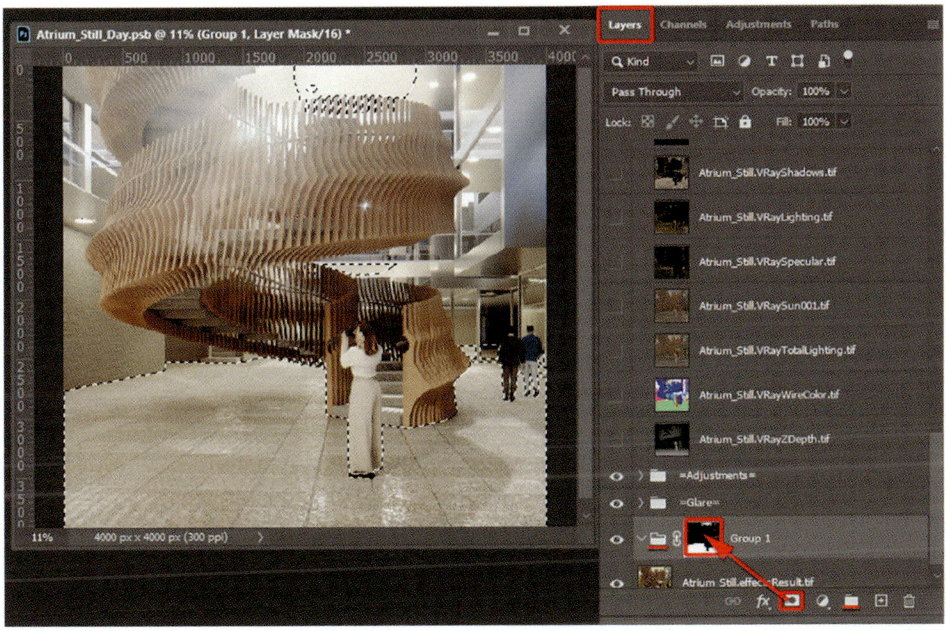

Create a new group and its adjacent mask

Name the new group as, =Floor=. To begin editing the floor material, copy and move the Diffuse element into the floor group.

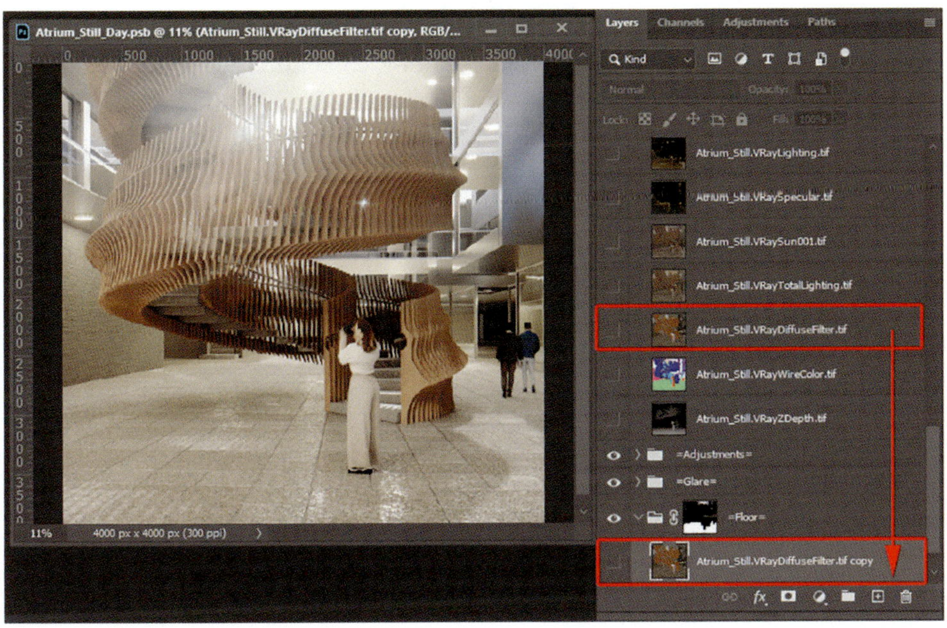

Copy and move the Diffuse element into the floor group

Enable the Diffuse layer visibility and reduce its opacity to about 46%.

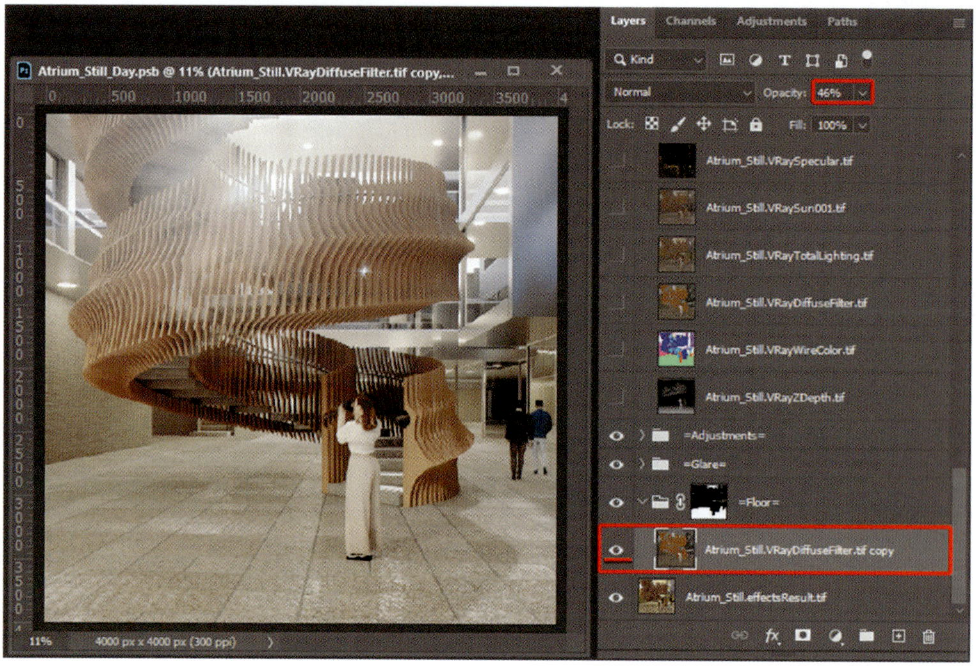

Enable the visibility of the Diffuse layer element and reduce its opacity to about 46%.

To add a bit of shine and highlights to the floor, copy and move the Specular layer into the floor group. Enable its visibility and change its blending mode to a Screen type.

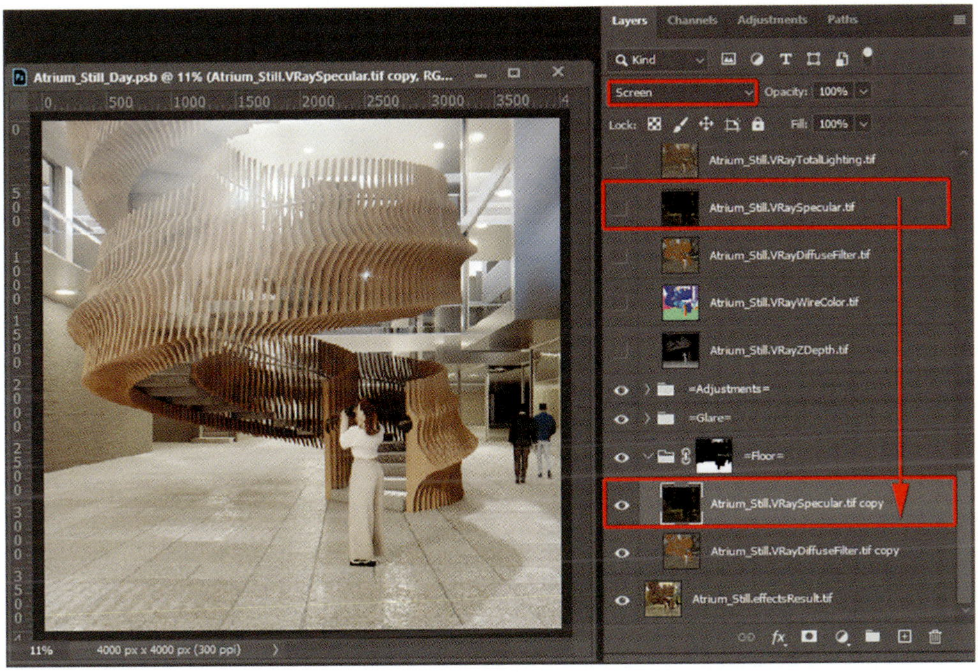

Copy and move the Specular layer followed by enabling its visibility and blending mode to Screen

Next, add the Levels adjustment layer, by clicking on its button.

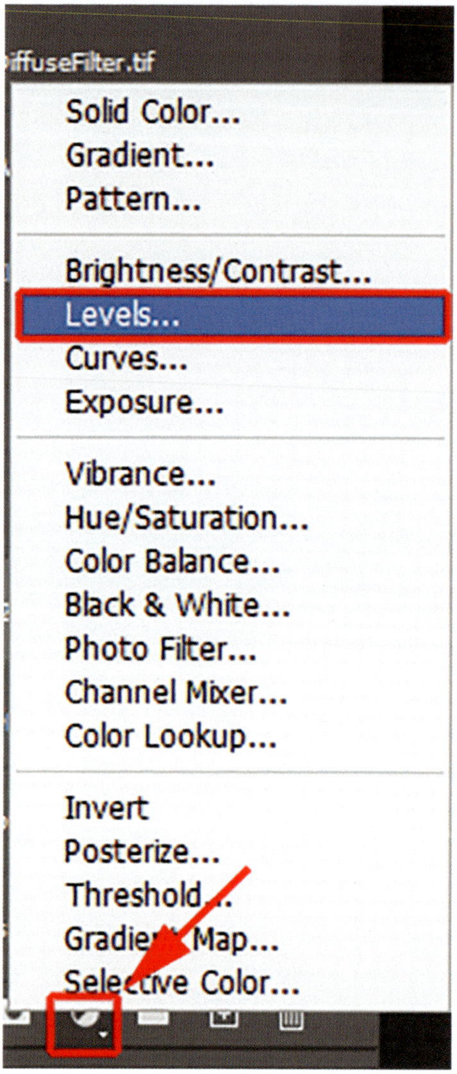

Create the Levels adjustment layer

In the RGB Levels Properties, move its middle point to about 0.50, and the right point to 185 to add a bit of contrast.

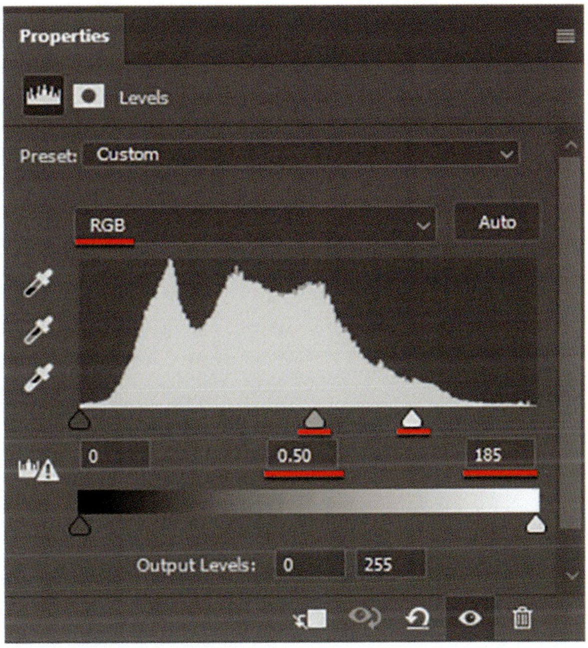

Adjust the RGB Levels Properties to add a bit of contrast

To control the saturation levels of the floor material, add the Hue/Saturation adjustment layer, and reduce its Master Saturation value to about –50.

NOTE

Because of the group mask, all changes being made inside the floor group are contained within it.

NOTE

While this value worked well, feel free to try different values, if necessary.

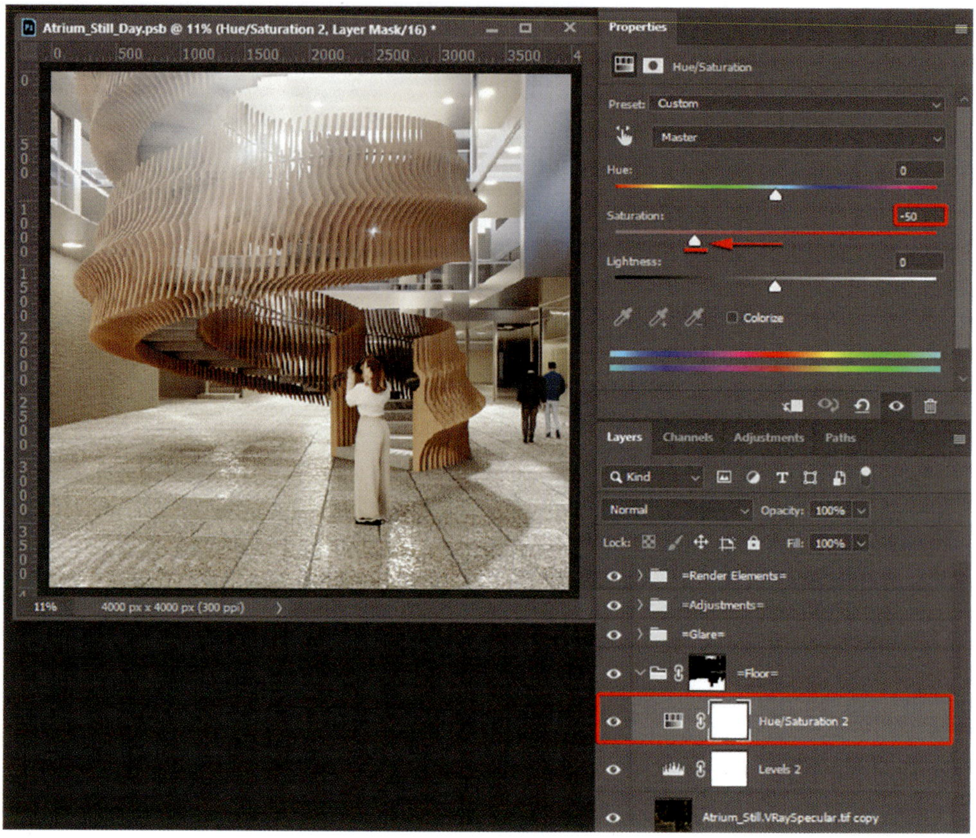

Add Hue/Saturation and reduce its Master Saturation value to about –50

The following step is to adjust the 3d people's color and contrast. To do so, let's start by enabling the visibility of the layer named, Atrium_Still.Alpha.tif.

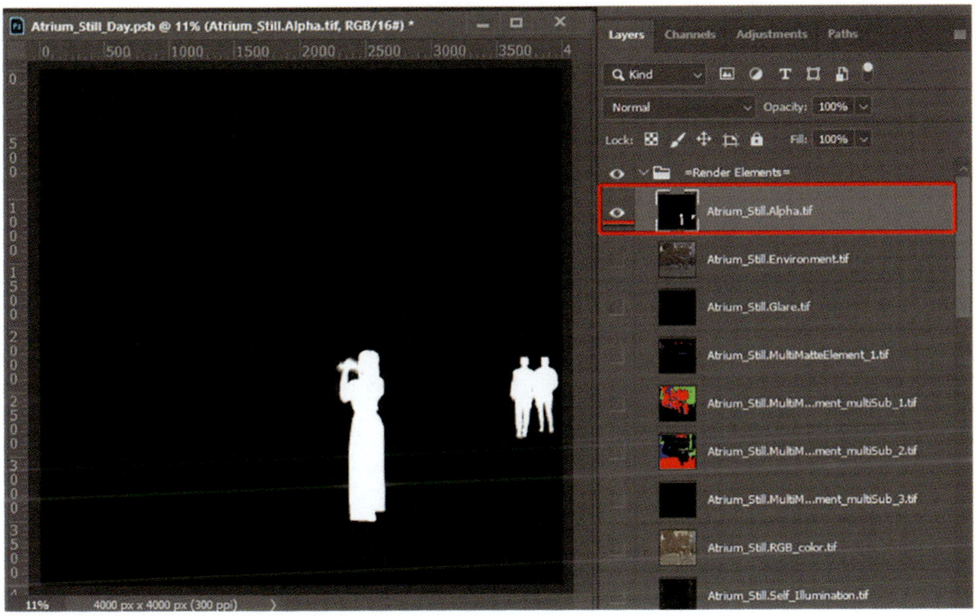

Turn on the visibility of layer named, Atrium_Still.Alpha.tif

While the layer is still selected, go to its Channels tab. To enable its selection, hold down the Ctrl key and left click on its RGB channel.

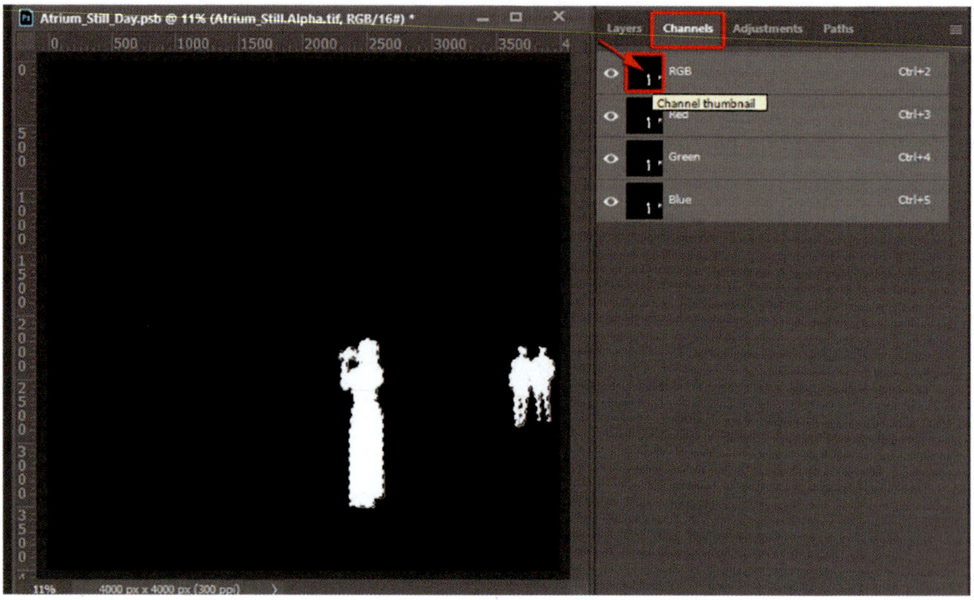

Hold down the Ctrl key and left click on its RGB channel to enable selection

Back on the Layers tab, while the selection is still on, turn off the Atrium_Still. Alpha.tif layer visibility.

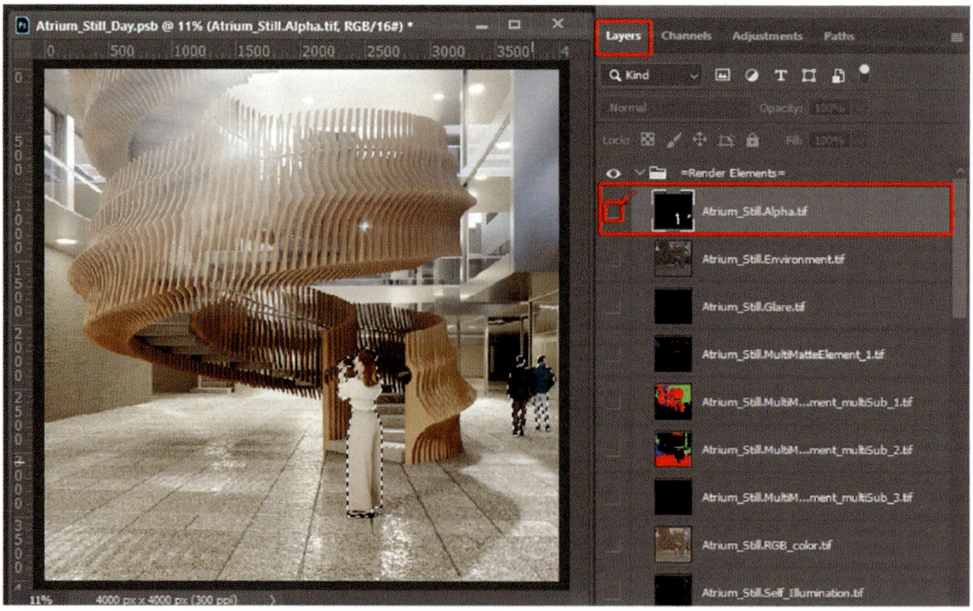

Turn off the, Atrium_Still.Alpha.tif layer visibility

Because we're only focusing on the selection of the lady, enable the Marquee tool (M) and hold down the Alt key.

You should see a minus sign. Draw around the area you want to subtract the selection from.

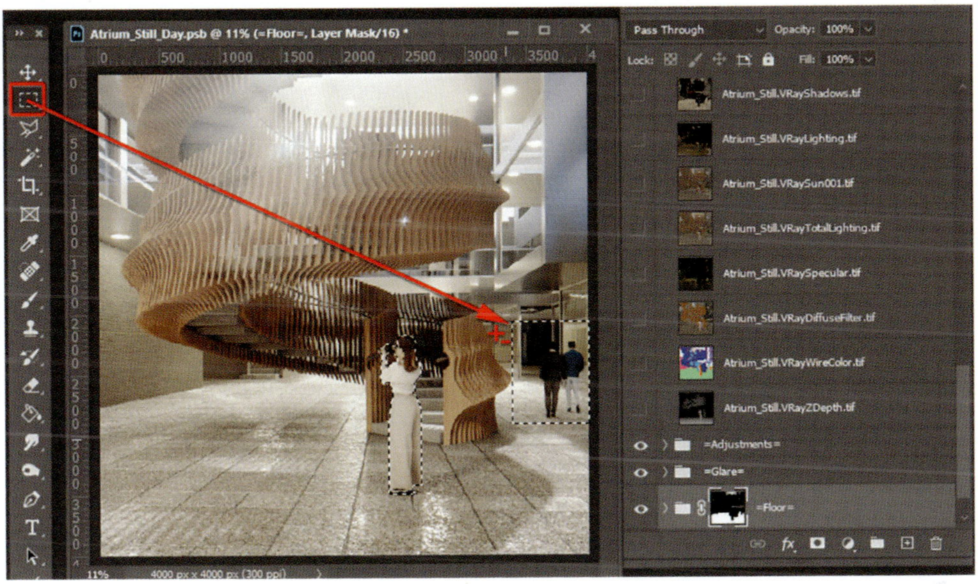

Hold down the Alt key and Draw around the area you want to subtract the selection from

While the selection of the lady is still on, create a new group and click on the mask button to create a group mask.

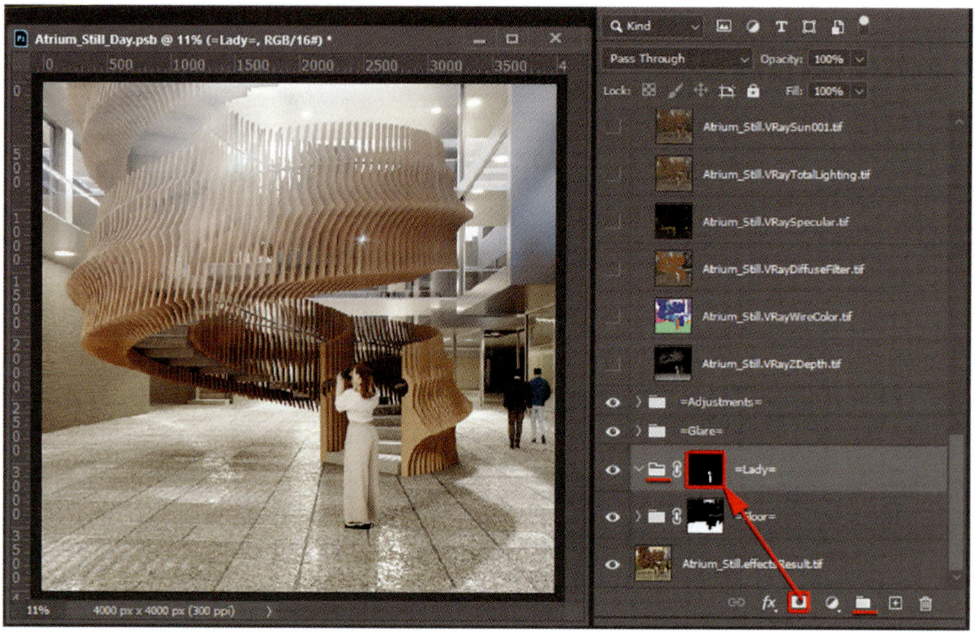

Create a new group and click on the mask button to create a group mask

To add a bit of contrast, add the Levels adjustment layer and move its middle point to about 0.50.

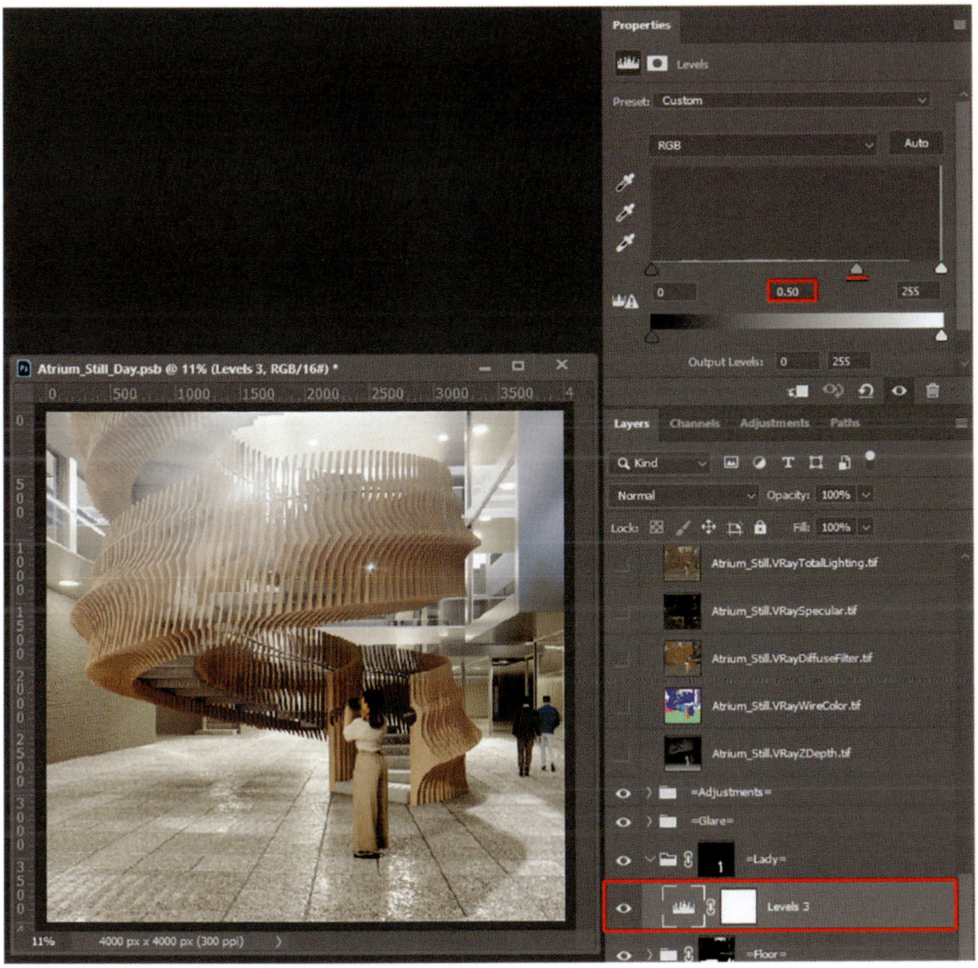

Create a new Levels adjustment layer and move its middle point to about 0.50

To match her color with the rest of the image, add a Hue/Saturation adjustment layer and reduce its Saturation value to about –50.

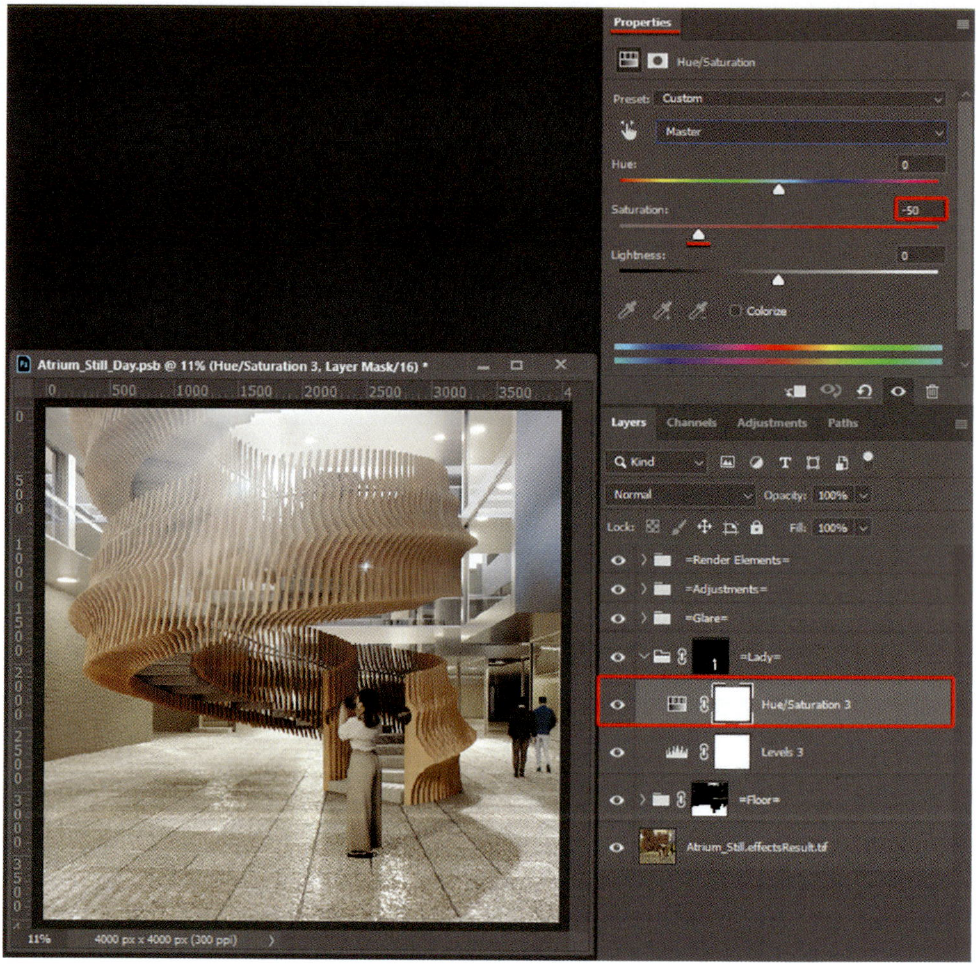

Add a Hue/Saturation adjustment layer and reduce its Saturation value to about –50

Once happy with the final tweaks, go to File and choose to Save as (Shift+Ctrl+S).

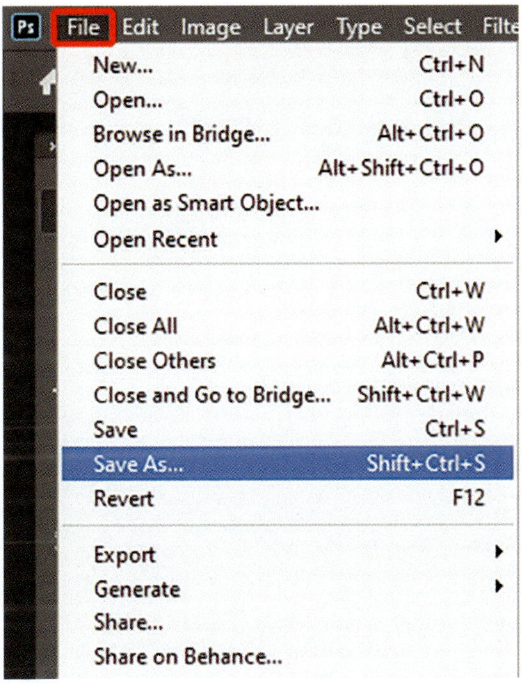

Go to File and choose to Save as (Shift+Ctrl+S)

Choose to Save as a TIFF file type and uncheck the Layers. In the TIFF Options, choose the option to Discard Layers and Save a Copy.

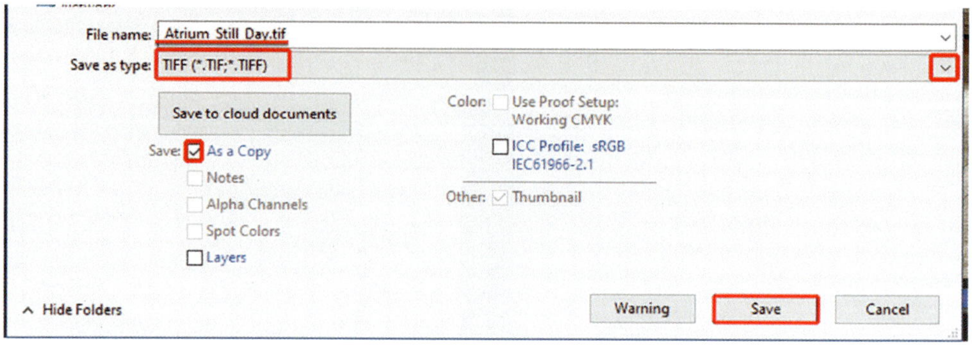

Choose to Save as a TIFF file type

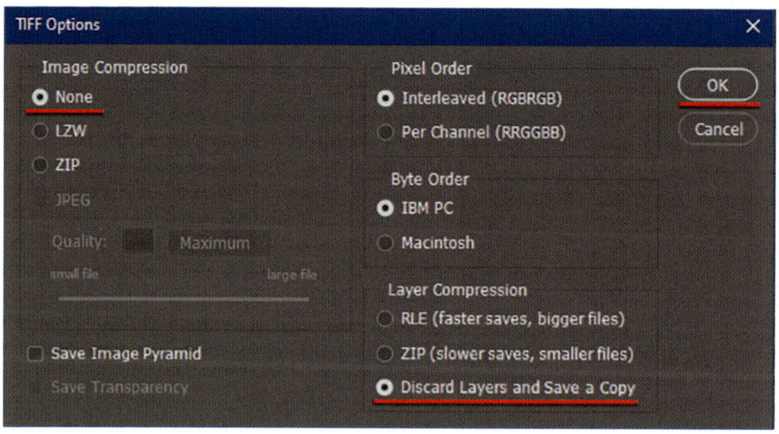

Choose the option to Discard Layers and Save a Copy

Finally, save the PSB file with all layers.

Conclusion

This chapter took users through the step-by-step process of loading the V-Ray Image file into the Frame buffer, how to use the LightMix and other VFB effects to tweak and save the rendered elements, followed by going into Photoshop and loading the pre-rendered layer elements into a stack, create groups and use MultiMatteElement to create masks.

In addition, users were shown how to use key render elements such as, reflections, specular and the diffuse filter to hence surfaces.

Finally, adjustments such as LUT and glare were used to help finalize the image.

11

Night Scene Pre-Production

11 Night Scene Pre-Production

Introduction

This chapter will take users through the usual methodical process of taking the brief from the client, along with their ideas, files, and their vision of the night/ dusk shot, followed by the meticulous process of collating mood boards with photo references for the final art direction.

Client Brief

For this night shot, the main brief was to highlight the effect of artificial lights around the main staircase, contrasted with the overall ambient light of the environment in order to achieve a more inviting and atmospheric look.

Photo References and/or Mood Board

The images below depict two of many photo references presented to the client.

Lighting/Color Suggestions

Photo references depicting lighting and color of night scenes

Conclusion

While this pre-production stage was notably straightforward, it is equally important to go through the process of selecting photo references that would help form an idea of the overall mood and light colors.

Finally, the photo references had to reflect the time of the day requested by the client (night).

DOI: 10.1201/9781315770802-11

12

Night Scene Lighting/Rendering

12 Night Scene Lighting/Rendering

Interior Night Scene

Introduction

Lighting an appealing interior night scene consists mainly of the ability to achieve the perfect balance between the blue tones often emitted by the diffused ambient/environment light, and the direct warm/yellow tones originating from the artificial lights.

The following tutorial will take users through the quick step-by-step process of turning a daylight interior scene into a night one.

NOTE

This chapter is a continuation of Staircase Atrium_ Final.max. Hence, the scene, camera, lighting, materials, and LUT files have already been created and set up.

Lighting

Let's start by opening the file under the name of, Staircase Atrium_Night_Start. max.

Before we begin working on the wood material, it's worth paying close attention to physical properties such as color, texture, grain, hardness and how it interacts/ reflects light, as depicted in the photo directly above.

To begin testing the lights, in the Common tab, reduce the Width and Height Output Size to 1000 pixels.

DOI: 10.1201/9781315770802-12

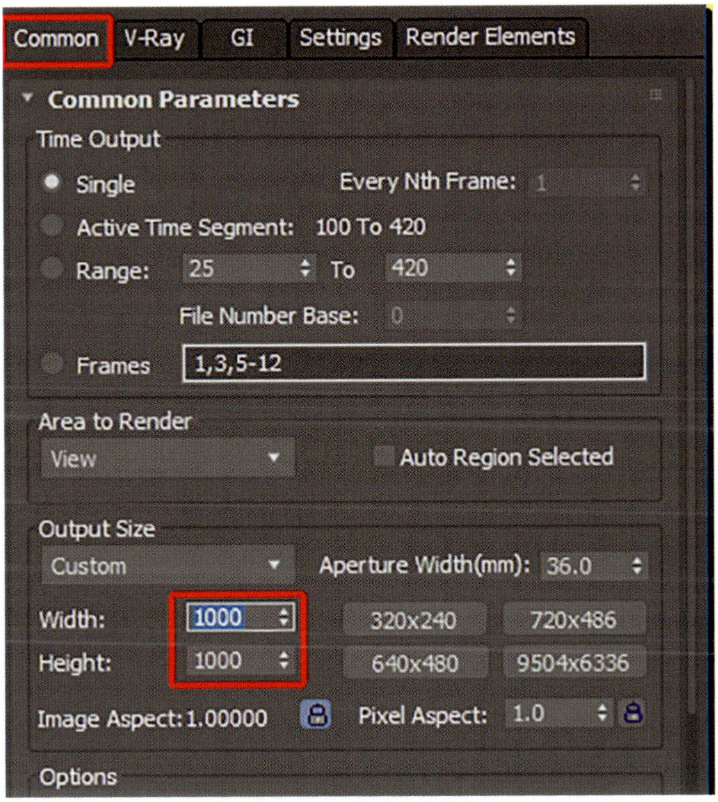

Reduce the Width and Height Output Size to 1000 pixels

In the V-Ray tab, under Frame buffer, disable the V-Ray raw image file function and the Separate render channels.

Also, under the Image sampler (Antialiasing), change the Type to Progressive and the Noise threshold to 0.01.

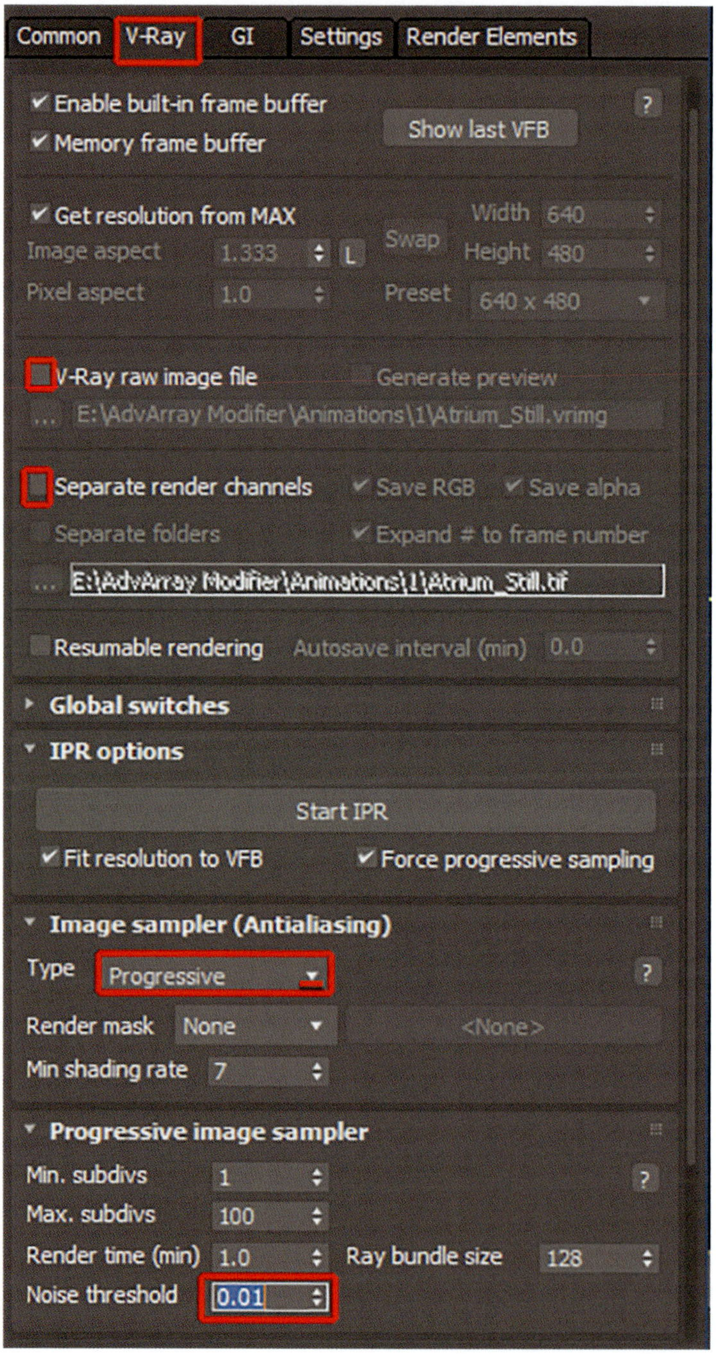

Disable the Frame buffer options and change the Image sampler to Progressive Type

Next, in the front viewport, select the VRaySun001 and move it down to about –2.09mm in Z axis.

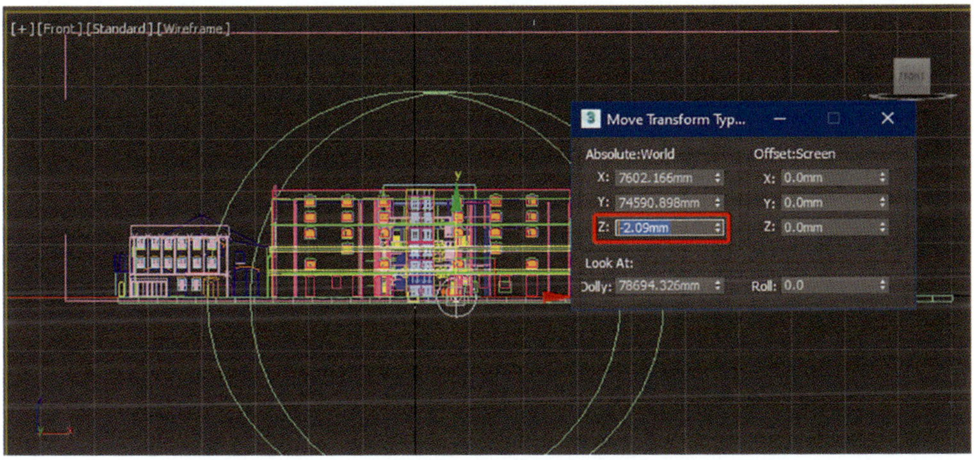

Move the VRaySun001 in Z axis to about –2.09mm

The following step is to create a Dome light to emulate diffused bluish light often seen at night. To do so, as previously done, under VRay, click on the VRayLight button and change its Type to Dome.

In the top viewport, click anywhere to create it.

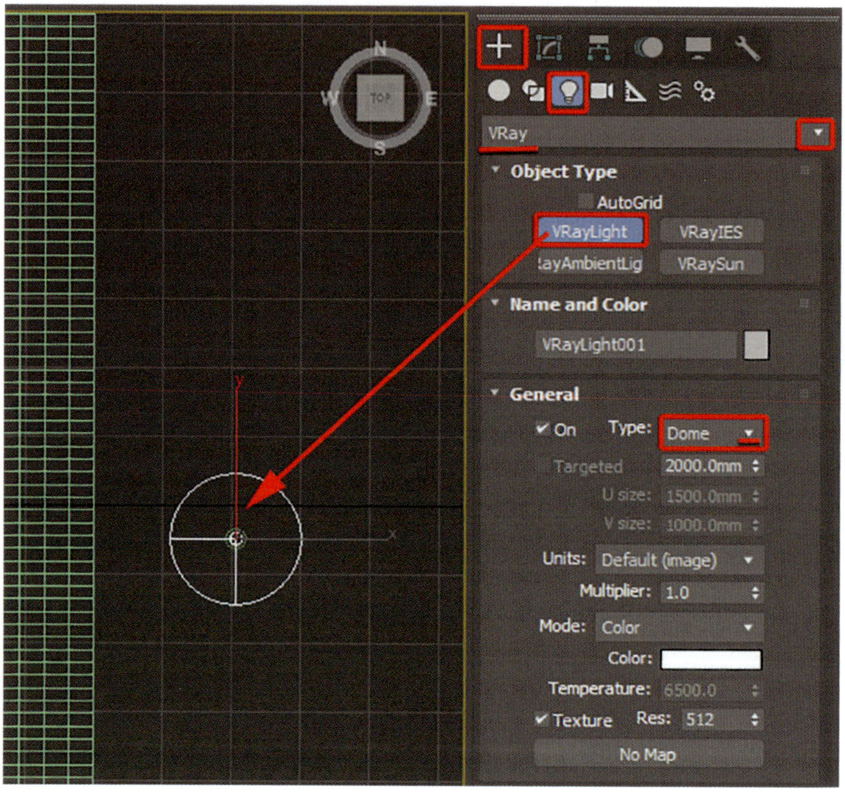

Click anywhere in the top viewport to create a VRay Dome light

While the VRayLight001 is selected, rename it as, VRayLight_Dome, and set its Multiplier to about 100.0 and the color to dark blue (R: 34, G: 63, B: 156, Hue: 160, Sat: 199, Value: 156).

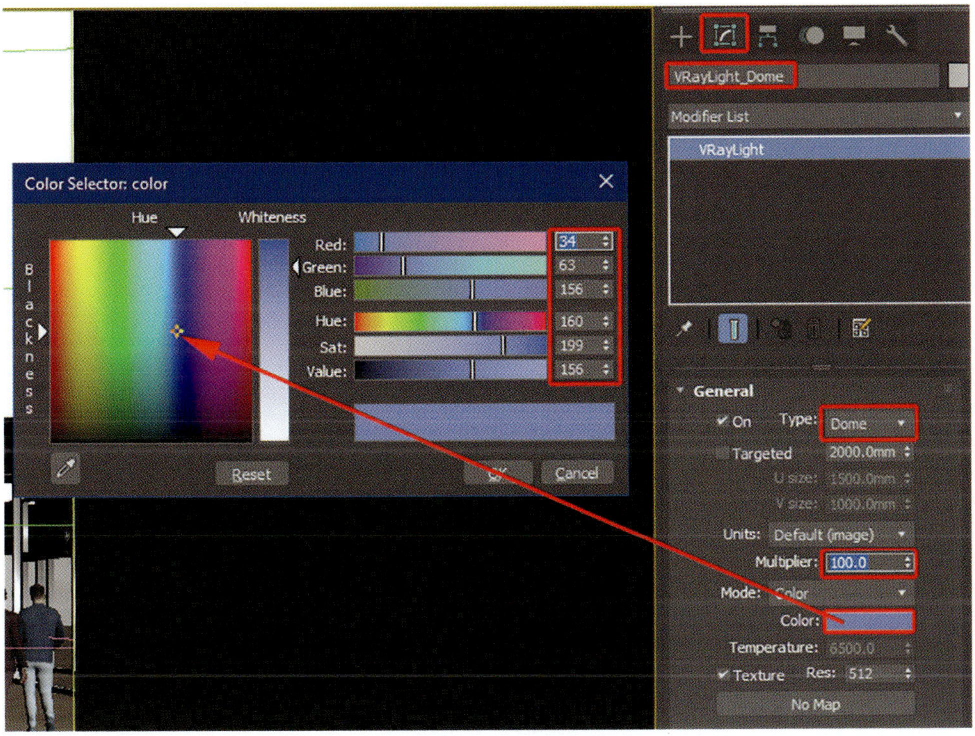

Set the Dome light Multiplier to 100.0 and the color to dark blue

Test render using the V-Ray Viewport IPR. The final result should be a dark tone of blue (cold) mixed with warm artificial lights.

Setting Up for Final Render

The following step is to revert back to some of the initial high render settings previously set for the daylight version of this Atrium scene.

Let's start by opening the V-Ray tab. Under Image sampler (Antialiasing), change it back to Bucket Type.

Under Bucket image sampler, change the Max subdivs to 10 and decrease the Noise threshold to 0.007.

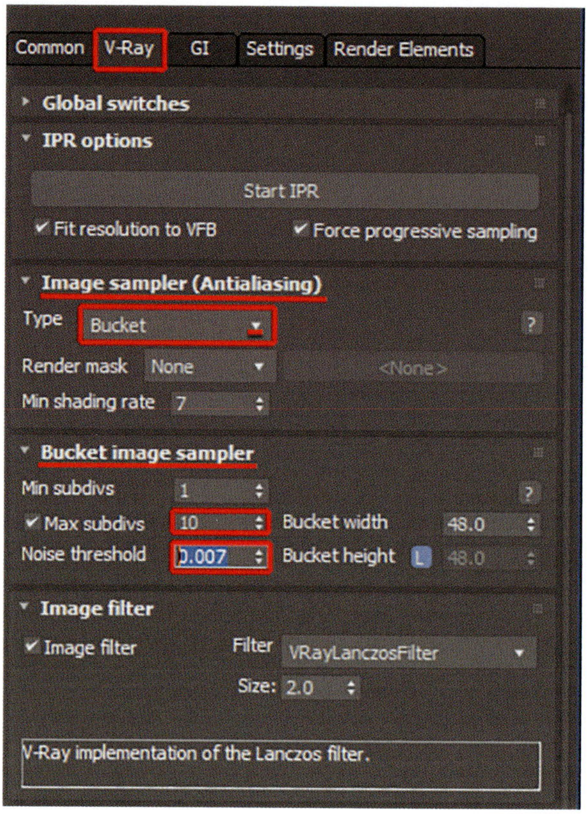

Change the Image sampler Type to Bucket, Max subdivs to 10, and Noise threshold to 0.007

NOTE

These parameters/values worked well. However, feel free to try different settings and values, if desired.

Under Frame buffer, re-enable the V-Ray raw image file function and click on its toggle to rename it as, Atrium_Still_Night_.vrimg. Keep the previous settings.

Also, enable the option to Separate render channels, Save RGB, Save alpha and Expand # to frame number. Finally, rename the TIF file as, Atrium_Still_Night_.tif, and keep its previous settings.

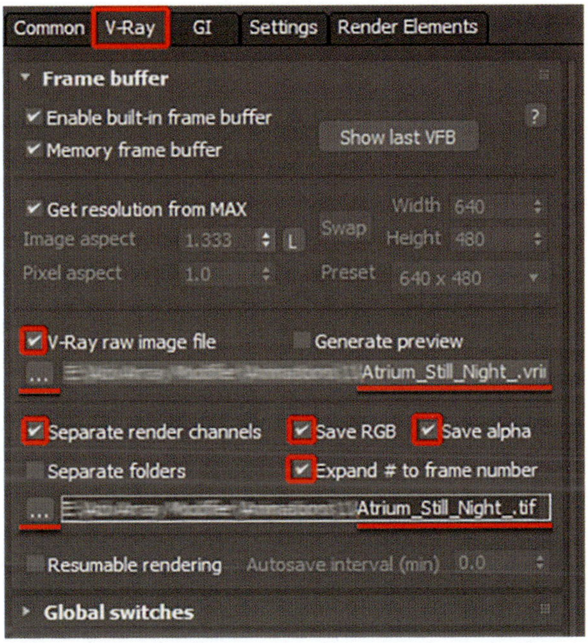

Re-enable the Frame buffer settings and rename the previous file names

Before sending the final render, open the Common tab. Under Output Size, set the Width and Height size to 4000 pixels and click to Render.

12 Night Scene Lighting/Rendering

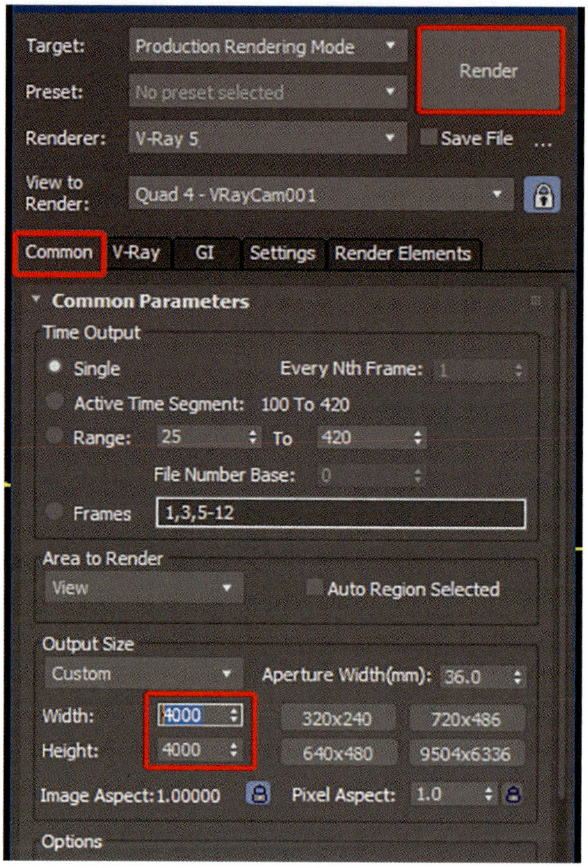

Set the Width and Height size to 4000 pixels and click to Render

Conclusion

This chapter focused on the intricacies of turning a daylight interior scene into a night one, by first lowering the position of the previous sunlight, followed by creating a dome light and tweaking its parameters to achieve an appealing interior night scene.

The final step was to switch back the final high-resolution settings in order to send the final render. The subsequent chapter will take users through the post-production process of using state-of-the-art techniques to finalize the image.

13

Night Scene Post-Production

13 Night Scene Post-Production

Introduction

The post-production process of a night scene will begin by using the V-Ray Frame Buffer (VFB) LightMix parameters to achieve the correct light mood and color, prior to stepping into Photoshop.

In Photoshop, users will learn the value of loading files into a stack, organize and name them into groups with masks, how to use Adjustment Layers, glare effects, render elements and much more.

V-Ray Frame Buffer (VFB)

Once the final high-resolution image is finished rendering, the next step is to use the VFB to tweak the lights and Lens effects.

DOI: 10.1201/9781315770802-13

As mentioned in the previous chapter, if you re-open 3DS Max and the final renders are not in your VFB, simply go to VFB File and choose to Load image named, Atrium_Still_Night_.vrimg.

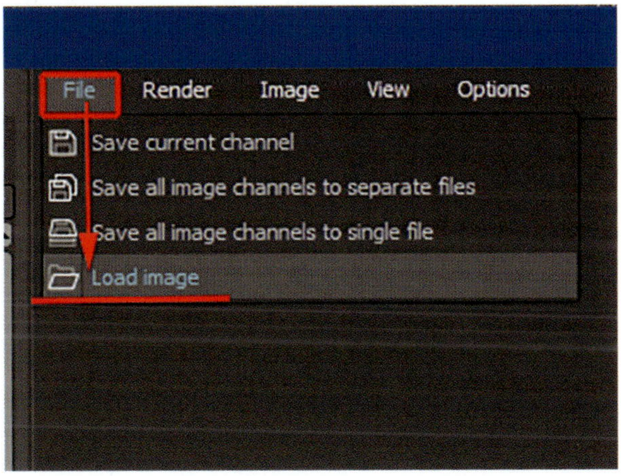

Go to VFB File and choose to Load image named, Atrium_Still_Night_.vrimg

To tweak the lights, select the Source: LightMix Layer. Under LightMix, increase the VRayLight_disc022 value to about 1.500 and the Self Illumination to 3.000. Also, change the color of VRayLight_Dome to blue.

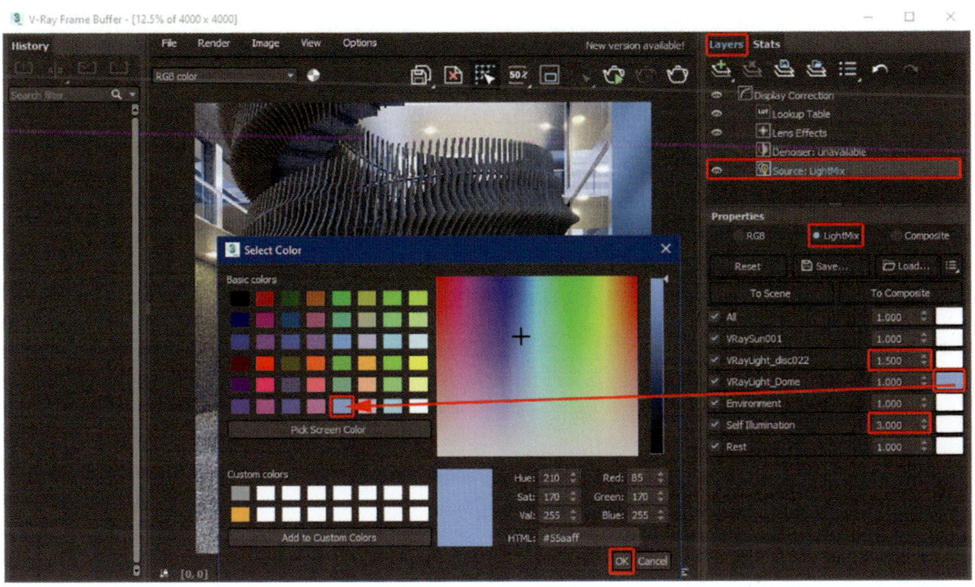

Increase the VRayLight_disc values, Self Illumination, and color values

NOTE

While these values and settings worked well, feel free to try different values and settings, if desired.

NOTE

While these values and settings worked well, feel free to try different values and settings, if desired.

Once happy with the results, in the VFB, click go to File and choose to Save all image channels to separate files.

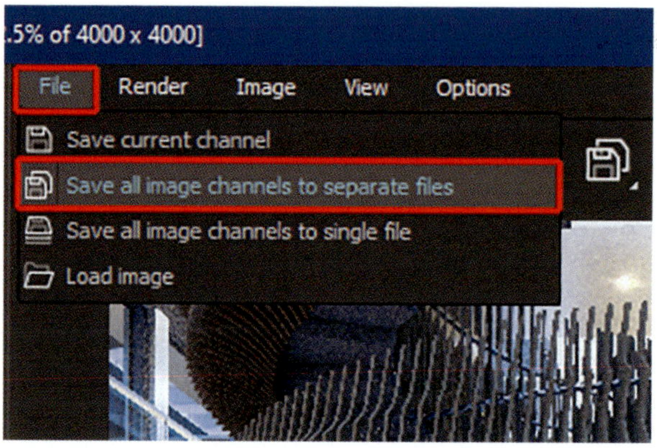

Click on the File and choose to Save all image channels to separate files

Create a new folder and save the channels as a TIF file, using the same parameters previously discussed.

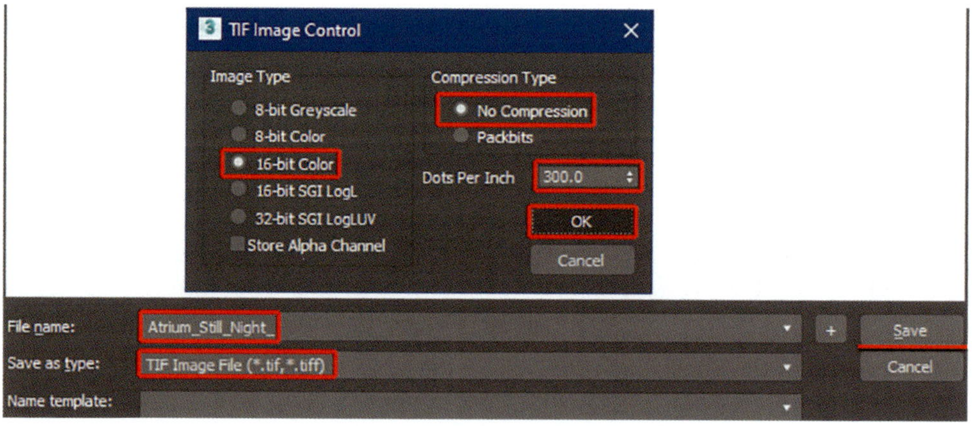

Save the channels as a TIF file, using the same parameters previously entered

Photoshop

To bring all the previously saved layers into a stack, in Photoshop, go to File>Scripts>Load Files into Stack.

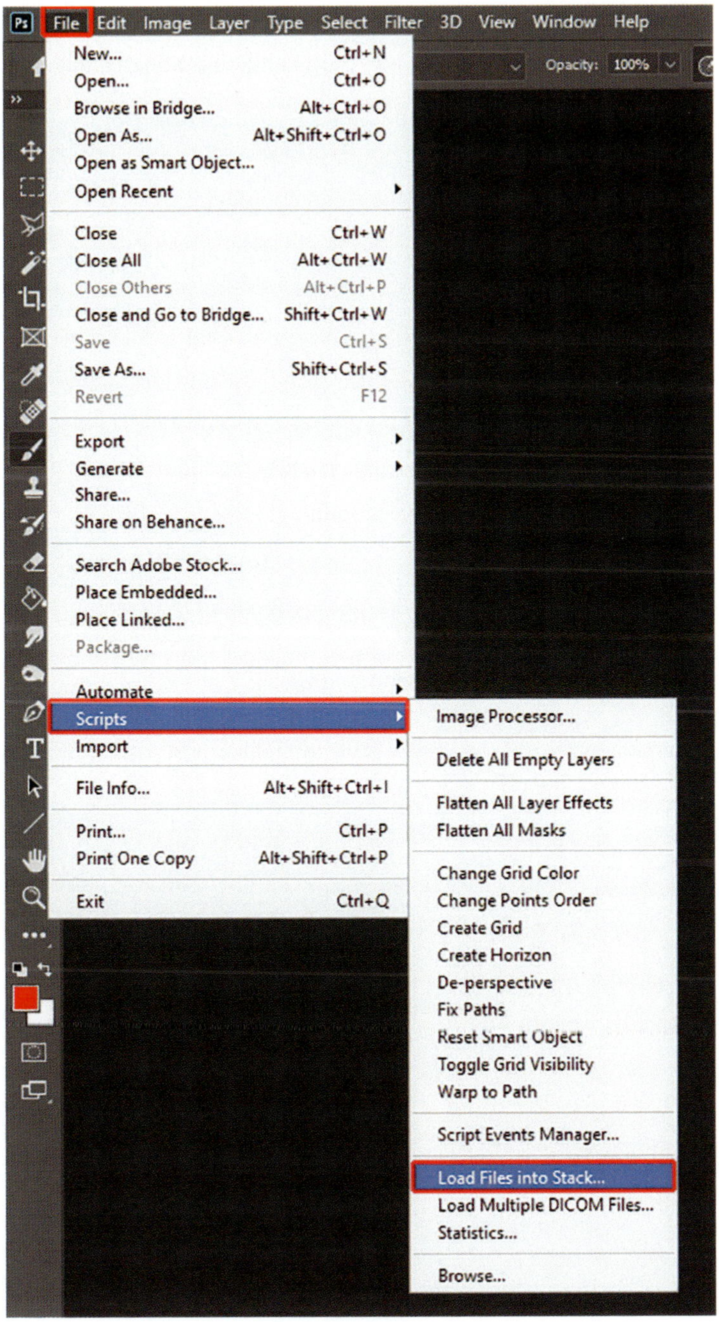

go to File>Scripts>Load Files into Stack

In the Load Layers dialog, click on the Browse button to locate the TIF files. Select all TIF files using Ctrl+Click or Select+Shift+Select.

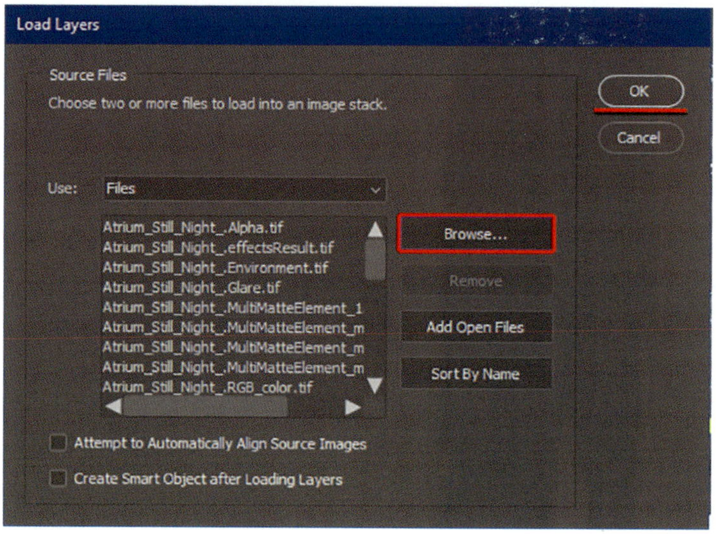

Use the Browse toggle to locate and load files

Once all TIF files are inside, click OK to Open and Load them into a stack.

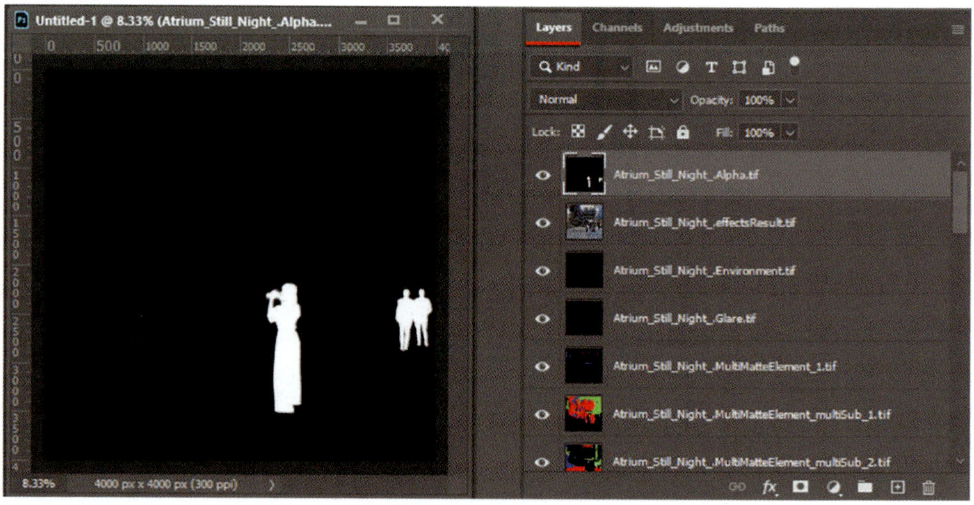

Loaded layers in a stack

Choose to Save the document as a PSB file format (Ctrl+S). Name it as, Atrium_Still_Night. Disable the option to Save As a Copy and enable the Layers function to keep layers.

As mentioned earlier, PSB file format allows users to save Photoshop files bigger than 2GB in size.

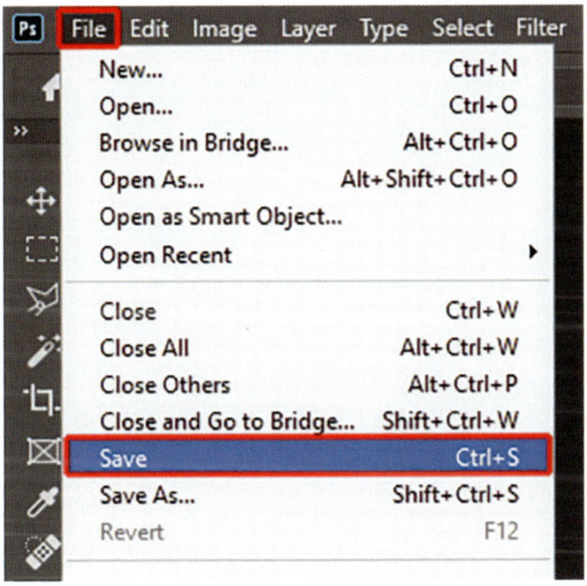

Save the Files as

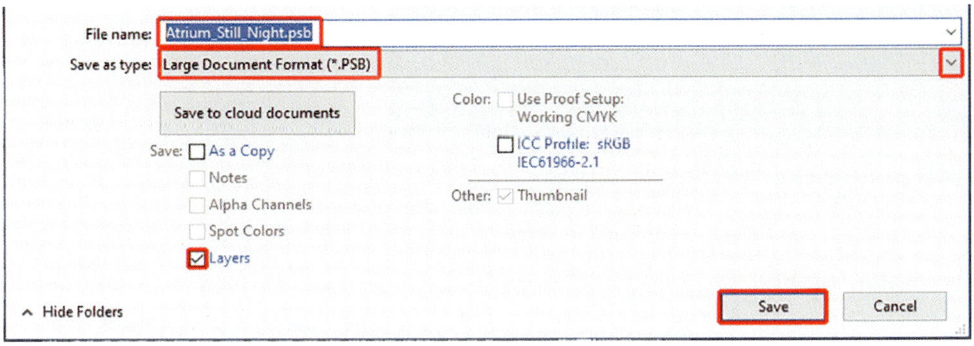

Save the document as a PSB file format

To begin organizing the layers, hold down the Alt key and click on the eye icon of the layer named, Atrium_Still_Night.effectsResult.tif.

All remaining layers should automatically become turned off as result.

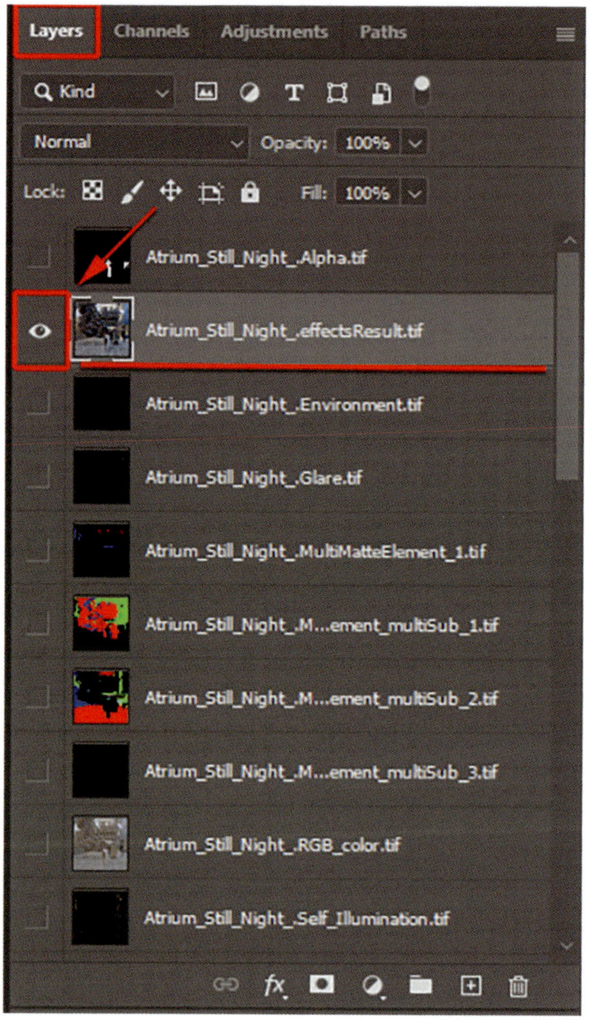

All layers but Atrium_Still.effectsResult.tif turned off automatically

The following step is to select and move the layer named, Atrium_Still_Night.effectsResult.tif to the bottom of the list. It's common practice to have the main layer at the bottom of the list before starting to add any subsequent layers and groups on top.

Move the layer to the bottom of the list

Select all the layers that are turned off using Select+Shift keys.

Select all the layers that are turned off

Next, click the button to Create a new group, followed by naming the new group as, =Render Elements=, and moving all the layers turned off inside the group. It's always good practice to organize layers in a document.

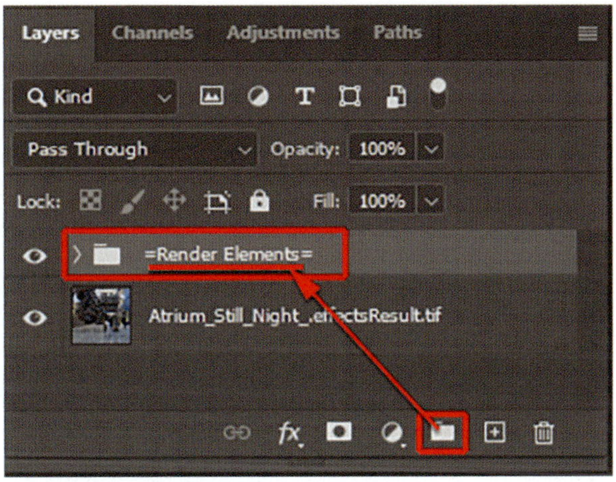

New group created and named with layers inside

To speed things up, let's open the previous PSB file named, Atrium_Still_Day.psb. Select the group named, =Adjustments=, followed by right clicking on it and choosing to Duplicate Group.

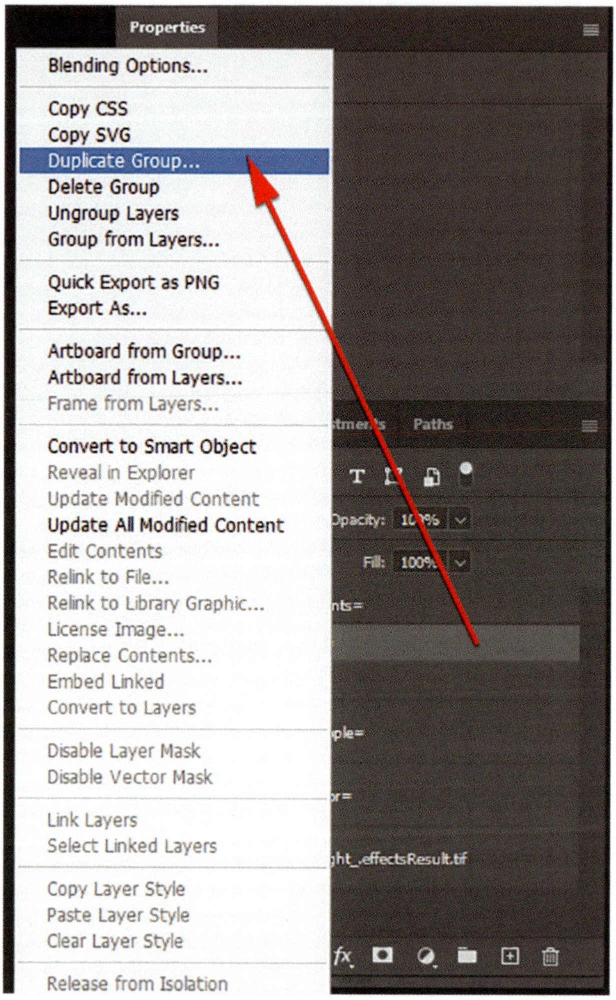

Select the Adjustments group, followed by right clicking and choosing to Duplicate Group

In the Duplicate Group dialog, choose the Destination Document to be, Atrium_Still_Night.PSB.

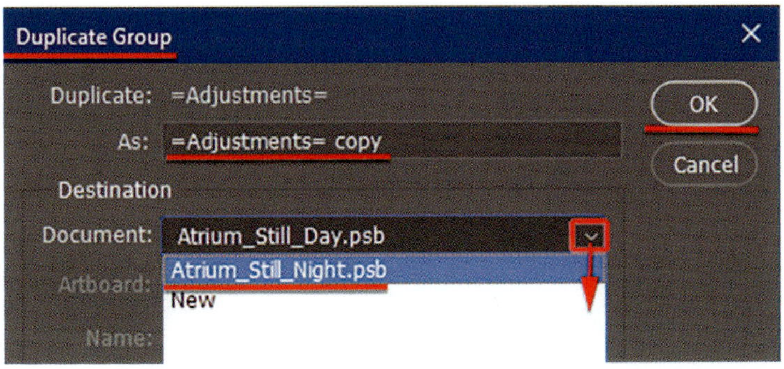

Choose the Destination Document to be, Atrium_Still_Night.PSB

In the Adjustments group, replace the previous VRayLighting layer with the new Atrium_Still_Night_VRayLighting. Copy it as previously done.

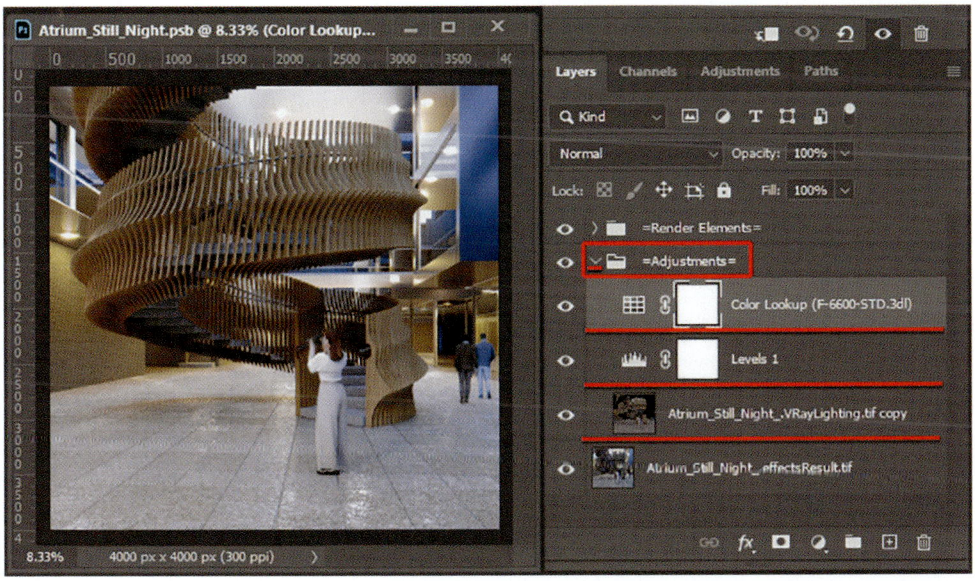

Replace the previous VRayLighting layer with the new Atrium_Still_Night_VRayLighting

Next, select the Levels adjustment layer (RGB) and move its middle point to about 0.80. Also, move its rightmost point to about 225.

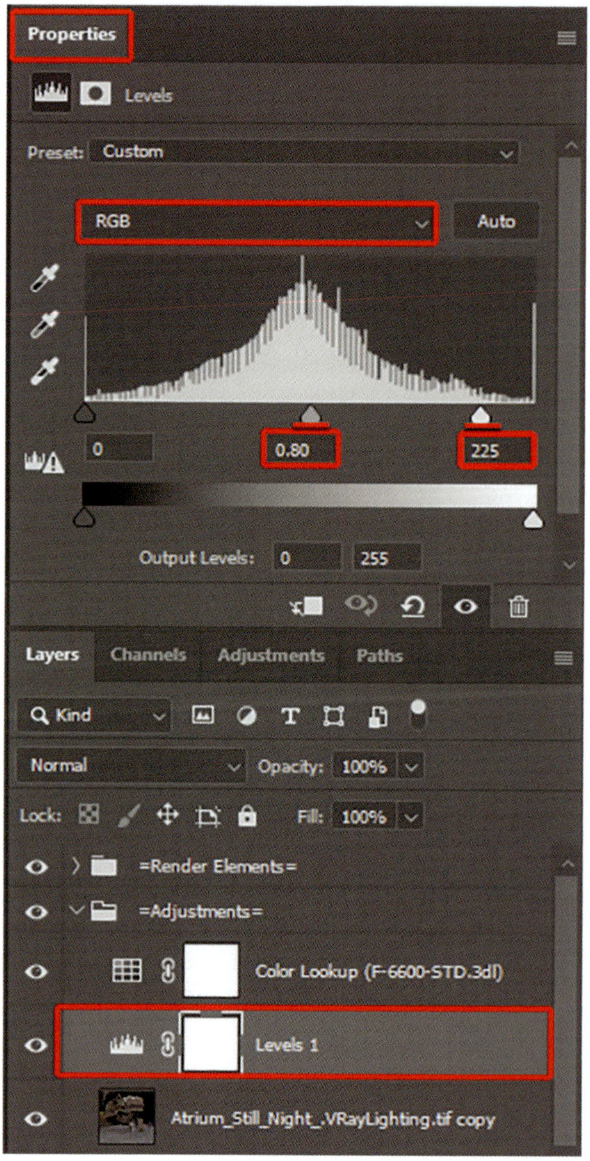

Tweak the RGB Levels adjustment layer

To adjust its color slightly, pick the Red channel and move the middle point to about 1.16.

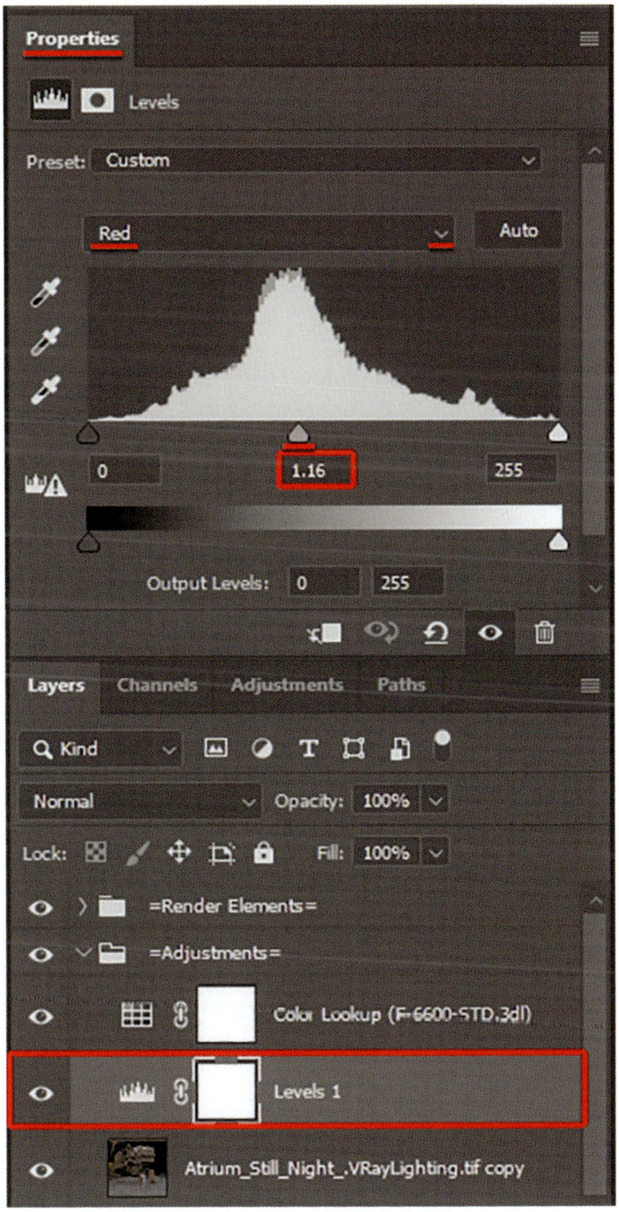

Pick the Red channel and move its middle point to about 1.16

Next, pick the Blue channel. Move the middle point to about 0.95, the right point to 220, and the left point to 46.

NOTE

While these values worked well, feel free to try different ones, if desired.

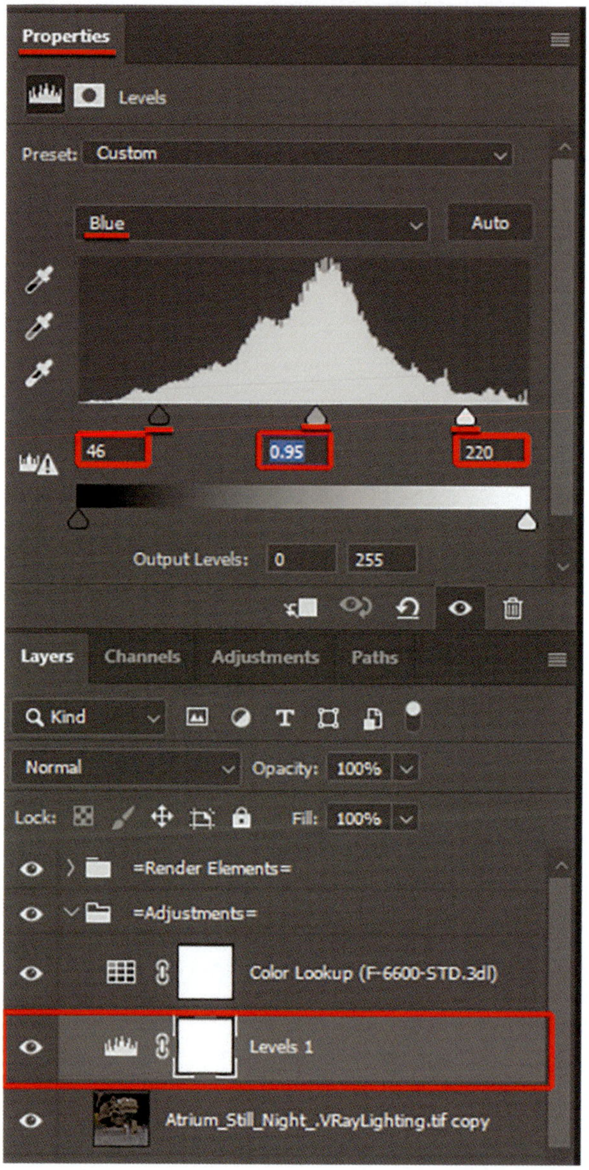

Move the Blue channel middle point to 0.95, the right point to 220, and the left point to 46

The following step is to duplicate the =Glare= group from the Atrium_Still_Day.psb document into the Atrium_Still_Night.psb as previously done.

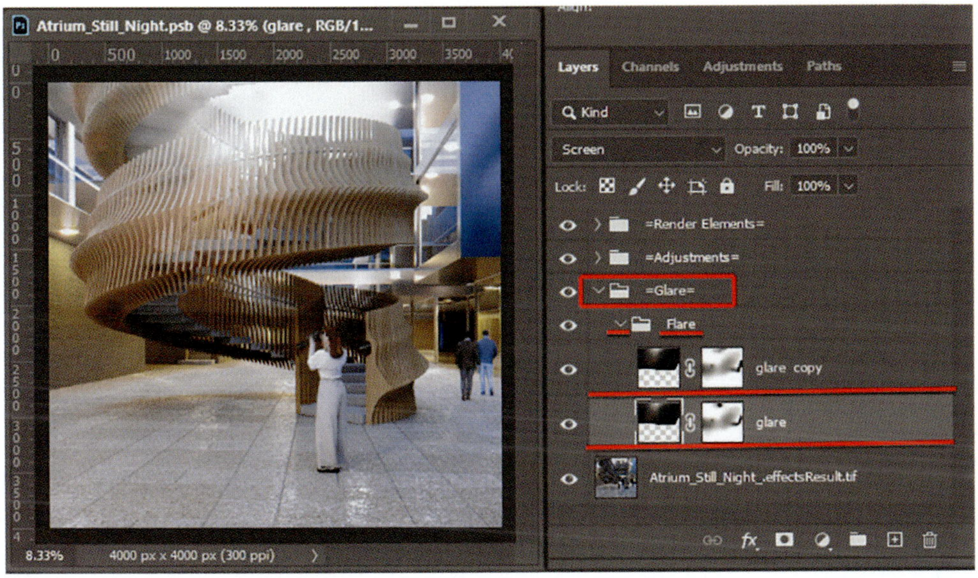

Duplicate the Glare group from the Atrium_Still_Day.psb into the Atrium_Still_Night.psb

Also, duplicate the =Lady= group from the Atrium_Still_Day.psb document into the Atrium_Still_Night.psb. Rename it as, People, and include the mask selection of the two people walking in the distance.

Select its Levels adjustment layer. Move the RGB middle point to about 0.47 and the left point to 9.

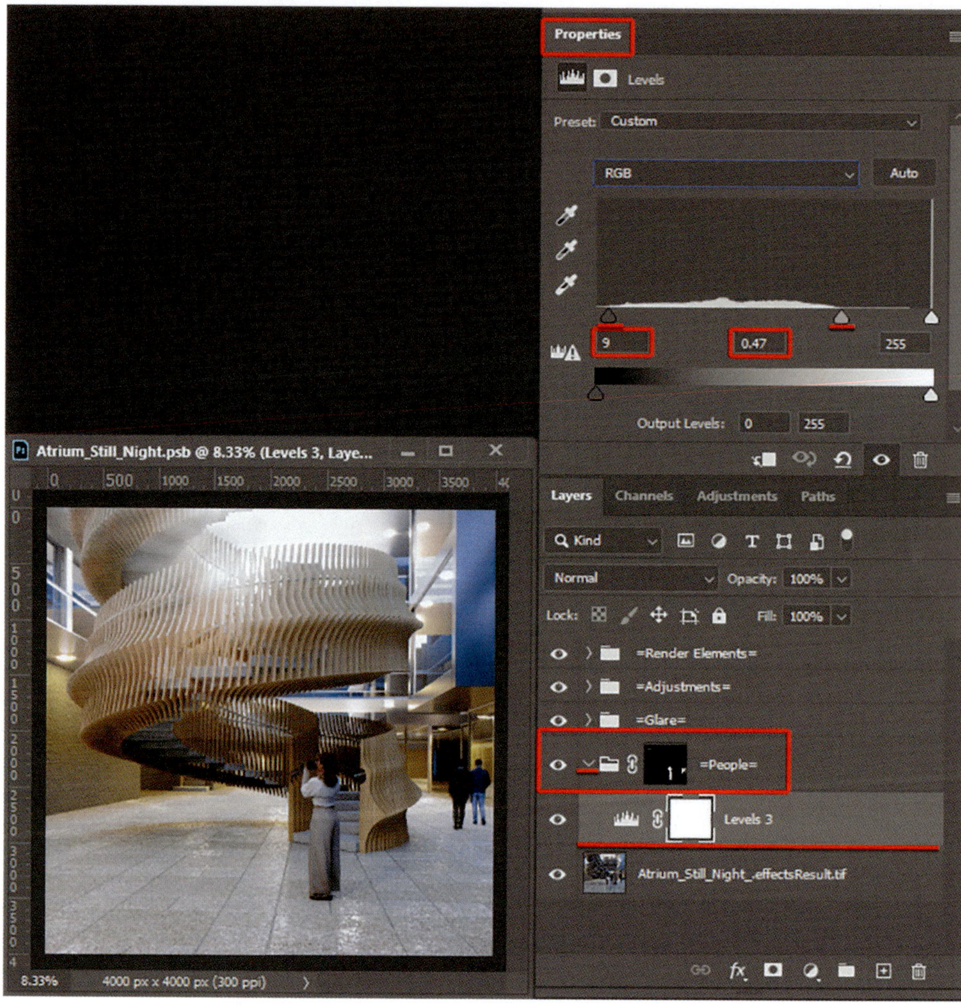

Duplicate the Lady group, followed editing its mask, renaming and tweaking its Levels values

Next, duplicate the =Floor= group. Delete the Hue/Saturation adjustment layer and replace the previous VRaySpecular with the new one from Atrium_Still_Night.psb.

Also, move the Levels middle point to about 0.50.

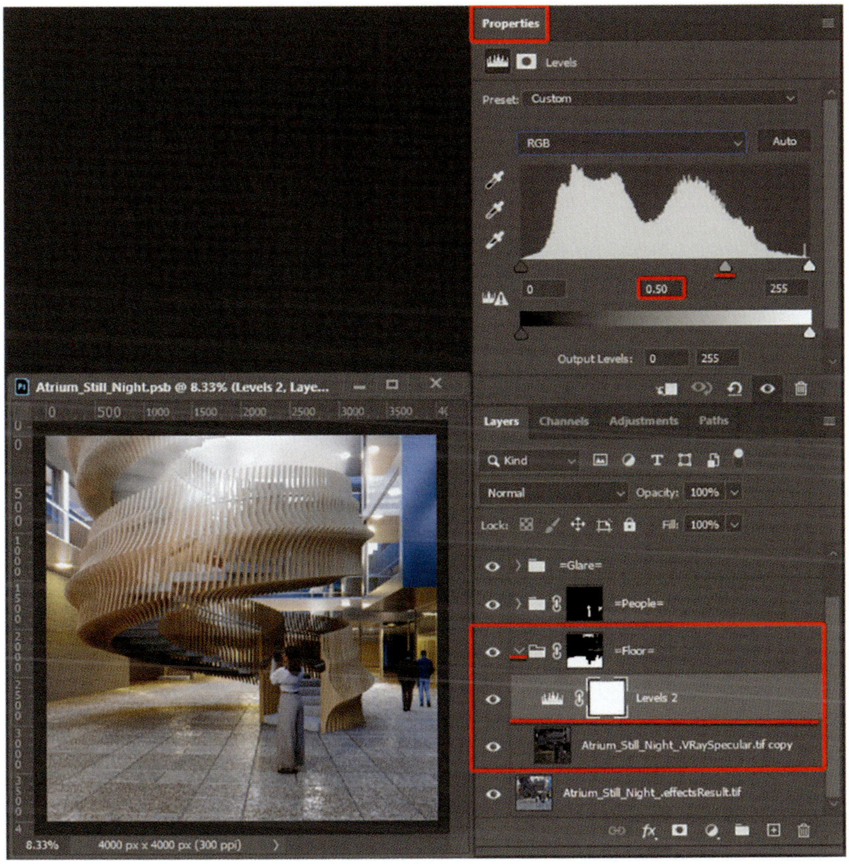

Duplicate the Floor group, tweak the Levels and replace the Specular element

Save the final image as a TIFF file format, using the previous parameters. In the TIFF Options, choose the option to Discard Layers and Save a Copy.

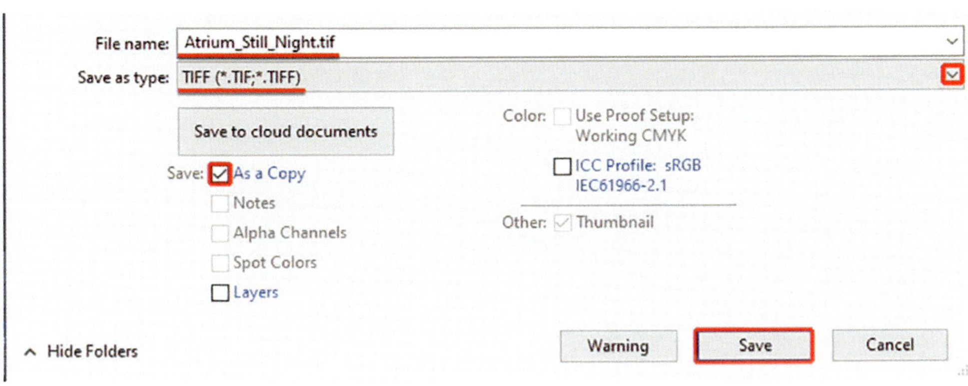

Save the final image as a TIFF file format

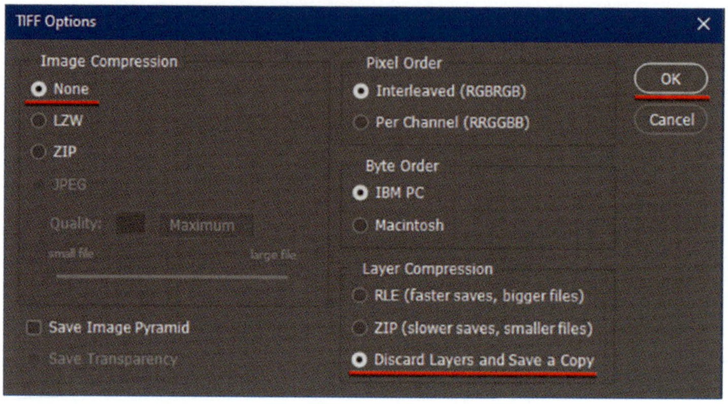

Choose the option to Discard Layers and Save a Copy

Finally, save the PSB file with all layers.

Conclusion

This chapter took users through the fascinating process of tweaking the LightMix parameters in the Frame buffer in order to achieve the desired night effect, prior to saving out the rendered elements. The following step focused mainly on the process of using Photoshop and the pre-rendered layer elements to enhance every aspect of the image.

Throughout the process, users were shown how to use key render elements to hence surfaces and the overall image.

Finally, post-production effects such as Levels, Hue/Saturation, LUT and glare were used to help finalize the shot.

14

Verified Views for Planning Applications

14 Verified Views

Final render of a Verified View with the proposed building

Introduction

Verified View/s methodology or Accurate Visual Representation (AVR) is an accurate Photomontage of a proposed design/building, using the Guidelines for Landscape and Visual Impact Assessment (GLVIA3).

In some countries, this process is called Certified Views or Aligned Views.

Verified Views are a crucial part of a series of documents an Architect or/and a Developer needs to submit to the planning authorities for permission to build, extend or simply change the facade of any proposed building.

Verified Views will provide the planning authorities with an accurate visual representation of the proposed building from the proposed views.

To create Verified Views, there are a series of steps one has to take in accordance with the Verified Views methodology.

Also, by law, your verified views methodology needs to be documented and included in the mandatory documentation for the planning application.

There will be documentation guidelines and portal links included in the resource files.

DOI: 10.1201/9781315770802-14

It's worth noting the initial proposed views may change depending on what's being seen. Therefore, it's important to plan the shots carefully ahead of time prior to visiting the physical site.

This chapter will take users through the intricacies of creating and submitting Verified Views for Planning Applications, using 3ds Max, V-Ray and Photoshop, while using accurate 3d context models from a company called Accucities.

Using accurate 3d context models of an existing site is a crucial part of the process to be included in the planning documentation.

Accucities are specialists in supplying 3D city models for planning applications. Their vast 3d library of city models consist of ready-made CAD models structured in 500 × 500 m tiles. Sites outside main city centers and specific countries can also be captured, by simply visiting their website and request it.

For more information about them, simply visit https://www.accucities.com/.

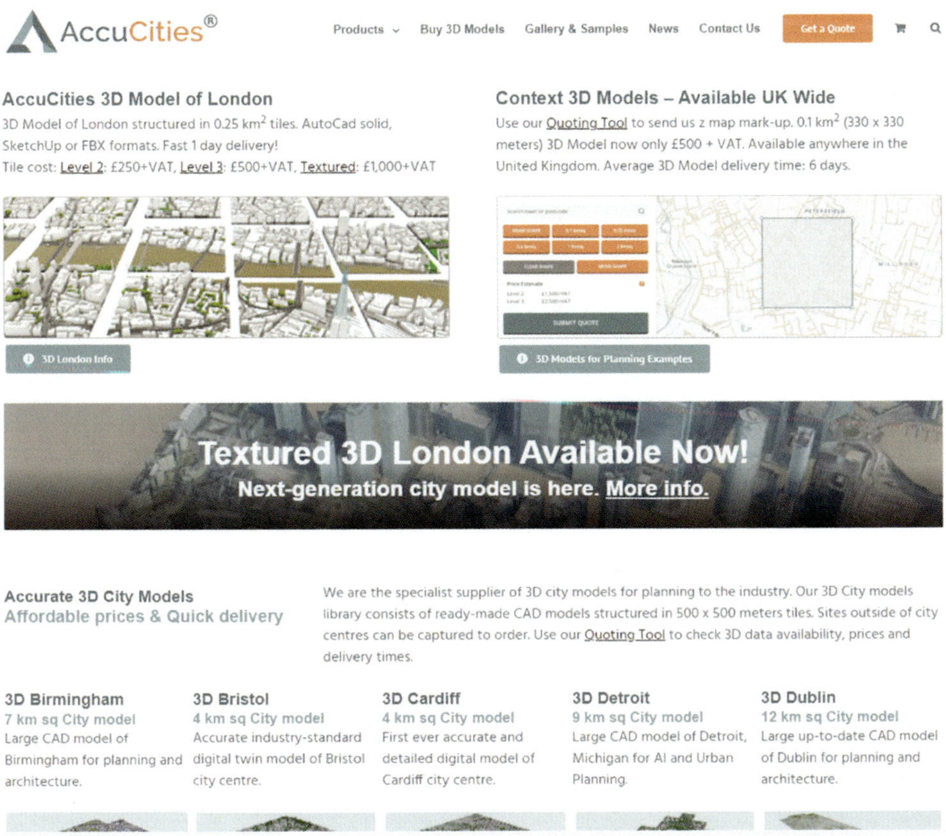

Accucities website

14 Verified Views

Let's start by opening a typical document depicting some of the proposed views by the client.

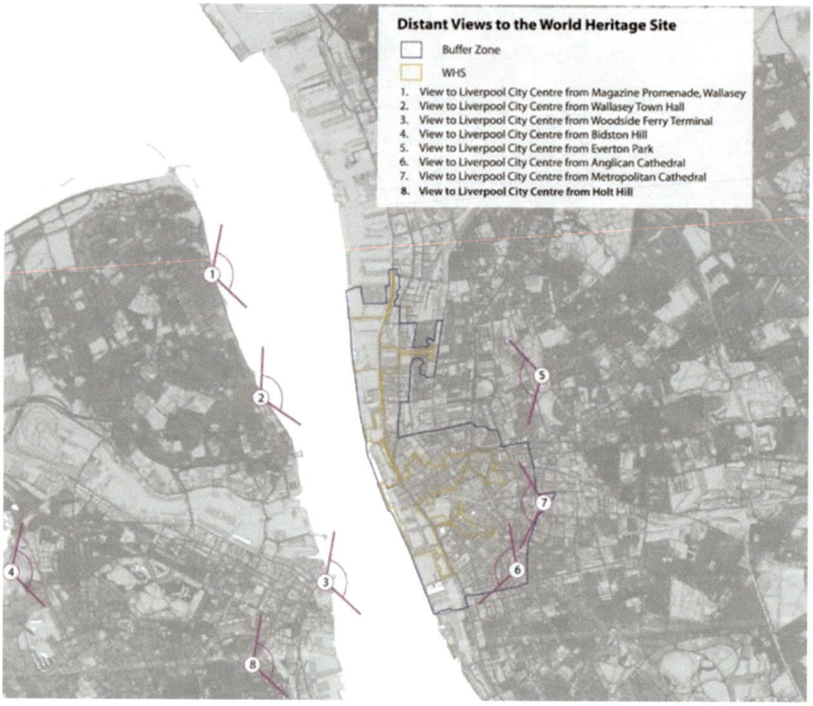

Typical document from a client depicting the initial proposed views

This document is an example of what an architect or a developer would often send to a 3d visualization specialist for a quotation. Users should also receive a 3d model block of the proposed building seen highlighted in orange, on the drawing map.

The proposed 3d building should come with its drawing coordinates of the ground Levels and heights on site.

Proposed 3d building with its drawing coordinates on site

Depending on how tall the proposed building is, the initial proposed views will include distant views as well as the standard close-up ones.

To start, once you receive the preliminary proposed views, simply go to Google maps and type in the street name of one of the views.

For this project, the name of the street was Newington butts. On Google maps, type in, Newington butts and zoom in to the area.

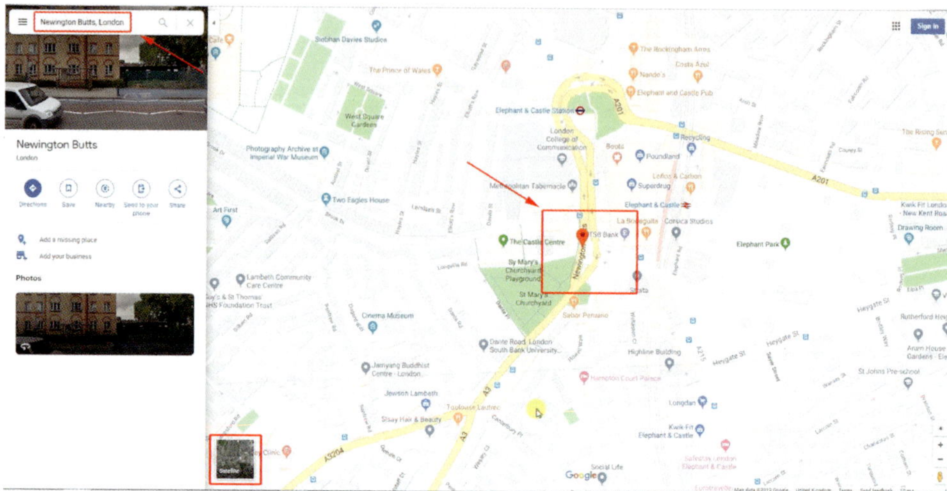

Newington butts typed in on Google maps

Next, click on the satellite thumbnail to see the satellite photography. Following that, click, drag and drop the yellow figure icon from the bottom right onto the desired area of the satellite photography.

Once dropped, users can quickly pan and zoom around the location using the mouse and scroll wheel.

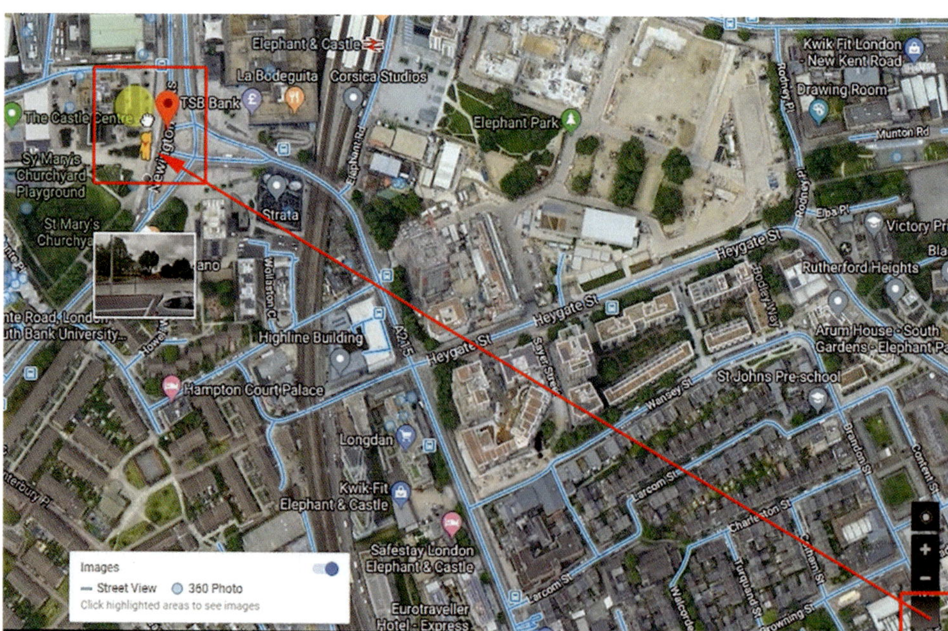

Yellow figure icon dropped onto the desired area of the satellite photography

This quick exercise often provides a quick preview of the proposed views.

Google Street View from Newington Butts looking toward the proposed building

Ultimately, to follow the planning guidelines and have a more accurate preview, users are required to have a 3d context model of the location, with the proposed 3d building inserted in, to see the real visual impact of the proposed building, from each of the proposed camera views.

3D context models are fundamental for the following reasons:

A They help planners and architects visualize the proposed camera views via CGIs and/or in VR (using Accucities VR app) prior to sending the surveyor and the photographer to the location.

This pre-visualization process will save planners and architects time and money, by eliminating any potential camera revisions that might occur, after sending the surveyor and the photographer to the physical location.

Accucities VR app

B It's quicker and easier to camera match against the survey data in 3d.

Having detailed and accurate context models makes it quicker, easier and more accurate to match the CG cameras against the survey points. Hence, creating more Accurate Visual Representations.

More often than not, some of the survey points seen in a photo might be focused on detailed areas of a building. if your 3d context model isn't accurate and doesn't include some of the details seen in the photo with survey points, the process of camera matching in 3d will become extremely laborious and less accurate.

For these reasons, it's exceptionally important to have detailed context models for close-up Accurate Visual Representations.

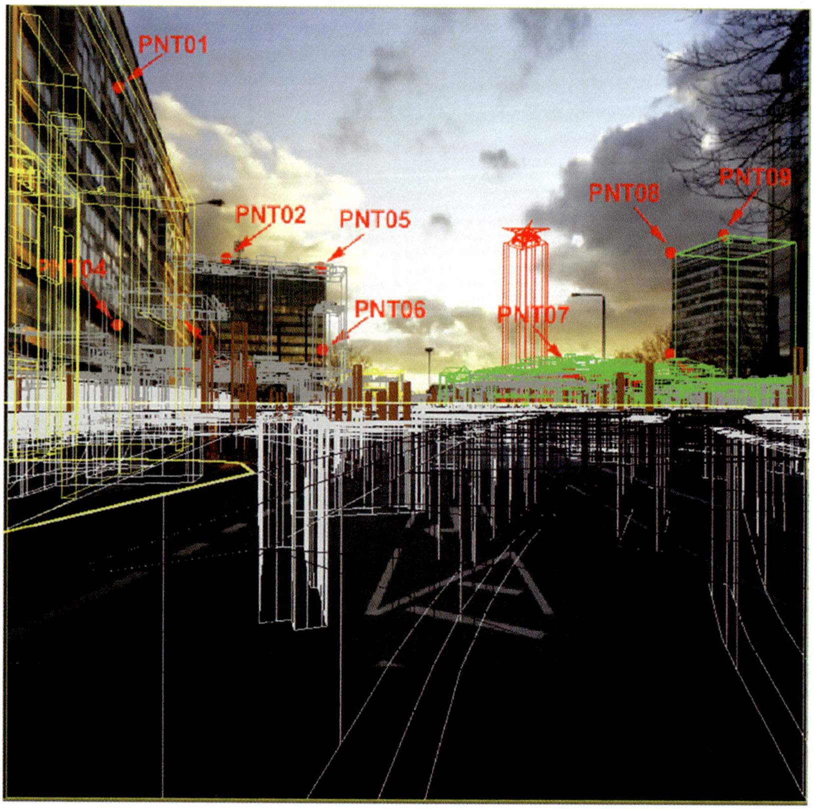

Survey points matched with Accucities 3d context models

Accucities provide users with four detail levels of accuracy: Level 1, Level 2, Level 3 and Level 4. For distant views, most companies use Level 2 context models.

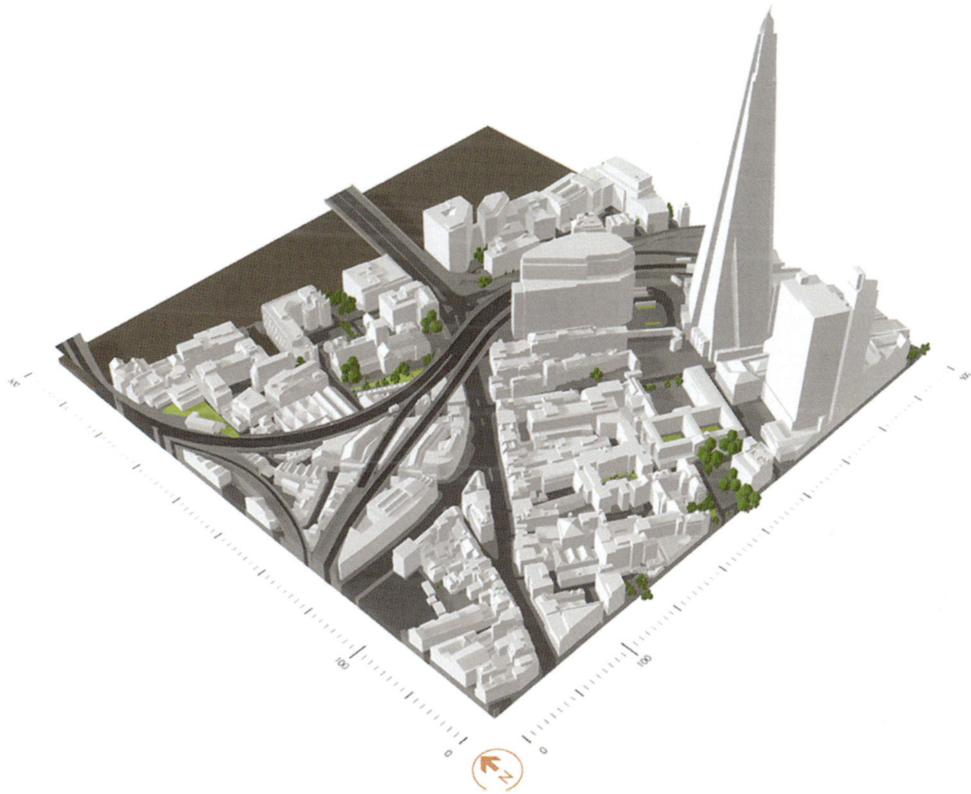

Accucities Level 2 context models

For close-ups, Level 3 is best suited.

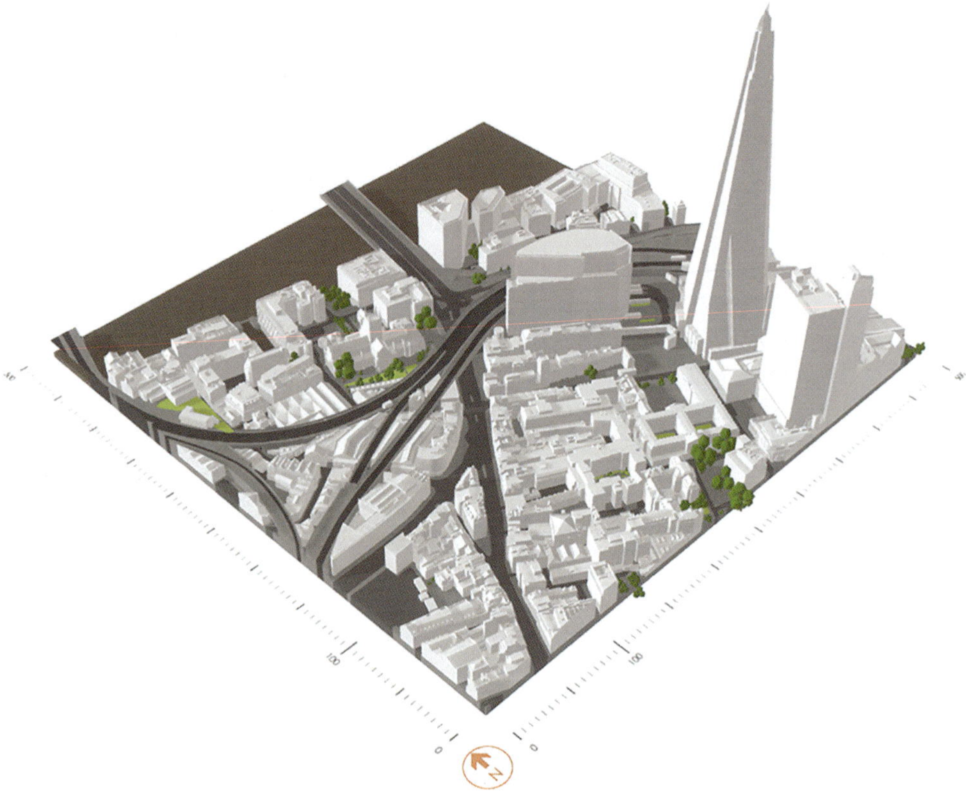

Accucities Level 3 context models

However, Level 4 comes with textures and facade details.

Accucities Level 4 context models

Level 3 and Level 4 models have a 15 cm accuracy on all axes.

3D context model files from Accucities are available in file formats such as SKP, CAD, FBX, 3ds Max, Autocad, Sketchup and Revit.

Furthermore, every 3d context model file/scene is uniquely organized in separate layers such as Buildings, Roads, Green spaces, Bridges, Rivers and Trees.

To acquire the 3d context model, simply visit https://www.accucities.com/.

As mentioned earlier, they provide the most accurate 3d context models of areas in the UK and abroad.

Once on the Accucities website, to buy 3d context model of a specific area, simply go to the Buy 3D Models tab, and click on the button to Get a Quote.

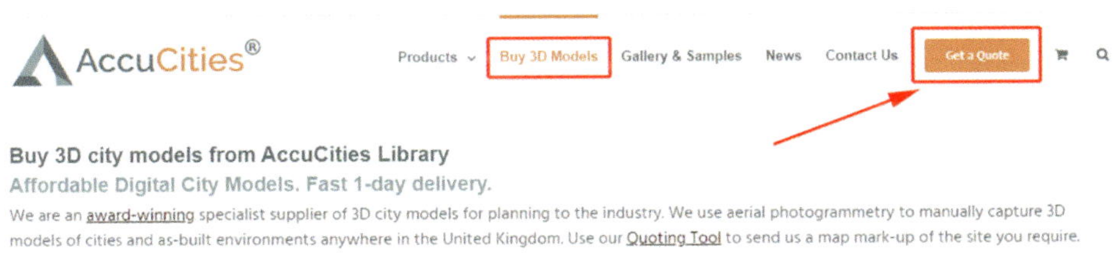

Accucities Buy 3D Models tab and the button to Get a Quote

In the Search town or postcode section, simply type in the desired area. As mentioned earlier, as an example we are going to the Newington butts area (9 Church yard road).

The area was automatically found. Zoom in to the desired area. Assuming you already know the areas you want to extract the 3d context model from, simply click on the button to, Draw Shape, and begin left clicking/drawing around the area to add points, and close the shape.

You should end up with a shape around the areas encompassing the proposed building and camera locations. There are also buttons to Edit Shape, Reset Map, Show Tiles and much more.

Once a shape is created (closed line) details of the Price and Delivery Estimates should be prompted on the left corner of the screen. Once satisfied, simply click on the Final Step: Enter Your details button.

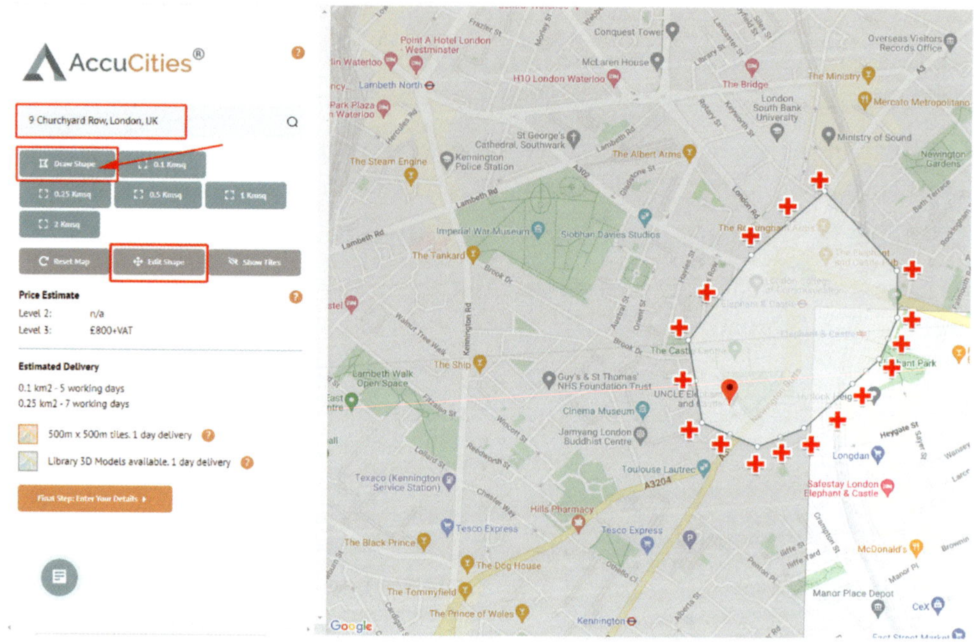

Get a Quote parameters

In the details section, users can enter their Name, Company, Email, telephone, Model Level Detail and Additional information, if desired.

In the Additional information section, users can emphasize things, such as file formats, etc.

Following that, simply click the button to, Submit Quote.

Users should receive a quotation reply shortly after, followed by the 3d context model.

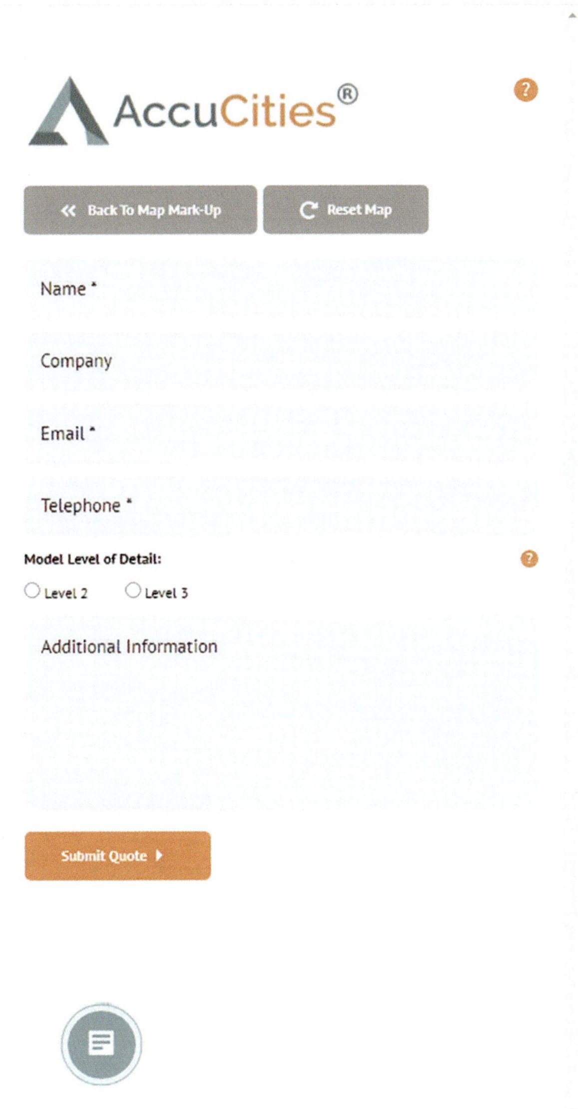

< User details section >

As mentioned earlier, the 3d context model and the proposed building are crucial to accurately preview each of the proposed views before sending the photographer and the surveyor on site. This precautionary measure and planning will help save time and money before sending the photographer and the surveyor on site.

In 3ds Max, merge the context model with the proposed 3d building already placed according to its drawing coordinates on the site plan referred to earlier. Before merging files, ensure the System Unit Setup of this Max file is exactly the same as the incoming one to ensure the scale is correct.

The System Unit Setup of the incoming file to be merged is in meters. To ensure this Max file is also in meters, click on the Customize button and choose the Units Setup option.

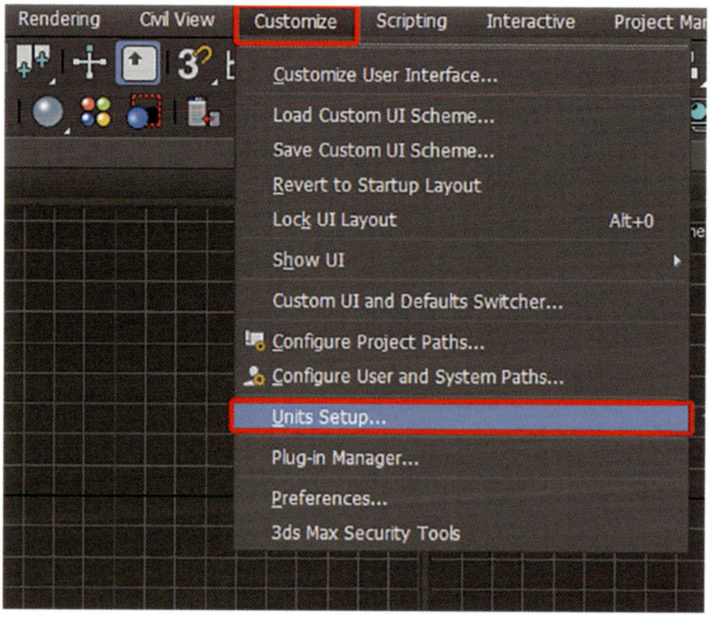

Click on the Customize button and choose the Units Setup option

Enable the Metric unit scale. It's worth noting that the functions in this dialog are for display purposes only and will not affect the scale of objects in the scene. Only the System Unit Setup parameters affect the scale of objects in the scene. Click on its toggle and ensure it's also set to meters, to be consistent with the incoming file to be merged.

As mentioned earlier, System Unit Setup parameters affect the physical scale of objects in this scene.

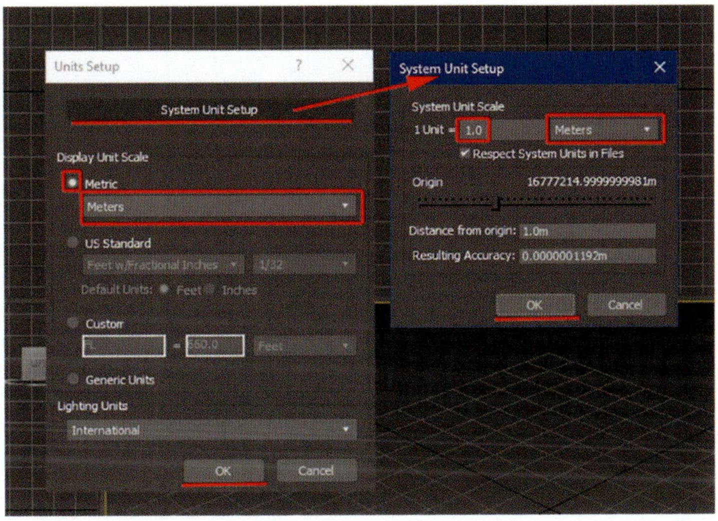

< Units Setup and System Unit Setup dialog parameters>

To merge the 3ds Max file with the context model and the proposed 3d building placed accurately in the scene, simply click on the File button, and choose to Import and Merge.

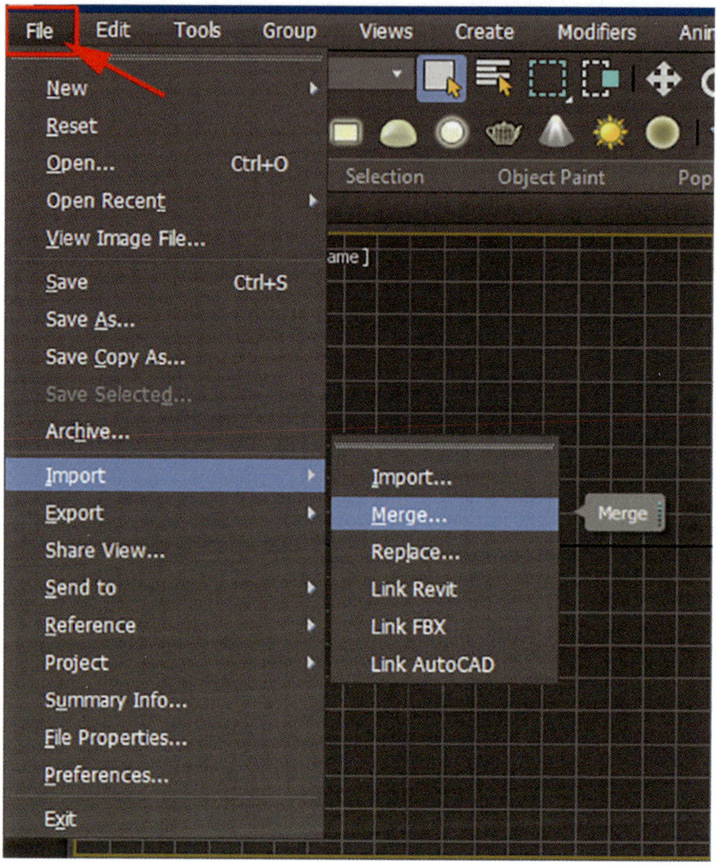

Click on the File button, choose to Import and to Merge

Next, select the relevant file to merge (Context to Merge.max). In the Merge dialog, click All and OK, to merge the entire list of objects.

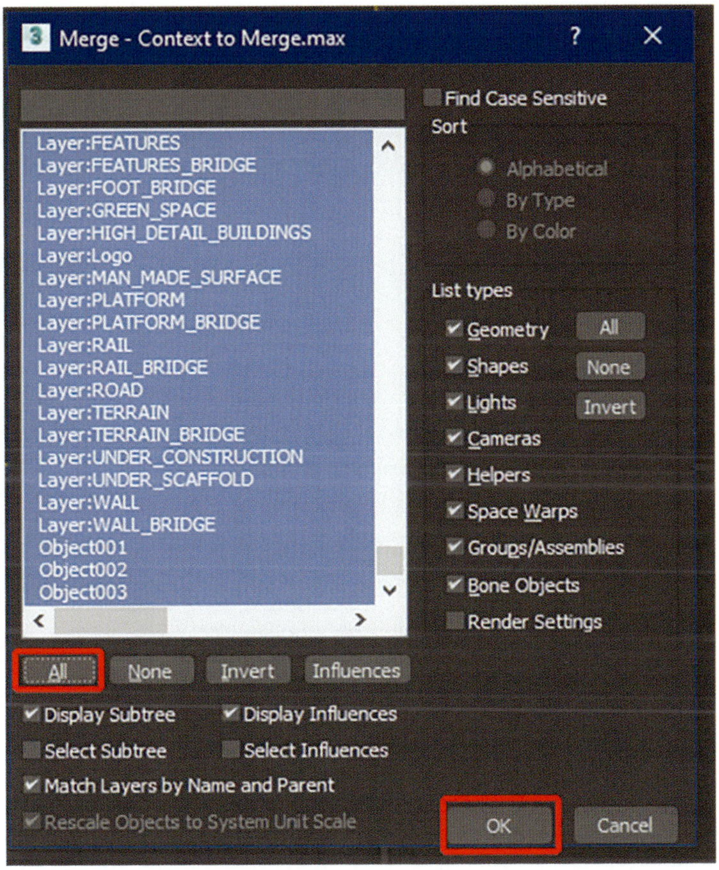

< In the Merge dialog, click All and OK, to merge the entire list of objects >

While all merged objects in the scene are selected by default, enable the Move tool (W), select one of the viewports and click Z on your keyboard to zoom closer to the selected objects. Repeat the same action in all viewports.

You should be able to see the entire context model and the proposed 3d building provided by the architect, accurately placed in scene according to the drawing coordinates referred to earlier.

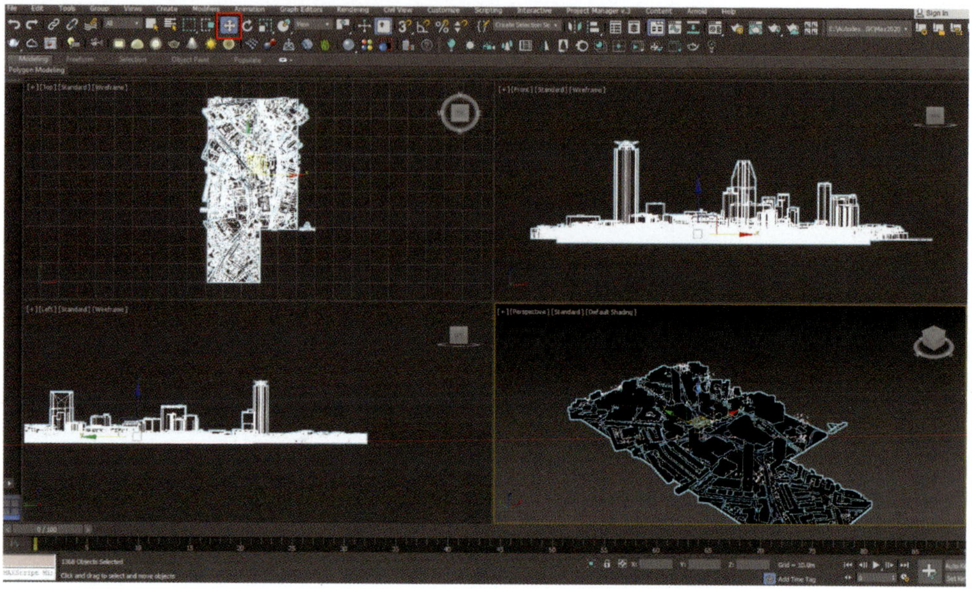

Entire context model and the proposed 3d building provided by the architect

To begin recreating one of the proposed camera views depicted in the drawing document, start by going to the create panel and clicking on the camera button.

Next, click on the camera button and its Target type. In the top viewport, click and drag the cursor point from the center of the context model toward the proposed building (in red), to create the first camera.

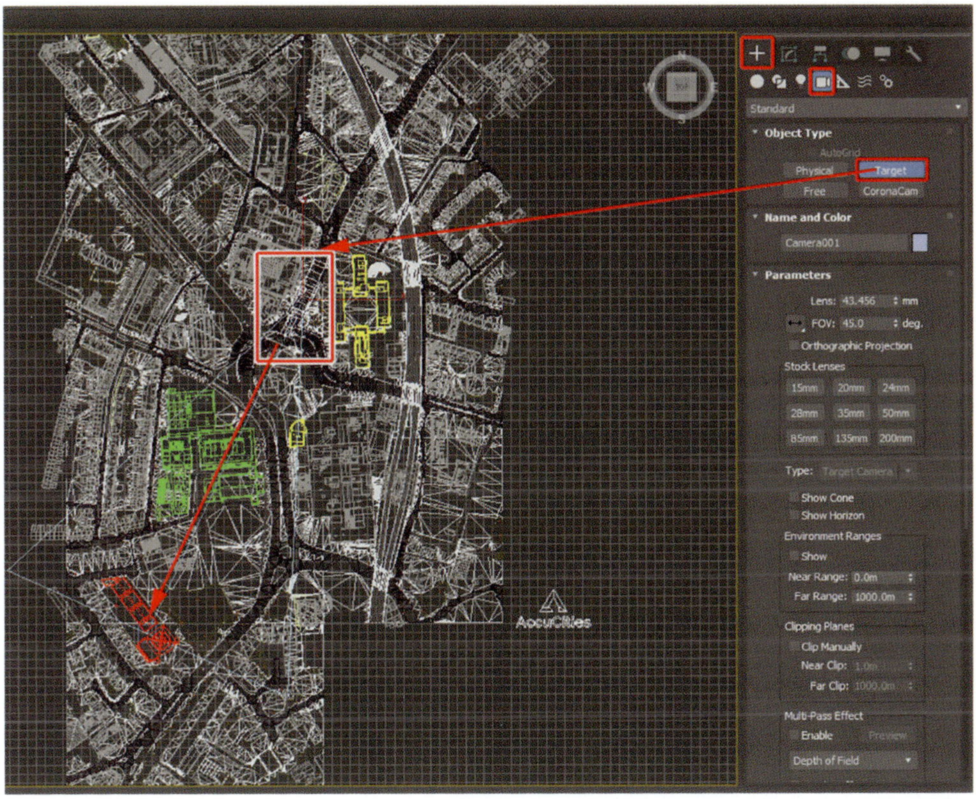

Click and drag the Target Camera cursor point in the Top viewport to create the first camera

Next, open the modify panel and change its Type to Free Camera. This is to have the flexibility to move and rotate the camera without being constrained by its target point. When the camera target is enabled, it's always going to be constrained by its target.

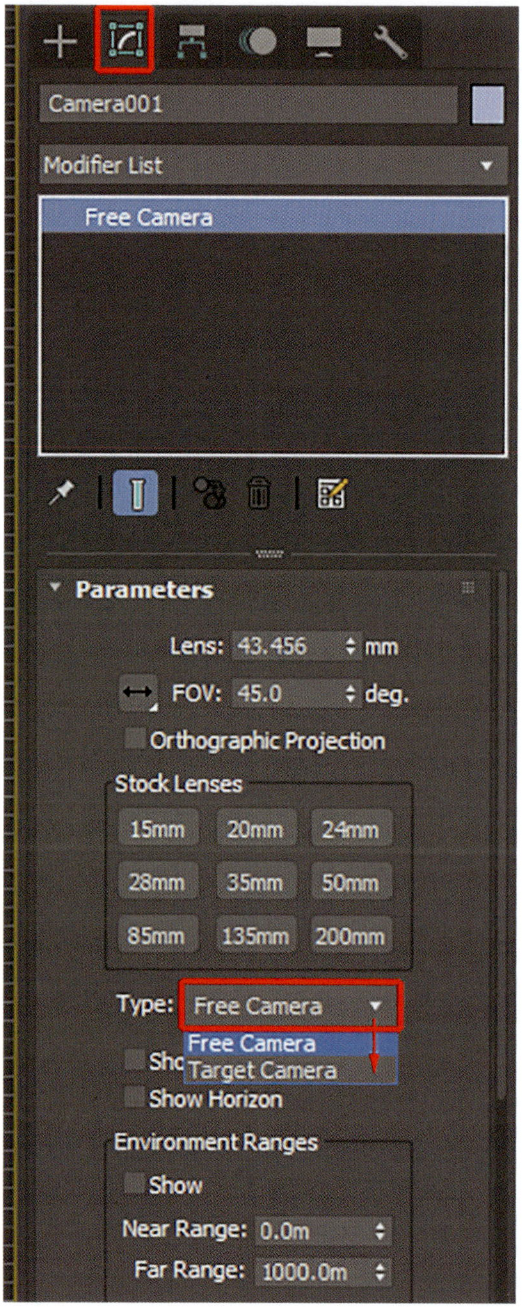

Open the modify panel and change its Type to Free Camera

To adjust the camera further, right click on the Move transform button to open its dialog. In Move transform (W), place the camera exactly at X: 531978.063 m; Y: 179156.313 m; and Z: 0.0 m.

In Rotate transform (E), place the camera exactly at X: –90.0; Y: 180; and Z: –24.732.

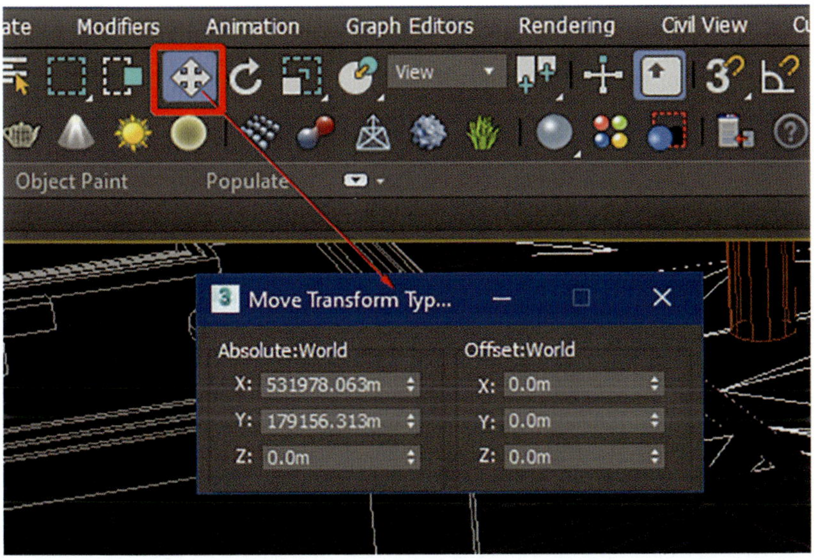

Right click on the Move transform button to open its dialog

Also, in the Perspective viewport, enable the function of Edge faces. This function helps users to see edges/segments of surfaces in shaded mode.

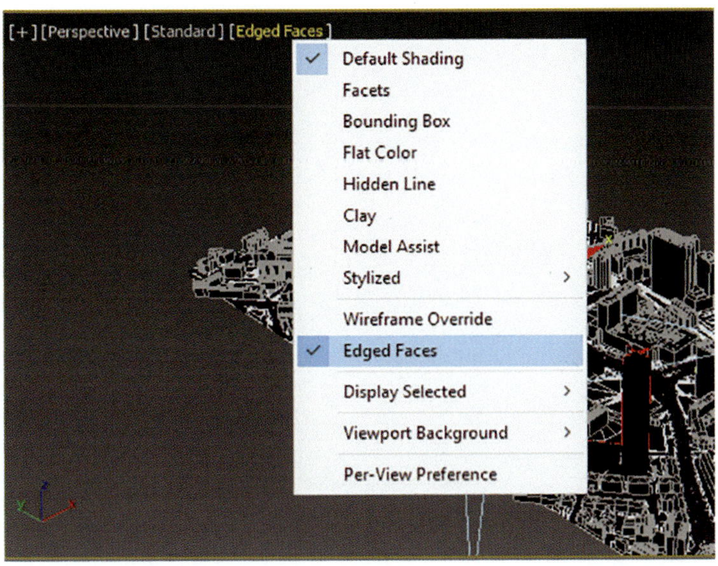

Enable the function to Edge faces in the Perspective viewport

Select the camera in the viewport and press the Z key on your keyboard to zoom into the selected camera.

Ensure the camera is currently touching the ground directly below. In the perspective viewport, place it exactly at Z: 4.419 m, Absolute: World section.

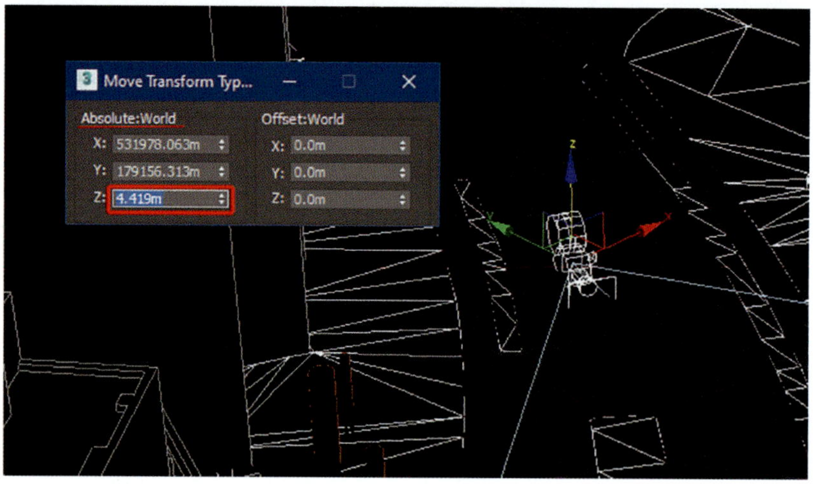

In the Perspective viewport, place the camera exactly at Z: 4.419 m

Next, Move it 1.64 m above the ground, by typing in 1.64 m in the Z Offset: World section.

1.64 meters is the standard camera height for photography (eye level).

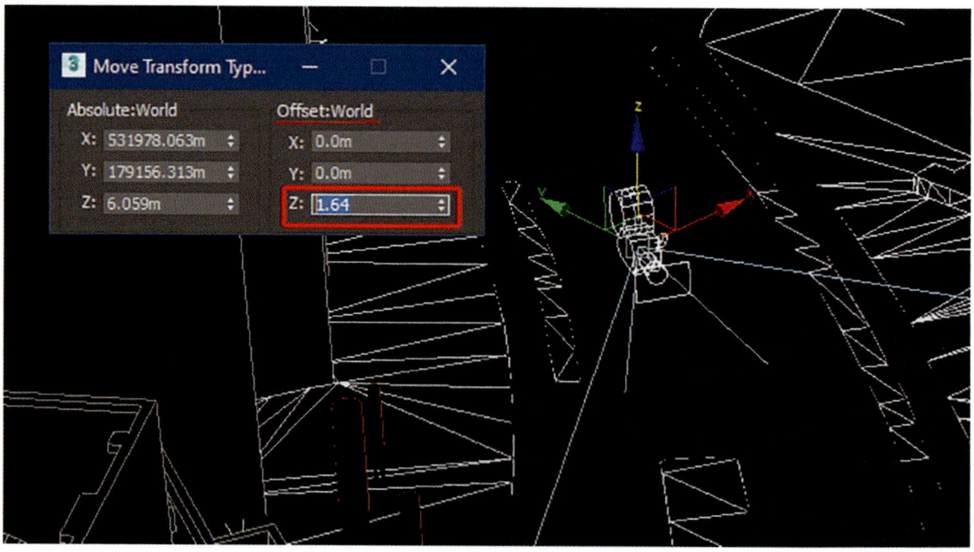

Move camera 1.64 m above the ground in the Z Offset: World section

This camera is being created and placed in a 3d space according to one of the proposed views depicted in the drawing reference. While the camera is selected the perspective viewport, press C on your keyboard to display the selected camera view.

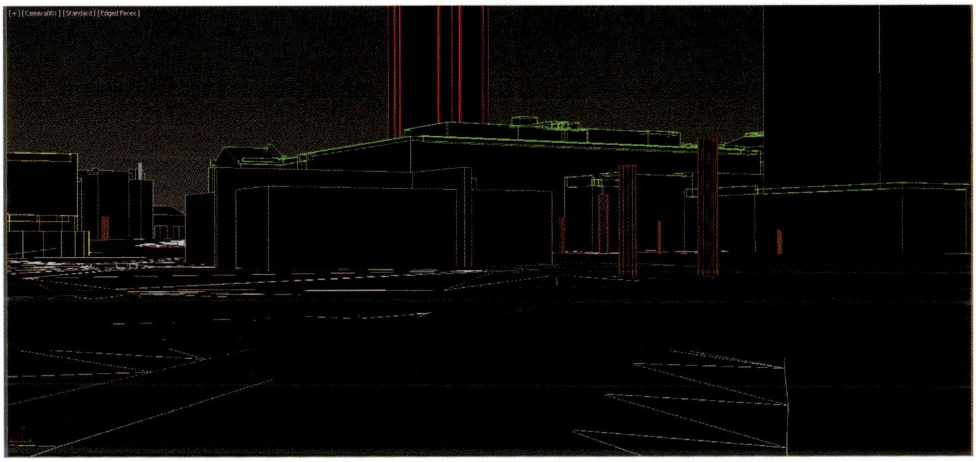

Camera enabled in the viewport

Following that, click on the camera text in the viewport and choose to Show Safe Frames from the dropdown list (Shift+F). This option allows you to see the exact areas to be rendered.

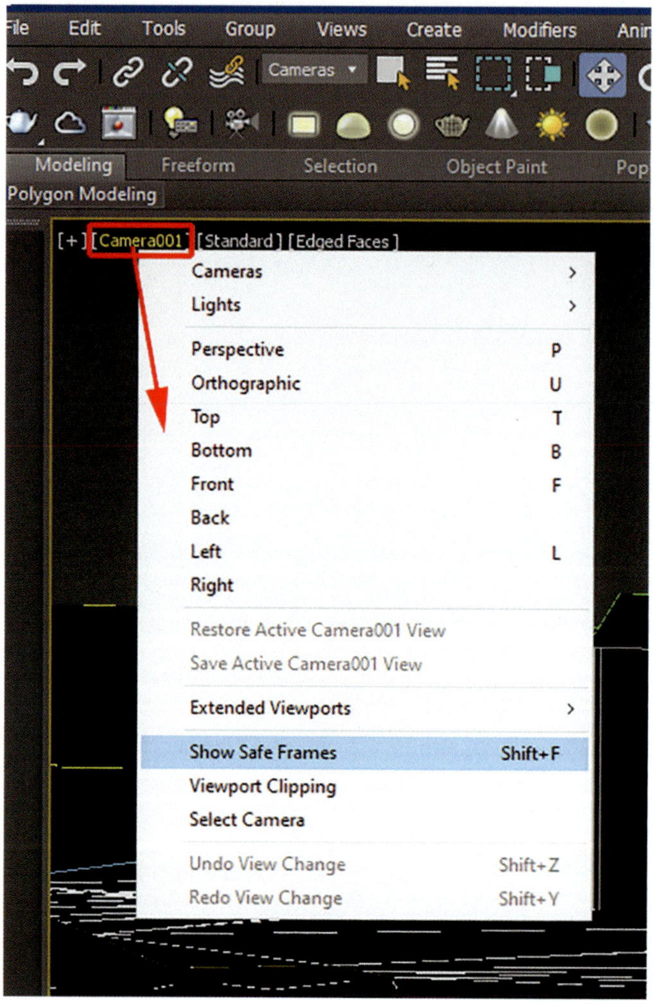

Show Safe Frames function enabled in the viewport (Shift+F)

As mentioned earlier, the tall red proposed building mass was accurately placed manually in the 3ds Max scene, along with the 3d context model. This was only possible because of the coordinates and drawings supplied by the architect, as referred to earlier.

To see more of the proposed building in the camera view, open the Modify panel while the camera is still selected, and change its lens to 30 mm.

This is one of the many reasons it is utterly important to plan each of the proposed views meticulously ahead of time before turning up on site to take photos and the survey points for the verified views.

Camera lens changed to 30 mm

This accurate and meticulous pre-planning methodology will also help the architects and the planning authorities make better-informed decisions about each of the proposed views with the proposed building and the context building in 3d.

In terms of pricing, it also reduces the total production costs dramatically, by preventing repeat visits to the site to take new photos and survey points.

To frame the camera view slightly better, open the Render Setup dialog (F10). Under the Common tab, change the Width and Height Output Size value to about 1200 pixels.

As mentioned earlier, this is a starting point to get the camera views approved by the architects/planners first, and direction to the photographer before he/she goes on site.

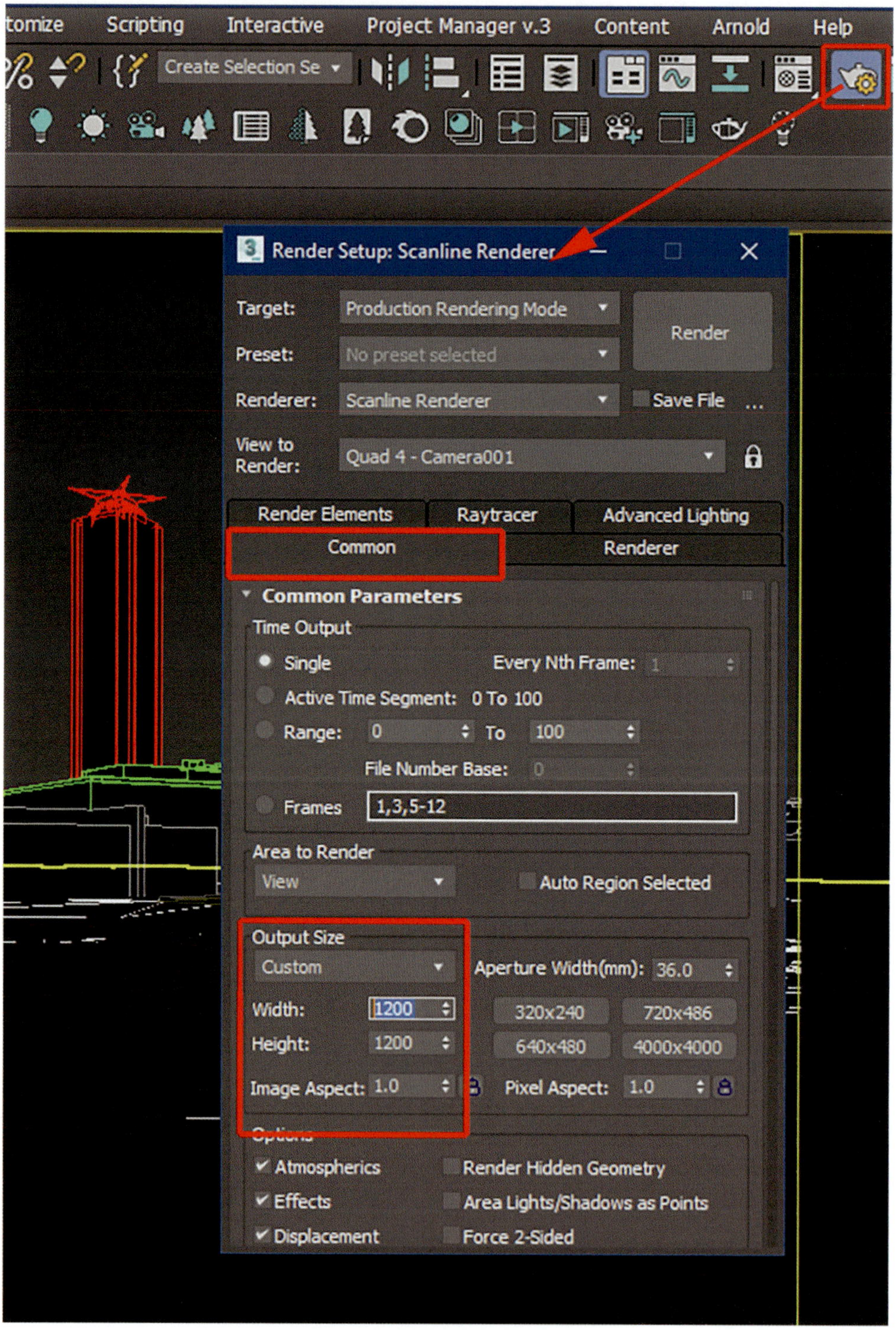

Width and Height Output Size value changed to about 1200 pixels

The following step is to create the first chalk render to be approved by the architect and planners. To start, click on the Renderer dropdown list and choose the V-Ray 5 renderer from the list.

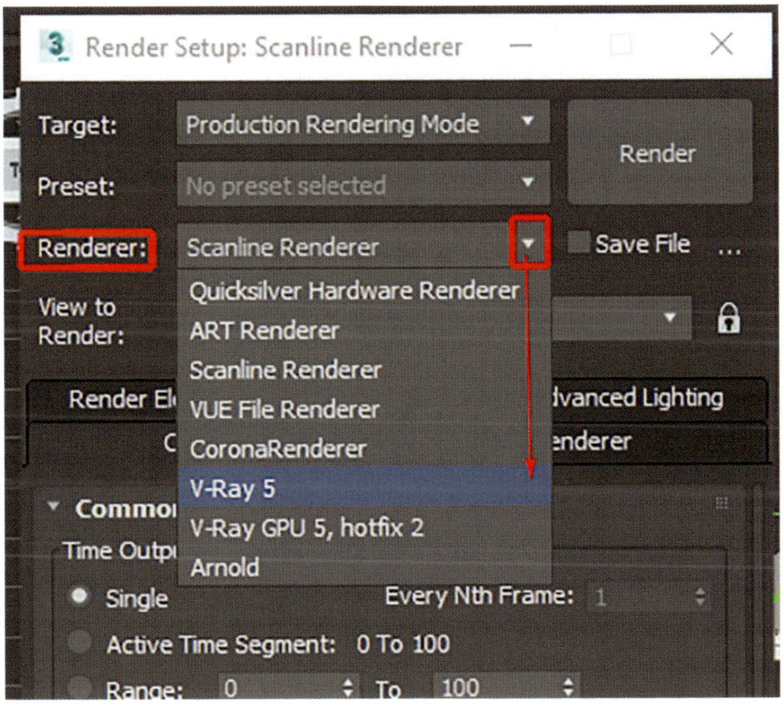

V-Ray 5 loaded from the renderer list

Once loaded, open the V-Ray tab. Under Progressive image sampler, keep the Min. subdivs as 1 and reduce the Max. subdivs to 7. Since these preliminary renders will be drafted, reducing their value will reduce the subdivision quality and the rendering times substantially.

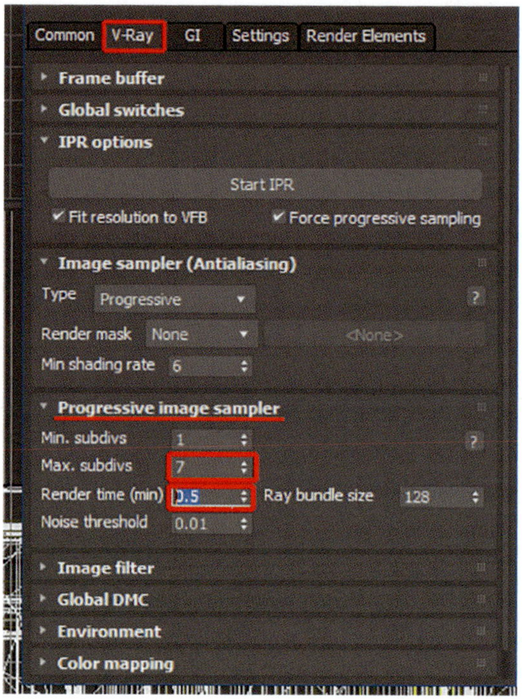

Keep the Min. subdivs as 1 and reduce the Max. subdivs to 7 to reduce the rendering times

Next, to add a chalk material to the overall scene, open the material editor first (M). Select an empty material slot and click on the Standard toggle to open the Material/Map Browser dialog.

Under V-Ray rollout, choose the VRayMtl procedural map from its list, and click OK to load it.

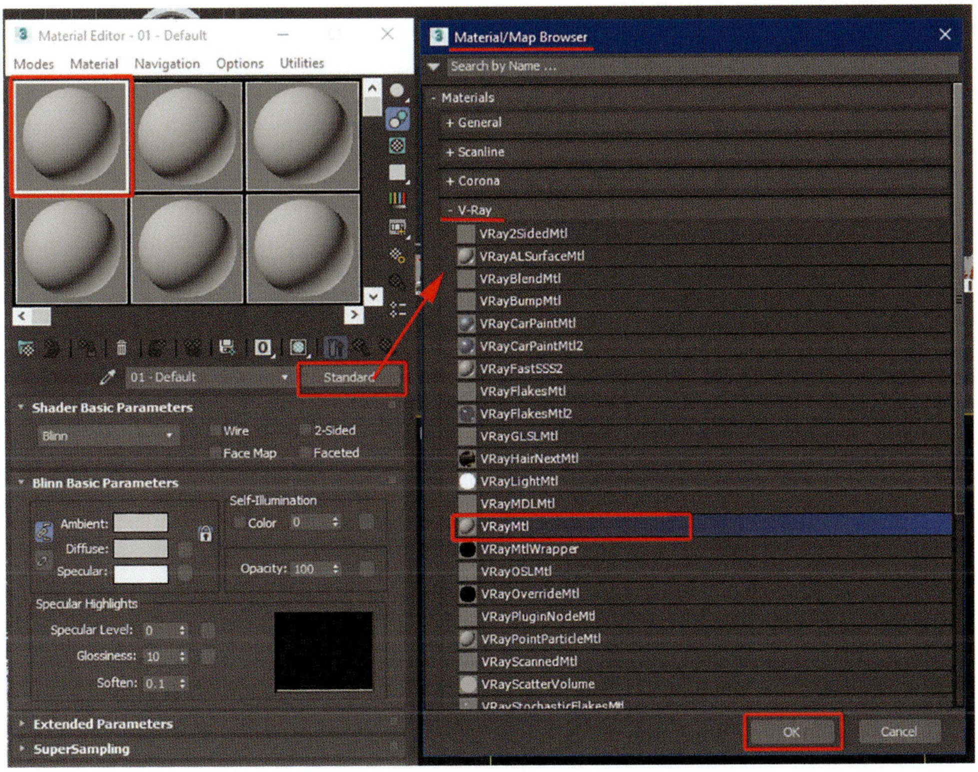

VRayMtl procedural map loaded from Material/Map Browser dialog

The following step is to extend the Global Switches parameters and enable the Override function. As mentioned earlier, this basic chalk render is mainly to get this camera view signed off by the architect and planner.

Drag and drop the material slot into the Override mtl toggle, and choose the Instance Method.

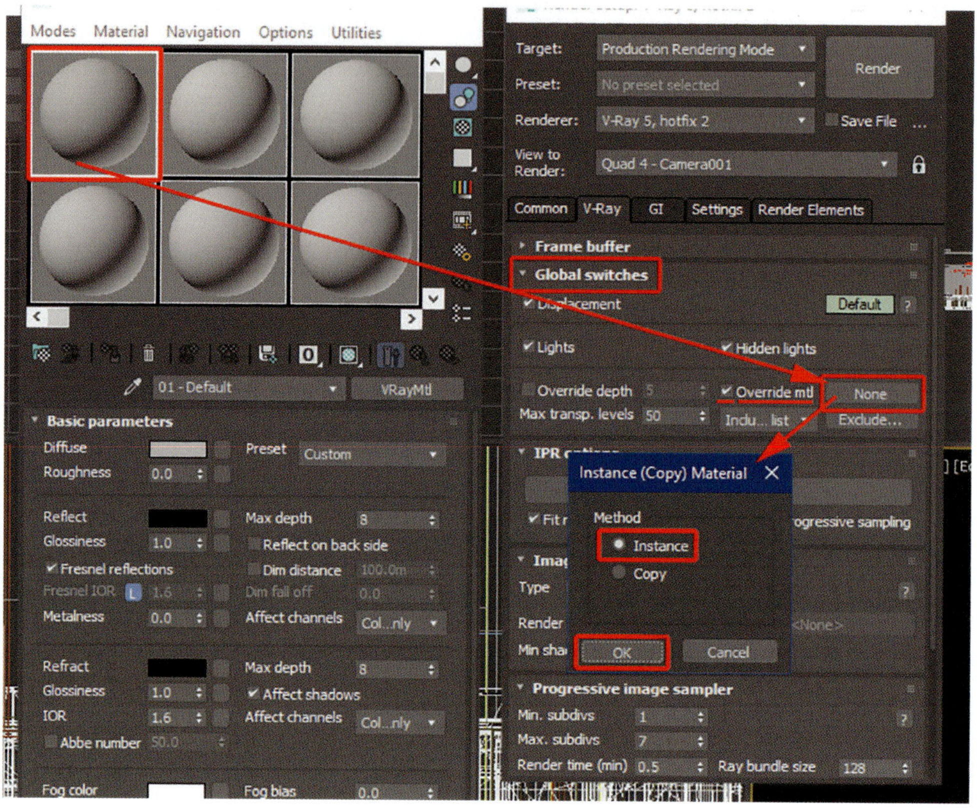

Material slot dragged and dropped into the Override mtl toggle

The subsequent step is to create the V-Ray sunlight, by enabling the Lights panel, selecting the VRaySun button, clicking and dragging the cursor in the top viewport to create it. Once prompted with the dialog message to automatically add VRaySky environment map, click Yes to accept it.

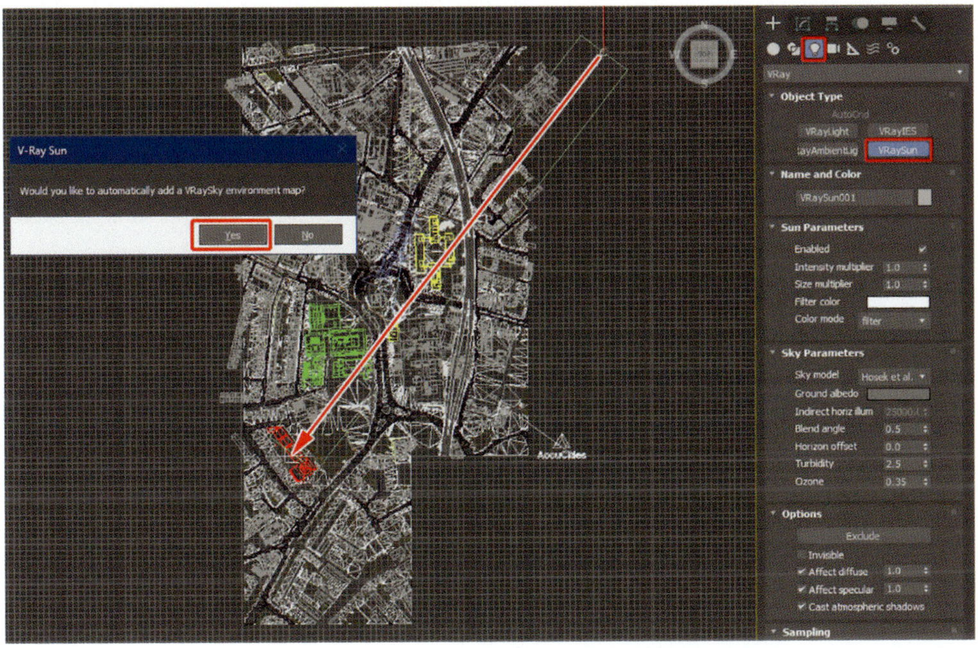

V-Ray sunlight and Sky created

To quickly adjust and preview the position of the sun in the viewport, go to the camera viewport and left click on the Standard text, followed by choosing the V-Ray Viewport IPR option from the dropdown list.

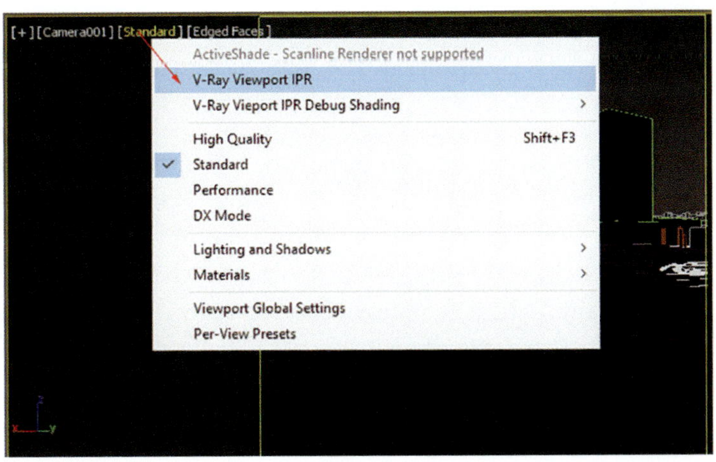

V-Ray Viewport IPR option enabled from the dropdown list

Next, open the Environment and Effects dialog (8) and load the VRay Exposure Control from its dropdown list. This is to prevent the preview in the viewport and render to be bleached out.

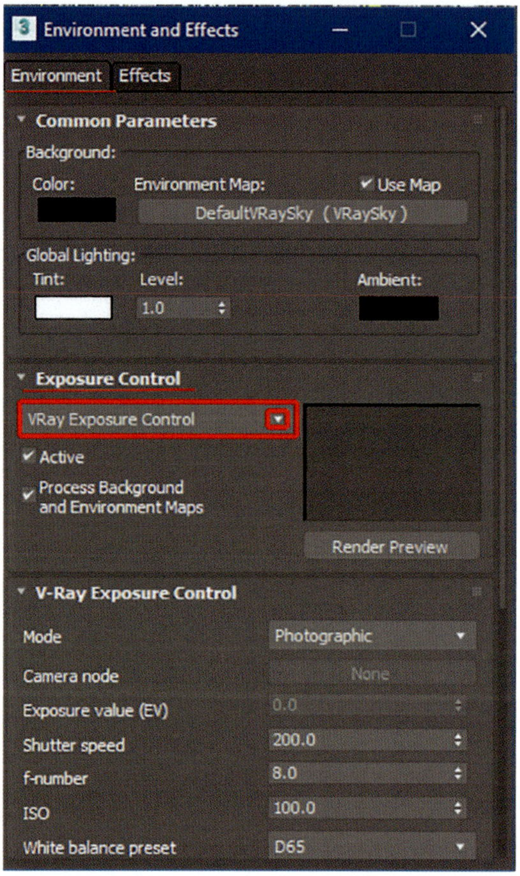

VRay Exposure Control enabled from the from the Environment and Effects dialog (8)

Begin moving the VRaySun head with the move tool (W) to find an appealing sun position that casts long shadows. Note: If the V-Ray Viewport IPR still looks too bright in the viewport, simply turn it off by going back to the camera viewport, left clicking on the Standard text, and choosing the V-Ray Viewport IPR option again. Repeat the same action to turn it back on again. It should work.

Use all four viewports to adjust the VRaySun position.

The final Absolute: World position/coordinates (W) of the Sun was: X 531702.813 m; Y: 179022.938 m; Z: 101.787 m; and Look at Dolly: 267.853 m.

The sun target was: X 531798.25 m; Y: 178794.297 m; and Z: 0.0 m.

V-Ray Viewport IPR in the camera viewport

This preliminary sun position is simply for the purpose of creating a chalk render to get this camera view signed off by the architects and planners. The following step is to increase the render settings to submit a higher quality chalk render for approval.

In the V-Ray tab, under Image sampler (Antialiasing), change the render Type to bucket. Under Bucket image sampler, change the Max subdivs to 7 and keep the remaining values.

Also, enable the function to use Separate render channels and click on its toggle to name the final render. Name it as Verified view chalk render, and choose the Save as type to be a TIF Image File format.

Next, click on the Setup toggle to open the TIF Image Control dialog. Change the Image Type to 16-bit Color, No Compression and 300 Dots Per Inch (DPI).

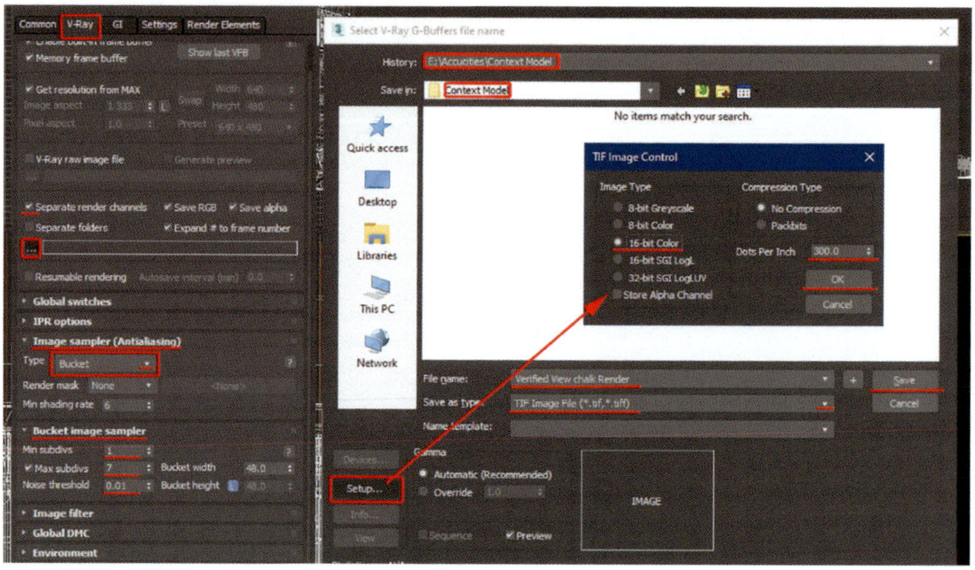

Setting up the chalk final render settings and Image Control

Before sending the final render, go to the Common tab and increase the Output Size to 3000×3000 pixels. Lock the Image Aspect padlock and the camera001 View to Render.

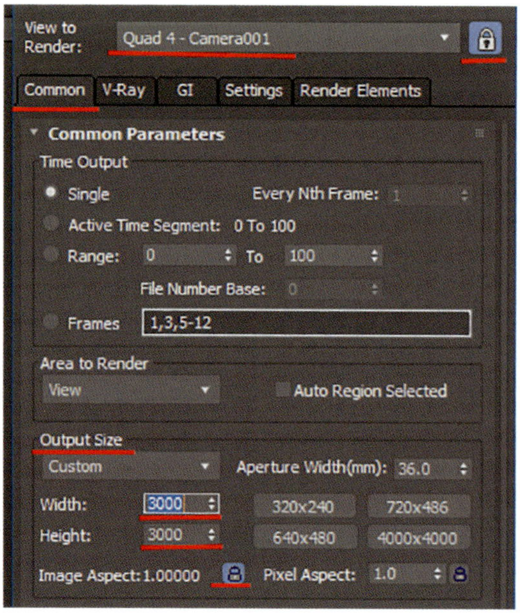

Increase the Output Size, lock the View to Render and Image Aspect

Final chalk render

Use Adobe Photoshop to help improve the final image slightly and get it signed off quicker. For this image, a LUT file was sufficient.

To apply the LUT file, in Photoshop, go to File, Scripts and choose the option to Load Files into Stack.

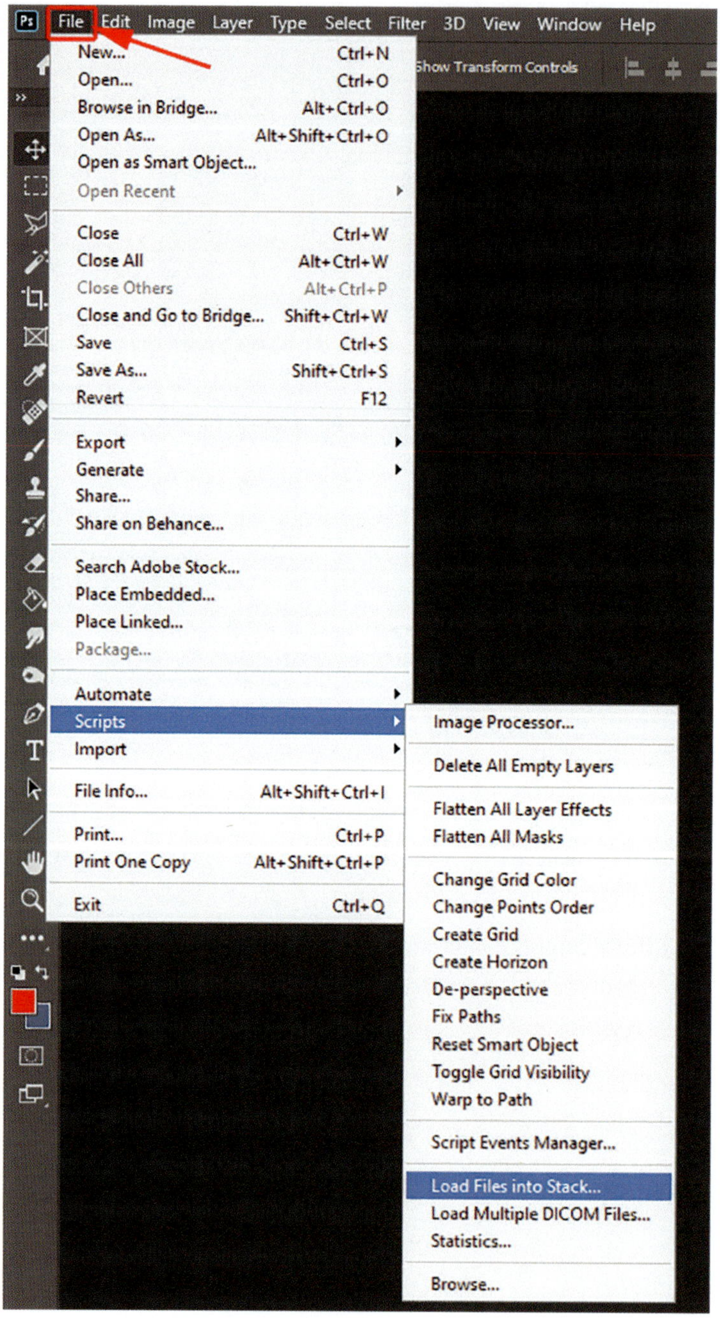

Choose the option to Load Files into Stack

In the Load Layers dialog, click on the Browse toggle to locate and load both TIFF files (RGB and Alpha elements). Once brought in, click OK to load them in Photoshop. Both TIFF files should load in a stack. Turn off the Alpha render element/layer.

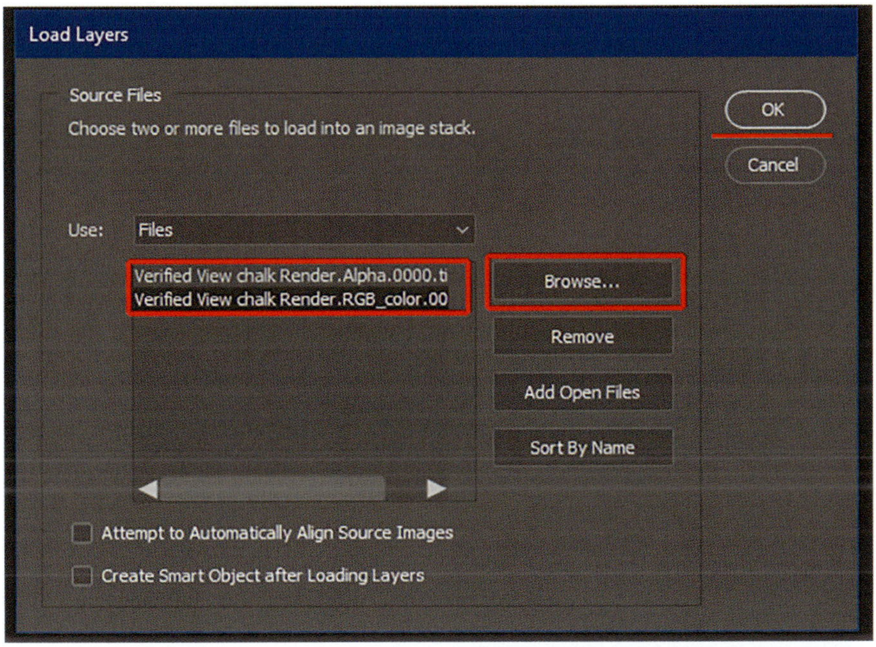

Load Layers dialog with the rendered files in

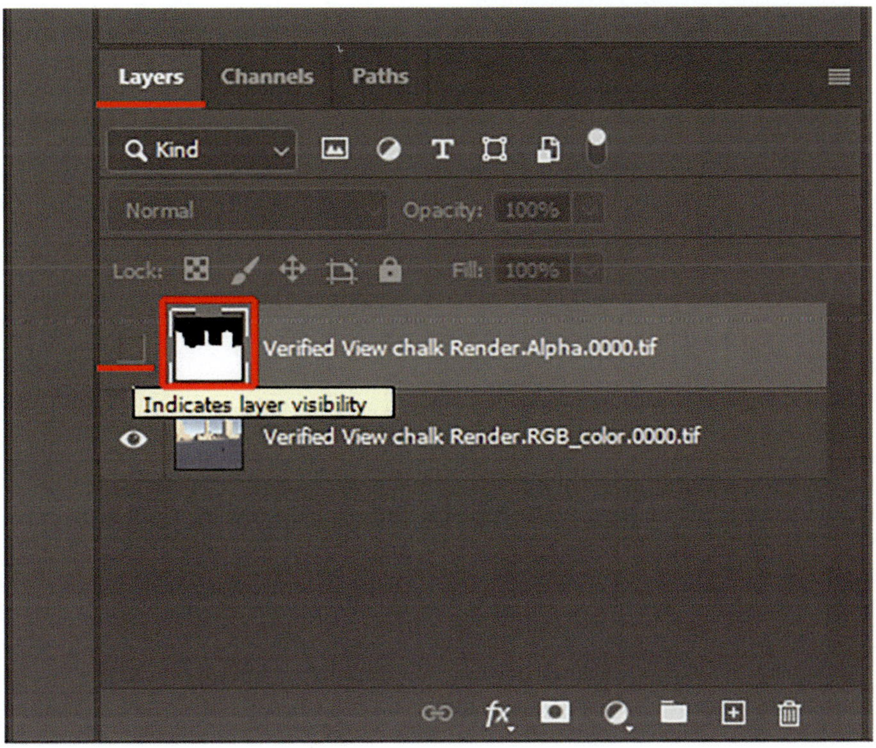

Files in a stack with the Alpha layer turned off

Next, click on the Adjustment layer button and choose the Color Lookup option from the list.

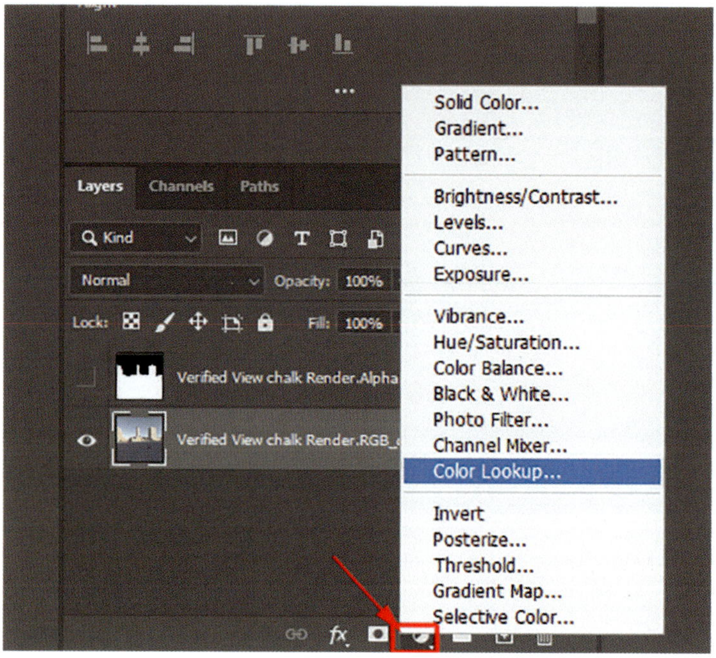

Choose the Color Lookup option from the list

The following step is to locate and choose a LUT file that will complement the current render. After a bit of trial and error, the LUT file named, C-8100-STD.3dl, worked well.

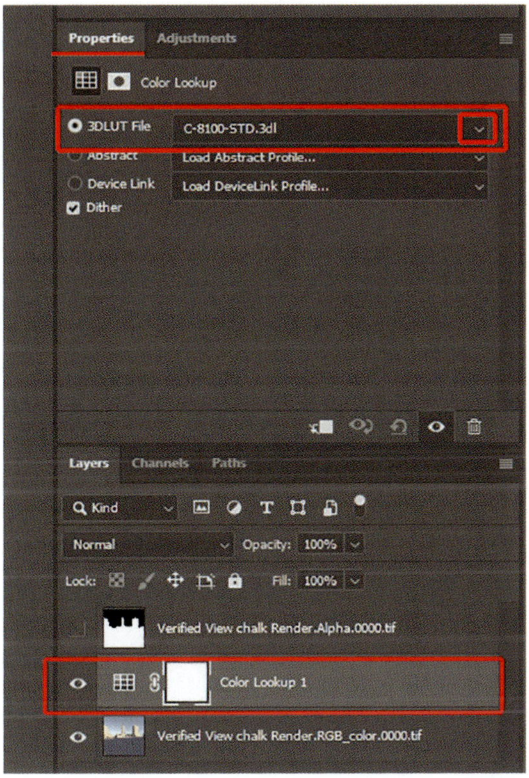

C-8100-STD.3dl file loaded under its Properties

Final chalk render with LUT applied

Once you're happy with the chalk render, simply save it by going to File and choosing the Save As option (Shift+Ctrl+S).

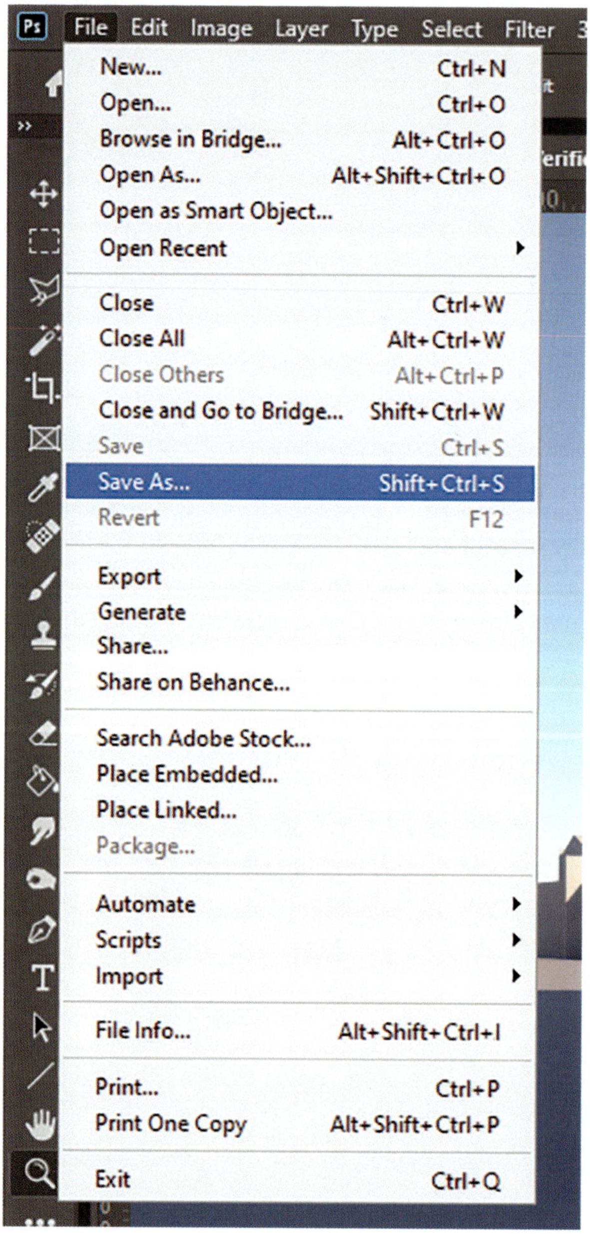

Choose the Save As option

Save the file as a Photoshop PSD file format first, in case you need to revisit the chalk render.

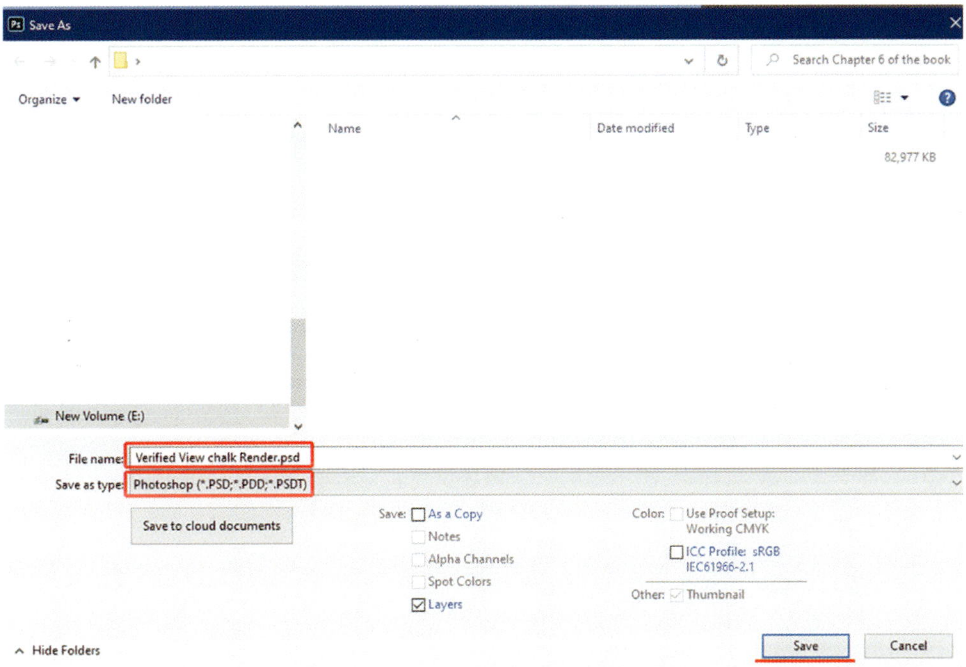

Save the file as a Photoshop PSD file format first

Next, choose to save it in the JPEG file format to be sent to the client. Set the quality to a maximum of 12 and OK to close the dialog.

Most clients often require between 5 and 20 verified views, depending on what's required. If you had that many proposed views, you would have had to go through the same process for each view, to get them all pre-approved before sending the photographer and the surveyor on site.

Once the chalk renders of the proposed views are signed off by the client, users need to organize a day for the photographer/Surveyor to go on site.

Before the photographers/surveyors go on-site, they often use an app called, Sun Surveyor. This app enables users to preview and plan the direction of the sun and its shadows on any given day and time, based on the geographical position.

To find out more about this app, simply Google sun surveyor. Sun surveyor also has a YouTube channel depicting how to quickly use the apps in less than 7 minutes.

14 Verified Views

Sun Surveyor website

Once everything is organized, the photographer/surveyor should make their way to the site with a tripod and all the necessary equipment required by the planning authorities

Below is a depiction of the equipment typically used by the photographer. The camera height is often set to about 1.60 m.

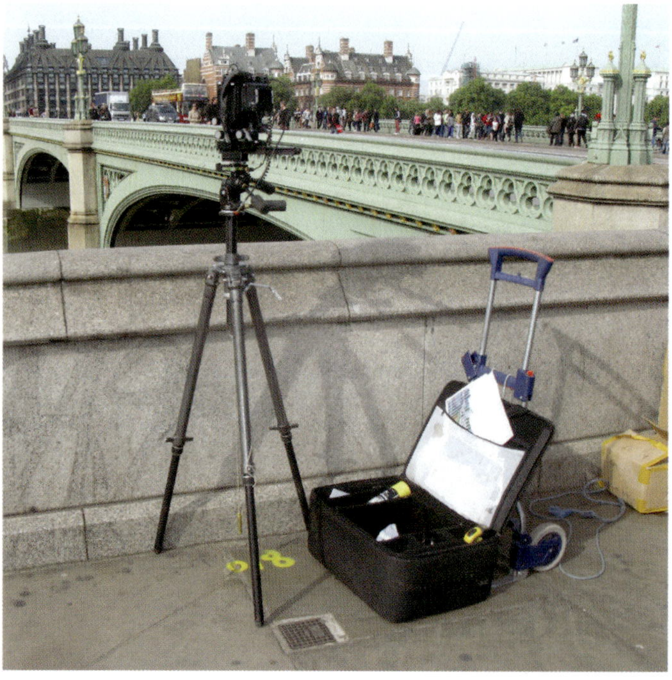

Photographer equipment typically used

AVR Photography Method Statement – Jeremy Young Photography

Careful consideration is given to achieving the best lighting for the chosen verified view.

The equipment is set up at the surveyed position with the aperture of the camera lens 1.60m. above the surveyed position. A plumb line is dropped from the camera shutter to the survey point and a tape is used to accurately measure the 1.60m. to the centre of the lens.

Vertical shift and time of day are recorded for each camera position, along with any other relevant information. Daylight exposures are usually in the region of $1/30^{th}$ sec. at f.11.5.

Images are captured as RAW files and processed using Capture One Pro 8.0.1, only colour balance and contrast are adjusted. A selected file is then opened in Adobe Photoshop CS6 and dust spots removed; otherwise the files are not altered. The selected file is outputted as a Tiff file with a resolution of 7216 x 5412 pixels at 360 dpi.

- Gitzo Tripod
- Arca Swiss F-Compact 6x9
- Phase One P45+ Digital Back
- Selection of Rodenstock / Schneider lenses from 28mm to 58mm

Photography documentation

NOTE

It's imperative that the camera is on a tripod for accuracy purposes, and to follow the planning guidelines. Before taking the final photo of each of the proposed views, by law, the photographer needs to mark up the location of the camera tripod, as required by the planning authorities. In addition, information about the camera details, view, date and time need to be accompanied with the final documentation. Below is an example of similar documents.

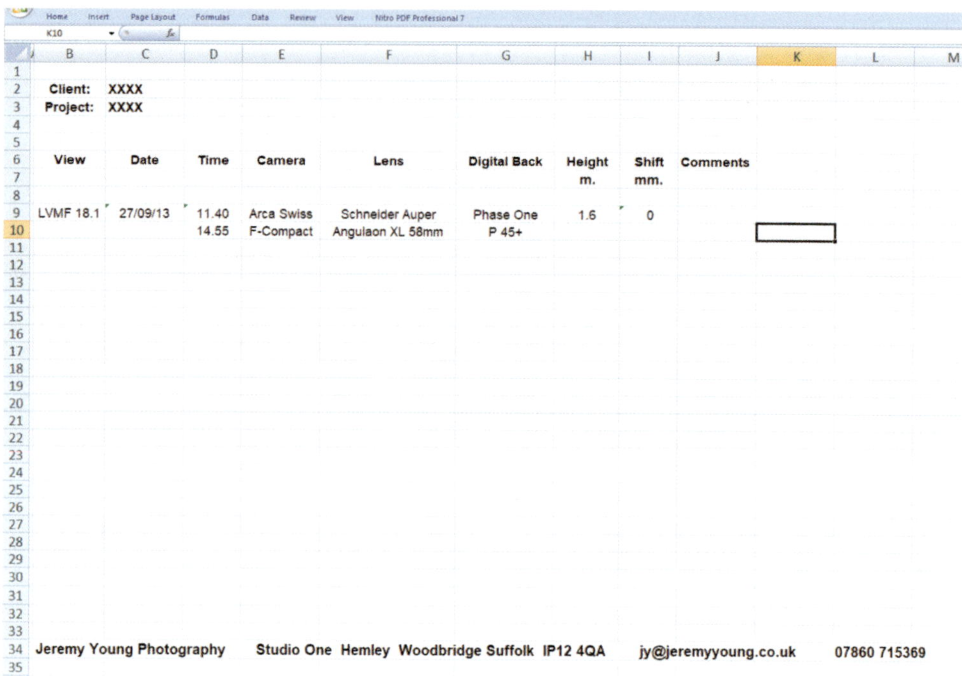

Client: XXXX
Project: XXXX

View	Date	Time	Camera	Lens	Digital Back	Height m.	Shift mm.	Comments
LVMF 18.1	27/09/13	11.40 14.55	Arca Swiss F-Compact	Schneider Auper Angulaon XL 58mm	Phase One P 45+	1.6	0	

Jeremy Young Photography Studio One Hemley Woodbridge Suffolk IP12 4QA jy@jeremyyoung.co.uk 07860 715369

Camera information, View, Date and Time

While the photographer is on-site, he/she can also take 360 HDR shots of each of the proposed views, to be later used for reflections and/or lighting. Most photographers use cameras such as Insta360 One X to do this. However, feel free to use any other cameras you're more comfortable with.

Once the photos of each of the proposed views are taken, the next step is to mark up the areas on each photo where users would ideally want the surveyor to take the survey points from. The photo below depicts an example of one of the shots created for GMJ design limited.

Site photo

Begin marking up the areas on the photo where the survey points should be taken. The more points on the photo, the more accurate the camera matching will be in 3ds Max.

The average number of surveys is between 10 and 20 points, per proposed view. To mark up the photo in Photoshop, simply enable the text tool, set the font size and begin typing in.

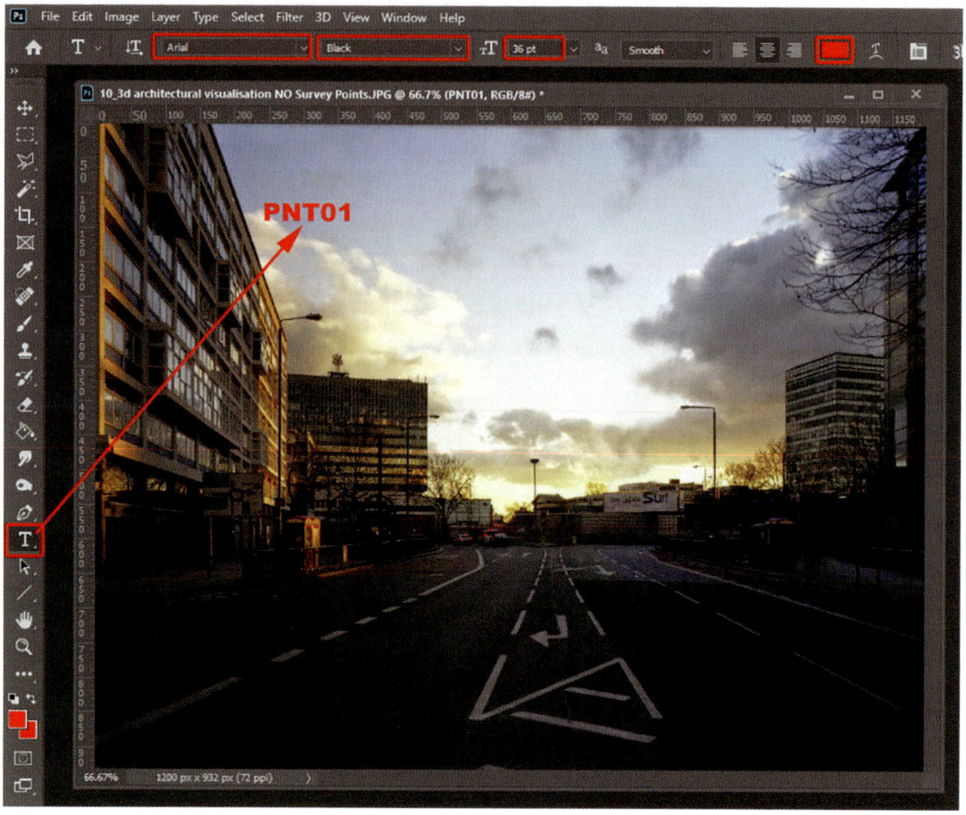

Enable the text tool, set the font size and begin typing in

To get the arrow pointing in a particular direction, simply enable the Line tool and click on its Option button. In Path Options, enable the End Arrowheads to get the direction. Next, click and drag the arrow to create it.

Create an arrow pointing down

To create a circle (Dot), simply click on the Marquee tool and choose the Elliptical shape from the list. Next, click and drag to create it.

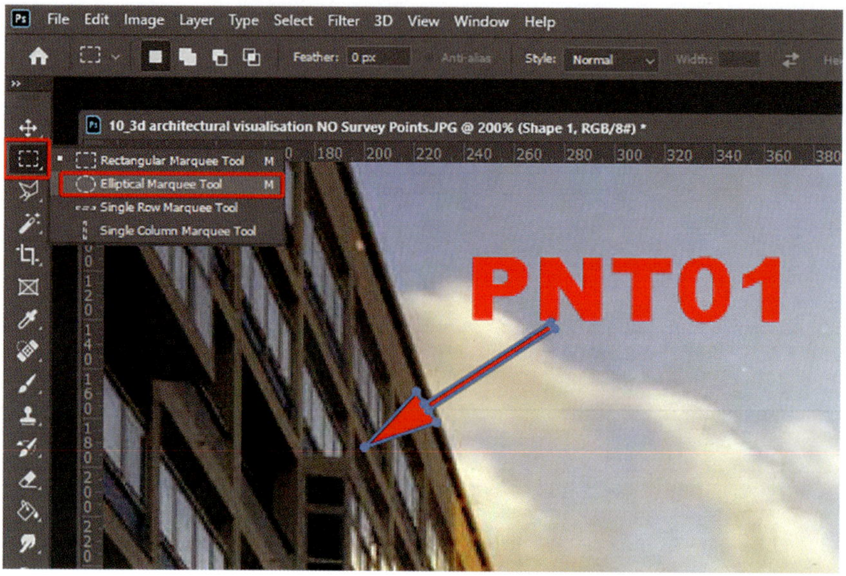

Click on the Marquee tool and choose the Elliptical shape

While the selection is still on, create a new layer by clicking on its button.

Create a new layer by clicking on its button

Next, enable the paint bucket tool, switch the background color to red and click on the circle selection again to fill it with a red color.

Red dot circle created

That's how users create each of the dots and text, to mark up the whole photo.

14 Verified Views

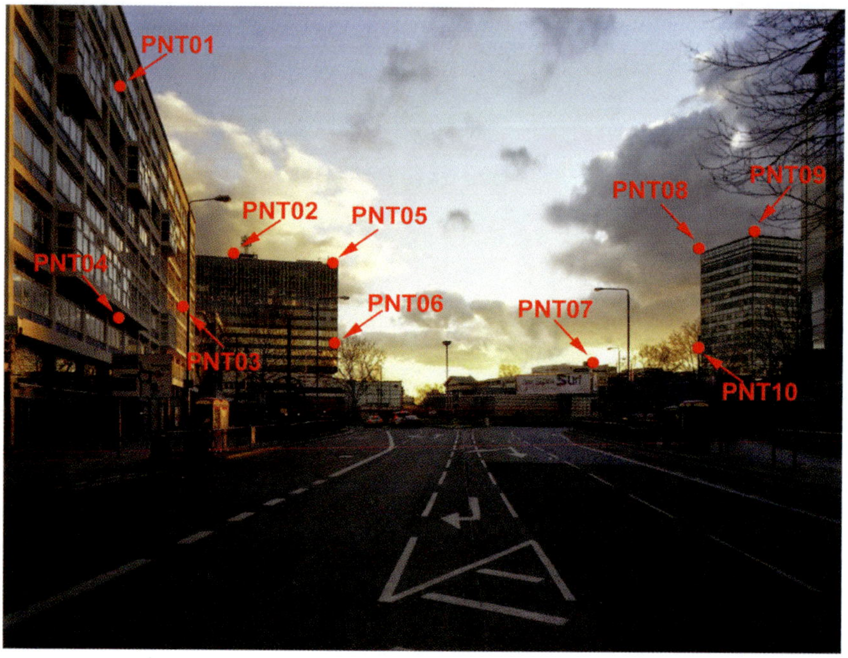

Marked-up photo

If there were ten separate proposed views/photos, users would have had to repeat the same process with all of them, prior to handing them over to the surveyor to be surveyed.

Some surveyors may end up surveying more points than the ones marked up on each photo, due to practicalities and for better accuracy. EDI surveys happen to be one of the best in the business.

They use some of the latest laser equipment for surveying. The surveyor will use some of the information previously provided by the photographer along with the marked-up photos to carry out the surveys.

On the surveyor's return, users should receive a series of photos depicting where each survey point was taken from, for each of the proposed views. It's worth mentioning that below are examples of what users would often receive from a surveyor.

As mentioned earlier, some of these points may differ slightly from the initial markups provided, because of practicalities and accuracy

Survey point PNT01

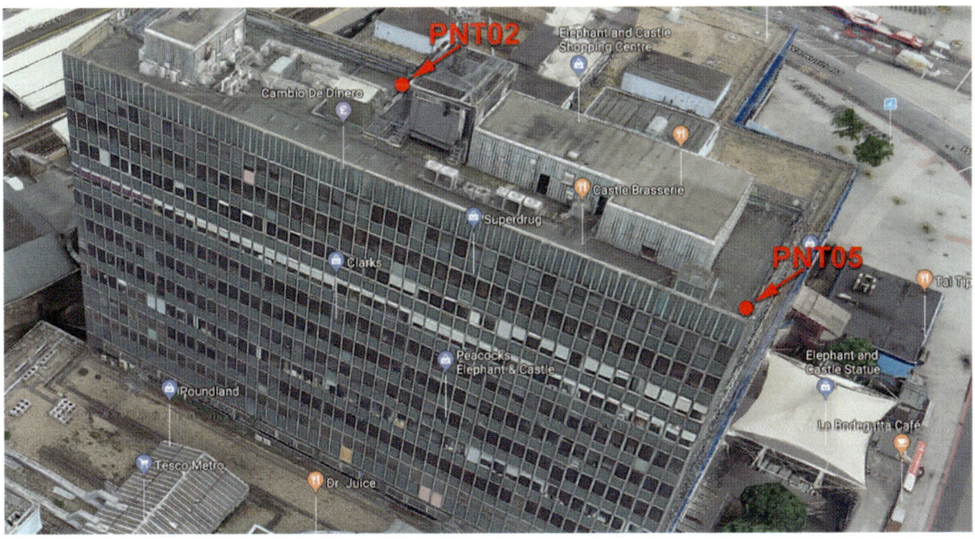

Survey point PNT02 and PNT05

Survey point PNT04

After double checking each of the new closed-up shots with survey points supplied by the surveyor, users might need to reposition the previously marked-up surveyed points accordingly, for each of the proposed views previously provided to the surveyor before going to the site.

After the new survey points have been matched accordingly in the Photoshop document, the following step is to recreate and match each survey point in a 3d scene, for each proposed view.

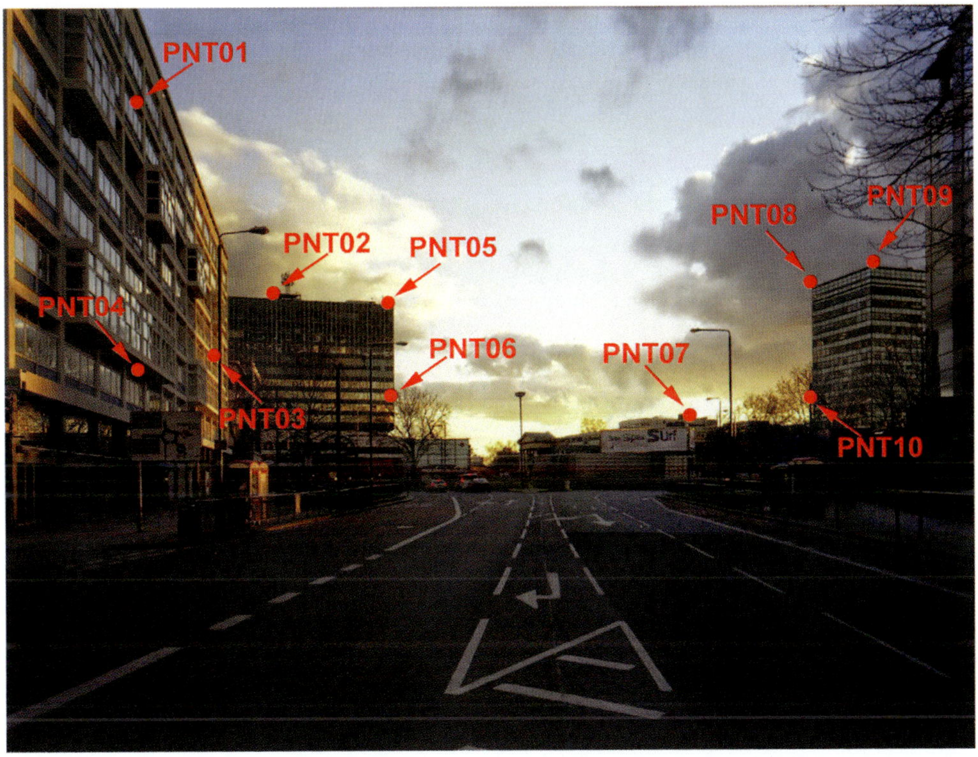

Survey points adjusted on the proposed view

Prior to saving this file as a jpeg and loading it in 3ds max, we need to create perspective lines in order to find the vanishing point and ensure the entire image is equally divided vertically. This process will make it easier to match the survey points and the camera in 3d.

Vanishing point is the point receding parallel lines viewed in perspective that appear to converge. To create the first perspective line in this photo, enable the Line tool as previously done.

In path options, disable the End arrowheads, and click/drag along the horizontal line of the far left top building to create the first line. A perspective line should be following the horizontal line of the far left top building.

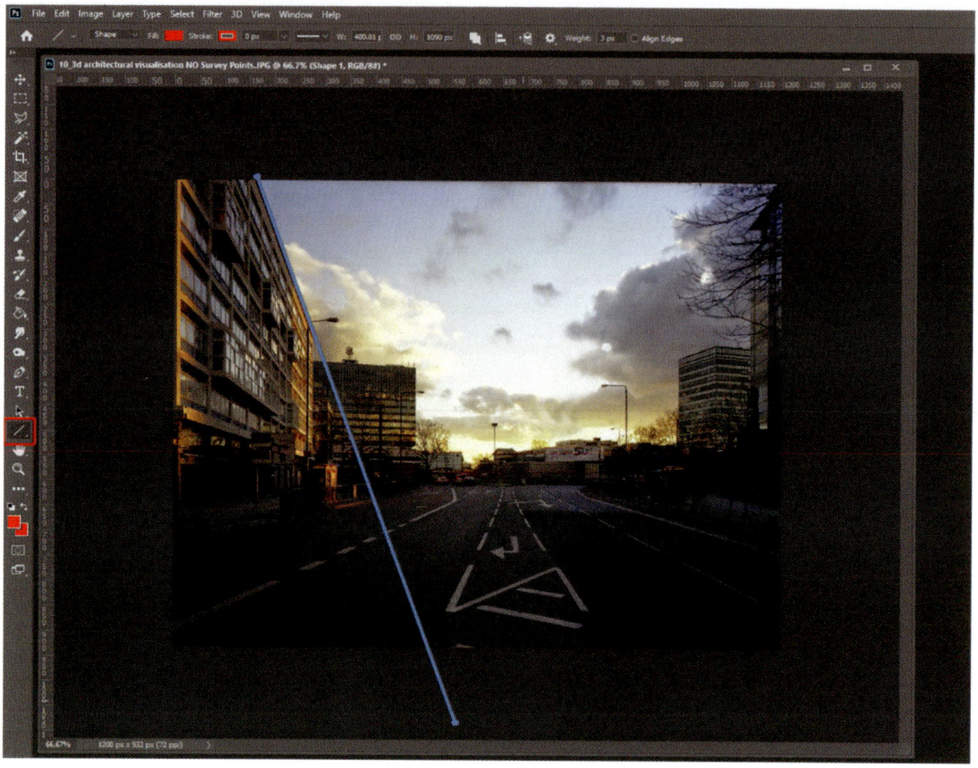

Line following along the far left top building

Next, create another perspective line from left to right following the horizontal line of the lower windows of the building on the far left side.

Second perspective line following the horizontal line of the lower windows of the building

Let's create few more lines to see where they all meet in middle. The vanishing point is where most perspective lines meet (the blue horizontal line in the middle).

The vanishing point where most perspective lines meet

To help match this camera perfectly in 3ds Max, the vanishing point needs to divide the image into two equal parts vertically. This methodology should also match the camera shift, if any was used.

Currently, the upper part of the vanishing point is not equally divided with the lower part of the photo. This is often a clear indication that camera shift was not used for this photo. To fix this and match the camera view perfectly in 3ds Max, enable the Crop tool.

The blue horizontal line in the middle (where most vanishing lines meet) is where the current center of the image is. To move it to the vanishing point, simply extend the document down with the Crop tool, by clicking and moving down the bottom handle of the Crop tool, until the middle point meets the center of the vanishing line.

The final result is the vanishing line dividing the image into two equal parts vertically. Which will be easier to match in 3ds max.

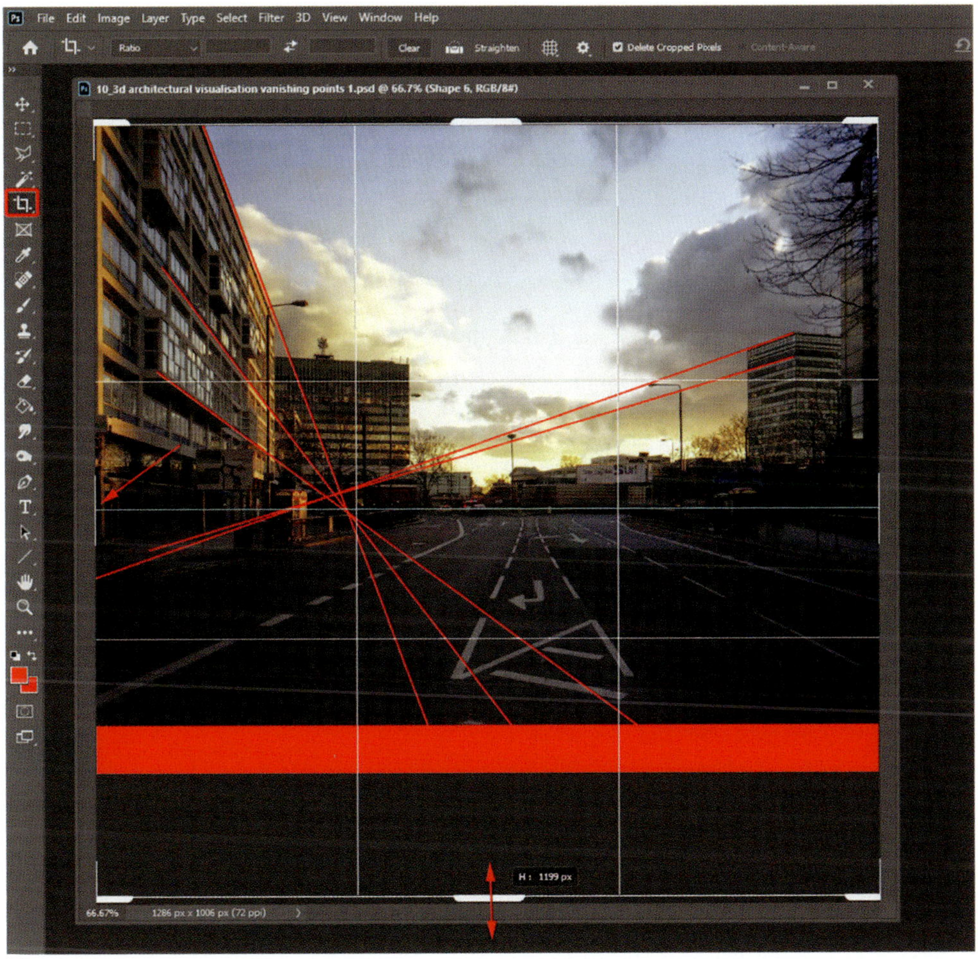

Document expanded vertically to center the vanishing point

Now that the document has been extended vertically, the following step is to tidy up the files and the survey points. To start, select the first layer of the document. Hold down the Ctrl key and select the rest of the perspective line layers.

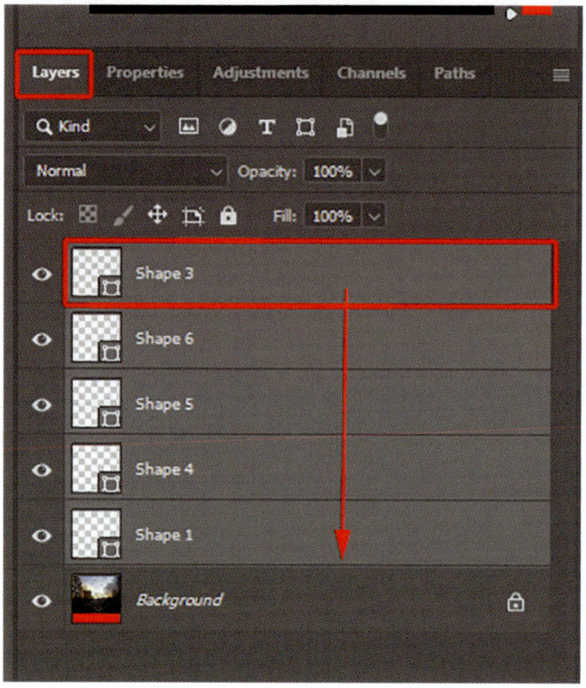

Multiple Photoshop layers selected

Next, click on the group button to create a new group folder and move all the selected layers inside. If you are using an older version of Photoshop, simply select and move the layers manually inside the group.

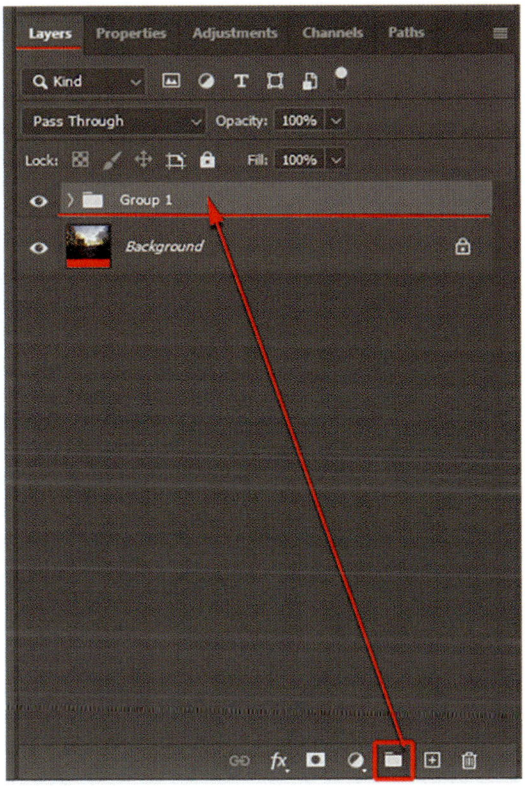

Group folder created

Rename the group as, Vanishing lines. Disable the group visibility by clicking on its eye icon and bring in the previous survey points created. Group the survey points and rename it as, Survey Points.

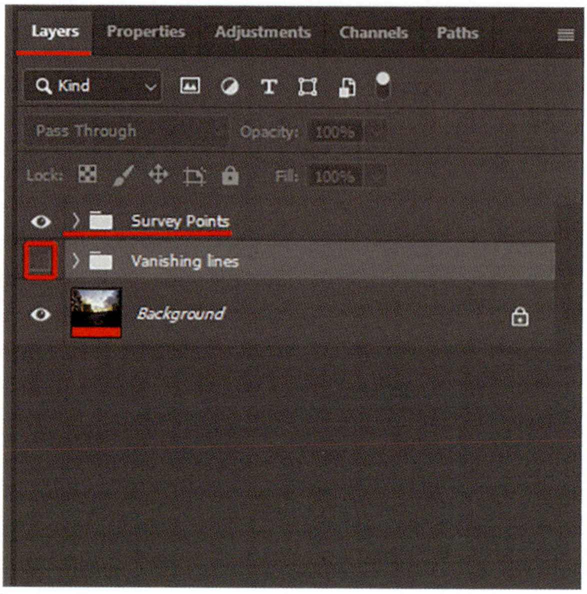

Vanishing lines and Survey Points in the same document

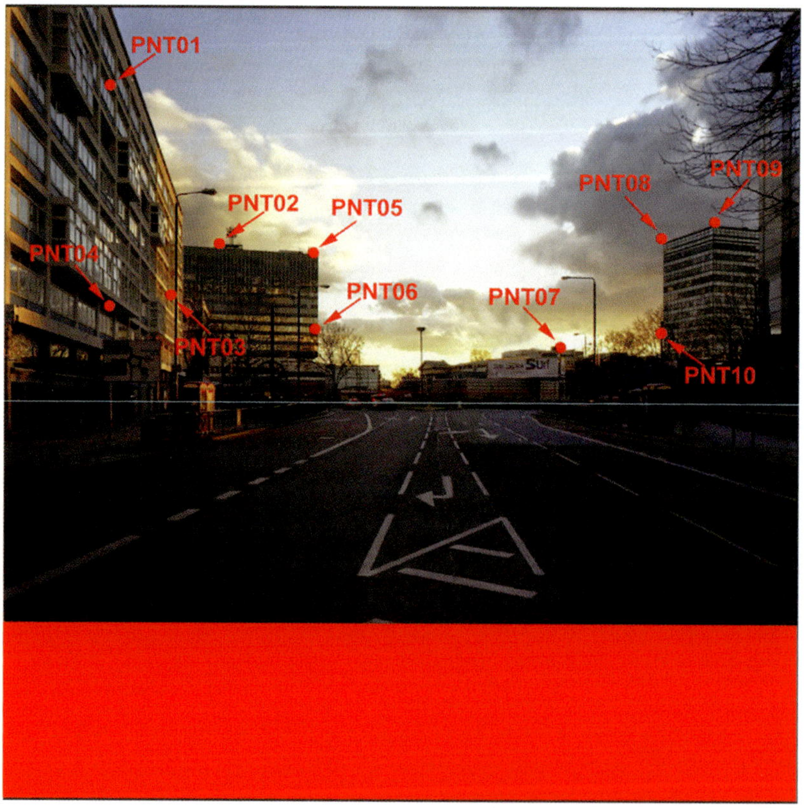

Image result of Vanishing lines and Survey Points in the same document

Save and rename this document as a jpeg. Following that, save the document as a PSD document, as a backup file to revisit, if necessary.

In addition to all the documents previously shown, once the survey is completed users should also receive an excel spreadsheet document depicting survey point coordinates for each of the proposed views in the world space. Below is an example of a survey spreadsheet document.

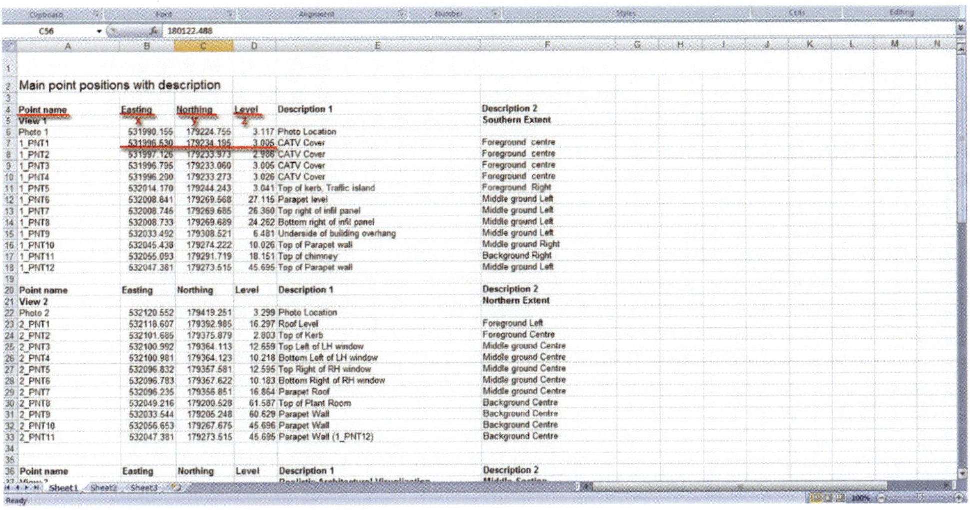

Main point positions with description

Point name	Easting	Northing	Level	Description 1	Description 2
View 1	X	Y	Z		Southern Extent
Photo 1	531990.156	179224.756	3.117	Photo Location	
1_PNT1	531996.530	179234.195	3.005	CATV Cover	Foreground centre
1_PNT2	531997.126	179233.973	2.986	CATV Cover	Foreground centre
1_PNT3	531996.795	179233.060	3.005	CATV Cover	Foreground centre
1_PNT4	531996.200	179233.273	3.026	CATV Cover	Foreground centre
1_PNT5	532014.170	179244.243	3.041	Top of kerb, Traffic island	Foreground Right
1_PNT6	532008.841	179269.568	27.115	Parapet level	Middle ground Left
1_PNT7	532008.746	179269.685	26.360	Top right of infil panel	Middle ground Left
1_PNT8	532008.733	179269.689	24.262	Bottom right of infil panel	Middle ground Left
1_PNT9	532033.492	179308.521	6.481	Underside of building overhang	Middle ground Left
1_PNT10	532045.438	179274.222	10.026	Top of Parapet wall	Middle ground Right
1_PNT11	532055.093	179291.719	18.151	Top of chimney	Background Right
1_PNT12	532047.381	179273.515	45.695	Top of Parapet wall	Middle ground Left
Point name	**Easting**	**Northing**	**Level**	**Description 1**	**Description 2**
View 2					**Northern Extent**
Photo 2	532120.552	179419.251	3.299	Photo Location	
2_PNT1	532118.607	179392.985	16.297	Roof Level	Foreground Left
2_PNT2	532101.685	179375.879	2.803	Top of Kerb	Foreground Centre
2_PNT3	532100.992	179364.113	12.659	Top Left of LH window	Middle ground Centre
2_PNT4	532100.981	179364.123	10.218	Bottom Left of LH window	Middle ground Centre
2_PNT5	532096.832	179357.581	12.595	Top Right of RH window	Middle ground Centre
2_PNT6	532096.783	179357.622	10.183	Bottom Right of RH window	Middle ground Centre
2_PNT7	532096.235	179356.851	16.864	Parapet Roof	Middle ground Centre
2_PNT8	532049.216	179200.528	61.587	Top of Plant Room	Background Centre
2_PNT9	532033.544	179205.248	60.629	Parapet Wall	Background Centre
2_PNT10	532056.653	179267.675	45.696	Parapet Wall	Background Centre
2_PNT11	532047.381	179273.515	45.695	Parapet Wall (1_PNT12)	Background Centre
Point name	**Easting**	**Northing**	**Level**	**Description 1**	**Description 2**

Spreadsheet document depicting survey point coordinates

This information will be required to go along with the planning application to help recreate each of the proposed views in 3d. Every single point comes with Easting, Northing and the Level coordinates.

The Level value represents the Z values in 3ds Max. The Northing value represents the Y values in 3ds Max. The Easting value represents the X values in 3ds max.

Top surveyors often provide users with survey points in a Cad 3d space or/ and 3ds Max format to be imported into a 3d scene for camera matching. Alternatively, users will have to create and enter the coordinate values of each of the survey points, manually.

For the purpose of this exercise, let's assume the surveyor didn't supply the survey points in 3d. In such cases, users would have had to open a new 3Ds Max scene first, followed by opening the previously extended image with survey points in 3ds Max, by clicking on the File toolbar and choosing the View image File option from the list.

NOTE

This survey document is unrelated to this project, and being used solely as a reference.

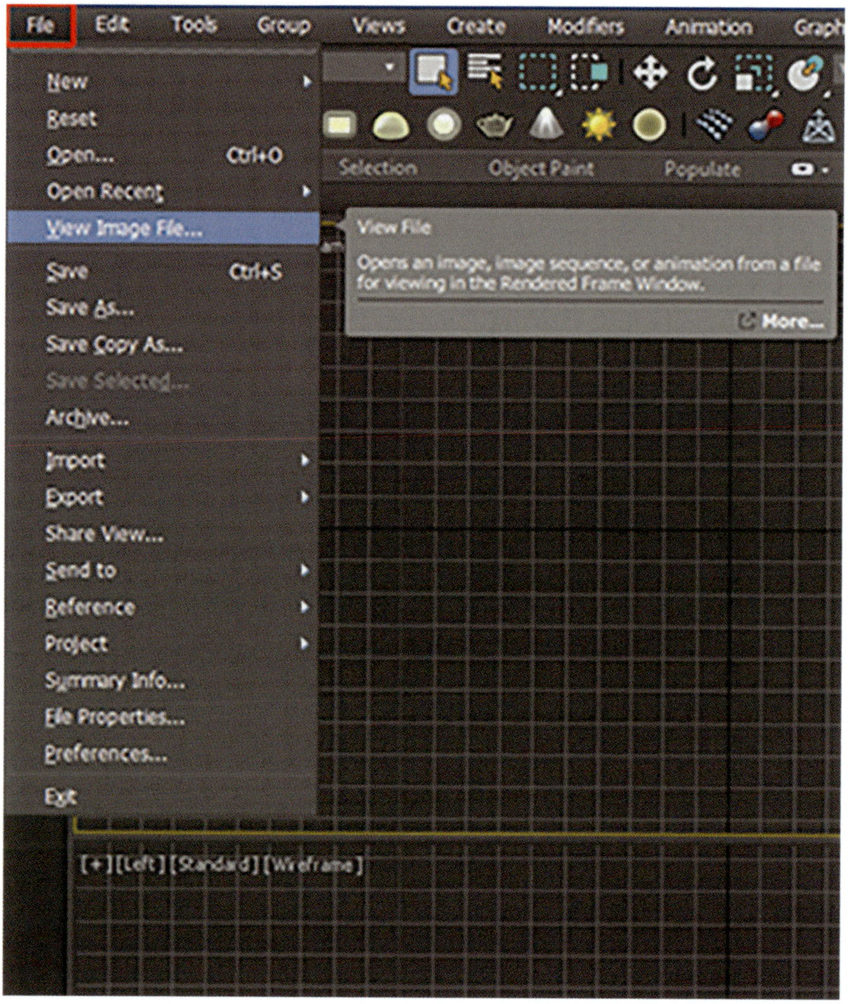

Choosing the View image File option from the list

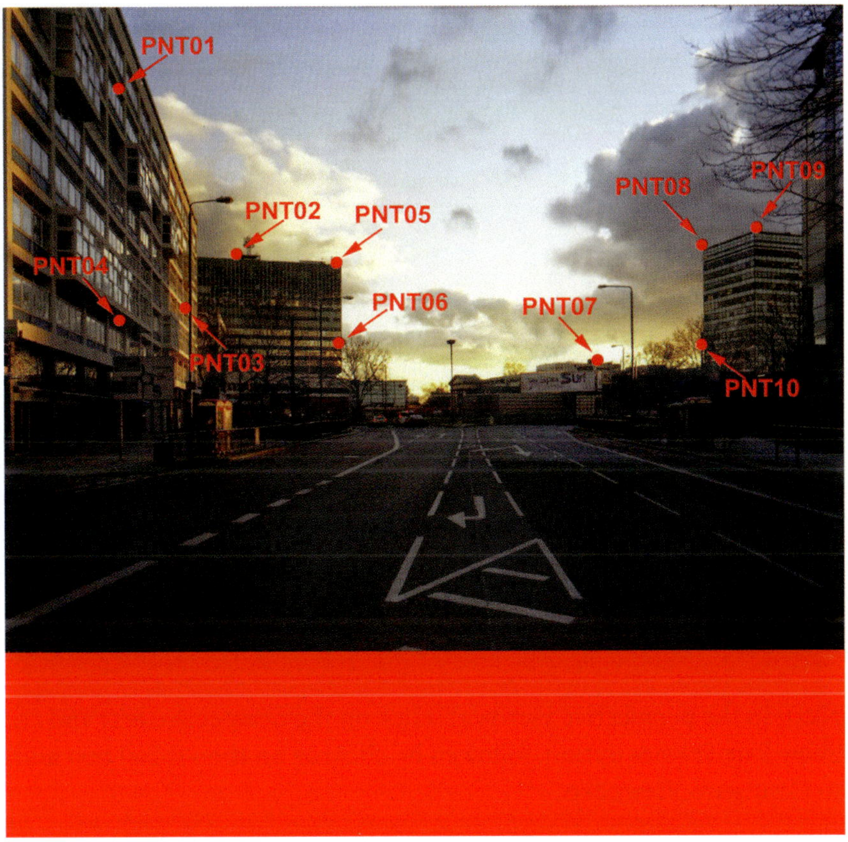

Extended image with survey points

The next step is to match the render output size with this new background image. To do so, click on the render setup button to open its dialog.

In the Output size group, type in the new Width and Height value taken from the extended image with the eyedropper sampling tool (right click on the page). Type in the new width and height values and lock it, by clicking on the image aspect padlock button.

NOTE

For the purpose of this exercise, we are currently working with smaller image sizes (1200 × 1200 pixels). However, in real projects, most of these images would have been in excess of 6000 pixels.

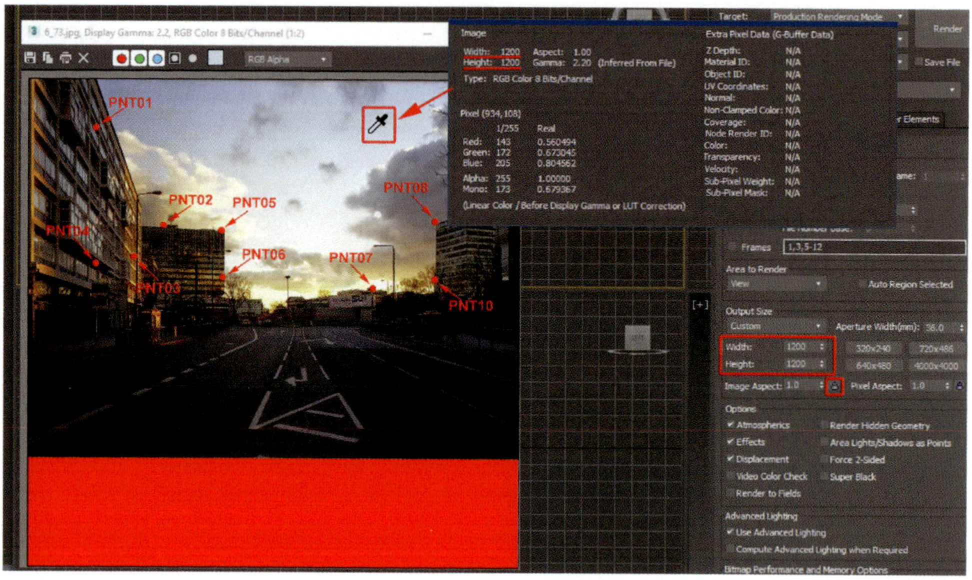

Width and Height value taken from automatic sampling tool

Next, in the perspective viewport, click on the perspective text and choose the Show Safe Frames option, followed by clicking on the + (plus) text and choosing to Configure Viewports.

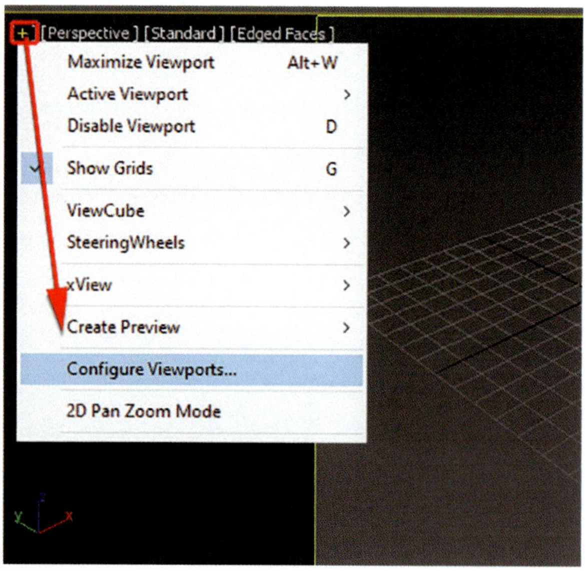

Click on the + (plus) text and choose to Configure Viewports

In its dialog, open the Background tab. Enable the Use files function and the Match Rendering Output option. Click on the Files toggle and choose the extended image with survey points.

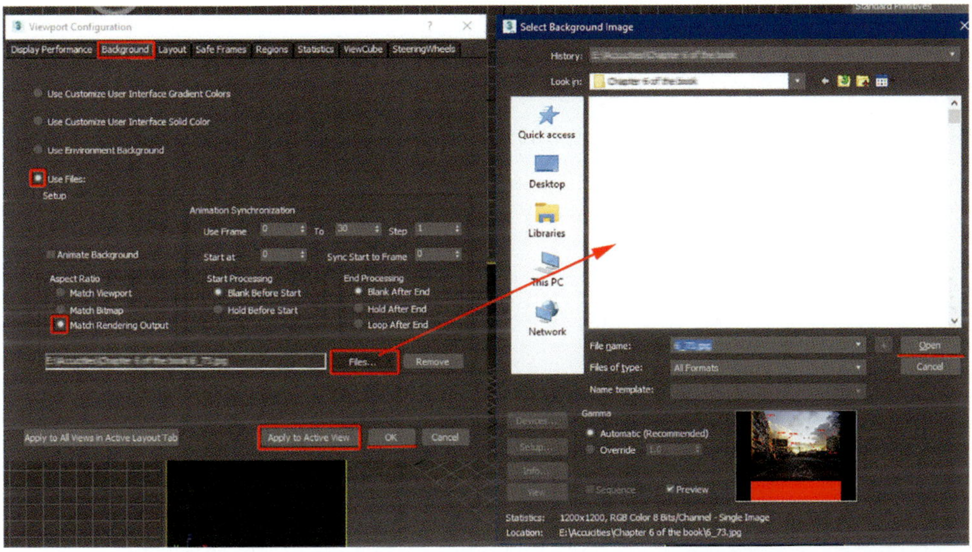

Click on the Files toggle and choose the extended image with survey points

Extended image with survey points loaded in the viewport

The next step is to begin creating the survey points in 3ds max based on their X, Y and Z coordinates. In the Create Command panel, click on the Helpers button and on the Point object, followed by clicking on the top viewport to create the first point.

Enable the Constant Screen Size option, to ensure it's always visible, regardless of its distance to the camera.

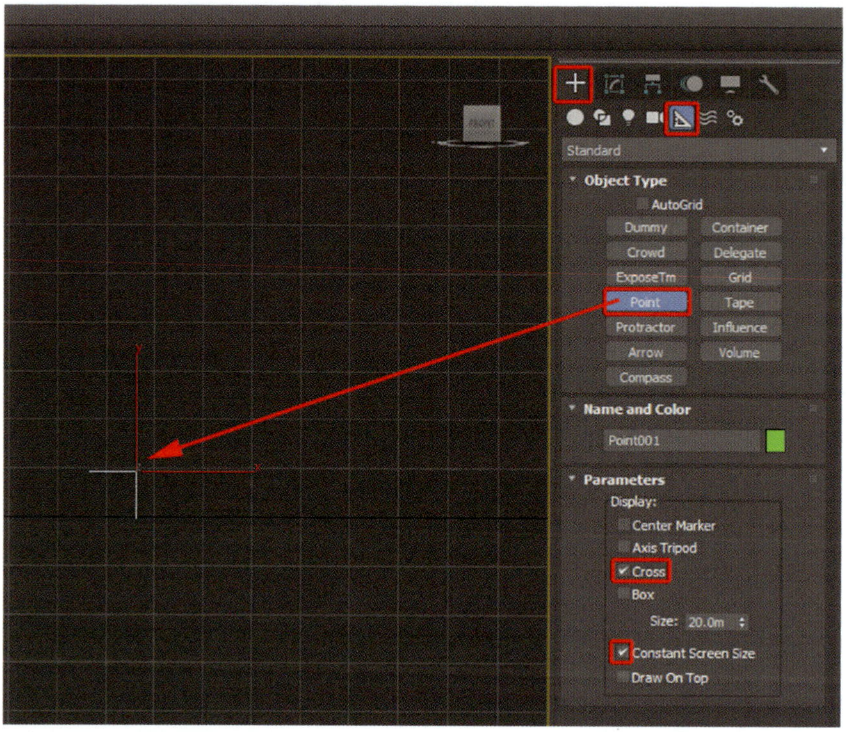

Helper point created in the Front viewport with Constant Size option enabled

Enable the Move tool and right click on it to open its dialog. Open the Units Setup and change the Display Unit Scale to Millimeters, to coincide with the values displayed in the spreadsheet.

As mentioned earlier, the Display Unit Scale is only for display purposes. Doesn't affect the physical scale of objects in the scene.

In the Perspective viewport, open the spreadsheet document, and begin copying and pasting the survey point values. Or simply type in the Easting, Northing and the Level values individually.

As mentioned earlier, the Easting coordinates are equivalent to the X values in 3d. The Northing coordinates are equivalent to the Y values in 3d. The Level coordinates are equivalent to the Z values in 3d.

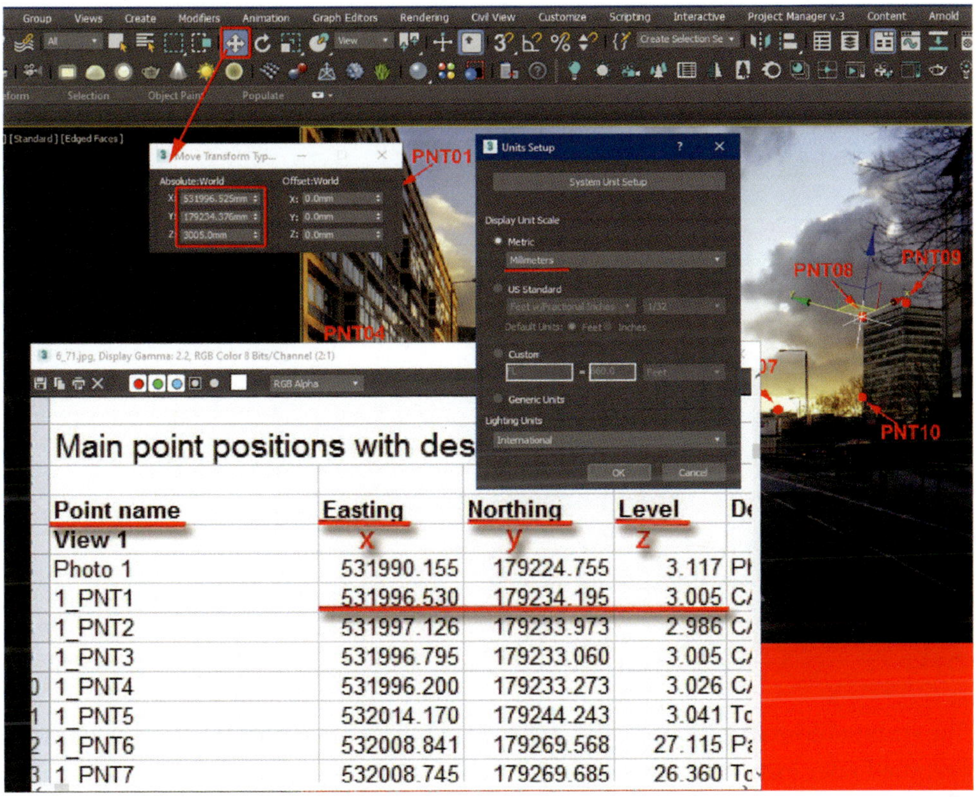

Easting, Northing and the Level values entered

The last three digits of the long coordinate value will always be slightly off, because the numerical values are too long for 3ds Max to compute and too far away from the 0.0.0 point. This tiny offset is so minute that, it will not make any visible difference in the overall accuracy of the survey position.

To expedite the process, there's a script available in the book resource files, under the name of, survey data 3ds max script.txt. The second line of the script clearly describes its function:

```
-- open the file as text, read mode
f = openFile "c:/surveypoints.csv" mode:"rt"

prefabPoint = point name:"dummy"

-- if it opened successfully (exists, etc)...
if f != undefined do
(
```

NOTE

After entering the first X, Y and Z coordinate values, in the top viewport, press the Z key on the keyboard to zoom in closer to the Point helper. Because there will be at least 10 survey points with X, Y and Z coordinates in each proposed View, the manual process can be extremely laborious.

```
while not eof f do
(
-- Read a line from the file
l = readline f
-- turn that line into an array of strings using commas as
delimiters
lf = filterString l ","
if (lf[1]!=undefined ) do
(
newPoint = instance prefabPoint
newPoint.name = lf[1]
x = lf[2] as float
y = lf[3] as float
z = lf[4] as float
newPoint.pos = [100*x,100*y,100*z]
)
)
close f
delete prefabPoint
)
```

The script automatically finds the excel spreadsheet file with a designated name and the folder location to extract the coordinates from. Users can either change the current excel file name to, survey points.csv and move it to the C drive as described in the script. Or, change the script functionality to match your file name and its location on your computer.

The script also creates each survey point automatically in your max scene, accurately. To do so, open the.txt file, select and copy the script it (Ctrl+C).

Inside 3ds Max, click on Scripting toolbar and choose the New Script option. Press Ctrl+V to paste the Text. Next, go to File and choose the Save as option.

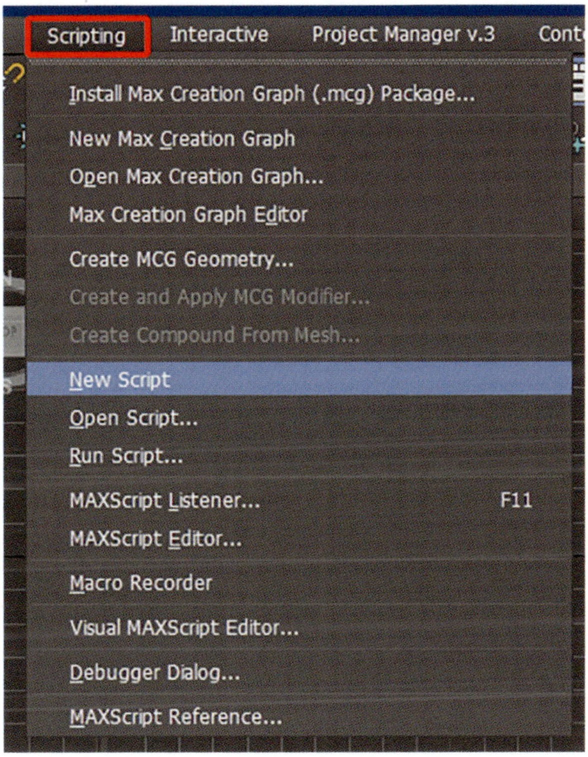

New Script option from Scripting toolbar

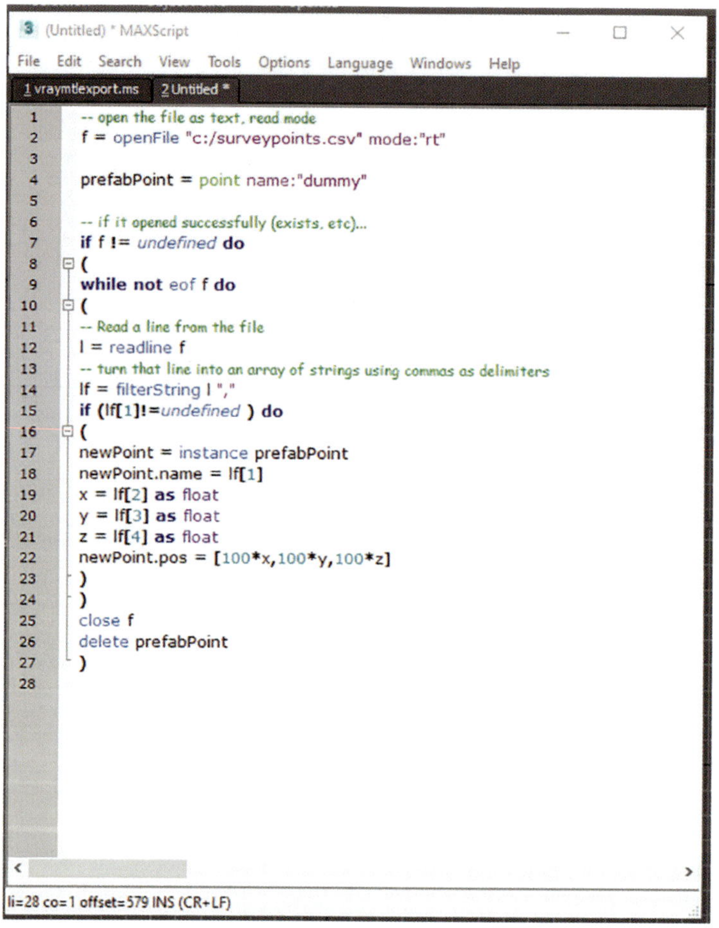

Script pasted onto the MaxScript dialog

Name the script as (Ctrl+Shift+S), Verified View script, and, click Save. Close the open New Script dialog.

Next, go to the Scripting toolbar and choose the Run Script option, followed by selecting the script.

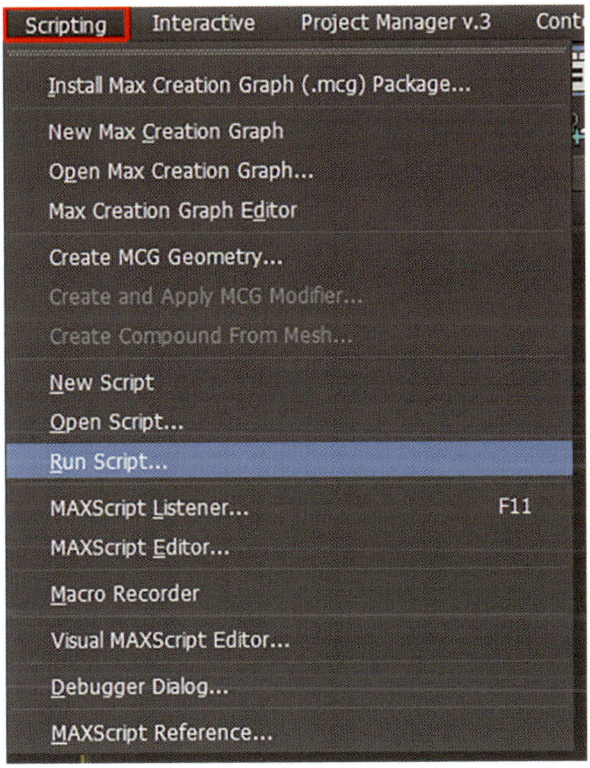

Choose the Run Script option

All survey points should be automatically created. Press Z on your keyboard to zoom close to them. As a reference point, the survey for the camera is always the furthest out, pointing toward the remaining surveys in the space.

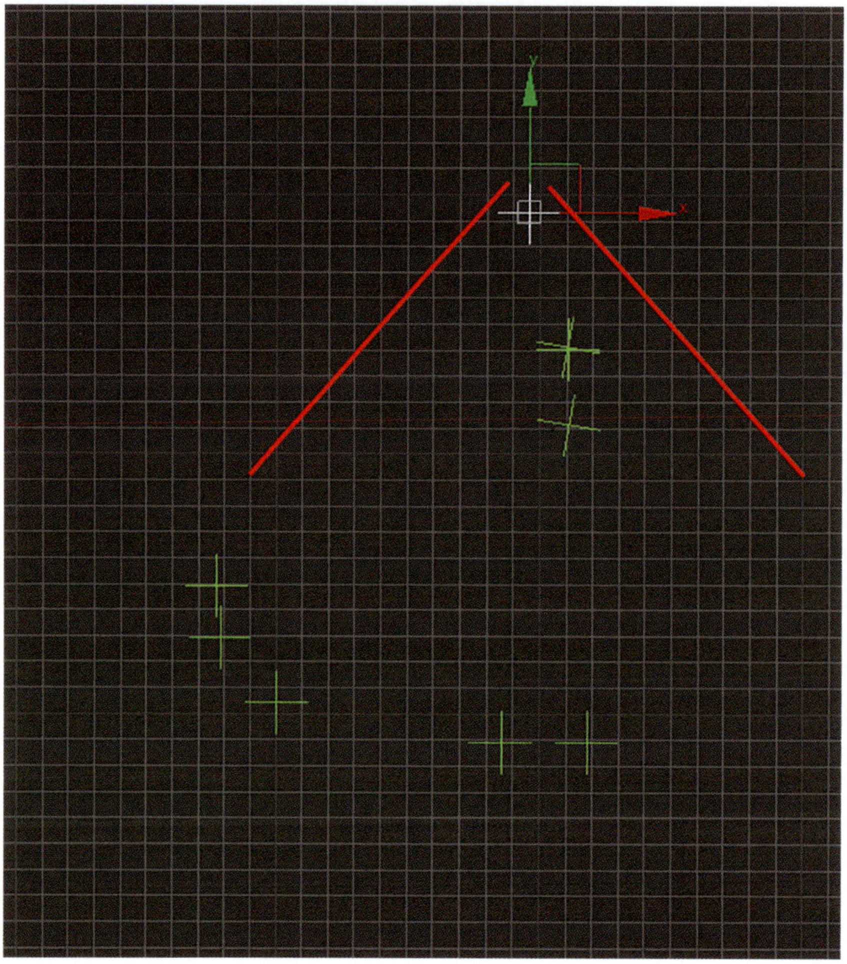

Surveys in the scene

The following step is to merge the previous 3d scene with the Accucities context model and camera previously set.

Once everything is merged, to start matching the camera, select both the camera and the survey Point011 (camera position survey). Use the Ctrl key for multiple selections.

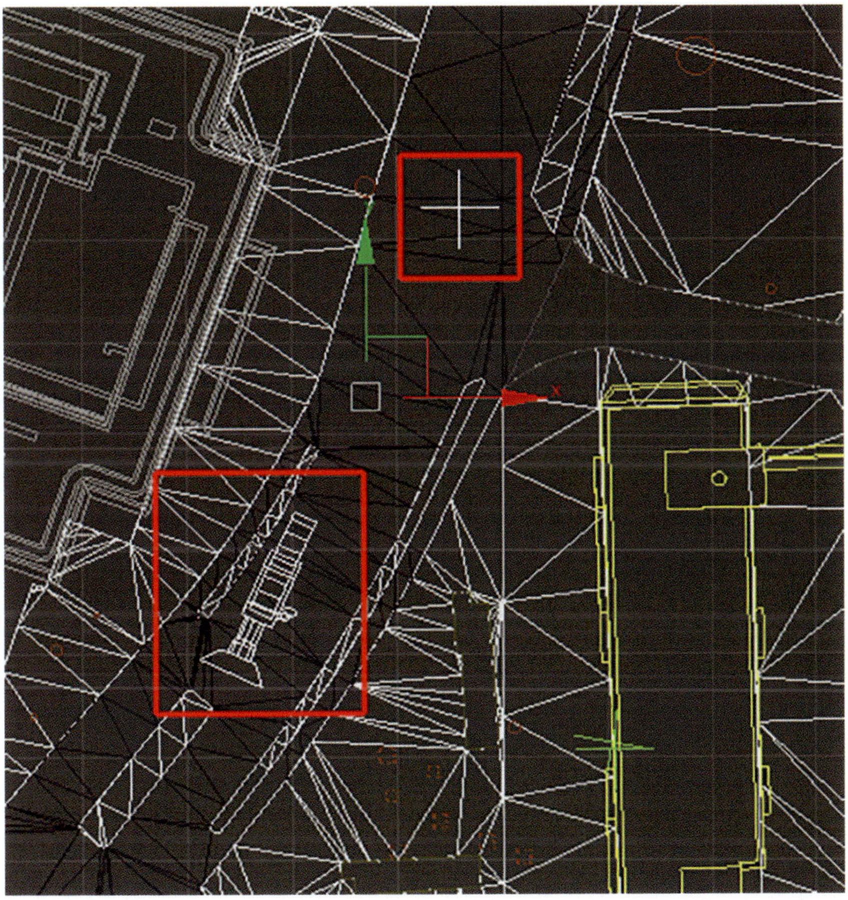

Select both the camera and the survey Point011

Isolate the selected objects (Alt+Q). Move the camera in X, Y and Z positions to where the survey Point011 is, and change its Lens to 26 mm, to coincide with the camera information provided by the photographer.

14 Verified Views

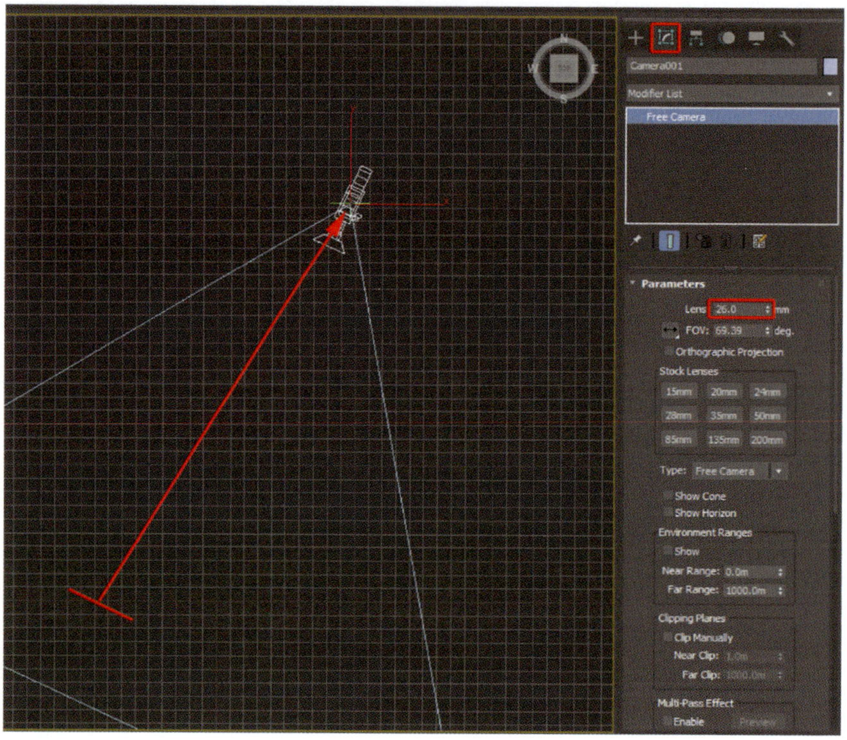

Camera moved in X, Y and Z positions to match the survey coordinates

Change its Type to Target Camera, and select the camera target.

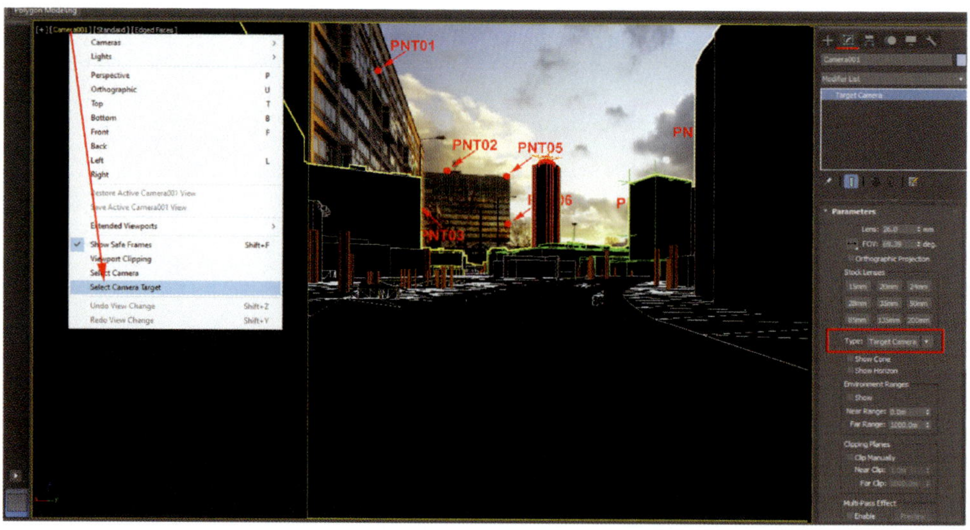

Camera Type changed and its Target selected

This is an example of one of the many documents a photographer would often provide you with.

In this one, you have the camera parameters, the date, time and other useful information to help you match the camera and the lighting accordingly.

To match the view accurately, simply move the camera target in X, Y and Z positions until the context and survey points are aligned with the background photo. To facilitate the process, turn the camera view to Wireframe and use the Move Transform dialog.

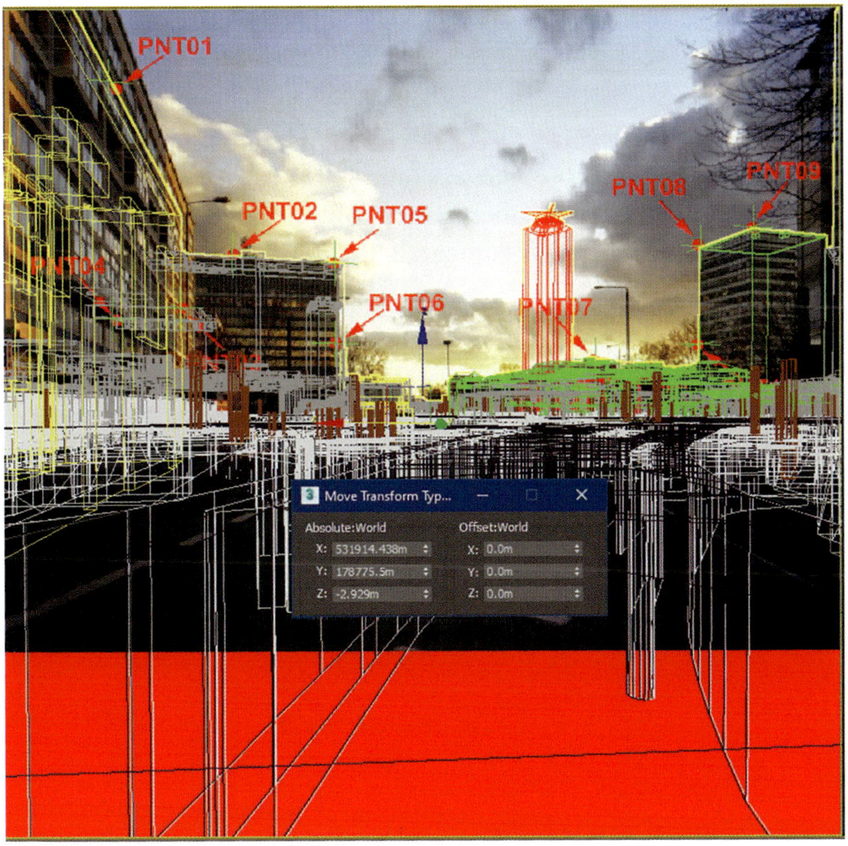

Camera view matched with Move Transform values from the camera target only

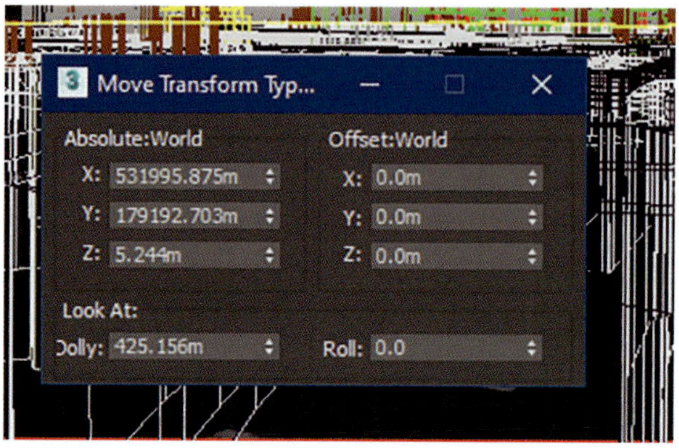

Move Transform values from the camera selection only

The next step is to create a Daylight system object to set up an accurate time and position of the sun. This photo was originally taken on June 5, 2016 at around 19:00 in London. As mentioned earlier, this information should also be provided by the photographer in a document.

To create the Daylight system object, open the Systems panel and click on the Daylight button. Next, left click and drag the cursor to create its compass. Release the left click and continue dragging the mouse to create the Daylight. Ensure the north of the compass is facing north as seen in the Accucities model.

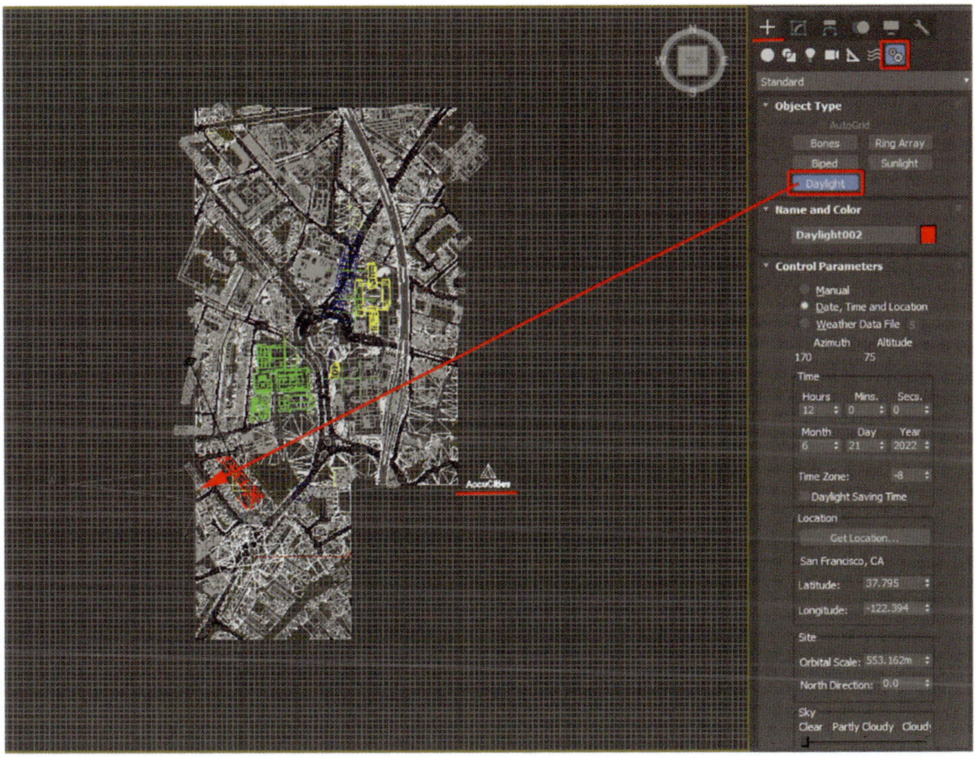

Daylight system object created in the scene

To set up an accurate time and position of the sun, open the Modify panel and change the Sunlight type to VRaySun. Disable the Skylight, because VRaySun already comes with its Skylight.

Under Sky Parameters, change the Sky model to Improved. This function automatically updates the sky effects depending on the sun position.

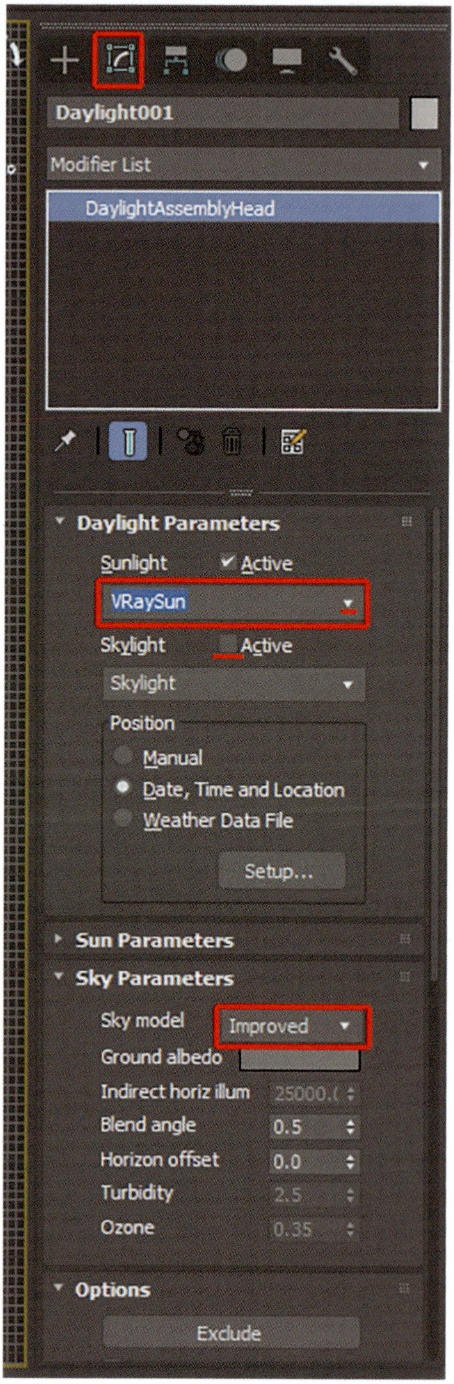

Daylight Parameters changed to VRaySun and Improved Sky model

Next, click on the Setup toggle. Under Control Parameters, set the Time to 19:00, Month 6 (June) and Year 2016. To set the location, click on the Get Location toggle and London.

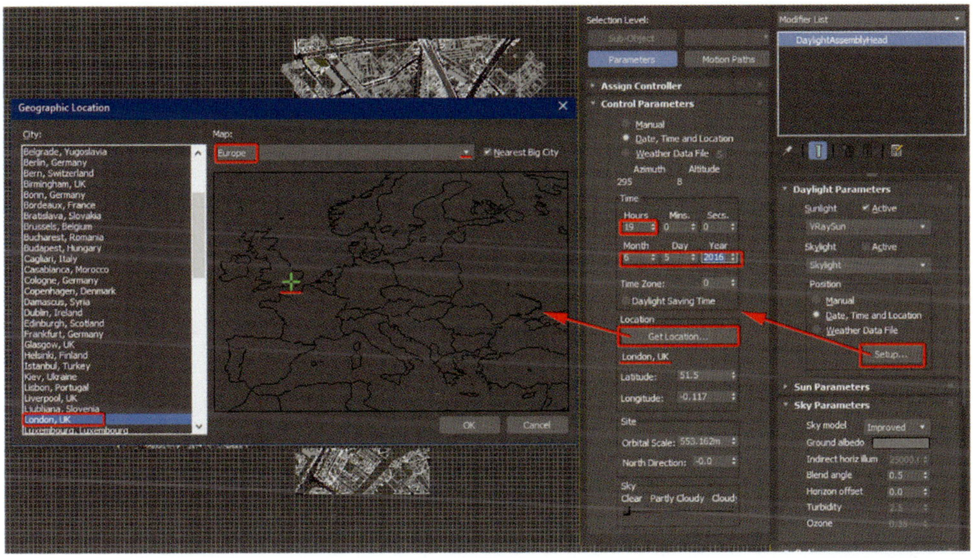

Daylight Control Parameters and Geographical Location

Override material the global material and do another test render using some of the previous render settings.

Test render with new DaylightSystem

The following step is to provide the client with the AVR 0 renders. AVR0s depict the outline of the proposed building overlaid against the photo.

Select the proposed building and isolate it (Alt+Q). Do another render.

As previously done, under V-Ray tab, click on the G-Buffer toggle to save the RGB and Alpha. Choose to save the render as a Tiff file format, with 16-bit, store alpha channel and 300 dpi. Name the render as AVR00.

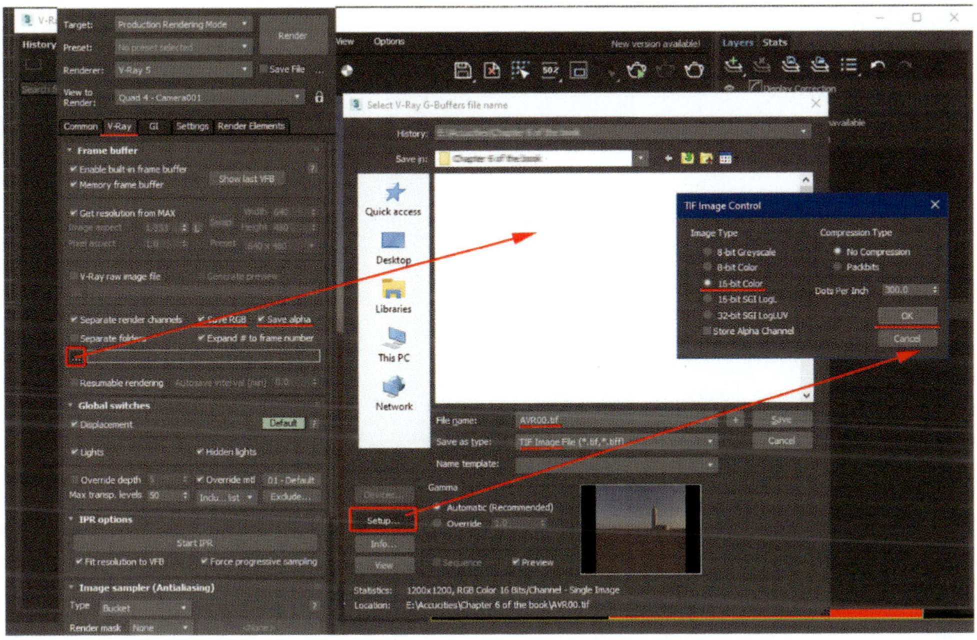

Save the isolated render as AVR00.TIF

In Photoshop, go to File, Scripts, and choose to Load Files into Stack.

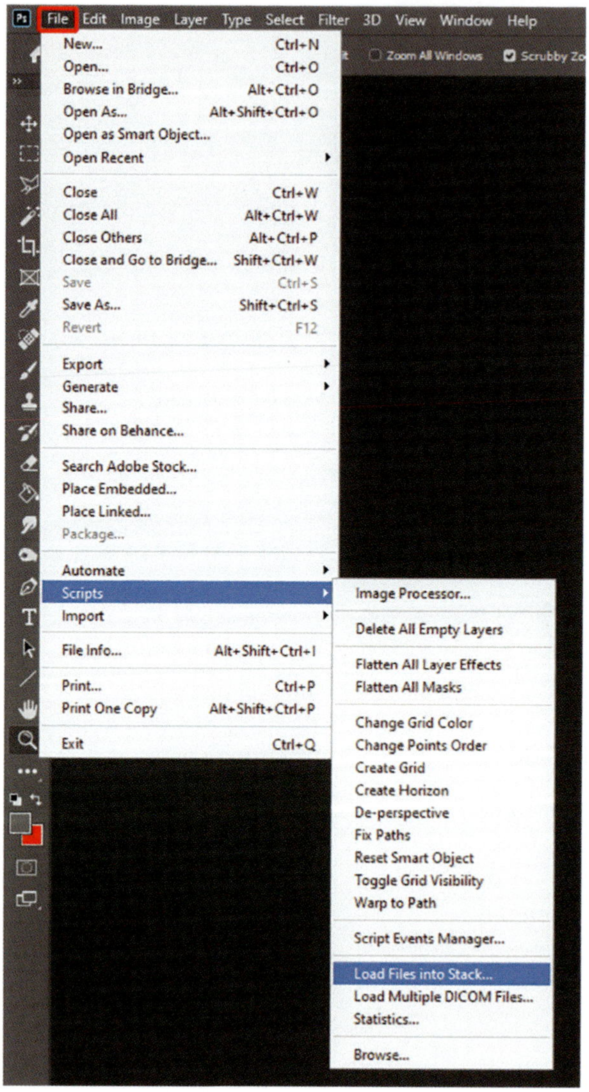

Choose to Load Files into Stack

To load multiple files, click on the Browse toggle to locate, select multiple files (Ctrl+Select) and open. Once multiple files are loaded, click OK to open them.

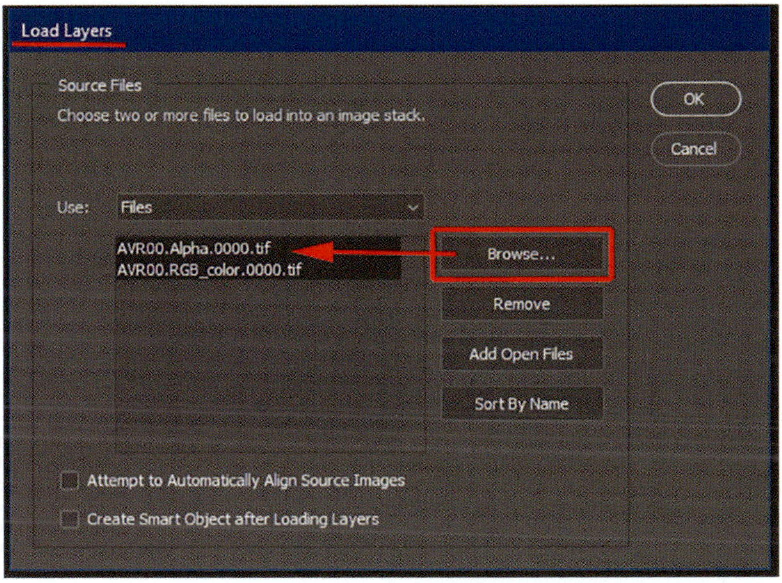

Open multiple files into the Load Layers dialog

Also, open the file named, Photo with Survey Points_ extended.psd. Next, Select the previous document with both rendered layers.

Select both pre-rendered TIFF layers using the Ctrl key, right click and choose to Duplicate Layers. In the Duplicate Layers dialog, choose the Destination Document to be, Photo with Survey Points_ extended.psd.

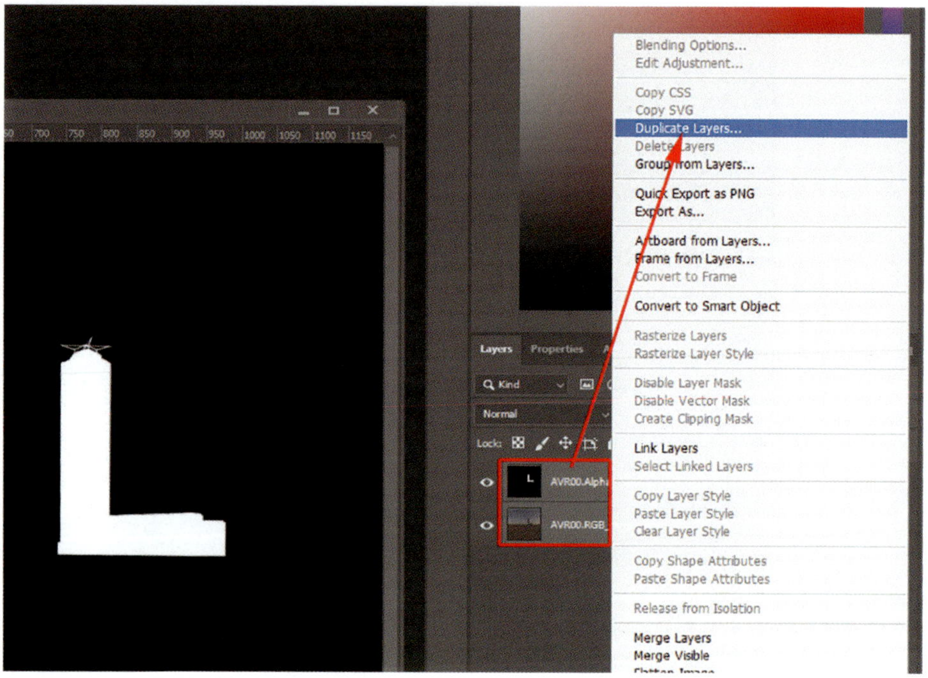

Choose to Duplicate Layers option

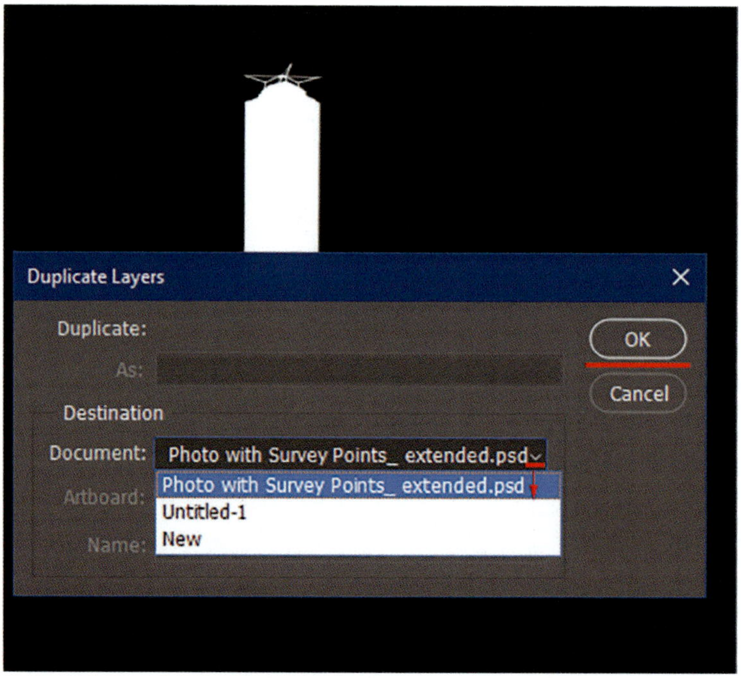

Choose the Destination Document

In the document, Photo with Survey Points_ extended.psd, ensure the duplicated layers are on top of all existing layers/groups.

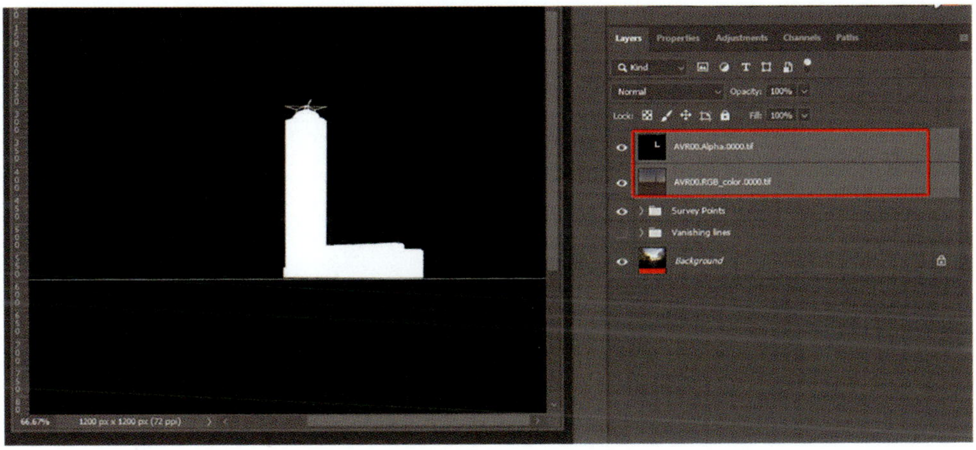

Duplicated layers on top of all existing layers/groups

To begin creating the AVR0, select the layer, AVR00.Alpha.0000.tif.

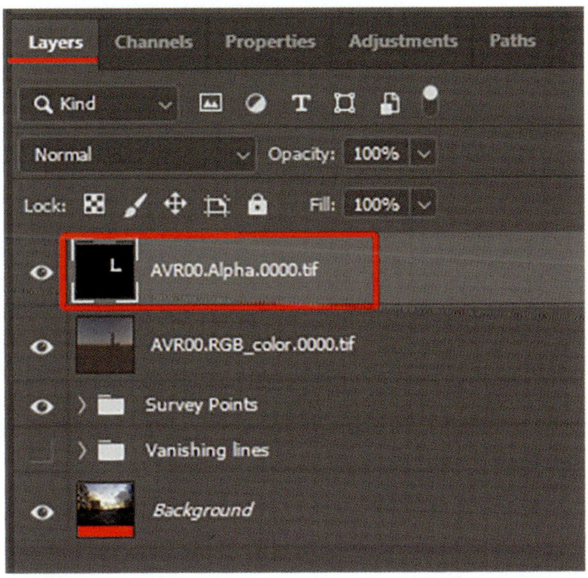

Layer AVR00.Alpha.0000.tif selected

Go to the Channels tab, hold down the Ctrl key and select the RGB. The Alpha selection should be enabled in the document.

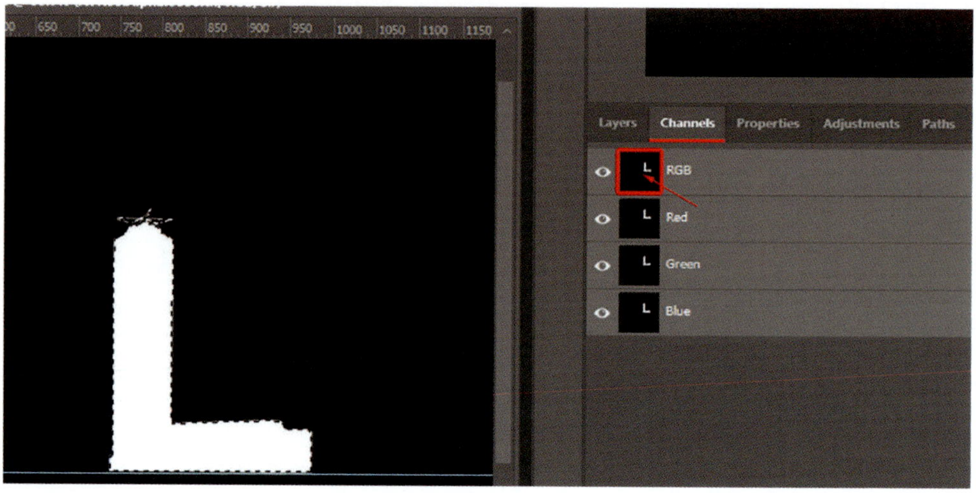

Hold down the Ctrl key and select the RGB channel

While the selection is on, go to the Select toolbar, Modify, and choose the Border option.

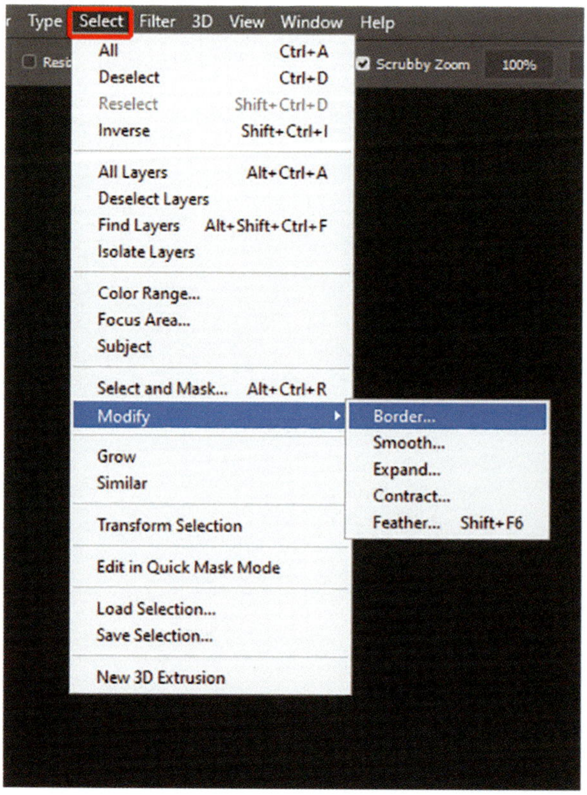

Choose the Border option

For the size of the document being used in this tutorial (1200 × 1200 pixels), the Width pixels was set to 2. Bigger documents would require bigger Width pixels.

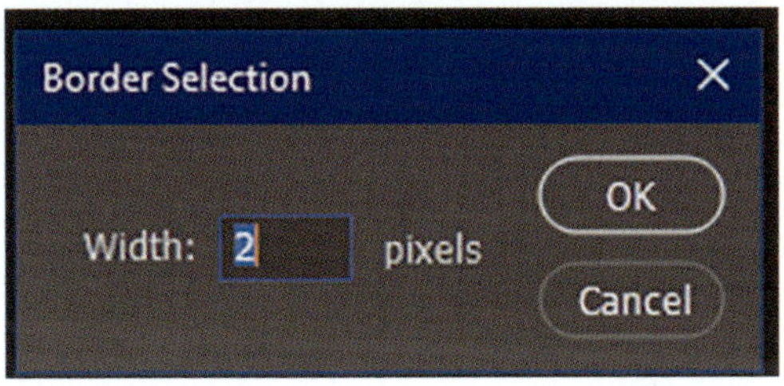

Border Selection Width pixels set to 2

While the boarder selection is on, under Layers tab, turn off the visibility of all layers by deselecting their eye icon. Following that, click the button to Create a new layer.

Turn off the visibility of all layers and Create a new layer

While the new layer is selected and border selection is still on, enable the brush tool (B) and begin brushing over the selection. Ensure not to brush over the foreground areas obstructing the proposed building.

Begin brushing over the border selection

NOTE

The Spacing function is the most important option for dotted brushes.

The areas where the proposed building is being obstructed by existing buildings in the foreground need to have dotted lines instead. To do so, while brush tool is selected (B), click on the brush settings toggle to open its panel.

Under Brush Settings, set the Size to around 40 px, Roundness to 10, Hardness to 100% and Spacing to 327%. These values worked best to paint dots on the vertical areas of the selection. Begin painting dots on the vertical areas of the selection.

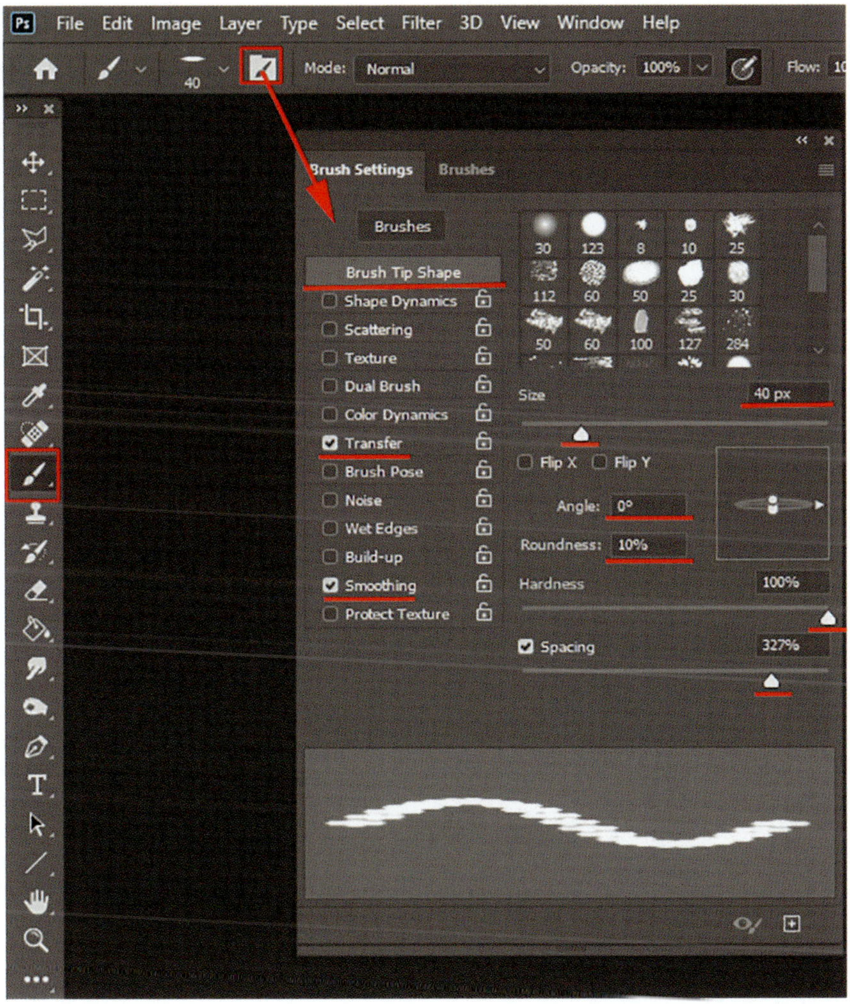

Brush Settings for dotted brush

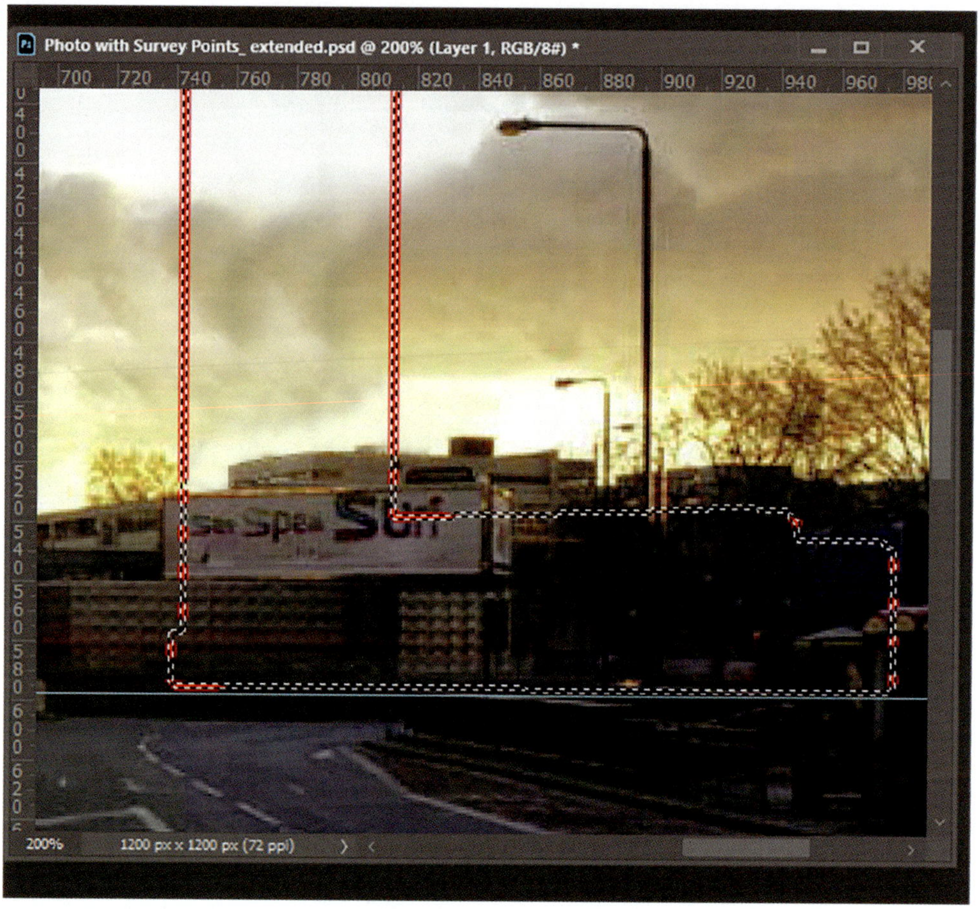

Begin brushing dots over the border selection

To brush dots on the vertical areas of the selection, set the Brush Settings Angle value to 90 degrees.

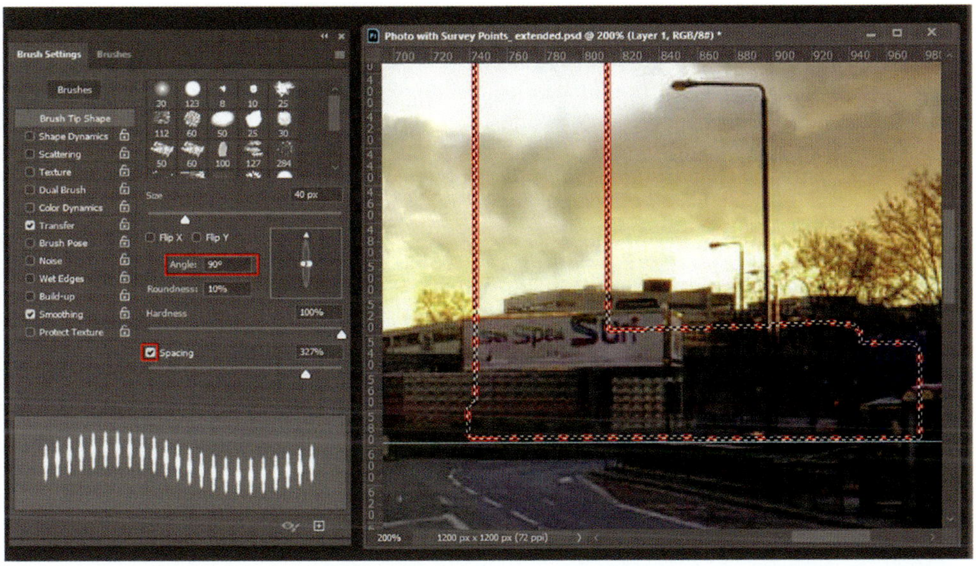

Set the Brush Settings Angle value to 90°C

Deselect the border selection and rename the new layer as, AVR0.

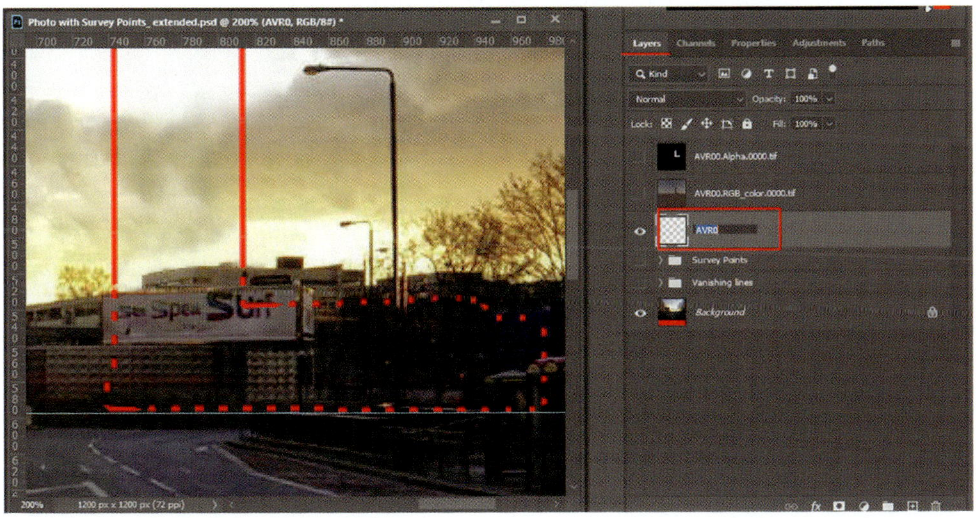

Rename the new layer as, AVR0

To edit the previous lines created on the AVR0 layer, simply create a layer mask by clicking on its button. An adjacent mask should appear on AVR0 layer.

The Background and Foreground colors should automatically change to black and white while the layer mask is selected. To brush away pixels while the layer mask is selected, ensure the black color is in the Foreground and begin brushing away pixels.

To have the opposite effect, ensure the white color is in the Foreground (X) and begin brushing away pixels.

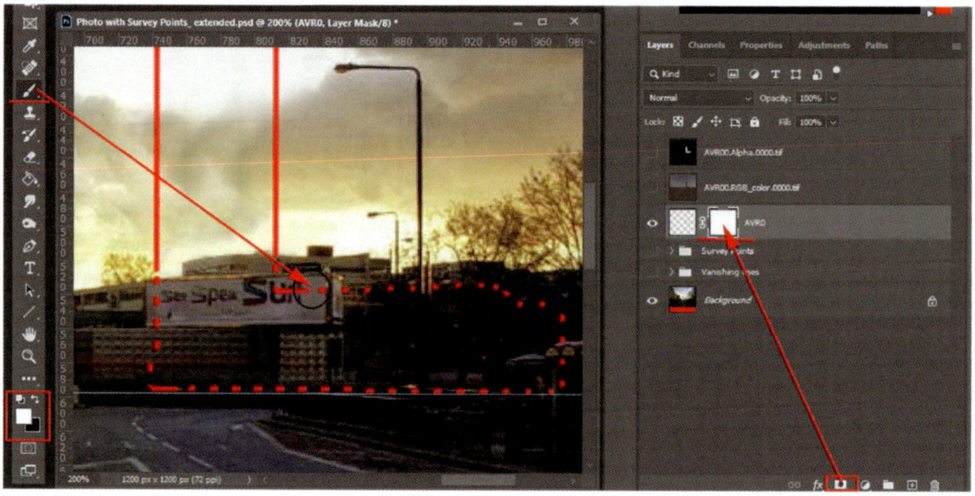

Create Layer mask and brush away pixels while the mask is selected

The following Layer to create is the AVR1. AVR1 consists of external and internal building outlines. To start, move the layer, AVR00.RGB_color.0000.tif, under the AVR0 layer. Also, enable its visibility.

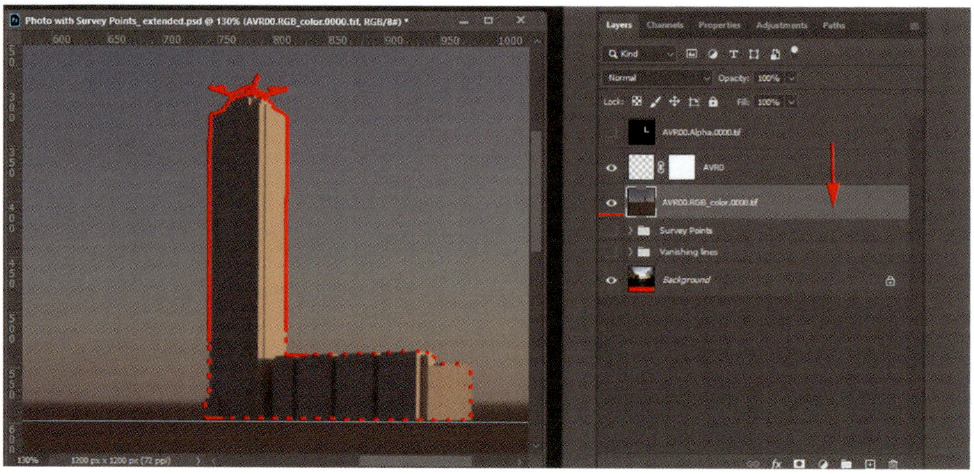

Enable the layer visibility and move it under AVR0 layer

Next, enable the Line tool (U) and begin drawing along the building's internal vertical lines.

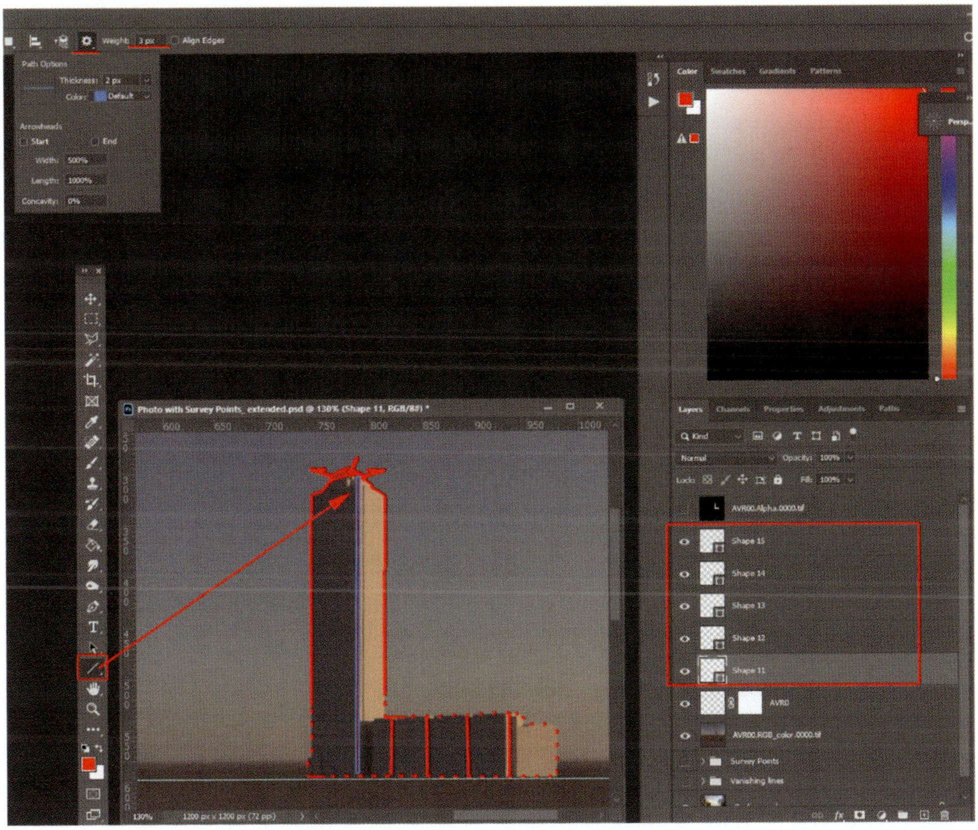

Internal vertical lines of the building drawn

Group the five new lines created and rename the group as, AVR1. To add dotted lines on the areas of the proposed building being obstructed, create a group mask as previously done. Set the brush accordingly and begin brushing away pixels with the Foreground color set to black (X).

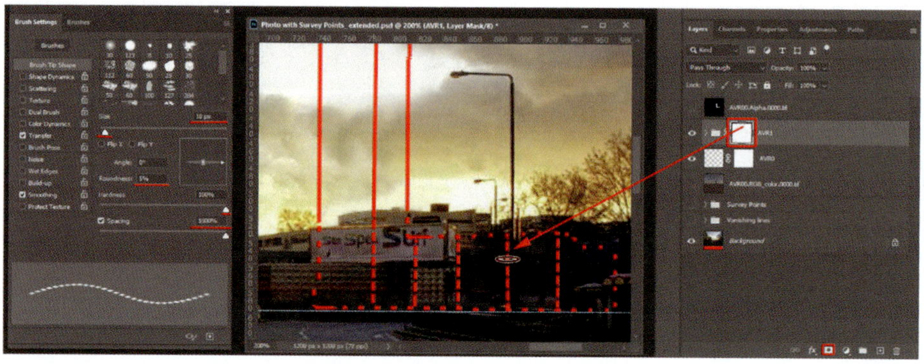

Five new lines grouped, edited and renamed as AVR1

The next step is to create the AVR2 image. AVR2 consists of a shaded/chalk render of the proposed building integrated with the background photo.

Let's start by creating a new group and renaming it as, AVR2.

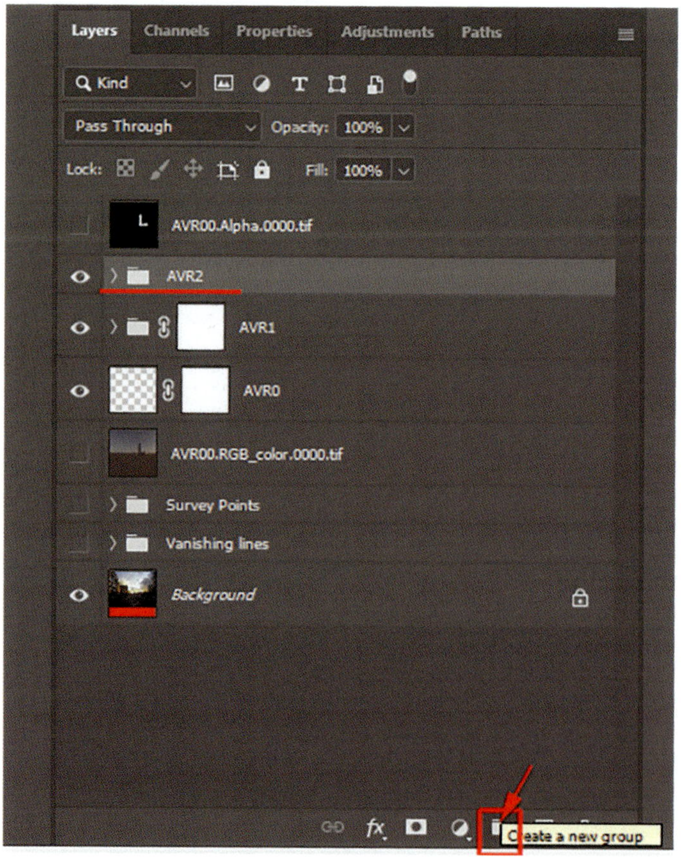

Create a new group and rename it as AVR2

The following step is to disable the visibility of AVR0 layer and AVR2 Group. Next, enable the building selection, using the previous steps. While the building selection is enabled, select the AVR2 Group.

Enable the building selection and select the AVR2 Group

While the selection is still on and the AVR2 Group is selected, click to create the group mask.

AVR2 Group mask created while the selection is on

Next, select the AVR00.RGB_color.0000.tif layer, hold down the Alt key and move it inside the AVR2 Group to copy it. Enable its visibility.

New layer copied and moved inside AVR2 Group

To integrate the chalk render perfectly into the background photography, select the AVR2 Group mask and enable the brush tool (B). Switch the Foreground color to black (X) Begin brushing away obstructed areas of the building.

Select the AVR2 Group mask and begin brushing away obstructed areas of the building

To adjust the brightness and contrast of the proposed building, start by creating a new subgroup and renaming it, Adjustment.

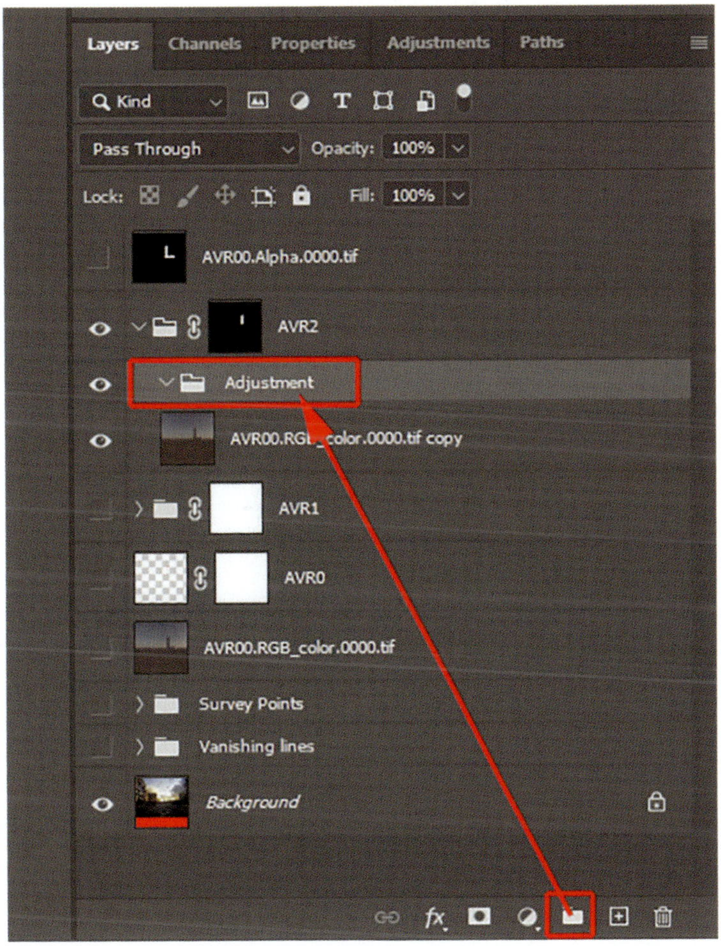

Create a new subgroup and rename it Adjustment

Next, add the Levels adjustment layer by clicking on its button.

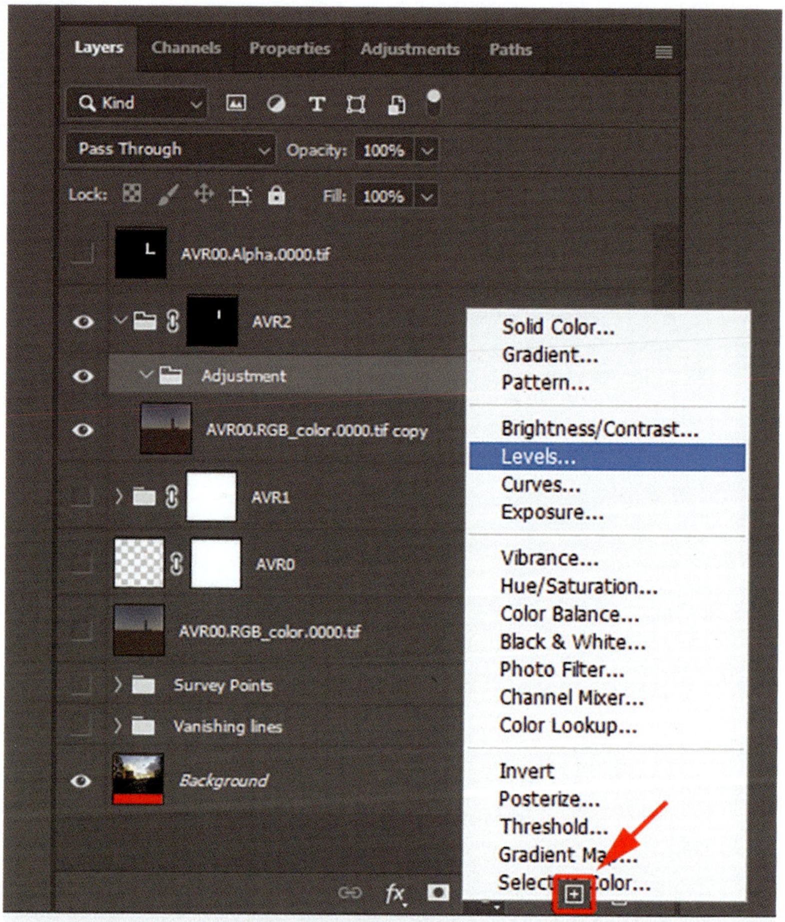

Add the Levels adjustment layer by clicking on its button

To begin adjusting the brightness of the building, move the Levels RGB middle point slightly to the right (0.84).

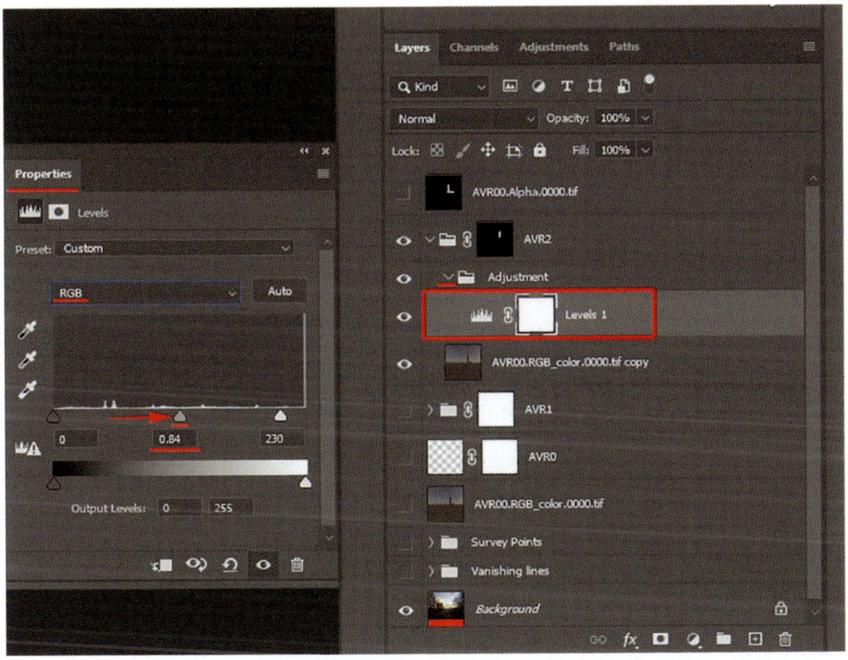

Move the Levels RGB middle point slightly to the right (0.84)

To adjust its color to match the background photo, choose the Blue color from the list and move its middle point toward the right, to add a bit of yellow tint.

Move the Levels Blue middle point slightly to the right to add a bit of yellow tint (0.87)

Create other subgroups with masked selections and adjustments for specific areas, using some of the techniques covered earlier. Ensure all subgroups are contained inside the main group, AVR2.

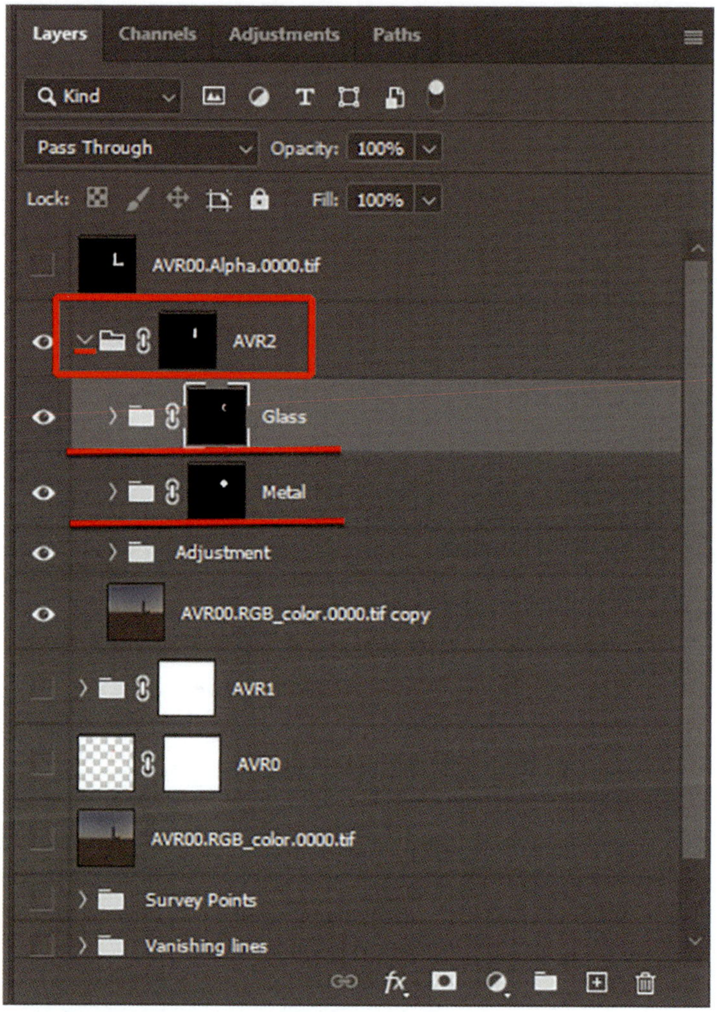

Create other subgroups with masked selections

Tidy up all the layers and groups in the document. Also, adjust the Levels RGB brightness slightly to blend the proposed building more seamlessly with the photo.

Create other subgroups with masked selections

AVR3 consists of the final high-resolution render with all the materials, lighting and Photoshop tweaked to perfection, using some of the techniques highlighted earlier.

Final AVR3

NOTE

If per chance you're having problems with the lighting, texturing, etc., due to how far from point 0.0.0 your 3d scene is, you may need to move the 3d scene closer to 0.0.0, for the purpose of rendering mainly. However, always keep the original files with surveys, camera matched and 3d context model intact as a separate file.

If you had ten proposed camera views, you would have had to repeat the entire process for every single camera view.

Index

Index

Index

Index

Index

Index

Index

Index

Index